401(k)
Answer Book

2000 Edition

401(k)
Answer Book

2000 Edition

EMJAY Corporation, a Wells Fargo Company

A PANEL PUBLICATION
ASPEN PUBLISHERS, INC.

This publication is designed to provide accurate and authoritative information in regard to the subject matter covered. It is sold with the understanding that the publisher is not engaged in rendering legal, accounting, or other professional services. If legal advice or other professional advice is required, the services of a competent professional should be sought.

> — From a *Declaration of Principles* jointly adopted by a Committee of the American Bar Association and a Committee of Publishers and Associations.

ISBN 0-7355-0484-9

Printed in the United States of America

About Panel Publishers

Panel Publishers—including the former Prentice Hall Law & Business, Little, Brown and Company's Professional Division, and Wiley Law Publications—is a leading publisher of authoritative and timely treatises, practice manuals, information services, and journals written by specialists to assist attorneys, financial and tax advisors, and other business professionals. Our mission is to provide practical, solution-based how-to information keyed to the latest legislative, judicial, and regulatory developments.

We offer publications in the areas of compensation and benefits, pensions, payroll, employment, civil rights, taxation, estate planning, and elder law.

Other Panel products on related topics include:

Books and Manuals
Annuities Answer Book
Nonqualified Deferred Compensation Answer Book*
Participant Directed Investment Answer Book
The Pension Answer Book*
Pension Distribution Answer Book*
Roth IRA Answer Book
SIMPLE, SEP, and SARSEP Answer Book

Periodicals and Electronic Products
401(k) Advisor
Journal of Deferred Compensation
Journal of Pension Benefits
Journal of Pension Planning and Compliance
Panel Pension Library on CD-ROM
Panel Pension Library Deluxe On-Line
Pension Plan Administrator

Companion volume of Forms and Worksheets available.

PANEL PUBLISHERS
A Division of Aspen Publishers, Inc.
Practical Solutions for Legal and Business Professionals
www.panelpublishers.com

SUBSCRIPTION NOTICE

This Panel product is updated on a periodic basis with supplements to reflect important changes in the subject matter. If you purchased this product directly from Panel, we have already recorded your subscription for the update service.

If, however, you purchased this product from a bookstore and wish to receive future updates and revised or related volumes billed separately with a 30-day examination review, please contact our Customer Service Department at 1-800-234-1660, or send your name, company name (if applicable), address, and the title of the product to:

Panel Publishers
A Division of Aspen Publishers, Inc.
7201 McKinney Circle
Frederick, MD 21704

Preface

Still the most popular and fastest growing private-sector defined contribution plan in the United States, 401(k) plans were once again available to nonprofit organizations in 1997. More than 29 million employees working for over 250,000 companies with over $1.5 trillion invested are covered by 401(k) plans. Among companies with more than 100 employees, 401(k) plan sponsorship grew by 92 percent from 1994 to 1998.

The *401(k) Answer Book, 2000 Edition,* is a comprehensive one-volume desk reference for pension administrators, benefits managers, fund managers, trustees, accountants, attorneys, human resources professionals, consultants, advisors, and anyone who must deal professionally with 401(k) plans. Each of the 21 chapters provides a tightly organized treatment of a single design feature or plan activity. Especially convenient to the user is the grouping of all material relating to nondiscrimination testing in chapters 9 through 12. As with past editions, the book provides a balance of formal qualification material with practical considerations for effective 401(k) plan design, administration, and communication.

The *2000 Edition* considers the implementation and implications of the IRS Restructuring and Reform Act of 1998 (IRRA), the Taxpayer Relief Act of 1997 (TRA '97), and the Small Business Job Protection Act of 1996 (SBJPA).

New topics and expanded material in the *2000 Edition* of the *401(k) Answer Book* include:

- Expanded material on 401(k) safe harbor plans
- Use of electronic technology satisfying disclosure requirements

- IRS Notice 99-1, which discusses paperless processing of benefit distributions
- Expanded material on EPCRS, including Table 19-1, which compares the programs under EPCRS
- ERISA Interpretive Bulletin 99-1, which extends many features of the Employee Plans Compliance Resolution System (EPCRS) to 403(b) plans
- IRS Notice 99-5, which deals with the fact that hardship withdrawals are no longer eligible rollover distributions
- Updated survey material concerning compliance with ERISA Section 404(c)
- Additional lessons for fiduciaries from the UNISYS case
- Recent judicial support for the Department of Labor position that ERISA preempts state escheat laws in handling benefits for participants who cannot be located
- The recent Department of Labor study on plan fees and expenses
- The impact of Revenue Procedure 99-23 on prior-year versus current-year actual contribution percentage (ACP) testing methods
- IRS Notice 99-11, which delays the required amendment date to conform plans to recent legislation

The *401(k) Answer Book, 2000 Edition* provides answers to such questions as:

- How is a SIMPLE IRA plan less flexible than a 401(k) plan?
- What are master and prototype plans?
- How should fiduciaries decide what investment options to provide?
- How effectively is plan sponsor liability limited when participants direct their own investments in accord with ERISA Section 404(c)?
- What happens when a plan loan is not timely repaid?
- How are excess contributions handled differently from excess aggregate contributions?

- How can IRS plan compliance programs be used to best advantage?

As with previous editions, the objective of this *2000 Edition* is to provide accessible, self-contained discussions addressing all aspects of 401(k) plan design and administration as well as the relationship of 401(k) plans with other types of retirement plans. Although the book is designed to be immediately useful both as a tutorial and as a reference, it is complemented by Panel Publisher's *401(k) Answer Book: Forms & Worksheets,* whose annual revisions provide a comprehensive, up-to-date set of tools based on the questions and answers given here.

The authors have made every attempt to ensure that the material in this book is current. However, given the regulatory and legislative environment, some rules may change by the time this book is in print.

Steven J. Franz
Joan C. McDonagh
John Michael Maier
William C. Kalke
Lisa R. Richardson
September 1999

About the Authors

STEVEN J. FRANZ has been with EMJAY since 1989. He is a 1976 graduate of the University of Wisconsin School of Law. He earned a Master of Law in Estate Planning from the University of Miami (Florida) School of Law in 1982 and is a member of the Wisconsin Bar Association.

Steve has over 17 years of experience in the employee benefits area. As EMJAY's Director of Compliance, Steve is responsible for plan documentation and the IRS determination letter process. He is a co-author of the *401(k) Answer Book: Forms & Worksheets*.

JOAN C. McDONAGH joined EMJAY in 1988, where she serves as EMJAY's Vice President, Secretary, and General Counsel. She received a JD from American University, Washington College of Law, in 1985 and subsequently practiced law in the employee benefits area. Joan's areas of expertise include ERISA compliance, with an emphasis on fiduciary requirements and qualified domestic relations orders.

Joan is a member of the Milwaukee, Wisconsin, and American Bar Associations and participates in the Tax Section and the Employee Benefits Committee, Subcommittee on Fiduciary Responsibility of the Real Property, Probate & Trust Law Section. She is also a member of the American Corporate Counsel Association and Wisconsin Retirement Plan Professionals, Ltd. She has written numerous articles on fiduciary issues related to qualified plan operation. She is a co-author of the *401(k) Answer Book: Forms & Worksheets*.

JOHN MICHAEL MAIER—President, has been with EMJAY since 1984. He received his law degree with distinction from the University of Wisconsin School of Law in 1984. He earned a Specialist in Pension Planning certificate from the American College School of Advanced Career Studies. He is currently Chief Operating Officer of EMJAY with general management responsibility for strategic and business planning and directs the Compliance and Legal departments.

He is a member of the Milwaukee, Wisconsin, and American Bar Associations and participates in the Tax and Business Law Sections and the Employee Benefits Committee of the Real Property, Probate & Trust Law Section; the American Corporate Counsel Association; the International Foundation of Employee Benefit Plans; and Wisconsin Retirement Plan Professionals, Ltd. He is a co-author of the *401(k) Answer Book: Forms & Worksheets* and the *Participant Directed Investment Answer Book.*

WILLIAM C. KALKE has been with EMJAY since 1992. Bill is an enrolled actuary with over 25 years of experience in the employee benefits area in both consulting and insurance company environments. He has lectured and written on the development of computer systems for the administration of defined contribution plans and has consulted on the design and implementation of 401(k) plans. He also holds a Series 6 Securities License.

Bill received a BA degree from Lawrence University and studied for four years in Princeton University's program in the History and Philosophy of Science. Prior to his employee benefits work, he taught philosophy at Duke University and the University of Wisconsin, Stevens Point. He is a member of the American Society of Pension Actuaries and a member of the American Academy of Actuaries. Bill serves as Consulting Actuary at EMJAY, where he also acts as business continuation planning coordinator. He is a co-author of the *401(k) Answer Book: Forms & Worksheets.*

LISA R. RICHARDSON serves as EMJAY's Associate Counsel. She received a law degree from the University of Minnesota Law School and was granted a Certified Employee Benefit Specialist (CEBS) designation from the International Foundation of Employee Benefit Plans and the Wharton School of the University of Pennsylvania.

Lisa is a member of the American and Wisconsin Bar Associations; the International Society of Certified Employee Benefit Specialists; the International Foundation of Employee Benefit Plans; and the Greater Milwaukee Employee Benefits Council. She has written numerous articles and conducted studies on a variety of employee benefit topics. She is a co-author of *Participant Directed Investment Answer Book.*

EMJAY Corporation, a Wells Fargo Company provides customized retirement planning solutions for plan sponsors and their participants throughout the United States. Located in Milwaukee, Wisconsin, EMJAY provides both bundled and unbundled services to assist employers with retirement strategies, including 401(k), profit sharing, money purchase, defined benefit, target, employee stock ownership, and new comparability plan needs. EMJAY administers more than 1,000 401(k) plans. EMJAY is a part of Wells Fargo's Institutional Trust Group. Wells Fargo is a diversified financial services company with more than $260 billion in employee benefit plan and institutional trust assets under administration serving 650,000 plan participants. Wells Fargo is among the 20 largest 401(k) providers in the country and was recently ranked #1 for client satisfaction.

How to Use This Book

The *401(k) Answer Book, 2000 Edition* is designed for professionals who need quick and authoritative answers to help them decide whether to install or continue a 401(k) plan, how to coordinate 401(k) plans with other plans, and how to comply with a vast number of federal requirements. This book uses straightforward language and avoids technical jargon whenever possible, but it also provides professionals with the tools to become conversant in the idiom of 401(k) plans. Citations to authority, particularly the Internal Revenue Code and its regulations, are provided as research aids for those who wish to pursue particular items in greater detail.

Format: The question-and-answer format breaks down complex subject areas into smaller segments. Introductory text provides an overview of the subject that is covered in detail in the questions and answers. Sample calculations furnish concrete aids to the decision-making process.

Numbering System: The questions are numbered consecutively within each chapter (e.g., Q 1:1, Q 1:2, Q 1:3).

Detailed List of Questions: The detailed List of Questions that follows the Table of Contents in the front of this book helps the reader to locate areas of immediate interest. This list serves as a detailed table of contents that provides both the question number and the page on which it appears.

Glossary: Because the pension area is replete with technical terms that have specific legal meaning, a special glossary, including abbreviations, follows the question-and-answer portion of this book.

Tables: Tables of all the regulatory source material referenced in the text and their appropriate question numbers have been included to facilitate easy access to the Internal Revenue Code; Treasury Regulations; ERISA and other federal statutes; cases; and miscellaneous agency rulings, opinions, and memoranda.

Index: At the back of this book is a comprehensive index.

Appendix A: Retirement Planning Tables: Retirement planning tables are included as an aid to determining income replacement ratios.

Appendix B: IRS Tables of Expected Return Multiples: Tables proscribed by the IRS for calculating minimum distributions are provided.

Use of Abbreviations: Because of the breadth of subject area, a number of terms and statutory references are abbreviated throughout the *401(k) Answer Book*. Among the most common of these short hand references are the following:

- COBRA—Consolidated Omnibus Budget Reconciliation Act of 1985, as amended
- Code or IRC—Internal Revenue Code of 1986, as amended (section references unless otherwise qualified refer to the IRC)
- DOL—U.S. Department of Labor
- ERISA—Employee Retirement Income Security Act of 1974, as amended
- IRRA—IRS Restructuring and Reform Act of 1998
- IRS—Internal Revenue Service
- PBGC—Pension Benefit Guaranty Corporation
- SBJPA—Small Business Job Protection Act of 1996
- TAMRA—Technical and Miscellaneous Revenue Act of 1988
- TRA '86—Tax Reform Act of 1986
- TRA '97—The Taxpayer Relief Act of 1997

For explanations of other abbreviations, please consult the Glossary.

Summary Table of Contents

Contents

Contents

Contents

List of Questions

l

1 Introduction

Over the last decade, 401(k) plans have evolved into one of the most popular employee benefits. A 401(k) plan may be a stand-alone plan or a feature of a profit sharing or stock bonus plan. When a 401(k) feature is incorporated into a plan, the plan is called a 401(k) plan or a cash or deferred arrangement (CODA). We will refer to such arrangements throughout this book as 401(k) plans. A 401(k) plan allows eligible employees the choice between receiving certain amounts in cash or directing the sponsoring employer to contribute these amounts to the qualified plan. Once contributed to the plan, these amounts are fully and immediately vested. However, distributions of these amounts are restricted by law. To retain its qualified status, the 401(k) plan must operate in a nondiscriminatory manner. In other words, the plan must not favor highly compensated over non-highly compensated employees. Rules relating to nondiscrimination will be discussed at length in chapters 9–12.

This chapter provides an overview of 401(k) plans, including their evolution, and pros and cons for employers and employees. We look at the extent to which 401(k) plans are used today and at the role of 401(k) plans as a benefit into the next century and summarize the impact of recent legislation.

HISTORY OF 401(k) PLANS

Q 1:1 What was the Internal Revenue Service's position on cash or deferred arrangements prior to the addition of Section 401(k) to the Internal Revenue Code?

Cash or deferred arrangements were a popular feature in profit sharing plans sponsored by a number of banks in the early to mid-1950s. Under this type of arrangement, an eligible employee could either elect to receive a portion of the profit sharing contribution in cash or to defer it in a profit sharing plan. The Internal Revenue Service (IRS) was somewhat wary of this arrangement but did issue some guidance in 1956. The IRS allowed for this arrangement if two requirements were met:

1. The participant made an irrevocable election to defer the profit sharing contribution before the close of the plan year for which the profit sharing contribution was made

2. More than half of the participants in the plan (who elected to defer) were among the lowest paid two thirds of all eligible employees.

[Rev Rul 56-497, 1956-2 CB 284]

The IRS later reaffirmed that this type of arrangement could be a qualified plan. Subsequently, it ruled that if such a plan met the nondiscrimination rules of Revenue Ruling 56-497, the deferred contributions would be exempt from the IRS doctrine of constructive receipt. [Rev Rul 63-180, 1963-2 CB 189] Further clarification of this position was issued in another revenue ruling in 1968. [Rev Rul 68-89, 1968-1 CB 402]

Despite these positive rulings, cash or deferred arrangements never became wildly popular. By the early 1970s, there were fewer than 1,000 plans in existence.

The IRS issued proposed regulations in 1972 that dramatically changed its previous position. Under the proposed regulations, salary reduction contributions would have been treated, for tax purposes, as if they had been received by the employee in cash. Although the regulations did not deal directly with the profit sharing deferral arrangements, they cast doubt on these arrangements. Conceptually, the IRS found it difficult to distinguish between the two types of deferrals.

Congress became concerned about the IRS stance in 1974. When Congress passed the Employee Retirement Income Security Act (ERISA), the act contained a provision that froze the existing tax status of cash or deferred arrangements until the end of 1976. Any such arrangements in existence on June 27, 1974, retained their tax-favored status. The moratorium was deferred twice, the last time until the end of 1979.

Q 1:2 How did the passage of Code Section 401(k) influence the growth of cash or deferred arrangements?

Congress followed up in 1978 when it passed the Revenue Act of 1978. Permanent provisions were added to the Internal Revenue Code, Section 401(k), effective for plan years beginning after December 31, 1979. The IRS issued proposed regulations in 1981 that sanctioned the use of salary reductions as a source of plan contributions. The floodgates were opened, as employers responded in 1982 with the adoption of new 401(k) plans and the conversion of existing thrift plans from after-tax contributions to pre-tax contributions.

The Tax Reform Act of 1984 (TRA '84) modified the rules for 401(k) plans in subtle ways. It eliminated the possibility of integrating 401(k) plans with Social Security. Nondiscrimination tests, which previously had been safe harbors, with an alternative of testing under the general qualified plan nondiscrimination rules, became mandatory. In addition, certain money purchase pension plans that allowed for salary reductions and were in existence before the passage of ERISA were grandfathered under this law.

Congress and the IRS became seriously concerned about the popularity of these plans in early 1986. The growth of 401(k) plans meant immediate revenue loss to the government, and many in government were concerned about the impact of 401(k) plans on the budget deficit. Some thought was given to repealing Code Section 401(k) entirely. Ultimately, in the Tax Reform Act of 1986 (TRA '86) Congress chose to tighten up the nondiscrimination rules and reduce the maximum annual amount that could be deferred in a 401(k) plan.

In 1991 the IRS issued final regulations that explain the statutory requirements of Section 401(k). These rules have changed very little since TRA '86. Subsequent chapters will deal with these regulations at length.

ADVANTAGES AND DISADVANTAGES OF 401(k) PLANS

Q 1:3 How does offering a 401(k) plan benefit the employer?

From the perspective of the sponsoring employer, there are a number of reasons to offer a 401(k) plan to employees. A 401(k) plan is a low-cost means of providing visible and appreciated retirement benefits to employees. It offers employees a real opportunity to participate actively in saving for retirement on a pre-tax basis. A sponsoring employer may use a 401(k) plan as its sole retirement plan or as a supplement to an existing plan. In larger organizations, a 401(k) plan is sometimes used to supplement an existing defined benefit plan.

For a cash-strapped employer, a 401(k) plan can help the employer address employee pressures for additional cash compensation without significant added cost and without jeopardizing employees' retirement income security. A matching contribution may provide the incentive for employees to save on a pre-tax basis. A discretionary match may be tied to company strategic compensation objectives. A 401(k) plan can also improve the participation and effectiveness of an existing thrift plan.

The plan may also be used as a vehicle to attract and retain qualified employees. To the extent the plan has discretionary employer contributions, the plan can be used to reward employees during years when the employer has reached its profitability objective. The

401(k) plan can improve morale and employee satisfaction, thereby improving productivity. If the 401(k) plan allows for the purchase of employer securities, this can increase an employee's sense of corporate identity.

Because of its inherent flexibility, the 401(k) plan can provide benefits to meet very different employee objectives. At little or no added cost, the 401(k) plan allows employees to take some responsibility for their own retirement savings.

For employers with existing retirement plans, a 401(k) plan can be a very attractive supplement. If an existing thrift plan is converted to a 401(k) plan, participation in the plan may be increased because employees now have an opportunity for pre-tax savings. To the extent that an employer is being pressured to increase benefit levels in a defined benefit plan, the addition of a 401(k) plan can be a low-cost substitute for benefit increases.

Q 1:4 How do competitive pressures motivate an employer to establish a 401(k) plan?

An employer operating in a highly competitive industry will be looking for a way to reduce costs to gain a competitive advantage. Such an employer may view the 401(k) plan as a vehicle for cost sharing, recognizing the need for employees to bear a portion of the cost of saving for their retirement.

In other cases, the benefit plans of competitors may be an employer's primary motivation for adopting a 401(k) plan. The design of a competitor's 401(k) plan can serve as the basis for incorporating features into a new 401(k) plan, including the level of match, the availability of investment options, loan and withdrawal features, and the frequency of reporting.

Q 1:5 What tax-related objectives may an employer have in establishing a 401(k) plan?

Some employers will set up a 401(k) plan with dual objectives: to provide employees with the opportunity for pre-tax deferral and the employers themselves with significant tax-deductible contributions. Such plans will generally set lower caps on deferral percentages to ensure that sufficient deductible employer contributions may be made and still meet the overall 15 percent of compensation contribution limit (see chapter 8).

Q 1:6 How can a 401(k) plan replace or supplement a defined benefit plan?

Employers with existing defined benefit plans may find that employees do not appreciate or understand the pension plan. Yet employers may be reluctant to terminate the plan out of concern for providing a minimum level of benefit security for their employees. The 401(k) plan in such a situation will need to be a highly visible plan. Attractive features such as a matching contribution, a wide range of investments, and loan or withdrawal options will help the plan to become more visible to employees. Frequent reports will also be an effective tool for maintaining the high profile of the 401(k) plan.

Employers with defined benefit plans may find their retirees dissatisfied with their current level of benefits. Cost-of-living adjustments can help to ease the concern of retirees, but significant benefit increases for existing employees may not be affordable. A 401(k) plan can be designed to supplement an existing defined benefit plan, with the employee and employer jointly bearing the cost.

Q 1:7 What type of employer is most likely to offer both a 401(k) and defined benefit plan?

According to a 1998 Buck Consultant's Study, *401(k) Plans—Survey Report on Plan Design,* organizations with larger employee populations are more likely to offer both plan types. Companies offering both a 401(k) plan and a defined benefit plan had, on average, twice as many employees as those offering only a 401(k) plan.

Q 1:8 Are there disadvantages to an employer in sponsoring a 401(k) plan?

The 401(k) plan does have some disadvantages from an employer's perspective. The administration of the plan can be costly and complex. Even larger employers who had previously maintained a staff to administer the plan are outsourcing functions to lower-cost providers. If the actual deferral percentage (ADP) test is not passed (as discussed in chapter 12), employee relations problems may result when highly compensated employees receive taxable refunds after the close of the plan year.

A 401(k) plan requires intensive communication throughout its life cycle. If the plan is not adequately communicated, the effectiveness of the 401(k) plan as an employee benefit will be lost. If the employer has an existing thrift plan, the communication must be carefully planned so that employees realize that the 401(k) plan is not a short-term capital accumulation vehicle.

Certain employers may find that the demographics of their employee base preclude the adoption of a 401(k) plan. In certain industries with high turnover, lower-paid employees may prefer cash. Since the success of a 401(k) plan is measured by the degree of participation of lower-paid employees, such a plan may be doomed to failure.

As plan sponsor, the employer must accept some fiduciary responsibility for the management of the plan and its assets. Though many plan functions can be delegated to others, the employer will inevitably be left with some responsibility (and corresponding potential liability) for the plan's operation.

Q 1:9 How does a 401(k) plan benefit employees?

From the employee's perspective, the 401(k) plan offers a unique opportunity to reduce current federal and state income taxes. The tax-sheltered aspects of the 401(k) plan make it an ideal vehicle for retirement savings. The ultimate tax paid by the employee may be lower, since the employee may find himself or herself in a lower bracket at retirement or when funds are withdrawn. In addition, the availability of special tax treatment (ten- and five-year income averaging and capital gains treatment) may also reduce the ultimate tax paid.

The 401(k) plan offers an employee a great deal of flexibility and choice: whether or not to defer, how much to defer, where to invest (if allowed by the plan), and when to change the deferral amount or investments. As an employee's circumstances change, different choices may be made. The availability of loans and hardship withdrawals means that invested funds can be used when personal financial circumstances change dramatically. The relative portability of a 401(k) plan allows an employee to change jobs without a significant loss in retirement benefits.

For an employee at a mid or high range of pay, the availability of deductible IRA contributions may be limited because of the existence of an employer's other qualified plan. The 401(k) plan will provide a very attractive option for deductible contributions through periodic savings.

Q 1:10 How may a 401(k) plan supplement an employee's personal savings program?

Employees covered by a qualified plan and at a middle range of pay may be precluded from making a deductible contribution to an IRA and so will find the 401(k) plan an attractive alternative. Even lower-paid employees will find the 401(k) plan an attractive and convenient means of saving through payroll deduction. In these types of plans, matching contributions may be low or non-existent—the primary objective is providing the opportunity for pre-tax savings.

Beginning in 1998, employees covered by a qualified plan may set up tax-sheltered Roth IRAs with joint income as high as $150,000 (see chapter 21).

Q 1:11 How is a 401(k) plan viewed by employees in a competitive environment?

In an era of global competition, layoffs can create tremendous pressure on households relying on dual incomes to maintain their lifestyles. If one spouse is laid off, the spouse who is currently employed will have a greater need for cash compensation and may be reluctant to commit any funds to a 401(k) plan. On the other hand, the presence of hardship withdrawal and loan features may provide the employee with the assurance that the funds are accessible in the event of financial difficulty.

Q 1:12 Are there disadvantages to an employee for participating in a 401(k) plan?

The employee may see some disadvantages in a 401(k) plan. Withdrawal rules will restrict access to funds before retirement or termination of employment. If funds are available before termination of employment, the 10 percent withdrawal penalty will significantly increase taxes on distribution. If the plan allows an employee to make investment choices, the employee may make poor ones and seriously undermine the value of retirement benefits in the 401(k) plan.

THE TAX POWER OF 401(k) PLANS

In considering whether to defer a portion of their current salaries in a 401(k) plan or similar program, employees must decide whether the deferral makes sense from a tax standpoint. If tax rates today are at their lowest point, does it make sense to defer today and pay more taxes tomorrow? The answer depends on a number of factors:

1. Rate of return on assets before taxes;

2. Rate of return on after-tax assets;

3. The increase in tax rates; and

4. The time at which tax rates will change.

This section analyzes different assumptions in demonstrating that tax deferral is generally the best alternative.

Q 1:13 In a stable tax environment, what are the advantages of accumulating money in a tax-deferred vehicle?

If tax rates remain stable or decline, it inevitably makes sense to accumulate money in a tax-deferred vehicle. Consider an employee who defers $2,000 per year for 20 years in a 401(k) plan or an IRA. The 20-year accumulation after taxes in the tax-deferred vehicle versus after-tax savings is shown below.

28 Percent Tax Bracket			
Interest Rate	*401(k) or Traditional IRA*	*After-Tax Savings*	*Difference*
6%	$ 52,971	$44,333	$ 8,638
8	65,897	51,625	14,272
10	82,476	60,339	22,137
12	103,756	70,760	32,996

Note. This table assumes that an individual is able to invest after-tax money as effectively as the 401(k) plan or IRA.

Q 1:14 Does it make sense to defer compensation in a rising tax environment?

Consider an employee who participates in a 401(k) plan and has an opportunity to receive a bonus currently or defer the bonus for a fixed number of years. Suppose the employee expects tax rates to rise from 33 percent to 50 percent in 15 years. Should the employee defer a bonus of $5,000 for 15 years?

The employee's alternatives are compared at interest rates of 6, 8, and 12 percent as follows.

At a 6 percent rate of return, there is little difference between after-tax savings and the 401(k) plan:

Year	401(k) Account	After-Tax Savings Account
0	$ 5,000	$3,350
15	$11,983	$6,051
Tax rate	50%	0%
After taxes	$ 5,991	$6,051
	Difference: $-60	

At 8 percent interest, the 401(k) plan is somewhat more favorable:

Year	401(k) Account	After-Tax Savings Account
0	$ 5,000	$3,350
15	$15,681	$7,331
Tax rate	50%	0%
After taxes	$ 7,930	$7,331
	Difference: $599	

At 12 percent interest, the 401(k) plan is clearly more favorable:

Year	401(k) Account	After-Tax Savings Account
0	$ 5,000	$ 3,350
15	$27,368	$10,686
Tax rate	50%	0%
After taxes	$13,684	$10,686
	Difference: $2,998	

The rate of return on tax-deferred savings is a critical element in determining whether it makes sense to defer money in a period when tax rates rise significantly.

Q 1:15 If an employee chooses to defer salary for a period of ten years, what impact will tax rate changes have?

The employee making a decision to defer a bonus for ten years may want to analyze whether it makes sense to defer if Congress raises tax rates at the end of ten years. Assuming that the employee is currently in a 33 percent tax bracket, tax rates would need to rise to the following levels to destroy the advantage of tax-deferred savings:

Earnings	Minimum Tax Bracket
6%	44.50%
8	47.70
10	50.60
12	53.35

If the employee is relatively pessimistic about future tax rates, a decision might be made to take the bonus currently.

Q 1:16 How does a 401(k) plan compare with an after-tax investment in a tax-deferred investment vehicle?

The comparison between a 401(k) plan and an after-tax investment is best illustrated by the following example.

Example. An employee who is 40 years old had the opportunity in 1991 to defer $8,475 in a 401(k) plan and would like to compare the after-tax accumulation (after 15 years) with a deferred annuity product. The employee is in the 33 percent tax bracket now, intends to retire at age 55, and anticipates that tax rates will increase to 40 percent after 10 years. The scheduled increase to the 401(k) limit is anticipated to rise at the rate of 4 percent per year.

Year	Tax Rate (Percentage)	401(k)	401(k) Accumulation	After-Tax Contribution	After-Tax Accumulation
1	33%	$ 8,475	$ 8,475	$ 5,678	$ 5,678
2	33	8,814	17,967	5,905	12,038
3	33	9,167	28,571	6,142	19,143
4	33	9,533	40,390	6,387	27,061
5	33	9,915	53,536	6,643	35,869
6	33	10,311	68,130	6,908	45,647
7	33	10,724	84,303	7,185	56,483
8	33	11,153	102,200	7,472	68,474
9	33	11,599	121,975	7,771	81,723
10	40	12,063	143,795	7,238	95,499
11	40	12,545	167,844	7,527	110,666
12	40	13,047	194,319	7,828	127,347
13	40	13,569	223,433	8,141	145,676
14	40	14,111	255,419	8,467	165,797
15	40	14,676	290,528	8,806	187,866
Total contribution:		$169,700		$108,098	
Total tax paid:			$116,211		$ 39,884
Available after tax		$174,317		$147,982	

Assumptions:
  Interest rate: 8%
  Annual cost of living adjustment: 4%

The accumulation in both plans is significant: $290,528 in the 401(k) plan versus $187,866 in the deferred annuity. If the employee retires at age 55 from the company, the 401(k) proceeds will not be subject to a 10 percent premature distribution tax. The accumulation of $290,528, if taken in a lump sum, will be subject to the 40 percent tax rate. The net available for the employee will be $174,317 after taxes.

On the other hand, if the employee puts the same amount (after tax) in a deferred annuity and withdraws the proceeds at age 55, the earnings will be subject to a 10 percent premature distribution tax. The total earnings of $79,768 will be subject to the 40 percent tax rate plus the 10 percent penalty rate. The net proceeds available to the employee from the deferred annuity will be $147,982, or $26,335 less than the amount available from the qualified plan.

All of the values in this example would be proportionately higher if the deferral were $10,000 instead of $8,475.

If the company makes a matching contribution to the 401(k) plan, the employee will be significantly further ahead by choosing to defer in the 401(k) plan.

Q 1:17 When might a company choose after-tax savings over a 401(k) plan?

In a small, closely held business, an owner may choose after-tax savings if the after-tax amount is greater than the amount that may be deferred in a 401(k) plan.

In the case of a larger business, an after-tax savings plan will make sense only if the 401(k) plan has poor participation and high administrative costs as a percentage of plan assets. Because of the significant economic advantages of accumulating funds in a tax-sheltered environment, it may make more sense to convince the employee group of the value of the 401(k) plan.

TYPES OF ENTITIES THAT MAY USE 401(k) PLANS

Q 1:18 What entities may adopt a 401(k) plan?

401(k) plans may be adopted by sole proprietorships, partnerships, limited liability companies (LLCs), or corporations (including

Subchapter S corporations). Beginning in 1987 and continuing through 1996, tax-exempt employers were not allowed to adopt 401(k) plans. Beginning in 1987, state and local governments or political subdivisions, agencies, or instrumentalities thereof, other than rural cooperatives, were not allowed to adopt 401(k) plans. A grandfather provision permits employers of tax-exempt entities or government units that maintained a 401(k) plan before 1986 to continue offering 401(k) plans to their current employees. [IRC § 401(k)(4)(B)]

Q 1:19 Can other types of cash or deferred arrangements be offered by governmental or tax-exempt employers?

Yes. Employees of the federal government can contribute to the Federal Thrift Savings Fund, which functions in many respects like a 401(k) cash or deferred arrangement. Employees of public schools or certain charitable or religious entities exempt from tax under Code Section 501(c)(3) may use individual salary reduction agreements to make contributions to an annuity contract (see chapter 21). [IRC §§ 402(g)(3)(C), 403(b)] Employees of state and local governments may be able to use similar salary reduction arrangements(see chapter 21). [IRC § 457]

Q 1:20 Will 401(k) be extended to government or tax-exempt employers?

The Small Business Job Protection Act of 1996 extended 401(k) plans to tax-exempt employers but not to government units. Government units often offer elective deferral of compensation to both employees and independent contractors through Section 457 plans (see chapter 21).

Q 1:21 What kinds of plans may offer a 401(k) feature?

Profit sharing plans, stock bonus plans (including ESOPs), rural cooperative plans, or pre-ERISA money purchase plans may include a 401(k) feature. [IRC § 401(k)(1); Treas Reg § 1.401(k)-1(a)(1)] Defined benefit plans or post-ERISA target or money purchase plans may not contain a 401(k) feature.

WHEN A 401(k) PLAN IS APPROPRIATE

Q 1:22 Does it make economic sense for a small business owner to establish or continue a qualified plan?

A plan design that will maximize the owner's portion of the total plan cost will also maximize the long-term effectiveness of the plan for a small, closely held business. Consider this case study in the following example.

Example. An owner of a small company with three employees set up a profit sharing plan several years ago when the maximum tax bracket was 50 percent. Now that tax rates have declined to 33 percent, the owner is wondering whether it makes sense to continue making tax-deductible contributions to the profit sharing plan.

The current profit sharing plan calls for employees to receive a pro rata share of the contribution based on their compensation. Last year, the company contributed 15 percent of pay to the plan and paid $3,500 in administrative fees:

Employee	Compensation	Contribution
Owner	$150,000	$22,500
B	30,000	4,500
C	20,000	3,000
	$200,000	$30,000

The total cost of the plan is $33,500 ($30,000 in contributions plus $3,500 in administrative fees), $22,500 of which is credited to the owner of the company.

If the owner had dissolved the profit sharing plan and taken a bonus of $33,500 instead, a net after-tax amount of $22,445 would have been available, or approximately the same amount as was deferred in the qualified plan for the owner.

Q 1:23　Are 401(k) plans appropriate for unincorporated businesses?

Yes. Unincorporated businesses may use 401(k) plans as a benefit program for employees. The calculations involved are more difficult, since the compensation of the self-employed individual (either a sole proprietor or partner) is reduced by the contributions made on behalf of common-law employees. Also, the self-employed individual's compensation must be reduced by one half of the Social Security contribution (SECA deduction).

Q 1:24　When is a 401(k) plan appropriate for a sole proprietorship?

A 401(k) plan is not a viable alternative unless the business has common-law employees. If there are no common-law employees, the sole proprietor need not have a 401(k) plan. A profit sharing, money purchase, or defined benefit plan will be a better option because in these a sole proprietor can control how much cash compensation is taken and how much can be deferred. Alternate plan designs will allow the sole proprietor the opportunity to defer far more than $10,000 (the 1999 deferral cap, adjusted for inflation, of a 401(k) plan). Based on the objectives of the sole proprietor, the following table indicates the appropriate design.

Objective	Plan Design
Up to 15% of pay, or $22,500	Profit sharing plan
Up to 25% of pay, or $30,000 (fixed commitment)	Money purchase plan
Greater than 25% of pay (depends on age of individual) (fixed commitment)	Defined benefit plan

Q 1:25　What are the considerations in designing a 401(k) plan for a partnership?

Complex rules govern partnerships that adopt 401(k) plans. In fact, the final regulations under Code Section 401(k) require that any plan that directly or indirectly permits a partner to vary the amount of contributions on his or her behalf will be considered a cash or deferred arrangement. The implications for a partnership are quite significant:

1. The annual contribution for each partner is subject to the 401(k) deferral cap of $10,000 (in 1999).

2. Until plan years beginning after December 30, 1997, matching contributions on behalf of each partner are treated as elective deferrals, subject to the 1999 deferral cap of $10,000 and non-discrimination testing.

3. Nondiscrimination testing must be performed.

4. Each partner must be 100 percent vested.

Thus, in designing a plan for a partnership, it is critical that the partners decide whether contributions should be variable for each partner. If contributions will be variable, a 401(k) plan is the only design available, with the resulting reduction in total contributions allocable to the partners.

Q 1:26 Can a limited liability company sponsor a 401(k) plan?

Yes. A limited liability company (LLC) is a business that operates with the flexibility and informality of a partnership and yet retains the personal liability protection associated with corporation share-holder interests. An LLC is designed to be taxed as a partner-ship. Members of the LLC (equivalent of partners or shareholders) receive and are taxed on company profits as earned income in the same manner as partners. For 401(k) plan purposes, "members" are treated like partners and nonmembers are treated like partner-ship employees.

Q 1:27 What are the 401(k) design considerations for a small or professional business?

Most qualified plans designed for small businesses (fewer than 20 employees) and professional firms (e.g., attorneys, accountants, engineers, physicians) will be top heavy (i.e., more than 60 percent of the benefits of the plan will be attributable to key employ-ees—see chapter 13). The impact of top heaviness on a 401(k) plan may be significant, since top-heavy minimum contributions may be required for non-key employees. Thus, the plan design should

take into account the fact that fixed employer contributions ranging from 3 percent to 7.5 percent of pay for non-key employees
may be required.

Beginning in 1997, 401(k) plans can avoid the top-heavy requirements if they qualify as SIMPLE 401(k) plans (see chapter 2).

MULTIEMPLOYER 401(k) PLANS

The terms of a collective bargaining agreement may call for the
establishment or maintenance of a 401(k) plan. If more than one
employer is required to contribute to the plan, it is treated as a multiemployer plan. The following section discusses design considerations for multiemployer 401(k) plans.

Negotiated 401(k) plans are generally started for one of two reasons: as a replacement for a terminating defined benefit plan or as a
supplement to an existing plan. The design features may be quite
different, depending on the reasons behind the start-up of the plan.

Q 1:28 Why do multiemployer units consider 401(k) plans?

Multiemployer defined benefit plans lost favor after Congress
passed the Multiemployer Pension Plan Amendments Act (MPPAA)
in 1980. A major drawback of the defined benefit approach was
its withdrawal liability feature: an individual employer attempting to withdraw from a multiemployer defined benefit plan would
be assessed a single sum withdrawal charge equal to the individual employer's pro rata share of the unfunded liability. This
made withdrawal from an underfunded plan expensive for an
employer and discouraged new employers from joining a multiemployer plan.

Favorable investment performance for many defined benefit plans
in the mid-1980s caused a number of plans to become well funded,
which encouraged the unions to request benefit increases. However,
employers were reluctant to grant increases because they feared
potential withdrawal liability. This left the union, the employers,
and the membership in a difficult situation. In many cases, this was
resolved by terminating the defined benefit plan and replacing it
with a defined contribution plan.

Q 1:29 In replacing a defined benefit plan, how is the 401(k) plan structured?

The replacement plan often is a profit sharing plan with a 401(k) feature attached to it. The primary emphasis is on replacing benefits lost by the termination of the defined benefit plan. Employer contributions are emphasized, and employee elective contributions are intended merely to supplement the retirement benefits provided by the terminated defined benefit plan and the new profit sharing plan.

Q 1:30 How is a supplemental 401(k) plan structured?

When a multiemployer group institutes a 401(k) plan as a supplement to an existing defined benefit plan, there is much less emphasis on employer contributions. Typically, employers are not interested in making any contributions at all to the 401(k) plan. When employer contributions are made, a common arrangement is that an employer will agree to contribute "x" cents per hour, and this money will be pooled. At the end of the year, the pooled money will be used to match a portion of the deferrals for each contributing employee.

Q 1:31 What design and administration features are unique to a multiemployer 401(k) plan?

There are a number of unique design and administrative features in a multiemployer 401(k) plan:

1. Nondiscrimination testing is performed on a planwide basis, making it critical that each employer provide accurate information relative to the plan members who are highly compensated.

2. The mobility of collectively bargained employees in certain industries, such as construction, makes the administration of the plan quite difficult. In a single-employer environment, these employees are simply considered to have terminated employment. In a multiemployer environment, the employees continue to be eligible and earn vesting credit.

3. Investment options may be designed to allow "socially responsible" investing; i.e., "union only" funds may be an option.

4. The collective bargaining agreement will specify the individual employer as responsible for administrative tasks, such as

maintaining employee deferral elections, withholding contributions, and forwarding contributions to the plan trustees.

5. Although delinquencies do not have an impact on an employee's benefit in a defined benefit plan, they are of critical importance in a 401(k) plan. Also, delinquencies are more likely
to occur in a multiemployer environment.

6. The handling of start-up costs may be difficult; in some
cases, the union may borrow money from the bank to cover
start-up costs.

Note: If start-up costs are deducted from trust assets, the rate of
return on investments in the first year may be negative or extremely low, creating a negative impression of the 401(k) plan on
the participants.

UTILIZATION OF 401(k) PLANS

This section deals with the use of 401(k) plans as employee benefit plans by large and small employers throughout the country.

Q 1:32 Overall, what percentage of companies in the United States offer 401(k) plans?

According to a 1998 survey conducted by the Spectrem Group for
the Society of Professional Administrators and Record Keepers
(SPARK), the percentage of companies offering 401(k) plans varies
with company size.

Number of Employees	Percentage with a 401(k) Plan
Fewer than 50	11%
50–100	28
100–500	34
500–1,000	70
1,000–5,000	81
More than 5,000	93

Q 1:33 What are the participation rates in 401(k) plans?

According to a 1997 survey by Hewitt Associates, LLC, *Survey Findings: 401(k) Trends and Experience,* average participation rates in 401(k) plans have risen from 75 percent in 1993 to 79 percent in 1997. Average participation rates may vary by plan size.

Number of Eligible Employees	Average Participation Rate
Fewer than 500	83%
500–999	86
1,000–4,999	80
5,000–9,999	78
10,000–14,999	74
15,000 or more	72

The average participation rate for salaried employees is 82 percent, compared with 79 percent for employees generally.

Q 1:34 Does the fact that a 401(k) plan offers a matching employer contribution noticeably affect 401(k) participation?

Yes. The Hewitt survey (see Q 1:33) shows much higher participation when a matching contribution is provided. Generally, participation rates were 62 percent in plans with no match and 80 percent in plans with a match. As is apparent from the following table, it is the existence of a match at all, and not the level of the match, that most heavily influences participation rates.

Match Level	Average Participation Rate
No match	62%
Any match	80
$0.25	75
$0.50	80
$1.00	84
Graded match	81
Based on length of service	85
Based on company performance	81

FUTURE OF 401(k) PLANS

What does the future hold for 401(k) plans? Will they continue to be a popular employee benefit? Will they eventually replace defined benefit plans as the primary employer-sponsored retirement plan vehicle? Will 401(k) plans become available to all employees? By looking at various trends—legislative, economic, and demographic—it is possible to make some reasonable guesses about 401(k) plans in the future.

Q 1:35 What demographic trends will affect 401(k) plans?

The workforce of the 1990s is vastly different from that of earlier decades. More women and minorities are present, with greater needs for flexible schedules and benefits. The workforce is aging, and with increased age comes an increased cost in benefits, particularly in health and defined benefit plans. The increased life expectancy of the average retiree has staggering implications in terms of future health care costs.

The workforce of the 1990s requires more active involvement in its benefit plans. Employees want more choice, and a greater percentage than ever before feel that they must bear a portion of the responsibility for providing retirement benefits for themselves. Few employees expect Social Security to be a major source of their retirement income. In fact, nearly one quarter of employees recently surveyed felt that Social Security would not be a factor at all.

Q 1:36 What economic trends will affect 401(k) plans?

The debate about health care costs and reform is forcing many employers to reevaluate their employee benefits. There is a great push to control costs and increase the bottom line while at the same time increasing productivity. Any means of leveraging employee benefits for financial gain will be a possibility for financially strapped companies: cost sharing by employees, reduction of benefits, and consolidation of retirement plans.

One important event in the early 1990s was the decline of certain insurance companies, including Executive Life and Mutual Benefit Life. Large numbers of 401(k) sponsors had money invested in the guaranteed insurance contracts of these companies. Although many plan sponsors have taken steps to ensure that participants will not lose money by replacing the lost dollars with additional contributions, the faith of plan participants in guaranteed investments has been seriously undermined.

Because of the favorable growth in the equity markets historically, the investment trend of the future should be more equity oriented. According to the Hewitt Survey (see Q 1:33) the percentage of plan assets invested in money market funds dropped from 25 percent in 1995 to 8 percent in 1997, while the percentage invested in equity index funds rose from 10 percent to 17 percent during that same period.

Q 1:37 What are the prospects for 401(k) plans?

With the publicity surrounding 401(k) plans and increased interest in sharing the responsibility for providing retirement benefits, employees of companies who do not sponsor a 401(k) plan will be clamoring for the addition of this plan to the benefits package. To the extent that the maximum 401(k) deferrals remain greater than IRA contributions, middle- and high-income employees will prefer 401(k) plans. Also, the relative availability of funds in a 401(k) plan through hardship withdrawals and loans makes the 401(k) plan an attractive alternative to an IRA.

Congress has recognized the need to simplify the retirement plan rules and to some extent has done so in the Small Business Job Protection Act of 1996 (discussed below). With simplicity will come less flexibility. The availability of special tax treatment on lump-sum distributions will disappear entirely.

The widespread popularity of 401(k) plans has greatly increased the interest of financial institutions in capturing these benefit dollars. The competition for dollars will increase, driving down the cost of administration, as many financial institutions subsidize administrative costs in their full service packages. Larger companies will try to outsource their benefits administration, as they critically evaluate the dollars spent for benefits.

Two other employee benefit programs, health insurance and defined benefit plans, will be competing with 401(k) plans for employers' benefit dollars. Health care costs for active employees and retirees will be steadily rising. As the baby boomer generation matures, the demand for defined benefit plans may start to rise and a resurgence of defined benefit plans could occur, for both the small and medium-sized employer.

Q 1:38 How has recent legislation affected 401(k) plans?

The trend of overall pension policy over the last decade has been to expand the availability of retirement plans to the workforce. Pension policy, in general, is that the federal government should not subsidize pensions for highly paid employees, and that if highly paid employees are covered, then a fair number of lower-paid employees must also be covered. The Tax Reform Act of 1986 (TRA '86) played a large role by tightening nondiscrimination standards, thus requiring more lower-paid employees to be benefited by employer-sponsored plans. When faster vesting is required, more employees become eligible for retirement plan benefits and expanded coverage is achieved.

The federal deficit will have a major impact on pension policy over the next decade. As legislators look for additional sources of revenue, the traditional tax-exempt status of qualified plans may be threatened. The concepts discussed include a flat income tax system, a trading tax, limited deductibility of pension contributions for employers, and an annual tax on retirement plan earnings. Although these may be viewed as viable short-term mechanisms for reducing the deficit, care must be taken to ensure that plan sponsors are not motivated to terminate their qualified plans. This would have the disastrous effect of reducing the retirement benefit security of employees in their retirement plans.

Until this past year, Congress has done little to encourage the continuation of defined benefit plans over the last decade. Increased complexity in the form of Omnibus Budget Reconciliation Acts of 1989 and 1990 (OBRA '89 and OBRA '90) has made plans more costly to administer. The increase in the reversion tax from 0 percent to 15 percent to a maximum now of 50 percent has made it more difficult to terminate defined benefit plans. The increase in the Pension Benefit Guaranty Corporation (PBGC) premiums from $1 per participant after the passage of ERISA in 1974 to an unlimited amount per participant has greatly reduced the attractiveness of these plans. For underfunded defined benefit plans, a potential additional premium of $53 or more per participant has caused many plan sponsors to cease future accruals and look to defined contribution plans as a source of future retirement funds for their employees. Though Congress is currently looking at ways to simplify defined benefit plans, the cost structure of these plans is likely to continue to limit their broad use by employers.

SMALL BUSINESS JOB PROTECTION ACT OF 1996 (SBJPA)

The Small Business Job Protection Act of 1996 (SBJPA) was signed into law by President Clinton on August 20, 1996. Subtitle D, Pension Simplification, contains a long list of provisions that will cumulatively have significant impact on the administration of 401(k) and other qualified plans for both large and small employers. SBJPA also contains increases in the minimum wage, which dominated discussion of the act in the popular press.

Q 1:39 How does SBJPA affect 401(k) plan distributions?

- Five-year income averaging for lump-sum distributions is repealed effective with taxable years beginning after December 31, 1999 (see chapter 15).

- The $5,000 exclusion of employees' death benefits is repealed for deaths after the date of enactment.

- A simplified method for taxing annuity distributions has been introduced.

- For non-5 percent owners, distributions can be delayed beyond age 70½ until actual retirement (see chapter 15).

- The minimum period for joint and survivor explanations before benefit commencement is reduced to seven days (see chapter 16).

- For limitation years beginning after December 31, 1999, the Section 415(e) combined plan limitation is repealed (see chapter 8).

- For distributions during 1997 through 1999, the tax on excess distributions (under Section 4980A) will not apply. (TRA '97 later repealed this tax entirely.)

Q 1:40 What salary deferral options did SBJPA introduce that do not require extensive nondiscrimination testing?

- SIMPLE IRA plans for employers with no more than 100 employees earning at least $5,000 for the prior year (see chapter 21)

- SIMPLE 401(k) plans for employers with no more than 100 employees earning at least $5,000 for the prior year (see chapter 2)

- Safe harbor formulas for 401(k) plans of any sponsor but not available until plan years beginning after December 31, 1998 (see chapter 2)

Q 1:41 How does SBJPA simplify the qualification and administration of 401(k) plans?

- Tax-exempt organizations and Indian tribal governments (but not other governmental bodies) are now eligible to sponsor 401(k) plans.

- The definition of *highly compensated employee* has been greatly simplified and the family aggregation rules have been repealed (see chapter 9).

- The 50 participant/40 percent participation rule no longer applies to 401(k) (or other defined contribution) plans (see chapter 10).

- An employer may choose to use prior year non-highly compensated employee data when performing the ADP and actual contribution percentage (ACP) tests, and the distribution of any excess contributions to highly compensated employees is now based on the amount of contributions rather than on deferral and contribution percentages (see chapter 12).

- Effective for years beginning after December 31, 1997, compensation for Code Section 415 shall include Section 401(k) deferrals, Section 125 salary reductions, and Section 457 deferrals (see chapter 8).

- The criterion for being a leased employee is changed from "duties historically performed" to "duties performed under the primary direction of or controlled by the recipient" (see chapter 9).

- Effective for plan years beginning after December 31, 1998, the ADP and ACP tests may exclude entirely non-highly compensated employees who have not met the minimum age and service participation requirements (see chapter 12).

Q 1:42 When must plan amendments required by SBJPA be adopted?

Amendments to plans required by SBJPA need not be made before the first day of the plan year beginning on or after January 1, 2000, provided that the plan is operated in accordance with the act before the enactment of the amendments and that such amendments, when made, apply retroactively as required by the act. [SBJPA § 1456; IRS Notice 99-11, 1999-8 IRB 56]

TAXPAYER RELIEF ACT OF 1997 (TRA '97)

On August 5, 1997, President Clinton signed into law the Taxpayer Relief Act of 1997 (TRA '97). Many of the provisions of this act are relevant to the issues discussed in this book. These provisions are summarized below and are also reflected throughout the book. Although in some cases these changes simplify plan administration or retirement planning for participants, many of the changes complicate planning by creating new options that must be taken into account.

Q 1:43 What changes did TRA '97 make to the IRA rules?

- *Penalty-free withdrawals can be made from individual retirement plans for higher education expenses.* Distributions from IRAs after December 31, 1997, for qualified higher education expenses that are incurred and paid after that date are exempt from the 10 percent additional tax on early distributions. Such education may be furnished to the taxpayer, the taxpayer's spouse, or the taxpayer's child or grandchild.

- *Education individual retirement accounts were created.* For taxable years beginning after December 31, 1997, up to $500 per year may be contributed to an education IRA for a named beneficiary. Although the contribution is made with after-tax money, no tax need be paid upon distributions for qualified higher education expenses for the named beneficiary provided the contributor's gross adjusted income does not exceed $95,000 ($150,000 if filing jointly). Such Education IRAs are completely separate from IRAs intended to provide retirement benefits.

- *Restoration of IRA deduction for certain taxpayers.* For taxable years beginning after December 31, 1997, IRA deductions are restored in two cases:

  1. An individual who is not an active participant in a retirement plan but whose spouse is an active participant will be able to fully deduct IRA contributions until joint income reaches $150,000.

  2. For an active participant in a retirement plan, the salary limit at which IRA deductibility phases out will increase according to the following schedule:

Year	Married Filing Joint Return	Unmarried Filing Individual Return
1998	$50,000	$30,000
1999	51,000	31,000
2000	52,000	32,000
2001	53,000	33,000
2002	54,000	34,000
2003	60,000	40,000
2004	65,000	45,000
2005	70,000	50,000
2006	75,000	50,000
2007	80,000	50,000

- *Establishment of nondeductible tax-free individual retirement accounts.* For taxable years beginning after December 31, 1997, taxpayers may establish Roth IRAs with after-tax dollars— qualifying distributions from Roth IRAs will be tax-free and exempt from the 10 percent early distribution tax (see chapter 21).

- *Distributions from certain IRAs may be used without penalty to purchase first homes.* Effective for payments and distributions in 1998 or later, IRA distributions up to a lifetime limit of $10,000 used to purchase a first home of the IRA owner, his or her spouse, or the child, grandchild, or ancestor of the owner or owner's spouse will be exempt from the 10 percent early distribution tax.

- *Certain bullion not treated as collectibles.* Beginning in 1998, IRAs may invest in gold, silver, or platinum U.S. coins and may invest in gold, silver, platinum, or palladium bullion of a fineness required for metals which may be delivered in satisfaction of a regulated futures contract.

Q 1:44 What changes did TRA '97 make to income and excise taxes that may affect 401(k) plans?

- *Maximum capital gains rates for individuals lowered.* Generally, the capital gains rate has been reduced from 28 percent to 20 percent for assets held at least 18 months. The reduced capital gains rate does not apply to sales of collectibles. Note, however, that distributions from 401(k) plans and IRAs are typically not eligible for capital gains treatment. A portion of a lump-sum distribution from a qualified plan is treated as a capital gain for those born before January 1, 1936, but it was already eligible for a grandfathered rate of 20 percent. Beginning in 2001, the capital gains rate for assets held at least five years is scheduled to reduce to 18 percent.

- *Cost-of-living adjustments relating to estate and gift tax provisions.* Beginning in 1998, the $600,000 exclusion amount used to calculate estate taxes will gradually increase, reaching $1,000,000 in 2006. Beginning in 1999, the $10,000 gift tax exclusion will be indexed for inflation increases in minimum $1,000 amounts. These changes should be taken into account by 401(k) plan participants as they plan for the distribution of their retirement plan benefits.

- *Repeal of excess distribution and excess retirement accumulation tax.* For distributions received in 1997 or later and for

decedents dying in 1997 or later, the 15 percent excess distribution and excess retirement accumulation taxes are repealed.
The excess distribution tax had already been waived by SBJPA
for tax years 1997 through 1999.

- *Increase in tax on prohibited transactions.* Effective for prohibited transactions occurring after August 5, 1997, the first-tier
  excise tax to be paid by any disqualified person participating
  in the prohibited transaction is increased from 10 percent to 15
  percent of the amount involved.

- *Basis recovery rules for annuities over more than one life.* Effective for annuity starting dates in 1998 or later, the number of
  anticipated payments where a monthly annuity is payable over
  more than one life is determined as follows, depending on the
  combined age of the annuitants:

Combined Age	Anticipated Payments
Not over 110	410 payments
Over 110 but not over 120	360 payments
Over 120 but not over 130	310 payments
Over 130 but not over 140	260 payments
Over 140	210 payments

- *Modification of 10 percent tax for nondeductible contributions.*
  Effective for taxable years beginning after December 31, 1997,
  an employer maintaining defined benefit and defined contribution plans that cover the same employees will not be subject to
  the 10 percent excise tax on nondeductible contributions so
  long as the contributions to the defined contribution plans do
  not exceed the greater of 6 percent of compensation or the sum
  of matching contributions and elective deferrals. Previous law
  provided an exception only up to 6 percent of compensation.

Q 1:45 What changes did TRA '97 make to 401(k) nondiscrimination rules?

- *Matching contributions of self-employed individuals not treated
  as elective employer contributions.* Prior to this change, such

matching contributions were treated by the IRS as elective contributions that counted against the elective deferral limit. This is especially relevant to partners sponsoring 401(k) plans (see Q 2:30). This change applies both to 401(k) plans and to SIMPLE IRA plans. In the case of 401(k) plans, the change is effective for plan years beginning after December 31, 1997. For SIMPLE IRA plans, the change is effective for years beginning after December 31, 1996.

- *Modification of 403(b) exclusion allowance to conform to 415 modifications.* Effective for years beginning after December 31, 1997, includible compensation under Section 403(b) plans includes all elective deferrals (per Section 402(g)(3) or Section 457) and any Section 125 contributions or deferrals. Also, the repeal of the 1.0 rule of Section 415(e), scheduled to take effect for years beginning after December 31, 1999, is extended to 403(b) plans.

- *Extension of moratorium on application of certain nondiscrimination rules to state and local governments.* The moratorium applying the following nondiscrimination rules to qualified retirement plans of state and local governments has been extended indefinitely:
  - Nondiscrimination requirements of Section 401(a)(4)
  - Minimum participation requirements of Section 401(a)(26)(H)
  - Minimum participation and coverage standards of Section 410
  - Cash or deferred arrangement participation and discrimination standards of Section 401(k)(3)
  - For tax-sheltered annuities, the nondiscrimination rules of Section 403(b)(12)

This change is effective August 5, 1997 and also retroactively for all taxable years before that date.

Q 1:46 What other TRA '97 changes impact 401(k) plans?

- *Pension accrued benefit distributable without consent increased to $5,000.* Effective for plan years beginning after August 5, 1997, a plan may provide for the lump sum cash-out of any participant whose vested accrued benefit does not exceed $5,000 without the consent of either the participant or the spouse. This is an increase from a limit of $3,500. This will benefit participants desiring lump-sum payments since it will cut significantly the paperwork and time delay needed to obtain a distribution.

- *Clarification of certain rules relating to employee stock ownership plans of S Corporations.* SBJPA extended to S Corporations the right to establish ESOPs. This section clarifies the application of a number of ESOP rules as they apply to plans sponsored by S Corporations. The section is effective for taxable years beginning after December 31, 1997.

- *Modification of prohibition of assignment or alienation.* Effective for judgments, orders, decrees, and settlement agreements on or after August 5, 1997, a participant's benefit under a qualified retirement plan may be offset under a judgment of conviction of a crime involving the plan or under judgments or settlements involving fiduciary violations in regard to the plan.

- *Elimination of paperwork burdens on plans.* Effective August 5, 1997, qualified plan administrators no longer need file with the DOL (unless requested) summary plan descriptions, plan descriptions, or summaries of modifications and changes. There is no change in the requirements that such documents be provided to plan participants. DOL filings are to cease immediately as of this date even if the event giving rise to the filing occurred before August 5, 1997.

- *Clarification of disqualification rules relating to acceptance of rollover contributions.* In order for the administrator of a plan receiving rollover contributions to reasonably conclude that the contribution is a valid rollover contribution, it shall not be necessary under IRS regulations for the distributing plan to have a determination letter from the IRS.

- *New technologies in retirement plans.* Not later than December 31, 1998, the IRS and DOL are directed to clarify the extent to which writing requirements for retirement plans may permit paperless transactions. Any final regulations shall not be effective until the first plan year beginning at least six months after the issuance of such final regulations. The IRS did release a notice of proposed rulemaking on this issue in December of 1998.

- *Diversification of Section 401(k) plan investments.* The ERISA

Section 407(a) rule that not more than 10 percent of the fair market value of plan assets may be employer securities and employer real property is extended to apply to non-ESOP elective deferrals (and allocable earnings) treated as a separate plan whenever the elective deferrals are required to be invested in employer securities or employer real property unless either the fair market value of all individual account plans maintained by the employer is no more than 10 percent of the fair market value of the assets of all retirement plans maintained by the employer, or the required investment for any year does not exceed 1 percent of any employee's compensation considered for elective deferrals. This extension applies to elective deferrals for plan years beginning after December 31, 1998.

IRS RESTRUCTURING AND REFORM ACT OF 1998 (IRRA)

On July 22, 1998, President Clinton signed into law the IRS Restructuring and Reform Act of 1998 (IRRA). In addition to its provisions relating to reform of the IRS, the act also contains a number of technical corrections and a few substantive changes dealing with retirement plans.

Q 1:47 What are the retirement plan related sections of the IRS Restructuring and Reform Act of 1998?

Section 3411(b). Extension of confidentiality privilege to non-attorneys. Effective with the enactment of IRRA, the privilege of confidentiality to tax advice is extended to any individual authorized under federal law to practice before the IRS (in addition to attorneys this could include certified public accountants, enrolled agents, and enrolled actuaries). The privilege may be asserted only in noncriminal tax proceedings before the IRS or in noncriminal tax proceedings in the federal courts where the IRS is a party to the proceedings.

The privilege applies only if the communication would be privileged between a taxpayer and an attorney—for example, information disclosed to an attorney for the purpose of preparing a tax return would not be privileged under present law. The privilege may not be asserted to prevent the disclosure of information to any other body than the IRS. The privilege does not extend to information that could be obtained by other means. If information is disclosed by the practitioner to a third party the privilege for that communication is considered to be waived. Also communication with respect to the participation of a corporation in a Code Section 6662(d)(2)(C)(iii) *tax shelter* is not privileged. (Such a *tax shelter* is defined to be any partnership, entity, plan, or arrangement a significant purpose of which is the avoidance or evasion of federal income tax.)

It is not clear whether this privilege applies to practitioner work-product, accountant's opinions on taxpayers financial statements, audit workpapers, or routine work involved in the adoption and administration of a retirement plan.

Section 3436(b). Distributions on account of an IRS levy. Effective for levies made after December 31, 1999, IRRA exempts distributions on account of an IRS levy on a retirement plan or IRA from the 10 percent tax on early withdrawals. However, this exemption does not apply to distributions made to make payments to the IRS when an IRS levy has not been made even if the payment is made to avoid a levy or to lift a levy on some other property.

Section 5001(a). Elimination of the 18-month holding period for capital gains. Effective for tax years after December 31, 1997, IRRA eliminates the 18-month holding period to qualify for the lowest capital gains rate, replacing it with the more traditional 12-month period. For taxpayers nearing retirement this may diminish somewhat the appeal of tax deferred savings via 401(k) plans versus aftertax savings whose earnings could now more easily qualify for capital gains treatment.

Section 6005(a). Adjusted gross income (AGI) phase-out range for deductible IRAs. Effective for IRAs established in 1998, deductible traditional IRAs phase out for active plan participants with AGIs ranging from $50,000–$60,000 (with the range gradually increasing to $80,000–$100,000 by 2007). IRRA clarifies that the phase-out for an active participant's spouse (who is not also an active participant) is joint AGI ranging from $150,000–$160,000.

Section 6005(b)(2). AGI conversion limit for Roth IRAs. Effective for tax years after December 31, 1997, IRRA clarifies that the

$100,000 AGI limit for conversions to Roth IRAs excludes the distribution of the converted amounts (though those amounts are included in AGI for tax payment purposes). IRRA also provides that this AGI conversion limit is not to include any deductible IRA contributions made during the year. See also the description of Section 7004(a) below.

Sections 6005(b)(3) and 6005(b)(5). Five-year holding period for Roth IRAs and distribution ordering rules. Effective for tax years beginning after December 31, 1997, IRRA establishes that there is only one five-year holding period for all Roth IRAs owned by a single taxpayer. In order for distributions from Roth IRAs to be excludable from taxes, the distribution must be made after this five-year holding period as well as satisfy other conditions.

IRRA also provides that if a distribution is made from a Roth IRA during this five-year holding period and the Roth IRA contained both contributions and conversion amounts, the distribution is to be treated as coming first from original Roth IRA contribution amounts, then from conversion amounts (in the order converted and beginning with amounts already includible in income), and last from earnings. For purposes of these ordering rules, all Roth IRAs, whether or not maintained in separate accounts, will be considered a single Roth IRA. Any conversion amounts thus withdrawn will be subject to the 10 percent early withdrawal penalty unless one of the exceptions under Section 72(t) applies (e.g., over age 59½).

Under these rules, recordkeeping for Roth IRAs will be much simpler if conversion amounts and original Roth IRA contribution amounts are not placed in the same Roth IRA account. This closes retroactively the loophole whereby the 10 percent early withdrawal tax on eligible rollover distributions could be avoided by rolling into a traditional IRA, converting to a Roth IRA, and then immediately withdrawing the converted amount.

Section 6005(b)(4). Four-year averaging for 1998 Roth IRA conversions. According to the Taxpayer Relief Act of 1997 (TRA '97), distributions during 1998 from traditional IRAs that were converted into Roth IRAs would be included in income ratably over the four-year period beginning with 1998. IRRA allows taxpayers to elect to include all of this income in 1998. Such an election may not be changed after the due date of the 1998 tax return. If no election is made, the income shall be averaged over four years.

IRRA also provides that if a distribution is made from the Roth IRA before the end of this four-year averaging period, the recognition of income must be accelerated. However, if the Roth IRA owner dies within the four-year period and the beneficiary of the Roth IRA is the owner's spouse, the spouse may elect to continue the Roth IRA and to recognize income according to the four-year schedule. If a partial withdrawal is made from the Roth IRA before the fourth year, the withdrawal must be included in income in addition to the amount already scheduled for inclusion (though the total included that year shall not exceed the remaining amount of the Roth IRA to be included).

> **Example.** Taxpayer Arnold has a nondeductible IRA with a value of $100 (and no other IRAs). The $100 consists of $75 of contributions and $25 of earnings. Arnold converts the IRA into a Roth IRA in 1998 and elects the four-year spread. As a result of the conversion, $25 is includible in income ratably over 4 years ($6.25 per year). The 10 percent early withdrawal tax does not apply to the conversion. At the beginning of 1999, the value of the account is $110, and Arnold makes a withdrawal of $10. The withdrawal is treated as attributable entirely to amounts that were includible in income due to the conversion. In the year of withdrawal, $16.25 is to be includible in income (the $6.25 includible in income in the year of withdrawal under the four-year rule plus $10, since $10 is less than the remaining taxable amount of $12.50). In the next year (2000), $2.50 is includible in income under the 4-year rule. No amount due to the conversion would be left to include in income in the fourth year (2001). [S Rep 105-174]

Sections 6005(b)(6) and 6005(b)(7). Correction of erroneous conversions to Roth IRAs. Conversion from a traditional IRA to a Roth IRA may only be made if the taxpayer's adjusted gross income for the year (before recognizing the conversion income) does not exceed $100,000. IRRA allows the owner of any IRA to make a trustee-to-trustee transfer of the contributions to that IRA along with any earnings attributable to the contributions to any other IRA by the due date (including extensions) of the taxpayer's tax return for the year of contribution. This allows taxpayers to undo erroneous conversions or to change between Roth IRA and traditional IRA contributions as they see fit. Such transfers will then be treated as having originally been made to the transferee plan (where they ended up) rather than to the transferor plan (from whence they came).

Sections 6005(b)(8) and 6005(b)(9). Relation of SEP and SIMPLE IRAs to Roth IRAs. Effective for tax years after December 31, 1997, IRRA clarified that the IRAs established under SEPs and under SIMPLE IRA plans may not be designated as Roth IRAs and that contributions to SEPs and to SIMPLE IRAs are not to be counted against the $2,000 annual limit for contributions to traditional and Roth IRAs.

Section 6005(c)(2). Hardship withdrawals will no longer be eligible rollover distributions. Effective for distributions after December 31, 1998, hardship withdrawals—per Code Section 401(k)(2)(B)(i)(IV)—will no longer be classified as eligible rollover distributions under Code Section 402(c)(4). This applies to hardship distributions from both 401(k) plans and 403(b) plans. Prior to this effective date, participants in employer sponsored retirement plans could avoid any early withdrawal tax applicable to such plans by rolling over hardship distributions to an IRA and withdrawing the funds from the IRA. IRRA modifies the rules relating to the ability to roll over hardship distributions in order to prevent such avoidance of the 10 percent early withdrawal tax. Since hardship distributions will no longer be eligible rollover distributions, they will no longer be subject to the 20 percent withholding applicable to eligible rollover distributions. In IRS Notice 99-5, transition relief was provided allowing plans to treat hardship distributions as eligible rollover distributions through December 31, 1999.

Section 6016(a)(1)(A). SIMPLE IRAs for noncollectively bargained employees. Effective for tax years beginning after December 31, 1996, IRRA clarifies that an employer's sponsoring a plan in which only collectively bargained employees may participate does not prevent it from also sponsoring a SIMPLE IRA plan for its noncollectively bargained employees.

Section 6016(a)(1)(B). SIMPLE IRAs following a merger or acquisition. Effective for tax years beginning after December 31, 1996, if an eligible sponsor of a SIMPLE IRA plan through merger or acquisition no longer meets the exclusive plan requirement, the 100 employee requirement, or the coverage requirement, IRRA provides that the sponsor shall continue to be treated as eligible to sponsor the SIMPLE IRA for a transition period beginning with the year of the merger or acquisition and continuing for the following two calendar years. However, the SIMPLE IRA cannot be significantly changed during this transition period and except for the merger or acquisition must continue to meet all other SIMPLE IRA requirements.

Section 6016(a)(2). Grandfathered rollovers from 403(b) to 401(k). Effective August 20, 1996, IRRA clarifies that amounts from 403(b)(7) custodial accounts of an Indian tribal government purchased before 1995 may be rolled over into a 401(k) plan. Under SBJPA it had not been clear that this exception applied to custodial accounts.

Section 6018(b). Return of excess contributions from a SIMPLE IRA. Effective for tax years beginning after December 31, 1996, IRRA clarifies that the return of excess contributions from a SIMPLE IRA plan are handled the same as the return of excess contributions from a SEP under Code Section 408(p)(2)(D)(i).

Section 7004(a). AGI conversion limit for Roth IRAs to exclude minimum required distributions. Effective for tax years beginning after 2004, IRRA provides that the $100,000 adjusted gross income Roth IRA conversion limit is to exclude any minimum required distributions from regular IRAs and from other qualified plans. Any minimum required IRA distributions will not themselves be eligible for conversion. Note the delayed effective date of this significant change. The technical corrections to the AGI conversion limit made by Section 6005(b)(2) (see above) are effective immediately.

RECENT DEVELOPMENTS

Q 1:48 How will Revenue Ruling 98-30, which authorized negative elections for 401(k) plans, affect 401(k) plan design?

In summer 1998, the IRS released Revenue Ruling 98-30 [1998-25 IRB 8], which gave a stamp of approval to negative elections for 401(k) plans. In a negative election 401(k) plan, a certain percentage or dollar amount of each eligible employee's compensation is automatically contributed to the 401(k) plan unless the employee designates a different amount or affirmatively elects not to contribute. Some employers view negative elections as a way to boost participation by lower paid employees that could allow for greater contributions by higher paid employees under the nondiscrimination testing (see chapter 12).

In Revenue Ruling 98-30, the IRS indicated it will allow negative elections as long as certain conditions are met:

- Employees must be notified of the negative election feature and their right to elect out of the feature before any deferrals are taken from pay.

- Any election to opt out must be implemented timely, but not later than the first pay payroll period beginning in the month in which the opt-out election is filed.

- Participants must be notified annually of their right to opt out.

Before a 401(k) plan adopts a negative election procedure it should consider carefully these issues:

- How should the automatic deferrals be invested? Some rule must be followed.

- The employer may well lose ERISA Section 404(c) protection with regard to the automatic deferral investments (see chapter 5).

- What is the effect of state wage garnishment laws? Are such laws preempted by ERISA?

- Is there a need to increase lower-paid employee contributions now that some employees who had been considered highly compensated are not highly compensated (see chapter 9)?

- Might a safe harbor 401(k) plan (see chapter 2) achieve the desired result?

Q 1:49 What other significant rulings have been released in 1998 and 1999?

- The IRS issued a proposed regulation and a notice (Notice 99-1) on the use of electronic technologies in retirement plans. (See chapters 15 and 18.)

- The DOL issued guidance on its expectations of plan fiduciaries relative to Y2K issues. This guidance is available at the Pension, Welfare, and Benefits Administration (PWBA) Web site, http://www.dol.gov/dol/pwba.

- The IRS released modifications to its voluntary compliance programs in Revenue Procedure 98-22 and Revenue Procedure 99-13. (See chapter 19.)

- The DOL published a booklet entitled, "A Look at 401(k) Plan Fees," which is available at the PWBA Web site listed above. (See chapter 4.)

- The IRS issued revised procedures for fulfilling notice, consent, and election requirements for plans subject to the survivor annuity rules in Treasury Regulations Sections 1.411(a)(11) and 1.417(e)(1). (See chapter 16.)

- The DOL issued proposed regulations regarding benefit claims procedures under ERISA Section 503. (See chapter 15.)

- In IRS Notice 99-11 [1999-8 IRB 56], the date for amending plan documents for GUSTI was delayed until the end of the first plan year beginning on or after January 1, 2000. (See chapter 3.)

2 401(k) Plan Design

After deciding to establish a 401(k) plan, an employer needs to consider the design of the plan. Some aspects of plan design involve options that can be chosen by the employer; other aspects, however, are mandated by law if the 401(k) plan is to be considered qualified for favorable tax treatment under the Internal Revenue Code (IRC). This chapter considers how employee demographics will affect plan design objectives and considers the design factors that most directly impact plan expenses and participation levels. It details the types of contributions, both employer and employee, that a 401(k) might contain and discusses the basic requirements a 401(k) plan must meet to be qualified. The chapter concludes with an explanation of the recently legislated SIMPLE and safe harbor 401(k) plan design options.

DESIGN OPTIONS AND OBJECTIVES

Q 2:1 What elements of employee demographics should be considered in designing a 401(k) plan?

The employee population must be considered in designing a 401(k) plan, including the size of the workforce; the ages, pay levels, and financial status of employees; and the rate of employee turnover. In some cases, the demographics of the workforce may make the 401(k) plan unfeasible. However, in most cases, special features will be incorporated into the 401(k) plan to accommodate the needs of the workforce.

Q 2:2 How does the size of the workforce affect 401(k) plan design?

The size of the workforce is a critical element. If fewer than 100 employees earning over $5,000 will be eligible to participate, a SIMPLE individual retirement account (IRA) plan (discussed in chapter 21) may make the most sense because it will have far fewer administrative requirements than a 401(k) plan or even a SIMPLE 401(k). If the higher employer contribution cost and inflexibility of a SIMPLE IRA plan are not attractive to the smaller employer, however, a 401(k) plan should be considered. Among the factors for a small company to consider in deciding between a 401(k) and a SIMPLE IRA plan are the possibility of passing the nondiscrimination tests (see chapter 12) and the cost of administration. The start-up costs of a 401(k) plan will be considerably higher on a per-participant basis. Moreover, the sophistication of the employer's payroll system will be a factor. An inadequate payroll system can cause significant administrative problems.

For the small but growing employer, size may not be an issue. If the employer projects significant growth in the workforce in future years, the 401(k) plan will be a good vehicle for attracting new employees. The start-up costs of the 401(k) plan can be a good investment for the future.

Q 2:3 How do the pay levels of employees affect 401(k) plan design?

The relative pay levels of the employee base are also important considerations. If employees generally receive low pay, the employer may have significant difficulty in attaining a sufficient level of participation. If a significant percentage of the employees are highly paid (for example, in a firm employing professionals), the plan should be designed to encourage participation of the lower-paid to allow highly paid professionals a reasonable level of salary deferral.

The pay level of employees is not the only factor, however. If significant numbers of employees are members of dual-income households, even the lower-paid spouse may be interested in making significant contributions. For example, the higher-paid spouse may be working for a company that does not offer a 401(k) plan, while the lower-paid spouse has a 401(k) plan available and may be interested in deferring the maximum allowed in the plan.

Q 2:4 What is the impact of employee turnover on 401(k) plan design?

The amount of employee turnover is another consideration in designing a 401(k) plan. In industries with high turnover, a vesting schedule may be attached to employer contributions. This can also be handled, to some extent, by the use of a one-year waiting period. The forfeitures that result when employees leave before becoming fully vested may be used to reduce future contributions or may be reallocated to the remaining participants. Reallocation can be an attractive feature and can be used to reward employees for long service. Also, the use of vesting schedules can help encourage

employees to remain in employment. A design that can help reduce turnover will be welcome, given the high cost of training
new employees.

Options That Impact Plan Expenses

**Q 2:5 What financial considerations should an employer take
into account before adopting a 401(k) plan?**

An employer considering the adoption of a 401(k) plan must take
its financial impact into account. The biggest portion of the cost of a
401(k) plan is employer contributions to the plan, whether they are
matching (see Qs 2:10–2:12 and 2:26–2:30), discretionary nonelective contributions (see Qs 2:13–2:14 and 2:31–2:50), or qualified
nonelective contributions (QNECs) (see Q 2:15 and chapter 12).
The employer needs to measure the level of its contributions on
both an initial and ongoing basis. The employer will incur other
costs as a result of adopting a 401(k) plan, including installation,
enrollment, administration, and compliance costs. Estimating these
costs will require decisions relative to the design, funding, and reporting frequency of the plan.

Q 2:6 How much will matching contributions cost?

It is useful to look at the cost of the match from two perspec-
tives: the maximum exposure of the employer and the expected
cost of the match. The maximum exposure of the employer is
the maximum dollar expenditure if 100 percent of eligible employees contributed at least an amount necessary to receive the maximum matching contribution. Generally, the employer will limit the
amount of an employee's salary deferral that will be matched; this
is called a *match cap*. The maximum exposure of the employer can
be computed by the following formula:

Covered payroll × matching percentage × match cap = Maximum exposure

> **Example.** Employer A has covered payroll of $1 million and
> wishes to provide a matching contribution of 25 percent of elec-
> tive contributions up to the first 4 percent of pay. The maximum
> cost Employer A would incur can be calculated as

$$\$1,000,000 \times 25\% \times 4\% = \$10,000$$

The maximum cost of the employer for the matching contribution is, therefore, $10,000, or 1 percent of payroll.

Q 2:7 How is the expected cost of the match computed?

The employer will not generally have experience to draw on, but it can be estimated that the participation rate will be approximately 75 percent if the 401(k) plan has a matching feature. This 75 percent estimate can be adjusted in later years when the actual participation rate is known. The estimated cost can then be obtained by multiplying the maximum cost by the expected participation rate.

Example. In the example above (see Q 2:6), the expected cost Employer A would incur would be

$$\$1,000,000 \times 25\% \times 4\% \times 75\% = \$7,500$$

Thus, $7,500, or 0.75 percent of payroll, is the expected cost of the employer for the matching contribution. The expected cost of the match will be a useful number for budgeting purposes, since this represents the amount that the employer anticipates spending.

Q 2:8 What other costs may be incurred in conjunction with a 401(k) plan?

In addition to matching contributions, the employer will incur other costs in setting up a 401(k) plan. The installation of a 401(k) plan can be a significant cost in itself, involving a consultant to design the plan, an attorney to draft the plan, and programmers to make changes to the payroll system or voice response unit. Installation costs can be reduced if a master or prototype plan, regional prototype plan, or volume submitter plan is used. (See chapter 3.) Also, if the employer uses an outside vendor for payroll processing, it is quite likely that payroll changes to accommodate 401(k) deferrals will be minimal.

Enrollment costs can also be a factor. Although the cost of enrollment materials and a consultant's time may be nominal, the cost to the employer of meetings for all employees could be substantial. Enrollment costs are highest at the time the plan is installed but will be ongoing as new employees become eligible for the plan. In some cases, re-enrollment meetings will be held to increase the participation of existing participants. Many employers have found that existing participants in the 401(k) plan can do an excellent job of "selling" the plan to their fellow employees.

Ongoing administrative costs should be factored in. The cost of participant recordkeeping can vary, ranging from as little as $10 per head to close to $50 or more per head, depending on the size of the employer, the investment choices allowed the participants, and the frequency of reports. The trustees' fees for trust recordkeeping may be nominal or substantial, depending on the type of investments used in the plan. In some cases, the administrative costs will be deducted from plan assets, thus minimizing the employer's direct costs. However, caution should be used in this approach, as this could have a significant impact on the rate of return realized by employees in a new 401(k) plan. If plan assets are substantial, impact on the rate of return should be minimal. If the employer chooses to pay fees directly, such costs will be tax-deductible.

Finally, the compliance costs should be taken into account. How will ongoing compliance with legislation and regulations be assured? Who will handle 401(k) and 401(m) nondiscrimination and top-heavy testing, and how much will it cost? The cost of coordinating benefit and contribution limits in the 401(k) and other benefit plans of the employer should not be overlooked.

Q 2:9 Should plan expenses be paid from plan assets?

Aggregate plan investment, administrative, and recordkeeping expenses range from 0.3 percent to 0.5 percent of plan assets for large plans to over ten times that amount for small plans (with less than $500,000 in assets). If expenses are paid from plan assets, they reduce the rate of return an average of 1 percent or 2 percent. This difference in rate of return over a 30-year period will reduce the value of the participant's account at retirement by almost one third. Expenses paid by the employer are a deductible expense and will cost about one third less than if paid out of plan assets. If the goal is to maximize retirement values, expenses should not be paid from plan assets. On the other hand, if the employer is under significant cash flow or cost control pressure, there may be no alternative but to pay expenses from the trust.

Options That Impact Plan Participation

Q 2:10 What is the impact of matching contributions on plan participation?

Two surveys confirm that matching contributions can have a significant impact on participation in the 401(k) plan. Massachusetts Mutual Life Insurance Co. of Springfield, Massachusetts, in its *401(k) Survey Report*, found that over 71 percent of all 401(k) plans provided matching contributions. The participation rate of non-highly compensated employees (NHCEs) increased markedly when the employer provided a matching contribution, as is shown below.

Rate of Match (percentage)	NHCE Participation Rate (percentage)
0	51
25	65
50	72
75	75
100	76

Hewitt Associates, in its survey *401(k) Plan Hot Topics, 1993*, reported similar findings: participation rates were 59 percent without a match and 77 percent when a matching contribution was made. It is interesting to note that participation does not substantially change when the match is increased beyond 50 percent.

Once the decision is made to make matching contributions, the employer must choose whether they will be fixed or discretionary (see Q 2:11) and whether matching contributions will be ongoing or made at year's end (see Q 2:12). These decisions will affect plan participation.

Q 2:11 Should matching contributions be fixed or discretionary?

According to the 1993 Hewitt survey (see Q 2:10), fewer than 20 percent of 401(k) plans that provide for matching contributions make them discretionary, or geared to the performance of the employer. The uncertainty as to whether a match will be made or about the level of the match does not provide a good incentive for employees to participate; a matching contribution will be most effective when the level is fixed. It may make sense to start with a modest match (e.g., 25 percent of the first 4 percent of pay) and then increase it in future years.

Q 2:12 Should matching contributions be ongoing or made at year's end?

According to the 1993 Hewitt survey (see Q 2:10), over 65 percent of matching contributions are made on an ongoing basis—that is, at the same time participant deferrals are made. This approach maximizes the visibility of matching contributions, as the employee will see them with each periodic report. It also becomes a valuable communication tool in encouraging employee participation.

Example. Employer B is installing a 401(k) plan with a matching contribution of 50 percent of the first 6 percent of pay. By setting the threshold of the match at 6 percent, the employer is encouraging lower-paid employees to contribute at least 6 percent to the plan. If the matching contributions are made on an ongoing basis, the 50 percent match may be viewed by employees as a guaranteed return of 50 percent on their 6 percent investment. Beyond this "guaranteed return" is the actual investment return, which should further enhance the value of the deferral.

If an employer chooses to have a discretionary match, this match will often occur at or after the end of the plan year, when profits are known.

Q 2:13 Why might an employer choose to make discretionary nonelective contributions to its 401(k) plan?

The employer may choose to supplement the employee elective contributions and matching contributions with discretionary nonelective contributions based on profitability or employer performance. More frequently, a 401(k) plan containing only elective contributions will be supplemented by discretionary nonelective contributions. The profit sharing element of discretionary nonelective contributions can provide significant performance incentives to participants.

Because the contribution is totally discretionary, the employer can contribute or not, depending on budgetary constraints.

Q 2:14 How does the employer make a choice between allocating funds to matching contributions or discretionary contributions?

Matching contributions will be contributed only to participants who choose to make elective contributions, while discretionary nonelective contributions will be allocated to all eligible employees. With limited resources, the employer may opt to direct more dollars to matching contributions (rather than discretionary) to reward the employees who make elective contributions to the 401(k) plan.

Methods for allocating discretionary nonelective contributions are discussed later in this chapter (see Qs 2:35–2:50).

Q 2:15 How may qualified nonelective contributions be used in a 401(k) plan?

Qualified nonelective contributions (QNECs) (discussed in depth in chapter 12) may be a feature in a 401(k) for a number of reasons:

1. The employer may wish to allow highly compensated employees (HCEs) the opportunity to defer a greater portion of their compensation by guaranteeing that the actual deferral percentage for non-highly compensated employees (NHCEs) will be equal to at least the level of the QNEC.

Example. Employer C is concerned that participation in the 401(k) plan will be low for NHCEs. By making a QNEC equal to 3 percent of pay for all NHCEs, Employer C will enable HCEs to defer at least 5 percent of pay. The 401(k) plan in this example should easily be able to satisfy the actual deferral percentage (ADP) test (discussed in chapter 12).

2. The QNEC may also be used to correct a problem with the ADP test. If it looks likely that the ADP test will not be met, a QNEC may be used to increase the actual deferral percentage for NHCEs. This will be, in many cases, a more viable alternative than refunding excess contributions to HCEs.

3. The QNEC may be used to provide top-heavy minimums for non-key employees in a top-heavy plan. Since non-key participants will generally have to be provided with a 3 percent of pay contribution from the employer, this may be done in the form of a QNEC. Using this approach will have a dual advantage: it will satisfy the top-heavy minimum requirement and assist the plan in passing the ADP test.

These strategies are actively being used by plans that have trouble complying with the ADP test due to the Section 401(a)(17) compensation cap ($160,000 for 1999).

Q 2:16 Is access to plan funds important to encourage participation in 401(k) plans?

Yes. A John Hancock survey, *Defined Contribution Plan Survey: Insights into Participant Behavior* (conducted for John Hancock Financial Services by the Gallup Organization in 1992 and confirmed in 1993) indicates that such access is critical to participation in savings plans. Some participants would either reduce their rate of contributions (11 percent) or stop contributing entirely (26 percent) if the funds were locked up until retirement. Although 98 percent of participants planned to use the money for retirement, 27 percent also planned to use the savings for educational expenses, and 27 percent felt they would want the funds available for medical expenses or other emergencies.

TYPES OF 401(K) PLAN CONTRIBUTIONS

Q 2:17 What types of contributions are generally found in a 401(k) plan?

A 401(k) plan will always include elective contributions (see Q 2:18) and may include bonus deferral contributions (see Q 2:25), matching contributions (see Q 2:26), or discretionary nonelective contributions (see Q 2:31).

Elective Contributions

Q 2:18 What is an *elective contribution?*

An *elective contribution* is a contribution made by an employer pursuant to an employee's cash or deferred election. [Treas Reg § 1.401(k)-1(g)(3)] Elective contributions are subject to discrimination testing under the actual deferral percentage (ADP) test. (See chapter 12.)

Q 2:19 What is a *cash or deferred election*?

A *cash or deferred election* is any election made by an employee to receive an amount in cash that is not currently available or to have that amount contributed to a 401(k) plan. [Treas Reg § 1.401(k)-1(a)(3)(i)]

Q 2:20 Is a one-time election to defer a specified amount or percentage of an employee's compensation considered a cash or deferred election?

Such an election will not be considered a cash or deferred election if it is irrevocable, is made upon commencement of employment or upon becoming a participant, and has never been made previously with respect to another plan (whether or not terminated) maintained by the employer. The election applies to the plan in question and any other plan of the employer that is currently maintained or adopted in the future. [Treas Reg § 1.401(k)-1(a)(3)(iv)]

Example. FLO Company sponsors a plan under which each employee, at the commencement of employment, must irrevocably specify what percentage or amount of his or her compensation will be contributed to the plan. Such an election will not be considered a cash or deferred election and the plan will not be considered a 401(k) plan. Contributions made pursuant to such an election will be considered nonelective contributions (see Q 2:31) and will be subject to the nondiscrimination rules applicable to nonelective contributions. (See chapter 11.)

Q 2:21 When is an amount considered currently available to an employee?

An amount is considered currently available if it has been paid to the employee or if the employee is currently able to receive the cash at his or her discretion. [Treas Reg § 1.401(k)-1(a)(3)(iii)]

Example. ABC Company establishes a calendar-year-end 401(k) plan on December 1, 1998. Dennis, a highly paid employee, wishes to defer $6,000 during the month of December. Dennis is compensated at the rate of $10,000 per month; therefore, he elects to defer 5 percent of his compensation, believing that his deferral election will apply to the compensation that he will have received throughout 1998 ($120,000). In fact, his deferral election can apply only to his $10,000 monthly December salary, since that is the only portion of his 1998 annual compensation not currently available. If Dennis wishes to make an elective contribution of $6,000 for 1998, his deferral election percentage must be 60 percent. Note that by contributing $6,000 during the month of December, Dennis does not violate the Section 415 limits on contributions to a 401(k) plan. A violation does not occur because compensation for the entire calendar year, not just December 1998, is considered when applying the Section 415 limits (see Q 8:20).

Q 2:22 When is an amount considered currently available to a partner in a 401(k) plan sponsored by a partnership?

A partner's compensation is deemed currently available on the last day of the partnership's taxable year. As a result, a partner's cash or deferred election must be made by the last day of that year. [Treas Reg § 1.401(k)-1(a)(6)(ii)(B)]

Example. The ABC partnership, which has a November 30 taxable year, sponsors a 401(k) plan with a calendar plan year. For the plan year ending December 31, 1998, a partner's compensation will be his or her compensation from the partnership for its taxable year ending November 30, 1998. A partner must make the cash or deferred election no later than November 30, 1998.

Q 2:23 Are there special limitations that apply to elective contributions?

Yes. Elective contributions must be 100 percent vested immediately and are subject to the limitations on distributions described in chapter 14. They are also subject to dollar and percentage limits explained in chapter 8.

Q 2:24 Are elective contributions considered employee contributions?

No. Elective contributions are treated as employer contributions, not employee contributions, for all purposes under the Internal Revenue Code. [Treas Reg § 1.401(k)-1(a)(4)(ii)]

Q 2:25 Are there special rules for elective contributions on bonuses?

Yes. Elective contributions may be made on bonus payments, and generally these are treated like any other elective contribution. However, there is a special rule that treats deferrals on bonuses paid within 2½ months after the end of a plan year as having been made within the plan year for purposes of discrimination testing. For this special rule to apply, the bonus must be attributable to services performed within the plan year. [Treas Reg § 1.401(k)-1(b)(4)] Elective contributions on bonuses are subject to discrimination testing under the ADP test. (See chapter 12.)

Matching Contributions

Q 2:26 What is a *matching contribution*?

A *matching contribution* is an employer contribution that is allocated on the basis of a participant's elective contribution or, less typically, a participant's employee after-tax contribution. [IRC § 401(m)(4)(A); Treas Reg § 1.401(m)-1(f)(12)] The rate of matching contribution may be specified in the plan document or may be determined at the discretion of the employer. It may be made on an ongoing basis, as elective contributions are paid into the 401(k) plan, or at or after the end of the plan year. Matching contributions, together with employee after-tax contributions, are subject to discrimination testing under the actual contribution percentage (ACP) test. (See chapter 12.)

Q 2:27 May matching contributions be made on a discretionary basis?

Yes. In some 401(k) plans, the employer will determine each plan year the rate (if any) of matching contributions for that year. If the rate of matching contributions is announced at the beginning of the year, the contributions will usually be made to the 401(k) plan on an ongoing basis and without regard to any minimum hours and/or last day requirements (see Qs 2:32 and 2:34). On the other hand, if the employer defers the decision until the end of the year or thereafter, the plan may require participants to satisfy either or both of these requirements in order to receive a matching contribution allocation.

Q 2:28 May matching contributions be made on a discretionary basis in a SIMPLE 401(k) plan?

No. Unless an employer elects to make a nonelective contribution of 2 percent of compensation, it is required to make matching contributions to a SIMPLE 401(k) plan on a dollar-for-dollar basis on elective contributions up to 3 percent of compensation. [IRC § 401(k)(11)] An employer cannot require a participant to complete a minimum number of hours of service or to be employed on any particular day of the plan year in order to be entitled to receive matching contributions. (See Qs 2:131–2:142 for further discussion of SIMPLE 401(k) plans.)

Q 2:29 May matching contributions be made on a discretionary basis in a safe harbor 401(k) plan under Code Section 401(k)(12)?

No. Unless an employer elects to make a nonelective contribution of 3 percent of compensation, an employer is required to make the matching contributions at the level set forth in Code Section 401(k)(12). Last day and/or minimum hours requirements for matching contributions are not permitted. (See Qs 2:143–2:163 for further discussion of safe harbor 401(k) plans.)

Q 2:30 May matching contributions be made on behalf of partners who participate in a 401(k) plan maintained by a partnership?

Yes, matching contributions may be made with respect to a partner's elective contributions, but, according to the regulations in effect through 1997, these matching contributions must be treated as elective contributions. [Treas Reg § 1.401(k)-1(a)(6)(iii)] The Internal Revenue Service (IRS) believes that this treatment is mandated by regulations under Code Section 404 that require that all contributions to a qualified plan on behalf of a partner be allocated, for deduction purposes, to that partner. The IRS position has, in effect, been reversed by the enactment of Section 1501 of the Taxpayer Relief Act of 1997 (TRA '97). Under this legislation, starting with plan years beginning after December 31, 1997, matching contributions for partners will no longer be treated as elective contributions.

Discretionary Nonelective Contributions

Q 2:31 What is a *discretionary nonelective contribution*?

A *discretionary nonelective contribution* in a 401(k) plan is an employer contribution that is allocated on the basis of compensation or in some manner other than on the basis of elective contributions or employee after-tax contributions. Discretionary nonelective contributions do not need to be included in any of the special nondiscrimination tests for 401(k) plans, but they are subject to the general nondiscrimination rules under Code Section 401(a)(4). (See chapter 11.) Discretionary nonelective contributions may sometimes be used to satisfy the ADP and ACP tests. (See Qs 12:15, 12:50.) A participant's right to receive an allocation of a discretionary nonelective contribution cannot depend on whether he or she has made elective contributions. [IRC § 401(k)(4)(A); Treas Reg § 1.401(k)-1(e)(6)]

> **Example.** Emily earns $35,000 and elects to contribute 10 percent of her compensation for the year. Emily's employer provides a matching contribution of 25 percent of the deferral amount and a discretionary nonelective contribution of 5 percent of pay. Emily's total allocation for the year is as follows:
>
> | | |
> |---|---:|
> | Elective contribution ($35,000 × 10%) | $3,500 |
> | Matching contribution ($3,500 × 25%) | 875 |
> | Discretionary contribution ($35,000 × 5%) | 1,750 |
> | Total contribution | $6,125 |

Q 2:32 What eligibility requirements may be imposed on a 401(k) participant for purposes of receiving a discretionary nonelective contribution allocation?

A minimum hours requirement of up to 1,000 hours may be imposed. For example, if a plan requires 1,000 hours of service, an active or terminated participant who works fewer than 1,000 hours will not be entitled to an allocation of discretionary nonelective contributions.

A requirement that the participant be employed on the last day of the plan year may also be imposed. This requirement would generally preclude any terminated employees from receiving a portion of the nonelective contribution.

Q 2:33 What eligibility requirements may be imposed on a 401(k) participant in the case of a SIMPLE 401(k) plan or a safe harbor 401(k) plan under Code Section 401(k)(12)?

A minimum hours requirement and/or last day requirement may not be imposed in the case of an employer that elects to make the 2 percent of compensation nonelective contribution to a SIMPLE 401(k) plan or the 3 percent of compensation nonelective contribution to a safe harbor 401(k) plan. All participants eligible to make elective contributions are entitled to the nonelective contribution; however, in the case of a SIMPLE 401(k) plan, a participant may be required to receive at least $5,000 of compensation (or such lesser amount designated by the employer) for the plan year. [IRC §§ 401(k)(11), 401(k)(12)] (SIMPLE and safe harbor 401(k) plans are discussed in detail at the end of this chapter.)

Q 2:34 What are the special concerns of a plan sponsor that imposes minimum hours and/or last day requirements?

Because the nonelective contribution portion of the plan is tested separately for coverage (see the definition of *plan* in chapter 9), care must be taken to ensure that the Section 410(b) coverage requirements are met. If a significant number of employees are excluded from an allocation of nonelective contributions, the plan may fail the coverage tests. (See chapter 10.)

Allocation Methods

Q 2:35 What methods of allocation of discretionary nonelective contributions are available to the sponsor of a 401(k) plan?

The nondiscrimination rules allow plan sponsors the choice of a design-based safe harbor formula or a formula that meets the requirements of the general test for defined contribution plans. (See

Qs 11:1 and 11:9.) [Treas Reg § 1.401(a)(4)-2] Generally, if a safe harbor formula is used, the plan sponsor is assured that the allocation of discretionary nonelective contributions will not discriminate in favor of highly compensated employees (HCEs). (See chapter 9.)

Q 2:36 What are the design-based safe harbor allocation methods?

There are three basic methods: proportional, integrated, and a points system. The proportional method will provide an allocation that is an equal percentage of pay, an equal dollar amount for each eligible participant, or an equal dollar amount for each uniform unit of service (not to exceed one week). (See Q 11:2.) The integrated method will allow the plan sponsor to take Social Security contributions into account by providing an allocation that is a greater percentage of pay for more highly paid participants. (See Qs 11:15–11:18.) The points system is more involved, as a nondiscrimination test must be performed on the allocations to demonstrate that the allocation does not discriminate in favor of HCEs. (See Qs 11:4–11:6.)

Q 2:37 How does the points system of allocation work?

The plan awards points for age, service, or both. Points may also be given for units of compensation, which cannot exceed $200 in value. Each employee must receive the same number of points for each year of age, for each year of service, and for each unit of compensation. If the plan grants points for years of service, it may limit the number of years of service taken into account. [Treas Reg § 1.401(a)(4)-2(b)(3)(i)(A)]

For each plan year, the average of the allocation rates for HCEs cannot exceed the average of the allocation rates for non-highly compensated employees (NHCEs) (the *average allocation test*). An employee's allocation rate is the amount allocated to the employee's account for a plan year expressed as either a percentage of compensation or a dollar amount. [Treas Reg § 1.401(a)(4)-2(b)(3)(i)(B)]

Q 2:38 What alternative formulas for allocation of discretionary nonelective contributions are available?

Any allocation formula that does not discriminate in favor of HCEs may be used. The general test for nondiscrimination must then be performed on an annual basis. (See Qs 11:9–11:14.) The employer must weigh the costs of performing this test annually with the results of the allocation to determine the value of using the general test.

For example, a points system formula could be used with compensation units of $1,000. Because each compensation unit exceeds $200, general testing must be performed to use this formula. On the other hand, if the points system formula does not satisfy the average allocation test (see Q 2:37), then general testing must also be performed.

Another alternative available to a 401(k) plan sponsor is the age-weighted allocation of nonelective contributions. Although the general test must be applied, an age-weighted allocation formula will, by reason of its nature, usually satisfy the requirements of the general test. (See Qs 2:39–2:50.)

Example. The following four illustrations show the results of allocating nonelective contributions under the various methods discussed here. For purposes of these illustrations, a small employer (with three employees) is used, but the concepts are equally applicable to larger employers.

1. *Proportional method.* ABC Company decides to contribute 5 percent of eligible payroll, or $8,000. Under a proportional allocation, all participants would receive an allocation equal to 5 percent of pay.

Name	Pay	Total Contribution	Percentage of Pay
Alice	$100,000	$5,000	5.00%
Brent	40,000	2,000	5.00
Cathy	20,000	1,000	5.00
Totals	$160,000	$8,000	

2. *Integrated method.* The plan uses an integration level of $55,500 (see Q 11:16). If $8,000 is contributed, the formula for allocation is 7.824 percent of compensation in excess of $55,500, plus 3.912 percent of compensation below that amount. The contribution is allocated as follows:

Name	Pay	Excess Pay	Excess Contribution	Base Contribution	Total Contribution	Percentage of Pay
Alice	$100,000	$44,500	$3,482	$2,171	$5,653	5.65%
Brent	40,000	0	0	1,565	1,565	3.91
Cathy	20,000	0	0	782	782	3.91
Totals	$160,000	$44,500	$3,482	$4,518	$8,000	

3. *Points method.* The plan provides one point for each $200 of compensation, one point for each year of age, and five points for each year of service. The total points for all participants amount to 1,000. Each point is, therefore, worth $8 calculated as $8,000/1,000.

Name	Age	Years of Service	Pay	Pay Points	Age Points	Service Points	Total Points	Total Contribution	Percentage of Pay
Alice	50	5	$100,000	500	50	25	575	$4,600	4.60%
Brent	40	10	40,000	200	40	50	290	2,320	5.80
Cathy	25	2	20,000	100	25	10	135	1,080	5.40
Totals			$160,000	800	115	85	1,000	$8,000	

4. *Age-weighted method.* $8,000 is contributed, and the plan uses 8.5 percent interest and UP 84 mortality as the basis for age-weighting. (See Qs 2:39–2:50.)

Name	Age	Pay	Total Contributions	Percentage of Pay
Alice	50	$100,000	$6,200	6.20%
Brent	40	40,000	1,200	3.00
Cathy	25	20,000	600	3.00
Totals		$160,000	$8,000	

Note: This plan is top heavy, and top-heavy minimums of 3 percent of compensation are provided for each non-key participant.

Q 2:39 How does an age-weighted formula differ from the design-based safe harbor formulas?

The key difference between an age-weighted formula and a design-based formula is that, in an age-weighted formula, the contributions are allocated to favor older employees. An age-weighted formula tests for nondiscrimination on the basis of benefits; that is, the discretionary nonelective contributions allocated to the accounts of participants are converted to equivalent benefits at normal retirement age, and testing is performed on the basis of those benefits.

Q 2:40 How does the conversion from contributions to benefits operate?

The cross-testing rules specify that, when testing defined contribution plans on a benefits basis, all allocated contributions and forfeitures must be converted to equivalent benefit accrual rates (EBARs). [Treas Reg § 1.401(a)(4)-8] The EBARs represent an annual annuity benefit as a percentage of compensation.

Example. An employer with two employees contributes $12,550 and allocates $11,690 to the older and $860 to the younger employee. By converting the contribution to a benefit for each employee, it can be demonstrated that the benefits are equivalent as a percentage (5 percent) of pay:

Age	Salary	Contribution	Accumulations	Annual Annuity	EBAR
50	$100,000	$11,690	$39,743	$5,000	5%
35	25,000	860	9,940	1,250	5
Totals	$125,000	$12,550	$49,683	$6,250	

Assumptions:
   Interest: 8.5%
   Mortality: Unisex Pension Table of 1984 (UP 84)
   Testing Age: 65

Q 2:41 How are the age-weighting factors determined?

A plan document containing an age-weighted formula must contain a table of age-weighting factors or a list of assumptions. The Section 401(a)(4) regulations contain a list of safe harbor mortality tables and specify that interest rates must be in the range of 7.5 percent to 8.5 percent. [Treas Reg § 1.401(a)(4)-8(b)(2)]

To ensure that an age-weighted formula satisfies the nondiscrimination tests, a table is set up that defines the contribution, as a percentage of compensation, for each age. This contribution can be translated into a benefit of 1 percent of compensation. Selected factors from such a table are shown below.

Age	Factor
55	3.515%
45	1.555
35	0.688
25	0.304

Assumptions:
  Interest: 8.5%
  Mortality: UP 84

Q 2:42 How is the contribution allocated to participants under an age-weighted formula?

To obtain the contribution allocation for each participant, it is necessary to take the following steps:

1. Determine the present value factor from the table;
2. Multiply the table factor by compensation; and
3. Allocate the contribution on a pro rata basis among the participants based on the result obtained in Step 2.

Example. Employer E wishes to make a discretionary nonelective contribution of 10 percent of pay, or $15,000, to its 401(k) plan. Using 8.5 percent interest and UP 84 mortality, the contribution would be allocated as follows:

Age	Salary	Factor	Allocation Base Salary × Factor	Allocated Contribution $15,000/$3,799 × Allocation Base
55	$ 90,000	3.515%	$3,164	$12,493
45	30,000	1.555	467	1,844
35	20,000	.688	138	545
25	10,000	.304	30	118
Totals	$150,000		$3,799	$15,000

Note. The total contribution of $15,000 is approximately 3.948 times the allocation base of $3,799. This factor can be applied to each individual's allocation base to obtain the allocated contribution.

Q 2:43 How does an age-weighted formula automatically satisfy the nondiscrimination tests?

Initially, the EBARs should be an equal percentage of compensation for each participant in the plan, since the allocation is based on a 1 percent EBAR for all participants. Because the EBARs for all HCEs should be exactly equal to the EBARs for all NHCEs, the plan will comply with the requirements of Code Section 401(a)(4).

Q 2:44 How are top-heavy minimums handled in a 401(k) plan containing an age-weighted formula?

If a plan or aggregated group of plans is top heavy (see chapter 13), and if the 401(k) plan document requires that minimum contributions be provided in the 401(k) plan, then top-heavy minimums must be allocated to all non-key employees. Because the age-weighted allocation formula will not automatically ensure that top-heavy minimums are made for non-key employees, employers must see that they are by using one of three basic methods:

1. *Top-off method.* The employer contributes additional amounts as necessary to bring non-key employees up to their minimum level of contributions:

Age	Salary	Contribution	Top-Heavy Minimum	Additional Requirements	Total Contributions
55	$ 90,000	$12,493			$12,493
45	30,000	1,844	$900		1,844
35	20,000	545	600	$ 55	600
25	10,000	118	300	182	300
Totals	$150,000	$15,000		$237	$15,237

Result: An extra $237 is contributed.

2. *Skim method.* Contributions are reduced for key employees and reallocated to non-key employees in an iterative fashion until all non-key employees receive their top-heavy minimums:

Age	Pay	Pass I Contributions	Pass II Contributions	Pass III Contributions
55	$ 90,000	$12,493	$12,344	$12,288
45	30,000	1,844	1,820	1,812
35	20,000	545	536	600
25	10,000	118	300	300
Totals	$150,000	$15,000	$15,000	$15,000

3. *Dual plan method.* Top-heavy minimums are allocated first to non-key and key employees alike; then the balance of the contribution is allocated under the age-weighted formula. The dual plan method is not looked upon favorably by the IRS, which believes that it is not possible to test segments of plans, one on a contributions basis and the other on a benefits basis. Its position is supported by the final Section 401(a)(4) regulations. However, it is possible to have two separate plans—one age-weighted and the other that provides only top-heavy minimums:

Age	Pay	Top-Heavy Minimum Portion	Age-Weighted Portion	Total
55	$ 90,000	$2,700	$ 8,746	$11,446
45	30,000	900	1,290	2,190
35	20,000	600	380	980
25	10,000	300	84	384
Totals	$150,000	$4,500	$10,500	$15,000

Q 2:45 How are EBARs tested?

To calculate EBARs, the 401(k) plan must specify a testing age for purposes of the cross-testing rules. [Treas Reg § 1.401(a)(4)-8] The uniform normal retirement age is deemed to be the testing age. In calculating EBARs, a 401(k) plan containing an age-weighted formula may not automatically satisfy the nondiscrimination rules for one of two reasons:

1. The top-heavy minimum provisions of Code Section 416 require that younger, non-key employees, who may also be highly compensated, receive top-heavy minimums. Their EBARs will be greater than those calculated for older NHCEs.

2. Older NHCEs may be limited based on the Code Section 415 25 percent of compensation limit. The result may be that their EBARs are less than the EBARs of HCEs.

Q 2:46 How can rate group restructuring help an age-weighted formula satisfy the nondiscrimination rules?

The Section 401(a)(4) regulations provide a potential solution, called rate group restructuring, to these problems. To apply restructuring, it is necessary to establish a rate group for each HCE (cornerstone employee). This rate group will consist of a cornerstone employee and all HCEs and NHCEs whose EBARs are greater than or equal to that of the cornerstone employee. Once the rate group is established, it is tested under the coverage rules of Code Section 410(b). (See chapter 10.) This method is illustrated by the following example.

Example. An NHCE, age 60, has an EBAR that is lower than the EBAR for the HCE:

Age	HCE?	Salary	Age-Weighted Contribution	EBAR
52	Yes	$150,000	$30,000	6.543%
30	No	35,000	1,170	6.543
23	No	25,000	750	10.455
21	No	20,000	600	12.308
60	No	20,000	5,000	4.258
Totals		$260,000	$37,520	

In this example, in order to allocate $30,000 to the HCE, the goal was to produce an EBAR of 6.543 percent of compensation for all employees. However, the 60-year-old maxed out at 25 percent of compensation, and the two employees in their 20s needed more to reach the top-heavy minimum. The EBAR for the 60-year-old employee is less than that for the HCE. The cornerstone employee is the only HCE, the 52-year-old. There is only one rate group, consisting of that HCE and three of four NHCEs (whose EBARs are greater than or equal to the EBAR of the only HCE). The ratio percentage test of Code Section 410(b) is satisfied, since the ratio of NHCE to HCE coverage (75 percent) is greater than 70 percent:

$$\frac{\text{NHCE \%}}{\text{HCE \%}} = \frac{3/4}{1/1} = 75\%$$

Q 2:47 When would an age-weighted formula be used in lieu of a design-based safe harbor formula or a defined benefit plan?

An age-weighted formula can be quite advantageous when compared with defined benefit plans or design-based safe harbor formulas for the following reasons:

- The employer has the flexibility to contribute between 0 percent and 15 percent of total payroll.
- Because the age-weighted formula is applied to contributions

made to a defined contribution plan, it is much easier to administer.

- Participants receive annual statements reflecting their account balances. This is much easier for employees to understand than accrued benefits in defined benefit plans expressed in terms of benefits commencing at normal retirement age.
- There is no need for an actuary or for filing a Form 5500, Schedule B. A 401(k) plan containing an age-weighted formula is not liable for PBGC premiums, nor are the complexities of FAS 87 reporting necessary.
- The contributions can be significantly higher as a percentage of compensation for older HCEs.

Q 2:48 What are the drawbacks of an age-weighted formula?

An age-weighted formula does have some disadvantages, including the following:

- If the plan is top heavy, care must be taken to ensure that top-heavy minimums are provided.
- There are some difficult communication issues in replacing a traditional allocation formula with an age-weighted formula because many participants will receive a smaller contribution as a percentage of compensation than in the past.
- An age-weighted formula can be more expensive to administer than traditional allocation formulas because of the additional cross-testing necessary to ensure nondiscrimination under Code Section 401(a)(4).
- The employer cannot contribute more than 15 percent of total payroll, or spend more than $30,000 or 25 percent of compensation for highly compensated employees.

Q 2:49 What are the uses of an age-weighted formula?

An age-weighted formula can be an effective plan design in a number of situations:

- It is ideal for a business with older highly paid principals who wish to receive a larger share of the profit sharing plan contribution.

- As a replacement for a terminating defined benefit plan, an age-weighted formula can reduce the benefits lost by older participants as a result of the conversion to a defined contribution plan.
- Age-weighted allocations, the addition of a vesting schedule, and reduced accessibility to funds can be viewed as significant advantages for an employer considering a conversion from a SEP to a 401(k) plan containing an age-weighted formula.

Q 2:50 How may fail-safe provisions be incorporated into a 401(k) plan containing an age-weighted allocation formula?

To ensure that the age-weighted formula does not fail under the general tests of Code Section 401(a)(4), fail-safe provisions should be inserted in the plan document. Two such provisions are available:

1. Default to a traditional profit sharing allocation in the event the general test is failed; or

2. Use the safe harbors provided in Treasury Regulations Section 1.401(a)(4)-2, which allow for unit weighting based on age and compensation. (See chapter 11.)

Transfer or Rollover of Benefits

Q 2:51 What methods exist for moving benefits from one plan or IRA to a 401(k) plan?

Currently, four methods can be used:

- A direct rollover (see Q 2:52)
- A 60-day rollover (see Q 2:53)
- A transfer (see Q 2:54)
- An elective transfer (see Q 2:55)

Q 2:52 What is a *direct rollover*?

A *direct rollover* is a distribution that, at the election of the participant, is transferred directly from the trustee of the distributing plan or IRA to the trustee of the receiving plan. (See Q 15:58.)

Q 2:53 What is a *60-day rollover*?

A *60-day rollover* is a distribution that is received by a participant and then deposited into another qualified plan within 60 days following the participant's receipt of the distribution. (See Q 15:62.)

Q 2:54 What is a *transfer*?

A *transfer* occurs when benefits are distributed directly from one plan trustee to another, and where participants do not have the right to elect immediate distribution. It generally occurs when a group of participants moves from one plan to another as a result of a plan merger, spin-off, or other transaction. (See Qs 2:58–2:60.)

Q 2:55 What is an *elective transfer*?

An *elective transfer* is the process whereby a participant who is entitled to receive a distribution elects to have his or her entire benefit transferred into a new plan. [Treas Reg § 1.411(d)-4, Q&A 3(b)(1)] An elective transfer is very similar in both process and effect to a direct rollover. However, in an elective transfer, 100 percent of a participant's vested account balance must be transferred, while in a direct rollover, a participant is entitled to roll over any portion of a distribution. Additionally, benefits that are not eligible rollover distributions (see Qs 15:49–15:50), such as after-tax employee contributions, can be transferred in an elective transfer process.

Q 2:56 What design considerations should govern whether a plan should accept rollover contributions?

Plans are not required to accept rollover contributions. A plan that accepts rollovers will generally need to account separately for rollover contributions and may have different distribution options available with respect to rollover accounts. For example, a plan might permit in-service withdrawal of a participant's rollover account for any purpose while limiting in-service withdrawals of other 401(k) plan accounts to hardship. Many plans will also permit participants to make their own investment decisions with respect to a rollover account. The only separate treatment for a rollover account that is required as a practical matter is separate accounting of those funds.

One advantage to an employer in accepting rollovers is that it may make the plan more attractive and may help to recruit new employees. It may also create flexibility in the event of a plan merger or consolidation.

Q 2:57 If a plan accepts rollover contributions, should any steps be taken to ensure that the contribution is eligible for rollover?

It makes sense for a plan administrator to obtain some assurance that a rollover contribution is valid—that is, that it came from a qualified plan or conduit IRA and that it was transferred either as a direct rollover or within 60 days after a participant received it. The risk in not taking these precautions is that the contribution will be considered an after-tax contribution subject to nondiscrimination testing under Code Section 401(m) and will be counted as an annual addition under Code Section 415.

Q 2:58 Are plans required to accept transfers?

No. Accepting transferred benefits is more complicated than accepting rollover contributions (see Q 2:59), and plans are not required to do so.

Q 2:59 What considerations are involved in accepting plan transfers?

Accepting transfers within plans of the same employer may provide flexibility should the employer wish to redesign or otherwise alter the plans it offers to employees. For this reason, many plans contain a feature permitting this type of transfer.

Accepting transfers from another employer's plan can serve a useful purpose. For example, for a company that is growing through acquisition, accepting transfers will provide flexibility and efficiency to the process of merging benefits for employees of a newly acquired company. However, there are also a number of pitfalls involved in accepting transferred benefits that may be difficult to overcome if the plan distributing benefits is from an unrelated employer.

Transferred benefits will generally carry with them any distribution options, including qualified joint and survivor annuity requirements and other optional forms of benefit, that existed in the distributing plan. Thus, an employer accepting transferred benefits may end up essentially operating two separate plans—one for the transferred benefits and another for existing and future benefits. The employer accepting the transfer will be required to review the documents of the distributing plan to identify all protected distribution options and then apply those options to the transferred benefits.

Q 2:60 How are transferred or rolled-over benefits counted for purposes of nondiscrimination testing?

Benefits that have been rolled over (in either a direct or 60-day rollover) or transferred pursuant to an elective transfer process (see Q 2:55) are not taken into account in determining whether contributions or benefits under a plan are nondiscriminatory (see chapter 11). [Treas Reg § 1.401(a)(4)-11(b)(1)] Other transferred benefits will be taken into account. For example, benefits transferred as a result of a plan merger will be counted for purposes of Section 401(a)(4) nondiscrimination testing.

BASIC QUALIFICATION REQUIREMENTS

Q 2:61 How do basic qualification requirements affect the design of a 401(k) plan?

401(k) plans, like other types of qualified plans, must meet the basic qualification requirements for retirement plans contained in Code Section 401(a). In addition, 401(k) plans must meet qualification rules that apply specifically to cash or deferred arrangements.

Q 2:62 What advantages accrue to a 401(k) plan that is qualified?

There are many advantages to having a qualified 401(k) plan. A 401(k) plan that meets the basic qualification rules will allow the employer to take a tax deduction for contributions to the plan, will cause investment earnings of the plan's assets to be exempt from current taxation, and will avoid current taxation to plan participants of amounts allocated to their accounts.

Formal Requirements

Q 2:63 Must the 401(k) plan be in writing?

Yes. Although some states do recognize the existence of an oral trust, a 401(k) plan will not be considered qualified unless it is established and operated in accordance with a definite written program. [Treas Reg § 1.401-1(a)(2)] The written document must include all provisions essential for qualification. [Rev Rul 74-466, 1974-2 CB 131] The plan document serves to define the rights and obligations of the plan sponsor, participants, and beneficiaries. It also forms the basis of any IRS determination that the plan is tax-qualified. (See Qs 3:19–3:24.)

Q 2:64 Does the plan have to be communicated to employees?

Yes. Internal Revenue Code provisions generally require that a plan be communicated to employees. [Treas Reg § 1.401-1(a)(2); Rev Rul 71-90, 1971-1 CB 115] Department of Labor (DOL) regulations also contain this requirement and detail the content and method for this communication. (See Qs 18:22, 18:23.)

Q 2:65 How are assets of the plan held?

All assets of a qualified plan must be held in a trust that is created and organized in the United States and maintained as a domestic trust. [IRC § 401(a); Treas Reg § 1.401-1(a)(3)(i)] However, foreign trusts may be entitled to some favorable tax treatment. [IRC § 402(e)(5)] DOL provisions generally prohibit a trustee or other fiduciary from maintaining the indicia of ownership of any assets that are not subject to the jurisdiction of the United States district courts. [ERISA § 404(b)] An exception from the trust requirement is carved out for plans that use custodial accounts held by a bank or other person satisfactory to the IRS, or annuity contracts issued by qualified insurance companies. [IRC § 401(f); ERISA § 403(a)]

Q 2:66 Can a 401(k) plan provide insurance benefits to participants?

A 401(k) plan must be established primarily to offer deferred compensation to employees. The plan will not violate this rule if it provides for incidental life, accident, or health insurance benefits. [Treas Reg § 1.401-1(b)(1)(ii)] Insurance benefits in a 401(k) plan will be considered incidental if the aggregate premiums paid for insurance benefits do not exceed 25 percent of the aggregate contributions and forfeitures that have been allocated to that participant. If ordinary life (for example, whole life) is purchased, the same rule is applied, using a 50 percent limit. The rationale for the increased limit is that only half the premium used to buy ordinary life insurance is used for the purchase of a death benefit. The rest is used to build deferred cash benefits. [Rev Rul 61-164, 1961-2 CB 99; IRS Pub 778]

Continuing Contributions

Q 2:67 Must the 401(k) plan be a permanent and continuing arrangement?

A plan will not be considered qualified if it appears from surrounding facts and circumstances that it was established as a temporary program. A profit sharing plan will be considered temporary if substantial and recurring contributions are not made. It will also be considered temporary if it is abandoned within a few years after it is established for reasons other than business necessity. A plan will be considered permanent, however, even though contributions are not made every year. The employer may also reserve the right to terminate the plan or discontinue contributions without jeopardizing its status as a permanent program. [Treas Reg § 1.401-1(b)(2)]

The issue of permanency is unlikely to arise in a 401(k) plan because contributions are likely to be made each year and contributions are not dependent on the employer's profits.

Q 2:68 Can the employer take back contributions that have been made to the 401(k) plan?

Under the terms of the trust, it must be impossible for any plan assets to be used for a purpose other than the exclusive benefit of employees and beneficiaries until all the plan's liabilities to employ-ees and beneficiaries have been satisfied. [IRC § 401(a)(2)] This rule generally bars the employer from recapturing any contributions made to the plan or other plan assets. It also prohibits a plan from covering nonemployees, such as certain limited partners or inde-pendent contractors. [Rev Rul 70-411, 1970-2 CB 91; Rev Rul 69-569, 1969-2 CB 91]

Q 2:69 Under what limited circumstances may contributions be returned to the employer without jeopardizing the qualified status of the 401(k) plan?

If a contribution is made in the first year of the plan and is con-tingent on the plan's receiving a favorable determination letter from the IRS, the contribution may be returned if the IRS denies the plan's qualified status and the contribution is returned within one year of that denial. [ERISA § 403(c)(2)(B); Rev Rul 91-4, 1991-1 CB 57]

If a contribution is made contingent on its tax deductibility and the IRS disallows the deduction, the contribution may be returned within one year of the disallowance. [ERISA § 403(c)(2)(C); Rev Rul 91-4, 1991-1 CB 57] A contribution may not be returned merely because the IRS could disallow it. An active disallowance by the IRS is required.

If a contribution is made as a result of a good-faith mistake of fact, it may be returned to the employer within one year of when the contribution was made. [ERISA § 403(c)(2)(A); Rev Rul 91-4, 1991-1 CB 57] Unintentionally making a payment that is in excess of the deductible limit for plan contributions (see Q 8:54) is not con-sidered a mistake of fact. [IRS Notice 89-52, 1989-1 CB 98, Q&A 16; Ltr Rul 9144041]

Assignment of Benefits

Q 2:70 May participants assign or alienate their benefits?

As a general rule, benefits under a 401(k) plan may not be as-signed or alienated or be subject to any type of garnishment, levy, or other legal or equitable process. [IRC § 401(a)(13); Treas Reg § 1.401(a)-13(b)] The Employee Retirement Income Security Act of

1974 (ERISA) generally preempts state laws relating to employee benefit plans, including state garnishment, levy, or other attachment proceedings. [ERISA § 514(a)] This corresponding ERISA rule helps the plan trustee avoid the situation of being compelled by a state court order to make a distribution to a creditor that would have the effect of disqualifying the entire plan.

Q 2:71 What exceptions to the anti-assignment rule are recognized by the IRS?

- A qualified domestic relations order may award a portion of a participant's benefit to his or her spouse, former spouse, child, or other dependent. (See Q 16:31.)

- Benefits may be pledged as security for a loan from a plan to a plan participant. [Treas Reg § 1.401(a)-13(d)(2)]

- A portion of future benefit payments may be assigned by a participant or beneficiary in pay status. The assignment must be voluntary and revocable, must not in the aggregate exceed 10 percent of any benefit payments, and must not have the purpose or effect of defraying administrative costs to the plan. [Treas Reg § 1.401(a)-13(d)(1)]

- A participant or beneficiary may make a revocable election to pay some or all of his or her benefit to a third party (including his or her employer). The third party must file a statement in writing with the plan administrator stating that he or she has no enforceable rights to any plan benefits that he or she has not already received. [Treas Reg § 1.401(a)-13(e)]

- A plan may make payments in response to a federal tax levy or judgment without jeopardizing the qualified status of the plan. [Treas Reg § 1.401(a)-13(b)(2)]

- The Taxpayer Relief Act of 1997 (TRA '97) added an exception that allows a participant's benefit to be offset by amounts due the plan pursuant to a court order or a settlement agreement with the DOL or Pension Benefit Guaranty Corporation (PBGC) against the participant for crimes or violations of ERISA involving the plan. This exception is effective for orders issued or settlement agreements entered into after August 5, 1997. [TRA '97 § 1502]

Q 2:72 Is there an exception to the anti-assignment rules for bankruptcy of the participant?

No. The United States Supreme Court resolved a long-standing question by holding that benefits in a plan subject to Title I of ERISA are not available to pay creditors in a bankruptcy proceeding. [Patterson v Shumate, 112 S Ct 2242 (1992)]

Under bankruptcy law the estate available for distribution to creditors includes all legal and equitable property interests owned by the debtor. [Bankruptcy Code § 541(a)] There is an exception from this rule for property held in a trust that restricts the transfer of trust property under applicable nonbankruptcy law. [Bankruptcy Code § 541(c)(2)] The Supreme Court ruled that ERISA's anti-alienation provisions constitute applicable nonbankruptcy law. Therefore, a participant's benefits in a qualified plan are not part of the bankruptcy estate and are thus not available to pay claims of creditors.

Several lower court cases have created exceptions to the *Patterson v. Shumate* ruling in cases where the only employees covered by a plan are owner-employees. However, these rulings should not have any impact on a 401(k) plan.

Q 2:73 Is there an exception to the anti-assignment rules for amounts owed to the employer?

There is no exception to the anti-assignment rules that permits an employer to withhold benefit payments otherwise due an employee as security for amounts owed by the employee to the employer. The Supreme Court has ruled that even if an employee embezzles funds from an employer, the employee's benefit in a qualified plan cannot be used to pay back the employer. [Guidry v Sheet Metal Workers National Pension Fund, 493 US 365 (1990)]

Merger or Consolidation

Q 2:74 What protection must participants have in the event of merger or consolidation?

A plan must provide that upon the merger or consolidation of the plan, each participant is entitled to receive benefits after the merger that are no less than the benefits he or she was entitled to before the merger. [IRC §§ 401(a)(12), 414(l); Treas Reg § 1.401(a)-12] As a practical matter, this requires that a merging plan allocate any contributions, forfeitures, or earnings and identify the account balance of each participant as of the date of the merger. (See chapter 20 for a detailed discussion of plan mergers.)

Nondiscrimination Rules

Q 2:75 What is the purpose of the nondiscrimination rules?

The purpose of the nondiscrimination rules is to limit the extent to which plan sponsors may maintain a 401(k) plan that exclusively or primarily benefits only highly compensated or key employees. The nondiscrimination rules are discussed in detail in chapters 9 through 13.

Q 2:76 What are the basic nondiscrimination requirements?

The Code gives the following four nondiscrimination requirements:

1. The plan must meet certain minimum standards concerning coverage of employees. (See chapter 10.)

2. The plan must not discriminate in favor of highly compensated employees with respect to contributions, benefits, or other rights and features of the plan. (See chapter 11.)

3. Elective contributions, matching contributions, and employee after-tax contribution must meet special nondiscrimination tests. (See chapter 12.)

4. A plan that is top heavy must meet additional rules concerning the vesting of benefits and minimum contributions or benefits. (See chapter 13.)

Compensation and Benefit Limits

Q 2:77 How much compensation can be used for calculating plan contributions or benefits?

There is a limit on the amount of compensation that can be taken into account for computing plan contributions and benefits and for applying nondiscrimination tests. The 1999 limit is $160,000. This amount will be adjusted for inflation in $10,000 increments. [IRC § 401(a)(17)]

Q 2:78 Is there a limit placed on the amount that can be contributed to a 401(k) plan?

Code Section 415 places annual limits on the amount that can be contributed to a plan on behalf of individual plan participants. These limits are discussed in detail in chapter 8.

Q 2:79 What are the basic limits for a 401(k) plan?

The amount of annual additions allocated to a participant cannot exceed the lesser of $30,000 or 25 percent of the participant's compensation. (See Qs 8:20–8:25.) [IRC § 415(c)]

Q 2:80 Are there special limits that apply to elective contributions?

There is an annual limit on the amount of elective contributions that may be made by an individual to the 401(k) plan. The 1999 limit is $10,000, and it will be adjusted for inflation in $500 increments. [IRC § 401(a)(30)]

Q 2:81 Do contributions need to be based on business profits?

Contributions to a 401(k) plan do not need to be based on profits or accumulated retained earnings. The Tax Reform Act of 1986 removed this requirement. [IRC § 401(a)(27)]

Distribution Requirements

Q 2:82 Are there basic qualification requirements relating to how benefits must be paid from a 401(k) plan?

Yes. A 401(k) plan must meet certain rules concerning when distributions of benefits must be made available (see Q 15:12) as well as minimum distribution requirements (see Q 15:20).

A 401(k) plan must provide for automatic survivor benefits payable to the surviving spouse of a participant in the form of a qualified joint and survivor annuity or a qualified preretirement survivor annuity unless an exception applies. (See chapter 16.)

Finally, there are restrictions on when the distribution of elective contributions can be made to participants. (See Q 14:47.)

Q 2:83 Must a participant have the option to make a direct rollover of a distribution to an IRA or other qualified plan?

A 401(k) plan must provide the option for a participant to elect to have an eligible rollover distribution made by means of a direct trustee-to-trustee transfer to an IRA or other qualified plan of the participant's choice. [IRC § 401(a)(31)] If a participant fails to choose a direct rollover, the plan administrator is required to withhold 20 percent of the distribution for income tax. [IRC § 3405(c)]

Eligibility Rights

Q 2:84 Can a 401(k) plan place restrictions on which employees may become plan participants?

Most 401(k) plans contain restrictions on who may become plan participants. For example, a plan may restrict participation to employees not covered by a collective bargaining agreement. Plans are free to impose restrictions of this kind; however, the resulting class of eligible employees must satisfy the Section 410(b) coverage rules. (See chapter 10.) Frequently, 401(k) plans restrict participation to those employees who satisfy minimum age and/or minimum service requirements, but such restrictions are subject to special rules.

Q 2:85 May a 401(k) plan require employees to reach a certain age before they can become plan participants?

Yes. A 401(k) plan may require employees to attain any age up to 21 before they may become participants in the plan. [IRC § 410(a)(1)(A)(i)]

Q 2:86 May a 401(k) plan exclude from participation any employee who has reached a specified age?

No. Maximum age conditions are not permitted. [IRC § 410(a)(2)]

Q 2:87 What length of service requirement may a 401(k) plan impose?

A 401(k) plan may require up to one year of service before allowing employees to make elective contributions. [Treas Reg § 1.401(k)-1(e)(5)] If a 401(k) plan also provides for employer contributions, employees can be required to complete up to two years of service before becoming entitled to receive those contributions. In that case, however, the law requires employees to be 100 percent vested in their accounts attributable to employer contributions. [IRC § 410(a)(1)(B)(i)]

Q 2:88 What is a *year of service*?

A *year of service* is any eligibility computation period during which an employee completes the number of hours of service specified in the plan. Not more than 1,000 hours may be specified for this purpose. [IRC § 410(a)(3)(A)]

Q 2:89 What is an *eligibility computation period*?

The initial *eligibility computation period* is the 12-month period beginning on the date on which an employee is credited with an hour of service (employment commencement date). Subsequent eligibility computation periods may be based on the 12-month periods beginning on the anniversaries of the employment commencement date. In the alternative, a plan may base subsequent eligibility computation periods on plan years beginning with the plan year in which occurs the first anniversary of the employment commencement date. [DOL Reg § 2530.202-2]

Example. Company A's 401(k) plan, which is a calendar-year plan, has a one-year minimum service requirement. Joe is hired June 15, 1998. During the initial eligibility computation period (June 15, 1998–June 14, 1999), he does not complete 1,000 hours of service. Under the plan, subsequent eligibility computation periods are based on the plan year, and during the 1999 plan year Joe completes more than 1,000 hours of service. As a result, Joe would become a participant on January 1, 2000 (assuming the plan has semiannual entry dates). Note that if the plan based subsequent eligibility computation periods on the anniversaries of the employment commencement date, then the earliest Joe could enter the plan would be July 1, 2000, which is the semiannual entry date following the second eligibility computation period (June 15, 1999–June 14, 2000).

Q 2:90 What is an *hour of service*?

Under Department of Labor (DOL) regulations, an *hour of service* must be credited for each of the following:

1. Each hour for which an employee is paid, or entitled to payment, for the performance of duties;

2. Each hour for which an employee is paid, or entitled to payment, on account of a period of time during which no duties are performed (whether or not employment has been terminated) as a result of vacation, holiday, illness, disability, layoff, jury duty, military duty, or leave of absence (not more than 501 hours of service are required to be credited on account of any single continuous period during which no duties are performed); and

3. Each hour for which back pay, irrespective of mitigation of damages, is either awarded or agreed to by the employer.

[DOL Reg § 2530.200b-2(a)]

The regulations set forth complicated rules for determining the number of hours of service for reasons other than the performance of duties and for the crediting of hours of service to computation periods. [DOL Reg §§ 2530.200b-2(b), 2530.200b-2(c)]

Q 2:91 Do the regulations provide other methods for determining hours of service?

Yes. Rather than counting actual hours of service, an employer may elect to use an equivalency method for determining hours of service. There are equivalencies based on hours worked, regular time hours, periods of employment, and earnings. [DOL Reg §§ 2530.200b-3(c), 2530.200b-3(d), 2530.200b-3(e), 2530.200b-3(f)]

Q 2:92 After an employee has satisfied the minimum age and/or service requirements under a 401(k) plan, when must participation commence?

Participation must commence no later than the earlier of the following dates:

1. The first day of the plan year beginning after the date on which the employee has satisfied the plan's minimum age and/or service requirements, or

2. The date six months after the date such requirements are satisfied.

[Treas Reg § 1.410(a)-4(b)(1)]

401(k) plans will generally specify two or more dates on which employees satisfying the minimum age and/or service requirements can enter the plan.

Example. A calendar-year plan provides that an employee may enter the plan on the first semiannual entry date, January 1 or July 1, after the employee has satisfied the plan's minimum age and service requirements. The employee satisfies those requirements on January 15, 1999, and consequently becomes a participant on July 1, 1999. The plan complies with the law because the employee is eligible to participate on July 1, 1999, which is earlier than the date by which the law would require participation to commence, July 15, 1999.

Q 2:93 May an employee waive participation?

An employee may waive participation if the plan so provides. Unless the waiver is irrevocable, any such waiver provision could attract the scrutiny of the IRS, which might argue that the ability to waive participation or to rescind a waiver on a year-by-year basis is tantamount to a cash or deferred election. It should also be noted that unless a waiver is irrevocable, an employee will be considered an eligible employee for purposes of performing the actual deferral percentage test and the actual contribution percentage test. (See Qs 12:2, 12:12, and 12:38.)

Q 2:94 May a 401(k) plan exclude part-time employees from plan participation?

No. In a field directive issued in November 1994, the IRS takes the position that the exclusion of part-time employees is, in effect, a service requirement that is subject to the limitations described in Q 2:87. According to the field directive, it does not matter that a 401(k) plan will satisfy the minimum coverage requirements (see chapter 10) after excluding part-time employees.

Example. GHI Company sponsors a 401(k) plan that requires one year of service (1,000 or more hours of service in an eligibility computation period) and excludes any employee who is regularly scheduled to work fewer than 30 hours per week. Bob has been a part-time employee (fewer than 30 hours per week) for five years but has completed more than 1,000 hours during each eligibility computation period (see Q 2:89). The 401(k) plan's exclusion of part-time employees has prevented Bob from becoming a plan participant even though he has completed five years of service. Because the part-time employee exclusion is treated as an indirect service requirement, GHI Company's 401(k) plan is subject to disqualification since it contains a length of service requirement in excess of that permitted under Code Section 410(a)(1).

Break-in-Service Rules

Q 2:95 If a participant terminates employment and is then rehired at a later date, is the plan allowed to ignore years of service completed by the participant before termination of employment?

Unless a plan contains a break-in-service rule that applies to the participant, all of an employee's years of service with an employer must be taken into account. (*Employer* is defined in chapter 9.) [Treas Reg § 1.410(a)-5(c)(1)]

Example 1. Company B sponsors a 401(k) plan that contains no break-in-service rules. Linda, a plan participant, terminates employment on July 15, 1998, and is rehired August 15, 2000. Linda's years of service prior to July 15, 1998, must be taken into account. Accordingly, Linda resumes participation in the plan on her date of rehire, August 15, 2000.

Example 2. The facts are the same as in Example 1, except that Linda, although satisfying the 401(k) plan's service requirement, was never a participant because she was a member of a collective bargaining unit not covered under the plan. As in Example 1, Linda is rehired, but she is now in a class of employees covered under the plan. Linda commences participation immediately on her date of rehire. Her previous years of service are taken into account even though they were earned while she was not in a class of employees eligible to participate in the plan.

Q 2:96 What are the break-in-service rules?

There are three break-in-service rules:

1. The one-year break-in-service rule (see Q 2:97);
2. The rule of parity (see Q 2:98); and
3. The two-year, 100 percent vested break-in-service rule (see Q 2:99).

Q 2:97 How does the one-year break-in-service rule operate?

Under this rule, a 401(k) plan may disregard years of service completed before a one-year break in service until the employee completes a year of service after the break. Upon completion of a year of service following the break, the employee's pre-break years of service are retroactively restored. With the restoration of pre-break years of service, the employee's participation commences retroactively to the date of rehire. Although retroactive participation may be feasible in the case of a non-401(k) plan, it is not in a 401(k) plan. This is because an employee cannot make elective contributions with respect to compensation already received. [Treas Reg § 1.410(a)-5(c)(3)]

Q 2:98 What is the *rule of parity*?

The *rule of parity* allows a plan to disregard pre-break years of service if a participant does not have a vested account balance and the number of consecutive one-year breaks in service equals or exceeds the greater of five or the number of years of service completed before the break. This rule will generally have little significance in a 401(k) plan as it will not apply to participants who have made

100 percent-vested elective contributions to the 401(k) plan. [IRC § 410(a)(5)(D)]

Q 2:99　How does the two-year, 100 percent vested break-in-service rule operate?

Under this rule, a plan that requires employees to complete two years of service as a condition of participation may, in the case of a participant who has not satisfied this service requirement, disregard a year of service completed before a one-year break in service. [IRC § 410(a)(5)(B)] Again, this rule is of little practical significance because the elective contribution portion of a 401(k) plan cannot have a minimum service requirement of greater than one year.

Q 2:100　What is a *one-year break in service?*

A *one-year break in service* is a computation period during which an employee fails to complete more than 500 hours of service. [DOL Reg § 2530.200b-4(a)(1)]

Q 2:101　What computation period is used for determining whether an employee incurs a one-year break in service?

The computation period used for this purpose is the computation period designated in the plan for measuring years of service after the initial eligibility computation period (see Q 2:89). [DOL Reg § 2530.200b-4(a)(2)]

Q 2:102　How do maternity or paternity leaves of absence affect the determination of whether an employee incurs a one-year break in service for purposes of eligibility?

Solely for the purpose of determining whether an employee has incurred a one-year break in service, an employee absent from work on account of a maternity or paternity leave of absence must be credited with up to 500 hours of service. The number of hours of service credited during the absence will be the number of hours of service that otherwise would normally have been credited or, if that number cannot be determined, eight hours of service per day. The hours will be credited to the computation period in which the absence begins if an employee would be prevented from incurring a one-year break in service; otherwise, they will be credited to the immediately following computation period. A maternity or paternity leave of absence is any absence from work as a result of the pregnancy of the employee, the birth of the employee's child, the placement of the employee's adopted child, or the caring for the child after its birth or placement. [IRC § 410(a)(5)(E)]

Additional hours are not explicitly required for unpaid leave under the Family and Medical Leave Act of 1993 (FMLA). However, the FMLA regulations do state that any period of unpaid FMLA leave shall not be treated as or counted toward a break in service for purposes of eligibility to participate in a retirement plan. [29 CFR § 825.215(d)(4)] In addition to maternity and paternity leave, FMLA leave can include up to 12 weeks during the course of a serious health condition affecting the employee or a family member.

Vesting Rules

Q 2:103 What is *vesting*?

Vesting refers to the extent to which a participant's interest in a 401(k) plan is nonforfeitable. Any portion of that interest that is not vested is subject to possible forfeiture.

Q 2:104 Are there circumstances that require a participant's entire interest in a 401(k) plan to be vested?

Yes. All of a participant's interest in a 401(k) plan must be 100 percent vested upon the participant's attainment of normal retirement age, upon the termination or partial termination of the plan, or upon the complete discontinuance of contributions to the plan. [Treas Reg §§ 1.411(a)-1(a)(1), 1.411(d)-2(a)(1)] Although this is not legally required, nearly all 401(k) plans will provide for 100 percent vesting upon a participant's death or disability.

Q 2:105 What does the term *normal retirement age* mean?

Normal retirement age means the earlier of:

1. The time specified by the 401(k) plan at which a participant reaches normal retirement age; or

2. The later of:

    The date a participant reaches age 65, or

    The first day of the plan year in which occurs the fifth anniversary of the date a participant commences participation in the plan.

[IRC § 411(a)(8); Treas Reg § 1.411(a)-7(b)]

Q 2:106 What kinds of contributions must always be 100 percent vested?

The following kinds of contributions must always be 100 percent vested:

- Elective contributions (see Q 2:18) [Treas Reg § 1.401(k)-1(c)]
- Qualified matching contributions (QMACs) (see Q 12:14) [Treas Reg § 1.401(k)-1(g)(13)(i)]
- Qualified nonelective contributions (QNECs) (see Q 12:14) [Treas Reg § 1.401(k)-1(g)(13)(ii)]
- After-tax employee contributions (see Q 12:47) [Treas Reg § 1.411(a)-1(a)(2)]
- Rollover contributions (see Qs 2:51–2:60)
- Nonelective and matching contributions in a SIMPLE 401(k) plan or safe harbor 401(k) plan (see Qs 2:131–2:163)

Q 2:107 What kinds of contributions are not subject to the 100 percent vesting requirement?

In a 401(k) plan that does not qualify as a SIMPLE plan or a safe harbor 401(k) plan, nonelective contributions (see Q 2:31) and matching contributions (see Q 2:26) are not required to be 100 percent vested at all times. Instead, these contributions must become vested under a vesting schedule at least as rapidly as under one of the two schedules below. [Treas Reg § 1.411(a)-3T(b) & (c)]

Years of Service	Vested Percentage
Fewer than 3	0%
3	20
4	40
5	60
6	80
7 or more	100
Fewer than 5	0%
5 or more	100

Q 2:108 What is a *year of service?*

A *year of service* means any vesting computation period during which an employee completes the number of hours of service specified in the plan. Not more than 1,000 hours may be specified for this purpose. [IRC § 411(a)(5)(A)] (See Q 2:90 for a discussion of the term *hour of service.*)

Q 2:109 What is a *vesting computation period?*

In most 401(k) plans the *vesting computation period* is the plan year. However, any 12-month period may be selected as long as it applies to all participants. [DOL Reg § 2530.203-2(a)]

Q 2:110 Is a 401(k) plan permitted to disregard any years of service when calculating a participant's vested percentage?

A 401(k) plan may disregard any years of service completed with respect to vesting computation periods ending before a participant's eighteenth birthday. [IRC § 411(a)(4)(A)] Years of service completed before an employer maintained a 401(k) plan or any predecessor plan may also be disregarded. [Treas Reg § 1.411(a)-5(b)(3)]

Q 2:111 What is a *predecessor plan?*

If a 401(k) plan is established within the five-year period immediately preceding or following the date another qualified plan terminates, then the other qualified plan is considered a *predecessor plan* to the 401(k) plan. [Treas Reg § 1.411(a)-5(b)(3)(v)]

Example. Employer X's qualified defined benefit plan terminated on January 1, 1995. Employer X establishes a 401(k) plan on January 1, 1999. The defined benefit plan is a predecessor plan with respect to the 401(k) plan because the 401(k) plan is established within the five-year period immediately following the date the defined benefit plan was terminated.

Q 2:112 For purposes of vesting, if a participant terminates employment and is then rehired at a later date, is the plan allowed to ignore years of service completed by the participant before termination of employment?

Unless a plan contains a break-in-service rule that applies to the participant, all of an employee's years of vesting service with an employer must be taken into account. (*Employer* is defined in chapter 9.) [Treas Reg § 1.411(a)-5(a)]

Example 1. Company B sponsors a 401(k) plan that contains no break-in-service rules and that applies a vesting schedule to the matching contributions made under the plan. Linda, a plan participant, terminates employment on July 15, 1998, and is rehired August 15, 2000. Linda's years of service prior to July 15, 1998, must be taken into account in determining the vested percentage in her account balance attributable to matching contributions.

Example 2. The facts are the same as in Example 1, except that Linda was never a participant in the 401(k) plan because she was a member of a collective bargaining unit not covered under the plan. As in Example 1, Linda is hired, but is now in a class of employees covered under the 401(k) plan. Linda's years of service completed before July 15, 1998, must be taken into account even though they were earned while she was not in a class of employees eligible to participate in the plan.

Q 2:113 What break-in-service rules may apply in determining an employee's vested percentage?

There are three break-in-service rules:

1. The one-year break-in-service rule (see Q 2:114);
2. The rule of parity (see Q 2:115); and
3. The five-year rule (see Q 2:116).

Q 2:114 For purposes of vesting, how does the one-year break-in-service rule operate?

Under this rule, a 401(k) plan may disregard years of service completed before a one-year break in service until the employee completes a year of service after the break. Upon completion of a year of service following the break, the employee's pre-break years of service may again be taken into account in determining the employee's vested percentage. [Treas Reg § 1.411(a)-6(c)(1)(i)]

Q 2:115 What is the rule of parity for vesting purposes?

The rule of parity allows a 401(k) plan to disregard pre-break years of service if a participant does not have a vested account balance under the plan and the number of consecutive one-year breaks in service equals or exceeds the greater of five or the number of years of service completed before the break. This rule will generally have little significance in a 401(k) plan as it will not apply to participants who have made 100 percent-vested elective contributions to the plan. [IRC § 411(a)(6)(D)]

Q 2:116 What is the *five-year rule*?

In the case of a participant who has incurred five consecutive one-year breaks in service, the *five-year rule* permits a 401(k) plan to disregard years of service completed after the break in determining the vested percentage of the participant's account balance attributable to contributions allocated before the break. [IRC § 411(a)(6)(C)]

Example. A 401(k) plan provides for nonelective contributions allocated in proportion to participant compensation. At the time she terminates employment, Betty has completed four years of service and is 50 percent vested in her account balance attributable to nonelective contributions. Betty incurs five consecutive one-year breaks in service and is then rehired. Any service completed after she returns cannot increase the vested percentage of her account balance attributable to nonelective contributions allocated to her account before her termination of employment.

Q 2:117 For purposes of vesting, what is a one-year break in service?

A one-year break in service is a vesting computation period during which an employee fails to complete more than 500 hours of service. [DOL Reg §§ 2530.200b-4(a)(1), 2530.200b-4(a)(3)]

Q 2:118 How do maternity or paternity leaves of absence affect the determination of whether an employee incurs a one-year break in service for purposes of vesting?

Solely for the purpose of determining whether an employee has incurred a one-year break in service, an employee absent from work on account of a maternity or paternity leave of absence must be credited with up to 500 hours of service. The number of hours of service credited during the absence will be the number of hours of service that otherwise would normally have been credited or, if that number cannot be determined, eight hours of service per day. The hours will be credited to the vesting computation period in which the absence begins, if an employee would be prevented from incurring a one-year break in service, or in the immediately following vesting computation period. A maternity or paternity leave of absence is any absence from work as the result of the pregnancy of the employee, the birth of the employee's child, the placement of the employee's adopted child, or the caring for the child after its birth or placement. [IRC § 411(a)(6)(E)]

Additional hours are not explicitly required for unpaid leave under the Family and Medical Leave Act of 1993 (FMLA). However, the FMLA regulations do state that any period of unpaid FMLA leave shall not be treated as or counted toward a break in service for purposes of vesting in a retirement plan. [29 CFR 825.215(d)(4)] In addition to maternity and paternity leave, FMLA leave can include up to 12 weeks for a serious health condition affecting the employee or a family member.

Q 2:119 Can a vesting schedule be amended to reduce a participant's vested percentage?

No. The vested percentage (as determined under the 401(k) plan prior to the amendment) of an employee who is a participant on the later of the date the amendment is adopted or the date the amendment is made effective cannot be reduced by reason of an amendment to the vesting schedule. [Treas Reg § 1.411(a)-8(a)]

Q 2:120 Do any participants have the right to have the vested percentage of their account balances determined under the previous vesting schedule?

Yes. Any participant with three or more years of service by the end of the election period has the right to select the previous vesting schedule. This election right, however, need not be provided to any participant whose vested percentage under the amended schedule would never be less than the percentage determined under the previous schedule. [Treas Reg §§ 1.411(a)-8T(b)(1), 1.411(a)-8T(b)(3)]

Q 2:121 What is the election period for selecting the previous vesting schedule?

The election period is a period beginning no later than the date on which the amended vesting schedule is adopted and ending on the latest of the following dates:

1. Sixty days after the amended vesting schedule is adopted;

2. Sixty days after the amended vesting schedule is made effective; or

3. Sixty days after a participant is provided a written notice of the amendment.

[Treas Reg § 1.411(a)-8T(b)(2)]

Q 2:122 Under what circumstance will the nonvested portion of a participant's account balance be forfeited?

The forfeiture of a participant's nonvested accounts will ordinarily occur only after the participant's termination of employment.

Q 2:123 When will the forfeiture occur?

The timing of the forfeiture depends on whether the plan has a cash out/buy back rule. For 401(k) plans without this rule, the non-vested portion of a participant's account balance is not forfeited until the participant incurs five consecutive one-year breaks in service. (See Q 2:116.) In the case of a 401(k) plan that contains the cash out/buy back rule, the forfeiture occurs at the time the participant receives all or any part of his or her vested interest in the plan.

Q 2:124 What is the *cash out/buy back rule?*

The *cash out/buy back rule* permits the forfeiture of a participant's nonvested account balance upon payment to the participant of the vested portion of his or her account balance. This rule will apply, however, only if two conditions are met:

1. The distribution is made no later than the close of the second plan year following the plan year in which the employee's termination of participation occurs; and

2. The plan contains a repayment provision.

[Treas Reg § 1.411(a)-7(d)(4)]

Q 2:125 How much may be forfeited?

The amount that may be forfeited depends upon the amount distributed to the participant. If the participant's entire vested account balance is distributed, then the entire nonvested portion of the account balance may be forfeited. If a participant receives less than all of his or her vested account balance, then only a portion of the nonvested account can be forfeited. That portion is determined by multiplying the nonvested account balance by the amount of distribution and then dividing by the vested account balance. [Treas Reg § 1.411(a)-7(d)(4)(iii)]

Q 2:126 What happens to forfeitures under a 401(k) plan?

The disposition of forfeitures depends on the terms of the 401(k) plan. They may, for example, be allocated as if they were additional employer nonelective contributions. On the other hand, they can be used to reduce matching contributions. Some plans provide that forfeitures attributable to nonelective contributions are to be reallocated and those attributable to matching contributions are to be used to reduce such contributions.

Repayment Rights

Q 2:127 What is the *plan repayment provision*?

Under the *plan repayment provision,* the nonvested portion of an employee's account balance that was previously forfeited must be restored to the employee upon repayment by the employee of the full amount previously distributed. A plan is not required to extend repayment rights to an employee until the employee is again covered under the plan. [Treas Reg § 1.411(a)-7(d)(4)(iv)]

Q 2:128 Must the previously forfeited amount that is restored to an employee be credited with interest from the date of the forfeiture?

No. [Treas Reg § 1.411(a)-7(d)(4)(v)]

Q 2:129 May the plan impose limits on the participant's repayment rights?

Yes. The 401(k) plan may provide that a participant's repayment rights expire at the earlier of the following:

1. Five years after the day the participant is reemployed; or

2. At the end of a period of five consecutive one-year breaks in service.

[Treas Reg § 1.411(a)-7(d)(4)(iv)(C)]

Example. John, a participant in GHI Company's 401(k) plan, receives a distribution of $10,000 following his termination of employment in 1995. The nonvested portion of his interest in the plan, $5,000, is forfeited under the plan's cash out/buy back rule. John is rehired on January 1, 2000, after incurring four consecutive one-year breaks in service. Because he has not incurred five consecutive one-year breaks in service, John's repayment rights are still in effect. His right of payment cannot lapse until January 1, 2005, five years after his date of reemployment.

Q 2:130 If repayment rights are exercised, what funds may be used to restore previously forfeited account balances?

The plan can restore previously forfeited account balances from plan earnings, current forfeitures, or employer contributions. [Treas Reg § 1.411(a)-7(d)(6)(iii)(C)]

SIMPLE 401(k) PLANS

Q 2:131 What is a *SIMPLE 401(k)* plan?

A *SIMPLE 401(k) plan* is a 401(k) plan under which an eligible employer no longer needs to be concerned with discrimination testing (see chapter 12) or with top-heavy rules (see chapter 13). [IRC §§ 401(k)(11) and 401(m)(10)] There is a trade-off, however. SIMPLE 401(k) plans mandate fixed levels of employer contribution, lower the elective deferral limit, and require 100 percent vesting of employer contributions.

SIMPLE 401(k) plans are similar to SIMPLE retirement account plans, which were also created by the Small Business Job Protection Act of 1996, but they also differ in important ways. (SIMPLE retirement account plans, also called SIMPLE IRA plans, are discussed in chapter 21.)

Q 2:132 Which employers are eligible to sponsor SIMPLE 401(k) plans?

Any employer that has 100 or fewer employees with at least $5,000 of compensation in the preceding calendar year is eligible to sponsor a SIMPLE 401(k) plan. Eligible employers include private tax-exempt organizations but not governmental employers. The Section 414 employer aggregation and leased employee rules apply in determining which employees to count. An employer that no longer satisfies the 100-employee rule may continue to sponsor a SIMPLE 401(k) plan during a two-year grace period.

Example. Because it had only 80 employees earning at least $5,000 during calendar year 1997, Small Company, Inc. decided to establish a SIMPLE 401(k) plan for the 1998 calendar year. During 1998 and 1999, Small Company, Inc. employed fewer than 100

$5,000-per-year employees. In 2000, however, the number of such employees exceeded 100. The grace period during which Small Company, Inc. may continue to maintain its SIMPLE 401(k) plan consists of the years 2001 and 2002.

Q 2:133 What dollar limit applies to elective contributions under a SIMPLE 401(k) plan?

Under a SIMPLE 401(k) plan, each employee may elect to defer up to $6,000 of compensation into the plan (subject to the Code Section 415 25 percent of pay limitation). This dollar limit is adjusted each year for inflation in $500 increments. This $6,000 amount is significantly less than the $10,000 permitted to be deferred during 1999 into a regular 401(k) plan. (See Q 8:19.)

Q 2:134 Under what conditions would the reduced elective deferral limit for SIMPLE 401(k) plans make sense?

In a 401(k) plan with low participation rates on the part of non-highly compensated employees, the nondiscrimination test that applies to elective contributions (see chapter 12) may prevent highly compensated employees from deferring the maximum permitted amount ($10,000 for 1999). Also, compensation levels, even for HCEs, may prevent the maximum amount from being deferred. (See Q 8:20.)

Q 2:135 What employer contributions are required to be made to a SIMPLE 401(k) plan?

An employer is required to provide a dollar-for-dollar match on salary deferrals up to 3 percent of compensation. However, in lieu of making the matching contribution, an employer may elect to make a nonelective contribution of 2 percent of compensation to all eligible employees. This election must be made and communicated to employees within a reasonable time before the sixtieth day before the beginning of the calendar year for which the election is effective. [IRC § 401(k)(11)(B)(ii)] When calculating the required matching or nonelective contributions, a SIMPLE 401(k) plan must cap compensation at the Code Section 401(a)(17) limit ($160,000 for 1999). (Compensation is not limited by Code Section 401(a)(17) when calculating matching contributions under a SIMPLE IRA plan.)

Q 2:136　May an employer contribute more than the amount required to be contributed to a SIMPLE 401(k) plan?

No. The limitation on the amount that can be contributed by an employer will make the SIMPLE 401(k) plan unattractive to employers that wish to contribute and deduct the maximum amount permitted under the law. (See Qs 8:46–8:55.)

Q 2:137　May employees eligible for a SIMPLE 401(k) plan also participate in other retirement plans of the sponsoring employer?

No. The existence of one or more other retirement plans covering any of the same eligible employees would eliminate the SIMPLE 401(k) plan as an option. For example, an employer with a money purchase plan providing a contribution rate of 10 percent of compensation cannot continue to maintain that plan and also provide a SIMPLE 401(k) plan to any of the same group of participants. Nor can the employer terminate the money purchase plan and provide the same 10 percent nonelective contribution rate under a SIMPLE 401(k) plan, since those contributions would be limited to 2 percent of compensation (see Q 2:135).

Q 2:138　What conditions, if any, can be placed on the receipt of matching contributions in a SIMPLE 401(k) plan?

No conditions are allowed; therefore, an employer must match elective contributions made by all eligible employees. Consequently, a SIMPLE 401(k) plan will not appeal to an employer whose existing 401(k) plan requires an employee to complete a specified number (not more than 1,000) of hours of service during the year and/or to be employed on the last day of the year in order to be entitled to a matching contribution. Of course, if conditions such as these are imposed in a non-SIMPLE 401(k) plan, the employer must be concerned about the 401(k) plan's meeting the Section 410(b) minimum coverage rules. (See chapter 10.)

Q 2:139 What conditions, if any, can be placed on the receipt of the 2 percent nonelective contribution in a SIMPLE 401(k) plan?

As with matching contributions, no hours of service and/or last day requirements are allowed. However, an employer may require a participant to have received $5,000 of compensation during the plan year (or any lesser amount specified by the employer) to be entitled to an allocation of the 2 percent nonelective contribution.

Q 2:140 Can a SIMPLE 401(k) plan have minimum age and service requirements that must be met before an employee can become a participant?

Yes. In this respect there is no difference between a regular 401(k) plan and a SIMPLE 401(k) plan. (See Qs 2:85–2:92.) Hence, employers adopting SIMPLE 401(k) plans can prevent part-time employees (less than 1,000 hours of service in an eligibility computation period) from becoming plan participants. This feature cannot be duplicated in a SIMPLE IRA plan because employees can be kept out of a SIMPLE IRA plan only if their compensation is below $5,000. (See chapter 21.)

Q 2:141 What special vesting rules apply to SIMPLE 401(k) plans?

A SIMPLE 401(k) plan must provide that employer contributions as well as elective contributions be 100 percent immediately vested. In a regular 401(k) plan, on the other hand, employer contributions can be made subject to a vesting schedule. (See Q 2:107.) If an employer has low employee turnover, the 100 percent immediate vesting requirement will probably not be of great concern. High turnover that consistently produces substantial forfeitures will make the SIMPLE 401(k) plan unattractive to employers with a high-turnover workforce.

Q 2:142 How can an employer establish a SIMPLE 401(k) plan or convert an existing 401(k) plan to a SIMPLE 401(k) plan?

This can be done by using an IRS-drafted model amendment that contains SIMPLE 401(k) plan provisions. The model amendment can be found in Revenue Procedure 97-9. [1997-1 CB 624] It is available only for sponsors of 401(k) plans that have received favorable opinion, notification, advisory, or determination letters that take into account the requirements of TRA '86. The model amendment also contains a model revocation clause that permits employers to revoke the SIMPLE provisions without terminating the plan.

SAFE HARBOR 401(k) PLANS

Q 2:143 What is a *safe harbor 401(k) plan?*

A *safe harbor 401(k) plan* is a 401(k) plan under which an employer will no longer be required to perform nondiscrimination testing of elective contributions or matching contributions. [IRC §§ 401(k)(12) and 401(m)(11)] To land within the safe harbor, a 401(k) plan must meet certain employer contribution requirements and, like a SIMPLE 401(k) plan, must provide for 100 percent immediate vesting of these contributions. Other limitations that apply to SIMPLE 401(k) plans—reduced elective deferral limits and exclusive plan requirements—do not apply to safe harbor 401(k) plans. This should make safe harbor 401(k) plans attractive to more employers than are attracted to the SIMPLE 401(k) option. The following questions and answers describe the benefits and myriad requirements of safe harbor 401(k) plans. [Notice 98-52, 1998-46 IRB 16]

Q 2:144 When can employers adopt a safe harbor 401(k) plan?

Employers are able to adopt safe harbor 401(k) plans starting with plan years beginning in 1999. The safe harbor design is available for both new and existing plans. For existing plans, plan amendments needed to implement the safe harbor provisions may be deferred until the date other Small Business Job Protection Act of 1996 (SBJPA) amendments are required (for calendar year plans, generally, December 31, 2000).

To satisfy the safe harbor rules, the plan year must be 12 months long or, in the case of the first plan year of a newly established plan, the plan year must be at least 3 months long (or any shorter period if established soon after the employer comes into existence). That requirement and the requirement that participant receive advance written notice of a safe harbor plan (see Q 2:145) will affect the determination of when a safe harbor 401(k) plan can be adopted.

A safe harbor plan will not be considered "newly established" if it is a *successor plan*. A plan is a *successor plan* if 50 percent or more of the eligible employees for the first plan year were eligible under another 401(k) plan of the employer in the prior year. [Notice 98-1, 1998-3 IRB 42] In that situation, the employer would have to wait to adopt 401(k) safe harbor provisions effective as of the next full plan year.

Q 2:145 What notice must be given to an employee eligible to participate in a safe harbor 401(k) plan?

Each eligible employee must be given written notice of rights and obligations under the safe harbor 401(k) plan within a reasonable period before the beginning of the plan year (or, in the year an employee becomes eligible, within a reasonable period before the employee becomes eligible). Giving such notice at least 30 days (and no more than 90 days) before the beginning of each plan year (for employees entering the plan on a day other than the first day of the plan year, during the 90-day period ending on the date of entry) is deemed to satisfy the timing requirement. A transitional rule provided that employee notices for the 1999 plan year were not required before March 1, 1999. Failure to comply with the notice requirement will cause the plan to lose its safe harbor status.

Q 2:146 What are the main advantages and disadvantages of adopting a safe harbor 401(k) plan?

By adopting a safe harbor 401(k) plan, a plan sponsor can avoid actual deferral percentage (ADP) testing of elective contributions and actual contribution percentage (ACP) testing of matching contributions. The ADP and ACP tests are used to determine whether the amount of elective contributions and matching and after-tax contributions discriminates in favor of highly compensated employees (HCEs) (see chapter 12). The plus of avoiding certain nondiscrimination testing must be weighed against these minuses: the required contributions under a safe harbor 401(k) plan can be costly, and the annual participant notice requirements can be cumbersome. [IRC §§ 401(k)(12), 401(m)(11)]

Generally speaking, employers that might benefit from a safe harbor design include the following:

- Employers with highly paid employees unable to contribute the full 401(k) dollar amount ($10,000 in 1999) because of low participation rates of the lower-paid employees

- Employers already making (or planning to make) employer contributions at or near the safe harbor levels

- Employers required to make top-heavy minimum contributions

- Employers with plans using a cross-tested profit sharing formula (i.e., the contribution allocation is tested under the general nondiscrimination test on the basis of projected benefits)

- Employers with relatively low employee turnover

Q 2:147 How is ADP testing avoided with a safe harbor design?

A 401(k) plan will satisfy the ADP test if the prescribed level of employer contributions is made on behalf of all eligible non-highly compensated employees (NHCEs) and if the employees are provided a timely notice describing their rights and obligations under the plan. The employer contributions must be required under the terms of the plan document.

Q 2:148 What employer contributions must be made to a safe harbor 401(k) plan?

Under a safe harbor 401(k) plan, an employer can elect to provide either of the following contributions:

1. A dollar-for-dollar match on elective contributions up to 3 percent of compensation and a 50 cents-on-the-dollar match on elective contributions between 3 percent and 5 percent of compensation (the *basic matching formula*); or

2. A 3 percent of compensation nonelective contribution.

Although an employer may match on a per-payroll basis, the employer must calculate the safe harbor match on the basis of the entire plan year compensation (i.e., provide for match "true-ups" in certain situations).

Q 2:149 Can other matching contribution formulas satisfy the safe harbor?

Yes. If the aggregate amount of matching contributions under an *enhanced matching formula* at any given rate of elective contributions is at least equal to the aggregate amount of matching contributions that would be made under the basic matching formula (see Q 2:148), then the alternative formula will satisfy the safe harbor.

An alternative formula will *not* satisfy the safe harbor, however, if the rate of matching contribution increases as the rate of elective contribution increases or if, at any rate of elective contributions, the rate of matching contributions that would apply with respect to any HCE who is an eligible employee is greater than the rate of matching contributions that would apply with respect to an NHCE who is an eligible employee and who has the same rate of elective contributions.

Q 2:150 How is ACP testing avoided with a safe harbor design?

A plan that satisfies the ADP test safe harbor will also satisfy the ACP test safe harbor if any of the following is true:

1. The plan provides safe harbor matching contributions using the basic matching formula (see Q 2:148) and no other matching contributions are provided under the plan;

2. The plan provides safe harbor matching contributions using an enhanced matching formula (see Q 2:149) under which matching contributions are only made with respect to elective contributions that do not exceed 6 percent of the employee's compensation and no other matching contributions are provided under the plan; or

3. The plan provides matching contributions, other than safe harbor matching contributions, and (a) the matching contributions are not made with respect to employee contributions or elective contributions that in the aggregate exceed 6 percent of the employee's compensation, (b) the rate of matching contributions does not increase as the rate of employee contributions or elective contributions increases, and (c) at any rate of employee contributions or elective contributions, the rate of matching contributions that would apply with respect to any

HCE who is an eligible employee is no greater than the rate of matching contributions that would apply with respect to an NHCE who is an eligible employee and who has the same rate of employee contributions or elective contributions.

A plan that satisfies the ADP test safe harbor with matching contributions under the basic matching formula or an enhanced matching formula will not cause the ADP test safe harbor to be failed merely because additional matching contributions may be made at the employer's discretion. The plan will fail to satisfy the ACP test safe harbor, however, if the plan provides for discretionary matching contributions on behalf of any employee that, in the aggregate, could exceed a dollar amount equal to 4 percent of the employee's compensation. Such limitation on matching contributions made at the employer's discretion does not apply to plan years beginning before January 1, 2000.

The following examples illustrate the requirements of the ACP test safe harbor rules:

Example 1. An employer's only plan, Plan M, satisfies the ADP test safe harbor using safe harbor matching contributions under the basic matching formula. No contributions, other than elective contributions and contributions under the basic matching formula, are made to Plan M. Because the Plan M satisfies the ADP test safe harbor using the basic matching formula and Plan M provides for no other matching contributions, Plan M automatically satisfies the ACP test safe harbor.

Example 2. Beginning January 1, 2000, Plan N satisfies the ADP test safe harbor using a 3 percent safe harbor nonelective contribution. Plan N also provides matching contributions equal to 50 percent of each eligible employee's elective contributions up to 6 percent of compensation. Matching contributions under Plan N are fully vested after three years of service. No other matching contributions are provided for under Plan N. The plan is maintained on a calendar-year basis, and all contributions for a plan year are made within 12 months after the end of the plan year. Based on these facts, Plan N satisfies the ACP test safe harbor with respect to matching contributions because the ADP test safe harbor is satisfied and because the matching contribution limitations (described in item 3, above) are not exceeded.

Example 3. The facts are the same as those in Example 2, except that Plan N also provides matching contributions equal to 50 percent of each eligible employee's employee contributions up to 6 percent of compensation. Plan N does *not* satisfy the matching contribution limitations because matching contributions can be made with respect to elective contributions and employee contributions that, in the aggregate, exceed 6 percent of compensation.

Example 4. The facts are the same as those in Example 2, except that Plan N also provides that Employer B, in its discretion, may make additional matching contributions up to 50 percent of each eligible employee's elective contributions that do not exceed 6 percent of compensation. Plan N does not fail to satisfy the ACP test safe harbor on account of discretionary matching contributions, because, under Plan N, the amount of discretionary matching contributions cannot exceed 4 percent of an employee's compensation.

Q 2:151 May an employer make additional contributions to a safe harbor 401(k) plan?

Yes. An employer that provides a safe harbor matching contribution could, for example, also make a profit sharing contribution to the safe harbor 401(k) plan.

Q 2:152 What special vesting rules apply to safe harbor 401(k) plans?

A safe harbor 401(k) plan must provide that the safe harbor matching or 3 percent-of-compensation nonelective contribution be 100 percent immediately vested. Any other employer contributions to a safe harbor 401(k) plan can be made subject to a vesting schedule (see Q 2:107).

Q 2:153 Can a safe harbor 401(k) plan have minimum age and service requirements that must be met before an employee can become a participant?

Yes. With regard to minimum age and service requirements, safe harbor 401(k) plans are the same as regular 401(k) plans (see Qs 2:85–2:92).

Q 2:154 Can any conditions be placed on the receipt of the matching contribution or the 3 percent nonelective contribution in a safe harbor 401(k) plan?

No. Once an employee has satisfied any minimum age and service requirements under the safe harbor 401(k) plan, the employer (see Q 2:153) must make the required contribution (match or 3 percent-of-compensation nonelective contribution) whether or not the participant is employed on the last day of the plan year or has completed 1,000 hours of service during the plan year.

Q 2:155 What restrictions, if any, can be placed on elective contributions made by participants in a 401(k) plan that provides safe harbor matching contributions?

In a 401(k) plan that provides safe harbor matching contributions, elective contributions by NHCEs may not be restricted, *except* in the manner described below:

1. A plan sponsor may limit the frequency and duration of periods in which eligible employees may make or change salary deferral elections under a plan, provided that, after receipt of the safe harbor notice, an employee has a reasonable opportunity (including a reasonable period) to make or change a cash or deferred election for the plan year—for such purposes, a 30-day period is deemed to be a reasonable period;

2. A plan sponsor may limit the amount of elective contributions that may be made by an eligible employee under a plan, provided that each NHCE who is an eligible employee is permitted (unless the employee is restricted under item 4, below) to make elective contributions in an amount that is at least sufficient to receive the maximum amount of matching contributions available under the plan for the plan year and is permitted to elect any lesser amount of elective contributions;

3. A plan sponsor may limit the types of compensation that may be deferred by an eligible employee under a plan, provided that each NHCE who is an eligible employee is permitted to make elective contributions under a definition of compensation that would be a reasonable definition of com-

pensation within the meaning of Treasury Regulations Section 1.414(s)-1(d)(2); and

4. A plan sponsor may limit the amount of elective contributions made by an eligible employee under a plan (a) because of the limitations under Code Section 402(g), the limit on elective deferrals ($10,000 in 1999), or Code Section 415, the overall limit on contributions (lesser of 25 percent of compensation or $30,000) or (b) because, on account of a hardship distribution, an employee's ability to make elective contributions has been suspended for 12 months.

Q 2:156 What compensation must be used for purposes of the safe harbor contributions?

Any definition of compensation that satisfies Code Section 414(s) can be used for purposes of the safe harbor matching and nonelective contributions; provided, however, a definition of compensation that excludes all compensation in excess of a specified dollar amount cannot be used (see chapter 9). An employer may limit the period used to determine compensation for a plan year to that portion of the plan year in which the employee is an eligible employee, provided that such a limit is applied uniformly.

Q 2:157 Is the dollar limit on elective deferrals reduced for safe harbor 401(k) plans?

No. The full elective deferral limit under Code Section 402(g) is available ($10,000 for 1999).

Q 2:158 Are employee after-tax contributions permitted in a safe harbor 401(k) plan exempt from nondiscrimination testing?

No. In a 401(k) plan that is not a safe harbor 401(k) plan, employer matching contributions and employee after-tax contributions are combined for purposes of the ACP test (see Q 12:40). If the 401(k) plan qualifies as a safe harbor 401(k) plan, however, only matching contributions are exempt from the ACP test. That is, after-tax contributions are not exempt from the ACP test.

Q 2:159 Is a safe harbor 401(k) plan exempt from the top-heavy rules?

No. Although a safe harbor 401(k) plan is not exempt from the top-heavy rules, the 3 percent-of-pay nonelective contributions made to meet the safe harbor can be credited toward an employer's top-heavy minimum contribution obligation. In contrast, the safe harbor matching contributions to a top-heavy safe harbor 401(k) plan cannot be used to help satisfy a minimum contribution obligation.

Q 2:160 Can the safe harbor nonelective contribution be counted in a cross-tested profit sharing formula or for purposes of permitted disparity?

The 3 percent-of-pay nonelective contribution can be counted in a cross-tested profit sharing formula, but cannot be used for purposes of permitted disparity (see Qs 11:15–11:25).

Q 2:161 Are in-service withdrawals of safe harbor matching and nonelective contributions permitted?

Only in some circumstances. Safe harbor matching and nonelective contributions are subject to the withdrawal restrictions of Code Section 401(k)(2)(B). Therefore, in-service withdrawals of safe harbor matching and nonelective contributions may be allowed on or after age 59½. In-service withdrawals of safe harbor contributions on account of financial hardship (or after a specified time period of being made) cannot, however, be permitted.

Q 2:162 What are some examples illustrating the various 401(k) safe harbor rules?

The following examples illustrate various rules that apply to safe harbor 401(k) plans.

Example 1. Beginning January 1, 1999, Employer A maintains Plan L covering employees (including HCEs and NHCEs) in Divisions D and E. Plan L is a 401(k) plan that provides for a required matching contribution equal to 100 percent of each eligible employee's elective contributions up to 4 percent of compensation. For purposes of the matching contribution formula, compensation is defined as all compensation within the meaning of Code Section 415(c)(3) (a definition that satisfies Code Section 414(s)). Also, each employee is permitted to make elective contributions from all compensation within the meaning of Code Section 415(c)(3) and may change an elective contribution election at any time. Plan L limits the amount of an employee's elective contributions consistent with Code Sections 402(g) and 415, and, in the case of a hardship distribution, suspends an employee's ability to make elective contributions for 12 months. All contributions under Plan L are 100 percent vested and are subject to the withdrawal restrictions of Code Section 401(k)(2)(B). Plan L provides for no other contributions, and Employer A maintains no other plans. Plan L is maintained on a calendar-year basis and all contributions for a plan year are made within 12 months after the end of the plan year.

Based on these facts, matching contributions under Plan L are safe harbor matching contributions because they are 100 percent vested, are subject to the withdrawal restrictions of Code Section 401(k)(2)(B), and are required to be made on behalf of each NHCE who is an eligible employee.

Plan L's formula is an enhanced matching formula because each NHCE who is an eligible employee receives matching contributions at a rate that, at any rate of elective contributions, provides an aggregate amount of matching contributions at least equal to the aggregate amount of matching contributions that would have been received under the basic matching formula, and the rate of matching contributions does not increase as the rate of an employee's elective contributions increases.

Plan L would satisfy the safe harbor for purposes of ADP testing if it also satisfied the safe harbor notice requirement. If the ADP test safe harbor applies, Plan L then also satisfies the ACP test safe harbor.

Example 2. The facts are the same as those in Example 1, except that instead of providing a required matching contribution equal to 100 percent of each eligible employee's elective contributions up to 4 percent of compensation, Plan L provides a matching contribution equal to 150 percent of each eligible employee's elective contributions up to 3 percent of compensation.

Plan L's formula is an enhanced matching formula, and it satisfies the safe harbor contribution requirement. Plan L would satisfy the ADP test safe harbor if it also satisfied the safe harbor notice requirement. If the ADP test safe harbor applies, Plan L then also satisfies the ACP test safe harbor.

Example 3. The facts are the same as those in Example 1, except that instead of permitting each employee to make elective contributions from compensation within the meaning of Code Section 415(c)(3), each employee's elective contributions under Plan L are limited to 15 percent of the employee's "basic compensation." Basic compensation is defined under Plan L as compensation within the meaning of Code Section 415(c)(3), but excluding bonuses and overtime pay. The definition of basic compensation under Plan L is a reasonable definition of compensation within the meaning of Treasury Regulations Section 1.414(s)-1(d)(2).

Plan L will not fail to satisfy the safe harbor contribution requirement merely because Plan L limits the amount of elective contributions and the types of compensation that may be deferred by eligible employees, provided that each NHCE who is an eligible employee may make elective contributions equal to at least 4 percent of the employee's compensation under Code Section 415(c)(3) (i.e., the amount of elective contributions that is sufficient to receive the maximum amount of matching contributions available under the plan).

Example 4. The facts are the same as those in Example 1, except that Plan L provides that only employees employed on the last day of the plan year will receive a safe harbor matching contribution. Plan L would not satisfy the safe harbor contribution requirement because safe harbor matching contributions are not made on behalf of all NHCEs who are eligible employees and who make elective contributions.

The result would be the same if, instead of providing safe harbor matching contributions under an enhanced formula, Plan L provides for a 3 percent safe harbor nonelective contribution that is restricted to eligible employees who are employed on the last day of the plan year.

Example 5. The facts are the same as those in Example 1, except that instead of providing safe harbor matching contributions under the enhanced matching formula to employees in both Divisions D and E, employees in Division E are provided safe harbor matching contributions under the basic matching formula, while matching contributions continue to be provided to employees in Division D under the enhanced matching formula.

The plan would fail to satisfy the safe harbor contribution requirement because the rate of matching contributions with respect to HCEs in Division D at a rate of elective contributions between 3 percent and 5 percent would be greater than that with respect to NHCEs in Division E at the same rate of elective contributions. For example, an HCE in Division D who would have a 4 percent rate of elective contributions would have a rate of matching contributions of 100 percent while an NHCE in Division E who would have the same rate of elective contributions would have a lower rate of matching contributions.

Q 2:163 May employees covered by a safe harbor 401(k) plan also participate in other retirement plans of the same employer?

Yes. Employees covered by a safe harbor 401(k) plan may also be covered under another qualified retirement plan maintained by their employer. Further, safe harbor contributions may be made to another defined contribution plan as if the contribution were made to the safe harbor 401(k) plan.

3 The 401(k) Plan Document

401(k) plans, like all qualified retirement plans, must be in writing (see chapter 2). The written plan requirement means that a 401(k) plan must be embodied in a formal plan document. This chapter describes the types of documents available to 401(k) plan sponsors and considers the merits of having the plan document reviewed and approved by the Internal Revenue Service (IRS).

PLAN DOCUMENT ALTERNATIVES

Q 3:1 What plan document alternatives are available to a 401(k) plan sponsor?

A plan sponsor adopting a 401(k) plan has four plan document alternatives:

1. Master or prototype plan;

2. Regional prototype plan;

3. Volume submitter plan; or

4. Individually designed document.

Determining what type of document to use will depend on the sponsor's needs for investment and design flexibility, the costs of document preparation and IRS review, and the costs of ongoing compliance with legislative and regulatory changes.

Master and Prototype Plans

Q 3:2 What are *master* and *prototype plans*?

Master and *prototype plans* are documents that have been reviewed and approved by the National Office of the IRS. The sponsors of master and prototype plans are limited to banks, insurance companies, credit unions, mutual funds, trade or professional organizations, or individuals approved by the IRS. [Rev Proc 89-9, 1989-1 CB 780] The preapproved documents consist of two parts: the basic plan and trust document (the trust document can also be a document wholly separate from the plan document), and the adoption agreement. The basic plan and trust document contains language that cannot be varied and describes the administrative provisions in the plan. The adoption agreement contains choices for the individual plan sponsor. Typical choices include vesting schedules, deferral percentage limitations, level of matching contributions, waiting periods, minimum age requirements, loan and withdrawal options, and distribution provisions.

Q 3:3 What is the difference between master and prototype plans?

Master and prototype plans are distinguished by the type of trustee used and the funding medium. Prototype plans have a separate funding medium for each adopting employer, and the adopting employer has the ability to designate a trustee or trustees for the plan; master plans are funded using a corporate trustee and a single funding medium for the joint use of all adopting employers. The corporate trustee is responsible for reporting the trust activity to the adopting employers.

Q 3:4   What are the available document options for master and prototype plans?

Most master and prototype plan sponsors offer both standardized and nonstandardized plans. The standardized document offers very limited design options. For example, a standardized document must grant a participant employed on the last day of the year an allocation of the employer's contribution without regard to the number of hours completed. Also, a standardized document must provide a terminated participant who works more than 500 hours in a plan year an allocation of the employer's contribution.

A nonstandardized plan allows the employer to vary the plan design to suit its needs more closely. For example, a nonstandardized document may require a participant to be employed on the last day of the year and/or to complete year of service (1,000 or more hours of service in a plan year) in order to receive an allocation.

Q 3:5   What are the advantages and disadvantages of standardized and nonstandardized plans?

The basic advantage of a standardized plan is that it is designed to satisfy automatically the Internal Revenue Code's minimum coverage and nondiscrimination requirements (see chapters 10 and 11). It is an ideal choice, therefore, for employers who have few employees and who, consequently, cannot take advantage of the last day and year of service design options available to nonstandardized plans (see Q 3:4). Because it is designed to satisfy the minimum coverage and nondiscrimination requirements, the standardized plan must cover all employees except for collective bargaining employees and nonresident aliens. This requirement is of little concern to an employer with few employees, but to an employer with a large, multilocation workforce, requiring all employees to participate in a single plan would usually not meet the employer's needs.

Q 3:6   Should a plan sponsor use a master or prototype plan?

The advantages of a plan sponsor's using a master or prototype document include minimal expenses for adoption and IRS review of the plan (if deemed necessary), and the ability to rely on the master or prototype plan sponsor for plan amendments to comply with legislative and regulatory changes. In addition, the master or prototype sponsor generally provides a summary plan description to be distributed to the participants, so that the adopting employer does not have to bear the expense of drafting this document.

The disadvantages are the loss of design flexibility and the inability to make changes not available on the adoption agreement. If a master or prototype plan is amended to use provisions not contained in the adoption agreement, the plan is considered individually designed, with the consequences described in Q 3:14. Also, the terms of the basic plan document may limit the use of funding vehicles to products offered by the master or prototype plan sponsor. A plan sponsor looking for funding flexibility should choose another document type, or at least recognize the need to change documents when funding vehicles are changed.

Regional Prototype Plan

Q 3:7 What is a *regional prototype plan*?

A *regional prototype plan* is a relatively new type of plan with features quite similar to prototype plans approved by the National Office of the IRS. It differs from a master or prototype plan since it is approved in the Cincinnati, Ohio, key district office. A regional prototype plan generally provides greater design and investment flexibility to the plan sponsor than a master or prototype document.

Q 3:8 What are the requirements for regional prototype sponsors?

The requirements are far less stringent than for master or prototype plans as the sponsor may be any individual, partnership, or corporation that has an established place of business and at least 30 clients within two regions of the IRS. [Rev Proc 89-13, 1989-1 CB 801]

Q 3:9 How does the format of a regional prototype plan differ from that of a master or prototype plan?

Regional prototype plans are similar in form to prototype plans, consisting of a basic plan document and an adoption agreement.

Both standardized and nonstandardized adoption agreements are available. As with the National Office master and prototype plans, summary plan descriptions are provided by the regional prototype sponsor. The basic difference is the investment flexibility gained by the individual plan sponsor; most regional prototypes allow a wide range of investments. However, like the National Office prototypes, an amendment to a regional prototype plan that elects options not available in the adoption agreement causes the plan to be treated as individually designed.

Q 3:10 What is a *mass submitter regional prototype*?

If the sponsor itself does not have at least 30 clients, the sponsor can use the mass submitter form of a regional prototype. This is a regional prototype, which is approved by the National Office of the IRS and must be used by at least 50 unaffiliated sponsors.

Regional prototypes are available to most third-party administrative firms, using either their own plan or the plan of a mass submitter.

Volume Submitter Plan

Q 3:11 What is a *volume submitter plan*?

A *volume submitter plan* is a single document (rather than a base document and a separate adoption agreement), the format of which is preapproved by the key district office of the IRS. Volume submitter plans, which are generally offered by law firms, offer greater flexibility to the individual plan sponsor. The procedure for document approval is to submit a specimen plan to the key district of the IRS. The volume submitter must certify that at least 30 employers within two key districts will be using the plan document.

Q 3:12 What is the format of a volume submitter plan?

By contrast with the National Office or regional prototype plans, any plan provisions that do not apply to the individual plan sponsor may be deleted from the individual plan document. Thus, the plan document is far more compact and easier to use. In fact, minor language changes are permitted to accommodate the needs of the individual plan sponsor. However, if major language changes are required, the individual plan sponsor needs to use an individually designed plan, with the consequences described in Q 3:14.

Q 3:13 How do volume submitter plans compare with master and prototype plans and with regional prototype plans?

Unlike these other types of plans, a volume submitter plan does not afford the plan sponsor the opportunity to choose a standardized plan. Each plan must be individually submitted to the IRS. However, the user fee is lower than for individually designed plans. As in the case of master and prototype plans, the adopting employer can rely on the volume submitter for plan amendments to comply with legislative and regulatory changes.

Individually Designed Plans

Q 3:14 What are the advantages and disadvantages of individually designed plans?

Individually designed plans offer the greatest flexibility to the plan sponsor in plan design and availability of investment products. They also require the greatest expense in legal fees and IRS user fees. The burden of ongoing compliance with legislative and regulatory changes falls on the plan sponsor, although legal counsel generally handles this function.

Plan amendments are also expensive, as substantial plan changes may need to be submitted to the IRS for approval. Finally, summary plan descriptions and summaries of material modifications require extra effort and expense on the part of the individual plan sponsor.

ADVANCE IRS APPROVAL

Q 3:15 Is it necessary to secure advance IRS approval of a 401(k) plan document?

It is not necessary but prudent to obtain IRS approval. The advantages of a tax-qualified 401(k) plan do not depend upon securing advance IRS approval. A 401(k) plan is qualified if, in its form and operation, it meets the various requirements of the Code. Nonetheless, prudence dictates that IRS approval be secured for most types of 401(k) plans.

Advantages of Qualification and Approval

Q 3:16 What are the advantages of tax qualification?

The advantages of tax qualification are as follows:

1. The employer receives a deduction for the taxable year in which contributions are made or are deemed made.
2. The contributions made by the employer and the earnings on those contributions are not includible in the income of employees until received.
3. The earnings generated by the trust are tax exempt.
4. Amounts received by employees may be eligible for special tax treatment.

Q 3:17 What is the primary advantage of obtaining IRS approval in advance?

The primary advantage of obtaining advance IRS approval is that the IRS will not retroactively withdraw its approval of a 401(k) plan if:

1. There is no misstatement or omission of material facts.
2. The facts at the time of 401(k) plan adoption are not materially different from the facts on which IRS approval is based.
3. There is no change in the applicable law.
4. The employer has acted in good faith in relying on previous IRS approval.

Q 3:18 What are the other advantages to obtaining IRS approval in advance?

A 401(k) plan that is timely submitted to the IRS has the opportunity to amend plan provisions that do not comply with the qualification requirements of the Code. It is also believed that IRS approval diminishes the likelihood that the plan will later be audited by the IRS. Finally, certain IRS programs for correcting operational errors are available only to plans with prior IRS approval (see chapter 19).

Determination Letter Application

Q 3:19 How do plan sponsors obtain IRS approval?

Plan sponsors obtain IRS approval by applying for a determination letter. The IRS has developed several application forms, depending upon the type of 401(k) plan being submitted. The following are the most commonly used forms:

- *Form 5300*—used with individually designed plans
- *Form 5303*—used with collectively bargained plans
- *Form 5307*—used with master/prototype plans, regional prototype plans, and volume submitter plans
- *Form 6406*—used for plan amendments

More detailed information about the determination letter process can be found in Revenue Procedure 99-6. [1999-1 IRB 187]

Q 3:20 Where is the determination letter application sent?

Until recently, an application was sent to the IRS key district director for the district in which the employer's principal place of business was located. Pursuant to an IRS plan for consolidation of the determination letter process, all applications are now sent to the Cincinnati, Ohio, key district office. Its address is:

Internal Revenue Service
P.O. Box 192
Covington, KY 41012-0192

Q 3:21 Does the IRS charge a fee for reviewing a determination letter application?

Yes. The IRS charges a user fee, the amount of which depends on the type of application form and whether the employer elects to demonstrate that the plan meets the Section 410(b) coverage rules by passing the average benefits test (see Q 10:17) or that the plan is nondiscriminatory in the amount of contributions on the basis of the Section 401(a)(4) general test (see Q 11:9). Following is a table showing the fees in effect as of 1999.

Application Form	Average Benefits Test or General Test Demonstration	User Fee
5300	No	$ 700
5300	Yes	1,250
5303	No	700
5303	Yes	1,250
5307	No	125
5307	Yes	1,000
6406	N/A	125

Q 3:22 Must employees be notified of a pending determination letter application?

Yes. Employees who are interested parties are entitled to receive notice. In general, an interested party is any employee eligible to participate in the 401(k) plan; however, under certain limited circumstances specified in the regulations, other employees may also be considered interested parties. [Treas Reg § 1.7476-1(b)] The notice informs the interested parties that the IRS application is pending and that they have a right to comment to the DOL and the IRS regarding the qualification of the plan. Rules relating to the content of the notice, its timing, and its manner of distribution can be found in Sections 17 and 18 of Revenue Procedure 99-6. [1999-1 IRB 187]

Q 3:23 Is there any type of plan for which a determination letter is not necessary to obtain the advantages of advance IRS approval?

Yes. In some cases, adopters of standardized master/prototype plans or regional prototype plans may rely on the favorable opinion or notification letters received by the sponsors of master/prototype or regional prototype plans. To have automatic reliance, the employer adopting the master/prototype or regional prototype plan must not maintain or have maintained any other plan except for a paired plan. [Rev Proc 89-13, 1989-1 CB 801, § 11; Rev Proc 89-9, 1989-1 CB 780, § 6]

Q 3:24 What are *paired plans*?

Paired plans are two or more standardized master/prototype plans or regional prototype plans maintained by the same sponsor that are designed to satisfy automatically the top-heavy requirements of Code Section 416 (see chapter 13) and the contribution limitations under Code Section 415 (see chapter 8).

4 Plan Services and Service Providers

The proper operation of a 401(k) plan requires both intensive transaction activity in processing ongoing contributions and a working understanding of complex legal rules. The burden on plan sponsors is increased by the fact that they are required to act as experts in matters involving the plan. As a result, most plan sponsors outsource some or all of the services needed to operate the 401(k) plan. This chapter discusses what services a 401(k) plan might need, what types of service providers can fulfill those needs, options for plan accounting, and how to analyze the fees charged by providers.

401(k) PLAN SERVICES

Q 4:1 What services are needed in operating a 401(k) plan?

- Named fiduciary services (see Q 4:2)
- Trustee services (see Q 4:3)
- Plan administrator services (see Q 4:4)
- Investment selection and management (see Q 4:5)
- Investment processing (see Qs 4:7–4:29)
- Recordkeeping for trust and financial statements (see Qs 4:7–4:29)
- Recordkeeping for participant statements (see Q 4:7–4:29)
- Plan design and consultation (see chapter 2)
- Plan Document and Summary Plan Description drafting and maintenance (see chapter 3)
- Legal compliance (see especially chapters 5, 8, 14, and 19)
- QDRO review and determination (see chapter 6)
- Participant communication and investment education (see chapter 7)
- Nondiscrimination testing (see chapters 9–13)
- Distribution processing and tax reporting (see chapters 15–17)
- 5500 preparation (see chapter 18)

Many of these functions are typically combined and handled by one service provider.

Q 4:2 What is the role of the *named fiduciary*?

Every plan document must clearly identify one or more persons to be the *named fiduciary* for the plan. [ERISA § 402(a)] If there is only one named fiduciary, that person or entity will be considered a fiduciary for all purposes under the plan. If there is more than one named fiduciary, the named fiduciaries can allocate responsibilities among themselves. The purpose of the named fiduciary designation is to clearly identify to participants and government agencies who is primarily responsible for the plan.

Q 4:3 What is the role of the *plan trustee*?

All plan assets must be held in a trust, and a *plan trustee* must be named. The trustee holds plan assets and is usually responsible for managing the plan's investments, although this function can be subject to the direction of another fiduciary, an investment manager, or plan participants. [ERISA § 403(a)] The plan trustee is usually responsible for processing contributions and investment transactions, preparing financial statements, and disbursing funds to participants or to pay fees and expenses of the trust.

Q 4:4 What is the role of the *plan administrator*?

A *plan administrator* is responsible for determining who is eligible to participate in the plan, determining what benefits are due under the plan, and responding to benefit claims and appeals. Plan administrators also have responsibilities dictated under the Internal Revenue Code (Code) and Employment Retirement Income Security Act of 1974 (ERISA) as follows:

1. Distribution of summary plan description, summary annual reports, and statement of vested benefits to participants and beneficiaries [ERISA § 101(a), 105(a)];

2. For plans with over 100 participants, engaging an independent qualified public accountant to audit the financial records of the plan [ERISA § 103(a)(3)(A)];

3. Maintenance of plan records for at least six years [ERISA §§ 107, 209];

4. Determination of whether a domestic relations order is qualified [ERISA § 206(d); IRC § 414(p)(6)]; and

5. Providing a written explanation of rollover and tax withholding election options, as well as an explanation of tax options with respect to distributions to recipients. [IRC § 401(f)]

Q 4:5 What is the role of an *investment manager*?

An *investment manager* for a plan must be either a registered investment adviser, bank, or a qualified insurance company. The manager must agree in writing to become a fiduciary with respect to a plan. [ERISA § 3(38)] An investment manager has the power to buy, sell, and manage the assets of the plan.

Q 4:6 Can the responsibilities of the plan administrator or trustee be delegated to others?

ERISA permits fiduciaries to allocate responsibilities among themselves. Nonfiduciaries can also be named to carry out some responsibilities. A common example is the situation in which recordkeeping or other administrative services are provided by a third party to a named plan administrator. [ERISA § 405(c)(1)]

The allocation of responsibilities can be described in the plan document, in contracts with service providers, or in records kept by plan officials.

Plan fiduciaries must act prudently when allocating or delegating responsibilities. They remain responsible for monitoring the performance of experts or advisers employed to assist them with their plan responsibilities.

SELECTING PLAN ADMINISTRATION SERVICES

Proper administration is a critical element in the maintenance of an effective 401(k) plan. If participants do not receive statements on a timely basis, their satisfaction with the plan will diminish and they may cease to participate. If nondiscrimination tests are not satisfied, refunds may need to be made to highly compensated employees; worse yet, the plan may lose its qualified status. If fees are excessive and charged to the participants, the impact on the rate of return of their investments will be significant.

Q 4:7 What choices does an employer have for plan administration services?

An employer has three choices for plan administration services:

1. In-house (see Qs 4:10–4:11);

2. Bundled administration (see Qs 4:12–4:13); or

3. Third-party administration (with or without a strategic alliance) (see Qs 4:14–4:16).

Q 4:8 What factors should an employer focus on when selecting administration services?

The overall objectives of the employer in choosing an administration method should be the following:

1. Ensuring that data are maintained accurately and processed on a timely basis;

2. Ensuring that participant information is readily accessible to both the employer and the employees;

3. Ascertaining that the recordkeeping is cost-effective and that the fees charged are reasonable (to maximize the earnings credited to participants' accounts); and

4. Assuring that routines are developed that demonstrate ongoing compliance with Internal Revenue Service (IRS) and Department of Labor (DOL) regulations.

Q 4:9 What factors add cost to 401(k) plan administration?

The employer should be aware that certain plan design features can add both complexity and cost to the administration of the 401(k) plan. Such features include different sources of contributions (e.g., after-tax employee contributions, rollovers, mandatory employee contributions), investment options for employees, self-directed brokerage accounts, frequent investment change dates, liberal withdrawal provisions, and loans. Although the employer may not wish to exclude this design flexibility from the plan, it should be aware of the impact on cost.

The structure of the employer may also add to the complexity and cost of plan administration. If the employer has different divisions or different locations, gathering employee data will take more effort. Similarly, employees who transfer from one division or location to another will require special administrative considerations. If the employer has different payroll systems for different locations, this will increase the handling effort. Last, the maintenance of other benefit plans will create additional administrative effort in coordinating the limitations and benefits.

The use of technology such as daily accounting, voice response units, or Internet functions can also increase 401(k) plan costs.

In-House Administration

Historically, larger employers with more than 1,000 employees have been more likely to choose to administer their 401(k) plans in-house. These employers can typically afford to maintain benefit professionals on their staffs. The employer implementing a 401(k) plan will need to consider whether the management information staff should develop an internal system for 401(k) administration or purchase a package as an adjunct to its payroll system.

Q 4:10 What are the advantages of in-house administration of a 401(k) plan?

One major advantage is control over the original source data. The employer always maintains certain basic employee information in individual human resources files: name, Social Security number, date of birth, date of employment, and pay information. If this information is passed on to a third party, updates or changes must be handled twice: once by the employer and once by the third party. As a result, errors can occur. The employer also has easiest access to information about the other benefit plans it provides for its employees, making the coordination between plans much simpler. Moreover, an employer who is concerned about the confidentiality of data may be reluctant to pass information on to a third party.

Q 4:11 What are the disadvantages of in-house administration of a 401(k) plan?

Outside recordkeepers have both the expertise and resources to keep abreast of changes in the law. In-house benefit administrators generally have other responsibilities and less ability to assess the impact of these changes on the recordkeeping system, since 401(k) administration will not be the employer's primary business focus. The employer also may find this to be the most expensive option; outside legal and consulting resources need to be retained and consulted with on a regular basis.

In addition to the compliance issues faced by in-house administrators, the increasing use of technology in servicing 401(k) plans makes it more difficult for in-house administrators to offer the types of services and features that many participants want. Features such as daily accounting, investment processing via telephone, or Internet access to plan information and transaction activity are generally too expensive for an individual employer to invest in.

Bundled Administration

Bundled, or "one-stop shopping," services are provided by a single firm, generally an investment firm, a bank, or an insurance company that provides recordkeeping services, investment management, trustee services, and employee communication in one package. The idea is to minimize the employer's involvement in the administration of the 401(k) plan.

Q 4:12 What are the advantages of bundled 401(k) administration?

When both the investment management and recordkeeping services are provided at the same place, there is no need to rely on outside parties (other than the employer) for information. The financial institution will have the information necessary to prepare participant statements when it receives payroll data from the employer. Since the financial data are readily available, more frequent reports may be provided to participants than in-house administrators could provide. Some of the larger bundled 401(k) administrators have been in the business for many years and have considerable expertise. One key advantage of a bundled package is often cost, since the packages are frequently designed to reduce or eliminate direct costs by paying administration costs through investment management fees.

Q 4:13 What are the disadvantages of bundled 401(k) administration?

The primary disadvantage is that the employer may not be pleased with the performance of the bundled administrator in all respects. For example, if the investment performance is poor, the employer will have to choose a different administrator to provide employees with different investment opportunities. Similarly, if the employer is pleased with the investment performance but not with the timing of delivery of participant statements, the employer will have to seek another administrator and a new set of plan documents. In some cases, the bundled administrator may subcontract for the recordkeeping functions, and this may delay the delivery of reports.

Moreover, a financial institution's motivation in establishing bundled services is to manage the assets of 401(k) plans. The administration of 401(k) plans is not its primary business. It also may be difficult for the employer to ascertain the true cost of administration since certain loads or contract charges may be built into the insurance or investment contract.

Third-Party Administration

The employer may consider contracting with a third-party administrator to handle the plan recordkeeping. Under such an arrangement, the employer will generally handle the trustee functions (or contract with an independent trustee) and will also select the investments for the plan. Thus, the employer may maintain contracts with several vendors for recordkeeping, investment management, and trustee services. Alternatively, the employer may contract with a third-party administrator who has formed a strategic alliance with one or more trustees and/or investment managers. In this case, the employer can receive the one-stop shopping benefits of bundled services, while still retaining the flexibility to change investments without changing administrators, or vice versa.

Q 4:14 What are the advantages of using a third-party administrator for a 401(k) plan?

If the employer is dissatisfied with the recordkeeping of the third-party administrator, it is not necessary to disrupt the plan investments or plan documents. Similarly, the recordkeeping will not be disrupted if plan investments are changed.

Like bundled administrators, most established third-party administrators have been in the 401(k) administration business for many years. In fact, many third-party administrators have worked with defined contribution plan administration since the passage of ERISA in 1974. Thus, third-party administrators have considerable expertise. Administration is generally their only business.

Q 4:15 What are the disadvantages of using a third-party administrator for a 401(k) plan?

Processing delays may occur, since third-party administrators must wait for participant data from the plan sponsor and financial data from the investment adviser or trustee. Also, the third-party administrator must rely on the data provided by other parties, increasing the possibility for error to be introduced in the process. Finally, unlike a bundled administrator, a third-party administrator cannot easily provide reports more frequently than monthly. Many of these problems can be avoided if the third-party administrator is in a strategic alliance with the trustee or other party responsible for providing financial data (see Q 4:16) or if the plan uses a daily valuation system (see Qs 4:23–4:29).

Q 4:16 What is a *strategic alliance?*

A *strategic alliance* is a group of two or more service providers to plans that have entered into an agreement that enables them to offer a unified package of services to plan sponsors. The most common example is an investment management company combined with a third-party administration company.

The main advantage for plan sponsors participating in a strategic alliance is cost savings. Typically, the asset management company will pay a portion of its asset management fee to the third-party administrator, thereby offsetting the plan's administrative costs.

Example. Assume a plan has $5 million in assets and 100 participants. It is paying 95 basis points, or $47,500, in investment management fees and $12,000 in plan administration fees, for a total annual cost of $59,500. It joins a strategic alliance in which the investment manager agrees to pay 15 of the 95 basis points to the administrator. The plan receives the same services, but saves $7,500 and pays an annual fee of $52,000.

Q 4:17 What questions should you ask before selecting a service provider?

- How has the provider demonstrated a long-term commitment to servicing retirement plans?

- How many clients does the provider have with plans similar to yours? Can you contact those clients?

- Will any services be outsourced? If so, where? What control will you have over those providers?

- What is the total fee the provider will receive for servicing your plan, including direct fees, indirect fees, and any soft-dollar arrangements?

- Is the provider's software year-2000 compliant? If not, what is the plan for becoming compliant?

- How does the provider keep abreast of changes in the law?

- Can the provider's services be customized to meet your current and anticipated future needs? At what cost?

- Has the provider been a defendant in litigation relating to the provision of retirement plan services?

- What is the average client duration?

Q 4:18 What are other employers choosing to do for plan administration services?

According to the 1997 Hewitt survey (see chapter 1), 79 percent of plans use an outside provider as the sole source of recordkeeping services, and another 15 percent share the task with an outside provider. The types of providers selected are as follows:

Benefit consulting firm	29%
Trust company/bank	13%
Mutual fund/investment firm	28%
Recordkeeping-only firm	6%
Insurance company	3%
Internal staff	6%
Shared responsibility	15%

ALLOCATION OF EARNINGS AND EXPENSES

In a 401(k) plan, the allocation of plan earnings and expenses to participants may occur as frequently as daily or as infrequently as annually. This allocation process, called a *valuation*, updates a participant's account balance for all activity that has occurred during a valuation period, including contributions, transfers, rollovers, withdrawals, earnings, and expenses.

Traditionally, a high percentage of 401(k) valuations were performed quarterly, although the current trend is toward more frequent valuations. A 1997 survey by Hewitt Associates (see Q 1:31) indicates that 71 percent of all 401(k) plans perform valuations daily, 11 percent perform them quarterly, 16 percent perform them monthly, and 2 percent perform them annually.

Q 4:19 What are the major methods of allocating earnings and expenses to the accounts of participants?

There are two basic methods: *balance forward accounting* and *daily*, or *on demand, valuation.* Balance forward accounting is a method of approximating a participant's share of gains, losses, and expenses; each participant's account shares proportionately in these. For example, if a participant's account balance represents 1 percent of the plan's assets, then 1 percent of gains, losses, and expenses will be allocated to that participant.

Daily, or on demand, valuation is more precise. Units of securities are allocated to a participant's account; subsequent earnings, gains, losses, and expenses attributable to these units can be directly computed and allocated to the participant by daily revaluing of the units.

Balance Forward Accounting

Historically, balance forward accounting has been the traditional method for allocating gains and losses to a participant's account in a defined contribution plan. This method has provided a reasonable allocation of gains and losses in most defined contribution plans where accounts are valued annually and employer contributions are deposited annually. As 401(k) plans increased in popularity, balance forward accounting was adapted to the increased frequency of valuation and deposits.

Q 4:20 How frequently are balance forward accounts valued?

Balance forward accounts must be valued at least annually, although semiannual, quarterly, or monthly valuations are common. The terms of the plan document will dictate the frequency of valuation. In some plan documents, accounts may be valued more frequently if a significant event occurs that would result in an inequitable allocation of earnings and expenses (e.g., a stock market crash or a participant's withdrawing a significant portion of the plan's assets). It makes sense to include this flexibility in the document, since an attempt to add it in conjunction with a distribution following a market fluctuation may be considered a violation of fiduciary duty. [Pratt v Maurice L Brown Co Employee Savings Plan, 9 EBC (BNA) 2380 (DC, KS 1988)]

Q 4:21 What methods are used for allocating earnings and expenses in balance forward accounting?

Four basic methods are used in balance forward accounting. Other methods do exist, but they are variations of the methods discussed in the following list. In all cases, an allocation basis is established. Earnings and expenses are then prorated, using the allocation basis. The four methods are described as follows:

1. *Regular defined contribution method.* Allocation basis is the account balance at the beginning of the valuation period.

2. *Adjusted balance method.* Allocation basis is the account balance at the beginning of the valuation period less cash-outs, less transfers, less one half of partial withdrawals, plus one half of contributions.

3. *Ending balance method.* Allocation basis is the account balance at the beginning of the valuation period less cash-outs, less transfers, less withdrawals, plus contributions.

4. *Time-weighted method.* Allocation basis is the account balance at the beginning of the valuation period plus additions (weighted for length of time in the fund), less subtractions (weighted for length of time in the fund).

Q 4:22 Which balance forward method will provide the most equitable allocation of a plan's earnings and expenses among participants?

None of the methods will provide an equitable allocation of earnings (or losses) in the event of dramatic market fluctuations. If the underlying investments in the fund are of the fixed income variety, then methods 2 and 4 will provide a reasonably equitable allocation of earnings.

Daily Valuation

Daily, or on demand, valuation is becoming increasingly popular. Hewitt Associates, in a series of surveys, found that only 6 percent of plans were valued daily in 1988, whereas 18 percent were valued daily in 1991, 29 percent in 1993, 38 percent in 1995, and 71 percent in 1997.

Daily valuation originated with mutual fund companies, which entered the 401(k) recordkeeping business in the mid-1980s. These companies brought with them the facility and expertise to handle daily valuation from their shareholder systems, since mutual funds are valued daily and statements for mutual fund shareholders can be provided as frequently as daily. With the market crash of 1987, 401(k) and other defined contribution plan sponsors began rethinking their approach to allocating gains and losses to participants. Also, the growth of participants' accounts in 401(k) plans (the average balance of a participant in a 401(k) plan today is over $39,000) has heightened participants' awareness and interest in the following:

- Moving fund balances at will
- Having increased access to current account balances
- Sharing equitably in investment results

The technological advances in automation now make daily valuation available to even small employers.

Q 4:23 What is *daily valuation?*

Daily valuation is a computerized system for tracking trust investment activity at the participant level. In a traditional balance forward system, account balances are tracked in dollars and updated on a periodic basis. In a daily valuation system, account balances are tracked in units, and the number of units allocated is updated whenever a transaction occurs. Participants can determine the value of their accounts on any day by multiplying their allocated number of units by the market price of the unit on that day. Earnings activity (e.g., dividends, capital gains, or market fluctuation) and account activity (e.g., contributions, loans, distributions, or hardship withdrawals) are all incorporated into either the daily market price or the number of units allocated to a participant's account.

Q 4:24 What are the advantages of daily valuation to the plan sponsor?

The plan sponsor has increased flexibility in the number of fund options that may be offered to participants. It can also receive financial reports and participant statements containing information that is days old, instead of two to six weeks old, as is the case under a balance forward system. Because there is no trust reconciliation work (i.e., reconciling fund values to participant allocations) and all activity is tracked as it occurs, a clean report can be produced usually within a day or two.

Q 4:25 What are the disadvantages of daily valuation to the plan sponsor?

The handling of non-daily priced funds, including guaranteed investment contracts (GICs) and common trust funds, is not easily adapted to daily valuation, and recordkeeping expenses for these types of investment products are generally greater. Some daily valuation systems are also restricted in their ability to handle funds from more than one mutual fund family, thus limiting a sponsor's investment options. With daily valuation, there is little error tolerance, as it is more difficult to correct errors than with balance forward accounting, where small errors can generally be absorbed in the gain/loss allocation. There is also a risk that participants may abuse their ability to switch funds daily and that the plan will consequently incur significant transaction charges. Owing to the intensity of transactions, daily valuation can be more costly from a systems usage standpoint.

Q 4:26 What are the advantages of daily valuation to the participant?

The participant enjoys a more equitable allocation of market experience. The participant benefits by more timely investment of elective contributions and timely and accurate exchanges and withdrawals. Account balance information becomes available on a daily basis, compared with a four-to-eight-week lag time for balance forward accounting. Distributions can often be processed more quickly, as the participant will not have to wait for completion of a valuation before benefits can be distributed.

Q 4:27 What are the disadvantages of daily valuation to the participant?

Historically, participants in 401(k) plans are poor market timers: the tendency is to sell when prices are low and buy when prices are high. Thus, a 401(k) participant who moves money frequently will likely make poor choices and adversely affect his or her retirement security. Heightened awareness of the 401(k) investments may discourage a long-term outlook on the plan's investments, and the individual may be less patient in weathering market lows. However, there is evidence that on average participants move money less often under daily valuation than when movements are restricted to a single day per quarter or per month.

Q 4:28 How can some of the disadvantages of daily valuation be avoided?

A plan can provide a daily valuation system that does not permit participants to make investment changes on a daily basis. Participants would still be able to access information about their accounts on a daily basis and distribution processing would be faster, but the employer could limit the number of times during a year that a participant can make investment changes.

Q 4:29 What is a *voice response unit*?

A *voice response unit* is often used as an adjunct to a daily valuation system. It enables participants to access information about their accounts and perform certain types of activity by using a Touch-Tone telephone. Participants are generally given a means to access the voice response unit through use of a code and then can receive information through a recording. Recent studies have shown that although many participants and plan sponsors want to have voice response, most participants seldom use it once it becomes available.

PAYMENT OF FEES AND EXPENSES

A plan sponsor incurs many expenses in adopting and maintaining a 401(k) plan. Implementing a plan may necessitate legal fees for drafting and submitting plan documents, IRS user fees in requesting a determination letter for the plan, and consulting fees for designing and communicating the plan. An ongoing plan incurs trustee fees, recordkeeping charges, compliance costs, and investment management fees. If the plan is terminated, additional charges may result.

Surprisingly, many plan sponsors do not know the total cost of their plans. A plan's total cost can be divided into two components: identifiable and performance costs. The plan sponsor may opt to pay those expenses directly and will generally receive a tax deduction for plan-related expenses. Alternatively, the expenses may be paid from plan assets and indirectly borne by plan participants.

Plan fees have garnered considerable media attention recently. Industry reports show overall plan fees vary widely and, particularly for smaller plans, are rising. In November of 1997, the DOL held a hearing on 401(k) plan fees to assess what action, if any, it should take to improve disclosure of 401(k) fees and expenses. In 1998 the DOL issued a report entitled "A Look at 401(k) Plan Fees" and also released the results of recent research on 401(k) fees in a report entitled "Study of 401(k) Plan Fees and Expenses."

Q 4:30 What are *identifiable costs*?

Identifiable costs are predictable costs that can be anticipated in the course of plan administration.

Q 4:31 What identifiable costs may be incurred in the operation of a participant directed plan?

Identifiable costs generally include the costs of administering the plan and investing plan assets. Administration costs will often include costs related to legal compliance, employee communication, recordkeeping, trust services, consulting, and audits. Because plan assets are typically managed by mutual fund companies, banks, brokerage companies, and insurance companies, investment management costs will include costs such as sales fees, management fees, contract fees, transaction fees, and 12b-1 fees. Costs can be a stated dollar amount or a percentage of plan assets. Stated dollar fees typically include a base fee and per participant fee.

Administration costs will vary depending on the complexity of plan administration. Investment management fees will vary depending on how plan assets are invested. Typically, investment management costs are a plan's largest cost component. The amount is often expressed as a percentage of assets. Sometimes investment management fees subsidize administration costs under a fee-sharing arrangement. Although many do, not all service providers disclose such arrangements to plan sponsors.

Q 4:32 Who pays a plan's identifiable costs?

Administration and investment management costs may be paid by plan sponsors, from plan assets, or by and from both. A plan sponsor opting to pay those costs directly will generally receive a tax deduction for the expenses. [Treas Reg § 1.404(a)-3(d)] If paid from plan assets, the costs are indirectly borne by plan participants. That is, as costs are shifted to the plan, plan expenses reduce the earnings credited to plan participants' accounts.

Although charging administration costs against plan assets is an attractive option to plan sponsors, they should be aware that participants are paying the costs with money that could otherwise have been compounding on a tax-deferred basis. Administration expenses of a large plan spread over thousands of participants may have little impact on participant accounts; that may not hold true in a smaller plan. Similarly, investment management costs can have a significant impact on participant accounts.

Q 4:33 What are *performance costs*?

Performance costs are unpredictable costs that may or may not occur in the course of plan administration. Obviously, they are not identifiable up front.

Q 4:34 What performance costs may be incurred in the operation of a participant directed plan?

Costs related to legal compliance problems (e.g., additional legal costs needed to avoid plan disqualification and various penalties for noncompliance) and substandard investment performance are examples of performance costs.

Q 4:35 Who pays a plan's performance costs?

Plan sponsors typically pay the costs related to legal compliance problems and operational defects. Plan participants bear costs of substandard investment performance. Careful selection of plan administrators and investment managers can diminish the probability that performance costs will occur.

Q 4:36 Why is it important for plan sponsors to calculate total plan costs, especially those borne by participants?

Years of strong stock market performance have made it too easy for plan sponsors to overlook the effect of total costs on participants' investment returns. Past performance, however, is no guarantee of future performance. If plan participants are forced to endure a long bear market, plan sponsors may find themselves in court explaining why, as fiduciaries, they neglected the effect of unreasonable plan costs on participants' retirement security.

Examining investment management costs is especially important. Not only are they commonly the largest cost component, but investment management costs are increasingly being paid by plan participants. By relying on mutual funds, for example, the cost of fund management is paid by the plan participant, thus automatically diminishing investment return. A plan sponsor should examine expenses (e.g., sales commissions, management fees, contract fees, transaction fees, 12b-1 fees) of fund options and analyze the impact expenses have on overall investment performance.

Carefully comparing and monitoring plan costs will minimize the potential of being sued for neglect when it comes to plan fees. Plan sponsors should be wary of promises made by investment managers that superior investment performance will offset costs borne by participants.

Q 4:37 How can a plan sponsor calculate a plan's total costs?

Making an accurate evaluation of plan costs mystifies many plan sponsors. A plan sponsor can determine identifiable costs given the right information. During the provider selection process, a plan sponsor should complete a fee worksheet for each of the various provider options. A fee worksheet can also be used to monitor plan costs on an ongoing basis. To get a sense of whether its plan's costs are higher or lower than industry standards, a plan sponsor should compare them to industry benchmarks.

Because they are not known up front, estimating future performance costs is difficult. A plan sponsor can, however, calculate those costs retrospectively. If, for example, the plan incurred additional costs related to an unintended legal compliance problem, that cost would be included in performance costs.

Though calculating costs is not an exact science, a plan sponsor can estimate costs of substandard investment performance by following these steps:

1. Determining the investment category of each investment option (e.g., money market fund, small-cap growth equity fund);

2. Finding the best performing fund, or applicable benchmark, in each category (preferably over a three- to five-year period);

3. Comparing each investment option to the best performing fund, or benchmark, in its investment category;

4. Multiplying the percentage each investment option is performing below the best-performing fund, or benchmark, by the plan assets invested in that option;

5. Finding the total costs of all investment options; and

6. Determining whether comparable levels of risk were taken to achieve the results.

Example. Awesome Company's 401(k) plan offers participants four investment options. Over the past five years, the money market fund has had an average annual return of 3 percent. The benchmark money market fund had an average annual return of 5 percent over the past five years. One million dollars of plan assets are invested in the money market fund. The estimated annual cost of substandard performance for that option is $20,000 (2% × $1,000,000).

Q 4:38 How do most plan sponsors allocate plan costs?

According to the Hewitt Associates survey Trends and Experience in 401(k) Plans, 1997, fees are paid as shown in Table 4-1.

The trend is toward shifting the operational costs of a 401(k) plan from the plan sponsor to the plan. As these costs are shifted to the plan, the plan participants will be affected, as any expenses will reduce the earnings credited to their account. The plan sponsor should be aware of what types of expenses can be shifted to the plan, in keeping with ERISA and the DOL's position (see Qs 4:39–4:44).

Q 4:39 How does ERISA treat the use of plan assets to pay administrative expenses?

ERISA expressly permits plan assets to be used to defray administrative expenses. [ERISA §§ 403, 404] The payment of reasonable

TABLE 4-1. Allocation of Plan Expenses

Plan Expenses	Percentage of Plans		
	Plan Pays	Employer Pays	Shared Expense
Audit fees	24	73	3
Internal administrative staff compensation	4	93	3
Employee communication	14	75	11
Investment management fees	56	39	5
Legal/design fees	9	85	6
Recordkeeping fees	35	58	7
Trustee fees	40	55	5
Investment education:	9	83	8
Other media	10	82	8
Other	24	61	15

administrative expenses from plan assets is an exception to the prohibited transaction rules. [ERISA § 408(b)(2)]

Q 4:40 What is the DOL's position on the use of plan assets to pay administrative expenses?

The DOL issued a letter in 1987 to Mr. Kirk F. Maldonado, discussing what types of expenses may be appropriate charges against plan assets. [PWPA Information Ltr, Mar 2, 1987] The letter establishes the general principle that payments cannot be made for the employer's benefit or to pay expenses that the employer could reasonably be expected to pay. The DOL opined that expenses related to settlor functions would not be appropriate charges against plan assets.

Q 4:41 What are *settlor functions*?

The DOL considers certain services provided in conjunction with the establishment, termination, or design of plans to be *settlor func-*

tions. Although it is not totally clear whether the following are set-tlor functions, the plan sponsor would be safer paying the following expenses directly, rather than from plan assets:

- Cost of a feasibility study for a 401(k) plan
- Cost of drafting and submitting plan documents to the IRS
- Cost of plan amendments
- Fees related to an economic analysis of whether or not to terminate the plan

Q 4:42 How should expenses be allocated in a plan?

Once it is determined that an expense may be properly charged to the 401(k) plan, it must then be determined how to allocate the cost to participants. Generally, all appropriate expenses are combined with plan earnings, gains, and losses, resulting in a net gain to be prorated among all participants. However, certain expenses may be directly attributable to an individual participant and should be properly charged to that participant alone.

Q 4:43 What types of expenses may be charged directly to a plan participant?

No express authority exists for charging all the fees in the following list directly to a plan participant; caution should be used. However, the DOL has not ruled unfavorably when these expenses are charged to the plan participant. If these fees are charged, the plan document should provide (and the summary plan description should disclose) that the following types of expenses will be charged directly to a participant's account:

- Loan fees
- Fees incurred by the plan participant on account of investment of a self-directed account
- Expenses related to hardship withdrawals

Reasonable procedures should be in place to inform participants that such charges will be made. Each participant should be periodically informed of actual expenses incurred. [DOL Reg § 2550.404c-1(b)(2)(ii)(A)]

A plan may not charge fees to a participant's account for the exercise of any right mandated by Title I of ERISA. For example, a plan may not charge a participant account for administrative expenses incurred in connection with a determination of the status of a domestic relations order (DRO) or the administration of a qualified domestic relations order (QDRO). [DOL Op 94-32A]

Q 4:44 Can an employer reimburse a plan for expenses paid by the plan?

Any reimbursement by an employer of expenses that were previously paid by a plan will be considered an additional contribution subject to both the aggregate deductible limit and the individual limits on allocations (see chapter 8). [Ltr Ruls 9124034, 9124035, 9124036, 9124037]

Q 4:45 Has the DOL taken any action with respect to plan fees and expenses?

Questions have been raised in the media and elsewhere with respect to fees and expenses being charged to 401(k) plans and their participants. Concern has been expressed that the robust market may be obscuring fees paid for plan investments. Though employees may direct investments, employers retain responsibility for selecting and monitoring the investment options. Employees may not understand the costs associated with investment options and plan services such as frequent trading capabilities. In response, the DOL held a public hearing on November 12, 1997, to consider the following:

1. Whether 401(k) plans are being overcharged for certain services;

2. Whether fees charged to plans are hidden;

3. Whether plan sponsors are doing enough to protect participants from excessive fees; and

4. Whether participants understand what fees and expenses are being charged to their accounts.

More specifically, the DOL asked for information with respect to the following questions:

- Are employers/plan sponsors being furnished with sufficient information to evaluate whether the fees and expenses associated with plan investments, investment options, and administrative services are reasonable? If not, what additional information should be provided to or requested by plan sponsors, and is it readily available? What steps are plan sponsors taking to ensure that the fees and expenses charted to the individual accounts of the participants are reasonable?

- Are plan participants being furnished with sufficient information about fees and expenses associated with the investment options offered under their plan to make informed investment decisions? What additional information should be provided to or requested by participants, and is it readily available?

- Is the information about services, fees, and expenses that is disclosed to participants regarding their accounts provided in a manner understandable to most participants? Is the disclosure automatic or upon request? If automatic, how often is the disclosure provided and to whom is it provided (plan sponsor, participants, or both)?

- How are the services and the respective fees included in a bundled fee arrangement disclosed? How are the fees and expenses with respect to each of the covered services in a bundled arrangement determined?

- What actions, if any, should the DOL take to improve consideration and disclosure of fees and expenses charged to 401(k) plans? If action is necessary, what information should be required to be disclosed? Would a uniform format for such disclosure be helpful to participants?

[62 Fed Reg 53802, October 16, 1997]

The DOL has released two reports addressing some of these issues (see Q 4:29).

Q 4:46 Are other DOL initiatives planned with respect to 401(k) fees?

The DOL hearings held on November 12, 1997 (see Q 4:45) are just one part of an overall examination of 401(k) plan fees. Other planned initiatives on 401(k) fees reportedly include the following:

- A research project to review existing data and to research practices relating to how 401(k) fees are paid by plans

- A special enforcement project to ensure that the 401(k) savings

4-23

of participants and beneficiaries are not eroded because of excessive or undisclosed fees paid from their 401(k) accounts (This project will be used to determine whether plan sponsors are meeting their fiduciary responsibility. The DOL will identify the fees 401(k) investment managers charge, the services they provide for those fees, and whether the fees are charged separately or netted with investment results.)

- A consumer publication to help employers and workers understand the costs associated with plan investments

[*Pension & Benefits Week,* Nov. 17, 1997, at 7–8]

Q 4:47 What is the DOL's position on fees paid by mutual fund companies to third-party service providers?

It has become a common practice for mutual funds to offer 12b-1 fees and other fees to third parties, such as recordkeepers, that provide services to defined contribution plans, including those that are participant directed. Mutual funds pay the fees to service providers because such arrangements reduce their administrative costs in providing services to shareholders. More important, referrals from service providers ensure access to a growing pool of assets in defined contribution plans. Plan service providers that receive fees from mutual funds often reduce fees paid by the plan for trustee, recordkeeping, and administrative services.

A service provider receiving fees from mutual funds in connection with plan investments raises issues under ERISA's "anti-kickback" provision prohibiting a fiduciary from receiving consideration from a party dealing with a plan in connection with a plan transaction. [ERISA § 406(b)(3)] Until recently, the DOL took the position that a person who is a fiduciary under ERISA may violate the anti-kickback prohibition merely by receiving a fee or other consideration from a party dealing with a plan. That position was particularly confusing to directed trustees, which are viewed by the DOL as fiduciaries but do not "cause" plans to invest in a particular mutual fund.

On May 22, 1997, the DOL released two advisory opinions addressing issues raised when mutual funds pay fees (including 12b-1 fees) to recordkeepers, trustees, and other plan service providers. The opinions describe different scenarios under which service providers might receive mutual fund fees and how they will be analyzed under ERISA. [DOL Adv Ops 97-15A, 97-16A] See Q 4:48. Frost National Bank and Aetna Life Insurance and Annuity Company requested the opinions.

Q 4:48 Under what circumstances, according to the DOL, can a service provider receive fees from mutual funds without violating ERISA's self-dealing and anti-cutback provisions?

In two advisory opinions [DOL Adv Ops 97-15A, 97-16A], the DOL generally took the position that as long as a service provider does not exercise any authority or control to "cause" a plan to invest in a mutual fund, it will not violate the self-dealing and anti-kickback prohibitions under ERISA Sections 406(b)(1) and 406(b)(3), respectively, by receiving fees from mutual funds in connection with plan investments. A trustee that advises plan fiduciaries regarding mutual funds in which to invest plan assets would have such authority or control. A directed trustee will be considered to have the requisite discretionary authority or control if it assists plans in selecting mutual funds to be plan investment options or reserves *unrestricted* authority to add, delete, and substitute funds on the mutual fund menu for a bundled program, or both. When a service provider is a fiduciary *and* causes the plan to invest in mutual funds that pay fees, the service provider must disclose any fee arrangements and offset any fees received, on a dollar-for-dollar basis, against other fees the plan is obligated to pay to avoid violating ERISA's self-dealing and anti-kickback provisions.

A nonfiduciary service provider that provides nondiscretionary administration and recordkeeping services will not be prohibited from receiving fees solely as a result of deleting or substituting a fund from a bundled program, provided that the appropriate plan fiduciary makes the decision to accept or reject the change. In that regard, the fiduciary must be provided advance notice of the change, including any changes in the fees received, and afforded a reasonable period to decide whether to accept or reject the change and, in the event of a rejection, secure a new service provider. The fees need not be offset.

Q 4:49 What is a reasonable amount for a 401(k) plan to pay for administration and investment services?

The most meaningful way to compare 401(k) plan costs is to look at total cost on either a per participant basis or according to the number of basis points on total plan assets. As a general rule, the smaller the plan, the higher the relative cost.

One of the reasons the DOL is looking at 401(k) plan fees is that there can be great disparity in both how fees are charged and the level of fee charged. In a recent survey by HR Investment Consultants, Roger Casey concluded that for a plan with 1,000 participants the average cost for investment services was 112 basis points (1.12 percent), with a range from 47 to 252 basis points. A survey conducted by Access Research suggests that plan administration costs are generally about $100 per year per participant but can go as low as $23 for plans with more than 5,000 employees.

Q 4:50 What were the major findings of the DOL's May 1998 study on 401(k) plan fees?

One of the key findings of the DOL's May 1998 study of 401(k) plan fees and expenses was that plan sponsors and participants do not fully understand how 401(k) plan fees are charged, and, as a result, may be paying more than they should in fees. The study relied on a report that concluded that 78 percent of plan sponsors do not know what they are paying for plan services and that this is in part a function of the fact that there are over 80 different ways that vendors charge fees for the same services. The DOL study quoted results from a 1997 survey done by Stephen J. Butler of Pension Dynamics, which obtained quotes from 17 different providers on a 401(k) plan with 100 participants and $2 million in assets. The quotes for annual fees ranged from $11,375 to $42,775. The DOL study also noted the following five items:

1. Total plan costs are determined substantially by investment-related expenses. Investment expenses typically constitute 75 to 90 percent of total plan expenses.

2. There are significant variations in observed investment fees across the full array of 401(k) plan service providers. For a given amount of assets in a plan, expensive providers can generate fees several times higher than lower-cost providers.

3. Plan sponsors have control over overall investment-related expenses. Within a diverse marketplace with thousands of available funds, there is substantial opportunity to pursue fee reduction strategies. To some extent, the literature suggests that one problem sponsors face is the appeal of "name-brand" retail mutual funds to many participants. This appeal is often reinforced by the free or low-cost communication and education services that sponsors can obtain from these providers.

4. The other major expense categories—recordkeeping and administration, processing of loans, and trustees' fees—exhibit wide variations in the level of providers' fees and the manner in which those fees are structured. Some providers charge relatively high per capita or per transaction fees for certain services, while providing other services at low or zero charge. Plan sponsors shopping for the best price for a given package of services must assess the total effect of all the components of the fee structure.

5. Larger plans enjoy potentially significant economies of scale. In the case of investment expenses, they have access to more providers offering a wide range of investment vehicles at lower cost. Very large plans may be able to reduce investment expenses even more through fee-reduction negotiations with the providers or use of lower-cost institutional accounts. In other expense categories, the combination of flat (or nearly flat) fees regardless of plan size, plus declining per capita charges in the basic administration fee, reduce per participant administrative costs among larger plans.

5 Fiduciary and Prohibited Transaction Rules

The establishment and management of a 401(k) plan involves numerous fiduciary responsibilities. Certain types of investment transactions carry such fiduciary risk that they are prohibited altogether. There are important steps that plan sponsors and other fiduciaries can take to manage the fiduciary liability arising out of the administration of a 401(k) plan.

FIDUCIARY ISSUES

Retirement plans are managed for the exclusive benefit of participants by plan officials called fiduciaries. A critical phase in the establishment of a 401(k) plan is the definition and allocation of plan responsibilities among the various fiduciaries. A typical 401(k) plan will involve the following fiduciaries:

- Named fiduciary
- Trustee
- Investment fiduciary
- Plan administrator

Who Is and Who Is Not a Fiduciary

Q 5:1 What is a *fiduciary*?

A *fiduciary* is a person who exercises any discretionary authority or control over the management of the plan or its assets, or who is paid to give investment advice regarding plan assets. The definition depends on the functions a person performs and not on the person's title. Plan service providers such as actuaries, attorneys, accountants, brokers, and recordkeepers are not fiduciaries unless they exercise discretion or are responsible for the management of the plan or its assets. [ERISA § 3(21); DOL Reg § 2509.75-8, D-2]

Q 5:2 What are some examples of services that can be provided to a plan without giving rise to fiduciary status?

Persons performing mere ministerial functions within guidelines established by others are not plan fiduciaries. Department of Labor (DOL) regulations list the following job functions as ministerial:

1. Applying rules to determine eligibility for participation or benefits;
2. Calculating service and pay for benefit purposes;
3. Preparing account statements or communications to employees;
4. Maintaining participants' work records;
5. Preparing reports required by government agencies;

6. Calculating benefits;

7. Explaining the plan to new participants and advising participants of their rights and options under the plan;

8. Collecting contributions and applying them according to plan provisions;

9. Preparing reports covering participants' benefits;

10. Processing claims; and

11. Making recommendations to others for decisions with respect to plan administration.

[DOL Reg § 2509.75-8, D-2]

Q 5:3 How is *investment advice* defined for the purpose of identifying fiduciary status?

A person gives *investment advice* to a plan when he or she does the following:

1. Makes recommendations as to valuing, buying, holding, or selling securities or other property, and

2. (a) Has, directly or indirectly, discretionary authority or control over buying or selling securities or other property for the plan, whether or not pursuant to an agreement, arrangement, or understanding, or
(b) Regularly renders advice to the plan pursuant to a mutual agreement, arrangement, or understanding that such advice will serve as a primary basis for plan investment decisions and that such advice will be based on the particular needs of the plan regarding such matters as investment policies or strategy, overall portfolio composition, or diversification of plan investments.

[DOL Reg § 2510.3-21(c)(1)]

Q 5:4 What is a *named fiduciary*?

A *named fiduciary* is one who has the ultimate authority to control and manage the operation and administration of the plan. This fiduciary must be specifically named or clearly identifiable in the plan document so that participants or other interested parties such as the Internal Revenue Service (IRS) or the DOL will be able to identify who is responsible for the plan and will be able to address issues to that person. [ERISA § 402(a)]

Q 5:5 Must a person consent to be a fiduciary to be treated as a fiduciary?

No. A person who has or actually exercises discretionary management or control will have fiduciary responsibility, regardless of whether that person explicitly consents to becoming a fiduciary. Fiduciary status is determined by a person's function rather than by his or her title.

It should be noted, however, that an investment manager or a qualified professional asset manager (QPAM) must explicitly consent to be a fiduciary in order to be appointed as one. Such explicit appointment or qualification is necessary to protect other fiduciaries and to enable the use of certain prohibited-transaction class exemptions. If an investment manager or a QPAM does not acknowledge that it is a fiduciary, it will not be an ERISA-qualified investment manager or QPAM. It will, however, still be a fiduciary and thus will be subject to liability under the Employment Retirement Income Security Act of 1974 (ERISA) if it performs fiduciary functions (e.g., investing plan assets using discretion).

Q 5:6 What is the trustee's responsibility?

The trustee collects and holds plan assets in trust for the participants. The trustee will also be responsible for managing the plan investments unless the plan expressly provides that the trustee is subject to direction from a named fiduciary or an investment manager. [ERISA § 403(a)]

Q 5:7 Can a fiduciary perform more than one function?

All of the fiduciary functions can be performed by one individual. It is sometimes the case with plans sponsored by smaller businesses that all discretionary actions and authority will be given to one person, usually the business owner. It is rare, however, for one person to have the necessary skills and knowledge to perform all of these functions at the standard to which fiduciaries are held. Often, such individual fiduciaries will engage experts to advise them in these various areas. In fact, if the fiduciary lacks the required expertise in an area, he or she must seek expert advice. The fiduciary will remain responsible for the quality of the decision.

Q 5:8 How are fiduciary responsibilities allocated?

Major functions are defined in the plan and trust document. Specific, detailed responsibilities are often developed and limited in service contracts or management agreements, or in the minutes and records of meetings of plan officials. These side letters and documents must not conflict with the express terms of the plan and trust. [ERISA §§ 402, 404(a)(1)(D)]

Funding Policy and Method

Q 5:9 How do fiduciaries decide how to invest plan assets?

Every plan is required to establish and carry out a funding policy and method consistent with the objectives of the plan. The funding policy and method serves as a guide to the fiduciary for evaluating a specific investment opportunity. [ERISA § 402(b)(1)] At a minimum, the fiduciary also gives appropriate consideration to the following questions:

1. How is the investment, as part of the portfolio, reasonably designed to further the purposes of the plan?
2. What is the risk of loss, and the opportunity for gain?
3. How does the investment affect the diversification of the portfolio?
4. Are the liquidity and current return sufficient to meet the expected cash flow needs of the plan?
5. What is the projected return of the portfolio compared with the funding objectives of the plan?

Q 5:10 Who develops the funding policy and method?

Typically, the funding policy is developed by a team. The investment manager brings knowledge of investment opportunities and a sense of realistic long-term market performance goals. The plan administrator or actuary brings information about the projected need to provide cash for anticipated benefit payments, as well as projections about the cash flow of future contributions. The named fiduciary usually has detailed knowledge about the employer's business objectives and resources, including a feel for what benefits are needed to attract and retain employees. In addition, legal advice helps to ensure that the policy says what it is intended to mean and documents the prudent actions of the fiduciary.

Q 5:11 What should a 401(k) plan investment policy cover?

Investment policies need to be flexible enough to adapt to an employer's specific situation and reflect the fiduciaries' attitudes and philosophies. For a typical 401(k) plan that allows participants a choice among investment funds, the policy should also recognize the participants' needs and goals. Further, the policy should deal with the number and types of funds to be made available. How many choices are enough? How many choices are too many?

The policy should also cover how any loan program will affect investments and whether the withdrawal program is consistent with the types of funds selected. For example, if participants are expected to access funds through loans or withdrawals, do the investment funds allow for such withdrawals without penalty?

Finally, the policy should deal with the regulatory issues, specifically the requirements of ERISA Section 404(c), discussed in chapter 6.

Q 5:12 What are the disadvantages of developing, consistently applying, and updating the funding policy and method?

There are none.

Fiduciary Selection

Q 5:13 What factors are important in selecting a fiduciary?

The selection of a fiduciary is, in itself, a fiduciary decision subject to the fiduciary standard of care. The named fiduciary should document the investigation and selection of a potential fiduciary or service provider. Answers to the following questions should be gathered and reviewed:

1.   What are the candidate's qualifications with respect to rele-

vant experience, education, credentials, licensing and registration, and reputation?

2. How will the candidate be compensated? Are the fees reasonable?

3. What specific services are covered in the service contract?

4. What provisions are made for monitoring and documenting
   performance?

5. Does the candidate have proper bonding and insurance
   coverage?

6. Are the financial and organizational resources of the candidate consistent with the scale and needs of the plan?

Q 5:14 What procedures should be followed when selecting a fiduciary?

Each fiduciary should acknowledge acceptance of fiduciary status
in writing. The plan document and service agreement should detail
the specific authority and responsibility of the fiduciary. Fiduciary
performance should be monitored, and the appointment should be
reviewed regularly.

Fiduciary Duties and Obligations

Q 5:15 What are the basic fiduciary duties and obligations?

A fiduciary must

1. Act in the exclusive retirement benefit interest of participants
   and control expenses of administration [ERISA § 404(a)];

2. Make decisions with the level of care that a prudent person
   familiar with retirement plans would use under the same circumstances [ERISA § 404(a)(1)(B)];

3. Diversify investments to minimize the risk of large losses
   [ERISA § 404(a)(1)(C)];

4. Use care to prevent co-fiduciaries from committing breaches
   and rectify the actions of others [ERISA § 405];

5. Hold plan assets within the jurisdiction of United States
   courts [ERISA § 404(b)];

6. Be bonded in the amount of 10 percent of funds handled up
   to a $500,000 maximum bond [ERISA § 412];

7. Act according to the terms of written plan documents unless the documents are in conflict with the provisions of ERISA [ERISA § 404(a)(1)(D)]; and

8. Not engage in prohibited transactions. [ERISA § 406]

Q 5:16 What is *adequate diversification*?

Adequate diversification cannot be reliably defined by a fixed percentage or allocation. The standard turns on a plan's facts and circumstances. Courts have upheld high concentrations of assets in a single investment or asset category where the concentration is consistent with a particular preplanned written investment policy or philosophy. General issues for fiduciaries to consider are

- Portfolio composition with respect to diversification
- Portfolio liquidity, current return, and anticipated cash flow
- Projected return of the portfolio relative to the funding objectives

The fiduciary should also consider the possible risk of loss of an investment, as well as the financial soundness of any insurance company or bank that issues an investment. Real estate loans should be documented with a credit check on the borrower as well as an appraisal of the borrower's property. [DOL Reg § 2550.404b-1]

Q 5:17 Who must be covered by an ERISA bond?

Every fiduciary of a plan and anyone else (plan official) who handles or has authority to handle plan assets must be bonded. [ERISA § 412(a)] The bond must provide a direct right of access in favor of the plan in the event the insured plan official takes plan assets. The bond coverage amount must be at least 10 percent of plan assets up to a maximum bond amount of $500,000. It is unlawful for anyone who is required to be bonded to handle plan assets without a bond. Likewise, it is unlawful for any fiduciary to allow another plan official to handle plan assets without being properly bonded. [ERISA § 412(b)]

Q 5:18 What happens if fiduciaries breach their duties?

Fiduciaries who breach their duties may be personally liable to make a plan whole for losses caused by their breaches. Losses can include lost-opportunity costs and, possibly, attorneys' fees and court costs. Co-fiduciaries may be jointly liable with a breaching fiduciary if the co-fiduciary knew of or should have known of the breach and failed to take steps to protect the plan. Fiduciaries can be removed from responsibility and barred from acting in a future fiduciary capacity with respect to any plan. [ERISA §§ 409, 502]

In addition to liability for plan losses, the IRS and the DOL can levy civil penalties. The IRS can levy a 15 percent prohibited transaction excise tax on a fiduciary who is party to a prohibited transaction—increased from 10 percent effective August 5, 1997, by the Taxpayer Relief Act of 1997 (TRA '97). This tax is reported on Form 5330. The DOL can levy a civil penalty of 20 percent of the amount recovered with respect to a plan. [IRC § 4975; ERISA § 502(1)]

Effective August 5, 1997, a participant's benefit may be offset by a settlement involving fiduciary violations. [TRA '97 § 1502]

Q 5:19 Can nonfiduciaries be held liable for a breach of fiduciary duty?

The United States Supreme Court has held that outside service providers, such as attorneys, actuaries, and other consultants, are not liable for fiduciary breach damages even where the nonfiduciary participated in the breach. [Mertens v Hewitt Assocs, 948 F 2d 607 (9th Cir 1991), aff'd, 113 S Ct 2063 (1993)] The DOL is seeking legislation to overturn the result.

Q 5:20 Can a fiduciary be liable for an unwitting violation of ERISA's fiduciary duties?

Yes. Even if a fiduciary is unaware that he or she is violating ERISA's fiduciary duties, the fiduciary can still be liable for the violation. The ERISA standard of conduct is an objective one: good faith is not sufficient.

Similarly, a fiduciary will be liable under ERISA for engaging in a prohibited transaction if he or she knew or should have known that the transaction was prohibited. [ERISA § 406(a)(1)] Under the Code, excise taxes will be imposed on a fiduciary for engaging in certain transactions as a disqualified person, even if he or she does not satisfy the "knows or should have known" standard. [IRC §§ 4975(c)(1)(E), 4975(c)(1)(F)]

Q 5:21 Can a fiduciary be liable for a breach of fiduciary duty that occurred before the fiduciary's appointment?

No. A fiduciary cannot be held liable for a breach of fiduciary duty that was committed before the fiduciary became a fiduciary. Although the fiduciary may not be liable for the original breach, if the fiduciary knows about it, he or she should take steps to remedy the situation. Failure to do so may constitute a subsequent independent breach of fiduciary duty by the successor fiduciary.

Q 5:22 Can a fiduciary be liable for failing to act?

Yes. A breach of fiduciary duty can occur by reason of omission as well as commission. Some fiduciary duties are affirmative in nature, and a fiduciary who fails to execute them risks liability. Similarly, a co-fiduciary can be liable for failing to take reasonable steps to correct another fiduciary's breach of duty.

Q 5:23 Can a nonfiduciary be liable to a plan on non-ERISA grounds?

Yes. Nonfiduciaries may be liable to a plan under various statutes or state-law negligence theories. For example, a plan may have a malpractice claim against an attorney who erred in representing the plan. Or a plan may have a securities fraud claim against a nonfiduciary broker who excessively trades or churns a plan account or misrepresents an investment sold to the plan. Some state law claims, however, are barred by ERISA's pre-emption clause, which pre-empts all state laws that relate to an employee benefit plan. [ERISA § 514(a)]

Q 5:24 Can a fiduciary be held liable for breaches committed by a co-fiduciary?

Yes. A fiduciary can be liable for the acts of a co-fiduciary if the fiduciary does any of the following:

1. Knowingly participates in or tries to conceal a co-fiduciary's breach;

2. Enables a co-fiduciary to commit a breach by failing to meet his or her specific fiduciary responsibilities; or

3. Knowing of a co-fiduciary's breach, fails to make a reasonable effort to remedy it.

[ERISA § 405(a)]

Q 5:25 What should a fiduciary do if a co-fiduciary commits a breach of duty?

A fiduciary must try to remedy a breach of duty by a co-fiduciary. For example, if an improper investment was made, the fiduciary might consider disposing of the asset. Alternatively, the fiduciary might notify the company or the plan participants of the breach, institute a lawsuit against the co-fiduciary, or bring the matter before the DOL. The fiduciary's resignation as a protest against the breach, without making reasonable efforts to prevent it, will not relieve the fiduciary of liability. [ERISA § 405(a)(3); DOL Reg § 2509.75-5, FR-10]

Q 5:26 Does ERISA authorize punitive damages to a beneficiary for breach of fiduciary duty?

No. The United States Supreme Court has held that punitive damages are not available to a beneficiary in an action against the plan fiduciary for an alleged breach of fiduciary duty. Remedies available to the beneficiary in such instances would include only recovery of the benefits owed, clarification of the beneficiary's right to present or future benefits, or removal of the breaching fiduciary. [Mass Mutual Life Ins Co v Russell, 473 US 134 (1985)]

Q 5:27 Does ERISA authorize the recovery of attorneys' fees and costs?

Yes. A court may in its discretion award reasonable attorneys' fees and costs to either party in an action by a participant, beneficiary, or fiduciary. [ERISA § 502(g)] The award of attorneys' fees is the exception rather than the rule.

Courts weigh the following factors in deciding whether to award fees and costs:

- Opponent's bad faith
- Opponent's ability to pay
- Deterrent effect on others in similar circumstances

- Whether action benefited all plan participants
- Relative merits of parties' positions

Q 5:28 What can fiduciaries do to minimize their liability risk?

Fiduciaries should accept only the responsibilities that they can carry out faithfully, exercise procedural due diligence in executing their duty, and document all their actions and decisions. Although fiduciaries are not expected to be clairvoyant when selecting investments or carrying out their other functions, they are expected to follow a process that ensures that their decisions are well informed and consistent with the plan's stated objectives at the time the decision is made.

A plan may not agree in advance to excuse a fiduciary from liability or indemnify the fiduciary. Fiduciary insurance may be provided by an errors-and-omissions policy or by indemnification by the sponsoring employer. [ERISA § 410]

Responsibility for investment decisions can be shifted to an investment manager or to plan participants where the participants are allowed to direct the investments in their accounts (see Qs 6:49–6:85). [ERISA §§ 401(c)(3), 405(d), 404(c)]

PROHIBITED TRANSACTIONS

There are certain investment transactions that the Department of Labor considers so fraught with potential to run afoul of the fiduciary requirement to act exclusively in the interests of plan participants that it prohibits the transaction altogether. It is important to bear in mind that these transactions are prohibited regardless of whether they prove to be good or bad investments for a plan, and regardless of the actual motive of the fiduciary making the investment decision.

Types of Prohibited Transactions

Q 5:29 What transactions are prohibited?

The Internal Revenue Code (Code) and ERISA contain outright prohibitions against direct or indirect economic transactions involving plan assets and parties related to the plan unless the transaction is covered by an exemption. The Code calls related parties *disqualified persons*. Under ERISA, they are referred to as *parties in interest*.

Prohibited transactions cover the direct or indirect sale, exchange, or lease of property; extension of credit; provision of goods or services; transfer or use of plan assets; and the investment in employer securities or employer real estate in excess of the legal limits. In addition, ERISA specifically prohibits fiduciaries from dealing with plan assets where the fiduciary has a conflict of interest. This includes self-dealing, acting on behalf of a party whose interest is adverse to the interests of the plan, or receiving a kickback from any other person in connection with a transaction involving plan assets. [ERISA § 406]

Q 5:30 What is a *party in interest* or *disqualified person*?

The definitions for both *party in interest* and *disqualified person* are complex and include plan fiduciaries, service providers, sponsoring employers, and those who control the employer, as well as individuals who are related to the foregoing by family or business ties.

Under ERISA, the following are parties in interest with respect to a plan (the Code definition for disqualified person is nearly identical):

1. Any fiduciary, counsel, or employee of the plan;

2. A person providing services to the plan;

3. An employer, any of whose employees are covered by the plan, and any direct or indirect owner of 50 percent or more of such employer;

4. A relative, namely, the spouse, ancestor, lineal descendant, or spouse of a lineal descendant of any of the persons described in items 1, 2, or 3 of this list;

5. An employee organization, any of whose members are covered by the plan;

6. A corporation, partnership, estate, or trust of which at least 50 percent is owned by any person or organization described in items 1, 2, 3, 4, or 5 of this list;

7. Officers, directors, 10 percent-or-more shareholders, and

employees of any person or organization described in items 2, 3, 5, or 6 of this list; and

8. A 10 percent-or-more partner of or joint venturer with any person or organization described in items 2, 3, 5, or 6 of this list.

[ERISA § 3(14)]

Prohibited Transaction Penalties and Corrections

Q 5:31 What penalties may be imposed on a party in interest or disqualified person for engaging in a prohibited transaction?

Under ERISA, a prohibited transaction is a breach of fiduciary duty. Any fiduciary who engages in a prohibited transaction is therefore personally liable for any losses to the plan (see Q 3:58) and must restore to the plan any profit made by the fiduciary through the use of the plan's assets. Also, a 20 percent civil penalty imposed by the DOL for certain breaches of fiduciary duty applies to prohibited transactions; however, the penalty is reduced by any penalty tax imposed under Code Section 4975. [ERISA §§ 409(a), 502(1)]

Under the Code, a penalty tax is imposed on a disqualified person for each year or part thereof that the transaction remains uncorrected. For prohibited transactions occurring before August 20, 1996, the tax is 5 percent. For prohibited transactions occurring after August 20, 1996, the tax is increased from 5 percent to 10 percent. [Small Business Job Protection Act of 1996 (SBJPA) § 1453] For transactions occurring after August 5, 1997, the tax is increased to 15 percent. [TRA '97] An additional tax equal to 100 percent of the amount involved is imposed if the prohibited transaction is not timely corrected. [ERISA §§ 4975(a), 4975(b)]

Q 5:32 How can a prohibited transaction be corrected?

A prohibited transaction can be corrected by undoing the transaction to the extent possible but in any event by placing the plan in a financial position no worse than the position it would have been in had the party in interest acted under the highest fiduciary standards. [IRC § 4975(f)(5)]

Common Prohibited Transactions

Q 5:33 What is the most likely type of prohibited transaction to occur in a 401(k) plan?

An employer's failure to timely remit salary deferral contributions to the plan trustee is the most frequent type of prohibited transaction to occur in a 401(k) plan.

Salary deferrals must be held in trust as soon as they become plan assets. Amounts paid by participants or withheld by the employer from participants' wages as contributions to a plan will be considered plan assets as of the earliest date on which the contributions can reasonably be segregated from the general assets of the employer. In any event, that date can be no later than 15 business days after the end of the month in which the contributions are received by the employer or would have been paid to the employee in cash if not withheld from wages. [DOL Reg § 2510.3-102(a) (effective Feb 3, 1997)] Furthermore, if contributions can reasonably be segregated from general company assets prior to this time limit, then the employer should place the assets in trust at such earlier time. Once salary deferral contributions become plan assets, their retention by the employer is treated by the IRS as a prohibited loan from the plan to the employer.

Example 1. The Widget Company employs 100 employees at one location. The payroll service updates salary deferral contributions and match with each biweekly paycheck. The administrator does not levy a surcharge for frequent remittances. Contributions should be sent to the trustee with each payroll.

Example 2. Worldwide Conglomerate, Inc. operates in every major city. Multiple payroll vendors provide service on a variety of different payroll frequencies. Reconciliation is manual. Deposits must be made to the trust by the fifteenth business day after the month in which any salary deferrals are withheld.

Example 3. Best Practices Corporation uses a daily valuation recordkeeping system. Payroll and census data are transmitted electronically. When payroll is prepared on a Tuesday before a Friday payday, a modem transmission is sent to the recordkeeper with the plan contribution data. The recordkeeper prepares the investment fund breakdown based on standing participant elections and directs the trustee to capture the contributions via automated clearing house withdrawal from the employer's checking account on payday. The contributions are then wired to the investment funds the same day as they are withheld from the employees' paycheck.

Q 5:34 How often should deposits be made to the trust?

Deferral contributions are commonly remitted to the trustee on a monthly or more frequent basis. Some payroll systems can segregate salary deferral and matching contributions automatically each pay date. In that case, deposits can be made at each payroll. More frequent deposits allow the plan to maximize the benefits of dollar cost averaging and reduce investment purchase risk. In addition, increased deposit frequency puts contributions to work sooner, earning in the tax-free trust. On the other hand, significant effort is involved in reconciling deferrals to elections and payroll; therefore, it may be more cost-effective to batch-process deposits on a monthly basis.

Q 5:35 May a fiduciary accept the contribution of property to a 401(k) plan?

A transfer of property to a pension plan that is used to satisfy a contribution obligation is a prohibited transaction. Further, a contribution of encumbered property to a plan is also a prohibited transaction. [Commissioner v Keystone Consol Indus Inc, 113 S Ct 2006 (1993)] However, a wholly discretionary contribution to a profit-sharing plan may be made in the form of unencumbered property. [DOL Op Ltrs 81-69A, 90-05A]

In a 401(k) plan, "in-kind" contributions may be made to the employer discretionary account. Strong arguments can be made that both salary deferral and matching contributions are employer obligations (except perhaps for a truly discretionary match) and that in-kind contributions made to satisfy these obligations would result in prohibited transactions.

Q 5:36 How do prohibited transactions occur in the design process?

The following are examples of situations where prohibited transactions occur during plan design:

- The plan hires the owner's spouse as paid investment adviser for the plan assets.

- The broker for the insurance contract used to fund the plan is the son of the sole director of the sponsoring employer.

- An insurance agent sells a contract without disclosing specific information about the payment of commissions required under the applicable class exemption.

- The plan contracts with a person to provide administrative services and agrees to pay him or her more than reasonable compensation.

Care should be taken during the plan design stage to avoid selection of fiduciaries, service providers, or investment structures that might result in prohibited transactions. Plans may wish to identify significant parties in interest from the outset and use the list to screen prospective investments for conflicts.

Q 5:37 How can prohibited transactions occur in setting up a plan checking account?

Most banks, trust companies, and other financial institutions run disbursement checks through a master controlled disbursement account. The master account generates collected balances from uncashed checks. The collected balances are invested in short-term interest-bearing securities. The institution keeps the earnings generated on the account as a fee. (The funds are generally not able to be precisely allocated back to the plan from which the check was cut.) In 1993 the DOL advised Tennessee banking regulators that such a practice is a prohibited transaction. [DOL Op Ltr 93-24A]

Q 5:38 Can a fiduciary receive compensation such as alliance or recordkeeping credits from third parties?

No. To the extent a service provider is a fiduciary, it is prohibited from receiving remuneration from anyone whose interests are adverse to the interests of the plan participants. The common practice of mutual fund groups, for example, to rebate part of the investment management fee to service providers for recordkeeping or sub-transfer agency functions has raised concerns at the DOL where the service provider has fiduciary discretion. [DOL Opinion Ltrs 97-15A,

97-16A]. According to the opinion letters, a fiduciary who receives alliance credits or similar compensation from third parties must apply the money as a direct dollar-for-dollar offset to the normal fees due the fiduciary. In addition, the existence of the arrangement and the amount of fees must be disclosed to the employer or other independent fiduciary who approves the arrangement.

Prohibited Transaction Exemptions

Q 5:39 What is a prohibited transaction exemption?

There are three kinds of exemptions from the prohibited transaction rules:

1. *Statutory exemption.* This is an exemption for routine transactions with low risk of abuse. For example, a plan may pay benefits to a fiduciary who is also a participant in accordance with the terms of the plan, or plan service providers may be paid fees from the plan as long as no more than reasonable compensation is paid. [ERISA § 408(b)]

2. *Class exemption.* The DOL has granted class exemptions for transactions that were not specifically defined in ERISA but are of a similar low-risk character. For example, insurance policies may be transferred between the plan and a party in interest if detailed procedural requirements are adhered to. [ERISA § 408(a)]

3. *Individual exemption.* An individual may apply to the DOL for an individual prohibited transaction exemption where he or she is able to demonstrate that an intended prohibited transaction is in the best interests of the plan. [ERISA § 408(a)]

MANAGING FIDUCIARY LIABILITY IN A 401(k) PLAN

There are a number of ways that fiduciaries and plans can protect themselves from the failure of a fiduciary to perform at the required level of skill and competence. Two major strategies are to insure against the risk and to limit or shift responsibility through allocation of duties to others. Insurance can be achieved through a formal insurance policy or by means of indemnification provisions in plan documents and service contracts. In participant-directed plans, a major objective often is to shift responsibility of asset allocation decisions to the plan participants. The use of a designated investment manager can also help to reduce investment risk. Finally, understanding the scope of the fiduciary role and practicing procedural due diligence in fulfilling that role can substantially reduce risk.

Fiduciary Insurance

It is beyond the scope of this book to provide a detailed discussion of the intricacies of fiduciary liability insurance policies. There is a helpful discussion of fiduciary liability insurance, including an analysis of common policy provisions and limitations, in Friedman, Albert, Schelberg, and Rattner, *ERISA Fiduciary Answer Book* (New York: Panel Publishers).

Plan sponsors should consider engaging an insurance agent with experience in writing this type of coverage and should also have the policies reviewed by ERISA counsel. Although many policy provisions are required by state insurance law, there is still significant opportunity to negotiate optional terms of coverage. Care should be taken to ensure that a policy covers the activities in which the plan and its fiduciaries in fact intend to engage.

Q 5:40 Can a plan purchase fiduciary liability insurance for itself or for plan fiduciaries?

Yes. The insurance contract must, however, permit recourse by the insurer against the fiduciary for the loss resulting from a breach of a fiduciary obligation by such fiduciary. [ERISA § 401(b)] Whether fiduciary liability insurance may cover fiduciaries for the 20 percent excise tax for fiduciary breaches under ERISA Section 502(1) is a matter of state law.

For a nominal sum, a fiduciary can purchase a nonrecourse rider to the policy. (A fiduciary should ensure that plan funds are not used for such purpose.) The nonrecourse rider provides that the insurance company waives its rights to proceed against the fiduciary. The fiduciary involved in purchasing insurance against fiduciary breaches for the plan must do his or her best to secure the most suitable coverage for the plan at no greater expenditure of plan assets than is necessary. [DOL News Rel 75-127 (Mar 4, 1975)]

Q 5:41 Can a fiduciary or an employer purchase insurance for the plan fiduciary to cover liability or losses resulting from the acts or omissions of the plan fiduciary?

Yes. A fiduciary can purchase insurance to cover his or her liability resulting from a breach of fiduciary duties, and an employer or an employee organization can purchase insurance for the plan fiduciary. [Mazur v Gaudet, 826 F Supp 188 (ED La 1992)] Here, by contrast with the situation in which the plan purchases the policy, the policy need not provide for recourse against the fiduciary. [ERISA § 410(b)]

Q 5:42 Can a plan fiduciary purchase from the same insurance company that insures the plan against fiduciary breaches a policy that protects the fiduciary from recourse lawsuits that the insurer can bring against the fiduciary?

Yes. A *linked* insurance policy—one that links low-cost insurance for an individual fiduciary purchased by a fiduciary (which protects the fiduciary against recourse lawsuits that the insurer can bring against the fiduciary) with high-cost insurance (which protects the plan against a fiduciary's breach) purchased by the plan—is legal as long as the plan fiduciary purchases the insurance policy prudently and solely in the interest of plan participants and beneficiaries. [DOL New Rel 75-127 (Mar 4, 1975)] The plan may not pay for such coverage.

Q 5:43 What is the purpose of fiduciary liability insurance?

Fiduciary liability insurance is designed to protect fiduciaries who, although acting in good faith, violate the complex fiduciary rules as expressed in federal rules, regulations, and court rulings. Fiduciaries also need additional protection from liability for acts of co-fiduciaries, especially where a fiduciary should have known of the breach by a co-fiduciary and failed to remedy the breach.

Q 5:44 Who can be covered under a fiduciary liability insurance policy?

Fiduciary liability insurance policies generally protect a wide range of plan fiduciaries (e.g., administrators, trustees, committees), the company sponsoring the plan (and, in many cases, its employees), and the plan itself from certain claims brought against it based on alleged fiduciary breaches. The fiduciaries covered are typically past, present, and future trustees of the trust under the plan, in-house plan administrators, and all plan and trust fund employees who are fiduciaries. In some cases, third-party plan administrators, arbitrators, and attorneys may also be protected by fiduciary liability insurance with respect to employee benefit issues arising under the plan.

Q 5:45 May fiduciary liability insurance policies cover fiduciaries for the 20 percent civil penalty applicable to fiduciary breaches under ERISA Section 502(1)?

ERISA Section 502(1) provides that a penalty of 20 percent of the amount payable pursuant to a court order or settlement agreement with the DOL may be assessed by the DOL for a breach of fiduciary duty. State insurance law must be reviewed to ascertain whether the 20 percent penalty may be covered by insurance.

Q 5:46 How should a plan fiduciary determine which insurance company to use to provide it with fiduciary liability insurance?

In recommending or choosing fiduciary liability insurance protection for the plan, a fiduciary must act prudently and solely in the interest of plan participants and beneficiaries. [DOL News Rel 75-127 (Mar 4, 1975)] A fiduciary involved in purchasing insurance against fiduciary breaches for the plan must therefore do his or her best to secure the most suitable coverage for the plan at no greater expenditure of plan assets than is necessary. In order to satisfy ERISA's requirements, the fiduciary should ascertain that the insurance company from which he or she wishes to purchase the policy has a satisfactory rating from a reputable rating agency.

Q 5:47 Can a plan purchase insurance to cover any losses to the plan resulting from a prohibited transaction?

Yes. A plan can carry insurance to protect itself from losses it incurs as the result of the misconduct of a fiduciary, including participation in a prohibited transaction. A plan may not, however, contain a provision that would relieve a fiduciary of liability for a prohibited transaction. [ERISA § 410]

Indemnification

Q 5:48 What is *indemnification*?

Indemnification is a promise to reimburse or hold a person harmless for acting in good faith. It can be important because fiduciary liability can attach to a fiduciary who acted on behalf of a plan in good faith. A plan fiduciary may wish to consider obtaining an indemnity from the plan sponsor in lieu of, or in addition to, fiduciary liability insurance. Indemnification is only as good as the financial viability of the company providing the indemnity.

Q 5:49 May a plan indemnify a fiduciary for liability for breach of duty?

No. ERISA prohibits the indemnification and exculpation of a fiduciary by a plan. Therefore, the plan may not agree to excuse the fiduciary from responsibility for fiduciary breaches. Similarly, plan assets may not be used to reimburse a fiduciary for liability it is found to have for its actions. A plan may, however, provide for indemnification of expenses of a fiduciary who successfully defends against a claim of breach of fiduciary duty. [Packer Eng'g, Inc v Kratville, No 91-2976 (7th Cir 1992)]

Q 5:50 May an employer who sponsors a plan, or an employee organization whose members are covered by the plan, indemnify a fiduciary?

Yes. ERISA permits the indemnification of a fiduciary by an employer who sponsors a plan or by an employee organization whose members are covered by a plan. The indemnification does not relieve the fiduciary of responsibility or liability for fiduciary breaches. Rather, it leaves the fiduciary fully responsible and liable, but permits another party to satisfy any liability incurred by the fiduciary. [DOL Reg § 2509.75-4]

Allocation of Responsibility to an Investment Manager

Q 5:51 Can fiduciary responsibility be delegated?

Yes. For example, the trust instrument can provide that one trustee has responsibility for one half of the plan assets and a second trustee has responsibility for the other half. Neither trustee would be liable for the acts of the other except under the co-fiduciary liability rule of ERISA Section 405(a). [ERISA § 405(b)]

Q 5:52 Who can qualify as an *investment manager* under ERISA?

An ERISA *investment manager* is a bank, insurance company, or registered investment adviser under the Investment Advisers Act of 1940 (Advisers Act) that acknowledges in writing that it is a fiduciary with respect to the plan and accepts the power to manage plan assets. [ERISA § 3(38)]

In selecting a registered investment adviser as an investment manager, therefore, a plan sponsor or fiduciary should ask about the adviser's registration status and inquire as to the amount of securities the adviser has under management.

Participant Direction of Investments—ERISA Section 404(c)

Q 5:53 Can an employer reduce or eliminate its fiduciary liability for investment decision making by giving participants investment control?

ERISA Section 404(c) says that if a participant is given control over the investment of his or her account, plan fiduciaries will not be held responsible for investment losses resulting from that exercise of control. There are very specific requirements, discussed more fully in chapter 6, that must be met before Section 404(c) can be claimed as a defense.

Even if a plan satisfies the requirements of Section 404(c), plan fiduciaries cannot completely eliminate liability for investment decision making. Plan fiduciaries in a Section 404(c) plan typically remain responsible for the selection and monitoring of funds available for investment, for prompt and accurate execution of transactions, and for providing adequate disclosure.

Q 5:54 Has ERISA Section 404(c) been tested as a defense in a lawsuit?

Yes. In *Meinhardt v. UNISYS Corp.* [74 F 3d 420 (3d Cir 1996)], the fiduciaries of the UNISYS plan claimed that ERISA Section 404(c) protected them from liability for failure to disclose information about a GIC fund invested in Executive Life annuity contracts. The plan participants could choose to invest among six funds and effect transfers monthly. However, there were restrictions on transfers involving the GIC fund depending on the destination of the transfer.

The case was based on the law in effect before the 1992 DOL regulations. The fiduciaries won summary judgment at the trial court level based on the participants' ability to control their accounts and general caveats about the lack of any guarantee in GIC funds. The appeals court reversed the trial court on general fiduciary principles of prudence, diversification, and disclosure and also dismissed the ERISA Section 404(c) defense because the fiduciaries had not disclosed negative information in their possession about the financial condition of Executive Life and because of the restrictions on the participants' ability to transfer out of the GIC fund.

The case was remanded to the trial court, which determined that the plan's fiduciaries had not breached their duties and that Section 404(c) was available as a defense. The case was again appealed, and the appellate court upheld the trial court's opinion on the basis of general fiduciary rules only—it did not rule on the ERISA Section 404(c) issue.

Q 5:55 What lessons can fiduciaries learn from the *UNISYS* case?

To protect themselves, fiduciaries need to act prudently and disclose material information to participants. Specific strategies can be used by fiduciaries to avoid repeating the errors the appellate court struggled with in *UNISYS*:

- Document the investment policy, procedure, and search process.
- Critically evaluate consultant recommendations.
- Compare and analyze alternatives.
- Identify and document the basis for decisions that reject recommendations of consultants or experts.

- Keep participant disclosure data up to date.

- Look long and hard at promised returns that are too good to be true—identify what additional risks support the potential returns.

- Exercise regular oversight according to a documented procedure and process—be prepared to take action.

- Do not give insiders access to information or opportunities to make changes that are not generally available to all participants.

Since the *UNISYS* case was resolved without creating any lasting authority on ERISA Section 404(c), its lessons will not be the final word on how that section should be applied. It remains, however, the only discussion of Section 404(c) by a court and, as such, is helpful in providing some direction for fiduciaries intending to rely on Section 404(c) as protection from fiduciary liability.

Managing Personal Liability

All plan fiduciaries will be left with some degree of responsibility for decision making, and for some the scope of that responsibility will be broad. It is essential for any fiduciary to review the plan document, service agreements with other providers, and any other documents necessary to understanding the exact scope and nature of the fiduciary role. Once that is understood, procedural due diligence should be applied to all decision making within that role.

Q 5:56 What is *procedural due diligence*?

Procedural due diligence is a process for making high-quality, prudent fiduciary decisions and documenting the decision-making process. In addition, use of procedural due diligence will help to ensure that the fiduciary is in a good position to defend himself or herself in the event that the prudent decision results in a bad outcome. Procedural due diligence in analyzing plan investment alternatives involves the following:

- Reading the investment documents, prospectus, proposed contracts, and disclosure materials and highlighting the costs (including fees or penalties for early liquidation), level of risk, and expected return

- Determining whether the fees associated with the investment are reasonable
- Demonstrating that the investment is reasonably designed to further the purposes of the plan and that it is consistent with the plan's funding policy and method
- Reviewing investment alternatives and, where appropriate, obtaining competitive bids
- Reviewing the historical performance of the investment and its sponsor, including checking any information available from a ratings service that covers the individual stock, mutual fund, or insurance company
- If necessary, hiring an expert to help in the decision-making process and consulting with advisers
- Having a qualified appraiser value investments in real estate, closely held stock, or other assets for which a market is not readily available to establish fair market value as of the date of purchase
- Making arrangements to receive regular information about the performance of the investment, reviewing the information promptly, and following up on material discrepancies
- Documenting all of the above and maintaining a file of reports, meeting notes, analyses, and legal documents

6 Investing Plan Assets

Most 401(k) plans give participants some degree of investment control over the assets in their account. The most common method is for the employer to designate a limited number of investment alternatives among which participants can elect to invest some or all of their accounts. An alternative is the fully directed plan in which participants can elect from a virtually unlimited universe of investments. Section 404(c) of the Employee Retirement Income Security Act of 1974 (ERISA) defines the method by which employers or other fiduciaries can be relieved of fiduciary liability for investment decision making by shifting that function to participants. There are also issues surrounding the investment of 401(k) plan assets in the stock of the company sponsoring the plan. A brief description of the characteristics of different investment alternatives is contained in this chapter. For a more complete analysis, including the risk and return characteristics of various investments, see *Participant Directed Investment Answer Book* (New York, Panel Publishers, 1999).

PRIMARY ASSET CLASSES

The three primary asset classes are stocks, bonds, and cash investments. Those broad asset classes are commonly divided into more narrow categories: for example, large-cap and small-cap stocks and corporate and government bonds. International stock and bond investments and real estate are also important asset classes. It is the primary asset classes that underlie most investment options in 401(k) plans. As in any long-term investment portfolio, which asset classes are included and how much is allocated to each asset class will generally dominate the return, with such factors as investment selection and market timing being less significant.

Stocks

Q 6:1 What is a *stock*?

A *stock* is a security that represents part ownership, or equity, in a corporation. Each share of stock is a claim on its proportionate stake in the company, some of which may be paid out as dividends. Of the three major asset classes, only stocks have historically provided both an income component and a significant long-term growth component. Investment professionals use the terms *equity* and *stock* interchangeably to refer to financial instruments that represent ownership interests in a company.

Q 6:2 What are *growth stocks*?

Growth stocks are stocks of companies whose earnings are expected to grow faster than average. Because of its potential for strong growth, a growth stock tends to be expensive relative to current earnings.

Q 6:3 What are *value stocks*?

Value stocks are stocks that tend to be inexpensive based on such various measures as current earnings, current cash flow, and book value. They are undervalued because they are from companies out of favor for some reason. A value investor seeks to identify companies poised for a turnaround that will result in rising earnings and higher stock prices.

Q 6:4 What are the risks and returns associated with stock ownership?

Historically, stocks have had the highest long-term average rate of return of the three major asset classes. To achieve such remarkable long-term results, investors are exposed to a degree of risk, which means that returns can vary greatly from year to year and that there is a chance of a significant loss of market value in any one year. Stocks have a higher expected risk than do bonds or cash investments.

The most significant risks associated with stock investing are market risk and business risk. An investor can, however, reduce inflation risk by having a portion of his or her portfolio invested in stocks. That is because stocks have over time outperformed inflation by a greater margin than other asset classes.

Bonds

Q 6:5 What is a *bond?*

A *bond* is a debt instrument issued by a corporation, government (federal, state, or local), or government agency interested in raising money. As fixed income investments, bonds pay stated interest at regular intervals until they mature, at which time investors receive the face value of the bond. Since bonds are issued with a fixed coupon rate and a fixed face value, their market value or purchase price must change to reflect changes in the interest climate—the market value must fall to return a higher yield and must increase to reflect a lower yield. Bonds that are purchased to yield a higher return than their coupon rate are said to be purchased *below par* or *at a discount,* while bonds that are purchased to yield a lower return than their coupon rate are said to be purchased *above par* or *at a premium.* Most long-term corporate bonds are secured by a pledge of collateral; unsecured, short-term corporate bonds are called *debentures.*

For most bonds, the interest rate that the issuer promises to pay the bondholder is called the *coupon rate.* The coupon rate on a bond is closely tied to its maturity, the credit quality of the issuing entity, and the general level of interest rates at the date of issue. Bondholders have a lending, or creditor, interest in the issuer as opposed to an ownership or equity interest.

Q 6:6 What are the risks and returns associated with investing in bonds?

Of the three major asset classes, bonds fall between cash investments and stocks on the risk and return spectrum. The risks most associated with bond investing are inflation risk, credit risk, and interest rate risk. It is important to remember that since bonds provide a fixed payment stream, their market value must fall when interest rates rise and must increase when interest rates decline. Thus, even the most secure of bonds—say, those issued by the United States Government—are subject to a loss in market value due to interest rate risk even if they present a negligible business risk of default.

Q 6:7 What types of bonds does the federal government issue?

The federal government issues four basic types of bonds:

1. *Treasury bills* with original maturities of 3, 6, or 12 months;
2. *Treasury notes* with original maturities ranging from 2 to 10 years;
3. *Treasury bonds* with maturities longer than 10 years; and
4. *Treasury Inflation-Protected Securities (TIPS)* also with maturities longer than 10 years but with a face value (and hence coupon payments) that changes with inflation.

Cash Investments

Q 6:8 What is meant by a *cash investment*?

A *cash investment* is a very short-term loan to a borrower with a very high credit rating. Examples of cash investments are short-term bank certificates of deposit (CDs), Treasury bills (T-bills), and commercial paper (i.e., short-term obligations of corporations with the highest credit ratings). Money market funds, which hold bank CDs, T-bills, and commercial paper, are also considered cash investments.

Q 6:9 What are the risks and returns associated with cash investments?

Cash investments generally have lower expected risk and return than bonds and stocks. The risk of losing principal in a cash investment is low because the borrowers are creditworthy and the loans are so short, typically one year or less. Having relatively low returns, however, exposes long-term investors to significant inflation risk.

INVESTMENT VEHICLES

With the exception of employer securities and plans with a self-directed option, investment options in 401(k) plans seldom include individual stocks and bonds directly. Rather, they include invest-ment vehicles that invest in a number of securities. The growth market for the financial services industry continues to be retire-ment plan assets, including those in 401(k) plans. In the battle for those assets, mutual fund companies have emerged as the domi-nant players.

Q 6:10 What are typical investment vehicles in 401(k) plans?

The typical investment vehicles in 401(k) plans include mutual funds, variable annuity contracts, guaranteed investment contracts (GICs), life insurance contracts, and employer stock. With limited exceptions, 401(k) plans do not offer individual securities as invest-ment options.

Mutual Funds

Q 6:11 What is a *mutual fund*?

A *mutual fund* is an investment company that pools the resources of many investors to purchase a portfolio of individual securities. The mutual fund is merely a structure, a "wrapper," containing vari-ous investments such as stocks, bonds, and cash. By owning shares (or units) of a mutual fund, shareholders own a fraction of each se-curity purchased by that mutual fund.

Q 6:12 What are the advantages of offering mutual funds in 401(k) plans?

There are many advantages to offering mutual funds in a 401(k) plan:

1. *Diversification.* Because the money of a participant is pooled with money from thousands of other investors, a mutual fund can invest in a wide array of securities.

2. *Professional management.* Decisions about buying and selling securities in a mutual fund are overseen by a professional in-vestment manager.

3. *Liquidity.* Shares in most mutual funds may be sold whenever an investor chooses.

4. *Convenience.* Shares can be conveniently purchased under many different arrangements, such as by mail or telephone or through stockbrokers, banks, or insurance agents.

5. *Information.* Shareholders receive regular reports on fund performance and, in many cases, other investment-related information. Extensive recordkeeping services help track transactions. Shareholders also have the ability to evaluate and monitor fund performance through newspapers, trade publications, and fund ratings services.

6. *Flexibility.* A mutual fund has the ability to accommodate large numbers of individual investors and accept cash inflows at irregular intervals.

Q 6:13 What are the disadvantages of offering mutual funds in 401(k) plans?

There are some disadvantages to mutual fund investing in 401(k) plans:

1. *No guarantees.* Unlike bank deposits (such as CDs), mutual funds are not insured or guaranteed by the Federal Deposit Insurance Corporation (FDIC) or any other federal agency. Even though mutual funds are regulated by the SEC and state securities regulators, they do not protect a fund from the risk of losing value.

2. *Manager risk.* Evidence suggests that few investment managers outperform the market on a consistent basis. Inasmuch as past performance is no guarantee of future performance, finding star performers in advance is difficult to do on a consistent basis. Even if a good manager is on board, there is still the danger that the investment manager will change his or her investment style or leave the fund altogether.

3. *Fees.* Although mutual funds can offer lower costs than would arise from buying individual securities through brokers, the combination of fees charged by mutual funds can be quite expensive. Funds that are sold through intermediaries such as brokers and insurance agents may entail fees in addition to those charged by the mutual fund.

Q 6:14 What are common types of mutual funds offered in 401(k) plans?

- Money market funds (see Q 6:15)
- Corporate/government bond funds (see Q 6:17)
- Balanced funds (see Q 6:18)
- Indexed stock funds (see Q 6:19)
- Growth and income stock funds (see Q 6:21)
- Growth stock funds (see Q 6:22)
- Aggressive growth stock funds (see Q 6:22)
- International stock funds (see Q 6:23)

Though their numbers are growing, two other types of mutual funds are less prevalent in 401(k) plans: asset allocation funds (see Q 6:24) and real estate funds (see Q 6:25).

Q 6:15 What is a *money market fund*?

A *money market fund* is a fund that invests in very short-term, high-quality loans such as Treasury bills, CDs, and commercial paper. Because money market funds are constantly buying and selling such loans, they earn a fluctuating rate of interest. The original investment, or principal, remains stable, though strictly speaking it is not guaranteed since there is always some business risk from the underlying investments.

Q 6:16 What is a *stable value fund*?

A *stable value fund* generally is a fund that offers stability of principal—that is, no fluctuation of principal as a result of market movements. Because of its stability of principal, a money market fund is sometimes called a stable value fund; however, the term *stable value fund* is more commonly used to refer to a fund that invests primarily in guaranteed investment contracts (GICs) with insurance companies or GIC alternatives with institutions such as banks—though the guarantee is only as good as the financial situation of the insurance company or other institution that provides it.

Q 6:17 What is a *corporate/government bond fund*?

A *corporate/government bond fund* is a fund that invests mainly in bond issues of various companies and bonds issued by the U.S. government, one of its agencies, or both.

Q 6:18 What is a *balanced fund*?

A *balanced fund* is a fund that invests in a relatively fixed combination of both stocks and bonds. The discretion an investment manager has to change the percentage of assets invested in stocks and bonds depends on the individual fund. The fund's prospectus may provide some insight into the leeway a manager has to change those percentages. If a manager has considerable freedom, a balanced fund may introduce a wild card to participants trying to maintain specific asset allocation strategies (e.g., 80 percent stocks and 20 percent bonds). Despite their popularity, balanced funds may not be a good investment option in a 401(k) plan for that reason. As a single investment, however, balanced funds can offer both income and growth, and they are a first step in controlling risk through diversification.

Q 6:19 What is an *index fund*?

An *index fund*, or passively managed fund, is one for which its manager, with the aid of computer software, structures a diversified portfolio whose holdings replicate those of a particular securities universe (i.e., a bond or stock index). An index fund essentially invests in all the stocks or bonds in the same proportion as they are represented in a market index. For example, an S&P 500 index fund buys the 500 stocks that make up the index. Other major indexes include the Russell 2000, which tracks the performance of the stocks of 2,000 small companies, and the Shearson Lehman Brothers Government and Corporate Bond index, which tracks the performance of investment-grade bonds.

Q 6:20 What is an *actively managed fund*?

An *actively managed fund* is one for which its manager actively analyzes individual holdings in an attempt to outperform a selected market index. Actively managed funds typically involve higher fees than index funds. Some studies suggest that, on average, actively managed funds do not outperform index funds sufficiently to cover the higher fees, though other studies support the opposite conclusion.

Q 6:21 What are *growth and income stock funds*?

Growth and income stock funds are funds that invest mainly in stocks of large- and medium-sized companies with a long history of steady growth and reliable dividends. Such funds seek to provide a balance between current dividend income and long-term growth. They tend to grow less rapidly, however, than pure growth funds (see Q 6:22). Growth and income funds are often called *value funds.*

Q 6:22 What are *growth* and *aggressive growth funds*?

A *growth fund* is a fund that invests in stock of companies whose earnings are expected to grow faster than average—that is, growth stocks. An *aggressive growth fund* is a fund that typically invests in smaller, less established companies having high growth potential but higher than average risk. Both types of funds are quite vulnerable to short-term market fluctuations.

Growth stocks tend to carry high price tags relative to current earnings. The market is willing to pay more for growth stocks because they are from companies with the potential for strong, consistent earnings growth that may be worth considerably more in the future. A growth stock fund manager determines if a stock's price is justified based on the company's potential for growth.

Q 6:23 What are the different types of international funds?

Funds that hold only non-U.S. securities are known as *international funds*; those that invest in both U.S. and non-U.S. securities are known as *global funds.* Funds that target a small group of neighboring foreign countries are called *regional funds,* and those that specialize in newer, less established markets are called *emerging market funds.* Within those broad categories, risks and returns will vary widely.

International funds can provide a source of diversification since markets outside the United States often move independently of the domestic markets. However, they also tend to be riskier for the same levels of return because of currency risk and higher risk of political instability and corruption within less well regulated markets. International funds also tend to carry higher investment fees than do domestic funds of comparable quality.

Asset Allocation Funds

Q 6:24 What are *asset allocation funds*?

Asset allocation funds (e.g., lifestyle funds, fund of funds, life-cycle funds) blend various funds into broad-based asset allocations that are appropriate for predefined investor profiles. Such blending is an investor-friendly attempt to match an investor with a fund that delivers an appropriate mix of risk and return. The goal of asset allocation funds is to offer a convenient way to get both professional asset allocation and broad diversification from one investment.

Given the importance of asset allocation decisions, offering asset allocation funds in 401(k) plans clearly has its advantages. That is especially true if participants lack the investment savvy to make proper asset allocation decisions. The drawback of such funds is that they typically have a double layer of fees: fees of the underlying funds plus fees related to operating and managing the asset allocation fund.

Real Estate Funds

Q 6:25 What are *real estate funds*?

Real estate funds are funds that invest primarily in real estate investment trusts (REITs), which are publicly traded securities representing ownership interests in real estate. Some REITs spread their holdings across a variety of properties—apartment buildings, offices, hotels, and so forth. Others concentrate in a single real estate category.

Despite their checkered past, real estate offerings can enhance portfolio diversification because of their low correlation with other asset classes. Historically, real estate investments have also been an effective hedge against inflation. That attribute, however, can vary dramatically depending on an investor's investment horizon.

Variable Annuities

Q 6:26 What is a *variable annuity contract*?

Some sponsors of 401(k) plans offer participants a menu of investment options under a variable annuity contract sold by an insurance company. Investments provided under such a contract may include a selection of proprietary investment portfolios, nonproprietary funds, or both. A variety of features and fees are associated with a variable annuity contract.

A *variable annuity contract* is a tax-deferred investment contract sold by an insurance company; contributions are invested in underlying investment options and converted to a lump sum or an income stream, typically at an investor's retirement. Variable annuity contracts typically offer a number of investment options, such as a money market portfolio, a bond portfolio, a stock portfolio, and other specialized portfolios (referred to as *subaccounts*). Many insurance companies manage their own investment portfolios. In addition, major mutual fund groups have spawned funds that are offered through variable annuity contracts, many being replicas of well-known funds.

Unlike those under a fixed annuity contract, payments under a variable annuity contract will depend on the performance of the underlying investment portfolios. Variable annuity contracts can be made on an individual or group basis.

The insurance-like feature of a variable annuity is the death benefit, which guarantees that a minimum amount will be left to one's survivors regardless of market conditions. Death benefit provisions will vary, but most will provide that the benefit expires once the holder turns a certain age (e.g., age 75).

A detailed description of the legislative and regulatory framework into which variable annuity products fall is complex and beyond the scope of this book. Most variable annuity contracts are offered through a two-tiered structure in which a *separated account* is used to invest in a number of underlying investment portfolios referred to as *subaccounts*. Separate accounts of insurance companies are creatures of and established pursuant to state law. Under federal securities law, separate accounts supporting variable annuity contracts are *securities* under the Securities Act and must be registered as investment companies under the 1940 Act (usually as *unit investment trusts*). An underlying fund offering shares to a separate account must likewise be registered under the 1940 Act and must register its shares under the Securities Act. From the standpoint of federal securities law, it is interesting to note that the Securities and Exchange Commission (SEC) appears to be focusing considerable attention on the sales practices associated with variable annuity products.

Q 6:27 What are some factors to consider when deciding whether to choose a variable annuity contract as an investment vehicle for a 401(k) plan?

A plan sponsor should ask the following questions when analyzing a variable annuity contract for its 401(k) plan:

- Is there an opportunity to provide participants a fund lineup that allows them to construct portfolios that fit their investment goals and risk profiles?
- How do the performance records of the underlying funds compare with those of other mutual funds in their peer groups?
- Have managers of the underlying funds employed consistent investment styles?
- What are the fees of the underlying funds?
- What is the annual insurance contract charge?
- Is there a surrender charge?
- Are there any fees for switching investment choices?
- How is the death benefit calculated, and at what age does it expire?
- How do the sponsoring insurance company's financial stability and claims-paying ability rate?
- What other services are being provided under the contract (e.g., administration, education, recordkeeping)?
- How do the cost and quality of overall services compare with those of other available options?

Guaranteed Investment Contracts (GICs)

Q 6:28 What is a *guaranteed investment contract*?

A *guaranteed investment contract* (GIC), a type of stable value investment, is a contract sold by an insurance company that guarantees the payment of a specified rate of interest on the amount of money invested for a specified period of time, usually for periods ranging from one to five years. The insurance company invests the moneys in a portfolio of securities usually structured to mature around the time the GIC is scheduled to expire. A GIC is issued as an obligation of the insurance company's general account.

Life Insurance

Q 6:29 What is a *life insurance contract*?

A *life insurance contract* is a contract in which an insurance company agrees to pay the contract owner a sum of money when the insured person dies. Although the primary purpose of a retirement plan is to pay retirement benefits, a plan may also provide incidental life insurance coverage for participants. No part of an individual retirement account (IRA) can be invested in life insurance contracts, so life insurance contracts held in a 401(k) plan cannot be rolled over into an IRA upon distribution. [IRC § 408(a)(3)]

ASSET ALLOCATION STRATEGY

The allocation of assets across different asset classes (e.g., stocks, bonds, and cash investments) has been shown to be responsible for over 90 percent of the variation of portfolio returns. In 401(k) plans, the importance of asset allocation cannot be overemphasized.

Q 6:30 What is *asset allocation*?

Asset allocation is the process of allocating assets across broad asset classes (e.g., stocks, bonds, and cash investments). Those broad asset classes can be further divided into more narrow categories. In the stocks category, for example, there may be large-cap stocks, small-cap stocks, and international stocks. The bond category might have long-term and short-term bonds and corporate and government bonds. Asset allocation differs from investment selection, which is selecting specific investments to hold within a particular asset class.

Q 6:31 Why is asset allocation important?

A well-known study found that asset allocation decisions can account for over 90 percent of the variation in a portfolio's performance. In other words, investment selection and market timing have far less impact than asset allocation decisions. Participants in 401(k) plans should dedicate much of their investment decision making to arriving at an appropriate asset allocation. That decision should not be obscured or downplayed because of its seeming simplicity. [Brinson, Singer, & Beebower, "Determinants of Portfolio Performance II: An Update," *Fin Analysts J*, May–June 1991, at 40–48]

Q 6:32 What does an asset allocation fund accomplish?

An asset allocation fund (e.g., lifestlye fund, fund of funds, life-cycle fund) invests in several different types of assets normally invested in separate funds. With an asset allocation fund, a portfolio manager makes the asset allocation decisions. In 401(k) plans, such funds can provide some assurance that participants, especially those ill equipped to make asset allocation decisions, will meet their investment objectives. Asset allocation funds do, however, have drawbacks (see Q 6:24).

EMPLOYER SECURITIES

The decision to offer employer securities as an investment option in a 401(k) plan is quite different from a decision to offer other investment options. Although offering employer securities can help align participants' interests with those of the company, plan sponsors must be extremely careful with such an arrangement. A major concern will be ensuring that the fiduciary rules of ERISA are met. If ERISA Section 404(c) protection is intended to extend to an employer stock option, special conditions must be satisfied. Ensuring that participant assets are adequately diversified—that is, not overly invested in employer stock—will also be a concern.

Federal and state securities law issues also arise whenever a plan invests in employer securities. Liquidity, voting, valuation, and other unique issues may surface as a result of a decision to offer employer stock in a 401(k) plan. Because of the complexities involved, a plan sponsor considering employer stock for its plan should consult attorneys specializing in ERISA and securities law.

Q 6:33 How can a plan sponsor offer employer stock in a 401(k) plan?

There are two ways to offer employer stock to plan participants:

1. Participants may be given the option to direct the investment of their accounts in, among other investment options, employer stock. Depending on the plan, the option may apply to only certain accounts, including elective contribution, match, profit sharing, after-tax, and rollover accounts.

2. Second, employer contributions (i.e., match and profit sharing contributions) may be made, or automatically invested, in employer stock. Under such an arrangement, participants may or may not be given the ability to transfer out of (and back into) employer stock allocated to their accounts.

Other basic design considerations may include:

• Whether the plan will allow distributions in employer stock

• Whether participant investment in employer stock will be limited to a certain percentage

• What voting rights participants will be given with respect to employer stock

• Whether ERISA Section 404(c) protection will be sought for participant investment in employer stock

• Whether to include a money market fund in the employer stock option to generate liquidity for payouts

• What method of accounting will be used (share or unit)

Q 6:34 Do special ERISA fiduciary rules apply to a plan investing in employer securities?

Yes. A plan fiduciary engages in a prohibited transaction (see chapter 5) if he or she causes a plan to acquire or hold employer securities and does not follow all of these requirements:

1. The plan may invest only in qualifying employer securities (see Q 6:35). [ERISA § 407(a)(1)(A)]

2. The plan may not have more than 10 percent of its assets invested in employer securities. [ERISA § 407(a)(2)] An eligible individual account plan (see Q 6:36) may, however, invest more than 10 percent if the plan explicitly provides for

the acquisition and holding of employer securities. [ERISA §§ 407(b)(1), 407(d)(3)(B)] For plan years beginning after December 31, 1998, no more than 10 percent of a participant's elective contributions can be required to be invested in employer securities. [ERISA § 407(b)(2)]

3. The plan's sale or acquisition of employer securities must be for adequate consideration (see Q 6:38), and no commission may be charged. [ERISA § 408(e)]

[ERISA §§ 406(a)(1)(E), 406(a)(2)]

As a general rule, a plan fiduciary must also act prudently and for the exclusive benefit of plan participants and beneficiaries. [ERISA § 404(a)] So, although a plan fiduciary might not engage in a prohibited transaction by offering employer stock, he or she might still violate ERISA's fiduciary duty requirements by, for example, offering the stock when it is no longer financially appropriate to do so. Plan fiduciaries would be wise to seek independent legal and investment advice to ensure compliance with ERISA's fiduciary standards.

Qualifying Employer Securities

Q 6:35 What is a *qualifying employer security*?

A *qualifying employer security* is a security issued by an employer (or an affiliate) of employees covered by the plan that is stock, a marketable obligation, or an interest in certain publicly traded partnerships. [ERISA §§ 407(d)(1), 407(d)(5)]

The term *marketable obligation* means a bond, debenture, note, certificate, or other evidence of indebtedness where the following conditions are met:

1. The obligation is acquired on the market either at the price prevailing on a national securities exchange (registered with the SEC) or, if not traded on such exchange, at a price not less favorable to the plan than the offering price as established by the current bid and asked prices (quoted by persons independent of the issuer), from an underwriter at a price not in excess of the public offering price and at which a substantial portion of the same issue is acquired by persons independent of the issuer, or directly from the issuer at a price not less favorable to the plan than the price paid currently for a sub-

stantial portion of the same issue by persons independent of the issuer;

2. Immediately after the obligation is acquired, no more than 25 percent of the aggregated amount of obligations issued in such issue and outstanding is held by the plan, and at least 50 percent of the aggregated amount is held by persons independent of the issuer; and

3. Immediately after the obligation is acquired, no more than 25 percent of the assets of the plan is invested in obligations of the employer or its affiliate.

[ERISA § 407(e)]

Stock interests acquired by a plan (other than an eligible individual account plan) after December 17, 1987, will be a qualifying employer security only if, immediately following the acquisition of such stock:

1. No more than 25 percent of the aggregate amount of stock of the same class issued and outstanding at the time of acquisition is held by the plan; and

2. At least 50 percent of such aggregate amount is held by persons independent of the issuer.

[ERISA § 407(f)(1)]

Plans holding stock that failed to meet the above requirements had until January 1, 1993, to divest themselves of such stock (provided that the stock was held since December 1, 1987, or acquired after December 17, 1987, but pursuant to a legally binding contract in effect on December 17, 1987, and so held at all times thereafter). [ERISA § 407(f)(2)]

Q 6:36 What is an *eligible individual account plan*?

An *eligible individual account plan* is an individual account plan (i.e., a defined contribution plan) that is one of the following:

1. A profit sharing, stock bonus, thrift, or savings plan (including a 401(k) plan);

2. An employee stock ownership plan (ESOP); or

3. A pre-ERISA money purchase pension plan invested primarily in employer securities.

The term does not include an individual retirement account or annuity. [ERISA § 407(d)(3)(A)] A plan will be treated as an eligible individual account plan only if such plan explicitly provides for the acquisition and holding of qualifying employer securities. [ERISA § 407(d)(3)(B)]

Q 6:37 What new restriction will apply to 401(k) plans investing in qualifying employer securities?

Eligible individual account plans, which would include 401(k) plans, are generally not subject to the 10 percent limit on investment in employer securities. For plan years beginning after December 31, 1998, however, the portion of a 401(k) plan consisting of employee salary deferrals, and earnings thereto, that is *required* to be invested in employer stock under the terms of the plan or at the direction of a person other than the participant will be treated as a separate plan subject to the 10 percent limit.

The restriction would not apply to 401(k) plans that permit participant investment of salary deferral contributions or to ESOPs. It also will not apply if the fair market value of all the employer's individual account plans is no more than 10 percent of the fair market value of all the employer's retirement plans, and it will not apply if no more than 1 percent of the employee's eligible compensation is required to be invested in employer securities. [PL 105-34 § 1524, amending ERISA § 407(b)]

Fair Market Value of Employer Stock

Q 6:38 What does it mean for a plan to purchase or sell employer securities for *adequate consideration*?

The acquisition or sale of qualifying employer securities is exempt from the prohibited transaction rules only if the acquisition or sale is for adequate consideration and no commission is charged. [ERISA § 408(e)] In the case of a security for which there is a generally recognized market, *adequate consideration* means the price of the security prevailing on a national securities exchange registered under Section 6 of the Securities Exchange Act of 1934, or, if the security is not traded on such a national securities exchange, a price not less favorable to the plan than the offering price for the security as established by the current bid and asked prices quoted by persons independent of the issuer and any party in interest. [ERISA § 3(18)(A)]

In the case of a security not freely tradable, *adequate considera-tion* means the fair market value of the security as determined in good faith by the trustee or named fiduciary, pursuant to the terms of the plan and the regulations promulgated by the Department of Labor (DOL). For such purpose, fair market value must be the price of a willing buyer and a willing seller in an arm's-length transaction determined as of the applicable date and reflected in a written docu-ment meeting the requirement of the DOL regulations. The good-faith component requires:

1. Objective standards of conduct;
2. Prudent investigation of circumstances prevailing at the time of the valuation;
3. Application of sound business principles of valuation; and
4. That the fiduciary making the valuation either be independ-ent of all parties (other than the plan) or be reliant on the re-port of an appraiser who is independent of all parties (other than the plan).

[Prop DOL Reg § 2510.3-18]

Q 6:39 Why is it important to properly value employer stock when it is offered as a plan investment option?

An accurate assessment of the fair market value is essential to a plan's ability to comply with the requirements set forth in the Inter-nal Revenue Code (Code) and ERISA. For instance, a prohibited transaction exemption may not apply unless the fair market value of assets is accurately determined.

Similarly, a failure to properly establish fair market value may cause:

1. An exclusive benefit violation under Code Section 401(a);
2. A violation of the limitation on benefits and contributions under Code Section 415;
3. An excess deduction under Code Section 404;
4. A violation of the minimum funding requirements under Code Section 412; or
5. A discrimination violation under Code Section 401(a)(4).

[Ann 92-182, 1992-52 IRB 45]

Although most investments held by a plan present minimal valuation problems (e.g., publicly traded employer stock and mutual funds), some investments such as closely held employer stock, real estate, and limited partnerships may receive special scrutiny. The Internal Revenue Service (IRS) monitors compliance with the valuation standards on Form 5500, which requires a statement of plan assets valued at fair market value. A valuation problem may exist, according to the IRS, if a plan reports assets with level values in successive years or if there is a sudden jump in plan asset values in the same year a large distribution is made to highly compensated employees.

Because amounts allocated or distributed to participants in a defined contribution plan must be ascertainable, such a plan must value its assets at least once a year in accordance with a method consistently followed and uniformly applied. [Rev Rul 80-155, 1980-1 CB 84] Furthermore, employer securities must be valued at the time of the transaction whenever acquired or sold. [Rev Rul 69-494, 1969-2 CB 88]

Voting Rights for Employer Stock

Q 6:40 Do companies give participants voting rights with respect to employer stock allocated to their accounts?

Some companies pass through voting of shares to participants to enforce the awareness of ownership. Some do not; instead, the plan trustee typically controls how shares are voted in its own discretion or at the direction of a named fiduciary. Alternatively, a properly appointed ERISA investment manager may control voting of shares. [ERISA § 401(a); DOL Reg § 2509.94-21] If ERISA Section 404(c) protection is desired, however, voting, tender, and similar rights must be passed through to the participants.

Special rules under the Code govern when voting must be passed through to participants in an ESOP. If an employer has securities that are readily tradable on an established securities exchange, voting on allocated shares must be passed through to plan participants. [IRC § 409(e)(2)] If the employer has securities that are not readily tradable, voting on allocated shares must be passed through to participants only with respect to major corporate matters (e.g., merger,

recapitalization, liquidation, sale of substantially all of the assets).
[IRC § 409(e)(3)]

The legal issue of whether pass-through voting protects a plan fiduciary, such as a plan trustee, from liability for results of the proxy
(or tender) decision was the subject of a recent appellate court decision. (Herman v NationsBank Trust Co, 126 F 3d 1354, 21 EBC
(BNA) 2061 (11th Cir 1997)]

Registration Requirements

Q 6:41 What registration requirements under federal securities laws arise when a 401(k) plan offers employer securities?

Under federal securities law, each offer or sale of an employer's
stock must be registered with the SEC, or there must be an applicable exemption from the registration requirement. [Securities Act of
1933, §§ 2(1), 3–4; 15 USC §§ 77b(1), 77c–77d] The rule applies
whether or not the employer's stock is publicly traded.

The SEC has taken the position that when a plan allows voluntary
employee contributions including salary deferrals to be invested in
employer stock, an individual employee's interest in that plan is a
security. That may subject the plan to securities registration, prospectus, and antifraud requirements, although, depending on the
employer and plan structure, there may be exemptions from some
of those requirements. If registration requirements apply, the *plan*
must be registered for SEC purposes. It is not enough that the stock
itself is registered. The plan is typically registered by means of an
abbreviated S-8 filing. [SEC Rel 33-6188, 45 Fed Reg 8960 (Feb 11,
1980)] If interests in the plan itself must be registered, annual financial reports on the plan may also need to be filed with the SEC. [SEC
Rule 15d-21, 17 CFR § 240.15d-21]

If a plan does not permit investment of voluntary employee contributions, registration is not required even if participants have the
right to direct investment of employer contributions and earnings
among various investments, including employer stock. Even though
employee interests in the plan may not be securities, however, the
underlying employer stock may be considered a security that must
be either registered or offered pursuant to an available exemption
from registration. Further, although a distribution of unregistered

stock from a plan to a participant in satisfaction of a benefit obligation does not require SEC registration, the participant may not be able then to sell the stock unless it is registered or falls within a securities law exemption. [SEC Rel 33-6188, Part V, C and Part VI, B, 45 Fed Reg 8976, 8977 (Feb 11, 1980)]

A registration exemption may not, however, provide an exemption from disclosure (antifraud) requirements and, in some cases, state registration. Unless it provides disclosures regarding its operations comparable to those provided to prospective investors by publicly traded companies, a privately held company may have a significant antifraud exposure. If a privately held company is not willing to provide such disclosures to employees (either because of cost or privacy concerns), offering its stock as an investment option is usually not recommended. Whatever the situation, it is best to seek advice from a securities law expert before offering employer stock.

Short-Swing Profit Rules

Q 6:42 How might the SEC short-swing profits rules apply to transactions involving publicly traded employer stock in a 401(k) plan?

The 1934 Securities Exchange Act imposes reporting requirements and liability on transactions in publicly traded employer stock by directors, executive officers, and more-than-10 percent shareholders of the employer (i.e., corporate insiders). [Securities Exchange Act of 1934 § 16, 15 USC § 78p] Section 16(a) requires corporate insiders to file certain periodic reports with the SEC of their ownership, including changes to that ownership. Under Section 16(b), liability is imposed on insiders for any profit derived from any purchase and sale (or sale and purchase) during the same six-month period; this is known as *short-swing profit liability*. The provisions were intended to prevent the misuse of insider information prohibited under Section 10(b) and SEC Rule 10b-5.

Example. To avoid short-swing profit liability, a participant insider electing into an employer stock alternative on January 1, 1998, would not be allowed to transfer shares out of that employer stock until July 1, 1998.

Transactions in employer stock should also be analyzed under other SEC trading rules, such as the prohibition on market manipulation.

Q 6:43 What is the principal SEC rule governing short-swing profit liability in employee benefit plans?

The principal rule applying to employee benefit plan transactions is SEC Rule 16b-3. These are the key features of Rule 16b-3:

1. Any transaction between the issuer (including the plan) and an insider involving employer stock is exempt from Section 16(b) if Rule 16b-3 is met;

2. Any transaction in company stock (other than a *discretionary transaction*) in a *tax-conditioned plan* shall be exempt from Section 16(b) without condition. Those transactions include the following:

   a. 401(k) plan purchases pursuant to elective deferrals;

   b. Elections to begin or cease participation or change contribution levels;

   c. In-service employer stock withdrawals (treated as only a change in the nature of beneficial ownership, other than cash distributions resulting from stock disposition); and

   d. Any transaction in connection with the participant's death, disability, retirement, or termination from employment;

3. A *discretionary transaction* in employer stock is exempt from Section 16(b) only if effected pursuant to an election made at least six months following the date of the most recent election, with respect to any plan of the issuer, that effected an "opposite way" discretionary transaction. For example, an intra-plan transfer *out* of employer stock would be exempt if the election occurred more than six months after an election to transfer assets *into* employer stock.

4. An intra-plan transfer *into* employer stock would be exempt if the election occurred more than six months following an intra-plan transfer *out* of employer stock or a plan loan funded through the sale of employer stock held in employer stock.

5. The timing of opposite-way discretionary transaction focuses

on the date of *elections* and not the dates the elections are effected by the plan. Elections for same-way discretionary transactions need not be separated by six months.

6. All tax-conditioned plan transactions, other than discretionary transactions, are completely exempt from Section 16(a) reporting.

[SEC Rule 16b-3, 17 CFR § 240.16b-3; SEC Rule 16a-4, 17 CFR § 240.16a-4]

Q 6:44 What is a *discretionary transaction* under SEC Rule 16b-3?

A *discretionary transaction* for purposes of SEC Rule 16b-3 is defined as a transaction pursuant to an employee benefit plan that:

1. Is at the volition of a plan participant;
2. Is not made in connection with the participant's death, disability, retirement, or termination of employment;
3. Is not required to be made available to a plan participant pursuant to a provision of the Code; and
4. Results in either an intra-plan transfer involving employer stock or a cash distribution funded by a volitional disposition of employer stock.

[SEC Rule 16b-3, 17 CFR § 240.16b-3]

Employer Stock Strategy

Q 6:45 What are the dangers of being heavily invested in employer stock?

Being heavily invested in a single security can carry high risk. With both job and retirement security tied to the performance of the same company, the risk is magnified. Proper diversification applies to investment in employer stock. Many plan participants are aware of the potential rewards associated with investing in employer stock but are unaware of the risks of being heavily invested in this stock.

Q 6:46 What are some general guidelines for including employer stocks as an investment option in a 401(k) plan?

The following are some general guidelines for including an employer stock investment alternative in a 401(k) plan with the least risk of creating compliance problems:

1. If the stock is not registered, offer the option of investing in employer stock only for matching or profit sharing accounts—not salary deferral, rollover, or after-tax accounts.

2. If the stock is not registered, make all distributions from the plan in the form of cash, not stock.

3. If the stock is not publicly traded, include a money market fund in the employer stock fund to generate the liquidity necessary to make payouts; the money market fund can also be used to hold contributions until a purchase date.

4. If the stock is not publicly traded, allow investments into and out of the fund on an annual basis only.

5. Work closely with the plan administrator to create a plan design that will match the type of stock and goals of the employer with the purchase availability and distribution options made available to participants under the plan.

6. In all situations, consult a securities law attorney and an ERISA attorney to ensure that all SEC filings, state and federal securities requirements, and other compliance issues are addressed.

401(k) STOCK OWNERSHIP PLANS (KSOPs)

Q 6:47 What is a *401(k) stock ownership plan (KSOP)*?

A *401(k) stock ownership plan,* commonly called a *KSOP,* is a stock bonus plan in which salary deferrals and/or employer matching contributions may be invested in employer stock. The primary benefit of a KSOP is that it enables participants to purchase employer stock on a pretax basis. A KSOP must comply with all the stock bonus plan rules as well as the 401(k) rules. [IRC § 401(k)(1)]

Q 6:48 What are the stock bonus rules that apply to KSOPs?

The following regulatory and Code provisions govern KSOPs:

1. The plan must be designed to invest primarily in employer securities, and benefits must be distributable in employer stock. [Treas Reg § 1.401-1(a)(2)(iii)]

2. The plan may provide a cash distribution option as long as the participants have the right to demand that a distribution be made in stock. [IRC § 409(h)]

3. Distribution of non-publicly traded securities from a plan are subject to the participants' right to sell the stock back to the employer. [IRC § 409(h)]

4. Participants have certain voting rights on employer stock. [IRC § 409(e)]

5. A stock bonus plan may be designed with ESOP features allowing the plan to borrow funds to purchase employer securities. [IRC § 4975(e)(7)]

6. Distributions must begin by the end of the plan year after the year a participant stops work because of normal retirement, death, or disability. Other distributions generally must be made by the end of the sixth plan year after the year the participant terminates employment; however, the plan may allow for the delay of payment for large account balances consisting of securities acquired with ESOP loans; [IRC § 409(o)]

7. A stock bonus ESOP plan that invests in non-publicly traded employer securities must have the valuation of those securities made by an independent appraiser. [IRC § 401(a)(28)]

PARTICIPANT DIRECTED PLANS AND ERISA SECTION 404(c)

Many 401(k) plans include an option for participants to choose how to invest the money in their plan accounts. Including this feature in plans with salary deferral accounts has a certain logic, since participants could have elected to have control of the money in the first place by opting to receive cash. Another key reason why participant direction is often offered is the protection from fiduciary liability that is available in participant directed plans. This section discusses the 1992 final Department of Labor (DOL) ERISA Section 404(c)regulations on how a participant directed plan must be designed and operated in order to take advantage of this fiduciary relief.

Q 6:49 What is a *participant directed plan*?

A *participant directed plan* is a plan in which each participant chooses how to invest the assets held in his or her account. Some of these plans are completely open-ended; that is, there are no limits placed on what a participant can invest in. This type of participant directed plan is not very common, since it is usually expensive and difficult to administer and requires a fairly high degree of investment knowledge on the part of plan participants. The advantage to a self-directed plan (see Qs 6:86–6:95) is that it increases the fiduciary protection available, since plan fiduciaries will not be responsible for selecting designated funds.

Most participant directed plans offer participants a choice among a limited group of funds designated by the employer. This type of arrangement is quite common in participant directed plans and is the type of plan design that the DOL Section 404(c) regulation focuses on. [DOL Reg § 2550.404c]

Q 6:50 What is the rule concerning protection from fiduciary liability in participant directed plans?

The statutory rule in ERISA Section 404(c) states that if a participant in a defined contribution plan exercises control over the assets in his or her account, a participant will not be considered a fiduciary by reason of that control, and no other fiduciary shall be held responsible for losses resulting from that control. This general rule has been interpreted in great detail in a 1992 DOL regulation. [ERISA § 404(c); DOL Reg § 2550.404c-1]

Q 6:51 Are participant directed plans required to comply with the DOL regulation?

No. Compliance with the DOL regulation is optional, and participant direction may be offered in a plan that does not satisfy the DOL regulation. [DOL Reg § 2550.404c-1(a)(2); 57 Fed Reg 46907]

Q 6:52 Are most 401(k) plan sponsors of participant directed plans electing to comply with the DOL regulation?

Yes. A Hewitt Associates survey titled *Trends and Experience in 401(k) Plans, 1995* surveyed 434 plans of medium-sized and large-sized employers (1,000 to 10,000 employees). Of those, 29 percent of plans indicated they were currently in compliance, 44 percent intended to comply, and 15 percent were considering compliance. Only 12 percent did not intend to comply.

According to a 1998 Buck Consultants survey, 84 percent of 646 401(k) plans reported being in compliance with ERISA Section 404(c), and only 4 percent had no intention of bringing their plans into compliance.

Q 6:53 What is the effect of having a participant directed plan that does not comply with the DOL regulation?

A noncomplying participant directed plan cannot rely on ERISA Section 404(c) as a defense in the event of an investment loss. In other words, plan fiduciaries cannot argue that they are not responsible for an investment loss because a participant made the investment decisions.

An employer cannot have a plan that almost satisfies the DOL regulation and still raise ERISA Section 404(c) as a defense. If the plan is not in full compliance with the regulation, plan fiduciaries will be judged according to the general ERISA fiduciary rules without any consideration of the impact of ERISA Section 404(c). [DOL Reg § 2550.404c-1(a)(2)]

Q 6:54 What are the general requirements of the DOL regulation on participant directed plans?

Under the DOL regulation, fiduciary protection is available in a participant directed plan only if the plan meets these requirements:

1. It permits participants to choose from a broad range of investment alternatives that meet certain criteria (see Q 6:58); if designated funds are used to satisfy the broad range requirement, at least three pooled or core funds must be selected.

2. It provides an opportunity for participants to exercise control over the assets in their accounts. For this opportunity to exist, the following conditions must be present:

    a. Participants are permitted to make transfers among investment alternatives with a frequency commensurate - with the volatility of the investments. For example, if three core funds are offered to satisfy the broad range requirement, a transfer option must be offered at least quarterly for all three core funds (see Qs 6:74–6:76).

    b. Participants are provided with sufficient information to permit informed investment decision making (see Qs 6:69–6:73).

    c. Participants can give investment instructions to an identified plan fiduciary who is obligated to comply with those instructions (see Q 6:77).

[DOL Reg § 2550.404c-1(b)]

Q 6:55 Must participants be able to select investments for all their accounts in a plan?

No. Participants need not be given the option to choose their own investments with respect to all accounts in a plan. It is very common for employers to offer choices for elective deferral accounts or for rollover accounts only, but not for employer-funded accounts. However, the protection from liability exists only in those accounts that satisfy the Section 404(c) regulation. [57 Fed Reg 46907] The right to direct investments is a protected benefit under Code Section 401(a)(4), so if this right is offered only with respect to limited accounts, it cannot be offered in a way that results in discrimination in favor of highly compensated employees. [Treas Reg § 1.401(a)(4)-4(e)(3)]

Q 6:56 Must all employees and beneficiaries be given the same rights to direct their accounts?

Not necessarily. The protection from fiduciary liability is available with respect to investment decisions made by any person with a benefit in the plan. This includes participants, beneficiaries, and alternate payees. [57 Fed Reg 46908] The plan can limit investment control to categories of people. [57 Fed Reg 46907] However, the right to direct investments is a protected benefit under Code Section 401(a)(4). Therefore, if this right is limited to a particular category of people, it cannot be limited in a way that discriminates in favor of highly compensated employees.

Q 6:57 How does a plan become a 404(c) plan?

No notice is required to be filed with the IRS or the DOL concerning a plan's intent to comply with the Section 404(c) regulation. The plan must simply comply with the requirements of the regulation. This includes giving notice to plan participants that the plan is designed to comply with ERISA Section 404(c) and that plan fiduciaries may be relieved of liability for investment losses. (See Q 6:70.) This notice is often considered the "trigger" establishing the date when Section 404(c) protection becomes available.

Broad Range of Investment Alternatives

Q 6:58 What is considered a broad range of investment alternatives?

The broad range requirement is satisfied if the following conditions are met:

1. Participants are given a reasonable opportunity to affect the level of return and degree of risk to which their accounts are subject.

2. Participants are given the opportunity to choose from at least three investment alternatives that satisfy the following:

    a. Each alternative is diversified; for example, if a fund invests only in assets within the same industry, it may not be considered adequately diversified.

    b. Each alternative is materially different in terms of risk and return characteristics.

    c. In the aggregate, the alternatives enable participants to achieve a portfolio with aggregate risk and return characteristics at any point within a range normally appropriate for the participants.

    d. Each of the three funds, when combined with other alternatives, tends to minimize through diversification the overall risk of loss.

3. Participants must have the opportunity to diversify so as to minimize the risk of large losses, taking into account the nature of the plan and the size of participant accounts.

[DOL Reg § 2550.404c-1(b)(3)(i)]

A plan that is self-directed—that is, one that permits participants to invest in any asset of their choice—automatically satisfies the broad range requirement. [57 Fed Reg 46921]

Q 6:59 What is an example of a group of funds that would satisfy the broad range requirement?

The number and types of funds needed to satisfy the broad range standard will vary depending on the age and income level of participants, the size of the funds selected, and the relative volatility of the funds. A typical example of three funds that meet the broad range standard are:

- Money market fund
- Bond fund
- Equity fund

Q 6:60 Will every plan be able to satisfy the broad range standard using three funds?

No. Three funds is the minimum for any plan. If a plan covers a diverse group of employees in terms of age or income levels, uses funds at either end of the volatility spectrum, or uses small or specialized funds, it may be necessary to offer more than three funds to satisfy the broad range standard. In a Hewitt Associates study titled *Trends and Experience in 401(k) Plans, 1997,* it was reported that on average 8 investment options are offered for elective contributions, up from 4.5 options reported in 1993 and 6.3 options in 1995.

Q 6:61 Can a fixed income investment satisfy the broad range requirement as one of the three core funds?

Yes. The regulation specifically permits fixed income investments to serve as core funds. [DOL Reg § 2550.404c-1(e)(1)] However, if a contract contains any type of early withdrawal fee, transfer restriction, equity-wash, or other similar restriction, those restrictions must not have the effect of limiting a participant's exercise of control. [57 Fed Reg 46919]

Q 6:62 Can individual stocks or other individual assets be used to satisfy the broad range requirement?

The regulation requires that all participants in the plan, regardless of the dollar amounts of their accounts and/or years to retirement, must have an opportunity to diversify. Therefore, unless all participants in a plan have very large accounts, the required diversification can be achieved only by using either an open-ended approach or designated pooled funds.

Q 6:63 What are the advantages of using pooled funds to satisfy the broad range requirement?

If a pooled fund is used, the underlying assets held in the fund will be considered plan assets for purposes of determining whether the diversification requirement is met. [DOL Reg § 2550.404c-1(b)(3)(ii)] Therefore, in a new plan or any plan in which participants have relatively small account balances, pooled funds will be the only means of achieving diversification under a designated investment approach.

Independent Exercise of Control

Q 6:64 When is a participant's exercise of control considered independent?

Whether a participant has exercised independent control is determined through a facts-and-circumstances analysis. The exercise of control will fail to be independent if any of the following conditions exists:

1. A plan fiduciary uses improper influence with respect to a transaction (e.g., a plan fiduciary offers some type of incentive to participants selecting a particular investment alternative).

2. A fiduciary has concealed material, nonpublic facts that he or she is not prohibited from revealing under any federal or state law not preempted by ERISA.

3. A fiduciary accepts instructions from a participant knowing him or her to be legally incompetent.

[DOL Reg § 2550.404c-1(c)(2)]

Q 6:65 How do the rules apply to a plan that uses investment managers?

A plan that conforms to ERISA Section 404(c) may permit participants to select an investment manager of their choice or, alternatively, permit them to select among a group of managers designated by the employer. In either situation, the investment manager will remain responsible for its decisions, and those decisions will not be considered the direct and necessary result of the participant's election to use that manager. However, the employer or other plan fiduciary will not be held responsible for the manager's decisions. If the employer designates a select group of managers, the employer will remain responsible for both selecting and monitoring the managers. [DOL Reg § 2550.404c-1(d)(2)(iii)]

Employer Securities under ERISA Section 404(c)

Q 6:66 Is ERISA Section 404(c) protection available for investment in employer securities?

Yes. Employer securities may be offered in a 401(k) plan, and ERISA Section 404(c) protection can extend to those investments. An employer security cannot function as one of the three core funds, however, since it is not a diversified investment.

Q 6:67 Are there any restrictions on the types of employer securities that can be offered in an ERISA Section 404(c) plan?

Yes. The securities offered must be qualifying securities under ERISA Section 407(d)(5). In addition, they must meet all of the following requirements:

1. The security must be either publicly traded or traded with sufficient frequency to permit prompt execution of participants' investment instructions.

2. Participants and beneficiaries investing in employer securities must receive all information that is provided to shareholder.

3. All voting, tender, and similar rights with respect to the securities must be passed through to participants.

[DOL Reg § 2550.404c-1(d)(2)(ii)(E)(4)]

Q 6:68 Are there any special procedures that must be followed in an ERISA Section 404(c) plan that offers employer securities?

Yes. The following procedures must all be followed:

1. The plan must have procedures in place concerning the purchase and sale of employer securities as well as the exercise of any voting, tender, or other rights that are designed to ensure the confidentiality of these transactions.

2. The plan must designate a fiduciary to ensure that the procedures are being followed and that, when required (as in procedure 3), an independent fiduciary is designated.

3. An independent fiduciary must be appointed in connection with any transaction involving employer securities whenever there is a potential for undue influence (e.g., in a tender offer situation or when there is competition for board of directors' positions). [DOL Reg §§ 2550.404c-1(d)(2)(ii)(E)(4)(viii), 2550.404c-1(d)(2)(ii)(E)(4)(ix); 57 Fed Reg 46926–27]

4. The plan must offer participants the ability to transfer funds out of employer securities and into any of the core funds available in the plan at a frequency commensurate with the volatility level of the employer security. (See Q 6:75.)

Disclosure Requirements

Q 6:69 What information must generally be provided to participants about the available investment alternatives?

Participants must generally be given sufficient information about the investment alternatives to make meaningful investment choices. If the plan is open-ended, plan fiduciaries need only disclose to participants the fact that any alternative is permitted and pass on any information that is received by the plan. If the plan uses designated funds, plan fiduciaries have an affirmative obligation to provide participants with information about those fund options. This obligation is not limited to just those investments intended to satisfy the broad range requirement. (See Q 6:58.) Participants must be given information on all available alternatives. Participants must also be given sufficient information to permit informed decision making with respect to any voting rights or other incidents of ownership that are passed on to them in connection with an investment. [DOL Reg § 2550.404c-1(b)(2)(i)(B); 57 Fed Reg 46909–46910]

Q 6:70 What specific information must always be given to participants?

In addition to satisfying the general standard described in Q 6:69, participants must automatically be given all of the following specific information:

1. An explanation that the plan is designed to be an ERISA Section 404(c) plan and that plan fiduciaries may be relieved of liability for any losses that are the direct and necessary result of the participant's investment instructions;

2. A description of the available investment alternatives:

   a. If the plan is open-ended, the disclosure can merely state that participants may invest in any administratively feasible option; however, even in a self-directed plan, plan fiduciaries must pass on copies of any prospectuses, financial reports, or similar materials that are furnished to the plan.

   b. If the plan uses designated fund options, the disclosure must include a general description of each alternative; this description must address the investment objectives, risk and return characteristics, and types and diversification of assets that make up the portfolio. Although this information is generally contained in a prospectus, many sponsors also provide it in a more understandable format.

3. The procedures for giving investment instructions, including any limitations on transfers or any restrictions on the exercise of voting, tender, or similar rights;

4. If a designated investment manager is used, the identification of the manager;

5. A description of any transaction fees (e.g., commissions, sales loads, deferred sales charges) that will be directly assessed against a participant's account;

6. The name, address, and telephone number of the plan fiduci-
    ary responsible for providing information to participants
    upon request (see Q 6:71) (the fiduciary may be identified
    by position—e.g., plan administrator, trustee—rather than
    by name);

7. If an investment alternative is subject to the 1933 Securities
    Act, a copy of the most recent prospectus on the security, to
    be provided either immediately before or immediately follow-
    ing a participant's initial investment in that alternative;

8. To the extent that voting, tender, or other similar rights are
    passed through to participants, all materials relating to the ex-
    ercise of these rights; and

9. If the plan permits investment in employer securities, a de-
    scription of the procedures for maintaining confidentiality of
    transactions as well as the name or title, address, and tele-
    phone number of the plan fiduciary responsible for monitor-
    ing compliance with these procedures.

[DOL Reg § 2550.404c-1(b)(2)(i)(B)(1)]

Q 6:71 What information are plan fiduciaries required to provide to participants upon request?

In addition to complying with the automatic disclosure rules described in Q 6:70, plan fiduciaries must also respond to participants'
requests for any of the following information:

1. A description of the annual operating expenses of each
    designated alternative, including any investment manage-
    ment fees, administrative fees, transaction costs, or any other
    type of fee that would reduce the rate of return to the par-
    ticipant (the disclosure should also include the aggregate
    amount of such expenses addressed as a percentage of aver-
    age net assets);

2. Copies of any prospectuses, financial statements, reports, or
    any other materials related to an investment alternative that
    are provided to the plan;

3. If a designated investment alternative consists of assets that

are plan assets (e.g., a fund managed by the employer), the following information:

a. A list of such assets;

b. The value of each such asset or the proportion of the investment alternative that it comprises; and

c. If the asset is a fixed-rate investment contract, the name of the issuer of the contract, the term of the contract, and the rate of return for the contract;

4. The value of shares or units in any designated investment alternative, as well as past and current investment performance of the alternative determined on a reasonable and consistent basis; and

5. The value of shares or units in designated investment alternatives held in the account of a participant—plans may establish reasonable procedures to limit the frequency of these requests.

[DOL Reg § 2550.404c-1(b)(2)(i)(B)(2); 57 Fed Reg 46912]

Q 6:72 As a practical matter, how can the disclosure requirements be satisfied?

The DOL suggests in its preamble to the regulation that the disclosure requirements with regard to information about specific investments can be satisfied by simply passing on information provided to the plan, as well as by giving participants access to the information contained in the 5500 annual filing. [57 Fed Reg 46912] This will probably hold true for investments, such as mutual funds, that generate prospectuses and financial reports. However, if an alternative is offered that does not generate this type of information, plan fiduciaries are still responsible for assuring that participants are provided with adequate information to permit informed decision making.

Additionally, the preamble to the regulation makes it clear that it is not sufficient simply to direct participants to the source of information. Fiduciaries are responsible for actually providing the information directly to participants. [57 Fed Reg 46910] Therefore, if a designated fund does not provide the information described in Qs 6:70–6:71, plan fiduciaries must supply it.

Q 6:73 Is an employer obligated to provide investment advice or investment education to participants?

No. The regulation specifically states that plan fiduciaries are not obligated to provide investment advice, nor are they obligated to assist participants in any way to understand prospectuses, financial reports, or other materials that are passed on to them. [DOL Reg § 2550.404c-1(c)(4); 57 Fed Reg 46913] An employer may have good reasons for wanting to give participants general information about long-term investing; this type of information may help participants achieve their investment goals and thereby reduce the possibility for participant claims in the future. However, there is nothing in the DOL regulation that requires employers or other plan fiduciaries to provide this type of education to participants. In June 1996 the DOL released Interpretive Bulletin 96-1 (discussed in detail in chapter 7), which provides guidance on how an employer can provide meaningful investment education to participants without giving investment advice that would cause it to become a fiduciary as defined by ERISA Section 3(21)(A).

Investment Change Frequency

Q 6:74 How frequently must participants be permitted to change their investment choices?

The general standard is that participants must be permitted to make investment changes with a frequency that is appropriate in light of the volatility of the investment. If the plan uses three designated core funds to satisfy the broad range requirement, transfers among those funds must be permitted at least quarterly. [DOL Reg § 2550.404c-1(b)(2)(ii)(C)]

Q 6:75 How do the change-frequency rules apply in a plan offering investment alternatives with different volatility levels?

If a plan offers quarterly changes for its three core funds and then adds an additional fund with a higher level of volatility, participants must have a meaningful ability to make transfers out of the more volatile fund. To satisfy this requirement, the plan must permit participants to move out of the more volatile fund and into either one of the three core funds, or an income-producing, low-risk, liquid fund, with the same degree of frequency that is available for the more volatile investment. [DOL Reg § 2550.404c-1(b)(2)(ii)(C)(2)] It should be noted that there is no corresponding requirement that a participant be able to move out of a core or income-producing fund and into the more volatile fund at a frequency consistent with that of the more volatile fund.

If the more volatile fund consists of employer securities, the participants must be able to transfer into any one of the core investment alternatives intended to satisfy the broad range requirement or, alternatively, into an income-producing, low-risk, liquid fund as frequently as they are permitted to give instructions with respect to employer securities. If the income-fund method is used, participants must be able to make transfers out of the income fund and into any one of the core funds at least quarterly. Again, the rule concerns itself only with a participant's ability to transfer out of the more volatile fund. The plan is not required to permit transfers into the employer security fund more frequently than quarterly. [DOL Reg § 2550.404c-1(b)(2)(ii)(C)(3)]

Q 6:76 Can a fund with transfer restrictions or transfer fees satisfy the rules concerning transfer frequency?

Yes. A fund that contains early withdrawal penalties, back-end commissions, an equity wash, or other restrictions on transfer will not automatically lose Section 404(c) protection because of the change-frequency requirement. [57 Fed Reg 46915] However, the charges or other restrictions must be reasonable in light of the investment and cannot have the effect of limiting a participant's actual ability to make investment changes in accordance with the regulation.

Investment Elections

Q 6:77 What procedures can be used to obtain investment elections?

Participants must have a reasonable opportunity to give investment instructions to an identified plan fiduciary obligated to comply with those instructions. The directions can be oral, written, or otherwise. However, the participant must have the opportunity to receive confirmation of the transaction in writing. The plan fiduciary can be identified either by name or by position (e.g., plan administrator or plan sponsor). [DOL Reg § 2550.404c-1(b)(2)(i)(A)]

Q 6:78 Can a default election be used for participants who fail to make an election?

The protection offered under ERISA Section 404(c) is available only for investments made as a result of a participant's affirmative election. Therefore, if a default option is used in a plan, the employer will remain responsible for transactions into that default fund. Once an affirmative election has been made by a participant, it may be given effect until affirmatively revoked. [57 Fed Reg 46918, 46923]

Q 6:79 May a fiduciary place any restrictions on what investment directions it will agree to execute?

Yes. Fiduciaries may decline to implement any of the following types of instructions:

1. Any instruction that would result in a prohibited transaction under ERISA;
2. Any instruction that would generate taxable income to a plan;
3. Any instruction that would be contrary to the plan document;
4. Any instruction that would cause the plan to maintain the indicia of ownership of assets held outside the jurisdiction of United States courts;
5. Any investment that would jeopardize the plan's tax-qualified status;
6. Any instruction that could result in a loss to the participant in excess of the participant's account balance; and
7. Any loan to a participant.

[DOL Reg § 2550.404c-1(d)(2)(ii)]

A plan may also impose reasonable restrictions on a participant's ability to make transfers. For example, it may require a minimum transfer of $100 or 5 percent of the amount to be invested. However, any such restriction must bear a reasonable relationship to the administrative costs involved and be applied on a consistent basis. A plan cannot place a maximum limit on the amount to be transferred. [DOL Reg § 2550.404c-1(b)2(ii)(C); 57 Fed Reg 46918]

Q 6:80 May fees associated with investment choices be charged directly to participants' accounts?

Yes. A plan may charge participants' accounts with any reasonable expenses of carrying out their investment instructions. Participants must be notified in advance that fees will be charged directly to their account. In addition, the plan must periodically inform participants of the actual expenses incurred in their individual accounts. [DOL Reg § 2550.404c-1(b)(2)(ii)(A)]

Fiduciary Liability

Q 6:81 What relief from liability is available to fiduciaries in an ERISA Section 404(c) plan?

Two consequences result from maintaining a complying Section 404(c) plan. One is that the participants and beneficiaries making investment decisions will not be considered plan fiduciaries simply by reason of controlling investment of their accounts. The other, more significant result is that other plan fiduciaries will not be held responsible for any loss that is a direct and necessary result of a participant's exercise of control. [DOL Reg § 2550.404c-1(d)] Generally, relief is offered from the prudence and diversification requirements of ERISA.

To take advantage of this fiduciary relief, two conditions must be present:

1. The plan must be designed as a Section 404(c) plan—in other words, it must offer a broad range of investment alternatives, offer quarterly change dates for its three core funds, provide the disclosure required in the regulation, and so forth.

2. The participant must have actually exercised control with respect to whatever transaction is at issue—the burden of proof in this circumstance is on the plan sponsor.

The transactional nature of the fiduciary relief creates the biggest gap in protection from fiduciary liability. It prevents plan fiduciaries from simply setting up an appropriate plan design for compliance with ERISA Section 404(c) and then relying on that section for fiduciary relief.

The potential always exists for exposure for individual transactions that are not executed properly or that, for any other reason, fail to meet the standards of ERISA Section 404(c).

Q 6:82 What liability can fiduciaries not avoid in participant directed plans?

Plan fiduciaries will remain responsible for any transactions of the type described in Q 6:79. If designated funds are used, fiduciaries will remain responsible for selecting and monitoring the funds to make sure they continue to satisfy the broad range and diversification requirements. [57 Fed Reg 46922]

Fiduciaries will also remain responsible for maintaining procedures to comply with the information disclosure requirements, as well as the special procedures required in the event employer securities are offered as an investment alternative. Finally, there is no relief from the IRS prohibited transaction rules.

Q 6:83 How do ERISA's fiduciary rules apply to participant directed plans that do not comply with ERISA Section 404(c)?

The DOL's position is that a participant's investment decisions in a plan that does not comply with ERISA Section 404(c) will be judged according to ERISA's general fiduciary rules. In other words, plan fiduciaries will be held responsible for a participant's investment choices as if those choices had been made by the plan fiduciary. It is unclear whether courts interpreting ERISA will follow that approach. Even if plan fiduciaries are held accountable for participants' investment decisions, the participants in a noncomplying Section 404(c) plan themselves will arguably become fiduciaries with respect to their accounts and will therefore share in the liability. Given this circumstance, it may be unlikely that participants will seek legal redress against other plan fiduciaries for investment losses resulting from their own investment decisions.

Q 6:84 Is compliance with the DOL's regulation worth the protection offered?

The answer to this question must be based on the circumstances of a particular plan. If a plan already offers three or more pooled funds that satisfy the broad range requirement, permits quarterly transfers, and has the ability to implement procedures to satisfy the disclosure requirements, it makes sense to comply. However, if a plan must add either funds or an investment change date, the administrative expense of compliance must be evaluated in comparison with the protection offered.

For employers who are either starting a new plan or considering adding the option of participant direction to an existing plan, a careful review of the employer's goals in adding this feature should be undertaken. The administrative costs of a participant directed plan will be higher than those of an employer or other fiduciary directed plan.

Participants historically have not performed well as investors, and the results of a John Hancock survey titled *Participant Attitudes on Retirement Saving* conducted in 1991, 1992, and 1993 suggested that although participants were shifting more toward investing in equities, the avalanche of investment education programs since 1992 had not had much of an impact on their basic investment knowledge. However, a 1998 Buck Consultants survey suggests that investment education is having an impact both in causing participants to be less conservative in their investment decisions and in causing them to increase their contribution level.

If the value sought to be achieved in offering participant direction is protection from fiduciary liability, the DOL regulation makes it clear that ERISA Section 404(c) compliance cannot be relied upon absolutely for that protection.

Q 6:85 What is the effective date of the final DOL ERISA 404(c) regulation?

The final DOL ERISA 404(c) regulation is effective with respect to transactions occurring on or after the second plan year beginning after October 12, 1992 (or January 1, 1994, for a calendar-year plan). For collectively bargained plans, the regulation is effective on the later of the general effective date or the date the last collective bargaining agreement ratified before October 13, 1992, terminates.

[DOL Reg § 2550.404c-1(g)] Since compliance with the regulation is optional, a plan sponsor can elect to comply at any later time and will receive ERISA Section 404(c) protection from the date compliance is achieved.

SELF-DIRECTED OPTIONS

A majority of employers find a menu of investment options adequate for most participants. Some employers are offering participants a wider range of investment options, however, through a self-directed option (also known as an open-ended option, a self-directed brokerage account, and an open-ended plan). So far, only a few companies offer a self-directed option, but that number appears to be slowly rising.

Q 6:86 What is a *self-directed option*?

A *self-directed option* is an option permitting participants to invest their plan assets in an unlimited number of investment options.

Q 6:87 How can a self-directed option be offered?

A self-directed option can be set up in two ways:

1. A *full brokerage account,* which allows participants to invest in any mutual fund, stock, or bond made available through the account; or

2. A *mutual fund window,* which allows participants to invest in any mutual fund made available but not in individual securities.

These accounts are set up with designated brokers or a broker of the participant's choice.

Self-directed accounts are often an added feature of a plan that already has a broad menu of investment options. For instance, the first level of a plan will consist of standard core options, and the second level will include self-directed accounts. In such an arrangement, the plan may or may not limit investment in the self-directed account to a certain percentage of plan assets. Alternatively, the plan can be entirely self-directed (i.e., a self-directed or open-ended plan). Participants typically pay an annual fee to maintain a self-directed account, as well as broker fees and commissions on trades. Historically, self-directed accounts have appealed to only a small portion of an employee population—for example, senior-level executives—though this may change as 401(k) balances grow larger.

Motivation for Self-Directed Options

Q 6:88 What might motivate an employer to offer a self-directed option or plan to participants?

An employer may choose to offer a self-directed plan, or add a self-directed option to a current plan, for the following reasons:

- To respond to employees who are demanding more and varied investment offerings
- To balance competing needs of employees who might need more investment options with those who might be confused by an unlimited number of investment offerings
- To avoid fiduciary liability associated with the selection of plan investment alternatives by declining to designate any investment options and making the self-directed feature the only investment option

Concerns Arising from Self-Directed Options

Q 6:89 What are some concerns associated with offering a self-directed option?

The following concerns have been associated with providing a self-directed option to employees:

- Administrative complications and increased costs
- Participants who are overwhelmed by, and ill-equipped to handle, unfettered investment options
- Discrimination issues under the "benefits, rights, and features" rules (see Q 6:92)
- Participant investment in inappropriate or troublesome assets
- Difficulty satisfying certain ERISA Section 404(c) requirements

Q 6:90 What administrative complications and increased costs are associated with self-directed accounts?

Self-directed accounts have the potential for introducing added administrative complications and costs. All trading is done at the participant level, rather than aggregated at the plan level as is done with menu plans. When participants use their own brokerage firms to custody their accounts, as many plans permit, assets are fragmented, thus complicating the plan's aggregate recordkeeping and reporting functions. The result may be delayed and, quite possibly, inaccurate reporting. Investment in assets that create valuation issues, such as limited partnerships, can also be problematic. Plan trustees will require fair values for those types of assets to comply with requirements under the Code and ERISA.

As for costs, there are fees charged for each brokerage account and additional costs for administration services. The increased investment and administrative costs of self-directed accounts can be significant. Although the additional costs are often passed through to participants, the employer (or other fiduciary) should carefully monitor such costs and make sure they are reasonable in light of services being provided. It may be true that the costs will be small relative to a large account balance; however, they may represent a substantial drag on earnings of a small account.

Q 6:91 Could some participants become overwhelmed by unlimited investment options in a self-directed environment?

Yes. In the self-directed environment, there is a potential that a number of participants will be overwhelmed by the sheer volume of investment possibilities and remain invested in the most conservative investment option. Plan sponsors may need to enhance their investment education programs (see chapter 7), especially if an employer intends to make the benefit available to a large employee population. 401(k) plans with a menu of investment options typically provide a more manageable investment decision-making forum and a reasonable framework for an ongoing investment education program. They may not, however, satisfy all the investment needs of a large and diverse workforce.

Q 6:92 When could a self-directed option create discrimination issues under the benefits, rights, and features rules?

Offering employees the option to self-direct investments could present discrimination issues under Code Section 401(a)(4). Under that section each benefit, right, or feature must be made available to employees on a nondiscriminatory basis. A right or feature would include a self-directed option because it can reasonably be expected to be of meaningful value to an employee. Therefore, the option must be available to non-highly compensated employees (NHCEs) in a manner that satisfies the *current availability* and *effective availability* tests (see Qs 11:30–11:36). [IRC § 401(a)(4); Treas Reg § 1.401(a)(4)-4(a)]

The current availability test is generally satisfied if, under the terms of the plan document, the option's availability to NHCEs satisfies the Section 410(b) coverage test. [Treas Reg § 1.401(a)(4)-4(b)] The effective availability test is a facts-and-circumstances determination as to whether availability substantially favors highly compensated employees (HCEs). [Treas Reg § 1.401(a)(4)-4(c)]

As is to be expected, problems arise if only HCEs are given the option to self-direct. If instead all employees are given the option, a plan may still fail to satisfy the effective availability test if NHCEs do not receive information about the option (including how to use it) (see Q 11:36). [Treas Reg § 1.401(a)(4)-4(c)(2), Ex 2] Requiring a minimum account balance or minimum investment amount could also cause problems under the effective availability test.

Q 6:93 What inappropriate or troublesome investments could result in self-directed accounts?

Self-directed accounts tend to confound an employer's ability to oversee plan investment. Unless certain safeguards are in place, there is the potential participants will invest in inappropriate or troublesome assets. For example, a plan fiduciary may be held liable if participant investment decisions result in a prohibited transaction, contravene the plan document, or cause the indicia of ownership of plan assets to be outside U.S. jurisdiction. [ERISA §§ 406; 404(a)(1)(D); 404(b) DOL Reg § 2550.404-1]

Free rein to invest in any asset, such as real estate and limited partnerships, could also create valuation problems. To comply with various requirements under ERISA and the Code, plan assets must be valued at least annually. If no fair market value is readily available, the assets will have to be appraised—a process that could be both costly and time consuming. [ERISA § 103; Rev Rul 80-155, 1980-1 CB 84]

Participant investment in collectibles (i.e., works of art, rugs, antiques, metals, gems, stamps, coins, and other tangible personal property specified by the IRS) should also be avoided. Certain types of investment could result in unrelated business taxable income (UBTI) for the plan. [IRC § 512]

Self-Directed Options and ERISA Section 404(c)

Q 6:94 What difficulties might arise for a plan sponsor seeking ERISA Section 404(c) protection for a self-directed option?

With access to unlimited investment options, a self-directed option will likely satisfy the broad-range-of-investment-alternatives requirement automatically. What is unclear is how the other requirements set forth above apply to self-directed options.

The market volatility rule generally provides that participants must be permitted to make investment changes with a frequency appropriate to market volatility. Allowing participants to switch their investments quarterly may be acceptable in a menu plan; it may not be for a plan with a self-directed option where there is access to investments with volatilities all over the board. Such a plan should permit investment transfers on a daily basis to satisfy the volatility rule.

An unrestricted investment option may make it difficult to ensure that participants are receiving the requisite ERISA Section 404(c) disclosure information. Much of the information can be disclosed in the summary plan description or a special form given to participants before investment elections are made. Often overlooked is the requirement that participants receive a prospectus immediately before or immediately following an initial investment in an investment alternative subject to the Securities Act. If a broker (or other service provider) fails to provide prospectuses when required, ERISA Section 404(c) relief may be jeopardized. Special arrangements must also be made to ensure that participants automatically receive prospectuses. In addition, provisions should be made to ensure that participants receive specified information from an identified plan fiduciary that is to be provided upon request. Much of that information will be accessible by the broker, who may or may not be a plan fiduciary.

Plan participants must, according to the regulations supporting ERISA Section 404(c), have a reasonable opportunity to give investment instructions to an identified fiduciary. Participants using a self-directed option often give investment instructions directly to the broker. A broker, however, may not be (or want to be) a plan fiduciary. It is unclear then whether the regulations would be satisfied if instructions are given directly to a nonfiduciary broker. Investment instructions may need to be funneled through a plan fiduciary.

Self-Directed Option Strategies

Q 6:95 How can a self-directed option be structured to minimize administrative complications, additional costs, and fiduciary liability exposure?

To minimize administrative complications, additional costs, and fiduciary liability exposure, careful consideration should be given to the following:

- Prohibiting investment in certain types of investments such as limited partnerships, collectibles, and real estate
- Selecting one or more brokers to serve as the plan's *designated brokers,* who agree to provide certain information (such as prospectuses) to participants and investment oversight
- Selecting brokers and service providers performing consolidated reporting functions that can be electronically linked
- Selecting a custodian to act as sole custodian for all brokerage accounts
- Establishing procedures for monitoring participant investment transactions
- Permitting daily investment transfers
- Offering the option to participants in a manner that will not

create discrimination issues and communicating how to use the option

- Conducting a cost/benefit analysis of a self-directed option and monitoring its costs on an ongoing basis

SELECTING AND MONITORING PLAN INVESTMENTS

The key criteria for selecting and monitoring plan investments are investment performance and manager style. A plan sponsor's basic concern is to ensure that each plan investment is generating sufficient returns given its risk level. That includes evaluating the effects fees have on returns. In addition, plan sponsors will want to analyze investment manager style and monitor changes that may occur in that style.

Plan sponsors have many sources of information for evaluating plan investments, including those that track investment performance, rate mutual funds, and identify trends in the marketplace. Some sources of information entail little or no expense—for example, mutual fund prospectuses and financial publications; others may involve more substantial costs—for example, independent ratings services and consultants.

Q 6:96 What are the major considerations in the investment selection process?

The ultimate goal in the investment selection process is to offer a menu of funds that give participants the ability to construct portfolios that fit their investment goals and risk profiles. To do that requires having several investment options with varying risk and return characteristics. It also means offering a variety of funds across different investment styles. Table 6-1 shows the factors plan sponsors consider to be most important when selecting investment options.

Offering several investment options can provide more investment opportunity; however, each option must be reviewed against others to determine that it is clearly distinct. Too many funds with similar risk and reward characteristics may not provide participants adequate opportunity to diversify. Participants faced with an over-

**TABLE 6-1. Factors Most Important
in Selection of Investment Options**

Factor	Percentage of Plans Ranking		
	Most Important	Second Most Important	Third Most Important
Investment performance (consistent with fund objectives)	92%	5%	1%
Investment fees/expense ratio	3	53	27
Employee support/communication	1	18	25
Name recognition of fund manager	< 1	12	17
Listing of fund value/return in newspaper	0	4	12
Employer access to fund manager	1	5	14
Other factors (e.g., manager credentials, investment diversity)	2	3	4

Note: 423 plans reporting "most important"; 417 plans reporting "second most important"; 405 plans reporting "third most important."
Source: 401(k) Trends and Experience, Hewitt Associates, 1997.

whelming array of investment options may also experience unnecessary confusion.

The investment options selected should have solid performance records and reasonable fees. Among other things, a plan's investment policy should have guidelines about the investment options to be made available, the selection criteria, including acceptable risk and return characteristics, and the monitoring process. (See chapter 5 for additional discussion of a plan's investment policy)

Q 6:97 How many and what types of investment options are typically offered in a 401(k) plan?

The average employer offers participants from five to eight investment options. A plan designed to comply with ERISA Section 404(c) must provide a minimum of three funds (see Qs 6:58–6:63). The typical mix includes funds investing mainly in stocks, bonds, or

**TABLE 6-2. Number of Investment Funds Available
for Participant Contributions by Plan Size (Percentage of Plans)**

Number of Funds	Plan Size by Number of Participants					All Plans
	1–49	50–199	200–999	1,000–4,999	5,000+	
One	5.8%	4.3%	3.3%	2.1%	1.5%	3.5%
Two	2.3	1.7	0.6	1.1	1.5	1.4
Three	3.5	3.5	5.9	4.3	6.1	4.7
Four	10.5	9.6	5.3	11.7	10.6	9.0
Five	17.4	27.8	19.1	12.8	12.1	18.7
Six	15.1	15.7	19.1	12.8	9.1	15.2
Seven	7.0	14.8	19.1	16.0	10.6	14.4
Eight	11.6	4.3	11.2	17.0	15.2	11.3
Nine	1.2	4.3	3.3	10.6	12.1	5.7
Ten and more	25.6	13.9	13.2	11.7	21.2	16.2
	100.0%	99.9%	100.1%	100.1%	100.0%	100.1%

Source: 40th Annual Survey of Profit Sharing and 401(k) Plans, Profit Sharing/
401(k) Council of America, reflecting 1996 Plan Year Experience, 1997.

cash; a balanced stock and bond fund; funds that mirror an index such as the S&P 500; GIC or stable value investment; an international stock fund; and, in some cases, shares of employer stock. Table 6-2 shows a real-life distribution of number and types of investment options across different-sized plans. Nearly all the plans surveyed (93.4 percent) allowed participants to direct the investment of their contributions.

Q 6:98 What are the key elements in an investment monitoring program?

The key elements in an investment monitoring program are setting performance objectives for each investment option, establish-

6-53

ing a review procedure, and incorporating those objectives and procedures in a written investment policy.

Q 6:99 Should investment performance be compared with the performance of other similar investments?

Yes. Besides being compared with benchmarks, investment performance should be compared with the performance of other investments with similar risk characteristics. That means, for example, comparing the performance of an aggressive growth fund with that of other aggressive growth funds. That is of particular importance in the case of actively managed portfolios. Unless the investment option is an index fund, investors should be compensated for taking on additional risk by selecting an actively managed portfolio. In other words, the objective of an actively managed portfolio should be to outperform, not just match, the market index. "Peer group"-type data can help put performance in the context of other actively managed portfolios. It is available from independent rating services such as Morningstar (see Q 6:101), software products, and various consulting firms.

Q 6:100 How often should investment performance be monitored?

Investment performance should be monitored at least quarterly; however, the trend is toward monthly performance reviews. Nonetheless, absent clear changes in investment management style or objectives, decisions to change funds should be based on performance over a longer period of time.

Q 6:101 What is the function of mutual fund independent ratings services?

Several independent ratings services provide comprehensive information about mutual funds, such as expense ratios, risk analysis, and performance figures. Morningstar is currently the most prominent source of comprehensive mutual fund information. It also tracks average performance of variable annuities.

Morningstar's *Principia* and *Principia Plus,* available by subscription, are computer software programs used by professionals to evaluate and compare mutual funds. Morningstar's binder product,

Morningstar Mutual Funds, contains similar but less detailed mutual fund information in printed form. *Morningstar Mutual Funds* is available by subscription and at the reference desks of most public libraries. Morningstar also produces a newsletter, *Morningstar Investor.*

The following are among the more frequently used mutual fund performance services:

Morningstar Mutual Funds
225 West Wacker Drive
Chicago, IL 60606
(312) 696-6000

Lipper Analytical Services, Inc.
47 Maple Street
Summit, NJ 07901
(908) 598-2220

CDA/Wiesenberger Investment Companies Services
1355 Piccard Drive, Suite 220
Rockville, MD 20850
(800) 232-2285

Value Line
220 East 42nd Street
New York, NY 10017-5891
(800) 284-7607

7 Participant Communication and Education

In a 401(k) plan, employees are asked to choose to give up current income in exchange for a future benefit. Depending on the demographics of the employee group, this may appear an unattractive choice. Lower-paid or younger employees may be less interested in tax benefits or retirement planning than they are in the availability of current income. For this reason, it is important to have an employee communication strategy that enables employees to understand the ways in which a 401(k) plan can benefit them. It is also important that employees understand basic information about the plan and how it operates.

For participant directed plans, investment education is an important part of an effective communications program. However, it is important that investment education not step over the line to become investment advice if the sponsor is to be shielded from fiduciary liability for poor participant investment decisions.

As part of the communication and education process, it is important that participants understand the basics of setting a retirement planning goal and be able to assess their progress in reaching that goal.

AN EFFECTIVE 401(k) COMMUNICATION PROGRAM

This section begins with employee communication strategy as it relates to an employee's general understanding of a 401(k) plan and concentrates on start-up administration and initial employee enrollment. It then provides a broader view of 401(k) communications as it relates to individual retirement planning. This section does not address communication required under the disclosure rules of the Employee Retirement Income Security Act (ERISA). That subject is discussed in detail in chapter 18.

Q 7:1 Why is initial communication important?

Employees who do not understand the benefits of a 401(k) plan are less likely to participate in and appreciate the value of the plan. The benefits of a 401(k) plan are not as obvious as those of a profit sharing or other type of plan that is funded entirely by employer contributions. Where employees are being asked to sacrifice current income by contributing to a 401(k) plan, it is critical that they understand how this sacrifice will benefit them in the long run.

Better communication can increase participation of lower-paid employees in the plan and permit the higher-paid employees to put in greater dollar amounts without violating the actual deferral percentage (ADP) test (see chapter 12). This result often serves an employer's goal of rewarding key executives.

Employees who understand how a 401(k) plan works are also more likely to plan realistically for their retirement. Since a 401(k) plan is designed to encourage employees to take some responsibility for their own retirement planning, it is important that they understand the relationship between current contributions and future retirement income.

Content of a Communication Program

Q 7:2 What is the most important information to be communicated in a 401(k) plan?

It is essential that key plan provisions such as eligibility, the availability of funds through loans or hardship withdrawals, and any limits on contributions (maximum or minimum) be communicated. A one-page plan summary can be of tremendous help in getting employees to focus on key provisions, rather than trying to get them to sift through a 30- or 40-page document.

The benefits of investing in a 401(k) plan, particularly when the plan is compared with IRA or after-tax savings accounts, must also be explained. Table 7-1 demonstrates the advantages of saving in a 401(k) plan versus a traditional or Roth individual retirement account (IRA).

Q 7:3 What additional information should be communicated if participants choose their own investments in the plan?

Some plans let participants choose their own investments, at least for their elective contributions. Most plans that offer this option limit the investment choices to three or more designated funds. However, the number of options that can be offered is unlimited, and a plan may offer completely open-ended investment choice. Participant directed plans are discussed in more detail in chapter 6.

TABLE 7-1. Advantages of Saving in a 401(k) Plan Versus an IRA

	IRA	401(k)
Limits	$2,000 annual limit (plus $2,000 spousal IRA)	$10,000 annual limit on employee contributions (adjusted for cost of living and subject to plan and individual limits)
Company match	None	Company match is common
Deposits	Usually single deposit	Deposits through convenient payroll deduction
Access	Limited tax-free access for first-time home buyers and some medical expenses	Depending on plan design can access through participant loans without paying penalty
Timing of tax savings	Tax deduction when return is filed for traditional IRA	Immediate tax reduction (tax withholding is reduced)
Use with other company plans	Traditional IRA may not be available on a tax-deductible basis if participating in a company plan at the same time; Roth IRA not available to higher income employees	Available even if participating in another company plan
Tax treatment at distribution	No special tax treatment for traditional IRA; Roth IRA escapes taxation for qualified distributions; rollover available once per 12-month period	Through 1999, special 5-year income averaging on lump-sum distributions after age 59½; rollover available on unlimited basis

Often, one of the goals in letting participants choose their own investments is to protect the employer from legal liability for the investment performance of participants' accounts. If employees are not given enough information about the investment choices offered, however, the employer will not be able to attain this objective. In addition, participants may become discouraged with the investment performance of their accounts if they do not understand the risks and benefits of the available funds or how to match those risks and benefits with their individual goals.

The information required to be provided to participants in a plan that intends to comply with the Department of Labor (DOL) regulation under ERISA Section 404(c) is described in chapter 6.

In all participant directed plans, employees may find the following information useful in making appropriate investment decisions:

1. The factors an individual should consider when making investment decisions;

2. The effect of a participant's age, income, years to retirement, and other individual factors on his or her investment decisions;

3. Whether a stable value fund is offered (e.g., a guaranteed investment contract (GIC) offered by an insurance company), what stable value means (e.g., it does not mean that it is impossible to lose money);

4. An explanation of why the most conservative option (e.g., a money market or a GIC) is not always the best investment choice in the long run; and

5. A historical analysis showing how different asset types (e.g., stocks, bonds, fixed income funds) have performed when measured in 5-, 10-, or 20-year cycles.

Employers who offer 401(k) plans are not necessarily investment experts and are often reluctant to discuss investment strategies with participants, particularly in a written format. Participants with no investment information may be more likely to "follow the market" (i.e., buy high and sell low) or to limit unnecessarily the investment growth of their accounts by investing all of it in the most conservative fund choice available. Given these tendencies, it is worthwhile to provide some basic information on investment planning so that the 401(k) plan will become an effective retirement savings vehicle for employees. If the employer is uncomfortable providing this information directly, it may be advisable to bring in an outside expert.

Q 7:4 Why must an effective 401(k) communications program go beyond the plan's reporting and disclosure requirements?

Following the government's reporting and disclosure requirements is important for maintaining the tax qualified status of a 401(k) plan, but fulfilling these requirements alone will not produce an effective employee benefit communications program. The plan document, the summary annual report, and the notice to interested parties are designed as legal documents and, as such, are far from being effective communication pieces. Even the summary plan description, written in laypersons' language, is at best a communications starting point. Annual benefit statements are not even part of the government's reporting and disclosure requirements.

Q 7:5 Can an effective 401(k) communications program present just the facts?

No. Although many facts about the design and operation of the 401(k) plan must be part of a communications program, to be effective, the program must go beyond the facts in a number of ways. It must put the facts in a context that relates to the perceived needs, wants, and even fears of the participants. It must do this in a way that both attracts and maintains their attention. A question and answer format is a good way to put facts into a context that participants can easily understand and use.

Just the facts would provide account balances and a list of investment options. But participants need to know more than this in order to use the plan effectively to provide for their retirements. Retirement planning involves future uncertainties and difficult decision making. Participants must be educated about these uncertainties and about the risks involved so that they are equipped to make good decisions.

Implementing a Communication Program

Q 7:6 What steps should be taken in order to implement an effective 401(k) communications program?

An effective 401(k) communications program is likely to involve the following steps:

1. Assess the information needs of the participants (see Q 7:7).

2. Set a measurable goal for the program (see Q 7:8).

3. Keep in mind the differing information needs among plan participants (see Q 7:9).

4. Structure the program to have:

    a. Multiple contacts (see Q 7:13),

    b. Multiple approaches (see Q 7:15), and

    c. Multiple messages (see Q 7:18).

5. Evaluate the effectiveness of the program (see Q 7:19).

6. Follow up to reinforce and further increase participant understanding (see Q 7:20).

Q 7:7 What are some methods for assessing the information needs of plan participants?

In a larger company, focus groups that discuss what participants know and what they would like to know are an effective way to assess their information needs. In a smaller company, informal discussion can serve a similar purpose. A formal information-needs survey can be an effective tool to assess information needs of any size group. Such a survey can also serve to enhance interest in the plan. A follow-up distribution of the results can serve as an additional communications contact.

The following are examples of questions that could be part of a benefits-needs survey:

1. How long do you think your retirement income will need to last?

    a. 1–5 years

    b. 6–10 years

    c. 11–15 years

    d. 16–20 years

    e. 21–25 years

    f. 26–30 years

    g. Don't know

2. I expect Social Security to provide me with an adequate retirement income.

   a. Agree strongly

   b. Agree somewhat

   c. Don't know

   d. Disagree somewhat

   e. Disagree strongly

3. I am confident that my 401(k) investments along with Social
   Security and other retirement savings will provide me with
   adequate retirement income.

   a. Agree strongly

   b. Agree somewhat

   c. Don't know

   d. Disagree somewhat

   e. Disagree strongly

4. If interest rates rise, what is the immediate impact on the
   value of a bond fund?

   a. Increase

   b. Decreases

   c. No direct impact

   d. Don't know

5. For investments that carry with them the risk of a loss of principal, how does this risk vary as you hold the investment for
   longer periods of time?

   a. Increases

   b. Decreases

   c. No direct impact

   d. Don't know

6. If you want $20,000 per year purchasing power beginning at
   age 65, and lasting for your life expectancy, about how much
   do you need to begin putting into your 401(k) plan each year
   from age 35, assuming that you can earn 8 percent on your
   investments and that future inflation averages 3 percent?

   a. $500

   b. $1,500

   c. $3,500

   d. Don't know

Q 7:8 What measurable goals might be set for a 401(k) communications program?

The goals chosen should relate to the needs of both the plan participants and the sponsor. A goal might be increased understanding as evidenced by a follow-up survey. Often the goal will be an increased number of participants, or participation at a higher level, or an increased number participating at levels above a company match. Greater diversity among investment choices or greater participation in equity investments might also be set as goals and can be readily measured.

Q 7:9 How might information needs differ among plan participants?

Information needs may well differ by age groups, or by management versus rank and file, or by salary level, or by education level, or by the type of work and other experience. As participants learn more about their 401(k) plan and how it can meet their retirement needs, their interests typically move along the spectrum: consumption, savings, investing, planning. An effective communications program must have at least these two aims: to present material relevant to the location of the participant along this spectrum, and to present material that will move the participant's interest along the spectrum.

Q 7:10 What is the best way to present retirement planning to the younger, consumption-oriented employee?

Younger participants without prior experience with a 401(k) plan are often focused on consumption rather than saving, investing, or planning. It may seem to them that their salary levels are not adequate to permit saving or they may be newly independent, focused on immediate wants, and feel that they have plenty of time "in the future" for retirement saving. For this group, it is important to emphasize the immediate tax advantages of a 401(k) plan and the gain from an employer match. Accessibility of 401(k) funds through loan or hardship withdrawal provisions will also be of interest.

Even a consumption-oriented group will have experience with the monthly budgeting needed to pay the rent or mortgage. Many will know teachers who are paid only nine months of the year but soon learn to budget for the year's fourth quarter. Everyone has jobs that are like that: individuals are paid for about three quarters of their adult life and need to budget for necessities during retirement in order to do well during life's fourth quarter. The impact of beginning retirement savings during life's first quarter rather than delaying until the second or third quarter will be an important concept for this group.

Example. What monthly savings are needed to produce $10,000 annual purchasing power at age 65, and how does the amount of savings vary by the age at which the savings begin?

Age When Savings Begin	Monthly Savings Needed
25	$ 147
35	267
45	530
55	1,378

Examples like the one shown in the above table are dramatic and attention getting. Monthly retirement savings must be more than 80 percent greater if savings begin at age 35 rather than age 25.

It is good to follow the example with a discussion of the assumptions involved. In this case, it was assumed that

- Salary keeps pace with 3 percent inflation.

- Tax-sheltered investments would average 8 percent returns pre-retirement and 6 percent post-retirement.

- The participant had better than male average life expectancy (which is the same as somewhat worse than female average life expectancy).

- Retirement spending was designed to allow for a 10 percent chance of outliving retirement savings.

The lesson of the example is that budgeting for retirement is much easier to achieve if begun during life's first quarter. The follow-up discussion of assumptions sets the stage for more investment education and more comprehensive retirement planning at a later time or later in the same presentation.

Q 7:11 What is the best way to move plan participants from a savings orientation to an investing orientation?

Use concrete examples of the significance that investment earnings have on retirement income, then follow up with a discussion of basic investment classes and the returns that historically have been achieved with each. This approach can also serve as an introduction to a retirement planning tool such as the tables in Appendix A (which are discussed in more detail later in this chapter).

For initial explorations of such a planning tool, it is best to concentrate on just one common case so that the participant is not overwhelmed with the variety of options available. Using the tables in Appendix A, a presenter should pick just one salary/inflation scenario and just one retirement age—for instance, that salary keeps pace with 3 percent inflation and planned retirement is at age 65 (although he or she should be sure to mention that this is just one example).

Q 7:12 How can an exploration using Table 1 from Appendix A introduce the importance of investment return for retirement planning?

Often a participant will be ready to move from a saving orientation to an investing orientation after a few years of plan participation when he or she has an account balance to invest. Table 1 from Appendix A speaks directly to this participant since it allows calculation of the salary replacement at retirement that can be derived from the current account balance. (See the section below on individual retirement planning for more information about using these retirement planning tables.)

Example. Sally, at age 40, has a 401(k) account about twice her annual salary. Assume her salary will keep pace with 3 percent inflation, that she has better than female average life expectancy, and that she plans to retire at age 65. Sally is given Table II-65-1 and is helped to locate the set of four numbers that applies to her situation—which are from the better-than-female-average section at the right of the table and from the row labeled "25 years to retirement." Sally then circles the four numbers that apply to her situation: 5.22 percent, 9.85 percent, 17.51 percent, and 31.65 percent. These tell her how much of her salary she can replace with an account balance equal to her salary if her pre-retirement returns are 4 percent, 6 percent, 8 percent, and 10 percent, respectively (with somewhat lower returns post-retirement). Sally has been earning about 6 percent on her investments. Since her account balance is twice her current salary, she can expect to replace about 19 percent (2 × 9.85%) of her salary at age 65 retirement if she continues to earn 6 percent pre-retirement.

It is important to follow up this example by drawing attention to the impact that higher rates of return would have. If Sally could earn 10 percent pre-retirement instead of 6 percent over the next 25 years, she would be able to replace about 62 percent (2 × 31.65%) of her income at retirement. An increase in investment return from 6 percent to 10 percent leads to more than a threefold increase in retirement income.

This is a natural lead-in to a discussion of what asset classes might be expected to return 10 percent rather than 6 percent over a 25-year investment horizon. Good investment education should also include a discussion of investment risk (variability) and how it relates to investment horizon. (See Qs 5:16–5:39.) Discussion of risk must emphasize that there is a trade-off between investment risk (which decreases significantly for investment horizons over ten years) and the risk of insufficient retirement income.

Retirement planning tools will be complex because of the number of assumptions that must be taken into account. It is important to teach use of the tools through simple explorations that focus the participants' attention on the tools and leave for later a detailed consideration of all the factors needed to develop a complete individual plan.

Q 7:13 What is meant by the statement that an effective 401(k) communications program will have multiple contacts, multiple approaches, and multiple messages?

Repetition is important for learning, and a 401(k) communications program must teach a number of complex concepts. This is accomplished best through a carefully structured program with multiple contacts through the year that reinforce one another and build upon the material presented earlier. Multiple approaches are important because different people learn in different ways. Also, the use of a variety of media and different types of participant interactions reinforces the message for each person.

The communications program must deal with the complexity of retirement planning using a 401(k) plan. Each contact must have one or two key messages, but no one contact can present all of the messages that must be communicated. The messages must interlock across contacts so that they reinforce what has already been communicated and at the same time provide an introduction to what will be presented in more detail in a later contact.

Q 7:14 How many yearly contacts are needed for an effective 401(k) communications program?

It depends. Many 401(k) plans provide quarterly reports to participants, which supplies a yearly base of four contacts. Another three or four contacts can provide a well-rounded program. This could involve two or three payroll stuffers using brochures that emphasize a key retirement planning or investing concept. Short articles in company newsletters can also introduce and reinforce these messages. Where the goal is a sizable increase in participation, two hour-long presentations and discussions will have strong impact.

Q 7:15 What are some of the multiple approaches that are parts of an effective 401(k) communications program?

Effective communications should involve both written and presented material. Material presented in person through videos or voice response telephone programs works well for getting participants' attention and for dramatizing messages in ways participants can remember. However, written material reinforces what has been presented and allows for reference at a later time.

Presentations are also important because they allow for participant interaction both through activities ("Circle the row on the table that applies to you") and through questions.

In order to move participants along the spectrum of consumption, savings, investing, and planning, it is important to give them tools that they can apply to answer questions they already have as well as to answer questions suggested by the material. Traditionally, these have been paper-and-pencil tools using tables such as those found in Appendix A. Computer programs that provide for similar planning as well as investment education are available, and many

Internet sites now make similar tools available online. Many of the mutual fund families provide such programs for little more than postage and handling or on the Internet as a way of advertising their services. Investment-independent programs are also available where computer software is sold—often for less than $50.

Q 7:16 How does the effectiveness of paper-and-pencil planning tools compare with that of computer-based planning tools?

Paper-and-pencil tools and computer-based tools can both play important roles in a complete 401(k) communications package. Paper-and-pencil tools can easily be used in a group setting to explore and illustrate planning and investment concepts. Individuals already familiar with computer technology may find a computer software approach to planning and education more attractive since it is more interactive and allows the illustration of many calculations in a short period of time. However, many plan participants will not be comfortable with computer technology and will better appreciate and be more willing to act upon the results of a paper-and-pencil calculation that they have worked through over a period of 30 or 40 minutes.

Q 7:17 What computer-based planning tools are available?

Many of the large mutual fund families offer user-friendly software that can assist in retirement planning. This software can usually be ordered by telephone for about $15.
Some examples are

- Vanguard, 800-876-1840; this can also be run on-line at http://www.vanguard.com

- Fidelity, 800-457-1768; this can be downloaded via the Internet from http://www.fidelity.com

- T-Rowe Price, 800-541-1472

Retirement planning packages are also available for around $50 from most software retailers. Examples include Quicken—Financial Planner, Ernst & Young—Prosper, Dow Jones—Plan Ahead, and Microsoft Money. As mentioned above, many World Wide Web sites also now include interactive retirement planning tools.

Q 7:18 How can the multiple messages involved in 401(k) communications be structured?

No one structure will work for all plans. However, some general guidelines are useful. The traditional enrollment meeting needs to cover the operation of the plan and introduce consumer-oriented employees to the benefits of tax-deferred retirement savings. A follow-up meeting of up to an hour in length can be structured to concentrate on the factors needed to develop a retirement income plan (importance of starting early; importance of investment return; retirement age, life expectancy, and the impact of inflation). A third type of meeting, also about an hour in length, can go into more detail about investment concepts (asset classes and their associated rewards and risks; risk measurement such as standard deviation, investment horizon, and asset allocation as tools for risk management). Each of these meetings should reinforce concepts already presented and lay the groundwork for concepts to be presented in later meetings. These meetings should be supplemented with written material such as newsletter articles or brochures used as payroll stuffers.

Q 7:19 How can the effectiveness of a 401(k) communication program be measured?

As discussed in Q 7:8, it is important to establish measurable goals as part of the design of an effective communication program. If the program includes a group meeting, hand out a questionnaire at the end asking participants to evaluate the material presented and ask for suggestions for future communications. In larger companies focus groups can be just as important for evaluating an ongoing program as for deciding what information is needed initially.

Q 7:20 What type of follow-up is needed for an effective 401(k) communications program?

A communications program over a period of several months can achieve the immediate goals that were set for it. However, it is typical to find that after a few months or a year have passed, participants will no longer remember many of the concepts they had begun to learn during the program. For example, the goal may have been to increase equity investments so that participants would better be able to meet retirement income goals. However, participants need to be reeducated yearly about the risks and rewards involved with equity investments. Otherwise, a year with a down market will lead them to question or even reverse sound investment decisions they made earlier.

Follow-up communication can be less extensive than the initial communications program, but each of the important messages needs to be recommunicated on an annual basis. Typically, a full-blown 401(k) communications program should be redone after a number of years, especially as the investment climate changes, as new participants enter, or as changes are made in plan design or investment options.

DEPARTMENT OF LABOR GUIDANCE
ON PARTICIPANT INVESTMENT EDUCATION

Under ERISA anyone who provides investment advice for a fee with respect to any moneys or property of an employee benefit plan becomes a fiduciary with respect to that plan. With the growth of participant directed individual account plans sponsors have increasingly relied upon ERISA Section 404(c) to avoid fiduciary liability and have looked to the Department of Labor (DOL) for guidance as to when investment education does not constitute investment advice.

Q 7:21 What guidance has the DOL provided as to whether investment education constitutes investment advice?

The DOL in June 1996 issued Interpretive Bulletin 96-1, titled Participant Investment Education. [61 Fed Reg (June 11, 1996)] This bulletin provides guidance as to which activities that have been designed to educate and assist participants and beneficiaries in making informed investment decisions will not, as such, cause persons engaged in such activities to become plan fiduciaries.

Investment Advice Under ERISA

Q 7:22 How is investment advice characterized under ERISA?

In the context of providing investment-related information to participants and beneficiaries of participant directed individual account plans, a person will be considered to be rendering investment advice only if both of the following items are true:

1. The person either renders advice as to the value of securities or other property, or makes recommendations as to the advisability of investing in, purchasing, or selling securities or other property; and

2. The person either has discretionary authority or control with respect to purchasing or selling securities or other property for the participant or beneficiary, or renders advice on a regular basis, pursuant to a mutual agreement that the person will render individualized advice based on the particular needs of the participant or beneficiary and that such advice will serve as a primary basis for the participant's or beneficiary's investment decisions with respect to plan assets.

[29 CFR § 2510.3-21(c)]

Q 7:23 What are the four examples of investment-related information and material that would not, in the view of the DOL, result in the rendering of investment advice under ERISA?

The DOL has determined that the furnishing of any of four categories of information and materials to a participant or beneficiary in a participant directed individual account retirement plan will not, as such, constitute investment advice under ERISA, irrespective of

- Who provides the information
- The frequency with which the information is shared
- The form in which the information and materials are provided (e.g., individual or group basis, in writing or orally, or via video or computer software)
- Whether the information in any one category is furnished alone or in combination with the other categories

The four categories of information are as follows:

1. Plan information (see Q 7:24);
2. General financial and investment information (see Q 7:26);

3. Asset allocation models (see Q 7:27); and

4. Interactive investment materials (see Q 7:29).

[29 CFR § 2509.96-1(d)]

Plan Information

Q 7:24 What does the DOL mean by *plan information,* and why does it not constitute investment advice?

By *plan information,* the DOL means information or materials that inform plan participants or beneficiaries about any of the following:

- Benefits of plan participation
- Benefits of increasing plan participation
- Impact of preretirement withdrawals on retirement income
- Terms of the plan
- Operation of the plan
- Investment alternatives under the plan (see Q 7:25)

Since this information relates to plan participation without reference to the appropriateness of any individual investment option for a particular participant or beneficiary, furnishing the information does not constitute rendering investment advice within the meaning of ERISA. [29 CFR § 2509.96-1(d)(1)]

Q 7:25 According to the DOL, what information about investment alternatives may be included as plan information?

According to the DOL, information about investment alternatives may include descriptions of investment objectives and philosophies, risk and return characteristics, historical return information, related prospectuses, and the generic asset class (e.g., equities, bonds, or cash) of the investment alternative. [29 CFR § 2509.96-1(d)(1)(ii)]

General Financial and Investment Information

Q 7:26 What does the DOL mean by *general financial and investment information,* and why does it not constitute investment advice?

By *general financial and investment information,* the DOL means information or materials that inform plan participants or beneficiaries about any of the following:

- General financial and investment concepts such as risk and return, diversification, dollar cost averaging, compounded return, and tax deferred investment
- Historic differences in rates of return among different asset classes (e.g., equities, bonds, or cash) based on standard market indices
- Effects of inflation
- Estimating future retirement income needs
- Determining investment time horizons
- Assessing risk tolerance

Since this general financial and investment information has no direct relationship to the investment alternatives available to participants and beneficiaries, furnishing it would not constitute rendering investment advice within the meaning of ERISA. [29 CFR § 2509.96-1(d)(2)]

Asset Allocation Models

Q 7:27 What does the DOL mean by *asset allocation models,* and why does providing them not constitute investment advice?

According to the DOL, *asset allocation models* are information and materials (such as pie charts, graphs, or case studies) made available to all plan participants and beneficiaries that provide asset allocation portfolios of hypothetical individuals with different time horizons and risk profiles. Because the asset allocation models would enable a participant or beneficiary to assess the relevance of any particular model to his or her individual situation, furnishing

7-19

the models would not constitute a recommendation and thus would not be investment advice within the meaning of ERISA. [29 CFR § 2509.96-1(d)(3)]

Q 7:28 What four conditions must asset allocation models satisfy in order to meet the DOL standard?

In order to meet the safe harbor of DOL Interpretive Bulletin 96-1, asset allocation models must meet all four of these conditions:

1. Such models must be based on generally accepted investment theories that take into account the historic returns of different asset classes (e.g., equities, bonds, or cash) over defined periods of time [29 CFR § 2509.96-1(d)(3)(i)];

2. All material facts and assumptions on which such models are based must accompany the models (e.g., retirement ages, life expectancies, income levels, financial resources, replacement income ratios, inflation rates, and rates of return) [29 CFR § 2509.96-1(d)(3)(ii)];

3. To the extent that an asset allocation model identifies any specific investment alternative available under the plan, the model must be accompanied by a statement indicating that other investment alternatives having similar risk and return characteristics may be available under the plan and identifying where information on those investment alternatives may be obtained [29 CFR § 2509.96-1(d)(3)(iii)]; and

4. The asset allocation models must be accompanied by a statement indicating that in applying particular asset allocation models to their individual situations, participants or beneficiaries should consider their other assets, income, and investments (e.g., equity in a home, IRA investment, savings accounts, and interests in other qualified and nonqualified plans) in addition to their investments in the plan. [29 CFR § 2509.96-1(d)(3)(iv)]

However, the status of the asset allocation model would not, in the view of the DOL, be affected by the fact that a plan offers only one investment alternative in a particular asset class identified in the model.

Interactive Investment Materials

Q 7:29 What does the DOL mean by *interactive investment materials*, and why does providing them not constitute investment advice?

According to the DOL, *interactive investment materials* include questionnaires, worksheets, software, and similar materials that provide a participant or beneficiary the means to estimate future retirement income needs and assess the impact of different asset allocations on retirement income. Because these materials enable participants and beneficiaries independently to design and assess asset allocation models, but otherwise do not differ from asset allocation models based on hypothetical assumptions, they would not constitute a recommendation and hence would not be investment advice within the meaning of ERISA. [29 CFR § 2509.96-1(d)(4)]

Q 7:30 What five conditions must interactive investment materials satisfy in order to meet the DOL standard?

In order to meet the safe harbor of DOL Interpretive Bulletin 96-1, interactive investment materials must meet all five of these conditions:

1. Such interactive materials must be based on generally accepted investment theories that take into account the historic returns of different asset classes (e.g., equities, bonds, or cash) over defined periods of time [29 CFR § 2509.96-1(d)(4)(i)];

2. There must be an objective correlation between the asset allocation generated by the materials and the information and data supplied by the participant or beneficiary [29 CFR § 2509.96-1(d)(4)(ii)];

3. All material facts and assumptions that may affect a participant or beneficiary's assessment of the different asset allocations must either accompany the interactive materials or be specified by the participant or beneficiary (e.g., retirement ages, life expectancies, income levels, financial resources, replacement income ratios, inflation rates, and rates of return) [29 CFR § 2509.96-1(d)(4)(iii)];

4. To the extent an asset allocation generated by the materials identifies any specific investment alternative available under the plan, the asset allocation must be accompanied by a statement indicating that other investment alternates having similar risk and return characteristics may be available under the plan and identifying where information on those investment alternatives may be obtained [29 CFR § 2509.96-1(d)(4)(iv)]; and

5. The interactive materials must either take into account or be accompanied by a statement indicating that, in applying particular asset allocation models to their individual situations, participants or beneficiaries should consider their other assets, income, and investments (e.g., equity in a home, IRA investment, savings accounts, and interests in other qualified and nonqualified plans) in addition to their investments in the plan. [29 CFR § 2509.96-1(d)(4)(v)]

Investment Education Versus Investment Advice

Q 7:31 Might there be other examples of investment education materials that would not constitute investment advice?

Yes. According to the DOL, there may be many other examples of investment education materials that would not constitute investment advice. Determination of whether any such information constitutes investment advice must be made by reference to the criteria set forth in 29 C.F.R. Section 2510.3-21(c)(1) and discussed in Q 7:22. [29 CFR § 2509.96-1(d)]

Q 7:32 Are the four types of investment education materials identified in DOL Interpretive Bulletin 96-1 safe harbors for avoiding the rendering of investment advice as defined by ERISA?

Only in a limited sense. The four types of investment education identified in DOL Interpretive Bulletin 96-1 will not in themselves constitute investment advice. However, any of them could be used in a context that would cross the line to become investment advice if they were accompanied by particular recommendations or otherwise interfered with a participant's or beneficiary's exercise of independent control in the selection of asset allocations under the plan.

Investment Education and Fiduciary Liability

Q 7:33 Is the selection by a plan sponsor or fiduciary of a person to provide the types of investment education identified in DOL Interpretive Bulletin 96-1 itself a fiduciary action?

Yes. As with any designation of a service provider to a plan, the designation of a person to provide investment education is an exercise of discretionary authority or control with respect to the management of the plan. Thus the persons making the designation must act prudently and solely in the interest of the plan participants and beneficiaries both in making the designation and in continuing it. [29 CFR § 2509.96-1(e)]

Q 7:34 In the context of an ERISA Section 404(c) plan, would the designation of a person to provide the types of investment education identified in DOL Interpretive Bulletin 96-1 give rise to fiduciary responsibility for investment losses resulting from a participant's or beneficiary's asset allocation choices?

No. According to the DOL, the designation of a person to provide investment education (or even the designation of a fiduciary to provide investment advice) would not by itself give rise to fiduciary responsibility for investment loss that was the direct and necessary result of a participant's or beneficiary's independent control over his or her asset allocation choices. [29 CFR § 2509.96-1(e)]

Impact of Interpretive Bulletin 96-1

Q 7:35 What features of DOL Interpretive Bulletin 96-1 are likely to be of most value to plan sponsors?

In Interpretive Bulletin 96-1 the DOL has clarified that extensive use of model portfolios and interactive materials for generating model portfolios can generally be used in investment education without crossing the line into investment advice. Moreover, these tools can be used in individual counseling sessions as well as in group presentations and can be used on a continuing basis. The DOL has made it clear that providing extensive investment education will not conflict with the protection from liability for loss provided by ERISA Section 404(c).

Q 7:36 What features of DOL Interpretive Bulletin 96-1 remain unclear or are likely to cause problems for plan sponsors?

DOL Interpretive Bulletin 96-1 introduces the notion of "objective correlation" between generated asset allocations and the data provided by the participant or beneficiary, but it is not clear what is meant by this. There is no discussion in the bulletin as to what constitutes generally accepted investment theories, and there is no agency (like the Financial Accounting Standards Board (FASB), which promulgates generally accepted accounting principles) to look to for clarification.

In practice it may be difficult to meet the disclosure-of-all-facts-and-assumptions requirement for model portfolios without so overwhelming the participant as to defeat the goal of effective education. Yet cutting back on this material could at some point result in crossing the line from education to advice. The bulletin provides little guidance as to the point where the participant's or beneficiary's independence becomes compromised, but that independence is crucial if investment education is not to become investment advice as defined by ERISA. The bulletin also does not address the question of whether staying within its framework will prevent the employer from being considered an investment adviser subject to securities law registration requirements.

INDIVIDUAL RETIREMENT PLANNING

This section describes and illustrates how to use the retirement planning tables in Appendix A. The tables can be used by an individual just entering a 401(k) plan or by someone who already has accumulated significant 401(k) retirement savings. Since retirement planning involves many factors that are unknown and can only be guessed at, the tables consider a variety of economic scenarios involving the relation of future salary and inflation. They also allow planning for a range of possible retirement ages and provide for four different life expectancies at retirement. The tables illustrate the impact of beginning retirement savings on persons in their twenties. Finally, the tables illustrate the importance that expected long-term return on investment has in retirement planning. The questions and answers in this section, along with the tables, also provide valuable information that can serve as a basis for educating 401(k) plan participants about investment choices and their significance for retirement planning.

The Four Types of Retirement Planning Tables

Q 7:37 What economic scenarios involving future salaries and inflation are considered in Appendix A?

The individual retirement planning tables in Appendix A are grouped according to four economic scenarios involving expectations for future salaries and inflation. These are shown in the title box at the top of each table and are identified by Roman numerals. The four scenarios are:

I. Level salary and no inflation

II. Salary keeps pace with low 3 percent inflation

III. Salary outpaces low 3 percent inflation

IV. Salary falls behind moderate 6 percent inflation

Q 7:38 What is meant in Appendix A by salary "falling behind" or "outpacing" inflation?

In the tables, *salary falling behind inflation* means a person's salary increases on average 1 percent per year less than inflation over the rest of his or her working life. Similarly, *salary outpacing inflation* means a person's salary increases on average 1 percent per year more than inflation over the rest of his or her life.

Q 7:39 What factors influence whether a person's future salary will fall behind, keep pace with, or outpace inflation?

Salary increases are generally regarded to have two components: the increase in salary levels for the entire workforce and increases due to an individual's increased productivity (as evidenced by greater job skill or promotion).

Through this century until about 1972, average wages outpaced inflation. During the last 20 years of this period, average wages outpaced inflation by a record 2 percent per year. However, during the period of higher inflation beginning in 1972 through 1982, average wages fell behind inflation by about 1 percent per year. Because of increased competition from developing countries, increased government regulation, and greater attention to ecological concerns, it may be that average wages will no longer outpace even low levels of inflation.

Individual productivity increases are often greatest during the earlier years of a person's career and level off during the last third or so because there is more to be learned in the early years.

Q 7:40 How can historic and current levels of inflation provide a guide to future inflation?

For the last century, inflation has varied greatly from year to year. During the 110 years from 1871 to 1981, stable prices with average inflation of 0.1 percent occurred only 16 percent of the time. Low to moderate inflation, averaging 1.4 percent, occurred 30 percent of the time, and rapid inflation, averaging 8.3 percent, occurred 29 percent of the time. Although recent experience makes it hard to believe, during this 110-year period deflation averaging negative 3.3 percent occurred 25 percent of the time. During the last decade, inflation has generally trended downward from a double-digit high of 10.2 percent in 1981 to current levels (in 1999) of somewhat under 2 percent.

From an even broader historic perspective, this last century's inflation has been unusually volatile. A study of cottage rents in England dating back to 1066 showed long periods (up to a century or more) of essentially level prices broken by periods of rapid inflation lasting only a few years to a decade. These periods of inflation usually occurred during times of rapid technological or political change. It may be that during our current times the pace of technological and political change continues at such a rate as to promote a low level of continued inflation. It would therefore seem prudent for retirement planners to expect low levels of inflation to continue and to consider the impact that moderate levels of inflation would have.

Q 7:41 What planned retirement ages are shown in the tables in Appendix A?

Appendix A provides tables for planned retirement ages of 59, 62, 65, 68, and 71. At about age 59, qualified retirement plan savings and IRA savings can be withdrawn without a 10 percent early withdrawal penalty. Age 62 is about the average retirement age for U.S. workers during recent years and is also the earliest age at which workers are eligible for Social Security retirement benefits. Age 65 has for many years been considered "normal retirement age" under many retirement plans and is the age by which benefits must fully vest under qualified plans.

Retirement ages as late as 68 and 71 should also be considered. Since retirement is no longer mandatory for most workers, more workers are retiring later. This is both practical, since more people are remaining healthy and productive later in life, and necessary, as longer life expectancies require greater amounts for retirement. Although workers retiring today receive full Social Security benefits at age 65, current law calls for normal retirement age under Social Security to increase gradually for workers born after 1937 until it reaches age 67 for workers born after 1959.

Q 7:42 What are the four types of retirement planning tables in Appendix A for each economic scenario and planned retirement age?

The four types of retirement planning tables are:

Table 1. Percent of Salary Replaced by a 401(k) Account Equal to Current Annual Salary

Table 2. Percent of Salary Replaced by a 401(k) Contribution of 1 percent of Current Annual Salary

Table 3. 401(k) Contribution (Percent of Current Salary) Needed to Replace 10 percent of Salary at Retirement

Table 4. Accumulation at Retirement (Multiple of Current Salary) for 10 percent Salary Replacement

Tables 1 and 2 begin with an in-place 401(k) savings plan and project the replacement ratio that is likely to result at planned retirement age. Table 3 works backward and allows the determination of the 401(k) contribution that would be needed to meet an established replacement ratio goal (see Q 7:45). Table 4 projects the accumulation needed to meet a replacement ratio goal.

Q 7:43 What additional factors are considered in each of the four types of retirement planning tables in Appendix A?

All four types of retirement planning tables in Appendix A also take into account probable life expectancy at retirement; expected return on 401(k) assets, both pre- and post-retirement; and the number of years remaining to retirement.

The tables all show four probable life expectancies at retirement:

- Same as Male Average
- Better Than Male Average
- Same as Female Average
- Better Than Female Average

(The columns labeled Better Than Male Average can also be used for Worse Than Female Average.)

The tables all show four patterns of expected return on 401(k) investments:

- 4 percent pre- and 4 percent post-retirement
- 6 percent pre- and 5 percent post-retirement
- 8 percent pre- and 6 percent post-retirement
- 10 percent pre- and 7 percent post-retirement

The tables show gross expected return; the "real" growth of purchasing power would be the return shown, less the rate of inflation.

Finally, the tables all show results for people at retirement age down to those as young as 50 years from planned retirement age.

Replacement Ratios at Retirement

Q 7:44 How is the adequacy of retirement benefits measured?

The use of replacement ratios to measure the adequacy of retirement benefits is quite common. A replacement ratio computed for employees at different levels of compensation can be used to measure the adequacy of current benefits and to compare the benefit package with those of other employers in the industry.

Q 7:45 What is a *replacement ratio*?

A *replacement ratio* is a ratio obtained by dividing total projected retirement income (including Social Security) by current pay at the time of retirement. Typical adequacy standards vary by income level and decline as income increases, as shown in the following table.

Gross Pay Prior to Retirement	Recommended Gross Replacement Ratio (percentage)	Replacement Ratio Excluding Employee Savings (percentage)
$ 15,000	75–85%	70–80%
20,000	70–80	65–75
25,000	65–75	60–70
40,000	60–70	55–65
60,000	60–70	50–60
80,000	60–70	45–55
100,000	55–65	40–50
150,000	50–60	40–50

Example. Company W has a defined benefit plan providing a benefit equal to 25 percent of pay. The company is concerned about the adequacy of its benefits programs. By reviewing the company benefits and projected Social Security benefits at normal retirement age, the company finds shortfalls at all thresholds of income:

7-29

Gross Pay	Defined Benefit Plan	Social Security[a]	Replacement Ratio (percentage)	Recommended Replacement Ratio (percentage)	Shortfall (percentage)
$ 15,000	$ 3,750	$ 4,500	55%	80%	25%
20,000	5,000	6,000	55	75	20
25,000	6,250	7,500	55	70	15
40,000	10,000	12,000	55	65	10
60,000	15,000	12,000	45	65	20
80,000	20,000	12,000	40	65	25
100,000	25,000	12,000	33	55	22
150,000	37,500	12,000	33	55	22

[a]Note: For illustration only—not intended to reflect current levels of Social Security.

Company W might consider installing a 401(k) plan with employer matching contributions to supplement the existing defined benefit plan and make up for the projected shortfalls in replacement income at retirement.

Q 7:46 What is an example of an expected replacement ratio at retirement?

The example in this answer uses Tables 1 and 2 under Scenario III. The example will also serve as a guide to using the tables.

Example. Betty is 45 and has a 401(k) balance equal to twice her current annual salary. Including the employer match, her current 401(k) contribution is 5 percent of salary. She plans to retire at 65 and expects her salary to outpace an inflation level of 3 percent. Her 401(k) assets are invested in a combination of a money market account and a bond fund that have been yielding about 4 percent. Betty exercises regularly, follows a sensible diet, and all four of her grandparents are still alive. She considers that her life expectancy at retirement will be better than the female average. Betty is 20 years from planned retirement.

Table III-65-1 (the numbers correspond to scenario number–age at retirement–table number), in the column for better than female average life expectancy and 4 percent pre- and post-retirement expected return, shows that 4.10 percent of salary will be replaced in 20 years by a 401(k) account equal to current salary. Since Betty has a 401(k) account of twice her current salary, this account balance can be expected to grow to replace 8.2 percent (2 times 4.10 percent) of her salary at retirement.

The corresponding column (the fourth from the right) in Table III-65-2, shows that 0.82 percent of salary at retirement will be replaced by each 1 percent of salary contributed for the next 20 years. Since Betty is contributing 5 percent of salary, her future 401(k) contributions can be expected to grow to replace 4.10 percent (5 times 0.82 percent) of her salary at retirement.

Betty's 401(k) savings plan can be expected to produce a total replacement ratio at age 65 of 12.30 percent (8.2 percent plus 4.10 percent). This means that at age 65 Betty can expect to retire and begin drawing 12.30 percent of her final year's salary from her retirement plan. If inflation averages 3 percent during her retirement and her assets continue to earn 4 percent, she can expect that on average her savings will last her for her expected lifetime.

Q 7:47 What does it mean to say that "on average" someone can expect his or her savings to last for his or her expected lifetime?

Averages have no meaning in any individual situation. Betty (see Q 7:46) has just one life to lead. "On average" means that if a large number of people in similar situations are tracked, a large number of them will be found to die before their "life expectancy," leaving retirement savings unspent, and a large number of them will be found to live longer than their life expectancy and run out of retirement savings before they die. Only a very few will find that their retirement savings closely match their needs during retirement.

Betty's 401(k) plan may allow her to buy an annuity from an insurance company that would guarantee payments for her entire life. However, such annuities would rarely provide for inflation protection. Very few people retiring with plans that do not require an annuity actually select one. Perhaps they believe that on their own they can invest money with a better return than the insurance company can realize; or they may suspect that only very healthy people buy annuities so that the rates are not a very good deal for people of average or below average health. Insurance company actuaries and underwriters long ago mastered the technique of charging less healthy people higher life insurance rates, but only a very few have begun to charge lower annuity rates to those same people.

Q 7:48 How can individual retirement planners manage the risk of outliving their retirement savings other than by buying an annuity?

Traditionally, the answer to this problem was to work for a large company that provided a defined benefit plan. However, for most workers, this is not an option. The best way to manage the risk of outliving the savings from a 401(k) is to plan conservatively. This has been done to some extent in the tables in Appendix A because they are built using conservative life expectancies. (The Appendix A tables are constructed using the 1983 Group Annuity Mortality Male Table (GAM83) with a six-year setback for females. However, the tables have been set back an additional five years to build in additional conservatism appropriate for use in individual (rather than large group) retirement planning and to anticipate improvement in life expectancy, especially for younger workers.)

For retirement at age 65, the tables in Appendix A show a male average life expectancy of 20.7 years and a female average of 25.7 years. In contrast, for all workers under Social Security, a recent actuarial study reported current life expectancy at 65 to be 15 years for males and 18.9 years for females. The study presented as an intermediate-level assumption improvements in life expectancy by 2050 that would increase this to 17.6 years for males and 21.7 years for females. The study's "pessimistic" projection showed increases by 2050 to 20 years for males and 24 years for females. However, this Social Security study covered all workers under Social Security and provides numbers appropriate for large group planning. Individuals who have exercised the discipline to generate 401(k) savings and who are now planning for retirement should likely use more conservative life expectancies, such as those built into the tables in Appendix A.

A retirement savings plan can also explicitly provide for a less than 50 percent risk of outliving savings. A technique for doing this is discussed in Qs 7:64 and 7:65.

Q 7:49 Can the Appendix A tables be used to determine how much retirement savings a retiree can afford to spend each year?

Yes. Table 1 can be used for this purpose. Each year, an individual may choose the appropriate inflation scenario, treat the current age as the planned retirement age, and choose the appropriate life expectancy class and the appropriate post-retirement expected return on savings. Then, the percentage shown at zero years to retirement is the percentage of savings that can reasonably be spent during the upcoming year. As long as the life expectancies in the tables remain conservative, the retiree can simply subtract 1 from the prior year's expectancy. This technique will automatically adjust for differences in actual return on assets or for major deviations of past inflation from expected values. If there have been no major deviations, a retiree could instead increase his or her last year's expenditures by the inflation rate, since retirement planning has allowed for inflation increases. (See Q 7:63 for calculations using intermediate retirement ages.)

Q 7:50 How much would a participant have to contribute to a 401(k) plan for the next 20 years to be likely to achieve a replacement ratio of 40 percent?

The answer to this question uses Scenario II, Table II-65-3.

Example. Tom at age 45 has finally gotten around to saving for retirement. He would like to retire at age 65 with a replacement ratio from his 401(k) plan of 40 percent. He expects his salary to keep pace with 3 percent inflation. Tom's health is about the same as the male average. Under male average life expectancy, it is found that the percentage of salary contribution needed 20 years from retirement depends significantly on the expected return from Tom's 401(k) investments. If his expected return is as low as 4 percent pre-retirement, he would need 33.56 percent (4 times 8.39 percent) savings for a replacement ratio of 40 percent. As Tom's expected pre-retirement return increases to 6 percent, 8 percent, or 10 percent, the required contribution rate drops to 24.8 percent, 18.36 percent, and 13.52 percent, respectively. The amount Tom could actually contribute would depend both on the design of his plan and on federal law and regulations.

If Tom had started saving for retirement at age 25, the dependence on rate of return would be even more dramatic. From age 25, Tom's contribution rate to achieve a 40 percent replacement ratio would have been 15.16 percent, 8.96 percent, 5.12 percent, and 2.88 percent for expected pre-retirement returns of 4 percent, 6 percent, 8 percent, and 10 percent, respectively. For savings that begin at age 25, a 2 percent increase in the expected return on investment will lower the needed 401(k) contribution rate by more than 40 percent.

Long-Term Investment Return

Q 7:51 What does experience indicate is the most reliable way to increase the expected return from long-term investments?

Experience indicates that different asset classes on average yield significantly different average return on investments. For example, during the 59 years from 1926 to 1985, when inflation increased by an average of 3.1 percent per year, long-term government bonds yielded on average 4.2 percent, 10- to 20-year corporate bonds yielded on average 4.9 percent, and the stocks making up the Standard & Poor's 500 index yielded on average 10 percent.

The results are similar for most periods as short as 10 to 15 years. Investment advisers generally agree that for long-term investments, common stocks will average an annual yield of about 10 percent, long-term bonds will average an annual yield of about 6.5 percent, and short-term treasuries (under 1 year) will average an annual yield of about 4.5 percent.

Using a long-term average inflation rate of 3 percent, these three asset classes can be expected to average annual real return after inflation of about 7 percent for common stocks, 3.5 percent for long-term bonds, and 1.5 percent for short-term Treasuries.

Q 7:52 Are there any disadvantages to investing solely in asset classes with higher expected average return on investment?

Yes. Experience shows that asset classes with higher average return on investment are also much riskier in the sense that the investment gain or loss varies more from year to year than does the gain or loss on lower-yielding investment classes.

A common way to measure the risk of variable return from year to year is with the statistic called standard deviation. For example, a report on various asset classes over a ten-year period might show results as follows:

Asset Class	Average Annual Return	Annual Standard Deviation
Short-term Treasuries	3.0%	3.0%
Intermediate bonds	4.5	5.5
Long-term bonds	5.5	8.3
Real estate	7.0	13.5
Large stocks	10.5	15.5
Small stocks	11.0	19.0

Q 7:53 How should a participant interpret the standard deviation of annual return when assessing the riskiness of an asset class?

About 68 percent of the time, the annual return can be expected to lie within one standard deviation of the average. About 95 percent of the time, the return should lie within two standard deviations, and over 99 percent of the time, the return should lie within three standard deviations. In other words, there is about a one in six chance that the return in any one year will be less than the average return by at least one standard deviation. Since this is the same odds as getting a one when rolling a single die, it is easy to understand that this would not be a very unlikely or surprising outcome.

There is about a 1 in 40 chance any year's return will be as much as 2 standard deviations below the average. Another way to illustrate risk is to show the lowest return over the last 40 or more years—this is often close to the average less 2 standard deviations.

Based on the table above (see Q 7:52), even though large stocks are expected to average 10.5 percent return, there is a 1 in 6 chance that any given year will have a return as low as (or lower than) negative 5 percent (10.5 percent average, less 15.5 percent standard deviation). There is also a 1 in 6 chance that the return in any given year will equal or exceed 26 percent, but most investors do not lie awake nights worrying that their stock investments will earn more than expected.

Q 7:54 How can long-term 401(k) investors manage the variable return risk that comes with higher-yielding asset classes such as stocks?

Precisely because retirement planning is long term, the short-term variability of annual return is less important than it would be with savings for short-term needs. As return is measured over longer periods of time, the variability decreases substantially. For example, in one study, an annual standard deviation of return measuring 7.2 percent fell to 4.6 percent after 10 years and fell even further, to 3.8 percent, after 15 years. Even at retirement, there is still a long-term investment horizon extending well beyond 10 or 15 years.

Investing across the individual enterprises that make up an asset class already lowers variability of return because of diversification. The risk that a single enterprise will lose money (or even fail) is called *business risk*. The risk that an entire class of investments will lose money in a given year is called *market risk*. The stock investments available under a 401(k) plan are typically mutual funds that already diversify to reduce business risk.

The principle of diversification can also be applied to reduce the market risk of any one class of assets. An investment portfolio comprising a mix of different asset class investments will have the same expected return as the average of the expected returns of the asset classes, but if the investment mix is properly chosen, the variability of the entire portfolio will be less than the variability of a single asset class with that expected return. This is true because experience shows that some asset class returns tend to increase and decrease somewhat out of phase with the increases and decreases in return of other asset classes.

Q 7:55 What is an example of a portfolio with an asset mix that achieves its investment objective while lowering risk?

Suppose that the goal is to achieve an expected return of 7 percent. Given the expected returns seen above (Q 7:52), a portfolio consisting of 100 percent real estate would have this expected return, but would have a high standard deviation (13.5 percent).

Computer programs are available that can calculate an optimum portfolio given the historical returns of each available asset class, optimum in the sense that it will have the desired expected return but will have a lower variability than any other possible asset mix for that group of asset classes. Such a portfolio for this example might contain 1 percent treasuries, 30 percent intermediate bonds, 16 percent long-term bonds, 27 percent real estate, 18 percent large stocks, and 8 percent small stocks. Such a portfolio then would have the required 7 percent expected return, but would typically have a standard deviation of about 7.2 percent, significantly lower than the real estate class standard deviation of 13.5 percent.

The Impact of Inflation

Q 7:56 If salaries are likely to keep pace with inflation, is it important to take inflation into account in retirement planning?

Yes, for two reasons. First, salaries keep pace with inflation only while the employee is working, while inflation continues into retirement. Second, during periods of inflation, more of an employee's investment is based on higher salaries late in his or her career, and there is less time for compound returns to build substantial retirement assets.

Example. Jane starts saving in her 401(k) plan at age 30 and plans to retire at age 65. She believes she will have a female average life expectancy and plans to maintain a high-return, low-risk balanced investment portfolio with an expected yield of 8 percent pre-retirement and 6 percent post-retirement. If Jane ignores inflation in her retirement planning and uses the tables in Scenario I for level salary and no inflation, she would conclude from Table I-65-2 that each 1 percent of 401(k) contribution would replace 13.68 percent of her salary at retirement. However, under Scenario II, where salary keeps pace with low 3 percent inflation, Table II-65-2 shows that each 1 percent of 401(k) contribution can be expected to replace 5.01 percent of her salary at retirement. This example demonstrates that the impact of even low levels of inflation on retirement planning is significant.

Q 7:57 What does experience show about the ability of various asset classes to keep pace with inflation?

Neither stocks nor bonds reliably maintain the same real return over inflation during different levels of inflation. For example, during the 110 years ending in 1981, the average yield of stocks during the periods of stable prices was 20.8 percent. During periods of low to moderate inflation, the average return on stocks fell to 13.8 percent, and during periods of rapid inflation, the average return on stocks fell again to 12.2 percent. Stocks tended to have returns higher than inflation on average, but inflation is disruptive to business plans, and, on average, the real return offered by stocks did fall significantly during periods of inflation.

During this 110 years, long-term bonds had an average yield of 4.9 percent during periods of stable prices. The average bond yield fell to 3.8 percent during low to moderate inflation and fell again to 3.1 percent during rapid inflation. As a result, bonds on average had negative real yields during periods of moderate or rapid inflation. However, during periods of deflation, bond yields averaged 5.2 percent while the average deflation was minus 3.3 percent.

Also during this 110 years, housing and farmland have on average increased their rate of return more than inflation during periods of increasing prices. During periods of stable prices, moderate inflation, and rapid inflation, housing had average total returns of 4 percent, 7.1 percent, and 12.1 percent, respectively. Farmland historically has done even better as an inflation hedge with total average yields of 4.2 percent, 12.4 percent, and 16.4 percent during periods of stable prices, moderate inflation, and rapid inflation. During the periods of average minus 3.3 percent deflation, housing had an average total yield of minus .4 percent, while farmland did much worse, with an average yield of minus 12.2 percent (see Q 7:40).

Other Sources of Retirement Income

Q 7:58 What sources of retirement income besides a 401(k) plan should be considered in planning for retirement?

During recent years, both Social Security and home ownership have been important sources of income during retirement. Retirees have often been able to sell a larger house for much more than they paid for it. After buying a smaller retirement house, they have been able to use the difference to provide income during retirement. As with a qualified retirement plan, the government provides significant tax savings for home ownership.

As indicated above (Q 7:57), housing has historically been a good investment during periods of inflation. During the 1970s and 1980s, the increased demand created by the baby boomers moving into the housing market has also contributed to higher yields. However, the country may now be moving into a period of low inflation when housing may do less well, and the demand for housing may decrease as the baby boom generation moves toward retirement.

Q 7:59 How can the tables in Appendix A be used to estimate the salary replacement ratio derived from the sale of a house at retirement?

Table 1 can be used to estimate the replacement ratio derived from the sale of a house at retirement by expressing the expected gain as a percentage of expected salary at retirement. However, since the tax status of money from a home sale is different from that of money drawn from a qualified retirement plan, this is a somewhat less precise estimate than Table 1 yields for 401(k) account balances.

Example. Rick expects to retire at age 68. After selling his house and buying a retirement home, he expects a gain of about two times his projected salary at age 68. Rick expects about 3 percent inflation and feels he has better-than-male-average life expectancy. He will invest his gain to yield about 6 percent before taxes. Table II-68-1 indicates that Rick can expect the gain from the sale of his house to replace about 13.4 percent (2 times 6.70 percent) of his income. (Note that this determination requires Rick to project what his salary is likely to be at retirement and uses the zero years to retirement row of Table 1.)

Q 7:60 What salary replacement ratio can be expected from Social Security?

Social Security replacement ratios vary by level of income and by age at retirement, as well as by time spent in the workforce and the pattern of past salary changes. In 1999 Social Security provided payments that replaced approximately these percentages of a typical worker's final year of salary:

Salary Level	Age 62	Age 65	Age 70
About $12,950	50%	60%	65%
About $28,500	35	45	50
About $66,000	20	25	30
About $122,000	10	13	14

This table is based on a worker's primary insurance amount. In addition to this amount, Social Security also typically provides half as much again for the worker's spouse (decreased by any Social Security benefits the spouse has earned directly).

This table is only a rough estimate of Social Security benefits under current law. It is important for all workers to request an Earnings and Benefit Estimate Statement from the Social Security Administration at least every three years. This is done by using Form SSA-7004-SM, which is available from local Social Security offices or by calling 800-772-1213. One may also request a benefit estimate from the Social Security Administration on the Internet at http://www.ssa.gov/. Social Security benefits depend on a worker's entire wage history, and, if reporting errors have been made, there is only a limited time to correct them.

Future Social Security levels will be subject to both political and economic forces. As the baby boomers move into retirement, retirees will continue to be a potent political lobby for continuing Social

Security payments at historic levels. However, as the percentage of the population that is retired increases, the taxes needed to continue Social Security at historic levels will also increase.

It is likely that Social Security payments, which are indexed for inflation, will continue to be an important source of retirement income for most Americans. However, even current law calls for some decrease in benefit levels for many people both through later Social Security Normal Retirement Age and through increased tax on Social Security benefits.

Encouraging Younger Workers to Participate

Q 7:61 What reasons can younger workers be given to encourage them to save in 401(k) plans when they believe they cannot afford it?

The following example uses Tables II-68-2 and III-68-3 from Appendix A.

Example. Jack is 28 and has just become eligible for his company's 401(k) plan that will match 25 percent of his deferrals up to 4 percent, but Jack feels he cannot afford to save for retirement at this time. If Jack has male average life expectancy and retires at age 68 after a career where his salary keeps pace with 3 percent inflation, a 1 percent deferral on his part (1.25 percent with company match) will provide for salary replacement of 10.73 percent (1.25 times 8.58 percent) at retirement (assuming 8 percent pre-retirement expected return). If Jack delays retirement savings until age 38, this 10.73 percent replacement ratio will require deferrals of about 1.8 percent, and a delay until age 48 would require a deferral of about 3.6 percent to achieve the same 10.73 percent replacement ratio that a 1 percent deferral can achieve at age 28. This result is calculated from Table II-68-3, which shows that a 10 percent replacement ratio requires a 4.17 percent deferral at 20 years from retirement, but only a 1.17 percent deferral 40 years from retirement when Jack is 28. This means for Jack that a deferral beginning at age 48 needs to be 3.56 times greater (4.17 percent divided by 1.17 percent) than one beginning at age 28 to achieve the same replacement ratio.

Because 401(k) deferrals reduce Jack's taxable income, each $1 of deferral will reduce Jack's take-home pay by only about $.80 (as-suming a 20 percent marginal tax bracket). Moreover, each $100 that Jack does not defer this year will leave $25 of salary match on the table.

A good time to begin (or increase) salary deferrals would be along with a salary increase. This will result in an increase in take-home pay, and over a period of only a few years will result in levels of 401(k) contribution that can be expected to provide substantial salary replacement ratios at retirement.

Additional Retirement Options

Q 7:62 Can the tables in Appendix A, which apply directly to retirement income for the life of the participant, be used to estimate replacement ratios for payments in other forms?

Yes, but only in one special case. The tables in Appendix A apply directly only to retirement income for the life of the partici-pant. However, they can also be used for retirement payments while both the participant and a beneficiary are alive where income would reduce by half at either death. (This is not the same as a 50 percent qualified joint and survivor annuity, which reduces pay-ments only upon the death of the participant, not upon the death of the beneficiary.)

The procedure is simplest for use with Table 3 in each scenario. First, calculate the required deferral percentage for the participant. Second, calculate a Table 3 deferral percentage using the same years to retirement as the participant but using the life expectancy and age at retirement of the beneficiary. The deferral percentage for in-come that reduces by half at the first of either death is the average of these two deferrals (calculated as their sum divided by two).

For Table 1 or Table 2 of each scenario, the procedure is some-what more complicated. From either Table 1 or Table 2, calculate the replacement ratio first for the participant, then for the benefici-ary (using the participant's years to retirement, but the life expec-tancy and retirement age of the beneficiary). Calculate the average of these two replacement ratios (as their sum divided by two). One last calculation is now needed: multiply the replacement ratios for the participant and beneficiary and divide the result by the average calculated in the step above. This result is the appropriate Table 1 or Table 2 replacement ratio for income that would reduce by 50 percent at the first of either death.

Example. Kim is 45 and plans to retire at 65 with better-than-male-average life expectancy. Kim's spouse is three years older with better-than-female-average life expectancy. Kim wants to know what deferral percentage is needed to provide a 10 percent salary replacement ratio where retirement income would reduce by 50 percent when either Kim or Kim's spouse dies. Kim expects salary to keep pace with 3 percent inflation and expects to earn 8 percent on pre-retirement 401(k) savings.

Under Table II-65-3, at 20 years from retirement, the deferral percentage for Kim alone is 4.59 percent. Using Table II-68-3, again at 20 years from retirement, the deferral percentage for Kim's spouse alone is 5.37 percent. The deferral percentage for income that reduces by 50 percent at the first of either's death is 4.98 percent (the sum 4.59 percent plus 5.37 percent divided by 2).

If Kim has an IRA balance equal to current income, what replacement ratio will this provide where retirement income is to reduce by 50 percent at the earlier of Kim's or Kim's spouse's death? Under Table II-65-1, the replacement ratio for Kim alone is 17.28 percent. According to Table II-68-1, the replacement ratio for Kim's spouse alone is 14.76 percent. The arithmetic average of these two is 16.02 percent. The replacement ratio for income that reduces by 50 percent at the first of either death is 15.92 percent (17.28 percent times 14.76 percent divided by the average 16.02 percent).

Intermediate Values

Q 7:63 How can the retirement planning tables in Appendix A be used for intermediate retirement ages or for intermediate expected investment return?

The tables in Appendix A provide for retirement ages of 59, 62, 65, 68, and 71 and for expected pre-retirement investment returns of 4 percent, 6 percent, 8 percent, and 10 percent. The tables can be used to provide reasonable estimates for intermediate retirement ages and intermediate expected returns.

For intermediate retirement ages, a participant can look up the result for the lower and for the higher retirement age, subtract the two results, and divide the difference by three. Then, the participant can add (or subtract) this third of the difference to (or from) the table value for the closer retirement age. This is easier to do than to describe—one should just remember that one will either add or subtract so that the intermediate age will have an intermediate result.

Example 1. Fred is retiring at age 66 with a 401(k) balance equal to 5.6 times salary. Fred has a life expectancy about the same as the female average and expects inflation of 3 percent and post-retirement returns between 5 percent and 6 percent. What replacement ratio range should Fred expect?

For 5 percent post-retirement returns, according to Table II-65-1, there is a replacement ratio at 0 years from retirement of 28.45 percent (5.6 times 5.08 percent). According to Table II-68-1 there is a replacement ratio of 30.91 percent (5.6 times 5.52 percent). The difference (30.91 percent less 28.45 percent) is 2.46 percent, and one third of this is 0.82 percent. The intermediate age 66 retirement replacement ratio is 29.27 percent (the age 65 value of 28.45 percent plus this one-third difference of 0.82 percent). The same procedure for 6 percent post-retirement returns produces an intermediate age 66 replacement ratio of 32.85 percent (intermediate between the age 65 value of 32.03 percent and the age 68 value of 34.50 percent). At age 66 retirement Fred can expect a replacement ratio range of about 28 percent to about 33 percent for expected returns ranging from 5 percent to 6 percent.

At Fred's age of 66 in the example above, the difference in replacement ratios for expected investment returns intermediate between 5 percent and 6 percent is small enough not to warrant more precise calculation. However, at younger pre-retirement ages, where the tables provide expected returns at only 2 percent intervals, intermediate expected return calculations are useful.

Example 2. Vic is 35 and plans to retire in 30 years with somewhat-worse-than-female-average life expectancy. Assuming salary keeps pace with 3 percent inflation and 8.75 percent pre-retirement expected return, what replacement ratio can Vic expect from 401(k) savings equal to current salary? From Table II-65-1 there is a replacement ratio of 25.52 percent for an 8 percent expected return and a replacement ratio of 49.17 percent for a 10 percent return. In this case, the difference is great enough for a precise intermediate calculation to be warranted. The difference between the 8 percent replacement ratio and the 10 percent replacement ratio is 34.39 percent. The intermediate value will be calculated by adding a portion of the 34.39 percent value to the replacement ratio for an 8 percent expected return. The portion is calculated by determining how far 8.75 percent is from 8 percent divided by how far 10 percent is from 8 percent. This portion is 0.375 (0.75 percent divided by 2 percent). Multiplying this 0.375 portion times the 34.39 percent difference produces 12.90 percent to be added to the 8 percent replacement ratio of 25.52 percent. This 8.75 percent replacement ratio is 38.42 percent (25.52 percent plus 12.9 percent).

This precise intermediate calculation procedure is more difficult to describe than it is to carry out. One should just remember to add or subtract the appropriate portion of the difference to or from the lower interest rate result to end up with an intermediate value. There is no need to keep track of pluses and minuses when calculating the differences.

By applying this procedure to Table 3, Vic in the example above can determine what deferral percentage is needed to produce a 10 percent replacement ratio at age 65 retirement in 30 years. Table II-65-3 figures show that the 8 percent return deferral percentage is 2.51 percent, and the 10 percent return deferral percentage is 1.61 percent. The intermediate deferral percentage calculation will subtract a portion of the difference from the 8 percent result. The difference is 0.9 percent (2.51 percent less 1.61 percent). The portion to subtract is the same 0.375 calculated for the Table 1 example (0.75 percent divided by 2 percent). Subtracting 0.34 percent (0.375 times 0.9 percent) from 2.51 percent leaves a 2.17 percent deferral percentage required for a 10 percent replacement ratio when the expected pre-retirement return is 8.75 percent. (As seen above, the difference in post-retirement return is much less significant than the difference in pre-retirement return, so it can be ignored in this calculation.)

This procedure for calculating intermediate values for a table is called interpolation. Interpolation can also be used between the tables in Scenarios I and II for retirement planning with salary that keeps pace with 1 or 2 percent inflation.

Managing Longevity Risk

Q 7:64 How does the risk of outliving retirement income decrease for years beyond life expectancy?

The best way for an individual to manage this risk is to build a measured amount of safety into his or her plan. Table 7-2 starts with the 50 percent risk "life expectancy" for retirement ages ranging from 59 to 71, then indicates the payment years needed to reduce the risk of outliving retirement income to 25 percent, 10 percent, 5 percent, and 1 percent. The two numbers shown are for average male mortality and average female mortality, respectively. For example, a male of average health retiring at age 65 would need to plan for payments for 36 years to reduce his risk to 5 percent. A female of average health retiring at age 68 and willing to settle for a 10 percent risk of outliving her retirement income would need to plan for 35 years of payments.

If a person considers himself or herself to be of better than average male/female health, he or she can add three years; if worse than average male/female health, he or she can subtract three years. It should be noted that females on average have much better than average male health and need to plan for about five to six more years of income.

Articles on retirement planning sometimes recommend as a rule of thumb to plan for retirement income that lasts ten years beyond

TABLE 7-2. Years (Male/Female) Needed for Each Risk Level of Outliving Retirement Income

Retirement Age	50% Risk	25% Risk	10% Risk	5% Risk	1% Risk
59	27/32	33/39	38/44	41/47	47/52
62	24/29	30/36	35/41	38/44	44/49
65	21/27	27/33	33/38	36/41	41/47
68	18/24	25/30	30/35	33/38	38/44
71	16/21	22/27	27/33	30/36	35/41

one's life expectancy. From the above table, it can be seen that adding ten years to the 50 percent risk comes very close to the years needed to lower the risk of outliving one's income to 10 percent. Another ten years would get the risk very close to zero.

Q 7:65 How can a plan for retirement savings explicitly lower the risk of outliving retirement savings?

Many retirement planning tools, including the tables in Appendix A, allow for income that will last for life expectancy. This means there is a 50 percent chance of outliving such savings, since 50 percent of the population can be expected to live longer than life expectancy. Tables 7-3 and 7-4 provide factors that can be used by females and males, respectively, to adjust a plan for retirement savings to allow for changing from a risk level of 50 percent to lower risk levels of 25 percent, 10 percent, 5 percent, or 1 percent.

Each table provides two factors: the benefit security discount (BSD) and the asset security multiplier (ASM). The BSD is used to calculate a reduced amount of benefit corresponding to a lower risk of outliving savings. The ASM is used to determine the increased amount of asset (or increased savings rate) that would be needed to lower the risk of outliving savings for a desired level of benefits.

Example 1. In Q 7:46, Betty had determined that 5 percent of salary going into her 401(k) plan would likely replace 4.10 percent of her salary at age 65 given that she had better-than-female-average life expectancy and that she expected to earn about 4 percent on her savings both before and after retirement during 3 percent average inflation. Since this result is based on life expectancy, it allows for a 50 percent risk that Betty would outlive her savings. Betty, however, would prefer to reduce the risk of outliving her savings to 5 percent. To do this, she needs to reduce the 4.10 percent replacement ratio by the Table 7-3 benefit security discount factor of 0.7056, so she now plans for a replacement ratio of 2.89 percent (4.10% × 0.7056). (The 0.7056 factor is found in Table 7-3, in the 4 percent post-retirement return section, in the row for age 65 retirement for above average life expectancy, and in the column for 5 percent risk.)

Example 2. In Q 7:50, Tom wanted a 40 percent replacement ratio at age 65 retirement and determined that this would require

Female Years Needed for Each
Risk Level of Outliving Retirement Income

(**Use left ret. age for avg. life expectancy)
(*Use right ret. age for above avg. life expectancy)

Ret. Age	50% Risk	25% Risk	10% Risk	5% Risk	1% Risk
62*	32 yrs	39 yrs	44 yrs	47 yrs	52 yrs
62 65	29 yrs	36 yrs	41 yrs	44 yrs	49 yrs
65 68	27 yrs	33 yrs	38 yrs	41 yrs	47 yrs
68**	24 yrs	30 yrs	35 yrs	38 yrs	44 yrs

4% Post Retirement Return
3% Inflation

Benefit Security Discount (BSD)

Ret. Age	50% Risk	25% Risk	10% Risk	5% Risk	1% Risk
62*	1.0000	0.8471	0.7680	0.7287	0.6734
62 65	1.0000	0.8318	0.7471	0.7056	0.6479
65 68	1.0000	0.8411	0.7472	0.7020	0.6291
68**	1.0000	0.8225	0.7213	0.6735	0.5976

Asset Security Multiplier (ASM)

Ret. Age	50% Risk	25% Risk	10% Risk	5% Risk	1% Risk
62*	1.0000	1.1805	1.3022	1.3724	1.4850
62 65	1.0000	1.2022	1.3385	1.4172	1.5434
65 68	1.0000	1.1890	1.3383	1.4245	1.5895
68**	1.0000	1.2158	1.3864	1.4848	1.6733

5% Post Retirement Return
3% Inflation

Benefit Security Discount (BSD)

Ret. Age	50% Risk	25% Risk	10% Risk	5% Risk	1% Risk
62*	1.0000	0.8710	0.8049	0.7724	0.7270
62 65	1.0000	0.8557	0.7837	0.7487	0.7005
65 68	1.0000	0.8620	0.7812	0.7425	0.6807
68**	1.0000	0.8433	0.7547	0.7130	0.6475

Asset Security Multiplier (ASM)

Ret. Age	50% Risk	25% Risk	10% Risk	5% Risk	1% Risk
62*	1.0000	1.1481	1.2423	1.2947	1.3755
62 65	1.0000	1.1687	1.2760	1.3356	1.4276
65 68	1.0000	1.1601	1.2801	1.3467	1.4690
68**	1.0000	1.1858	1.3251	1.4024	1.5444

Table 7-3. Female Longevity Security

To lower the risk of outliving benefits from 50%, multiply:

Derived benefit levels by the
Benefit Security Discount (BSD)

Required assets or contributions by the
Asset Security Multiplier (ASM)

6% Post Retirement Return
3% Inflation

Benefit Security Discount (BSD)

Ret. Age	50% Risk	25% Risk	10% Risk	5% Risk	1% Risk
62*	1.0000	0.8922	0.8379	0.8115	0.7752
62 65	1.0000	0.8771	0.8168	0.7878	0.7484
65 68	1.0000	0.8810	0.8122	0.7796	0.7283
68**	1.0000	0.8624	0.7855	0.7498	0.6942

Asset Security Multiplier (ASM)

Ret. Age	50% Risk	25% Risk	10% Risk	5% Risk	1% Risk
62*	1.0000	1.1209	1.1935	1.2323	1.2901
62 65	1.0000	1.1401	1.2243	1.2693	1.3362
65 68	1.0000	1.1351	1.2313	1.2827	1.3731
68**	1.0000	1.1595	1.2730	1.3337	1.4405

7% Post Retirement Return
3% Inflation

Benefit Security Discount (BSD)

Ret. Age	50% Risk	25% Risk	10% Risk	5% Risk	1% Risk
62*	1.0000	0.9106	0.8666	0.8456	0.8172
62 65	1.0000	0.8961	0.8462	0.8226	0.7911
65 68	1.0000	0.8979	0.8400	0.8130	0.7712
68**	1.0000	0.8798	0.8137	0.7834	0.7371

Asset Security Multiplier (ASM)

Ret. Age	50% Risk	25% Risk	10% Risk	5% Risk	1% Risk
62*	1.0000	1.0982	1.1539	1.1826	1.2236
62 65	1.0000	1.1160	1.1818	1.2156	1.2641
65 68	1.0000	1.1137	1.1905	1.2300	1.2967
68**	1.0000	1.1367	1.2290	1.2765	1.3566

Male Years Needed for Each
Risk Level of Outliving Retirement Income

(**Use left ret. age for avg. life expectancy)
(*Use right ret. age for above avg. life expectancy)

Ret. Age	50% Risk	25% Risk	10% Risk	5% Risk	1% Risk
62*	27 yrs	33 yrs	38 yrs	41 yrs	47 yrs
62 65	24 yrs	30 yrs	35 yrs	38 yrs	44 yrs
65 68	21 yrs	27 yrs	33 yrs	36 yrs	41 yrs
68**	18 yrs	25 yrs	30 yrs	33 yrs	38 yrs

4% Post Retirement Return
3% Inflation

Benefit Security Discount (BSD)

Ret. Age	50% Risk	25% Risk	10% Risk	5% Risk	1% Risk
62*	1.0000	0.8411	0.7472	0.7020	0.6291
62 65	1.0000	0.8225	0.7213	0.6735	0.5976
65 68	1.0000	0.7998	0.6726	0.6251	0.5614
68**	1.0000	0.7439	0.6344	0.5847	0.5195

Asset Security Multiplier (ASM)

Ret. Age	50% Risk	25% Risk	10% Risk	5% Risk	1% Risk
62*	1.0000	1.1890	1.3383	1.4245	1.5895
62 65	1.0000	1.2158	1.3864	1.4848	1.6733
65 68	1.0000	1.2504	1.4867	1.5998	1.7811
68**	1.0000	1.3443	1.5763	1.7103	1.9250

5% Post Retirement Return
3% Inflation

Benefit Security Discount (BSD)

Ret. Age	50% Risk	25% Risk	10% Risk	5% Risk	1% Risk
62*	1.0000	0.8620	0.7812	0.7425	0.6807
62 65	1.0000	0.8433	0.7547	0.7130	0.6475
65 68	1.0000	0.8203	0.7071	0.6651	0.6091
68**	1.0000	0.7666	0.6675	0.6227	0.5644

Asset Security Multiplier (ASM)

Ret. Age	50% Risk	25% Risk	10% Risk	5% Risk	1% Risk
62*	1.0000	1.1601	1.2801	1.3467	1.4690
62 65	1.0000	1.1858	1.3251	1.4024	1.5444
65 68	1.0000	1.2190	1.4142	1.5036	1.6417
68**	1.0000	1.3045	1.4982	1.6058	1.7719

Table 7-4. Male Longevity Security

To lower the risk of outliving benefits from 50%, multiply:

Derived benefit levels by the
Benefit Security Discount (BSD)

Required assets or contributions by the
Asset Security Multiplier (ASM)

6% Post Retirement Return
3% Inflation

Benefit Security Discount (BSD)

Ret. Age	50% Risk	25% Risk	10% Risk	5% Risk	1% Risk
62*	1.0000	0.8810	0.8122	0.7796	0.7283
62 65	1.0000	0.8624	0.7855	0.7498	0.6942
65 68	1.0000	0.8395	0.7395	0.7028	0.6545
68**	1.0000	0.7880	0.6989	0.6591	0.6077

Asset Security Multiplier (ASM)

Ret. Age	50% Risk	25% Risk	10% Risk	5% Risk	1% Risk
62*	1.0000	1.1351	1.2313	1.2827	1.3731
62 65	1.0000	1.1595	1.2730	1.3337	1.4405
65 68	1.0000	1.1912	1.3522	1.4229	1.5280
68**	1.0000	1.2691	1.4307	1.5171	1.6456

7% Post Retirement Return
3% Inflation

Benefit Security Discount (BSD)

Ret. Age	50% Risk	25% Risk	10% Risk	5% Risk	1% Risk
62*	1.0000	0.8979	0.8400	0.8130	0.7712
62 65	1.0000	0.8798	0.8137	0.7834	0.7371
65 68	1.0000	0.8571	0.7696	0.7379	0.6968
68**	1.0000	0.8080	0.7287	0.6936	0.6488

Asset Security Multiplier (ASM)

Ret. Age	50% Risk	25% Risk	10% Risk	5% Risk	1% Risk
62*	1.0000	1.1137	1.1905	1.2300	1.2967
62 65	1.0000	1.1367	1.2290	1.2765	1.3566
65 68	1.0000	1.1667	1.2994	1.3551	1.4351
68**	1.0000	1.2376	1.3724	1.4418	1.5412

401(k) savings of 13.52 percent, assuming he had average male life expectancy and could earn 10 percent pre-retirement and 7 percent post-retirement during 3 percent average inflation. Since this result is based on life expectancy, it allows for a 50 percent risk that Tom will outlive his savings. Tom would like to reduce this risk to 10 percent. To do this, he finds the appropriate asset security multiplier of 1.2994 from Table 7-4 and concludes that his savings rate would have to be 17.57 percent (13.52% × 1.2994). (This asset security multiplier is from the 7 percent post-retirement return section of Table 7-2 and uses the retirement age 65 row (average life expectancy) and the 10 percent risk column.)

Retirement Plan Accumulation

Q 7:66 Can the tables in Appendix A be used to determine what retirement plan accumulation will be needed to meet a given replacement ratio goal?

Yes. In each scenario in Appendix A, Table 4 will determine what accumulation at retirement age will be needed for any given salary replacement goal. The Table 4 entries give the multiple of current salary needed to replace 10 percent of final salary at retirement. Each Table 4 is laid out in the same way as the other three types of tables in Appendix A: by years from retirement, then across the page for the four life-expectancy groups (same and better than male average and same and better than female average), then within each life expectancy group by expected investment return (both pre- and post-retirement).

Example. Joyce is 25 years old and is planning to retire at age 68. She would like to replace 50 percent of her salary with her 401(k) accumulation. Assuming her $25,000 salary will outpace 3 percent inflation, and that she can earn 8 percent pre-retirement and 6 percent post-retirement, how much will she need to accumulate to meet her 50 percent replacement goal?

Using Table III-68-4, 43 years from retirement, average female mortality, and 8 percent pre- and 6 percent post-retirement returns, Joyce's accumulation will be 8.76 times her current salary for every 10 percent salary replacement. Since her replacement goal is 50 percent (or 5 × 10%), her accumulation will be

$1,095,000 ($25,000 × 8.76 × 5). It should be noted that this allows for a 50 percent chance of outliving her retirement savings. Joyce could apply an asset security multiplier from Table 7-3 to adjust the needed accumulation to accommodate a lower risk level.

This last example illustrates the importance of emphasizing salary replacement rather than accumulation in retirement planning. Even with fairly low 3 percent inflation, Joyce will need to accumulate over $1,000,000 to replace just 50 percent of her $25,000 salary.

If this were the starting point of Joyce's savings plan, this might seem like an overwhelming goal. However, these are inflated dollars, and knowing this accumulation amount does not provide a plan for meeting this goal. It is better to begin to plan using Table 3 from Appendix A since that directly tells an individual what savings rate is needed to achieve his or her income replacement goal without the distraction of dealing with inflated dollar amounts. However, once planning has been done in terms of replacement ratios and salary savings as a percentage of current salary, it is of interest to compare the accumulation that will result with current accumulations. This is the most important use of Table 4.

8 Contribution Limits

401(k) plans, like other qualified plans, are subject to restrictions on the amounts that can be contributed to them. These restrictions apply at both the employer level and the participant level. At the employer level the restriction takes the form of a limitation on the maximum amount of plan contributions that are deductible by the employer. At the participant level the law limits the total amounts—*annual additions*—that can be allocated to a participant under all plans maintained by the employer. The law also caps the amount of elective contributions that can be made by an employee during any calendar year whether to the plans of a single employer or to the plans of more than one employer. This chapter explains these restrictions and their often complex interrelationships.

LIMITS ON ELECTIVE CONTRIBUTIONS

Q 8:1 Is the amount of elective contributions to a 401(k) plan subject to limitation?

Yes. However, before 1987 there was no limit on the amount of elective contributions that an employee could make to the plan other than the limits on annual additions imposed by Code Section 415 (see Q 8:20). Consequently, participants could defer up to the lesser of $30,000 or 25 percent of compensation. The Tax Reform Act of 1986 (TRA '86) placed an annual cap on the amount of *elective deferrals* (see Q 8:3) that can be made by any individual. That cap, originally $7,000 but adjusted periodically to reflect cost-of-living increases, is $10,000 for 1999. (See Q 8:19 for a discussion of the reduced annual cap for 401(k) plans that are considered SIMPLE 401(k) plans.)

Q 8:2 For what period does the annual cap apply?

The annual cap applies to the participant's taxable year, which, in most cases, will be the calendar year. Thus, a participant's elective deferrals for the taxable year cannot be greater than the annual cap in effect for that year. [Treas Reg § 1.402(g)-1(d)(1)]

Q 8:3 What are *elective deferrals?*

Elective deferrals consist of elective contributions made to 401(k) plans, to salary reduction simplified employee pensions (SARSEPs) under Code Section 408(k)(6), and to Section 408(p) SIMPLE retirement plans. Salary reduction contributions made to a Section 403(b) annuity contract are also considered elective deferrals, but salary reduction contributions made to a Section 457 plan are not. (See chapter 21.) [Treas Reg § 1.402(g)-1(b)]

Example. From January 1, 1999, to June 30, 1999, when he terminated his employment with a not-for-profit hospital, John contributed $5,000 to a 403(b) annuity contract. On July 1, 1999, he became an employee of ABC Company, which sponsors a 401(k) plan. His participation in the 401(k) plan commenced August 1, 1999. The maximum amount of elective contribution he can make to ABC Company's 401(k) plan for the balance of 1999 is $5,000 ($10,000 minus $5,000 of contributions made to the 403(b) annuity).

Q 8:4 Was there a special limitation that applied to elective deferrals under a 403(b) annuity contract?

Yes. Prior to 1996, elective deferrals of $9,500 could be made annually to a Section 403(b) annuity. Now that the annual 401(k) plan deferral cap exceeds $9,500, the same deferral cap limit applies to both 403(b) plans and 401(k) plans, although 403(b) plans also allow for additional catch-up contributions under some circumstances (see chapter 21).

Excess Deferrals

Q 8:5 What happens if the participant's elective deferrals for the taxable year exceed the annual cap?

If a participant has *excess deferrals* (the amount by which a participant's elective deferrals exceed the annual cap) based only on the elective contributions made to a single 401(k) plan, then the plan must return the excess deferrals to the participant by April 15 of the following year. [Treas Reg §§ 1.401(a)-30, 1.402(g)-1(e)(1)] It could happen, however, that a participant has excess deferrals as a result of making elective contributions to 401(k) plans, SARSEPs, SIMPLE retirement plans, and 403(b) annuity contracts of different employers. If the 401(k) plan so provides, the participant may notify the plan of the amount of excess deferrals allocated to it no later than April 15 (or any earlier date specified in the plan). The plan is then required to distribute to the participant no later than April 15 the amount of the excess deferrals allocated to the 401(k) plan by the participant. [Treas Reg § 1.402(g)-1(e)(2)]

Example. Steve is 62 and participates in Employer Y's 401(k) plan. In January 1998 Steve withdraws $5,000 from the 401(k) plan. From February through September, Steve defers $1,200 per month. On October 1, Steve leaves Employer Y and becomes employed by Employer Z (unrelated to Y). During the remainder of 1998, Steve defers $1,800 under Z's 401(k) plan. In January 1999 Steve realizes that he has deferred a total of $11,400 in 1998 and therefore has a $1,400 excess deferral ($11,400 minus $10,000, the applicable limit for 1998). Assuming at least one of the 401(k) plans permits corrective distributions, Steve has until April 15, 1999 (or such earlier date specified in the plan) to request a distribution of excess deferrals. The $5,000 withdrawal did not correct the excess deferral because it occurred before the excess deferral was made (see Q 8:7).

Corrective Distributions

Q 8:6 Is a plan required to permit the distribution of excess deferrals if the excess deferrals arise from elective contributions made to 401(k) plans, SARSEPs, SIMPLE retirement plans, and 403(b) annuity contracts of different employers?

No. [Treas Reg § 1.402(g)-1(e)(4)]

Q 8:7 Must a 401(k) plan wait until after the end of the participant's taxable year before a corrective distribution of excess deferrals can be made?

No. A plan may provide that an individual with excess deferrals may receive a corrective distribution during the taxable year in which the excess deferral occurs. The corrective distribution must occur after the excess deferral is made and must be treated by both the employer and the participant as a corrective distribution. [Treas Reg § 1.402(g)-1(e)(3)]

Q 8:8 If an excess deferral is distributed, must the income allocable to the excess deferrals be distributed as well?

Yes. [Treas Reg § 1.402(g)-1(e)(2)(ii)]

Q 8:9 What is the income allocable to excess deferrals?

The income allocated to excess deferrals is the amount of the allocable gain or loss for the taxable year of the participant. If the plan so provides, it also includes the allocable gain or loss for the *gap period,* which is the period between the end of the participant's taxable year and the date of distribution. [Treas Reg § 1.402(g)-1(e)(5)(i)]

Q 8:10 How is income allocable to excess deferrals determined?

Any reasonable method may be used, provided that the method is not discriminatory, is consistently used for all participants and for all corrective distributions, and is used by the plan for allocating income to participants' accounts. The regulations, however, provide for an alternate method for allocating income. Under this alternative, the income for the taxable year (and the gap period if the plan so provides) allocable to elective deferrals is multiplied by a fraction. The numerator of the fraction is the amount of excess deferrals; the denominator is the amount of the account balance attributable to elective deferrals as of the beginning of the taxable year plus the employee's elective deferrals for the taxable year (and for the gap period if gap-period income is allocated). [Treas Reg §§ 1.402(g)-1(e)(5)(ii), 1.402(g)-1(e)(5)(iii)]

Example. Omicron Company sponsors a 401(k) plan, and Linda has an excess deferral of $1,000 for the 1998 calendar year. The 401(k) plan does not have a gap-period income provision. To determine the amount of income allocable to the excess deferral, Omicron will use the alternate method under the regulations. Following are the data needed to calculate the income for the calendar year allocable to Linda's excess deferral.

Income allocated to Linda's elective deferral account for 1998:	$ 5,000
Value of elective contribution account on January 1, 1998:	$75,000
Amount of elective contributions made during 1998:	$11,000

The income for 1998 allocable to Linda's excess deferral is $58.14 calculated as $1,000/($75,000 + $11,000) × $5,000.

Q 8:11 How is allocable income determined for the gap period?

Gap-period income allocable to excess deferrals may be determined under any reasonable method, including the alternate method described in Q 8:10, or may be determined pursuant to a safe harbor method. Under the safe harbor method, income allocable to excess deferrals for the gap period is equal to 10 percent of the income allocable to excess deferrals for the preceding taxable year under the alternate method described in Q 8:10 times the number of calendar months that have elapsed since the end of the taxable year. A corrective distribution made on or before the fifteenth day of a month will be treated as made on the last day of the preceding month; after the fifteenth day, a distribution is treated as made on the first day of the next month. [Treas Reg § 1.402(g)-1(e)(5)(iv)]

> **Example.** The facts are the same as in the example in Q 8:10, except that Linda receives the excess deferral on February 20, 1999. The 401(k) plan provides for the calculation of gap-period income and uses the IRS alternate method in making this calculation. The amount of gap-period income is $11.63, determined by multiplying the 1998 income allocable to Linda's excess deferral ($58.14) by 20 percent. Twenty percent is used because the distribution made on February 20, 1999, is deemed made on March 1, 1999. Thus, the number of calendar months that are considered to have elapsed since the end of 1998 is two.

Q 8:12 Are excess deferrals still treated as employer contributions?

In general, excess deferrals are treated as employer contributions. However, if a non-highly compensated employee (NHCE) makes elective deferrals in excess of the annual cap to one or more plans of the same employer (see definition of *employer* in chapter 9), then the excess deferrals are not taken into account in calculating that NHCE's actual deferral ratio. (See Q 12:4.) Also, excess deferrals that are distributed to a participant, including a participant who is a highly compensated employee (HCE), will not be considered annual additions under Code Section 415 (see Q 8:22). [Treas Reg § 1.402(g)-1(e)(1)(ii)] This contrasts with the distribution of excess contributions, which continue to be treated as Section 415 annual additions (see Q 12:28). (As explained in chapter 12, *excess contributions* are the amount by which elective contributions for an HCE exceed the amounts permitted by the actual deferral percentage (ADP) nondiscrimination test of Code Section 401(k).

Q 8:13 How does the distribution or recharacterization of excess contributions affect the amount of excess deferrals that may be distributed to an employee?

The amount of excess deferrals that may be distributed to an employee for a taxable year is reduced by any excess contributions previously distributed or recharacterized with respect to the employee for the plan year beginning with or within the taxable year. (See Q 12:18.) In the event of a reduction, the amount of excess contributions includible in the gross income of the employee and reported as a distribution of excess contributions is in turn reduced by the amount of the reduction. [Treas Reg § 1.402(g)-1(e)(6)]

Example. Beth is an HCE who makes elective contributions of $10,000 to Employer Z's 401(k) plan during the plan year ending December 31, 1998. To satisfy the ADP test for the 1998 plan year, Beth receives a $2,500 distribution of excess contributions in January 1999. In February, Beth notifies Employer Z that she made elective deferrals of $2,200 in 1998 under the 401(k) plan of a different employer and requests distribution of the excess deferral from the 401(k) plan of Employer Z. Since a $2,500 excess contribution has already been distributed to Beth, no additional amount needs to be distributed to her. When reporting these distributions, Employer Z must treat $2,200 of the $2,500 distributed as a distribution of excess deferrals; the $300 balance is treated as a distribution of excess contributions.

Q 8:14 Is employee or spousal consent required for a distribution of excess deferrals and allocable income?

No. [Treas Reg § 1.402(g)-1(e)(7)]

Tax Treatment

Q 8:15 What is the tax treatment of corrective distributions to employees?

Because the amount of excess deferrals is includible in the participant's gross income for the taxable year in which the excess deferral is made, a corrective distribution of excess deferrals is not included in the participant's gross income for the distribution year. However, the income allocable to excess deferrals is included in the participant's gross income for the taxable year in which it is distributed. [Treas Reg § 1.402(g)-1(e)(8)(i)]

Q 8:16 Are corrective distributions of excess deferrals (plus allocable income) subject to excise taxes?

No. [Treas Reg § 1.402(g)-1(e)(8)(i)]

Q 8:17 May a corrective distribution of excess deferrals and allocable income be applied toward an employee's minimum distribution requirement under Code Section 401(a)(9)?

No. [Treas Reg § 1.402(g)-1(e)(9)]

Failure to Correct

Q 8:18 What happens if excess deferrals are not corrected?

It depends on how they arise. If excess deferrals arise out of elective deferrals made to one or more plans maintained by the same employer (see definition of *employer* in chapter 9), then the qualification of the plan is at risk. This is because Code Section 401(a)(30) provides that a plan cannot accept elective contributions in excess of the annual cap. If, on the other hand, the excess deferrals arise out of elective deferrals made to plans maintained by unrelated employers, the excess deferral will be included in gross income twice: in the taxable year in which the excess deferral was contributed, and in the taxable year in which the excess deferral is ultimately distributed to the participant. [Treas Reg § 1.402(g)-1(e)(8)(iii)]

SIMPLE 401(k) Plans

Q 8:19 What is the annual cap on elective contributions to a SIMPLE 401(k) plan?

The annual cap for 1999 is $6,000, an amount that will be adjusted in the future for cost-of-living increases. The law is at present unclear about what happens if a participant has excess deferrals based only on the elective contributions made to a single SIMPLE 401(k) plan. The mechanism for returning excess deferrals as explained in Q 8:5 does not appear to apply to SIMPLE 401(k) plans. Perhaps, in this situation, the 401(k) plan will lose its SIMPLE status and will be required to satisfy the actual deferral percentage test (see Q 12:2) and to provide for top-heavy minimum contributions. However, excess deferrals resulting from elections to 401(k) plans, SARSEPs, SIMPLE retirement plans, and 403(b) annuity contracts of different employers can be returned as explained above in Q 8:5.

Example. Jim, who is a participant in Employer O's 401(k) plan, defers $7,000 between January 1, 1998, and June 30, 1998. On July 1, 1998, Jim leaves Employer O and commences employment with Employer N (unrelated to Employer O). Jim is allowed to participate immediately in Employer N's SIMPLE 401(k) plan, and he defers $6,000 during the last six months of 1998. In January 1999 Jim realizes that he has deferred a total of $13,000 in 1998 and therefore has a $3,000 excess deferral ($13,000 minus $10,000, the applicable limit for 1998). Assuming that at least one of the 401(k) plans permits corrective distributions, Jim has until April 15, 1999, to receive a distribution of excess deferrals plus allocable income.

CODE SECTION 415—ANNUAL ADDITION LIMITS

Q 8:20 How does Code Section 415 limit annual additions to a 401(k) plan?

Code Section 415 limits the annual additions that may be allocated to an individual's account in any limitation year. The limitation year is the calendar year unless another 12-month period is designated in the plan document. For 1999, the maximum annual addition is the lesser of 25 percent of compensation or $30,000.

Q 8:21 Is the $30,000 limit indexed for inflation?

Yes, the $30,000 limit is indexed for inflation. However, under the General Agreement on Tariffs and Trade (GATT) pension provisions, the dollar limit must always be a multiple of $5,000 and will always be rounded to the next lowest multiple of $5,000. [IRC § 415(d)]

Annual Additions

Q 8:22 What are *annual additions*?

Annual additions include the following:

1. Elective contributions;
2. Matching contributions;
3. Employer nonelective contributions;
4. Employee mandatory and voluntary contributions;
5. Employer contributions to other defined contribution plans, including money purchase plans, ESOPs, and profit sharing plans;
6. Forfeitures allocated to a participant's account from nonvested or partially vested terminated participants;
7. Amounts allocated to a Section 401(h) individual medical account, which is part of a qualified pension plan maintained by the employer; and
8. Employer contributions for a key employee allocated to a separate account under a welfare benefit plan for post-retirement medical benefits.

[IRC §§ 415(c)(2), 415(l), 419A(d)(2)]

The annual additions described at (7) and (8) count only toward the dollar limit. They do not count toward the 25 percent of compensation limit. When determining an employee's annual additions, contributions to all defined contribution plans maintained by the same employer must be aggregated. See chapter 9 for the definition of *employer.*

Compensation under Code Section 415

Q 8:23 What is considered compensation for purposes of the 25 percent of compensation limit?

Generally, total compensation earned during the limitation year from the employer maintaining the plan is considered. Specifically, the following items are included:

1. The employee's wages, salaries, fees for professional services,

and other amounts received for personal services, to the extent that such amounts are includible in gross income;

2. For a self-employed individual, earned income;

3. Taxable amounts that result from employer-provided accident and health insurance benefits and medical reimbursement plan benefits;

4. Moving expenses paid by the employer that are not deductible by the employee;

5. The value of a nonqualified stock option granted to an employee to the extent includible in gross income; and

6. The amount includible in gross income upon making an election to be taxed on the value of restricted property.

[Treas Reg § 1.415-2(d)(2)]

The following items are specifically excluded from compensation for purposes of Code Section 415:

1. Employer contributions to a qualified plan and to a nonqualified plan of deferred compensation to the extent not includible in gross income;

2. Employer contributions to a simplified employee pension plan and, presumably, to a SIMPLE retirement plan;

3. Distributions from a deferred compensation plan, unless such distributions are from an unfunded nonqualified plan (in which case they may be treated as compensation);

4. Contributions made by an employer toward the purchase of an annuity contract under Code Section 403(b) (tax-sheltered annuity contracts);

5. Amounts realized from the exercise of a nonqualified stock option or when restricted stock or property held by an employee either becomes freely transferable or is no longer subject to a substantial risk of forfeiture;

6. Amounts realized from the sale, exchange, or other disposition of stock acquired under a qualified stock option; and

7. Amounts that receive special tax benefits, such as premiums for group term life insurance, to the extent that such benefits are not includible in gross income of the employee.

[Treas Reg § 1.415-2(d)(3)]

Q 8:24 Are there other definitions of compensation that satisfy Code Section 415?

Yes. The regulations provide for three alternatives:

1. The short list definition, which treats as compensation for Section 415 purposes only the items included in (1) and (2) of the first paragraph in Q 8:23 [Treas Reg § 1.415-2(d)(10)];

2. The W-2 definition, under which compensation for Section 415 purposes is the amount of compensation that would be reported on Form W-2 [Treas Reg § 1.415-2(d)(11)(i)];

3. The federal income tax withholding definition, under which compensation for Section 415 purposes is the amount of compensation subject to federal income tax withholding under Code Section 3401(a). [Treas Reg § 1.415-2(d)(11)(ii)]

Table 9-1 in chapter 9 shows which items of remuneration are treated as Section 415 compensation.

Q 8:25 Are elective contributions treated as compensation for purposes of Code Section 415?

For limitation years beginning after December 31, 1997, elective contributions will be treated as compensation for purposes of Code Section 415. Also considered compensation will be other amounts that are treated as elective deferrals (see Q 8:3) or that are deferred by the employee into a Section 125 cafeteria plan or a Section 457 plan. [IRC § 415(c)(3)]

Plan Design

Q 8:26 How should a 401(k) plan be designed to ensure that the Section 415 limits are not violated?

The plan should contain some fail-safe language, such as the following, that provides for inadvertent violations of this limit:

> Amounts in excess of this limit will be reallocated to the remaining participants. To the extent that every participant in the plan has reached his or her limit, any remaining amounts shall be placed in a suspense account and reallocated in the next year.

If the 401(k) plan is designed carefully, there should be little chance that the annual additions limitation will be violated in a plan year.

Correcting a Violation

Q 8:27 Can a violation of the Section 415 limits be corrected by returning salary deferral contributions?

Yes. If the 401(k) plan has a provision so permitting, a Section 415 violation can be corrected in this way. According to the regulations, this corrective mechanism is available only if the violation results from any one of the following:

1. Allocation of forfeitures;
2. A reasonable error in estimating a participant's compensation;
3. A reasonable error in determining the amount of elective contributions that may be made under Code Section 415; or
4. Other limited facts and circumstances that the IRS determines justify the use of this corrective mechanism.

[Treas Reg § 1.415-6(b)(6)]

Matching contributions attributable to the returned elective contributions of highly compensated employees will result in the plan's providing a higher rate of matching contributions to highly compensated employees. This disparity in matching rates may present an issue under the Section 401(a)(4) nondiscrimination regulations regarding the availability of benefits, rights, and features. (See Qs 11:26–11:30.)

Q 8:28 What are the tax implications of elective contributions that are returned to a participant to correct a Section 415 violation?

The tax consequences of returned elective contributions are as follows:

1. The distribution is includible in income for the taxable year distributed.
2. The distribution cannot carry out any basis (after-tax contributions, PS-58 costs, etc.) a participant may have in the 401(k) plan.

3. The distribution is not subject to the additional income tax on premature distributions under Code Section 72(t).

4. The distribution is not considered wages for Federal Insurance Contributions Act (FICA) and Federal Unemployement Tax Act (FUTA) purposes.

5. No consent (by either the participant or the spouse) is required.

6. The distribution is subject to voluntary withholding under Code Section 3405. However, it is not considered an eligible rollover distribution.

7. The returned elective contributions are not counted toward the annual limit on elective contributions (see previous section, *Limits on Elective Contributions*) and are not treated as elective contributions for purposes of the actual deferral percentage test or as matching contributions for purposes of the actual contribution percentage test. (See *Actual Deferral Percentage (ADP) Test* and *Actual Contribution Percentage (ACP) Test* in chapter 12.)

[Treas Reg 1.415-6(b)(6)(iv); Rev Proc 92-93, 1992-2 CB 505]

Maximum Deferral Percentage

Q 8:29 What is the maximum deferral percentage in a 401(k) plan?

If the 401(k) plan will consist only of elective contributions, the maximum deferral percentage is 25 percent (see *Limits on Elective Contributions* in the previous section). For limitation years beginning before January 1, 1998, the maximum percentage in this case would have been 20 percent. The lower maximum percentage for pre-1998 limitation years reflected the Code's requirement that elective contributions be subtracted from compensation for purposes of applying the annual additions limit. Thus, the 25 percent limitation was applied after reducing compensation by the amount of the elective contribution.

Example. For the limitation year beginning January 1, 1997, Alfred's annual pay was $40,000. Alfred elects to defer 20 percent of pay into the 401(k) plan, or $8,000 ($40,000 × 20%). For purposes of computing the Section 415 limit, Alfred's compensation was $40,000 less the $8,000 elective contribution, or $32,000. The maximum annual additions limit was the lesser of 25 percent of pay or $30,000. Computing this limit for Alfred yielded a limit of $8,000 ($32,000 × 25%).

Q 8:30 What is the maximum deferral percentage if a 401(k) plan also provides a matching contribution?

If the 401(k) plan provides a matching contribution, the maximum deferral percentage should be reduced by the amount of the match. The formula for determining the maximum deferral is shown below:

Maximum deferral percentage = 25% − matching percentage

Example. ABC Company establishes a 401(k) plan and provides for a matching contribution of 50 percent of the first 6 percent of pay. Thus, the maximum match would be equal to 3 percent of pay (50% × 6%). The maximum deferral percentage that ABC Company should set is computed as follows:

$$
\begin{aligned}
\text{Maximum deferral percentage} &= 25\% - \text{matching percentage} \\
&= 25\% - 3\% \\
&= 22\%
\end{aligned}
$$

Boris elects to defer the maximum of 22 percent of pay. Boris earns $30,000 and is also eligible for the maximum match of 3 percent of pay. Boris' contributions in the 401(k) are broken down as follows:

Deferral amount (22% × $30,000):	$6,600
Matching amount (3% × $30,000):	900
Total contribution:	$7,500

Q 8:31 Should the maximum deferral percentage be reduced in a plan that provides discretionary nonelective contributions?

Yes. If the employer's 401(k) plan has a provision for discretionary nonelective contributions, the maximum deferral percentage should be reduced by taking the maximum expected percentage of employer contributions into account. Although this is not required, it makes good sense from an employee relations standpoint. If the employee is allowed to defer the maximum 25 percent of pay, then no employer contribution may be allocated to the employee. Thus, the employee is penalized for electing the maximum deferral percentage.

Q 8:32 How is the maximum deferral percentage computed in a 401(k) plan with a discretionary nonelective contribution?

The formula for determining the maximum deferral percentage is similar to the formula discussed above (see Q 8:30):

Maximum deferral percentage = 25% – matching percentage
– discretionary percentage

Example. Employer C is installing a 401(k) plan with a matching contribution of 25 percent of the first 4 percent of pay plus a discretionary nonelective contribution. Employer C anticipates that the maximum potential nonelective contribution in any year will be 5 percent of pay. The maximum deferral percentage is computed as follows:

Maximum deferral percentage = 25% – matching percentage
– discretionary percentage
= 25% – 1% – 5%
= 19%

Donald elects to defer the maximum, which is 19 percent of pay. Donald's annual pay is $50,000. Donald is also eligible for the maximum match of 1 percent of pay. This year, Employer C elects to make a discretionary contribution of 5 percent of pay. Donald's contributions in the 401(k) plan are broken down as follows:

Deferral amount (19% × $50,000):	$ 9,500
Matching amount (1% × $50,000):	500
Discretionary amount (5% × $50,000):	2,500
Total contribution:	$12,500

The Section 415 limit for Donald is 25 percent of $50,000, or $12,500.

Combined Plan Limits

Q 8:33 Should the design of an employer's 401(k) plan take into account the other retirement plans maintained by the employer?

Yes. It is vital that the employer coordinate the design of a 401(k) plan with other benefit plans. In some cases, the other benefit plans may need to be amended so that participants are not adversely affected by virtue of electing to participate in the 401(k) plan. The maximum percentage that an employee may defer in a 401(k) plan may need to be scaled back to ensure that an employee's benefit or contribution in another plan is not reduced. Furthermore, the 401(k) plan needs to be carefully designed so that it fits within the employer's overall objectives for the total benefits package.

Q 8:34 How is the maximum deferral percentage computed when the employer has other defined contribution plans?

The following formula may be applied in calculating the maximum deferral percentage:

Maximum deferral percentage = 25% − matching percentage
− discretionary percentage
− other DC plan percentage

Example. Employer E adopts a money purchase plan that provides an annual contribution equal to 7.5 percent of pay. The match in the 401(k) plan is equal to 25 percent of the first 6 percent of pay. Employer E does not provide for a discretionary nonelective contribution in the 401(k) plan. The maximum deferral percentage is computed as follows:

Maximum deferral percentage = 25% − 1.5% − 0 − 7.5%
= 16%

Frank elects to defer 16 percent of pay. Frank earns $36,000 annually. Frank's contributions in both the money purchase and the 401(k) plans are broken down as follows:

Deferral amount (16% × $36,000):	$5,760
Matching amount (1.5% × $36,000):	540
Money purchase amount (7.5% × $36,000):	2,700
Total contribution:	$9,000

The Section 415 limit for Frank is 25 percent of $36,000, or $9,000.

If the other defined contribution plan or the discretionary none-lective contribution is integrated with Social Security, the maximum deferral percentages will generally need to be calculated on an individual basis, since the contribution (as a percentage of compensation) will not be uniform for all participants.

It is also important to note that these maximum deferral percentage formulas generally apply only to lower-paid employees. Employees earning more than $40,000 will generally be limited by the annual deferral cap ($10,000 in 1998).

Q 8:35 Will an employer's defined benefit plan have an impact on the design of a 401(k) plan?

Yes. Until 2000 Code Section 415(e) also limits the maximum benefits and contributions that may be provided to an individual who participates in both a defined contribution plan and a defined benefit plan.

Q 8:36 What is the Section 415 limitation for a defined benefit plan?

The limit is the lesser of $130,000 (as indexed for 1999) or 100 percent of the participant's average annual compensation for the three consecutive highest paid years. [IRC § 415(b)(1)] The dollar limit of $130,000 is the maximum annual benefit payable to a participant who has reached Social Security retirement age in 1999. The dollar limit is reduced for a participant who begins to receive benefits before attaining Social Security retirement age; the dollar limit is increased if benefits commence after Social Security retirement age. [IRC §§ 415(b)(1)(C), 415(b)(1)(D)]

If the participant has fewer than ten years of participation in the plan, the dollar limit of $130,000 is reduced by one tenth for each year of participation less than ten. If the participant has fewer than ten years of service at normal retirement age, then the 100 percent limit is reduced by one tenth for each year of service less than ten. [IRC § 415(b)(5)]

Q 8:37 What is the Social Security retirement age?

Social Security retirement age is the age at which full benefits are payable from Social Security. For purposes of Code Section 415, these ages are rounded to the nearest integer and depend on the individual's date of birth, as shown below.

Year of Birth	Social Security Retirement Age
1937 or earlier	65
1938–1954	66
1955 or later	67

Q 8:38 How do the 415 limits operate when an employee has participated in two or more plans of the same employer?

The maximum benefits and contributions that may be provided to an employee who participates in both a defined benefit plan and a defined contribution plan are further limited. [IRC § 415(e)] The employer must establish a defined benefit fraction and a defined contribution fraction, and the sum of these fractions cannot exceed 1.

Even if the sponsor has terminated the defined benefit plan and distributed its assets, the defined benefit fraction continues to exist. Similarly, all prior defined contribution plans are taken into account in computing the defined contribution fraction. These rules were designed to ensure that plan sponsors could not avoid their imposition by terminating a plan and accumulating significantly larger retirement benefits for participants.

For limitation years beginning after December 31, 1999, the Small Business Job Protection Act of 1996 (SBJPA) eliminates the combined limit that applies to employers who have sponsored both defined benefit and defined contribution plans.

Q 8:39 How is the defined benefit fraction computed?

The defined benefit fraction consists of the following:

Numerator: The participant's projected annual benefit under all defined benefit plans of the employer, determined as of the close of the limitation year. For purposes of this calculation, the participant's current pay level is used, without adjustment for future salary increases. It is also assumed that the participant continues to work and to earn benefits from the present until normal retirement age. [IRC § 415(e)(2)(A)]

Denominator: The lesser of:

1. *The defined benefit dollar limit in effect for the limitation year (1999 limit, $130,000) multiplied by 1.25.* If the participant's normal retirement age is earlier than Social Security retirement age, the dollar limit will be reduced. If the participant's normal retirement age is later than Social Security retirement age, the dollar limit will be increased. If the participant is projected to have fewer than ten years of service at normal retirement age, then the dollar limit is reduced by one tenth for each year of service less than ten.

OR

2. *One hundred percent of the participant's average compensation in the three consecutive highest-paid years, multiplied by 1.4.* If the participant is projected to have fewer than ten years of service at normal retirement age, then the 100 percent limit is reduced by one tenth for each year of service less than ten. [IRC § 415(e)(2)(B)]

Q 8:40 How is the defined contribution fraction computed?

The defined contribution fraction is computed on a cumulative basis for all years of service with the employer, including a predecessor employer that previously maintained the plan. [IRC § 414(a)(1)] The numerator and denominator are determined as follows:

Numerator: The sum of all annual additions to the participant's account in all defined contribution plans of the employer since the inception of the plan. [IRC § 415(e)(3)(A)]

Denominator: The lesser of the following:

1. The defined contribution dollar limit in effect for each limitation year multiplied by 1.25; or

2. Twenty-five percent of the participant's compensation for the limitation year multiplied by 1.4.

Once the results are obtained for a limitation year, the results are summed for each limitation year. [IRC § 415(e)(3)(B)]

Q 8:41 Are there transition rules for the computation of the defined benefit and defined contribution fractions?

Yes. Since the Tax Equity and Fiscal Responsibility Act (TEFRA) and TRA '86 successively reduced the benefit and contribution limits, transitional rules were available to plans whose participants exceeded the limits. These transition rules essentially allowed a "fresh start" by reducing the defined contribution numerator to the point that the sum of the defined benefit and defined contribution fractions equaled one.

Q 8:42 Is the computation of the combined limit fraction affected if the plans are top heavy?

If the plans are top heavy (see chapter 13), the defined benefit and defined contribution fractions are computed using 1 rather than 1.25 in the denominators. [IRC § 416(h)(1)] If the plan elects to "buy back" the use of 1.25 in the denominator, the price is extra minimum contributions or benefits. The extra minimum contribution will generally be 7.5 percent of compensation in the defined contribution plan, if the defined benefit plan is still in existence. If the defined benefit plan no longer exists, the extra minimum contribution will be 4 percent of compensation. If the extra minimum benefit is provided, the minimum benefit in the defined benefit plan will be an annual accrual of 3 percent of average annual compensation for a maximum period of ten years. However, if the plans become super top-heavy (more than 90 percent of the benefits and contributions are attributable to key employees), the buy back rule is not available, and 1 must be used in the denominator. [IRC § 416(h)(2)]

Q 8:43 What happens if the fractions exceed 1?

In most cases, the plans will provide that the projected annual benefit from the defined benefit plan is to be reduced if the limit is exceeded. In some cases, however, the plan document will provide that the annual additions to the defined contribution plan will be reduced if the limit is exceeded. This will generally be the case when the defined benefit plan no longer exists. The 401(k) plan could provide first that discretionary nonelective contributions are not allocated to the participant if the limits are exceeded and that the amount not allocated to the participant be reallocated to the remaining participants. (See Q 8:26.) Alternatively, the 401(k) plan could provide first that salary deferral contributions be returned to the affected participant if it is determined that one of the circumstances listed at Q 8:27 applies.

Q 8:44 What employers are affected by the overall Section 415 benefit and contribution limits?

This is generally a concern only for sponsors of top-heavy plans (see Q 8:42). However, if annual additions are approaching $30,000 and annual benefits are close to the maximum permitted, the combined limit should be computed even in a large plan. The combined limit is generally applicable only to the highest-paid employees. The fractions should be computed at the time the 401(k) plan is installed to determine which individuals might be affected by the combined plan limits, and annually thereafter for affected individuals.

CODE SECTION 404—DEDUCTION LIMITS

Q 8:45 What deduction limits are applicable to a 401(k) plan?

Because a 401(k) plan is usually a type of profit sharing plan, contributions will be subject to the deductibility rules for profit sharing plans.

Maximum Deductible Amount

Q 8:46 What is the maximum annual amount deductible for a 401(k) plan?

In general, the maximum deductible amount for a taxable year of the employer is 15 percent of the compensation paid during the taxable year to the participants under the plan. [IRC § 404(a)(3)(A)(i)] If an employer maintains two or more profit sharing plans, they will be treated as a single plan for purposes of applying the 15 percent limit. [IRC § 404(a)(3)(A)(iv)]

Example. Employer XYZ maintains a 401(k) plan as well as a profit sharing plan covering the same employees. Contributions to the 401(k) plan amount to 7 percent of participant compensation. If Employer XYZ wishes to contribute the maximum deductible amount, it can make a contribution to the profit sharing plan equal to 8 percent of compensation.

Q 8:47 Is the maximum deductible amount determined with respect to each participant, or is it determined on an aggregate basis?

The maximum deductible amount is determined on an aggregate basis. Thus, it does not matter that a particular participant's allocation of contributions in a 401(k) plan is greater than 15 percent of his or her compensation. What does matter is that the total amount contributed to the 401(k) plan not exceed 15 percent of the aggregate compensation of the participants benefiting under the plan. [Treas Reg § 1.404(a)-9(c)]

Q 8:48 Are elective contributions treated as employer contributions for purposes of the deduction limit?

Yes. [Treas Reg § 1.401(k)-1(a)(4)(ii)]

Compensation under Code Section 404

Q 8:49 What does the term *compensation* mean?

According to the regulations, *compensation* means all compensation paid or accrued during the taxable year. However, compensation does not include contributions made to a 401(k) plan, including elective contributions made at the election of employees. [Treas Reg § 1.404(a)-9(b)] The change made by Section 1434 of the Small Business Job Protection Act of 1996 to treat elective contributions as compensation for purposes of Code Section 415 apparently does not apply for purposes of determining the 15 percent limit. Finally, the plan's definition of compensation is not relevant in determining the maximum deductible amount. [Rev Rul 80-145, 1980-1 CB 89]

Example. Under a 401(k) plan, participants are not allowed to defer any portion of a bonus, and bonuses are not taken into account in allocating nonelective contributions. Compensation not including bonuses is $1 million; bonuses for the year are $500,000. The maximum deductible amount for the taxable year is $225,000 ($1,500,000 × 15%)

Q 8:50 Is there a limit on the amount of compensation that may be taken into account in determining the maximum deductible amount?

Under Code Section 404(l), the amount of compensation that may be taken into account with respect to any participant is limited to $150,000 ($160,000 for taxable years beginning after 1996). This limit is adjusted in increments of $10,000, as explained at Q 9:110.

In addition, for taxable years beginning before 1997, an HCE (see chapter 9) who was a 5 percent owner or one of the ten most highly compensated HCEs and his or her spouse and any child who had not reached age 19 before the close of the taxable year were treated as a single employee for purposes of this limit. This was known as *family aggregation.* [IRC § 404(l)] The family aggregation rules were repealed for tax years beginning after 1996.

Example. Claire owns 100 percent of ABC Company, which sponsors a 401(k) plan. The compensation of the employees of ABC Company for its taxable year beginning July 1, 1996, is as follows:

Employee	Relationship to Claire	Compensation	Subject to Family Aggregation
Claire		$180,000	Yes
Dave	Husband	75,000	Yes
Derek	Son (over 19)	75,000	No
Danny	Son (under 19)	5,000	Yes
Vincent	None	100,000	No
N1	None	30,000	No
N2	None	25,000	No
N3	None	24,000	No
N4	None	23,000	No
N5	None	20,000	No

Claire's compensation of $180,000 is aggregated with Dave's and Danny's compensation ($180,000 + $75,000 + $5,000 = $260,000) and limited to $150,000 for the 1996 tax year. Hence, the maximum deductible amount for the 1996 tax year is $67,050 [($150,000 + $75,000 + $100,000 + $30,000 + $25,000 + $24,000 + $23,000 + $20,000) × 15%]. If the compensation amounts are identical for the taxable year beginning July 1, 1997, the maximum deductible amount is $80,550 [($160,000 + $75,000 + $75,000 + $5,000 + $100,000 + $30,000 + $25,000 + $24,000 + $23,000 + $20,000) × 15%]. This amount is greater than the 1996 maximum deductible amount on account of the elimination of family aggregation.

Q 8:51 In determining the maximum deductible amount, may the employer take into account the compensation of all employees, or just those who are plan participants?

Only the compensation of those participants who benefit under the 401(k) plan may be taken into account. [Rev Rul 65-295, 1965-2 CB 148] The cited revenue ruling does not deal specifically with a

401(k) plan. Presumably, the compensation of a participant who elects not to make contributions would still be taken into account.

Q 8:52 Is the maximum deductible amount determined on the basis of the plan year or the taxable year of the employer?

The maximum deductible amount is determined with reference to compensation paid or accrued during the taxable year of the employer, not the plan year. This fact is of little significance when the plan year and taxable year are identical. It can be troublesome, however, if these periods are not the same.

> **Example.** Omicron, which has a June 30 taxable year, sponsors a 401(k) plan that is administered on a calendar-year basis. In addition to the elective contributions made under the plan, Omicron makes matching contributions as well as discretionary nonelective contributions, which are allocated on December 31 in proportion to participant compensation for the plan year ending on that date. Omicron makes elective and matching contributions throughout its fiscal year ending June 30, 1999. It also makes a nonelective contribution on June 30, 1999, to be allocated on December 31, 1999. Even though the nonelective contribution made on June 30, 1999, will be allocated on December 31, 1999, in proportion to 1999 calendar-year compensation, its deductibility—when added to the elective and matching contributions made during the taxable year ending June 30, 1999—will be based on the compensation paid or accrued to participants for that taxable year.

Nondeductible Contributions

Q 8:53 What happens if more than the maximum deductible amount is contributed to a 401(k) plan?

If contributions to a 401(k) plan exceed the maximum deductible amount for the taxable year, the employer is obligated to pay an excise tax equal to 10 percent of the nondeductible amount. [IRC § 4972] Any excess amount can be deducted in a succeeding taxable year if the excess amount plus the contributions made in the succeeding taxable year are not greater than 15 percent of the compensation paid to participants in the succeeding taxable year. [IRC § 404(a)(3)(A)(ii)]

Example. Alpha contributes $180,000 to its 401(k) plan. Aggregate participant compensation for the year is $1 million. As a result, Alpha has made a nondeductible contribution of $30,000 ($180,000 – (15% × $1,000,000)), which will result in an excise tax liability of $3,000 (10% × $30,000). In the succeeding year, aggregate compensation is $1.5 million and contributions for that year again total $180,000. The $30,000 nondeductible contribution is fully deductible in the succeeding year because $210,000 ($30,000 + $180,000) is less than $225,000, the maximum deductible amount for the succeeding year ($1,500,000 × 15%).

Q 8:54 May an employer avoid the excise tax on nondeductible contributions by withdrawing them before the end of the taxable year?

No. Absent a good faith mistake of fact (see Q 2:69), contributions made to a plan cannot be returned without jeopardizing its qualified status. [IRC § 401(a)(2); Notice 89-52, 1989-1 CB 98, Q&A 16]

Q 8:55 May a 401(k) plan take advantage of the fact that in prior taxable years amounts contributed to the plan were less than the maximum deductible amount?

For 401(k) plans that were not in existence before 1987, the answer is no. If a 401(k) plan was maintained before 1987, the amount by which the maximum deductible amount in any pre-1987 taxable year exceeded the amount actually contributed (referred to as a *pre-'87 limitation carryforward*) may be used to increase the maximum deductible amount for a current taxable year. However, the pre-'87 limitation carryforward cannot cause the maximum deductible amount to exceed 25 percent of compensation for the current taxable year. [IRC § 404(a)(3)(A)(v)]

Example. MNO Company has maintained a 401(k) plan since 1984 and has a pre-'87 limitation carryforward of $100,000. In the current year, the aggregate compensation of the participants benefiting under the plan is $500,000. The maximum deductible amount, taking into account the pre-'87 limitation carryforward, is therefore $125,000 ($500,000 × 25%). If MNO makes a contribution of $100,000, that amount will be deductible and the amount of the pre-'87 limitation carryforward will be reduced to $75,000 ($100,000 − ($100,000 − [$500,000 × 15%]) = $75,000).

Timing of Deductions

Q 8:56 For what taxable year are contributions to a 401(k) plan deductible?

As a general rule, contributions are deductible for the taxable year in which they are paid. The fact that an employer may be an accrual basis taxpayer is not relevant. The one exception to the general rule treats contributions as having been paid on the last day of the taxable year if the contributions are paid no later than the tax return due date (including extensions) for that taxable year. [IRC § 404(a)(6)]

Q 8:57 Can an employer deduct elective and matching contributions for a taxable year if they are attributable to compensation earned by plan participants in the succeeding taxable year?

No. According to the IRS, these contributions are not deductible in the previous taxable year because they do not relate to compensation paid in that taxable year. [Rev Rul 90-105, 1990-2 CB 69]

Example. SRT Company, which is a calendar-year taxpayer, sponsors a 401(k) plan that is administered on a calendar-year basis. SRT Company makes elective contributions and matching contributions in January 1999. These contributions are attributable to compensation paid to participants in that month. Although these contributions were paid before the tax return due date for 1998, they are not deductible for that year. They are deductible in 1999 because they relate to compensation paid in that year.

Design Considerations

Q 8:58 How should the 15 percent deductible limit be taken into account in the design of the plan?

In designing a 401(k) plan, the 15 percent deductible limit should be taken into account. In the aggregate, the sum of elective contributions, matching contributions, and nonelective contributions must not exceed 15 percent of the pay of eligible participants. [IRC § 404(a)(3)(A)(i)] Generally, this will not be a major concern to an employer who maintains only a 401(k) plan; however, if the employer discretionary nonelective contribution is greater than 5 percent of pay, the 401(k) deferral percentage limits should be reduced to take the deductibility limits into account. If the employer maintains another profit sharing plan in addition to the 401(k) plan, the aggregated plans, as pointed out in Q 8:46, are subject to the 15 percent of pay limit.

Q 8:59 What is the deductible limit if the employer also has a defined benefit plan?

Generally speaking, deductibility is limited to 25 percent of pay, which applies on an aggregate basis when at least one employee is covered by both a 401(k) plan and a defined benefit plan. If the employer has a defined benefit plan that requires an annual contribution in excess of 25 percent of pay, the annual contribution to the defined benefit plan will be fully deductible. [IRC § 404(a)(7)(A)] However, any contribution to the 401(k) plan will not be deductible and may be subject to the 10 percent excise tax for nondeductible contributions. [IRC § 4972] An employer with a defined benefit plan that requires contributions in excess of 25 percent of pay will not be a good candidate for a 401(k) plan.

Q 8:60 May an employer with an existing profit sharing plan set up a 401(k) plan?

An employer that regularly makes an annual contribution equal to 15 percent of pay into a profit sharing plan is not a likely candidate for a 401(k) plan. However, if the employer is willing to scale back the discretionary profit sharing contribution, a 401(k) plan may be used in conjunction with the profit sharing plan.

Q 8:61 How are the limits coordinated if the employer has a money purchase or target plan?

An employer that maintains a money purchase or target plan with modest contributions of 10 percent of pay or less may be able to add a 401(k) plan. However, considerable care should be exercised in reviewing the individual Section 415 limits.

9 Data for Nondiscrimination Testing

This chapter and the three chapters that follow set forth the nondiscrimination tests a 401(k) plan must pass to ensure that the plan does not unduly favor highly compensated employees (HCEs). The data for performing these tests must be assembled correctly. Crucial to the data collection are certain terms and concepts that are explained in this chapter.

Because 401(k) plans are established and maintained by employers, the chapter starts by discussing who is considered to be the employer when the Internal Revenue Code's nondiscrimination rules are applied. The chapter then defines the term *plan,* which, for purposes of applying the nondiscrimination rules, differs from the commonsense notion of what a 401(k) plan is. Following that, the chapter defines and discusses other terms that will be important in applying the Code's nondiscrimination rules:

- Who are considered *employees*?
- Which employees are considered *HCEs*?
- What is *compensation*?

WHO IS THE EMPLOYER?

To prevent taxpayers from avoiding nondiscrimination and other qualification requirements through the use of multiple entities, rules have been developed that require certain related entities to be treated as a single employer for purposes of these requirements. Where there is sufficient common ownership to form a *controlled group* of corporations, the employees are treated as employed by a single employer. Similar controlled group rules also apply to groups consisting of at least one noncorporate employer. Even where there may not be sufficient common ownership to form a controlled group, other rules require the aggregation of members of an *affiliated service group*. Although aggregation of related entities is the general rule, it is possible for multiple entities (and even parts of a single entity) to be treated as separate employers if the *qualified separate lines of business* (QSLOB) rules are satisfied.

Controlled Groups

Q 9:1 Must business entities under common control be aggregated as a single employer when applying the nondiscrimination and other qualification requirements?

Yes, provided the entities meet the definition of a *controlled group* as set forth in Code Sections 414(b) and 414(c).

Q 9:2 How many kinds of controlled groups are there?

In general, there are two kinds of controlled groups:

1. A parent-subsidiary controlled group; and
2. A brother-sister controlled group.

[Treas Reg §§ 1.414(c)-2(a), 1.1563-1(a)]

Q 9:3 What is a *parent-subsidiary controlled group*?

A *parent-subsidiary controlled group* consists of one or more chains of organizations in which a controlling interest in each of the organizations, except for the common parent, is owned by another organization. [Treas Reg §§ 1.414(c)-2(b)(1), 1.1563-1(a)(2)(i)]

Q 9:4 What is a *controlling interest*?

For a corporation, a *controlling interest* means ownership of stock possessing at least 80 percent of the total combined voting power of all classes of stock entitled to vote, or at least 80 percent of the total value of shares of all classes of stock. In the case of a trust or estate, it means ownership of an actuarial interest of at least 80 percent of the trust or estate. Finally, in the case of a partnership, a controlling interest means ownership of at least 80 percent of the profits or capital interest of the partnership. [Treas Reg §§ 1.414(c)-2(b)(2), 1.1563-1(a)(2)(i)]

Example. The ABC Partnership owns stock possessing 80 percent of the total combined voting power of all the classes of stock of S Corporation entitled to vote. S Corporation owns 80 percent of the profits interest in the DEF Partnership. The ABC Partnership is the common parent of a controlled group consisting of the ABC Partnership, S Corporation, and the DEF Partnership. The result would be the same if the ABC Partnership, rather than S Corporation, owned 80 percent of the profits interest in the DEF Partnership.

Q 9:5 What is a *brother-sister controlled group*?

A *brother-sister controlled group* consists of two or more organizations satisfying two requirements:

1. The same five or fewer persons who are individuals, estates, or trusts own a controlling interest (see Q 9:4) in each organization.

2. Taking into account the ownership of each such person only to the extent ownership is identical with respect to each organization, such persons are in effective control of each such organization.

The persons whose ownership is considered for purposes of the controlling-interest requirement in (1) above must be the same persons whose ownership is considered for purposes of the effective-control requirement in (2) above. [Treas Reg §§ 1.414(c)-2(c)(1), 1.1563-1(a)(3)(i)]

Q 9:6 What constitutes *effective control*?

In the case of a corporation, *effective control* means owning stock possessing more than 50 percent of the total combined voting power of all classes of stock entitled to vote, or more than 50 percent of the total value of shares of all classes of stock. For a trust or estate, it means owning an actuarial interest of more than 50 percent of the trust or estate. Finally, in the case of a partnership, effective control means owning more than 50 percent of the profits or capital interest of the partnership. [Treas Reg §§ 1.414(c)-2(c)(2), 1.1563-1(a)(3)(i)]

Example 1. The outstanding stock of corporations P, Q, R, S, and T, which have only one class of stock outstanding, is owned by the following unrelated individuals:

	Corporations				
	P	*Q*	*R*	*S*	*T*
Individuals	*(Percentage)*	*(Percentage)*	*(Percentage)*	*(Percentage)*	*(Percentage)*
A	55%	51%	55%	55%	55%
B	45	49			
C			45		
D				45	
E					45
Totals	100%	100%	100%	100%	100%

Corporations P and Q are members of a brother-sister controlled group. Although the effective-control requirement is met for all five corporations, corporations R, S, and T are not members of the controlled group because a controlling interest in each of those corporations is not owned by the same five or fewer persons whose stock ownership is considered for purposes of the effective-control requirement.

Example 2. The outstanding stock of corporations U and V, which have only one class of stock outstanding, is owned by the following unrelated individuals:

	Corporations	
Individuals	*U (Percentage)*	*V (Percentage)*
A	12%	12%
B	12	12
C	12	12
D	12	12
E	13	13
F	13	13
G	13	13
H	13	13
Totals	100%	100%

Any group of five of the shareholders will have effective control of the stock in each corporation. However, U and V are not members of a brother-sister controlled group because a controlling interest in each corporation is not owned by the same five or fewer persons.

Q 9:7 In determining whether organizations are members of a controlled group, may certain interests be disregarded?

Yes. In the case of a corporation, for example, treasury stock and nonvoting stock that is limited and preferred as to dividends are disregarded. [Treas Reg §§ 1.414(c)-3(a), 1.1563-2(a)] Other interests are disregarded only if certain conditions are satisfied first.

Q 9:8 What interests may be disregarded?

All the following interests may be disregarded:

1. An interest held by a plan of deferred compensation covering certain U.S. citizens and residents who are employees of
   a foreign affiliate. [See IRC § 406(a)(3)] This exclusion applies to parent-subsidiary controlled groups only. [Treas Reg
   §§ 1.414(c)-3(b)(3), 1.1563-2(b)(2)(i)]

2. An interest held by a qualified plan. This exclusion applies to
   brother-sister controlled groups only. [Treas Reg §§ 1.414(c)-
   3(c)(2), 1.1563-2(b)(4)(i)]

3. An interest held by an individual who is a principal owner,
   officer, partner, or fiduciary of the parent. This exclusion applies to parent-subsidiary controlled groups only. [Treas Reg
   §§ 1.414(c)-3(b)(4), 1.1563-2(b)(2)(ii)] (See the example at
   the end of this answer.)

4. An interest held by an employee if the interest is subject to
   conditions that run in favor of the organization or a common
   owner of the organization and that substantially restrict or
   limit the employee's right to dispose of the interest. This exclusion applies to both parent-subsidiary and brother-sister
   controlled groups. [Treas Reg §§ 1.414(c)-3(b)(5), 1.414(c)-
   3(c)(3), 1.1563-2(b)(2)(iii), 1.1563-2(b)(4)(ii)]

5. An interest held by a controlled organization exempt from tax
   under Code Section 501(c)(3). This exclusion applies to both
   parent-subsidiary and brother-sister controlled groups. [Treas
   Reg §§ 1.414(c)-3(b)(6), 1.414(c)-3(c)(4), 1.1563-2(b)(2)(iv),
   1.1563-2(b)(4)(iii)]

For purposes of determining whether a group of organizations is a
parent-subsidiary controlled group, these interests are disregarded
only if such group would be considered a parent-subsidiary controlled group if the test for a controlling interest (see Q 9:4) is based
on 50 percent rather than 80 percent. [Treas Reg §§ 1.414(c)-
3(b)(1), 1.1563-2(b)(1)] For purposes of determining whether a
group of organizations is a brother-sister controlled group, these interests are disregarded only if the same five or fewer persons who
are individuals, estates, or trusts own a controlling interest in each

organization based on 50 percent rather than 80 percent. [Treas Reg §§ 1.414(c)-3(c)(1), 1.1563-2(b)(3)]

Example. ABC Partnership owns 70 percent of both the capital and profits interests in the DEF Partnership. The remaining capital and profits interests in DEF are owned as follows: 4 percent by A (a general partner in ABC) and 26 percent by D (a limited partner in ABC). On first impression, ABC and DEF do not form a parent-subsidiary controlled group because ABC does not own at least 80 percent of DEF. But ABC does own at least 50 percent of DEF; thus, as explained in (3) above, the capital and profits interests in DEF owned by A and D, who are partners in ABC, are disregarded for purposes of determining whether ABC and DEF are members of a parent-subsidiary controlled group. By disregarding A's and D's interests in DEF, ABC is considered to own 100 percent of the capital and profits interests in DEF. Accordingly, ABC and DEF are members of a parent-subsidiary controlled group.

Q 9:9 Who is a *principal owner*?

A *principal owner* is an individual who owns 5 percent or more of the parent organization. [Treas Reg §§ 1.414(c)-3(d)(2), 1.1563-2(b)(2)(ii)]

Q 9:10 Who is an *officer*?

An *officer* is an individual who serves in any one of the following capacities for the parent organization: president, vice president, general manager, treasurer, secretary, comptroller, or any other individual who performs duties corresponding to those performed by individuals in those capacities. [Treas Reg §§ 1.414(c)-3(d)(3), 1.1563-2(b)(2)(ii)]

Q 9:11 When will an employee's interest in an organization be considered subject to conditions that substantially restrict the right to dispose of that interest?

Substantial restrictions exist if another person has preferential rights to the acquisition of the employee's interest. A right of first refusal in favor of the other person is an example of such a restriction. However, in some cases, an employee's interest in an organization will not be considered substantially restricted if the conditions apply to all owners of the organization. [Treas Reg §§ 1.414(c)-3(d)(6), 1.1563-2(b)(4)(ii)]

Constructive Ownership Rules

In determining whether organizations are members of a controlled group, a plan must take into account not only the interests in an organization that are directly owned, but also those that are indirectly or constructively owned. Under the constructive ownership rules, an interest held by a person in an organization will, under certain circumstances, be attributed to another person. There are three basic forms of attribution: (1) option, (2) entity, and (3) family.

Q 9:12 What is the *option attribution rule?*

Under the *option attribution rule,* a person who has an option to acquire an outstanding interest in an organization will be considered to own that interest. [Treas Reg §§ 1.414(c)-4(b)(1), 1.1563-3(b)(1)] The option attribution rule takes precedence over all other attribution rules. (See Example 3 in Q 9:20.) [Treas Reg §§ 1.414(c)-4(c)(3), 1.1563-3(c)(3)]

Q 9:13 What is the *entity attribution rule?*

Under the *entity attribution rule,* a person will be treated as the owner of an interest in an organization held by a partnership, estate, trust, or corporation.

Q 9:14 Under what circumstances will an interest in an organization held by a partnership be attributed to another person?

An interest in an organization owned, directly or indirectly, by a partnership will be considered owned by any partner having an interest of 5 percent or more in either the profits or capital interest of the partnership. A partner's attributed ownership will be in proportion to the partner's interest in the profits or capital of the partnership, whichever proportion is larger. [Treas Reg §§ 1.414(c)-4(b)(2), 1.1563-3(b)(2)]

Example. A, B, and C, unrelated individuals, are partners in the

ABC Partnership. The partners' interests in the capital and profits of ABC are as follows:

Partner	Capital (Percentage)	Profits (Percentage)
A	36%	25%
B	60	71
C	4	4

The ABC Partnership owns the entire outstanding stock (100 shares) of X Corporation. A is considered to own the stock of X owned by the ABC Partnership in proportion to his interest in capital (36 percent) or profits (25 percent) of the ABC Partnership, whichever proportion is larger. Therefore, A is considered to own 36 shares (100 × 36%) of X stock. Since B has a greater interest in the profits of the partnership than in the capital, B is considered to own X stock in proportion to his interest in such profits. Therefore, B is considered to own 71 shares (100 × 71%) of X stock. Because C does not have an interest of 5 percent or more in either the capital or profits of the ABC Partnership, he is not considered to own any shares of X stock.

Q 9:15 Under what circumstances will an interest in an organization held by a corporation be attributed to another person?

An interest in an organization owned, directly or indirectly, by a corporation will be considered owned by a shareholder owning 5 percent or more in value of the stock of the corporation. The shareholder's ownership will be proportionate to the value of the stock owned by the shareholder relative to the total value of all stock in the corporation. [Treas Reg §§ 1.414(c)-4(b)(4), 1.1563-3(b)(4)]

Q 9:16 Under what circumstances will an interest in an organization held by an estate or trust be attributed to another person?

An interest in an organization owned, directly or indirectly, by an estate or trust will be considered owned by a beneficiary of the estate or trust if the beneficiary has an actuarial interest of 5 percent or more in the estate or trust. A beneficiary's attributed ownership in the organization will be in proportion to the beneficiary's actuarial interest in the estate or trust. [Treas Reg §§ 1.414(c)-4(b)(3), 1.1563-3(b)(3)]

Q 9:17 What is the *family attribution rule?*

Under the *family attribution rule,* an interest held by the spouse of an individual will generally be attributed to that individual. [Treas Reg §§ 1.414(c)-4(b)(5)(i), 1.1563-3(b)(5)(i)] The family attribution rule also deals with children, grandchildren, parents, and grandparents.

Q 9:18 When will an interest in an organization owned by a spouse not be attributed to an individual?

Spousal attribution will not occur if four conditions are satisfied:

1. The individual does not, at any time during the year, directly own any interest in the organization.
2. The individual is not a member of the board of directors, a fiduciary, or an employee of the organization, and does not participate in the management of the organization at any time during the year.
3. Not more than 50 percent of the organization's gross income is derived from unearned income.
4. The spouse's interest in the organization is not subject to conditions that substantially restrict or limit the spouse's right to dispose of the interest and that run in favor of the individual or the individual's children who have not attained age 21.

[Treas Reg §§ 1.414(c)-4(b)(5)(ii), 1.1563-3(b)(5)(ii)]

Q 9:19 Under what circumstances will an individual's interest in an organization be attributed to a lineal ascendant or descendant?

An individual will be considered to own an interest in an organization owned, directly or indirectly, by his or her child who has not reached age 21. Similarly, if an individual has not reached age 21, that individual will be considered to own an interest in an organization owned, directly or indirectly, by his or her parents. [Treas Reg §§ 1.414(c)-4(b)(6)(i), 1.1563-3(b)(6)(i)]

If an individual has effective control of an organization (see Q 9:6), then that individual will be considered to own any interest in the organization owned, directly or indirectly, by his or her parents, grandparents, grandchildren, and children who have reached age 21. [Treas Reg §§ 1.414(c)-4(b)(6)(ii), 1.1563-3(b)(6)(ii)]

Example. F owns directly 40 percent of the profits interest of the DEF Partnership. His son, M, 20 years of age, owns directly 30 percent of the profits interest of DEF, and his other son, A, 30 years of age, owns directly 20 percent of the profits interest. The remaining 10 percent of the profits interest and 100 percent of the capital interest of DEF are owned by an unrelated person. The attribution of ownership for each individual is determined as follows: F owns 40 percent of the profits interest in DEF directly and is considered to own the 30 percent of profits interest owned directly by M. Consequently, F is treated as owning 70 percent of the profits interest of DEF and, as a result, is in effective control of DEF. With effective control of DEF, F is also considered to own the 20 percent profits interest of DEF owned by his adult son, A. Accordingly, F is considered to own a total of 90 percent of the profits interest in DEF.

Minor son, M, owns 30 percent of the profits interest in DEF directly, and is considered to own the 40 percent profits interest owned directly by his father, F. However, M is not considered to own the 20 percent profits interest of DEF owned directly by his brother, A, and constructively by F, because an interest constructively owned by F by reason of family attribution is not considered as owned by him for purposes of making another member of his family the constructive owner of such interest (see Q 9:20). Therefore, M is considered to own a total of 70 percent of the profits interest of the DEF Partnership.

Adult son, A, owns 20 percent of the profits interest in DEF directly. A is not in effective control of DEF because F's profits interest is not attributed to A. Accordingly, A is considered to own only the 20 percent profits interest in DEF that he owns directly.

Q 9:20 Is there any limit on the number of times an interest in an organization may be attributed?

In general, no. Consequently, an interest constructively owned by a person will be treated as actually owned by the person for the purpose of attributing that ownership to another. However, an interest constructively owned by an individual as a result of the operation of the family attribution rules cannot be reattributed to another family member. [Treas Reg §§ 1.414(c)-4(c)(1), 1.414(c)-4(c)(2), 1.1563-3(c)(1), 1.1563-3(c)(2)]

> **Example 1.** A, 30 years of age, has a 90 percent interest in the capital and profits of DEF Partnership. DEF owns all the outstanding stock of Corporation X, and X owns 60 shares of the 100 outstanding shares of Corporation Y. The 60 shares of Y constructively owned by DEF by reason of the corporation attribution rule are treated as actually owned by DEF for purposes of applying the partnership attribution rule. Therefore, A is considered as owning 54 shares of the Y stock (90 percent of 60 shares).

> **Example 2.** Assume the same facts as in Example 1. Assume further that B, who is 20 years of age and the brother of A, directly owns 40 shares of Y stock. Although the stock of Y owned by B is considered as owned by C (the father of A and B), under the family attribution rule, such stock may not be treated as owned by C for purposes of making A the constructive owner of such stock.

> **Example 3.** Assume the same facts as in Examples 1 and 2. Further assume that C has an option to acquire the 40 shares of Y stock owned by his son, B. In this case, the 40 shares owned by B may be attributed to A because under the precedence given to the option attribution rule (see Q 9:12), C is considered to own the 40 shares by reason of option attribution and not by reason of family attribution. Because A is in effective control of Y, the 40 shares of Y stock constructively owned by C are reattributed to A. A is therefore considered to own a total of 94 shares of Y stock.

Significance of Controlled Groups

Q 9:21 What employee benefit requirements are affected by the controlled group rules?

If two or more organizations are members of the same controlled group, then the employees of all such members will be treated as if they were employed by a single employer when applying the following qualification requirements:

1. General qualification requirements under Code Section 401;

2. Minimum participation and coverage standards under Code Section 410;

3. Minimum vesting standards under Code Section 411;

4. Limitations on benefits and contributions under Code Section 415; and

5. Special rules for top-heavy plans under Code Section 416.

[IRC §§ 414(b), 414(c)]

It should be noted that for purposes of applying Code Section 415, a controlling interest in a parent-subsidiary controlled group will be based on ownership of more than 50 percent rather than 80 percent (see Q 9:4). [IRC § 415(h)]

Affiliated Service Groups

Even in cases where there may not be sufficient common ownership to form a controlled group, the employees of an *affiliated service group* are treated, for various employee benefit requirements, as if they were employed by a single employer.

Q 9:22 What are the types of affiliated service groups?

There are three types of affiliated service groups. One type consists of a first service organization (FSO) and one or more A-organizations (A-orgs). [IRC § 414(m)(2)(A)] The second consists of an FSO and one or more B-organizations (B-orgs). [IRC § 414(m)(2)(B)] The third variety is composed of a management organization and any organization that is the recipient of the management-type services provided by it. [IRC § 414(m)(5)]

Q 9:23 What is a *first service organization*?

A *first service organization*, or an FSO, is a service organization. [Prop Treas Reg § 1.414(m)-2(a)] However, a corporation that is not a professional service corporation under state law cannot be treated as an FSO with respect to any A-orgs. [Prop Treas Reg § 1.414(m)-1(c)]

Q 9:24 What is an *organization*?

An *organization* includes a sole proprietorship, partnership, corporation, or any other type of entity regardless of its ownership format. [Prop Treas Reg § 1.414(m)-2(e)]

Q 9:25 What is a *service organization*?

An organization will be considered a *service organization* if capital is not a material income-producing factor for the organization. Generally, capital will be considered a material income-producing factor if a substantial portion of the gross income of the business is attributable to the employment of capital in the business, as reflected in substantial investments in inventories, plant, and equipment. However, capital is not a material income-producing factor if the gross income of the business consists primarily of fees, commissions, and other compensation for personal services rendered. Any organization engaged in any one of the following fields will be deemed a service organization: health, law, engineering, architecture, accounting, actuarial science, performing arts, consulting, and insurance. [Prop Treas Reg §§ 1.414(m)-2(f)(1), 1.414(m)-2(f)(2)]

Q 9:26 What is an *A-org*?

An *A-org* is a service organization that is a partner or shareholder in an FSO (regardless of the percentage interest it owns, or constructively owns, in the FSO) and regularly performs services for the FSO or is regularly associated with the FSO in performing services for third persons. [Prop Treas Reg § 1.414(m)-2(b)]

Example. Attorney N is incorporated, and the corporation is a partner in a law firm. Attorney N and his corporation are regularly associated with the law firm in performing services for third persons. Considering the law firm as an FSO, the corporation is an A-org because it is regularly associated with the law firm in performing services for third persons. Accordingly, the corporation and the law firm constitute an affiliated service group.

Q 9:27 How does one determine whether a service organization regularly performs services for an FSO or is regularly associated with an FSO in performing services for third persons?

This determination is made on the basis of all relevant facts and circumstances. The proposed regulations indicate that one relevant factor is the amount of income derived by the service organization from performing services for the FSO or from performing services for third persons in association with the FSO. [Prop Treas Reg § 1.414(m)-2(b)(2)]

Q 9:28 What is a *B-org*?

An organization will be considered a *B-org* if three requirements are satisfied:

1. A significant portion of the business of the organization is the performance of services for the FSO, for one or more A-orgs determined with respect to the FSO, or for both.

2. The services are of a type historically performed by employees in the service field of the FSO or the A-orgs.

3. Ten percent or more of the interest in the organization is owned, directly or indirectly, in the aggregate by persons who are highly compensated employees (HCEs) (see Qs 9:74–9:96) of the FSO or the A-orgs.

[IRC § 414(m)(2)(B); Prop Treas Reg § 1.414(m)-2(c)(1)]

Q 9:29 What constitutes a significant portion of the business of the organization?

The performance of services for an FSO, for one or more A-orgs, or for both, will be considered a significant portion of the business of an organization if the total receipts percentage is 10 percent or more. On the other hand, the performance of services for an FSO, for one or more A-orgs, or for both will not be considered a significant portion of the business of an organization if the service receipts percentage is less than 5 percent. If neither of these mechanical tests applies, then the determination will be based on all relevant facts and circumstances. [Prop Treas Reg §§ 1.414(m)-2(c)(2)(i), 1.414(m)-2(c)(2)(ii), 1.414(m)-2(c)(2)(iii)]

Q 9:30 What is the *service receipts percentage?*

The *service receipts percentage* is the ratio of the gross receipts of the organization derived from performing services for an FSO, for one or more A-orgs, or for both, to the total gross receipts of the organization derived from performing services. This ratio is the greater of the ratio for the year for which the determination is being made, or for the three-year period including that year and the two preceding years. [Prop Treas Reg § 1.414(m)-2(c)(2)(iv)]

Q 9:31 What is the *total receipts percentage?*

The *total receipts percentage* is calculated in the same manner as the service receipts percentage, except that gross receipts in the denominator of the ratio are determined without regard to whether such gross receipts are derived from performing services. [Prop Treas Reg § 1.414(m)-2(c)(2)(v)]

Example. The income of Corporation X is derived from both performing services and other business activities. The amount of its receipts derived from performing services for Corporation Z and the total receipts for all other customers are set forth below.

Origin of Income		Corporation Z	All Customers
Year 1	Services	$ 4,000	$100,000
	Other		20,000
	Total		120,000
Year 2	Services	9,000	150,000
	Other		30,000
	Total		180,000
Year 3	Services	42,000	200,000
	Other		40,000
	Total		240,000

In year 1 (the first year of existence of Corporation X), the service receipts percentage for Corporation X (for its business with Corporation Z) is less than 5 percent ($4,000/$100,000, or 4 percent). Thus, performing services for Corporation Z will not be considered a significant portion of the business of Corporation X.

In year 2, the service receipts percentage is the greater of the ratio for that year ($9,000/$150,000, or 6 percent) or for years 1 and 2 combined ($13,000/$250,000, or 5.2 percent), which is 6 percent. The total receipts percentage is the greater of the ratio for that year ($9,000/$180,000, or 5 percent) or for years 1 and 2 combined ($13,000/$300,000, or 4.3 percent), which is 5 percent. Because the service receipts percentage is greater than 5 percent and the total receipts percentage is less than 10 percent, whether performing services for Corporation Z constitutes a significant portion of the business of Corporation X is determined by the facts and circumstances.

In year 3, the service receipts percentage is the greater of the ratio for that year ($42,000/$200,000, or 21 percent) or for years 1, 2, and 3 combined ($55,000/$450,000, or 12.2 percent), which is 21 percent. The total receipts percentage is the greater of the ratio for year 3 ($42,000/$240,000, or 17.5 percent) or for years 1, 2, and 3 combined ($55,000/$540,000, or 10.1 percent), which is 17.5 percent. Because the total receipts percentage is greater than 10 percent and the service receipts percentage is not less than 5 percent, a significant portion of the business of Corporation X is considered to be the performance of services for Corporation Z.

Q 9:32 When will services be considered of a type historically performed by employees in the service field of the FSO or A-orgs?

Services will be considered of a type historically performed by employees in a particular service field if it was not unusual for the services to be performed by employees of organizations in that service field (in the United States) on December 13, 1980. [Prop Treas Reg § 1.414(m)-2(c)(3)]

Q 9:33 Under what circumstances will multiple affiliated service groups be aggregated?

Multiple affiliated service groups will be aggregated and treated as one affiliated service group if the affiliated service groups have a common FSO. [Prop Treas Reg § 1.414(m)-2(g)]

Q 9:34 What constructive ownership rules apply in determining whether an A-org has an ownership interest in an FSO or whether a 10 percent interest in a B-org is held by the HCEs of the FSO, A-org, or both?

The constructive ownership rules of Code Section 318(a) apply for this purpose. [IRC § 414(m)(6)(B)]

Q 9:35 In the case of a management-type affiliated service group, when is an organization considered a *management organization*?

An organization will be considered a *management organization* if the principal business of the organization is to perform, on a regular and continuing basis, management functions for a recipient organization. [IRC § 414(m)(5)] Proposed regulations, which were withdrawn in April 1993, contained complicated rules for determining whether the principal business of the organization is the performance of management functions. [Prop Treas Reg § 1.414(m)-5(b)]

Q 9:36 What are considered *management functions*?

The Code does not define management functions. According to the now defunct proposed regulations, *management functions* include only those activities and services historically performed by employees such as determining, implementing, or supervising (or providing advice or assistance in accomplishing) any of the following:

1. Daily business operations;
2. Personnel;
3. Employee compensation and benefits; or
4. Organizational structure and ownership.

[Prop Treas Reg § 1.414(m)-5(c)(1)]

Q 9:37 What employee benefit requirements are affected by the affiliated service group rules?

If two or more organizations are members of the same affiliated service group, the employees of all such members will be treated as if they were employed by a single employer when applying any of the following employee benefit requirements:

1. Minimum participation and coverage standards under Code Section 410;

2. The nondiscrimination requirements under Code Section 401(a)(4);

3. Minimum vesting standards under Code Section 411;

4. Limitations on benefits and contributions under Code Section 415;

5. The $150,000 (as adjusted) cap on compensation under Code Section 401(a)(17);

6. Special rules for top-heavy plans under Code Section 416; or

7. For plan years beginning before 1997 in the case of defined contribution plans, the minimum participation rules under Code Section 401(a)(26).

[IRC § 414(m)(4)]

Qualified Separate Lines of Business (QSLOBs)

Generally, all employees of corporations that are members of the same controlled group of corporations and all employees of trades or businesses under common control are treated as employed by a single employer for purposes of applying nondiscrimination and other qualification requirements. Similarly, all employees of members of an affiliated service group are considered employed by a single employer. Generally, the minimum participation rules, with respect to plan years of defined contribution plans beginning before 1997, and the minimum coverage rules (discussed in chapter 10) are applied only after the application of these controlled group and affiliated service group provisions. There is an exception to this general rule, however, in the case of the controlled group rules. If an employer operates two or more qualified separate lines of business (QSLOBs), the minimum participation and coverage rules can be applied separately to each QSLOB. At the end of this section, Flow-chart 9-1 outlines the operation of the QSLOB rules.

Q 9:38 What is a *qualified separate line of business*?

A *qualified separate line of business* (QSLOB) is a line of business that is also a separate line of business and that meets the following requirements:

1. The separate line of business has 50 employees. [Treas Reg § 1.414(r)-4(b)]

2. The employer notifies the IRS on Form 5310-A that it is apply-ing the QSLOB rules. [Treas Reg § 1.414(r)-4(c)]

3. The separate line of business passes administrative scrutiny. [Treas Reg § 1.414(r)-1(b)(2)]

Q 9:39 What is a *line of business*?

A *line of business* (LOB) is a portion of the employer identified by the property and services sold to customers in the ordinary course of the conduct of a trade or business. [Treas Reg §§ 1.414(r)-2(a), 1.414(r)-2(b)(2)]

Q 9:40 How does an employer designate LOBs?

An employer must first identify all property and services pro-vided to customers. Then the employer may designate which prop-erty and services will be provided by each LOB. [Treas Reg § 1.414(r)-2(b)(1)] All such property and services must be assigned to an LOB. [Treas Reg § 1.414(r)-2(b)(3)(i)]

Q 9:41 Must an LOB provide only one type or related types of property and services?

No. The employer may combine dissimilar types of property or services within one LOB. [Treas Reg § 1.414(r)-2(b)(3)(ii)]

Example. Employer A is a domestic conglomerate engaged in the manufacture and sale of consumer food and beverage prod-ucts and the provision of data processing services to private industry. Employer A also owns and operates a regional com-muter airline, a professional basketball team, a pharmaceutical manufacturer, and a leather-tanning company. Employer A apportions all the property and services it provides to its customers among three LOBs, one providing all its consumer food and beverage products, a second providing all its data processing services, and a third providing all the other property and services provided to customers through Employer A's regional commuter airline, professional basketball team, pharmaceutical manufacturer, and leather-tanning company. Even though the third LOB includes dissimilar types of property and services that are otherwise unrelated to one another, Employer A is permitted to combine these in a single LOB. Thus, Employer A has three LOBs.

Q 9:42 Is an employer required to combine within one LOB all property or services of a related type?

No. An employer may designate two or more LOBs that provide related or the same types of property or services. However, the employer's designation must be reasonable. Designations would be reasonable, for example, if the product or services of related types or the same type are manufactured, prepared, or provided in different geographic areas, in different levels in the chain of commercial distribution (wholesale or retail), in different types of transactions (sale or lease), or for different types of customers (government or private). A designation would be unreasonable, for example, if two types of related property or services are not provided separately to customers, or if one type of property or service is ancillary to another. [Treas Reg § 1.414(r)-2(b)(3)(iii)]

Example 1. Employer B is a diversified engineering firm offering civil, chemical, and aeronautical engineering services to government and private industry. Employer B provides no other property or services to its customers. Employer B operates the aeronautical engineering services portion of its business as two separate divisions, one serving federal government customers and the other serving customers in private industry. Employer B apportions all the property and services it provides to its customers among four LOBs, one providing all its civil engineering services, a second providing all its chemical engineering services, a third providing aeronautical engineering services to federal government customers, and a fourth providing aeronautical engineering services to customers in private industry. Even though the third and fourth

LOBs include the same type of service (i.e., aeronautical engineering services), Employer B is permitted to separate its aeronautical engineering services into two LOBs, since they are provided to different types of customers.

Example 2. Among its other business activities, Employer C manufactures industrial diesel generators. At no additional cost to its buyers, Employer C warrants the proper functioning of its diesel generators for a one-year period following sale. Pursuant to its warranty, Employer C provides labor and parts to repair or replace any components that malfunction within the one-year warranty period. Because Employer C does not provide the industrial diesel generators and the warranty repair services and replacement parts separately to its customers, it would be unreasonable for Employer C to separate this property and these services in different LOBs.

Q 9:43 What is a *separate line of business*?

A *separate line of business* (SLOB) is an LOB that is organized and operated separately from the remaining businesses of the employer. [Treas Reg § 1.414(r)-3(a)] A SLOB must meet all four of the following requirements:

1. The LOB must be formally organized as a separate organizational unit or group of separate organizational units. An organizational unit is a corporation, partnership, division, or other unit having a similar degree of organizational formality. [Treas Reg § 1.414(r)-3(b)(2)]
2. The LOB must be a separate profit center or group of separate profit centers. [Treas Reg § 1.414(r)-3(b)(3)]
3. The LOB must have its own, separate workforce. [Treas Reg § 1.414(r)-3(b)(4)]
4. The LOB must have its own, separate management. [Treas Reg § 1.414(r)-3(b)(5)]

Q 9:44 When does an LOB have its own, separate workforce?

An LOB has its own, separate workforce only if at least 90 percent of the employees who provide services to the LOB are substantial-service employees (see Q 9:45) with respect to the LOB and are not substantial-service employees with respect to any other line of business. [Treas Reg § 1.414(r)-3(b)(4)]

Q 9:45 What is a *substantial-service employee?*

An employee is a *substantial-service employee* with respect to an LOB if at least 75 percent of the employee's services are provided to that LOB. In addition, if an employee provides at least 50 percent of his or her services to an LOB, the employer may treat the employee as a substantial-service employee. [Treas Reg § 1.414(r)-11(b)(2)]

Q 9:46 When is an employee considered to provide services to an LOB?

An employee is considered to provide services to an LOB if more than a negligible portion of the employee's services contribute to the production of the property or services provided by the LOB. [Treas Reg § 1.414(r)-3(c)(5)(i)]

Q 9:47 How does an employer determine what percentage, if any, of an employee's services are provided to an LOB?

The most recent version of the final regulations does not provide any guidance. The initial version of the regulations provided that the employer must make these determinations in a manner that is reasonably reliable with respect to all employees and uniform with respect to similarly situated employees.

Example. Employer A's first LOB manufactures and sells construction machinery, its second LOB manufactures and sells agricultural equipment, and its third LOB manufactures and sells tires. As part of these LOBs, Employer A operates construction machinery, agricultural equipment, and tire factories on the same site. Employer A's facilities at this site include a health clinic and a fitness center that serve the employees of the construction machinery, agricultural equipment, and tire factories. Employee O is a nurse in the health clinic and Employee P is a fitness instructor in the fitness center. Both employees therefore provide services to Employer A's construction machinery LOB, agricultural equipment LOB, and tire factory LOB. In addition, Employer A determines that approximately 33 percent of the services of Employee O and Employee P are provided to each of Employer A's

LOBs. As a result, neither Employee O nor Employee P provides at least 75 percent of their respective services to any of Employer A's LOBs. Therefore, Employee O and Employee P are not substantial-service employees with respect to any of Employer A's three LOBs.

Q 9:48 When does an LOB have its own, separate management?

An LOB has its own, separate management if at least 80 percent of the employees who are top-paid employees with respect to an LOB are substantial-service employees. [Treas Reg § 1.414(r)-3(b)(5)]

Q 9:49 Who are the top-paid employees?

An employee is a top-paid employee with respect to an LOB if the employee is not a substantial-service employee with respect to any other LOB and is among the top 10 percent by compensation of those employees who provide services to that LOB. In determining top-paid employees, an employer must disregard all employees who provide less than 25 percent of their services to the LOB. [Treas Reg § 1.414(r)-11(b)(3)]

Example. Employer D operates four LOBs. One of its LOBs is a machine tool shop. Sixty of Employer D's employees provide at least 25 percent of their services to the machine tool shop. Of the 6 employees who constitute the top 10 percent by compensation of those 60 employees, 4 are substantial-service employees with respect to the LOB. Only 67 percent (4/6) of the top-paid employees with respect to the machine tool shop LOB are substantial-service employees with respect to that LOB. Therefore, the machine tool shop LOB does not satisfy the separate management requirement because less than 80 percent of the top-paid employees are substantial-service employees.

Q 9:50 How does a SLOB satisfy the administrative-scrutiny requirement?

A SLOB satisfies the administrative-scrutiny requirement if it satisfies a statutory safe harbor or one of several regulatory safe harbors. A SLOB that does not satisfy a safe harbor may still satisfy the administrative-scrutiny requirement if the IRS so determines. [Treas Reg §§ 1.414(r)-5(a), 1.414(r)-6]

Q 9:51 How does a SLOB satisfy the statutory safe harbor?

A SLOB satisfies the statutory safe harbor if the HCE percentage ratio of a SLOB is at least 50 percent and not more than 200 percent. [Treas Reg § 1.414(r)-5(b)(1)] A SLOB is deemed to satisfy the statutory safe harbor if at least 10 percent of all HCEs provide services to the SLOB and do not provide services to any other SLOBs. [Treas Reg § 1.414(r)-5(b)(4)]

Q 9:52 What is the *HCE percentage ratio*?

The *HCE percentage ratio* is a fraction, the numerator of which is the percentage of employees of the SLOB who are HCEs and the denominator of which is the percentage of all employees of the employer who are HCEs. [Treas Reg § 1.414(r)-5(b)(2)] (For the definition of HCE see Qs 9:74–9:96.)

Example. Employer B operates three SLOBs: a dairy products manufacturer, a candy manufacturer, and a chain of housewares stores. Employer B employs a total of 1,000 employees, 100 of whom are HCEs. Thus, the percentage of all employees of Employer B who are HCEs is 10 percent. The distribution of HCEs and non-highly compensated employees (NHCEs) among Employer B's SLOBs is as follows.

	Employer-wide	Dairy Products	Candy Mfg	Housewares Stores
Number of employees	1,000	200	500	300
Number of HCEs	100	5	50	45
Number of NHCEs	900	195	450	255
HCE percentage	10 (100/1,000)	2.5 (5/200)	10 (50/500)	15 (45/300)
HCE percentage ratio	N/A	25 (2.5/10)	100 (10/10)	150 (15/10)

Because the HCE percentage ratio for the dairy products LOB is less than 50 percent, it does not satisfy the requirements of the statutory safe harbor. However, because Employer B's other two SLOBs (candy manufacturing and housewares stores) each have an HCE percentage ratio that is no less than 50 percent and no greater than 200 percent, they each satisfy the statutory safe harbor. To qualify its dairy products SLOB as a QSLOB, Employer B may be able to apply one of the regulatory safe harbors or seek an individual determination by the IRS. Employer B could also combine the dairy products LOB with either of its other LOBs.

Q 9:53 What are the regulatory safe harbors?

There are five regulatory safe harbors:

1. *The different industries safe harbor.* This safe harbor applies if the products and services of the SLOB fall exclusively within one or more industry categories established by the IRS. [Treas Reg § 1.414(r)-5(c)]

2. *The mergers and acquisitions (M&A) safe harbor.* This safe harbor applies if an employer acquires an LOB that, after the acquisition, constitutes a SLOB. This safe harbor may be used for up to four years after the acquisition. [Treas Reg § 1.414(r)-5(d)]

3. *The industry segments safe harbor.* This safe harbor applies if a SLOB is reported as one or more industry segments (SIC code) on annual reports required to be filed under U.S. securities laws. [Treas Reg § 1.414(r)-5(e)]

4. *The average benefits safe harbor.* This safe harbor applies in two situations. If a SLOB has an HCE percentage ratio of less than 50 percent, the safe harbor applies if the average benefits provided to the SLOB's NHCEs are not less than the average benefits provided to other NHCEs. If a SLOB has an HCE percentage ratio of more than 200 percent, the safe harbor applies if the average benefits provided to the SLOB's HCEs are not greater than the average benefits provided to other HCEs. [Treas Reg § 1.414(r)-5(f)]

5. *The minimum or maximum benefits safe harbor.* This safe harbor operates to provide minimum benefits to NHCEs of a

SLOB with an HCE percentage ratio of less than 50 percent. On the other hand, if a SLOB's HCE percentage ratio is greater than 200 percent, the safe harbor operates to place maximums on the benefits accrued by HCEs of the SLOB. [Treas Reg § 1.414(r)-5(g)]

Q 9:54 How are employees allocated to a QSLOB?

All substantial-service employees of a QSLOB must be assigned to that QSLOB. [Treas Reg § 1.414(r)-7(b)(2)(i)] All residual shared employees (see Q 9:55) must be assigned to a QSLOB under one of the following three allocation methods:

1. *Dominant line of business method of allocation.* Under this method, all residual shared employees are assigned to the QSLOB to which at least 50 percent of the substantial-service employees of the employer are allocated. In some circumstances, this percentage can be reduced to 25 percent. [Treas Reg § 1.414(r)-7(c)(2)]

2. *Pro rata method of allocation.* Under this method, the number of residual shared employees to be assigned to a QSLOB will be in proportion to the substantial-service employees allocated to that QSLOB. This determination is done separately for HCEs and NHCEs. After the number of residual shared employees to be assigned to the QSLOB is determined, the employer may choose which residual shared employees will be allocated to the QSLOB. [Treas Reg § 1.414(r)-7(c)(3)]

3. *HCE percentage ratio method of allocation.* This method is similar to the pro rata method except that the number of residual shared employees to be assigned to a QSLOB is determined solely with reference to the percentage of the employer's HCEs that have already been assigned to a QSLOB. [Treas Reg § 1.414(r)-7(c)(4)]

Q 9:55 What is a *residual shared employee*?

A *residual shared employee* with respect to an LOB is an employee who provides services to an LOB but who is not a substantial-service employee with respect to any LOB. [Treas Reg § 1.414(r)-11(b)(4)]

Flowchart 9-1. Qualified Separate Lines of Business (QSLOBs)

START

Line of Business § 1.414(r)-2

Determine all Property and services provided to customers and designate portion thereof provided by the line of business

Separate Line of Business § 1.414(r)-3

Separate organizational unit? — Yes
Separate financial accountability? — Yes
Separate employee workforce? — Yes
Separate management? — Yes

No / No / No / No → This is not a QSLOB. Return to start and redesignate lines of business

Qualified Separate Line Business § 1.414(r)-4, 5 & 6

50 employees? — Yes → Notice to secretary? — Yes
No / No →

Administrative scrutiny requirement options

Statutory safe harbor? — Yes
or
SIC code safe harbor? — Yes
or
FAS 14 safe harbor? — Yes
or
M & A safe harbor? — Yes
or
Average benefits safe harbor? — Yes
or
Min/max benefits safe harbor? — Yes
or
Individual determination? — Yes
No →

This is a QSLOB

Are all property and services provided exclusively by QSLOBS? — Yes
No
Return to start and determine if other portions of employer are QSLOBS

Employer is treated as operating QSLOBs under Section 414(r)!

END

WHAT IS A PLAN?

Nondiscrimination rules are applied to plans. The word *plan* in this context is a term of art and may differ from the commonsense notion of what a plan is. The determination of a plan for purposes of applying the nondiscrimination rules is a two-step process. First, separate asset pools are identified. Second, each separate asset pool is broken into two or more parts under the mandatory disaggregation rules. Each of the resulting parts is considered a plan.

Q 9:56 What is a *separate asset pool?*

Under the regulations, a *separate asset pool* exists if all plan assets are available to pay benefits to participants and their beneficiaries. It remains a separate asset pool even though there are several distinct benefit structures or multiple documents. A separate asset pool is not affected by the fact that two or more employers—whether affiliated or not—make contributions or that assets are invested in several trusts or annuity contracts. [Treas Reg § 1.414(l)-1(b)(1)]

> **Example.** Company A sponsors a 401(k) plan covering its two divisions, C and D. The contributions made by Division C's employees are invested in a trust separate from the trust maintained for employees of Division D. Benefits are payable only from the trust established for the division for which an employee works. In this example, Company A would be treated as maintaining two separate asset pools.

Q 9:57 Is more than one separate asset pool created if participants have the right to direct the investment of their own account balances?

No. Also, multiple asset pools are not created merely because assets are invested in individual insurance or annuity contracts. [Treas Reg §§ 1.401(k)-1(g)(11)(i), 1.410(b)-7(b)]

Q 9:58 What are the mandatory disaggregation rules?

The mandatory disaggregation rules operate to divide a separate asset pool into two or more parts. Each resulting part is considered a plan to which the nondiscrimination rules are applied.

Q 9:59 Under what circumstances are the mandatory disaggregation rules applied?

The mandatory disaggregation rules are applied under any of the six circumstances described below.

1. *Plans benefiting collective bargaining employees.* A plan that benefits both collective bargaining employees and employees not included in a collective bargaining unit is treated as two plans. If more than one collective bargaining unit is covered, a separate plan is deemed to exist for each collective bargaining unit. Under the Section 401(k) regulations, however, at the employer's option, two or more collective bargaining units may be treated as a single collective bargaining unit as long as the combination of units is determined on a basis that is reasonable and is reasonably consistent from year to year. This disaggregation rule is not mandatory for purposes of applying the Section 401(a)(26) minimum participation requirements to pre-1997 plan years, thus making it easier for a plan to satisfy these requirements. [Treas Reg §§ 1.401(a)(26)-2(d)(2)(i), 1.401(k)-1(g)(11)(ii)(B), 1.410(b)-7(c)(4)(ii)(B)]

Example. Company A sponsors a 401(k) plan that covers employees who are members of collective bargaining units X, Y, and Z. The plan also covers nonunion employees of Company A. For purposes of applying the Section 410(b) minimum coverage requirements, the plan is considered to be four separate plans. In applying the special nondiscrimination rules that apply to elective contributions, Company A may treat the plan as four separate plans or may combine two or all three collective bargaining units so that the combined units are treated as a separate plan. Company A may, but is not required to, treat the plan as four separate plans for purposes of applying the Section 401(a)(26) minimum participation requirements to pre-1997 plan years.

2. *Plans benefiting employees of qualified separate lines of business (QSLOBs).* If an employer is treated as operating QSLOBs, a plan covering the employees of two or more QSLOBs will be treated as consisting of as many plans as the employer has QSLOBs. (See Q 9:38.) [Treas Reg §§ 1.401(a)(26)-2(d)(1)(iv), 1.401(k)-1(g)(11)(i), 1.410(b)-7(c)(4)(ii)(A)] This mandatory disaggregation rule does not apply, however if the plan is tested under the special rule for employer-wide plans. (See chapter 10.)

3. *Multiple-employer plans.* A plan that is maintained by two or more employers that are not members of the same controlled group or affiliated service group and that benefits only non-collective bargaining employees is subdivided into as many plans as there are employers maintaining the plan. [Treas Reg §§ 1.401(a)(26)-2(d)(1)(ii)(A), 1.401(k)-1(g)(11)(ii)(C), 1.410(b)-7(c)(4)(ii)(C)]

> **Example.** Alpha and Omega maintain a 401(k) plan for their nonunion employees. There is a certain amount of common ownership but not enough to cause Alpha and Omega to be considered part of the same controlled group. For purposes of applying all nondiscrimination rules, the 401(k) plan will be treated as two plans, one maintained by Alpha and the other by Omega.

4. *Multiemployer plans.* A plan maintained by multiple, unrelated employers for the benefit of their collective bargaining employees will be treated as a single plan. However, if the plan also covers non-collective bargaining employees, the portion of the plan covering those employees will be treated as a separate plan. [Treas Reg §§ 1.401(a)(26)-2(d)(1)(ii)(B), 1.401(k)-1(g)(11)(ii)(C)]

5. *Plans of different contribution types.* A plan must be disaggregated on the basis of the types of contributions made to it. The part of a plan that provides for elective contributions under Code Section 401(k) will be treated as a separate plan for purposes of the minimum coverage and nondiscrimination rules. The part of a plan that provides for employer matching contributions, employee after-tax contributions, or both, is similarly treated as a separate plan. Finally, if a plan provides for nonelective contributions (for example, discretionary profit-sharing contributions), that portion of the plan will also be treated as a separate plan. [Treas Reg § 1.410(b)-7(c)(1)] It should be noted that mandatory disaggregation on the basis of contribution type does not apply for purposes of the minimum participation rules.

> **Example.** Beta Company sponsors a 401(k) plan under which elective contributions made by employees are matched by Beta Company. Beta Company also makes discretionary profit-sharing contributions. For purposes of the minimum coverage and nondiscrimination requirements, this plan is treated as three separate plans.

6. *ESOPs and non-ESOPs.* The portion of a plan that is an employee stock ownership plan (ESOP) and the portion of a plan that is not are treated as separate plans. [Treas Reg §§ 1.401(a)(26)-2(d)(1)(i), 1.401(k)-1(g)(11)(i), 1.410(b)-7(c)(2)]

WHO IS AN EMPLOYEE?

401(k) plans, like all other qualified plans, are established and maintained by employers for the exclusive benefit of employees. Since 1962, the advantages of qualified plans have been extended to self-employed individuals—partners in partnerships and sole proprietors. The potential pool of qualified plan participants was expanded in 1982 to require employers, under certain circumstances, to cover individuals who were not its employees as a result of the leased-employee rules.

Q 9:60 Are self-employed individuals considered employees?

Yes. Self-employed individuals (partners in partnerships and sole proprietors) are deemed employees of the businesses they own under Code Section 401(c).

Q 9:61 Are leased employees considered employees?

During the late 1970s and early 1980s, Congress became concerned about employers' excluding employees from retirement plans through leased-employee arrangements. Under these arrangements, employers would dismiss their employees, who would then become employees of leasing organizations. Leasing organizations would then contract with employers for the services of their former employees.

In response to these arrangements, Congress passed the leased-employee rules. In general, these rules require employers to take into account leased employees for various employee benefit requirements. For example, an individual who is a leased employee must be treated as an employee when the minimum participation and coverage rules are applied. (See chapter 10.) Also, a leased employee will be considered an employee for purposes of identifying an employer's HCEs.

Example. LMN Company, which sponsors a 401(k) plan for its employees, has made the top-paid group election described in Q 9:88. During the look-back year ending December 31, 1998, LMN Company has 40 employees and 80 leased employees who cannot be excluded under the provisions described in Q 9:84. The maximum number of employees in the top-paid group is 24 (120 × 20%) because leased employees must be treated as if they were employees for this purpose. If the leased employees were not considered employees, the maximum number of employees in the top-paid group would be 8 (40 × 20%).

Since 1988, the primary guidance in the leased employee area was provided through proposed regulations. In April 1993, however, these regulations were withdrawn. In this section reference will be made to these now-withdrawn proposed regulations where the law or Notice 84-11 (which is the sole IRS guidance in this area) fails to elaborate upon certain employee leasing rules.

Q 9:62 What is the definition of a *leased employee*?

A *leased employee* is any individual who provides services to a recipient in a capacity other than as an employee of the recipient and with respect to whom the following three requirements are met:

1. The services of the individual are provided pursuant to one or more agreements between the recipient and a leasing organization.

2. The individual has performed services for the recipient on a substantially full-time basis for a period of at least one year.

3. The individual's services are performed under the primary direction or control of the recipient.

Prior to 1997, the employee leasing rules required that the services performed for the recipient be of a type that were historically performed by employees in the business field of the recipient. With the passage of the Small Business Job Protection Act of 1996 (SBJPA), the historical-performance requirement was replaced by the primary-direction-or-control requirement in item 3 above.

Q 9:63 Must an agreement between the recipient and a leasing organization be in writing?

The agreement need not be in writing. According to the now-withdrawn proposed regulations, an agreement includes any mutual understanding that the leasing organization will provide individuals to perform services for the recipient. The regulation also states that an agreement will be deemed to exist with respect to an individual if a leasing organization receives or is entitled to receive payment from the recipient in exchange for providing the individual performing services for the recipient. [Prop Reg § 1.414(n)-1(b)(5); Notice 84-11, Q&A 6]

Q 9:64 When is an individual considered to have performed services on a substantially full-time basis for a period of at least one year?

An individual is considered to have performed services on a substantially full-time basis for a period of at least one year if the individual is credited with

1. At least 1,500 hours of service; or

2. At least 75 percent of the average number of hours of service credited during the same period to employees of the recipient who perform similar services for the recipient.

In determining whether this requirement is satisfied, Notice 84-11 looks to any period of 12 consecutive months. The withdrawn regulation was more specific. Under it the period for determining hours of service is based on the 12-month period beginning on the date an individual first performs services for the recipient or any subsequent plan year of the recipient's plan as illustrated in the example below. [Prop Reg § 1.414(n)-1(b)(10)(i); Notice 84-11, Q&A 7]

Example. Dr. Jones employs three nurses; Richard, Sue, and Bob, who work 2,000, 1,800, and 1,200 hours, respectively, per year. Thus, the average number of hours of service performed by Dr. Jones's nurse-employees is 1,667. On July 15, 1998, Dr. Jones contracts with a leasing organization for the services of nurse Jane. During the 12-month period ending July 15, 1999, Jane completes 1,200 hours of service. Jane is not a leased employee at the end of this initial 12-month period because 1,200 hours of service is less than 1,500 hours and is also less than 75 percent of the average number of hours of service worked by employee nurses in Dr. Jones's office (1,667 hours × 75% = 1,250 hours). Dr. Jones's 401(k) plan has a calendar plan year. During calendar year 1999, Jane completes 1,400 hours of service. On December 31, 1999, Jane becomes a leased employee because 1,400 hours of service is greater than 75 percent of the average number of hours of service worked by the employee nurses.

Q 9:65 Is there an alternative way to determine whether an individual is considered substantially full-time?

Under the withdrawn proposed regulations, a recipient may treat any individual who has more than 1,000 hours of service during the period for determining hours of service (see Q 9:64) as substantially full-time. Using this alternative eliminates the need to determine who, if any, of the employees of the recipient are performing services similar to those provided by the individual. [Prop Reg § 1.414(n)-1(b)(10)(ii)]

Q 9:66 When will an individual cease to be considered a leased employee?

The withdrawn proposed regulations (but not Notice 84-11, which does not deal with this question) provided that an individual will cease to be considered a leased employee if the number of consecutive nonqualifying years equals or exceeds the greater of five or the total number of qualifying years. A nonqualifying year is a year during which the individual works fewer than 501 hours of service for the recipient. [Prop Reg § 1.414(n)-1(b)(13)]

Example. Larry has performed services for Dr. Bob substantially full-time since May 1, 1992. On December 31, 1997, Larry ceases to perform services for Dr. Bob, who maintains a calendar-year plan. As of December 31, 1997, Larry has six qualifying years (1993–1997, plus the period May 1, 1992–May 1, 1993). Larry resumes performing services for Dr. Bob on January 1, 2000. Larry is considered a leased employee on January 1, 2000, because the number of qualifying years (six) exceeds the number of nonqualifying years (two: 1998 and 1999).

Q 9:67 When will services be considered performed under the primary direction or control of the recipient?

According to the committee reports to SBJPA Section 1454, whether services are performed by an individual under primary direction or control by the recipient depends on the facts and circumstances. In general, primary direction and control means that the recipient exercises the majority of direction and control over the individual. Factors that are relevant in determining whether primary direction or control exists include whether the individual is required to comply with instructions of the recipient about when, where, and how he or she is to perform the services, whether the services must be performed by a particular person, whether the individual is subject to the supervision of the recipient, and whether the individual must perform services in the order or sequence set by the recipient.

Factors that generally are not relevant in determining whether direction or control exists include whether the recipient has the right to hire or fire the individual and whether the individual also works for others.

Q 9:68 What was the *historical-performance test* for leased employees?

The *historical-performance test,* which, as pointed out in Q 9:62, no longer applies for plan years beginning after 1996, determines whether the services provided by individuals to recipients are the types of services that have been historically performed by employees in the business field of the recipient. Services are considered historically performed by employees in a particular business field if it was not unusual for services of such type to be performed by employees of persons in that particular business field in the United States on September 3, 1982. If a particular business field did not exist on September 3, 1982, the determination will be made by analogy to similar business fields in existence on September 3, 1982. The historical-performance test will be considered satisfied, however, if services were performed in a particular business field by employees of a recipient. In that case, the historical-performance test will be considered satisfied for the period beginning on the date these services were first performed by an employee and ending on the date five years after these services are no longer performed by any employee. [Prop Reg § 1.414(n)-1(b)(12)]

Q 9:69 Must a leased employee be an employee of the leasing organization?

According to the withdrawn proposed regulations, the answer to this question is no. For example, an independent contractor who performs services for a recipient could be considered a leased employee. [Prop Reg § 1.414(n)-1(b)(1)] Some commentators have suggested, however, that an independent contractor cannot be a leased employee because the language of the statute requires the leased employee and the leasing organization to be two different persons.

Q 9:70 If an individual is considered a leased employee, is it necessary to cover the individual under the recipient's 401(k) plan?

It is not necessary to cover a leased employee under the recipient's 401(k) plan. However, unless the leased employee is covered by a safe harbor plan (see Q 9:72), he or she must be taken into account for various employee benefit requirements, including the minimum participation and coverage requirements. [IRC § 414(n)(3)]

> **Example.** ABC Company sponsors a 401(k) plan covering its 10 HCEs and 200 NHCEs. ABC Company also uses the services of 40 leased employees, all of whom are considered NHCEs. Although the leased employees are not covered by ABC Company's 401(k) plan, they must be taken into account in determining whether the 401(k) plan satisfies the minimum coverage requirements. Accordingly, the percentage of NHCEs benefiting under the plan is 83.33 percent (200/240). The 401(k) plan satisfies the ratio percentage test because the percentage of NHCEs benefiting under the 401(k) plan (83.33 percent) is greater than 70 percent of the percentage of HCEs benefiting under the plan (100 percent).

Q 9:71 May leased employees be disregarded if the leasing organization maintains a retirement plan for them?

Leased employees may be disregarded by the recipient if the leased employees are covered by a safe harbor plan and they do not constitute more than 20 percent of the recipient's non-highly compensated workforce. [IRC § 414(n)(5)]

Q 9:72 What is a *safe harbor plan*?

A *safe harbor plan* is a money purchase plan (see Glossary), maintained by the leasing organization, that meets all of the following requirements:

1. The plan provides for immediate participation.

2. Contributions are provided at a rate of at least 10 percent of compensation—compensation means compensation as defined for purposes of determining who is an HCE (see Q 9:94).

3. Contributions are provided to an individual whether or not the individual is employed by the leasing organization on the last day of the plan year and regardless of the number of hours of service.

4. The plan provides for immediate vesting.

[IRC § 414(n)(5); Prop Treas Reg § 1.414(n)-2(f)(1)]

Q 9:73 Who is considered part of the recipient's non-highly compensated workforce?

A recipient's non-highly compensated workforce consists of NHCEs who are either leased employees or employees of the recipient who have performed services for the recipient on a substantially full-time basis for at least one year. [IRC § 414(n)(5)(C)(ii)]

WHO IS A HIGHLY COMPENSATED EMPLOYEE?

The application of nondiscrimination rules requires employees to be categorized as either highly compensated or non-highly compensated pursuant to objective rules. The rules for determining HCEs were greatly simplified starting with plan years beginning in 1997.

Q 9:74 Who is a *highly compensated employee*?

An employee is a *highly compensated employee* (HCE) for a plan year only if the employee performs services for the employer during the determination year. (See Q 9:95.) In addition, the employee must be a member of at least one specified employee group (see Qs 9:75, 9:76). [IRC § 414(q)(1); Treas Reg § 1.414(q)-1T, Q&A 3(a)]

Q 9:75 What were these specified groups of employees for plan years beginning before 1997?

There were four separate groups of employees. Membership in any one of these groups would cause an employee to be an HCE for any plan year beginning before 1997:

1. The employee was a 5 percent owner (see Q 9:82) at any time during the determination year or look-back year.

2. The employee received compensation in excess of $75,000 during the determination year or look-back year.

3. The employee received compensation in excess of $50,000 during the determination year or look-back year and was a member of the top-paid group for the determination year or look-back year.

4. The employee was an includible officer (see Q 9:91) at any time during the determination year or look-back year.

An employee would be considered a member of one or more of the groups described in (2), (3), or (4) for a determination year only if the employee was one of the 100 employees receiving the most compensation during the determination year. [Treas Reg § 1.414(q)-1T, Q&As 3(a)(1), 3(a)(2)]

Q 9:76 What are these specified groups of employees for plan years beginning after 1996?

There are two separate groups of employees. Membership in either of these groups will cause an employee to be an HCE for any plan year beginning after 1996:

1. The employee is a 5 percent owner at any time during the determination year or look-back year; or

2. The employee receives compensation in excess of $80,000 (indexed) during the look-back year and, at the election of the employer, is a member of the top-paid group during the look-back year.

Example. ABC Company sponsors a 401(k) plan with a plan year beginning each April 1. For the look-back year ending March 31, 1999, Joe received $90,000 in compensation. For the plan year beginning April 1, 1999, Joe is considered a highly compensated employee because his compensation for the look-back year ending March 31, 1999, exceeded $80,000.

Q 9:77 Were the $75,000 and $50,000 thresholds adjusted?

Yes. These dollar thresholds were indexed at the same time and in the same manner as the defined benefit dollar limit under Code Section 415(b). For 1995 and 1996, the $75,000 threshold was $100,000. The $50,000 threshold was $66,000 for both 1995 and 1996. [Treas Reg § 1.414(q)-1T, Q&A 3(c)(1)] The following table shows the dollar thresholds in effect since 1986.

Year	$75,000 Threshold	$50,000 Threshold
1986	$ 75,000	$50,000
1987	75,000	50,000
1988	78,353	52,235
1989	81,720	54,480
1990	85,485	56,990
1991	90,803	60,535
1992	93,518	62,345
1993	96,368	64,245
1994	99,000	66,000
1995	100,000	66,000
1996	100,000	66,000

Q 9:78 How is the $80,000 threshold adjusted?

The $80,000 threshold will be indexed at the same time and in the same manner as the defined benefit dollar limit under Code Section 415(b). This dollar threshold will always be a multiple of $5,000 and will always be rounded to the next lower multiple of $5,000.

The base period for the indexation of the $80,000 threshold is the calendar quarter ending September 30, 1996. [IRC § 414(q)(1)]

Q 9:79 How are the dollar thresholds applied to a determination or look-back year?

The indexed $75,000 and $50,000 threshold amounts for a determination year or a look-back year were determined with reference to the calendar year in which the determination year or the look-back year began. [Treas Reg § 1.414(q)-1T, Q&A 3(c)(2)] The $80,000 threshold for the look-back year is determined in the same way.

Example. The determination and look-back years of a plan began on December 1, 1996, and December 1, 1995, respectively. The $75,000 threshold was $100,000 for both the determination year and the look-back year. The $50,000 threshold for each of those years was $66,000.

Q 9:80 Is the determination of HCEs limited to the employees of the entity sponsoring the plan?

No. All employers required to be aggregated under the controlled group and affiliated service group are treated as a single employer. [Treas Reg § 1.414(q)-1T Q&A 6(a)] For example, if Employee A receives $45,000 from Company X and $45,000 from Company Y during a look-back year beginning in 1999, Employee A will be considered an HCE even though only Company X sponsors a 401(k) plan. HCEs are determined before the operation of the QSLOB rules. (See Q 9:38.) [Treas Reg § 1.414(q)-1T, Q&A 6(c)]

Q 9:81 Who are considered employees in the determination of HCEs?

Employees are any individuals who perform services for the employer and include both common-law employees and self-employed individuals treated as employees under Code Section 401(c)(1). [Treas Reg § 1.414(q)-1T, Q&A 7(a)] Leased employees must also be treated as employees unless the leased employee is covered by a safe harbor plan (see Q 9:72) and is not otherwise covered by a qualified plan maintained by the employer. [Treas Reg § 1.414(q)-1T, Q&A 7(b)]

Q 9:82 Who is a *5 percent owner*?

An employee is considered a *5 percent owner* if at any time during a look-back year or a determination year an employee owns or is considered to own (applying attribution rules under Code Section 318) more than 5 percent of the value of the outstanding stock of a corporation or stock having more than 5 percent of the total combined voting power of all stock of the corporation. If the employer is not a corporation, a 5 percent owner is any employee owning more than 5 percent of the capital or profits interest of the employer. The controlled group and affiliated service group rules are disregarded in determining a 5 percent owner. [Treas Reg § 1.414(q)-1T, Q&A 8]

Example. An affiliated service group consists of a law firm partnership with 100 partners, each of which is a professional corporation owned by a single attorney. Although each professional corporation, and, by attribution, each attorney-owner, has only a 1 percent interest in the law partnership, each attorney-owner will be treated as a 5 percent owner because each attorney-owner owns 100 percent of his or her professional corporation.

Q 9:83 What is the *top-paid group*?

The *top-paid group* is the highest paid 20 percent of the employer's nonexcludable employees. (See Q 9:84.) For plan years beginning before 1997, the top-paid group was determined separately for the determination year and the look-back year. [Treas Reg § 1.414(q)-1T, Q&A 9(a)]

Q 9:84 How is the number of employees in the top-paid group determined?

The starting point is to determine the total number of employees who perform services for the employer during the year. From that number, the employer may subtract the number of employees who are in the following categories:

1. Employees who have not completed six months of service by the end of the year (for this purpose, service in the immediately preceding year is taken into account);

2. Employees who normally work fewer than 17½ hours per week during the year;

3. Employees who normally work fewer than seven months during the year;

4. Employees who are not age 21 by the end of the year;

5. Employees who are nonresident aliens with no U.S.-source earned income; and

6. Employees who are covered by a collective bargaining agreement. This exclusion applies, however, only if 90 percent or more of the employees are covered under collective bargaining agreements and the plan does not benefit employees covered under such agreements.

An employer may elect to modify these exclusions by requiring shorter periods of service or a lower age. In fact, these exclusions may be eliminated altogether. Also, the employer may ignore the collective bargaining employee exclusion. The ability to modify or ignore these exclusions must be provided for in the plan document. Exclusions must also be uniformly applied to all other retirement plans with plan years beginning in the same calendar year. [Treas Reg § 1.414(q)-1T, Q&A 9(b)]

Q 9:85 When is an employee considered to normally work fewer than 17½ hours per week?

An employee is deemed to normally work fewer than 17½ hours per week if the employee works fewer than 17½ hours per week for 50 percent or more of the total weeks worked by the employee. Any week during which an employee does not work is not taken into account. [Treas Reg § 1.414(q)-1T, Q&A 9(e)]

Q 9:86 When is an employee considered to normally work fewer than seven months during the year?

The determination as to whether an employee normally works fewer than seven months during the year is based on the employer's customary experience in prior years. An employee who works on one day during a month is deemed to have worked that month. [Treas Reg § 1.414(q)-1T, Q&A 9(f)]

Worksheet 9-1. How to Determine Membership in the Top-Paid Group

APPLIES TO: Plan years beginning after 1996.
TOP-PAID GROUP: Highest-paid 20 percent of employees.
EMPLOYEES: Anyone (other than nonresident aliens with no U.S.-source income) who performed services during the look-back year. May exclude any of the following:

- Employed fewer than six months at the end of the year
- Normally works fewer than 17½ hours per week
- Normally works fewer than seven months
- Has not attained age 21 at the end of the year
- Collective bargaining employees (but only if such employees make up 90 percent or more of the employees and no such employees are covered by the plan)

Plan Year 12/31/99   Look-back Year 12/31/98

                                            Dollar Limitation $80,000

Total employees   75

Employed < 6 mos   −   8

Work < 17½ hrs/wk   −   2

Work < 7 mos   −   0

Not age 21   −   3

Collective bargaining   −   0

Employees subject to test   =   62

                                              ×   20%

Number of employees who can be in the
  top-paid group (rounding down)   =   12

EMPLOYEES WHO EARN MORE THAN THE DOLLAR LIMITATION
DURING THE LOOK-BACK YEAR RANKED IN ORDER OF TOTAL
COMPENSATION (includes any employee who may have been excluded
in determining number of employees in top-paid group):

Look-back Year

Mary	$105,000
Bill	87,500
Tom	81,000

The employees who are considered HCEs are those employees (not more
than the number of employees who can be in the top-paid group, as
determined above) whose total compensation is the highest.

Q 9:87 How are the particular employees who will make up the top-paid group selected?

After the number of employees in the top-paid group has been determined, those employees with the highest compensation are identified. The exclusions used in determining the number of employees in the top-paid group are not applicable. [Treas Reg § 1.414(q)-1T, Q&A 9(c)]

Example. Mix-Max Company sponsors a 401(k) plan and, for purposes of determining HCEs, requires membership in the top-paid group. Jane is hired on July 15, 1998, and makes $105,000 during the look-back year ending December 31, 1998. Because she has worked fewer than six months as of December 31, 1998, Jane is excluded in determining the number of employees in the top-paid group. However, as long as her compensation places her in the top 20 percent of employees for the look-back year when ranked on the basis of compensation, she is considered an HCE for the plan year beginning January 1, 1999.

Worksheet 9-1 can be used to identify the employees who are in the top-paid group for a plan year beginning after 1996.

Q 9:88 How does an employer make an election to require membership in the top-paid group?

Code Section 414(q) does not prescribe a procedure for making this election. The IRS has indicated that an election to require membership in the top-paid group is not irrevocable and may be changed without prior IRS approval. According to the IRS, however, the plan document must reflect the election, and any change in the election must be accomplished through a plan amendment. [IRS Notice 97-45]

Q 9:89 Under what circumstances would an employer want to make the election to require membership in the top-paid group?

The election to require membership in the top-paid group may be advantageous to a company with a large number of HCEs.

Example. Mega Law Firm employs 200 employees, 100 of whom are attorneys consisting of 20 shareholders and 80 associates.

Each attorney in the firm has compensation in excess of $80,000. Without an election to require membership in the top-paid group, all 100 attorneys would be considered HCEs. If, however, the election is made, only the highest-paid 40 attorneys would be treated as HCEs (assuming that all of the shareholders would be among this top-paid 40).

Q 9:90 Who is an *officer*?

The determination of whether an employee is an officer is based on all the facts and circumstances, including, for example, the source of authority, the term for which appointed or elected, and the nature and extent of duties. Titles are not relevant. In general, an *officer* will be an administrative executive who is in regular and continued service. [Treas Reg §§ 1.414(q)-1T, Q&A 10(a), 1.416-1, Q&A T-13]

Q 9:91 Who was an *includible officer*?

An *includible officer* (see Q 9:75) was an employee who, at any time during the determination or look-back year, was an officer and received compensation in excess of 50 percent of the Section 415 defined benefit dollar limitation in effect for the year. The Section 415 defined benefit dollar limit in effect for a year was the limit in effect for the calendar year in which the determination or look-back year began. Fifty percent of the Section 415 defined benefit dollar limitation for 1997 was $62,500. [Treas Reg § 1.414(q)-1T, Q&A 10(a)]

Q 9:92 Was there a limit on the number of employees who could be considered includible officers?

Yes. Depending on the total number of employees, the limit was determined as follows:

Number of Employees	Maximum Number of Includible Officers
500 or more employees	50
30 or more employees but fewer than 500 employees	10% of the number of employees
Fewer than 30 employees	3

The number of employees for a year was the total number of employees who actually performed services during the year. The exclusions that applied to determine the number of employees in the top-paid group also applied here. [IRC § 414(q)(8); Treas Reg § 1.414(q)-1T, Q&A 10(b)]

Example. ABC Company employed 600 individuals during the look-back year ending December 31, 1995; however, only 400 of those employees had six months of service by the end of the look-back year. The maximum number of includible officers for the 1995 look-back year was 40 (400 × 10%).

Q 9:93 What happened if no officers had compensation for a year in excess of 50 percent of the Section 415 defined benefit dollar limit?

In this case, the officer with the greatest amount of compensation was considered an includible officer. The fact that an employee was an HCE by being a 5 percent owner did not change the determination of who was an includible officer. [Treas Reg § 1.414(q)-1T, Q&A 10(c)]

Example. Dom owns 100 percent of Company A and is one of two officers. Gerry is the other officer. Dom and Gerry have compensation of $45,000 and $40,000, respectively, for the determination year ending December 31, 1996. Dom is an HCE for the 1996 plan year because he is a 5 percent owner. Dom is also considered Company A's sole includible officer because Dom's compensation is greater than Gerry's.

Worksheet 9-2 can be used to identify those employees who were considered includible officers for plan years beginning before 1997.

Q 9:94 How is *compensation* defined for purposes of determining the group of HCEs?

Compensation means compensation as defined for purposes of Code Section 415. (See chapter 8.) It also includes elective contributions to 401(k) plans, SIMPLE retirement plans, and salary reduction simplified employee pension (SARSEP) plans and elective deferrals under a cafeteria plan. [IRC § 414(q)(4)]

Q 9:95 What are the determination and look-back years?

Generally, the determination year is the plan year and the look-back year is the 12-month period immediately preceding the plan year. For plan years beginning before 1997, an employer could elect to use the calendar year ending within the plan year as the look-back year, in which case the determination year became the short period (referred to as the lag period) from the end of the look-back year to the end of the plan year. If the plan year was a calendar year, there was no lag period. In that case, the regulations indicated that the determination of HCEs would be based solely on the single look-back calendar year. [Treas Reg § 1.414(q)-1T, Q&As 14(a), 14(b)(1)]

Example 1. A 401(k) plan had a plan year that ended on June 30. For the plan year ending June 30, 1996, the employer made the calendar-year-calculation election described previously. As a result, the look-back year was the calendar year ending December 31, 1995. The six-month lag period running from January 1, 1996, to June 30, 1996, then became the determination year.

Example 2. The facts are the same as in Example 1, except that the plan year ended December 31, 1996. Because the plan year was the calendar year, there was no lag period. 1996 became the look-back year and there was no determination year. Hence, in determining HCEs for 1996, the employer would use 1996 data only. It would not have been necessary to look at 1995 data. If the calendar-year election had not been made, the determination of HCEs for 1996 would be based on 1996 data (the determination year) and 1995 data (the look-back year).

For plan years beginning after 1996, a calendar-year election can also be made. [IRS Notice 97-45] A post-1996 election utilizes the calendar year beginning in the look-back year. According to Notice 97-45, this election applies only to the $80,000 (indexed) test.

Example 3. A 401(k) plan has a plan year that ends on March 31. For the plan year ending March 31, 2000, the employer makes the calendar-year-calculation election. As a result, the look-back year for determining whether an employee is an HCE by reason of having compensation in excess of $80,000 is the calendar year ending December 31, 1999. The calendar-year-calculation election does not apply in determining whether an employee is an HCE by rea-

Worksheet 9-2. How to Determine When an Officer Is Considered a Highly Compensated Employee

APPLIES TO: Plan years beginning before 1997.
OFFICER: Anyone who performs officer duties and/or has officer authority, whether or not he or she has the title of officer.

- Must be determined separately for the determination year as well as the look-back year. An officer is an HCE for a plan year if his or her total compensation for the applicable year (determination or look-back) is one half of the defined benefit dollar limit in effect at the beginning of such applicable year.

- Maximum number of officers who can be considered HCEs is the greater of three employees or 10 percent of the employees, but in no event more than 50 employees.

EMPLOYEES: Anyone (other than nonresident aliens with no U.S.-source income) who performed services during the applicable year. May exclude any of the following:

- Persons employed fewer than six months at the end of the year
- A person who normally works fewer than 17½ hours per week
- A person who normally works fewer than seven months
- A person who has not attained age 21 at the end of the year
- Collective bargaining employees (but only if such employees make up 90 percent or more of the employees and no such employees are covered by the plan)

Plan Year 12/31/96	Determination Year Dollar Limitation	12/31/96 $60,000	Look-back Year Dollar Limitation	12/31/95 $60,000
Total employees		85		75
Employed < 6 mos	–	10	–	8
Work < 17½ hrs/wk	–	2	–	2
Work < 7 mos	–	0	–	0
Not age 21	–	5	–	3
Collective bargaining	–	0	–	0
	=	68	=	62

Employees subject to test (rounding down)

68 × 10% = 6   62 × 10% = 6

If the product is less than 3, the maximum number of officers is 3. If the product is greater than 3, the maximum number of officers is 10 percent of the employees, but in no event more than 50.

OFFICERS WHO EARNED MORE THAN ONE HALF THE DEFINED BENEFIT DOLLAR LIMIT DURING THE APPLICABLE YEAR RANKED IN ORDER OF TOTAL COMPENSATION:

Determination Year		Look-back Year	
Mary	$120,000	Mary	$105,000
Tom	70,000	Tom	65,000
		Larry	61,000

The officers who are considered HCEs are those (not more than the number previously determined) whose total compensation is the highest. If no officer earns more than one half of the defined benefit dollar limit during an applicable year, the officer with the greatest amount of compensation is an HCE.

son of being a 5 percent owner. Thus, an employee will be a 5 percent owner if he or she owns more than 5 percent of the employer at any time during the look-back year ending March 31, 1999, or the determination year ending March 31, 2000.

A post-1996 calendar-year election is not irrevocable and may be changed without IRS approval. However, according to Notice 97-45, the plan document must reflect the election, and any change in the election must be accomplished by plan amendment.

Q 9:96 If the calendar-year-calculation election was made for plan years beginning before 1997, what effect did the election have on the determination of HCEs for the lag period?

For the lag period, the $75,000 and $50,000 thresholds, as well as the 50 percent defined benefit dollar limit, were multiplied by a fraction, the numerator of which was the number of calendar months in the lag period and the denominator of which was 12. [Treas Reg § 1.414(q)-1T, Q&A 14(b)(2)]

Flowcharts 9-2(a) and 9-2(b) summarize the steps used in determining HCEs for plan years beginning on or after January 1, 1997, or earlier.

WHAT IS COMPENSATION?

An employee's compensation is a key factor in the application of the Section 401(a)(4) nondiscrimination rules. In applying these rules to elective contributions and to employer matching and employee after-tax contributions, a plan must calculate ratios for each employee, which are based in part on the employee's compensation. (See chapter 12.) The amount of nonelective contributions allocated to an employee, expressed as a percentage of compensation, is the basis for determining whether the allocation is nondiscriminatory. (See chapter 11.) A plan is not free to use any definition of compensation when applying the Section 401(a)(4) nondiscrimination rules. In applying these rules, the plan must use a definition of compensation that is nondiscriminatory under Code Section 414(s).

Flowchart 9-2(a). Determining HCEs for plan years beginning on or after January 1, 1997

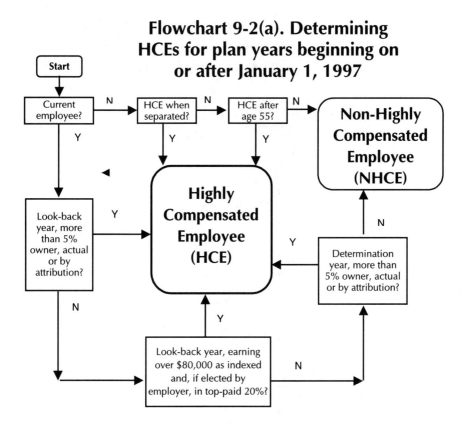

Flowchart 9-2(b). Determining HCEs for plan years beginning before January 1, 1997

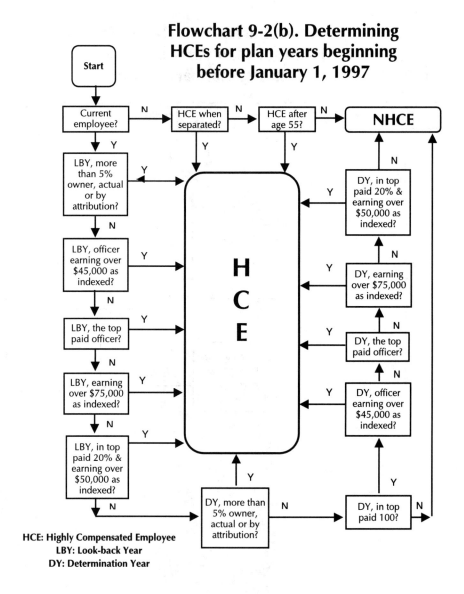

HCE: Highly Compensated Employee
LBY: Look-back Year
DY: Determination Year

Q 9:97 What definitions of compensation will automatically satisfy Code Section 414(s)?

Any definition of compensation that satisfies Code Section 415(c)(3) will automatically satisfy Code Section 414(s)—see chapter 8 for the definition of compensation under Code Section 415(c)(3). The regulations under Code Section 414(s) also provide for a safe harbor alternative definition. Under the safe harbor, a plan starts with a definition of compensation that satisfies Code Section 415(c)(3), reduced by the following categories of compensation:

1. Reimbursements or other expense allowances;

2. Cash and noncash fringe benefits;

3. Moving expenses;

4. Deferred compensation; and

5. Welfare benefits.

[Treas Reg §§ 1.414(s)-1(c)(2), 1.414(s)-1(c)(3)]

See Table 9-1 at the end of this section for a comparison of the definitions of compensation that automatically satisfy Code Section 414(s).

Q 9:98 Can a definition of compensation that includes amounts not includible in gross income satisfy Code Section 414(s)?

Yes. A definition of compensation will automatically satisfy Code Section 414(s) even though it is modified to include all of the following amounts not includible in gross income:

1. Cafeteria plan deferrals under Code Section 125;

2. Elective contributions under a 401(k) plan; and

3. Elective contributions under a salary reduction SEP or a SIMPLE retirement account.

[IRC § 402(k); Treas Reg § 1.414(s)-1(c)(4)]

For plan years beginning after 1997, the above amounts, though not includible in gross income, will automatically be treated as compensation under Code Section 415(c)(3)(D).

Q 9:99 If a plan excludes from the definition of compensation any portion of the compensation of an HCE, does the plan's definition of compensation continue to automatically satisfy Code Section 414(s)?

Yes. The plan's definition of compensation automatically satisfies Code Section 414(s) whether the exclusion applies to some or all HCEs. [Treas Reg § 1.414(s)-1(c)(5)]

Q 9:100 If a plan's definition of compensation does not automatically satisfy Code Section 414(s), how does the plan demonstrate that its definition still satisfies Code Section 414(s)?

A definition of compensation will satisfy Code Section 414(s) if the definition meets three requirements:

1. The definition must not by design favor HCEs.
2. The definition must be reasonable.
3. The definition must be nondiscriminatory.

[Treas Reg § 1.414(s)-1(d)(1)]
The regulations address only the last two requirements; they are silent with respect to the first requirement.

Q 9:101 When is a definition of compensation reasonable?

A definition of compensation is considered reasonable if it would otherwise automatically satisfy Code Section 414(s) except that it excludes certain types of irregular or additional compensation. According to the regulations, these types of compensation include overtime pay, shift differential and call-in premiums, bonuses, and any one of the categories of compensation excludable in determining the alternative safe harbor definition. (See Q 9:97.) A reasonable definition may include all or less than all of the amounts listed at Q 9:98. [Treas Reg § 1.414(s)-1(d)(2)(ii)]

Q 9:102 Is a definition of compensation considered reasonable if it excludes a specified percentage of each employee's compensation?

No. However, a definition of compensation is considered reasonable if it excludes all compensation in excess of a specified dollar amount. [Treas Reg § 1.414(s)-1(d)(2)(iii)]

Q 9:103 What is the nondiscrimination requirement?

A definition of compensation is nondiscriminatory if the average percentage of total compensation included under the plan's definition of compensation for HCEs as a group does not exceed by more than a de minimis amount the average percentage calculated in the same way for NHCEs. [Treas Reg § 1.414(s)-1(d)(3)(i)]

Q 9:104 How are average percentages determined?

The first step is to determine a compensation percentage for each employee in a group by dividing that employee's compensation, as defined in the plan, by the employee's total compensation, which is an amount determined under any definition of compensation that satisfies Code Section 415(c)(3), with or without the modification described at Q 9:98 for plan years beginning before January 1, 1998, but which does not exceed the Section 401(a)(17) limit (see Q 9:109). Total compensation for an HCE does not include any amount excluded as described in Q 9:99 unless the exclusion applies consistently in defining the compensation of all highly compensated employees. The average of the separately calculated individual compensation percentages is the average percentage for a group. [Treas Reg §§ 1.414(s)-1(d)(3)(ii), 1.414(s)-1(d)(3)(iv)(A)]

Example. ABC Company sponsors a plan under which bonuses and overtime pay are excluded. Is this plan's definition of compensation nondiscriminatory on the basis of these facts?

Employee	Plan Compensation	Total Compensation	Inclusion Percentage
HCE 1	$100,000	$120,000	83.3%
HCE 2	95,000	110,000	86.4
HCE 3	95,000	105,000	90.5
NHCE 1	30,000	35,000	85.7
NHCE 2	25,000	30,000	83.3
NHCE 3	24,000	25,000	96.0
NHCE 4	22,000	24,000	91.7
NHCE 5	22,500	23,000	97.8
NHCE 6	19,000	20,000	95.0

The average percentage for the HCE group is 86.7 percent, and the average percentage for the NHCE group is 91.6 percent. Because the average percentage of the NHCE group is greater, the plan's definition of compensation is considered nondiscriminatory.

Q 9:105 May other methods be used for determining average percentages?

Yes. Other reasonable methods to determine average percentages for either or both groups are permitted. The regulations point out, however, that any other method cannot be used if it can be reasonably expected to create a significant variance from the average percentage determined under the method described in Q 9:104. A significant variance could occur, for example, if several employees in a group have significantly higher compensation. [Treas Reg § 1.414(s)-1(d)(3)(iv)(B)]

Example. The facts are the same as in the example in Q 9:104, except that ABC Company computes the average percentage for NHCEs by aggregating the plan compensation for the members of this group and dividing that number by the aggregate total compensation of the NHCEs.

$$\frac{(30,000 + 25,000 + 24,000 + 22,000 + 22,500 + 19,000)}{(35,000 + 30,000 + 25,000 + 24,000 + 23,000 + 20,000)} = 90.8\%$$

Because 90.8 percent is not significantly different from 91.6 percent (as computed in the example in Q 9:104), the method illustrated in this example for determining the average percentage is reasonable.

Q 9:106 How does a plan determine whether the average percentage of total compensation for the HCE group exceeds by more than a de minimis amount the average percentage of total compensation for the NHCE group?

According to the regulations, a plan may take into account the differences between the percentages in prior periods in determining whether the difference in percentages for the current period is more than a de minimis amount. In addition, a plan may ignore an isolated instance of more than a de minimis amount between percentages that occurs because of an extraordinary unforeseeable event (for example, overtime payments to employees of a public utility on account of a major hurricane). A de minimis amount is not quantified by the regulations. Rather, it is the result of a determination made by the plan and based on the applicable facts and circumstances. [Treas Reg § 1.414(s)-1(d)(3)(v)]

Q 9:107 Are there special rules that apply to self-employed individuals?

If a plan uses a definition of compensation that does not satisfy Code Section 415(c)(3), a self-employed individual's compensation for purposes of Code Section 414(s) is the total earned income of the self-employed individual multiplied by the average percentage of total compensation included under the plan's definition of compensation for NHCEs as a group. [Treas Reg § 1.414(s)-1(g)(1)]

Q 9:108 Must a plan use a definition of compensation that satisfies Code Section 414(s) in calculating contributions under the plan?

A plan is not required to use a definition of compensation that satisfies Code Section 414(s) in determining contributions under the plan. However, whether contributions allocated under a plan satisfy the Section 401(a)(4) nondiscrimination rules must be tested on the basis of a compensation definition that does satisfy Code Section 414(s). [Treas Reg § 1.414(s)-1(a)(2)]

Example. Omega Corporation sponsors a 401(k) plan that allows employees to defer a specified percentage of their compensation. Lynn, an NHCE, elects to defer 5 percent ($1,000) of her base pay of $20,000. Her deferral percentage does not apply, however, to the $2,000 of overtime pay received by Lynn, because the plan's definition of compensation does not allow deferrals with respect to overtime pay. Bob, an HCE, also elects to defer 5 percent, but his deferral percentage applies to his total compensation of

TABLE 9-1. Compensation Definitions That Satisfy Code Section 414(s)

	"Long List" Code Section 415	"Short List" Code Section 415	Code Section 3401(a)	W-2	Section 414(s) Safe Harbor Exclusion[a]
Direct pay	Yes	Yes	Yes	Yes	
Reimbursements, expense allowances, and taxable fringes	Yes	Yes	Yes	Yes	Exclude
Section 911 earned income	Yes	Yes	Yes[b]	Yes	
Includible Section 105(h) short-term disability pay (sick pay)	Yes	No	Yes	Yes	Exclude[c]
Long-term disability pay	Yes	No	Yes	Yes	Exclude
Deductible moving expense	No	No	No	No	
Nondeductible moving expense	Yes	No	Yes	Yes	Exclude
Nonqualified stock option at grant (if taxable on option privilege)	Yes	No	Yes	Yes	
Nonqualified stock option taxable at exercise	No	No	Yes	Yes	
Section 83(b) elections	Yes	No	Yes	Yes	

Section 83 property vesting	No	No	Yes	Yes	
Unfunded deferred compensation payouts while employed (if plan so provides)	Yes	Yes	Yes	Yes	Exclude
Disqualifying disposition of qualified stock option	No	No	No[d]	No[d]	
Taxable group-term life insurance	Yes	Yes	No	Yes	Exclude
Nontaxable dependent care, education assistance, Section 132 fringe benefits	No	No	No	No	
Meals or lodging under Section 119	No	No	No	No	

a The Section 414(s) safe harbor can be used with any of the preceding four methods, but with the adjustments noted. Note that all of the adjustments must be made; an employer cannot elect to exclude only some of the excludable items.

b Section 3401(a)(8) excludes certain Section 911 earned income from "wages," but the regulation disregards exclusions based on the nature or location of work.

c The short-term disability is disregarded only if it is deemed to constitute a "welfare benefit."

d The IRS has said that disqualifying dispositions of Section 423 options constitute "wages" for income tax withholding. [See Ltr Ruls 8920040, 8921027]

9-61

$90,000, including a bonus of $20,000. Because it excludes over-time pay, the plan's definition of compensation favors HCEs by design, does not satisfy Code Section 414(s), and cannot be used in performing the actual deferral percentage (ADP) test (see chapter 12). Consequently, in order to perform the ADP test, the plan must use a definition of compensation meeting the requirements of Code Section 414(s). If total compensation is used for this purpose, then Lynn's deferral ratio is 4.55 percent ($1,000/$22,000).

Q 9:109 Is there a limit on the amount of compensation that may be taken into account?

Under Code Section 401(a)(17), the amount of compensation that may be taken into account is limited to $150,000. [IRC § 401(a)(17)(A)]

Q 9:110 Is the $150,000 limit on compensation subject to adjustment?

Yes. The Section 401(a)(17) limit will be adjusted in increments of $10,000. The adjustment will occur in the calendar year in which the previous Section 401(a)(17) limit, when adjusted annually in the same manner as the defined benefit dollar limit under Code Section 415(b), is more than $10,000 greater than the previous unadjusted Section 401(a)(17) limit. An adjustment in the Section 401(a)(17) limit is effective with respect to plan years beginning in the calendar year in which the adjustment occurs. [IRC § 401(a)(17)(B)]

Example. Company Y sponsors a 401(k) plan with a calendar plan year. The Section 401(a)(17) limit for 1999 is $160,000. By 2000 the $150,000 limit, as adjusted annually in the same manner as the defined benefit dollar limit under Code Section 415(b), is $171,500. As a result, in 2000 the Section 401(a)(17) limit is $170,000. The Section 401(a)(17) limit will remain $170,000 until the limit, as adjusted under Code Section 415(b), equals or exceeds $180,000.

The following table shows the Section 401(a)(17) limit in effect since 1994:

Year	Section 401(a)(17) Limit
1994	$150,000
1995	150,000
1996	150,000
1997	160,000
1998	160,000
1999	160,000

Q 9:111 Were there special rules that applied to HCEs and their family members?

Yes. For plan years beginning before 1997, an HCE who was a 5 percent owner or one of the ten most highly compensated employees and the HCE's spouse and any child who had not reached age 19 before the close of the year were treated as a single employee for purposes of the Section 401(a)(17) limit. Most plans allocated the Section 401(a)(17) limit in proportion to the compensation of the HCE and the family members. [IRC § 401(a)(17)]

> **Example.** Dick owns 100 percent of Company C. His spouse, Sharon, is an employee. Dick's compensation for the year is $300,000 and Sharon's compensation is $100,000. Their pro rata shares of the Section 401(a)(17) limit for 1996 were $112,500 ($300,000/$400,000 × $150,000) and $37,500 ($100,000/$400,000 × $150,000), respectively.

Note that additional family members were aggregated for purposes of applying coverage and nondiscrimination rules to pre-1997 plan years. (See chapters 10 and 12.)

For plan years beginning after 1996, Section 1431 of the Small Business Job Protection Act of 1996 eliminates the Section 401(a)(17) family aggregation rules.

Q 9:112 What are the purposes for which the Section 401(a)(17) limit applies?

The Section 401(a)(17) limit applies for three purposes:

1. A plan may not base the allocation of contributions on compensation in excess of the Section 401(a)(17) limit [Treas Reg § 1.401(a)(17)-1(b)(1)];

2. The amount of compensation taken into account in applying nondiscrimination rules cannot exceed the Section 401(a)(17) limit [Treas Reg § 1.401(a)(17)-1(c)(1)]; and

3. An employer may not determine the maximum deductible amount to a 401(k) plan by taking into account compensation in excess of the Section 401(a)(17) limit. [IRC § 404(l)]

10 Participation and Coverage Testing

To qualify for tax-favored status, a 401(k) plan must meet standards of minimum coverage. For plan years beginning after 1996, 401(k) plans no longer need meet the minimum participation rules; however, for some years in the future it may still be necessary to review or correct past 401(k) plan practice to assure that these rules were satisfied when they applied.

MINIMUM PARTICIPATION

The minimum participation rules were added to the Internal Revenue Code (Code) effective with plan years beginning in 1989. Before 1989 an employer was free to establish different plans for different groups of employees as long as the plans were comparable to one another. Congress believed, however, that the comparability rules were unduly complex and unevenly applied and that they permitted benefit disparities that too greatly favored highly compensated employees (HCEs). After 1989, many plans were terminated or merged with other plans of employers to satisfy the minimum participation rules.

For plan years beginning after 1996, the minimum participation rules no longer apply to defined contribution plans, including 401(k) plans, although they continue to apply to defined benefit plans and have even been strengthened.

Minimum Participation Rules

Q 10:1 What were the minimum participation rules as they applied to 401(k) plans for plan years beginning before January 1, 1997?

A 401(k) plan satisfied the minimum participation rules for plan years beginning before 1997 only if it benefited at least the lesser of 50 employees of the employer or 40 percent of the employees of the employer. [Treas Reg § 1.401(a)(26)-2(a)]

Q 10:2 What was considered to be a plan?

The minimum participation rules were applied to each 401(k) plan, as that term is defined in chapter 9, but with two modifications. First, a single 401(k) plan that covered both an employer's collective bargaining and its non-collective bargaining employees was not automatically treated as separate plans. In this situation, a single 401(k) plan might have been treated as separate plans if the employer so elected. Second, a 401(k) plan was not disaggregated to reflect the different types of contributions that might have been made to a 401(k) plan.

Q 10:3 Who was considered to be the employer?

For purposes of the minimum participation rules, the employer was the entity sponsoring the 401(k) plan and all other entities that were aggregated with it under Code Sections 414(b), 414(c), and 414(m). [Treas Reg § 1.401(a)(26)-8]

Q 10:4 When was an employee treated as benefiting under a 401(k) plan?

An employee was treated as benefiting under a 401(k) plan if the employee was eligible to make elective contributions. An employee was considered eligible even though his or her eligibility to make elective contributions had been suspended on account of a hardship distribution, a loan, or an election not to participate. An employee who was not eligible to make elective contributions because of the limits imposed by Code Section 415 was still treated as benefiting under the plan. [Treas Reg § 1.401(a)(26)-5(a)(1)]

Disregarding Certain Employees

Q 10:5 Could a 401(k) plan disregard certain employees in applying the minimum participation rules?

Yes. In applying the minimum participation rules, the 401(k) plan was allowed to disregard certain employees as follows:

1. *Age and service conditions.* A 401(k) plan could exclude all employees who had not satisfied the plan's age and service conditions. An employee was not treated as meeting those conditions until the date on which the employee entered the plan. This exclusion was available only if none of the employees who failed to satisfy these conditions were benefiting under the plan. [Treas Reg § 1.401(a)(26)-6(b)(1)]

> **Example.** ABC Company established a 401(k) plan on July 1, 1995. The plan year ended on December 31; consequently, the first plan year was a short plan year ending December 31, 1995. The plan required an employee to complete a year of service before the employee was eligible to participate. However, ABC Company waived the service requirement for any employee employed on July 1, 1995. Carol was hired on June 15, 1995, and was consequently eligible to make elective contributions on July 1, 1995.

For purposes of applying the minimum participation rules to the 1995 plan year, no employee could be disregarded under the plan's one-year-of-service requirement because there was an employee, Carol, who did not satisfy the one-year-of-service requirement but who was benefiting under the plan.

2. *Air pilots and nonresident aliens.* Air pilots covered by collective bargaining agreements and nonresident aliens who had no U.S.-source earned income were considered excludable employees. Also, certain nonresident aliens who had U.S.-source earned income could be excluded if a treaty so provided. [Treas Reg §§ 1.401(a)(26)-6(b)(2), 1.401(a)(26)-6(b)(3)]

3. *Collective bargaining employees.* Employees who were covered by a collective bargaining agreement (see Q 10:33) could be treated as excludable employees when testing a 401(k) plan covering only non-collective bargaining employees. [Treas Reg § 1.401(a)(26)-6(b)(4)]

4. *Non-collective bargaining employees.* Employees not covered by a collective bargaining agreement could be treated as excludable employees when testing a 401(k) plan covering only collective bargaining employees. [Treas Reg § 1.401(a)(26)-6(b)(5)]

5. *Employees of qualified separate lines of business (QSLOBs).* When applying the minimum participation rules to a 401(k) plan that benefited the employees of a QSLOB, the employees of other QSLOBs were considered excludable employees. Employees of other QSLOBs were not disregarded, however, if the plan was tested under the special rule for employer-wide plans. (See Q 10:15.) [Treas Reg § 1.401(a)(26)-6(b)(8)]

Testing for Minimum Participation

Q 10:6 How was a 401(k) plan tested to determine whether it satisfied the minimum participation rules?

Code Section 401(a)(26) required the minimum participation rules to be satisfied on each day of the plan year. However, the final regulations provided an alternative simplified testing method. Under this method, the 401(k) plan was treated as satisfying Code Section 401(a)(26) for a plan year if the 401(k) plan satisfied the minimum participation rule on any one day of the plan year. However, the day selected must have been reasonably representative of the employer's workforce and the plan's coverage. A 401(k) plan did not have to be tested on the same day each plan year. [Treas Reg §§ 1.401(a)(26)-7(a), 1.401(a)(26)-7(b)]

Example. A calendar-year 401(k) plan was tested on December 31, 1995, to determine whether it satisfied the minimum participation rules for 1995. For the 1996 plan year, the employer could select January 1, 1996, as the testing day if that day was reasonably representative of the employer's workforce and the plan's coverage during 1996.

Correcting Minimum Participation Failure

Q 10:7 What happened if a 401(k) plan failed to satisfy the minimum participation rules?

The sanction for failing to satisfy the minimum participation rules was directed at HCEs. In the case of a failure, an HCE was required to include in gross income the value of the HCE's vested account balances (other than any value attributable to the HCE's own basis in the plan resulting from after-tax contributions, PS-58 costs, and taxable loans) as of the close of the plan year in which the failure occurred. [IRC § 402(b)(2)]

Q 10:8 Was there any way to correct a failure retroactively?

Yes. The August 1993 final regulations under Code Section 401(a)(4) contain a mechanism for retroactive correction, which, as explained in more detail at Qs 10:39–10:41, involved making contributions on behalf of additional nonhighly compensated employees (NHCEs). This retroactive correction method could be avoided if potential minimum participation problems were detected and cured before the end of the plan year.

Example. ABC Company sponsored a 401(k) plan covering the employees of its Alpha Division. The employees of its Beta Division were not covered by the plan. For years, employment at the Alpha Division was higher than at the Beta Division; consequently, the minimum participation rules were easily satisfied. However, employment at the two divisions shifted so that the 401(k) plan benefited fewer than 40 percent of ABC Company's nonexcludable employees. (Assume that ABC Company was a small company and that the 50-employee component of the minimum participation rule did not apply.) To ensure that the 401(k) plan satisfied Code Section 401(a)(26), ABC Company needed to extend the coverage of the 401(k) plan to the employees of the Beta Division. This had to be accomplished before the end of the plan year.

Automatically Satisfying Minimum Participation

Q 10:9 Did any 401(k) plans automatically satisfy the minimum participation rules?

The final regulations allowed the types of 401(k) plans described below to automatically satisfy Code Section 401(a)(26).

1. *Plans not benefiting HCEs.* To qualify for this exception for a plan year, a 401(k) plan must have satisfied all of the following requirements:

- The 401(k) plan must not have been a top-heavy plan.
- The 401(k) plan must not have benefited any HCEs.
- The 401(k) plan must not have been combined with any other plan to enable the other plan to satisfy the minimum coverage rules under Code Section 410(b). A plan was not considered combined with another plan for this purpose even though it was combined with another plan under the Section 410(b) average benefit percentage test. (See Q 10:26.)

[Treas Reg § 1.401(a)(26)-1(b)(1)]

2. *Multiemployer plans.* The portion of a multiemployer 401(k) plan covering collective bargaining employees automatically satisfied Code Section 401(a)(26). The portion of a multiemployer 401(k) plan that benefited employees who were not collective bargaining employees was treated as a separate plan. (See the definition of *plan* in chapter 9.) This deemed-separate plan had to satisfy the minimum participation rules by itself unless the multiemployer 401(k) plan benefited at least 50 employees (whether or not these employees were members of a collective bargaining unit). [Treas Reg § 1.401(a)(26)-1(b)(2)]

3. *Certain acquisitions or dispositions.* The final regulations provided a transition period for the 401(k) plans of an employer involved in an asset or stock acquisition, merger, or other similar transaction involving a change in the employer of the employ-

ees of a trade or business. During the transition period, the minimum participation rules were automatically satisfied. The transition period began on the date of the acquisition or disposition and ended on the last day of the plan year following the plan year in which the acquisition or disposition occurred. [Treas Reg § 1.401(a)(26)-1(b)(5)]

Example. ABC Company purchased the stock of a corporation that maintained a 401(k) plan for that corporation's 35 employees. After the acquisition, the 401(k) plan of the purchased corporation covered fewer than 40 percent of ABC Company's nonexcludable employees. If the acquisition occurred on August 15, 1995, and the 401(k) plan had a calendar year, then the 401(k) plan was automatically treated as satisfying the minimum participation rules until the last day of the transition period, December 31, 1996.

MINIMUM COVERAGE

The minimum coverage rules require employers to make a 401(k) plan available to a cross section of employees. Certain plans automatically satisfy the coverage rules, but most others must meet either of two tests: the ratio percentage test or the average benefits test. The minimum coverage rules are applied to each plan as that term is defined in chapter 9. There are rules, however, that permit or require plans to be combined before the minimum coverage rules are applied. The employer, for purposes of the coverage rules, is considered to be the entity sponsoring the plan and all other entities required to be aggregated with it, as explained in greater detail in chapter 9.

Automatically Satisfying Minimum Coverage

Q 10:10 What types of 401(k) plans automatically satisfy the Code Section 401(b) minimum coverage rules?

Four types of 401(k) plans automatically satisfy the minimum coverage rules:

1. A plan maintained by an employer that has no non-highly compensated employees (NHCEs) at any time during the plan year [Treas Reg § 1.410(b)-2(b)(5)];

2. A plan that benefits no HCEs during the plan year [Treas Reg § 1.410(b)-2(b)(6)];

3. A plan that benefits only collective bargaining employees [Treas Reg § 1.410(b)-2(b)(7)];

4. During the transition period described in Q 10:9, a plan of an employer involved in an asset or stock acquisition, merger, or other similar transaction involving a change in the employer of the employees of a trade or business. [Treas Reg § 1.410(b)-2(f)]

Example. Acme maintains a 401(k) plan that covers both its collective and non-collective bargaining employees. The 401(k) plan provides for elective contributions only. For purposes of the minimum coverage rules, the 401(k) plan is treated as two plans, one covering the collective bargaining employees and the other covering the non-collective bargaining employees. (See definition of *plan* in chapter 9.) The plan covering the collective bargaining employees automatically satisfies the coverage rules. Note that if the 401(k) plan also provided for matching contributions and employer nonelective contributions, the 401(k) plan would be treated as if it consisted of six separate plans. The three plans covering the collective bargaining employees would automatically satisfy the minimum coverage rules.

Ratio Percentage Test

Q 10:11 What is the *ratio percentage test*?

The *ratio percentage test* is a test that requires that the percentage of NHCEs benefiting under the plan be at least 70 percent of the percentage of HCEs benefiting under the plan. [Treas Reg § 1.410(b)-2(b)(2)]

Example 1. ABC Company maintains a 401(k) plan that benefits 70 percent of its NHCEs and 100 percent of its HCEs. The 401(k) plan satisfies the ratio percentage test because the percentage of NHCEs benefiting under the plan (70 percent) is 70 percent of the percentage of HCEs benefiting under the plan (100 percent).

Example 2. XYZ Company maintains a 401(k) plan that benefits 40 percent of its NHCEs and 60 percent of its HCEs. The 401(k) plan does not satisfy the ratio percentage test because the percentage of NHCEs benefiting under the plan (40 percent) is 66.67 percent of the percentage of HCEs benefiting under the plan (60 percent).

Q 10:12 What does it mean to benefit under a 401(k) plan?

The definition of benefiting depends on the portion of the 401(k) plan being tested. (See definition of *plan* in chapter 9.) In the case of the portion of the 401(k) plan attributable to elective contributions, benefiting means being eligible to make elective contributions. Similarly, being eligible to make employee contributions or to receive an allocation of matching contributions constitutes benefiting under the Section 401(m) portion of the plan. Employees are considered eligible even though eligibility to make elective contributions and employee contributions and to receive matching contributions has been suspended owing to a hardship distribution, a loan, or an election not to participate. [Treas Reg § 1.410(b)-3(a)(2)(i)] With respect to that portion of a 401(k) plan attributable to nonelective contributions, the minimum coverage rules require employees to actually receive an allocation of contributions or forfeitures before they are considered to be benefiting. [Treas Reg § 1.401(b)-3(a)(1)] An employee who would otherwise benefit under a 401(k) plan but for the limits imposed by Code Section 415 is still treated as benefiting. [Treas Reg § 1.410(b)-3(a)(2)(ii)]

Q 10:13 Are there special rules that apply to HCEs in determining whether they benefit under the plan?

Not any longer. For purposes of applying the minimum coverage rules to plan years beginning before 1997, an HCE who was a 5 percent owner or one of the ten most highly paid HCEs and the family members of the HCE were treated as a single HCE. If the HCE or any one of the family members benefited under the plan, the deemed-single HCE was treated as benefiting. The family members of an HCE were the spouse of the HCE, the HCE's lineal ancestors and their spouses, and the HCE's lineal descendants and their spouses. [Treas Reg § 1.410(b)-8(b)]

Example. RQS Company sponsors a 401(k) plan covering only the employees of Division A. RQS Company is owned equally by Chris and Mary, who are not related. Chris and her husband, Jeff, are employed by Division A, whereas Mary is employed by Division B and, consequently, is not benefiting under the plan. The percentage of HCEs benefiting under the plan for the plan year ending December 31, 1996, is 50 percent. It is 50 percent, rather than 66.67 percent, because Chris, who is an HCE owning 50 percent of RQS Company, and Jeff are treated as a single HCE for purposes of applying the minimum coverage rules to pre-1997 plan years.

For plan years beginning after 1996, the Small Business Job Protection Act of 1996 eliminated this family aggregation rule.

Q 10:14 May 401(k) plans be combined to satisfy the ratio percentage test?

401(k) plans may be combined only if they have the same plan years. Generally, portions of plans that are required to be treated as separate plans (see definition of *plan* in chapter 9) cannot be combined (nor can an employer combine two or more plans that would be disaggregated if they were portions of the same plan). If an employer treats two or more plans as a single plan for purposes of the ratio percentage test, it must treat them as a single plan for purposes of applying all other nondiscrimination rules. [Treas Reg § 1.410(b)-7(d)]

Example 1. ABC Company maintains a 401(k) plan covering its salaried and office clerical employees and maintains a defined benefit plan for its collective bargaining employees. No plan is maintained for ABC Company's noncollective bargaining hourly employees. The 401(k) plan cannot be aggregated with the defined benefit plan for purposes of satisfying the ratio percentage test. Aggregation is not allowed because plans established for collective bargaining employees cannot be aggregated with plans established for employees who are not covered by a collective bargaining agreement.

Example 2. Employer X maintains two 401(k) plans, one for its salaried employees and the other for its non-collective bargaining hourly employees. Employer X decides to treat the two plans as a single plan for purposes of satisfying the ratio percentage test. Because the plans have been aggregated, they must be treated as one plan in applying the nondiscrimination rules. (See chapters 11 and 12.) Consequently, the actual deferral percentage test for determining whether elective contributions are discriminatory in amount will be applied as if the two 401(k) plans were one. If either or both of the plans provide for matching and/or employee contributions, the actual contribution percentage test will be applied as if the two plans were one. Any nonelective contributions to the plans will be tested under the Section 401(a)(4) nondiscrimination rules as if the two plans were one. Finally, the benefits, rights, or features provided under the plans will be tested as if the plans were one plan.

Q 10:15 Is there an exception to the rule that 401(k) plans that are required to be treated as separate plans cannot be combined for purposes of the ratio percentage test?

Yes. Normally, a 401(k) plan covering the employees of two or more QSLOBs must be treated as consisting of as many plans as there are QSLOBs. (See definition of *plan* in chapter 9.) However, this disaggregation rule may be ignored and the ratio percentage test satisfied if the plan, when tested on an employer-wide basis, benefits 70 percent of the employer's NHCEs. If a plan is tested on an employer-wide basis, other nondiscrimination rules are also applied on that basis. [Treas Reg § 1.414(r)-1(c)(2)(ii)]

Example. Employer A maintains a 401(k) plan covering all three of its QSLOBs. Tested on an employer-wide basis, the plan benefits 70 percent of Employer A's NHCEs; thus, the rules requiring the plan to be treated as three separate plans (one for each QSLOB) may be ignored. Because the plan is tested on an employer-wide basis, the nondiscrimination rules are also applied on that basis. For example, the actual deferral percentage test, used to determine whether elective contributions are discriminatory in amount, will take into account all employees of Employer A. (See "Actual Deferral Percentage Test" in chapter 12.) If the 401(k) plan had not been tested on an employer-wide basis, an actual deferral percentage test would have to be conducted separately with respect to each QSLOB.

Q 10:16 If an employer that is divided into QSLOBs maintains a 401(k) plan that is tested on an employer-wide basis, may that plan be combined with any other plan maintained by the employer to demonstrate that the other plan satisfies the ratio percentage test?

No. [Treas Reg § 1.410(b)-7(d)(4)]

Example. Employer A is divided into two QSLOBs. Employer A maintains a 401(k) plan that benefits all of its employees and that is considered to satisfy the ratio percentage test on an employer-wide basis. Employer A also maintains a defined benefit plan that benefits the salaried and office clerical employees of QSLOB 1. The defined benefit plan does not benefit 70 percent of Employer A's NHCEs when tested on an employer-wide basis. In determining whether the defined benefit plan satisfies the ratio percentage test, the defined benefit plan may not be combined with that portion of the 401(k) plan that benefits the employees of QSLOB 1.

Average Benefits Test

Q 10:17 What is the *average benefits test*?

The *average benefits test* consists of two separate tests, both of which must be satisfied. The two tests are the nondiscriminatory classification test (see Qs 10:18–10:25) and the average benefit percentage test (see Qs 10:26–10:31). [Treas Reg § 1.410(b)-2(b)(3)]

Nondiscriminatory Classification Test

Q 10:18 What is the *nondiscriminatory classification test*?

The *nondiscriminatory classification test* is a test that requires the 401(k) plan to benefit a class of employees established by the employer that is both reasonable and nondiscriminatory. [Treas Reg § 1.410(b)-4(a)]

Q 10:19 What is a *reasonable classification*?

A *reasonable classification* is one established under objective business criteria that identify the group of employees who are eligible to participate in the 401(k) plan. Reasonable classifications include job categories, nature of compensation (salaried or hourly), and geographic location. A list of named employees eligible to participate in the plan would not be considered a reasonable classification. [Treas Reg § 1.410(b)-4(b)]

Q 10:20 What is a *nondiscriminatory classification* of employees?

A *classification* is automatically considered *nondiscriminatory* if the 401(k) plan's ratio percentage (the percentage determined by dividing the percentage of NHCEs benefiting under the plan by the percentage of HCEs benefiting under the plan) is greater than or equal to the safe harbor percentage. [Treas Reg § 1.410(b)-4(c)(2)] If the plan's ratio percentage is less than the safe harbor percentage, a classification can still be considered nondiscriminatory if

1. The plan's ratio percentage is greater than or equal to the plan's unsafe harbor percentage; and

2. The classification, based on all relevant facts and circumstances, is determined by the IRS to be nondiscriminatory.

[Treas Reg § 1.410(b)-4(c)(3)]

Q 10:21 What is the *safe harbor percentage*?

A 401(k) plan's *safe harbor percentage* is 50 percent reduced by three quarters of a percentage point for each whole percentage point by which the NHCE concentration percentage is greater than 60 percent. [Treas Reg § 1.410(b)-4(c)(4)(i)]

Q 10:22 What is the *unsafe harbor percentage*?

A 401(k) plan's *unsafe harbor percentage* is 40 percent reduced by three quarters of a percentage point for each whole percentage point by which the NHCE concentration percentage is greater than 60 percent. In no event, however, can the unsafe harbor percentage be less than 20 percent. [Treas Reg § 1.410(b)-4(c)(4)(ii)]

TABLE 10-1. Safe and Unsafe Harbor Percentages

NHCE Concentration Percentage	Safe Harbor Percentage	Unsafe Harbor Percentage
0–60%	50.00%	40.00%
61	49.25	39.25
62	48.50	38.50
63	47.75	37.75
64	47.00	37.00
65	46.25	36.25
66	45.50	35.50
67	44.75	34.75
68	44.00	34.00
69	43.25	33.25
70	42.50	32.50
71	41.75	31.75
72	41.00	31.00
73	40.25	30.25
74	39.50	29.50
75	38.75	28.75
76	38.00	28.00
77	37.25	27.25
78	36.50	26.50
79	35.75	25.75
80	35.00	25.00
81	34.25	24.25
82	33.50	23.50
83	32.75	22.75
84	32.00	22.00
85	31.25	21.25

TABLE 10-1   (continued)

NHCE Concentration Percentage	Safe Harbor Percentage	Unsafe Harbor Percentage
86	30.50	20.50
87	29.75	20.00
88	29.00	20.00
89	28.25	20.00
90	27.50	20.00
91	26.75	20.00
92	26.00	20.00
93	25.25	20.00
94	24.50	20.00
95	23.75	20.00
96	23.00	20.00
97	22.25	20.00
98	21.50	20.00
99	20.75	20.00

Q 10:23   What is the *NHCE concentration percentage*?

An employer's *NHCE concentration percentage* is the percentage of all employees of the employer who are NHCEs. This percentage is determined by taking into account only nonexcludable employees. (See Q 10:32.) [Treas Reg § 1.410(b)-4(c)(4)(iii)]

Table 10-1 shows the safe and unsafe harbor percentages for any given NHCE concentration percentage.

Q 10:24   What facts and circumstances will be taken into account in determining whether a classification under a 401(k) plan will be considered nondiscriminatory?

The regulations cite several examples of facts and circumstances that will be taken into account in determining whether a classification is nondiscriminatory:

1. The underlying business reason for the classification. The greater the business reason for the classification, the more likely the classification is nondiscriminatory. Reducing the employer's cost of providing retirement benefits is not a relevant business reason.

2. The percentage of the employer's employees benefiting under the plan. The higher the percentage, the more likely the classification is nondiscriminatory.

3. Whether the number of employees benefiting under the plan in each salary range is representative of the number of employees in each salary range of the employer's workforce. In general, the more representative the percentages of employees benefiting under the plan in each salary range, the more likely the classification is nondiscriminatory.

4. The difference between the plan's ratio percentage and the safe harbor percentage. The smaller the difference, the more likely the classification is nondiscriminatory.

5. The extent to which the plan's average benefit percentage exceeds 70 percent. (See Q 10:27.)

[Treas Reg § 1.410(b)-4(c)(3)(ii)]

Example 1. Employer A has 200 nonexcludable employees. Of those employees, 120 are NHCEs and 80 are HCEs. Employer A maintains a 401(k) plan that benefits 60 NHCEs and 72 HCEs. Thus, the plan's ratio percentage is 55.56 percent [(60/120)/(72/80) = 0.5556], which is below the percentage (70 percent) necessary to satisfy the ratio percentage test. Employer A's NHCE concentration percentage is 60 percent (120/200); thus, Employer A's safe harbor percentage is 50 percent, and its unsafe harbor percentage is 40 percent. (See Table 10-1.) Because the plan's ratio percentage is greater than the safe harbor percentage, the plan's classification is considered nondiscriminatory.

Example 2. Employer B has 10,000 nonexcludable employees. Of those employees, 9,600 are NHCEs and 400 are HCEs. Employer B maintains a 401(k) plan that benefits 500 NHCEs and 100 HCEs. Thus, the plan's ratio percentage is 20.83 percent [(500/9,600)/(100/400) = 0.2083], which is below the percentage necessary (70 percent) to satisfy the ratio percentage test.

Employer B's NHCE concentration percentage is 96 percent (9,600/ 10,000); thus, the plan's safe harbor percentage is 23 percent, and its unsafe harbor percentage is 20 percent. Because the plan's ratio percentage (20.83 percent) is above the unsafe harbor percentage (20 percent) and below the safe harbor percentage (23 percent), the IRS may determine that the classification is nondiscriminatory after considering all the facts and circumstances.

Q 10:25 May 401(k) plans be combined to satisfy the nondiscriminatory classification test?

Yes, 401(k) plans may be combined in the same way as they are for purposes of satisfying the ratio percentage test. (See Q 10:14.) [Treas Reg § 1.410(b)-7(d)]

Average Benefit Percentage Test

Q 10:26 What is the *average benefit percentage test?*

The *average benefit percentage test* is one that requires the average benefit percentage of the 401(k) plan for the plan year to be at least 70 percent. [Treas Reg § 1.410(b)-5(a)]

Q 10:27 How is the average benefit percentage calculated?

The average benefit percentage is determined by dividing the actual benefit percentage of the NHCEs in plans in the testing group for the testing period by the actual benefit percentage of the HCEs in plans in the testing group for the testing period. (See Q 10:30 for the definition of the testing period.) [Treas Reg § 1.410(b)-5(b)]

Q 10:28 How is the actual benefit percentage of each group calculated?

The actual benefit percentage of a group of employees (highly compensated or non-highly compensated) for a testing period is the average of the employee benefit percentages, calculated separately with respect to each employee of the group, for the testing period. If nonexcludable employees are not benefiting under a plan, their employee benefit percentages are zero. [Treas Reg § 1.410(b)-5(c)]

Q 10:29 What is the *testing group*?

The *testing group* consists of the 401(k) plan being tested and all other plans that could be combined with the plan for purposes of satisfying the ratio percentage test or the nondiscriminatory classification test (the same-plan-year requirement does not apply, however). (See Qs 10:14, 10:25.) The rules requiring disaggregation on the basis of types of contributions are also ignored (see definition of *plan* in chapter 9). Consequently, elective contributions and matching contributions (but not employee after-tax contributions) are included in determining an employee's benefit percentage. In addition, the rules requiring disaggregation of the ESOP and non-ESOP portions of a plan are not taken into account. Finally, the portions of plans benefiting the employees of the same QSLOB are combined even though one or more of the plans may have been tested on an employer-wide basis. (See Q 10:16.) [Treas Reg §§ 1.410(b)-5(d)(3)(i), 1.410(b)-7(e)(1)]

> **Example.** Employer X is treated as operating two QSLOBs: QSLOB 1 and QSLOB 2. Employer X maintains the following plans:
>
> 1. Plan A, the portion of Employer X's employer-wide 401(k) plan that benefits all non-collectively bargained employees of QSLOB 1;
>
> 2. Plan B, the portion of Employer X's employer-wide 401(k) plan that benefits all non-collectively bargained employees of QSLOB 2;
>
> 3. Plan C, a defined benefit plan that benefits all hourly, non-collectively bargained employees of QSLOB 1;
>
> 4. Plan D, a defined benefit plan that benefits all collectively bargained employees of QSLOB 1;
>
> 5. Plan E, an ESOP that benefits all non-collectively bargained employees of QSLOB 1; and
>
> 6. Plan F, a profit sharing plan that benefits all salaried, non-collectively bargained employees of QSLOB 1.

Assume that Plan F does not satisfy the ratio percentage test but satisfies the nondiscriminatory classification test. Therefore, to satisfy the minimum coverage rules, Plan F must satisfy the average benefit percentage test. The plans in the testing group used to determine whether Plan F satisfies the average benefit percentage test are Plans A, C, E, and F. Plan B is not included in the testing group because it is maintained by QSLOB 2. Plan D is not included in the testing group because it is maintained for the benefit of collective bargaining employees.

Q 10:30 What is the testing period for the average benefit percentage calculation?

An employee's benefit percentage (see Q 10:28) is determined on the basis of plan years ending in the same calendar year. These plan years, in the aggregate, are considered the testing period. [Treas Reg § 1.410(b)-5(d)(3)(ii)]

Q 10:31 How is an employee's benefit percentage calculated?

The rules for determining an employee's benefit percentage can be quite complicated, but, in general, an employee's benefit percentage is calculated by dividing employer-provided benefits or contributions by a participant's compensation for a plan year ending in the testing period. If there are both defined benefit and defined contribution plans in the testing group, either contributions must be converted to equivalent benefits or benefits must be converted to equivalent contributions. [Treas Reg § 1.410(b)-5(d)(5)]

Example. Company X has a 401(k) plan with a discretionary nonelective contribution feature that fails the ratio percentage test under Code Section 410(b). The nondiscriminatory classification test is passed, so the average benefit percentage test must be conducted based on all employer-provided benefits.

The employee benefit percentages or allocation rates are computed for two sample employees on a contribution basis by dividing the employer contribution by compensation:

Employee	Employer-Provided Contribution	Compensation	Allocation Rate
Y	$1,500	$20,000	7.5%
Z	6,000	60,000	10.0

Note: The employer-provided contribution may include elective, matching, and nonelective contributions.

The allocation rates may be adjusted to take Social Security into account. The adjustment will vary, depending on whether the employee earns more than the taxable wage base.

- For employees whose plan year compensation does not exceed taxable wage base: lesser of A rate or B rate:

  A rate = 2 × unadjusted allocation rate (UAR)
  B rate = UAR + permitted disparity rate (PDR)

- For employees whose plan year compensation exceeds taxable wage base: lesser of C rate or D rate:

$$C\text{ rate} = \frac{\text{Allocation}}{\text{Compensation} - \frac{1}{2}\text{ taxable wage base (TWB)}}$$

$$D\text{ rate} = \frac{\text{Allocation} + (\text{PDR} \times \text{TWB})}{\text{Compensation}}$$

- For Employee Y, who earns less than the maximum taxable wage base of $55,500, the adjusted allocation rate is the lesser of

  A rate = 2 × 7.5% = 15%
  B rate = 7.5% + 5.7% = 13.2%

  Employee Y's adjusted allocation rate is 13.2%.

- For Employee Z, who earns more than the maximum taxable wage base of $55,500, the adjusted allocation rate is the lesser of:

$$C\text{ rate} = \frac{6,000}{60,000 - (\frac{1}{2} \times 55,500)}$$

$$= \frac{6,000}{32,250} = 18.6\%$$

$$D\text{ rate} = \frac{6,000 + (0.057 \times 55,500)}{60,000}$$

$$= \frac{9,163.50}{60,000} = 15.3\%$$

Employee Z's adjusted allocation rate is 15.3%.

Rather than computing allocation rates, the plan sponsor may convert the contributions to benefits by computing equivalent benefit accrual rates. Two methods are allowed: an annual method (using the annual allocation to the participant's account) and the accrued-to-date method (using the participant's account balance).

The annual method will convert the contributions to benefits using the following steps:

1. Determine the dollar amount of allocation;
2. Convert to a single life annuity benefit at testing age; and
3. Express the single life annuity benefit as a percentage of compensation. Note: This is called an equivalent accrual rate (EAR).

Using testing age 65, 8.5 percent interest, and UP-1984 mortality, the equivalent accrual rates are computed as follows:

Employee	Y (Age 35)	Z (Age 55)
Annual allocation	$ 1,500	$ 6,000
Converted benefit	$ 2,115	$ 1,707
Compensation	$20,000	$60,000
EAR	10.6%	2.8%

Note: Permitted disparity has not been imputed.

The accrued-to-date method uses the account balance and testing service (the number of years in which a contribution was allocated to the participant) to obtain an equivalent accrual rate:

1. Determine adjusted allocation:
$$\frac{\text{Account balance}}{\text{Testing service}}$$
2. Convert to a single life annuity benefit at testing age; and
3. Express benefit as a percentage of compensation.

Using testing age 65, 8.5 percent interest, and UP 1984 mortality, the equivalent accrual rates are computed as follows:

Employee	Y (Age 35)	Z (Age 55)
Account balance	$35,000	$120,000
Testing service	10 yrs	12 yrs
Adjusted allocation	$ 3,500	$ 10,000
Converted benefit	$ 5,090	$ 2,845
Compensation	$20,000	$ 60,000
EAR	25.4%	4.7%

Note: Permitted disparity has not been imputed.

Disregarding Certain Employees

Q 10:32 Can a 401(k) plan disregard certain employees in applying the minimum coverage rules?

Yes. In applying the minimum coverage rules, certain employees may be excluded. These exclusions are applied with reference to the 401(k) plan that is being tested. If, for example, two or more plans are combined, whether permissively, as in the case of the ratio percentage or nondiscriminatory classification tests, or mandatorily, as in the case of the average benefit percentage test, the exclusions are applied to this deemed-single plan. [Treas Reg § 1.410(b)-6(a)(2)]

Q 10:33 Which employees may be excluded?

The employees described below may be excluded in applying the minimum coverage rules:

1. *Age and service conditions.* A 401(k) plan may exclude all employees who have not satisfied the plan's age and service eligibility conditions until the date on which employees enter the plan. This exclusion is available, however, only if no employee who does not satisfy these conditions is benefiting under the plan. [Treas Reg § 1.410(b)-6(b)(1)]. If a plan has two or more age and service eligibility conditions, only those employees who fail to satisfy all the different sets of age and service conditions are excludable. [Treas Reg § 1.410(b)-6(b)(2)]

Example. ABC Company maintains Plan A for salaried employees and Plan B for hourly employees. Plan A has no minimum age or service condition. Plan B has no minimum age condition but requires one year of service. ABC Company treats Plans A and B as a single plan for purposes of the ratio percentage test. Because Plan A does not impose minimum age and service conditions, all employees of ABC Company automatically satisfy the minimum age and service conditions of Plan A. Therefore, no employees can be excluded for purposes of satisfying the ratio percentage test.

2. *Air pilots and nonresident aliens.* Air pilots covered by collective bargaining agreements and nonresident aliens who have no U.S.-source earned income are considered excludable employees. Also, certain nonresident aliens who have U.S.-source earned income may be excluded if a treaty so provides. [IRC § 410(b)(3)(B); Treas Reg § 1.410(b)-6(c)]

3. *Collective bargaining employees.* Employees who are covered by a collective bargaining agreement are treated as excludable employees when testing a plan covering only noncollective bargaining employees. [Treas Reg § 1.410(b)-6(d)] A collective bargaining employee is an employee who is included in a unit of employees covered by an agreement that the Secretary of Labor finds to be a collective bargaining agreement between employee representatives and one or more employers, provided there is evidence that retirement benefits were the subject of good-faith bargaining between employee representatives and the employer or employers. [Treas Reg § 1.410(b)-6(d)(2)(i)] However, an employee will not be considered a collective bargaining employee if 50 percent of the membership of the organization to which he or she belongs consists of owners, officers, or executives of employers. [IRC § 7701(a)(46)] In addition, an employee will not be considered covered under a collective bargaining agreement if more than 2 percent of the employees who are covered under the agreement are professionals. [Treas Reg §§ 1.410(b)-6(d)(2)(iii)(B)(1), 1.410(b)-9]

4. *Employees of QSLOBs.* When applying the minimum coverage rules to a 401(k) plan that benefits the employees of a QSLOB, the employees of other QSLOBs are considered excludable employees. This exclusion does not apply, however, in determining whether a plan satisfies the nondiscriminatory classification test. [Treas Reg

§ 1.410(b)-6(e)] Also, this exclusion is disregarded if a plan is tested on an employer-wide basis. (See Q 10:15.)

5. *Certain terminating employees.* An employee may be treated as an excludable employee for a plan year with respect to a plan if all of the following requirements are met:

- The employee does not benefit under the plan for the plan year.

- The employee is eligible to participate in the plan.

- The plan has a minimum service requirement or a requirement that an employee be employed on the last day of the plan year (last-day requirement) for an employee to receive an allocation for the plan year.

- The employee fails to receive an allocation under the plan solely because of the failure to satisfy the minimum service or last-day requirement.

- The employee is not employed on the last day of the plan year and is credited with no more than 500 hours of service.

[Treas Reg § 1.410(b)-6(f)]

Example. Employer X has 30 employees who are eligible to participate under a 401(k) plan that also provides for discretionary, nonelective contributions. The plan requires 1,000 hours of service to receive an allocation of nonelective contributions. Ten employees do not receive an allocation because of their failure to complete 1,000 hours of service. Three of the ten employees who fail to satisfy the minimum service requirement complete 500 or fewer hours of service and terminate their employment. Two of the employees complete more than 500 but fewer than 1,000 hours of service and terminate their employment. The remaining five employees do not terminate employment. The three terminated employees who complete 500 or fewer hours of service are treated as excludable employees for the portion of the plan year they are employed. The other seven employees who do not receive an allocation are taken into account for purposes of the minimum coverage rules, but are treated as not benefiting under the nonelective contribution portion of the plan.

Testing for Minimum Coverage

Q 10:34 How is a 401(k) plan tested to determine whether it satisfies the minimum coverage rules?

The regulations set forth three methods for determining whether a 401(k) plan satisfies the minimum coverage rules:

1. The daily testing method;
2. The quarterly testing method; and
3. The annual testing method.

The last of these methods must be used by those portions of a 401(k) plan attributable to elective contributions and to matching and employee contributions. (See definition of *plan* in chapter 9.) The annual testing method must also be used to apply the average benefit percentage test. [Treas Reg § 1.410(b)-8(a)]

Q 10:35 What is the *daily testing method*?

The *daily testing method* is a method under which the employer must show that a 401(k) plan satisfies the ratio percentage or non-discriminatory classification test on each day of the plan year. Only individuals employed on that day are taken into account. [Treas Reg § 1.410(b)-8(a)(2)]

Q 10:36 What is the *quarterly testing method*?

The *quarterly testing method* is a method under which the employer must show that the 401(k) plan satisfies the ratio percentage test or nondiscriminatory classification test on at least one day in each quarter of the plan year. The days selected must be reasonably representative of the plan's coverage over the entire plan year. Only individuals employed on the dates selected are taken into account. [Treas Reg § 1.410(b)-8(a)(3)]

Q 10:37 What is the *annual testing method*?

The *annual testing method* is a method under which the employer must show that the minimum coverage rules are satisfied on the last day of the plan year, taking into account all individuals who were employed on any day during the plan year. [Treas Reg § 1.410(b)-8(a)(4)]

Correcting Minimum Coverage Failure

Q 10:38 What happens if a 401(k) plan fails to satisfy the minimum coverage rules?

The sanction for failing to satisfy the minimum coverage rules is directed at HCEs. In the case of a failure, an HCE must include in gross income the value of the HCE's vested account balances (other than any value attributable to the HCE's own basis in the plan resulting from after-tax contributions, PS-58 costs, and taxable loans) as of the close of the plan year in which the failure occurs. [IRC § 401(b)(2)]

Q 10:39 Is there any way to correct retroactively a failure to satisfy the minimum coverage rules?

Yes. Final regulations under Code Section 401(a)(4) issued in August 1993 allow plans to be amended retroactively to satisfy the minimum coverage rules. In the case of the portion of the plan attributable to elective contributions, retroactive correction is accomplished by making qualified nonelective contributions (see Q 12:14) to nonexcludable NHCEs who were not considered eligible employees (see Q 12:12) for the plan year in question. Similarly, if the portion of a 401(k) plan attributable to matching contributions and employee contributions does not satisfy the minimum coverage rules, qualified nonelective contributions can be made on behalf of nonexcludable NHCEs who were not considered eligible employees (see Q 12:48) for the plan year in question. [Treas Reg § 1.401(a)(4)-11(g)(3)(vii)]

Example. Employer M maintains an elective-contribution-only 401(k) plan for the employees of Division A. For its plan year ending December 31, 1999, the 401(k) plan does not cover the employees of Division B. The QSLOB rules do not apply. After the end of the 1999 plan year, the plan administrator determines that the 401(k) plan can satisfy neither the ratio percentage test nor the nondiscriminatory classification test. To satisfy the minimum coverage rules, Employer M amends the 401(k) plan to provide for qualified nonelective contributions on behalf of the nonex-cludable Division B NHCEs.

Q 10:40 What level of qualified nonelective contributions must be provided to these NHCEs?

The amount to be provided to each nonexcludable NHCE equals his or her compensation for the plan year in question multiplied by the actual deferral percentage (see Q 12:3) of the group of NHCEs who were eligible employees under the 401(k) plan. [Treas Reg § 1.401(a)(4)-11(g)(3)(vii)]

Example. In the example in Q 10:39, the actual deferral percentage of the NHCE group for the 1999 plan year was 4 percent. Hence, Employer M must provide to each nonexcludable Division B NHCE an amount equal to 4 percent of his or her 1999 compensation.

Q 10:41 By when must a 401(k) plan be amended to correct retroactively a failure to satisfy the minimum coverage rules?

The 401(k) plan must be amended, and the amendment must be implemented, no later than the fifteenth day of the tenth month after the close of the plan year. [Treas Reg § 1.401(a)(4)-11(g)(3)(iv)] For example, in the case of a plan year ending December 31, 1999, the corrective amendment must be made and implemented by October 15, 2000.

Q 10:42 Does the method of retroactive correction discussed in Qs 10:39–10:41 apply to the nonelective contribution portion of a 401(k) plan?

Yes. In this case, however, correction does not require that qualified nonelective contributions be made on behalf of NHCEs. All that is required is a timely amendment (see Q 10:41) that brings in a sufficient number of employees to satisfy the minimum coverage rules.

11 General Nondiscrimination Testing

Like other qualified plans, a 401(k) plan will retain its qualified status only if the contributions or benefits under the plan do not discriminate in favor of highly compensated employees (HCEs). (See chapter 9 for the definition of *highly compensated employee*.) This chapter discusses what tests are applied in determining whether the amount of employer nonelective contributions (such as profit sharing contributions) is discriminatory. The special tests that apply to elective (deferral) contributions, matching contributions, and employee after-tax contributions are covered in chapter 12. This chapter also explains the interaction of the permitted disparity rules with the antidiscrimination requirement. Finally, this chapter addresses the rules for determining whether benefits, rights, and features under the plan discriminate in favor of HCEs.

TESTING OF EMPLOYER NONELECTIVE CONTRIBUTIONS

As discussed in chapter 12, the ADP and ACP tests are used to determine whether the amount of elective (deferral) contributions and matching and employee after-tax contributions (both mandatory and voluntary) made under a 401(k) plan discriminates in favor of HCEs. Employer nonelective contributions other than matching contributions must also be nondiscriminatory in amount. Profit sharing contributions are a common example of such nonelective contributions.

Under the final Section 401(a)(4) regulations, a plan may be designed to ensure that nonelective contributions to a 401(k) plan are allocated on a nondiscriminatory basis. (See Qs 11:1–11:8.) However, if a plan does not contain a design-based safe harbor formula for allocating nonelective contributions, the plan must satisfy the Section 401(a)(4) general test on either a contributions or an equivalent benefits basis. (See Qs 11:9–11:14.)

The Design-Based Safe Harbor

Q 11:1 What is the *design-based safe harbor*?

A 401(k) plan will satisfy the *design-based safe harbor* for nonelective contributions if the plan contains a uniform allocation formula (see Q 11:2) or the plan is a uniform point system plan (see Q 11:4). [Treas Reg § 1.401(a)(4)-2(b)(1)]

Q 11:2 What is a *uniform allocation formula*?

A *uniform allocation formula* is a formula that allocates the same percentage of compensation or the same dollar amount to each employee in the plan. A plan that determines allocations based on the same dollar amount for each uniform unit of service (not to exceed one week) will also be considered to have a uniform allocation formula. An allocation formula is still considered uniform even if the plan takes into account permitted disparity under Code Section 401(l). (See Qs 11:15–11:18.) [Treas Reg § 1.401(a)(4)-2(b)(2)]

11-2

Q 11:3 What is considered compensation for purposes of applying a uniform allocation formula?

A uniform allocation formula that takes into account compensation must use a definition of compensation that is nondiscriminatory under Code Section 414(s). (See the discussion of *compensation* in chapter 9.) Generally, compensation paid during the plan year will be used for this purpose, but the regulations do permit the use of compensation paid during any 12-month period ending within the plan year. The plan may also provide that only compensation paid during the portion of a plan year that an employee is a participant will be taken into account. [Treas Reg § 1.401(a)(4)-12]

Q 11:4 What is a *uniform point system plan*?

A *uniform point system plan* is a plan under which each employee's allocation of nonelective contributions is determined by multiplying the contribution to be allocated by a fraction. The numerator of the fraction is the employee's points for the year, and the denominator of the fraction is the points of all employees. A uniform point system plan must also satisfy a nondiscrimination test. [Treas Reg § 1.401(a)(4)-2(b)(3)]

Q 11:5 How are an employee's points determined?

The plan must award points for either age or service and may award points for both. Points may also be granted for units of compensation. Each employee must receive the same number of points for each year of age, for each year of service, and for each unit of compensation. The unit of compensation must be the same for all employees and cannot exceed $200. If a plan grants points for years of service, the plan may impose a limit on the number of years of service taken into account. [Treas Reg § 1.401(a)(4)-2(b)(3)(i)(A)]

Q 11:6 What nondiscrimination test must be satisfied before a plan can be considered a uniform point system plan?

For each plan year, the average of the allocation rates for HCEs cannot exceed the average of the allocation rates for NHCEs. An employee's allocation rate is the amount allocated to the employee's account for a plan year expressed as either a percentage of compensation or a dollar amount. [Treas Reg § 1.401(a)(4)-2(b)(3)(i)(B)]

Example. A 401(k) plan provides for nonelective contributions that are allocated pursuant to a uniform point system formula. The plan grants each employee ten points for each year of service and one point for each $100 of compensation. For the plan year, total allocations are $69,700, and total points for all employees in the plan are 6,970. Each employee's allocation for the plan year is set forth in the following table.

Employee	Years of Service	Plan Year Compensation	Credits	Amount of Allocation	Rate
H1	10	$150,000	1,600	$16,000	10.7
H2	5	150,000	1,550	15,500	10.3
H3	30	100,000	1,300	13,000	13.0
H4	3	100,000	1,030	10,300	10.3
N1	10	40,000	500	5,000	12.5
N2	5	35,000	400	4,000	11.4
N3	3	30,000	330	3,300	11.0
N4	1	25,000	260	2,600	10.4
Total			6,970	$69,700	

For the plan year, the average allocation rate for the HCEs in the plan (H1–H4) is 11.1 percent [(10.7% + 10.3% + 13.0% + 10.3%)/4], and the average allocation rate for NHCEs in the plan (N1–N4) is 11.3 percent [(12.5% + 11.4% + 11.0% + 10.4%)/4]. Because the average of the allocation rates for the HCEs in the plan does not exceed the average of the allocation rates for the NHCEs, the plan will be treated as a uniform point system plan for the plan year.

Q 11:7 Will an allocation of nonelective contributions that is conditioned on employment on the last day of the plan year cause an allocation formula to lose its status as a design-based safe harbor formula?

No. A 401(k) plan that contains a last-day requirement for sharing in an allocation of nonelective contributions will still be considered a design-based safe harbor formula. Similarly, a plan requiring a minimum number of hours of service in order to obtain an allocation will not affect the formula's safe harbor status. [Treas Reg § 1.401(a)(4)-2(b)(4)(iii)] However, 401(k) plans containing these requirements may find it more difficult to pass the minimum coverage rules because participants not receiving allocations on account of these requirements are likely to be treated as not benefiting. (See Q 10:12.)

Q 11:8 Will an allocation formula be considered a design-based safe harbor formula if a participant who is a non-key employee receives only a top-heavy minimum contribution?

Yes, but only if the nonelective contribution component of the 401(k) plan satisfies the Section 410(b) coverage rules when the non-key employee who receives only a top-heavy minimum contribution is treated as not benefiting (see the discussion of the minimum coverage rules in chapter 10). [Treas Reg § 1.401(a)(4)-2(b)(4)(vi)(D)(3)] If the 401(k) plan cannot satisfy the minimum coverage rules under these circumstances, the allocation formula loses its status as a design-based safe harbor formula, and the nonelective contribution portion of the 401(k) plan must satisfy the general nondiscrimination test. (See Q 11:9.)

Example. Somba Corporation sponsors a top-heavy 401(k) plan that provides for nonelective contributions allocated in proportion to the compensation paid to all those participants who are employed on the last day of the plan year and who complete 1,000 or more hours of service during the plan year. Somba makes a nonelective contribution equal to 6 percent of pay. All of its HCEs receive a 6 percent allocation, and each of 12 NHCEs receives a 6 percent allocation. The remaining 3 NHCEs receive only a top-heavy minimum contribution equal to 3 percent of pay because they have not completed 1,000 or more hours of service during the year. The plan's allocation formula is considered a design-based safe harbor because the 401(k) plan, after treating the participants who receive only a top-heavy minimum contribution as not benefiting, has a ratio percentage of 80 percent, a percentage that is in excess of the ratio percentage (70 percent) necessary to satisfy the ratio percentage test under Code Section 410(b). (See Qs 10:12–10:16.)

The General Nondiscrimination Test

Q 11:9 What is the *general nondiscrimination test?*

The *general nondiscrimination test* is a test requiring that each rate group under the plan satisfy the minimum coverage rules as if the rate group were a separate plan. [Treas Reg § 1.401(a)(4)-2(c)(1)]

Q 11:10 What is a *rate group?*

A *rate group* exists for each HCE and consists of that HCE and all other employees who have allocation rates greater than or equal to the allocation rate for that HCE. [Treas Reg § 1.401(a)(4)-2(c)(1)]

Q 11:11 What is an employee's *allocation rate?*

An employee's *allocation rate* is the amount allocated to an employee's account for the plan year expressed as either a percentage of compensation (as discussed at Q 11:13) or a dollar amount. [Treas Reg § 1.401(a)(4)-2(c)(2)(i)]

Q 11:12 What amounts are taken into account in determining allocation rates?

The amounts taken into account are the nonelective contributions (other than matching contributions) allocated to an employee's account for the plan year. Forfeitures are also included if allocated in the same way as nonelective contributions. Earnings, expenses, gains, and losses allocable to an account are not taken into account. [Treas Reg § 1.401(a)(4)-2(c)(2)(ii)]

Q 11:13 How does a rate group satisfy the minimum coverage rules?

Each rate group must satisfy the minimum coverage rules as if the rate group were a separate plan. However, in applying these rules, the following exceptions apply:

1. A rate group cannot be permissibly aggregated with another rate group for purposes of satisfying the ratio percentage test or the nondiscriminatory classification test.

2. If the rate group is being tested under the nondiscriminatory classification test, the rate group is deemed to satisfy the reasonable classification requirement. (See Q 10:19.)

3. If the rate group is being tested under the nondiscriminatory classification test, there will not be a facts-and-circumstances determination in the event that the rate group's ratio percentage (see Qs 10:20–10:24) is less than the safe harbor percentage but greater than or equal to the unsafe harbor percentage. Instead, the facts and circumstances requirement will be considered satisfied if the ratio percentage of the rate group is greater than or equal to the lesser of:

    a. The ratio percentage of the plan; or

    b. The midpoint between the safe and unsafe harbor percentages for the plan.

4. If a rate group is being tested under the average benefit percentage test, the rate group will be treated as satisfying this test if the plan of which it is a part satisfies this test.

[Treas Reg § 1.401(a)(4)-2(c)(3)]

Example. Employer Y has six nonexcludable employees, all of whom benefit under its 401(k) plan, which also provides for nonelective profit sharing contributions. The HCEs in the plan are H1 and H2, and the NHCEs are N1–N4. For the plan year, H1 and N1–N3 have an allocation rate of 5 percent of compensation. For the same plan year, H2 has an allocation rate of 7.5 percent of compensation, and N4 has an allocation rate of 8 percent of compensation.

The plan has two rate groups. Rate group 1 consists of H1 and all those employees who have an allocation rate greater than or equal to H1's allocation rate (5 percent). Thus, rate group 1 consists of H1, H2, and N1–N4. Rate group 2 consists of H2 and all those employees who have an allocation rate greater than or equal to H2's allocation rate (7.5 percent). Thus, rate group 2 consists of H2 and N4.

Rate group 1 satisfies the ratio percentage test under the minimum coverage rules because the ratio percentage of the rate group is 100 percent—that is, 100 percent (the percentage of all NHCEs who are in the rate group) divided by 100 percent (the percentage of all HCEs who are in the rate group).

Rate group 2 does not satisfy the ratio percentage test because the ratio percentage of the rate group is 50 percent—that is, 25 percent (the percentage of all NHCEs who are in the rate group) divided by 50 percent (the percentage of all HCEs who are in the rate group).

However, rate group 2 satisfies the nondiscriminatory classification test under the minimum coverage rules because the rate group is deemed to satisfy the reasonable classification requirement and the ratio percentage of the rate group (50 percent) is greater than the safe harbor percentage applicable to the plan—safe harbor percentage from Table 10-1 would be 45.5 percent based on an NHCE concentration percentage of 66.7 percent (4/6).

If the plan satisfies the average benefit percentage test (see Qs 10:26–10:31), rate group 2 will also be treated as satisfying that test. In that case, the plan satisfies the general nondiscrimination test because each rate group under the plan satisfies the minimum coverage rules as if each rate group were a separate plan.

Q 11:14 Is the general nondiscrimination test required to be satisfied on the basis of allocation rates?

No. In applying the general nondiscrimination test, a plan may substitute equivalent accrual rates for allocation rates. Equivalent accrual rates are determined by converting nonelective contributions and forfeitures allocated to employees into actuarially equivalent benefits. The ability to convert nonelective contributions into benefits is the basis for age-weighted profit sharing plans (see Q 2:40). [Treas Reg § 1.401(a)(4)-8(b)]

PERMITTED DISPARITY

The permitted disparity rules allow relatively higher retirement plan allocations on behalf of higher-paid employees as a way of recognizing that lower-paid employees receive relatively higher Social Security benefits. This section presents the basic permitted disparity rules, considers how permitted disparity can be used, and ends with the rules covering use of permitted disparity in more than one plan.

Basic Permitted Disparity Rules

Q 11:15 What is *permitted disparity*?

Permitted disparity is the allocation of nonelective contributions at different rates on compensation above and below the plan's integration level. [Treas Reg § 1.401(l)-2(a)(1)] It is allowed under Code Section 401(l) as a way of recognizing the Social Security contributions made by the employer on behalf of the plan's participants. Traditionally, permitted disparity was known as integration with Social Security, or simply integration. The rate of contribution on compensation below the integration level is called the *base contribution percentage*. [Treas Reg § 1.401(l)-1(c)(4)] The rate of contribution on compensation above the integration level is the *excess contribution percentage*. [Treas Reg § 1.401(l)-1(c)(15)]

Q 11:16 What is the *integration level*?

The *integration level* is a dollar amount that is either specified in the plan or determined under a formula contained in the plan. The integration level cannot exceed the Social Security taxable wage base in effect at the beginning of the plan year. [Treas Reg § 1.401(1)-2(d)]

Q 11:17 What is the maximum disparity permitted between the excess contribution percentage and the base contribution percentage?

The excess contribution percentage may not be more than two times the base contribution percentage. In no event, however, may the excess contribution percentage exceed the base benefit percentage by the greater of:

1.   5.7 percent; or

2.   The percentage rate of tax under Code Section 3111(a), in effect as of the beginning of the plan year, that is attributable to the old age insurance portion of the Old Age, Survivors and Disability Insurance provisions of the Social Security Act (currently approximately 5.1 percent).

[Treas Reg § 1.401(l)-2(b)]

The percentage determined from (1) or (2) above may need to be reduced, as described at Q 11:18.

Example. UV Company sponsors a 401(k) plan under which it may make nonelective contributions that are allocated taking into account the permitted disparity rules. The integration level of the plan is the Social Security taxable wage base. UV Company makes a nonelective contribution for the 1999 plan year. If the allocation results in an excess contribution percentage of 6 percent, then the base contribution percentage must be no less than 3 percent. (The excess contribution percentage cannot be more than two times the base contribution percentage.) If the allocation results in an excess contribution percentage of 12 percent, the base contribution percentage must be no less than 6.3 percent. (The excess contribution percentage cannot exceed the base contribution percentage by more than 5.7 percentage points.)

Q 11:18   When will a reduction be required in the percentage determined from (1) or (2) of Q 11:17?

A reduction will be required unless the integration level of the plan is either of the following:

1.   The Social Security taxable wage base; or

2.   A dollar amount that is equal to or less than 20 percent of the Social Security taxable wage base.

If the integration level is otherwise, then the excess contribution percentage cannot exceed the base contribution percentage by more than the percentage determined from the table below.

Integration Level	Percentage
Greater than 20 percent of the taxable wage base, but not more than 80 percent of the taxable wage base	4.3%
Greater than 80 percent of the taxable wage base, but less than the taxable wage base	5.4

[Treas Reg § 1.401(l)-2(d)(4)]

Example. The facts are the same as in the example in Q 11:17, except that the integration level is 40 percent of the Social Security taxable wage base. If the allocation results in an excess contribution percentage of 6 percent, the base contribution percentage must be no less than 3 percent. (The excess contribution percentage cannot be more than twice the base contribution percentage.) If the allocation results in an excess contribution percentage of 12 percent, then the base contribution percentage must be no less than 7.7 percent. (The excess contribution percentage cannot exceed the base contribution percentage by more than 4.3 percentage points.)

How Permitted Disparity Is Used

Q 11:19 Under what circumstances should permitted disparity be used?

Whether the employer should use permitted disparity in allocating nonelective contributions depends on two issues: the objectives of the employer and the degree to which permitted disparity is or was used in other plans of the employer.

Q 11:20 Why would an employer use permitted disparity?

Employers who wish to make a larger contribution (as a percentage of pay) for higher-paid employees than for lower-paid employees will want to use permitted disparity. Permitted disparity takes into account the regressive Social Security taxes under which the employer contributes a larger percentage of pay for employees earning less than the maximum taxable wage base ($72,600 in 1999).

Example 1. Two employees earn $40,000 and $120,000, respectively. The 1999 FICA contributions made by their employer are shown below:

Employee	Pay	FICA	Percentage of Pay
A	$ 40,000	$3,060	7.65%
B	120,000	6,241	5.20

As a percentage of pay, Employee B is credited with a FICA contribution of 5.20 percent, which is far less than Employee A's contribution of 7.65 percent.

An employer may also want to use permitted disparity to take into account the fact that an HCE is unable to defer as large a percentage of pay as an NHCE.

Example 2. Employee H earns $20,000 and opts to defer 15 percent of pay, or $3,000, into a 401(k) plan. Employee J earns $100,000 and is able to defer only 10 percent of pay for 1999, or $10,000. Employee K earns $36,000 and is able to defer 15 percent of pay, or $5,400. Employer L may wish to use permitted disparity to partially make up the difference to Employee J.

Q 11:21 How does permitted disparity work?

The operation of permitted disparity is best illustrated by example.

Example. Employer L wishes to make a nonelective contribution equal to slightly less than 4 percent of pay of all participants. Employees H, J, and K are the only participants in the plan. The plan's integration level is 81 percent of the maximum taxable wage base of $72,600. In this case, the formula for allocating the nonelective contribution is equal to 3 percent of total pay plus 3 percent of total pay in excess of $58,806. The nonelective contribution is allocated as shown below:

Employee	Total Compensation	Excess Compensation	Excess 3%	Base 3%	Total Contribution	Percentage of Pay
J	$100,000	$41,194	$1,236	$3,000	$4,236	4.24%
K	36,000	0	0	1,080	1,080	3.00
H	20,000	0	0	600	600	3.00
Totals	$156,000	$41,194	$1,236	$4,680	$5,916	

J is thus receiving a greater contribution as a percentage of pay than K or H, making up partially for the fact that Employer L made a larger FICA contribution (as a percentage of pay) to H and K.

Permitted Disparity in More Than One Plan

Q 11:22 Can permitted disparity be used in more than one plan of the employer?

Yes. However, if an employee is covered by two or more plans, each of which uses permitted disparity, an annual overall limit prevents the overuse of permitted disparity in the plans.

Q 11:23 How is the annual overall limit for permitted disparity computed?

For each employee a fraction is computed for each plan in which the employee is a participant. The fraction is computed as follows:

$$\frac{\text{Actual disparity in the plan}}{\text{Maximum permitted disparity}}$$

The fractions are then summed for each employee. The annual overall limit is met if the sum of these fractions does not exceed 1. [Treas Reg § 1.401(l)-5(b)]

Example. Company M has a money purchase plan with a formula equal to 3 percent of pay plus 3 percent of pay in excess of the maximum taxable wage base. The disparity fraction for the money purchase plan is:

$$\frac{\text{Actual disparity}}{\text{Maximum permitted disparity}} = \frac{3\%}{5.7\%} = 0.5263$$

If Company M wishes to use permitted disparity in its 401(k) plan, the sum of the disparity fractions cannot exceed 1.0. Since 0.5263 is "used up," 0.4737 is the allowable disparity fraction in the 401(k) plan.

$$\frac{\text{Actual disparity}}{\text{Maximum permitted disparity}} = 0.4737$$

$$\frac{\text{Actual disparity}}{5.7\%} = 0.4737$$

$$\text{Actual disparity} = 0.4737 \times 5.7\%$$

$$= 2.7\%$$

Company M could use a formula of 2.7 percent of total pay plus 2.7 percent of pay in excess of the maximum taxable wage base to allocate the nonelective contribution in the 401(k) plan.

Q 11:24 What is the *cumulative disparity limit*?

The *cumulative disparity limit* is a limit providing that the sum of an employee's annual disparity fractions cannot exceed 35. This limit applies, however, only in the case of an employee who benefits after 1993 in a defined benefit plan that uses permitted disparity. [Treas Reg § 1.401(l)-5(c)(1)]

Q 11:25 What is the practical implication of these limits on the use of permitted disparity?

The practical implication of these limits is that an employer designing a 401(k) plan will generally not be able to use permitted disparity in the 401(k) plan if the employer has other defined benefit or defined contribution plans that use permitted disparity.

NONDISCRIMINATORY AVAILABILITY OF BENEFITS, RIGHTS, AND FEATURES

Until now we have been concerned with whether employee non-elective contributions under the plan are nondiscriminatory in amount. The focus of this section of the chapter shifts to the question of whether benefits, rights, and features under the 401(k) plan are provided on a nondiscriminatory basis. To resolve this question, it is necessary to examine the "availability" to employees of a benefit, right, or feature.

Q 11:26 What are *benefits, rights, and features?*

Benefits, rights, and features consist of all optional forms of benefits, ancillary benefits, and other rights and features. [Treas Reg § 1.401(a)(4)-4(a)]

Q 11:27 What is an *optional form of benefit?*

An *optional form of benefit* is a distribution alternative available for the payment of an employee's account balance. A distribution alternative is different from another distribution alternative if the difference results from variations in payment schedule, timing, commencement, medium of distribution, election rights, or the portion of the benefit to which the distribution alternative applies. [Treas Reg § 1.401(a)(4)-4(e)(1)(i)]

Q 11:28 What is an *ancillary benefit?*

In the case of a 401(k) plan, an *ancillary benefit* means any incidental life insurance or health insurance benefits provided under the plan. [Treas Reg § 1.401(a)(4)-4(e)(2)]

Q 11:29 What are *other rights or features?*

Other rights or features are those that are not part of optional forms of benefits or ancillary benefits and that can reasonably be expected to have more than insignificant value. (The term *insignificant value* is not defined in the regulations.) The regulations provide examples of other rights or features:

- Plan loan provisions (other than a provision relating to a distribution of an employee's account balance upon loan default, which is considered an optional form of benefit)
- The right to direct investments
- The right to a particular form of investment
- The right to purchase additional ancillary benefits
- The right to make each rate of elective contributions
- The right to make each rate of employee contributions
- The right to receive each rate of matching contributions
- The right to make rollover contributions

[Treas Reg § 1.401(a)(4)-4(e)(3)]

Q 11:30 When are benefits, rights, and features provided on a nondiscriminatory basis?

Benefits, rights, and features under the plan are provided on a nondiscriminatory basis when they satisfy the current availability requirement and the effective availability requirement. [Treas Reg § 1.401(a)(4)-4(a)]

Current Availability

Q 11:31 How is the current availability requirement satisfied?

The current availability requirement is satisfied if the benefit, right, or feature is currently available to a group of employees that satisfies either the ratio percentage test or the nondiscriminatory classification test. (See discussion of minimum coverage rules in chapter 10.) [Treas Reg § 1.401(a)(4)-4(b)(1)]

Q 11:32 When is a benefit, right, or feature considered currently available to an employee?

Whether or not a benefit, right, or feature is currently available to an employee is based on the current facts and circumstances with respect to the employee. Unless an exception applies, the fact that an employee may, in the future, be eligible for a benefit, right, or feature does not cause the benefit, right, or feature to be currently available. [Treas Reg § 1.401(a)(4)-4(b)(2)]

Q 11:33 What conditions on the availability of benefits, rights, or features may be disregarded in determining current availability?

For purposes of determining the current availability of optional forms of benefits (but not ancillary benefits or other rights or features), age and service conditions may be disregarded. However, age and service conditions cannot be ignored if they must be met within a certain period. In that case, the plan is allowed to project the age and service of employees to the last date by which the conditions must be satisfied. [Treas Reg § 1.401(a)(4)-4(b)(2)(ii)(A)]

Example 1. Employer A maintains a 401(k) plan for its sole HCE and nine NHCEs. The HCE is age 65, and all of the NHCEs are under age 50. The plan provides that elective contributions may be withdrawn on or after the attainment of age 59½. The plan satisfies the current availability requirement because the optional form of benefit (the right to withdraw elective contributions at age 59½) is considered currently available to all employees. The age 59½ condition is disregarded.

Example 2. The facts are the same as in Example 1, except that the right to withdraw will be available only for a period of one year. The plan does not satisfy the current availability requirement because none of the NHCEs will meet the age 59½ condition by the end of the one-year period.

Example 3. The facts are the same as in Example 1, except that it is the right to direct investments that is made available to any employee who reaches age 59½. The plan does not satisfy the current availability requirement because the age 59½ condition cannot be disregarded in the case of other rights or features.

Q 11:34 Are there other conditions that may be disregarded?

Any conditions on the availability of a benefit, right, or feature such as termination of employment, death, satisfaction of a specified health condition (or failure to meet such condition), disability, hardship, or family status are disregarded. Also disregarded are plan provisions requiring mandatory payouts for employees whose account balances are less than $5,000 (or a lesser specified amount), plan provisions requiring an employee's account balance to be less than a specified dollar amount, and plan provisions requiring account balances large enough to support a minimum participant loan amount. It should be noted that these conditions may be disregarded whether they apply to optional forms of benefits, ancillary benefits, or other rights or features. [Treas Reg §§ 1.401(a)(4)-4(b)(2)(ii)(B), 1.401(a)(4)-4(b)(2)(ii)(C), 1.401(a)(4)-4(b)(2)(ii)(D), 1.401(a)(4)-4(b)(2)(ii)(E)]

Q 11:35 What happens if a benefit, right, or feature is prospectively eliminated?

A benefit, right, or feature that is prospectively eliminated but that is retained with respect to benefits accrued prior to the date of elimination will satisfy the current availability requirement in the future as long as the current availability requirement is met as of the date of elimination. This rule applies, however, only if there are no changes in the terms of the benefit, right, or feature after the elimination date. In addition, in the case of optional forms of benefit, the employee's accrued benefit as of the elimination date must be credited with gains or losses subsequent to the elimination date. [Treas Reg § 1.401(a)(4)-4(b)(3)]

Effective Availability

Q 11:36 What is the *effective availability requirement*?

The *effective availability requirement* is the requirement that a 401(k) plan, in light of all facts and circumstances, not substantially favor HCEs as the group of employees to whom the benefit, right, or feature is effectively available. [Treas Reg § 1.401(a)(4)-4(c)]

> **Example.** Employer Z amends its 401(k) plan on June 30, 1999, to provide for a single-sum optional form of benefit for employees who terminate employment with Employer Z after June 30, 1999, and before January 1, 2000. The availability of this single-sum op-

tional form of benefit is conditioned on the employee's having a particular disability at the time of termination of employment. The only employee of the employer who meets this disability requirement at the time of the amendment and thereafter through December 31, 1999, is an HCE. The disability condition is disregarded in determining the current availability of the single-sum optional form of benefit. Nevertheless, under these facts, the group of employees to whom the single-sum optional form of benefit is effectively available substantially favors HCEs.

12 ADP and ACP Testing

As explained in chapter 10, a 401(k) plan must satisfy a minimum coverage test and, for plan years beginning before 1997, a minimum participation test. In addition, the amount of contributions or benefits under a plan must not discriminate in favor of highly compensated employees (HCEs). The amount of elective (deferral) contributions under a 401(k) plan is not considered discriminatory if the plan satisfies the *actual deferral percentage* (ADP) test (see Qs 12:2–12:37). Similarly, any employer matching and employee after-tax contributions (both voluntary and mandatory) are not discriminatory in amount if the plan meets the *actual contribution percentage* (ACP) test (see Qs 12:38–12:68). (For a comparison of the ADP and ACP tests, see Table 12-1 at the end of this chapter.) Note that employer matching contributions are often referred to simply as matching contributions and that employee after-tax contributions are often referred to simply as employee contributions.

If a 401(k) plan provides for both elective contributions and either employee or matching contributions, the plan must prevent multiple use of the *alternative limit* (see Qs 12:69–12:74). All other employer contributions (such as nonelective profit sharing contributions) are tested for discrimination on the basis of the general nondiscrimination regulations as explained in chapter 11.

AVOIDING ADP AND ACP TESTING

Q 12:1 Can a 401(k) plan avoid ADP and ACP testing?

For plan years beginning after 1996, a 401(k) plan can avoid ADP testing and ACP testing of matching contributions if the 401(k) plan qualifies as a SIMPLE 401(k) plan (see chapter 2). [IRC §§ 401(k)(11), 401(m)(10)] This testing can also be avoided for plan years beginning in 1999 if the 401(k) plan qualifies as a safe harbor 401(k) plan (see chapter 2). [IRC §§ 401(k)(12), 401(m)(11)]

THE ACTUAL DEFERRAL PERCENTAGE (ADP) TEST

Q 12:2 How do elective contributions to a 401(k) plan satisfy the actual deferral percentage (ADP) test?

Elective contributions under a 401(k) plan will satisfy the ADP test if at least one of the following tests is met:

1. The ADP of the group of eligible HCEs is not more than 125 percent of the ADP of the eligible non-highly compensated employees (NHCEs); or

2. The ADP of the eligible HCEs is not more than two percentage points greater than the ADP of the eligible NHCEs, and the ADP of the eligible HCEs is not more than two times the ADP of the eligible NHCEs.

[Treas Reg § 1.401(k)-1(b)(2)]

The following table combines these two tests to show the maximum ADP for HCEs, given an ADP for NHCEs:

ADP for NHCEs	ADP for HCEs	Rule Used
1	2	Times 2
2	4	Plus 2
3	5	Plus 2
4	6	Plus 2
5	7	Plus 2
6	8	Plus 2
7	9	Plus 2
8	10	Times 1.25
9	11.25	Times 1.25
10	12.50	Times 1.25

Example 1. If the ADP of the NHCEs is 1.23 percent, the ADP of the HCEs can be no greater than 1.23 times 2, or 2.46 percent.

Example 2. If the ADP of the NHCEs is 7.43 percent, the ADP of the HCEs can be no greater than 7.43 plus 2, or 9.43 percent.

Example 3. If the ADP of the NHCEs is 9.87 percent, the ADP of the HCEs can be no greater than 9.87 times 1.25, or 12.34 percent.

Q 12:3 How is the ADP for a group of eligible employees calculated?

The ADP for a group of eligible employees (see Q 12:12) is the average of the actual deferral ratios of the eligible employees in that group. The ADP and actual deferral ratios are calculated to the nearest hundredth of a percentage point. [Treas Reg § 1.401(k)-1(g)(1)(i)]

Prior-Year versus Current-Year Testing Method

Q 12:4 How is an eligible employee's actual deferral ratio determined?

The actual deferral ratio of an eligible employee who is an HCE is the amount of his or her elective contributions for the current plan year divided by the eligible employee's compensation for the current plan year. For plan years beginning before January 1, 1997, the actual deferral ratios of NHCEs were calculated in the same way. However, starting with plan years beginning in 1997, the actual deferral ratios and the ADP of NHCEs will be based on the elective contributions and compensation for the preceding plan year. A 401(k) plan that performs the ADP test using NHCE data from the preceding plan year is using the *prior-year testing method.* [IRC § 401(k)(3)(A)(ii); IRS Notice 98-1, 1998-3 IRB 42]

Q 12:5 Can an employer elect to calculate NHCE actual deferral ratios and ADP using current-plan-year data?

Yes. An employer that makes this election is using the *current-year testing method.* [IRC § 401(k)(3)(A)(ii); IRS Notice 98-1] Once made, this election cannot be revoked after 2000 unless the current-year testing method has been used for each of the five plan years preceding the plan year of revocation. However, employers may elect to use the current-year testing method in any plan year beginning before 2000 and may revoke the election in the subsequent plan year. [IRS Notice 98-1, 1998-3 IRB 42; Rev Proc 99-23, 1999-16 IRB 5]

Example. Tip Top Corporation sponsors a 401(k) plan administered on a December 31 plan year. For the plan year ending December 31, 1998, the ADP of the NHCEs was 5.2 percent. Unless Tip Top elects to use the current-year testing method, the ADP of the NHCEs for the 1999 plan year will be 5.2 percent (regardless of whether the composition of the NHCE group has changed for 1999). Thus, the maximum ADP of the HCEs (based on elective contributions and compensation for the 1999 plan year) will be 7.2 percent.

Q 12:6 Is IRS approval required to use the current-year testing method?

IRS approval is not required for either making or revoking an election to use the current-year testing method. Nor is there any IRS filing requirement. According to the IRS, however, the plan document must reflect the election and any change in the election must be accomplished through a plan amendment. [IRS Notice 98-1, 1998-3 IRB 42]

Special Adjustments

Q 12:7 Is a 401(k) plan permitted to take into account other types of contributions along with elective contributions in determining actual deferral ratios?

Under the regulations, *qualified matching contributions* (QMACs) and *qualified nonelective contributions* (QNECs) may be treated as elective contributions for purposes of the ADP test (see Q 12:14). [Treas Reg § 1.401(k)-1(g)(1)(ii)(A)] However, elective contributions treated as matching contributions for purposes of the ACP test (see Q 12:50) are not taken into account in calculating an eligible employee's actual deferral ratio. [Treas Reg § 1.401(k)-1(b)(4)(ii)]

Q 12:8 Is the ADP of the NHCEs adjusted if an eligible employee who was an NHCE during the prior plan year is an HCE during the current plan year?

No. An adjustment is not required in this situation. In addition, an adjustment is not required if an eligible employee who was an NHCE during the prior plan year is not an eligible employee during the current plan year. [IRS Notice 98-1, 1998-3 IRB 42]

Q 12:9 How is the ADP of the NHCEs calculated for the initial plan year of a 401(k) plan?

For the initial year, the ADP of the NHCEs is deemed to be 3 percent unless the employer elects to calculate the actual deferral ratios and ADP of the NHCEs using the current-year testing method. An employer is free to revoke this election for the plan year following the initial year. [IRS Notice 98-1, 1998-3 IRB 42]

Q 12:10 Are there circumstances under which the actual deferral ratio of an HCE will be computed differently?

Yes. One of those circumstances arises when an HCE is eligible to participate in two or more 401(k) plans in which the HCE can make elective contributions. In that case, the actual deferral ratio of the HCE will be calculated by treating all the 401(k) plans as one plan. [Treas Reg § 1.401(k)-1(g)(1)(ii)(B)]

Example. Employer X maintains two 401(k) plans, one covering its salaried and office clerical employees and the other covering all its employees. Mary, an HCE, elects in each plan to defer 4 percent of her $100,000 in total compensation. For purposes of each 401(k) plan, Mary's actual deferral ratio is 8 percent calculated as ($4,000 + $4,000)/$100,000.

Q 12:11 In what other circumstance will the actual deferral ratio of an HCE be computed differently?

For plan years beginning before 1997, an HCE who was a 5 percent owner or one of the ten most highly compensated employees was subject to the family aggregation rules. Under these rules, elective contributions, QMACs and QNECs that were treated as elective contributions for purposes of the ADP test, and compensation of the HCE and of any family members who were eligible employees were combined to form a single actual deferral ratio. Family members were defined as the HCE's spouse, lineal ascendants and their spouses, and lineal descendants and their spouses. [Treas Reg § 1.401(k)-1(g)(1)(ii)(C)]

Example 1. Jim owned 100 percent of a company that maintained a 401(k) plan. Jim and certain family members were participants in the 401(k) plan. Their elective contributions and compensation for the 1996 plan year were as follows:

Name	Relation to Jim	Elective Contributions	Compensation
Jim	—	$ 7,000	$100,000
Jan	Spouse	3,000	30,000
Joan	Daughter (age 30)	0	20,000
Stan	Son-in-law	4,000	50,000
		$14,000	$200,000

The combined actual deferral ratio for Jim and his family members was 7 percent calculated as $14,000/$200,000. If the only other eligible HCE had an actual deferral ratio of 5 percent, the ADP for the HCE group would be 6 percent calculated as (5% + 7%)/2.

Example 2. The facts were the same as in Example 1, except that Jim's compensation was $300,000. Because of the Section 401(a)(17) limitation (see Qs 9:109–9:112), Jim's and Jan's compensation for 1996 was limited to $150,000. The combined actual deferral ratio for Jim and his family members was 6.36 percent calculated as $14,000/($150,000 + $20,000 + $50,000). The ADP for the HCE group was 5.68 percent calculated as (5% + 6.36%)/2.

For plan years beginning after 1996, the Small Business Job Protection Act of 1996 (SPJPA) eliminated this family aggregation rule.

Eligible Employees

Q 12:12 Who are considered eligible employees?

Employees are considered eligible if they are directly or indirectly eligible to make elective contributions under the 401(k) plan for all or any portion of the plan year. Employees are considered eligible even if their right to make elective contributions has been temporarily suspended on account of a plan loan or distribution, or because of an election not to participate in the plan. However, an employee

is not considered an eligible employee if, upon beginning employment or upon first becoming eligible to participate in the plan, an
employee makes a onetime election not to participate in the plan or
any other 401(k) plan maintained (whether presently or in the
future) by the employer. [Treas Reg § 1.401(k)-1(g)(4)]

Calculating Actual Deferral Ratios

**Q 12:13 What is considered *compensation* for purposes of
calculating actual deferral ratios?**

The definition of *compensation* used in determining actual deferral ratios must be one that is nondiscriminatory under Internal
Revenue Code (Code) Section 414(s). (See discussion of compensation in chapter 9, Qs 9:97–9:112.) Generally, compensation paid
during the plan year with respect to which the actual deferral ratio
is being calculated will be used for this purpose, but the regulations
do permit the use of compensation paid during the calendar year
ending within the plan year. The plan may also provide that only
compensation paid during the portion of a plan year or calendar
year that an employee is an eligible employee will be taken into account. [Treas Reg § 1.401(k)-1(g)(2)]

> **Example.** Joe becomes eligible to participate in his employer's
> 401(k) plan on July 1, 1999, which is one of two entry dates for
> the plan year ending December 31, 1999. Joe elects to contribute
> 4 percent of his compensation to the plan. Joe makes $20,000
> during the final six months of the year; he makes $18,000 during
> the first six months. If the plan provides that compensation will
> be counted from the entry date, Joe's actual deferral ratio will be
> 4 percent. On the other hand, if the plan uses compensation for
> the entire plan year, Joe's actual deferral ratio will be 2.11 percent
> calculated as (20,000 × 4%)/38,000.

See Q 12:4 for a discussion of the change in the calculation of actual deferral ratios for NHCEs that is effective beginning with 1997
plan years.

Q 12:14 What are *QMACs* and *QNECs*?

QMACs are matching contributions that are 100 percent vested at
all times and that are subject to the same restrictions on distributa-

bility as are elective contributions. *QNECs* are employer nonelective contributions, other than matching contributions, that satisfy these same requirements. These requirements must be satisfied by QMACs and QNECs even though they are not taken into account for purposes of the ADP test and, in the case of QNECs, for purposes of the ACP test. [Treas Reg § 1.401(k)-1(g)(13)]. To be taken into account in determining actual deferral ratios and ADPs, QMACs and QNECs must be made no later than 12 months after the plan year to which they relate. [Treas Reg § 1.401(k)-1(f)(6)(i); IRS Notice 98-1, 1998-3 IRB 42] This rule applies even in the case of a 401(k) plan using the prior-year testing method.

> **Example.** Employer J maintains a 401(k) plan with a calendar plan year. In performing the ADP test for the plan year ending December 31, 1998, Employer J elects to use the prior-year testing method. In the preceding plan year ending December 31, 1997, the ADP of the NHCEs was 5 percent. Thus, the maximum ADP of the HCE group for the plan year ending December 31, 1998, is 7 percent. Because Employer J failed to monitor the salary deferral elections of its HCEs, Employer J discovers on December 31, 1998, that the 1998 ADP of its HCEs is 8 percent. If Employer J decides to correct the failed ADP test by making QNECs on behalf of its NHCEs, the QNEC contributions must be made on December 31, 1998. Note that if the 401(k) plan uses the current-year testing method, the QNEC deadline will be December 31, 1999.

Q 12:15 Under what circumstances may QMACs and QNECs be taken into account for purposes of the ADP test?

All or any portion of the QMACs and QNECs made with respect to employees who are eligible to make elective contributions may be treated as elective contributions for purposes of the ADP test. As a condition of using QNECs for purposes of the ADP test, the allocation of nonelective contributions, including QNECs used for this purpose, must be nondiscriminatory. Also, the allocation of nonelective contributions, excluding QNECs used to satisfy the ADP test and the ACP test, must be nondiscriminatory. [Treas Reg § 1.401(k)-1(b)(5)] QMACs that are treated as elective contributions for purposes of the ADP test may not be taken into account in determining whether the ACP test is satisfied. [Treas Reg § 1.401(m)-1(b)(4)(ii)(B)]

Example. Employer D maintains a profit sharing plan under which employees may make elective contributions. The following amounts are contributed under the plan:

1. Six percent of each employee's compensation. These contributions are not QNECs.

2. Two percent of each employee's compensation. These contributions are QNECs.

3. Elective contributions, if any, made by the employees.

Employer D elects to use the current-year testing method in performing the ADP test. For the 1999 plan year, the compensation, elective contributions, and actual deferral ratios of employees M through S are as follows:

Employee	Compensation	Elective Contributions	Actual Deferral Ratio
M	$150,000	$4,500	3%
N	150,000	3,000	2
O	60,000	1,800	3
P	40,000	0	0
Q	30,000	0	0
R	20,000	0	0
S	20,000	0	0

Both types of nonelective contributions are made for all employees.

The elective contributions alone do not satisfy the ADP test because the ADP for the HCE group, consisting of Employees M and N, is 2.5 percent calculated as (3% + 2%)/2, and the ADP for the NHCE group is 0.6 percent calculated as (3% + 0% + 0% + 0% + 0%)/5. However, the 2 percent QNECs may be taken into account in applying the ADP test. The 6 percent nonelective contributions may not be taken into account because they are not QNECs.

If the 2 percent QNECs are taken into account, the ADP for the HCE group is 4.5 percent calculated as (5% + 4%)/2, and the ADP for the NHCE group is 2.6 percent calculated as (5% + 2%

+ 2% + 2% + 2%)/5. Because 4.5 percent is not more than two percentage points greater than 2.6 percent, and not more than two times 2.6, the ADP test is satisfied.

Correcting ADP Test Failures

Q 12:16 What happens if the ADP test for a plan year is not satisfied?

If the ADP test for a plan year is not satisfied, the portion of the 401(k) plan attributable to elective contributions—and, most likely, the plan in its entirety—will no longer be qualified. The regulations, however, provide several mechanisms for correcting an ADP test that does not meet the requirements of the law. These mechanisms are as follows:

1. The employer makes QNECs or QMACs that are treated as elective contributions for purposes of the ADP test and that, when combined with elective contributions, cause the ADP test to be satisfied.
2. Excess contributions are recharacterized.
3. Excess contributions and allocable income are distributed.
4. The portion of the 401(k) plan attributable to elective contributions is restructured.

A plan may use any one or more of these correction methods. [Treas Reg §§ 1.401(k)-1(f)(1)(i), 1.401(k)-1(f)(1)(ii), 1.410(b)-7(c)(3)]

Q 12:17 Are there correction methods that are not permissible?

It is impermissible for excess contributions to remain unallocated or to be placed in a suspense account for allocation in future plan years. [Treas Reg § 1.401(k)-1(f)(1)(iii)]

Determining Excess Contributions

Q 12:18 How were excess contributions determined for plan years beginning before 1997?

The excess contribution for an HCE was the amount by which the HCE's elective contributions had to be decreased so that the HCE's actual deferral ratio would cause the ADP test to be satisfied. The HCE with the highest actual deferral ratio was reduced first. If, after reducing this HCE's actual deferral ratio to the actual deferral ratio of the HCE with the second-highest actual deferral ratio, the ADP test was still not satisfied, then the actual deferral ratio of these two HCEs is reduced further. This process was repeated until the ADP test was satisfied. [Treas Reg § 1.401(k)-1(f)(2)]

Example. Y Corporation maintains a 401(k) plan. The plan year is the calendar year. For the 1996 plan year, all 12 of Y's employees are eligible to participate in the plan. The employees' compensation, elective contributions, and actual deferral ratios are shown in the following table.

Employee	Compensation	Elective Contributions	Actual Deferral Ratios
A	$150,000	$6,000	4.00%
B	140,000	7,000	5.00
C	70,000	7,000	10.00
D	65,000	6,500	10.00
E	42,000	2,100	5.00
F	35,000	3,500	10.00
G	28,000	2,800	10.00
H	28,000	2,800	10.00
I	21,000	700	3.33
J	21,000	0	0
K	21,000	0	0
L	20,000	0	0

Employees A–D are HCEs. Employees E–L are NHCEs. The ADP for the HCE group is 7.25 percent calculated as (4% + 5% + 10% + 10%)/4, and the ADP for the NHCE group is 4.79 percent calculated as (5% + 10% + 10% + 10% + 3.33% + 0% + 0% + 0%)/8. The ADP test is not met. Y Corporation will not contribute QMACs or QNECs to the plan.

The ADP for the HCE group must be reduced to 6.79 percent. This is done by reducing the actual deferral ratio of the HCEs with the highest actual deferral ratio (Employees C and D) to 9.08 percent since (9.08% + 9.08% + 4% + 5%)/4 = 6.79%. This makes Employee C's maximum elective contribution $6,356 calculated as $70,000 × 9.08%. This requires a distribution or recharacterization of $644 calculated as $7,000 − $6,356. Employee D's elective contribution must be reduced by $598 [$6,500 − (9.08% × $65,000)] to $5,902 through distribution or recharacterization.

Q 12:19 How was the excess contribution determined for pre-1997 plan years in the case of an HCE subject to family aggregation?

The first step was to reduce, if necessary, the combined actual deferral ratio of the HCE and family members to that actual deferral ratio that would cause the plan to satisfy the ADP test. Once the amount of the excess contribution was determined (see Q 12:18), the excess contribution was allocated among the family members in proportion to the amount of the HCE's and each family member's elective contributions. [Treas Reg § 1.401(k)-1(f)(5)(ii)]

Example. Jim and his three family members have a combined actual deferral ratio of 7 percent. The compensation and elective contributions of Jim and his family members are as follows:

Name	Contribution	Compensation
Jim	$ 7,000	$100,000
Jan	3,000	30,000
Joan	0	20,000
Stan	4,000	50,000
	$14,000	$200,000

To satisfy the ADP test, the combined actual deferral ratio of the family group must be reduced to 6 percent. Consequently, the amount of the excess contribution is $2,000 calculated as

$14,000 – (6% × $200,000). The excess contribution of $2,000 will be allocated among family members as follows:

Jim	($7,000/$14,000) × $2,000 =	$1,000
Jan	($3,000/$14,000) × $2,000 =	$ 429
Joan	($0/$14,000) × $2,000 =	$ 0
Stan	($4,000/$14,000) × $2,000 =	$ 571
		$2,000

With SBJPA's elimination of family aggregation for plan years beginning in 1997, the process described above will no longer apply.

Q 12:20 How are excess contributions determined for plan years beginning after 1996?

The amount of excess contributions is determined in the same way that it is determined for pre-1997 plan years (by using the leveling process described in Q 12:18). What differs is the manner in which the excess contributions are allocated. In pre-1997 plan years, they were allocated to the HCEs whose actual deferral ratios were reduced. For plan years after 1996, they are allocated on the basis of the amount of elective contributions, starting with the HCE with the largest amount of elective contributions. [IRC § 401(k)(8)(C); IRS Notice 97-2, 1997-1 CB 348]

Example. The facts are the same as in the example in Q 12:18, except that the plan year ends December 31, 1998, and that Corporation Y has elected to use the current year testing method to calculate the actual deferral ratios and ADP of the NHCEs. The total excess contributions for the plan year are $1,242 (Employee C's $644 plus Employee D's $598). The first $1,000 of the excess contributions is allocated to Employees B and C, who each have $7,000 of elective contributions. After this initial allocation, $242 of excess contributions remains to be allocated. This remaining amount is allocated equally among Employees B, C, and D. After this second allocation, all excess contributions will have been allocated in the following amounts:

Employee	Allocated Excess Contributions
A	$ 0.00
B	580.67
C	580.67
D	80.66
	$1,242.00

The amount of excess contributions as allocated above must then be distributed or recharacterized.

Recharacterizing Excess Contributions

Q 12:21 What happens when excess contributions are recharacterized?

Excess contributions that are recharacterized are includible in the employee's gross income on the earliest dates any elective contributions would have been received had the employee elected to receive the elective contributions in cash. Although includible in gross income, recharacterized excess contributions are generally treated as employer contributions. However, they will be treated as employee contributions for purposes of the ACP test. [Treas Reg § 1.401(k)-1(f)(3)(ii)] It should be noted that the recharacterization of excess contributions as employee contributions will often result in a failure to satisfy the ACP test. Consequently, these recharacterized excess contributions will ultimately be distributed to correct the ACP test.

Q 12:22 What requirements must be met before recharacterization is permitted?

A plan must not only provide for recharacterization as a correction method for excess contributions but must also provide for employee contributions. The regulations indicate that the amount of recharacterized excess contributions plus employee contributions cannot exceed the maximum amount of employee contributions permitted under the plan. [Treas Reg § 1.401(k)-1(f)(3)(iii)(B)]

Q 12:23 When is recharacterization deemed to have occurred?

Recharacterization is deemed to have occurred on the date on which the last of the HCEs with excess contributions is notified that his or her excess contributions are to be recharacterized. Excess contributions may not be recharacterized more than 2½ months after the plan year to which the excess contributions relate. [Treas Reg § 1.401(k)-1(f)(3)(iii)(A)]

Distributing Excess Contributions

Q 12:24 How does the corrective distribution rule work?

The corrective distribution rule requires that excess contributions and income allocable to those contributions be distributed to the appropriate HCEs after the close of the plan year, but no later than 12 months thereafter. [Treas Reg § 1.401(k)-1(f)(4)]

Q 12:25 What is the income allocable to excess contributions?

The income allocable to excess contributions is the amount of the allocable gain or loss for the plan year. If the plan so provides, it also includes the allocable gain or loss for the *gap period,* which is the period between the end of the plan year and the date of distribution. [Treas Reg § 1.401(k)-1(f)(4)(ii)(A)]

Q 12:26 How is income allocable to excess contributions determined?

Any reasonable method may be used, provided the method is not discriminatory, is consistently used for all participants and for all corrective distributions, and is used by the plan for allocating income to participants' accounts. The regulations, however, provide for an alternate method of allocating income. Under this alternative, the income for the plan year (and the gap period if the plan so provides) allocable to elective contributions, and QMACs and QNECs treated as elective contributions, is multiplied by a fraction. The numerator of the fraction is the amount of excess contributions, and the denominator is the sum of the account balances attributable to elective contributions and QMACs and QNECs treated as elective contributions as of the beginning of the plan year plus the employee's elective contributions and QMACs and QNECs treated as elective contributions for the plan year (and for the gap period if gap-period income is allocated). [Treas Reg §§ 1.401(k)-1(f)(4)(ii)(B), 1.401(k)-1(f)(4)(ii)(C)]

Example. Omicron Company sponsors a 401(k) plan. Linda, an HCE, will receive an excess contribution of $1,000 for the plan year ending June 30, 1999. The 401(k) plan does not have a gap-period income provision. To determine the amount of income allocable to the excess contribution, Omicron will use the alternate method under the regulations. The following data elements are needed to calculate the income for the plan year allocable to her excess contribution:

1. Income allocated to Linda's elective contribution
   account for the plan year ending June 30, 1999: $ 5,000

2. Value of elective contribution account on
   July 1, 1998: $75,000

3. Amount of elective contributions for the plan
   year ending June 30, 1999: $ 8,000

The income for the plan year ending June 30, 1999, allocable to Linda's excess contribution is $60.24 calculated as $1,000/($75,000 + $8,000) × $5,000.

Q 12:27 How is allocable income determined for the gap period?

Gap-period income allocable to excess contributions may be determined under any reasonable method as described in Q 12:26 or may be determined pursuant to a safe harbor method. Under the safe harbor method, income on excess contributions for the gap period is equal to 10 percent of the income allocable to excess contributions for the preceding plan year under the alternate method described in Q 12:26 times the number of calendar months that have elapsed since the end of the plan year. A corrective distribution made on or before the fifteenth day of a month will be treated as made on the last day of the preceding month. A distribution made after the fifteenth day is treated as made on the first day of the next month. [Treas Reg § 1.401(k)-1(f)(4)(ii)(D)]

12-17

Q 12:28 Are excess contributions that are distributed still treated as employer contributions?

Yes. For example, a distributed excess contribution continues to be treated as an annual addition for purposes of Code Section 415. [Treas Reg § 1.401(k)-1(f)(4)(iv)] This contrasts with the distribution of excess deferrals that will not be considered Section 415 annual additions. (See Q 8:12.)

Q 12:29 Is employee or spousal consent required for a distribution of excess contributions and allocable income?

No. [Treas Reg § 1.401(k)-1(f)(4)(iii)]

Q 12:30 What is the tax treatment of corrective distributions to employees?

The tax treatment of a corrective distribution depends on when the distribution is made. A corrective distribution made within 2½ months after the end of the plan year is includible in the employee's gross income on the earliest dates any elective contributions made by the employee during the plan year would have been received by the employee had the employee originally elected to receive cash. A corrective distribution made more than 2½ months after the end of the plan year will be includible in gross income for the taxable year in which it is distributed. The same rules apply to any income allocable to excess contributions. However, if the total amount of excess contributions and excess aggregate contributions (see Q 12:53) for a plan year is less than $100, the amount of any corrective distribution will be includible in the year distributed, regardless of whether it is made within 2½ months after the end of the plan year. [Treas Reg §§ 1.401(k)-1(f)(4)(v)(A), 1.401(k)-1(f)(4)(v)(B)]

Q 12:31 Are corrective distributions of excess contributions (plus income) subject to the additional income tax for distributions made before age 59½?

No. [Treas Reg § 1.401(k)-1(f)(4)(v)(A)]

Q 12:32 Can a corrective distribution of excess contributions and allocable income be applied toward an employee's minimum distribution requirement under Code Section 401(a)(9)?

No. [Treas Reg § 1.401(k)-1(f)(4)(vi)]

Q 12:33 What happens if excess contributions (plus allocable income) are not distributed within 12 months after the end of the plan year?

If excess contributions and allocable income are not distributed within the 12-month period following the plan year in which the excess contributions arose, the portion of the plan attributable to elective contributions will no longer be qualified for that plan year and all later plan years during which the excess contribution is not corrected. Elective contributions, in this case, would be includible in an employee's gross income at the time the cash would have been received but for the employee's election. For all other purposes, elective contributions would be treated as employer nonelective contributions subject to the separate nondiscrimination rules that apply to nonelective contributions. [Treas Reg § 1.401(k)-1(f)(6)(ii)] The adverse consequences indicated above may be avoided, however, if this error is corrected as described in chapter 19.

Q 12:34 What happens if excess contributions (plus allocable income) are distributed within 12 months after the end of the plan year but more than 2½ months thereafter?

In this case, the employer will be subject to a 10 percent excise tax on the amount of excess contributions. [IRC § 4979] The excise tax can be avoided, however, if the employer makes QMACs or QNECs, or both, thereby enabling the plan to satisfy the ADP test. [Treas Reg § 1.401(k)-1(f)(6)(i)] As pointed out in Q 12:14, in 401(k) plans using the prior-year testing method in performing the ADP test, QMACs and QNECs must be made no later than 12 months after the end of the prior plan year.

Restructuring for ADP Testing

Q 12:35 Under what circumstances can a 401(k) plan be restructured to show that the ADP test is satisfied?

A 401(k) plan that does not use the statutory minimum age or service eligibility conditions (age 21 and one year of service) under Code Section 410(a) may be restructured. [Treas Reg § 1.401(k)-1(b)(3)(ii)]

Q 12:36 How is the 401(k) plan restructured?

Restructuring is accomplished by treating the portion of the 401(k) plan attributable to elective contributions as two component plans for ADP testing purposes. The first component plan consists of those eligible employees who have met the statutory minimum age and service eligibility conditions; the second consists of those eligible employees who have not met the statutory minimum conditions but who have met the 401(k) plan's less restrictive age and service conditions. By segregating the younger and shorter-service eligible employees (who are likely to be NHCEs and to defer at lower rates) from the remaining eligible employees, the 401(k) plan may be able to demonstrate that the ADP test is satisfied by showing that each component plan satisfies this test.

Example. A 401(k) plan with no age and service requirements allows any employee to begin participating on his or her date of hire. The ADP of the eligible HCEs, all of whom have met the statutory minimum age and service conditions, is 6 percent, and that of the eligible NHCEs is 3 percent, as calculated below using the current-year testing method:

Eligible NHCEs	Actual Deferral Ratio	Met Statutory Minimum Age and Service Conditions
A	6	Yes
B	5	Yes
C	4	Yes
D	3	Yes
E	4	No
F	0	No
G	2	No
H	0	No

Without the benefit of restructuring, the 401(k) plan does not satisfy the ADP test because the ADP of the NHCEs, which is 3 percent [(6% + 5% + 4% + 3% + 4% + 0% + 2% + 0%)/8], is less than 4 percent, the minimum percentage necessary to pass the test. However, with restructuring, only the NHCEs who have met the statutory minimum age and service conditions need be taken into account. The ADP of that group (NHCEs A–D) is 4.5 percent [(6% + 5% + 4% + 3%)/4], a percentage large enough to cause the 401(k) plan to satisfy the ADP test.

Q 12:37 How did the Small Business Job Protection Act of 1996 affect the ability of a 401(k) plan to use restructuring?

Beginning with post-1998 plan years, only the first component of the plan (consisting of those eligible employees who have met the statutory minimum age and service eligibility conditions) will be subject to ADP testing. However, HCEs who have not met the statutory minimums must be included in determining the ADP of the HCE group. [IRC § 401(k)(3)(F)] It is not entirely clear how restructuring will work if the actual deferral ratios and ADPs of NHCEs are determined using the prior-year testing method.

THE ACTUAL CONTRIBUTION PERCENTAGE (ACP) TEST

Q 12:38 How do employer matching and employee after-tax contributions to a 401(k) plan satisfy the actual contribution percentage (ACP) test?

The employer matching and employee contributions to a plan must satisfy either of the following tests:

1. The ACP of the group of eligible HCEs cannot be more than 125 percent of the ACP of the eligible NHCEs; or

2. The ACP of the eligible HCEs cannot be more than two percentage points greater than the ACP of the eligible NHCEs, and the ACP of the eligible HCEs cannot be more than two times the ACP of the eligible NHCEs.

[Treas Reg § 1.401(m)-1(b)(1)]

The following table combines these rules to show the maximum ACP for HCEs, given an ACP for NHCEs:

ACP for NHCEs	ACP for HCEs	Rule Used
1	2	Times 2
2	4	Plus 2
3	5	Plus 2
4	6	Plus 2
5	7	Plus 2
6	8	Plus 2
7	9	Plus 2
8	10	Times 1.25
9	11.25	Times 1.25
10	12.50	Times 1.25

See Table 12-1, at the end of this chapter, for a comparison of the ACP and ADP tests.

Example 1. If the ACP of the NHCEs is 1.23 percent, the ACP of the HCEs can be no greater than 1.23 times 2, or 2.46 percent.

Example 2. If the ACP of the NHCEs is 7.87 percent, the ACP of the HCEs can be no greater than 7.87 plus 2, or 9.87 percent.

Example 3. If the ACP of the NHCEs is 10.98 percent, the ACP of the HCEs can be no greater than 10.98 times 1.25, or 13.73 percent.

Q 12:39 How is the ACP for a group of eligible employees calculated?

The ACP for a group of eligible employees is the average of the actual contribution ratios of the eligible employees in that group. The ACP as well as actual contribution ratios must be calculated to the nearest hundredth of a percentage point. [Treas Reg § 1.401(m)-1(f)(1)(i)]

Actual Contribution Ratios

Q 12:40 How is an eligible employee's actual contribution ratio determined?

In general, an eligible employee's actual contribution ratio is the sum of employer matching and employee contributions allocated to the employee's account divided by the employee's compensation. Recharacterized excess contributions (see Q 12:21) are also taken into account in determining an employee's actual contribution ratio. [Treas Reg § 1.401(m)-1(b)(4)(i)(B)] However, matching contributions treated as elective contributions for purposes of the ADP test are disregarded. [Treas Reg § 1.401(m)-1(b)(4)(ii)(B)] In addition, matching contributions that are forfeited because the elective or employee contributions to which they relate are treated as excess contributions, excess aggregate contributions, or excess deferrals (see Q 8:5) are not taken into account. [Treas Reg § 1.401(m)-1(b)(4)(ii)(C)] (See Q 12:61.) It should be noted, however, that if the ACP test is not satisfied, plan provisions calling for the distribution and/or forfeiture of excess aggregate contributions (see Q 12:53) are implemented first before determining whether matching contributions must be forfeited. [IRS Ann 94-101, § 442.43]

Example. Employer T maintains a 401(k) plan that provides for a fully vested matching contribution. Under the plan, Employer T will contribute 50 cents for each $1 of elective contributions. Employee A, whose compensation is $100,000, is the only HCE of Employer T. Employee A makes elective contributions of $7,000 and, consequently, receives a matching contribution of $3,500. Because the plan does not satisfy the ADP test, Employee A's actual deferral ratio must be reduced to 5 percent. The plan does, however, satisfy the ACP test.

The plan provides for the distribution of excess contributions; hence, $2,000 (plus allocable income) is distributed to Employee A. After the distribution of excess contributions, the effective rate of matching contribution for Employee A is 70 percent ($3,500 of matching contributions divided by $5,000, the amount of elective contributions remaining after distribution of the excess contributions). Employee A's rate of matching contributions is discriminatory because it is higher than the rate of matching contributions provided to NHCEs under the plan (50 percent). To achieve nondiscrimination, $1,000 of the $3,500 of matching contributions made on Employee A's behalf must be forfeited.

Prior-Year versus Current-Year Testing Method

Q 12:41 How has the Small Business Job Protection Act of 1996 changed the way actual contribution ratios are determined?

Starting with plan years beginning in 1997, the actual contribution ratios and the ACP of NHCEs will be based on contributions and compensation for the preceding plan year (the prior-year testing method). Alternatively, an employer may elect to use current plan year data, the current-year testing method. [IRC § 401(m)(2)(A); IRS Notice 98-1] Once made, however, this election cannot be revoked after 2000 unless the current-year testing method had been used for each of the five plan years preceding the plan year of revocation. However, employers may elect to use the current-year testing method in any plan year beginning before 2000 and may revoke the election in the subsequent plan year. [IRS Notice 98-1, 1998-3 IRB 42; Rev Proc 99-23, 1999-16 IRB 5]

Q 12:42 Is IRS approval required to use the current-year testing method?

IRS approval is not required for either making or revoking an election to use the current-year testing method. Nor is there any IRS filing requirement. According to the IRS, however, the plan document must reflect the election, and any change in the election must be accomplished through a plan amendment. [IRS Notice 98-1, 1998-3 IRB 42]

Special Adjustments

Q 12:43 Is the ACP of the NHCEs adjusted if an eligible employee who was an NHCE during the prior plan year is an HCE during the current plan year?

No. An adjustment is not required in this situation. Also, an adjustment is not required if an eligible employee who was an NHCE during the prior plan year is not an eligible employee during the current plan year. [IRS Notice 98-1, 1998-3 IRB 42]

Q 12:44 How is the ACP of the NHCEs calculated for the initial plan year of a 401(k) plan?

For the initial plan year, the ACP of the NHCEs is deemed to be 3 percent unless the employer elects to calculate the actual contribution ratios and ACP of the NHCEs using the current-year testing method. An employer is free to revoke this election for the plan year following the initial plan year. [IRS Notice 98-1, 1998-3 IRB 42]

Q 12:45 Are there circumstances under which the actual contribution ratio of an HCE will be computed differently?

Yes. One of those circumstances arises when an HCE is eligible to participate in two or more plans of an employer to which matching and employee contributions are made. In that case, the actual contribution ratio of an HCE will be calculated by treating all plans in which the HCE is eligible to participate as one plan. (See Q 12:10.) [Treas Reg § 1.401(m)-1(f)(1)(ii)(B)]

Q 12:46 In what other circumstance will the actual contribution ratio of an HCE be computed differently?

For plan years beginning before 1997, an HCE who was a 5 percent owner or one of the ten most highly compensated HCEs was subject to the family aggregation rules. Under these rules, employee contributions and matching contributions, as well as elective contributions and QNECs that were treated as matching contributions for purposes of the ACP test (see Q 12:50), recharacterized excess contributions, and compensation of the HCE and of any family members who were eligible employees were to be combined to form a single actual contribution ratio. Family members were defined as the HCE's spouse, lineal ascendants and their spouses, and lineal descendants and their spouses. (See Q 12:11.) [Treas Reg § 1.401(m)-1(f)(1)(ii)(C)]

For plan years beginning after 1996, the Small Business Job Protection Act of 1996 (SPBJPA) eliminated this family aggregation rule.

Employee Contributions of Eligible Employees

Q 12:47 What contributions are considered *employee contributions?*

An *employee contribution* is either a mandatory or a voluntary contribution that is treated as an after-tax employee contribution. Recharacterized excess contributions are treated as employee contributions. Employee contributions do not include loan payments, buybacks to restore previously forfeited amounts, or transfers directly from another plan. [Treas Reg § 1.401(m)-1(f)(6)]

Q 12:48 Who are considered *eligible employees?*

Eligible employees are those who are directly or indirectly eligible to make employee contributions or to receive an allocation of matching contributions for a plan year. Employees are considered eligible even if their right to make employee contributions or to receive matching contributions has been temporarily suspended on account of a plan loan or distribution, or because of an election not to participate in the plan. However, an employee is not considered an eligible employee if, upon beginning employment or upon first becoming eligible to participate in the plan, the employee makes a onetime election not to participate in the plan or any other plan maintained (whether presently or in the future) by the employer. [Treas Reg § 1.401(m)-1(f)(4)]

Calculating Actual Contribution Ratios

Q 12:49 What is considered *compensation* for purposes of calculating actual contribution ratios?

The definition of *compensation* used in determining actual contribution ratios must be one that is nondiscriminatory under Code Section 414(s). (See discussion of "compensation" in chapter 9, Qs 9:97–9:112.) Generally, compensation paid during the plan year with respect to which the actual contribution ratio is being calculated will be used for this purpose, but the regulations do permit the use of compensation paid during the calendar year ending within the plan year. The plan may also provide that only compensation paid during the portion of a plan year or calendar year that an employee is eligible will be taken into account. [Treas Reg § 1.401(m)-1(f)(2)]

See Q 12:41 for a discussion of the change in the calculation of actual contribution ratios for NHCEs that was effective beginning with 1997 plan years.

Q 12:50 Under what circumstances may elective contributions and QNECs be treated as matching contributions for purposes of the ACP test?

All or any portion of the elective contributions and QNECs made with respect to employees who are eligible employees under the plan may be treated as matching contributions for purposes of the ACP test. If QNECs are treated as matching contributions, two requirements must be met. First, the allocation of the nonelective contributions, including QNECs treated as matching contributions for purposes of the ACP test, must be nondiscriminatory. Second, the allocation of nonelective contributions, excluding QNECs treated as matching contributions for purposes of the ACP test and as elective contributions for purposes of the ADP test, must be nondiscriminatory. [Treas Reg § 1.401(m)-1(b)(5)] If any portion of elective contributions is treated as matching contributions for purposes of the ACP test, that portion may not be taken into account in determining whether the ADP test is satisfied. [Treas Reg § 1.401(k)-1(b)(4)(ii)]

Example 1. Employer P maintains a 401(k) plan to which elective contributions, QNECs, employee contributions, and matching contributions are made and with respect to which the current-year testing method is employed. For the 1999 plan year, the contributions are shown in the following table.

	QNECs	Elective Contributions	Employee/Matching Contributions
HCE	0%	6%	6%
NHCE	3	3	3

The QNECs may be used in the ADP test, the ACP test, or a combination of the two. If Employer P treats one third of the QNECs as elective contributions and two thirds as matching contributions, the ADPs for the HCEs and NHCEs are 6 percent and 4 percent, respectively, and satisfy the 200 percent/2 percentage point part of the ADP test. Similarly, the ACPs for the two groups are 6 percent and 5 percent, respectively, and satisfy the 125 percent part of the ACP test.

Example 2. Employer P maintains a 401(k) plan to which elective contributions, QNECs, employee contributions, and matching contributions are made and with respect to which the current-year testing method is employed. For the 1999 plan year, the QNECs, elective contributions, and employee and matching contributions are shown in the following table:

	QNECs	Elective Contributions	Employee/Matching Contributions
HCE	3%	5%	6%
NHCE	3	4	2

The elective contributions satisfy the ADP test. The employee and matching contributions, however, do not meet the ACP test. Employer P may not use any QNECs of the NHCEs to meet the ACP test because the remaining QNECs would discriminate in favor of the HCEs. However, Employer P could make additional QNECs or matching contributions of 2 percent of compensation on behalf of the NHCEs. Alternatively, Employer P could treat all QNECs for all employees and elective contributions equal to 1 percent of compensation for NHCEs as matching contributions and make additional QNECs of 1.2 percent of compensation on behalf of NHCEs. The ACPs for HCEs and NHCEs would then be 9 percent and 7.2 percent, respectively, thus satisfying the 125 percent part of the ACP test. The ADPs for the two groups would be 5 percent and 3 percent, respectively, which would satisfy the 200 percent/ 2 percentage point part of the ADP test.

Correcting ACP Test Failures

Q 12:51 What happens if the ACP test for a plan year is not satisfied?

If the ACP test for a plan year is not satisfied, the plan will no longer be qualified. However, the regulations provide the following five mechanisms for correcting an ACP test that does not meet the requirements of the law:

1. The employer makes QNECs that are treated as matching contributions for purposes of the ACP test and that, when combined with employee and matching contributions, cause the ACP test to be satisfied.

2. Elective contributions are treated as matching contributions for purposes of the ACP test and, when combined with employee and matching contributions, cause the ACP test to be satisfied.

3. Excess aggregate contributions and allocable income are distributed.

4. If the plan so provides, excess aggregate contributions, to the extent attributable to nonvested matching contributions, and allocable income are forfeited.

5. The portion of the 401(k) plan attributable to employee and matching contributions is restructured.

A plan may use any one or more of these correction methods. [Treas Reg §§ 1.401(m)-1(e)(1)(i), 1.401(m)-1(e)(1)(ii), 1.401(m)-1(b)(3)(ii)]

Example. Employer H maintains a 401(k) plan under which elective contributions up to 8 percent of compensation are matched on a dollar-for-dollar basis. The plan provides for the vesting of matching contributions at the rate of 20 percent per year of service. It also provides for the distribution of excess contributions plus allocable income. Employee A, whose compensation for the plan year is $100,000, is the only HCE, and she is 60 percent vested in matching contributions at the end of the 1999 plan year. The ADPs and ACPs for Employee A and the NHCE group are as follows:

	ADP	ACP
Employee A	8%	8%
NHCEs	4	4

To satisfy the ADP test, Employee A's actual deferral ratio must be reduced to 6 percent, resulting in a corrective distribution of $2,000 calculated as (8% – 6%) × $100,000 plus any allocable income. To satisfy the ACP test (and, as well, the restriction on the multiple use of the alternative limit), Employee A's actual contribution ratio must be reduced to 5 percent. The amount of Employee A's excess aggregate contribution is $3,000 calculated as (8% – 5%) × $100,000. The plan has two options available in disposing of Employee A's excess aggregate contribution of $3,000:

1. The plan may provide for the distribution to Employee A of $1,800, which represents the vested portion of her matching contribution, and for the forfeiture of the $1,200 balance. These amounts are in proportion to her vested and nonvested interests in all matching contributions.

2. The plan may provide for the distribution to Employee A of $3,000, thus leaving the nonvested matching contributions in the plan. If this option is selected, the plan would have to apply one of the formulas contained at Treasury Regulations Section 1.411(a)-7(d)(5) in determining the vested percentage of her remaining matching contributions.

Q 12:52 Are there correction methods that are not permissible?

It is impermissible for excess aggregate contributions to remain unallocated or to be placed in a suspense account for allocation in future plan years. Also, excess aggregate contributions may not be corrected by forfeiting vested matching contributions, recharacterizing matching contributions, or not making matching contributions required under the terms of the plan. [Treas Reg § 1.401(m)-1(e)(1)(iii)] Finally, any method of distributing excess aggregate contributions must not be discriminatory. [Treas Reg § 1.401(m)-1(e)(4)]

Determining Excess Aggregate Contributions

Q 12:53 How were excess aggregate contributions determined for plan years beginning before 1997?

The excess aggregate contribution for an HCE was the amount by which the HCE's employee and matching contributions had to be reduced so that the employee's actual contribution ratio would cause the ACP test to be satisfied. The HCE with the highest actual contribution ratio was reduced first. If, after reducing this HCE's actual contribution ratio to the actual contribution ratio of the HCE with the second-highest actual contribution ratio, the ACP test was still not satisfied, the actual contribution ratio of these two HCEs was reduced further. This process was repeated until the ACP test was satisfied. [Treas Reg § 1.401(m)-1(e)(2)].

Q 12:54 How was the excess aggregate contribution determined for pre-1997 plan years in the case of an HCE subject to family aggregation?

The first step was to reduce, if necessary, the combined actual contribution ratio of the HCE and family members to that actual contribution ratio that would cause the plan to satisfy the ACP test. Once the amount of the excess aggregate contribution was determined (see Q 12:53), then the excess aggregate contribution was allocated among the family members in proportion to the amount of the HCE's and each family member's employee and matching contributions. (See Q 12:19.) [Treas Reg § 1.401(m)-1(e)(2)(iii)]

Q 12:55 How are excess aggregate contributions determined for plan years beginning after 1996?

The amount of excess aggregate contributions is determined in the same way that it is determined for pre-1997 plan years (by using the leveling process described in Q 12:53). What differs is the manner in which the excess aggregate contributions are allocated. In pre-1997 plan years, they were allocated to the HCEs whose actual contributions ratios were reduced. In post-1996 plan years, they are allocated on the basis of the amount of matching contributions and employee contributions starting with the HCE with the largest amount of these contributions. (See Q 12:20.) [IRC § 401(m)(6)(C); IRS Notice 97-2, 1997-1 CB 348]

Q 12:56 If a 401(k) plan provides for the recharacterization of excess contributions as employee contributions, how will this affect the calculation of excess aggregate contributions?

The amount of excess aggregate contributions for an HCE is calculated after determining the amount of excess contributions recharacterized as employee contributions. [Treas Reg § 1.401(m)-1(e)(2)(ii)]

Example. Employee A is the only HCE in a 401(k) plan maintained by Employer X. The 401(k) plan provides a fully vested matching contribution equal to 50 percent of elective contributions. The 401(k) plan is a calendar-year plan and corrects excess contributions by recharacterization. For the 1999 plan year, Employee A's compensation is $58,333, Employee A's elective contributions are $7,000, and Employee A's matching contributions are $3,500. The ADPs and ACPs of Employee A and the NHCEs are shown below:

	ADP	ACP
Employee A	12%	6%
NHCEs	8	4

In February 2000, Employer X determines that Employee A's actual deferral ratio must be reduced to 10 percent to satisfy the ADP test. As a result, $1,167 calculated as $7,000 – (10% × $58,333) of Employee A's elective contributions is recharacterized as employee contributions. After recharacterization, Employee A's actual contribution ratio is 8 percent ($3,500 in matching contributions plus $1,167 in recharacterized elective contributions, divided by $58,333 in compensation). Since Employee A's actual contribution ratio must be limited to 6 percent to satisfy the ACP test, the plan must distribute $1,167 calculated as ($3,500 + $1,167) – (6% × $58,333) or all of Employee A's recharacterized excess contributions. Because Employee A's elective contributions after recharacterization total $5,833, the amount of Employee A's matching contribution allocation must be reduced to $2,917 calculated as $5,833 × 50% to avoid discrimination. The $583 difference between the matching contributions initially allocated ($3,500) and the amount permitted thereafter ($2,917) must be forfeited.

Distributing Excess Aggregate Contributions

Q 12:57 How does the corrective distribution rule work?

The corrective distribution rule requires that excess aggregate contributions and the income allocable to those contributions be distributed to the appropriate HCEs after the close of the plan year, but not later than 12 months thereafter. [Treas Reg § 1.401(m)-1(e)(3)]

Q 12:58 What is the income allocable to excess aggregate contributions?

The income allocable to excess aggregate contributions is the amount of the allocable gain or loss for the plan year. If the plan provides, it also includes the allocable gain or loss for the gap period, which is the period between the end of the plan year and the date of distribution. [Treas Reg § 1.401(m)-1(e)(3)(ii)(A)]

Q 12:59 How is income allocable to excess aggregate contributions determined?

Any reasonable method may be used, provided the method is not discriminatory, is consistently used for all participants and for all corrective distributions, and is used by the plan for allocating income to participants' accounts. The regulations, however, provide for an alternative method of allocating income. Under this alternative, the income for the plan year (and the gap period if the plan so provides) allocable to employee contributions, matching contributions, and elective contributions and QNECs treated as matching contributions is multiplied by a fraction. The numerator of the fraction is the amount of excess aggregate contributions. The denominator of the fraction is the sum of the account balances attributable to employee contributions, matching contributions, and elective contributions and QNECs treated as matching contributions as of the beginning of the plan year plus employee contributions, matching contributions, and elective contributions and QNECs treated as matching contributions for the plan year (and for the gap period if gap-period income is allocated) (see Q 12:26). [Treas Reg §§ 1.401(m)-1(e)(3)(ii)(B), 1.401(m)-1(e)(3)(ii)(C)]

Q 12:60 How is allocable income determined for the gap period?

Gap-period income allocable to excess aggregate contributions may be determined under any reasonable method as described in Q 12:59 or may be determined pursuant to a safe harbor method. Under the safe harbor method, income on excess aggregate contributions for the gap period is equal to 10 percent of the income allocable to excess aggregate contributions for the preceding plan year under the alternate method times the number of calendar months that have elapsed since the end of the plan year. A corrective distribution made on or before the fifteenth day of a month will be treated as made on the last day of the preceding month. A distribution made after the fifteenth day is treated as made on the first day of the next month. [Treas Reg § 1.401(m)-1(e)(3)(ii)(D)]

Q 12:61 When is a method of distributing excess aggregate contributions considered discriminatory?

If excess contributions are recharacterized or distributed, a 401(k) plan must be sure that the level of matching contributions is non-discriminatory. For example, if a plan matches elective contributions on a dollar-for-dollar basis, each dollar of elective contribution that is distributed or recharacterized must result in a forfeiture of a dollar of matching contribution. On the other hand, if the match is made only on elective contributions of up to 6 percent of compensation, no matching contributions are required to be forfeited if an HCE receives a distribution of excess contributions which results in the reduction of the HCE's actual deferral ratio from 8 percent to 7 percent. [Treas Reg § 1.401(m)-1(e)(4)] However, as pointed out in Q 12:40, the IRS takes the position that whether the level of matching contributions is discriminatory is determined only after giving effect to distributions and/or forfeitures required in order to satisfy the ACP test.

Q 12:62 How are corrective distributions and forfeited matching contributions treated for tax purposes?

To the extent attributable to matching contributions, excess aggregate contributions, including forfeited matching contributions, are treated as employer contributions for purposes of Code Section 404. A forfeited matching contribution is considered an annual addition under Code Section 415 with respect to the HCE whose excess aggregate contribution includes the forfeited matching contribution. That same forfeited matching contribution, when allocated to the accounts of other participants, will also be considered a Section 415 annual addition with respect to those other participants. [Treas Reg § 1.401(m)-1(e)(3)(iv)]

Q 12:63 What is the tax treatment of corrective distributions to employees?

The tax treatment of corrective distributions to employees depends on when the distribution is made. A corrective distribution made within 2½ months after the end of the plan year is includible, to the extent attributable to matching contributions, in the employee's gross income for the taxable year of the employee ending with or within the plan year in which the excess aggregate contribution arose. A corrective distribution made more than 2½ months after the end of the plan year will be includible, to the extent attributable to matching contributions, in gross income for the taxable year in which distributed. The same rules apply to any income allocable to excess aggregate contributions. However, if the total amount of excess contributions and excess aggregate contributions for a plan year is less than $100, excess aggregate contributions and any allocated income will be includible in the year distributed regardless of when the corrective distribution is actually made. [Treas Reg § 1.401(m)-1(e)(3)(v)]

Q 12:64 Are corrective distributions of excess aggregate contributions (plus income) subject to the additional income tax for distributions made before age 59½?

No. [Treas Reg § 1.401(m)-1(e)(3)(v)(A)]

Q 12:65 Can a corrective distribution of excess aggregate contributions and allocable income be applied toward an employee's minimum distribution requirement under Code Section 401(a)(9)?

No. [Treas Reg § 1.401(m)-1(e)(3)(vi)]

Q 12:66 Is employee or spousal consent required for a corrective distribution of excess aggregate contributions and allocable income?

No. [Treas Reg § 1.401(m)-1(e)(3)(iii)]

Q 12:67 What happens if a plan fails to make a corrective distribution of excess aggregate contributions and allocable income?

If a plan fails to make a corrective distribution during the 12-month period following the plan year in which the excess aggregate contribution arose, the plan will be disqualified for that plan year and for all subsequent plan years in which the excess aggregate contribution remains in the plan. (But see chapter 19, which describes procedures for avoiding these consequences by correcting the error.) If a corrective distribution is made before the end of the 12-month period but more than 2½ months after the end of the plan year, the employer will be subject to a 10 percent excise tax on the amount of the excess aggregate contributions. The excise tax can be avoided, however, if the employer makes QNECs enabling the plan to satisfy the ACP test. [Treas Reg § 1.401(m)-1(e)(5)] To be taken into account in performing the ACP test, QNECs must be made no later than 12 months after the plan year to which they relate. [IRS Notice 98-1, 1998-3 IRB 42] Thus, in 401(k) plans using the prior-year testing method in performing the ACP test, QNECs must be made no later than 12 months after the end of the prior plan year. (See Q 12:14.)

Restructuring for ACP Testing

Q 12:68 Under what circumstances can a 401(k) plan be restructured to show that the ACP test is satisfied?

The portion of the 401(k) plan attributable to employee and matching contributions can be restructured in the same way as the elective contribution portion of the 401(k) plan, as explained in Qs 12:35 and 12:36.

NO MULTIPLE USE OF THE ALTERNATIVE LIMIT

Q 12:69 What is *multiple use of the alternative limit* in performing the ADP and ACP test?

When a 401(k) plan also provides for matching or employee contributions, it is not enough to show that the ADP and ACP tests are satisfied. The plan must also prevent the use of the alternative limit in both tests. The *alternative limit* means use of either the "times 2" rule or the "plus 2" rule as described in Qs 12:2 and 12:38.

Q 12:70 When does multiple use of the alternative limit occur?

Four conditions must be present before multiple use of the alternative limit occurs:

1. At least one HCE is eligible to make elective contributions and to make employee contributions or receive an allocation of matching contributions.
2. The sum of the ADP and ACP for the HCE group exceeds the aggregate limit. (See Q 12:72.)
3. The ADP for the HCE group is more than 125 percent of the ADP for the NHCE group.
4. The ACP for the HCE group is more than 125 percent of the ACP for the NHCE group.

[Treas Reg § 1.401(m)-2(b)(1)]

Example. Employer E maintains a 401(k) plan that also provides for matching contributions. The ADPs and ACPs for a plan year are as follows:

	ADP	ACP
HCE	3.6	1.69
NHCE	1.8	1.35

12-37

The ADP of the HCE group exceeds the 1.25 limit (1.25 × 1.8% = 2.25%) but not the alternative limit (2% + 1.8%, but not more than twice 1.8%, or 3.6%). The ACP of the HCE does not exceed the 1.25 limit (1.25 × 1.35% = 1.69%). Accordingly, the plan satisfies both the ADP and ACP tests. Because the ACP of the HCE group does not exceed the 1.25 limit, the fourth condition is not present. Therefore, there is no multiple use of the alternative limit.

Q 12:71 Is the multiple-use test applied before or after the operation of the ADP and ACP tests?

A multiple-use test is applied after the operation of these tests. [Treas Reg § 1.401(m)-2(b)(1)] As a result, the test is applied only after the use of QNECs and QMACs to satisfy the ADP test and the use of QNECs and elective contributions to satisfy the ACP test.

Q 12:72 What is the *aggregate limit*?

The *aggregate limit* is the greater of (1) or (2) below:

1. The sum of
    a. 125 percent of the greater of the ADP or ACP for the NHCE group, and
    b. 2 percentage points plus the lesser of the ADP or ACP for the NHCE group, but in no event more than twice the lesser of the ADP or ACP for the NHCE group; or
2. The sum of
    a. 125 percent of the lesser of the ADP or ACP for the NHCE group, and
    b. 2 percentage points plus the greater of the ADP or ACP for the NHCE group, but in no event more than twice the greater of the ADP or ACP for the NHCE group.

[Treas Reg § 1.401(m)-2(b)(3)]

Example. Assume that Employer G maintains a 401(k) plan under which the ADPs of the HCE and NHCE groups are 5.5 percent and 4 percent, respectively. The 401(k) plan also provides for matching contributions, and the ACPs for the two groups are

4.2 percent and 3 percent, respectively. The multiple use of the alternative limit is tested as follows:

1.	Greater of the ADP and ACP for NHCEs	4.00%
2.	1.25 × (1)	5.00%
3.	Lesser of the ADP and ACP for NHCEs	3.00%
4.	(3) + 2 percentage points	5.00%
5.	(2) + (4)	10.00%
6.	1.25 × (3)	3.75%
7.	(1) + 2 percentage points	6.00%
8.	(6) + (7)	9.75%
9.	Aggregate limit: greater of (5) or (8)	10.00%

In this case, the sum of the ADP and the ACP for the HCE group is 9.7 percent calculated as 4.2% + 5.5%, which is less than the aggregate limit of 10 percent. Therefore, there is no multiple use of the alternative limit.

Q 12:73 How is multiple use of the alternative limit corrected?

Multiple use of the alternative limit must be corrected by reducing the ADP or ACP of the HCE group or some combination of the two, as specified in the plan document. However, in lieu of a reduction, an employer may make QNECs. (But see Qs 12:14 and 12:50.) Presumably, restructuring would also be an available alternative. (See Qs 12:35, 12:68.) [Treas Reg § 1.401(m)-2(c)(1)]

Q 12:74 How will a reduction be handled?

The reduction of the ADP, ACP, or some combination of the two, as specified in the plan, will be done in the same manner as the ADP or ACP is reduced in order to satisfy the ADP or ACP test. The ADP, ACP, or both, as the case may be, will be reduced until there is no multiple use of the alternative limit. The employer may reduce the actual deferral ratios and/or actual contribution ratios of only those HCEs that are eligible to make elective contributions and to make employee contributions or receive an allocation of matching contributions, if this method is specified in the plan.

[Treas Reg § 1.401(m)-2(c)(3)] It is not clear, though, how this alternative would work as a result of the change in the method for determining and then allocating excess contributions and excess aggregate contributions for plan years beginning after 1996. (See Qs 12:20 and 12:55).

Example. All employees of Employer Q are eligible to participate in a 401(k) plan that also provides for matching and employee contributions. The plan provides that multiple use of the alternative limit will be corrected by reducing the ACP for the HCE group. Employees X and Y are HCEs. Each receives compensation of $100,000, defers $6,000, receives a $3,000 matching contribution, and makes employee contributions of $3,000. The ADPs and ACPs for the employee groups for the plan year are shown below.

	ADP	ACP
HCE	6%	6%
NHCE	4	4

The aggregate limit and amount required to be corrected are determined as follows:

Step 1. Determination of Aggregate Limit

1. Greater of the ADP and ACP for NHCEs	4.0%
2. 1.25 × (1)	5.0%
3. Lesser of the ADP and ACP for NHCEs	4.0%
4. (3) + 2 percentage points	6.0%
5. (2) + (4)	11.0%
6. 1.25 × (3)	5.0%
7. (1) + 2 percentage points	6.0%
8. (6) + (7)	11.0%
9. Aggregate limit: greater of (5) or (8)	11.0%

Step 2. Calculation of Correction Amount

10. ADP of HCEs   6.0%

11. Maximum permitted ACP of HCEs (9) – (10)   5.0%

12. Amount taken into account in determining actual
contribution ratio of Employee X $6,000

13. Maximum amount permitted without use of
alternative limit—(11) × compensation of
Employee X $5,000

14. Excess aggregate contribution (12) – (13) $1,000

An identical calculation is used to determine the excess aggregate contribution of Employee Y.

TABLE 12-1.   Comparison of ADP and ACP Tests

Feature	ADP Test	ACP Test
Name of test	Actual deferral percentage	Actual contribution percentage
Required by Code Section	401(k)(3)	401(m)(2)
When applicable—the tests do not apply after 1996 to 401(k) plans that qualify as SIMPLE plans and after 1998 to 401(k) plans that are considered safe harbor plans under Code Section 401(k)(12)	Any 401(k) plan year when both HCEs and NHCEs are eligible to make elective contributions (i.e., deferrals)	Any plan year when both HCEs and NHCEs are eligible either to receive employer matching contributions or to make after-tax contributions
Which contributions to test—for plan years beginning after 1996, use NHCE contributions for the preceding plan year unless the employer elects to use data for the cur-	• Include elective contributions (deferrals) allocated as of a date within the plan year • For HCEs, include elective contributions to all other 401(k) plans of the employer for which the HCE is eligible • Include any QNECs or QMACs treated as elective contributions (QNECs and	• Include employer matching contributions • Include employee after-tax contributions (including any excess contributions under the ADP test recharacterized as employee after-tax contributions) • For HCEs, include matching contributions and employee after-tax contributions to all other plans of the employer

	ADP	ACP
rent year (note that QNECs and QMACs are employer non-elective and matching contributions, respectively, qualified as fully vested, and subject to Section 401(k) distribution restrictions).	QMACs used to pass the ADP test may not also be used to pass the ACP test) • Exclude any QMACs to NHCEs used to satisfy the top-heavy minimum contribution requirements • Exclude any elective contributions used to satisfy the ACP test • Exclude contributions under a onetime, irrevocable election made at the time of hire or first eligibility	for which the HCE is eligible • Include any elective contributions or QNECs treated as matching contributions and any QMACs not used to satisfy the ADP test • Exclude matching contributions to NHCEs used to satisfy the top-heavy minimum contribution requirements
What compensation to test against—for plan years beginning after 1996 use NHCE compensation for the preceding plan year unless the employer elects to use compensation for the current year	By employer choice: • Can use either plan-year compensation or compensation for the calendar year ending within the plan year • May elect to exclude compensation earned when the participant was not yet eligible	Same choices as ADP
Family aggregation (only for plan years beginning before 1997)	Contributions and compensation of family members of 5 percent owner HCEs and ten top-paid HCEs are aggregated and treated as being for a single HCE	Same as ADP

(continued)

12-43

TABLE 12-1. Comparison of ADP and ACP Tests (*continued*)

Feature	ADP Test	ACP Test
Calculation of each employee's actual deferral or contribution ratio	The *actual deferral ratio* is the sum of the employee's elective contributions and any other included amounts, divided by the employee's compensation, rounded to the nearest hundredth of a percentage point	The *actual contribution ratio* is the sum of the employee's matching and after-tax contributions and any other included amounts, divided by the employee's compensation, rounded to the nearest hundredth of a percentage point
Calculation of actual deferral or contribution percentage for the HCE group and for the NHCE group	For the group of HCEs and for the group of NHCEs, calculate the ADP as the average of each group's individual actual deferral ratios (in the average, remember to include eligible employees with a zero ratio)	For the group of HCEs and for the group of NHCEs, calculate the ACP as the average of each group's individual actual contribution ratios (in the average, remember to include eligible employees with a zero ratio)
Primary and alternative limit (multiple use by both the ADP and the ACP of the alternative limit is generally prohibited when the sum of the ADP and ACP for the HCE group exceeds the aggregate limit as defined in Q 12:72)	• If ADP of NHCEs exceeds 8 percent, ADP of HCEs must not exceed 1.25 times ADP of NHCEs (primary limit) • If ADP of NHCEs is between 2 percent and 8 percent, ADP of HCEs must not exceed ADP of NHCEs plus 2 percent (part of the alternative limit) • If ADP of NHCEs is less than 2 percent, ADP of HCEs must not exceed two times ADP of NHCEs (other part of the alternative limit)	• If ACP of NHCEs exceeds 8 percent, ACP of HCEs must not exceed 1.25 times ACP of NHCEs (primary limit) • If ACP of NHCEs is between 2 percent and 8 percent, ACP of HCEs must not exceed ACP of NHCEs plus 2 percent (part of the alternate limit) • If ACP of NHCEs is less than 2 percent, ACP of HCEs must not exceed two times ACP of NHCEs (other part of the alternate limit)

Determination of excess amounts	Beginning with the HCE with the largest actual deferral ratio, reduce deferral ratios until the test is passed; the amounts identified by this leveling process are called *excess contributions*—for plan years beginning after 1996, these amounts are allocated beginning with the HCE who has the largest deferral amount	After any excess contributions have been recharacterized and beginning with the HCE with the largest actual contribution ratio, reduce contribution ratios until the test is passed; the amounts identified by this leveling process are called *excess aggregate contributions*—for plan years beginning after 1996, these amounts are allocated beginning with the HCE who has the largest contribution amount
Permissible methods to correct initial failure of the test	• Distribute excess contributions • Recharacterize excess contributions as employee after-tax contributions • Treat QNECs or QMACs as elective contributions • Restructure the 401(k) plan if eligibility requirements are less restrictive than allowed under law OR • Any combination of the above (an HCE can be allowed to choose between recharacterization and distribution)	• Forfeit nonvested excess aggregate contributions if permitted by the plan • Treat either elective contributions or QNECs as matching contributions • Distribute excess aggregate contributions • Restructure the 401(k) plan if eligibility requirements are less restrictive than allowed under law OR • Any combination of the above

(continued)

12-45

TABLE 12-1. Comparison of ADP and ACP Tests (*continued*)

Feature	ADP Test	ACP Test
Impermissible methods to correct initial failure of the test	• Cannot place excess contributions in a suspense account	• Cannot recharacterize excess aggregate contributions • Cannot place excess aggregate contributions in a suspense account • Cannot fail to make required matching contributions to HCEs • Cannot forfeit vested contributions of HCEs
Failure to correct within 2½ months after close of tested plan year	Employer penalty of 10 percent of the excess contributions (unless additional QNECs or QMACs are treated as eligible, even if made more than 2½ months after close of tested plan year)	Same as ADP except that penalty is based on amount of excess aggregate contributions
Failure to correct within 12 months after close of tested plan year	Disqualification of the 401(k) cash or deferred arrangement for the tested plan year and for any following year until corrected	Disqualification of the plan for the tested plan year and for any following year until corrected
Limits on recharacterization of excess contributions as employee after-tax contributions	• Must be recharacterized within 2½ months after close of tested plan year • The plan must allow for employee after-tax contributions • Amounts recharacterized must not ex-	Not applicable

	ceed the amount of elective contributions on behalf of the HCE for the plan year	Same as APD
Distribution of excess amounts	• Must include fund earnings • Still treated as employer contributions under Code Section 404 and as annual additions under Code Section 415 • No spousal consent is required • Do not count as early distributions under Code Section 72(t) • Do not count toward the minimum required distributions under Code Section 401(a)(9)	Same as APD
When distributions must be included in income	• If distributed within 2½ months of close of tested plan year, include as income in the year deferred; however, if the sum of excess contributions and excess aggregate contributions is less than $100, include as income in the year of distribution • If distributed more than 2½ months after close of tested plan year, include as income in the year of distribution	Same as ADP

12-47

13 Top-Heavy Rules

When more than 60 percent of the benefits of 401(k) plans are attributable to key employees, the plans are subject to additional requirements. These plans, referred to as *top-heavy plans,* must provide minimum contributions to non-key employees. If a 401(k) plan provides for contributions other than elective contributions, the account balances attributable to those contributions must vest at an accelerated rate. As of 1997, however, 401(k) plans that are considered SIMPLE plans (see chapter 2) are not subject to top-heavy minimum contribution and vesting requirements.

TOP-HEAVY TESTING

Q 13:1 What issues must be considered in determining whether a 401(k) plan is top heavy?

In determining whether a 401(k) plan is top heavy, the employer must consider the following issues:

1. Who is the *employer*?
2. What is the determination date for the plan year?
3. Which employees are key employees or former key employees?
4. Which former employees have not performed services during the last five years?
5. Which plans of the employer must be aggregated or may be aggregated?
6. What is the value of accrued benefits under the plan?

[Treas Reg § 1.416-1, Q&A T-1(a)]

Q 13:2 How does a plan become top heavy?

A plan becomes top heavy if the present value of accrued benefits for key employees is more than 60 percent of the present value of accrued benefits of all employees. A plan that is part of a required aggregation group (see Q 13:5) will also be considered top heavy if the sum of the accrued benefits for key employees under all plans of the employer in the required aggregation group is more than 60 percent of the sum of the accrued benefits for all employees. [Treas Reg § 1.416-1, Q&As T-1(c) & T-9]

Q 13:3 Who is considered the *employer*?

For purposes of the top-heavy rules, the *employer* is considered to be the entity sponsoring the 401(k) plan and all other entities that are aggregated with it under Code Sections 414(b), 414(c), and 414(m) (discussed in chapter 9). [Treas Reg § 1.416-1, Q&A T-1(b)]

Q 13:4 Who is considered an *employee*?

An *employee* is an individual currently or formerly employed by the employer. [Treas Reg § 1.416-1, Q&A T-1(d)] Leased employees (see chapter 9) are treated as employees. [IRC § 414(n)(3)(B)]

Aggregation Groups

Q 13:5 What is a *required aggregation group?*

A *required aggregation group* includes each plan of the employer in which a key employee participates during the plan year containing the determination date (see Q 13:21) or any of the four preceding plan years (the *determination period*). Also included in a required aggregation group is any plan of an employer that, during the determination period, enables another plan in which a key employee participates to satisfy the minimum coverage rules (see chapter 10). [Treas Reg § 1.416-1, Q&A T-6]

Q 13:6 What is a *permissive aggregation group?*

A *permissive aggregation group* consists of all plans of the employer that are required to be aggregated, plus any other plan of the employer that is not part of the required aggregation group. A plan or plans cannot be added to form a permissive aggregation group unless such plan (or plans) and the plans required to be aggregated together satisfy the nondiscrimination requirements of Code Section 401(a)(4). [Treas Reg § 1.416-1, Q&A T-7]

Q 13:7 If more than 60 percent of the sum of the accrued benefits under all plans of the employer in the permissive aggregation group are attributable to key employees, which plans will be considered top heavy?

Only those plans that are part of the required aggregation group are considered top heavy. [Treas Reg § 1.416-1, Q&A T-11]

Example. Plans W, X, Y, and Z form a permissive aggregation group, but only plans Y and Z are required to be aggregated. It is determined that more than 60 percent of the sum of the accrued benefits under the four plans forming the permissive aggregation group are attributable to key employees. As a result, plans Y and Z are considered top heavy. Plans W and X will not be considered top heavy; consequently, the special minimum contribution and vesting rules for top-heavy plans will not apply to them.

Q 13:8 If 60 percent or less of the sum of the accrued benefits under all plans of the employer in the permissive aggregation group are attributable to key employees, will any of the plans required to be aggregated be considered top heavy?

No. [Treas Reg § 1.416-1, Q&A T-11]

Key Employee

Q 13:9 Who is considered a *key employee*?

A *key employee* is any employee (including any deceased employee) who at any time during the determination period is:

1. An includible officer (see Q 13:13);
2. A top ten owner (see Qs 13:17–13:18);
3. A 5 percent owner (see Q 13:10); or
4. A 1 percent owner (see Q 13:11) having annual compensation from the employer greater than $150,000.

[Treas Reg § 1.416-1, Q&A T-12]

Q 13:10 Who is a *5 percent owner*?

An employee is considered a *5 percent owner* if at any time during a plan year in the determination period an employee owns or is considered to own (applying attribution rules under Code Section 318 as modified under Code Section 416(i)(1)(B)(iii)(I)) more than 5 percent of the value of the outstanding stock of a corporation, or stock having more than 5 percent of the total combined voting power of all stock of the corporation. If the employer is not a corporation, a 5 percent owner is any employee owning more than 5 percent of the capital or profits interest of the employer. [Treas Reg § 1.416-1, Q&A T-17] The controlled group and affiliated service group rules are disregarded in determining a 5 percent owner. [Treas Reg § 1.416-1, Q&A T-20]

Example. An affiliated service group consists of a law firm partnership with 100 partners, each of which is a professional corporation owned by a single attorney. Although each professional corporation, and, by attribution, each attorney-owner, has only a 1 percent interest in the law partnership, each attorney-owner will be treated as a 5 percent owner because each attorney-owner owns 100 percent of his or her professional corporation.

Q 13:11 Who is a *1 percent owner*?

A *1 percent owner* is determined in exactly the same way as a 5 percent owner, except that 1 percent is substituted for 5 percent. [Treas Reg § 1.416-1, Q&A T-16] Although the controlled group and affiliated service group rules are disregarded in determining a 1 percent owner, they are taken into account in determining whether an employee has $150,000 in compensation for a plan year in the determination period. [Treas Reg § 1.416-1, Q&A T-20]

Example. An individual owns 2 percent of the value of a professional corporation, which in turn owns a one tenth of 1 percent interest in a partnership. The entities are part of an affiliated service group. The individual performs services for the professional corporation and for the partnership. The individual receives compensation of $125,000 from the professional corporation and $26,000 from the partnership. The individual is considered a key employee because she has a 2 percent interest in the professional corporation and because her combined compensation from both the professional corporation and the partnership is more than $150,000.

Q 13:12 Who is an *officer*?

In general, an *officer* is an administrative executive who is in regular and continued service. The determination of whether an employee is an officer is based on all the facts and circumstances, including, for example, the source of authority, the term for which appointed or elected, and the nature and extent of duties. Titles are not relevant. An individual's status as an officer will be determined on the basis of the responsibilities to the employer for which the individual is directly employed. The fact that an officer's employer may be a member of a controlled group or an affiliated service group is disregarded. [Treas Reg § 1.416, Q&A T-13]

Q 13:13 Who is an *includible officer*?

An *includible officer* is an employee who, at any time during a plan year in the determination period, is an officer and receives compensation in excess of 50 percent of the Section 415 defined benefit dollar limitation in effect for the plan year. The Section 415 defined benefit dollar limit in effect for a plan year is the limit in effect for the calendar year in which such plan year ends. [IRC § 416(i)(1)(A)(i)] For example, an officer who earns more than $65,000 in a plan year that ends in 1999 will be an includible officer.

Q 13:14 Is there a limit on the number of includible officers who can be considered key employees?

Yes. Depending on the number of employees (including leased employees), the limit is determined as follows:

Number of Employees	Maximum Number of Includible Officers
500 or more employees	50
30 or more employees, but fewer than 500 employees	10% of the number of employees
Fewer than 30 employees	3

Q 13:15 How is the number of employees determined?

The number of employees is determined by selecting that plan year in the determination period in which the greatest number of individuals performed services for the employer. That number is determined only after excluding the following categories of employees:

1. Employees who have not completed six months of service by the end of the year (for this purpose, service in the immediately preceding year is taken into account);
2. Employees who normally work fewer than 17½ hours per week during the year (see Q 9:85);
3. Employees who normally work fewer than seven months during the year (see Q 9:86);
4. Employees who are not age 21 by the end of the year;
5. Employees who are nonresident aliens with no U.S.-source earned income; and
6. Employees who are covered by a collective bargaining agree-

ment. This exclusion applies, however, only if 90 percent or more of the employees are covered under collective bargaining agreements and the plan does not benefit employees covered under such agreements.

[IRC §§ 414(q)(8), 416(i)(1)(A); Treas Reg §§ 1.414(q)-1T, Q&A 9(b), 1.416-1, Q&A T-14]

Q 13:16 If the number of includible officers is greater than the maximum number of includible officers who can be considered key employees, which includible officers will be treated as key employees?

The includible officers who will be treated as key employees will be those includible officers who have the greatest amount of compensation during a plan year in the determination period in which they are includible officers. [Treas Reg § 1.416-1, Q&A T-14]

Example. EFG Company is testing to see if its plan is top heavy for the 1999 plan year. In each year from 1994 through 1998 it has more than 500 employees. Assume that (1) because of rapid turnover among officers, the individuals who are officers each year are different from the individuals who are officers in any preceding year, and (2) all officers are includible officers. Under the limitations, only a total of 50 includible officers would be considered key employees by virtue of being officers in testing for top heaviness for the 1999 plan year. Further, the 50 includible officers considered key employees under this test would be determined by selecting the 50 out of 250 individuals (50 different includible officers each year) who had the highest annual plan-year compensation during the 1994–1998 period (while officers).

Q 13:17 How are the *top ten owners* determined?

An employee is considered a *top ten owner* if the employee's interest in the employer, during any of the plan years in the determination period in which the employee is eligible to be a top ten owner, is among the ten largest interests owned by employees during the determination period. [Treas Reg § 1.416-1, Q&A T-19(a)] If two or more employees have the same ownership interest, the employee having the greatest amount of compensation during the plan year will be treated as having the largest interest in the employer. [Treas Reg § 1.416-1, Q&A T-19(b)]

Q 13:18 Who is eligible to be a top ten owner?

An employee is eligible to be a top ten owner if the employee meets both of the following requirements:

1. The employee has annual compensation for any plan year in the determination period greater than the Section 415 defined contribution plan dollar limit for the calendar year in which such plan year ends; and

2. The employee owns (applying attribution rules under Code Section 318 as modified under Code Section 416(i)(1)(B)(iii)(I)) at any time during such plan year more than a ½ percent interest in the employer.

[Treas Reg § 1.416-1, Q&A T-19(a)]

If an employee's ownership interest changes during a plan year in the determination period, the employee's ownership interest is the largest interest owned at any time during the plan year. [Treas Reg § 1.416-1, Q&A T-19(b)] The controlled group and affiliated service group rules are disregarded in determining whether an employee owns a ½ percent interest [Treas Reg § 1.416-1, Q&A T-20]

Q 13:19 What is considered *compensation* for purposes of determining key employees?

Compensation means compensation as defined for purposes of Code Section 415. It also includes elective contributions to 401(k) plans, SARSEPs, SIMPLE retirement accounts, and elective deferrals under a cafeteria plan. [IRC § 416(i)(1)(D)]

Determination Date

Q 13:20 When is the top-heavy determination for a plan year made?

The top-heavy determination for a plan year is made on the determination date. When two or more plans constitute an aggregation group, the plan years taken into account are those whose determination dates fall within the same calendar year. [Treas Reg § 1.416-1, Q&As T-22 & T-23]

Q 13:21 What is the *determination date* for a plan year?

The *determination date* for a plan year is the last day of the preceding plan year. In the case of a plan's initial plan year, the determination date is the last day of such plan year. [Treas Reg § 1.416-1, Q&A T-22]

> **Example.** Beta Corporation maintains Plan A and Plan B, each containing a key employee. Plan A's plan year commences July 1 and ends June 30. Plan B's plan year is the calendar year. For Plan A's plan year commencing July 1, 1999, the determination date is June 30, 1999. For Plan B's plan year commencing January 1, 2000, the determination date is December 31, 1999. These plans are required to be aggregated. (See Q 13:5.) For each plan, as of their respective determination dates, the present values of the accrued benefits for key employees and all employees are separately determined. Since the two determination dates, June 30, 1999, and December 31, 1999, fall within the same calendar year, the present values of accrued benefits as of each of these dates are combined to determine whether the group is top heavy. If, after combining the two present values, the required aggregation group is top heavy, Plan A will be top heavy for the plan year commencing July 1, 1999, and Plan B will be top heavy for the 2000 calendar year.

Present Value of Accrued Benefits

Q 13:22 How is the present value of accrued benefits determined in a defined contribution plan?

The present value of accrued benefits as of the determination date for any individual is the participant's account balance as of that date. (Technically, the regulations provide that account balances are determined as of the most recent valuation date occurring within the 12-month period ending on the determination date. For most plans, however, the determination date, because it is the last day of the plan year, will be a valuation date.) Contributions made after the determination date but allocated as of that date are not taken into account unless either of these conditions exists:

1. The plan is a money purchase, target benefit, or other defined contribution plan subject to minimum funding requirements under Code Section 412; or

2. The plan is a 401(k) plan or other profit sharing or stock bonus plan, and a top-heavy determination is being made for the initial plan year.

[Treas Reg § 1.416-1, Q&A T-24]

Q 13:23 How is the present value of accrued benefits determined in a defined benefit plan?

In general, the present value of accrued benefits as of the determination date for any individual is determined as of the most recent valuation date occurring within the 12-month period ending on the determination date. It should be noted that if a defined benefit plan's valuation date is the first day of a plan year, the determination of whether a plan is top heavy for a plan year is based on a valuation date occurring one year before the plan year begins.

Example. An employer sponsors a defined benefit plan maintained on a calendar-year basis and valued annually on the first day of the plan year. The determination date for the plan year beginning January 1, 2000, is December 31, 1999. The determination of the present value of accrued benefits will be based on the valuation occurring on January 1, 1999.

Special rules apply for determining the present value of accrued benefits for the first two plan years of a defined benefit plan. [Treas Reg § 1.416-1, Q&A T-25]

Q 13:24 What actuarial assumptions are used in determining the present value of accrued benefits in a defined benefit plan?

The actuarial assumptions must be set forth in the defined benefit plan and they must be reasonable, but they need not be the same as those used for minimum funding purposes or for determining actuarially equivalent optional forms of benefit. The present value of a participant's accrued benefit must be computed using an interest rate assumption and a post-retirement mortality assumption. A pre-retirement mortality assumption may be used, but withdrawal and salary scale assumptions may not. [Treas Reg § 1.416-1, Q&A T-26]

Q 13:25 Are accrued benefits attributable to employee contributions taken into account?

Yes; however, account balances attributable to voluntary deductible employee contributions are disregarded. [Treas Reg § 1.416-1, Q&A T-28]

Q 13:26 What effect do distributions to participants have on the determination of the present value of accrued benefits?

In general, distributions made during the determination period are added to the present value of accrued benefits. Distributions occurring after the most recent valuation date but before the determination date are disregarded for this purpose. (This is likely to be an issue only for defined benefit plans.) Also disregarded are certain distributions that are rolled over to a related plan. (See Q 13:28.) Distributions include all distributions, even those of an employee's own contributions. [Treas Reg § 1.416-1, Q&A T-30]

Q 13:27 What effect do distributions to beneficiaries of deceased participants have on the determination of the present value of accrued benefits?

Distributions made during the determination period and paid by reason of death are also taken into account; however, in the case of a defined benefit plan, the distribution is taken into account only to the extent of the present value of the participant's accrued benefit determined immediately before death. [Treas Reg § 1.416-1, Q&A T-31]

Example. AMO Company maintains a defined benefit plan on a calendar-year basis. The plan provides a pre-retirement death benefit equal to 100 times a participant's projected monthly normal retirement benefit. In 1999, Doug's widow, Sara, receives a death benefit of $200,000. Immediately prior to his death, the present value of Doug's accrued benefit under the plan is

$100,000. For purposes of determining whether the plan is top heavy, only $100,000 will be treated as having been distributed to Sara.

Q 13:28 How are rollovers and plan-to-plan transfers handled?

It depends on whether they are related. A rollover or plan-to-plan transfer is considered related if it is not initiated by the participant or if it is made between plans of the same employer (as defined in chapter 9); it is considered unrelated if it is initiated by the employee and is made between plans maintained by different employers.

If a rollover or plan-to-plan transfer is related, then it will not be treated as a distribution from the transferor plan. Instead, the rollover or plan-to-plan transfer will become part of a participant's present value of accrued benefits under the transferee plan. If a rollover or plan-to-plan transfer is unrelated, then it will be treated as a distribution from the transferor plan, but it will not be taken into account under the transferee plan. [Treas Reg § 1.416-1, Q&A 32]

Example. John terminates his employment with Employer X. At his request, the 401(k) plan in which John participated makes a direct rollover to the 401(k) plan of his new employer, Y, which is unrelated to Employer X. This rollover is unrelated; consequently, it will be treated as a distribution from the 401(k) plan of Employer X and will not be treated as part of John's accrued benefit under the 401(k) plan of Employer Y.

Q 13:29 Are the accrued benefits of certain participants disregarded for purposes of determining whether a plan is top heavy?

There are two occasions when accrued benefits are disregarded:

1. The participant was previously a key employee but is now a non-key employee. [IRC § 416(g)(4)(B)]

2. The participant has not performed services for the employer during the determination period. [IRC § 416(g)(4)(E)]

MINIMUM VESTING

Q 13:30 What special vesting requirements apply to top-heavy plans?

If a 401(k) plan becomes top heavy, account balances attributable to employer contributions must vest at a rate that is at least as rapid as one of the following schedules:

Schedule 1	
Years of Service	Vested Percentage
Fewer than 2	0%
2	20%
3	40%
4	60%
5	80%
6 or more	100%

Schedule 2	
Years of Service	Vested Percentage
Fewer than 3	0%
3 or more	100%

As explained in Q 2:106, account balances attributable to elective contributions, qualified nonelective contributions (QNECs), and qualified matching contributions (QMACs) are always 100 percent vested. In addition, safe harbor employer contributions under a 401(k) safe harbor plan are 100 percent vested at all times (see Q 2:157). Thus, the above schedules are relevant only if a 401(k) plan provides for other kinds of employer contributions. [Treas Reg § 1.416-1, Q&A V-1]

Q 13:31 What service may be disregarded in determining a participant's vested percentage?

Any service permitted to be disregarded under the regular vesting rules (see Qs 2:110–2:112) may be disregarded in determining a participant's vested percentage in a top-heavy plan. [Treas Reg § 1.416-1, Q&A V-2]

Q 13:32 Does a top-heavy vesting schedule apply only to that portion of a participant's account balance accrued after a plan becomes top heavy?

No. The top-heavy vesting schedule applies to the participant's entire account balance. However, a top-heavy vesting schedule will not apply to a participant who does not have an hour of service after the plan becomes top heavy. [Treas Reg § 1.416-1, Q&A V-3]

Q 13:33 What happens if a 401(k) plan is no longer top heavy?

If a plan is no longer top heavy, the rules relating to changes in vesting schedule apply. (See Qs 2:119–2:120.) [Treas Reg § 1.416-1, Q&A V-7] It should be noted that some plans, in order to reduce administrative complexity, will retain the top-heavy vesting schedule even if the plan is no longer top heavy.

MINIMUM CONTRIBUTIONS

Q 13:34 What special contribution requirements apply to top-heavy plans?

If a 401(k) plan becomes top heavy, non-key employees must be provided with a minimum contribution. In general, the minimum contribution will be equal to 3 percent of compensation. [Treas Reg § 1.416-1, Q&A M-7]

Q 13:35 What is *compensation* for purposes of determining a non-key employee's minimum contribution?

For this purpose, *compensation* has the same meaning as it does under Code Section 415. (See Qs 8:23–8:24.) The minimum contribution is generally based on compensation for the plan year, although the regulations permit the use of compensation for the calendar year ending within the plan year. [Treas Reg § 1.416-1, Q&A M-7]

Q 13:36 Are allocated forfeitures taken into account in determining whether a non-key employee has received a minimum contribution?

Yes. [Treas Reg § 1.416-1, Q&A M-7]

Q 13:37 Is the top-heavy minimum contribution always 3 percent of compensation?

No. A lower minimum is permitted when the allocation of contributions and forfeitures on behalf of any key employee is less than 3 percent of compensation. In that event, the minimum contribution is the largest percentage of compensation allocated to any key employee. There is, however, an exception to this rule. The top-heavy minimum remains at 3 percent of compensation if the 401(k) plan enables a defined benefit plan in the same required aggregation group to satisfy the minimum coverage rules under Code Section 410(b). [Treas Reg § 1.416-1, Q&A M-7]

Example 1. ABC Company maintains a top-heavy 401(k) plan that provides for elective contributions only. M is the only key employee to defer more than 3 percent of compensation. The top-heavy minimum contribution for non-key employees is 3 percent of compensation.

Example 2. The facts are the same as in Example 1, except that M defers only 2 percent of his compensation, which is the largest rate of deferral by any key employee in the plan. The top-heavy minimum contribution for non-key employees is 2 percent of compensation.

Example 3. The facts are the same as in Example 2, except that ABC Company sponsors a defined benefit plan that is required to be aggregated with the 401(k) plan (see Q 13:5) and that satisfies the minimum coverage rules under Code Section 410(b) only when aggregated with the 401(k) plan. The top-heavy minimum contribution for non-key employees is 3 percent of compensation.

Q 13:38   Are elective contributions made on behalf of key employees taken into account in determining whether a key employee's allocation of contributions and forfeitures constitutes 3 percent of compensation?

Yes. [Treas Reg § 1.416-1, Q&A M-20] The examples in Q 13:37 illustrate this point.

Q 13:39   What amounts are taken into account in determining whether a participant has received a top-heavy minimum?

Except as noted below, all employer contributions and forfeitures allocated to a participant are taken into account. [Treas Reg § 1.416-1, Q&A M-7] QNECs, whether or not treated as elective contributions or matching contributions for purposes of the ADP and ACP tests (see chapter 12), and safe harbor nonelective contributions under a 401(k) safe harbor plan (see Q 2:155) may also be taken into account. [Treas Reg § 1.416-1, Q&A M-18; Notice 98-52, 1998-46 I.R.B. 16] However, neither elective contributions made on behalf of non-key employees nor safe harbor matching contributions under a safe harbor 401(k) plan can be applied toward top-heavy minimums. [Treas Reg § 1.416-1, Q&A M-20; Notice 98-52, 1998-46 I.R.B. 16] Non-safe harbor matching contributions made on behalf of non-key employees may be applied toward top-heavy minimums, but any such matching contributions applied for this purpose can no longer be taken into account under the ADP or ACP test. Such matching contributions would be tested under the general Section 401(a)(4) nondiscrimination rules. (See discussion immediately preceding Q 11:1.) [Treas Reg § 1.416-1, Q&A M-19].

Q 13:40   Which non-key employees must receive a minimum contribution?

Those non-key employees who are participants in a 401(k) plan and who are employed on the last day of the plan year must receive a top-heavy minimum. A non-key employee is entitled to a minimum contribution even if the non-key employee fails to complete the number of hours of service (typically 1,000) required by the plan for an allocation of nonelective contributions. [Treas Reg § 1.416-1, Q&A M-10]

Q 13:41 If an employer maintains a 401(k) plan and another defined contribution plan, must both plans provide top-heavy minimums for non-key employees who participate in both?

No. As long as one plan provides the top-heavy minimum contribution for a non-key employee who participates in both plans, the other plan does not have to provide a minimum contribution. [Treas Reg § 1.416-1, Q&A M-8]

Q 13:42 What happens if non-key employees participate in both a 401(k) plan and a defined benefit plan?

As in Q 13:41, two top-heavy minimums are not required. The regulations provide four different methods for determining top-heavy minimums in this situation:

1. Provide for the defined benefit top-heavy minimum (generally a benefit at normal retirement age equal to 2 percent of average annual compensation per year of service up to a maximum of 20 percent of average annual compensation);

2. Provide that the defined benefit top-heavy minimum will be offset by the benefits provided under the 401(k) plan [See Rev Rul 76-259, 1976-2 CB 111] (presumably, account balances attributable to elective contributions and matching contributions cannot be used as an offset);

3. Demonstrate that benefits under the defined benefit plan and the 401(k) plan are providing benefits in the aggregate that are comparable to the defined benefit minimums (as explained in (2) above, elective contributions and matching contributions cannot be taken into account); or

4. Provide for a top-heavy minimum contribution of 5 percent of compensation in the 401(k) plan.

[Treas Reg § 1.416-1, Q&A M-12]

TOP-HEAVY STRATEGY

A newly established 401(k) plan may be top heavy from its inception, possibly to the surprise and chagrin of an employer who had viewed the plan as a vehicle for elective contributions only. Top heaviness can result, for example, from the requirement that distributions from a terminated plan be taken into account in testing the new 401(k) plan. (See Q 13:26.) This section explains how an employer may cope with the resulting top-heavy minimum contribution requirements or avoid them altogether.

Q 13:43 Is there a minimum contribution requirement for a top-heavy 401(k) plan that provides for elective contributions only?

Yes, there can be a minimum contribution requirement if a key employee makes elective contributions to the 401(k) plan. (See Q 13:38.) Consequently, if no key employee makes elective contributions, there will be no top-heavy minimum contribution obligation. The lack of participation by key employees may also hasten the day the 401(k) plan is no longer top-heavy because the present value of accrued benefits attributable to key employees will decline relative to that of non-key employees. (See Q 13:2.)

Q 13:44 Can the top-heavy plan rules be avoided by converting a 401(k) plan to a SIMPLE plan?

Yes. Although a SIMPLE 401(k) plan is not subject to the top-heavy plan rules, their nonapplication comes at a cost. First, eligible employers under a SIMPLE 401(k) plan must provide either a dollar for dollar matching contribution on elective contributions up to 3 percent of pay or a 2 percent of pay nonelective contribution. Second, any employer contribution must be 100 percent vested immediately. Note that in theory, an employer could avoid matching contributions if no non-key employee elected to participate in the SIMPLE 401(k) plan. Also, the 2 percent nonelective contribution, if elected by the employer, is less than the minimum contribution (generally 3 percent of pay) under the top-heavy rules.

Q 13:45 If an employer makes a discretionary profit sharing contribution, can each non-key employee's allocation of that contribution be credited toward the top-heavy minimum contribution obligation?

Yes. If the allocation of the profit sharing contribution results in each non-key employee's receiving the top-heavy minimum (see Qs 13:34–13:37), no additional amount need be contributed.

Q 13:46 Can an employer matching contribution be used to satisfy the top-heavy minimum contribution obligation?

As explained in Q 13:39, this is possible. However, use of matching contributions for top-heavy purposes may make it difficult or even impossible to satisfy the ACP test that applies to matching contributions.

Q 13:47 Is there any other type of employer contribution that can be used to satisfy the top-heavy rules?

Yes. 401(k) plans that fail the ADP test, the ACP test, or both will sometimes satisfy these tests by making qualified nonelective contributions (QNECs) as defined at Q 12:14. In addition to performing that function, QNECs that are allocated to non-key employees will count toward fulfilling the employer's top-heavy minimum contribution obligation.

14 Participant Loans, Hardship Withdrawals, and In-Service Distributions

In the case of most companies, a successful 401(k) plan requires significant participation from lower-paid employees. Many employees, however, may be reluctant to commit funds to the 401(k) plan if they have no savings or other resources with which to respond to unanticipated financial demands. One common way to address that concern is to provide access to funds in the 401(k) plan through loans, hardship withdrawals, or other distributions while a participant is actively employed. This chapter discusses the rules and design considerations involved when including loans, hardship withdrawals, or in-service distribution provisions in the 401(k) plan document.

PARTICIPANT LOANS

Participant loans provide a means for participants to access their 401(k) account balances without incurring tax liability. There are two sets of rules that must be complied with when designing and implementing a participant loan program. The Department of Labor (DOL) provisions of the Employee Retirement Income Security Act of 1974 (ERISA) dictate how loans must be structured to avoid treatment as a prohibited transaction. The Internal Revenue Code (Code) dictates how loans must be structured to avoid treatment as a taxable distribution. This section discusses both the DOL and the Code rules, as well as other issues related to participant loans.

Q 14:1 Who may borrow money from his or her 401(k) plan account?

A plan generally may permit participants to borrow against their 401(k) plan accounts. Many plan sponsors include this option in their 401(k) plans to encourage a higher rate of participation by lower-paid employees. A 1997 survey by Hewitt & Associates, *Trends and Experience in 401(k) Plans,* indicates that 90 percent of all 401(k) plans allow for participant loans.

Participant loans cannot be made to any owner-employee, which includes a sole proprietor, a 5 percent shareholder of a Subchapter S corporation, or a partner with an ownership interest of at least 10 percent. Any loan to an owner-employee is a prohibited transaction. [IRC §§ 4975(d), 401(c)(3); ERISA § 408(d)] If a participant is not an owner-employee when a loan is taken out but becomes one before the loan is repaid (e.g., if a corporation changes from C to S status), the amount of the loan outstanding on the date the participant becomes an owner-employee will be treated as a prohibited transaction. [DOL Op 84-44A]

Department of Labor Regulation of Participant Loans

Q 14:2 What are the purpose and general content of the DOL rules?

A loan from a plan to a participant falls within the definition of a prohibited transaction under ERISA. [ERISA § 406(a)(1)(B)] (The prohibited transaction rules are discussed more fully in chapter 5.)

A statutory exemption provides the means to avoid treatment as a prohibited transaction as long as certain conditions are met. To qualify for this exemption, loans must satisfy all of the following:

- Be made available to all participants and beneficiaries on a reasonably equivalent basis (see Q 14:3)
- Not be made available to highly compensated employees in an amount greater than the amount available to other employees (see Q 14:4)
- Be made in accordance with specific provisions that are set forth in the plan (see Q 14:5)
- Bear a reasonable rate of interest (see Qs 14:6, 14:7)
- Be adequately secured (see Qs 14:8, 14:9)

[ERISA § 408(b)(1); DOL Reg § 2550.408b-1]

Loan Availability

Q 14:3 When is a loan available to all participants on a reasonably equivalent basis?

The plan sponsor can place some restrictions on loan availability without running afoul of the reasonably equivalent rule. The following are some examples of acceptable restrictions:

1. A plan can effectively make loans available to active employees without making them available to most terminated participants or plan beneficiaries. This is done by making loans available only to parties in interest to the plan. [Treas Reg § 1.401(a)(4)-10(c); DOL Op 89-30A]

2. The availability of loans can be restricted to particular purposes, such as hardship. However, the restriction must be consistent with the interest of participants and cannot operate in a way that makes loans unavailable to large numbers of participants. Also, any such restrictions cannot be designed to benefit the employer, fiduciary, or other party in interest. For example, a plan cannot restrict the availability of loans to situations where the loan proceeds are used to make a capital investment in the plan sponsor. [DOL Reg § 2550.408b-1(a)(4), Ex 2]

3. A sponsor can limit loans to a threshold dollar amount. The Internal Revenue Service (IRS) has approved a safe harbor minimum threshold of up to $1,000. [Treas Reg § 1.401(a)(4)-4(b)(2)(ii)(E); DOL Reg § 2550.408b-1(b)(2)]

A plan sponsor cannot restrict loans based on factors upon which a commercial lender would not rely. For example, the sponsor may not take into account race, color, religion, sex, age, national origin, or job performance issues unrelated to the creditworthiness of the employee. [DOL Reg § 2550.408b-1(b)(1)]

Q 14:4 When are loans made available to highly compensated employees in amounts greater than what is available to other employees?

This is a facts-and-circumstances determination. The general rule is that the loan program cannot exclude large numbers of employees. [DOL Reg § 2550.408b-1(c)(1)] For example, if the sponsor sets a minimum service limit that results in only 20 percent of employees qualifying for a loan, the loan program will be considered to favor highly compensated employees improperly. It is permissible to vary the loan amount with the size of account balances. For example, a plan might limit loans to 50 percent of an employee's vested account balance. [DOL Reg § 2550.408b-1(c)(2)]

Loan Terms and Provisions

Q 14:5 What provisions concerning loans must be in the plan document?

The plan document must include the following provisions:

1. The identity of the person authorized to administer the participant program;
2. The procedure for applying for loans;
3. The standards for approving or denying loans;
4. Any limitations on loan types or loan amounts;
5. The procedures used to determine a reasonable rate of interest;
6. The types of collateral that can be used to secure participant loans; and

7. The events constituting default and the steps necessary to preserve plan assets in the event of default.

This information may be contained either in the plan document itself or in the loan application forms. It must be contained in the summary plan description (as described in chapter 18). [DOL Reg § 2550.408b-1(d); 54 Fed Reg 30523]

Q 14:6 What is a reasonable rate of interest for participant loans?

The interest rate chosen must be consistent with interest rates charged by commercial lenders for a loan made under similar circumstances. [DOL Reg § 2550.408b-1(e)] The DOL's view is that there is no justification for using below-market interest rates on participant loans. According to the testimony of a DOL expert, rates considered reasonable by the DOL for loans secured by a participant's account balance range from a certificate of deposit rate plus 2 percent to the prime rate plus 1 percent. [McLaughlin v Rowley, 698 F Supp 1333 (ND Tex 1988)] A 1998 survey by the Profit Sharing/401(k) Council of America found that 84 percent of 401(k) plans use the prime rate plus a percentage, while only about 7.5 percent rely on local commercial lending rates.

Q 14:7 Must the plan interest rate be reviewed each time a new loan is taken out?

Yes. The DOL regulations state that the reasonable rate of interest standard must be looked at each time a loan is originated, renewed, renegotiated, or modified. [DOL Reg § 2550.408b-1(a)(3)(ii)] Therefore, a plan sponsor cannot simply choose a rate at the time the plan is set up and use that rate continuously. Rates must be reviewed and updated as often as necessary to ensure that they remain consistent with commercial lending practices.

Q 14:8 When is a loan considered adequately secured?

The general rule is that the security must be adequate to ensure that all principal and interest on the loan will be paid. The type and amount of collateral must be comparable to what a commercial lender would require in an arm's-length transaction. [DOL Reg § 2550.408b-1(f)(1)]

Q 14:9 Can a participant's account balance be used to secure the loan?

Yes. Up to 50 percent of the present value of a participant's account balance can be used to secure a loan. This is measured at the time the loan is made. [DOL Reg § 2550.408b-1(f)(2)] Therefore, if a participant borrows one half of his or her account balance and then takes a hardship distribution before the loan is repaid, he or she will still be in compliance with this rule.

Q 14:10 Must the plan examine the creditworthiness of each borrower?

No. The DOL does not require plan sponsors to review financial statements or other indications of creditworthiness of each participant who wants a loan. [54 Fed Reg 30522–30525]

Q 14:11 Are there any restrictions on how a loan is used by a participant?

No. In fact, as long as the employer does not place any restrictions on use of the loan that would benefit itself, a fiduciary, or other party in interest, there is no reason why a participant cannot independently make the decision to use loan proceeds in a way that would benefit the employer or other restricted party. [DOL Reg § 2550.408b-1(a)(4), Ex 6]

Q 14:12 Can a participant loan be made to a fiduciary involved in administering the loan program?

Yes, but the DOL will look on such a loan with special scrutiny. The loan must be made according to strict objective criteria. When the fiduciary borrows from his or her own account, an independent plan representative should approve the loan. [54 Fed Reg 30520] For example, if the plan trustee is the person authorized to approve participant loans and he or she is seeking approval for a loan, that approval should come from the plan administrator or some other representative of the plan.

Q 14:13 Does the DOL impose any other restrictions on participant loans?

Yes. The parties to a loan agreement must intend to repay the loan. [DOL Reg § 2550.408b-1(a)(3)(i)] For this reason, it is important that the plan be diligent in collecting amounts due on participant loans. Many employers use payroll deductions for loan repayments to avoid collection problems.

Furthermore, the general fiduciary rules concerning plan investments that require prudence and diversification must be adhered to when making an investment in a participant loan. [DOL Op 81-12A]

Q 14:14 What are the consequences of failing to satisfy the DOL loan rules?

The loan will be considered a prohibited transaction (see chapter 5). Also, if the loan results in a loss to the plan, the fiduciary responsible for plan investments may be held personally liable to the plan for the loss. [ERISA § 409(a)] A disqualifying loan may also disqualify the plan by violating the anti-alienation rule discussed in Q 2:70. [Treas Reg § 1.401(a)-13(d)(2); Rev Rul 89-14, 1989-1 CB 111]

Taxation of Participant Loans

Q 14:15 How may taxation of participant loans be avoided?

Loans from a plan to a plan participant would generally be treated as distributions under Code Section 72(p)(1) and are taxable in whole or in part under Code Section 72(e). [Prop Treas Reg § 1.72(p)-1, Q&A 1(a)] The following three conditions must be met in order to avoid taxation of a participant loan at the time the loan is made:

1. The loan must be paid in full within five years, unless the loan is used to acquire a principal residence of the participant. [IRC §72(p)(2)(B)]

2. The loan must require substantially level amortization of principal and interest, with payments required at least quarterly.

For example, a loan for a five-year term that requires payments of interest only until the end of the term, and a balloon payment at the end, does not qualify. [IRC § 72(p)(2)(C)]

3. The loan is limited to a dollar limit equal to the lesser of (a) or (b):

(a) $50,000, reduced by:

The highest outstanding balance of loans during the one-year period ending on the day before the date a loan is to be made; less

The outstanding balance of loans on the date the loan is to be made.

(b) The greater of:

One half of a participant's vested accrued benefit; or

$10,000. [IRC § 72(p)(2)(A)]

Generally, if no other plan loans are outstanding, a participant may borrow up to the following amounts:

Vested Account Balance	Maximum Loan Amount
$10,000 or less	Entire vested account balance
$10,001–$20,000	$10,000
$20,001–$100,000	50% of vested account
Over $100,000	$50,000

If the participant has a loan outstanding and wants a new loan, or has repaid a loan within the 12 months preceding his or her request for a new loan, the loan amount is determined as demonstrated in the following example.

Example. Michael, whose vested accrued benefit is $150,000, has a $20,000 loan balance currently. The highest outstanding loan balance for the prior 12-month period is $28,000. Michael's nontaxable loan limit is $42,000, calculated as follows:

Limited to lesser of (a) or (b):

(a) $50,000, reduced by:

> Highest outstanding balance for prior 12 months ($28,000); less

> Outstanding balance on date of new loan ($20,000) = $42,000

(b) Greater of:

> One half of vested accrued benefit (½ × $150,000 = $75,000); or

> $10,000 = $75,000

Since (a) = $42,000 and (b) = $75,000, the nontaxable loan limit—the lesser of (a) or (b)—is $42,000.

Michael could borrow up to $22,000, calculated as $42,000 – $20,000.

In determining the dollar limit, the employer must aggregate all vested accrued benefits and all loans from any other plans of the employer or related company under Code Sections 414(b), 414(c), and 414(m). (For the definition of *employer* see chapter 9.)

Q 14:16 What loans are subject to these rules?

Any loan made, modified, extended, or renegotiated on or after January 1, 1987, is subject to these rules.

Q 14:17 If a loan fails to meet these requirements, what taxes apply?

A loan that fails to meet these requirements is treated as a deemed distribution and under these rules will be subject to regular income tax as well as the 10 percent additional tax imposed by Code Section 72(t) on premature distributions. (See Qs 17:59–17:60.) [Prop Treas Reg § 1.72(p)-1, Q&A 11(b)] It should be noted that the premature distribution tax does not apply to distributions to participants who have attained age 59½. A loan that becomes taxable but that is not offset against a participant's account balance is not an eligible rollover distribution (see Qs 15:49–15:50) and therefore is not subject to the 20 percent withholding requirement. [Treas Reg § 1.402(c)-2, Q&A 4(d)]

Q 14:18 How much of the loan is taxed if the requirements are not met?

The answer depends on which rule is violated and when the violation occurs. If a loan by its terms does not require repayment within five years or does not call for quarterly payments of principal and interest, then the entire amount of the loan will be deemed a distribution. [Prop Treas Reg § 1.72(p)-1, Q&A 4(a)] If the loan exceeds the dollar limit, then only the amount in excess of the limit is deemed distributed. [Prop Treas Reg § 1.72(p)-1, Q&A 4(a)] If the loan terms are in compliance but the loan goes into default, then the amount of principal and interest remaining upon default or at the end of any grace period allowed by the plan administrator is deemed distributed. A grace period can continue up to the last day of the calendar quarter following the calendar quarter in which a default occurs. [Prop Treas Reg § 1.72(p)-1, Q&A 10(a)]

Other Loan Rules

Q 14:19 If some or all of a loan is treated as a distribution, does that portion of the loan still need to be repaid?

Yes. A promissory note will still be considered effective and a trustee's obligation to preserve the asset represented by the plan loan will remain in effect even though some or all of the loan amount is taxed to the participant. The rules in Code Section 72(p) apply only to the question of whether or not a loan is taxable. They do not govern treatment of the loan in other circumstances.

Q 14:20 If a participant defaults on a loan payment secured by his or her account balance, should the account balance be reduced?

Yes, but only with respect to that part of a participant's account balance not attributable to elective contributions. Foreclosure to reduce a participant's account balance is considered a distribution under the plan, and any distribution of elective contributions that occurs for reasons other than separation from service, hardship, disability, or attainment of age 59½ would disqualify the plan. [Treas

Reg § 1.401(k)-1(d)] To meet the qualification requirements, the plan sponsor must wait until a distribution event occurs before it actually forecloses on a participant's elective contribution account balance. The fact that the plan sponsor is required to wait does not mean that the loan is not adequately secured as long as it is reasonably anticipated that no loss of principal or interest will occur. [54 Fed Reg 30526]

Q 14:21 Can a plan distribute a loan to a terminated participant?

Yes. Upon termination of employment, a plan can distribute a loan to a participant as part of the benefit distribution. A participant would then be entitled to substitute cash for the outstanding loan amount and roll over the entire amount. [Ltr Rul 8103063] Loans can also be transferred from one qualified plan to another without any adverse tax consequences. [Ltr Rul 8950008] Distributed loans or loan offsets are eligible rollover distributions. (See Qs 15:49–15:50.) However, the plan does not need to offer a rollover option for loan distributions. [Treas Reg § 1.401(a)(31)-1, Q&A-15]. Distributed loans cannot be rolled over into an IRA (see chapter 21).

Q 14:22 How does an employer determine whether a loan is being used to buy a principal residence?

There is no clear guidance as to what level of proof is required before an employer can extend the five-year term. A very conservative approach would be to issue the check jointly to the participant and the seller of the property, or, alternatively, to an escrow agent who can disburse only upon the closing. A more liberal and less cumbersome approach is to rely on a signed statement from the participant that the loan proceeds will be used to purchase a principal residence within a stated short period of time. The plan administrator could also require a copy of the purchase contract.

Q 14:23 What is a plan administrator's obligation when a taxable distribution has occurred?

The plan administrator must report the amount of the deemed distribution on a Form 1099R at the close of the participant's taxable year.

Q 14:24 If a participant who has filed bankruptcy has an outstanding loan in the plan, what happens to the loan?

The Bankruptcy Code prohibits creditors from attempting to collect any payment from a debtor once the bankruptcy has been filed. [Bankruptcy Code § 362] Generally, the plan administrator should cease all efforts at collecting the plan loan (including repayment through payroll deduction) while a bankruptcy is pending. There may be some exceptions to this general rule prohibiting collection, depending on the type of collateral used for the loan and the steps that have been taken by the plan to secure its rights in that collateral. The terms of the plan document may preserve the plan's right to offset the outstanding loan balance from a participant's distribution. However, the offset amount cannot include any interest accruals after the date a bankruptcy is filed. For this reason, it may make sense to segregate the loan to the bankrupt's account.

The rules concerning the taxability of participant loans (see Qs 14:15–14:23) continue to apply in bankruptcy. That is, if a required payment is not made by the end of the grace period, if any (see Q 14:18), the entire principal and interest will be deemed distributed for tax purposes.

Q 14:25 Are participant loans subject to federal truth-in-lending disclosure rules?

Yes. If a plan makes 25 or more plan loans in the current or prior calendar year (or 5 or more loans secured by a dwelling), it must make federal truth-in-lending disclosures. [12 CFR § 226.2(a)(17)]

Q 14:26 Is interest paid on a participant loan deductible?

After 1992, interest paid on a participant loan is generally not deductible. If the loan is secured by the participant's principal residence, the interest is deductible as long as the participant is not a key employee. (See Q 13:9.) [IRC § 72(p)(3); Ltr Rul 8933018]

Q 14:27 Can fees incurred to set up and administer a participant loan be charged to that participant's account?

Yes. However, caution must be used to ensure that imposing the fee does not result in the exclusion of large numbers of employees. [54 Fed Reg 30522]

Q 14:28 Is spousal consent needed to make a participant loan?

If the plan is subject to spousal annuity requirements (see chapter 16), the employee's spouse must give written consent to any loan secured by the employee's account balance. This rule does not apply if the total account balance serving as security for the loan does not exceed $5,000. (For plan years beginning before August 6, 1997, the $5,000 limit was $3,500.) If consent is required, it must be given within 90 days before the date the loan is made. [Treas Reg § 1.401(a)-20, Q&A 24(a)(1)]

Q 14:29 Can an employer eliminate or change its loan program?

The features of an employer's loan program are not protected optional forms of benefits subject to the anti-cutback rules of Code Section 411(d)(6). [Treas Reg § 1.411(d)-4, Q&As 1(d)(4), 2(b)(2)(vii)] The features of a loan program are subject to the rule prohibiting discrimination in favor of highly compensated employees. Therefore, a plan can freely change or eliminate its loan program as long as the changes do not cause the features of the loan program to become less available to non-highly compensated employees.

HARDSHIP WITHDRAWALS OF ELECTIVE CONTRIBUTIONS

Participants in a 401(k) plan may be permitted to withdraw their elective deferral contributions because of hardship without separating from service or otherwise becoming eligible for distribution from the plan. Hardship withdrawals are an optional plan feature.

Q 14:30 Is allowing for hardship withdrawals of elective contributions likely to increase 401(k) plan participation?

Many sponsors choose to include this feature in their plans because of a belief that it encourages higher levels of participation by lower-paid employees, which will help the plan pass the actual deferral percentage (ADP) test (see chapter 12). In fact, according to a 1997 survey conducted by Hewitt Associates LLC, *Trends and Experience in 401(k) Plans,* the average participation rate was no higher in 401(k) plans that allow for hardship withdrawals than in plans that don't.

Q 14:31 When is a distribution of elective contributions considered made on account of a hardship?

A distribution is considered made on account of a hardship if it is made in response to an immediate and heavy financial need (the *events test*), and it is necessary to satisfy that need (the *needs test*). [Treas Reg § 1.401(k)-1(d)(2)] The regulation provides two different standards for determining whether these tests are satisfied: the *general standard* (also called the facts-and-circumstances standard) and the *safe harbor standard*. It is not necessary to use the same standard to determine whether both tests are satisfied.

The Events Test

Q 14:32 How is the general standard applied to the events test?

The regulation's guidance on this question is limited to a direction that all relevant facts and circumstances be considered. The regulations do point out that whether a need can be foreseen or the fact that it is voluntarily incurred is generally not relevant. [Treas Reg § 1.401(k)-1(d)(2)(iii)(A)]

Q 14:33 How is the safe harbor standard applied to the events test?

The events test is considered satisfied if a distribution is made for any of the following reasons:

1. Payment of medical care expenses previously incurred by the participant or the participant's spouse or dependents; expenses necessary to obtain medical care are also covered;

2. Costs related to the purchase of a participant's principal residence (not including mortgage payments);

3. Payment of tuition, related educational fees, and room and board expenses for the next 12 months of post-secondary education for the participant or the participant's spouse, children, or dependents; and

4. Payments necessary to prevent eviction from or foreclosure on a mortgage on the participant's principal residence.

[Treas Reg § 1.401(k)-1(d)(2)(iv)(A)]

The Needs Test

Q 14:34 How is the general standard applied to the needs test?

The needs test is satisfied if, based on all the facts and circumstances, a distribution is needed to relieve the participant's financial need. In determining whether that need exists, the plan is required to consider whether the need can be relieved through other resources reasonably available to the employee. This determination, however, would require intruding into the personal financial circumstances of employees. As a result, the regulations offer an escape hatch. Under the regulations, the needs test is considered satisfied if the employer, in the absence of actual knowledge to the contrary, relies on the participant's written statement that his or her financial need cannot be satisfied through any of the following:

1. Reimbursement or compensation by insurance or otherwise;

2. Liquidation of the participant's assets;

3. Ceasing contributions under the plan;

4. Other distributions or nontaxable loans from plans maintained by the employer or any other employer; or

5. Borrowing from commercial sources on reasonable commercial terms.

[Treas Reg § 1.401(k)-1(d)(2)(iii)(B)]

Q 14:35 How is the safe harbor standard applied to the needs test?

The needs test is considered satisfied if all the following requirements are met:

1. The amount of the distribution does not exceed the amount necessary to relieve the financial need;

2. The participant has obtained all distributions (other than hardship distributions) and all nontaxable loans from all plans maintained by the employer;

3. The annual cap on elective deferrals (see Qs 8:1–8:3) for the participant's taxable year following the taxable year in which the hardship distribution occurs is reduced by the amount of elective contributions made by the participant during the taxable year in which the hardship distribution occurs; and

4. The participant does not make elective contributions and employee contributions to the plan and all other plans maintained by the employer (see Q 14:36) for at least 12 months after the hardship distribution is received.

[Treas Reg § 1.401(k)-1(d)(2)(iv)(B)]

Example. FGH Corporation sponsors a 401(k) plan that allows for hardship withdrawals. The plan determines, on the basis of the safe harbor standard, that John satisfies the events and needs tests. John receives a hardship distribution of $5,000 on June 15, 1999. As a result, John cannot resume making elective contributions until June 15, 2000. In addition, the annual cap for 2000 is reduced by the amount of elective contributions made by John during 1999.

Q 14:36 What is meant by the phrase *all other plans maintained by the employer*?

All other plans maintained by the employer means all qualified and nonqualified plans of deferred compensation including stock option, stock purchase or similar plans, or a cash or deferred arrangement that is part of a Section 125 cafeteria plan. However, the phrase does not include defined benefit plans to which paricipants make mandatory contributions. [Treas Reg § 1.401(k)-1(d)(2)(iv)(B)]

Safe Harbor Standard versus General Standard

Q 14:37 What is the best standard to use?

Each plan sponsor must reach its own conclusion as to what standard will work best. The advantage to using the safe harbor standard rather than the general standard is that the employer avoids needing to dig into and police a participant's personal financial situation. The disadvantage is that it is less flexible in terms of when hardship distributions will be available, making the plan less attractive to employees. Many employers also feel that the inability to make salary deferral contributions for one year following a hardship withdrawal under the safe harbor rules is a major deterrent to using the safe harbor "amount necessary" method.

Q 14:38 May an employer combine the standards?

It is possible to use a combination of the safe harbor and the general facts and circumstances standards. It is also possible for an employer to use the safe harbor standard for one part of the test (e.g., the circumstances creating a financial need) and the general facts and circumstances standard for the other part of the test. For example, an employer may specify the circumstances creating a financial need and include all the safe harbor events but also include additional events. If an employer uses this combined method, it will not have to review independently requests for hardship withdrawals where the event is one of the four contained in the safe harbor rules. However, for additional events that do not fall within the safe harbor rules, it will have to do an independent review under the general facts and circumstances test.

Tax Consequences

Q 14:39 What tax consequences apply to hardship withdrawals of elective contributions?

Hardship distributions are subject to ordinary income tax and to the 10 percent excise tax on distributions prior to age 59½. For this reason, it is often more advantageous for a participant to access his or her account through a plan loan rather than a hardship withdrawal.

Prior to 1999, hardship distributions were considered eligible rollover distributions subject to mandatory 20 percent income tax withholding unless rolled over into another qualified plan or an IRA. (See chapter 15 for a discussion of eligible rollover distributions). The IRS Restructuring and Return Act of 1998 (IRRA) changed this rule so that hardship distributions made after December 31, 1998, are no longer considered eligible rollover distributions, and a participant can elect out of income tax withholding without rolling the distribution over. Because of the administrative time and effort involved in amending forms and procedures to comply with this new rule, the IRS, in Notice 99-5, provided transitional relief by allowing plan sponsors the choice to apply either the old or the new rules through the end of 1999. Beginning on January 1, 2000, the new rules will apply in all plans. [IRS Notice 99-5, 1999-3 IRB 10]

Q 14:40 May a plan take into account federal, state, or local income taxes and penalties that may be payable as a result of a hardship withdrawal?

Yes. Income taxes and penalties may be taken into account for the purpose of determining whether the needs test is satisfied. [Treas Reg §§ 1.401(k)-1(d)(2)(iii)(B), 1.401(k)-1(d)(2)(iv)(B)]

Other Withdrawal Issues

Q 14:41 Is there a limit on the amount of a hardship withdrawal?

Yes. A hardship distribution cannot exceed the participant's withdrawal basis, which is the participant's total elective contributions as of the date of withdrawal reduced by amounts previously distributed on account of hardship. If the plan so provides, a participant's withdrawal basis may be increased by the amount of income attributable to elective contributions, the amount of qualified matching contributions (QMACs) and qualified nonelective contributions (QNECs) used to satisfy the ADP test (see Q 12:15), and the amount of income attributable to such QMACs and QNECs. These amounts include only those credited to a participant's account during any plan year ending before July 1, 1989. [Treas Reg § 1.401(k)-1(d)(2)(ii)]

Q 14:42 Do the rules that restrict the accessibility of elective contributions apply to any other kinds of contributions made under a 401(k) plan?

Yes. QNECs and QMACs, which may be used to satisfy the ADP or actual contribution percentage (ACP) test, are subject to these rules. (See Qs 14:41, 12:14.) [Treas Reg § 1.401(k)-1(g)(13)]

IN-SERVICE DISTRIBUTIONS

Q 14:43 In general, when may 401(k) accounts be distributed?

Unlike simplified employee pensions and SIMPLE retirement accounts (see chapter 21), where funds held for a participant may be withdrawn by the participant at any time, 401(k) plans are subject to rules that restrict a participant's access to his or her 401(k) plan accounts. All 401(k) plans may provide that a participant's accounts may be distributed upon retirement, death, disability, or separation from service. [Treas Reg §§ 1.401-1(b)(1)(ii), 1.401(k)-1(d)(1)(i)]

Whether accounts are accessible in other situations depends on the type of contribution used to fund a particular account. In general, accounts attributable to elective contributions are, under the law, less accessible to participants than accounts funded with other types of employer contributions.

Q 14:44 Under what circumstances other than retirement, death, disability, or separation from service may employer nonelective contributions be distributed?

According to the regulations, funds may be distributed after a fixed number of years, the attainment of a stated age, or upon the occurrence of some event such as layoff or illness. [Treas Reg § 1.401-1(b)(1)(ii)] These regulations apply to a 401(k) plan that is part of a profit sharing or stock bonus plan. A 401(k) plan that is part of a pre-ERISA money purchase plan may not allow distributions under these circumstances.

Q 14:45 What is considered a *fixed number of years*?

The IRS believes that contributions must be held in a plan for two years before they can be considered held for a fixed number of years. [Rev Rul 71-295, 1971-2 CB 184] According to the IRS, this two-year period runs from the date contributions are actually made and not from the date as of which they are deemed made under Code Section 404(a)(6).

Example. ABC Company, which is a calendar-year taxpayer, maintains a 401(k) plan administered on a calendar-year basis. ABC makes a nonelective contribution on March 1, 1999, which is deemed made and allocated as of December 31, 1998, under Code Section 404(a)(6). Under the plan, participants are allowed on January 10, 2001, to withdraw contributions allocated to them on December 31, 1998. According to the IRS, the plan provision violates the two-year rule because the contributions are withdrawn less than two years after they are actually made.

The IRS has indicated that the two-year rule can be disregarded if there has been a significant deferral of compensation. In a revenue ruling, the IRS permitted the withdrawal of all funds (even contributions made within two years of the withdrawal) where the right to

withdraw was extended only to employees who had been participants for 60 months. [Rev Rul 68-24, 1968-1 CB 150]

Q 14:46 Can distributions of employer nonelective contributions be made on account of hardship?

Yes. Although not specified in the regulations, the IRS has allowed a plan provision permitting withdrawal of employer contributions on account of hardship. According to the IRS, the term
hardship must be defined, the rules relating to hardship distributions must be uniformly and consistently applied, and the portion
distributed cannot exceed the participant's vested account. [Rev Rul
71-224, 1971-1 CB 124] This revenue ruling would not apply to a
401(k) plan that is part of a pre-ERISA money purchase plan.

Q 14:47 Under what circumstances, other than retirement, death, disability, or separation from service, may amounts attributable to elective contributions be distributed?

Amounts attributable to elective contributions may be distributed
under the following circumstances:

1. Attainment of age 59½ (profit sharing or stock bonus plan
   only);

2. Hardship as discussed in Qs 14:30–14:42 (profit sharing or
   stock bonus plan only);

3. Termination of the plan (see chapter 20);

4. Sale or other disposition of substantially all (at least 85 percent of) assets used by a corporation in a trade or business to
   an unrelated corporation; or

5. Sale or other disposition by a corporation of its interest in a
   subsidiary to an unrelated individual or entity.

[Treas Reg §§ 1.401(k)-1(d)(1)(ii), 1.401(k)-1(d)(1)(iii), 1.401(k)-
1(d)(1)(iv), 1.401(k)-1(d)(1)(v)]

15 Distributions Subsequent to Termination of Employment

A 401(k) plan participant who terminates employment with a vested account balance wants the answers to three questions: (1) When can I receive my benefits? (2) How will those benefits be paid to me? (3) Can tax deferral be maintained? The answers to the first two questions depend upon what optional forms of benefit are available under the plan. In large part, what is available is decided by the employer at the time the plan is established. The employer's decisions, however, must be made within a legal framework that places limits on the employer's ability to dictate when and how benefits will be paid. The answer to the third question depends on the rules relating to the rollover of 401(k) plan distributions to qualified plans and to individual retirement accounts. Although this chapter concentrates on distributions subsequent to termination of employment, it also points out cases where the distribution rules have special significance for hardship withdrawals. For additional information on hardship withdrawals and other in-service distributions, see chapter 14.

OPTIONAL FORMS OF BENEFIT

Q 15:1 What is an *optional form of benefit*?

An *optional form of benefit* is a distribution alternative available under a plan. It includes any plan provision that affects the timing of a distribution, the payment schedule for a distribution, the medium of distribution (e.g., cash or in kind), any election rights related to distributions, and when distributions commence. [Treas Reg § 1.401(a)(4)-4(e)(1)]

Example 1. Employer A has a plan that permits distributions in the form of a lump sum, joint and survivor annuity, or installments. All benefits in excess of $10,000 are deferred until normal retirement age. In-service hardship withdrawals of elective contributions are permitted. Distribution can be made in the form of cash or employer stock. Each one of these distribution features is a separate optional form of benefit subject to the rules discussed in Q 15:3.

Example 2. Employer ABC's plan requires that employees of Division A defer benefits in excess of $5,000. Division B employees are required to defer all benefits. These are two separate optional forms of benefits, since they differ as to the portion of the benefit to which the option applies.

Q 15:2 What are not optional forms of benefits?

The following are examples of plan features that are not optional forms of benefits:

- Ancillary life insurance protection
- Accident or health insurance benefits
- Social Security supplements
- The availability of loans
- The right to make elective deferrals or after-tax employee contributions
- The right to direct investments
- The right to a particular form of investment
- Contribution, valuation, and allocation dates
- Procedures for distributing benefits
- Rights that derive from administrative and operational provisions

[Treas Reg § 1.401(a)(4)-4(e)(2)&(3)]

Q 15:3 What rules apply to optional forms of benefits?

The availability of optional forms of benefits cannot discriminate in favor of highly compensated employees [Treas Reg § 1.401(a)(4)-4] (see Qs 11:26–11:36) and cannot be subject to employer discretion. [Treas Reg § 1.411(d)-4, Q&A 4(a)] Also, optional forms of benefits cannot be reduced or eliminated with respect to benefits that have already been accrued. [Treas Reg § 1.411(d)-4, Q&A 2(a)(1)]

Q 15:4 Does an employer have discretion over what optional forms of benefits will be made available to individual participants?

No. The availability of any optional form of benefit cannot be subject to employer discretion. For example, a plan cannot permit some participants to take an immediate lump-sum distribution while prohibiting others from doing so based on a subjective determination made by the employer. [Treas Reg § 1.411(d)-4, Q&A 4]

Q 15:5 Is employer discretion prohibited under all circumstances?

No. A plan can apply objective criteria as a condition for a distribution option and permit the employer the limited discretion of determining whether these criteria are met. [Treas Reg § 1.411(d)-4, Q&As 4(b) & 6(a)] For example, a plan may permit distributions in the event of disability and let the plan administrator decide whether a participant is disabled based on a written definition of disability contained in the plan.

Anti-Cutback Rules

Q 15:6 Can optional forms of benefits be reduced or eliminated by plan amendment?

The general rule is that an employer cannot eliminate or reduce optional forms of benefits with respect to benefits that have already been accrued. [Treas Reg § 1.411(d)-4, Q&A 2(a)] For example, if an employer maintains a plan that permits immediate lump-sum distributions and wants to amend the plan to require deferral of any lump-sum distributions until normal retirement age, the employer will not be able to apply the deferral provision to any benefits that had accrued while the older, more liberal plan provision was in place. The deferral provision can apply only to benefits that accrue after the later of the date the amendment is adopted or the date it becomes effective. This is known as the anti-cutback rule. [Treas Reg § 1.411(d)-4, Q&A 2(a)(1)]

Q 15:7 Are any other plan features subject to the anti-cutback rule?

Yes. Early retirement benefits or retirement-type subsidies are subject to the same anti-cutback rule as optional forms of benefits. [IRC § 411(d)(6)]

Q 15:8 Are there any exceptions to the anti-cutback rule?

Yes. The regulations include a number of exceptions to the anti-cutback rule, one of the most significant of which permits a plan to add a provision requiring the cash-out of benefits of $5,000 or less. [Treas Reg § 1.411(d)-4, Q&A 2(b)(2)(v)] Another exception permits a 401(k) plan that is not subject to the joint and survivor annuity rules under Section 417 to eliminate an installment option upon plan termination. [Treas Reg § 1.411(d)-4, Q&A 2(b)(2)(vi)] A 401(k) plan may also amend or eliminate its hardship distribution provisions without violating the anti-cutback rule. [Treas Reg § 1.411(d)-4, Q&A 2(b)(2)(x)]

Q 15:9 Can an employer avoid the anti-cutback rules through an employee waiver?

No. An employee cannot waive the protection afforded under the anti-cutback rules. [Treas Reg § 1.411(d)-4, Q&A 3(a)(3)]

Q 15:10 What should an employer consider when designing distribution features in a new plan?

An employer's main concern at the time a plan is established should be to avoid including distribution options or other protected features of a plan that it may desire to eliminate later. For example, if an employer is concerned that once benefits in a plan build up to a substantial level, the immediate availability of those funds to a terminated participant may enable that participant to set up a competing business, it may want to include a deferral provision at the time the plan is established, even though the concern is not an immediate one. A plan can always be amended to liberalize distribution options without running afoul of the anti-cutback rules. It is far more problematic to eliminate or reduce these options, since it will require the plan to have a dual tracking system that applies the more permissive features for benefits accrued prior to the date of the reduction and applies the more restrictive features to benefits accrued after the amendment becomes effective.

Q 15:11 What should an employer consider when terminating a plan or transferring benefits?

The anti-cutback rules cannot be avoided simply by transferring benefits to another plan in connection with a plan merger or otherwise. For example, if a 401(k) plan that provides for an immediate, lump-sum payment option on termination of employment merges into a profit sharing plan, participants' rights to retain this optional form of benefit with respect to their 401(k) plan account balances cannot be eliminated. The rules concerning protected benefits in plan terminations and mergers, as well as ways to avoid a dual tracking system for transferred benefits, are discussed in chapter 20.

Postponement of Benefits

Q 15:12 How long may a 401(k) plan delay the payment of benefits to a participant?

A 401(k) plan may be designed to delay the payment of benefits until 60 days after the close of the plan year in which the latest of the following events occurs:

1. The participant's attainment of age 65 or, if earlier, the normal retirement age specified in the plan;

2. The tenth anniversary of the date an employee's participation in the plan commenced (many commentators believe that the statute must be corrected so that the triggering event is the fifth anniversary, which would be consistent with the change made in 1986 to the definition of *normal retirement age* in Code Section 411(a)(8));

3. The participant's termination of service with the employer; or

4. If permitted in the plan, the date specified in an election by the participant.

[Treas Reg § 1.401(a)-14(a)]

Q 15:13 Does an early retirement provision in the 401(k) plan accelerate the payment of benefits?

Yes. If there is an early retirement provision, a participant who terminates employment before satisfying the age requirement for early retirement, but after satisfying the service requirement, must be allowed to begin receiving benefits at the time the participant satisfies the age requirement. [Treas Reg § 1.401(a)-14(c)]

Example. DEF Company maintains a 401(k) plan that permits participants to retire early at age 60 after completing 5 years of service. Joe terminates employment at age 40 after completing 15 years of service. The 401(k) plan must allow Joe to commence receiving benefits when he reaches age 60.

Q 15:14 What requirements must be met by a participant who is allowed to elect to delay the payment of benefits?

The election must be in writing, must be signed by the participant, and must describe when benefits will begin and in what form they will be paid. Any election must not violate the Section 401(a)(9) minimum distribution rules discussed in Qs 15:23–15:34. [Treas Reg § 1.401(a)–14(b)]

Q 15:15 Are there circumstances under which plan provisions delaying the payment of benefits are superseded?

Yes. The payment of benefits must commence by the required beginning date under the Section 401(a)(9) minimum distribution rules even if the required beginning date is earlier than the dates listed in Q 15:12. Also, benefits cannot commence without the consent of the participant if the date determined by one of the methods listed in Q 15:12 occurs when benefits are considered immediately distributable under Code Section 411(a)(11). (See Q 15:20.) [Treas Reg § 1.411(a)-11(c)]

Example. QRS Company sponsors a 401(k) plan that is administered on a calendar-year basis and that has a normal retirement age of 60. Jane retires in 1999 upon attaining age 60 and after having participated in the plan for more than ten years. Although Code Section 401(a)(14) requires the payment of benefits to commence by March 1, 2000, the participant consent rules in Code Section 411(a)(11) take precedence. Accordingly, benefits may not be paid to Jane on March 1, 2000, without her previous consent. Her consent would be required until she reaches age 62, when benefits are no longer considered immediately distributable under Code Section 411(a)(11).

Q 15:16 What conditions must be satisfied before a participant's consent is considered valid?

A participant's consent is not considered valid unless a participant receives the following:

1. A general description of the material features of the forms of benefits provided under the plan;

2. An explanation of the relative values of these forms of benefits; and

3. A notice of his or her right to defer payment of benefits.

[Treas Reg § 1.411(a)-11(c)(2)(i)]

This notice must be provided no less than 30 days and no more than 90 days before the date on which benefits are to be paid. In the case of a 401(k) plan that is not subject to the Section 401(a)(11) joint and survivor rules, the 30-day requirement will be considered satisfied, even if benefits are paid less than 30 days after notice is provided, as long as the notice makes clear that the participant has 30 days after the notice is provided to make a decision. (See Q 15:70.) [Treas Reg § 1.411(a)-11(c)(2)(iii)] The immediately preceding sentence also applies to a 401(k) plan that is subject to the Section 401(a)(11) joint and survivor rules as long as benefits are not paid until 7 days after the date notice is given. [Treas Reg § 1.417(e)-1(b)(3)(ii)] Under the current regulations, a participant's consent must be in writing and must not be made before the participant receives the notice. [Treas Reg § 1.411(a)-11(c)(2)(ii)]

Q 15:17 How do recently proposed Treasury regulations affect the notice and consent requirements described in Q 15:16?

The proposed regulations would permit participant consent to be given electronically. They would also allow electronic delivery of the notice. Finally, plans would be allowed to provide the notice more than 90 days before a distribution if the plan provides a summary notice within 90 days of the distribution. [Prop Treas Reg § 1.411(a)–11(c)(2)(iii) and (f)]

The proposed regulation is a part of recently released IRS guidance that interprets how the notice and consent requirements apply to electronically administered retirement plans. In this guidance the

IRS confirmed that there are no specific Code requirements regarding the use of electronic media for participant enrollments, contribution elections, investment elections, beneficiary designations (other than designations requiring spousal consent), electing direct rollovers, and plan and account information inquiries. [IRS Notice 99-1, 1999-2 IRB 8]

Q 15:18 What information must be included in the summary notice?

The summary notice must advise the participant of the right, if any, to defer receipt of the distribution; must set forth a summary of the distribution options under the plan; must refer the participant to the most recent occasion on which the notice was provided (and, in the case of a notice provided in any document containing information in addition to the notice, must identify that document and must indicate where the notice may be found in that document); and must advise the participant that, upon request, a copy of the full notice will be provided without charge.

Q 15:19 What form must the notice and consent take?

The notice of a participant's rights may be provided either on a written paper document or through an electronic medium reasonably accessible to the participant. A notice or summary provided through an electronic medium must be provided under a system that satisfies the following requirements:

1. The system must be reasonably designed to provide the notice or summary in a manner no less understandable to the participant than a written paper document.

2. At the time the notice or summary is provided, the participant must be advised that he or she may request and receive the notice on a written paper document, and, upon request, that document must be provided to the participant at no charge.

The required consent may be given either on a written paper document or through an electronic medium reasonably accessible to the participant. A consent given through an electronic medium must be given under a system that satisfies the following requirements:

1. The system must be reasonably designed to preclude any individual other than the participant from giving the consent;

2. The system must provide the participant with a reasonable opportunity to review and to confirm, modify, or rescind the terms of the distribution before the consent to the distribution becomes effective; and

3. The system must provide the participant, within a reasonable time after the consent is given, a confirmation of the terms (including the form) of the distribution either on a written paper document or through an electronic medium under a system that satisfies the requirements of Code Section 411(a)(11).

[IRS Notice 99-1, 1999-2 IRB 8]

Example 1: E-Mail Consent and Confirmation. A qualified plan (Plan A) permits participants to request distributions by e-mail. Under Plan A's system for such transactions, a participant must enter his or her account number and personal identification number (PIN); this information must match that in Plan A's records in order for the transaction to proceed. If a participant changes his or her PIN, the participant may not proceed with a transaction until Plan A has sent confirmation of the change to the participant. If a participant requests a distribution from Plan A by e-mail, the plan administrator provides the participant with a notice by e-mail. The plan administrator also advises the participant that he or she may request the notice on a written paper document and that, if the participant so requests, the written paper document will be provided at no charge. To proceed with the distribution by e-mail, the participant must acknowledge receipt, review, and comprehension of the notice and must consent to the distribution within the time required under Code Section 411(a)(11). Within a reasonable time after the participant's consent, the plan administrator, by e-mail, sends confirmation of the distribution to the participant and advises the participant that he or she may request the confirmation on a written paper document that will be provided at no charge. Plan A does not fail to satisfy the notice or consent requirement of Code Section 411(a)(11) merely because the notice and consent are provided other than through written paper documents.

Example 2: E-Mail Consent and Written Confirmation. The facts are the same as in Example 1, except that, instead of sending a confirmation of the distribution by e-mail, the plan administrator, within a reasonable time after the participant's consent, sends the participant an account statement for the period that includes information reflecting the terms of the distribution. Plan A does not fail to satisfy the consent requirement of Code Section 411(a)(11) merely because the consent is provided other than through a written paper document.

Example 3: Web Site Consent and Confirmation. A qualified plan (Plan B) permits participants to request distributions through its web site (Internet or intranet). Under Plan B's system for such transactions, a participant must enter his or her account number and personal identification number (PIN); this information must match that in Plan B's records in order for the transaction to proceed. If a participant changes his or her PIN, the participant may not proceed with a transaction until Plan B has sent confirmation of the change to the participant. A participant may request a distribution from Plan B by following the applicable instructions on the Plan B web site. After the participant has requested a distribution, the participant is automatically shown a page on the web site containing the notice. Although this page of the web site may be printed, the page also advises the participant that he or she may request the notice on a written paper document and that, if the participant so requests, the written paper document will be provided at no charge. To proceed with the distribution through the web site, the participant must acknowledge review and comprehension of the notice and must consent to the distribution within the time required under Code Section 411(a)(11). The web site requires the participant to review and confirm the terms of the distribution before the transaction is completed. After the participant has given consent, the Plan B web site confirms the distribution to the participant and advises the participant that he or she may request the confirmation on a written paper document that will be provided at no charge. Plan B does not fail to satisfy the notice or consent requirement of Code Section 411(a)(11) merely because the notice and consent are provided other than through written paper documents.

Example 4: Automated Phone System. A qualified plan (Plan C) permits participants to request distributions through its automated telephone system. Under Plan C's system for such transactions, a participant must enter his or her account number and personal identification number (PIN); this information must match that in Plan C's records in order for the transaction to proceed. If a participant changes his or her PIN, the participant may not proceed with a transaction until Plan C has sent confirmation of the change to the participant. Plan C provides only the following distribution options: a lump sum or annual installments over 5, 10, or 20 years. A participant may request a distribution from Plan C by following the applicable instructions on the automated telephone system. After the participant has requested a distribution, the automated telephone system reads the notice to the participant. The automated telephone system also advises the participant that he or she may request the notice on a written paper document and that, if the participant so requests, the written paper document will be provided at no charge. Before proceeding with the distribution transaction, the participant must acknowledge comprehension of the notice and must consent to the distribution within the time required under Code Section 411(a)(11). The automated telephone system requires the participant to review and confirm the terms of the distribution before the transaction is completed. After the participant has given consent, the automated telephone system confirms the distribution to the participant and advises the participant that he or she may request the confirmation on a written paper document that will be provided at no charge. Because Plan C has relatively few and simple distribution options, the provision of the notice over the automated telephone system is no less understandable to the participant than a written paper notice. Plan C does not fail to satisfy the notice or consent requirement of Code Section 411(a)(11) merely because the notice and consent are provided other than through written paper documents.

Example 5: Automated Phone System with Transfer to a Customer Service Representative. The facts are the same as in Example 4, except that, pursuant to Plan C's system for processing such transactions, a participant who so requests is transferred to a customer service representative whose conversation with the participant is recorded. The customer service representative provides the notice from a prepared text and processes the participant's distribution in accordance with predetermined instructions of the plan administrator. Plan C does not fail to satisfy the notice or consent requirement of Code Section 411(a)(11) merely because the notice and consent are provided other than through written paper documents.

Involuntary Distributions

Q 15:20 Under what circumstances may a 401(k) plan compel a participant to commence receiving benefits?

Under the law, a 401(k) plan may provide that a participant's vested account balance be paid immediately and in the form of a single sum if the vested account balance does not exceed $5,000. If the participant's vested account balance is greater than $5,000, a participant's consent is required for any distribution that is immediately distributable. [Treas Reg §§ 1.411(a)-11(c)(3), 1.411(a)-11(c)(4)] A distribution is considered immediately distributable at any time before the later of the following dates:

1. The date on which the participant attains the plan's normal retirement age; or

2. The date on which the participant attains age 62.

[Treas Reg § 1.411(a)-11(c)(4)]

Example. XYZ Company sponsors a 401(k) plan that has a normal retirement age of 65. Frank terminates employment when he is 55. His vested account balance exceeds $5,000. Any distribution to Frank is considered immediately distributable until he reaches his normal retirement age of 65 (since this is later than age 62); consequently, Frank's consent is required if distribution is made before he reaches age 65.

For plan years beginning before August 6, 1997, single sum cash-outs could occur so long as the participant's vested account balance did not exceed $3,500. [TRA '97 § 1071]

Q 15:21 Is a beneficiary's consent required in the event of a participant's death?

No. A 401(k) plan is not required to obtain the consent of a participant's beneficiary before benefit payments commence. [Treas Reg § 1.411(a)-11(c)(5)]

Q 15:22 Is an alternate payee's consent required in the case of a qualified domestic relations order (QDRO)?

The consent of the alternate payee is not required unless the QDRO itself requires the alternate payee's consent. [Treas Reg § 1.411(a)-11(c)(6)]

MINIMUM DISTRIBUTION REQUIREMENTS

The payment of benefits cannot be postponed indefinitely. Whether or not the plan grants participants the right to determine when benefits are payable, benefits must commence no later than the participants' required beginning date.

Required Beginning Date

Q 15:23 How long may a participant defer benefits in a 401(k) plan?

Before December 31, 1996, a participant must have begun receiving distributions from a qualified plan by April 1 of the calendar year after reaching age 70½. For example, a participant who turned age 70½ before July 1, 1994, must have begun receiving benefits under a 401(k) plan before April 1, 1995.

Effective for years beginning after December 31, 1996, the required beginning date for a participant who is not a 5 percent owner is the April 1 of the calendar year following the later of the calendar year in which he or she reaches age 70½ or the calendar year in which the participant retires. The old rule continues to apply to 5 percent owners. [IRC § 401(a)(9)(C)]

Q 15:24 Can a participant who is no longer required to receive a minimum distribution elect to stop receiving post-70½ distributions?

Yes. The IRS has issued guidelines making it clear that participants who are not 5 percent owners and who turned age 70½ in 1996 or later are not required to take distributions until their required beginning date. [IRS Notice 97-45, 1997-33 IRB 7] Notice 97-45 also permits plans to allow non-5 percent owners who turned age 70½ before 1996 to elect to stop receiving minimum distributions. Elections to stop and then recommence minimum distributions may, in the case of a 401(k) plan subject to the Section 417(a)(11) joint and survivor rules, require spousal consent. [IRS Notice 97-45, 1997-33 IRB 7, Q&A 8]

Q 15:25 Can a plan cease making post-70½ distributions not required under the new law without amending the plan document?

Prior to 1997, all qualified plan documents provided for participants turning 70½ to commence distributions regardless of whether they were 5 percent owners and/or actively employed. This distribution right falls within the protection of Code Section 411(d)(6), which prohibits a plan from eliminating a distribution option with respect to benefits accrued prior to the amendment date. The IRS has stated that a plan can be retroactively amended to allow participants not required to take a distribution under the new minimum distribution rules to elect out of the distribution without violating Code Section 411(d)(6), provided the amendment is made by the last day of the plan year beginning on or after January 1, 2000. [Rev Proc 99-23, 1999-16 IRB 5] The IRS has also taken the position that the right to receive an in-service distribution at age 70½ can be eliminated entirely for active, non-5 percent owners who reach age 70½ after December 31, 1998. [Prop Reg § 1.411(d)-4, Q&A 10]

Q 15:26 Who is a *5 percent owner* for minimum distribution purposes?

A participant is considered a *5 percent owner* if he or she is a 5 percent owner for the plan year ending in the calendar year in which he or she attains age 70½. According to the law, a 5 percent owner is to be determined for this purpose in the same way as it is determined for top-heavy purposes (see Q 13:10). [IRC § 401(a)(9)(C)(ii)(I)]

Q 15:27 Is there any exception to the rules establishing an employee's required beginning date?

Yes. If an employee made an election under Section 242(b) of the Tax Equity and Fiscal Responsibility Act of 1982 (TEFRA), then an employee's required beginning date is the date established under the TEFRA election. An IRS notice sets forth the requirements that must have been satisfied for a valid TEFRA election. [Notice 83-23, 1983-2 CB 418]

Q 15:28 What happens if a participant revokes an election made under TEFRA Section 242(b)(2)?

If a participant revokes an election made under TEFRA Section 242(b)(2) by electing to receive a distribution earlier than provided in the election form, then "catch-up" distributions must be made by December 31 of the calendar year following the calendar year of revocation. [Prop Treas Reg § 1.401(a)(9)-1, Q&A J-4]

Example. A participant who owns 50 percent of the stock of the employer had made an election under TEFRA Section 242(b) to defer receipt of benefits until age 80. In 1999, at age 75, the participant elects to receive a partial distribution of $10,000. Since his election was effectively revoked, the participant must catch up for any distributions not made after attainment of age 70½. The participant turned 70½ in 1994 and should have received distributions for the years 1994 through 1998. The revocation rules require that catch-up distributions for the years 1994 through 1998 be made by December 31, 2000.

Q 15:29 In the case of a participant who dies before his or her required beginning date, what is the date by which post-death benefits must begin?

The required beginning date for post-death benefits depends on whether the plan employs either or both of two rules permitted under the law:

1. The five-year rule (see Q 15:30); or

2. The designated beneficiary rule (see Q 15:33).

[Prop Treas Reg § 1.401(a)(9)-1, Q&A C-1(a)]

Q 15:30 What is the *five-year rule*?

The *five-year rule* is a rule by which the employee's entire interest in a 401(k) plan must be distributed no later than December 31 of the calendar year containing the fifth anniversary of the employee's death. [Prop Treas Reg § 1.401(a)(9)-1, Q&A C-2] The five-year rule always applies to a beneficiary that is not a designated beneficiary. A designated beneficiary may also be subject to the five-year rule if the plan so provides, or if the designated beneficiary elects the five-year rule pursuant to an election permitted under the plan. [Prop Treas Reg § 1.401(a)(9)-1, Q&As C-4(b)&(c)]

Q 15:31 Who is a *designated beneficiary*?

A *designated beneficiary* is an individual who is entitled, upon the death of an employee, to all or any portion of the employee's interest in the plan, and who is designated as a beneficiary under the plan either by the plan's terms or, if the plan so provides, by an election of the employee. A designated beneficiary need not be specified by name in order to be a designated beneficiary as long as the individual who is to be the beneficiary can be ascertained. [Prop Treas Reg § 1.401(a)(9)-1, Q&A D-2]

Example. Gamma Corporation's 401(k) plan permits a participant to designate a beneficiary to receive the participant's account balance upon his or her death. In the absence of a valid designation, the plan provides that the participant's spouse will be the beneficiary. Bob, who, at the time of his death, was married to Jane, died without having designated a beneficiary. Under the plan's terms, Jane will be the beneficiary. Even though Jane is not specifically named as Bob's beneficiary, she is considered a designated beneficiary for purposes of the minimum distribution rules because at the time of Bob's death it is possible to ascertain that Jane is the beneficiary under the terms of the plan.

Q 15:32 May an estate or trust be considered a designated beneficiary?

An estate cannot be a designated beneficiary. [Prop Treas Reg § 1.401(a)(9)-1, Q&A D-2A(a)] A trust itself cannot be a designated beneficiary, but individuals who are beneficiaries of the trust are treated as designated beneficiaries if the trust meets the following requirements:

1. It is valid under state law or would be valid but for the fact that there is no trust corpus;

2. It is irrevocable, or it will, by its terms, become irrevocable on the participant's death;

3. Its beneficiaries are identifiable under the trust instrument; and

4. A copy of the trust instrument or a certified list of beneficiaries is provided to the plan.

[Prop Treas Reg § 1.401(a)(9)-1, Q&As D-5 & D-7]

Q 15:33 What is the *designated beneficiary rule*?

The *designated beneficiary rule* is a rule by which payment of the employee's interest in the plan must begin no later than December 31 of the calendar year immediately following the calendar year in which the employee died. The designated beneficiary rule is available only to designated beneficiaries or trusts whose beneficiaries are treated as designated beneficiaries as discussed in Q 15:32. The designated beneficiary rule requires that the employee's interest be paid over the life of the designated beneficiary or over a period not exceeding the life expectancy of the designated beneficiary. [Prop Treas Reg § 1.401(a)(9)-1, Q&As C-1(a) & C-3(a)]

Q 15:34 What happens if the designated beneficiary is the employee's surviving spouse?

In the case of a designated beneficiary who is a surviving spouse, the required beginning date under the designated beneficiary rule is determined differently. The required beginning date is the later of:

1. December 31 of the calendar year immediately following the calendar year in which the employee died; or

2. December 31 of the calendar year in which the employee would have attained age 70½.

[Prop Treas Reg § 1.401(a)(9)-1, Q&A C-3(b)]

Payment Options

Q 15:35 What payment options may be offered by a 401(k) plan?

Except as otherwise required by the Section 401(a)(11) joint and survivor rules, a 401(k) plan is free to offer as few or as many payment options as desired. For example, a 401(k) may provide that benefits are payable as a single sum only. On the other hand, a 401(k) plan can provide a whole panoply of payment options from single sums to annuity contracts. No matter which payment options are offered, the amounts paid under these distribution options must satisfy the minimum distribution rules.

Q 15:36 Must distributions that are made to an employee before an employee's required beginning date satisfy the minimum distribution rules?

No. [Prop Treas Reg § 1.401(a)(9)-1, Q&A B-3A]

Q 15:37 Over what length of time may an employee receive his or her interest in the plan?

An employee's interest in the plan may be paid over the life of the employee (or the joint lives of the employee and a designated beneficiary), or over a period not extending beyond the life expectancy of the employee (or the joint life and last survivor expectancy of the employee and designated beneficiary). [IRC § 401(a)(9)(A)] It should be noted, however, that an election made under TEFRA Section 242 can provide for a longer period of payment. (See Q 15:27.)

Q 15:38 If an employee's interest in the plan will be paid out over a period of time not exceeding the employee's life expectancy (or joint life and last survivor expectancy), what amount is required to be paid each calendar year?

The amount required to be paid each calendar year must at least equal the quotient obtained by dividing the value of the employee's interest in the plan by the applicable life expectancy. The first calendar year for which a distribution is required is the calendar year immediately preceding the calendar year containing his or her required beginning date. The minimum distribution for that calendar year must be made by the required beginning date. (See Q 15:23.) The minimum distribution for any subsequent calendar year must be made by December 31 of that year. [Prop Treas Reg § 1.401(a)(9)-1, Q&A F-1]

Example. Diane, a 5 percent owner and a participant in a 401(k) plan, reaches age 70½ in 1998. The minimum distribution for calendar year 1998 must be made on or before April 1, 1999, her required beginning date. The minimum distribution for calendar year 1999 is due no later than December 31, 1999.

Q 15:39 What is the applicable life expectancy used in determining the amount of the minimum distribution?

The applicable life expectancy is either the life expectancy of the employee or the joint life and last survivor expectancy of the employee and the designated beneficiary. The applicable life expectancy is calculated using the employee's (and, if applicable, the designated beneficiary's) attained age as of the employee's birthday (and, if applicable, the designated beneficiary's birthday) in the calendar year immediately preceding the calendar year containing his or her required beginning date. [Prop Treas Reg § 1.401(a)(9)-1, Q&A E-1(a)] Life expectancies are determined under the expected return multiples in Tables V and VI of Treasury Regulations Section 1.72-9, which are reprinted in Appendix B. [Prop Treas Reg § 1.401(a)(9)-1, Q&As E-3 & E-4]

Example. Rick, a participant in a 401(k) plan, retired in 1995. Because he attained 70½ during 1999, he is required to receive a minimum distribution no later than April 1, 2000. Rick turned 71 on December 1, 1999, and his designated beneficiary, Fran, was 68 on December 15, 1999. The applicable life expectancy for purposes of calculating his initial minimum distribution is 21.2, based on their ages of 71 and 68.

Q 15:40 How is the applicable life expectancy determined in succeeding calendar years?

Unless life expectancies are recalculated, the applicable life expectancy is the applicable life expectancy for the preceding calendar year reduced by one. [Prop Treas Reg § 1.401(a)(9)-1, Q&A F-1(d)] In the example at Q 15:39, if life expectancies are not recalculated, the applicable life expectancy for purposes of calculating the 2000 minimum distribution would be 20.2, calculated as 21.2 – 1.

Q 15:41 Under what circumstances may life expectancies be recalculated?

If the 401(k) plan provides, the life expectancy of the employee and the employee's spouse, if the spouse is the designated beneficiary, may be redetermined annually. [Prop Treas Reg § 1.401(a)(9)-1, Q&As E-6–E-8] In the example at Q 15:39, if Fran is Rick's spouse and their life expectancies are being recalculated, then the applicable life expectancy for purposes of calculating the 2000 minimum distribution would be 20.3 (based on their ages of 72 and 69).

Q 15:42 Can an employee minimize the amount of the required minimum distribution by designating a substantially younger beneficiary?

No. When a nonspouse designated beneficiary is more than ten years younger than the employee, the applicable life expectancy is determined under a table that assumes the beneficiary is only ten years younger than the employee. [Prop Treas Reg § 1.401(a)(9)-2, Q&A 4(a)] These tables do not apply, however, if the designated beneficiary is the spouse. [Prop Treas Reg § 1.401(a)(9)-2, Q&A 7(a)]

Example. John, a non-5 percent owner participant in a 401(k) plan, retires in 1999, having reached the age of 75 by the end of that year. John's designated beneficiary is his grandson, Mark, who turns 20 in 1999. The joint life and last survivor expectancy of John and Mark is 61.9. However, because Mark is more than ten years younger than John, the divisor for determining the amount of John's minimum distribution for 1999 is 26.2, a number based on the tables in Proposed Treasury Regulation Section 1.401(a)(9)-2

Q 15:43 What is the value of an employee's interest for purposes of calculating the minimum distribution for a calendar year?

The value of an employee's interest is the employee's account balance as of the last valuation date in the calendar year (valuation calendar year) immediately preceding the calendar year for which a minimum distribution is being made, with the following adjustments:

1. The account balance is increased by contributions or forfeitures allocated as of dates in the valuation calendar year after the valuation date; and

2. The account balance is decreased by distributions made in the valuation calendar year after the valuation date.

[Prop Treas Reg § 1.401(a)(9)-1, Q&As F-5(a)–F-5(c)]

Example. FGH Company maintains a 401(k) plan that has an annual valuation date of May 31. On May 31, 1999, the value of Judy's account balance under the plan is $50,000. Between June 1, 1999, and December 31, 1999, Judy, who is 73 and who is not a 5 percent owner, makes elective contributions of $2,000. She also withdraws $10,000 on November 15, 1999. Judy retires during calendar year 2000; thus, her required beginning date is April 1, 2001. The value of her interest in the 401(k) plan for purposes of calculating her 2000 minimum distribution is $42,000, calculated as ($50,000 + $2,000) − $10,000.

Q 15:44 If an employee dies after the required beginning date but before the employee's entire interest has been distributed, how must the remaining interest in the plan be distributed?

The employee's remaining interest in the plan must be distributed to the employee's beneficiary at least as rapidly as under the method in effect at the employee's death. [Prop Treas Reg § 1.401(a)(9)-1, Q&A B-4]

Q 15:45 How are required minimum distributions reported?

Required minimum distributions are taxable as ordinary income and reported on Form 1099-R. They are not eligible rollover distributions (see Q 15:50). To the extent the participant has a cost basis, the exclusion ratio would be applied (see Q 17:36).

Distributions to actively employed participants who are over 70½ and who are not 5 percent owners are no longer considered required minimum distributions. As a result, distributions to participants in this category are considered eligible rollover distributions (see Q 15:49) unless they fall within another exception to that rule. [IRS Notice 97-75, 1997-51 IRB 18]

ROLLOVER RULES

Q 15:46 What is a *rollover*?

A *rollover* is a tax-free transfer of cash or other property from a qualified plan into an individual retirement account (IRA) or another qualified plan. A participant in a 401(k) plan may defer the tax on a distribution by rolling it over. [IRC § 402(c)(1)] In some cases, distributions are rolled into an IRA that, in effect, serves as a conduit when the proceeds are subsequently rolled over into another qualified plan. A rollover into a qualified plan is permitted only if the plan document of the receiving plan allows for rollovers.

Q 15:47 How did the Unemployment Compensation Act of 1992 change the rollover rules?

The Unemployment Compensation Act of 1992, which is effective for all distributions occurring on or after January 1, 1993, significantly broadened the availability of rollovers. Under prior rules, rollovers were available only on qualified total distributions or on partial distributions that met certain rules. Under the new law, any eligible rollover distribution (see Qs 15:49–15:50), including certain periodic or installment distributions, is eligible for rollover. Also, rollovers are no longer restricted to distributions occurring due to particular events. See Qs 15:82–15:85 for additional information on the Unemployment Compensation Act of 1992.

Eligible Rollover Distribution

Q 15:48 What distributions are eligible for tax-free rollover?

Any distribution that fits within the definition of an eligible rollover distribution (Qs 15:49–15:50) can be rolled over. There are no longer any restrictions based on the amount of the benefit distributed or the reason for the distribution.

Q 15:49 What is an *eligible rollover distribution?*

An *eligible rollover distribution* is a distribution of all or any portion of the balance to the credit of an employee's account in a qualified plan. [IRC § 402(c)(4); Treas Reg § 1.402(c)-2, Q&A 3]

Q 15:50 Are there any exceptions to the general rule defining eligible rollover distributions?

Yes. The following distributions are not considered eligible rollover distributions:

1. Any distribution to the extent it is required under the minimum distribution rules of Code Section 401(a)(9) (see Q 15:53);

2. Any distribution that is part of a series of substantially equal periodic payments made not less frequently than annually over the life (or life expectancy) of the employee, the joint lives (or joint life and last survivor expectancy) of the employee and his or her designated beneficiary, or for a period of ten years or more (see Q 15:51);

3. The portion of any distribution that is not included in gross income, including any portion of a distribution excluded from gross income under the Section 101(b) $5,000 death benefit exclusion for participants who died on or before August 20, 1996;

4. Section 401(k) elective deferrals that are returned as a result of Section 415 limitations (see Qs 8:27–8:28);

5. Corrective distributions of excess contributions, excess defer-

rals, or excess aggregate contributions, as well as the income allocable to those corrective distributions;

6. Loans that are treated as distributions under Code Section 72(p) or that are considered deemed distributions by reason of default (see Qs 14:15–14:23);

7. Dividends on employee stock ownership plan (ESOP) stock either paid to participants or used to repay an ESOP loan [IRC § 404(k)];

8. The cost of life insurance coverage (PS-58 costs); and

9. Any other item designated by the IRS in any revenue ruling, notice, or other guidance of general applicability.

[IRC § 402(c)(4); Treas Reg § 1.402(c)-2, Q&As 3, 4, & 14]

Although net unrealized appreciation in employer securities is excluded from gross income under Code Section 402(e)(4), the amount of net unrealized appreciation may be treated as an eligible rollover distribution. [Treas Reg § 1.402(c)-2, Q&A 3]

Effective December 31, 1998, the law provides that hardship withdrawals (see chapter 14) will no longer be classified as eligible rollover distributions. [IRRA § 6005(c)(2)] However, because of the formidable administrative problems presented by the change, the IRS, under Notice 99-5, will allow participants to roll over hardship withdrawals of elective contributions until December 31, 1999.

Q 15:51 How is it determined that a distribution is part of a series of substantially equal periodic payments?

The determination that a payment is part of a series of substantially equal periodic payments is made at the time payments begin without taking into account contingencies that have not yet occurred. For example, if payment is being made in the form of a joint and survivor annuity, whereby the amount of the payment will increase in the event the beneficiary predeceases the participant, those payments are still considered a series of payments that are not eligible rollover distributions. [Treas Reg § 1.402(c)-2, Q&A 5(a)] In determining whether payments are substantially equal, Social Security supplements are disregarded. [Treas Reg § 1.402(c)-2, Q&A 5(b)]

Q 15:52 What happens if, while an employee is receiving substantially equal periodic payments that are not eligible rollover distributions, the amount of the payment changes?

If there is a change in the amount of the payment, a new determination must be made as to whether the remaining payments are eligible rollover distributions, without taking into account payments that were made prior to this change. [Treas Reg § 1.402(c)-2, Q&A 5(c)] If the payment is an isolated payment that is substantially smaller or larger than other payments in the series, that payment may be considered an eligible rollover distribution even though all prior and subsequent distributions are not eligible rollover distributions. [Treas Reg § 1.402(c)-2, Q&A 6]

Q 15:53 When is a distribution considered a minimum distribution under Code Section 401(a)(9) that is not an eligible rollover distribution?

For each calendar year, all distributions will be treated as required distributions under Code Section 401(a)(9) until the total minimum distribution amount has been met for that calendar year. If the full amount of a required minimum distribution is not distributed in a calendar year, the amount that was required but not distributed is added to the amount of the minimum distribution for the next calendar year. [Treas Reg § 1.402(c)-2, Q&A 7]

> **Example.** A participant's required minimum distribution in a given calendar year is $1,000, and the participant receives four quarterly distributions of $400 each. The first two distributions and $200 of the third distribution are not eligible rollover distributions. However, $200 of the third distribution and the final $400 distribution are eligible rollover distributions.

The Small Business Job Protection Act of 1996 (SPJPA) amended Code Section 401(a)(9) so that active employees who are not 5 percent owners are no longer required to take minimum distributions. Many 401(k) plans will give such active employees the option not to begin receiving distributions until they retire. If an employee nonetheless elects to receive or to continue to receive minimum distributions, these distributions will not be considered required minimum distributions and will be treated as eligible rollover distributions unless another exception applies. [IRS Notice 97-75, 1997-51 IRB 18]

Direct Rollover Option

Q 15:54 What options must be offered regarding the tax treatment of eligible rollover distributions?

An individual receiving an eligible rollover distribution must be given the option to have the distribution paid directly to an eligible retirement plan (see Q 15:59) in a direct rollover. [IRC § 401(a)(31)(A)] This is required for the plan to maintain its tax-qualified status. Additionally, with a distribution of $500 or more, the distributee must be given the opportunity to have a portion of the distribution rolled over to an eligible retirement plan and the remainder distributed in cash, subject to withholding. [Treas Reg § 1.401(a)(31)-1, Q&A 9]

Q 15:55 Are there any restrictions that can be placed on a distributee's right to elect direct rollover on eligible rollover distributions?

Yes. If the amount of all eligible rollover distributions during a year is reasonably expected to total less than $200, the distributee need not be offered the option of a direct rollover. The plan may simply cash out the participant, and no withholding is required. [Treas Reg §§ 1.401(a)(31)-1, Q&A 11, 31.3405(c)-1, Q&A 14]

If the amount of the eligible rollover distribution is less than $500, a plan may also require that the distribution cannot be divided. The entire amount distributed must be either rolled over or distributed in cash. If a distribution is divided, the plan may also require that the amount to be directly rolled over must be at least $500. [Treas Reg § 1.401(a)(31)-1, Q&A 9]

Q 15:56 Can property other than cash be rolled over?

Yes. Property generally is eligible for rollover. The only restriction arises from the ability of the recipient plan or IRA to accept the property. For example, insurance policies cannot be rolled into an IRA.

A distributee has two choices with regard to rolling over property other than cash: he or she may simply transfer title to the new trustee, or the distributee may sell the property and transfer the proceeds to the new trustee. [IRC § 402(c)(6)]

Q 15:57 Must a direct rollover option be offered on a loan offset amount that is an eligible rollover distribution?

No. A plan need not offer participants the option of rollover for a loan offset amount. (See Q 15:86.) [Treas Reg § 1.401(a)(31)-1, Q&A 15]

Q 15:58 What is a *direct rollover*?

A *direct rollover* is a distribution that is made directly from the trustee of the distributing plan to the trustee of the recipient eligible retirement plan. The distribution does not pass through the participant or other distributee. [Treas Reg § 1.401(a)(31)-1, Q&A 3]

Q 15:59 What is an *eligible retirement plan*?

An *eligible retirement plan* is an individual retirement account under Code Section 408(a), an individual retirement annuity described in Code Section 408(b), an annuity plan described in Code Section 403(a), or a qualified plan that accepts rollover distributions. [IRC § 401(a)(31); Treas Reg § 1.402(c)-2, Q&A 2]

Q 15:60 Are plans required to permit direct rollovers of eligible rollover distributions?

Yes. A plan will lose its tax-qualified status if it does not offer the option of a direct rollover on any eligible rollover distribution. [IRC § 401(a)(31); Treas Reg § 1.401(a)(31)-1, Q&A 1]

Q 15:61 Are plans required to accept direct rollovers of eligible rollover distributions?

No. A plan can refuse to accept rollovers altogether or limit the circumstances under which it will accept rollovers. For example, a plan might accept rollovers only from other plans of the same employer, or only of certain types of assets. [Treas Reg § 1.401(a)(31)-1, Q&A 13]

Rollover of Cash Distributions

Q 15:62 If a distributee elects to receive a cash distribution, can he or she later roll over that distribution?

Yes. The old rules concerning rollover availability within 60 days following receipt of a distribution continue to apply. Under these rules, the rollover must be accomplished within 60 days of the date of distribution, with no extensions available. [Treas Reg § 1.402(c)-2, Q&A 11] The amount that is actually rolled over will be exempt from income tax. However, if the distributee does not make up the amount that was withheld from the plan distribution, that amount will be subject to income tax and, if applicable, the additional income tax on early distributions.

> **Example.** A participant receives a distribution of $10,000 and elects to receive it in cash. The plan withholds 20 percent, or $2,000, and makes a payment to the participant of $8,000. Within 60 days of receiving the $8,000, the participant decides to deposit it into an IRA. The $8,000 deposited will not be subject to income tax. The $2,000 withheld will be included in the participant's taxable income. The participant can avoid taxation on the $2,000 by depositing a total of $10,000 in the IRA, using assets other than the plan distribution to make up the $2,000 difference. [Treas Reg § 1.402(c)-2, Q&A 11]

Direct Rollover Election

Q 15:63 Is the rollover option available to all distributees?

No. All plan participants, as well as the spouses of deceased participants, must be given the option to roll over eligible rollover distributions. A former spouse who is an alternate payee under a QDRO also has a rollover option. However, a spouse of a deceased participant can elect rollover only to an individual retirement account or an individual retirement annuity, and not to a qualified plan. Nonspouse beneficiaries do not have a rollover option. [Treas Reg § 1.402(c)-2, Q&A 12]

Q 15:64 How is a direct rollover elected?

The plan administrator is required to notify recipients of their right to a direct rollover and to provide forms and procedures to accomplish the rollover. (See Qs 15:68–15:72.)

Q 15:65 Is spousal consent needed on a direct rollover election?

Yes. If the distribution is subject to the survivor annuity rules (see Qs 16:1–16:30), then spousal consent is needed on a direct rollover election.

Q 15:66 Must distributees be given the option to roll over into more than one eligible retirement plan?

No. A plan administrator is not required (but is permitted) to allow distributees to divide eligible rollover distributions into more than one plan. [Treas Reg § 1.401(a)(31)-1, Q&A 10]

Q 15:67 How is a direct rollover accomplished?

A trustee can transfer benefits in a direct rollover using any reasonable means. Reasonable means include wire transfers and mailing a check to the new trustee. If there is no trustee (such as in an individual retirement annuity), the check or wire should be directed to the custodian of the plan or the issuer of the contract. [Treas Reg § 1.401(a)(31)-1, Q&A 3] A direct rollover can also be accomplished by sending a check to the distributee with instructions to deliver it to the trustee of the eligible retirement plan. If this method is used, the check must be made payable to the named trustee as trustee of the named plan. The check must also indicate for whose benefit it is. [Treas Reg § 1.401(a)(31)-1, Q&A 4]

Direct Rollover Procedures

Q 15:68 May the plan administrator impose procedures or limitations on direct rollover elections?

The plan administrator may prescribe reasonable procedures for electing a direct rollover. These procedures may include a requirement that the recipient provide adequate information or documentation that the distribution is being directed to an eligible retirement plan. However, the plan administrator cannot require information or documentation that would effectively eliminate the distributee's ability to elect direct rollover. For example, the plan administrator cannot require an attorney's opinion that the plan receiving the rollover is an eligible retirement plan. [Treas Reg § 1.401(a)(31)-1, Q&A 6]

Q 15:69 Is notice of the direct rollover option required?

Yes. Plan administrators must provide participants with a written explanation of their right to elect a direct rollover and the tax consequences of not doing so. Certain other tax information is also required. This notice must be provided within a reasonable period of time before a participant makes an eligible rollover distribution. [Treas Reg § 1.402(f)-1, Q&A 1]

Q 15:70 What is a reasonable period of time for providing notice?

Notice must be provided to plan participants no less than 30 days and no more than 90 days before a distribution is made. For distributions not subject to spousal consent requirements, however, if, after receiving the notice, a participant makes an affirmative election, the distribution may be made immediately without violating the reasonable time requirement. The plan administrator must clearly indicate to the participant that he or she has an opportunity to consider a decision regarding rollover for at least 30 days after notice is provided. [Treas Reg § 1.402(f)-1, Q&A 2] For distributions subject to the spousal consent requirements of Code Sections 401(a)(11) and 417, the 30-day notice period can be waived as long as benefits are not paid until 7 days after the date notice is given. [Treas Reg § 1.417(e)-1(b)(3)(ii)] Recently proposed regulations would liberalize the notice requirement and permit the notice to be provided through an electronic medium (see Qs 15:17–15:19). [Prop Treas Reg § 1.402(f)-1, Q&A 2 & 3]

Q 15:71 What information must the notice contain?

The notice must explain the rules under which the participant may have the distribution paid in a direct rollover to an eligible retirement plan, the rules requiring the withholding of income tax if it is not paid in a direct rollover, the rules under which the participant will not be subject to tax if the distribution is rolled over to an eligible retirement plan within 60 days of the distribution, and any other special tax rules that might apply (e.g., five-year averaging or capital gains treatment). Also, if the payment is one in a series and the plan administrator intends to apply the initial election to subsequent payments, this must be explained in the notice. [Treas Reg §§ 1.402(f)-1, Q&As 1&3, 1.401(a)(31)-1, Q&A 12]

Q 15:72 Is there a model notice that can be used to assure compliance with Code Section 402(f)?

Yes. The IRS provides a model notice in IRS Notice 92-48. [1992-2 CB 377] A plan administrator who provides this model notice will be deemed to have complied with the requirements of Code Section 402(f). [Treas Reg § 1.402(f)-1, Q&A 1(b)]

Q 15:73 May a plan administrator implement a default option for participants who fail to make a rollover election?

Yes. If a participant has received the required notice and explanation of the direct rollover option and the reasonable time period has passed (see Q 15:70), the plan administrator may implement a default election. The default option can be either to cash the participant out after withholding 20 percent or to implement a direct rollover. [Treas Reg § 1.401(a)(31)-1, Q&A 7]

Q 15:74 May the plan administrator establish a cutoff date after which a rollover election cannot be revoked?

Yes; however, the deadline must not be more restrictive than the deadline used in the plan for permitting changes in electing a form of distribution. [Treas Reg § 1.401(a)(31)-1, Q&A 8]

Q 15:75 How do the notice and election rules apply to eligible rollover distributions that are paid in periodic installments?

A plan may treat a participant's rollover election with respect to the initial payment in a series of periodic payments as applying to all subsequent payments. The employee must be permitted to revoke that election at any time and must receive an explanation that the election will apply to all future payments unless revoked. [Treas Reg § 1.401(a)(31)-1, Q&A 12] The employee must be provided with a notice concerning his or her right to a direct rollover prior to the first payment and then annually for as long as payments continue. [Treas Reg § 1.402(f)-1, Q&A 3]

Q 15:76 How is a direct rollover distribution reported for income tax purposes?

A direct rollover distribution must be reported on Form 1099-R. For purposes of 1099-R reporting, it is treated as a distribution that is immediately rolled over. [Treas Reg § 31.3405(c)-1, Q&A 16]

Q 15:77 Is a direct rollover considered a transfer of benefits to which the optional form of benefit rules apply?

No. A direct rollover is treated as though the employee elected a cash distribution and later rolled it over. Therefore, the rule requiring the carryover of certain distribution rights (see Qs 15:1–15:11) on transferred benefits does not apply to amounts directly rolled over. [Treas Reg § 1.401(a)(31)-1, Q&A 14]

Rollover Strategies

Q 15:78 What are the advantages of a rollover?

The major advantage of a rollover is the postponement of tax, since the distribution will accumulate earnings on a tax-deferred basis. When distributions are ultimately paid from the eligible retirement plan, the distributee may be in a lower tax bracket, or tax rates may be lower, which would maximize the ultimate benefits received.

Another advantage of rollover to an IRA is that distribution from the IRA is not subject to the mandatory 20 percent income tax withholding requirement. (See Q 15:83.) Distributees from an IRA can generally elect out of income tax withholding.

Q 15:79 What are the disadvantages of a rollover?

If a distribution is rolled over to an IRA, the recipient will lose the ability to elect the special tax treatment available for qualified plan distributions occurring before 2000. There is no opportunity, therefore, to elect capital gains treatment for a portion of a distribution or to use income averaging.

An additional disadvantage to distributees who are alternate payees pursuant to a QDRO (see Q 16:31) is the potential imposition of the 10 percent additional income tax on early distributions. (See Q 17:59.) Distributions from a qualified plan to an alternate payee are exempt from this tax, but distributions from an IRA are not.

WITHHOLDING ON DISTRIBUTIONS

Most 401(k) plan distributions are subject to income tax withholding. The Unemployment Compensation Act of 1992 significantly changed the withholding rules on 401(k) plan distributions occurring after December 31, 1992. This section discusses these withholding rules, including procedures for notifying recipients and for reporting and paying withheld taxes. For additional discussion of the Unemployment Compensation Act of 1992 and its effect on rollovers see Qs 15:46–15:79.

Some distributions from 401(k) plans were not affected by the

Unemployment Compensation Act of 1992. The pre-1992 withholding rules, discussed at Qs 15:98–15:102, continue to apply to these distributions.

Q 15:80 Is withholding required on contributions to a 401(k) plan?

No. Federal income tax withholding is not required on elective contributions or any other type of 401(k) plan contribution.

Q 15:81 Is withholding required on distributions from a 401(k) plan?

Yes. Federal income tax withholding is required on distributions from a 401(k) plan. [IRC §§ 3405(a), 3405(b), 3405(c)]

Unemployment Compensation Act of 1992

Q 15:82 How did the withholding rules change for plan distributions occurring after December 31, 1992?

Under prior rules, participants could generally elect not to have income tax withheld from a distribution. If participants did not elect out of withholding, the rate of withholding varied, depending on the type of distribution involved (i.e., periodic, nonperiodic, or qualified total distribution).

The Unemployment Compensation Act of 1992 significantly altered the withholding rules on most distributions from qualified plans. The Act defined a new term: *eligible rollover distribution.* (See Qs 15:49–15:50.) Recipients of eligible rollover distributions can no longer elect out of withholding. Withholding can be avoided only by making a direct rollover (see Q 15:58) to an eligible retirement plan (see Q 15:59). The rate of withholding on all eligible rollover distributions that are not rolled over is 20 percent. [IRC § 3405(c)(1)(B)] For distributions that are not eligible rollover distributions, the pre-1993 rules continue to apply. (See Qs 15:98–15:102.)

Q 15:83 What is the amount of income tax withholding required on eligible rollover distributions?

The amount of withholding on all eligible rollover distributions is 20 percent of the amount of cash and the fair market value of other property received in a distribution. [Treas Reg § 31.3405(c)-1, Q&A 11] This is true regardless of whether the distribution is made in a single sum or in a series of periodic payments that are still considered eligible rollover distributions.

Q 15:84 May a participant elect out of withholding on an eligible rollover distribution?

No. The only way to avoid income tax withholding on an eligible rollover distribution is to have it transferred in a direct rollover. It is no longer an option to receive cash without a deduction for income tax withholding. [Treas Reg § 31.3405(c)-1, Q&A 2]

Q 15:85 Are hardship withdrawals subject to mandatory withholding?

It depends on the source of the withdrawal. Hardship withdrawals of contributions other than elective contributions are considered eligible rollover distributions subject to 20 percent withholding. Starting in 1999, however, hardship withdrawals of elective contributions will not be considered eligible rollover distributions and, as a result, the pre-1993 rules (see Qs 15:98–15:102) apply. [IRRA § 6005(c)(2)] Because of the formidable administrative problems presented by this change, the IRS, under Notice 99-5, will allow administratorsk and participants to treat hardship withdrawals of elective contributions as eligible rollover distributions during 1999. [IRS Notice 99-5, 1999-3 IRB 10]

Loan Offset Amount

Q 15:86 Are participant loans subject to the new withholding rules?

A participant loan that complies with the requirements of Code Section 72(p) is not considered a taxable distribution and therefore is not an eligible rollover distribution subject to withholding. The regulations also indicate that in the event a participant loan becomes taxable because of a default or failure to comply with Code Section 72(p), the amount of the outstanding loan is still not considered an eligible rollover distribution. [Treas Reg § 1.402(c)-2, Q&A 4]

When a loan is distributed as an offset to the participant's account balance, the amount of the offset is considered an eligible rollover distribution subject to 20 percent withholding. [Treas Reg § 1.402(c)-2, Q&A 9] This is true regardless of whether the participant's employment is terminated at the time the offset occurs. For example, if the plan document permits an offset upon loan default such that the participant's account is actually reduced by the amount of the outstanding loan, that offset will be considered an eligible rollover distribution.

Q 15:87 How is the 20 percent withholding requirement applied to a distribution that includes a loan offset amount?

The amount of the cash and property distributed, plus the amount of the loan offset, is subject to 20 percent withholding. Any amount that the employee elects to have directly rolled over to an eligible retirement plan is not subject to 20 percent withholding. [Treas Reg § 31.3405(c)-1, Q&A 11]

Example. Employee A has an account balance of $10,000, of which $3,000 is invested in a plan loan. Employee A elects to receive $2,000 as a cash distribution and to have $5,000 rolled to an eligible retirement plan. The amount subject to withholding is $5,000 (the amount of the loan offset plus the amount of the cash distribution). Therefore, the amount of the withholding is $1,000 and the employee will receive only $1,000 in cash.

Q 15:88 Is there any limit on the amount of withholding required for a loan offset amount that is an eligible rollover distribution?

Yes. The amount withheld cannot exceed the sum of cash and the fair market value of any property (other than employer securities) received by a participant. [Treas Reg § 31.3405(c)-1, Q&A 11]

Example. Employee A has an account balance of $10,000, of which $3,000 is invested in a plan loan. Employee A elects to have her entire $7,000 distribution directly rolled over to an eligible retirement plan. Even though the $3,000 loan offset amount is considered an eligible rollover distribution, no withholding is required since Employee A received no cash or property from which to withhold the tax.

Other Special Distributions

Q 15:89 How do the 20 percent withholding rules apply to distributions of property?

If property other than employer securities is distributed as part of an eligible rollover distribution, the fair market value of the property is subject to 20 percent withholding. If the distribution does not include enough cash to satisfy the withholding requirement, the plan has two options: it can sell part of the property prior to the distribution to satisfy withholding, or it can permit the payee to remit to the plan administrator enough cash to satisfy the withholding requirement. [Treas Reg §§ 31.3405(c)-1, Q&A 9, 35.3405-1, Q&A F-2]

Q 15:90 How do the withholding rules apply to the distribution of employer securities?

The maximum amount that can be withheld in a distribution is the sum of the cash distributed plus the fair market value of property, other than employer securities, received in the distribution. [Treas Reg § 31.3405(c)-1, Q&A 11] Therefore, if only employer securities are distributed, no withholding is required.

If employer securities and cash are received in a single distribution, then the cost basis of those securities will be subject to 20 percent withholding, assuming there is sufficient cash to pay that withholding. For example, if an employee receives a distribution consisting of employer securities with a cost basis of $3,000 and $5,000 in cash, 20 percent withholding will be applied against the entire $8,000 distribution. The employee will receive the employer securities plus $3,400 in cash. [Treas Reg § 31.3405(c)-1, Q&As 11&12]

Q 15:91 Do the withholding rules apply to distributions from IRAs?

No. The 20 percent withholding requirement applies only to eligible rollover distributions from qualified plans under Section 401(a) and Section 403(b) annuities. [IRC §§ 402(c)(8), 3405(c)(3)]. Therefore, a participant has the ability to avoid the 20 percent withholding requirement by electing a direct rollover to an IRA and then taking a distribution from that IRA. The IRA distribution would be subject to regular income tax, the early distribution tax if the recipient is under age 59½, and, possibly, fees associated with the transaction.

Responsibility for Withholding

Q 15:92 Who is responsible for enforcing the mandatory 20 percent withholding?

The plan administrator is generally responsible for satisfying the notice requirement and for withholding 20 percent of any eligible rollover distribution that is not directly rolled over. The plan administrator can shift this responsibility to the payor. [Treas Reg § 31.3405(c)-1, Q&As 4 & 5]

Q 15:93 Will the plan administrator be responsible for taxes, interest, or penalties if a direct rollover is elected, but the rollover fails?

The plan administrator will be liable in this circumstance only if it does not reasonably rely on adequate information provided by the distributee. The plan administrator is not required to verify independently the accuracy of information, as long as it is not clearly erroneous on its face. [Treas Reg § 31.3405(c)-1, Q&A 7]

Q 15:94 What constitutes adequate information on which a plan administrator can rely to avoid taxes, interest, and penalties?

To avoid tax liability on a direct rollover that fails, the plan administrator must have been furnished with the name of the eligible retirement plan to receive the distribution; a representation from the distributee that the recipient plan is an IRA or a qualified plan; and any information necessary to permit the plan administrator to accomplish the direct rollover (i.e., the name and address of the recipient trustee). [Treas Reg § 31.3405(c)-1, Q&A 7]

The plan administrator can reasonably conclude that the distributing plan is a qualified plan even if it does not have a favorable determination letter from the IRS. [TRA '97 § 1509]

Implementation of Mandatory Withholding

Q 15:95 What is the effective date of the mandatory withholding rules?

The withholding rules apply to any distributions occurring after December 31, 1992.

Q 15:96 When were plans required to be amended to reflect the mandatory withholding rules?

Plans had to be amended on or before the last day of the first plan year beginning on or after January 1, 1994. [Treas Reg § 1.401(a)(31)-1, Q&A 18]

Q 15:97 Are all plan distributions subject to the mandatory withholding rules?

No. Only eligible rollover distributions (see Qs 15:49–15:50) are subject to the new rules. Distributions that are not eligible rollover distributions, such as the distribution of death benefits to a nonspouse beneficiary, or minimum distributions required by Code Section 401(a)(9), are subject to the old rules described in Qs 15:98–15:102.

Distributions Not Eligible for Rollover

Q 15:98 What withholding rules apply to distributions from a qualified plan that are not eligible rollover distributions?

Distributions that are not eligible rollover distributions are subject to the old withholding rules described in Qs 15:98–15:112. [Treas Reg § 31.3405(c)-1, Q&A 1] Therefore, distributees can elect out of withholding altogether without rolling over the distribution. Also, the rate of withholding varies depending on the type of distribution involved.

Q 15:99 What amounts are subject to withholding under the old rules?

No withholding is required on nonperiodic distributions (see Q 15:105) of $200 or less. [Treas Reg § 35.3405-1, Q&A F-7] For other distributions, any cash and the value of any property distributed from a plan are subject to withholding unless the payor reasonably believes that an amount is not includible in gross income. [IRC § 3405(e)] For example, if the payor knows that a portion of the distribution represents after-tax employee contributions or a loan that was previously taxed as a distribution, those amounts are not subject to the withholding requirement.

If the distribution is of property other than cash, the payor must use a valuation made within one year of the distribution as the basis for determining the withholding amount. If the employee does not elect out of the withholding requirement, he or she can simply pay the amount of tax to the payor in lieu of selling a portion of the property, thereby satisfying the withholding requirement. [Treas Reg § 35.3405-1, Q&As F-1 & F-2]

Q 15:100 Are there special rules for withholding on distributions of employer securities?

Yes. The distribution of employer securities is not subject to the withholding requirement. [IRC § 3405(e)(8)] The appreciation on employer securities distributed from a qualified plan is not subject to income tax until the securities are sold. Relief from the withholding provisions protects payees from being forced to sell securities that would otherwise qualify for this income tax deferral just to satisfy the withholding requirement.

Q 15:101 Is aggregation with amounts distributed from another plan of the employer required?

No. The payor is not required to aggregate 401(k) plan distributions with distributions from other plans when computing and reporting withholding. The payor may elect to aggregate; however, the payee has a separate right to elect out of withholding for each plan distribution. [IRC § 3405(e)(9)]

Q 15:102 What rate of withholding applies to 401(k) plan distributions under the old rules?

The rate of withholding depends on the type of distribution involved as well as on elections made by the payee. There are separate rules for periodic and nonperiodic distributions (see Qs 15:103–15:106).

Periodic Distributions

Q 15:103 What is a *periodic distribution*?

Any distribution that is taxable under Code Section 72 and is either paid under an annuity contract or is one of a series of payments payable over a period of more than one year is a *periodic distribution*. [Treas Reg § 35.3405-1, Q&As A-9 & B-8] It is not necessary that the payments be of equal amounts or that they be made at regular intervals. However, a payment cannot be treated as a periodic distribution unless the frequency of payments is known. [Treas Reg § 35.3405-1, Q&A B-7]

Q 15:104 What is the rate of withholding for periodic distributions?

The rate of withholding on periodic distributions is determined by the payee on a withholding certificate, Form W-4P. If the payee does not submit a withholding certificate, the rate of withholding should be determined as if the payee were married and claiming three exemptions. [IRC § 3405(a)(4)]

Q 15:105 What is a *nonperiodic distribution*?

A *nonperiodic distribution* is any taxable distribution from a plan that is not a periodic distribution. (See Q 15:103.) [IRC § 3405(e)(3)]

Q 15:106 What is the rate of withholding required on nonperiodic distributions?

The rate of withholding on nonperiodic distributions is 10 percent. [IRC § 3405(b)]

Electing Out of Withholding

Q 15:107 Who may elect not to have a withholding taken from a 401(k) plan distribution?

Any payee who receives a distribution in the United States that is not an eligible rollover distribution (see Qs 15:49–15:50) may elect out of the withholding requirement. The right to make this election applies whether the distribution is periodic or nonperiodic. The only payees who cannot elect out of withholding are those with foreign addresses. For the rules concerning withholding on distributions to foreign payees, see Q 15:113.

Q 15:108 Is the plan administrator required to notify payees of their right to elect out of withholding?

Yes. Payees must be notified of their right to elect out of the withholding requirement. The time for providing this notification varies depending upon the type of distribution. (See Qs 15:110–15:111.) Payees of periodic distributions must also be notified of their right to renew or revoke a withholding election at least once per calendar year. [IRC § 3405(e)(10)(B)] Any election not to have withholding apply will remain in effect until revoked. [Treas Reg § 35.3405-1, Q&A D-1] Recently proposed regulations would permit the notice to be provided through an electronic medium (see Qs 15:17–15:19). [Prop Treas Reg § 35.3405-1, Q&A D-35]

Q 15:109 What information must be contained in the withholding notice?

The notice must inform payees of their right to elect out of withholding and tell them how to revoke any prior election. It must inform the payee that any prior election will continue to apply until it is revoked and must also advise the payee that penalties could be incurred if the amount of tax withheld is less than that required under the estimated tax payment requirements of Code Section 6654. [Treas Reg § 35.3405-1, Q&A D-18]

Q 15:110 When must notice be given on periodic distributions?

Payees receiving periodic distributions must receive notice of their right to elect out not earlier than six months before the first payment and not later than the date of the first payment. After the initial notification, notice must also be provided at least once each calendar year thereafter. [IRC § 3405(e)(10)(B)(i)] Failure to provide timely notice will subject the plan administrator to a penalty tax of $10 per failure, not to exceed $5,000. [IRC § 6652(h)]

If the amount of the annual payment is expected to be less than

$5,400, the payer can notify the payee that no tax will be withheld unless a withholding certificate is filed. [Treas Reg § 35.3405-1, Q&A D-5]

Q 15:111 When must notice be given for nonperiodic distributions?

Notice of withholding on nonperiodic distributions must be given no earlier than six months before the distribution and no later than a time that gives the payee a reasonable period within which to elect not to have withholding apply. [Treas Reg § 35.3405-1, Q&A D-9] The "reasonable period of time" requirement is met if notice is given at the time the application for benefits is provided to the payee. [Treas Reg § 35.3405-1, Q&A D-10] Failure to provide timely notice will subject the plan administrator to a penalty tax of $10 per failure, not to exceed $5,000. [IRC § 6652(h)]

Q 15:112 What withholding elections should be given effect by the payor?

Any time a participant clearly indicates his or her desire to elect out of the withholding requirement, that election should be given effect. [Treas Reg § 35.3405-1, Q&As D-22 & D-26]

The payor of a periodic distribution may require the payee to elect out of withholding up to 30 days before the first payment is due. [Treas Reg § 35.3405-1, Q&A D-11] However, if the payment is a nonperiodic one, the payer must honor any election made up to the time of distribution. [Treas Reg § 35.3405-1, Q&A, D-12] If the payment is a periodic one, any withholding election or revocation of a prior election must be given effect no later than 31 days after it is received, if periodic payments have not yet begun. If the payments have begun, it must be given effect on the January 1, May 1, July 1, or October 1 that is at least 30 days after the request is received. [Treas Reg § 35.3405-1, Q&A B-3]

A withholding election will not be given effect if the taxpayer does not properly disclose his or her taxpayer identification number. [IRC § 3405(e)(12)]

Withholding Procedures and Penalties

Q 15:113 Is withholding required on distributions to participants with foreign addresses?

Yes. A flat 30 percent rate of withholding is required on distributions to payees with foreign addresses, and those payees may not elect out of this withholding requirement. However, if the payee certifies under penalty of perjury that he or she is not a U.S citizen, resident alien, or tax-avoiding expatriate, withholding can be avoided. [IRC § 3405(e)(13); IRS Notice 87-7, 1987-1 CB 420]

Q 15:114 How are withheld income taxes reported to the Internal Revenue Service?

Withheld income taxes are reported on IRS Form 945. In general, the return is due one month after the end of each calendar year. However, if deposits have been made on time in full payment of the withheld income taxes, the return may be filed by February 10. [Treas Reg § 31.6071(a)-1(a)(1)]

Q 15:115 Are deposits of federal income tax withholding required?

Yes. Withheld income taxes must be deposited with either a financial institution qualified as a depository for federal taxes or a federal reserve bank. The amount of the income tax withheld will determine the frequency of deposits required. For example, if the total income tax withheld is less than $500 for the year, the withheld income tax may be paid over at the time the return is filed. At the other end of the spectrum, if the accumulated withheld income tax reaches $100,000 within the deposit period, the withheld income taxes must be deposited by the close of the next banking day. [IRC § 6302(g); Treas Reg § 31.6151-1(a)] Employers with income and employment tax obligations (i.e., amounts reported on IRS Forms 945, 941, 941-M, 941-PR, 941-SS, 943, and CT-1) of more than $50,000 in a prior year must, according to current regulations, make deposits electronically through the Electronic Federal Tax Payment System.

Q 15:116 Must withheld amounts be reported to the payee?

Yes. Payees must be informed of any amounts withheld on Form 1099-R.

Q 15:117 Are there penalties for failing to withhold, report, or pay federal taxes?

Yes. Civil penalties may apply for late filing of a return [IRC § 6651(a)], failing to deposit taxes when due [IRC § 6656], or failing to pay tax due after payment has been demanded by the IRS. [IRC § 6651(d)] Additional penalties may apply if a failure is willful or due to fraud. [IRC §§ 6663, 6672] If the violation is done with a corrupt motive or an intent to disobey the law, criminal penalties may also apply. [IRC §§ 7201, 7202, 7203, 7204, 7205, 7206, 7207]

16 Spousal Rights

This chapter deals with the legal protections that are extended to the spouse of a 401(k) plan participant. Protection is afforded in two contexts. First, benefits are provided upon death to a surviving spouse unless during the participant's lifetime these benefits are waived by the participant with the consent of his or her spouse. Second, a spouse can be awarded all or any part of a participant's interest in a 401(k) plan upon the dissolution of the marriage.

SURVIVOR ANNUITY REQUIREMENTS

Q 16:1 What plans are subject to the survivor annuity requirements?

A 401(k) pre-ERISA money purchase plan is always subject to these requirements. A 401(k) profit sharing or stock bonus plan is subject to the survivor annuity requirements unless all of the following conditions are satisfied:

1. The plan provides that upon death, the participant's entire vested account balance is payable to the participant's surviving spouse unless the surviving spouse consents to the designation of another beneficiary. (See Q 16:29.)

2. The participant elects not to have his or her account balance paid over the participant's lifetime as would be the case if a life annuity contract is purchased. (This requirement does not apply if the plan does not offer life annuities as a payment option.)

3. The 401(k) plan is not a transferee plan as to the participant.

[Treas Reg § 1.401(a)-20, Q&A 3(a)]

Q 16:2 What is a *transferee plan*?

A 401(k) plan is considered a *transferee plan* if it receives—through merger, spin-off, or other similar transfer—benefits from a plan subject to the survivor annuity requirements. However, a 401(k) plan is not considered a transferee plan if these benefits come into the 401(k) plan as a result of a rollover contribution and, presumably, although there is no regulatory guidance, as a result of an elective transfer under Treasury Regulation Section 1.411(d)-4, Q&A 3(b). [Treas Reg § 1.401(a)-20, Q&A 5(a)]

Q 16:3 If a 401(k) plan is a transferee plan, do the survivor annuity requirements apply to all plan participants?

No. The survivor annuity requirements apply only to the participants whose benefits are transferred to the 401(k) plan. [Treas Reg § 1.401(a)-20, Q&A 5(a)]

Q 16:4 If a 401(k) plan is a transferee plan with respect to a participant, do the survivor annuity requirements apply to that participant's entire account balance?

The general rule is that a participant's entire account balance is subject to the survivor annuity requirements. However, if a separate account is maintained for the benefits transferred to the plan, then the survivor annuity requirements apply only to the transferred benefits. [Treas Reg § 1.401(a)-20, Q&A 5(b)]

Qualified Pre-Retirement Survivor Annuity (QPSA) and Qualified Joint and Survivor Annuity (QJSA)

Q 16:5 What are the survivor annuity requirements?

If a participant dies before the annuity starting date, benefits must be paid to the surviving spouse in the form of a qualified pre-retirement survivor annuity (QPSA). If a participant survives until the annuity starting date, the participant's account balance must be used to purchase a qualified joint and survivor annuity (QJSA). [Treas Reg § 1.401(a)-20, Q&A 8(a)]

Q 16:6 What is a *qualified pre-retirement survivor annuity* (QPSA)?

A *qualified pre-retirement survivor annuity* (QPSA) is an immediate annuity for the life of the surviving spouse purchased with not less than 50 percent of the value of the participant's account balance determined as of the date of death. [Treas Reg § 1.401(a)-20, Q&A 20]

Q 16:7 What is a *qualified joint and survivor annuity* (QJSA)?

In the case of a married participant, a *qualified joint and survivor annuity* (QJSA) is an immediate annuity for the life of the participant with a survivor annuity for the life of the spouse. The amount of the survivor annuity cannot be less than 50 percent and not more than 100 percent of the amount of the annuity that is payable during the joint lives of the participant and spouse. [IRC § 417(b)] In the case of an unmarried participant, the QJSA is an immediate annuity for the life of the participant. [Treas Reg § 1.401(a)-20, Q&A 25(a)]

Q 16:8 What is the *annuity starting date*?

The *annuity starting date* is the first day of the first period for which an account is payable as an annuity or any other form. [Treas Reg § 1.401(a)-20, Q&A 10(b)]

Example. Employee A retires and elects to receive his 401(k) account balance in the form of a life annuity commencing April 1. Because of administrative delays, Employee A's April 1 payment is not received until April 15. April 1 is still considered the annuity starting date.

Q 16:9 When must payments under a QPSA commence?

The 401(k) plan must permit the surviving spouse to begin receiving payments under a QPSA within a reasonable time after the participant's death. [Treas Reg § 1.401(a)-20, Q&A 22(b)]

Q 16:10 When must payments under a QJSA commence?

The 401(k) plan must permit the participant to begin receiving payments under a QJSA when the participant attains the earliest retirement age under the plan. [Treas Reg § 1.401(a)-20, Q&A 17(a)] It should be noted that this rule, in effect, supersedes the rules contained in Section 401(a)(14) and discussed at Q 15:12, which set forth the latest possible time a plan may delay the commencement of benefits. Payments under a QJSA, however, cannot be made while benefits are considered immediately distributable (see Q 15:20), unless the participant's consent is obtained. [Treas Reg § 1.417(e)-1(b)(1)]

Q 16:11 What is the *earliest retirement age*?

The *earliest retirement age* under a 401(k) plan is the earliest age at which a participant may elect to receive benefits under the plan. In no event, however, may the earliest retirement age be later than the early retirement age determined under the provisions of the plan or, if there is no early retirement provision, the plan's normal retirement date. [Treas Reg § 1.401(a)-20, Q&A 17(b)]

Example. Beta Corporation sponsors a 401(k) plan under which participants who separate from service cannot receive benefits until they reach age 50. Fred, age 40, terminates employment with a vested account balance under the plan. The earliest retirement age under the plan with respect to Fred is age 50, the age at which he can elect to receive benefits.

Waivers

Q 16:12 May a participant waive the QPSA and/or QJSA?

Yes. With the consent of the participant's spouse, a participant may waive either or both of these benefits during the election period applicable to each benefit. [Treas Reg § 1.401(a)-20, Q&A 8(b)]

Q 16:13 What requirements must be met by a participant's waiver of the QPSA?

A participant's waiver of the QPSA must specify the nonspouse beneficiaries who will receive benefits upon the participant's death. [Treas Reg § 1.401(a)-20, Q&A 31(a)]

Q 16:14 What requirements must be met by a participant's waiver of the QJSA?

A participant's waiver of the QJSA must specify the nonspouse beneficiaries who will receive benefits upon the participant's death. In addition, the waiver must specify the form of benefit the participant will receive in lieu of the QJSA. [Treas Reg § 1.401(a)-20, Q&A 31(a) & (b)]

Q 16:15 When may a participant waive the QPSA?

In general, a participant may waive the QPSA only after the first day of the plan year in which the participant reaches age 35. A plan may allow a participant to waive the QPSA before then if the previous waiver becomes invalid at the beginning of the plan year in which the participant reaches age 35. A participant must then execute a new waiver in order to avoid the QPSA requirement. [Treas Reg § 1.401(a)-20, Q&A 33(b)]

Q 16:16 Are there special rules that apply to terminated participants?

Yes. A participant who separates from service before age 35 is allowed to waive the QPSA any time after the date of separation. [IRC § 417(a)(6)] In this case, the rule described in Q 16:15 that automatically revokes a previously made waiver does not apply.

Example. Joe is 27 when he separates from service. The 401(k) plan in which he participates does not allow the payment of benefits until a participant reaches 45. Joe can waive the QPSA even though he is not yet 35. In addition, when Joe reaches age 35, his waiver will not be automatically revoked.

Q 16:17 When may a participant waive the QJSA?

A participant may waive the QJSA no earlier than 90 days before the annuity starting date. [IRC § 417(a)(6)(A); Treas Reg § 1.417(e)-1(b)(3)]

Written Explanation

Q 16:18 Must a 401(k) plan provide a written explanation of the survivor annuity requirements?

Yes. A plan must provide to each participant a written explanation containing the following information:

1. The terms and conditions of the QJSA or QPSA;

2. The participant's right to make, and the effect of, an election to waive the QJSA or QPSA;

3. The spouse's right to consent to the participant's waiver;

4. The participant's right to make, and the effect of, a revocation of a previously made election to waive the QJSA or QPSA; and

5. A general description of the conditions and other material features of the plan's other forms of benefit and their relative values.

[IRC § 417(a)(3); Treas Reg § 1.401(a)-20, Q&A 36]

Q 16:19 When must the written explanation of the QPSA be provided to participants?

The answer to this question depends on the particular circumstance of each participant. For most participants, this explanation must be given sometime during the period beginning on the first day of the plan year in which the participant reaches age 32 and ending on the last day of the plan year in which the participant reaches age 34. If an individual becomes a participant after this period, then the period runs from the date one year before the individual becomes a participant until the date one year after participation commences. In the case of an individual who separates from service before age 35 (see Q 16:16), the explanation must be given during the one-year period following the participant's separation from service. [Treas Reg § 1.401(a)-20, Q&A 35]

Q 16:20 When must the written explanation of the QJSA be provided to participants?

According to the Code, the written explanation must be provided within a reasonable period before the annuity starting date. [IRC § 417(a)(3)(A)] Most plans will incorporate the required explanation into benefit election forms given to participants.

Spouse's Consent

Q 16:21 What requirements must a spouse's consent satisfy?

The spouse's consent must be in writing, must acknowledge the effect of a participant's waiver, and must be witnessed by a plan representative or notary public. [IRC § 417(a)(2)(A)] The consent must specify the nonspouse beneficiaries who will receive benefits upon the participant's death. It must also specify, in the case of a participant's waiver of a QJSA, the particular optional form of benefit selected by the participant. [Treas Reg § 1.401(a)-20, Q&A 31(a) & (b)]

Q 16:22 If a participant revokes a prior waiver and then elects again during the election period to waive the survivor annuity requirements, must the spouse's consent be obtained again?

In general, the answer is yes. The spouse's consent is also required if, during the election period, the participant changes the beneficiary to whom benefits are payable on death or if the participant selects an optional form of benefit different from the one selected when the QJSA was originally waived. [Treas Reg § 1.401(a)-20, Q&A 31(a) & (b)] Spousal consent may not be required, however, if the spouse's original consent permits the participant to change beneficiaries or other forms of benefit without further consent of the spouse. The spouse's relinquishment of consent rights may be total or limited. [Treas Reg § 1.401(a)-20, Q&A 31(c)]

> **Example.** Darlene waives the QPSA and names her mother, Joan, as her beneficiary. Darlene's husband, Jim, consents to the waiver and to the naming of any other beneficiary as long as that beneficiary is a child of Darlene's. At a later date, Darlene names her father as beneficiary. This change can be made only if Jim consents.

Q 16:23 Is the spouse's consent revocable?

Whether the spouse's consent is revocable depends on the provisions of the plan. [Treas Reg § 1.401(a)-20, Q&A 30] Most 401(k) plans that are subject to the survivor annuity requirements provide that a spouse's consent cannot be revoked.

Q 16:24 Does a spouse's consent to the waiver of the survivor annuity requirements apply to a subsequent spouse?

Except in the case of a loan secured by a participant's account balance, the answer is no. [Treas Reg § 1.401(a)-20, Q&A 29]

Loans

Q 16:25 How do the survivor annuity requirements apply to loans?

If a 401(k) plan is subject to the survivor annuity requirements at the time of the loan and the participant's account balance is pledged as security for the loan, then spousal consent must be obtained. Spousal consent must be obtained no earlier than 90 days before the participant's account balance is pledged. The spouse's consent must be in writing, must acknowledge the effect of the loan, and must be witnessed by a plan representative or notary public. [Treas Reg § 1.401(a)-20, Q&A 24(a)]

Q 16:26 Is spousal consent required if, after the loan is obtained, the 401(k) plan becomes subject to the survivor annuity requirements or a single participant marries?

No. In addition, the consent of a spouse is effective with respect to any subsequent spouse. [Treas Reg § 1.401(a)-20, Q&A 24(b)]

Q 16:27 What happens if a secured loan is outstanding at the time the QJSA or QPSA is payable?

The account balance of the participant will first be reduced by the outstanding amount of the loan. [Treas Reg § 1.401(a)-20, Q&A 24(d)]

Example. At the time of her death, Karen was an active participant in a 401(k) plan with an account balance of $40,000. There was also outstanding a $10,000 loan secured by her account balance. The QPSA was not waived prior to her death; accordingly, Karen's husband, Dan, is entitled to a QPSA with a value of no less than $15,000, calculated as ($40,000 – $10,000) × 50%.

Special Circumstances

Q 16:28 Is spousal consent required if a plan representative is satisfied that there is no spouse or that the spouse cannot be located?

No. Spousal consent is also not required if the participant is legally separated or the participant has been abandoned (within the meaning of local law) and the participant has a court order to that effect. If a spouse is legally incompetent, the spouse's legal guardian, including the participant, may give consent. [Treas Reg § 1.401(a)-20, Q&A 27]

Q 16:29 If a 401(k) plan is not subject to the survivor annuity requirements because it provides that a participant's vested account balance is payable in full, upon the participant's death, to the participant's surviving spouse, when must the participant's account balance be paid to the surviving spouse?

The participant's account balance must be available to the participant's spouse within a reasonable period of time after the participant's death; availability within 90 days will be deemed reasonable. If benefits are not available within this 90-day period, reasonableness, according to the regulations, will be based on the particular facts and circumstances, unless, under the plan, the surviving spouse is treated less favorably than other participants entitled to distributions. In that event, availability is deemed unreasonable. (See Q 16:1.) [Treas Reg § 1.401(a)-20, Q&A 3(b)(1)]

Q 16:30 May a participant waive the spousal death benefit applicable to 401(k) plans not subject to the survivor annuity requirements?

Yes. A participant may waive the spousal death benefit at any time, including any point in time prior to the first day of the plan year in which the participant reaches age 35. A participant's waiver is effective, however, only if the spouse consents to the waiver. A spouse's consent must satisfy the same requirements that apply to the consent of a participant's waiver of the QPSA. (See Q 16:21.) [Treas Reg § 1.401(a)-20, Q&As 32 & 33]

QUALIFIED DOMESTIC RELATIONS ORDERS (QDROs)

Qualified domestic relations orders (QDROs) are an exception to the general rule that prohibits benefits in a qualified plan from being assigned or alienated. The QDRO rules grew out of a recurring controversy between state courts, which were attempting to award qualified plan benefits in divorce proceedings, and plan trustees, who were concerned that compliance with these orders would place them in violation of the anti-assignment rules and disqualify the plan. Enacted in 1984, the QDRO rules now make clear what a plan administrator's or trustee's obligations are when an order dividing benefits is received. This section discusses those rules.

Q 16:31 What is a *qualified domestic relations order* (QDRO)?

A *qualified domestic relations order* (QDRO) is a domestic relations order that creates a right for an alternate payee to receive some or all of a participant's benefits in a qualified plan. [IRC § 414(p)(1)(A)]

Q 16:32 What is a *domestic relations order* (DRO)?

A *domestic relations order* (DRO) is a judgment, decree, or other order made pursuant to a state domestic relations law that relates to the provision of child support, alimony, or marital property rights (including the division of community property). [IRC § 414(p)(1)(B)] For example, a stipulation signed by both parties in a divorce attempting to award retirement plan benefits is not a domestic relations order. However, a court order incorporating and approving that stipulation is a domestic relations order subject to the QDRO rules.

Q 16:33 Who can be an alternate payee?

An alternate payee must be the spouse, former spouse, child, or other dependent of a participant. [IRC § 414(p)(8)] For example, a QDRO could not award benefits to a participant's grandchild who was not living with the participant.

QDRO Terms

Q 16:34 What terms must be contained in a QDRO?

A QDRO must clearly specify the following information:

1. The name and last known mailing address of the participant and each alternate payee awarded benefits in the order. However, if the plan administrator has independent knowledge of this information, the order cannot be rejected for failing to provide it. [S Rep No 98-575 98th Cong, 2d Sess 20 (1984)]

2. The amount or percentage of benefits to be paid the alternate payee, or the manner in which such amount or percentage is to be determined. This requirement generally prohibits a

QDRO from using plan benefits as collateral for a separate obligation, as opposed to being the primary source of payment.
For example, a QDRO can require payment in the amount of
$5,000 to an alternate payee; it cannot, however, require that
a participant's benefit serve as collateral in the event of default on a promissory note in the amount of $5,000 from a
participant to the alternate payee. In the latter situation, there
is simply no way for the plan administrator to determine how
much of the participant's benefit is affected by the order at
any given point in time.

3. The number of payments or the period to which the order ap-
    plies. This generally requires that the order specify whether
    payments will be paid as a lump sum, as an annuity, in in-
    stallments, and so forth.

4. The plan to which the order applies.

[IRC § 414(p)(2)]

Q 16:35 What terms cannot be contained in a QDRO?

A QDRO cannot contain any provision that requires a plan to provide any type or form of benefit or any option not otherwise provided under the plan. For example, a QDRO may not require that a
segregated, self-directed account be established for an alternate
payee if the plan does not permit participants and beneficiaries to
segregate and direct the investments of their accounts.

A QDRO may not contain a provision that would require the plan
to pay increased benefits. For example, a QDRO may not award an
alternate payee a dollar amount that is in excess of a participant's
vested account balance.

Finally, a QDRO may not require a plan to pay to one alternate
payee benefits that have already been awarded to another alternate
payee in a separate QDRO. [IRC § 414(p)(3)]

Review and Qualification of a Domestic Relations Order (DRO)

Q 16:36 What is the plan administrator's responsibility when a DRO is received?

The plan administrator must promptly notify the participant and
alternate payee that an order has been received and inform them of

the plan's procedures for reviewing orders. Within a reasonable period of time, the plan administrator must determine whether the order is qualified. This determination must also be communicated to the participant and alternate payee. [IRC § 414(p)(6)] According to the DOL, the plan administrator's cost for reviewing and responding to a QDRO may not be charged to the individual account of the participant and/or alternate payee. [DOL Adv Op 94-32A]

Q 16:37 Can the plan make payments to a participant while an order is under review?

A plan administrator cannot pay to a participant any amounts that would be payable to an alternate payee if the order were qualified. These amounts must be separately accounted for and must be held back from distribution for an 18-month period beginning on the date the first payment would be required under the order. [IRC § 414(p)(7)]

Plan Provisions

Q 16:38 Does a plan need to contain any specific provisions concerning QDROs?

No. A plan must have reasonable procedures for reviewing domestic relations orders, but this information need not be contained in the plan document. No other plan documentation is required to achieve compliance with the QDRO rules. [Treas Reg § 1.401(a)-13(g)(2)] As discussed in Q 16:41, a plan may want to include a provision permitting immediate payment to alternate payees. This avoids the administrative task of carrying alternate payee accounts and providing disclosure to alternate payees.

Tax Consequences

Q 16:39 What are the tax consequences of distributions to alternate payees?

If the alternate payee is the spouse or former spouse of a participant, the distribution is taxed to the alternate payee. [IRC § 402(e)(1)(A)] If the alternate payee is not a spouse or former spouse, the distribution is taxed to the participant.

The 10 percent additional income tax that generally applies to distributions made before a participant attains age 59½ does not apply to any distribution to a spousal alternate payee. [IRC § 72(t)(2)(C)]

An alternate payee who is the spouse or former spouse of a participant may roll over his or her distribution [IRC § 402(e)(1)(B)] and, until 2000, may also take advantage of income averaging if he or she is otherwise eligible. [IRC § 402(d)(4)(J)]

Special Circumstances

Q 16:40 Should a plan administrator distribute benefits to a participant if he or she knows a QDRO is being drafted, but it has not been received?

This situation can present a dilemma for a plan administrator since the optional form of benefit rules (see Qs 15:1–15:11) and the plan document may require the immediate lump-sum payment of benefits to the participant. In many circumstances where an order might be pending, the participant will not have a divorce decree yet and therefore will not be able to take a lump sum without his or her spouse's consent because of the survivor annuity rules. However, if this is not the case, the decision is a difficult one. The legislative history of the QDRO rules suggests that whenever a plan administrator is on notice that a QDRO is being sought, payment to a participant may be delayed for a reasonable period of time. [Conf Rep No 99-841, 99th Cong, 2d Sess II-858 (1986)] If a "hold" procedure will be used, it should be reflected in the plan's written QDRO procedures. [Schoonmaker v Amoco Corp Employee Savings Plan, 16 EBC (BNA) 1646 (7th Cir 1993)]

Q 16:41 What rights does an alternate payee have?

An alternate payee is generally treated as a plan beneficiary and is entitled to receive a summary plan description, an annual benefit statement, and other information available under ERISA's disclosure rules. (See chapter 18.) [ERISA § 206(d)(3)(J)] A QDRO may also award survivor annuity rights to an alternate payee. [IRC § 414(p)(5)] To the extent such rights are awarded, the rights of any subsequent spouse of a participant will be limited.

It is not always clear from the plan document whether an alternate payee is entitled to receive loans and/or hardship distributions or to direct the investment of his or her account to the same extent participants are given these rights. Many plan sponsors avoid this issue by providing for immediate distribution to alternate payees. If an alternate payee's benefit will remain in a plan, it makes sense to give investment control to the alternate payee to the same extent it is available to plan participants.

Q 16:42 If a plan changes administrators, should any QDROs be reapproved by the new administrator?

No. Once a determination has been made by a plan administrator that an order is qualified, any successor plan administrator is bound by that determination. [Rep No 98-575 98th Cong, 2d Sess 20 (1984)]

Q 16:43 When can benefits be distributed to an alternate payee?

The answer to this question will vary depending on the terms of the plan and the QDRO. A 401(k) plan may contain a provision permitting immediate distribution to alternate payees once an order is approved. If this provision is in the plan and the order calls for immediate distribution, benefits may be paid right away. [Treas Reg § 1.401(a)-13(g)(3)]

If the plan does not contain this special provision, an order can still require payment to be made to an alternate payee when a participant attains age 50, even if the participant has not terminated employment. [IRC § 414(p)(4)] It is not necessary for there to be any special provision in the plan to permit this distribution; it is only necessary that this language be contained in the QDRO.

It is possible that an order will not take advantage of either of these early distribution options. In that event, payment will be permitted at whatever point called for in the order after the participant becomes eligible for a distribution.

Q 16:44 What is the consequence of making payment pursuant to a domestic relations order that is not qualified?

Any such payment will be considered a violation of the anti-assignment and alienation rules contained in Code Section 401(a)(13) and will provide a basis for disqualifying the entire plan.

Q 16:45 What happens if the form of benefit specified in a QDRO is no longer available at the time distribution occurs?

Legislative history suggests that if an alternate payee is awarded a right to a particular form of benefit in a QDRO that is later eliminated either through plan amendment or change of law, the alternate payee is still entitled to receive that form of benefit unless it would adversely affect a participant's right to his or her benefits. [S Rep No 99-313 99th Cong, 2d Sess 20 (1986), Report of the Senate Committee on Finance on the Tax Reform Act of 1986, 1105]

17   Taxation of 401(k) Plans

This chapter focuses on the tax reporting and payment requirements of 401(k) plans. Federal withholding is covered, from both a contribution and a distribution standpoint. Internal Revenue Service (IRS) forms are discussed, including tax reporting of distributions from 401(k) plans. Also covered are some planning strategies for reducing or eliminating income tax on 401(k) distributions.

PAYROLL TAXES

Employers that maintain 401(k) plans are subject to a number of requirements concerning the withholding, reporting, and payment of federal taxes. Some of these requirements apply at the time elective contributions to a plan are made, some apply at the time distributions from the plan are made, and others must be attended to on a quarterly and/or annual basis. Table 17-1 provides an overview of the deadlines for collecting, paying, and reporting these taxes.

TABLE 17-1. Deadlines for Collecting, Paying, and Reporting Federal Taxes

	FICA	FUTA	FIT
Elective contributions	Taxable	Taxable	Exempt
Other contributions	Exempt	Exempt	Exempt
Distributions	Exempt	Exempt	Taxable
Withholding on distributions	None	None	Required unless payee elects a direct rollover
IRS reporting	Annually on Form 941	Quarterly on Form 940 or 940EZ	Annually on Form 1099-R or W-2G
Participant reporting of withheld amounts	Annually on Form W-2	None	Annually on Form 1099-R or W-2G

Federal Insurance Contributions Act (FICA)

Q 17:1 What is the *FICA tax*?

The *FICA tax* is a tax authorized by the Federal Insurance Contributions Act (FICA), an offshoot of the Social Security Act, enacted in 1935. Its purpose is to provide retirement and welfare benefits to people who are no longer employed. [21 USC §§ 3101–3128, subtitle C] The employer and the employee each pay equal portions of the FICA tax, which is collected by the IRS.

Q 17:2 What amounts are subject to FICA withholding?

Elective contributions to a 401(k) plan are subject to FICA withholding at the time the contributions are made. [IRC § 3121(v)(1)(A)] However, matching contributions or profit sharing contributions are not subject to FICA withholding, either at the time the contributions are made or at the time a distribution is made to a participant. [IRC § 3121(a)(5)(A)]

Example. Erin earns $30,000 and elects to contribute $2,000 of that to her 401(k) plan. Erin's employer makes a matching contribution to her account of $1,000. Although Erin's obligation for payment of federal income tax will be based on earnings of $28,000, her FICA tax obligation will be based on $30,000. She will, however, avoid both federal income and FICA tax on the $1,000 matching contribution made to her account.

Q 17:3 Which employees are subject to FICA tax withholding?

Generally, FICA tax is due on amounts paid to any common-law employee or corporate officer for services performed in the United States. [IRC § 3121(d)] Since the Employee Retirement Income Security Act of 1974 (ERISA) requires that qualified plans be offered for the benefit of employees, as a general rule, anyone who is a plan participant will be subject to FICA tax. Self-employed individuals are subject to the Self-Employment Contributions Act (SECA), which imposes taxes similar to those imposed on common-law employees under FICA. [IRC § 1401]

Q 17:4 How is the FICA tax computed?

The FICA tax is composed of two elements: Old-Age, Survivor, and Disability Insurance (OASDI) and Hospital Insurance (HI). For 1990 and thereafter, the employer and the employee each pay 6.2 percent of wages for OASDI and 1.45 percent of wages for HI, for a total rate of 7.65 percent each. [IRC §§ 3101(a), 3101(b), 3111(a), 3111(b)]

Example. Assume the amount of wages subject to FICA is $1,000. The amounts owed are as follows.

	Employer Portion	Employee Portion
OASDI	$62.00	$62.00
HI	14.50	14.50
Total	76.50	76.50

Total FICA tax due: $153.00

Q 17:5 How is FICA tax collected?

The employee portion of the FICA tax on elective contributions is deducted from an employee's pay at the time the payment is issued. [IRC § 3102(a)] The employer will be liable for the employee portion of the tax, in addition to the employer portion, whether or not the tax is collected from the employee. [IRC § 3102(b); Treas Reg § 31.3102-1(c)]

Q 17:6 How is the FICA tax paid?

Deposits of collected FICA withholdings must be made to a financial institution qualified as a depository for federal taxes or to a federal reserve bank. The frequency of required deposits depends on the amount of tax withheld by the employer: the larger the amount withheld, the more frequently deposits are required. Some employers are required to make deposits daily, while others may do so as infrequently as quarterly. [Treas Reg § 31.6302(c)-1(a)]

Q 17:7 How is the FICA tax reported?

FICA taxes are reported quarterly on IRS Form 941. Employees who have FICA tax withheld must be furnished with IRS Form W-2, Wage and Tax Statement, on an annual basis. [IRC § 6051(a); Treas Reg § 31.6051-1(a)(1)(i)]

Federal Unemployment Tax Act (FUTA)

Q 17:8 What is the *FUTA tax*?

The *FUTA tax* is a tax imposed by the Federal Unemployment Tax Act (FUTA) on employers to fund cash benefits to former employees undergoing temporary periods of unemployment. [23 USC §§ 3301–3311, subtitle C] Like the FICA tax, these amounts are paid to the IRS. Unlike FICA, this tax is collected from employers only, so there is no withholding requirement on amounts paid to employees.

The Unemployment Insurance Program is a joint federal and state program. As such, credits may be available on amounts due the federal government under FUTA for payments that have been made to state unemployment funds. [IRC § 3302(a)(1)]

Q 17:9 What amounts are subject to FUTA?

As with FICA, elective contributions to a 401(k) plan are subject to FUTA tax, but matching or profit sharing contributions and plan distributions are not. [IRC §§ 3306(b)(5)(A), 3306(r)(1)(A)] The maximum amount of wages paid to an employee during any calendar year that may be subject to FUTA tax is currently $7,000, but this amount may be periodically adjusted through legislative amendment. [IRC § 3306(b)(1)]

Q 17:10 Which employees' wages are subject to the FUTA tax?

All wages paid to common-law employees and corporate officers who perform services in the United States and wages paid for services performed by a citizen of the United States as an employee of an American employer are subject to the FUTA tax. [IRC § 3306(c)] There is no tax comparable to FUTA that applies to net employment income earned by self-employed individuals.

Q 17:11 How is the FUTA tax computed?

For calendar years 1988–1998, the FUTA tax rate is 6.2 percent. [IRC § 3301(1)] After 1998, the rate will be reduced to 6 percent. [IRC § 3301(2)] Credits against this tax may be available for payments made to a state unemployment fund, as well as for employers with an historically low incidence of unemployment. [IRC §§ 3302(a)(1), 3302(b)]

Q 17:12 How is the FUTA tax reported?

FUTA taxes are reported annually to the IRS on Form 940 or 940EZ, which is due on January 31 for the prior calendar year. [IRS Pub. 15]

Since there is no obligation for employees to pay any portion of the FUTA tax, there is also no corresponding obligation on the part of employers to collect FUTA tax from wages.

Q 17:13 How is the FUTA tax paid?

If the employer's FUTA tax liability exceeds $100 in any calendar quarter, deposits must be made to an authorized financial institution or a federal reserve bank. [Treas Reg § 31.6302(c)-3(a)(2)] In calculating the $100 limit, the employer may assume that the maximum credit is available so that the tax rate applied (prior to 1995) is 0.8 percent. For example, if the total amount of wages subject to FUTA tax in a calendar quarter was $10,000, the employer would not be required to make a deposit during that quarter since, by applying a tax rate of 0.8 percent, the total FUTA tax obligation would be only $80.

TAXATION AND REPORTING OF DISTRIBUTIONS

One of the major advantages of a qualified plan is that contributions are not taxed when made to the plan, only when distributed to the participant. In some cases, the distribution may not be in cash; the participant will then be taxed on the value of the benefit. This section deals with the federal tax treatment of distributions from 401(k) plans and how such distributions are reported. Most distributions are reported on Form 1099-R, but certain excise taxes are reported on personal or estate tax returns. If the distribution is an eligible rollover distribution, tax may be deferred by rolling it over to an eligible retirement plan. Additional information concerning the tax treatment of eligible rollover distributions can be found in chapter 15.

Lump-Sum Distributions

Q 17:14 How are distributions generally paid from 401(k) plans?

Distributions from most 401(k) plans are generally made in the form of a single sum. If a single sum qualifies as a lump-sum distribution, then favorable tax treatment may be available to the participant. If the distribution does not qualify as a lump-sum distribution, the entire distribution is taxable as ordinary income in the year of receipt.

Q 17:15 How is a *lump-sum distribution* defined?

A distribution will qualify as a *lump-sum distribution* if it meets the following requirements:

1. The distribution or distributions are made within one year (the recipient's taxable year is used for purposes of these rules);

2. The distribution represents the balance to the credit of the employee;

3. The distribution is made on account of death, attainment of age 59½, separation from service (applicable only to common-law employees), or disability (applicable only to self-employed individuals) [IRC § 402(d)(4)(A)]; and

4. The participant has participated in the plan for five or more taxable years. (Beneficiaries of death proceeds are exempt from this requirement.) The number of tax years of participation in the plan completed prior to the taxable year of termination is counted for this purpose. [IRC § 402(d)(4)(F)]

Q 17:16 Do distributions as a result of termination of a 401(k) qualify for lump-sum treatment?

A notable omission from the list of qualified lump-sum distribution events is a distribution on account of termination of the plan. These distributions are not entitled to favorable treatment for purposes of the lump-sum distribution rules unless the participant has attained age 59½.

Q 17:17 What plans are considered in determining whether a 401(k) distribution qualifies for lump-sum treatment?

All similar plans are aggregated for lump-sum purposes, including all 401(k) and profit sharing plans of the employer. [IRC § 402(d)(4)(C)] Defined benefit, money purchase, stock bonus, and target plans need not be considered when determining whether a single-sum distribution from a 401(k) plan constitutes a lump-sum distribution.

Q 17:18 What constitutes the *balance to the credit* of a participant?

The definition of the *balance to the credit* of a participant is critical in the determination of whether a distribution qualifies as a lump sum. The general meaning of *balance to the credit* in a 401(k) plan is the vested account balance. However, all 401(k) and profit sharing plans of the employer must be treated as one plan. [IRC § 402(d)(4)(C)] Thus, if an employee receives a distribution of his or her vested balance from a 401(k) plan but not from the profit sharing plan, the 401(k) distribution does not qualify as the balance to the credit of the employee.

The balance to the credit does not include amounts payable to an alternate payee under a qualified domestic relations order (QDRO). [IRC § 402(d)(4)(H)] The balance to the credit includes all amounts in the participant's account as of the time of the first distribution received after the event that triggers the distribution. A participant receiving installment payments after separation from service may elect a single sum in a later year, but the single sum will not qualify as the balance to the credit of the participant. [Prop Treas Reg § 1.402(e)-2(d)(1)(ii)(C)]

Q 17:19 How do subsequent payments affect the lump-sum treatment of a prior distribution?

After a participant's account has been distributed, incidental amounts may be credited to the account as a result of calculation errors, additional earnings, forfeiture reallocations, or year-end contributions. These incidental payments do not destroy the lump-sum treatment of amounts received in a prior taxable year. However, the incidental payment itself is taxable as ordinary income in the calendar year received. [Prop Treas Reg § 1.402(e)-2(d)(1)(ii)((B)]

Q 17:20 What tax options are available to a participant who qualifies for lump-sum treatment?

Special treatment is available to a participant who is over the age of 59½ and has been a participant in the plan for at least five taxable years prior to the year of distribution. This treatment is available only once. [IRC § 402(d)(4)(B)]

Four options are available to an individual in this situation:

1. Five-year forward income averaging can be done on the entire distribution (not available after 1999). (See Q 17:25.)

2. Ordinary income tax can be paid on the entire distribution.

3. The distribution may be rolled over to an IRA or another qualified plan, where taxation would be deferred until funds are withdrawn.

4. A portion of the distribution can be rolled over and the remainder received in cash and subject to ordinary income tax.

Q 17:21 Does an alternate payee in a QDRO qualify for lump-sum treatment?

If lump-sum treatment is available to a participant, a payment to an alternate payee who is the spouse or former spouse of a participant under a QDRO of the total sum due under the terms of the QDRO will also qualify as a lump-sum distribution [IRC § 402(d)(4)(J)]

Q 17:22 How did the Tax Reform Act of 1986 protect favorable treatment for older participants?

The Tax Reform Act of 1986 (TRA '86) grandfathered certain individuals who were 50 or over on January 1, 1986. These individuals have a choice of five-year forward income averaging at the rates in the calendar year of distribution or ten-year forward income averaging based on 1986 rates. Capital gains treatment would be available at a flat 20 percent rate on any pre-1974 accumulation. Under Section 1401 of the Small Business Job Protection Act of 1996 (SBJPA) five-year forward income averaging will no longer be available after 1999. Ten-year averaging under the grandfather rule will remain available.

Q 17:23 What items can be excluded from taxation in a lump-sum distribution?

If the participant has an investment in the contract (cost basis), certain items are excluded from taxation. These items would include after-tax voluntary or mandatory employee contributions, PS-58 costs (explained in Q 17:46), the net unrealized appreciation in employer securities, and loans that have become taxable under Internal Revenue Code (Code) Section 72(p). [IRC § 402(d)(4)(D)] However, the earnings related to after-tax employee contributions are includible as taxable items. To the extent 401(k) excess deferrals have remained in the plan and have been previously taxed, that money is once again taxed when distributed.

Q 17:24 Do small lump-sum distributions qualify for any additional favorable treatment?

To the extent forward income averaging is available, the minimum distribution allowance (MDA) will serve to further reduce the amount of tax on a lump-sum distribution. This applies to distributions of less than $70,000. The MDA is calculated in two steps:

1. The lesser of $10,000 or 50 percent of the taxable distribution,

2. Minus 20 percent of the excess over $20,000.

[IRC § 401(d)(1)(C)]

An example of the calculation of the MDA is shown below.

Example. Participant receives a lump-sum distribution of $50,000. The amount of this distribution that is not subject to federal tax is the MDA. The allowance is:

1. Lesser of

    $10,000 or

    $(½ \times \$50,000) = \$25,000$
    ($10,000 is the result)

2. Reduced by 20 percent of ($50,000 – $20,000) = $6,000
    (1) – (2) = MDA
    $10,000 – $6,000 = $4,000

As a result, $4,000 will not be subject to federal tax; the remaining $46,000 will be subject to federal tax.

Q 17:25 How is the tax on a lump-sum distribution computed?

The following steps are taken in computing the tax with five-year income averaging:

1. Subtract the minimum distribution allowance from the total taxable amount.

2. Divide the net result by 5.

3. Compute the tax using the tax table for single individuals.

4. Multiply the result by 5.

An example of the calculation is shown below.

1. Distribution: $45,000
    MDA:

    Lesser of (a) $10,000 or

    (b) $½ \times \$45,000 = \$22,500$
    Reduced by 20% × ($45,000 – $20,000) = $5,000
    MDA = $10,000 – $5,000 = $5,000
    Taxable distribution: $45,000 – $5,000 = $40,000

2. Divide by 5:
    $40,000/5 = $8,000

3. Calculate ordinary income tax on $8,000:
   15% × $8,000 = $1,200

4. Multiply result by 5:
   5 × $1,200 = $6,000

If ordinary income tax is paid on the distribution without applying income averaging or the MDA, the total tax is $9,396 (1999 single return tax rates). The tax savings from the special treatment results in a savings of $3,396 to the taxpayer.

Q 17:26 Must prior distributions be considered in computing the tax on a lump-sum distribution?

Not any longer. Prior to passage of the Unemployment Compensation Act of 1992, there was a six-year look-back rule that required that prior lump-sum distributions be aggregated in determining the tax on the current year's distribution. The impact of the rule was to increase the tax rate applied to the current year's distribution. This multiple distribution rule was eliminated when Code Section 402 was revised pursuant to the Unemployment Compensation Act of 1992.

Q 17:27 What is the impact on future election rights if an individual makes a lump-sum election as a beneficiary?

If an individual receives a lump-sum distribution as a beneficiary of a participant in a qualified plan, any election made in the capacity of a beneficiary does not affect a subsequent election by the individual in his or her capacity as a participant in a qualified plan.

Q 17:28 How are lump-sum distributions reported?

Lump-sum distributions are reported on Form 1099-R. If the participant has a cost basis, such basis will be reported on this form. In addition, any portion of the distribution attributable to pre-1974 participation will also be reported on Form 1099-R.

Employer Securities

Q 17:29 Does a participant in a 401(k) plan receive any favorable treatment when receiving employer securities in a distribution?

Yes. The net unrealized appreciation (the difference between the market value of the security at the time distributed from the plan and the cost basis of the security) is not subject to tax until the employer securities are sold. In the case of a distribution other than a lump-sum distribution (determined without regard to the five-year participation rule described in Q 17:20), this treatment applies only to employer securities attributable to employee after-tax contributions. The cost basis of the securities is included in taxable income at the time of the distribution. [IRC § 402(e)(4)]

Q 17:30 How are *employer securities* defined?

Employer securities are shares of stock, bonds, or debentures issued by a corporation sponsoring the plan. Employer securities include securities of a parent or subsidiary corporation. [IRC § 402(e)(4)(E)]

Q 17:31 What options does a participant have after receiving employer securities?

A participant who receives employer stock in a distribution has four options:

1. Roll the stock into an IRA.
2. Sell the stock and roll the proceeds into the IRA.
3. Keep the stock, pay tax on the cost basis, and sell the stock later for potential capital gains treatment.
4. Keep the stock and pay tax on the market value of the stock at the time of distribution.

The participant may not keep the stock and substitute its value with cash to roll over to an IRA.

Distributions on Death

Q 17:32 How is the beneficiary taxed on proceeds received from a 401(k) plan?

Death benefits are generally paid to the beneficiary of a deceased participant in a lump sum. In effect, the tax treatment available to the participant is extended to the beneficiary. The investment in the contract (cost basis) will not be taxable to the beneficiary. If the participant is eligible for capital gains and income averaging treatment, this treatment is also available to the beneficiary. The five-year participation requirement does not apply to the beneficiary.

For participants who died on or before August 20, 1996, there was a $5,000 employee death benefit exclusion available to the beneficiary. This exclusion was eliminated by SBJPA Section 1402.

Q 17:33 How are life insurance proceeds treated in a death payout?

If part of the death benefit includes the proceeds of a life insurance policy, a portion of the proceeds is income tax free to the beneficiary. The difference between the face amount of the life insurance and the cash surrender value is treated as life insurance proceeds and is not subject to tax. Two conditions must be satisfied to ensure this tax treatment: the premiums must be paid with pre-tax dollars, and PS-58 costs (discussed in Q 17:46) must be reported on an annual basis. The cash surrender value of the insurance contract plus the side fund proceeds will be taxable to the beneficiary. [Treas Reg § 1.72-16(c)]

Q 17:34 May a beneficiary roll over death proceeds to an individual retirement account (IRA)?

If the beneficiary of the participant is a spouse or a former spouse receiving benefits pursuant to a QDRO and the distribution is an eligible rollover distribution (see Qs 15:46–15:47), rollover treatment is available. [IRC §§ 402(c)(9), 402(e)(1)]

Installment Distributions

Q 17:35 How are installment distributions from a 401(k) plan taxed?

Installment distributions (made over a fixed period of time or in a fixed amount) are generally taxable as ordinary income when received. Likewise, payments in annuity form are treated as ordinary income when received. To the extent that a participant has a cost basis (investment in the contract) in the plan, an exclusion ratio is set up for each annual series of payments, which results in a portion of the payments being tax free. If the installment distribution is an eligible rollover distribution (see Qs 15:49–15:50), it can be rolled over to an eligible retirement plan and thus avoid current income taxation.

Q 17:36 How is the exclusion ratio computed?

The exclusion ratio is computed as follows [IRC § 72(b)(1)]:

$$\text{Investment in the contract} = \frac{\text{Percentage of tax-free annual income}}{\text{Expected return}}$$

This percentage of the annual income is tax free. Once the investment in the contract is recovered, the entire annual payment thereafter will be subject to ordinary income tax. [IRC § 72(b)(2)] If an individual dies before recovering the entire investment in the contract, a deduction may be taken on the last income tax return of the individual. [IRC § 72(b)(3)(A)]

Prior law allowed treatment of the first three years' worth of payments as the investment in the contract if the entire cost basis could be recovered within the three-year period. TRA '86 removed this provision from the Code.

Example. Rosemary retires at age 62 with an account balance of $150,000 and opts to receive ten annual installments. Her investment in the contract is $30,000, the amount of the after-tax voluntary contributions. Using the exclusion ratio calculation above, the portion of each annual installment that is income tax free is computed as follows:

$$\frac{\$30,000}{\$150,000} = 20\%$$

Thus, 20 percent of each annual installment is excluded from income tax. Once the entire $30,000 is used, no further offsets are available.

SBJPA Section 1403 simplifies the method for determining the portion of each installment not includible in gross income when payments are made in the form of an annuity.

The cost-basis recovery on periodic payments from qualified plans is simplified for annuities starting after November 18, 1996, but not when the primary annuitant has attained age 75, unless there are fewer than five years guaranteed.

The cost-basis recovery is now calculated under a method similar to the simplified general method, though with a larger number of expected payments for each age range. The exclusion amount from each payment is the investment in the contract divided by the number of anticipated payments determined as follows:

Age of Primary Annuitant on Start Date	Number of Anticipated Payments
Not over 55	360
Over 55, not over 60	310
Over 60, not over 65	260
Over 65, not over 70	210
Over 70	160

Q 17:37 How are installment distributions reported?

Installment distributions are reported on Form 1099-R.

In-Service Withdrawals

Q 17:38 How are withdrawals from a 401(k) plan taxed while a participant is actively employed?

In-service withdrawals are taxable as ordinary income when received and generally are treated as installment distributions. If the participant is under age 59½ and does not qualify for any of the exceptions, the participant is subject to a 10 percent premature withdrawal penalty (see Q 17:59).

Q 17:39 Will a participant's cost basis from after-tax contributions be excluded from tax in a withdrawal?

If the participant's account balance includes voluntary or mandatory contributions, the basis recovery rules will allow a portion of the in-service withdrawal to be treated as a nontaxable item. Before TRA '86, employee after-tax contributions could be recovered first in an in-service withdrawal; once the employee contributions were recovered, the balance would be treated as taxable.

Q 17:40 How did TRA '86 change the basis recovery rules?

In an attempt to discourage the use of retirement plans for purposes other than retirement, TRA '86 changed the basis recovery rules, effective for withdrawals made after July 1, 1986. The rules provide a pro rata recovery of the employee's cost basis. The following ratio is applied to each withdrawal to determine the nontaxable amount:

$$\frac{\text{Investment in contract}}{\text{Vested account balance}} \times \text{withdrawal amount} = \text{Amount not taxed}$$

Example. A participant has a vested account balance in a 401(k) plan of $5,000. Voluntary after-tax contributions (exclusive of earnings) of $1,000 have been made. If the participant withdraws $2,000 for hardship purposes, it will be taxed as follows:

$$\frac{\$1,000}{\$5,000} \times \$2,000 = \$400$$

$400 is recovered tax free and the balance, or $1,600, is taxable as ordinary income. [IRC § 72(e)]

Q 17:41 Should voluntary and mandatory contributions be accounted for separately?

The taxable amount can be minimized if voluntary and mandatory contributions are accounted for separately from employer contributions and elective contributions. The reason for favorable treatment is that the account balance considered in the recovery ratio would then consist only of the after-tax employee contributions plus earnings. [IRC § 72(d)]

Example. A participant has an account balance of $5,000. It consists of $2,700, representing voluntary after-tax contributions plus earnings, and $2,300, representing elective contributions plus earnings. Voluntary after-tax contributions of $1,000 have been made. If the participant withdraws $2,000 from his voluntary account, the basis recovery rules are applied as follows:

$$\frac{\text{Investment in contract}}{\text{Vested account balance}} \times \text{withdrawal amount} = \text{Amount not taxed}$$

$$\frac{\$1,000}{\$2,700} \times \$2,000 = \$740.74$$

$740.74 is tax free, and the remaining $1,259.26 is taxable as ordinary income.

Q 17:42 How did TRA '86 preserve the old basis recovery rules for certain plans?

TRA '86 provided a grandfather rule to exempt certain plans from the new basis recovery rules. If a plan contained voluntary or mandatory contributions and, on May 5, 1986, allowed for withdrawal of these contributions before separation from service, then the basis recovery rules do not apply to pre-1987 after-tax contributions. [IRC § 72(e)(8)(D)]

Q 17:43 How do the grandfathered basis recovery rules work?

The following steps would be taken to determine the taxable amount of an in-service withdrawal under the grandfather rules:

Step I. Grandfather rule:

1. Determine current amount of pre-1987 after-tax contributions, exclusive of earnings.

2. If distribution is less than or equal to the current balance of pre-1987 after-tax contributions, the entire amount is not taxable.

3. If distribution is more than the current balance of pre-1987 after-tax contributions, taxation of excess is determined in Steps II and III.

Step II. Pro rata taxation of remaining distribution, if any (up to the amount of total post-1986 after-tax contributions plus earnings thereon):

1. Remaining portion of distribution (up to the amount of total post-1986 after-tax contributions plus earnings thereon), multiplied by

2. Post-1986 after-tax contributions, exclusive of earnings, divided by

3. Post-1986 after-tax contributions, plus earnings thereon equals

4. Amount that is not taxable.

Step III. Remainder of distribution, if any:

1. The remainder of the distribution, if any, is fully taxable, except to the extent there is other basis in the account balance (for example, PS 58 costs or loans treated as distributions). In that case, a pro rata calculation must be done as follows:

2. Remainder of distribution after Steps I and II, multiplied by

3. Remaining basis in account balance after Steps I and II, divided by

4. Total account balance, less amounts subject to Steps I and II.

Example

$10,000 distribution

$ 8,000 pre-1987 after-tax contributions, exclusive of earnings

$ 4,000 post-1986 after-tax contributions, exclusive of earnings

$ 1,250 earnings on after-tax contributions

Step I. Grandfather rule (not taxable):

$ 8,000

Step II. Amount subject to pro rata rule:

$2,000 (amount of post-1986 after-tax
contributions included in distribution) $\times$

$$\frac{\$4,000 \text{ (post-1986 after-tax contributions)}}{\$5,250 \text{ (post-1986 after-tax contributions plus earnings}} =$$

$1,524 not taxable; $476 taxable

Q 17:44 How are in-service withdrawals reported?

In-service withdrawals are taxable as ordinary income and re-ported on Form 1099-R. To the extent the participant has a cost basis, the exclusion ratio would be applied to reduce the tax-able amount.

LIFE INSURANCE

Q 17:45 How is life insurance in a 401(k) plan taxed?

If life insurance benefits are provided in a 401(k) plan, the term cost of this life insurance protection is includible annually in the employee's gross income. This treatment applies for each year in which deductible employer contributions or trust income is applied to purchase life insurance protection. [Treas Reg § 1.72-16(b)] The types of contracts included in a 401(k) plan that are subject to this treatment would include group permanent, term, whole life, and universal life. The employee will be taxed on the cost of the insur-ance protection if either the proceeds are payable to the estate or designated beneficiary, or the proceeds are payable to the trustee but the trustee is required to pay the proceeds to the employee's estate or designated beneficiary. [Treas Reg § 1.72-16(b)(1)]

Q 17:46 How is the taxable cost of life insurance computed?

The taxable cost of life insurance is determined by subtracting the cash value at the end of the policy year from the face amount of life insurance. One-year term premium rates are then applied at the insured's age to this difference, otherwise known as the *amount at risk.* The rates published in Revenue Ruling 55-747, called *PS-58 rates,* are the applicable rates for purposes of this calculation. However, if the insurance company rates for individual one-year term policies available to all standard risks are lower, these insurance company rates may be used. [Rev Rul 66-110, 1966-1 CB 12]

Example. A participant in a 401(k) plan uses 20 percent of his elective contributions to pay premiums each month. The face amount or death benefit provided in the insurance contract is $100,000. At the end of the policy year, the cash value is $2,500. If the participant is age 60 at the end of the policy year, the applicable rate from the PS-58 Table is $20.73 per thousand. The taxable cost of life insurance is computed as follows:

Life insurance face amount:	$100,000.00
Cash value:	− 2,500.00
Amount at risk:	$97,500.00
Premium per thousand dollars:	× $20.73
Taxable amount:	$2,021.18

Q 17:47 How is survivor whole life taxed?

A number of 401(k) plans use a special type of life insurance protection called *survivor whole life,* or *second-to-die,* life insurance. This type of life insurance protection pays death proceeds only after the death of the last surviving spouse. Since the payment of proceeds is contingent upon the deaths of two individuals, premium rates are substantially lower, and greater life insurance protection can be provided. Likewise, in determining the current taxation of these contracts, a lower government table can be used, the US Life Table 38. [Information letter from Norman Greenberg, Chief of the Actuarial Branch, Department of Treasury] If the participant's spouse dies while the policy is held in the 401(k) plan, the PS-58 rates would be applicable thereafter.

Q 17:48 How is the taxable cost of life insurance protection reported?

The taxable cost of life insurance must be reported annually on Form 1099-R.

LOANS

Q 17:49 When do participant loans become taxable to a participant?

Participant loans in 401(k) plans can generate taxable income to the participant if principal and interest payments are not made on a timely basis. Furthermore, if a participant loan exceeds the Tax Equity and Fiscal Responsibility Act of 1982 (TEFRA) limits (the lesser of 50 percent of the account balance or $50,000, as discussed in chapter 14), or if it fails to satisfy the requirements of Code Section 72 (p) by its terms, immediate taxation can result. [IRC § 72(p)]

Q 17:50 If a participant loan becomes taxable, does the obligation to the 401(k) plan still exist?

Yes. From the trustee's perspective, the fact that all or a portion of the loan is taxed to the participant does not remove the participant's obligation to the plan. The participant is still responsible for paying interest on the loan and repaying principal.

Q 17:51 May a participant loan ever be converted to a distribution?

Yes. If the plan permits withdrawals after age 59½ and the participant is older than 59½, the outstanding loan may be converted to a distribution and no further obligation to the plan will exist. If the loan is still outstanding at the time of retirement or severance of employment, the obligation may be extinguished by reducing the participant's account balance by the outstanding loan. It is important to note that the loan will not be taxed twice. Once the loan is treated as taxable, it represents part of the participant's cost basis (investment in the contract). (See Q 17:23.)

Q 17:52 How is a taxable loan reported?

The amount of the default or the amount in excess of the TEFRA limits is reported on Form 1099-R in the year of default or in the year the excess loan is made.

DISTRIBUTION OF EXCESS DEFERRALS

Q 17:53 How are excess deferrals taxed to a participant in a 401(k) plan?

Excess deferrals result from elective deferrals in a calendar year in excess of the annual cap. For 1999, the deferral cap is $10,000. Both the excess deferral and the income applicable to the excess deferral must be included in income. The excess deferral amount is taxable in the calendar year in which the deferral was made; the income, however, is taxable in the year in which it is distributed.

Example. A participant defers $10,500 for calendar year 1999 when the deferral cap is $10,000. The plan returns $500 plus earnings on February 15, 2000. The $500 is includible in income in 1999. The income earned on the $500 excess deferral for 1999 is $50. Since the $500 is returned before April 15, 2000, $50 is includible in 2000 taxable income. (See Qs 17:55–17:58 for requirements relating to the timing of return of excess deferrals.) Both items are reportable on separate Forms 1099-R. Both items would be reported on 2000 forms, even though the excess deferral is taxable in 1999.

Q 17:54 What happens if the plan has a net investment loss and the earnings attributable to the excess deferral are negative?

If the excess deferral has a loss attributable to the plan's loss, the total excess deferral is still taxable in the year of deferral; the loss, however, would be reported in the year of distribution. Employers must give participants a separate statement instructing that the excess deferral (unadjusted for the loss) must be included in line 7 of Form 1040. [IRS Notice 89-32, 1989-1 CB 671] The loss is reported as a negative number under Other Income, but for the year of distribution, not the year of the excess deferral.

DISTRIBUTION OF EXCESS CONTRIBUTIONS

Q 17:55 How are excess contributions in a 401(k) plan taxed to the participant?

Excess contributions result from plans that fail to satisfy the actual deferral percentage (ADP) test. If excess contributions plus earnings are distributed within 2½ months following the close of the plan year, the highly compensated employee reports certain amounts in gross income in the taxable year in which the first elective contributions of that plan year were made. The reportable amounts consist of the excess contribution plus earnings allocable to the excess contribution. (Most individuals use the calendar year as their taxable year; however, some individuals do use noncalendar taxable years.) If the excess is distributed after 2½ months, but within 12 months after the close of the plan year, the entire amount is taxable in the calendar year received. [Treas Reg § 1.401(k)-1(f)(4)(v)]

> **Example.** A plan year begins July 1, 1998, and ends June 30, 1999. On August 1, 1999, the plan administrator determines that $1,000 must be refunded to a highly compensated employee. The income earned on $1,000 for the plan year that ended June 30, 1999, is $150. Thus, $1,150 is reported as income in calendar year 1998 if the income and the excess contribution are refunded by September 15, 1999. If not, $1,150 is reported as income in 1999 if distributed after that date. Both the excess contribution and the income must be reported on a 1999 Form 1099-R, even though $1,150 is taxable in 1998. Since $1,150 is taxable in 1998, the individual must refile his or her 1998 personal tax return.

Q 17:56 Is there an exception for small amounts of excess contributions?

Yes. The Technical and Miscellaneous Revenue Act of 1988 (TAMRA) provided a de minimis distribution rule that applies if the sum of excess contributions and excess aggregate contributions is less than $100 and distributed with income within 2½ months after the close of the plan year. Such excess contributions are taxed in the year of distribution rather than the taxable year in which the first elective contributions of the plan year were made. [Treas Reg § 1.401(k)-1(f)(4)(v)(B)]

Q 17:57 How are excess contributions in a 401(k) plan taxed to the employer?

If excess contributions are distributed more than 2½ months following the close of the plan year (but before the close of the next plan year), the employer is subject to a 10 percent excise tax. [Treas Reg § 1.401(k)-1(f)(6)(i)] If excess contributions are not distributed within 12 months following the close of the plan year, the plan is subject to disqualification. [Treas Reg § 1.401(k)-1(f)(6)(ii)]

Q 17:58 How are excess aggregate contributions taxed?

Excess aggregate contributions are contributions resulting from a plan that has failed to satisfy the Section 401(m) test. To the extent that they are fully vested matching contributions or voluntary after-tax contributions, such contributions are treated in the same manner as excess contributions resulting from the failure to satisfy the ADP test. However, if the excess aggregate contributions consist of matching contributions that are not fully vested, the unvested portion is reallocated to the accounts of the other participants. The vested portion of the match, plus earnings attributable to the vested portion, is refunded to the employee and reported on Form 1099-R.

OTHER TAXES

Up to this point, the focus has been on federal income tax on distributions from 401(k) plans. Certain distributions from 401(k) plans may be subject to additional income tax if distributions occur before age 59½. Other distributions may be subject to excise tax if they are delayed beyond age 70½ (see, however, Q 15:23). Even if distributions commence on a timely basis at age 70½, excise taxes may be levied if distributions are either too small or too large. This section deals with the rules relating to the computation of these taxes, the exceptions to those rules, and how the taxes are paid.

Premature Distributions

Q 17:59 What is the penalty on premature distributions?

Distributions received from a 401(k) plan before the participant reaches age 59½ are subject to a 10 percent additional income tax. [IRC § 72(t)] If the distribution is rolled over to an IRA, this penalty tax will not apply.

Q 17:60 What are the exceptions to the premature distribution penalty?

There are a number of exceptions to the general rule:

1. *Death.* Distribution made to a beneficiary or estate of the participant after the participant's death;

2. *Disability.* If the participant meets a special definition of disability by virtue of being unable to "engage in any substantial gainful activity by reason of a medically determinable physical or mental impairment which can be expected to result in death or to be of long-continued and indefinite duration"; [IRC § 72(m)(7)]

3. *Substantially equal periodic payments.* If payments are made in at least annual installments over the life (or life expectancy) of the participant or the joint lives of the participant and designated beneficiary (discussed in more detail later at Qs 17:79–17:81; [IRC § 72(t)(2)(A)(iv)]

4. *Attainment of age 55.* If the participant separates from service after attaining age 55;

5. *Medical expenses.* If payments are made for medical care, but not in excess of amounts allowable as a deduction under Section 213;

6. *QDRO.* If payments are made to an alternate payee under a QDRO;

7. *401(k) excesses.* If excess deferrals, excess contributions, or excess aggregate contributions plus earnings are refunded to a participant on a timely basis;

8. *ESOP dividends.* If dividends are distributed in cash to ESOP participants; and

9. *PS-58 costs.* If the taxable cost of life insurance is reported annually by a participant.

[IRS Notice 89-25, 1989-1 CB 662]

Q 17:61 How is the premature distribution penalty reported?

If none of the exceptions listed in Q 17:60 applies, the distribution is reported on Form 1099-R as a premature distribution and is subject to a 10 percent additional income tax. The employer is not responsible for withholding this tax. The participant computes the 10 percent penalty by completing Form 5329 (Part I), if required, and entering the result on Form 1040 under "Tax on qualified retirement plans, including IRAs."

Minimum Required Distributions

Q 17:62 What is the penalty for failure to distribute minimum distributions as required?

If a 401(k) plan sponsor fails to distribute the minimum required distribution to a participant who is over age 70½ and who is a 5 percent owner or has terminated employment, an excise tax of 50 percent of the shortfall is imposed on the participant (see, however, Q 15:23). The tax is imposed on the participant during the taxable year that begins with or within the calendar year for which the distribution is required. [Prop Treas Reg § 54.4974-2, Q&A-1] The excise tax may be waived if it is established that the shortfall was due to reasonable error and that reasonable steps are being taken to remedy it. [Prop Treas Reg § 54.4974-2, Q&A 8]

Q 17:63 How is the minimum distribution penalty reported?

The excise tax is reported on Form 5329 (Part III) and entered on Form 1040 under "Tax on qualified retirement plans, including IRAs."

Excess Distributions and Accumulations

Q 17:64 What were the *excess distributions* and *excess accumulations excise taxes*?

A 15 percent *excess distribution excise tax* on annual distributions exceeding certain limits was in effect from 1986 through 1996. It has been repealed for distributions received after December 31, 1996.

The *excess accumulations excise tax*, which imposed a 15 percent excise tax on death benefits exceeding a certain limit, was repealed by the Taxpayer Relief Act of 1997 (TRA '97).

Federal Estate Tax

Q 17:65 How are 401(k) death distributions treated for federal estate tax purposes?

The treatment of qualified plan assets for federal estate tax purposes has varied considerably over the years. Prior to the passage of TEFRA in 1982, amounts attributable to employer contributions enjoyed an unlimited estate tax exclusion.

The Deficit Reduction Act of 1984 (DEFRA) removed the estate tax exclusion completely. DEFRA provided for the grandfathering of certain estates in pay status as of December 31, 1984. To avail themselves of the $100,000 exclusion, beneficiaries had to make an irrevocable election to receive benefits before July 18, 1984.

Q 17:66 What are the estate tax implications if the spouse is named as beneficiary of the 401(k) plan proceeds?

From a practical standpoint, the proceeds of a 401(k) plan resulting from the death of a participant are subject to federal estate tax. However, if the spouse is named as the beneficiary of the proceeds, there is an unlimited marital deduction. Upon the death of the spouse, the proceeds would then be subject to federal estate tax.

Q 17:67 How much is the federal estate tax?

Depending on the size of the total estate, the tax may be from 18 percent to 55 percent of the retirement plan proceeds. [IRC § 2001(c)]

FILING REQUIREMENTS FOR DISTRIBUTIONS

Q 17:68 What are the reporting rules for distributions from 401(k) plans?

All taxable distributions from 401(k) plans are reported on Form 1099-R. Form W-2 was previously used to report installments, periodic payments, or partial distributions, but, effective in 1991, Form 1099-R is the sole form used for distribution reporting. If the distribution is less than $1, Form 1099-R does not need to be filed. The individual who receives Form 1099-R must attach it to Form 1040 if federal income tax is withheld. Copy B is used for these purposes. The reporting of distributions from 401(k) plans is also required in some states.

Q 17:69 What is the penalty for failure to file Form 1099-R?

The penalty for failure to file Form 1099-R on a timely basis is $25 per day, up to a maximum of $15,000. [IRC § 6652(e)]

Q 17:70 When must a plan administrator file Form 1099-R on magnetic media?

A payor that prepares more than 250 1099-R forms must submit the information to the IRS on magnetic media. It is necessary to obtain approval of the particular magnetic format from the IRS 30 days before the due date of the return. Form 4419 is used for these purposes. It is not necessary to reapply for approval each year. If filing on magnetic media presents a hardship to the payor, it may request a waiver on Form 8508 if filed 45 days before the due date of the return. Failure to file on magnetic media results in a penalty of $50 per return.

Q 17:71 What are the rules for filing paper returns?

For payors filing fewer than 250 forms, certain requirements must be met. The forms themselves are printed by the IRS. The first copy is headlined in red. Photocopies may not be used. The forms are two to a sheet and should not be cut or separated, and no stapling, tearing, or taping is allowed. Pinfeed holes on the forms are not allowed. Copy A is submitted to the IRS. When providing the paper return to the payee, a statement should be provided that indicates the following: "This information is be-ing furnished to the IRS." Form 1096 is used to transmit paper copies to the IRS.

Q 17:72 How are 1099-R forms corrected?

If it becomes necessary to correct a Form 1099-R, the payor must complete the entire form, not just the corrected items. If more than 250 corrections are needed, the payor must file on magnetic media. If fewer than 250 corrections are done, the corrections should be submitted with Form 1096.

DISTRIBUTION PLANNING

Employees who are thinking about retiring will need to make a number of important decisions about the payment of their retire-ment benefits. Some of the decisions will be tax motivated, since the employee wishes to maximize the amount left after paying federal and state taxes. Other decisions will be driven by the indi-vidual's family and financial situation, health, and established retire-ment objectives. The individual's view of the future will enter into the decisions as well: the health of the economy, the impact of the budget deficit, and anticipated changes in future tax laws. Last, the broad range of investment opportunities available to the individual at retirement can be a significant factor in the decision-making process.

Distribution planning is not just for the wealthy trying to avoid federal income and estate taxes. As 401(k) plans grow in popular-ity and the funds accumulate, many individuals will find their 401(k) plan the most significant part of their retirement savings program. This section is concerned with techniques that may prove useful in deferring, minimizing, or avoiding taxes on 401(k) plan distributions.

Utilizing Rollovers

Q 17:73 How is a rollover advantageous to an individual?

An individual who receives an eligible rollover distribution (see Qs 15:49–15:50) from a 401(k) plan may choose to defer taxation on all or a portion of the distribution by rolling the proceeds over into an IRA. Once the distribution is rolled over, no funds will be required to be withdrawn until the individual reaches age 70½. If the individual dies before reaching age 70½, distributions must commence to the designated beneficiary no later than December 31 of the calendar year following the calendar year of death, or the entire IRA must be distributed by December 31 of the year that includes the fifth anniversary of the individual's death. The only exception to this rule exists for a spouse, in which case distributions can be deferred until the year the individual would have attained age 70½.

SBJPA did not change the minimum distribution rules for IRAs as it did for retirement plans.

Q 17:74 May a rollover be made by an individual who is over age 70½?

Yes, but if the individual is over age 70½ at the time the rollover is made, distributions must begin immediately over the individual's life expectancy or the joint life expectancy of the individual and designated beneficiary. This option may prove to be useful for an older participant in a 401(k) plan who has retired but does not wish to receive 401(k) plan proceeds in a lump sum.

Q 17:75 When may a partial distribution be rolled over?

If a distribution is not a life annuity and is not in installments extending past ten years, there is no longer any relevant distinction between partial distributions and total distributions as they affect the ability to roll over the proceeds. The distribution of any portion of a participant's account can constitute an eligible rollover distribution that can be rolled into an IRA or another qualified plan. [Treas Reg § 1.402(c)-2T, Q&A 3]

Utilizing Lump Sums

Q 17:76 What are the tax advantages of a lump-sum distribution?

A 401(k) plan may allow a participant to choose whether the account balance is to be paid in a single sum or installments. If a single sum is chosen, the individual must determine whether favorable tax treatment is available. If the individual was at least 50 on January 1, 1986, he or she can choose whether five- or ten-year income averaging is more favorable. If the individual participated in the plan before 1974, a portion of the distribution may be entitled to capital gains treatment. Currently, the capital gains portion would be taxed at a 20 percent rate. Depending on the amount of the distribution, it may be more advantageous to income average the entire distribution. However, as the amount of the distribution increases, the tax advantage of continuing deferrals may outweigh the tax advantage of income averaging.

Five-year income averaging will no longer be available for tax years beginning after 1999. [SBJPA § 1401]

Q 17:77 Should an eligible individual choose ten- or five-year income averaging?

Based on 1999 single return tax rates (and 1986 tax rates for ten-year income averaging), a lump-sum distribution would be taxed as follows:

Amount of Distribution	1986 Ten-Year Averaging (%)	1999 Five-Year Averaging (%)
$ 50,000	$ 5,870 (11.75)	$ 7,500 (15.00)
100,000	14,470 (14.47)	15,000 (15.00)
250,000	50,770 (20.30)	53,265 (21.31)
500,000	143,680 (28.75)	128,848 (25.78)
1,000,000	382,210 (38.22)	309,335 (30.13)

Note: The illustration above does not take into account any potential capital gains treatment.

Avoiding the Premature Distribution Tax

Q 17:78 How may the 10 percent premature distribution tax be avoided if the participant is not deceased or disabled?

A 10 percent penalty is imposed on distributions taken before age 59½, with certain exceptions discussed in Q 17:60. If the participant retires after attaining age 55, the 10 percent penalty tax will not be imposed. For a younger participant, the tax may be avoided after severing employment by beginning to take distributions in annual installments.

Q 17:79 What conditions must be satisfied to avoid this tax?

A number of requirements need to be met to satisfy the annual installment exception in Q 17:78:

1. Each distribution must be part of a series of substantially equal periodic payments made over the life (or joint lives) of the participant (and participant's beneficiary).
2. Distributions must commence after separation from service.
3. Distributions may not be later modified (other than by reason of death or disability) before the later of:
    a. The end of the five-year period after benefits commence; or
    b. After attainment of age 59½.

[IRC § 72(t)(2)(A)(iv)]

Q 17:80 How are equal periodic payments computed?

The requirement that distributions be part of a series of substantially equal periodic payments can be met by using one of three possible methods:

1. The principles used for determining minimum distributions after attainment of age 70½ can be applied (discussed in chapter 15).
2. The annual payment can be determined by amortizing the individual's account balance over the number of years equal to his or her life expectancy or joint life expectancy using the IRS tables prescribed under the Section 401(a)(9) regulations and using a reasonable interest rate.
3. The annual payment can be determined by dividing the individual's account balance by an annuity factor (using reasonable interest and mortality factors).

[IRS Notice 89-25, 1989-1 CB 662]

Example. A single individual, age 50, severs employment and has a vested account balance of $1,278,000 in 1999. The individual wishes to receive annual installments from the 401(k) plan without incurring a 10 percent premature distribution tax. The individual can choose one of three methods of distribution:

1. Use the IRS tables with single life expectancy factor of 33.1 (See Appendix B). A joint life expectancy factor could also be used if the participant had a designated beneficiary. The 1999 distribution would be equal to:

$$\frac{\$1,278,000}{33.1} = \$38,610$$

2. Amortize the account balance over 33 years at 8 percent:

$$\frac{\$1,278,000}{12.435} = \$102,774$$

3. Annuitize the account balance, using 8 percent interest and the widely used UP-1984 Mortality Table:

$$\frac{\$1,278,000}{10.6509} = \$119,990$$

The individual looking to maximize the distribution would probably choose option 3. No change could be made in the distribution until the individual attains age 59½.

Q 17:81 Is this exception also available for amounts in an IRA?

Yes. The participant can qualify for the annual installment exception even though the 401(k) plan may not allow for installment payments. The participant would elect a lump-sum distribution, roll the proceeds into the IRA, and commence distributions under the above rules.

Distributions versus Accumulations

Q 17:82 What are the disadvantages of accelerating the payment of retirement benefits?

By taking larger distributions earlier, the participant may be incurring a larger ongoing tax liability, since the earnings on the funds withdrawn from the 401(k) plan will be subject to income tax. However, the current tax liability could be reduced through the use of tax-sheltered accumulation vehicles such as municipal bonds, real estate, life insurance, or annuity products.

Q 17:83 Why may it be advantageous to continue to accumulate funds in a 401(k) plan?

An individual should compare the use of the qualified plan as a wealth accumulation vehicle with other investment alternatives. As a general rule, wealth can be accumulated on the most tax-favorable basis inside a qualified plan or IRA.

Example. An individual has retired at age 60 in 1998 with $750,000 in a 401(k) plan. If the individual takes a lump-sum distribution in 1998, it will not be subject to the 15 percent excise tax. Using 1998 rates and five-year income averaging, the approximate federal tax on the distribution would be $211,888, or 28.25 percent of the distribution. The net amount left for investment would be:

Taxable distribution:	$ 750,000
Taxes:	− 211,888
Net after taxes:	$ 538,112

If this is invested at 6 percent (after taxes and assuming the individual has other resources to live on), the net accumulation in 25 years (at age 85) would be:

Net after taxes:	$ 538,112
Accumulation factor (6% interest per year for 25 years):	× 4.29187
	$2,309,507

If this individual left the funds in the 401(k) until attainment of age 70½ and then started taking distributions over her single life expectancy, the net after-tax accumulation at age 85 would be $2,532,335. This assumes that tax rates increase from their present level to 40 percent by age 70½. Over $200,000 more is available to this individual by keeping the funds within a qualified plan until age 70½.

18 Reporting and Disclosure

The Employment Retirement Income Security Act of 1974 (ERISA) details the various reporting and disclosure requirements for qualified plans. Title I contains the Department of Labor (DOL) requirements, which are applicable to all employee benefit plans. Title II contains the Internal Revenue Service (IRS) reporting requirements, which are applicable to all tax-qualified plans, including 401(k) plans. Title IV contains the Pension Benefit Guaranty Corporation (PBGC) reporting requirements, which are generally not applicable to 401(k) plans. This chapter discusses the IRS and DOL reporting requirements for 401(k) plans, as well as the requirements for providing information to participants.

IRS AND DOL FORM 5500 REPORTING

Q 18:1 Who is responsible for reporting information to the IRS and the DOL?

The plan administrator who is designated in the plan document is responsible for IRS and DOL reporting. If the plan document does not designate a plan administrator, the plan sponsor or person responsible for the control, disposition, or management of plan assets must handle the reporting. [ERISA § 3(16)(A); Treas Reg § 1.414(g)-1(b)(4)]

Q 18:2 What is the basic IRS reporting requirement?

The 5500 series (5500, 5500-C/R, or 5500-EZ) must be filed for each year in which the plan has assets. [IRC § 6058] If the plan has 100 or more participants, Form 5500 should be filed. If the plan covers a sole owner, a sole owner and spouse, or only partners in a partnership, then Form 5500-EZ may be filed. [IRS Ann 86-125] Form 5500-EZ is not available to businesses that are members of controlled groups, affiliated service groups, or groups that employ leased employees. For other plans with fewer than 100 participants, the C portion of Form 5500-C/R is completed in the first year of the plan, once every three years thereafter, and in the final year. The R portion of the form is a brief registration statement filed in the interim years. [DOL Reg § 2520.103-1(c)] However, the C portion may be filed in any year, which would begin a new three-year cycle.

Q 18:3 What are the exceptions to the basic reporting rules?

If a plan has between 80 and 120 participants, it is only necessary to file what was filed in the previous year. [DOL Reg § 2520.103-1(d)] Thus, a plan with 110 participants that filed Form 5500-C/R for the last plan year may file Form 5500-C/R for the current plan year, instead of Form 5500. If a plan is eligible to file Form 5500-EZ, no reporting is necessary while plan assets are less than $100,000. All plans of the employer must be aggregated for purposes of the $100,000 limit. [IRS Ann 90-16] Beginning in 1995, once a plan files with over $100,000 in assets, it must continue to file even if assets drop below $100,000.

Q 18:4 Is there an audit requirement?

Yes. A certified public accountant or licensed public accountant must conduct an audit of the plan's financial statements and schedules. [ERISA § 103(a)(3)(A)] The accountant must not have a financial interest in the plan or the plan sponsor, and the audit must express an opinion on the financial statements and schedules, as well as the accounting principles and practices used by the plan. [DOL Reg § 2520.103-1(b)(5)] Plans with fewer than 100 participants are exempt from this requirement, although there have been congressional efforts to eliminate this exemption. [DOL Reg § 2520.103-1(b)] In addition, any plan that qualifies for filing Form 5500C/R is also exempt from the audit requirement. [DOL Reg §§ 2520.104-46(d), 2520.104-41]

The opinion of the auditor need not extend to any statement or information prepared and certified by a bank or similar institution or an insurance carrier. [DOL Reg § 2520.103-8] This exemption is not available for financial statements prepared by securities brokerage firms. [DOL Adv Op 93-21A]

Q 18:5 What schedules are attached to the 5500 series?

• *Schedule A, Insurance Information* contains information about insurance products used in the funding of the plan. These products include individual life insurance or annuity contracts, as well as group annuity or deposit administration contracts. Information disclosed on Schedule A includes premiums paid during the policy year, commissions paid to insurance agents, and financial information for group contracts. Schedule A does not need to be completed if the employer is filing Form 5500-EZ.

• *Schedule P, Annual Return of Fiduciary of Employee Benefit Trust,* is an optional form that may be filed by every trustee of a qualified plan. Filing this form starts the running of the statute of limitations for the taxable year of the trust. [IRC § 6501] The statute of limitations will run for both the filing of Form 5500 and any prohibited transactions disclosed on Form 5500. If problems with the Form 5500 or disclosed prohibited transactions are not acted upon by the IRS or the DOL before the statute of limitations expires, the employer should not be penalized. An employer who is not required to file Form 5500-EZ because plan assets are less than $100,000 may wish to consider filing Form 5500-EZ and Schedule P, since starting

the statute of limitations running could diminish the tax consequences to the employer if the IRS later retroactively disqualifies the
plan. Schedule P also satisfies the Section 6033(a) requirement that
a qualified trust file an annual report.

• *Schedule SSA, Annual Registration Statement Identifying Separated Participants with Deferred Vested Benefits,* is filed for each
plan year in which one or more participants with deferred vested
rights separates from service. This registration statement is for-
warded by the IRS to the Social Security Administration. Then,
in the year in which the participant becomes entitled to receive
the benefits of the plan, the Social Security Administration notifies the participant that benefits are due. [IRC § 6057; Treas Reg
§ 301.6057-1] Failure to file the SSA may result in a penalty of $1 per
day of delinquency for each participant, up to a maximum of
$5,000. [IRC § 6652(d)(1)]

• *Schedule C, Service Provider and Trustee Information,* is filed if
a plan is required to file Form 5500 and if any service provider receives more than $5,000 during the plan year. [ERISA § 103(c)]
Service providers include auditors, contract administrators, investment managers, recordkeepers, and trustees. If any of the service
providers have been terminated during the plan year, the reason for
the change must be disclosed on Schedule C.

• *Schedule E, ESOP Annual Information,* is filed for any employee stock ownership plan (ESOP). This form also applies to an
ESOP permitting elective contributions. The form has a number of
questions about ESOP loans and dividends and requests a list of the
classes of stock owned by the ESOP. [IRC § 6047(e)]

• *Schedule G, Financial Schedules,* is an optional means of providing information that may be required by item 27 of Form 5500.

If the plan's assets are held in a bank's common or collective fund
or an insurance carrier's pooled separate account, the 5500 filing
should include either a copy of the annual statement of assets and
liabilities of the account or trust or certification that the plan administrator has received a copy of the statement and that the bank or insurance carrier has filed the statement directly with the DOL. [DOL
Reg §§ 2520.103-3, 2520.103-4] Currently, assets held by any of
these entities are not subject to the audit requirement. However,
this exception has come under attack and may be eliminated.

Q 18:6 What revisions have been proposed for the Form 5500 series?

In September of 1997, the DOL announced proposed revisions to the Form 5500 series filings. Originally, the proposal was to take effect for 1998 plan years (with filings beginning in 1999). However, as the result of comments received, the DOL announced in February of 1998 that the revised forms would not take effect until 1999 plan years (with filings beginning in 2000).

The proposed revision was developed jointly by the DOL, IRS, and PBGC with an aim of simplifying filings and allowing for more efficient handling of the filings by the government agencies. The current Form 5500 and Form 5500-C/R are to be combined into a single one page Form 5500, which will act as a registration form for the filing and a checklist of which schedules are being attached. Financial information that had appeared on Form 5500 or Form 5500-C will appear on the newly designed Schedules FIN (Financial Information) and FIN-SP (Financial Information—Small Plan).

Other new schedules include Schedule PEN (Pension Plan Information) and Schedule Q (Qualified Pension Plan Coverage Information). Existing schedules that are being revised include Schedule A (Insurance Information), Schedule C (Service Provider Information), and Schedule G (Financial Transactions). Where applicable, Schedule G will no longer be optional. Schedule E (ESOP Annual Information), Schedule P (Trust Fiduciary Information), and Schedule SSA (Separated Participants with Deferred Vested Benefits) are not expected to be revised.

The revisions do not address Form 5500-EZ.

Q 18:7 What is the due date for filing the Form 5500 series?

The plan must file the Form 5500 series and accompanying schedules by the last day of the seventh month following the close of the plan year. [Treas Reg § 301.6058-1(a)(4)] An extension of 2½ months may be obtained by filing Form 5558 before the due date of the Form 5500 series. As an alternative, Form 5500 may be automatically extended (without filing Form 5558) for 2½ months if the following requirements are met:

1. The employer maintaining the plan has obtained an extension for filing its federal tax return; and

2. The plan year coincides with the employer's taxable year.

In this case, it would only be necessary to attach a copy of the federal tax return extension to the Form 5500 filing.

Q 18:8 What are the penalties for late filing of the Form 5500 series?

The DOL has authority to assess penalties of up to $1,000 per day. [ERISA § 502(c)(2)] The penalty period begins from the due date of filing, regardless of any extensions obtained, and generally continues to the date a satisfactory return is filed. The penalty should reflect the materiality of the failure and should also take into account the willfulness of the failure and the good faith and diligence exercised by the plan administrator. [DOL Reg § 2560.502(c)-2] This penalty applies to plan years beginning on or after January 1, 1988.

The IRS may assess a penalty of $25 per day up to $15,000. The penalty begins to run on the due date of the return. If an extension has been filed, the penalty begins to run on the extended due date. It applies to plan years beginning on or after September 2, 1974. [IRC § 6652(e)]

Q 18:9 What is the DOL's current enforcement policy?

In the Federal Register, April 27, 1995, the DOL announced its Delinquent Filer Voluntary Compliance (DFVC) Program for late filers or nonfilers of Form 5500 returns. Under the program, plan administrators who wish to file previously unfiled reports due for 1988 and thereafter can do so during a grace period that began April 27, 1995. The DOL intends the DFVC program to be of indefinite duration. The penalty under DFVC is $50 per day. For returns filed within 12 months of a due date, the maximum penalty is $2,500 for Form 5500 filers and $1,000 for 5500-C/R filers. If the return is more than 12 months late, the maximums are $5,000 and $2,000, respectively. Plan administrators who fail to take advantage of the grace period and/or fail to file timely reports in the future may be assessed a penalty of $300 per day up to an annual maximum of $30,000. Once a plan administrator has been notified of a failure to file, DFVC is no longer available. IRS late filing penalties continue to apply in full to DFVC filers. Further information on DFVC can be obtained from the DOL by calling (202) 214-8776.

Q 18:10 Are incomplete filings subject to these penalties?

Yes. An annual report that has been rejected for lack of material information will be treated as having not been filed. Material information is defined as information necessary to process, verify, or analyze the annual report. However, under the DOL rules, once the plan administrator is notified that a filing has been rejected for lack of material information, it has 45 days in which to cure the problem by filing a satisfactory report. If such a report is filed, no penalty will be assessed. [DOL Reg § 2560.502(c)-2(b)(3)]

Failure of an insurer to provide timely Schedule A information will not excuse a late filing. The proper procedure is to complete and file Schedule A to the extent possible, noting the deficiencies, the name of the insurance carrier, and the steps being taken to secure adequate information. Upon receipt of the missing information, an amended return should be filed.

Although the regulations do not specify what a plan administrator should do in the event an employer or other person fails to provide necessary information, it makes sense to follow a similar procedure.

Q 18:11 May late filing penalties be appealed to the DOL?

Yes. Under DOL rules, the plan administrator has 30 days from the date it is served with a notice of assessment in which to file a statement of reasonable cause. It must be a written statement setting forth all the facts alleged to support a claim of reasonable cause and must declare that the statement is being made under penalty of perjury. [DOL Reg § 2560.502(c)-2(e)]

The DOL will take into account the degree of willfulness involved and any facts indicating good faith and diligence on the part of the plan administrator. The DOL penalty period will be delayed from the day after the plan administrator receives notice of intent to assess a penalty until the day after the DOL serves the plan administrator with its notice of determination on the reasonable cause submission.

Q 18:12 May late filing penalties be appealed to the IRS?

Yes. The IRS rules also contain a reasonable-cause exception. The IRS clearly recognizes as reasonable cause filing in the wrong district, reliance on erroneous information provided by an IRS employee, serious illness or death of the taxpayer or someone in the immediate family, unavoidable absence of the taxpayer, destruction by fire or casualty of the taxpayer's business records, or failure of the IRS to provide assistance by means of blank forms or advice following a written or in-person request by the taxpayer. If none of the above situations applies, the standard will be whether a reasonable person of ordinary prudence and intelligence would consider that the facts show a reasonable cause for delay and clearly indicate no willful intent to disobey the filing requirement. The IRS does not have express authority to waive only a portion of the penalty. [IRM-Administration, 7(10)91.3; IRS, DOL, and PBGC Revision of Annual Information Return/Reports, 54 Fed Reg § 8631 (Mar 1, 1989)]

Q 18:13 Who is responsible for payment of the penalties?

The DOL penalty is assessed against the plan administrator. [DOL Reg § 2560.502(c)-2(a)] The IRS penalty is assessed against the plan administrator or employer. [Treas Reg § 301.6652-3(a)(3)] In both cases, the penalty is the personal liability of the plan administrator or employer and therefore is not deductible from plan assets as an administrative expense.

Q 18:14 Are there any criminal penalties for failure to file annual reports?

Yes. Criminal penalties may be imposed for willful violations of the reporting requirements: $5,000 for an individual and $100,000 for any other type of entity. [ERISA § 501] In addition, one year's imprisonment could be imposed. The penalty for making false statements is a $10,000 fine, five years' imprisonment, or both.

Q 18:15 Where should the Form 5500 series forms be filed?

The annual report should be filed with the appropriate Internal Revenue Service Center listed below.

If the principal office of the plan sponsor or the plan administrator is located in:	*Use this Internal Revenue Service Center address:*
Connecticut, Delaware, District of Columbia, Foreign Address, Maine, Maryland, Massachusetts, New Hampshire, New Jersey, New York, Pennsylvania, Puerto Rico, Rhode Island, Vermont, or Virginia	Holtsville, NY 00501-0044
Alabama, Alaska, Arkansas, California, Florida, Georgia, Hawaii, Idaho, Louisiana, Mississippi, Nevada, North Carolina, Oregon, South Carolina, Tennessee, or Washington	Atlanta, GA 39901-0044
Arizona, Colorado, Illinois, Indiana, Iowa, Kansas, Kentucky, Michigan, Minnesota, Missouri, Montana, Nebraska, New Mexico, North Dakota, Ohio, Oklahoma, South Dakota, Texas, Utah, West Virginia, Wisconsin, or Wyoming	Memphis, TN 37501-0024
All Form 5500-EZ filers	Memphis, TN 37501-0024

The IRS is responsible for forwarding the information to the DOL and the Social Security Administration.

Q 18:16 Can Form 5500 be filed electronically?

Yes. Qualified tax return filers can file Forms 5500, 5500-C/R, or 5500-EZ and related schedules on magnetic tapes, floppy disks, or electronically. Plans using this method must also file IRS Form 8453-E. If magnetic or electronic media are being used to file, then Form 8453-E should be sent to the following address:

Internal Revenue Service
Attention: EFU (EPMF)
Stop 37
P.O. Box 30309, A.M.F.
Memphis, TN 38130

SPECIAL FILING ISSUES

Q 18:17 What filing is required of a plan that is merging, consolidating, or transferring assets?

Form 5310A must be filed with the IRS for some plans involved in a transfer of assets or liabilities, or any merger or consolidation. The filing is due no later than 30 days prior to the date of the transfer. [IRS § 6058(b)] The penalty for failure to file is $25 per day, with a maximum penalty of $15,000. [IRC §§ 6058, 6652(c)] No filing is required if the transaction involves plans of the same type (i.e., two or more defined contribution plans, or two or more defined benefit plans) and the requirements of Treasury Regulation Section 1.414(1) are met.

Q 18:18 What filing is required of a plan that is terminating?

No special filing is required. The plan sponsor must indicate on the Form 5500 series filing that it is a final return. It is possible to get an IRS determination that a plan is qualified upon termination. This is done by filing IRS Form 5310 and accompanying Form 6088. Requesting an IRS determination may involve some delay in the termination process, and it does not prevent the IRS from auditing the plan or disqualifying it for years prior to the termination. It is a procedure that is most often used when large account balances are rolled or transferred to an IRA or another qualified plan. An IRS determination in this circumstance provides some assurance that the transfer or rollover will be considered a nontaxable event.

Q 18:19 What filing is required to notify the IRS of a change in plan status?

If a plan changes its name or if the name or address of the plan administrator changes, the IRS must be notified on the 5500 series filing for the year the change occurred. [IRC § 6057(b)] Failure to comply with this rule may result in a penalty of $1 per day of delinquency, up to a maximum of $1,000. [IRC § 6652(d)(2)]

Q 18:20 What filing is required to report excise taxes?

Form 5330, Return of Excise Taxes Related to Employee Benefit Plans, is filed to report any prohibited transactions or excise taxes.

Among the events reported on Form 5330 are prohibited transactions, nondeductible contributions, excess contributions to 401(k) plans, and certain ESOP dispositions. The penalty tax is computed and should be remitted when the form is filed. The due date, generally, is the same date for filing the Form 5500 series. However, in the case of 401(k) excess contributions, Form 5330 is due on the last day of the fifteenth month after the close of the plan year. A separate Form 5558 must be filed to request an extension of time for filing Form 5330, and an estimated excise tax payment should accompany it.

Q 18:21 What other reports does the DOL require?

Prior to August 5, 1997, in addition to the Form 5500 series, the DOL has required that the following reports be prepared:

1. Summary plan descriptions;
2. Summary of material modifications; and
3. Supplementary or terminal reports.

[ERISA § 101(a)]

Plans that are exempt from Title I (plans covering only owners or sole owner and spouse) are not required to prepare the DOL reports. [DOL Reg §§ 2510, 3.(b) and (c)]

Effective August 5, 1997, the Taxpayer Relief Act of 1997 (TRA '97) eliminated the requirement to file summary plan descriptions and summaries of material modifications with the DOL. These documents need only be provided to the DOL upon request.

SUMMARY PLAN DESCRIPTION (SPD)

Q 18:22 What is a *summary plan description* (SPD)?

A *summary plan description* (SPD) describes the provisions of the plan as well as the participants' rights under the plan. The SPD must be written in a style and format that is comprehensible to the average participant. The level of comprehension and education of the typical plan participant should be taken into account. Technical jargon should be avoided, as well as long, complex sentences.

Clarifying examples and illustrations, clear cross-references, and a table of contents should be included. [DOL Reg § 2520.102-2]

Q 18:23 What types of information must be included in the SPD?

The SPD must provide the following information:

1. The type of plan;
2. The identification number of the plan;
3. The responsible fiduciaries;
4. A description of the eligibility, vesting, and benefit accrual features;
5. A description of the break-in-service rules;
6. The plan's normal retirement age;
7. The plan's provisions describing any conditions that must be met before a participant is eligible to receive benefits;
8. If the plan provides joint and survivor benefits, any requirements necessary to reject these benefits;
9. Any circumstances under which benefits may be denied, lost, or forfeited;
10. The sources of contributions to the plan and the method by which the contribution is calculated;
11. The funding media used for the accumulation of assets;
12. The procedures to be used in making a claim for benefits; and
13. A statement of ERISA rights.

[ERISA § 102(b)]

Q 18:24 Are there any special requirements if participants do not speak English?

If a significant number of participants are literate only in the same non-English language, the plan administrator must attach a notice to the English-language SPD. This notice, written in the non-English language common to these participants, must offer assistance to participants in their own language. The assistance offered must include the name of a contact at the office of the plan administrator. This requirement is applicable in the following situations:

1. If the plan covers fewer than 100 participants and at least 25 percent of all plan participants are literate only in the same non-English language; or

2. If the plan covers 100 or more participants and the lesser of:

   a. 500 or more participants, or

   b. 10 percent or more of all plan participants are literate only in the same non-English language.

[DOL Reg § 2520.102-2(c)]

It is interesting to note that the DOL regulations do not address the issue of participants who are illiterate.

Q 18:25 Who is entitled to receive an SPD?

All plan participants and beneficiaries entitled to receive benefits must receive an SPD. [ERISA § 102(a)(1)]

Q 18:26 What is the timing for receipt of the SPD?

The SPD must be distributed no later than 120 days after the plan becomes subject to the reporting and disclosure requirements of Title I of ERISA. If a new plan does not become effective until the IRS issues a favorable determination letter, then the SPD must be distributed within 120 days following receipt of the favorable determination letter. [DOL Reg § 2520.104a-2(a)]

Future participants must receive an SPD within 90 days after becoming participants. In the case of beneficiaries entitled to death benefits, the SPD must be received within 90 days after commencement of benefits. [DOL Reg § 2520.104b-2(a)]

Q 18:27 Should the SPD be filed with the DOL?

No. The Taxpayer Relief Act of 1997 eliminated the requirement to file the SPD with the DOL. The SPD must be made available to the DOL upon request. [TRA '97 § 1503]

Q 18:28 How should the SPD be distributed to participants?

The plan administrator must be reasonably sure that participants and beneficiaries actually receive the SPD. The SPD may be hand-delivered at the workplace or mailed using first-class mail. If second- or third-class mail is used, return and forwarding postage should be guaranteed and address correction requested. Any returns should be sent back by first-class mail or personally delivered at the workplace.

Another option is to include the SPD as a special insert in a company periodical or publication, if the distribution list is current and comprehensive. A prominent notice should be placed on the front page of the periodical advising readers that the issue contains important information about rights under the plan. The notice should also advise the reader that the SPD should be read and retained for future reference.

It is not acceptable merely to place copies of the material in a location frequented by plan participants. [DOL Reg § 2520.104b-1(b)(1)]

Q 18:29 When should an SPD be updated?

If the plan has been amended, an updated SPD should be provided no later than five years after the date of the most recent SPD. There is a 210-day grace period to complete the updated SPD. [DOL Reg § 2520.104b-1(b)(1)]

If the plan has not been amended, an updated SPD should be provided no later than ten years after the date of the most recent SPD. There is also a 210-day grace period for the completion of this updated SPD. [DOL Reg § 2520.104b-2(b)(2)]

SUMMARY OF MATERIAL MODIFICATIONS (SMM)

Q 18:30 When must participants be notified of any changes in the plan through a summary of material modifications (SMM)?

A summary of material modifications (SMM) must be provided to participants and beneficiaries within 210 days after the close of the plan year in which the sponsor adopts the amendment. [DOL Reg § 2520.104a-4] The definition of *material* cannot be found in ERISA or the regulations. However, the general view is that any amendment that changes the information found in the SPD is material and must be disclosed in the SMM.

An SMM does not need to be prepared if an updated SPD is

prepared and distributed within 210 days after the close of the plan year in which a material modification occurred. [DOL Reg § 2520.104b-3(b)]

Q 18:31 What information must be provided in the SMM?

The SMM has no prescribed format. Like the SPD, the information must be in simple, understandable language comprehensible to the average participant. [DOL Reg § 2520.104b-3(b)]

Q 18:32 What are the consequences of failing to provide participants with an SPD or SMM on a timely basis?

No specific penalty applies for failing to provide participants with an SPD or SMM on a timely basis. However, when participants are not provided with this information, a court may hold them not bound to the terms of the SPD or SMM.

Q 18:33 What are the benefits of including a disclaimer in the SPD?

The SPD is only an outline of the governing plan document and as such does not contain all the terms and conditions affecting the operation of the plan. Most SPDs contain a disclaimer stating that the larger plan document is the controlling authority and should be consulted as an aid to interpreting the SPD. This disclaimer is useful in situations where there may be a conflict between the SPD or SMM and the plan document. However, use of the disclaimer will not protect the plan from liability in all situations where such a conflict exists. The best protection is to make sure that SPDs are accurate and that any changes that may affect participants' rights or benefit amounts are communicated in a timely fashion in an SMM.

SUMMARY ANNUAL REPORT (SAR)

Q 18:34 What must be included in a *summary annual report* (SAR)?

The basic information provided in the summary annual report (SAR) must include:

1. The name of the plan and employer identification number (EIN);

2. The period covered by the annual report;

3. A basic financial statement of the plan; and

4. A notice advising the participant that a copy of the full annual report is available on request, that the individual may obtain additional information regarding the annual report, and that the individual may inspect the annual report at a designated location of the employer or at the DOL.

[DOL Reg § 2520.104b-10(d)(3)]

An SAR must be furnished annually to each participant.

Q 18:35 Is the SAR required for plans that file Form 5500-C/R?

Yes. However, in a year in which the R portion of the form is completed, the participant need only receive a copy of the Form 5500-C/R with a notice that the participant may request a copy of Schedule A and has the right to inspect the documents at a designated location of the employer or at the DOL. [DOL Reg § 2520.104b-10(d)]

Q 18:36 What if the plan has non-English speaking participants?

As in the case of the SPD requirements (see Q 18:24), notice that assistance is available must be provided in the non-English language. [DOL Reg § 2520.104b-10(e)]

INDIVIDUAL PARTICIPANT STATEMENTS

Q 18:37 Must a participant receive an annual statement of his or her account balance in the 401(k) plan?

No. The DOL requires only that the plan administrator furnish annual statements of account balances to participants and beneficiaries who submit a written request for information regarding their account balances and vested status in the plan. [ERISA § 105(a)]

From a practical standpoint, administrators of 401(k) plans will provide such information on an automatic basis at least annually. If participants are furnished this information on an annual basis, the plan administrator is not obligated to respond to written requests from participants for this information. [DOL Prop Reg § 2520.105-2(a)(6)]

Q 18:38 Must a terminated participant receive a statement of his or her account balance in the 401(k) plan?

Yes. The plan administrator must furnish a benefit statement within 180 days after the close of the plan year in which the participant terminates employment. If the participant has no nonforfeitable benefits under the plan, a statement of nonvested status must be provided. [DOL Prop Reg § 2520.105-2(b)]

Q 18:39 What other documents may a participant request?

The participant may request a copy of the latest annual report, terminal report, collective bargaining agreements, trust agreements, or any other document under which the plan is established or operated. [ERISA § 104(b)(2)]

Q 18:40 May the plan administrator charge for providing the participant with requested reports or documents?

The plan administrator may not charge participants or beneficiaries for providing the SPD, updated SPD, SAR, SMM, or individual benefit statements. However, the plan administrator may impose a reasonable charge (for actual costs incurred) of up to 25 cents per page for furnishing additional copies of the SPD, updated SPD, or SMM, or for requested copies of the latest annual report, terminal report, collective bargaining agreements, trust agreements, or any other document under which the plan is established or operated. [DOL Reg § 2520.104b-30]

Q 18:41 What is the time limit for responding to a participant's request for information?

A plan administrator must supply information required to be disclosed under ERISA within 30 days of when a request for the information is received. [ERISA § 502(c)(1)]

Q 18:42 What are the consequences of failing to provide requested information in a timely manner?

The plan administrator may be required to pay the requesting participant an amount up to $100 per day from the date of the request. This penalty will not be imposed if the reason for delay is beyond the control of the plan administrator. [ERISA § 502(c)]

USE OF ELECTRONIC TECHNOLOGY

Q 18:43 What is meant by *paperless administration*?

Paperless administration refers to a system in which information is prepared, stored, and communicated in electronic form instead of on paper. In light of various technological advances and the growth of computer use, plan administrators are experiencing the evolution of paperless administration. To some extent, paperless administration is currently accomplished though the use of interactive voice response (IVR) systems, kiosks, personal computers, and the Internet and intranets.

Various modes of electronic communication allow participants and beneficiaries to access benefit information at times convenient to them. In some cases, paperless administration can lead to significant cost savings for plan sponsors by reducing costly paper flow and errors and increasing plan participation.

Q 18:44 What are some of the legal issues associated with paperless administration?

Although the use of electronic communication has great potential, plan sponsors must consider the legal implications of paperless administration. There are three main legal issues:

1. Written consent and notification requirements;

2. Satisfying disclosure requirements under ERISA; and

3. Security of participant transactions and confidentiality of personal information.

Q 18:45 What are issues that arise from ERISA disclosure requirements?

When a plan administrator is required by ERISA to furnish materials either by direct operation of law or on individual request, the administrator must use measures reasonably calculated to ensure actual receipt by plan participants and beneficiaries. Material required to be furnished must be sent by a method likely to result in full distribution. In-hand delivery to an employee at his or her work site is acceptable. It is not acceptable merely to place copies of the material in a location frequented by plan participants. [DOL Reg § 2520.104b-1(b)(1)]

Presumably, the disclosure requirements were intended to ensure actual receipt of, and continuous access to, plan information by participants and beneficiaries. It should follow that disclosure of such material electronically would be permitted as long as those goals are satisfied.

Q 18:46 What guidance did the DOL recently release concerning the use of electronic technologies for complying with ERISA's disclosure requirements?

On January 28, 1999, the DOL published guidance on the use of electronic technologies for satisfying ERISA's disclosure requirements. The proposed rules establish a safe harbor method for furnishing summary plan descriptions, summary of material modifications, and summary annual reports using electronic media. The disclosure requirements are generally deemed satisfied if:

1. The administrator takes appropriate and necessary measures to ensure that the system for furnishing documents results in actual receipt by participants of transmitted information and documents (e.g., uses return-receipt electronic mail feature or conducts periodic reviews or surveys to confirm receipt of transmitted information);

2. Electronically delivered documents are prepared and furnished in a manner consistent with ERISA's applicable style, format, and content requirements;

3. Each participant is provided notice, through electronic means or in writing, apprising the participant of the document(s) to be furnished electronically, the significance of the document (e.g., the document describes changes in the benefits provided by the plan), and the participant's rights to request and receive, free of charge, a paper copy of each such document; and

4. Upon request of any participant, the administrator furnishes, free of charge, a paper copy of any document delivered to the participant through electronic media.

The furnishing of documents through electronic media satisfies the disclosure requirements only with respect to participants:

1. Who have the ability at their work site to effectively access documents furnished in electronic form; and

2. Who have the opportunity at their work site to readily convert furnished documents from electronic form to paper form free of charge.

[64 Fed Reg 4505 (Jan 28, 1999)]

Q 18:47 What standards apply to the use of electronic media for the maintenance and retention of records required by ERISA?

ERISA contains requirements for the maintenance of records for reporting and disclosure purposes and for determining the benefits to which participants and beneficiaries are or may become entitled. [ERISA §§ 107, 209] The record maintenance and retention requirements of ERISA will be satisfied when using electronic media if the following is the case:

1. The electronic recordkeeping system has reasonable controls to ensure the integrity, accuracy, authenticity, and reliability of the records kept in electronic form;

2. The electronic records are maintained in reasonable order and in a safe and accessible place and in such manner as they may be readily inspected or examined (e.g., the recordkeeping system should be capable of indexing, retaining, preserving, retrieving, and reproducing the electronic records);

3. The electronic records are readily convertible into legible and readable paper copy as may be needed to satisfy reporting and disclosure requirements or any other obligation under Title 1 of ERISA;

4. The electronic recordkeeping system is not subject, in whole or in part, to any agreement or restriction that would, directly or indirectly, compromise or limit a person's ability to comply with any reporting and disclosure requirement or any other obligation under Title 1 of ERISA; and

5. Adequate records management practices are established and implemented (e.g., following procedures for labeling of electronically maintained or retained records, providing a secure storage environment, creating backup electronic copies and selecting an off-site storage location, observing a quality assurance program evidenced by regular evaluations of the electronic recordkeeping system including periodic checks of electronically maintained or retained records; and retaining paper copies of records that cannot be clearly, accurately, or completely transferred to an electronic recordkeeping system).

All electronic records must exhibit a high degree of legibility and readability when displayed on a video display terminal and when reproduced in paper form. Original paper records may be disposed of any time after they are transferred to an electronic recordkeeping system that complies with the above requirements, except such original records may not be discarded if they have legal significance or inherent value as original records such that an electronic reproduction would not constitute a duplicate record (e.g., notarized documents, insurance contracts, stock certificates, and documents executed under seal). [64 Fed Reg 4505 (Jan 28, 1999)]

19 Correcting 401(k) Plan Qualification Errors

The size of this book is an indication of how complicated it is to set up and administer a 401(k) plan properly. Even well-intentioned plan sponsors with good advisers can make inadvertent errors that could result in plan disqualification. The Internal Revenue Service (IRS) has, over the years, introduced a variety of programs designed to promote compliance without resorting to the sanction of disqualification. These programs have recently been consolidated into the Employee Plans Compliance Resolution System (EPCRS).

Q 19:1 What is the impact of plan disqualification?

The IRS, from its perspective, wants to promote full compliance with all its rules and regulations. The primary tool that it has for accomplishing this is the threat of plan disqualification, which results in loss of the employer's deduction for any contributions to the plan, taxation of trust income, and taxation of individual participants for contributions made on their behalf. The consequences of disqualifying a plan are both serious and far-reaching in that the tax bite is felt not only by the plan sponsor and key personnel, who may have been involved in the error that caused the disqualification, but also by all rank-and-file employees who participated in the plan. Perhaps for that reason, the IRS has typically disqualified fewer than 100 plans per year.

EMPLOYEE PLANS COMPLIANCE RESOLUTION SYSTEM (EPCRS)

Q 19:2 What is the *Employee Plans Compliance Resolution System* (EPCRS)?

Beginning in 1991, the IRS started introducing various programs designed to promote full compliance while using sanctions that fall short of the full tax impact of plan disqualification. These programs have now been consolidated and are referred to as the *Employee Plans Compliance Resolution System* (EPCRS). [Rev Proc 98-22, 1998-12 IRB 11]

Q 19:3 What programs does the IRS offer under EPCRS to avoid plan disqualification?

Under EPCRS, four IRS programs are available for solving plan qualification defects. They are as follows:

1. *Administrative Policy Regarding Self-Correction (APRSC)*;

2. *Voluntary Compliance Resolution (VCR)* Program;

3. *Walk-In Closing Agreement Program (Walk-In CAP)*—also known as *Voluntary CAP*; and

4. *Audit Based Closing Agreement Program (Audit CAP)*—also known as *Correction upon Audit, Examination CAP* or even *I Got Caught CAP*.

Q 19:4 What common features apply to all programs under EPCRS?

Common to all the programs under EPCRS is that a qualification failure is not considered corrected unless full correction is made with respect to all participants and beneficiaries and for all taxable years.

Q 19:5 What principles are to be taken into account in determining whether full correction is accomplished?

In determining whether full correction is accomplished, a plan must use a correction method that is reasonable and appropriate and that should restore the plan to the position that it would have been in had the qualification failure not occurred. Restoring the plan to this position also means the restoration of current and former participants and beneficiaries to the benefits and rights they would have had if the qualification failure had not occurred.

Q 19:6 Is there only one reasonable and appropriate correction method for a qualification failure?

No, there may be more than one such method. Whether a particular correction method is reasonable and appropriate should be determined taking into account relevant facts and circumstances and the following principles:

1. The correction method should, to the extent possible, resemble one already provided for in the Internal Revenue Code.

2. The correction method for a qualification failure relating to nondiscrimination should provide benefits to non-highly compensated employees.

3. The correction method should keep assets in the plan except to the extent the Internal Revenue Code permits corrective distributions to participants or beneficiaries or the return of assets to the employer.

4. The correction method should not violate any other qualification requirement.

Q 19:7 Are there any exceptions to full correction?

In general, no. The inconvenience and burden of full correction are generally insufficient to relieve the employer of its responsibility to fully correct qualification failures. But full correction may not be required in certain situations because it is unreasonable and not feasible. Such situations include the following:

1. Reasonable estimates of benefits are allowed if it is not possible to make a precise calculation or the probable difference between the approximate and precise amount of benefits is insignificant and the administrative cost of determining the precise amount of benefits would significantly exceed that difference.

2. Corrective distribution of benefits of $20 or less is not required if the cost of processing and delivering the distribution exceeds the amount of the distribution.

3. Corrective distributions are not required if the participant or beneficiary cannot be located.

ADMINISTRATIVE POLICY REGARDING SELF-CORRECTION (APRSC)

Q 19:8 What qualification defects are covered by the APRSC program?

The APRSC program is designed to cover qualification defects that arise from the failure to operate a plan in accordance with its terms. The APRSC program is not available to cure qualification issues arising from defects in the plan document (for example, a failure to amend for Tax Equity and Fiscal Responsibility Act of 1982 (TEFRA), Deficit Reduction Act of 1984 (DEFRA), or Retirement Equity Act of 1984 (REA)). It is also not available for qualification issues that arise because of a shift in demographics (for example, creating a problem with the minimum coverage rules under Internal Revenue Code Section 410(b)). Finally, the APRSC program cannot be used to correct operational failures that are egregious or that relate to the diversion of assets.

Q 19:9 Is there a deadline for correcting operational defects under the APRSC program?

It depends. For failures that are considered significant the operational defect must be corrected by the end of the second plan year following the plan year in which the defect arose. Failures treated as insignificant can be corrected after this deadline.

Q 19:10 What factors are considered in determining whether or not an operational failure is insignificant?

The factors to be considered include but are not limited to the following:

1. Whether other failures occurred during the period being examined;

2. The percentage of plan assets and contributions involved in the failure;

3. The number of years the failure occurred;

4. The number of participants affected versus the total number of participants;

5. The number of participants affected versus the total number of participants that could have been affected;

6. Whether correction was made within a reasonable time after the failure's discovery; and

7. The reason for the failure.

Q 19:11 Must a plan have a favorable IRS letter in order to take advantage of the APRSC program?

Yes. In order to correct significant operational failures the plan must have a favorable IRS letter. A favorable IRS letter is, in the case of an individually designed plan (including a volume submitter plan), a current favorable determination letter. Adopters of master or prototype plans and regional prototype plans will be considered to have favorable letters if the sponsors of these plans have received current favorable opinion or notification letters.

Q 19:12 Is there any other condition that must be met before the APRSC program can be used to correct an operational failure?

Yes. Prior to the defect, the plan must have had established practices and procedures (whether formal or informal) that were reasonably designed to promote and facilitate overall compliance but in which, because of an oversight or mistake in applying them or because of their inadequacy, operational violations occurred.

Q 19:13 Is the APRSC program available if the plan is being audited by the IRS?

It is available but, in general, the APRSC program can be used only to correct insignificant operational failures once the plan is being audited by the IRS.

Q 19:14 What procedures are used to take advantage of the APRSC program?

Except for insignificant defects, the APRSC program is designed to be initiated by the plan sponsor or the plan administrator, without IRS involvement, with respect to any plan eligible for the APRSC program.

Q 19:15 What is the cost of using APRSC?

No sanctions or penalties are payable to the IRS in connection with use of the APRSC program. The only cost to the plan sponsor is the cost of correcting the defect.

VOLUNTARY COMPLIANCE RESOLUTION (VCR) PROGRAM

Q 19:16 What qualification defects are covered by the VCR program?

The VCR program is designed to cover qualification defects that arise in the operation of a plan. Typical examples include failure to comply with the Section 415 limits, failure to make top-heavy minimum contributions, or failure to satisfy the ADP or ACP tests. VCR is not available to cure qualification issues arising from defects in the plan document (for example, failure to amend for TEFRA, DEFRA, and REA). It is also not available to cure any violations of the exclusive benefit rule (e.g., misuse or diversion of plan assets), or for egregious violations such as consistently covering only highly compensated employees.

Q 19:17 Is there a deadline for correcting operational defects under the VCR program?

No, there is no deadline. However, the VCR program is not available if the plan is being audited by the IRS.

Q 19:18 Must a plan have a favorable IRS letter in order to take advantage of the VCR program?

Yes, a favorable IRS letter is required.

Q 19:19 Must a plan have established practices and procedures in effect in order to utilize the VCR program?

No. In this respect it differs from the APRSC program.

Q 19:20 How does the standardized VCR program (SVP) differ from the regular VCR program?

The SVP program differs from the regular VCR program in that it currently applies to only seven types of operational errors. These are as follows:

1. Failure to make minimum top-heavy contributions;
2. Failure to meet the ADP test, ACP test, or multiple-use test;
3. Failure to distribute elective deferrals in excess of the Code Section 402(g) limit;
4. Exclusion of eligible employees from plan participation;
5. Violations of the Code Section 415(c) annual additions limit;
6. Failure to obtain spousal consent to a distribution; and
7. Violations of the Code Section 401(a)(9) minimum distribution rule.

SVP requires the employer to use a method specified in Appendix A of Revenue Procedure 98-22 to correct the violation. There is no option (as there is in the regular VCR program) to negotiate a method of correction.

Q 19:21 What procedures are used to take advantage of the VCR program?

The plan sponsor initiates the program by preparing an application to the IRS that contains all the information described in Section 12.03 of Revenue Procedure 98-22. Essentially, the plan sponsor must describe the defect and the correction and explain why the problem will not recur.

The IRS will respond to a VCR application with a compliance statement that addresses the operational failure and the terms of its correction and that contains the IRS's agreement not to disqualify the plan on account of the operational failure described in the compliance statement. Within 30 days after the statement is issued, a plan sponsor that agrees with the statement must send a signed acknowledgment letter to the IRS. If this acknowledgment is made, the plan sponsor has 150 days after the issuance of the compliance statement to correct the operational failure.

Q 19:22 What is the cost of using the VCR program?

The cost of using SVP is $350 for all plans. The cost of using the regular VCR program varies with the number of participants in the plan and the value of plan assets. For plans with no more than 1,000 participants, the fee is $500 if assets of the plan are no more than $500,000, and $1,250 if assets of the plan exceed $500,000. For plans with more than 1,000 but fewer than 10,000 participants, the application fee is $5,000. For plans with 10,000 or more participants, the application fee is $10,000. The fee must be paid by the sponsor and not by the plan or its participants.

In addition to paying these fees, the plan sponsor must fully correct all qualification defects for all years in which the disclosed defects occurred, not limited to the three-year period the IRS has to disqualify a plan under the statute of limitations.

Use of the VCR program will not provide the plan sponsor with relief from any excise taxes, nor is there any relief from ERISA's Title

I fiduciary conduct provisions. These factors must be considered in reviewing the decision to use VCR and in analyzing the costs involved.

WALK-IN CLOSING AGREEMENT PROGRAM (WALK-IN CAP)

Q 19:23 What qualification defects are covered by Walk-In CAP?

Walk-In CAP may be used by a plan sponsor to correct operational failures that are not eligible for correction under APRSC or VCR. It is also available to correct qualification issues that arise from defects in the plan document or from a demographic shift that leads to a failure to satisfy Code Section 410(b). Walk-In CAP is not available, however, for operational failures that relate to the diversion or misuse of plan assets. It is also not available if the plan is being audited by the IRS.

Q 19:24 What procedures are used to take advantage of the Walk-In CAP program?

Walk-In CAP is initiated by the plan sponsor with an application containing all the information described in Section 12.03 of Revenue Procedure 98-22. As with VCR, the plan sponsor must describe the defect and explain why the problem will not recur. If the plan sponsor agrees to correct the failures identified in its application, the IRS will enter into a closing agreement with the plan sponsor. The closing agreement, which is binding upon both the IRS and the plan sponsor, will provide that plan disqualification will not occur as a result of the defect described in the closing agreement.

Q 19:25 Can Walk-In Cap be used to correct an operational defect by a plan amendment that conforms the terms of the plan to its past operation?

Yes—under appropriate circumstances Revenue Procedure 98-22 indicates that a retroactive amendment is possible. The circumstances under which such amendments will be permitted will be fleshed out in future IRS guidance.

Q 19:26 What is the cost of using Walk-In CAP?

The fee for Walk-In CAP is determined in accordance with the table below. The table contains a graduated range of fees based on the number of participants in the plan. Each range includes a minimum amount (which is the VCR fee that would apply if the defect were handled under the VCR program—see Q 19:22), a maximum amount, and a presumptive amount. Factors described in Section 13.05(2) of Revenue Procedure 98-22 determine where the actual fee falls within each range.

Number of Participants	Fee Range	Presumptive Amount
10 or fewer	VCR fee to $4,000	$ 2,000
11 to 50	VCR fee to $8,000	4,000
51 to 100	VCR fee to $12,000	6,000
101 to 300	VCR fee to $16,000	8,000
301 to 1,000	VCR fee to $30,000	15,000
Over 1,000	VCR fee to $70,000	35,000

In addition to the IRS fee, the plan sponsor may need to pay amounts into the plan in order to correct the errors identified in the closing agreement.

AUDIT BASED CLOSING AGREEMENT PROGRAM (AUDIT CAP)

Q 19:27 Under what circumstances will Audit CAP be used?

Audit CAP is available to a plan sponsor if the qualification defect (other than an insignificant operational error that can be handled through APRSC) is discovered by the IRS during an audit. All defects that may be corrected under Walk-In CAP (see Q 19:23) may be corrected under Audit CAP. If the plan sponsor corrects the qualification failures identified by the IRS, pays a sanction, and enters into a closing agreement with the IRS, then the IRS will not disqualify the plan on account of the qualification defect.

Q 19:28 How is the amount of the Audit CAP sanction determined?

The amount of the sanction is a negotiated percentage of the full amount of the tax liability that would be due the IRS if the plan were disqualified for the years open under the statute of limitations (known as the *maximum payment amount*). In other words, it will include taxes based on the loss of the employer's deduction for plan contributions, taxes on trust earnings, taxes on individual employees for inclusion of plan contributions in their taxable compensation, and any penalties and interest that would accrue on any of these amounts. The negotiated percentage is to bear a reasonable relationship to the nature, extent, and severity of the failures and must not be excessive. Section 15.02 of Revenue Procedure 98-22 cites examples of the factors that will be taken into account in arriving at the negotiated percentage.

TABLE 19-1. Comparison of Programs under EPCRS

Feature	APRSC	VCR	Walk-in CAP	Audit CAP
Also known as	N/A	N/A	Voluntary CAP	Examination CAP
Defects subject to correction	**Program I:** Self-identified significant but nonegregious operational defects within last two years if plan has IRS letter **Program II:** Insignificant defects found by agent or employer (meeting most of seven factors)	Self-identified non-egregious operational defects if plan has IRS letter	Self-identified defects, generally in form or demographics	Defects found by agent
Available for operational defects that relate to the diversion or misuse of plan assets?	No	No	No	No
Available once an IRS audit has commenced?	Yes, but only under Program II	No	No	Yes
Must there have been policies and procedures in effect prior to the defect's occurring?	Yes	No	No	No

Correction	For all years make plan and participants whole; document correction but do not report to IRS	For all years make plan and participants whole (in a way subject to negotiation) within 150 days of compliance letter	For all years make plan and participants whole; may be able to amend plan to conform to operation under certain circumstances	For all years make plan and participants whole as required by IRS
Results in	IRS can second-guess correction on examination	Written compliance letter from IRS	Written closing agreement with IRS	Written closing agreement with IRS
Fee or sanction	None	User fee between $350 & $10,000 based on plan size	Sanction based on Rev. Proc. 98-22 table of presumed amounts and ranges	Negotiated sanction based on deduction on nonvested contributions, tax on trust, employee tax on vested contributions, and mitigating factors
Variation	N/A	Standard VCR Program (SVP) applies to seven listed types of errors with specified nonnegotiable correction methods (fee always $350)	N/A	N/A

20 Plan Terminations, Mergers, and Spin-offs

An employer may wish to terminate its 401(k) plan for a number of reasons, including the closing or selling of a business, a change in goals for the employer's benefit programs, or the establishment of a new plan. An employer may also wish to consolidate its plans, combine its plan with that of another employer, or divide a single plan into separate plans for subsidiaries or divisions. This section discusses how to accomplish those goals. It also discusses when an involuntary or partial termination of a plan will be considered to have occurred.

PLAN TERMINATIONS

Q 20:1 How is an employer's ability to terminate a 401(k) plan restricted?

Employers are generally free to terminate a 401(k) plan at any time, and the authority to terminate a plan is usually incorporated into the plan document. The only restriction on this freedom is the rule requiring a plan to be a permanent, not a temporary, program. (See chapter 2.) Under this rule, if a plan is terminated for any reason other than business necessity within a few years after it has taken effect, it may not be considered a qualified plan. [Treas Reg § 1.401-1(b)(2)] The regulation is silent as to what constitutes "a few years."

Q 20:2 How does an employer terminate its 401(k) plan?

The decision to terminate a plan is generally done through corporate resolution or other similar authorization. In a 401(k) plan, there is no requirement that participants be notified in advance of the termination, although employees may view the change more favorably if they are kept informed.

There is also no requirement to notify the Internal Revenue Service (IRS) or the Department of Labor (DOL) that the termination of a 401(k) plan is intended.

A single-employer plan may request an IRS determination that the plan is qualified at the time of termination by filing IRS Form 5310; multiemployer plans must use IRS Form 5303. The filing of a Form 5310 or 5303 will usually result in a delay of the plan termination process; therefore, it is not always an attractive option. It is used most frequently when there are large account balances that will be rolled over to an IRA or another qualified plan. In this circumstance, the delay involved may be worth the assurance that the money distributed will continue to be treated as nontaxable.

Regardless of whether an IRS determination is requested, the employer must continue filing annual reports for the plan until such time as all assets are distributed to participants. The annual report for the final year of the plan must indicate that it is the last year of filing. For employers with fewer than 100 participants, a Form 5500-C must be filed for the final year of the plan.

Q 20:3 What is the impact of a plan termination on participants' benefits in the plan?

When a plan is terminated, all benefits must become 100 percent vested as of the date of the termination. [IRC § 411(d)(3); Treas Reg § 1.411(d)-2(a)(1)] For example, even if a plan has a vesting schedule applied to its matching contributions so that a participant is not 100 percent vested until he or she has earned seven years of service, all funds held in a participant's matching account will become 100 percent vested at plan termination regardless of how many years of service have been earned.

Q 20:4 What is the date of termination for purposes of applying the 100 percent vesting rule?

Generally, an employer can dictate the date a plan is considered terminated. [Treas Reg § 1.411(d)-2(c)(3)] This information is usually contained in the resolution to terminate the plan.

Q 20:5 How do the nondiscrimination rules apply to plan termination?

The effect of any plan termination must be nondiscriminatory. [Treas Reg § 1.401(a)(4)-1(b)(4)] For example, a corporation may, in the course of winding down its business affairs, distribute benefits to terminated participants who have left the company in connection with the wind-down. If, after distributing benefits to non-highly compensated employees, the corporation then makes a discretionary profit sharing contribution to the few remaining employees, all of whom are highly compensated, the plan will violate the nondiscrimination rule.

Q 20:6 May benefits always be distributed when a plan terminates?

No. A 401(k) plan may not distribute elective contributions to participants upon plan termination if the employer maintains a successor plan. [Treas Reg § 1.401(k)-1(d)(3)]

Q 20:7 What is a *successor plan*?

Except as noted below, a *successor plan* is a defined contribution plan that exists at the time the 401(k) plan is terminated or within the 12-month period following the distribution of the 401(k) plan's assets. Employee stock ownership plans (ESOPs) and simplified employee pension plans (SEPs), however, are not considered successor plans. It is likely, too, that SIMPLE retirement accounts will not be considered successor plans. Any other defined contribution plan is not considered a successor plan if fewer than 2 percent of the employees eligible to participate in the 401(k) plan at the time of its termination are eligible to participate in such other defined contribution plan within 12 months before or after the 401(k) plan's termination. [Treas Reg § 1.401(k)-1(d)(3)]

Q 20:8 How must a distribution on plan termination be paid?

A distribution must be in the form of a lump-sum payment. (See Q 2:10.) [Treas Reg § 1.401(k)-1(d)(5)]

Q 20:9 When may a distribution of elective contributions be made on account of the sale or disposition of assets or subsidiaries?

Elective contributions may be distributed only if the seller maintains the 401(k) plan after the disposition. Also, the purchaser must not maintain the same 401(k) plan after the disposition. A purchaser is treated as maintaining the 401(k) plan of the seller if the purchaser adopts the 401(k) plan or if assets of the 401(k) plan are transferred to a plan of the purchaser. Assets of the 401(k) plan are not considered transferred to a plan of the purchaser if the assets are transferred as a result of a rollover contribution or an elective transfer under Treasury Regulations Section 1.411(d)-4, Q&A 3(b)(1). [Treas Reg § 1.401(k)-1(d)(4)(i)]

Q 20:10 Are there other requirements relating to the distribution of elective contributions on account of the sale or other disposition of assets or subsidiaries?

Yes. Distribution of elective contributions can be made only to participants who become employees of the purchaser. [Treas Reg § 1.401(k)-1(d)(4)(ii)] In addition, distribution must be made no later than the end of the second calendar year following the calendar year in which the disposition occurs. [Treas Reg § 1.401(k)-1(d)(4)(iii)] Finally, any distribution must be in the form of a lump-sum payment. A lump-sum payment is the distribution of the participant's account balance under the seller's 401(k) plan within a single taxable year of the participant. [Treas Reg § 1.401(k)-1(d)(5)]

Example. XYZ Company sponsors a 401(k) plan covering the employees of its two divisions, A and B. XYZ Company sells the assets of Division B on February 15, 1998. The 401(k) plan has until

December 31, 2000, to make lump-sum payments to those participants who were employees of Division B.

Q 20:11   What options does an employer have if benefits cannot be distributed upon plan termination?

If the employer cannot distribute plan assets, it will have to either continue the 401(k) plan or merge it into another plan. If the 401(k) plan is frozen (i.e., amended to eliminate all contributions), the employer must still file annual reports, keep the plan document up to date and in compliance with any changes in the law, and continue to make any top-heavy contributions (see chapter 13). These requirements make continuing a frozen plan an unattractive alternative for most employers.

An employer generally may not solve a distribution problem by purchasing annuity contracts for plan participants designed to pay benefits at a time when the successor plan rules would no longer apply. The optional form of benefit rules prevent an employer from eliminating any distribution options or features through the purchase of annuity contracts. [Treas Reg § 1.411(d)-4, Q&A 2(a)(3)(ii)] Since most annuity contracts do not carry with them all the distribution features available in a qualified plan, this option is not generally available to solve a distribution limitation in a 401(k) plan.

Q 20:12   What options does a plan administrator have if a participant cannot be located?

Unlocatable participants in a terminated plan, which is attempting to distribute all its assets, present a significant problem. An ongoing plan can forfeit benefits payable to an unlocatable participant as long as the plan provides for reinstatement of that benefit if a claim is later made. [Treas Reg § 1.411(a)-4(b)(6)] However, since a terminating plan cannot provide reinstatement rights, forfeiture does not appear to be an option that would be accepted by the IRS in a qualified plan.

The best solution to the problem is to locate the participant. If the person cannot be found through co-workers, family, or friends, there are other search services available. Local Social Security offices will assist in locating missing participants. The IRS offers a "Humane Locator Service," whereby it will attempt to notify missing participants that a benefit is due them. There are also commercial locator services available that will find missing persons for a fee.

If all efforts to locate a participant fail, there is no clear guidance on what the employer should do. The DOL and the IRS have suggested at various times that benefits of $5,000 or less can be distributed to a bank account in the name of the participant, and benefits in excess of $5,000 can be used to purchase an annuity contract in the name of the participant. However, as a practical matter, these options are usually not available since banks and annuity providers run into their own problems carrying assets for people who cannot be located. State escheat is another potential option and is usually governed by state statute. The DOL has stated publicly that in its view escheat is not an option because state escheat laws are preempted by Section 514(a) of the Employee Retirement Income Security Act of 1974 (ERISA). There appears to be judicial support for the department's position, at least in states where the funds turned over remain available to the participant. [Commonwealth Edison Co v Vega, Case No 98-2417 (7th Cir 1999)]

PARTIAL TERMINATION

Q 20:13 What is a *partial termination*?

A *partial termination* occurs when a group of employees who were covered by a plan are excluded by either plan amendment or severance from service with the employer. [Treas Reg § 1.411(d)-2(b)(1)]

Q 20:14 What is the effect of a partial termination?

If a plan is partially terminated, all affected participants become 100 percent vested in their accounts. [IRC § 411(d)(3); Treas Reg § 1.411(d)-2(a)(1)(i)] It should be noted that 100 percent vesting in a partial termination is required only for affected participants—that is, participants who were actually excluded or who separated from service in connection with the event. [Treas Reg § 1.411(d)-2(b)(3)]

Example. Company A sells off Division X, and a partial plan termination results. Only employees of Division X will be entitled to 100 percent vesting of their accounts; other employees of Company A who remain in the plan after the sale will be subject to the plan's regular vesting schedule.

Q 20:15 Are there plan events other than termination or partial termination that may require 100 percent vesting?

Yes. If a plan completely discontinues contributions, 100 percent vesting may be required. [Treas Reg § 1.411(d)-2(a)(1)(ii)] A temporary freezing of benefits, however, will generally not trigger 100 percent vesting. [Treas Reg § 1.411(d)-2(d)(1)]

Q 20:16 How does an employer decide when a partial termination has occurred?

It is often very difficult for an employer to determine whether a partial termination has occurred and, if it has, when it occurred. The general rule is that the existence of a partial termination is a facts-and-circumstances determination to be made by the Tax Commissioner. [Treas Reg § 1.411(d)-2(b)(1)] Some guidance has been developed over the years on this issue, but it still remains an individual determination. As a general guideline, if a significant percentage of employees are excluded from a plan in connection with a major corporate event, a partial termination may occur. [Rev Rul 72-439, 1972-2 CB 223; Rev Rul 73-284, 1973-2 CB 139; Weil v Terson Retirement Plan Comm, 577 F Supp 781 (SDNY), rev'd, 750 F 2d 10 (2d Cir 1984)]

The IRS has indicated that if more than 20 percent of participants turn over in a particular year, partial termination is a consideration, while if 50 percent or more turn over, partial termination is a strong possibility. [IRS Doc 6678 (dated April 1981) Explanation for Worksheet Form 6677, Plan Termination Standards] The IRS has also indicated that employees who leave voluntarily and not as a result of any employer-initiated action are not counted in deciding whether a partial termination has occurred. [GCM 39344 (Oct 16, 1984)]

If an employer wants to be sure that it has handled a partial termination or potential partial termination correctly, the only reliable method is to apply for an IRS determination on whether a particular set of facts constitutes a partial termination. For a 401(k) plan, this request is made using IRS Form 5300.

MERGERS AND SPIN-OFFS

Q 20:17 What is a *merger*?

A merger occurs whenever two or more plans are combined into a single plan. [Treas Reg § 1.414(l)-1(b)(2)] For example, if an employer maintains a profit sharing plan and a 401(k) plan and wishes to combine them into a single plan to save administrative costs, the plans would undergo a merger to achieve that result.

Q 20:18 What rules apply to the allocation of benefits in a merger?

When two or more defined contribution plans are merged, the following conditions must be met:

1. The sum of account balances in each plan as of the date of the merger must equal the fair market value of the entire plan's assets;

2. The assets of each plan must be combined to form the assets of the merged plan; and

3. Immediately after the merger, each participant in the surviving plan must have an account balance equal to the sum of the account balances the participant had in the plans immediately prior to the merger.

[Treas Reg § 1.414(l)-1(d)]

Q 20:19 What is a *spin-off*?

A *spin-off* is the splitting of a single plan into two or more plans. For example, if Corporation A sells Division 5 to Corporation B, that portion of Corporation A's plan covering the employees of Division 5 could be spun off to merge with a plan maintained by Corporation B. [Treas Reg § 1.414(l)-1(b)(4)]

Q 20:20 What rules apply to the allocation of assets in a spin-off?

If defined contribution plans undergo a spin-off, the following rules apply to the allocation of assets:

1. The sum of account balances for each participant in the resulting plans must equal the account balance for that participant in the plan before the spin-off; and

2. The assets in each plan immediately after the spin-off must equal the sum of account balances for all participants in that plan.

[Treas Reg § 1.414(l)-1(m)]

Q 20:21 What procedures are involved in a merger or spin-off?

A spin-off or merger transaction usually begins with a corporate resolution outlining how the transaction will occur. All plans involved in the transaction will have to be reviewed to determine what amendments are necessary, and a date must be selected for the transaction. The plans must undergo a valuation of assets and the allocation of all funds to participants on that date so that compliance with the rules discussed in Qs 20:18 and 20:20 can be determined.

No federal filing is required when a plan is merged. In a 401(k) plan, no notification to participants in advance of a merger or spin-off is required, although as a practical matter an employer may want to keep its employees informed. If plans are merging, the disappearing plan must file a final return (Form 5500 or 5500-C) in the year of the merger.

The plan sponsor need not request an IRS determination letter on a merged or spun-off plan, but if it wishes to do so, it can request the IRS's determination by filing IRS Form 5300 or 5307.

Q 20:22 What plan provisions should be reviewed when merging or spinning off plans?

A number of problems can arise in the context of a merger or spin-off when the plans involved do not contain identical provisions concerning benefits and other features. For example, if the plans involved have different vesting schedules or eligibility requirements or inconsistent plan years, amendments may have to be made to the merged or spun-off plan to ensure that participants do not lose valuable rights and are credited with appropriate levels of service in the resulting plan.

To the extent that the distribution options or other optional forms of benefits (see Qs 15:1, 15:10) in the involved plans are different, measures will have to be taken to ensure that no optional forms of benefits are eliminated or reduced as a result of the transaction. [Treas Reg § 1.411(d)-4, Q&A 2(a)(3)]

Example. Plan A, which permits immediate lump-sum distribution of benefits, is merged into Plan B, which requires deferral of any lump-sum payments until normal retirement age. Plan B will have to retain the right for participants in Plan A to take an immediate lump-sum distribution of benefits accrued up to the date of the merger.

Q 20:23 What special distribution concerns are involved in mergers or spin-offs of 401(k) plans?

If a 401(k) plan is merged into a non-401(k) plan and benefits are transferred in connection with that merger, care must be taken to ensure that elective contributions transferred to the merged plan do not become available for immediate distribution to active employees. The 401(k) regulations prevent an employer from avoiding the restriction on in-service withdrawals of elective contributions through the merger or transfer of benefits. [Treas Reg § 1.401(k)-1(d)(6)(iv)]

If a 401(k) plan is accepting transferred benefits from a non-401(k) plan, a key issue for review is whether the plan transferring benefits contains a qualified joint and survivor annuity requirement that is not contained in the 401(k) plan. The survivor annuity requirements also must survive any merger or transfer. [Treas Reg § 1.401(a)-20, Q&A 5]

Q 20:24 How can the problem of monitoring and harmonizing distribution options be avoided?

The problem of monitoring and harmonizing distribution options can be avoided by liberalizing the surviving plan so that it encompasses the most liberal distribution features of all the original plans. If this option is chosen, care must also be taken to preserve survivor annuity requirements, if applicable, as well as restrictions on in-service withdrawals of elective contributions.

Q 20:25 Is the IRS considering offering relief from distribution option concerns?

Yes. In Notice 98-29 [1998-22 IRB 8] the IRS requested comment on several proposals that would relieve surviving plans in a merger from the obligation to preserve all distribution options that were available in the disappearing plan. The DOL's current proposals include the option to maintain a lump sum and one extended-payment option, to be able to eliminate distribution options that are not utilized by participants, or to be able to eliminate any distribution option after a specified period of time.

Q 20:26 What special considerations are there when a merger or spin-off occurs in connection with a corporate acquisition or divestiture?

A merger or spin-off that occurs in connection with the purchase or sale of a company will often involve some consideration of whether the minimum coverage requirements will continue to be met after the transaction takes place. Employers are given some time to adjust to these changes through plan redesign or other methods. Under these rules, as long as each plan meets the minimum coverage requirements prior to the transaction, it will continue to be considered in compliance with these rules throughout the plan year in which the transaction takes place and in the following plan year. [IRC § 410(b)(6)(C)]

21 401(k) Plan Alternatives

A number of qualified and nonqualified arrangements may be used by plan sponsors or individuals as an alternative to a 401(k) plan. As discussed in chapter 1, an employer may not be eligible to set up a 401(k) plan for its employees and, in other cases, a 401(k) plan may not provide the desired benefit security for employees. For small employers interested in maximizing benefits or contributions for key employees, a 401(k) plan may not make sense.

Employees given the opportunity to participate in a 401(k) plan must weigh a number of factors and consider the alternatives. Depending on level of pay, a larger deferral might be available to them in an individual retirement arrangement (IRA). Specific features of the 401(k) plan can have an impact on an employee's decision as well: the level of employer matching contributions, availability of withdrawals or loans, and investment choices are all significant factors. Chapter 1 also considers whether the employee may view after-tax savings as a practical alternative to participating in a 401(k) plan.

This chapter explores a number of alternatives to 401(k) plans, discusses the availability of these plans to different types of employers, and presents the features of these alternatives, as well as their relative advantages and disadvantages. Not all the options are discussed here; traditional defined benefit and defined contribution plans are not addressed, since it is assumed that the reader is familiar with the traditional alternatives. At the end of each section, the discussed alternative is compared with a 401(k) plan. Table 21-6 compares the features of 401(k) plans with all the alternatives.

INDIVIDUAL RETIREMENT ARRANGEMENTS (IRAs)

Individual retirement arrangements (IRAs) were established by the Employee Retirement Income Security Act of 1974 (ERISA) to allow eligible employees to make deductible contributions that accumulate on a tax-deferred basis to be used for retirement benefits. Unlike a 401(k) plan or the other arrangements discussed in this chapter, an IRA may be set up by an individual. IRAs may also be sponsored by an employer, but it is far more likely that employees will set up their own IRAs. Originally, IRAs were available only to employees who did not participate in a qualified plan, but they were made available to all employees by the Economic Recovery Tax Act of 1981 (ERTA). The Tax Reform Act of 1986 (TRA '86), however, imposed significant restrictions on the availability and tax advantages of this arrangement. The Taxpayer Relief Act of 1997 (TRA '97) created an additional form of IRA (the Roth IRA), contributions to which are nondeductible but from which qualifying distributions are tax-free. The original form of IRA is now being called a traditional IRA.

For additional information on IRAs, see Panel Publishers' *Individual Retirement Account Answer Book* and *Roth IRA Answer Book*.

Traditional IRAs

Q 21:1 How much may an individual contribute to an IRA?

An individual may make a deductible traditional IRA contribution of as much as $2,000 annually. [IRC § 219(b)(1)] If contributions are made to a separate IRA for the individual's spouse, then as much as $4,000 in total may be contributed. Prior to 1997 this total amount was $2,250. However, if the individual (or spouse prior to 1998) is covered by a qualified plan and adjusted gross income exceeds certain thresholds, the deduction is scaled back, even if the benefit earned in the qualified plan is less than the IRA contribution that would have been allowed. Contributions may be made to an IRA at any time before the individual tax return is due (not including extensions). The amount of the allowable deduction claimed for a traditional IRA is limited, as shown in Table 21-1. Beginning in 1998, deductible IRA contributions can be made wholly independent of the spouse's active participation in a qualified retirement plan. [TRA '97 § 301]

Under The Taxpayer Relief Act of 1997, these income limits for traditional IRAs are scheduled to increase. The Taxpayer Relief Act of 1997 established significantly higher salary limits in the new

**TABLE 21-1. Limitations on
Allowable Deductions to Traditional IRAs**

Description of Employee	Availability of Deduction
Employee (and spouse prior to 1988) not covered by a company plan	Full IRA deduction
Employee (or spouse) covered by plan but with 2000 adjusted gross income not greater than: $52,000 (married) $32,000 (single) $0 (married, filing separately)	Full IRA deduction
Employee (or spouse) covered by a company plan with 2000 adjusted gross income of: $62,000 or more (married) $42,000 or more (single) $10,000 or more (married, filing separately)	No IRA deduction (nondeductible IRA instead)
Employee (or spouse prior to 1988) covered by a company plan with 2000 adjusted gross income between: $52,000 and $62,000 (married) $32,000 and $42,000 (single) $0 and $10,000 (married, filing separately)	Prorated IRA deduction (nondeductible IRA for the difference between the partial and full amount)

after-tax Roth IRAs for contributions independent of active plan participant status (see Q 21:11). Beginning in 1998, the total that may be contributed to both a traditional and a Roth IRA is $2,000 for the taxpayer and $2,000 for the spouse.

Q 21:2 How is a prorated IRA deduction calculated?

The prorated IRA deduction is calculated using the following formula:

$$\frac{\text{Maximum IRA deduction} \times (\text{highest number in the range of the bracket } - \text{ adjusted gross income})}{\$10,000}$$

Thus, for a single taxpayer with a 2000 adjusted gross income of $33,000, the high range in the bracket is $42,000 and the deductible contribution is calculated as follows:

$$\frac{\$2,000 \times (\$42,000 - \$33,000)}{\$10,000} = \$1,800$$

Prorated IRA deductions are rounded to the next highest $10. If an employee has a prorated deduction greater than zero, a minimum deduction of $200 is allowed. [IRC § 219(g)(2)]

Q 21:3 When is an individual considered "covered by a plan" for purposes of making deductible traditional IRA contributions?

Employees are considered covered by a plan if they are active participants in their employer's qualified plan. [IRC § 219(g)(5)] The term *active participant* is defined as follows:

- *In a defined benefit plan.* An employee is an active participant if the employee is eligible to participate in the plan at any time during the calendar year. No employee can avoid active participant status by waiving the right to participate.

- *In a money purchase or target pension plan.* An employee is an active participant if any employer contribution or forfeiture is required to be allocated to the participant's account for the plan year ending with or within the employee's taxable year.

- *In a profit sharing plan.* An employee is an active participant if any employer contribution or forfeiture is actually allocated to the participant's account during the employee's taxable year. A contribution is added to an employee's account on the later of either the date it is made or the date it is allocated. For example, if a contribution is made after the close of the plan year, the employee will be an active participant during the calendar year in which the contribution is made.

- *In a 401(k) plan.* An employee who makes elective deferrals is considered an active participant. An individual who is eligible but does not defer is not considered an active participant.

- *In a Section 403(b) plan (but not a Section 457 plan).* An employee who makes elective deferrals is considered an active participant.

- *In any plan.* An employee who makes voluntary or mandatory employee contributions is an active participant.

[IRS Notice 87-16, 1987-1 CB 446]

An individual is considered covered even if he or she has terminated nonvested during the year and forfeited all benefits earned.

Q 21:4 What is a *spousal IRA?*

A *spousal IRA* is a traditional or Roth IRA set up by a working spouse on behalf of a spouse earning less than $2,000 per year. A deduction may be taken up to the maximum total of $4,000 for the worker's own and the spousal IRA if both individuals file a joint return. The spouse must have no earned income or alimony or must elect to be treated as having no compensation for the taxable year. [IRC § 219(c)(1)] The contribution may be split between the spouses in any manner. However, no more than $2,000 may be contributed to one spouse's account. [IRC § 219(c)(2)] If one spouse is over the age of 70½, a traditional spousal IRA of $2,000 will be allowed, assuming that the other spouse is under the age of 70½. Spousal Roth IRAs can be made at any age so long as the taxpayer has sufficient earned income.

Q 21:5 If both spouses are employed, how much may each contribute to an IRA?

If both individuals are employed and each earns in wages more than $2,000, a $2,000 IRA contribution may be made for each.

Q 21:6 When may nondeductible contributions be made to a traditional IRA?

If an individual is not eligible to make a deductible contribution, or is not eligible to deduct the entire $2,000, a nondeductible contribution may be made to a traditional IRA. [IRC § 408(o)(2)] The nondeductible contribution is limited to the lesser of $2,000 or 100 percent of compensation. Although the contribution itself does not reduce taxable income, income on the account is tax-deferred until funds are withdrawn from the IRA. At that time, the nondeductible contributions are returned tax free and earnings are taxed as ordinary income. The individual must designate on Form 8606 whether contributions are deductible or nondeductible. In many situations it will be advantageous to make contributions to a Roth IRA (see the next section) rather than make nondeductible contributions to a traditional IRA.

Roth IRAs

Q 21:7 What is a *Roth IRA*?

A *Roth IRA* is similar to a traditional IRA except that contributions are always made with after-tax dollars and no tax is due for qualifying distributions. Roth IRAs were created by the Taxpayer Relief Act of 1997 and may be established for the first time for tax years beginning in 1998. Final Regulations for Roth IRA become effective February 3, 1999. [Treas Reg § 1.408A]

Q 21:8 What is a *qualifying distribution* from a Roth IRA?

Qualifying distributions from Roth IRAs are those made after a five year period beginning with the first year for which a Roth IRA contribution was made and which satisfy at least one of the following conditions:

1. The IRA owner is 59½ or older;
2. The IRA owner has died or become disabled; or
3. To pay for certain first-time home buyer expenses up to a lifetime limit of $10,000.

The IRS Restructuring and Reform Act of 1998 (IRRA) clarified that there is only one five-year holding period for all Roth IRAs owned by any one taxpayer. [IRRA § 6005(b)(2)]

IRRA also provides that if a distribution is made from a Roth IRA during this five-year holding period and the Roth IRA contained both contributions and conversion amounts, the distribution is to be treated as coming first from original Roth IRA contribution amounts, then from conversion amounts (in the order converted and beginning with amounts already includible in income), and last from earnings. For purposes of these ordering rules, all Roth IRAs, whether or not maintained in separate accounts, will be considered a single Roth IRA. Any conversion amounts thus withdrawn will be subject to the 10 percent early withdrawal penalty unless one of the exceptions under Code Section 72(t) applies (e.g., over age 59½). Under the rules, recordkeeping for Roth IRAs will be much simpler if conversion amounts and original Roth IRA contribution amounts are not placed in the same Roth IRA account. This closes retroactively the loophole whereby the 10 percent early withdrawal tax on eligible rollover distributions could be avoided by rolling into a traditional IRA, converting to a Roth IRA, and then immediately withdrawing the converted amount. [IRRA §§ 6005(b)(3), 6005(b)(5)]

Q 21:9 May nonqualifying distributions be made from a Roth IRA?

Yes. However, distributed earnings will be subject to both income tax and a 10 percent early withdrawal penalty tax. Unlike early distributions from traditional IRAs, early distributions from Roth IRAs are considered to be made first from the after-tax cost basis, which would not be subject either to income tax or to the 10 percent penalty. This is one of the ways in which a Roth IRA is a more flexible savings tax shelter than a traditional IRA.

Q 21:10 Must required distributions from Roth IRAs begin at age 70½?

No. Provided either the original owner or the spouse is still alive, there is no required distribution date for Roth IRAs. In fact, provided the taxpayer continues to have earned income, additional Roth IRA contributions can be made after age 70½. This is another way that a Roth IRA is a more flexible savings tax shelter than a traditional IRA.

Q 21:11 How much may be contributed to a Roth IRA?

Up to $2,000 per year can be contributed to a Roth IRA. Another $2,000 could be contributed to a spousal Roth IRA. These amounts must be reduced by any contributions made to a traditional IRA for the same year. Contributions to Roth IRAs can be made regardless of whether the taxpayer is covered by a qualified retirement plan. However, to contribute to a Roth IRA, adjusted gross income for the year must be under $160,000 (phasing out from $150,000) for married taxpayers filing jointly and under $110,000 (phasing out from $95,000) for single taxpayers. Married taxpayers filing separately are not eligible for Roth IRA contributions. These are the limits for 1999—they will be indexed for inflation.

Q 21:12 Does a Roth IRA provide for the opportunity of greater tax savings than a traditional IRA?

Yes. Even though the maximum annual contribution to a Roth IRA is the same $2,000 as to a traditional IRA, these dollars produce greater tax savings because they are after tax. Consider the following examples:

Example 1. Dick starts with $2,000 before taxes—all of which he contributes to a traditional deductible IRA so no taxes are currently due. He invests for 25 years until he is 60, with a tax-sheltered return of 8 percent which yields $13,697. If he then takes a distribution and pays taxes at a 30 percent rate, he will have $9,588 after taxes.

Example 2. Jane also starts with $2,000 before taxes. She plans to contribute to a Roth IRA, so she first must pay taxes on this income, which, at the same 30 percent rate Dick paid, leaves $1,400 to go into the Roth IRA. She invests for the same 25 years until age 60, with the same tax-sheltered return of 8 percent which yields $9,588. No taxes will be due if she then withdraws the funds, since this will be a qualifying distribution from the Roth IRA.

These examples illustrate the mathematical result that if you assume tax rates will be the same now as at distribution, there is no difference between the after-tax amounts at distribution, whether the same pre-tax income is invested in a Roth IRA or a traditional IRA. In effect, the Roth IRA locks in the current tax rate so that it will produce a higher yield than a traditional IRA if tax rates increase but a lower yield if tax rates fall between now and distribution.

However, Jane in example 2 is not limited to contributing only $1,400 to the Roth IRA. She can, if she can afford it, contribute up to $2,000 of after-tax dollars. This would give her $13,697 tax free after 25 years. This illustrates that even though both Roth IRAs and traditional IRAs allow the same nominal $2,000 annual contribution, because the Roth IRA is made with after-tax dollars it allows for a greater tax shelter.

Q 21:13 Can a traditional IRA be converted to a Roth IRA?

Yes, provided the adjusted gross income of the taxpayer or taxpayer and spouse for the year of conversion does not exceed $100,000. To make the conversion, a deemed distribution must be made from the traditional IRA and any amount of the distribution that has not previously been taxed must be included in income for the year (though there would be no 10 percent early withdrawal penalty on amounts transferred to a Roth IRA). The $100,000 limit applies before the deemed distribution and excludes any deductible IRA contribution made for the year. Also, for tax years after 2004, IRRA provides that the $100,000 conversion limit excludes any minimum required distributions from traditional IRAs and from other qualified plans. [IRRA § 7004(a)] Even after a conversion is made the taxpayer could undo it by a trustee-to-trustee transfer by the due date with extensions of the taxpayer's return. [IRRA §§ 6005(b)(6), 6005(b)(7)] For transfers made during 1998, the taxable distribution could have been recognized in income over four years, or the taxpayer could elect to recognize all of this income in 1998. (See also example in Q 1:47.) [IRRA § 6005(b)(4)].

If funds from outside the IRA distribution can be used to pay the taxes due on the distribution, such a conversion in effect increases substantially the effectiveness of the tax shelter. If you are under 59½, you should consider a transfer to a Roth IRA only if you can afford to pay the additional taxes that year with non-IRA assets, as this would avoid the 10 percent early distribution penalty on IRA assets used to pay the taxes.

Example. Jim transfers a $40,000 traditional IRA to a Roth IRA and pays $12,000 (30 percent) in additional taxes. In 15 years at an 8 percent tax-sheltered investment return, this would grow to $126,887 available as a tax-free qualifying distribution from the Roth IRA. If instead, Jim kept the $40,000 in the traditional IRA and invested the $12,000 in taxable savings, after 15 years at 8 percent pre-tax return the $40,000 traditional IRA would also have grown to $126,887, which, after 30 percent taxes were paid, would yield as an after-tax distribution $88,821. Meanwhile, assuming the same 30 percent tax rate each year, the $12,000 taxable savings would have grown to an after-tax amount of $27,173. Thus the total after-tax amount derived from continuing the traditional IRA and making taxable savings would be $115,994 ($88,821 plus $27,173), significantly less than the Roth IRA after-tax amount of $126,887.

Q 21:14 Should a traditional IRA be converted to a Roth IRA?

It depends. If taxes at distribution are likely to be no higher than taxes today, and if the taxes due at the conversion can be paid with other assets, then the conversion probably makes sense. Even if taxes may be somewhat higher at distribution than they are today, the conversion may still make sense because of the greater tax shelter gained by the conversion (see the previous example), and because the Roth IRA does not require distributions to begin at 70½ and thus allows for a greater tax shelter beyond that time. The Roth advantage is, of course, dependent on Congress' retaining the tax exemption for qualifying distributions many years into the future.

Q 21:15 Can a 401(k) distribution be rolled over directly into a Roth IRA?

No. However, it can be rolled over directly into a traditional IRA and then converted to a Roth IRA.

Q 21:16 Should a Roth IRA be considered by a participant in a 401(k) plan?

Yes—though if there is a match in the 401(k) plan, the Roth IRA should usually be considered only after the employee has made sufficient elective contributions to qualify for the full match. The Roth IRA may offer greater investment flexibility and may allow penalty-free distribution toward the purchase of a first home. However, the 401(k) but not the Roth IRA may offer loans and would provide better protection of assets in the event of personal bankruptcy. Many states provide traditional IRA assets with protection in bankruptcy but have not extended that protection to Roth IRAs.

IRA Funding

Q 21:17 How is an IRA funded?

Both traditional and Roth IRAs can be funded by three different vehicles: individual retirement accounts, individual retirement annuities, and individual retirement bonds.

Q 21:18 What is an *individual retirement account*?

An *individual retirement account* is set up in the form of either a trust or a custodial account, with a few restrictions. Life insurance may not be used in the funding of an individual retirement account, nor may individual retirement accounts be commingled with qualified trust assets. [IRC § 408(a)] However, in a custodial IRA, virtually any other type of funding vehicle is available: stocks, bonds, mutual funds, and U.S. gold and silver coins (but not other collectibles). This flexibility is also found in distribution options: an individual may take a single sum, regular installments, or sporadic distributions. Beginning in 1998, certain forms of bullion and additional coin types can be IRA investments. [TRA '97 § 304]

Q 21:19 What are *individual retirement annuities*?

Individual retirement annuities are annuity contracts offered by life insurance companies. Typically, an individual flexible premium annuity from a legally licensed life insurance company is used. [IRC § 408(b)] It is critical that the premiums be flexible to accommodate adjustments in levels of contributions. However, there is little flexibility in distribution options: the contract will generally allow only single-sum withdrawals, annuity options, or regular, periodic installments.

Q 21:20 What are *individual retirement bonds*?

Individual retirement bonds are federal government bonds issued under Chapter 31 of the United States Code. Although some existing IRAs once used this type of vehicle, these bonds are no longer issued and are no longer available to taxpayers for current IRA contributions.

Q 21:21 May an employer sponsor an IRA program for its employees?

Yes. The contribution made by the employer to the employee's IRA will be deductible by the employer and will be taxable to the employee and subject to Federal Insurance Contributions Act (FICA) and Federal Unemployment Tax Act (FUTA) taxes. The employee may deduct the IRA contribution under the rules described earlier in Qs 21:1–21:5. [IRC § 408(c)] In ERISA Interpretive Bulletin 99-1, the DOL issued safe harbor regulations clarifying the conditions under which an employer-sponsored IRA program is not an ERISA pension plan.

IRA Versus 401(k) Plan

Q 21:22 How do IRAs compare with 401(k) plans, and in what situations may an employer choose one over the other?

Deductible traditional IRAs compare with 401(k) plans in the following features:

- *Limits.* The maximum contribution allowed to an IRA is $2,000 or $4,000 for a spousal IRA. The 1998 annual limit on employee deferrals in a 401(k) plan is $10,000. If no employee wishes to defer more than $2,000, an IRA would be the most appropriate vehicle.

- *Deposits.* IRAs are generally funded through a single annual deposit. 401(k) plans are funded via deposits made through payroll deductions.

- *Withdrawals.* There is generally a 10 percent penalty on withdrawals from an IRA prior to age 59½, though the after-tax amounts contributed to a Roth IRA can be withdrawn without penalty. A 401(k) plan will provide more accessibility of funds to employees before age 59½, since hardship withdrawals for nondeductible major medical expenses and other permitted events are available without penalty with a 401(k) plan. Beginning in 1998 penalty-free withdrawals may be made from IRAs for higher education expense and for purchase of a first home. [TRA '97 §§ 203, 303]

- *Timing of tax savings.* The employee will receive a tax deduction for the IRA when Form 1040 is filed. In the case of a 401(k) plan, an immediate tax savings will be realized, since federal and state income tax withholding will be reduced.

- *Use with other company plans.* If the individual exceeds certain income thresholds, a deductible traditional IRA will not be available to an employee who is participating in a qualified plan. If the employer has another qualified plan, a 401(k) will be more effective in providing tax-deductible contributions for such a higher-income employee.

- *Tax treatment at distribution.* When amounts are withdrawn from a traditional IRA, the withdrawals are taxed at ordinary income tax rates. Under a 401(k) plan, special five- or ten-year income tax averaging on lump-sum distributions after age 59½ may be available (though this is scheduled to phase out). Rollover to an IRA to further defer taxation is also available under a 401(k) plan.

- *Excess contributions.* Excess contributions to an IRA are taxed at a 6 percent penalty unless the excess amount plus earnings is withdrawn before the due date of the tax return. In a 401(k) plan, deferrals that exceed the 1999 annual limit of $10,000 must be withdrawn before the due date of the individual's return. If the excess amounts are not withdrawn, the individual will be taxed both in the current year and upon later withdrawal from the 401(k) plan.

- *Distribution commencement date.* The minimum distribution requirements are similar for a traditional IRA and for a 401(k) plan: distributions must commence from a traditional IRA no later than April 1 following the calendar year in which the individual turns 70½. In a 401(k) plan the same rules apply to 5 percent owner participants. Other 401(k) participants may delay distributions beyond age 70½ until retirement. There is no minimum distribution requirement for Roth IRAs.

- *Nondiscrimination rules.* An employer-sponsored IRA may discriminate in favor of highly compensated employees (HCEs). [IRC § 408(c)] If the $2,000 cap is not an issue, an employer-sponsored IRA may better meet the sponsor's objectives than a 401(k) plan.

SIMPLIFIED EMPLOYEE PENSIONS (SEPs)
AND SALARY REDUCTION SEPs (SARSEPs)

Simplified employee pensions (SEPs) were created by the Revenue Act of 1978 to provide small employers with an incentive to establish retirement plans for their employees. Contribution limits were raised in 1981 with the passage of the ERTA. Virtual parity with qualified plans was attained in 1982 with the passage of the Tax Equity and Fiscal Responsibility Act of 1982 (TEFRA).

Compared with qualified plans, SEPs can minimize an employer's administrative responsibilities. Under a SEP arrangement, an employer simply makes tax-deductible contributions to an employee's tax-deferred traditional IRA account. These contributions may be significantly greater than the $2,000 maximum IRA contribution but must not discriminate in favor of HCEs.

The salary reduction SEP (SARSEP) more closely resembles a 401(k) plan but was available only to employers with 25 or fewer employees. New SARSEPs may not be established after 1996, although existing SARSEPs may be continued.

For additional information on SEPs and SARSEPs, see Panel Publishers' *SIMPLE, SEP, and SARSEP Answer Book.*

Q 21:23 What is the maximum amount an employer can deduct for a SEP?

An employer's maximum deduction in a SEP arrangement for any employee is limited to 15 percent of covered payroll. If the SEP is maintained on a calendar-year basis, contributions are deductible for the employer's taxable year within which the calendar year ends. If the SEP is maintained on the employer's taxable year, contributions are deductible for that period. [IRC § 404(h)(1)(A)]

Contributions may be made at any time up to the due date of the employer's tax return. In addition, the plan may be set up at any time before the employer's tax return is due. This contrasts with a qualified plan, which must be set up by the last day of the employer's fiscal year.

Q 21:24 Must a SEP be aggregated with other plans of the employer?

Yes. A SEP must be aggregated with any 401(k), stock bonus, or profit sharing plans of the employer. All such plans are subject to an aggregate limit of 15 percent of covered payroll. [IRC § 404(h)(2)] If the employer maintains both a SEP and a pension plan (such as a money purchase or defined benefit plan), the aggregate deductible limit between the SEP and the pension plan is 25 percent of covered compensation. [IRC § 404(h)(3)] For purposes of the maximum benefit and contribution limits (discussed in chapter 8), a SEP is treated as a defined contribution plan.

Q 21:25 What are the basic SEP requirements?

A SEP arrangement requires that a formal plan document be adopted. This document must specify the requirements for an employee to receive the contribution and must also specify how employees' contributions will be computed. [Prop Treas Reg § 1.408-7(b)] Contributions must bear a uniform relationship to compensation. [IRC § 408(k)(3)(c)] Life insurance is not allowed as an investment under a SEP. Since SEP contributions must be invested in one or more IRAs, all the usual IRA investment options and restrictions apply.

The IRAs established under SEPs may not be designated as Roth IRAs, and contributions to SEPs are not to be counted against the $2,000 annual IRA contribution limit. [IRRA §§ 6005(b)(8), 6005(b)(9)]

For any employee, the maximum compensation taken into account could not exceed $235,840 for 1993. The limit was reduced to $150,000 for 1994 through 1996, but has increased to $160,000 for 1997, where it remained for 1998 and 1999. Contributions must be made for all eligible employees in a controlled or affiliated service group (discussed in chapter 9). This contrasts with qualified plans, in which a group may be carved out if the plan will meet the minimum coverage and participation requirements (discussed in chapter 10).

Q 21:26 Who is eligible to participate in a SEP?

Eligible employees must include those who meet the following requirements:

1. Attained age 21;
2. Worked for the employer during any three of the last immediately preceding five years; and

3. Received at least $400 (1999 indexed limit) in pay for the current year.

[IRC § 408(k)(2)]

A SEP may exclude employees subject to a collective bargaining agreement and nonresident aliens.

Q 21:27 May a SEP be integrated with Social Security?

Yes. Disparity under Internal Revenue Code Section 401(1) (discussed in chapter 5) is allowed in a SEP arrangement. [IRC § 408(k)(3)(D)] The employer may effectively credit employees who earn more than the maximum taxable wage base with a contribution of up to 5.7 percent in excess of the wage base.

Example. Company B has an integrated SEP, integrated at the 1998 maximum taxable wage base of $68,400. There are three eligible participants earning a total of $161,500. Company B wishes to contribute $24,000 to the plan. The contribution would be allocated as follows:

Employee	Salary	Salary in Excess of $68,400	5.7% × Excess Salary	Salary-Based Allocation	Total SEP Contribution
#1	$105,500	$37,100	$2,115	$14,297	$16,412
#2	36,500	–0–	–0–	4,946	4,946
#3	19,500	–0–	–0–	2,642	2,642
Totals	$161,500	$37,100	$2,115	$21,885	$24,000

It should be noted, though, that any SEP contribution exceeding 15 percent of salary would be included in the employee's W-2 income. [IRC § 402(h)(2)] In this example, the contribution for employee #1 is 15.56 percent of salary.

Q 21:28 When may funds be withdrawn from a SEP arrangement?

Employees may make withdrawals from a SEP arrangement at any time, since contributions are made directly to an individual's

IRA, and the funds must be accessible to employees at all times. Furthermore, future contributions may not be conditioned on the employee's continuing to maintain the funds in the SEP account. [IRC § 408(k)(4)] Contributions to the SEP become 100 percent vested immediately.

Q 21:29 Do the top-heavy rules of Code Section 416 apply?

Yes. The top-heavy rules of Code Section 416, as discussed in chapter 13, do apply. [IRC § 408(k)(1)(B)] If the SEP arrangement (or any other qualified plan of the employer) is top heavy, then top-heavy minimum contributions must be made.

Q 21:30 What is the tax treatment of SEP contributions?

Contributions by the employer are treated the same as if contributed to a qualified plan. They are not included in an employee's W-2 income and are not subject to federal, state, or FICA withholding. [IRC § 402(h)(1)] When contributions are withdrawn from a SEP, they are taxed to the employee in the same manner as other IRA withdrawals.

Q 21:31 May a SEP include a salary reduction feature?

Salary reduction SEPs (SARSEPs) could be established only prior to January 1, 1997, and only for employers with 25 or fewer employees. SARSEPs established before that date can be maintained and may admit new members. Maximum deferrals under SARSEPs are indexed, with the 1999 maximum at $10,000. At least 50 percent of those eligible must elect some deferral. SARSEP deferrals must satisfy a nondiscrimination test similar to the actual deferral percentage (ADP) test for 401(k) plans. SARSEPs with any deferrals by key employees are generally considered top heavy.

Q 21:32 What are the similarities between a SEP and a SARSEP?

A SARSEP has many provisions in common with a SEP. The eligibility requirements and deductibility limits are identical, as are the funding deadlines. [Treas Reg § 1.408-7(b)] Vesting of contributions is 100 percent immediate, and there are few administrative requirements for either type of plan, although a SARSEP sponsor must ensure that the federal, state, and FICA withholdings are done correctly. With both types of plans, funds are immediately accessible to employees once they are deposited into the individual's IRA. The features of all three plan types—SEP, SARSEP, and 401(k)—are outlined in Table 21-2.

Q 21:33 How does a 401(k) plan with an age-weighted formula compare with a SEP?

A 401(k) plan with an age-weighted formula (see chapter 2) has some significant advantages over SEPs: the weighting of contributions in favor of older HCEs is one of these. In addition, a vesting schedule can be used that will result in forfeitures for employees who terminate before becoming fully vested. Finally, accessibility of funds is a critical issue. In a SEP plan, funds are accessible immediately once the contribution is made (although the employee will be responsible for the 10 percent premature withdrawal penalty and be immediately taxed). In-service withdrawals can be prohibited or limited in a 401(k) plan.

Q 21:34 When might an employer choose to use a SEP over a 401(k) plan?

Because of its minimal reporting and disclosure requirements, an employer who wishes to have a truly simple plan might choose a SEP. Further, if the employer wishes to spend an identical percentage of pay for each eligible employee, the SEP is the best vehicle. Minimal reporting and disclosure requirements will make the SEP attractive.

On the other hand, an employer who wishes to involve employees in its retirement plan will probably choose a 401(k) plan because of the ability of employees to defer a portion of their pay. Matching employer contributions can encourage participation in the 401(k) plan. Also, in a 401(k) plan, relatively larger contributions as a percentage of pay may be made for HCEs; this may be very attractive to an employer. Finally, an employer who wants to limit the accessibility of funds to encourage saving for retirement will favor the adoption of the 401(k) plan.

TABLE 21-2. Comparison of SEPs and SARSEPs with 401(k) Plans

Feature	SEP	SARSEP	401(k)
Maximum eligibility requirements	Age 21; worked 3 of past 5 years; earned at least $400 (1999 amount)	Same as SEP	Age 21 and 1 year of service
Coverage	All eligible must participate	50% of those eligible must participate; maximum 25 or fewer eligible employees in preceding plan year	Follows Section 410(b) rules regarding nondiscrimination
Employer deduction limit	15% of covered payroll	Same	Same
Maximum employee contributions	Not applicable; employer contributions only	Employee salary deferral—lesser of 15% compensation or $10,000 (1999 limit)	Lesser of 15% of compensation or $10,000 (1999 limit)

Vesting	100% immediate	100% immediate	Vesting schedule permitted (on employer contributions)
IRS reporting	Form 5305A-SEP establishes model plan	Same as SEP—though new SARSEPs may not be established after 1996	Annual form 5500 reports required
Access to deposited funds	Contributions are deposited as IRAs; subject to IRA rules; 10% IRS penalty for premature distribution	Same as SEP	Withdrawals permitted under certain circumstances—retirement, hardship, etc. Loans if employer allows. 10% IRS penalty for premature distribution
Plan documents	IRS Model; Master or Prototype	Same as SEP	Master or Prototype; individually designed
Tax treatment of distributions	Ordinary income	Same as SEP	Generally, ordinary income (10-year income averaging in some circumstances)

SIMPLE IRA PLANS

SIMPLE retirement account plans, also commonly called SIMPLE IRA plans, were created by the Small Business Job Protection Act of 1996 and could be established beginning January 1, 1997. Like SARSEPs, they allow pre-tax salary deferrals to be contributed to traditional IRAs (though with a lower maximum), but, unlike SARSEPs, they are available to a broader class of sponsors, do not require discrimination testing, and are exempt from both the top-heavy rules and Section 415 limitations. SIMPLE IRA plans mandate fixed levels of employer contributions, which must be 100 percent immediately vested. For more information on SIMPLE IRA plans, see also Panel Publishers' *SIMPLE, SEP, and SARSEP Answer Book.* SIMPLE IRA plans have similarities to SIMPLE 401(k) plans, but they also have important differences. SIMPLE 401(k) plans are discussed in chapter 2. See Table 21-3 for a comparison of SIMPLE IRA plans with both SIMPLE 401(k) plans and regular 401(k) plans.

Q 21:35 Which employers are eligible to establish SIMPLE IRA plans?

Any employer that has 100 or fewer employees with at least $5,000 of compensation in the preceding calendar year is eligible to sponsor a SIMPLE IRA plan. Eligible employers include private tax-exempt organizations and also governmental employers. (Governmental employers are not eligible to establish SIMPLE 401(k) plans.) The employer aggregation and leased employee rules of Code Section 414 apply to SIMPLE IRA plans. An employer no longer satisfying the 100-employee rule may continue to sponsor a SIMPLE IRA during a two-year grace period. (See also Q 21:43.) [IRS Notice 97-6, 1997-1 CB 353, Q&As B-1, B-2, B-4, B-5]

Q 21:36 What is the annual limit on the amount of salary reduction that an employee may elect under a SIMPLE IRA plan?

For 1999, the maximum deferral under a SIMPLE IRA plan remains at $6,000. This amount will be adjusted annually to reflect changes in the consumer price index, rounded down in $500 increments. Employees must be given a 60-day period prior to the beginning of the plan year to enter into a salary reduction agreement for the year, though an employer may provide additional or longer election periods. The employee must be given the right to terminate the salary reduction agreement at any time during the year. Other than the $6,000 limit, no restrictions may be placed on the amount an employee may defer. SIMPLE IRA plans are not subject to Section 415 limits, so an employee may defer more than 25 percent of compensation. [IRS Notice 97-6, 1997-1 CB 353, Q&As D-3, E-1, E-2, E-3]

The return of any excess contributions from a SIMPLE IRA plan is handled the same as the return of excess contributions from a SEP under Code Section 408(p)(2)(D)(i). [IRRA § 6018(b)]

Q 21:37 What employer matching contribution is generally required under a SIMPLE IRA plan?

Under a SIMPLE IRA plan, an employer is generally required to make a contribution on behalf of each eligible employee in an amount equal to the employee's salary reduction contributions, up to a limit of 3 percent of the employee's compensation for the calendar year. This 3 percent limit can be reduced for a calendar year at the employer's election subject to these three limitations:

1. The limit is not reduced below 1 percent of compensation;

2. The limit is not reduced for more than two years of five; and

3. Employees are notified of the reduced limit within a reasonable period before the 60-day period during which employees can enter into salary reduction agreements.

[IRS Notice 97-6, 1997-1 CB 353, Q&A D-5]

Matching contributions are calculated without regard to the $160,000 indexed limitation under Code Section 401(a)(17), and the match plus the deferral is not subject to the Section 415 percentage limitation.

Example. Ellyn's compensation is $200,000, and she elects to defer $6,000 under her company's SIMPLE IRA plan. The company matches 3 percent of her compensation, or $6,000, for a total contribution of $12,000.

Matching contributions must be made without regard to the number of hours the employee works during the year, whether the employee actually earns $5,000 in compensation, or whether the employee is employed on the last day of the plan year.

Q 21:38 May an employer make nonelective contributions instead of matching contributions to a SIMPLE IRA plan?

Yes. As an alternative to making the matching contributions discussed in Q 21:37, an employer may make nonelective contributions equal to 2 percent of each eligible employee's compensation for the entire calendar year (where compensation is capped at the $160,000 indexed limit under Code Section 401(a)(17)). This nonelective contribution must be made whether or not an employee has elected to make salary reduction contributions, and no minimum hour or last day requirement may be applied. The employer may, but is not required to, limit nonelective contributions to eligible employees who have at least $5,000 (or some lower amount) of compensation during the year. The employer must notify eligible employees that this 2 percent nonelective contribution will be made instead of matching contributions within a reasonable period of time before the 60-day election period during which employees can enter into salary reduction agreements. [IRS Notice 97-6, 1997-1 CB 353, Q&A D-6]

Q 21:39 Which employees must be eligible to participate in a SIMPLE IRA plan?

All employees who received at least $5,000 in compensation from the employer during any two preceding calendar years (whether or not consecutive) and who are reasonably expected to receive at least $5,000 in compensation during the calendar year must be eligible to participate. No additional age or minimum hours of service requirements may be imposed. The employer may exclude employees under a collective bargaining agreement, nonresident aliens with no domestic income from the employer, and certain airline employees. Less restrictive conditions can be applied. [IRS Notice 97-6, 1997-1 CB 353, Q&As C-1, C-2]

Q 21:40 Can contributions under a SIMPLE IRA plan be made to any type of IRA?

No. The contributions must be made to a SIMPLE IRA, which is a traditional IRA to which the only contributions allowed are those contributions under a SIMPLE IRA plan and rollovers or transfers from another SIMPLE IRA. Once amounts have been contributed to a SIMPLE IRA, an employer may not impose any withdrawal restrictions. [IRS Notice 97-6, 1997-1 CB 353, Q&As A2, F2]

IRRA clarifies that IRAs established under a SIMPLE IRA plan may not be designated as Roth IRAs and that contributions to SIMPLE IRAs are not to be counted against the $2,000 annual IRA contribution limit.

Q 21:41 Must contributions under a SIMPLE IRA plan be nonforfeitable?

Yes. All contributions must be fully vested when made. [IRS Notice 97-6, 1997-1 CB 353, Q&A F-1]

Q 21:42 What are the tax consequences when amounts are distributed from a SIMPLE IRA?

Generally, the same tax results apply to distributions from a SIMPLE IRA as to distributions from a traditional IRA; however, there is a special rule for distributions from a SIMPLE IRA during the two-year period beginning when the employee first participated in any SIMPLE IRA plan maintained by the employer. During this two-year period, the early distribution tax under Code Section 72(t) is increased from 10 percent to 25 percent unless the distribution is rolled over to another SIMPLE IRA. Tax-free trustee-to-trustee transfers can be made during the two-year period but only to another SIMPLE IRA. After this two-year period, trustee-to-trustee transfers and rollovers can be made to any IRA. [IRS Notice 97-6, 1997-1 CB 535, Q&As I-2, I-3]

Q 21:43 Can an employer make contributions under a SIMPLE IRA plan for a calendar year if it maintains another qualified retirement plan?

No. Neither the employer nor a predecessor employer may maintain a qualified plan under which any of its employees receives an allocation of contributions or has an increase in benefit accrual for any plan year beginning or ending in that calendar year. Rollovers and forfeitures are disregarded except to the extent forfeitures replace otherwise required contributions. Qualified retirement plans include SEPs and plans described under Code Sec-

TABLE 21-3. Comparison of SIMPLE IRA Plans with SIMPLE 401(k) and Regular 401(k) Plans

Feature	SIMPLE IRA	SIMPLE 401(k)	Regular 401(k)
Eligible employers	100 or fewer employees making $5,000 in prior year (2-year grace period)	Same as SIMPLE IRA, except no governmental	Any, except governmental
Types of contributions	Employee deferrals Employer match or nonelective	Employee deferrals Employer match or nonelective	Employee deferrals Employer match Employer fixed or discretionary
Other qualified plans	No	No (unless for employees not covered by the SIMPLE 401(k))	Yes
401(k)/401(m) discrimination testing	No	No	Yes
Top-heavy testing	No	No	Yes
Elective deferral limit	$6,000 (1999)	$6,000 (1999)	$10,000 (1999)
Level of match	100% of first 3% (not subject to $160,000 cap)	100% of first 3% (subject to $160,000 cap)	Any (subject to Section 401(m) test)

21-26

Match alternative	With notice may reduce cap to 1% in 2 of 5 years or make 2% nonelective contribution	With notice may make 2% nonelective contribution	Any (subject to Section 401(m) test)
Subject to Section 415 limits	No	Yes	Yes
Eligibility requirements	No minimum age or service Earned $5,000 in any 2 prior years and expected to earn $5,000 this year	Minimum age 21 1 year service/1,000 hours	Same as SIMPLE 401(k)
Vesting	100% immediate	100% immediate	Graded schedules allowed
Withdrawals	No restrictions; 10% pre-59½ penalty (25% in first 2 years)	Can restrict; 10% pre-59½ penalty	Same as SIMPLE 401(k)
Form 5500 reporting	No	Yes	Yes
Investment restrictions	No loans No life insurance	None	None

21-27

tions 401(a), 403(a), 403(b), and 457(b). [IRS Notice 97-6, Q&A B-3, 1997-2 IRB 26]

IRRA clarifies that an employer's sponsoring another qualified plan in which only collectively bargained employees may participate does not prevent it from sponsoring a SIMPLE IRA plan for its noncollectively bargained employees. [IRRA § 6016(a)(1)(A)] If any eligible sponsor through merger or acquisition no longer meets the exclusive plan requirement, the 100-employee requirement, or the coverage requirement, the sponsor shall continue to be treated as eligible to sponsor a SIMPLE IRA for a transition period beginning with the year of acquisition or merger and continuing for the following two years. [IRRA § 6016(a)(1)(B)]

Q 21:44 What are the annual reporting requirements for the employer sponsor of a SIMPLE IRA plan?

The employer must report on Form W-2 whether the employee is an active participant in the SIMPLE IRA plan and must show the amount of the participant's annual salary reduction contribution. No other employer reports are required. As with any IRA, the trustee must report annually to the participant the account balance as of the end of the year and the account activity during the year. No Form 5500 reporting is required for a SIMPLE IRA plan.

Q 21:45 Why might an eligible employer choose to establish a SIMPLE IRA plan rather than a regular 401(k)?

Unlike a regular 401(k) plan, a SIMPLE IRA plan requires no complicated plan document, nor does it involve the plan sponsor in ongoing administration and annual Form 5500 federal reporting. The 2 percent nonelective contribution option is less than the contribution that would be required under a top-heavy 401(k) plan.

Q 21:46 What are the disadvantages of a SIMPLE IRA plan compared with a regular 401(k) plan?

A SIMPLE IRA plan is much less flexible than a regular 401(k) plan. The contributions are fixed within narrow limits, and no discretionary profit sharing contribution can be made. No contributions can be made to other qualified plans. Eligibility cannot be limited to specific groups of employees. No vesting schedule is allowed on employer contributions. The maximum deferral limit is much lower: $6,000 for a SIMPLE IRA versus $10,000 in 1998 for a 401(k) plan.

Q 21:47 How are SIMPLE IRA plans being received by small businesses?

SIMPLE IRA plans have been selling well. In a 1997 poll commissioned by T. Rowe Price, of 179 business owners with between 5 and 35 employees, 51 percent that already had a retirement plan were aware of SIMPLE IRA plans, as were 33 percent of those without another plan. Of those who were aware of SIMPLE IRA plans, 22 percent were considering adopting one.

Generally, employers are showing much more interest in SIMPLE IRA plans than in SIMPLE 401(k) plans. The latter retain much of the administrative complexity of a regular 401(k) and provide little beyond greater investment flexibility and withdrawal restrictions over a SIMPLE IRA plan. Table 21-3 provides a comparison of SIMPLE IRA plans with both SIMPLE 401(k) plans and regular 401(k) plans.

CASH BALANCE PLANS

A cash balance plan is a hybrid of a defined benefit plan and a defined contribution plan. The defined benefit element of the cash balance plan operates similarly to a career average defined benefit plan (see Q 21:51). The defined contribution element operates similarly to a money purchase plan in providing a ledger "contribution" that is a fixed percentage of pay and ledger "account balances" that are updated annually (see Q 21:49).

Cash balance plans were introduced in 1985 by Lawrence T. Brennan of Kwasha Lipton, who designed such a plan at Bank America for approximately 60,000 employees. These plans, which have proved to be quite popular, are also known by other names, including guaranteed account balance plans, individual account pension plans, lump-sum pension plans, and pension equivalent reserve credit plans.

Defined benefit plans have lost favor with many employers because employees do not understand or appreciate the complex benefit formulas associated with them, administrative costs are increasing due to complex benefit regulations and increasing PBGC premiums, and contribution levels vacillate due to an overload of government regulation. Although TRA '86 has accelerated the vesting requirements, vesting in defined benefit plans is generally slower than in defined contribution plans. Furthermore, defined benefit plans are not responsive to changing demographics and the current mobility of the workforce. Employees who leave after a short period with the employer may receive minimal benefits that are often not paid until attainment of the plan's normal retirement age, and many defined benefit plans do not provide a lump-sum option (which would give employees the opportunity to invest proceeds from the plan at their own discretion). Another significant disadvantage of defined benefit plans is the inequity between younger and older employees.

Defined contribution plans also have their shortcomings. In these plans, the employees bear the investment risk, leaving the employer open to fiduciary concerns, as discussed in chapter 6. Additionally, the benefits of an employee under a defined contribution plan cannot be increased to take past service or age into account.

Except for profit sharing plans, defined contribution plans have little funding flexibility. Generally, profit sharing plans do not provide annuity options.

Cash balance plans are designed to address the weaknesses of both the defined benefit plan and the defined contribution plan. In short, cash balance plans respond to the diversity of the workforce and changes in demographic patterns by providing greater benefits to shorter-term employees (5 to 15 years of service) than the more traditional defined benefit type of plan.

Features of Cash Balance Plans

Q 21:48 What are the defined benefit features in a cash balance plan?

Defined benefit features in a cash balance plan include the following:

- Benefits are guaranteed (employer, not employee, bears the investment risk).

- The plan is subject to minimum funding standards [IRC § 412] and coverage by the Pension Benefit Guaranty Corporation (PBGC).

- The benefits in the plan are limited under Code Section 415 using defined benefit limits.

Q 21:49 What are the defined contribution features in a cash balance plan?

The defined contribution features include a benefit defined in terms of a hypothetical account balance and a hypothetical annual contribution for each participant. Interest is credited to the account based on a minimum rate as specified in the plan, although an employer may choose to provide a higher interest credit than that minimum. Usually, the vested portion of the account balance is made available upon termination.

Advantages of Cash Balance Plans

Q 21:50 What are the advantages of cash balance plans to the employer?

Cash balance plans combine the best features of defined benefit and defined contribution plans. A cash balance plan provides benefit security to an employee, since both the interest credited to the theoretical account balance and contributions are guaranteed. Because it is a defined benefit plan, flexibility in funding is available to the employer through the use of actuarial cost methods that generate minimum and maximum contribution levels. Also, since the cash balance plan is a type of career average plan, it allows for cost control, as compared with a final-average-pay defined benefit plan. The plans are simple to operate, provide a stable level of pension costs as a percentage of payroll, and can be used to attract younger employees.

Q 21:51 What is the difference between a career average defined benefit plan and a final pay plan?

A career average defined benefit plan uses an employee's entire earnings history to compute benefits, while a final pay plan uses average pay over a shorter period—often three or five years. As a comparison, consider two defined benefit plans, each providing a benefit equal to 1 percent of pay. One uses a career average for benefit calculation purposes, but the other uses final average pay.

Example. A 35-year-old employee earns $15,000 and receives 5 percent salary increases annually. His total career earnings will be $996,583. The benefit payable at age 65 from the career average plan would be calculated as follows:

$$\text{Career earnings} \times 1\% = \text{Annual benefit}$$
$$\$996,583 \times 1\% = 9,966$$

If the final pay plan uses a five-year average, the same employee's highest five-year average would be $56,135. The benefit payable at age 65 would be calculated as follows:

$$\text{Final average} \times 1\% \times \text{total service} = \text{Annual benefit}$$
$$\$56,135 \times 1\% \times 30 = \$16,841$$

The final pay plan provides a benefit that is almost 70 percent higher than the career average plan. Thus, the cost of providing benefits will be significantly lower under the career average plan.

Q 21:52 What are the advantages of a cash balance plan to employees?

With a cash balance plan, each employee has an individual portable account balance, which is a tangible, visible benefit. Contributions are made on an age-neutral basis, so that the inherent discrimination against younger employees that may be found in a defined benefit plan does not exist. The availability of a lump-sum benefit provides an employee with greater control over retirement options.

Disadvantages of Cash Balance Plans

Q 21:53 What are the disadvantages of a cash balance plan?

Some disadvantages may arise from the specifics of each plan or from the employer's circumstances and investment strategy:

1. If retirement benefits in a cash balance plan are structured to provide roughly the same retirement benefits as an existing defined

benefit plan, the cash balance plan will not be a mechanism for cost saving. If the company has high employee turnover, there will be large cash outlays as employees terminate employment. Also, since in a cash balance plan the employer bears the investment risk, earnings less than the plan's stated guaranteed interest rate will cause the plan's cost to increase. Depending on the level of the PBGC interest rates, the possibility also exists that a plan may have to pay out more than an individual's account balance at termination of employment, although the IRS has proposed guidance that would allow for plan designs that would eliminate this possibility. [Notice 96-8, 1996-6 IRB 23]

Note. The plan may need to pay an amount greater than the account balance because the plan document must specify interest rates used to convert account balances into an accrued monthly benefit. However, required rates must be used to convert the accrued benefit into a lump sum. If the required rates are lower than the plan's specified rates, an amount greater than the account balance may need to be paid.

2. Another disadvantage of cash balance plans is higher actuarial fees. As defined benefit plans, cash balance plans require an annual actuarial valuation. In addition, the Financial Accounting Standards Board, in Statement 87 (FAS 87), has prescribed a specific funding method for the reporting of pension costs, assets, and liabilities on the plan sponsor's financial statements. This report, furnished annually by the employer's pension actuary, involves calculations that are separate and distinct from the actuarial valuation that is used for Schedule B of Form 5500. Since actuarial calculations are more complex than in a traditional defined benefit plan, cash balance plans have higher actuarial fees.

3. For a given level of cost, a cash balance plan provides higher benefits for younger, shorter-service employees and lower benefits for older, longer-service employees than does a traditional defined benefit plan. As a result, a cash balance plan does not encourage and reward long service. This disadvantage can be overcome to some extent by providing "contribution" levels that vary by service—for example:

- A 3 percent contribution for 0 to 5 years of service
- A 4 percent contribution for 6 to 10 years of service
- A 5 percent contribution for 11 to 15 years of service

- A 6 percent contribution for 16 to 20 years of service
- A 7 percent contribution for years of service beyond 20

The contribution formula could also vary by age or by both age and service, although a formula that varies by age may be harder to explain and justify to participants. Any such graded formula must satisfy the backloading rules of Code Section 411(b) as well as the nondiscrimination rules of Code Section 401(a)(4).

4. Finally, the plan sponsor is still subject to PBGC reporting requirements. This generally means that the employer will be required to pay PBGC premiums. (Variable rate premiums are now nearly 1 percent of the unfunded liability.) The liability to the PBGC for underfunding the plan could subject up to 30 percent of the employer's net worth to attachment if the plan terminated.

Conversion to a Cash Balance Plan

Q 21:54 How might an existing defined benefit plan be converted to a cash balance plan?

The first step is to set up a starting account balance for each employee equal to the present value of the accrued benefit in the defined benefit plan. A percentage of pay (theoretical contribution) will then be credited to each individual's account each year. This, in fact, could be looked upon as a career average pension plan that provides a fixed annuity benefit at retirement. Upon termination of employment, the employee would receive the choice of a lump-sum distribution or an annuity. To ensure that older employees do not lose benefits in the transition, prior benefits may be grandfathered for employees who have attained a certain age at the time of the conversion.

Communication at the time of conversion is crucial in this plan. It is critical that employees appreciate the value of the new program. Younger employees who have significant service will need an explanation of why their opening account balances are so much lower than those of older employees. Older employees who may suffer a loss in projected benefits as a result of the conversion will also need to be dealt with.

In fact, most cash balance plans were created as conversions from existing (often overfunded) defined benefit plans. A cash balance plan may not be appropriate as a startup plan because it costs more to administer than a comparable defined contribution plan and exposes the employer to greater potential liability.

Q 21:55 How would an existing profit sharing or money purchase plan be converted to a cash balance plan?

The existing account balance of the participant in the defined contribution plan would be treated as the opening balance in the cash balance plan. A percentage of pay would then be credited to the account balance each year, as well as interest at the rate defined in the plan document. Generally, contributions may be graded upward depending on age and/or service.

Cash Balance Plan Design

Q 21:56 How are the interest credits in a cash balance plan determined?

The plan will state the minimum interest to be credited to participants' account balances; however, the plan sponsor may grant a larger amount. Interest is credited annually, although more frequent credits may occur. The purpose of crediting interest more frequently is to provide reports to participants more often and heighten the visibility of the program.

Q 21:57 What benefit options are available?

A variety of benefit options are available. The design of the cash balance plan is such that a lump-sum distribution is the most frequently elected option. To discourage employees from quitting in order to cash out their retirement benefits, a plan sponsor may consider restricting lump-sum distributions to participants who have attained early or normal retirement age. However, if the required interest rates are low, the account balance may need to be topped off to provide the minimum statutory guarantees. (See Q 21:53.)

As another option, loans may be provided in a cash balance plan. However, many experts believe that this is contrary to the purposes of the pension plan.

Q 21:58 What types of vesting schedules are used in cash balance plans?

Vesting will frequently be more rapid in a cash balance plan than in a traditional defined benefit plan. The result may be a more liberal graded schedule that provides for 100 percent vesting in five years, or a cliff vesting schedule for vesting within three years.

Q 21:59 What are the nondiscrimination requirements of a cash balance plan?

A cash balance plan can demonstrate that nondiscriminatory amounts are provided by using the defined benefit general test (see Q 11:9). [Treas Reg § 1.401(a)(4)-3(c)] Alternatively, accruals can be converted to equivalent allocations under the cross-testing rules. [Treas Reg § 1.401(a)(4)-8(c)(2)]

A safe harbor for cash balance plans is provided under the cross-testing rules. [Treas Reg § 1.401(a)(4)-8(c)(3)] The basic requirements are as follows:

1. The plan must be an accumulation plan—that is, a plan that uses an employee's compensation over his or her entire career.

2. The accrued benefit must be calculated by projecting the hypothetical account balance forward to normal retirement age at the interest rate specified in the plan and converting it to an annuity.

3. Hypothetical allocations must satisfy one of two tests:

   The defined contributions safe harbor, which provides the same amount or percentage of pay (permitted disparity may be used); or

   The general test, taking only hypothetical allocations into account (see chapter 11).

4. Interest credits must be either between 7.5 percent and 8.5 percent or a variable interest rate using current Treasury issues or PBGC interest rates.

5. Past service credits must be granted on a uniform basis, and the hypothetical allocations must have satisfied the safe harbor rules if the plan provision had been in place in the past.

6. Hypothetical interest credits must be granted if a partici-

pant delays commencement of benefits after normal retirement age.

Cash Balance Plan Versus 401(k) Plan

Q 21:60 When would it be advantageous for an employer to use a cash balance plan?

A cash balance plan can be used effectively in a number of situations. The first is an overfunded defined benefit plan, where the plan sponsor may be looking at a potential 50 percent reversion tax if the plan is terminated and assets revert to the employer. By converting to a cash balance plan, the excess assets in the pension plan can be "recovered" by using the surplus assets to fund future contributions to the cash balance plan. The result is that the possibility of reversion upon termination of the plan is reduced or eliminated.

It can also be advantageous to convert an existing defined benefit plan that employees do not consider valuable. Generally, a defined benefit plan represents one of an employer's largest expenditures. A plan sponsor seeking to improve the value of the pension plan without jeopardizing the guarantee of benefits may substitute a cash balance plan. This will provide real and substantial benefits for younger and short-service employees. The focus of these plans is on a target group with 5 to 15 years of service rather than on older, longer-service employees.

A third application of the cash balance plan is as a replacement for an ineffective profit sharing plan. The benefit security of the cash balance plan is often very appealing to the workforce, particularly if the investment experience in the profit sharing plan has been less than favorable in past years.

Q 21:61 When might a cash balance plan be used as an alternative to a 401(k) plan?

A cash balance plan differs significantly from a 401(k) plan in that the employer bears the investment risk. The cash balance plan reduces exposure to fiduciary liability and may be viewed as a viable alternative for a paternalistic employer concerned about the unfavorable impact of poor investment performance in a 401(k) plan on an employee's retirement benefits. An employer with an overfunded defined benefit plan will generally find a cash balance plan to be a more effective vehicle for using up surplus assets. If the employer terminates the plan, the maximum amount of the surplus that could be transferred to a 401(k) plan (if it satisfies the requirements for a qualified replacement plan under the Omnibus Budget Reconciliation Act (OBRA '90)) is 25 percent of the surplus. The balance, or 75 percent of the surplus, would be returned to the employer and be subject to a 20 percent excise tax. A cash balance plan, however, could use up to 100 percent of the surplus of an overfunded defined benefit plan with no penalty.

RETIREMENT BONUS PLANS

A retirement bonus plan (also known as a lump-sum plan or a life cycle plan) resembles a cash balance plan in that the benefit is defined as a lump sum payable upon termination of employment. However, instead of being defined as a hypothetical account balance, the bonus plan benefit is defined as accumulated bonus credits times final average salary. Although retirement bonus plans have only rarely been used in the United States, they are quite common in parts of Asia.

Q 21:62 What are the features of a retirement bonus plan?

The accrued benefit is defined as accumulated credits times final average salary. For example, if the credit were 10 percent per year, after 20 years the accumulated credit would be 200 percent and the lump-sum benefit would be 200 percent of final average pay. Because it is a defined benefit plan, a retirement bonus plan is subject to the minimum funding standards of ERISA and requires an enrolled actuary to perform annual valuations. The employer, not the employee, bears the investment risk. The benefits are covered by the PBGC and are limited under Code Section 415 using defined benefit limits.

Q 21:63 What are the advantages of a retirement bonus plan to the employer?

Like those of a cash balance plan, the features of a retirement bonus plan are easy to communicate to employees, who can readily understand and appreciate the value of the benefit they are accruing. It is simpler to administer than a cash balance plan since there is no need to define an interest rate for accruals and no need to maintain hypothetical account balances for each employee. Although the employer bears the investment risk, the employer also will benefit through lower contributions from any investment gains.

Q 21:64 What are the disadvantages of a retirement bonus plan to the employer?

Retirement bonus plans share the same disadvantages discussed in Q 21:53 for cash balance plans.

Q 21:65 How do retirement bonus plans compare with cash balance plans?

A cash balance plan is a career average plan, but a retirement bonus plan is a final pay plan. If the interest rate credited under a cash balance plan were to happen to be the same as the salary increase rate for an employee, then a retirement bonus plan would produce the same lump sum as a comparable cash balance plan. For fast-track employees, the salary increase rate would likely exceed the interest crediting rate, so a retirement bonus plan allows the employer to direct more of the benefit to such fast-track employees.

Q 21:66 What are the advantages of a retirement bonus plan to the employee?

Like a cash balance plan, a retirement bonus plan is easy to understand and produces a portable account balance that accumulates on an age-neutral basis.

Q 21:67 What are the disadvantages of a retirement bonus plan to the employee?

Although the retirement bonus plan is relatively easy to understand, there is still room for misunderstanding. A retirement bonus plan that credits 10 percent of pay per year of service will sound to the employee very similar to a 10 percent of pay money purchase plan. However, during periods of low to moderate inflation, pay increases for most employees are likely to be significantly less than the interest that could be earned on a money purchase account balance. In this case, the employee may believe the retirement bonus plan is more valuable as a benefit than it is likely to be.

FLOOR PLANS

A floor plan is actually a combination of two plans: a defined benefit plan coordinated with a defined contribution plan in order to provide a minimum level of benefits for all participating employees. Sometimes known as a floor offset plan, this approach is less costly for an employer than maintaining two separate plans. Mechanically, the benefit provided by the defined benefit plan is reduced by the actuarial present value of the vested account balance in the defined contribution plan. Typically, profit sharing plans will be used more frequently than money purchase plans as the defined contribution plan in a floor arrangement. Good investment performance will generally mean that the defined contribution provides all or a large portion of the benefits for participants. If the plans have poor investment results, the defined benefit plan will end up providing the minimum guarantee.

Q 21:68 What is the position of the IRS on floor plans?

In 1969, the IRS found floor plans unacceptable. [Rev Rul 69-502, 1969-2 CB 89] It was not until 1976 that the IRS reversed its position, finding them acceptable if they met certain requirements. [Rev Rul 76-259, 1976-2 CB 111] The current IRS position is that a floor plan is acceptable if:

1. Definitely determinable benefits are provided;
2. The plan specifies the actuarial basis for conversion of the defined contribution account balances;
3. The defined benefit formula meets the accrual rules of Code Section 411;
4. In converting the defined contribution account balances to benefits, vested account balances plus prior withdrawals are used; and
5. The plans are set up on such a basis as to preclude employer discretion.

Q 21:69 Why might an employer set up a floor plan?

A floor plan may be instituted to help achieve certain objectives of the employer. One objective may be to cut back an overly generous defined benefit program. Another objective might be to provide maximum benefits to older, highly compensated employees. A floor plan can also ease the transition from a defined benefit plan to a defined contribution plan by providing a minimum floor of benefits to older employees. The reverse may also be the case: a floor plan can be set up to supplement an existing profit sharing plan by providing guaranteed benefits.

Design of a Floor Plan

Q 21:70 What are the design features of a floor plan?

Floor plan arrangements always consist of two separate plans, and it is critical to have uniform provisions in both plans: eligibility, vesting (generally cliff), early retirement, death benefits, plan withdrawals, optional forms of benefits, and employee contributions. Since the defined contribution account balances are used to offset the benefits provided in the defined benefit plan, employee investment direction is generally not allowed. The account balances used for the offsets in the defined contribution plan must represent employer contributions only. Employee salary deferrals cannot be used to offset the employer-provided benefits. Joint and survivor annuity options must be provided in the defined contribution plan, even if it is a profit sharing plan otherwise not required to provide this option. Floor plans can be integrated under Code Section 401(l). If the aggregated plans are top heavy, top-heavy minimum benefits or contributions must be provided. In addition, the combined plan limitations of Code Section 415 must be applied.

Q 21:71 How do the minimum coverage and participation rules apply to floor plans?

A floor plan will satisfy the minimum participation rules of Code Section 401(a)(26) if the employee either accrues a benefit during the year or would have accrued a benefit if the offset were disregarded. Both plans must be maintained by the same employer, and all three of the following conditions must be satisfied:

1. The account balance accrued under the defined contribution plan is used to offset or reduce the benefits under the defined benefit plan;

2. The employees who benefit under the plan being tested also benefit under the other plan on a reasonable and uniform basis; and

3. The contributions under the defined contribution plan that are used to offset or reduce the benefits under the defined benefit plan are not used to offset or reduce that employee's benefits under any other plan or any other formula.

[Treas Reg § 1.401(a)(26)-5(a)(2)]

The minimum coverage rules are applied to each plan separately. An employee is treated as benefiting under the plan even if the offset results in no accrual for the year.

Q 21:72 How does a plan sponsor demonstrate that a floor plan provides nondiscriminatory benefits and contributions?

The defined contribution part of the floor plan should be able to demonstrate that nondiscriminatory amounts are provided by using the defined contribution safe harbors. (See chapter 5.) [Treas Reg § 1.401(a)(4)-2(b)] The defined benefit part of the floor plan tests under the general test on a benefits basis [Treas Reg § 1.401(a)(4)-3(c)] or uses the cross-testing rules by converting the accruals to equivalent allocation rates. [Treas Reg § 1.401(a)(4)-8(c)]

A floor plan may use a special safe harbor in testing for nondiscrimination. [Treas Reg § 1.401(a)(4)-8(d)] The floor plan must satisfy these conditions:

1. The defined contribution plan must not be an ESOP, 401(k), or 401(m) plan.

2. The defined benefit and defined contribution plans must both cover the same employees.

3. The vested portion of the defined benefit plan must be reduced by all or a part of the actuarial equivalent of the defined contribution account balance. (An interest rate greater than 8.5 percent cannot be used.)

4. One of the following must apply:

a. The defined benefit plan satisfies general uniformity conditions and the unit credit safe harbor without taking the offset into account. The defined contribution plan can satisfy any defined contribution safe harbor test or the general nondiscrimination test. OR

b. The defined contribution plan satisfies the general uniformity conditions and the unit allocation safe harbor. (See chapter 2.) The defined benefit plan can then use the general defined benefit safe harbor or general nondiscrimination test (before taking offset into account).

5. No employee contributions may be used in the offset.

Advantages and Disadvantages of a Floor Plan

Q 21:73 What are the advantages of floor plans?

A floor plan combines the best features of a defined benefit plan and a defined contribution plan. It provides employees with the security of a guaranteed benefit, and it allows the employer flexibility in funding. The employees will benefit by favorable experience while being insulated against poor performance by the minimum floor benefits.

A floor plan can provide meaningful benefits to older, longer-service employees. When an employer switches the emphasis to a defined contribution plan, the result will primarily benefit younger employees, while the defined benefit plan will benefit the older employees. A floor plan can also be used to provide a higher benefit to employees with rapid salary increases.

Q 21:74 What are the disadvantages of floor plans?

Floor plans are complex and require annual actuarial valuations. In fact, PBGC premiums are required for each participant, even if the projected benefits provided under the defined benefit plan are zero. FAS 87 reporting is also required, and anomalies may result in that the accumulated benefit obligation (ABO) may be greater than the projected benefit obligation (PBO). The actuarial valuation needs to take into account the projected future contributions to the defined contribution plan. This may result in a difficult forecast, since the level of future profit sharing plan contributions is uncertain.

Further, the complexity of floor plans can make communication to the employees extremely difficult; special care must be taken in designing the benefit statement.

Operation of a Floor Plan

Q 21:75 How does a floor plan work?

Consider the following:

Example 1. A defined benefit plan has a formula of 50 percent of final average pay, reduced for fewer than 25 years of service, and accrued fractionally over all years of service. In addition, profit sharing plan contributions have averaged 5 percent of pay since the profit sharing plan was set up ten years ago.

Alex retires at age 65 after 25 years of service. The account balance in the profit sharing plan is $19,500. Alex's final average pay is $30,000.

Converting the account balance to a benefit (using 8 percent conversion factors) will yield a benefit of approximately $2,400 per year. Thus, the profit sharing plan will provide $2,400 per year, and the defined benefit plan will provide the balance.

The benefit provided by the defined benefit formula is calculated as follows:

$$\text{Final average pay} \times \text{benefit formula} = \text{Benefit}$$
$$\$30,000 \times 50\% = \$15,000$$

This $15,000 benefit is then reduced by the $2,400 provided by the defined contribution plan. $12,600 ($15,000 − $2,400) is provided by the defined benefit plan.

Example 2. Beverly leaves employment at age 35 after working for ten years. Beverly's account balance in the profit sharing plan is $15,000. Beverly's final average pay is $40,000.

Converting the profit sharing plan account balance of $15,000 to a benefit at age 65 will yield approximately $18,420 per year at age 65. The accrued benefit in the defined benefit plan is computed as follows:

21-44

Final average pay × benefit formula × accrued benefit ratio = Accrued benefit

$40,000 × 50% × 10 / 40 = $5,000 per year

Thus, the benefit Beverly is entitled to in the defined benefit plan is completely offset by Beverly's account balance in the profit sharing plan.

Floor Plan Versus 401(k) Plan

Q 21:76 When might an employer use a floor plan as an alternative to a 401(k) plan?

An employee population that has little or no interest in deferring pay may cause an employer to consider other retirement plan alternatives. The floor plan benefit can provide a minimum level of benefit security for the employee population. The defined contribution element of the plan could provide significant benefits for the younger portion of the group, while the defined benefit portion could provide a satisfactory threshold of benefits for the older group.

NONQUALIFIED DEFERRED COMPENSATION PLANS

Nonqualified deferred compensation plans are unsecured contractual commitments by an employer to an employee to pay compensation in future tax years. The primary motivation for offering these plans is to provide tax-deferred benefits to a select group of key or highly paid employees. If properly structured, a nonqualified deferred compensation plan is not subject to qualified plan rules.

For additional information see Panel Publishers' *Nonqualified Deferred Compensation Answer Book* in the Panel Answer Book Series.

Q 21:77 Why have nonqualified plans grown in popularity?

Over the past decade, changes have been made in qualified plan rules that enhance the attractiveness of nonqualified plans:

- The drop in Section 415 limits imposed by TEFRA in 1982 and TRA '86 has significantly decreased the maximum benefit that may be provided from $136,425 in 1982 to $125,000 in 1997. The maximum contribution in a defined contribution plan has decreased over the same time from $45,475 to $30,000.

- TRA '86 imposed a compensation cap that is indexed annually and has dropped from $235,840 in 1993 to $160,000 for 1998. This is the maximum amount of compensation that can be taken into account for purposes of computing benefits under a qualified plan.

- TRA '86 dropped the maximum yearly salary deferral in a 401(k) plan from $30,000 in 1986 to $10,000 in 1998.

- TRA '86 also imposed faster vesting requirements and tougher nondiscrimination rules under Code Section 401(a)(4).

- TRA '86 imposed a reduction in the degree of integration permitted in a qualified plan.

- TRA '86 imposed 15 percent excess distribution and excess accumulation taxes on employees or their beneficiaries who receive large amounts from qualified plans. (These have since been repealed by TRA '97.)

The result of these changes is that the costs to employers of pension benefits for rank-and-file employees are increasing, while at the same time employers have less discretion and control over the plans. Therefore, HCEs will receive reduced benefits and consequently pay higher taxes.

Types of Nonqualified Plans

Q 21:78 What types of nonqualified plans are available?

Nonqualified deferred compensation plans are of two basic types: salary reduction arrangements and salary continuation plans. In a salary reduction arrangement, employees voluntarily choose to defer a portion of their salary or future bonus, which is a form of tax-deferred savings. A salary continuation plan is an "add-on" benefit, used to provide supplemental benefits above and beyond those provided in the qualified plan. This benefit is provided in addition to the employee's salary and other compensation.

Use and Design of Nonqualified Plans

Q 21:79 How are nonqualified deferred compensation plans used?

Nonqualified deferred compensation can be used effectively in a number of different circumstances to:

- Provide retirement or death benefits to key employees without the need to cover all employees in a qualified plan

- Provide supplemental benefits or contributions to executives who are currently receiving the maximum benefits or contributions under Code Section 415 in their qualified plans

- Provide certain key executives with benefits individually tailored to the needs of the employee and the employer—an example would be recruiting a senior executive who would not qualify for full benefits provided by the company's defined benefit plan as a result of a shorter service period

- Recruit, retain, and reward key personnel—this feature can allow many closely held companies to compete with publicly held corporations in attracting and retaining qualified executives

- Create incentives to encourage the early retirement of certain executives

Q 21:80 Can all employers use nonqualified deferred compensation plans?

Not all employers can effectively use nonqualified deferred compensation. It is generally not an effective way to compensate owner employees. Also, there should be a high probability that the corporation will be financially sound for the long term for the nonqualified plan to provide meaningful benefits.

Q 21:81 What requirements must be met by a nonqualified deferred compensation plan?

A nonqualified deferred compensation plan must meet the following requirements:

- The plan must be established and maintained by the employer primarily for the purpose of providing deferred compensation for a select group of management or highly compensated employees;
- The plan must be unfunded;
- The plan must be in writing; and
- The Department of Labor (DOL) must be notified of the implementation of the plan.

Note. Highly compensated employee is not defined for nonqualified plans in the same manner as it is for qualified plans. The highly compensated employee definition for qualified plans is discussed in chapter 9. The DOL is responsible for providing regulations that define the term *select group of management* or *highly compensated employees* for nonqualified plans. As of this date, such regulations have not been issued.

The employer will receive a deduction for the benefits only when they are actually provided to the employee. If a tax-deferred vehicle such as life insurance is used, the employer may ultimately receive a deduction greater than the actual contribution paid to the plan.

Advantages and Disadvantages of Nonqualified Plans

Q 21:82 What are the advantages of a nonqualified deferred compensation plan to the employer?

Nonqualified deferred compensation plans provide a number of advantages to the employer. A key advantage is the flexibility in plan design afforded the employer: a select group of employees can be covered by the plan, benefits can be individually tailored, and contributions and benefits can be made at the discretion of the employer. A nonqualified deferred compensation plan requires significantly less paperwork than a qualified plan: its administration is simpler, no government approval is required, and annual filing of 5500s is not needed. Nonqualified deferred compensation plans are also not covered by the PBGC.

Furthermore, the vesting rules of qualified plans do not apply. As a result, the nonqualified deferred compensation plan may provide that benefits are forfeited if the executive leaves employment before attaining a specified age. Funds can generally be recovered by the employer if the plan is not used to pay benefits to executives who have forfeited their benefits under the nonqualified plan.

Q 21:83 What are the advantages of a nonqualified plan to the employee?

For the employee, a nonqualified deferred compensation plan provides an opportunity for substantial wealth accumulation. The current deferral of income tax can result in significant tax savings, and death benefits provide protection for the individual's family. Further, funds can be available to the executive in the event of financial hardship.

Q 21:84 What are the disadvantages of a nonqualified plan to the employer?

A nonqualified deferred compensation plan defers the tax deduction on contributions until benefits actually commence. Thus, the earnings on the funds set aside to pay for the nonqualified deferred compensation plan may be immediately taxable to the corporation.

Q 21:85 What are the disadvantages of a nonqualified plan to the employee?

From the employee's viewpoint, nonqualified deferred compensation is not as secure as qualified plan benefits: essentially, a nonqualified plan is an unsecured promise to pay benefits. In addition, the employee's deferral of compensation in a nonqualified plan could result in a reduction of benefits in other plans, depending on their definition of compensation. For example, the pension plan may provide a benefit of 25 percent of pay, using a definition of average Form W-2 pay over the highest three years. Income deferred in a nonqualified plan will not be included on Form W-2, so an employee's benefits may be reduced as a result of the deferral. Also, if future tax rates are higher, deferring taxes currently may not make sense. This issue is discussed in greater detail in chapter 1.

Tax Traps of Nonqualified Plans

Q 21:86 What are the tax traps of nonqualified deferred compensation plans?

To avoid immediate taxation to the employee, a nonqualified plan must fulfill two major requirements. First, the plan must be structured to avoid both constructive receipt (see Q 21:87) and the provision of an economic benefit (see Q 21:88) currently to the employee. Second, care must be taken to avoid having the plan treated as "funded" under ERISA. These two requirements are discussed in the questions that follow.

Q 21:87 What is the *doctrine of constructive receipt*?

The *doctrine of constructive receipt* provides that amounts due from the employer are includible in income of the employee as soon as:

1. The money is available to the employee;
2. The employer is ready and willing to pay;
3. The right to receive the money is unrestricted; and
4. The failure of the employee to receive money results from the employee's own choice.

[Rev Rul 60-31, 1960-1 CB 174]

Q 21:88 What is the *economic benefit doctrine*?

The *economic benefit doctrine* provides that an employee is currently taxable (before actual or constructive receipt) whenever there is payment in kind, or where the employer makes an equivalent amount of cash available to the employee. This doctrine provides that the employee will not be taxed until funds are beyond the reach of the corporation and its creditors, and the employee runs no substantial risk of forfeiture. [IRC § 83(c)]

Q 21:89 What arc the consequences if a nonqualified plan is treated as "funded" under ERISA?

As can be seen in Table 21-4, it is important to avoid creating a "funded" plan under the ERISA definition. If the employer sets aside money or property for the employee's account in an irrevocable trust that restricts access to the funds by the employer and creditors, the following problems result:

1. The plan is considered funded and is taxable to the employee as soon as the employee's rights are substantially vested; and

2. The plan is subject to ERISA vesting and fiduciary requirements on qualified plans.

The features of qualified and nonqualified plans are compared in Table 21-4.

Benefit Security in Nonqualified Plans

Q 21:90 How can an employer enhance the benefit security of an employee in a nonqualified deferred compensation plan?

Since the plan assets in a nonqualified deferred compensation plan are accessible to the employer and the employer's creditors, employees are justifiably concerned about the safety of the benefits promised. Potential concerns can include the possibility of a hostile takeover, doubts about the company's financial capacity to pay benefits ultimately, and the possible need to litigate to enforce benefit payments. A technique to deal with these concerns that has been used effectively and has been approved in a number of private letter rulings by the IRS is called a rabbi trust (see Q 21:91).

Q 21:91 What is a *rabbi trust*?

A *rabbi trust* is so named because the original trust was created by a synagogue for the benefit of a rabbi. In a rabbi trust, an independent trustee holds the assets of the plan apart from the corporation but not from the corporation's creditors. The irrevocable trust holds the assets that will be used to satisfy all or a portion of the employer's obligation. This avoids a cash flow drain when payments are made to the employee. Some disadvantages of the rabbi trust approach include the following:

- The employer loses the ability to recapture assets.
- The rate of return on plan assets may be less than the rate of

TABLE 21-4. Comparison of Qualified and Nonqualified Plans

	Qualified Plans	Nonqualified Plans	
		Unfunded	Funded
Taxation:			
Company	Immediate deduction	Deferred	Deduction when vested
Employee	Deferred	Deferred	Deduction when vested
Earnings	Deferred	Taxable to company	Taxable to employee when vested
Plan assets	Trustee or insured (PBGC guarantee)	Available to employer or general contractors	Trusteed or insured
Coverage	ERISA tests	Select group only	Any group
Vesting	ERISA	Not subject to ERISA	ERISA
Reporting	Full ERISA requirements	DOL notification letter	Full ERISA requirements
Lump-sum benefits:			
Penalty tax	10% tax under age 59½ unless rollover to IRA	No penalty tax	No penalty tax
Five-year averaging	Permitted until 2000	Not permitted	Not permitted
15% excess distribution tax	Repealed	No tax	No tax
FICA wages	Excluded, except 401(k)	Includible, vested	Includible, vested
Pay limits	$160,000 maximum (1999)	No limit	No limit

return would have been had the assets been reinvested in the business.

- The employee is still not protected against the risk of employer insolvency.

Nonqualified Plan Versus 401(k) Plan

Q 21:92 When might a nonqualified plan be used as an alternative to a 401(k) plan?

An employer may give up on a 401(k) plan if it is unable to achieve significant employee participation. HCEs may become disgruntled with the plan if they cannot shelter as much as they want or if they are forced to receive a refund of their deferrals. In this situation, the employer may terminate the 401(k) plan (or cease to allow employee deferrals) and adopt a nonqualified plan, since a nonqualified plan would generally allow HCEs to defer any portion of their pay they wish.

Rather than terminating the 401(k) plan, the employer may supplement it with a nonqualified plan. HCEs who are unable to defer the amount they wish in the 401(k) plan would be able to defer the difference in the nonqualified plan. If participation of the NHCEs increases in the future, additional amounts may be deferred by HCEs in the 401(k) plan, and the nonqualified plan will become less important in supplementing retirement benefits.

SECTION 403(b) PLANS—TAX-SHELTERED ANNUITIES (TSAs)

A Section 403(b) plan is a deferred tax arrangement, available to employees of certain types of organizations, in which the employee may exclude amounts from gross income that are either premiums paid on an insurance contract or amounts paid to a custodian of a mutual fund. The employer may also contribute on behalf of the employee; in many cases, this takes the form of a matching contribution. The employee's salary reduction is capped at a maximum of $10,000 annually (1999 indexed value).

For additional information on tax-sheltered annuities, see Panel Publishers' *403(b) Answer Book*.

Design of Section 403(b) Plans

Q 21:93 What types of organizations may provide Section 403(b) plans?

An organization that is tax exempt under Code Section 501(c)(3) is eligible to set up a Section 403(b) plan. [IRC § 403(b)(1)(A)(i)] This includes nonprofit organizations whose purposes are religious, charitable, scientific, literary, educational, or safety testing. In addition, certain state and local hospitals are eligible for a Section 403(b) plan [Rev Rul 67-290, 1967-2 CB 198], as are public school systems. [IRC § 403(b)(1)(A)(ii)] Only employees of these types of organizations are eligible to make 403(b) contributions; independent contractors are specifically excluded. [Rev Rul 66-274, 1966-2 CB 446]

Section 1450 of the Small Business Job Protection Act of 1996 (SBJPA) provides that any 403(b) annuity contract purchased in a plan year beginning before 1995 will be treated as purchased by an employer eligible to maintain a Section 403(b) plan.

Q 21:94 What funding vehicles may be used in a Section 403(b) plan?

Three basic mechanisms are available for funding a Section 403(b) plan. The first and most widely used is an annuity contract. This contract can be an individual or group contract that provides fixed retirement benefits to the contract holder. A variable annuity is also permitted. [Rev Rul 68-116, 1968-1 CB 177] The second type of funding vehicle is a retirement endowment contract, which provides incidental life insurance protection. The cost of life insurance, or PS-58 cost, is taxable on an annual basis to the participant. [Ltr Rul 9007001] (See chapter 17.) The third type of funding vehicle is a regulated investment company (mutual fund). In this case, a custodian is required, and it must be a bank, insured federal credit union, or savings and loan. [IRC § 403(b)(7)]

Q 21:95 Who makes contributions to a Section 403(b) plan?

An employer sponsoring a Section 403(b) plan may make contributions on behalf of an employee to a 403(b) annuity. In this case, the amount is treated as additional compensation to the employee. The usual situation is that the employee makes contributions to the Section 403(b) plan via salary reductions. It is critical that the salary reduction agreement be written and legally binding as a contract between the employer and the employee. However, the contract may be terminated at any time with respect to amounts that are not yet earned by the employee. [Treas Reg § 1.403(b)-1(b)(3)] Until passage of SBJPA, only one agreement could be executed per year.

Almost all employees must be eligible to make deferrals to a Section 403(b) plan essentially from their date of hire.

Q 21:96 Must Section 403(b) deferrals be treated as annual additions along with contributions to a qualified plan?

It depends. If the Section 403(b) sponsoring organization also sponsors a qualified plan, then rank-and-file employees do not need to treat their Section 403(b) deferrals as annual additions along with contributions to the qualified plan. The situation is unclear for HCEs who also exercise control of the sponsoring organization. However, for Section 403(b) participants who control a separate company that sponsors a qualified plan, their Section 403(b) contributions do need to be treated as annual additions along with qualified plan contributions. Also, participants who elect option C to satisfy Code Section 415 must treat their Section 403(b) deferrals as annual additions with contributions on their behalf to other qualified plans of the sponsor. [Treas Reg §§ 1.415-7(h), 1.415-8(d)]

Q 21:97 What provisions are found in Section 403(b) plans?

Section 403(b) plans must contain the following provisions:

- A key feature of Section 403(b) plans is that the accounts of the employee are nonforfeitable. [IRC § 403(b)(1)(C)] The employee ordinarily owns the contract and can surrender, borrow, or exercise any ownership rights in it. The contract provisions must require that it not be transferred.

- Minimum distribution requirements under Code Section 401(a)(9) apply. Thus, distributions must commence by the later of April 1 following the calendar year in which the individual attains age 70½ or retirement (see chapter 15). [IRC § 403(b)(10)]

- Withdrawal restrictions apply to salary deferrals: distributions are not available until death, age 59½, separation from service, disability, or financial hardship. [IRC § 403(b)(11)]
- Section 403(b) plans are not subject to the top-heavy rules of Code Section 416.
- Loans are allowed, subject to the qualified plan rules (see chapter 14). [Ltr Rul 8741069]
- Rollovers are permitted to IRAs or to another Section 403(b) plan, although not to a qualified plan. [IRC § 403(b)(8)(A)(ii)]

Q 21:98 How do the minimum participation and coverage rules apply to Section 403(b) plans?

Special rules apply to Section 403(b) plans for plan years beginning after 1988. If contributions other than salary reductions are made, the qualified plan rules relating to minimum participation, coverage, and nondiscrimination apply. [IRC § 403(b)(12)(A)(i)] In looking at the coverage and participation requirements, certain employees may be excluded: nonresident aliens; employees working fewer than 20 hours per week; and employees who are deferring salary in a Section 457 plan, 401(k) plan, or another Section 403(b) plan.

Q 21:99 What are the requirements for a Section 403(b) plan that contains only salary deferrals?

If a plan has only salary reduction contributions, the rules of TRA '86 require that all employees must be eligible to make salary deferrals. A minimum requirement of $200 may be established. [IRC § 403(b)(12)(A)(ii)] However, governmental plans were exempt from these requirements until 1993 [Treas Reg §§ 1.401(a)(4)-13(b), 1.401(a)(26)-9(b)(1), 1.410(b)-2(e)], and churches are exempt from these nondiscrimination requirements permanently. [IRC § 403(b)(1)(D)] Safe harbor alternatives are available for employers who make nonmatching contributions. [IRS Notice 89-23, 1989-1 CB 654] The purpose of these safe harbors is to allow a certain amount of disparity between the contributions for HCEs and NHCEs.

Q 21:100 What requirements must be met if the employer makes matching contributions to a Section 403(b) plan?

Matching employer contributions that are made on account of employee deferral are subject to nondiscrimination testing under Code Section 401(m) (described in chapter 5). Excess aggregate contributions resulting from the failure to satisfy the test must be returned with earnings within 12 months following the close of the plan year; the penalty for failure to do so is plan disqualification. If such excess contributions are not returned within 2½ months following the close of the plan year, there is a 10 percent penalty tax imposed on the employer. A vesting schedule may be attached to the matching contributions.

If a plan runs afoul of the Section 401(m) test, it is not possible to aggregate it with any qualified plan to demonstrate nondiscrimination under the Section 401(a)(4) rules. This is expressly prohibited by the Section 401(a)(4) regulations, since matching contributions may not be included in general Section 401(a)(4) testing.

Q 21:101 What is the limit on elective deferrals?

The cap on the salary reduction amount is $10,000 for 1999. [IRC § 402(g)(4)] This amount will be indexed now that the current 401(k) deferral limit has exceeded $9,500. This aggregate limit of $10,000 includes the following salary reduction contributions: Sections 403(b), 401(k) deferrals, and SARSEP contributions. For example, an individual who contributes $2,000 to a 401(k) plan may also contribute $8,000 to a Section 403(b) plan. [IRS Notice 87-13, 1987-1 CB 432]

Q 21:102 What "catch up" provisions are available?

A special increased limit allows employees to catch up on past years in which the maximum Section 403(b) contribution was not made. This increased limit is available to employees who have completed 15 years of service with an educational organization, hospital, home health service agency, church, convention or association of churches, or health and welfare service agency. [IRC § 402(g)(8)] The limit is increased above $10,000 by the lesser of:

1. $3,000;

2. $15,000, less amounts previously used; or

3. $5,000, multiplied by the number of years of service, less elective deferrals the organization made on behalf of the employee for prior years.

[IRC § 402(g)(8)]

Q 21:103 Are contributions subject to an overall limit?

Yes. Employer contributions and employee salary deferrals are limited under Code Section 403(b)(2) by the *maximum exclusion allowance*. This percentage limit on aggregate contributions to a Section 403(b) plan can be determined by the following formula:

(20% of includible compensation × years of service) − prior contributions

Includible compensation is defined as salary after deduction of the Section 403(b) contribution. This calculation can become very complex for part-time employees. The maximum employer and employee contributions are limited by Code Section 415 to the lesser of 25 percent of includible compensation or $30,000.

Audit Environment for Section 403(b) Plans

Q 21:104 How has the audit environment been changing for Section 403(b) plans?

Until as recently as 1993, it was rare for a Section 403(b) plan to be audited. In 1993 the IRS decided to spot check the level of Section 403(b) compliance and audited 33 hospitals and 16 colleges and universities. None of the plans audited were in full compliance with Section 403(b) rules. The IRS has now targeted 403(b) plans for audit activity and has indicated that all future IRS audits of tax-exempt organizations will include an examination of their Section 403(b) plans. This suggests that loss of the plan's tax-exempt status could be the result of clear, egregious errors in administering a Section 403(b) plan. In May 1999 the IRS completed final 403(b) examination guidelines (chapter 13 of *Employee Plans Examination Guidelines Handbook*). [IRM 7(10) 54]

Q 21:105 What were the most common Section 403(b) defects found in the recent IRS audits?

The most common defect was the ineligibility of the sponsoring organization. Section 403(b) plans are available only to public educational organizations and Section 501(c)(3) nonprofit organizations. But the IRS found that other types of organizations, such as water authorities, trade associations, and Native American tribes, had been sold these plans. Another common defect was miscalculation of the maximum exclusion allowance, especially for part-time employees.

Q 21:106 What is the significance of IRS Announcement 95-33 for Section 403(b) plans?

IRS Announcement 95-33 contained proposed audit guidelines for Section 403(b) plans. It provided little in the way of new guidance, but it is important reading for plan sponsors as it indicates the areas the IRS will be looking at during an audit. Careful study of it will help sponsors find problems through self-examination. The announcement lists likely defects and gives some suggestions for correcting them. Early responses to the audit guidelines expressed disappointment that more guidance was not included and that the IRS intended to hold sponsors to some 30-year-old rules that are out of step with changes in other retirement plan areas.

Q 21:107 What common Section 403(b) plan defects are discussed in IRS Announcement 95-33?

Some common defects of special interest under the proposed audit guidelines are:

1. Sponsorship by an ineligible organization—for example, nonprofits that are not Section 503(c)(3) organizations or governmental entities that do not qualify as educational institutions;

2. Participation by ineligible individuals—for example, independent contractors (often physicians) or elected or appointed officials such as trustees or school board members;

3. Ineligible funding vehicles—for example, annuity contracts not sold by insurance companies or annuity contracts that are transferable (can be sold, assigned, or pledged as col-

lateral) or that do not contain the appropriate early distribution restrictions and incidental life insurance limits, custodial accounts not sponsored by a bank or other approved trustee under Code Section 401(f), and custodial accounts that invest in other than regulated investment companies (e.g., mutual funds);

4. Improper salary reduction election form—for example, failure to be irrevocable for amounts earned while the agreement is in effect, application to amounts earned before the document is effective, and, prior to 1996, more than one election made in a single calendar year;

5. Failure to satisfy all three of the contribution limits—for example, deferral of more than $10,000 per year (taking into account allowable catch-up deferrals), cumulative deferrals exceeding the maximum exclusion allowance (the exclusion allowance applies to both elective and nonelective deferrals), and deferrals in excess of the chosen Section 415 limitation method;

6. Failure to correct excess deferrals in a timely fashion—for example, failure to distribute by April 15 of the next tax year and failure to distribute earnings on the excess deferrals;

7. Failure to meet all the requirements for nonelective deferrals (which are not subject to the $10,000 limit)—for example, the election is not irrevocable if there is any time at which it can be terminated;

8. Clear violations of the nondiscrimination requirements—for example, failure to provide for universal eligibility for salary reduction and matching contributions that do not satisfy the actual contribution percentage (ACP) test;

9. Failure to make required minimum distributions—for example, after April 1 of the later of the year of retirement or the year in which the participant turns 70½ (except for church or government plans)—and combining Section 403(b) accounts with other types of plans to satisfy the distribution requirements;

10. Loans that fail to meet the requirements regarding amount,

repayment period, amortization, or employer and plan aggregation;

11. Violation of the early distribution restrictions of Code Section 403(b)(11)—for example, nonhardship withdrawals prior to separation, disability, death, or age 59½; and

12. Failure to allow direct transfers to an eligible plan to terminated participants and failure to withhold 20 percent of distributions made directly to participants.

Q 21:108 What steps can Section 403(b) sponsors take to prepare for an audit under the Announcement 95-33 guidelines?

1. Study the 403(b) portion of Announcement 95-33 carefully—although not a complete list of requirements, it does indicate the areas of special interest to the IRS and is clearly written with many examples.

2. Review all documents that govern operation of the plan.

3. Review all administrative procedures, especially those dealing with areas likely to be of special interest to the IRS.

4. Understand the responsibilities of third-party vendors involved in the administration of the plan, and prepare internal manuals documenting the role of all parties involved—remember, the plan sponsor is ultimately responsible for seeing that all requirements are followed.

TSA Voluntary Correction (TVC) Program

Q 21:109 What is the *TSA Voluntary Correction (TVC) program?*

The *TSA Voluntary Correction (TVC) program* was introduced by Revenue Procedure 95-24 [1995-1 CB 694] and greatly expanded by Revenue Procedure 99-13. [1999-51 IRB 52]] 403(b) plans may now correct excess contributions through distribution under the Administrative Policy Regarding Self-Correction (APRSC) (see chapter 19). Under TVC and Audit CAP (see chapter 19), upon payment of a negotiated sanction, the sponsor receives written assurance from the IRS that the corrections are acceptable and that the IRS will not pursue revocation of income tax exclusion with regard to the corrected defects.

Q 21:110 What must be included in a TVC submission?

In order to qualify for TVC, the sponsor must identify the defects, propose steps to correct them for all affected years, and obtain the cooperation of any third parties involved in the corrections. The TVC submission must include:

1. A complete description of the defects and the years affected, including years closed to IRS examination;

2. A description of all relevant administrative procedures;

3. An explanation of how and why the defects arose;

4. A description of the proposed methods for correcting the defects, including specific calculations for all affected employees;

5. Calculation of the total sanction amount that could arise from the defects;

6. A description of the measures proposed to ensure that the same defects do not occur again;

7. A list of any other Section 403(b) plans, qualified plans, or SEPs sponsored by the employer;

8. A statement that the plan is not known to be under or selected for IRS examination;

9. The location of the employer's key district office;

10. A statement that all entities involved have agreed to cooperate in correcting the defects;

11. The first two pages of the most recent Form 5500 submission or, if none, comparable information;

12. A copy of all relevant plan documents and agreements;

13. A statement that the employer is eligible to sponsor a Section 403(b) plan;

14. Signature on the submission by the employer or representa-

tive who meets the power of attorney requirements of Revenue Procedure 95-4 [1995-1 CB 397];

15. The following statement signed by the employer (not a representative): "Under penalties of perjury, I declare that I have examined this submission, including accompanying documents, and to the best of my knowledge and belief, the facts presented in support of the TVC request are true, correct, and complete";

16. The appropriate voluntary correction fee; and

17. The label "TVC Program" in the upper right hand corner of the letter.

Mail the submission to IRS, Attention: CP:E:EP:TVC, PO Box 14073, Ben Franklin Station, Washington, DC 20044.

The information submitted is subject to the confidentiality of Code Section 6103, and the corrective statement is not a determination letter per Code Section 6110.

Q 21:111 What is the amount of the TVC voluntary correction fee?

The fee is $500 for fewer than 25 employees, $1,250 for between 25 and 1,000 employees, $5,000 for between 1,001 and 9,999 employees, and $10,000 for 10,000 or more employees. This submission fee will be credited toward the amount of the negotiated sanction under the program.

Q 21:112 What determines the amount of the negotiated sanction?

In the typical case, the IRS will begin the negotiations at 40 percent of the total sanction amount. It is then the sponsor's obligation to present reasons for reducing the sanction. The sanction could for good reasons be reduced to as little as the voluntary correction fee already paid.

Factors that can influence the amount of sanction include the severity of the defects, the number and type of employees involved, the number of rank-and-file participants that would be hurt if the tax exclusions are lost, the extent to which the employer's procedures already in place found the error, and the cost of the correction.

Q 21:113 What is expected of an acceptable corrective measure under TVC?

The suggested corrective measures must be acceptable to the IRS, and the IRS reserves the right to propose alternative corrective steps. In general, acceptable corrections will accomplish the following:

1. Restore both active and terminated participants to the benefit levels they would have had if the defects had not occurred (appropriate steps must be taken to locate all affected terminated employees);

2. Bring the plan into conformity with all governing documents, though correction may also require amending documents to correct defects;

3. Generally, keep assets in the plan;

4. Adjust for investment earnings and forfeitures as well as allocations due to compensation changes;

5. Provide corrective contributions from the employer only;

6. Subject corrective contributions for prior years to the exclusion allowance for the year in which they were made, but to the Section 415 limits for the year to which they relate;

7. Not reduce the benefit to which any participant is entitled; and

8. Report corrections on Form 1099-R or W-2 as appropriate.

Q 21:114 What Section 403(b) defects are eligible for the expanded TVC program?

Under Revenue Procedure 99-13, TVC covers most failures not eligible or suitable for correction under APRSC that are not under examination by the IRS (except certain fiduciary failures that are not covered under any IRS program). The failures are divided into three groups:

1. *Eligibility failures* (the first two are significant expansions of TVC):

    • Establishment by an ineligible organization (assets can remain in the tax-sheltered arrangement provided contributions to it cease by the date of the TVC filing)

- Failure to purchase an appropriate annuity contract or custodial account

- Violation of the nontransferability requirement

2. *Operational failures* such as:

- Failure to satisfy Section 403(b)(12)(A)(ii) requirements on the availability of salary reduction contributions

- Failure to satisfy Section 401(m) nondiscrimination requirements on matching contributions

- Failure to satisfy Section 401(a)(17) limits on compensation to be recognized

- Failure to satisfy the distribution requirements of Sections 403(b)(7) and 403(b)(11)

- Failure to satisfy the incidental death benefit rules of Section 403(b)(10)

- Failure to pay minimum required distributions under Section 403(b)(10)

- Failure to give employees the right to elect a direct rollover under Section 403(b)(10), including failure to give meaningful notice of such right

- Failure to satisfy the elective deferral limit under Section 403(b)(1)(E)

- Failure involving contributions or allocations of excess amounts

- Other failures resulting in the loss of Section 403(b) status that are not a demographic failure, an eligibility failure, or a failure related to the purchase of annuities or contributions to custodial accounts on behalf of individuals not employed by the employer

3. *Demographic failures*

- Failure to satisfy the nondiscrimination requirements of Section 401(a)(4)

- Failure to satisfy the nondiscrimination requirements of Section 410(b)

Q 21:115 What 403(b) defects are not covered by either APRSC or TVC?

Misuse or diversion of plan assets is not covered under any part of the expanded TVC program. However, a number of defects that cannot be handled under either APRSC or TVC as described above can now be handled under Walk-In CAP (see chapter 19), including specifically operational, demographic, or eligibility failures uncovered during an audit.

Q 21:116 How does TVC compare with the voluntary correction programs for qualified plans?

TVC is closer in spirit to the closing agreement program (CAP) than it is to the voluntary compliance program (VCR). As with the former, the final sanction must be negotiated and may be significantly higher than the submission fee. Because there is no determination letter program for Section 403(b) plans, the IRS did not feel that it had enough knowledge of existing situations and so did not have the assurance to set a fee-only correction program for Section 403(b) plans similar to VCR.

Using a Section 403(b) Plan with a Qualified Plan

Q 21:117 How may a Section 403(b) plan be used in conjunction with a qualified plan?

Since 401(k) plans are generally not available to certain plan sponsors, it is possible to combine a Section 403(b) plan with a qualified plan under Code Section 401(a). The basic concept is to use the Section 403(b) plan for salary deferrals and to use the qualified plan for employer contributions. The advantage to this approach is twofold: (1) the qualified plan could use permitted disparity, and (2) the employer would have considerably more investment flexibility.

Beginning in 1997, nonprofit organizations and American Indian tribes may sponsor 401(k) plans, although 401(k) plans remain unavailable to government entities. Note that nonprofits that are not 401(c)(3) organizations remain ineligible for 403(b) tax-sheltered annuity plans, though they may now adopt 401(k) plans.

Section 403(b) Plan Versus 401(k) Plan

Q 21:118 How does a Section 403(b) plan compare with a 401(k) plan?

A key difference between Section 403(b) plans and 401(k) plans is that deferral amounts are not subject to nondiscrimination testing in a Section 403(b) plan. Matching contributions under both plan types are subject to nondiscrimination testing under Code Section 401(m). Catch-up provisions may allow an employee to contribute significantly more to a Section 403(b) plan than to a 401(k) plan. The minimum distribution rules in a Section 403(b) plan are virtually identical to those in a 401(k) plan. However, favorable tax treatment is not available to participants in Section 403(b) plans, as amounts distributed from such a plan are taxable as ordinary income when received. The investments in a Section 403(b) plan are limited to annuity contracts and mutual funds, while a 401(k) plan may use individual securities, group annuity contracts, and a host of other investment options.

TRA '86 applied many other qualified plan rules to Section 403(b) plans. Among them are the Section 410(b) coverage rules, the Section 401(a)(26) minimum participation rules, the Section 401(a)(17) compensation rules, the nondiscrimination rules of Code Sections 401(a)(4) and 401(a)(5), and the rollover and withholding rules of Code Section 401(a)(31). In a Section 403(b) plan prior to 1997, only one annual adjustment can be made in the elective deferral amount, whereas many annual changes may be made to elective deferrals in a Section 401(k) plan.

A 401(k) plan allows exclusion from eligibility for age and service, but no such exclusions are allowed under a Section 403(b) plan. However, a Section 403(b) plan is allowed to exclude those working fewer than 20 hours per week, students who also teach, participants in a Section 457 plan, those who have made a onetime election to participate in a government plan instead of the Section 403(b) plan, employees of a religious order subject to a vow of poverty, and professors normally at another school who are temporarily teaching at a particular institution.

Beginning in 1998, compensation as defined under Section 403(b) includes all elective deferrals or Section 457 plan deferrals as well as Section 125 contributions. Also, the scheduled repeal of Section 415(e) (the 1.0 rule) is extended to Section 403(b) plans. [TRA '97 § 1504]

Q 21:119 Must a Section 403(b) plan adopt a plan document and have it approved by the IRS?

Traditionally, many Section 403(b) arrangements have not had formal plan documents; rather, the only documentation was the individual annuity contract. However, by the last day of the plan year beginning on or after January 1, 1996, all Section 403(b) plans must be "amended" to comply with the relevant provisions of TRA '86. There is no determination letter process for 403(b) plans, although Section 403(b) plan documents may be submitted to the IRS for private letter rulings.

Q 21:120 Are Section 403(b) plans subject to Title I of ERISA?

It depends. Governmental and church plans are not subject to Title I. For Section 501(c)(3) sponsors of 403(b) plans, if they simply act as a conduit for employee deferrals, make no other contributions, and impose no limits on the choice of investment vehicles, they may avoid Title I coverage. [DOL Reg § 2510.3-2(f)] If a Section 403(b) plan is subject to Title I, then it would be required to make annual Form 5500 filings, to send each participant an annual Summary Annual Report, and to conform to disclosure requirements. However, 5500 filings are simpler for a Section 403(b) plan than for a 401(k) plan. According to a DOL representative, independent CPA audits are not required, and Schedule A need never be filed.

Q 21:121 When might an employer use a Section 403(b) plan as an alternative to a 401(k) plan?

The rules on eligible employers will generally dictate whether a Section 403(b) or 401(k) plan is used. (See Q 21:93 and chapter 1.) Beginning in 1997, Section 501(c)(3) nonprofits may sponsor either Section 403(b) plans or 401(k) plans. Section 403(b) plans may allow higher deferrals but may also be more complex to administer correctly.

SECTION 457 PLANS

The effect of Code Section 457 is to shelter deferred compensation and income attributable to the deferred amounts from current taxation. The amounts are deferred from tax until paid or otherwise made available to the participant or beneficiary. [IRC § 457(a)] To achieve this deferral of income, the plan must be maintained by an eligible employer and comply with the specific provisions of Code Section 457.

Under a Section 457 plan maintained by an eligible employer, an employee or independent contractor may elect to defer annually the lesser of $8,000 (as indexed for 1998) or 33.33 percent of compensation. The amounts are set aside by the employer and invested. The employee is then taxed on the deferred amounts and income earned when such amounts are paid or made available under the terms of the plan.

Under a Section 457 plan for governmental employers, there are no discrimination rules, minimum vesting or participation standards, or disclosure requirements. Section 1505 of TRA '97 extended indefinitely the moratorium on the application of certain nondiscrimination rules to state and local government retirement plans. These plans are nonqualified plans exempt from Title I of ERISA. Although Code Section 457 was extended to nonprofit employers by TRA '86, no parallel change was made under ERISA. Therefore, the practical availability to nonprofits is restricted. The plan funds are subject to the rights of the eligible employer's creditors.

Plan funds are available to the employee no earlier than upon separation from service or in the case of an unforeseeable emergency. In addition, Section 457 plans must meet minimum distribution rules (e.g., the age 70½ rules). The Section 457 distribution rules are slightly more restrictive than the qualified plan rules and are effective after 1988.

The IRS has indicated that it considers the regulations under Code Section 457 to be outdated and has stated that new regulations may be forthcoming.

For more information on Section 457 plans, see Panel Publishers' *457 Answer Book.*

Design of Section 457 Plans

Q 21:122 What types of employers are eligible for Section 457 plans?

Eligible employers are state governments or agencies or subdivisions thereof [IRC § 457(e)(1)(A)] or any nongovernmental organizations exempt from income taxes, defined in Code Sections 501 through 528, and especially Code Section 501(c). [IRC § 457(e)(1)(B)] Examples of these tax-exempt organizations are civic organizations and local associations of employees; religious, charitable, scientific, literary, and educational organizations; business leagues; certain credit unions; and mutual insurance funds.

Q 21:123 Who is eligible to make deferrals in a Section 457 plan?

Eligible participants include employees and can also include independent contractors of eligible employers. [IRC § 457(e)(2)] Participants may defer taxable compensation only for the performance of services. [IRC §§ 457(e)(2), 457(e)(5)]

Q 21:124 Are there exemptions from Section 457 coverage?

Yes. Deferral arrangements that were in writing by August 16, 1986, or the deferrals of which began before 1987 are exempt from the Section 457 requirements, although any increases under the arrangements would be subject to Code Section 457. Also exempt are nonelective deferrals to nonemployees, although all contractors with the same relationship to the payer must be covered under the same plan with no individual differences. [IRC § 457(e)(12)(A)] Deferred compensation arrangements for state judges do not generally fall under Section 457 rules.

Q 21:125 What are the deferral limits in a Section 457 plan?

The deferral is subject to a ceiling equal to the lesser of $8,000 (for 1999) or one third of includible compensation—that is, net of salary deferrals. [IRC § 457(b)(2)] This limitation is reduced by any of the following deferral amounts: Section 403(b) deferrals, 401(k) elective deferrals, and SARSEP deferrals. [IRC § 457(c)(2)]

Q 21:126 How is the $8,000 dollar limited applied?

The $8,000 dollar limit is applied per individual across all employers.

Q 21:127 How is the 33⅓ percent limit applied?

The 33⅓ percent limit must be applied separately to the compensation from each employer.

Q 21:128 Can deferrals into a Section 457 plan exceed the $8,000/33⅓ percent limits?

Yes. There are catch-up provisions, as discussed in Q 21:129. Also, deferrals can exceed the usual limits and remain nontaxable to the employee provided they remain "non-vested"—that is, subject to the future performance of substantial services. [IRC § 457(f)] Some Section 457 plans allow the employee to irrevocably postpone the vesting date to some fixed or determinable future time. If this can be done repeatedly, it is referred to as rolling vesting. The IRS has indicated suspicion of such rolling vesting arrangements, and this issue may be addressed in forthcoming regulations.

Q 21:129 Are there catch-up provisions in Section 457 plans?

Yes. The ceiling amount may be increased, if the plan so provides, for one or more of the last three taxable years ending before the participant attains normal retirement age. [IRC § 457(b)(3)] In that case, the ceiling per year is the lesser of $15,000 or the sum of the ceiling that normally applies for a year (i.e., $8,000 or one third of compensation) and the unused ceiling amounts from prior taxable years. [IRC § 457(b)(3)(B)] This unused ceiling is analogous to the profit sharing secondary limit of qualified plans or the exclusion allowance concept used in limiting deferrals in tax-sheltered annuities (TSAs).

Q 21:130 How is the allowable catch-up contribution computed?

The allowable catch-up contribution amounts are determined by the following four steps:

1. Compute the participant's available deferral ceiling.

2. Take into account the aggregation of contribution to 401(k)s, Section 403(b) tax-sheltered annuities (TSAs), and SEPs.

3. Subtract the actual deferral amounts.

4. Carry forward the balance until the participant nears retirement age.

[IRC §§ 457(c), 457(b)(3)(B)(ii)]

For each of the three taxable years prior to the year in which the participant attains normal retirement age, a new ceiling limit is computed. Any ceiling amount not used in the first of these three years is carried forward to the next, and so forth.

Q 21:131 When may the deferral amount be changed?

A further requirement is that deferral agreements are effective only for a month if executed prior to the beginning of the month. [IRC § 457(b)(4)] For new employees, a plan may provide for deferral during a month if the salary reduction agreement is executed on or before the first day of employment. [Treas Reg § 1.457-2(g)]

Q 21:132 Who owns and holds the assets of a Section 457 plan?

Historically, all deferrals, investments, and income attributable to deferrals remained solely the property of the employer. Assets could not be restricted to pay only plan benefits and were subject to the claims of the employer's general creditors. [IRC § 457(b)(6)] Funds remained the property of the employer until distributed to participants or beneficiaries. However, as with other nonqualified plans, the assets could be held in a rabbi trust.

For Section 457 plans established after August 20, 1996, amounts deferred must be held in a trust or in a custodial account or annuity contract for the exclusive benefit of employees. Plans already in existence must have met this requirement by January 1, 1999. Such trusts will be tax sheltered and may better prevent the assets from being subject to claims of the employer's creditors. [SBJPA § 1448]

Q 21:133 May the employee direct the investment of his or her Section 457 assets?

Yes. The participant may, if the plan provides, direct the investment of those assets.

Q 21:134 May Section 457 assets be invested in life insurance policies?

Yes. However, the employer must retain all incidents of ownership in the policies; the employer must be the sole beneficiary of the policies; and the employer must be under no obligation to transfer the policy or its proceeds to the participant or the participant's beneficiary. Any death benefit proceeds would be taxed under deferred compensation rules. [H Rep No 95-1445 (PL 95-600) 53]

Presumably, this will change under the trust requirement of Section 1448 of SBJPA (see Q 21:132).

Distributions from Section 457 Plans

Q 21:135 What are the distribution requirements of a Section 457 plan?

The distribution rules provide that deferred amounts and income will be made available no earlier than upon:

- Separation from service
- The occurrence of an unforeseeable emergency for the participant [IRC § 457(d)(1)(A)]
- The calendar year when the participant attains age 70½ [IRC § 457(d)(1)(A)(i)]
- After 1996, account balances not exceeding $3,500 may be distributed to in-service employees in some circumstances. [SBJPA § 1447]

[IRC §§ 457(b)(5), 457(d)]

Q 21:136 What is the latest that benefits may commence?

Under post-TRA '86 rules, distributions are required to begin no later than the April 1 following the later of the year of retirement or the calendar year in which the employee attains age 70½. [IRC § 401(a)(9)(C)] In the case of distribution beginning before a participant's death, at least two thirds of the amount payable must be scheduled to be paid over the life expectancy of the participant, determined at the time distributions begin. [IRC § 457(d)(2)(B)(i)(I)] Any amount not actually distributed to the participant by the time he or she dies must be paid at least as rapidly as the method of distribution being used at the date of death. [IRC § 457(d)(2)(B)(i)(II)]

Q 21:137 After a participant dies, how soon must benefits be distributed?

If a distribution has not begun before a participant dies, then the entire amount must be paid over a period of not more than 15 years. Payments may be made over the life expectancy of the spouse, however, if the spouse is the beneficiary. [IRC § 457(d)(2)(B)(ii)] Benefits payable over a period of more than one year must be made on a substantially nonincreasing basis and must be paid at least annually. [IRC § 457(d)(2)(C)]

Q 21:138 May participants be cashed out upon separation from service?

A cash-out rule allows a participant to receive a lump sum within 60 days of election if the total amount payable is $3,500 or less. No additional amounts may be deferred under the plan. [IRC § 457(e)(9)] The regulations require true separation from service in order to receive benefits. The participant, not the employer, has discretion over receipt of the cash-out.

Q 21:139 May amounts be transferred between Section 457 plans?

A tax-free transfer of a participant's account balance from one eligible plan to another is allowed. [IRC § 457(e)(10)] This is analogous to the qualified plan trust-to-trust transfer rules and is not a rollover provision. In other words, a participant may not receive a lump sum from a Section 457 plan and roll it tax free to another Section 457 plan. Further, amounts received from a Section 457 plan are not eligible for rollover or transfer to an IRA or any qualified plan. [Rev Rul 86-103, 1986-2 CB 62]

Q 21:140 How is *separation from service* defined in a Section 457 plan?

Separation from service for a common-law employee is the same as in the qualified plan context. If an employee would be separated for qualified lump-sum distribution purposes, as defined under Code Section 402(e)(4)(A)(iii), a distribution would be available from the Section 457 plan. [Treas Reg § 1.457-2(h)(2)]

Separation from service becomes complicated in the Section 457 context when dealing with independent contractors. The IRS is concerned that a contractor may achieve short-term deferral and access to deferrals by simply delaying periodic renewal of a long-term contract. To combat this perceived potential abuse, the regulations provide a facts-and-circumstances analysis of an independent contractor's "good faith and complete termination of the contractual relationship." [Treas Reg §§ 1.457-2(h)(3)(ii)(A), 1.457-2(h)(3)(ii)(B)]

Q 21:141 Are hardship withdrawals from a Section 457 plan permitted?

Yes, but the unforeseeable emergency test used for Section 457 plans is stricter than the qualified plan hardship distribution rules. To provide the option, a plan must define *unforeseeable emergency* as severe financial hardship to a participant resulting from:

1. The sudden and unexpected illness or accident of the participant or dependents;

2. The loss of a participant's property due to casualty; or

3. Other similar extraordinary and unforeseeable circumstances that result from events beyond a participant's control.

[Treas Reg § 1.457-2(h)(4)]

Unforeseeable emergency requires a facts-and-circumstances analysis. Even if the determination is made that an unforeseeable emergency exists, a Section 457 plan is prohibited from making a distribution to the extent that the hardship is or may be relieved through reimbursement, compensation, or insurance; by liquidation of assets (unless the liquidation would itself cause severe hardship); or by stopping deferrals under the plan. The purchase of a home and payment of college expenses are specifically listed as examples of what is not an unforeseeable emergency. [Treas Reg § 1.457-2(h)(4)] In any event, the amount of the emergency withdrawal is limited to what is reasonably required to satisfy the emergency need. [Treas Reg § 1.457-2(h)(5)]

Q 21:142 How are distributions from a Section 457 plan taxed?

A distribution from an eligible Section 457 plan is taxed to the recipient as ordinary income. There is no special tax treatment such as partial rollover, capital gains treatment, or ten- or five-year forward averaging. The only favorable tax treatment for Section 457 distributions is the plan-to-plan transfer option. On the other hand, there are no early distribution penalty taxes [IRC § 72(t)(1)], excess contribution taxes [IRC § 4979], excess distribution tax [IRC § 4980A], or prohibited transaction excise tax. [IRC § 4975(e)] However, nonprofits could potentially have prohibited transactions under ERISA. (See Q 5:29.)

A 50 percent required minimum distribution excise tax [IRC § 4974] is effective as of 1989. (See Q 17:62.)

Violations of Section 457

Q 21:143 What happens if a Section 457 plan does not meet the requirements?

The consequences of violating Section 457 provisions are as follows:

1. The plan ceases to be an eligible plan; and

2. Participants are taxed on deferrals and income attributable to them when there is no longer a substantial risk of forfeiture.

[IRC § 457(f)(3)(b)]

The recognition of income triggers payroll taxes as well as income taxes. Section 457 plans are deferred compensation plans rather than retirement or pension plans. Distributions are generally wages and may be subject to payroll taxes similar to traditional nonqualified deferred compensation arrangements. Deferrals to ineligible plans are subject to payroll tax at the time the employee's rights to benefits are no longer subject to a substantial risk of forfeiture. Deferrals under an eligible plan, however, are wages for payroll tax purposes when paid or made available to participants or beneficiaries. [IRC § 3121(v)(3)]

Table 21-5 compares the features of Section 457 and 401(k) plans.

TABLE 21-5. Comparison of Section 457 and 401(k) Plans

	457	*401(k)*
Maximum deferral	Lesser of 33⅓% of includible compensation. or $8,000 (for 1999)	Lesser or 25% of compensation, or $10,000 (for 1999)
Catch-up	Yes	No
Coordination	403(b) 401(k) SEP Not defined benefit	All retirement plans 403(b) SEP
Distributions	Ordinary income	5-year averaging (until 2000)
Rollovers	457 only	IRA; or another qualified plan
Vesting	Property of employer until distribution	100% vesting
Discrimination test	No	Yes
Eligibility	All employees and independent contractors	Age 21 1-year wait
Funds held by	Trust by 1999	Trust
Withdrawals	Unforeseeable emergency	After 59½ or hardship
Excise tax on early withdrawal	No	Yes

Section 457 Plan Versus 401(k) Plan

Q 21:144 When might an employer use a Section 457 plan as an alternative to a 401(k) plan?

The type of entity will determine whether the employer is eligible for a Section 457 plan or a 401(k) plan (see Q 21:122).

TABLE 21-6. Comparison of Retirement Savings Alternatives

	401(k) Plan	IRA	SEP	SIMPLE IRA	Cash Balance Plan	Floor Plan	Age-Weighted PS Plan	403(b) Plan	457 Plan	NQDC Plan	After-Tax Savings
Eligibility											
Minimum age	21	None	21	None	21	21	21	None	None	None	None
Waiting period	1 year	None	Worked 3 of last 5 years Earned more than $400	None	1 year, 2 years if 100% vested	1 year, 2 years if 100% vested	1 year, 2 years if 100% vested	None	None	None	None
Employee deferral limit	$10,000	$2,000 or $4,000	N/A	$6,000	0	0	0	$10,000 + catch-up	$8,000 + catch-up	No limit	0
Vesting schedule	Permitted on employer contribution	100%	100%	100%	Permitted	Permitted	Permitted	Permitted on employer contribution	100%	Permitted	N/A
Employer deduction	15% of payroll	N/A	Lesser of 15% of payroll or $30,000	Lesser of 100% of pay or $12,000	Actuarially determined	Actuarially determined up to 25% of payroll	15% of payroll	As compensation	As compensation	When benefits are paid	N/A
Eligible employers	All, except government units	N/A	All	Up to 100 employees earning at least $5,000	All	All	All	Public schools; nonprofit hospitals; 501(c)(3) corporations	Government units; tax-exempt	All, except government units	N/A

Taxation of lump-sum distributions	Income averaging until 2000	Ordinary income (except Roth IRA)	Ordinary income	Ordinary income	Income averaging until 2000	Income averaging until 2000	Ordinary income	Ordinary income	Ordinary income	Ordinary income	N/A
Required minimum distribution (50% penalty)	Over life expectancy or joint life	Over life expectancy or joint life (except Roth IRA)	Over life expectancy or joint life	Over life expectancy or joint life	Over life expectancy or joint life	Over life expectancy or joint life	Over life expectancy or joint life	Over life expectancy or joint life	⅔ over life expectancy	N/A	N/A
Premature withdrawals	10% penalty	10% penalty	10% penalty	10% penalty (25% first 2 years)	10% penalty	10% penalty	10% penalty	10% penalty	N/A	N/A	N/A
Investment options	ERISA fiduciary standards	No insurance No collectibles; no loans	No insurance No collectibles; no loans	No insurance No collectibles; no loans	ERISA fiduciary standards	ERISA fiduciary standards	ERISA fiduciary standards	Annuity contracts, mutual funds	No restrictions	No restrictions	No restrictions
Annual IRS reporting	Form 5500	Form 5498	Form 5305A SEP	W-2	Form 5500	Form 5500	Form 5500	None	None	None	None
FICA tax applies	Yes	Yes	No	Yes	No	No	No	Yes	Yes	Yes	Yes
Subject to PBGC & actuarial valuation	No	No	No	No	Yes	Yes	No	No	No	No	No

21-79

Appendix A
Retirement Planning Tables*

Scenarios

Each scenario includes these four tables

Table 1. Percent of Salary Replaced by a 401(k) Account Equal to Current
Annual Salary

Table 2. Percent of Salary Replaced by a 401(k) Contribution of 1 Percent
of Current Salary

Table 3. 401(k) Contribution (Percent of Current Salary) Needed to Replace
10 Percent of Salary at Retirement

Table 4. Accumulation at Retirement (Multiple of Current Salary) for 10 Percent
Salary Replacement

*See chapter 7.

I. Retirement Planning with Level Salary & No Inflation
Planned Retirement Age 59

Table 1 - Percent of Salary Replaced by a 401(k) Account Equal to Current Annual Salary I-59-1

Probable Life Expectancy at Retirement

Yrs. to Ret.	25.7 (Same as Male Avg.)				28.3 (Better than Male Avg.)				31 (Same as Female Avg.)				33.8 (Better than Female Avg.)				Yrs. to Ret.
	4% / 4%	6% / 5%	8% / 6%	10% / 7%	4% / 4%	6% / 5%	8% / 6%	10% / 7%	4% / 4%	6% / 5%	8% / 6%	10% / 7%	4% / 4%	6% / 5%	8% / 6%	10% / 7%	
	Expected Return (Pre-Retirement/Post-Retirement)								(Pre-Retirement/Post-Retirement)				Expected Return				
0	6.48	7.20	7.94	8.70	6.12	6.85	7.60	8.36	5.82	6.55	7.31	8.08	5.56	6.30	7.06	7.85	0
1	6.74	7.63	8.58	9.57	6.37	7.26	8.20	9.20	6.05	6.94	7.89	8.89	5.78	6.68	7.63	8.64	1
2	7.01	8.09	9.26	10.53	6.62	7.69	8.86	10.12	6.29	7.36	8.52	9.78	6.01	7.08	8.24	9.50	2
3	7.29	8.58	10.00	11.58	6.88	8.16	9.57	11.13	6.54	7.80	9.21	10.76	6.25	7.50	8.90	10.45	3
4	7.58	9.09	10.80	12.74	7.16	8.64	10.33	12.24	6.80	8.27	9.94	11.84	6.50	7.95	9.61	11.50	4
5	7.89	9.64	11.67	14.01	7.45	9.16	11.16	13.47	7.08	8.77	10.74	13.02	6.76	8.43	10.38	12.64	5
6	8.20	10.21	12.60	15.41	7.74	9.71	12.05	14.82	7.36	9.29	11.60	14.32	7.03	8.93	11.21	13.91	6
7	8.53	10.83	13.61	16.95	8.05	10.30	13.02	16.30	7.65	9.85	12.52	15.76	7.31	9.47	12.11	15.30	7
8	8.87	11.48	14.70	18.65	8.38	10.91	14.06	17.93	7.96	10.44	13.53	17.33	7.60	10.04	13.08	16.83	8
9	9.22	12.17	15.88	20.51	8.71	11.57	15.19	19.72	8.28	11.07	14.61	19.06	7.91	10.64	14.12	18.51	9
10	9.59	12.90	17.15	22.56	9.06	12.26	16.40	21.69	8.61	11.73	15.78	20.97	8.22	11.28	15.25	20.36	10
11	9.98	13.67	18.52	24.82	9.42	13.00	17.71	23.86	8.95	12.43	17.04	23.07	8.55	11.96	16.47	22.40	11
12	10.38	14.49	20.00	27.30	9.80	13.78	19.13	26.25	9.31	13.18	18.40	25.37	8.90	12.67	17.79	24.64	12
13	10.79	15.36	21.60	30.03	10.19	14.60	20.66	28.87	9.68	13.97	19.88	27.91	9.25	13.43	19.21	27.11	13
14	11.22	16.28	23.33	33.04	10.60	15.48	22.31	31.76	10.07	14.81	21.47	30.70	9.62	14.24	20.75	29.82	14
15	11.67	17.26	25.19	36.34	11.02	16.41	24.10	34.94	10.47	15.70	23.18	33.77	10.01	15.09	22.41	32.80	15
16	12.14	18.29	27.21	39.97	11.46	17.39	26.02	38.43	10.89	16.64	25.04	37.15	10.41	16.00	24.20	36.08	16
17	12.62	19.39	29.38	43.97	11.92	18.44	28.11	42.27	11.33	17.64	27.04	40.86	10.82	16.96	26.14	39.68	17
18	13.13	20.55	31.74	48.37	12.40	19.54	30.36	46.50	11.78	18.70	29.20	44.95	11.26	17.98	28.23	43.65	18
19	13.65	21.79	34.27	53.20	12.89	20.72	32.78	51.15	12.25	19.82	31.54	49.45	11.71	19.06	30.49	48.02	19
20	14.20	23.09	37.02	58.52	13.41	21.96	35.41	56.27	12.74	21.01	34.06	54.39	12.17	20.20	32.93	52.82	20
21	14.77	24.48	39.98	64.38	13.95	23.28	38.24	61.89	13.25	22.27	36.79	59.83	12.66	21.41	35.56	58.10	21
22	15.36	25.95	43.18	70.81	14.50	24.67	41.30	68.08	13.78	23.60	39.73	65.81	13.17	22.70	38.41	63.91	22
23	15.97	27.51	46.63	77.90	15.08	26.15	44.60	74.89	14.33	25.02	42.91	72.39	13.69	24.06	41.48	70.30	23
24	16.61	29.16	50.36	85.68	15.69	27.72	48.17	82.38	14.91	26.52	46.34	79.63	14.24	25.50	44.80	77.33	24
25	17.28	30.91	54.39	94.25	16.32	29.39	52.02	90.62	15.50	28.11	50.05	87.60	14.81	27.03	48.38	85.07	25
26	17.97	32.76	58.74	103.68	16.97	31.15	56.19	99.68	16.12	29.80	54.05	96.36	15.40	28.65	52.25	93.57	26
27	18.69	34.73	63.44	114.05	17.65	33.02	60.68	109.64	16.77	31.59	58.38	105.99	16.02	30.37	56.43	102.93	27
28	19.43	36.81	68.51	125.45	18.35	35.00	65.53	120.61	17.44	33.48	63.05	116.59	16.66	32.19	60.95	113.23	28
29	20.21	39.02	74.00	138.00	19.09	37.10	70.78	132.67	18.14	35.49	68.09	128.25	17.33	34.13	65.83	124.55	29
30	21.02	41.36	79.91	151.80	19.85	39.33	76.44	145.94	18.86	37.62	73.54	141.08	18.02	36.17	71.09	137.00	30
31	21.86	43.84	86.31	166.98	20.64	41.69	82.55	160.53	19.62	39.88	79.42	155.18	18.74	38.34	76.78	150.70	31
32	22.74	46.47	93.21	183.67	21.47	44.19	89.16	176.58	20.40	42.27	85.77	170.70	19.49	40.64	82.92	165.77	32
33	23.65	49.26	100.67	202.04	22.33	46.84	96.29	194.24	21.22	44.81	92.64	187.77	20.27	43.08	89.55	182.35	33
34	24.59	52.22	108.72	222.24	23.22	49.65	103.99	213.67	22.07	47.49	100.05	206.55	21.08	45.67	96.72	200.59	34
35	25.57	55.35	117.42	244.47	24.15	52.63	112.31	235.03	22.95	50.34	108.05	227.21	21.93	48.41	104.46	220.64	35
36	26.60	58.67	126.82	268.92	25.12	55.79	121.30	258.54	23.87	53.37	116.70	249.93	22.80	51.31	112.81	242.71	36
37	27.66	62.19	136.96	295.81	26.12	59.13	131.00	284.39	24.82	56.57	126.03	274.92	23.71	54.39	121.84	266.98	37
38	28.77	65.92	147.92	325.39	27.17	62.68	141.48	312.83	25.82	59.96	136.11	302.41	24.66	57.65	131.59	293.68	38
39	29.92	69.88	159.75	357.93	28.25	66.44	152.80	344.11	26.85	63.56	147.00	332.65	25.65	61.11	142.11	323.04	39
40	31.12	74.07	172.53	393.72	29.38	70.43	165.03	378.52	27.92	67.37	158.76	365.92	26.68	64.78	153.48	355.35	40
41	32.36	78.51	186.33	433.09	30.56	74.65	178.23	416.38	29.04	71.41	171.46	402.51	27.74	68.67	165.76	390.88	41
42	33.65	83.22	201.24	476.40	31.78	79.13	192.49	458.01	30.20	75.70	185.18	442.76	28.85	72.79	179.02	429.97	42
43	35.00	88.22	217.34	524.04	33.05	83.88	207.89	503.81	31.41	80.24	200.00	487.03	30.01	77.15	193.34	472.97	43
44	36.40	93.51	234.73	576.44	34.38	88.91	224.52	554.20	32.67	85.06	216.00	535.74	31.21	81.78	208.81	520.27	44
45	37.86	99.12	253.50	634.09	35.75	94.25	242.48	609.62	33.97	90.16	233.27	589.31	32.45	86.69	225.51	572.29	45
46	39.37	105.07	273.78	697.50	36.90	99.90	261.88	670.58	35.33	95.57	251.94	648.24	33.75	91.89	243.55	629.52	46
47	40.95	111.37	295.69	767.25	38.67	105.90	282.83	737.64	36.74	101.30	272.09	713.07	35.10	97.40	263.04	692.48	47
48	42.58	118.05	319.34	843.97	40.21	112.25	305.45	811.40	38.21	107.38	293.86	784.37	36.51	103.25	284.08	761.72	48
49	44.29	125.14	344.89	928.37	41.82	118.99	329.89	892.54	39.74	113.82	317.37	862.81	37.97	109.44	306.81	837.90	49
50	46.06	132.65	372.48	1021.21	43.50	126.13	356.28	981.79	41.33	120.65	342.76	949.09	39.49	116.01	331.35	921.68	50

Appendix A

I. Retirement Planning with Level Salary & No Inflation
Planned Retirement Age 59

Table 2 - Percent of Salary Replaced by a 401(k) Contribution of 1% of Current Salary

I-59-2

Probable Life Expectancy at Retirement

Yrs. to Ret.	25.7 (Same as Male Avg.)				28.3 (Better than Male Avg.)				31 (Same as Female Avg.)				33.8 (Better than Female Avg.)				Yrs. to Ret.
	4% / 4%	6% / 5%	8% / 6%	10% / 7%	4% / 4%	6% / 5%	8% / 6%	10% / 7%	4% / 4%	6% / 5%	8% / 6%	10% / 7%	4% / 4%	6% / 5%	8% / 6%	10% / 7%	
	Expected Return				(Pre-Retirement/Post-Retirement)				(Pre-Retirement/Post-Retirement)				Expected Return				
0	0.00	0.00	0.00	0.00	0.00	0.00	0.00	0.00	0.00	0.00	0.00	0.00	0.00	0.00	0.00	0.00	0
1	0.06	0.07	0.08	0.09	0.06	0.07	0.08	0.08	0.06	0.07	0.07	0.08	0.06	0.06	0.07	0.08	1
2	0.13	0.15	0.17	0.18	0.12	0.14	0.16	0.18	0.12	0.13	0.15	0.17	0.11	0.13	0.15	0.16	2
3	0.20	0.23	0.26	0.29	0.19	0.22	0.25	0.28	0.18	0.21	0.24	0.27	0.17	0.20	0.23	0.26	3
4	0.28	0.32	0.36	0.40	0.26	0.30	0.34	0.39	0.25	0.29	0.33	0.38	0.24	0.28	0.32	0.36	4
5	0.35	0.41	0.47	0.53	0.33	0.39	0.45	0.51	0.32	0.37	0.43	0.49	0.30	0.36	0.41	0.48	5
6	0.43	0.50	0.58	0.67	0.41	0.48	0.56	0.65	0.39	0.46	0.54	0.62	0.37	0.44	0.52	0.61	6
7	0.51	0.60	0.71	0.83	0.48	0.57	0.68	0.79	0.46	0.55	0.65	0.77	0.44	0.53	0.63	0.74	7
8	0.60	0.71	0.84	0.99	0.56	0.68	0.81	0.96	0.54	0.65	0.78	0.92	0.51	0.62	0.75	0.90	8
9	0.69	0.83	0.99	1.18	0.65	0.79	0.95	1.14	0.62	0.75	0.91	1.10	0.59	0.72	0.88	1.07	9
10	0.78	0.95	1.15	1.39	0.73	0.90	1.10	1.33	0.70	0.86	1.06	1.29	0.67	0.83	1.02	1.25	10
11	0.87	1.08	1.32	1.61	0.83	1.03	1.26	1.55	0.78	0.98	1.22	1.50	0.75	0.94	1.18	1.45	11
12	0.97	1.21	1.51	1.86	0.92	1.16	1.44	1.79	0.87	1.10	1.39	1.73	0.83	1.06	1.34	1.68	12
13	1.08	1.36	1.71	2.13	1.02	1.29	1.63	2.05	0.97	1.24	1.57	1.98	0.92	1.19	1.52	1.93	13
14	1.19	1.51	1.92	2.43	1.12	1.44	1.84	2.34	1.06	1.38	1.77	2.26	1.02	1.32	1.71	2.20	14
15	1.30	1.68	2.16	2.76	1.23	1.59	2.06	2.66	1.16	1.52	1.98	2.57	1.11	1.47	1.92	2.49	15
16	1.41	1.85	2.41	3.13	1.34	1.76	2.30	3.01	1.27	1.68	2.22	2.91	1.21	1.62	2.14	2.82	16
17	1.54	2.03	2.68	3.53	1.45	1.93	2.56	3.39	1.38	1.85	2.47	3.28	1.32	1.78	2.38	3.18	17
18	1.66	2.23	2.97	3.97	1.57	2.12	2.84	3.81	1.49	2.02	2.74	3.69	1.42	1.95	2.65	3.58	18
19	1.79	2.43	3.29	4.45	1.69	2.31	3.15	4.28	1.61	2.21	3.03	4.14	1.54	2.13	2.93	4.02	19
20	1.93	2.65	3.63	4.98	1.82	2.52	3.48	4.79	1.73	2.41	3.34	4.63	1.65	2.32	3.23	4.50	20
21	2.07	2.88	4.00	5.57	1.96	2.74	3.83	5.35	1.86	2.62	3.68	5.17	1.78	2.52	3.56	5.03	21
22	2.22	3.12	4.40	6.21	2.10	2.97	4.21	5.97	1.99	2.84	4.05	5.77	1.90	2.73	3.92	5.61	22
23	2.37	3.38	4.84	6.92	2.24	3.22	4.63	6.65	2.13	3.08	4.45	6.43	2.03	2.96	4.30	6.25	23
24	2.53	3.66	5.30	7.70	2.39	3.48	5.07	7.40	2.27	3.33	4.88	7.15	2.17	3.20	4.72	6.95	24
25	2.70	3.95	5.81	8.56	2.55	3.76	5.55	8.23	2.42	3.59	5.34	7.95	2.31	3.46	5.16	7.72	25
26	2.87	4.26	6.35	9.50	2.71	4.05	6.07	9.13	2.58	3.87	5.84	8.83	2.46	3.73	5.65	8.57	26
27	3.05	4.59	6.94	10.53	2.88	4.36	6.64	10.13	2.74	4.17	6.38	9.79	2.62	4.01	6.17	9.51	27
28	3.24	4.93	7.57	11.68	3.06	4.69	7.24	11.22	2.91	4.49	6.97	10.85	2.78	4.32	6.74	10.54	28
29	3.43	5.30	8.26	12.93	3.24	5.04	7.90	12.43	3.08	4.82	7.60	12.02	2.94	4.64	7.35	11.67	29
30	3.63	5.69	9.00	14.31	3.43	5.41	8.61	13.76	3.26	5.18	8.28	13.30	3.12	4.98	8.00	12.92	30
31	3.85	6.11	9.80	15.83	3.63	5.81	9.37	15.22	3.45	5.55	9.01	14.71	3.30	5.34	8.71	14.29	31
32	4.06	6.55	10.66	17.50	3.84	6.22	10.20	16.82	3.65	5.95	9.81	16.26	3.48	5.72	9.48	15.79	32
33	4.29	7.01	11.59	19.33	4.05	6.67	11.09	18.59	3.85	6.38	10.67	17.97	3.68	6.13	10.31	17.45	33
34	4.53	7.50	12.60	21.35	4.28	7.13	12.05	20.53	4.06	6.82	11.59	19.85	3.88	6.56	11.21	19.27	34
35	4.77	8.02	13.68	23.58	4.51	7.63	13.09	22.67	4.28	7.30	12.59	21.91	4.09	7.02	12.17	21.28	35
36	5.03	8.58	14.86	26.02	4.75	8.16	14.21	25.02	4.51	7.80	13.67	24.18	4.31	7.50	13.22	23.49	36
37	5.30	9.16	16.13	28.71	5.00	8.71	15.43	27.60	4.75	8.34	14.84	26.68	4.54	8.02	14.35	25.91	37
38	5.57	9.79	17.50	31.67	5.26	9.31	16.74	30.45	5.00	8.90	16.10	29.43	4.78	8.56	15.57	28.58	38
39	5.86	10.45	18.98	34.92	5.53	9.93	18.15	33.57	5.26	9.50	17.46	32.46	5.02	9.14	16.88	31.52	39
40	6.16	11.14	20.57	38.50	5.82	10.60	19.68	37.02	5.53	10.14	18.93	35.78	5.28	9.75	18.30	34.75	40
41	6.47	11.89	22.30	42.44	6.11	11.30	21.33	40.80	5.81	10.81	20.52	39.44	5.55	10.39	19.84	38.30	41
42	6.79	12.67	24.16	46.77	6.42	12.05	23.11	44.96	6.10	11.52	22.23	43.47	5.82	11.08	21.49	42.21	42
43	7.13	13.50	26.17	51.53	6.73	12.84	25.04	49.55	6.40	12.28	24.09	47.89	6.11	11.81	23.28	46.51	43
44	7.48	14.38	28.35	56.77	7.06	13.68	27.12	54.58	6.71	13.08	26.09	52.77	6.41	12.58	25.22	51.24	44
45	7.84	15.32	30.70	62.54	7.41	14.57	29.36	60.13	7.04	13.93	28.25	58.12	6.72	13.40	27.31	56.44	45
46	8.22	16.31	33.23	68.88	7.76	15.51	31.78	66.22	7.38	14.84	30.58	64.02	7.05	14.27	29.56	62.17	46
47	8.62	17.36	35.97	75.85	8.14	16.51	34.40	72.93	7.73	15.79	33.10	70.50	7.39	15.18	32.00	68.46	47
48	9.03	18.48	38.93	83.53	8.52	17.57	37.23	80.30	8.10	16.81	35.82	77.63	7.74	16.16	34.63	75.39	48
49	9.45	19.66	42.12	91.97	8.93	18.69	40.29	88.42	8.48	17.88	38.76	85.47	8.10	17.19	37.47	83.00	49
50	9.89	20.91	45.57	101.25	9.34	19.88	43.59	97.34	8.88	19.02	41.93	94.10	8.48	18.29	40.54	91.38	50

A-3

I. Retirement Planning with Level Salary & No Inflation
Planned Retirement Age 59

Table 3 - 401(k) Contribution (% of Current Sal.) Needed to Replace 10% of Sal. at Retirement   I-59-3

Probable Life Expectancy at Retirement

Yrs. to Ret.	25.7 (Same as Male Avg.)				28.3 (Better than Male Avg.)				31 (Same as Female Avg.)				33.8 (Better than Female Avg.)				Yrs. to Ret.
	4%/4%	6%/5%	8%/6%	10%/7%	4%/4%	6%/5%	8%/6%	10%/7%	4%/4%	6%/5%	8%/6%	10%/7%	4%/4%	6%/5%	8%/6%	10%/7%	
	Expected Return (Pre-Retirement/Post-Retirement)								(Pre-Retirement/Post-Retirement)				Expected Return				
0																	0
1	154.30	138.87	125.92	114.95	163.39	146.04	131.64	119.57	171.94	152.67	136.84	123.69	179.98	158.78	141.55	127.37	1
2	75.64	67.41	60.54	54.74	80.09	70.90	63.29	56.94	84.28	74.11	65.79	58.90	88.22	77.08	68.05	60.65	2
3	49.43	43.62	38.79	34.73	52.34	45.87	40.55	36.12	55.08	47.95	42.15	37.37	57.66	49.87	43.60	38.48	3
4	36.34	31.74	27.94	24.77	38.48	33.38	29.21	25.76	40.49	34.90	30.37	26.65	42.38	36.30	31.41	27.44	4
5	28.49	24.63	21.46	18.83	30.17	25.91	22.44	19.58	31.75	27.08	23.32	20.26	33.23	28.17	24.13	20.86	5
6	23.26	19.91	17.16	14.90	24.63	20.94	17.94	15.50	25.92	21.89	18.65	16.03	27.13	22.76	19.29	16.51	6
7	19.54	16.54	14.11	12.12	20.69	17.40	14.75	12.60	21.77	18.19	15.34	13.04	22.79	18.92	15.86	13.43	7
8	16.75	14.03	11.84	10.05	17.73	14.76	12.38	10.46	18.66	15.43	12.86	10.82	19.53	16.04	13.31	11.14	8
9	14.58	12.08	10.08	8.47	15.44	12.71	10.54	8.81	16.25	13.29	10.96	9.11	17.01	13.82	11.33	9.38	9
10	12.85	10.54	8.69	7.21	13.61	11.08	9.09	7.50	14.32	11.58	9.45	7.76	14.99	12.05	9.77	7.99	10
11	11.44	9.28	7.56	6.20	12.12	9.75	7.91	6.45	12.75	10.20	8.22	6.67	13.35	10.61	8.50	6.87	11
12	10.27	8.23	6.64	5.38	10.87	8.66	6.94	5.59	11.44	9.05	7.21	5.78	11.98	9.41	7.46	5.96	12
13	9.28	7.35	5.86	4.69	9.83	7.73	6.12	4.88	10.34	8.09	6.37	5.04	10.82	8.41	6.58	5.19	13
14	8.44	6.61	5.20	4.11	8.93	6.95	5.44	4.27	9.40	7.26	5.65	4.42	9.84	7.56	5.85	4.55	14
15	7.71	5.97	4.64	3.62	8.16	6.27	4.85	3.76	8.59	6.56	5.04	3.89	8.99	6.82	5.21	4.01	15
16	7.07	5.41	4.15	3.20	7.49	5.69	4.34	3.33	7.88	5.95	4.51	3.44	8.25	6.18	4.67	3.54	16
17	6.51	4.92	3.73	2.84	6.89	5.18	3.90	2.95	7.26	5.41	4.05	3.05	7.59	5.63	4.19	3.14	17
18	6.02	4.49	3.36	2.52	6.37	4.73	3.52	2.62	6.70	4.94	3.65	2.71	7.02	5.14	3.78	2.79	18
19	5.58	4.11	3.04	2.25	5.90	4.33	3.18	2.34	6.21	4.52	3.30	2.42	6.50	4.70	3.42	2.49	19
20	5.18	3.78	2.75	2.01	5.49	3.97	2.88	2.09	5.77	4.15	2.99	2.16	6.04	4.32	3.09	2.22	20
21	4.83	3.47	2.50	1.80	5.11	3.65	2.61	1.87	5.38	3.82	2.71	1.93	5.63	3.97	2.81	1.99	21
22	4.51	3.20	2.27	1.61	4.77	3.37	2.37	1.67	5.02	3.52	2.47	1.73	5.26	3.66	2.55	1.78	22
23	4.21	2.95	2.07	1.45	4.46	3.11	2.16	1.50	4.70	3.25	2.25	1.55	4.92	3.38	2.32	1.60	23
24	3.95	2.73	1.89	1.30	4.18	2.87	1.97	1.35	4.40	3.00	2.05	1.40	4.61	3.12	2.12	1.44	24
25	3.70	2.53	1.72	1.17	3.92	2.66	1.80	1.22	4.13	2.78	1.87	1.26	4.32	2.89	1.94	1.30	25
26	3.48	2.35	1.57	1.05	3.69	2.47	1.65	1.10	3.88	2.58	1.71	1.13	4.06	2.68	1.77	1.17	26
27	3.28	2.18	1.44	0.95	3.47	2.29	1.51	0.99	3.65	2.40	1.57	1.02	3.82	2.49	1.62	1.05	27
28	3.09	2.03	1.32	0.86	3.27	2.13	1.38	0.89	3.44	2.23	1.44	0.92	3.60	2.32	1.48	0.95	28
29	2.91	1.89	1.21	0.77	3.08	1.98	1.27	0.80	3.25	2.07	1.32	0.83	3.40	2.16	1.36	0.86	29
30	2.75	1.76	1.11	0.70	2.91	1.85	1.16	0.73	3.07	1.93	1.21	0.75	3.21	2.01	1.25	0.77	30
31	2.60	1.64	1.02	0.63	2.75	1.72	1.07	0.66	2.90	1.80	1.11	0.68	3.03	1.87	1.15	0.70	31
32	2.46	1.53	0.94	0.57	2.61	1.61	0.98	0.59	2.74	1.68	1.02	0.61	2.87	1.75	1.05	0.63	32
33	2.33	1.43	0.86	0.52	2.47	1.50	0.90	0.54	2.60	1.57	0.94	0.56	2.72	1.63	0.97	0.57	33
34	2.21	1.33	0.79	0.47	2.34	1.40	0.83	0.49	2.46	1.47	0.86	0.50	2.58	1.52	0.89	0.52	34
35	2.09	1.25	0.73	0.42	2.22	1.31	0.76	0.44	2.33	1.37	0.79	0.46	2.44	1.42	0.82	0.47	35
36	1.99	1.17	0.67	0.38	2.11	1.23	0.70	0.40	2.22	1.28	0.73	0.41	2.32	1.33	0.76	0.43	36
37	1.89	1.09	0.62	0.35	2.00	1.15	0.65	0.36	2.10	1.20	0.67	0.37	2.20	1.25	0.70	0.39	37
38	1.79	1.02	0.57	0.32	1.90	1.07	0.60	0.33	2.00	1.12	0.62	0.34	2.09	1.17	0.64	0.35	38
39	1.71	0.96	0.53	0.29	1.81	1.01	0.55	0.30	1.90	1.05	0.57	0.31	1.99	1.09	0.59	0.32	39
40	1.62	0.90	0.49	0.26	1.72	0.94	0.51	0.27	1.81	0.99	0.53	0.28	1.89	1.03	0.55	0.29	40
41	1.55	0.84	0.45	0.24	1.64	0.88	0.47	0.25	1.72	0.93	0.49	0.25	1.80	0.96	0.50	0.26	41
42	1.47	0.79	0.41	0.21	1.56	0.83	0.43	0.22	1.64	0.87	0.45	0.23	1.72	0.90	0.47	0.24	42
43	1.40	0.74	0.38	0.19	1.49	0.78	0.40	0.20	1.56	0.81	0.42	0.21	1.64	0.85	0.43	0.21	43
44	1.34	0.70	0.35	0.18	1.42	0.73	0.37	0.18	1.49	0.76	0.38	0.19	1.56	0.79	0.40	0.20	44
45	1.27	0.65	0.33	0.16	1.35	0.69	0.34	0.17	1.42	0.72	0.35	0.17	1.49	0.75	0.37	0.18	45
46	1.22	0.61	0.30	0.15	1.29	0.64	0.31	0.15	1.36	0.67	0.33	0.16	1.42	0.70	0.34	0.16	46
47	1.16	0.58	0.28	0.13	1.23	0.61	0.29	0.14	1.29	0.63	0.30	0.14	1.35	0.66	0.31	0.15	47
48	1.11	0.54	0.26	0.12	1.17	0.57	0.27	0.12	1.23	0.60	0.28	0.13	1.29	0.62	0.29	0.13	48
49	1.06	0.51	0.24	0.11	1.12	0.54	0.25	0.11	1.18	0.56	0.26	0.12	1.23	0.58	0.27	0.12	49
50	1.01	0.48	0.22	0.10	1.07	0.50	0.23	0.10	1.13	0.53	0.24	0.11	1.18	0.55	0.25	0.11	50

Appendix A

I. Retirement Planning with Level Salary & No Inflation
Planned Retirement Age 59

Table 4 - Accumulation at Retirement (Multiple of Current Sal.) for 10% Sal. Replacement

I-59-4

Probable Life Expectancy at Retirement

Yrs. to Ret.	25.7 (Same as Male Avg.)				28.3 (Better than Male Avg.)				31 (Same as Female Avg.)				33.8 (Better than Female Avg.)				Yrs. to Ret.
	4%/4%	6%/5%	8%/6%	10%/7%	4%/4%	6%/5%	8%/6%	10%/7%	4%/4%	6%/5%	8%/6%	10%/7%	4%/4%	6%/5%	8%/6%	10%/7%	
	Expected Return				(Pre-Retirement/Post-Retirement)				(Pre-Retirement/Post-Retirement)				Expected Return				
0	1.54	1.39	1.26	1.15	1.63	1.46	1.32	1.20	1.72	1.53	1.37	1.24	1.80	1.59	1.42	1.27	0
1	1.54	1.39	1.26	1.15	1.63	1.46	1.32	1.20	1.72	1.53	1.37	1.24	1.80	1.59	1.42	1.27	1
2	1.54	1.39	1.26	1.15	1.63	1.46	1.32	1.20	1.72	1.53	1.37	1.24	1.80	1.59	1.42	1.27	2
3	1.54	1.39	1.26	1.15	1.63	1.46	1.32	1.20	1.72	1.53	1.37	1.24	1.80	1.59	1.42	1.27	3
4	1.54	1.39	1.26	1.15	1.63	1.46	1.32	1.20	1.72	1.53	1.37	1.24	1.80	1.59	1.42	1.27	4
5	1.54	1.39	1.26	1.15	1.63	1.46	1.32	1.20	1.72	1.53	1.37	1.24	1.80	1.59	1.42	1.27	5
6	1.54	1.39	1.26	1.15	1.63	1.46	1.32	1.20	1.72	1.53	1.37	1.24	1.80	1.59	1.42	1.27	6
7	1.54	1.39	1.26	1.15	1.63	1.46	1.32	1.20	1.72	1.53	1.37	1.24	1.80	1.59	1.42	1.27	7
8	1.54	1.39	1.26	1.15	1.63	1.46	1.32	1.20	1.72	1.53	1.37	1.24	1.80	1.59	1.42	1.27	8
9	1.54	1.39	1.26	1.15	1.63	1.46	1.32	1.20	1.72	1.53	1.37	1.24	1.80	1.59	1.42	1.27	9
10	1.54	1.39	1.26	1.15	1.63	1.46	1.32	1.20	1.72	1.53	1.37	1.24	1.80	1.59	1.42	1.27	10
11	1.54	1.39	1.26	1.15	1.63	1.46	1.32	1.20	1.72	1.53	1.37	1.24	1.80	1.59	1.42	1.27	11
12	1.54	1.39	1.26	1.15	1.63	1.46	1.32	1.20	1.72	1.53	1.37	1.24	1.80	1.59	1.42	1.27	12
13	1.54	1.39	1.26	1.15	1.63	1.46	1.32	1.20	1.72	1.53	1.37	1.24	1.80	1.59	1.42	1.27	13
14	1.54	1.39	1.26	1.15	1.63	1.46	1.32	1.20	1.72	1.53	1.37	1.24	1.80	1.59	1.42	1.27	14
15	1.54	1.39	1.26	1.15	1.63	1.46	1.32	1.20	1.72	1.53	1.37	1.24	1.80	1.59	1.42	1.27	15
16	1.54	1.39	1.26	1.15	1.63	1.46	1.32	1.20	1.72	1.53	1.37	1.24	1.80	1.59	1.42	1.27	16
17	1.54	1.39	1.26	1.15	1.63	1.46	1.32	1.20	1.72	1.53	1.37	1.24	1.80	1.59	1.42	1.27	17
18	1.54	1.39	1.26	1.15	1.63	1.46	1.32	1.20	1.72	1.53	1.37	1.24	1.80	1.59	1.42	1.27	18
19	1.54	1.39	1.26	1.15	1.63	1.46	1.32	1.20	1.72	1.53	1.37	1.24	1.80	1.59	1.42	1.27	19
20	1.54	1.39	1.26	1.15	1.63	1.46	1.32	1.20	1.72	1.53	1.37	1.24	1.80	1.59	1.42	1.27	20
21	1.54	1.39	1.26	1.15	1.63	1.46	1.32	1.20	1.72	1.53	1.37	1.24	1.80	1.59	1.42	1.27	21
22	1.54	1.39	1.26	1.15	1.63	1.46	1.32	1.20	1.72	1.53	1.37	1.24	1.80	1.59	1.42	1.27	22
23	1.54	1.39	1.26	1.15	1.63	1.46	1.32	1.20	1.72	1.53	1.37	1.24	1.80	1.59	1.42	1.27	23
24	1.54	1.39	1.26	1.15	1.63	1.46	1.32	1.20	1.72	1.53	1.37	1.24	1.80	1.59	1.42	1.27	24
25	1.54	1.39	1.26	1.15	1.63	1.46	1.32	1.20	1.72	1.53	1.37	1.24	1.80	1.59	1.42	1.27	25
26	1.54	1.39	1.26	1.15	1.63	1.46	1.32	1.20	1.72	1.53	1.37	1.24	1.80	1.59	1.42	1.27	26
27	1.54	1.39	1.26	1.15	1.63	1.46	1.32	1.20	1.72	1.53	1.37	1.24	1.80	1.59	1.42	1.27	27
28	1.54	1.39	1.26	1.15	1.63	1.46	1.32	1.20	1.72	1.53	1.37	1.24	1.80	1.59	1.42	1.27	28
29	1.54	1.39	1.26	1.15	1.63	1.46	1.32	1.20	1.72	1.53	1.37	1.24	1.80	1.59	1.42	1.27	29
30	1.54	1.39	1.26	1.15	1.63	1.46	1.32	1.20	1.72	1.53	1.37	1.24	1.80	1.59	1.42	1.27	30
31	1.54	1.39	1.26	1.15	1.63	1.46	1.32	1.20	1.72	1.53	1.37	1.24	1.80	1.59	1.42	1.27	31
32	1.54	1.39	1.26	1.15	1.63	1.46	1.32	1.20	1.72	1.53	1.37	1.24	1.80	1.59	1.42	1.27	32
33	1.54	1.39	1.26	1.15	1.63	1.46	1.32	1.20	1.72	1.53	1.37	1.24	1.80	1.59	1.42	1.27	33
34	1.54	1.39	1.26	1.15	1.63	1.46	1.32	1.20	1.72	1.53	1.37	1.24	1.80	1.59	1.42	1.27	34
35	1.54	1.39	1.26	1.15	1.63	1.46	1.32	1.20	1.72	1.53	1.37	1.24	1.80	1.59	1.42	1.27	35
36	1.54	1.39	1.26	1.15	1.63	1.46	1.32	1.20	1.72	1.53	1.37	1.24	1.80	1.59	1.42	1.27	36
37	1.54	1.39	1.26	1.15	1.63	1.46	1.32	1.20	1.72	1.53	1.37	1.24	1.80	1.59	1.42	1.27	37
38	1.54	1.39	1.26	1.15	1.63	1.46	1.32	1.20	1.72	1.53	1.37	1.24	1.80	1.59	1.42	1.27	38
39	1.54	1.39	1.26	1.15	1.63	1.46	1.32	1.20	1.72	1.53	1.37	1.24	1.80	1.59	1.42	1.27	39
40	1.54	1.39	1.26	1.15	1.63	1.46	1.32	1.20	1.72	1.53	1.37	1.24	1.80	1.59	1.42	1.27	40
41	1.54	1.39	1.26	1.15	1.63	1.46	1.32	1.20	1.72	1.53	1.37	1.24	1.80	1.59	1.42	1.27	41
42	1.54	1.39	1.26	1.15	1.63	1.46	1.32	1.20	1.72	1.53	1.37	1.24	1.80	1.59	1.42	1.27	42
43	1.54	1.39	1.26	1.15	1.63	1.46	1.32	1.20	1.72	1.53	1.37	1.24	1.80	1.59	1.42	1.27	43
44	1.54	1.39	1.26	1.15	1.63	1.46	1.32	1.20	1.72	1.53	1.37	1.24	1.80	1.59	1.42	1.27	44
45	1.54	1.39	1.26	1.15	1.63	1.46	1.32	1.20	1.72	1.53	1.37	1.24	1.80	1.59	1.42	1.27	45
46	1.54	1.39	1.26	1.15	1.63	1.46	1.32	1.20	1.72	1.53	1.37	1.24	1.80	1.59	1.42	1.27	46
47	1.54	1.39	1.26	1.15	1.63	1.46	1.32	1.20	1.72	1.53	1.37	1.24	1.80	1.59	1.42	1.27	47
48	1.54	1.39	1.26	1.15	1.63	1.46	1.32	1.20	1.72	1.53	1.37	1.24	1.80	1.59	1.42	1.27	48
49	1.54	1.39	1.26	1.15	1.63	1.46	1.32	1.20	1.72	1.53	1.37	1.24	1.80	1.59	1.42	1.27	49
50	1.54	1.39	1.26	1.15	1.63	1.46	1.32	1.20	1.72	1.53	1.37	1.24	1.80	1.59	1.42	1.27	50

I. Retirement Planning with Level Salary & No Inflation
Planned Retirement Age 62

Table 1 - Percent of Salary Replaced by a 401(k) Account Equal to Current Annual Salary   I-62-1

Probable Life Expectancy at Retirement

Yrs. to Ret.	23.2 (Same as Male Avg.)				25.7 (Better than Male Avg.)				28.3 (Same as Female Avg.)				31 (Better than Female Avg.)				Yrs. to Ret.
	4% / 4%	6% / 5%	8% / 6%	10% / 7%	4% / 4%	6% / 5%	8% / 6%	10% / 7%	4% / 4%	6% / 5%	8% / 6%	10% / 7%	4% / 4%	6% / 5%	8% / 6%	10% / 7%	
	Expected Return				(Pre-Retirement/Post-Retirement)				(Pre-Retirement/Post-Retirement)				Expected Return				
0	6.92	7.63	8.36	9.11	6.48	7.20	7.94	8.70	6.12	6.85	7.60	8.36	5.82	6.55	7.31	8.08	0
1	7.19	8.09	9.03	10.02	6.74	7.63	8.58	9.57	6.37	7.26	8.20	9.20	6.05	6.94	7.89	8.89	1
2	7.48	8.57	9.76	11.03	7.01	8.09	9.26	10.53	6.62	7.69	8.86	10.12	6.29	7.36	8.52	9.78	2
3	7.78	9.09	10.54	12.13	7.29	8.58	10.00	11.58	6.88	8.16	9.57	11.13	6.54	7.80	9.21	10.76	3
4	8.09	9.63	11.38	13.34	7.58	9.09	10.80	12.74	7.16	8.64	10.33	12.24	6.80	8.27	9.94	11.84	4
5	8.41	10.21	12.29	14.68	7.89	9.64	11.67	14.01	7.45	9.16	11.16	13.47	7.08	8.77	10.74	13.02	5
6	8.75	10.82	13.27	16.14	8.20	10.21	12.60	15.41	7.74	9.71	12.05	14.82	7.36	9.29	11.60	14.32	6
7	9.10	11.47	14.33	17.76	8.53	10.83	13.61	16.95	8.05	10.30	13.02	16.30	7.65	9.85	12.52	15.76	7
8	9.47	12.16	15.48	19.53	8.87	11.48	14.70	18.65	8.38	10.91	14.06	17.93	7.96	10.44	13.53	17.33	8
9	9.84	12.89	16.72	21.49	9.22	12.17	15.88	20.51	8.71	11.57	15.19	19.72	8.28	11.07	14.61	19.06	9
10	10.24	13.67	18.06	23.64	9.59	12.90	17.15	22.56	9.06	12.26	16.40	21.69	8.61	11.73	15.78	20.97	10
11	10.65	14.49	19.50	26.00	9.98	13.67	18.52	24.82	9.42	13.00	17.71	23.86	8.95	12.43	17.04	23.07	11
12	11.07	15.36	21.06	28.60	10.38	14.49	20.00	27.30	9.80	13.78	19.13	26.25	9.31	13.18	18.40	25.37	12
13	11.52	16.28	22.75	31.46	10.79	15.36	21.60	30.03	10.19	14.60	20.66	28.87	9.68	13.97	19.88	27.91	13
14	11.98	17.25	24.57	34.61	11.22	16.28	23.33	33.04	10.60	15.48	22.31	31.76	10.07	14.81	21.47	30.70	14
15	12.46	18.29	26.53	38.07	11.67	17.26	25.19	36.34	11.02	16.41	24.10	34.94	10.47	15.70	23.18	33.77	15
16	12.95	19.39	28.66	41.87	12.14	18.29	27.21	39.97	11.46	17.39	26.02	38.43	10.89	16.64	25.04	37.15	16
17	13.47	20.55	30.95	46.06	12.62	19.39	29.38	43.97	11.92	18.44	28.11	42.27	11.33	17.64	27.04	40.86	17
18	14.01	21.78	33.42	50.67	13.13	20.55	31.74	48.37	12.40	19.54	30.36	46.50	11.78	18.70	29.20	44.95	18
19	14.57	23.09	36.10	55.73	13.65	21.79	34.27	53.20	12.89	20.72	32.78	51.15	12.25	19.82	31.54	49.45	19
20	15.15	24.47	38.98	61.31	14.20	23.09	37.02	58.52	13.41	21.96	35.41	56.27	12.74	21.01	34.06	54.39	20
21	15.76	25.94	42.10	67.44	14.77	24.48	39.98	64.38	13.95	23.28	38.24	61.89	13.25	22.27	36.79	59.83	21
22	16.39	27.50	45.47	74.18	15.36	25.95	43.18	70.81	14.50	24.67	41.30	68.08	13.78	23.60	39.73	65.81	22
23	17.05	29.15	49.11	81.60	15.97	27.51	46.63	77.90	15.08	26.15	44.60	74.89	14.33	25.02	42.91	72.39	23
24	17.73	30.90	53.04	89.76	16.61	29.16	50.36	85.68	15.69	27.72	48.17	82.38	14.91	26.52	46.34	79.63	24
25	18.44	32.75	57.28	98.73	17.28	30.91	54.39	94.25	16.32	29.39	52.02	90.62	15.50	28.11	50.05	87.60	25
26	19.18	34.72	61.86	108.61	17.97	32.76	58.74	103.68	16.97	31.15	56.19	99.68	16.12	29.80	54.05	96.36	26
27	19.94	36.80	66.81	119.47	18.69	34.73	63.44	114.05	17.65	33.02	60.68	109.64	16.77	31.59	58.38	105.99	27
28	20.74	39.01	72.16	131.41	19.43	36.81	68.51	125.45	18.35	35.00	65.53	120.61	17.44	33.48	63.05	116.59	28
29	21.57	41.35	77.92	144.56	20.21	39.02	74.00	138.00	19.09	37.10	70.78	132.67	18.14	35.49	68.09	128.25	29
30	22.43	43.83	84.17	159.01	21.02	41.36	79.91	151.80	19.85	39.33	76.44	145.94	18.86	37.62	73.54	141.08	30
31	23.33	46.46	90.90	174.91	21.86	43.84	86.31	166.98	20.64	41.69	82.55	160.53	19.62	39.88	79.42	155.18	31
32	24.26	49.25	98.17	192.40	22.74	46.47	93.21	183.67	21.47	44.19	89.16	176.58	20.40	42.27	85.77	170.70	32
33	25.23	52.20	106.02	211.64	23.65	49.26	100.67	202.04	22.33	46.84	96.29	194.24	21.22	44.81	92.64	187.77	33
34	26.24	55.33	114.51	232.81	24.59	52.22	108.72	222.24	23.22	49.65	103.99	213.67	22.07	47.49	100.05	206.55	34
35	27.29	58.65	123.67	256.09	25.57	55.35	117.42	244.47	24.15	52.63	112.31	235.03	22.95	50.34	108.05	227.21	35
36	28.38	62.17	133.56	281.70	26.60	58.67	126.82	268.92	25.12	55.79	121.30	258.54	23.87	53.37	116.70	249.93	36
37	29.52	65.90	144.24	309.87	27.66	62.19	136.96	295.81	26.12	59.13	131.00	284.39	24.82	56.57	126.03	274.92	37
38	30.70	69.86	155.78	340.86	28.77	65.92	147.92	325.39	27.17	62.68	141.48	312.83	25.82	59.96	136.11	302.41	38
39	31.93	74.05	168.25	374.94	29.92	69.88	159.75	357.93	28.25	66.44	152.80	344.11	26.85	63.56	147.00	332.65	39
40	33.21	78.49	181.71	412.43	31.12	74.07	172.53	393.72	29.38	70.43	165.03	378.52	27.92	67.37	158.76	365.92	40
41	34.53	83.20	196.24	453.68	32.36	78.51	186.33	433.09	30.56	74.65	178.23	416.38	29.04	71.41	171.46	402.51	41
42	35.92	88.19	211.94	499.05	33.65	83.22	201.24	476.40	31.78	79.13	192.49	458.01	30.20	75.70	185.18	442.76	42
43	37.35	93.48	228.90	548.95	35.00	88.22	217.34	524.04	33.05	83.88	207.89	503.81	31.41	80.24	200.00	487.03	43
44	38.85	99.09	247.21	603.85	36.40	93.51	234.73	576.44	34.38	88.91	224.52	554.20	32.67	85.06	216.00	535.74	44
45	40.40	105.04	266.99	664.23	37.85	99.12	253.50	634.09	35.75	94.25	242.48	609.62	33.97	90.16	233.27	589.31	45
46	42.02	111.34	288.35	730.65	39.37	105.07	273.78	697.50	37.18	99.90	261.88	670.58	35.33	95.57	251.94	648.24	46
47	43.70	118.02	311.41	803.72	40.95	111.37	295.69	767.25	38.67	105.90	282.83	737.64	36.74	101.30	272.09	713.07	47
48	45.44	125.10	336.33	884.09	42.58	118.05	319.34	843.97	40.21	112.25	305.45	811.40	38.21	107.38	293.86	784.37	48
49	47.26	132.61	363.23	972.50	44.29	125.14	344.89	928.37	41.82	118.99	329.89	892.54	39.74	113.82	317.37	862.81	49
50	49.15	140.56	392.29	1069.75	46.06	132.65	372.48	1021.21	43.50	126.13	356.28	981.79	41.33	120.65	342.76	949.09	50

Appendix A

I. Retirement Planning with Level Salary & No Inflation
Planned Retirement Age 62

Table 2 - Percent of Salary Replaced by a 401(k) Contribution of 1% of Current Salary I-62-2

Probable Life Expectancy at Retirement

Yrs. to Ret.	23.2 (Same as Male Avg.)				25.7 (Better than Male Avg.)				28.3 (Same as Female Avg.)				31 (Better than Female Avg.)				Yrs. to Ret.
	4%/4%	6%/5%	8%/6%	10%/7%	4%/4%	6%/5%	8%/6%	10%/7%	4%/4%	6%/5%	8%/6%	10%/7%	4%/4%	6%/5%	8%/6%	10%/7%	
	Expected Return (Pre-Retirement/Post-Retirement)								(Pre-Retirement/Post-Retirement)				Expected Return				
0	0.00	0.00	0.00	0.00	0.00	0.00	0.00	0.00	0.00	0.00	0.00	0.00	0.00	0.00	0.00	0.00	0
1	0.07	0.08	0.08	0.09	0.06	0.07	0.08	0.09	0.06	0.07	0.08	0.08	0.06	0.07	0.07	0.08	1
2	0.14	0.16	0.17	0.19	0.13	0.15	0.17	0.18	0.12	0.14	0.16	0.18	0.12	0.13	0.15	0.17	2
3	0.22	0.24	0.27	0.30	0.20	0.23	0.26	0.29	0.19	0.22	0.25	0.28	0.18	0.21	0.24	0.27	3
4	0.29	0.33	0.38	0.42	0.28	0.32	0.36	0.40	0.26	0.30	0.34	0.39	0.25	0.29	0.33	0.38	4
5	0.37	0.43	0.49	0.56	0.35	0.41	0.47	0.53	0.33	0.39	0.45	0.51	0.32	0.37	0.43	0.49	5
6	0.46	0.53	0.61	0.70	0.43	0.50	0.58	0.67	0.41	0.48	0.56	0.65	0.39	0.46	0.54	0.62	6
7	0.55	0.64	0.75	0.86	0.51	0.60	0.71	0.83	0.48	0.57	0.68	0.79	0.46	0.55	0.65	0.77	7
8	0.64	0.76	0.89	1.04	0.60	0.71	0.84	0.99	0.56	0.68	0.81	0.96	0.54	0.65	0.78	0.92	8
9	0.73	0.88	1.04	1.24	0.69	0.83	0.99	1.18	0.65	0.79	0.95	1.14	0.62	0.75	0.91	1.10	9
10	0.83	1.01	1.21	1.45	0.78	0.95	1.15	1.39	0.73	0.90	1.10	1.33	0.70	0.86	1.06	1.29	10
11	0.93	1.14	1.39	1.69	0.87	1.08	1.32	1.61	0.83	1.03	1.26	1.55	0.78	0.98	1.22	1.50	11
12	1.04	1.29	1.59	1.95	0.97	1.21	1.51	1.86	0.92	1.16	1.44	1.79	0.87	1.10	1.39	1.73	12
13	1.15	1.44	1.80	2.23	1.08	1.36	1.71	2.13	1.02	1.29	1.63	2.05	0.97	1.24	1.57	1.98	13
14	1.27	1.60	2.03	2.55	1.19	1.51	1.92	2.43	1.12	1.44	1.84	2.34	1.06	1.38	1.77	2.26	14
15	1.38	1.78	2.27	2.90	1.30	1.68	2.16	2.76	1.23	1.59	2.06	2.66	1.16	1.52	1.98	2.57	15
16	1.51	1.96	2.54	3.28	1.41	1.85	2.41	3.13	1.34	1.76	2.30	3.01	1.27	1.68	2.22	2.91	16
17	1.64	2.15	2.82	3.69	1.54	2.03	2.68	3.53	1.45	1.93	2.56	3.39	1.38	1.85	2.47	3.28	17
18	1.77	2.36	3.13	4.16	1.66	2.23	2.97	3.97	1.57	2.12	2.84	3.81	1.49	2.02	2.74	3.69	18
19	1.91	2.58	3.47	4.66	1.79	2.43	3.29	4.45	1.69	2.31	3.15	4.28	1.61	2.21	3.03	4.14	19
20	2.06	2.81	3.83	5.22	1.93	2.65	3.63	4.98	1.82	2.52	3.48	4.79	1.73	2.41	3.34	4.63	20
21	2.21	3.05	4.22	5.83	2.07	2.88	4.00	5.57	1.96	2.74	3.83	5.35	1.86	2.62	3.68	5.17	21
22	2.37	3.31	4.64	6.51	2.22	3.12	4.40	6.21	2.10	2.97	4.21	5.97	1.99	2.84	4.05	5.77	22
23	2.53	3.59	5.09	7.25	2.37	3.38	4.84	6.92	2.24	3.22	4.63	6.65	2.13	3.08	4.45	6.43	23
24	2.70	3.88	5.58	8.06	2.53	3.66	5.30	7.70	2.39	3.48	5.07	7.40	2.27	3.33	4.88	7.15	24
25	2.88	4.19	6.11	8.96	2.70	3.95	5.81	8.56	2.55	3.76	5.55	8.23	2.42	3.59	5.34	7.95	25
26	3.06	4.51	6.69	9.95	2.87	4.26	6.35	9.50	2.71	4.05	6.07	9.13	2.58	3.87	5.84	8.83	26
27	3.26	4.86	7.31	11.04	3.05	4.59	6.94	10.53	2.88	4.36	6.64	10.13	2.74	4.17	6.38	9.79	27
28	3.46	5.23	7.97	12.23	3.24	4.93	7.57	11.68	3.06	4.69	7.24	11.22	2.91	4.49	6.97	10.85	28
29	3.66	5.62	8.70	13.54	3.43	5.30	8.26	12.93	3.24	5.04	7.90	12.43	3.08	4.82	7.60	12.02	29
30	3.88	6.03	9.48	14.99	3.63	5.69	9.00	14.31	3.43	5.41	8.61	13.76	3.26	5.18	8.28	13.30	30
31	4.10	6.47	10.32	16.58	3.85	6.11	9.80	15.83	3.63	5.81	9.37	15.22	3.45	5.55	9.01	14.71	31
32	4.34	6.94	11.23	18.33	4.06	6.55	10.66	17.50	3.84	6.22	10.20	16.82	3.65	5.95	9.81	16.26	32
33	4.58	7.43	12.21	20.25	4.29	7.01	11.59	19.33	4.05	6.67	11.09	18.59	3.85	6.38	10.67	17.97	33
34	4.83	7.95	13.27	22.37	4.53	7.50	12.60	21.35	4.28	7.13	12.05	20.53	4.06	6.82	11.59	19.85	34
35	5.09	8.50	14.41	24.70	4.77	8.02	13.68	23.58	4.51	7.63	13.09	22.67	4.28	7.30	12.59	21.91	35
36	5.37	9.09	15.65	27.26	5.03	8.58	14.86	26.02	4.75	8.16	14.21	25.02	4.51	7.80	13.67	24.18	36
37	5.65	9.71	16.99	30.08	5.30	9.16	16.13	28.71	5.00	8.71	15.43	27.60	4.75	8.34	14.84	26.68	37
38	5.95	10.37	18.43	33.17	5.57	9.79	17.50	31.67	5.26	9.31	16.74	30.45	5.00	8.90	16.10	29.43	38
39	6.25	11.07	19.99	36.58	5.86	10.45	18.98	34.92	5.53	9.93	18.15	33.57	5.26	9.50	17.46	32.46	39
40	6.57	11.81	21.67	40.33	6.16	11.14	20.57	38.50	5.82	10.60	19.68	37.02	5.53	10.14	18.93	35.78	40
41	6.90	12.59	23.48	44.46	6.47	11.89	22.30	42.44	6.11	11.30	21.33	40.80	5.81	10.81	20.52	39.44	41
42	7.25	13.43	25.45	48.99	6.79	12.67	24.16	46.77	6.42	12.05	23.11	44.96	6.10	11.52	22.23	43.47	42
43	7.61	14.31	27.57	53.98	7.13	13.50	26.17	51.53	6.73	12.84	25.04	49.55	6.40	12.28	24.09	47.89	43
44	7.98	15.24	29.86	59.47	7.48	14.38	28.35	56.77	7.06	13.68	27.12	54.58	6.71	13.08	26.09	52.77	44
45	8.37	16.23	32.33	65.51	7.84	15.32	30.76	62.54	7.41	14.57	29.36	60.13	7.04	13.93	28.25	58.12	45
46	8.77	17.28	35.00	72.15	8.22	16.31	33.23	68.88	7.76	15.51	31.78	66.22	7.38	14.84	30.58	64.02	46
47	9.20	18.40	37.88	79.46	8.62	17.36	35.97	75.85	8.14	16.51	34.40	72.93	7.73	15.79	33.10	70.50	47
48	9.63	19.58	41.00	87.50	9.03	18.48	38.93	83.53	8.52	17.57	37.23	80.30	8.10	16.81	35.82	77.63	48
49	10.09	20.83	44.36	96.34	9.45	19.66	42.12	91.97	8.93	18.69	40.29	88.42	8.48	17.88	38.76	85.47	49
50	10.56	22.16	47.99	106.06	9.89	20.91	45.57	101.25	9.34	19.88	43.59	97.34	8.88	19.02	41.93	94.10	50

A-7

I. Retirement Planning with Level Salary & No Inflation
Planned Retirement Age 62

Table 3 - 401(k) Contribution (% of Current Sal.) Needed to Replace 10% of Sal. at Retirement   I-62-3

Probable Life Expectancy at Retirement

Yrs. to Ret.	23.2 (Same as Male Avg.)				25.7 (Better than Male Avg.)				28.3 (Same as Female Avg.)				31 (Better than Female Avg.)				Yrs. to Ret.
	4%/4%	6%/5%	8%/6%	10%/7%	4%/4%	6%/5%	8%/6%	10%/7%	4%/4%	6%/5%	8%/6%	10%/7%	4%/4%	6%/5%	8%/6%	10%/7%	
	Expected Return				(Pre-Retirement/Post-Retirement)				(Pre-Retirement/Post-Retirement)				Expected Return				
0																	0
1	144.58	131.04	119.56	109.74	154.30	138.87	125.92	114.95	163.39	146.04	131.64	119.57	171.94	152.67	136.84	123.69	1
2	70.87	63.61	57.48	52.26	75.64	67.41	60.54	54.74	80.09	70.90	63.29	56.94	84.28	74.11	65.79	58.90	2
3	46.32	41.16	36.83	33.15	49.43	43.62	38.79	34.73	52.34	45.87	40.55	36.12	55.08	47.95	42.15	37.37	3
4	34.05	29.96	26.53	23.65	36.34	31.74	27.94	24.77	38.48	33.38	29.21	25.76	40.49	34.90	30.37	26.65	4
5	26.69	23.25	20.38	17.97	28.49	24.63	21.46	18.83	30.17	25.91	22.44	19.58	31.75	27.08	23.32	20.26	5
6	21.80	18.79	16.30	14.22	23.26	19.91	17.16	14.90	24.63	20.94	17.94	15.50	25.92	21.89	18.65	16.03	6
7	18.31	15.61	13.40	11.57	19.54	16.54	14.11	12.12	20.69	17.40	14.75	12.60	21.77	18.19	15.34	13.04	7
8	15.69	13.24	11.24	9.60	16.75	14.03	11.84	10.05	17.73	14.76	12.38	10.46	18.66	15.43	12.86	10.82	8
9	13.66	11.40	9.57	8.08	14.58	12.08	10.08	8.47	15.44	12.71	10.54	8.81	16.25	13.29	10.96	9.11	9
10	12.04	9.94	8.25	6.89	12.85	10.54	8.69	7.21	13.61	11.08	9.09	7.50	14.32	11.58	9.45	7.76	10
11	10.72	8.75	7.18	5.92	11.44	9.28	7.56	6.20	12.12	9.75	7.91	6.45	12.75	10.20	8.22	6.67	11
12	9.62	7.77	6.30	5.13	10.27	8.23	6.64	5.38	10.87	8.66	6.94	5.59	11.44	9.05	7.21	5.78	12
13	8.70	6.94	5.56	4.47	9.28	7.35	5.86	4.69	9.83	7.73	6.12	4.88	10.34	8.09	6.37	5.04	13
14	7.90	6.24	4.94	3.92	8.44	6.61	5.20	4.11	8.93	6.95	5.44	4.27	9.40	7.26	5.65	4.42	14
15	7.22	5.63	4.40	3.45	7.71	5.97	4.64	3.62	8.16	6.27	4.85	3.76	8.59	6.56	5.04	3.89	15
16	6.62	5.10	3.94	3.05	7.07	5.41	4.15	3.20	7.49	5.69	4.34	3.33	7.88	5.95	4.51	3.44	16
17	6.10	4.64	3.54	2.71	6.51	4.92	3.73	2.84	6.89	5.18	3.90	2.95	7.26	5.41	4.05	3.05	17
18	5.64	4.24	3.19	2.41	6.02	4.49	3.36	2.52	6.37	4.73	3.52	2.62	6.70	4.94	3.65	2.71	18
19	5.23	3.88	2.88	2.15	5.58	4.11	3.04	2.25	5.90	4.33	3.18	2.34	6.21	4.52	3.30	2.42	19
20	4.86	3.56	2.61	1.92	5.18	3.78	2.75	2.01	5.49	3.97	2.88	2.09	5.77	4.15	2.99	2.16	20
21	4.52	3.28	2.37	1.71	4.83	3.47	2.50	1.80	5.11	3.65	2.61	1.87	5.38	3.82	2.71	1.93	21
22	4.22	3.02	2.16	1.54	4.51	3.20	2.27	1.61	4.77	3.37	2.37	1.67	5.02	3.52	2.47	1.73	22
23	3.95	2.79	1.96	1.38	4.21	2.95	2.07	1.45	4.46	3.11	2.16	1.50	4.70	3.25	2.25	1.55	23
24	3.70	2.58	1.79	1.24	3.95	2.73	1.89	1.30	4.18	2.87	1.97	1.35	4.40	3.00	2.05	1.40	24
25	3.47	2.39	1.64	1.12	3.70	2.53	1.72	1.17	3.92	2.66	1.80	1.22	4.13	2.78	1.87	1.26	25
26	3.26	2.22	1.50	1.01	3.48	2.35	1.57	1.05	3.69	2.47	1.65	1.10	3.88	2.58	1.71	1.13	26
27	3.07	2.06	1.37	0.91	3.28	2.18	1.44	0.95	3.47	2.29	1.51	0.99	3.65	2.40	1.57	1.02	27
28	2.89	1.91	1.25	0.82	3.09	2.03	1.32	0.86	3.27	2.13	1.38	0.89	3.44	2.23	1.44	0.92	28
29	2.73	1.78	1.15	0.74	2.91	1.89	1.21	0.77	3.08	1.98	1.27	0.80	3.25	2.07	1.32	0.83	29
30	2.58	1.66	1.06	0.67	2.75	1.76	1.11	0.70	2.91	1.85	1.16	0.73	3.07	1.93	1.21	0.75	30
31	2.44	1.55	0.97	0.60	2.60	1.64	1.02	0.63	2.75	1.72	1.07	0.66	2.90	1.80	1.11	0.68	31
32	2.31	1.44	0.89	0.55	2.46	1.53	0.94	0.57	2.61	1.61	0.98	0.59	2.74	1.68	1.02	0.61	32
33	2.18	1.35	0.82	0.49	2.33	1.43	0.86	0.52	2.47	1.50	0.90	0.54	2.60	1.57	0.94	0.56	33
34	2.07	1.26	0.75	0.45	2.21	1.33	0.79	0.47	2.34	1.40	0.83	0.49	2.46	1.47	0.86	0.50	34
35	1.96	1.18	0.69	0.40	2.09	1.25	0.73	0.42	2.22	1.31	0.76	0.44	2.33	1.37	0.79	0.46	35
36	1.86	1.10	0.64	0.37	1.99	1.17	0.67	0.38	2.11	1.23	0.70	0.40	2.22	1.28	0.73	0.41	36
37	1.77	1.03	0.59	0.33	1.89	1.09	0.62	0.35	2.00	1.15	0.65	0.36	2.10	1.20	0.67	0.37	37
38	1.68	0.96	0.54	0.30	1.79	1.02	0.57	0.32	1.90	1.07	0.60	0.33	2.00	1.12	0.62	0.34	38
39	1.60	0.90	0.50	0.27	1.71	0.96	0.53	0.29	1.81	1.01	0.55	0.30	1.90	1.05	0.57	0.31	39
40	1.52	0.85	0.46	0.25	1.62	0.90	0.49	0.26	1.72	0.94	0.51	0.27	1.81	0.99	0.53	0.28	40
41	1.45	0.79	0.43	0.22	1.55	0.84	0.45	0.24	1.64	0.88	0.47	0.25	1.72	0.93	0.49	0.25	41
42	1.38	0.74	0.39	0.20	1.47	0.79	0.41	0.21	1.56	0.83	0.43	0.22	1.64	0.87	0.45	0.23	42
43	1.31	0.70	0.36	0.19	1.40	0.74	0.38	0.19	1.49	0.78	0.40	0.20	1.56	0.81	0.42	0.21	43
44	1.25	0.66	0.33	0.17	1.34	0.70	0.35	0.18	1.42	0.73	0.37	0.18	1.49	0.76	0.38	0.19	44
45	1.19	0.62	0.31	0.15	1.27	0.65	0.33	0.16	1.35	0.69	0.34	0.17	1.42	0.72	0.35	0.17	45
46	1.14	0.58	0.29	0.14	1.22	0.61	0.30	0.15	1.29	0.64	0.31	0.15	1.36	0.67	0.33	0.16	46
47	1.09	0.54	0.26	0.13	1.16	0.58	0.28	0.13	1.23	0.61	0.29	0.14	1.29	0.63	0.30	0.14	47
48	1.04	0.51	0.24	0.11	1.11	0.54	0.26	0.12	1.17	0.57	0.27	0.12	1.23	0.60	0.28	0.13	48
49	0.99	0.48	0.23	0.10	1.06	0.51	0.24	0.11	1.12	0.54	0.25	0.11	1.18	0.56	0.26	0.12	49
50	0.95	0.45	0.21	0.09	1.01	0.48	0.22	0.10	1.07	0.50	0.23	0.10	1.13	0.53	0.24	0.11	50

I. Retirement Planning with Level Salary & No Inflation
Planned Retirement Age 62

Table 4 - Accumulation at Retirement (Multiple of Current Sal.) for 10% Sal. Replacement   I-62-4

Probable Life Expectancy at Retirement

	23.2 (Same as Male Avg.)				25.7 (Better than Male Avg.)				28.3 (Same as Female Avg.)				31 (Better than Female Avg.)				
Yrs. to Ret.	4% / 4%	6% / 5%	8% / 6%	10% / 7%	4% / 4%	6% / 5%	8% / 6%	10% / 7%	4% / 4%	6% / 5%	8% / 6%	10% / 7%	4% / 4%	6% / 5%	8% / 6%	10% / 7%	Yrs. to Ret.
	Expected Return				(Pre-Retirement/Post-Retirement)				(Pre-Retirement/Post-Retirement)				Expected Return				
0	1.45	1.31	1.20	1.10	1.54	1.39	1.26	1.15	1.63	1.46	1.32	1.20	1.72	1.53	1.37	1.24	0
1	1.45	1.31	1.20	1.10	1.54	1.39	1.26	1.15	1.63	1.46	1.32	1.20	1.72	1.53	1.37	1.24	1
2	1.45	1.31	1.20	1.10	1.54	1.39	1.26	1.15	1.63	1.46	1.32	1.20	1.72	1.53	1.37	1.24	2
3	1.45	1.31	1.20	1.10	1.54	1.39	1.26	1.15	1.63	1.46	1.32	1.20	1.72	1.53	1.37	1.24	3
4	1.45	1.31	1.20	1.10	1.54	1.39	1.26	1.15	1.63	1.46	1.32	1.20	1.72	1.53	1.37	1.24	4
5	1.45	1.31	1.20	1.10	1.54	1.39	1.26	1.15	1.63	1.46	1.32	1.20	1.72	1.53	1.37	1.24	5
6	1.45	1.31	1.20	1.10	1.54	1.39	1.26	1.15	1.63	1.46	1.32	1.20	1.72	1.53	1.37	1.24	6
7	1.45	1.31	1.20	1.10	1.54	1.39	1.26	1.15	1.63	1.46	1.32	1.20	1.72	1.53	1.37	1.24	7
8	1.45	1.31	1.20	1.10	1.54	1.39	1.26	1.15	1.63	1.46	1.32	1.20	1.72	1.53	1.37	1.24	8
9	1.45	1.31	1.20	1.10	1.54	1.39	1.26	1.15	1.63	1.46	1.32	1.20	1.72	1.53	1.37	1.24	9
10	1.45	1.31	1.20	1.10	1.54	1.39	1.26	1.15	1.63	1.46	1.32	1.20	1.72	1.53	1.37	1.24	10
11	1.45	1.31	1.20	1.10	1.54	1.39	1.26	1.15	1.63	1.46	1.32	1.20	1.72	1.53	1.37	1.24	11
12	1.45	1.31	1.20	1.10	1.54	1.39	1.26	1.15	1.63	1.46	1.32	1.20	1.72	1.53	1.37	1.24	12
13	1.45	1.31	1.20	1.10	1.54	1.39	1.26	1.15	1.63	1.46	1.32	1.20	1.72	1.53	1.37	1.24	13
14	1.45	1.31	1.20	1.10	1.54	1.39	1.26	1.15	1.63	1.46	1.32	1.20	1.72	1.53	1.37	1.24	14
15	1.45	1.31	1.20	1.10	1.54	1.39	1.26	1.15	1.63	1.46	1.32	1.20	1.72	1.53	1.37	1.24	15
16	1.45	1.31	1.20	1.10	1.54	1.39	1.26	1.15	1.63	1.46	1.32	1.20	1.72	1.53	1.37	1.24	16
17	1.45	1.31	1.20	1.10	1.54	1.39	1.26	1.15	1.63	1.46	1.32	1.20	1.72	1.53	1.37	1.24	17
18	1.45	1.31	1.20	1.10	1.54	1.39	1.26	1.15	1.63	1.46	1.32	1.20	1.72	1.53	1.37	1.24	18
19	1.45	1.31	1.20	1.10	1.54	1.39	1.26	1.15	1.63	1.46	1.32	1.20	1.72	1.53	1.37	1.24	19
20	1.45	1.31	1.20	1.10	1.54	1.39	1.26	1.15	1.63	1.46	1.32	1.20	1.72	1.53	1.37	1.24	20
21	1.45	1.31	1.20	1.10	1.54	1.39	1.26	1.15	1.63	1.46	1.32	1.20	1.72	1.53	1.37	1.24	21
22	1.45	1.31	1.20	1.10	1.54	1.39	1.26	1.15	1.63	1.46	1.32	1.20	1.72	1.53	1.37	1.24	22
23	1.45	1.31	1.20	1.10	1.54	1.39	1.26	1.15	1.63	1.46	1.32	1.20	1.72	1.53	1.37	1.24	23
24	1.45	1.31	1.20	1.10	1.54	1.39	1.26	1.15	1.63	1.46	1.32	1.20	1.72	1.53	1.37	1.24	24
25	1.45	1.31	1.20	1.10	1.54	1.39	1.26	1.15	1.63	1.46	1.32	1.20	1.72	1.53	1.37	1.24	25
26	1.45	1.31	1.20	1.10	1.54	1.39	1.26	1.15	1.63	1.46	1.32	1.20	1.72	1.53	1.37	1.24	26
27	1.45	1.31	1.20	1.10	1.54	1.39	1.26	1.15	1.63	1.46	1.32	1.20	1.72	1.53	1.37	1.24	27
28	1.45	1.31	1.20	1.10	1.54	1.39	1.26	1.15	1.63	1.46	1.32	1.20	1.72	1.53	1.37	1.24	28
29	1.45	1.31	1.20	1.10	1.54	1.39	1.26	1.15	1.63	1.46	1.32	1.20	1.72	1.53	1.37	1.24	29
30	1.45	1.31	1.20	1.10	1.54	1.39	1.26	1.15	1.63	1.46	1.32	1.20	1.72	1.53	1.37	1.24	30
31	1.45	1.31	1.20	1.10	1.54	1.39	1.26	1.15	1.63	1.46	1.32	1.20	1.72	1.53	1.37	1.24	31
32	1.45	1.31	1.20	1.10	1.54	1.39	1.26	1.15	1.63	1.46	1.32	1.20	1.72	1.53	1.37	1.24	32
33	1.45	1.31	1.20	1.10	1.54	1.39	1.26	1.15	1.63	1.46	1.32	1.20	1.72	1.53	1.37	1.24	33
34	1.45	1.31	1.20	1.10	1.54	1.39	1.26	1.15	1.63	1.46	1.32	1.20	1.72	1.53	1.37	1.24	34
35	1.45	1.31	1.20	1.10	1.54	1.39	1.26	1.15	1.63	1.46	1.32	1.20	1.72	1.53	1.37	1.24	35
36	1.45	1.31	1.20	1.10	1.54	1.39	1.26	1.15	1.63	1.46	1.32	1.20	1.72	1.53	1.37	1.24	36
37	1.45	1.31	1.20	1.10	1.54	1.39	1.26	1.15	1.63	1.46	1.32	1.20	1.72	1.53	1.37	1.24	37
38	1.45	1.31	1.20	1.10	1.54	1.39	1.26	1.15	1.63	1.46	1.32	1.20	1.72	1.53	1.37	1.24	38
39	1.45	1.31	1.20	1.10	1.54	1.39	1.26	1.15	1.63	1.46	1.32	1.20	1.72	1.53	1.37	1.24	39
40	1.45	1.31	1.20	1.10	1.54	1.39	1.26	1.15	1.63	1.46	1.32	1.20	1.72	1.53	1.37	1.24	40
41	1.45	1.31	1.20	1.10	1.54	1.39	1.26	1.15	1.63	1.46	1.32	1.20	1.72	1.53	1.37	1.24	41
42	1.45	1.31	1.20	1.10	1.54	1.39	1.26	1.15	1.63	1.46	1.32	1.20	1.72	1.53	1.37	1.24	42
43	1.45	1.31	1.20	1.10	1.54	1.39	1.26	1.15	1.63	1.46	1.32	1.20	1.72	1.53	1.37	1.24	43
44	1.45	1.31	1.20	1.10	1.54	1.39	1.26	1.15	1.63	1.46	1.32	1.20	1.72	1.53	1.37	1.24	44
45	1.45	1.31	1.20	1.10	1.54	1.39	1.26	1.15	1.63	1.46	1.32	1.20	1.72	1.53	1.37	1.24	45
46	1.45	1.31	1.20	1.10	1.54	1.39	1.26	1.15	1.63	1.46	1.32	1.20	1.72	1.53	1.37	1.24	46
47	1.45	1.31	1.20	1.10	1.54	1.39	1.26	1.15	1.63	1.46	1.32	1.20	1.72	1.53	1.37	1.24	47
48	1.45	1.31	1.20	1.10	1.54	1.39	1.26	1.15	1.63	1.46	1.32	1.20	1.72	1.53	1.37	1.24	48
49	1.45	1.31	1.20	1.10	1.54	1.39	1.26	1.15	1.63	1.46	1.32	1.20	1.72	1.53	1.37	1.24	49
50	1.45	1.31	1.20	1.10	1.54	1.39	1.26	1.15	1.63	1.46	1.32	1.20	1.72	1.53	1.37	1.24	50

I. Retirement Planning with Level Salary & No Inflation
Planned Retirement Age 65

Table 1 - Percent of Salary Replaced by a 401(k) Account Equal to Current Annual Salary   I-65-1

Probable Life Expectancy at Retirement

Yrs. to Ret.	20.7 (Same as Male Avg.)				23.2 (Better than Male Avg.)				25.7 (Same as Female Avg.)				28.3 (Better than Female Avg.)				Yrs. to Ret.
	4%/4%	6%/5%	8%/6%	10%/7%	4%/4%	6%/5%	8%/6%	10%/7%	4%/4%	6%/5%	8%/6%	10%/7%	4%/4%	6%/5%	8%/6%	10%/7%	
	Expected Return				(Pre-Retirement/Post-Retirement)				(Pre-Retirement/Post-Retirement)				Expected Return				
0	7.45	8.16	8.89	9.63	6.92	7.63	8.36	9.11	6.48	7.20	7.94	8.70	6.12	6.85	7.60	8.36	0
1	7.75	8.65	9.60	10.60	7.19	8.09	9.03	10.02	6.74	7.63	8.58	9.57	6.37	7.26	8.20	9.20	1
2	8.06	9.17	10.37	11.66	7.48	8.57	9.76	11.03	7.01	8.09	9.26	10.53	6.62	7.69	8.86	10.12	2
3	8.38	9.72	11.20	12.82	7.78	9.09	10.54	12.13	7.29	8.58	10.00	11.58	6.88	8.16	9.57	11.13	3
4	8.72	10.31	12.10	14.10	8.09	9.63	11.38	13.34	7.58	9.09	10.80	12.74	7.16	8.64	10.33	12.24	4
5	9.07	10.93	13.07	15.51	8.41	10.21	12.29	14.68	7.89	9.64	11.67	14.01	7.45	9.16	11.16	13.47	5
6	9.43	11.58	14.11	17.07	8.75	10.82	13.27	16.14	8.20	10.21	12.60	15.41	7.74	9.71	12.05	14.82	6
7	9.81	12.28	15.24	18.77	9.10	11.47	14.33	17.76	8.53	10.83	13.61	16.95	8.05	10.30	13.02	16.30	7
8	10.20	13.01	16.46	20.65	9.47	12.16	15.48	19.53	8.87	11.48	14.70	18.65	8.38	10.91	14.06	17.93	8
9	10.61	13.79	17.78	22.72	9.84	12.89	16.72	21.49	9.22	12.17	15.88	20.51	8.71	11.57	15.19	19.72	9
10	11.03	14.62	19.20	24.99	10.24	13.67	18.06	23.64	9.59	12.90	17.15	22.56	9.06	12.26	16.40	21.69	10
11	11.47	15.50	20.73	27.49	10.65	14.49	19.50	26.00	9.98	13.67	18.52	24.82	9.42	13.00	17.71	23.86	11
12	11.93	16.43	22.39	30.23	11.07	15.36	21.06	28.60	10.38	14.49	20.00	27.30	9.80	13.78	19.13	26.25	12
13	12.41	17.41	24.18	33.26	11.52	16.28	22.75	31.46	10.79	15.36	21.60	30.03	10.19	14.60	20.66	28.87	13
14	12.91	18.46	26.12	36.58	11.98	17.25	24.57	34.61	11.22	16.28	23.33	33.04	10.60	15.48	22.31	31.76	14
15	13.42	19.57	28.21	40.24	12.46	18.29	26.53	38.07	11.67	17.26	25.19	36.34	11.02	16.41	24.10	34.94	15
16	13.96	20.74	30.46	44.27	12.95	19.39	28.66	41.87	12.14	18.29	27.21	39.97	11.46	17.39	26.02	38.43	16
17	14.52	21.98	32.90	48.69	13.47	20.55	30.95	46.06	12.62	19.39	29.38	43.97	11.92	18.44	28.11	42.27	17
18	15.10	23.30	35.53	53.56	14.01	21.78	33.42	50.67	13.13	20.55	31.74	48.37	12.40	19.54	30.36	46.50	18
19	15.70	24.70	38.37	58.92	14.57	23.09	36.10	55.73	13.65	21.79	34.27	53.20	12.89	20.72	32.78	51.15	19
20	16.33	26.18	41.44	64.81	15.15	24.47	38.98	61.31	14.20	23.09	37.02	58.52	13.41	21.96	35.41	56.27	20
21	16.98	27.75	44.76	71.29	15.76	25.94	42.10	67.44	14.77	24.48	39.98	64.38	13.95	23.28	38.24	61.89	21
22	17.66	29.42	48.34	78.42	16.39	27.50	45.47	74.18	15.36	25.95	43.18	70.81	14.50	24.67	41.30	68.08	22
23	18.37	31.19	52.21	86.26	17.05	29.15	49.11	81.60	15.97	27.51	46.63	77.90	15.08	26.15	44.60	74.89	23
24	19.10	33.06	56.39	94.89	17.73	30.90	53.04	89.76	16.61	29.16	50.36	85.68	15.69	27.72	48.17	82.38	24
25	19.87	35.04	60.90	104.38	18.44	32.75	57.28	98.73	17.28	30.91	54.39	94.25	16.32	29.39	52.02	90.62	25
26	20.66	37.14	65.77	114.81	19.18	34.72	61.86	108.61	17.97	32.76	58.74	103.68	16.97	31.15	56.19	99.68	26
27	21.49	39.37	71.03	126.30	19.94	36.80	66.81	119.47	18.69	34.73	63.44	114.05	17.65	33.02	60.68	109.64	27
28	22.35	41.73	76.71	138.93	20.74	39.01	72.16	131.41	19.43	36.81	68.51	125.45	18.35	35.00	65.53	120.61	28
29	23.24	44.24	82.85	152.82	21.57	41.35	77.93	144.56	20.21	39.02	74.00	138.00	19.09	37.10	70.78	132.67	29
30	24.17	46.89	89.48	168.10	22.43	43.83	84.17	159.01	21.02	41.36	79.91	151.80	19.85	39.33	76.44	145.94	30
31	25.14	49.70	96.63	184.91	23.33	46.46	90.90	174.91	21.86	43.84	86.31	166.98	20.64	41.69	82.55	160.53	31
32	26.15	52.69	104.37	203.40	24.26	49.25	98.17	192.40	22.74	46.47	93.21	183.67	21.47	44.19	89.16	176.58	32
33	27.19	55.85	112.71	223.74	25.23	52.20	106.02	211.64	23.65	49.26	100.67	202.04	22.33	46.84	96.29	194.24	33
34	28.28	59.20	121.73	246.11	26.24	55.33	114.51	232.81	24.59	52.22	108.72	222.24	23.22	49.65	103.99	213.67	34
35	29.41	62.75	131.47	270.73	27.29	58.65	123.67	256.09	25.57	55.35	117.42	244.47	24.15	52.63	112.31	235.03	35
36	30.59	66.52	141.99	297.80	28.38	62.17	133.56	281.70	26.60	58.67	126.82	268.92	25.12	55.79	121.30	258.54	36
37	31.81	70.51	153.35	327.58	29.52	65.90	144.24	309.87	27.66	62.19	136.96	295.81	26.12	59.13	131.00	284.39	37
38	33.08	74.74	165.61	360.34	30.70	69.86	155.78	340.86	28.77	65.92	147.92	325.39	27.17	62.68	141.48	312.83	38
39	34.41	79.22	178.86	396.37	31.93	74.05	168.25	374.94	29.92	69.88	159.75	357.93	28.25	66.44	152.80	344.11	39
40	35.78	83.97	193.17	436.01	33.21	78.49	181.71	412.43	31.12	74.07	172.53	393.72	29.38	70.43	165.03	378.52	40
41	37.21	89.01	208.63	479.61	34.53	83.20	196.24	453.68	32.36	78.51	186.33	433.09	30.56	74.65	178.23	416.38	41
42	38.70	94.35	225.32	527.57	35.92	88.19	211.94	499.05	33.65	83.22	201.24	476.40	31.78	79.13	192.49	458.01	42
43	40.25	100.01	243.34	580.32	37.35	93.48	228.90	548.95	35.00	88.22	217.34	524.04	33.05	83.88	207.89	503.81	43
44	41.86	106.02	262.81	638.36	38.85	99.09	247.21	603.85	36.40	93.51	234.73	576.44	34.38	88.91	224.52	554.20	44
45	43.53	112.38	283.83	702.19	40.42	105.09	266.99	664.23	37.86	99.12	253.50	634.09	35.75	94.25	242.48	609.62	45
46	45.28	119.12	306.54	772.41	42.02	111.34	288.35	730.65	39.37	105.07	273.78	697.50	37.18	99.90	261.88	670.58	46
47	47.09	126.27	331.06	849.65	43.70	118.02	311.41	803.72	40.95	111.37	295.69	767.25	38.67	105.90	282.83	737.64	47
48	48.97	133.84	357.55	934.62	45.44	125.10	336.33	884.09	42.58	118.05	319.34	843.97	40.21	112.25	305.45	811.40	48
49	50.93	141.87	386.15	1028.08	47.26	132.61	363.23	972.50	44.29	125.14	344.89	928.37	41.82	118.99	329.89	892.54	49
50	52.97	150.39	417.05	1130.89	49.15	140.56	392.29	1069.75	46.06	132.65	372.48	1021.21	43.50	126.13	356.28	981.79	50

Appendix A

I. Retirement Planning with Level Salary & No Inflation
Planned Retirement Age 65

Table 2 - Percent of Salary Replaced by a 401(k) Contribution of 1% of Current Salary — I-65-2

Probable Life Expectancy at Retirement

Yrs. to Ret.	20.7 (Same as Male Avg.)				23.2 (Better than Male Avg.)				25.7 (Same as Female Avg.)				28.3 (Better than Female Avg.)				Yrs. to Ret.
	4% / 4%	6% / 5%	8% / 6%	10% / 7%	4% / 4%	6% / 5%	8% / 6%	10% / 7%	4% / 4%	6% / 5%	8% / 6%	10% / 7%	4% / 4%	6% / 5%	8% / 6%	10% / 7%	
	Expected Return				(Pre-Retirement/Post-Retirement)				(Pre-Retirement/Post-Retirement)				Expected Return				
0	0.00	0.00	0.00	0.00	0.00	0.00	0.00	0.00	0.00	0.00	0.00	0.00	0.00	0.00	0.00	0.00	0
1	0.07	0.08	0.09	0.10	0.07	0.08	0.08	0.09	0.06	0.07	0.08	0.09	0.06	0.07	0.08	0.08	1
2	0.15	0.17	0.18	0.20	0.14	0.16	0.17	0.19	0.13	0.15	0.17	0.18	0.12	0.14	0.16	0.18	2
3	0.23	0.26	0.29	0.32	0.22	0.24	0.27	0.30	0.20	0.23	0.26	0.29	0.19	0.22	0.25	0.28	3
4	0.32	0.36	0.40	0.45	0.29	0.33	0.38	0.42	0.28	0.32	0.36	0.40	0.26	0.30	0.34	0.39	4
5	0.40	0.46	0.52	0.59	0.37	0.43	0.49	0.56	0.35	0.41	0.47	0.53	0.33	0.39	0.45	0.51	5
6	0.49	0.57	0.65	0.74	0.46	0.53	0.61	0.70	0.43	0.50	0.58	0.67	0.41	0.48	0.56	0.65	6
7	0.59	0.69	0.79	0.91	0.55	0.64	0.75	0.86	0.51	0.60	0.71	0.83	0.48	0.57	0.68	0.79	7
8	0.69	0.81	0.95	1.10	0.64	0.76	0.89	1.04	0.60	0.71	0.84	0.99	0.56	0.68	0.81	0.96	8
9	0.79	0.94	1.11	1.31	0.73	0.88	1.04	1.24	0.69	0.83	0.99	1.18	0.65	0.79	0.95	1.14	9
10	0.89	1.08	1.29	1.54	0.83	1.01	1.21	1.45	0.78	0.95	1.15	1.39	0.73	0.90	1.10	1.33	10
11	1.01	1.22	1.48	1.79	0.93	1.14	1.39	1.69	0.87	1.08	1.32	1.61	0.83	1.03	1.26	1.55	11
12	1.12	1.38	1.69	2.06	1.04	1.29	1.59	1.95	0.97	1.21	1.51	1.86	0.92	1.16	1.44	1.79	12
13	1.24	1.54	1.91	2.36	1.15	1.44	1.80	2.23	1.08	1.36	1.71	2.13	1.02	1.29	1.63	2.05	13
14	1.36	1.72	2.15	2.69	1.27	1.60	2.03	2.55	1.19	1.51	1.92	2.43	1.12	1.44	1.84	2.34	14
15	1.49	1.90	2.41	3.06	1.38	1.78	2.27	2.90	1.30	1.68	2.16	2.76	1.23	1.59	2.06	2.66	15
16	1.63	2.10	2.70	3.46	1.51	1.96	2.54	3.28	1.41	1.85	2.41	3.13	1.34	1.76	2.30	3.01	16
17	1.77	2.30	3.00	3.91	1.64	2.15	2.82	3.69	1.54	2.03	2.68	3.53	1.45	1.93	2.56	3.39	17
18	1.91	2.52	3.33	4.39	1.77	2.36	3.13	4.16	1.66	2.23	2.97	3.97	1.57	2.12	2.84	3.81	18
19	2.06	2.76	3.69	4.93	1.91	2.58	3.47	4.66	1.79	2.43	3.29	4.45	1.69	2.31	3.15	4.28	19
20	2.22	3.00	4.07	5.52	2.06	2.81	3.83	5.22	1.93	2.65	3.63	4.98	1.82	2.52	3.48	4.79	20
21	2.38	3.27	4.48	6.17	2.21	3.05	4.22	5.83	2.07	2.88	4.00	5.57	1.96	2.74	3.83	5.35	21
22	2.55	3.54	4.93	6.88	2.37	3.31	4.64	6.51	2.22	3.12	4.40	6.21	2.10	2.97	4.21	5.97	22
23	2.73	3.84	5.41	7.66	2.53	3.59	5.09	7.25	2.37	3.38	4.84	6.92	2.24	3.22	4.63	6.65	23
24	2.91	4.15	5.94	8.53	2.70	3.88	5.58	8.06	2.53	3.66	5.30	7.70	2.39	3.48	5.07	7.40	24
25	3.10	4.48	6.50	9.47	2.88	4.19	6.11	8.96	2.70	3.95	5.81	8.56	2.55	3.76	5.55	8.23	25
26	3.30	4.83	7.11	10.52	3.06	4.51	6.69	9.95	2.87	4.26	6.35	9.50	2.71	4.05	6.07	9.13	26
27	3.51	5.20	7.77	11.67	3.26	4.86	7.31	11.04	3.05	4.59	6.94	10.53	2.88	4.36	6.64	10.13	27
28	3.72	5.59	8.48	12.93	3.46	5.23	7.97	12.23	3.24	4.93	7.57	11.68	3.06	4.69	7.24	11.22	28
29	3.95	6.01	9.24	14.31	3.66	5.62	8.70	13.54	3.43	5.30	8.26	12.93	3.24	5.04	7.90	12.43	29
30	4.18	6.45	10.07	15.85	3.88	6.03	9.48	14.99	3.63	5.69	9.00	14.31	3.43	5.41	8.61	13.76	30
31	4.42	6.92	10.97	17.53	4.10	6.47	10.32	16.58	3.85	6.11	9.80	15.83	3.63	5.81	9.37	15.22	31
32	4.67	7.42	11.93	19.38	4.34	6.94	11.23	18.33	4.06	6.55	10.66	17.50	3.84	6.22	10.20	16.82	32
33	4.93	7.95	12.98	21.41	4.58	7.43	12.21	20.25	4.29	7.01	11.59	19.33	4.05	6.67	11.09	18.59	33
34	5.21	8.51	14.10	23.65	4.83	7.95	13.27	22.37	4.53	7.50	12.60	21.35	4.28	7.13	12.05	20.53	34
35	5.49	9.10	15.32	26.11	5.09	8.50	14.41	24.70	4.77	8.02	13.68	23.58	4.51	7.63	13.09	22.67	35
36	5.79	9.73	16.64	28.82	5.37	9.09	15.65	27.26	5.03	8.58	14.86	26.02	4.75	8.16	14.21	25.02	36
37	6.09	10.39	18.06	31.79	5.65	9.71	16.99	30.08	5.30	9.16	16.13	28.71	5.00	8.71	15.43	27.60	37
38	6.41	11.10	19.59	35.07	5.95	10.37	18.43	33.17	5.57	9.79	17.50	31.67	5.26	9.31	16.74	30.45	38
39	6.74	11.84	21.25	38.67	6.25	11.07	19.99	36.58	5.86	10.45	18.98	34.92	5.53	9.93	18.15	33.57	39
40	7.08	12.64	23.04	42.64	6.57	11.81	21.67	40.33	6.16	11.14	20.57	38.50	5.82	10.60	19.68	37.02	40
41	7.44	13.47	24.97	47.00	6.90	12.59	23.48	44.46	6.47	11.89	22.30	42.44	6.11	11.30	21.33	40.80	41
42	7.81	14.36	27.05	51.79	7.25	13.43	25.45	48.99	6.79	12.67	24.16	46.77	6.42	12.05	23.11	44.96	42
43	8.20	15.31	29.31	57.07	7.61	14.31	27.57	53.98	7.13	13.50	26.17	51.53	6.73	12.84	25.04	49.55	43
44	8.60	16.31	31.74	62.87	7.98	15.24	29.86	59.47	7.48	14.38	28.35	56.77	7.06	13.68	27.12	54.58	44
45	9.02	17.37	34.37	69.26	8.37	16.23	32.33	65.51	7.84	15.32	30.70	62.54	7.41	14.57	29.36	60.13	45
46	9.46	18.49	37.21	76.28	8.77	17.28	35.00	72.15	8.22	16.31	33.23	68.88	7.76	15.51	31.78	66.22	46
47	9.91	19.68	40.27	84.00	9.20	18.40	37.88	79.46	8.62	17.36	35.97	75.85	8.14	16.51	34.40	72.93	47
48	10.38	20.95	43.58	92.50	9.63	19.58	41.00	87.50	9.03	18.48	38.93	83.53	8.52	17.57	37.23	80.30	48
49	10.87	22.28	47.16	101.84	10.09	20.83	44.36	96.34	9.45	19.66	42.12	91.97	8.93	18.69	40.29	88.42	49
50	11.38	23.70	51.02	112.13	10.56	22.16	47.99	106.06	9.89	20.91	45.57	101.25	9.34	19.88	43.59	97.34	50

A-11

I. Retirement Planning with Level Salary & No Inflation
Planned Retirement Age 65

Table 3 - 401(k) Contribution (% of Current Sal.) Needed to Replace 10% of Sal. at Retirement   I-65-3

Probable Life Expectancy at Retirement

	20.7 (Same as Male Avg.)				23.2 (Better than Male Avg.)				25.7 (Same as Female Avg.)				28.3 (Better than Female Avg.)				
	4% / 4%	6% / 5%	8% / 6%	10% / 7%	4% / 4%	6% / 5%	8% / 6%	10% / 7%	4% / 4%	6% / 5%	8% / 6%	10% / 7%	4% / 4%	6% / 5%	8% / 6%	10% / 7%	
Yrs. to Ret.	Expected Return				(Pre-Retirement/Post-Retirement)				(Pre-Retirement/Post-Retirement)				Expected Return				Yrs. to Ret.
0																	0
1	134.18	122.49	112.46	103.80	144.58	131.04	119.56	109.74	154.30	138.87	125.92	114.95	163.39	146.04	131.64	119.57	1
2	65.77	59.46	54.07	49.43	70.87	63.61	57.48	52.26	75.64	67.41	60.54	54.74	80.09	70.90	63.29	56.94	2
3	42.98	38.47	34.64	31.36	46.32	41.16	36.83	33.15	49.43	43.62	38.79	34.73	52.34	45.87	40.55	36.12	3
4	31.60	28.00	24.96	22.37	34.05	29.96	26.53	23.65	36.34	31.74	27.94	24.77	38.48	33.38	29.21	25.76	4
5	24.77	21.73	19.17	17.00	26.69	23.25	20.38	17.97	28.49	24.63	21.46	18.83	30.17	25.91	22.44	19.58	5
6	20.23	17.56	15.33	13.45	21.80	18.79	16.30	14.22	23.26	19.91	17.16	14.90	24.63	20.94	17.94	15.50	6
7	16.99	14.59	12.60	10.94	18.31	15.61	13.40	11.57	19.54	16.54	14.11	12.12	20.69	17.40	14.75	12.60	7
8	14.56	12.38	10.57	9.08	15.69	13.24	11.24	9.60	16.75	14.03	11.84	10.05	17.73	14.76	12.38	10.46	8
9	12.68	10.66	9.01	7.64	13.66	11.40	9.57	8.08	14.58	12.08	10.08	8.47	15.44	12.71	10.54	8.81	9
10	11.18	9.29	7.76	6.51	12.04	9.94	8.25	6.89	12.85	10.54	8.69	7.21	13.61	11.08	9.09	7.50	10
11	9.95	8.18	6.76	5.60	10.72	8.75	7.18	5.92	11.44	9.28	7.56	6.20	12.12	9.75	7.91	6.45	11
12	8.93	7.26	5.93	4.85	9.62	7.77	6.30	5.13	10.27	8.23	6.64	5.38	10.87	8.66	6.94	5.59	12
13	8.07	6.49	5.23	4.23	8.70	6.94	5.56	4.47	9.28	7.35	5.86	4.69	9.83	7.73	6.12	4.88	13
14	7.34	5.83	4.64	3.71	7.90	6.24	4.94	3.92	8.44	6.61	5.20	4.11	8.93	6.95	5.44	4.27	14
15	6.70	5.26	4.14	3.27	7.22	5.63	4.40	3.45	7.71	5.97	4.64	3.62	8.16	6.27	4.85	3.76	15
16	6.15	4.77	3.71	2.89	6.62	5.10	3.94	3.05	7.07	5.41	4.15	3.20	7.49	5.69	4.34	3.33	16
17	5.66	4.34	3.33	2.56	6.10	4.64	3.54	2.71	6.51	4.92	3.73	2.84	6.89	5.18	3.90	2.95	17
18	5.23	3.96	3.00	2.28	5.64	4.24	3.19	2.41	6.02	4.49	3.36	2.52	6.37	4.73	3.52	2.62	18
19	4.85	3.63	2.71	2.03	5.23	3.88	2.88	2.15	5.58	4.11	3.04	2.25	5.90	4.33	3.18	2.34	19
20	4.51	3.33	2.46	1.81	4.86	3.56	2.61	1.92	5.18	3.78	2.75	2.01	5.49	3.97	2.88	2.09	20
21	4.20	3.06	2.23	1.62	4.52	3.28	2.37	1.71	4.83	3.47	2.50	1.80	5.11	3.65	2.61	1.87	21
22	3.92	2.82	2.03	1.45	4.22	3.02	2.16	1.54	4.51	3.20	2.27	1.61	4.77	3.37	2.37	1.67	22
23	3.66	2.61	1.85	1.31	3.95	2.79	1.96	1.38	4.21	2.95	2.07	1.45	4.46	3.11	2.16	1.50	23
24	3.43	2.41	1.68	1.17	3.70	2.58	1.79	1.24	3.95	2.73	1.89	1.30	4.18	2.87	1.97	1.35	24
25	3.22	2.23	1.54	1.06	3.47	2.39	1.64	1.12	3.70	2.53	1.72	1.17	3.92	2.66	1.80	1.22	25
26	3.03	2.07	1.41	0.95	3.26	2.22	1.50	1.01	3.48	2.35	1.57	1.05	3.69	2.47	1.65	1.10	26
27	2.85	1.92	1.29	0.86	3.07	2.06	1.37	0.91	3.28	2.18	1.44	0.95	3.47	2.29	1.51	0.99	27
28	2.69	1.79	1.18	0.77	2.89	1.91	1.25	0.82	3.09	2.03	1.32	0.86	3.27	2.13	1.38	0.89	28
29	2.53	1.66	1.08	0.70	2.73	1.78	1.15	0.74	2.91	1.89	1.21	0.77	3.08	1.98	1.27	0.80	29
30	2.39	1.55	0.99	0.63	2.58	1.66	1.06	0.67	2.75	1.76	1.11	0.70	2.91	1.85	1.16	0.73	30
31	2.26	1.44	0.91	0.57	2.44	1.55	0.97	0.60	2.60	1.64	1.02	0.63	2.75	1.72	1.07	0.66	31
32	2.14	1.35	0.84	0.52	2.31	1.44	0.89	0.55	2.46	1.53	0.94	0.57	2.61	1.61	0.98	0.59	32
33	2.03	1.26	0.77	0.47	2.18	1.35	0.82	0.49	2.33	1.43	0.86	0.52	2.47	1.50	0.90	0.54	33
34	1.92	1.18	0.71	0.42	2.07	1.26	0.75	0.45	2.21	1.33	0.79	0.47	2.34	1.40	0.83	0.49	34
35	1.82	1.10	0.65	0.38	1.96	1.18	0.69	0.40	2.09	1.25	0.73	0.42	2.22	1.31	0.76	0.44	35
36	1.73	1.03	0.60	0.35	1.86	1.10	0.64	0.37	1.99	1.17	0.67	0.38	2.11	1.23	0.70	0.40	36
37	1.64	0.96	0.55	0.31	1.77	1.03	0.59	0.33	1.89	1.09	0.62	0.35	2.00	1.15	0.65	0.36	37
38	1.56	0.90	0.51	0.29	1.68	0.96	0.54	0.30	1.79	1.02	0.57	0.32	1.90	1.07	0.60	0.33	38
39	1.48	0.84	0.47	0.26	1.60	0.90	0.50	0.27	1.71	0.96	0.53	0.29	1.81	1.01	0.55	0.30	39
40	1.41	0.79	0.43	0.23	1.52	0.85	0.46	0.25	1.62	0.90	0.49	0.26	1.72	0.94	0.51	0.27	40
41	1.34	0.74	0.40	0.21	1.45	0.79	0.43	0.22	1.55	0.84	0.45	0.24	1.64	0.88	0.47	0.25	41
42	1.28	0.70	0.37	0.19	1.38	0.74	0.39	0.20	1.47	0.79	0.41	0.21	1.56	0.83	0.43	0.22	42
43	1.22	0.65	0.34	0.18	1.31	0.70	0.36	0.19	1.40	0.74	0.38	0.19	1.49	0.78	0.40	0.20	43
44	1.16	0.61	0.32	0.16	1.25	0.66	0.33	0.17	1.34	0.70	0.35	0.18	1.42	0.73	0.37	0.18	44
45	1.11	0.58	0.29	0.14	1.19	0.62	0.31	0.15	1.27	0.65	0.33	0.16	1.35	0.69	0.34	0.17	45
46	1.06	0.54	0.27	0.13	1.14	0.58	0.29	0.14	1.22	0.61	0.30	0.15	1.29	0.64	0.31	0.15	46
47	1.01	0.51	0.25	0.12	1.09	0.54	0.26	0.13	1.16	0.58	0.28	0.13	1.23	0.61	0.29	0.14	47
48	0.96	0.48	0.23	0.11	1.04	0.51	0.24	0.11	1.11	0.54	0.26	0.12	1.17	0.57	0.27	0.12	48
49	0.92	0.45	0.21	0.10	0.99	0.48	0.23	0.10	1.06	0.51	0.24	0.11	1.12	0.54	0.25	0.11	49
50	0.88	0.42	0.20	0.09	0.95	0.45	0.21	0.09	1.01	0.48	0.22	0.10	1.07	0.50	0.23	0.10	50

Appendix A

I. Retirement Planning with Level Salary & No Inflation
Planned Retirement Age 65

Table 4 - Accumulation at Retirement (Multiple of Current Sal.) for 10% Sal. Replacement　　I-65-4

Probable Life Expectancy at Retirement

Yrs. to Ret.	20.7 (Same as Male Avg.)				23.2 (Better than Male Avg.)				25.7 (Same as Female Avg.)				28.3 (Better than Female Avg.)				Yrs. to Ret.
	4%/4%	6%/5%	8%/6%	10%/7%	4%/4%	6%/5%	8%/6%	10%/7%	4%/4%	6%/5%	8%/6%	10%/7%	4%/4%	6%/5%	8%/6%	10%/7%	
	Expected Return				(Pre-Retirement/Post-Retirement)				(Pre-Retirement/Post-Retirement)				Expected Return				
0	1.34	1.22	1.12	1.04	1.45	1.31	1.20	1.10	1.54	1.39	1.26	1.15	1.63	1.46	1.32	1.20	0
1	1.34	1.22	1.12	1.04	1.45	1.31	1.20	1.10	1.54	1.39	1.26	1.15	1.63	1.46	1.32	1.20	1
2	1.34	1.22	1.12	1.04	1.45	1.31	1.20	1.10	1.54	1.39	1.26	1.15	1.63	1.46	1.32	1.20	2
3	1.34	1.22	1.12	1.04	1.45	1.31	1.20	1.10	1.54	1.39	1.26	1.15	1.63	1.46	1.32	1.20	3
4	1.34	1.22	1.12	1.04	1.45	1.31	1.20	1.10	1.54	1.39	1.26	1.15	1.63	1.46	1.32	1.20	4
5	1.34	1.22	1.12	1.04	1.45	1.31	1.20	1.10	1.54	1.39	1.26	1.15	1.63	1.46	1.32	1.20	5
6	1.34	1.22	1.12	1.04	1.45	1.31	1.20	1.10	1.54	1.39	1.26	1.15	1.63	1.46	1.32	1.20	6
7	1.34	1.22	1.12	1.04	1.45	1.31	1.20	1.10	1.54	1.39	1.26	1.15	1.63	1.46	1.32	1.20	7
8	1.34	1.22	1.12	1.04	1.45	1.31	1.20	1.10	1.54	1.39	1.26	1.15	1.63	1.46	1.32	1.20	8
9	1.34	1.22	1.12	1.04	1.45	1.31	1.20	1.10	1.54	1.39	1.26	1.15	1.63	1.46	1.32	1.20	9
10	1.34	1.22	1.12	1.04	1.45	1.31	1.20	1.10	1.54	1.39	1.26	1.15	1.63	1.46	1.32	1.20	10
11	1.34	1.22	1.12	1.04	1.45	1.31	1.20	1.10	1.54	1.39	1.26	1.15	1.63	1.46	1.32	1.20	11
12	1.34	1.22	1.12	1.04	1.45	1.31	1.20	1.10	1.54	1.39	1.26	1.15	1.63	1.46	1.32	1.20	12
13	1.34	1.22	1.12	1.04	1.45	1.31	1.20	1.10	1.54	1.39	1.26	1.15	1.63	1.46	1.32	1.20	13
14	1.34	1.22	1.12	1.04	1.45	1.31	1.20	1.10	1.54	1.39	1.26	1.15	1.63	1.46	1.32	1.20	14
15	1.34	1.22	1.12	1.04	1.45	1.31	1.20	1.10	1.54	1.39	1.26	1.15	1.63	1.46	1.32	1.20	15
16	1.34	1.22	1.12	1.04	1.45	1.31	1.20	1.10	1.54	1.39	1.26	1.15	1.63	1.46	1.32	1.20	16
17	1.34	1.22	1.12	1.04	1.45	1.31	1.20	1.10	1.54	1.39	1.26	1.15	1.63	1.46	1.32	1.20	17
18	1.34	1.22	1.12	1.04	1.45	1.31	1.20	1.10	1.54	1.39	1.26	1.15	1.63	1.46	1.32	1.20	18
19	1.34	1.22	1.12	1.04	1.45	1.31	1.20	1.10	1.54	1.39	1.26	1.15	1.63	1.46	1.32	1.20	19
20	1.34	1.22	1.12	1.04	1.45	1.31	1.20	1.10	1.54	1.39	1.26	1.15	1.63	1.46	1.32	1.20	20
21	1.34	1.22	1.12	1.04	1.45	1.31	1.20	1.10	1.54	1.39	1.26	1.15	1.63	1.46	1.32	1.20	21
22	1.34	1.22	1.12	1.04	1.45	1.31	1.20	1.10	1.54	1.39	1.26	1.15	1.63	1.46	1.32	1.20	22
23	1.34	1.22	1.12	1.04	1.45	1.31	1.20	1.10	1.54	1.39	1.26	1.15	1.63	1.46	1.32	1.20	23
24	1.34	1.22	1.12	1.04	1.45	1.31	1.20	1.10	1.54	1.39	1.26	1.15	1.63	1.46	1.32	1.20	24
25	1.34	1.22	1.12	1.04	1.45	1.31	1.20	1.10	1.54	1.39	1.26	1.15	1.63	1.46	1.32	1.20	25
26	1.34	1.22	1.12	1.04	1.45	1.31	1.20	1.10	1.54	1.39	1.26	1.15	1.63	1.46	1.32	1.20	26
27	1.34	1.22	1.12	1.04	1.45	1.31	1.20	1.10	1.54	1.39	1.26	1.15	1.63	1.46	1.32	1.20	27
28	1.34	1.22	1.12	1.04	1.45	1.31	1.20	1.10	1.54	1.39	1.26	1.15	1.63	1.46	1.32	1.20	28
29	1.34	1.22	1.12	1.04	1.45	1.31	1.20	1.10	1.54	1.39	1.26	1.15	1.63	1.46	1.32	1.20	29
30	1.34	1.22	1.12	1.04	1.45	1.31	1.20	1.10	1.54	1.39	1.26	1.15	1.63	1.46	1.32	1.20	30
31	1.34	1.22	1.12	1.04	1.45	1.31	1.20	1.10	1.54	1.39	1.26	1.15	1.63	1.46	1.32	1.20	31
32	1.34	1.22	1.12	1.04	1.45	1.31	1.20	1.10	1.54	1.39	1.26	1.15	1.63	1.46	1.32	1.20	32
33	1.34	1.22	1.12	1.04	1.45	1.31	1.20	1.10	1.54	1.39	1.26	1.15	1.63	1.46	1.32	1.20	33
34	1.34	1.22	1.12	1.04	1.45	1.31	1.20	1.10	1.54	1.39	1.26	1.15	1.63	1.46	1.32	1.20	34
35	1.34	1.22	1.12	1.04	1.45	1.31	1.20	1.10	1.54	1.39	1.26	1.15	1.63	1.46	1.32	1.20	35
36	1.34	1.22	1.12	1.04	1.45	1.31	1.20	1.10	1.54	1.39	1.26	1.15	1.63	1.46	1.32	1.20	36
37	1.34	1.22	1.12	1.04	1.45	1.31	1.20	1.10	1.54	1.39	1.26	1.15	1.63	1.46	1.32	1.20	37
38	1.34	1.22	1.12	1.04	1.45	1.31	1.20	1.10	1.54	1.39	1.26	1.15	1.63	1.46	1.32	1.20	38
39	1.34	1.22	1.12	1.04	1.45	1.31	1.20	1.10	1.54	1.39	1.26	1.15	1.63	1.46	1.32	1.20	39
40	1.34	1.22	1.12	1.04	1.45	1.31	1.20	1.10	1.54	1.39	1.26	1.15	1.63	1.46	1.32	1.20	40
41	1.34	1.22	1.12	1.04	1.45	1.31	1.20	1.10	1.54	1.39	1.26	1.15	1.63	1.46	1.32	1.20	41
42	1.34	1.22	1.12	1.04	1.45	1.31	1.20	1.10	1.54	1.39	1.26	1.15	1.63	1.46	1.32	1.20	42
43	1.34	1.22	1.12	1.04	1.45	1.31	1.20	1.10	1.54	1.39	1.26	1.15	1.63	1.46	1.32	1.20	43
44	1.34	1.22	1.12	1.04	1.45	1.31	1.20	1.10	1.54	1.39	1.26	1.15	1.63	1.46	1.32	1.20	44
45	1.34	1.22	1.12	1.04	1.45	1.31	1.20	1.10	1.54	1.39	1.26	1.15	1.63	1.46	1.32	1.20	45
46	1.34	1.22	1.12	1.04	1.45	1.31	1.20	1.10	1.54	1.39	1.26	1.15	1.63	1.46	1.32	1.20	46
47	1.34	1.22	1.12	1.04	1.45	1.31	1.20	1.10	1.54	1.39	1.26	1.15	1.63	1.46	1.32	1.20	47
48	1.34	1.22	1.12	1.04	1.45	1.31	1.20	1.10	1.54	1.39	1.26	1.15	1.63	1.46	1.32	1.20	48
49	1.34	1.22	1.12	1.04	1.45	1.31	1.20	1.10	1.54	1.39	1.26	1.15	1.63	1.46	1.32	1.20	49
50	1.34	1.22	1.12	1.04	1.45	1.31	1.20	1.10	1.54	1.39	1.26	1.15	1.63	1.46	1.32	1.20	50

A-13

I. Retirement Planning with Level Salary & No Inflation
Planned Retirement Age 68

Table 1 - Percent of Salary Replaced by a 401(k) Account Equal to Current Annual Salary

I-68-1

Probable Life Expectancy at Retirement

	18.3 (Same as Male Avg.)				20.7 (Better than Male Avg.)				23.2 (Same as Female Avg.)				25.7 (Better than Female Avg.)			
	4% / 4%	6% / 5%	8% / 6%	10% / 7%	4% / 4%	6% / 5%	8% / 6%	10% / 7%	4% / 4%	6% / 5%	8% / 6%	10% / 7%	4% / 4%	6% / 5%	8% / 6%	10% / 7%
Yrs. to Ret.	Expected Return				(Pre-Retirement/Post-Retirement)				(Pre-Retirement/Post-Retirement)				Expected Return			Yrs. to Ret.
0	8.12	8.83	9.55	10.29	7.45	8.16	8.89	9.63	6.92	7.63	8.36	9.11	6.48	7.20	7.94	8.70	0
1	8.44	9.36	10.32	11.32	7.75	8.65	9.60	10.60	7.19	8.09	9.03	10.02	6.74	7.63	8.58	9.57	1
2	8.78	9.92	11.14	12.45	8.06	9.17	10.37	11.66	7.48	8.57	9.76	11.03	7.01	8.09	9.26	10.53	2
3	9.13	10.52	12.04	13.70	8.38	9.72	11.20	12.82	7.78	9.09	10.54	12.13	7.29	8.58	10.00	11.58	3
4	9.50	11.15	13.00	15.07	8.72	10.31	12.10	14.10	8.09	9.63	11.38	13.34	7.58	9.09	10.80	12.74	4
5	9.88	11.82	14.04	16.58	9.07	10.93	13.07	15.51	8.41	10.21	12.29	14.68	7.89	9.64	11.67	14.01	5
6	10.27	12.52	15.16	18.23	9.43	11.58	14.11	17.07	8.75	10.82	13.27	16.14	8.20	10.21	12.60	15.41	6
7	10.68	13.28	16.37	20.06	9.81	12.28	15.24	18.77	9.10	11.47	14.33	17.76	8.53	10.83	13.61	16.95	7
8	11.11	14.07	17.68	22.06	10.20	13.01	16.46	20.65	9.47	12.16	15.48	19.53	8.87	11.48	14.70	18.65	8
9	11.56	14.92	19.10	24.27	10.61	13.79	17.78	22.72	9.84	12.89	16.72	21.49	9.22	12.17	15.88	20.51	9
10	12.02	15.81	20.63	26.69	11.03	14.62	19.20	24.99	10.24	13.67	18.06	23.64	9.59	12.90	17.15	22.56	10
11	12.50	16.76	22.28	29.36	11.47	15.50	20.73	27.49	10.65	14.49	19.50	26.00	9.98	13.67	18.52	24.82	11
12	13.00	17.77	24.06	32.30	11.93	16.43	22.39	30.23	11.07	15.36	21.06	28.60	10.38	14.49	20.00	27.30	12
13	13.52	18.83	25.99	35.53	12.41	17.41	24.18	33.26	11.52	16.28	22.75	31.46	10.79	15.36	21.60	30.03	13
14	14.06	19.96	28.06	39.08	12.91	18.46	26.12	36.58	11.98	17.25	24.57	34.61	11.22	16.28	23.33	33.04	14
15	14.62	21.16	30.31	42.99	13.42	19.57	28.21	40.24	12.46	18.29	26.53	38.07	11.67	17.26	25.19	36.34	15
16	15.21	22.43	32.73	47.29	13.96	20.74	30.46	44.27	12.95	19.39	28.66	41.87	12.14	18.29	27.21	39.97	16
17	15.81	23.78	35.35	52.02	14.52	21.98	32.90	48.69	13.47	20.55	30.95	46.06	12.62	19.39	29.38	43.97	17
18	16.45	25.20	38.18	57.22	15.10	23.30	35.53	53.56	14.01	21.78	33.42	50.67	13.13	20.55	31.74	48.37	18
19	17.10	26.71	41.24	62.94	15.70	24.70	38.37	58.92	14.57	23.09	36.10	55.73	13.65	21.79	34.27	53.20	19
20	17.79	28.32	44.53	69.24	16.33	26.18	41.44	64.81	15.15	24.47	38.98	61.31	14.20	23.09	37.02	58.52	20
21	18.50	30.02	48.10	76.16	16.98	27.75	44.76	71.29	15.76	25.94	42.10	67.44	14.77	24.48	39.98	64.38	21
22	19.24	31.82	51.94	83.78	17.66	29.42	48.34	78.42	16.39	27.50	45.47	74.18	15.36	25.95	43.18	70.81	22
23	20.01	33.73	56.10	92.16	18.37	31.19	52.21	86.26	17.05	29.15	49.11	81.60	15.97	27.51	46.63	77.90	23
24	20.81	35.75	60.59	101.37	19.10	33.06	56.39	94.89	17.73	30.90	53.04	89.76	16.61	29.16	50.36	85.68	24
25	21.64	37.89	65.43	111.51	19.87	35.04	60.90	104.38	18.44	32.75	57.28	98.73	17.28	30.91	54.39	94.25	25
26	22.51	40.17	70.67	122.66	20.66	37.14	65.77	114.81	19.18	34.72	61.86	108.61	17.97	32.76	58.74	103.68	26
27	23.41	42.58	76.32	134.93	21.49	39.37	71.03	126.30	19.94	36.80	66.81	119.47	18.69	34.73	63.44	114.05	27
28	24.35	45.13	82.43	148.42	22.35	41.73	76.71	138.93	20.74	39.01	72.16	131.41	19.43	36.81	68.51	125.45	28
29	25.32	47.84	89.02	163.26	23.24	44.24	82.85	152.82	21.57	41.35	77.93	144.56	20.21	39.02	74.00	138.00	29
30	26.33	50.71	96.15	179.59	24.17	46.89	89.48	168.10	22.43	43.83	84.17	159.01	21.02	41.36	79.91	151.80	30
31	27.39	53.75	103.84	197.55	25.14	49.70	96.63	184.91	23.33	46.46	90.90	174.91	21.86	43.84	86.31	166.98	31
32	28.48	56.98	112.14	217.30	26.15	52.69	104.37	203.40	24.26	49.25	98.17	192.40	22.74	46.47	93.21	183.67	32
33	29.62	60.40	121.12	239.03	27.19	55.85	112.71	223.74	25.23	52.20	106.02	211.64	23.65	49.26	100.67	202.04	33
34	30.80	64.02	130.80	262.93	28.28	59.20	121.73	246.11	26.24	55.33	114.51	232.81	24.59	52.22	108.72	222.24	34
35	32.04	67.86	141.27	289.23	29.41	62.75	131.47	270.73	27.29	58.65	123.67	256.09	25.57	55.35	117.42	244.47	35
36	33.32	71.94	152.57	318.15	30.59	66.52	141.99	297.80	28.38	62.17	133.56	281.70	26.60	58.67	126.82	268.92	36
37	34.65	76.25	164.78	349.97	31.81	70.51	153.35	327.58	29.52	65.90	144.24	309.87	27.66	62.19	136.96	295.81	37
38	36.04	80.83	177.96	384.96	33.08	74.74	165.61	360.34	30.70	69.86	155.78	340.86	28.77	65.92	147.92	325.39	38
39	37.48	85.68	192.19	423.46	34.41	79.22	178.86	396.37	31.93	74.05	168.25	374.94	29.92	69.88	159.75	357.93	39
40	38.98	90.82	207.57	465.81	35.78	83.97	193.17	436.01	33.21	78.49	181.71	412.43	31.12	74.07	172.53	393.72	40
41	40.54	96.27	224.18	512.39	37.21	89.01	208.63	479.61	34.53	83.20	196.24	453.68	32.36	78.51	186.33	433.09	41
42	42.16	102.04	242.11	563.62	38.70	94.35	225.32	527.57	35.92	88.19	211.94	499.05	33.65	83.22	201.24	476.40	42
43	43.84	108.16	261.48	619.99	40.25	100.01	243.34	580.32	37.35	93.48	228.90	548.95	35.00	88.22	217.34	524.04	43
44	45.60	114.65	282.40	681.99	41.86	106.02	262.81	638.36	38.85	99.09	247.21	603.85	36.40	93.51	234.73	576.44	44
45	47.42	121.53	304.99	750.18	43.53	112.38	283.83	702.19	40.40	105.04	266.99	664.23	37.86	99.12	253.50	634.09	45
46	49.32	128.83	329.39	825.20	45.28	119.12	306.54	772.41	42.02	111.34	288.35	730.65	39.37	105.07	273.78	697.50	46
47	51.29	136.56	355.74	907.72	47.09	126.27	331.06	849.65	43.70	118.02	311.41	803.72	40.95	111.37	295.69	767.25	47
48	53.34	144.75	384.20	998.49	48.97	133.84	357.55	934.62	45.44	125.10	336.33	884.09	42.58	118.05	319.34	843.97	48
49	55.48	153.43	414.93	1098.34	50.93	141.87	386.15	1028.08	47.26	132.61	363.23	972.50	44.29	125.14	344.89	928.37	49
50	57.70	162.64	448.13	1208.18	52.97	150.39	417.05	1130.89	49.15	140.56	392.29	1069.75	46.06	132.65	372.48	1021.21	50

Appendix A

I. Retirement Planning with Level Salary & No Inflation
Planned Retirement Age 68

Table 2 - Percent of Salary Replaced by a 401(k) Contribution of 1% of Current Salary   I-68-2

Probable Life Expectancy at Retirement

Yrs. to Ret.	18.3 (Same as Male Avg.) 4%/4%	6%/5%	8%/6%	10%/7%	20.7 (Better than Male Avg.) 4%/4%	6%/5%	8%/6%	10%/7%	23.2 (Same as Female Avg.) 4%/4%	6%/5%	8%/6%	10%/7%	25.7 (Better than Female Avg.) 4%/4%	6%/5%	8%/6%	10%/7%	Yrs. to Ret.
	Expected Return (Pre-Retirement/Post-Retirement)				(Pre-Retirement/Post-Retirement)				(Pre-Retirement/Post-Retirement)				Expected Return				
0	0.00	0.00	0.00	0.00	0.00	0.00	0.00	0.00	0.00	0.00	0.00	0.00	0.00	0.00	0.00	0.00	0
1	0.08	0.09	0.10	0.10	0.07	0.08	0.09	0.10	0.07	0.08	0.08	0.09	0.06	0.07	0.08	0.09	1
2	0.17	0.18	0.20	0.22	0.15	0.17	0.18	0.20	0.14	0.16	0.17	0.19	0.13	0.15	0.17	0.18	2
3	0.25	0.28	0.31	0.34	0.23	0.26	0.29	0.32	0.22	0.24	0.27	0.30	0.20	0.23	0.26	0.29	3
4	0.34	0.39	0.43	0.48	0.32	0.36	0.40	0.45	0.29	0.33	0.38	0.42	0.28	0.32	0.36	0.40	4
5	0.44	0.50	0.56	0.63	0.40	0.46	0.52	0.59	0.37	0.43	0.49	0.56	0.35	0.41	0.47	0.53	5
6	0.54	0.62	0.70	0.79	0.49	0.57	0.65	0.74	0.46	0.53	0.61	0.70	0.43	0.50	0.58	0.67	6
7	0.64	0.74	0.85	0.98	0.59	0.69	0.79	0.91	0.55	0.64	0.75	0.86	0.51	0.60	0.71	0.83	7
8	0.75	0.87	1.02	1.18	0.69	0.81	0.95	1.10	0.64	0.76	0.89	1.04	0.60	0.71	0.84	0.99	8
9	0.86	1.01	1.19	1.40	0.79	0.94	1.11	1.31	0.73	0.88	1.04	1.24	0.69	0.83	0.99	1.18	9
10	0.97	1.16	1.38	1.64	0.89	1.08	1.29	1.54	0.83	1.01	1.21	1.45	0.78	0.95	1.15	1.39	10
11	1.09	1.32	1.59	1.91	1.01	1.22	1.48	1.79	0.93	1.14	1.39	1.69	0.87	1.08	1.32	1.61	11
12	1.22	1.49	1.81	2.20	1.12	1.38	1.69	2.06	1.04	1.29	1.59	1.95	0.97	1.21	1.51	1.86	12
13	1.35	1.67	2.05	2.52	1.24	1.54	1.91	2.36	1.15	1.44	1.80	2.23	1.08	1.36	1.71	2.13	13
14	1.49	1.86	2.31	2.88	1.36	1.72	2.15	2.69	1.27	1.60	2.03	2.55	1.19	1.51	1.92	2.43	14
15	1.63	2.06	2.59	3.27	1.49	1.90	2.41	3.06	1.38	1.78	2.27	2.90	1.30	1.68	2.16	2.76	15
16	1.77	2.27	2.90	3.70	1.63	2.10	2.70	3.46	1.51	1.96	2.54	3.28	1.41	1.85	2.41	3.13	16
17	1.92	2.49	3.22	4.17	1.77	2.30	3.00	3.91	1.64	2.15	2.82	3.69	1.54	2.03	2.68	3.53	17
18	2.08	2.73	3.58	4.69	1.91	2.52	3.33	4.39	1.77	2.36	3.13	4.16	1.66	2.23	2.97	3.97	18
19	2.25	2.98	3.96	5.27	2.06	2.76	3.69	4.93	1.91	2.58	3.47	4.66	1.79	2.43	3.29	4.45	19
20	2.42	3.25	4.37	5.89	2.22	3.00	4.07	5.52	2.06	2.81	3.83	5.22	1.93	2.65	3.63	4.98	20
21	2.60	3.53	4.82	6.59	2.38	3.27	4.48	6.17	2.21	3.05	4.22	5.83	2.07	2.88	4.00	5.57	21
22	2.78	3.83	5.30	7.35	2.55	3.54	4.93	6.88	2.37	3.31	4.64	6.51	2.22	3.12	4.40	6.21	22
23	2.97	4.15	5.82	8.19	2.73	3.84	5.41	7.66	2.53	3.59	5.09	7.25	2.37	3.38	4.84	6.92	23
24	3.17	4.49	6.38	9.11	2.91	4.15	5.94	8.53	2.70	3.88	5.58	8.06	2.53	3.66	5.30	7.70	24
25	3.38	4.84	6.99	10.12	3.10	4.48	6.50	9.47	2.88	4.19	6.11	8.96	2.70	3.95	5.81	8.56	25
26	3.60	5.22	7.64	11.24	3.30	4.83	7.11	10.52	3.06	4.51	6.69	9.95	2.87	4.26	6.35	9.50	26
27	3.82	5.62	8.35	12.46	3.51	5.20	7.77	11.67	3.26	4.86	7.31	11.04	3.05	4.59	6.94	10.53	27
28	4.06	6.05	9.11	13.81	3.72	5.59	8.48	12.93	3.46	5.23	7.97	12.23	3.24	4.93	7.57	11.68	28
29	4.30	6.50	9.93	15.30	3.95	6.01	9.24	14.32	3.66	5.62	8.70	13.54	3.43	5.30	8.26	12.93	29
30	4.55	6.98	10.82	16.93	4.18	6.45	10.07	15.85	3.88	6.03	9.48	14.99	3.63	5.69	9.00	14.31	30
31	4.82	7.49	11.79	18.73	4.42	6.92	10.97	17.53	4.10	6.47	10.32	16.58	3.85	6.11	9.80	15.83	31
32	5.09	8.03	12.82	20.70	4.67	7.42	11.93	19.38	4.34	6.94	11.23	18.33	4.06	6.55	10.66	17.50	32
33	5.38	8.59	13.95	22.87	4.93	7.95	12.98	21.41	4.58	7.43	12.21	20.25	4.29	7.01	11.59	19.33	33
34	5.67	9.20	15.16	25.26	5.21	8.51	14.10	23.65	4.83	7.95	13.27	22.37	4.53	7.50	12.60	21.35	34
35	5.98	9.84	16.46	27.89	5.49	9.10	15.32	26.11	5.09	8.50	14.41	24.70	4.77	8.02	13.68	23.58	35
36	6.30	10.52	17.88	30.79	5.78	9.73	16.64	28.82	5.37	9.09	15.65	27.26	5.03	8.58	14.86	26.02	36
37	6.63	11.24	19.40	33.97	6.09	10.39	18.06	31.79	5.65	9.71	16.99	30.08	5.30	9.16	16.13	28.71	37
38	6.98	12.00	21.05	37.47	6.41	11.10	19.59	35.07	5.95	10.37	18.43	33.17	5.57	9.79	17.50	31.67	38
39	7.34	12.81	22.83	41.32	6.74	11.84	21.25	38.67	6.25	11.07	19.99	36.58	5.86	10.45	18.98	34.92	39
40	7.71	13.66	24.75	45.55	7.08	12.64	23.04	42.64	6.57	11.81	21.67	40.33	6.16	11.14	20.57	38.50	40
41	8.10	14.57	26.83	50.21	7.44	13.47	24.97	47.00	6.90	12.59	23.48	44.46	6.47	11.89	22.30	42.44	41
42	8.51	15.54	29.07	55.33	7.81	14.36	27.05	51.79	7.25	13.43	25.45	48.99	6.79	12.67	24.16	46.77	42
43	8.93	16.56	31.49	60.97	8.20	15.31	29.31	57.07	7.61	14.31	27.57	53.98	7.13	13.50	26.17	51.53	43
44	9.37	17.64	34.11	67.17	8.60	16.31	31.74	62.87	7.98	15.24	29.86	59.47	7.48	14.38	28.35	56.77	44
45	9.83	18.78	36.93	73.99	9.02	17.37	34.37	69.26	8.37	16.23	32.33	65.51	7.84	15.32	30.70	62.54	45
46	10.30	20.00	39.98	81.49	9.46	18.49	37.21	76.28	8.77	17.28	35.00	72.15	8.22	16.31	33.23	68.88	46
47	10.79	21.29	43.27	89.74	9.91	19.68	40.27	84.00	9.20	18.40	37.88	79.46	8.62	17.36	35.97	75.85	47
48	11.31	22.65	46.83	98.82	10.38	20.95	43.58	92.50	9.63	19.58	41.00	87.50	9.03	18.48	38.93	83.53	48
49	11.84	24.10	50.67	108.81	10.87	22.28	47.16	101.84	10.09	20.83	44.36	96.34	9.45	19.66	42.12	91.97	49
50	12.39	25.64	54.82	119.79	11.38	23.70	51.02	112.13	10.56	22.16	47.99	106.06	9.89	20.91	45.57	101.25	50

I. Retirement Planning with Level Salary & No Inflation
Planned Retirement Age 68

Table 3 - 401(k) Contribution (% of Current Sal.) Needed to Replace 10% of Sal. at Retirement I-68-3

Probable Life Expectancy at Retirement

	18.3 (Same as Male Avg.)				20.7 (Better than Male Avg.)				23.2 (Same as Female Avg.)				25.7 (Better than Female Avg.)				
	4% / 4%	6% / 5%	8% / 6%	10% / 7%	4% / 4%	6% / 5%	8% / 6%	10% / 7%	4% / 4%	6% / 5%	8% / 6%	10% / 7%	4% / 4%	6% / 5%	8% / 6%	10% / 7%	
Yrs. to Ret.	Expected Return				(Pre-Retirement/Post-Retirement)				(Pre-Retirement/Post-Retirement)				Expected Return				Yrs. to Ret.
0																	0
1	123.17	113.26	104.66	97.16	134.18	122.49	112.46	103.80	144.58	131.04	119.56	109.74	154.30	138.87	125.92	114.95	1
2	60.38	54.98	50.32	46.27	65.77	59.46	54.07	49.43	70.87	63.61	57.48	52.26	75.64	67.41	60.54	54.74	2
3	39.46	35.58	32.24	29.35	42.98	38.47	34.64	31.36	46.32	41.16	36.83	33.15	49.43	43.62	38.79	34.73	3
4	29.01	25.89	23.23	20.94	31.60	28.00	24.96	22.37	34.05	29.96	26.53	23.65	36.34	31.74	27.94	24.77	4
5	22.74	20.09	17.84	15.92	24.77	21.73	19.17	17.00	26.69	23.25	20.38	17.97	28.49	24.63	21.46	18.83	5
6	18.57	16.24	14.27	12.59	20.23	17.56	15.33	13.45	21.80	18.79	16.30	14.22	23.26	19.91	17.16	14.90	6
7	15.59	13.49	11.73	10.24	16.99	14.59	12.60	10.94	18.31	15.61	13.40	11.57	19.54	16.54	14.11	12.12	7
8	13.37	11.44	9.84	8.50	14.56	12.38	10.57	9.08	15.69	13.24	11.24	9.60	16.75	14.03	11.84	10.05	8
9	11.64	9.86	8.38	7.16	12.68	10.66	9.01	7.64	13.66	11.40	9.57	8.08	14.58	12.08	10.08	8.47	9
10	10.26	8.59	7.22	6.10	11.18	9.29	7.76	6.51	12.04	9.94	8.25	6.89	12.85	10.54	8.69	7.21	10
11	9.13	7.56	6.29	5.24	9.95	8.18	6.76	5.60	10.72	8.75	7.18	5.92	11.44	9.28	7.56	6.20	11
12	8.20	6.71	5.52	4.54	8.93	7.26	5.93	4.85	9.62	7.77	6.30	5.13	10.27	8.23	6.64	5.38	12
13	7.41	6.00	4.87	3.96	8.07	6.49	5.23	4.23	8.70	6.94	5.56	4.47	9.28	7.35	5.86	4.69	13
14	6.73	5.39	4.32	3.47	7.34	5.83	4.64	3.71	7.90	6.24	4.94	3.92	8.44	6.61	5.20	4.11	14
15	6.15	4.87	3.85	3.06	6.70	5.26	4.14	3.27	7.22	5.63	4.40	3.45	7.71	5.97	4.64	3.62	15
16	5.64	4.41	3.45	2.70	6.15	4.77	3.71	2.89	6.62	5.10	3.94	3.05	7.07	5.41	4.15	3.20	16
17	5.20	4.01	3.10	2.40	5.66	4.34	3.33	2.56	6.10	4.64	3.54	2.71	6.51	4.92	3.73	2.84	17
18	4.80	3.66	2.79	2.13	5.23	3.96	3.00	2.28	5.64	4.24	3.19	2.41	6.02	4.49	3.36	2.52	18
19	4.45	3.35	2.53	1.90	4.85	3.63	2.71	2.03	5.23	3.88	2.88	2.15	5.58	4.11	3.04	2.25	19
20	4.14	3.08	2.29	1.70	4.51	3.33	2.46	1.81	4.86	3.56	2.61	1.92	5.18	3.78	2.75	2.01	20
21	3.85	2.83	2.08	1.52	4.20	3.06	2.23	1.62	4.52	3.28	2.37	1.71	4.83	3.47	2.50	1.80	21
22	3.60	2.61	1.89	1.36	3.92	2.82	2.03	1.45	4.22	3.02	2.16	1.54	4.51	3.20	2.27	1.61	22
23	3.36	2.41	1.72	1.22	3.66	2.61	1.85	1.31	3.95	2.79	1.96	1.38	4.21	2.95	2.07	1.45	23
24	3.15	2.23	1.57	1.10	3.43	2.41	1.68	1.17	3.70	2.58	1.79	1.24	3.95	2.73	1.89	1.30	24
25	2.96	2.06	1.43	0.99	3.22	2.23	1.54	1.06	3.47	2.39	1.64	1.12	3.70	2.53	1.72	1.17	25
26	2.78	1.91	1.31	0.89	3.03	2.07	1.41	0.95	3.26	2.22	1.50	1.01	3.48	2.35	1.57	1.05	26
27	2.62	1.78	1.20	0.80	2.85	1.92	1.29	0.86	3.07	2.06	1.37	0.91	3.28	2.18	1.44	0.95	27
28	2.47	1.65	1.10	0.72	2.69	1.79	1.18	0.77	2.89	1.91	1.25	0.82	3.09	2.03	1.32	0.86	28
29	2.33	1.54	1.01	0.65	2.53	1.66	1.08	0.70	2.73	1.78	1.15	0.74	2.91	1.89	1.21	0.77	29
30	2.20	1.43	0.92	0.59	2.39	1.55	0.99	0.63	2.58	1.66	1.06	0.67	2.75	1.76	1.11	0.70	30
31	2.08	1.34	0.85	0.53	2.26	1.44	0.91	0.57	2.44	1.55	0.97	0.60	2.60	1.64	1.02	0.63	31
32	1.96	1.25	0.78	0.48	2.14	1.35	0.84	0.52	2.31	1.44	0.89	0.55	2.46	1.53	0.94	0.57	32
33	1.86	1.16	0.72	0.44	2.03	1.26	0.77	0.47	2.18	1.35	0.82	0.49	2.33	1.43	0.86	0.52	33
34	1.76	1.09	0.66	0.40	1.92	1.18	0.71	0.42	2.07	1.26	0.75	0.45	2.21	1.33	0.79	0.47	34
35	1.67	1.02	0.61	0.36	1.82	1.10	0.65	0.38	1.96	1.18	0.69	0.40	2.09	1.25	0.73	0.42	35
36	1.59	0.95	0.56	0.32	1.73	1.03	0.60	0.35	1.86	1.10	0.64	0.37	1.99	1.17	0.67	0.38	36
37	1.51	0.89	0.52	0.29	1.64	0.96	0.55	0.31	1.77	1.03	0.59	0.33	1.89	1.09	0.62	0.35	37
38	1.43	0.83	0.48	0.27	1.56	0.90	0.51	0.29	1.68	0.96	0.54	0.30	1.79	1.02	0.57	0.32	38
39	1.36	0.78	0.44	0.24	1.48	0.84	0.47	0.26	1.60	0.90	0.50	0.27	1.71	0.96	0.53	0.29	39
40	1.30	0.73	0.40	0.22	1.41	0.79	0.43	0.23	1.52	0.85	0.46	0.25	1.62	0.90	0.49	0.26	40
41	1.23	0.69	0.37	0.20	1.34	0.74	0.40	0.21	1.45	0.79	0.43	0.22	1.55	0.84	0.45	0.24	41
42	1.18	0.64	0.34	0.18	1.28	0.70	0.37	0.19	1.38	0.74	0.39	0.20	1.47	0.79	0.41	0.21	42
43	1.12	0.60	0.32	0.16	1.22	0.65	0.34	0.18	1.31	0.70	0.36	0.19	1.40	0.74	0.38	0.19	43
44	1.07	0.57	0.29	0.15	1.16	0.61	0.32	0.16	1.25	0.66	0.33	0.17	1.34	0.70	0.35	0.18	44
45	1.02	0.53	0.27	0.14	1.11	0.58	0.29	0.14	1.19	0.62	0.31	0.15	1.27	0.65	0.33	0.16	45
46	0.97	0.50	0.25	0.12	1.06	0.54	0.27	0.13	1.14	0.58	0.29	0.14	1.22	0.61	0.30	0.15	46
47	0.93	0.47	0.23	0.11	1.01	0.51	0.25	0.12	1.09	0.54	0.26	0.13	1.16	0.58	0.28	0.13	47
48	0.88	0.44	0.21	0.10	0.96	0.48	0.23	0.11	1.04	0.51	0.24	0.11	1.11	0.54	0.26	0.12	48
49	0.84	0.41	0.20	0.09	0.92	0.45	0.21	0.10	0.99	0.48	0.23	0.10	1.06	0.51	0.24	0.11	49
50	0.81	0.39	0.18	0.08	0.88	0.42	0.20	0.09	0.95	0.45	0.21	0.09	1.01	0.48	0.22	0.10	50

I. Retirement Planning with Level Salary & No Inflation
Planned Retirement Age 68

Table 4 - Accumulation at Retirement (Multiple of Current Sal.) for 10% Sal. Replacement   I-68-4

Probable Life Expectancy at Retirement

Yrs. to Ret.	18.3 (Same as Male Avg.)				20.7 (Better than Male Avg.)				23.2 (Same as Female Avg.)				25.7 (Better than Female Avg.)				Yrs. to Ret.
	4% / 4%	6% / 5%	8% / 6%	10% / 7%	4% / 4%	6% / 5%	8% / 6%	10% / 7%	4% / 4%	6% / 5%	8% / 6%	10% / 7%	4% / 4%	6% / 5%	8% / 6%	10% / 7%	
	Expected Return				(Pre-Retirement/Post-Retirement)				(Pre-Retirement/Post-Retirement)				Expected Return				
0	1.23	1.13	1.05	0.97	1.34	1.22	1.12	1.04	1.45	1.31	1.20	1.10	1.54	1.39	1.26	1.15	0
1	1.23	1.13	1.05	0.97	1.34	1.22	1.12	1.04	1.45	1.31	1.20	1.10	1.54	1.39	1.26	1.15	1
2	1.23	1.13	1.05	0.97	1.34	1.22	1.12	1.04	1.45	1.31	1.20	1.10	1.54	1.39	1.26	1.15	2
3	1.23	1.13	1.05	0.97	1.34	1.22	1.12	1.04	1.45	1.31	1.20	1.10	1.54	1.39	1.26	1.15	3
4	1.23	1.13	1.05	0.97	1.34	1.22	1.12	1.04	1.45	1.31	1.20	1.10	1.54	1.39	1.26	1.15	4
5	1.23	1.13	1.05	0.97	1.34	1.22	1.12	1.04	1.45	1.31	1.20	1.10	1.54	1.39	1.26	1.15	5
6	1.23	1.13	1.05	0.97	1.34	1.22	1.12	1.04	1.45	1.31	1.20	1.10	1.54	1.39	1.26	1.15	6
7	1.23	1.13	1.05	0.97	1.34	1.22	1.12	1.04	1.45	1.31	1.20	1.10	1.54	1.39	1.26	1.15	7
8	1.23	1.13	1.05	0.97	1.34	1.22	1.12	1.04	1.45	1.31	1.20	1.10	1.54	1.39	1.26	1.15	8
9	1.23	1.13	1.05	0.97	1.34	1.22	1.12	1.04	1.45	1.31	1.20	1.10	1.54	1.39	1.26	1.15	9
10	1.23	1.13	1.05	0.97	1.34	1.22	1.12	1.04	1.45	1.31	1.20	1.10	1.54	1.39	1.26	1.15	10
11	1.23	1.13	1.05	0.97	1.34	1.22	1.12	1.04	1.45	1.31	1.20	1.10	1.54	1.39	1.26	1.15	11
12	1.23	1.13	1.05	0.97	1.34	1.22	1.12	1.04	1.45	1.31	1.20	1.10	1.54	1.39	1.26	1.15	12
13	1.23	1.13	1.05	0.97	1.34	1.22	1.12	1.04	1.45	1.31	1.20	1.10	1.54	1.39	1.26	1.15	13
14	1.23	1.13	1.05	0.97	1.34	1.22	1.12	1.04	1.45	1.31	1.20	1.10	1.54	1.39	1.26	1.15	14
15	1.23	1.13	1.05	0.97	1.34	1.22	1.12	1.04	1.45	1.31	1.20	1.10	1.54	1.39	1.26	1.15	15
16	1.23	1.13	1.05	0.97	1.34	1.22	1.12	1.04	1.45	1.31	1.20	1.10	1.54	1.39	1.26	1.15	16
17	1.23	1.13	1.05	0.97	1.34	1.22	1.12	1.04	1.45	1.31	1.20	1.10	1.54	1.39	1.26	1.15	17
18	1.23	1.13	1.05	0.97	1.34	1.22	1.12	1.04	1.45	1.31	1.20	1.10	1.54	1.39	1.26	1.15	18
19	1.23	1.13	1.05	0.97	1.34	1.22	1.12	1.04	1.45	1.31	1.20	1.10	1.54	1.39	1.26	1.15	19
20	1.23	1.13	1.05	0.97	1.34	1.22	1.12	1.04	1.45	1.31	1.20	1.10	1.54	1.39	1.26	1.15	20
21	1.23	1.13	1.05	0.97	1.34	1.22	1.12	1.04	1.45	1.31	1.20	1.10	1.54	1.39	1.26	1.15	21
22	1.23	1.13	1.05	0.97	1.34	1.22	1.12	1.04	1.45	1.31	1.20	1.10	1.54	1.39	1.26	1.15	22
23	1.23	1.13	1.05	0.97	1.34	1.22	1.12	1.04	1.45	1.31	1.20	1.10	1.54	1.39	1.26	1.15	23
24	1.23	1.13	1.05	0.97	1.34	1.22	1.12	1.04	1.45	1.31	1.20	1.10	1.54	1.39	1.26	1.15	24
25	1.23	1.13	1.05	0.97	1.34	1.22	1.12	1.04	1.45	1.31	1.20	1.10	1.54	1.39	1.26	1.15	25
26	1.23	1.13	1.05	0.97	1.34	1.22	1.12	1.04	1.45	1.31	1.20	1.10	1.54	1.39	1.26	1.15	26
27	1.23	1.13	1.05	0.97	1.34	1.22	1.12	1.04	1.45	1.31	1.20	1.10	1.54	1.39	1.26	1.15	27
28	1.23	1.13	1.05	0.97	1.34	1.22	1.12	1.04	1.45	1.31	1.20	1.10	1.54	1.39	1.26	1.15	28
29	1.23	1.13	1.05	0.97	1.34	1.22	1.12	1.04	1.45	1.31	1.20	1.10	1.54	1.39	1.26	1.15	29
30	1.23	1.13	1.05	0.97	1.34	1.22	1.12	1.04	1.45	1.31	1.20	1.10	1.54	1.39	1.26	1.15	30
31	1.23	1.13	1.05	0.97	1.34	1.22	1.12	1.04	1.45	1.31	1.20	1.10	1.54	1.39	1.26	1.15	31
32	1.23	1.13	1.05	0.97	1.34	1.22	1.12	1.04	1.45	1.31	1.20	1.10	1.54	1.39	1.26	1.15	32
33	1.23	1.13	1.05	0.97	1.34	1.22	1.12	1.04	1.45	1.31	1.20	1.10	1.54	1.39	1.26	1.15	33
34	1.23	1.13	1.05	0.97	1.34	1.22	1.12	1.04	1.45	1.31	1.20	1.10	1.54	1.39	1.26	1.15	34
35	1.23	1.13	1.05	0.97	1.34	1.22	1.12	1.04	1.45	1.31	1.20	1.10	1.54	1.39	1.26	1.15	35
36	1.23	1.13	1.05	0.97	1.34	1.22	1.12	1.04	1.45	1.31	1.20	1.10	1.54	1.39	1.26	1.15	36
37	1.23	1.13	1.05	0.97	1.34	1.22	1.12	1.04	1.45	1.31	1.20	1.10	1.54	1.39	1.26	1.15	37
38	1.23	1.13	1.05	0.97	1.34	1.22	1.12	1.04	1.45	1.31	1.20	1.10	1.54	1.39	1.26	1.15	38
39	1.23	1.13	1.05	0.97	1.34	1.22	1.12	1.04	1.45	1.31	1.20	1.10	1.54	1.39	1.26	1.15	39
40	1.23	1.13	1.05	0.97	1.34	1.22	1.12	1.04	1.45	1.31	1.20	1.10	1.54	1.39	1.26	1.15	40
41	1.23	1.13	1.05	0.97	1.34	1.22	1.12	1.04	1.45	1.31	1.20	1.10	1.54	1.39	1.26	1.15	41
42	1.23	1.13	1.05	0.97	1.34	1.22	1.12	1.04	1.45	1.31	1.20	1.10	1.54	1.39	1.26	1.15	42
43	1.23	1.13	1.05	0.97	1.34	1.22	1.12	1.04	1.45	1.31	1.20	1.10	1.54	1.39	1.26	1.15	43
44	1.23	1.13	1.05	0.97	1.34	1.22	1.12	1.04	1.45	1.31	1.20	1.10	1.54	1.39	1.26	1.15	44
45	1.23	1.13	1.05	0.97	1.34	1.22	1.12	1.04	1.45	1.31	1.20	1.10	1.54	1.39	1.26	1.15	45
46	1.23	1.13	1.05	0.97	1.34	1.22	1.12	1.04	1.45	1.31	1.20	1.10	1.54	1.39	1.26	1.15	46
47	1.23	1.13	1.05	0.97	1.34	1.22	1.12	1.04	1.45	1.31	1.20	1.10	1.54	1.39	1.26	1.15	47
48	1.23	1.13	1.05	0.97	1.34	1.22	1.12	1.04	1.45	1.31	1.20	1.10	1.54	1.39	1.26	1.15	48
49	1.23	1.13	1.05	0.97	1.34	1.22	1.12	1.04	1.45	1.31	1.20	1.10	1.54	1.39	1.26	1.15	49
50	1.23	1.13	1.05	0.97	1.34	1.22	1.12	1.04	1.45	1.31	1.20	1.10	1.54	1.39	1.26	1.15	50

I. Retirement Planning with Level Salary & No Inflation
Planned Retirement Age 71

Table 1 - Percent of Salary Replaced by a 401(k) Account Equal to Current Annual Salary   I-71-1

Probable Life Expectancy at Retirement

Yrs. to Ret.	16 (Same as Male Avg.)				18.3 (Better than Male Avg.)				20.7 (Same as Female Avg.)				23.2 (Better than Female Avg.)				Yrs. to Ret.
	4% / 4%	6% / 5%	8% / 6%	10% / 7%	4% / 4%	6% / 5%	8% / 6%	10% / 7%	4% / 4%	6% / 5%	8% / 6%	10% / 7%	4% / 4%	6% / 5%	8% / 6%	10% / 7%	
	Expected Return				(Pre-Retirement/Post-Retirement)				(Pre-Retirement/Post-Retirement)				Expected Return				
0	8.94	9.65	10.38	11.11	8.12	8.83	9.55	10.29	7.45	8.16	8.89	9.63	6.92	7.63	8.36	9.11	0
1	9.30	10.23	11.21	12.22	8.44	9.36	10.32	11.32	7.75	8.65	9.60	10.60	7.19	8.09	9.03	10.02	1
2	9.67	10.84	12.10	13.45	8.78	9.92	11.14	12.45	8.06	9.17	10.37	11.66	7.48	8.57	9.76	11.03	2
3	10.05	11.50	13.07	14.79	9.13	10.52	12.04	13.70	8.38	9.72	11.20	12.82	7.78	9.09	10.54	12.13	3
4	10.46	12.19	14.12	16.27	9.50	11.15	13.00	15.07	8.72	10.31	12.10	14.10	8.09	9.63	11.38	13.34	4
5	10.88	12.92	15.25	17.90	9.88	11.82	14.04	16.58	9.07	10.93	13.07	15.51	8.41	10.21	12.29	14.68	5
6	11.31	13.69	16.47	19.69	10.27	12.52	15.16	18.23	9.43	11.58	14.11	17.07	8.75	10.82	13.27	16.14	6
7	11.76	14.51	17.78	21.66	10.68	13.28	16.37	20.06	9.81	12.28	15.24	18.77	9.10	11.47	14.33	17.76	7
8	12.23	15.38	19.21	23.82	11.11	14.07	17.68	22.06	10.20	13.01	16.46	20.65	9.47	12.16	15.48	19.53	8
9	12.72	16.31	20.74	26.20	11.56	14.92	19.10	24.27	10.61	13.79	17.78	22.72	9.84	12.89	16.72	21.49	9
10	13.23	17.29	22.40	28.82	12.02	15.81	20.63	26.69	11.03	14.62	19.20	24.99	10.24	13.67	18.06	23.64	10
11	13.76	18.32	24.20	31.71	12.50	16.76	22.28	29.36	11.47	15.50	20.73	27.49	10.65	14.49	19.50	26.00	11
12	14.31	19.42	26.13	34.88	13.00	17.77	24.06	32.30	11.93	16.43	22.39	30.23	11.07	15.36	21.06	28.60	12
13	14.88	20.59	28.22	38.36	13.52	18.83	25.99	35.53	12.41	17.41	24.18	33.26	11.52	16.28	22.75	31.46	13
14	15.48	21.82	30.48	42.20	14.06	19.96	28.06	39.08	12.91	18.46	26.12	36.58	11.98	17.25	24.57	34.61	14
15	16.10	23.13	32.92	46.42	14.62	21.16	30.31	42.99	13.42	19.57	28.21	40.24	12.46	18.29	26.53	38.07	15
16	16.74	24.52	35.55	51.06	15.21	22.43	32.73	47.29	13.96	20.74	30.46	44.27	12.95	19.39	28.66	41.87	16
17	17.41	25.99	38.40	56.17	15.81	23.78	35.35	52.02	14.52	21.98	32.90	48.69	13.47	20.55	30.95	46.06	17
18	18.11	27.55	41.47	61.79	16.45	25.20	38.18	57.22	15.10	23.30	35.53	53.56	14.01	21.78	33.42	50.67	18
19	18.83	29.20	44.79	67.97	17.10	26.71	41.24	62.94	15.70	24.70	38.37	58.92	14.57	23.09	36.10	55.73	19
20	19.59	30.95	48.37	74.76	17.79	28.32	44.53	69.24	16.33	26.18	41.44	64.81	15.15	24.47	38.98	61.31	20
21	20.37	32.81	52.24	82.24	18.50	30.02	48.10	76.16	16.98	27.75	44.76	71.29	15.76	25.94	42.10	67.44	21
22	21.18	34.78	56.42	90.46	19.24	31.82	51.94	83.78	17.66	29.42	48.34	78.42	16.39	27.50	45.47	74.18	22
23	22.03	36.87	60.93	99.51	20.01	33.73	56.10	92.16	18.37	31.19	52.21	86.26	17.05	29.15	49.11	81.60	23
24	22.91	39.08	65.80	109.46	20.81	35.75	60.59	101.37	19.10	33.06	56.39	94.89	17.73	30.90	53.04	89.76	24
25	23.83	41.42	71.07	120.40	21.64	37.89	65.43	111.51	19.87	35.04	60.90	104.38	18.44	32.75	57.28	98.73	25
26	24.78	43.91	76.75	132.45	22.51	40.17	70.67	122.66	20.66	37.14	65.77	114.81	19.18	34.72	61.86	108.61	26
27	25.77	46.54	82.89	145.69	23.41	42.58	76.32	134.93	21.49	39.37	71.03	126.30	19.94	36.80	66.81	119.47	27
28	26.80	49.34	89.53	160.26	24.35	45.13	82.43	148.42	22.35	41.73	76.71	138.93	20.74	39.01	72.16	131.41	28
29	27.88	52.30	96.69	176.28	25.32	47.84	89.02	163.26	23.24	44.24	82.85	152.82	21.57	41.35	77.93	144.56	29
30	28.99	55.44	104.42	193.91	26.33	50.71	96.15	179.59	24.17	46.89	89.48	168.10	22.43	43.83	84.17	159.01	30
31	30.15	58.76	112.78	213.30	27.39	53.75	103.84	197.55	25.14	49.70	96.63	184.91	23.33	46.46	90.90	174.91	31
32	31.36	62.29	121.80	234.64	28.48	56.98	112.14	217.30	26.15	52.69	104.37	203.40	24.26	49.25	98.17	192.40	32
33	32.61	66.02	131.54	258.10	29.62	60.40	121.12	239.03	27.19	55.85	112.71	223.74	25.23	52.20	106.02	211.64	33
34	33.92	69.99	142.07	283.91	30.80	64.02	130.80	262.93	28.28	59.20	121.73	246.11	26.24	55.33	114.51	232.81	34
35	35.27	74.19	153.43	312.30	32.04	67.86	141.27	289.23	29.41	62.75	131.47	270.73	27.29	58.65	123.67	256.09	35
36	36.68	78.64	165.71	343.53	33.32	71.94	152.57	318.15	30.60	66.52	141.99	297.80	28.38	62.17	133.56	281.70	36
37	38.15	83.35	178.96	377.88	34.65	76.25	164.78	349.97	31.81	70.51	153.35	327.58	29.52	65.90	144.24	309.87	37
38	39.68	88.36	193.28	415.67	36.04	80.83	177.96	384.96	33.08	74.74	165.61	360.34	30.70	69.86	155.78	340.86	38
39	41.26	93.66	208.74	457.24	37.48	85.68	192.19	423.46	34.41	79.22	178.86	396.37	31.93	74.05	168.25	374.94	39
40	42.91	99.28	225.44	502.96	38.98	90.82	207.57	465.81	35.78	83.97	193.17	436.01	33.21	78.49	181.71	412.43	40
41	44.63	105.23	243.48	553.26	40.54	96.27	224.18	512.39	37.21	89.01	208.63	479.61	34.53	83.20	196.24	453.68	41
42	46.42	111.55	262.95	608.58	42.16	102.04	242.11	563.62	38.70	94.35	225.32	527.57	35.92	88.19	211.94	499.05	42
43	48.27	118.24	283.99	669.44	43.84	108.16	261.48	619.99	40.25	100.01	243.34	580.32	37.35	93.48	228.90	548.95	43
44	50.20	125.33	306.71	736.39	45.60	114.65	282.40	681.99	41.86	106.02	262.81	638.36	38.85	99.09	247.21	603.85	44
45	52.21	132.85	331.25	810.02	47.42	121.53	304.99	750.18	43.53	112.38	283.83	702.19	40.40	105.04	266.99	664.23	45
46	54.30	140.83	357.75	891.03	49.32	128.83	329.39	825.20	45.28	119.12	306.54	772.41	42.02	111.34	288.35	730.65	46
47	56.47	149.28	386.37	980.13	51.29	136.56	355.74	907.72	47.09	126.27	331.06	849.65	43.70	118.02	311.41	803.72	47
48	58.73	158.23	417.28	1078.14	53.34	144.75	384.20	998.49	48.97	133.84	357.55	934.62	45.44	125.10	336.33	884.09	48
49	61.08	167.73	450.66	1185.96	55.48	153.43	414.93	1098.34	50.93	141.87	386.15	1028.08	47.26	132.61	363.23	972.50	49
50	63.52	177.79	486.71	1304.55	57.70	162.64	448.13	1208.18	52.97	150.39	417.05	1130.89	49.15	140.56	392.29	1069.75	50

I. Retirement Planning with Level Salary & No Inflation
Planned Retirement Age 71

Table 2 - Percent of Salary Replaced by a 401(k) Contribution of 1% of Current Salary   I-71-2

Probable Life Expectancy at Retirement

	16 (Same as Male Avg.)				18.3 (Better than Male Avg.)				20.7 (Same as Female Avg.)				23.2 (Better than Female Avg.)				
	4% / 4%	6% / 5%	8% / 6%	10% / 7%	4% / 4%	6% / 5%	8% / 6%	10% / 7%	4% / 4%	6% / 5%	8% / 6%	10% / 7%	4% / 4%	6% / 5%	8% / 6%	10% / 7%	
Yrs. to Ret.	Expected Return				(Pre-Retirement/Post-Retirement)				(Pre-Retirement/Post-Retirement)				Expected Return				Yrs. to Ret.
0	0.00	0.00	0.00	0.00	0.00	0.00	0.00	0.00	0.00	0.00	0.00	0.00	0.00	0.00	0.00	0.00	0
1	0.09	0.10	0.10	0.11	0.08	0.09	0.10	0.10	0.07	0.08	0.09	0.10	0.07	0.08	0.08	0.09	1
2	0.18	0.20	0.22	0.23	0.17	0.18	0.20	0.22	0.15	0.17	0.18	0.20	0.14	0.16	0.17	0.19	2
3	0.28	0.31	0.34	0.37	0.25	0.28	0.31	0.34	0.23	0.26	0.29	0.32	0.22	0.24	0.27	0.30	3
4	0.38	0.42	0.47	0.52	0.34	0.39	0.43	0.48	0.32	0.36	0.40	0.45	0.29	0.33	0.38	0.42	4
5	0.48	0.54	0.61	0.68	0.44	0.50	0.56	0.63	0.40	0.46	0.52	0.59	0.37	0.43	0.49	0.56	5
6	0.59	0.67	0.76	0.86	0.54	0.62	0.70	0.79	0.49	0.57	0.65	0.74	0.46	0.53	0.61	0.70	6
7	0.71	0.81	0.93	1.05	0.64	0.74	0.85	0.98	0.59	0.69	0.79	0.91	0.55	0.64	0.75	0.86	7
8	0.82	0.96	1.10	1.27	0.75	0.87	1.02	1.18	0.69	0.81	0.95	1.10	0.64	0.76	0.89	1.04	8
9	0.95	1.11	1.30	1.51	0.86	1.01	1.19	1.40	0.79	0.94	1.11	1.31	0.73	0.88	1.04	1.24	9
10	1.07	1.27	1.50	1.77	0.97	1.16	1.38	1.64	0.89	1.08	1.29	1.54	0.83	1.01	1.21	1.45	10
11	1.21	1.45	1.73	2.06	1.09	1.32	1.59	1.91	1.01	1.22	1.48	1.79	0.93	1.14	1.39	1.69	11
12	1.34	1.63	1.97	2.38	1.22	1.49	1.81	2.20	1.12	1.38	1.69	2.06	1.04	1.29	1.59	1.95	12
13	1.49	1.82	2.23	2.73	1.35	1.67	2.05	2.52	1.24	1.54	1.91	2.36	1.15	1.44	1.80	2.23	13
14	1.64	2.03	2.51	3.11	1.49	1.86	2.31	2.88	1.36	1.72	2.15	2.69	1.27	1.60	2.03	2.55	14
15	1.79	2.25	2.82	3.53	1.63	2.06	2.59	3.27	1.49	1.90	2.41	3.06	1.38	1.78	2.27	2.90	15
16	1.95	2.48	3.15	4.00	1.77	2.27	2.90	3.70	1.63	2.10	2.70	3.46	1.51	1.96	2.54	3.28	16
17	2.12	2.72	3.50	4.51	1.92	2.49	3.22	4.17	1.77	2.30	3.00	3.91	1.64	2.15	2.82	3.69	17
18	2.29	2.98	3.89	5.07	2.08	2.73	3.58	4.69	1.91	2.52	3.33	4.39	1.77	2.36	3.13	4.16	18
19	2.47	3.26	4.30	5.69	2.25	2.98	3.96	5.27	2.06	2.76	3.69	4.93	1.91	2.58	3.47	4.66	19
20	2.66	3.55	4.75	6.36	2.42	3.25	4.37	5.89	2.22	3.00	4.07	5.52	2.06	2.81	3.83	5.22	20
21	2.86	3.86	5.23	7.11	2.60	3.53	4.82	6.59	2.38	3.27	4.48	6.17	2.21	3.05	4.22	5.83	21
22	3.06	4.19	5.75	7.93	2.78	3.83	5.30	7.35	2.55	3.54	4.93	6.88	2.37	3.31	4.64	6.51	22
23	3.27	4.54	6.32	8.84	2.97	4.15	5.82	8.19	2.73	3.84	5.41	7.66	2.53	3.59	5.09	7.25	23
24	3.49	4.90	6.93	9.83	3.17	4.49	6.38	9.11	2.91	4.15	5.94	8.53	2.70	3.88	5.58	8.06	24
25	3.72	5.30	7.59	10.93	3.38	4.84	6.99	10.12	3.10	4.48	6.50	9.47	2.88	4.19	6.11	8.96	25
26	3.96	5.71	8.30	12.13	3.60	5.22	7.64	11.24	3.30	4.83	7.11	10.52	3.06	4.51	6.69	9.95	26
27	4.21	6.15	9.06	13.46	3.82	5.62	8.35	12.46	3.51	5.20	7.77	11.67	3.26	4.86	7.31	11.04	27
28	4.47	6.61	9.89	14.91	4.06	6.05	9.11	13.81	3.72	5.59	8.48	12.93	3.46	5.23	7.97	12.23	28
29	4.73	7.11	10.79	16.52	4.30	6.50	9.93	15.30	3.95	6.01	9.24	14.32	3.66	5.62	8.70	13.54	29
30	5.01	7.63	11.76	18.28	4.55	6.98	10.82	16.93	4.18	6.45	10.07	15.85	3.88	6.03	9.48	14.99	30
31	5.30	8.18	12.80	20.22	4.82	7.49	11.79	18.73	4.42	6.92	10.97	17.53	4.10	6.47	10.32	16.58	31
32	5.60	8.77	13.93	22.35	5.09	8.03	12.82	20.70	4.67	7.42	11.93	19.38	4.34	6.94	11.23	18.33	32
33	5.92	9.40	15.15	24.70	5.38	8.59	13.95	22.87	4.93	7.95	12.98	21.41	4.58	7.43	12.21	20.25	33
34	6.24	10.06	16.46	27.28	5.67	9.20	15.16	25.26	5.21	8.51	14.10	23.65	4.83	7.95	13.27	22.37	34
35	6.58	10.76	17.88	30.12	5.98	9.84	16.46	27.89	5.49	9.10	15.32	26.11	5.09	8.50	14.41	24.70	35
36	6.94	11.50	19.42	33.24	6.30	10.52	17.88	30.79	5.78	9.73	16.64	28.82	5.37	9.09	15.65	27.26	36
37	7.30	12.28	21.07	36.68	6.63	11.24	19.40	33.97	6.09	10.39	18.06	31.79	5.65	9.71	16.99	30.08	37
38	7.68	13.12	22.86	40.46	6.98	12.00	21.05	37.47	6.41	11.10	19.59	35.07	5.95	10.37	18.43	33.17	38
39	8.08	14.00	24.80	44.61	7.34	12.81	22.83	41.32	6.74	11.84	21.25	38.67	6.25	11.07	19.99	36.58	39
40	8.49	14.94	26.88	49.18	7.71	13.66	24.75	45.55	7.08	12.64	23.04	42.64	6.57	11.81	21.67	40.33	40
41	8.92	15.93	29.14	54.21	8.10	14.57	26.83	50.21	7.44	13.47	24.97	47.00	6.90	12.59	23.48	44.46	41
42	9.37	16.98	31.57	59.75	8.51	15.54	29.07	55.33	7.81	14.36	27.05	51.79	7.25	13.43	25.45	48.99	42
43	9.83	18.10	34.20	65.83	8.93	16.56	31.49	60.97	8.20	15.31	29.31	57.07	7.61	14.31	27.57	53.98	43
44	10.32	19.28	37.04	72.53	9.37	17.64	34.11	67.17	8.60	16.31	31.74	62.87	7.98	15.24	29.86	59.47	44
45	10.82	20.54	40.11	79.89	9.83	18.78	36.93	73.99	9.02	17.37	34.37	69.26	8.37	16.23	32.33	65.51	45
46	11.34	21.86	43.42	87.99	10.30	20.00	39.98	81.49	9.46	18.49	37.21	76.28	8.77	17.28	35.00	72.15	46
47	11.88	23.27	47.00	96.90	10.79	21.29	43.27	89.74	9.91	19.68	40.27	84.00	9.20	18.40	37.88	79.46	47
48	12.45	24.76	50.86	106.70	11.31	22.65	46.83	98.82	10.38	20.95	43.58	92.50	9.63	19.58	41.00	87.50	48
49	13.04	26.35	55.04	117.48	11.84	24.10	50.67	108.81	10.87	22.28	47.16	101.84	10.09	20.83	44.36	96.34	49
50	13.65	28.02	59.54	129.34	12.39	25.64	54.82	119.79	11.38	23.70	51.02	112.13	10.56	22.16	47.99	106.06	50

I. Retirement Planning with Level Salary & No Inflation
Planned Retirement Age 71

Table 3 - 401(k) Contribution (% of Current Sal.) Needed to Replace 10% of Sal. at Retirement   I-71-3

Probable Life Expectancy at Retirement

Yrs. to Ret.	16 (Same as Male Avg.)				18.3 (Better than Male Avg.)				20.7 (Same as Female Avg.)				23.2 (Better than Female Avg.)				Yrs. to Ret.
	4%/4%	6%/5%	8%/6%	10%/7%	4%/4%	6%/5%	8%/6%	10%/7%	4%/4%	6%/5%	8%/6%	10%/7%	4%/4%	6%/5%	8%/6%	10%/7%	
	Expected Return				(Pre-Retirement/Post-Retirement)				(Pre-Retirement/Post-Retirement)				Expected Return				
0																	0
1	111.87	103.61	96.36	89.99	123.17	113.26	104.66	97.16	134.18	122.49	112.46	103.80	144.58	131.04	119.56	109.74	1
2	54.84	50.29	46.33	42.85	60.38	54.98	50.32	46.27	65.77	59.46	54.07	49.43	70.87	63.61	57.48	52.26	2
3	35.84	32.54	29.68	27.19	39.46	35.58	32.24	29.35	42.98	38.47	34.64	31.36	46.32	41.16	36.83	33.15	3
4	26.34	23.68	21.39	19.39	29.01	25.89	23.23	20.94	31.60	28.00	24.96	22.37	34.05	29.96	26.53	23.65	4
5	20.65	18.38	16.43	14.74	22.74	20.09	17.84	15.92	24.77	21.73	19.17	17.00	26.69	23.25	20.38	17.97	5
6	16.87	14.85	13.14	11.66	18.57	16.24	14.27	12.59	20.23	17.56	15.33	13.45	21.80	18.79	16.30	14.22	6
7	14.16	12.34	10.80	9.48	15.59	13.49	11.73	10.24	16.99	14.59	12.60	10.94	18.31	15.61	13.40	11.57	7
8	12.14	10.47	9.06	7.87	13.37	11.44	9.84	8.50	14.56	12.38	10.57	9.08	15.69	13.24	11.24	9.60	8
9	10.57	9.02	7.72	6.63	11.64	9.86	8.38	7.16	12.68	10.66	9.01	7.64	13.66	11.40	9.57	8.08	9
10	9.32	7.86	6.65	5.65	10.26	8.59	7.22	6.10	11.18	9.29	7.76	6.51	12.04	9.94	8.25	6.89	10
11	8.30	6.92	5.79	4.86	9.13	7.56	6.29	5.24	9.95	8.18	6.76	5.60	10.72	8.75	7.18	5.92	11
12	7.45	6.14	5.08	4.21	8.20	6.71	5.52	4.54	8.93	7.26	5.93	4.85	9.62	7.77	6.30	5.13	12
13	6.73	5.49	4.48	3.67	7.41	6.00	4.87	3.96	8.07	6.49	5.23	4.23	8.70	6.94	5.56	4.47	13
14	6.12	4.93	3.98	3.22	6.73	5.39	4.32	3.47	7.34	5.83	4.64	3.71	7.90	6.24	4.94	3.92	14
15	5.59	4.45	3.55	2.83	6.15	4.87	3.85	3.06	6.70	5.26	4.14	3.27	7.22	5.63	4.40	3.45	15
16	5.13	4.04	3.18	2.50	5.64	4.41	3.45	2.70	6.15	4.77	3.71	2.89	6.62	5.10	3.94	3.05	16
17	4.72	3.67	2.86	2.22	5.20	4.01	3.10	2.40	5.66	4.34	3.33	2.56	6.10	4.64	3.54	2.71	17
18	4.36	3.35	2.57	1.97	4.80	3.66	2.79	2.13	5.23	3.96	3.00	2.28	5.64	4.24	3.19	2.41	18
19	4.04	3.07	2.33	1.76	4.45	3.35	2.53	1.90	4.85	3.63	2.71	2.03	5.23	3.88	2.88	2.15	19
20	3.76	2.82	2.11	1.57	4.14	3.08	2.29	1.70	4.51	3.33	2.46	1.81	4.86	3.56	2.61	1.92	20
21	3.50	2.59	1.91	1.41	3.85	2.83	2.08	1.52	4.20	3.06	2.23	1.62	4.52	3.28	2.37	1.71	21
22	3.27	2.39	1.74	1.26	3.60	2.61	1.89	1.36	3.92	2.82	2.03	1.45	4.22	3.02	2.16	1.54	22
23	3.06	2.20	1.58	1.13	3.36	2.41	1.72	1.22	3.66	2.61	1.85	1.31	3.95	2.79	1.96	1.38	23
24	2.86	2.04	1.44	1.02	3.15	2.23	1.57	1.10	3.43	2.41	1.68	1.17	3.70	2.58	1.79	1.24	24
25	2.69	1.89	1.32	0.91	2.96	2.06	1.43	0.99	3.22	2.23	1.54	1.06	3.47	2.39	1.64	1.12	25
26	2.52	1.75	1.21	0.82	2.78	1.91	1.31	0.89	3.03	2.07	1.41	0.95	3.26	2.22	1.50	1.01	26
27	2.38	1.63	1.10	0.74	2.62	1.78	1.20	0.80	2.85	1.92	1.29	0.86	3.07	2.06	1.37	0.91	27
28	2.24	1.51	1.01	0.67	2.47	1.65	1.10	0.72	2.69	1.79	1.18	0.77	2.89	1.91	1.25	0.82	28
29	2.11	1.41	0.93	0.61	2.33	1.54	1.01	0.65	2.53	1.66	1.08	0.70	2.73	1.78	1.15	0.74	29
30	1.99	1.31	0.85	0.55	2.20	1.43	0.92	0.59	2.39	1.55	0.99	0.63	2.58	1.66	1.06	0.67	30
31	1.89	1.22	0.78	0.49	2.08	1.34	0.85	0.53	2.26	1.44	0.91	0.57	2.44	1.55	0.97	0.60	31
32	1.78	1.14	0.72	0.45	1.96	1.25	0.78	0.48	2.14	1.35	0.84	0.52	2.31	1.44	0.89	0.55	32
33	1.69	1.06	0.66	0.40	1.86	1.16	0.72	0.44	2.03	1.26	0.77	0.47	2.18	1.35	0.82	0.49	33
34	1.60	0.99	0.61	0.37	1.76	1.09	0.66	0.40	1.92	1.18	0.71	0.42	2.07	1.26	0.75	0.45	34
35	1.52	0.93	0.56	0.33	1.67	1.02	0.61	0.36	1.82	1.10	0.65	0.38	1.96	1.18	0.69	0.40	35
36	1.44	0.87	0.52	0.30	1.59	0.95	0.56	0.32	1.73	1.03	0.60	0.35	1.86	1.10	0.64	0.37	36
37	1.37	0.81	0.47	0.27	1.51	0.89	0.52	0.29	1.64	0.96	0.55	0.31	1.77	1.03	0.59	0.33	37
38	1.30	0.76	0.44	0.25	1.43	0.83	0.48	0.27	1.56	0.90	0.51	0.29	1.68	0.96	0.54	0.30	38
39	1.24	0.71	0.40	0.22	1.36	0.78	0.44	0.24	1.48	0.84	0.47	0.26	1.60	0.90	0.50	0.27	39
40	1.18	0.67	0.37	0.20	1.30	0.73	0.40	0.22	1.41	0.79	0.43	0.23	1.52	0.85	0.46	0.25	40
41	1.12	0.63	0.34	0.18	1.23	0.69	0.37	0.20	1.34	0.74	0.40	0.21	1.45	0.79	0.43	0.22	41
42	1.07	0.59	0.32	0.17	1.18	0.64	0.34	0.18	1.28	0.70	0.37	0.19	1.38	0.74	0.39	0.20	42
43	1.02	0.55	0.29	0.15	1.12	0.60	0.32	0.16	1.22	0.65	0.34	0.18	1.31	0.70	0.36	0.19	43
44	0.97	0.52	0.27	0.14	1.07	0.57	0.29	0.15	1.16	0.61	0.32	0.16	1.25	0.66	0.33	0.17	44
45	0.92	0.49	0.25	0.13	1.02	0.53	0.27	0.14	1.11	0.58	0.29	0.14	1.19	0.62	0.31	0.15	45
46	0.88	0.46	0.23	0.11	0.97	0.50	0.25	0.12	1.06	0.54	0.27	0.13	1.14	0.58	0.29	0.14	46
47	0.84	0.43	0.21	0.10	0.93	0.47	0.23	0.11	1.01	0.51	0.25	0.12	1.09	0.54	0.26	0.13	47
48	0.80	0.40	0.20	0.09	0.88	0.44	0.21	0.10	0.96	0.48	0.23	0.11	1.04	0.51	0.24	0.11	48
49	0.77	0.38	0.18	0.09	0.84	0.41	0.20	0.09	0.92	0.45	0.21	0.10	0.99	0.48	0.23	0.10	49
50	0.73	0.36	0.17	0.08	0.81	0.39	0.18	0.08	0.88	0.42	0.20	0.09	0.95	0.45	0.21	0.09	50

Appendix A

I. Retirement Planning with Level Salary & No Inflation
Planned Retirement Age 71

Table 4 - Accumulation at Retirement (Multiple of Current Sal.) for 10% Sal. Replacement   I-71-4

Probable Life Expectancy at Retirement

Yrs. to Ret.	16 (Same as Male Avg.)				18.3 (Better than Male Avg.)				20.7 (Same as Female Avg.)				23.2 (Better than Female Avg.)				Yrs. to Ret.
	4% / 4%	6% / 5%	8% / 6%	10% / 7%	4% / 4%	6% / 5%	8% / 6%	10% / 7%	4% / 4%	6% / 5%	8% / 6%	10% / 7%	4% / 4%	6% / 5%	8% / 6%	10% / 7%	
	Expected Return				(Pre-Retirement/Post-Retirement)				(Pre-Retirement/Post-Retirement)				Expected Return				
0	1.12	1.04	0.96	0.90	1.23	1.13	1.05	0.97	1.34	1.22	1.12	1.04	1.45	1.31	1.20	1.10	0
1	1.12	1.04	0.96	0.90	1.23	1.13	1.05	0.97	1.34	1.22	1.12	1.04	1.45	1.31	1.20	1.10	1
2	1.12	1.04	0.96	0.90	1.23	1.13	1.05	0.97	1.34	1.22	1.12	1.04	1.45	1.31	1.20	1.10	2
3	1.12	1.04	0.96	0.90	1.23	1.13	1.05	0.97	1.34	1.22	1.12	1.04	1.45	1.31	1.20	1.10	3
4	1.12	1.04	0.96	0.90	1.23	1.13	1.05	0.97	1.34	1.22	1.12	1.04	1.45	1.31	1.20	1.10	4
5	1.12	1.04	0.96	0.90	1.23	1.13	1.05	0.97	1.34	1.22	1.12	1.04	1.45	1.31	1.20	1.10	5
6	1.12	1.04	0.96	0.90	1.23	1.13	1.05	0.97	1.34	1.22	1.12	1.04	1.45	1.31	1.20	1.10	6
7	1.12	1.04	0.96	0.90	1.23	1.13	1.05	0.97	1.34	1.22	1.12	1.04	1.45	1.31	1.20	1.10	7
8	1.12	1.04	0.96	0.90	1.23	1.13	1.05	0.97	1.34	1.22	1.12	1.04	1.45	1.31	1.20	1.10	8
9	1.12	1.04	0.96	0.90	1.23	1.13	1.05	0.97	1.34	1.22	1.12	1.04	1.45	1.31	1.20	1.10	9
10	1.12	1.04	0.96	0.90	1.23	1.13	1.05	0.97	1.34	1.22	1.12	1.04	1.45	1.31	1.20	1.10	10
11	1.12	1.04	0.96	0.90	1.23	1.13	1.05	0.97	1.34	1.22	1.12	1.04	1.45	1.31	1.20	1.10	11
12	1.12	1.04	0.96	0.90	1.23	1.13	1.05	0.97	1.34	1.22	1.12	1.04	1.45	1.31	1.20	1.10	12
13	1.12	1.04	0.96	0.90	1.23	1.13	1.05	0.97	1.34	1.22	1.12	1.04	1.45	1.31	1.20	1.10	13
14	1.12	1.04	0.96	0.90	1.23	1.13	1.05	0.97	1.34	1.22	1.12	1.04	1.45	1.31	1.20	1.10	14
15	1.12	1.04	0.96	0.90	1.23	1.13	1.05	0.97	1.34	1.22	1.12	1.04	1.45	1.31	1.20	1.10	15
16	1.12	1.04	0.96	0.90	1.23	1.13	1.05	0.97	1.34	1.22	1.12	1.04	1.45	1.31	1.20	1.10	16
17	1.12	1.04	0.96	0.90	1.23	1.13	1.05	0.97	1.34	1.22	1.12	1.04	1.45	1.31	1.20	1.10	17
18	1.12	1.04	0.96	0.90	1.23	1.13	1.05	0.97	1.34	1.22	1.12	1.04	1.45	1.31	1.20	1.10	18
19	1.12	1.04	0.96	0.90	1.23	1.13	1.05	0.97	1.34	1.22	1.12	1.04	1.45	1.31	1.20	1.10	19
20	1.12	1.04	0.96	0.90	1.23	1.13	1.05	0.97	1.34	1.22	1.12	1.04	1.45	1.31	1.20	1.10	20
21	1.12	1.04	0.96	0.90	1.23	1.13	1.05	0.97	1.34	1.22	1.12	1.04	1.45	1.31	1.20	1.10	21
22	1.12	1.04	0.96	0.90	1.23	1.13	1.05	0.97	1.34	1.22	1.12	1.04	1.45	1.31	1.20	1.10	22
23	1.12	1.04	0.96	0.90	1.23	1.13	1.05	0.97	1.34	1.22	1.12	1.04	1.45	1.31	1.20	1.10	23
24	1.12	1.04	0.96	0.90	1.23	1.13	1.05	0.97	1.34	1.22	1.12	1.04	1.45	1.31	1.20	1.10	24
25	1.12	1.04	0.96	0.90	1.23	1.13	1.05	0.97	1.34	1.22	1.12	1.04	1.45	1.31	1.20	1.10	25
26	1.12	1.04	0.96	0.90	1.23	1.13	1.05	0.97	1.34	1.22	1.12	1.04	1.45	1.31	1.20	1.10	26
27	1.12	1.04	0.96	0.90	1.23	1.13	1.05	0.97	1.34	1.22	1.12	1.04	1.45	1.31	1.20	1.10	27
28	1.12	1.04	0.96	0.90	1.23	1.13	1.05	0.97	1.34	1.22	1.12	1.04	1.45	1.31	1.20	1.10	28
29	1.12	1.04	0.96	0.90	1.23	1.13	1.05	0.97	1.34	1.22	1.12	1.04	1.45	1.31	1.20	1.10	29
30	1.12	1.04	0.96	0.90	1.23	1.13	1.05	0.97	1.34	1.22	1.12	1.04	1.45	1.31	1.20	1.10	30
31	1.12	1.04	0.96	0.90	1.23	1.13	1.05	0.97	1.34	1.22	1.12	1.04	1.45	1.31	1.20	1.10	31
32	1.12	1.04	0.96	0.90	1.23	1.13	1.05	0.97	1.34	1.22	1.12	1.04	1.45	1.31	1.20	1.10	32
33	1.12	1.04	0.96	0.90	1.23	1.13	1.05	0.97	1.34	1.22	1.12	1.04	1.45	1.31	1.20	1.10	33
34	1.12	1.04	0.96	0.90	1.23	1.13	1.05	0.97	1.34	1.22	1.12	1.04	1.45	1.31	1.20	1.10	34
35	1.12	1.04	0.96	0.90	1.23	1.13	1.05	0.97	1.34	1.22	1.12	1.04	1.45	1.31	1.20	1.10	35
36	1.12	1.04	0.96	0.90	1.23	1.13	1.05	0.97	1.34	1.22	1.12	1.04	1.45	1.31	1.20	1.10	36
37	1.12	1.04	0.96	0.90	1.23	1.13	1.05	0.97	1.34	1.22	1.12	1.04	1.45	1.31	1.20	1.10	37
38	1.12	1.04	0.96	0.90	1.23	1.13	1.05	0.97	1.34	1.22	1.12	1.04	1.45	1.31	1.20	1.10	38
39	1.12	1.04	0.96	0.90	1.23	1.13	1.05	0.97	1.34	1.22	1.12	1.04	1.45	1.31	1.20	1.10	39
40	1.12	1.04	0.96	0.90	1.23	1.13	1.05	0.97	1.34	1.22	1.12	1.04	1.45	1.31	1.20	1.10	40
41	1.12	1.04	0.96	0.90	1.23	1.13	1.05	0.97	1.34	1.22	1.12	1.04	1.45	1.31	1.20	1.10	41
42	1.12	1.04	0.96	0.90	1.23	1.13	1.05	0.97	1.34	1.22	1.12	1.04	1.45	1.31	1.20	1.10	42
43	1.12	1.04	0.96	0.90	1.23	1.13	1.05	0.97	1.34	1.22	1.12	1.04	1.45	1.31	1.20	1.10	43
44	1.12	1.04	0.96	0.90	1.23	1.13	1.05	0.97	1.34	1.22	1.12	1.04	1.45	1.31	1.20	1.10	44
45	1.12	1.04	0.96	0.90	1.23	1.13	1.05	0.97	1.34	1.22	1.12	1.04	1.45	1.31	1.20	1.10	45
46	1.12	1.04	0.96	0.90	1.23	1.13	1.05	0.97	1.34	1.22	1.12	1.04	1.45	1.31	1.20	1.10	46
47	1.12	1.04	0.96	0.90	1.23	1.13	1.05	0.97	1.34	1.22	1.12	1.04	1.45	1.31	1.20	1.10	47
48	1.12	1.04	0.96	0.90	1.23	1.13	1.05	0.97	1.34	1.22	1.12	1.04	1.45	1.31	1.20	1.10	48
49	1.12	1.04	0.96	0.90	1.23	1.13	1.05	0.97	1.34	1.22	1.12	1.04	1.45	1.31	1.20	1.10	49
50	1.12	1.04	0.96	0.90	1.23	1.13	1.05	0.97	1.34	1.22	1.12	1.04	1.45	1.31	1.20	1.10	50

II. Retirement Planning where Salary Keeps Pace with Low 3% Inflation
Planned Retirement Age 59

Table 1 - Percent of Salary Replaced by a 401(k) Account Equal to Current Annual Salary   II-59-1

Probable Life Expectancy at Retirement

Yrs. to Ret.	25.7 (Same as Male Avg.)				28.3 (Better than Male Avg.)				31 (Same as Female Avg.)				33.8 (Better than Female Avg.)				Yrs. to Ret.
	4%/4%	6%/5%	8%/6%	10%/7%	4%/4%	6%/5%	8%/6%	10%/7%	4%/4%	6%/5%	8%/6%	10%/7%	4%/4%	6%/5%	8%/6%	10%/7%	
	Expected Return				(Pre-Retirement/Post-Retirement)				(Pre-Retirement/Post-Retirement)				Expected Return				
0	4.47	5.08	5.72	6.40	4.10	4.71	5.36	6.03	3.79	4.40	5.05	5.73	3.52	4.13	4.78	5.47	0
1	4.51	5.23	6.00	6.83	4.14	4.85	5.62	6.45	3.83	4.53	5.29	6.12	3.56	4.25	5.02	5.84	1
2	4.55	5.38	6.29	7.30	4.18	4.99	5.89	6.88	3.86	4.66	5.55	6.54	3.59	4.38	5.26	6.24	2
3	4.60	5.54	6.60	7.79	4.22	5.14	6.18	7.35	3.90	4.80	5.82	6.98	3.63	4.50	5.51	6.66	3
4	4.64	5.70	6.92	8.32	4.26	5.29	6.48	7.85	3.94	4.94	6.10	7.45	3.66	4.63	5.78	7.12	4
5	4.69	5.86	7.25	8.89	4.30	5.44	6.79	8.39	3.98	5.08	6.40	7.96	3.70	4.77	6.06	7.60	5
6	4.73	6.03	7.61	9.49	4.35	5.60	7.12	8.96	4.02	5.23	6.71	8.50	3.73	4.91	6.36	8.12	6
7	4.78	6.21	7.97	10.14	4.39	5.76	7.47	9.56	4.06	5.38	7.03	9.08	3.77	5.05	6.66	8.67	7
8	4.82	6.39	8.36	10.83	4.43	5.93	7.83	10.21	4.09	5.54	7.37	9.70	3.81	5.20	6.99	9.26	8
9	4.87	6.58	8.77	11.56	4.47	6.10	8.21	10.91	4.13	5.70	7.73	10.36	3.84	5.35	7.33	9.89	9
10	4.92	6.77	9.19	12.35	4.52	6.28	8.60	11.65	4.17	5.86	8.11	11.06	3.88	5.51	7.68	10.56	10
11	4.97	6.96	9.64	13.19	4.56	6.46	9.02	12.44	4.22	6.03	8.50	11.81	3.92	5.67	8.05	11.28	11
12	5.01	7.17	10.10	14.09	4.61	6.65	9.46	13.29	4.26	6.21	8.91	12.62	3.96	5.83	8.44	12.04	12
13	5.06	7.38	10.59	15.04	4.65	6.84	9.92	14.19	4.30	6.39	9.35	13.48	3.99	6.00	8.85	12.86	13
14	5.11	7.59	11.11	16.07	4.69	7.04	10.40	15.16	4.34	6.58	9.80	14.39	4.03	6.17	9.28	13.74	14
15	5.16	7.81	11.65	17.16	4.74	7.25	10.90	16.19	4.38	6.77	10.27	15.37	4.07	6.35	9.73	14.67	15
16	5.21	8.04	12.21	18.33	4.79	7.46	11.43	17.29	4.42	6.96	10.77	16.42	4.11	6.54	10.20	15.67	16
17	5.26	8.27	12.80	19.57	4.83	7.67	11.99	18.47	4.47	7.17	11.29	17.53	4.15	6.73	10.70	16.74	17
18	5.31	8.51	13.43	20.90	4.88	7.90	12.57	19.72	4.51	7.38	11.84	18.72	4.19	6.93	11.22	17.87	18
19	5.36	8.76	14.08	22.32	4.93	8.13	13.18	21.06	4.55	7.59	12.42	20.00	4.23	7.13	11.76	19.09	19
20	5.42	9.02	14.76	23.84	4.97	8.36	13.82	22.50	4.60	7.81	13.02	21.36	4.27	7.33	12.33	20.39	20
21	5.47	9.28	15.48	25.46	5.02	8.61	14.49	24.03	4.64	8.04	13.65	22.81	4.31	7.55	12.93	21.77	21
22	5.52	9.55	16.23	27.19	5.07	8.86	15.19	25.66	4.69	8.27	14.31	24.36	4.36	7.77	13.56	23.25	22
23	5.58	9.83	17.01	29.04	5.12	9.12	15.93	27.40	4.73	8.51	15.01	26.02	4.40	7.99	14.22	24.83	23
24	5.63	10.11	17.84	31.02	5.17	9.38	16.70	29.27	4.78	8.76	15.73	27.79	4.44	8.23	14.91	26.52	24
25	5.68	10.41	18.70	33.13	5.22	9.65	17.51	31.26	4.83	9.02	16.50	29.68	4.48	8.47	15.63	28.33	25
26	5.74	10.71	19.61	35.38	5.27	9.94	18.36	33.38	4.87	9.28	17.30	31.69	4.53	8.71	16.39	30.25	26
27	5.80	11.02	20.56	37.79	5.32	10.22	19.25	35.65	4.92	9.55	18.14	33.85	4.57	8.97	17.18	32.31	27
28	5.85	11.34	21.56	40.36	5.37	10.52	20.18	38.08	4.97	9.83	19.02	36.15	4.62	9.23	18.01	34.51	28
29	5.91	11.67	22.60	43.10	5.43	10.83	21.16	40.67	5.02	10.11	19.94	38.61	4.66	9.49	18.89	36.85	29
30	5.97	12.01	23.70	46.03	5.48	11.14	22.19	43.43	5.06	10.41	20.90	41.24	4.71	9.77	19.80	39.36	30
31	6.02	12.36	24.85	49.16	5.53	11.47	23.26	46.38	5.11	10.71	21.92	44.04	4.75	10.06	20.76	42.04	31
32	6.08	12.72	26.06	52.51	5.59	11.80	24.39	49.54	5.16	11.02	22.98	47.03	4.80	10.35	21.77	44.90	32
33	6.14	13.09	27.32	56.08	5.64	12.14	25.58	52.91	5.21	11.34	24.10	50.23	4.84	10.65	22.83	47.95	33
34	6.20	13.47	28.64	59.89	5.69	12.50	26.82	56.51	5.26	11.67	25.26	53.65	4.89	10.96	23.94	51.21	34
35	6.26	13.86	30.03	63.96	5.75	12.86	28.12	60.35	5.31	12.01	26.49	57.30	4.94	11.28	25.10	54.69	35
36	6.32	14.27	31.49	68.31	5.81	13.24	29.48	64.45	5.37	12.36	27.78	61.19	4.99	11.61	26.31	58.41	36
37	6.38	14.68	33.02	72.96	5.86	13.62	30.91	68.83	5.42	12.72	29.12	65.35	5.04	11.94	27.59	62.38	37
38	6.45	15.11	34.62	77.92	5.92	14.02	32.41	73.51	5.47	13.09	30.53	69.80	5.08	12.29	28.93	66.62	38
39	6.51	15.55	36.30	83.21	5.98	14.43	33.98	78.51	5.52	13.47	32.02	74.54	5.13	12.65	30.33	71.15	39
40	6.57	16.00	38.06	88.87	6.03	14.85	35.63	83.85	5.58	13.86	33.57	79.61	5.18	13.02	31.80	75.99	40
41	6.63	16.47	39.90	94.92	6.09	15.28	37.36	89.55	5.63	14.27	35.20	85.03	5.23	13.40	33.34	81.16	41
42	6.70	16.94	41.84	101.37	6.15	15.72	39.17	95.64	5.69	14.68	36.91	90.81	5.28	13.79	34.96	86.68	42
43	6.76	17.44	43.87	108.26	6.21	16.18	41.07	102.15	5.74	15.11	38.69	96.98	5.34	14.19	36.66	92.57	43
44	6.83	17.95	46.00	115.63	6.27	16.65	43.06	109.09	5.80	15.55	40.57	103.58	5.39	14.60	38.43	98.87	44
45	6.90	18.47	48.23	123.49	6.33	17.13	45.15	116.51	5.85	16.00	42.54	110.62	5.44	15.02	40.33	105.59	45
46	6.96	19.00	50.57	131.89	6.39	17.63	47.34	124.44	5.91	16.47	44.60	118.14	5.49	15.46	42.25	112.77	46
47	7.03	19.56	53.02	140.85	6.46	18.15	49.63	132.90	5.97	16.94	46.76	126.18	5.55	15.91	44.30	120.44	47
48	7.10	20.13	55.59	150.43	6.52	18.67	52.04	141.93	6.02	17.44	49.03	134.76	5.60	16.37	46.45	128.63	48
49	7.17	20.71	58.29	160.66	6.58	19.22	54.57	151.59	6.08	17.95	51.41	143.92	5.65	16.85	48.70	137.38	49
50	7.24	21.32	61.11	171.59	6.65	19.78	57.21	161.89	6.14	18.47	53.90	153.71	5.71	17.34	51.07	146.72	50

II. Retirement Planning where Salary Keeps Pace with Low 3% Inflation
Planned Retirement Age 59

Table 2 - Percent of Salary Replaced by a 401(k) Contribution of 1% of Current Salary II-59-2

Probable Life Expectancy at Retirement

Yrs. to Ret.	25.7 (Same as Male Avg.)				28.3 (Better than Male Avg.)				31 (Same as Female Avg.)				33.8 (Better than Female Avg.)				Yrs. to Ret.
	4% / 4%	6% / 5%	8% / 6%	10% / 7%	4% / 4%	6% / 5%	8% / 6%	10% / 7%	4% / 4%	6% / 5%	8% / 6%	10% / 7%	4% / 4%	6% / 5%	8% / 6%	10% / 7%	
	Expected Return				(Pre-Retirement/Post-Retirement)				(Pre-Retirement/Post-Retirement)				Expected Return				
0	0.00	0.00	0.00	0.00	0.00	0.00	0.00	0.00	0.00	0.00	0.00	0.00	0.00	0.00	0.00	0.00	0
1	0.04	0.05	0.06	0.06	0.04	0.05	0.05	0.06	0.04	0.04	0.05	0.06	0.04	0.04	0.05	0.05	1
2	0.09	0.10	0.12	0.13	0.08	0.10	0.11	0.12	0.08	0.09	0.10	0.12	0.07	0.08	0.10	0.11	2
3	0.14	0.16	0.18	0.21	0.12	0.15	0.17	0.19	0.11	0.14	0.16	0.18	0.11	0.13	0.15	0.18	3
4	0.18	0.21	0.25	0.28	0.17	0.20	0.23	0.27	0.15	0.18	0.22	0.25	0.14	0.17	0.21	0.24	4
5	0.23	0.27	0.32	0.37	0.21	0.25	0.30	0.35	0.19	0.23	0.28	0.33	0.18	0.22	0.26	0.31	5
6	0.27	0.33	0.39	0.46	0.25	0.30	0.36	0.43	0.23	0.28	0.34	0.41	0.22	0.27	0.32	0.39	6
7	0.32	0.39	0.46	0.55	0.30	0.36	0.43	0.52	0.27	0.34	0.41	0.49	0.25	0.32	0.39	0.47	7
8	0.37	0.45	0.54	0.65	0.34	0.42	0.51	0.61	0.31	0.39	0.48	0.58	0.29	0.37	0.45	0.56	8
9	0.42	0.51	0.63	0.76	0.38	0.48	0.59	0.72	0.35	0.45	0.55	0.68	0.33	0.42	0.52	0.65	9
10	0.47	0.58	0.71	0.88	0.43	0.54	0.67	0.83	0.40	0.50	0.63	0.78	0.37	0.47	0.60	0.75	10
11	0.52	0.65	0.81	1.00	0.47	0.60	0.76	0.94	0.44	0.56	0.71	0.89	0.41	0.53	0.67	0.85	11
12	0.57	0.72	0.90	1.13	0.52	0.67	0.85	1.07	0.48	0.62	0.80	1.01	0.45	0.58	0.75	0.97	12
13	0.62	0.79	1.00	1.27	0.57	0.73	0.94	1.20	0.52	0.68	0.89	1.14	0.49	0.64	0.84	1.09	13
14	0.67	0.86	1.11	1.42	0.61	0.80	1.04	1.34	0.57	0.75	0.98	1.27	0.53	0.70	0.93	1.22	14
15	0.72	0.94	1.22	1.58	0.66	0.87	1.14	1.49	0.61	0.81	1.08	1.42	0.57	0.76	1.02	1.35	15
16	0.77	1.02	1.34	1.75	0.71	0.94	1.25	1.66	0.65	0.88	1.18	1.57	0.61	0.83	1.12	1.50	16
17	0.82	1.10	1.46	1.94	0.75	1.02	1.37	1.83	0.70	0.95	1.29	1.74	0.65	0.89	1.22	1.66	17
18	0.87	1.18	1.59	2.13	0.80	1.09	1.49	2.01	0.74	1.02	1.40	1.91	0.69	0.96	1.33	1.82	18
19	0.93	1.26	1.72	2.34	0.85	1.17	1.61	2.21	0.79	1.10	1.52	2.10	0.73	1.03	1.44	2.00	19
20	0.98	1.35	1.86	2.57	0.90	1.25	1.74	2.42	0.83	1.17	1.64	2.30	0.77	1.10	1.56	2.19	20
21	1.03	1.44	2.01	2.80	0.95	1.34	1.88	2.65	0.88	1.25	1.77	2.51	0.82	1.17	1.68	2.40	21
22	1.09	1.54	2.17	3.06	1.00	1.42	2.03	2.89	0.92	1.33	1.91	2.74	0.86	1.25	1.81	2.62	22
23	1.14	1.63	2.33	3.33	1.05	1.51	2.18	3.14	0.97	1.41	2.05	2.98	0.90	1.33	1.94	2.85	23
24	1.20	1.73	2.50	3.62	1.10	1.60	2.34	3.42	1.02	1.50	2.20	3.24	0.95	1.41	2.09	3.10	24
25	1.26	1.83	2.68	3.93	1.15	1.70	2.51	3.71	1.07	1.59	2.36	3.52	0.99	1.49	2.24	3.36	25
26	1.31	1.93	2.86	4.26	1.21	1.79	2.68	4.02	1.11	1.68	2.53	3.82	1.04	1.57	2.39	3.64	26
27	1.37	2.04	3.06	4.62	1.26	1.89	2.86	4.36	1.16	1.77	2.70	4.14	1.08	1.66	2.56	3.95	27
28	1.43	2.15	3.26	4.99	1.31	2.00	3.06	4.71	1.21	1.86	2.88	4.47	1.13	1.75	2.73	4.27	28
29	1.49	2.26	3.48	5.40	1.37	2.10	3.26	5.09	1.26	1.96	3.07	4.84	1.17	1.84	2.91	4.62	29
30	1.55	2.38	3.71	5.83	1.42	2.21	3.47	5.50	1.31	2.06	3.27	5.22	1.22	1.94	3.10	4.98	30
31	1.61	2.50	3.94	6.29	1.48	2.32	3.69	5.93	1.36	2.17	3.48	5.63	1.27	2.04	3.30	5.38	31
32	1.67	2.63	4.19	6.78	1.53	2.44	3.92	6.40	1.41	2.27	3.70	6.07	1.31	2.14	3.50	5.80	32
33	1.73	2.75	4.45	7.31	1.59	2.55	4.17	6.89	1.47	2.38	3.93	6.54	1.36	2.24	3.72	6.25	33
34	1.79	2.88	4.73	7.87	1.64	2.68	4.42	7.42	1.52	2.50	4.17	7.05	1.41	2.35	3.95	6.73	34
35	1.85	3.02	5.01	8.47	1.70	2.80	4.69	7.99	1.57	2.61	4.42	7.58	1.46	2.46	4.19	7.24	35
36	1.91	3.16	5.31	9.11	1.76	2.93	4.97	8.59	1.62	2.73	4.69	8.16	1.51	2.57	4.44	7.79	36
37	1.98	3.30	5.63	9.79	1.82	3.06	5.27	9.24	1.68	2.86	4.96	8.77	1.56	2.68	4.70	8.37	37
38	2.04	3.45	5.96	10.52	1.87	3.20	5.58	9.92	1.73	2.99	5.25	9.42	1.61	2.80	4.98	8.99	38
39	2.10	3.60	6.30	11.30	1.93	3.34	5.90	10.66	1.79	3.12	5.56	10.12	1.66	2.93	5.27	9.66	39
40	2.17	3.75	6.67	12.13	1.99	3.48	6.24	11.44	1.84	3.25	5.88	10.87	1.71	3.05	5.57	10.37	40
41	2.24	3.91	7.05	13.02	2.05	3.63	6.60	12.28	1.90	3.39	6.22	11.66	1.76	3.18	5.89	11.13	41
42	2.30	4.08	7.45	13.97	2.11	3.78	6.97	13.18	1.95	3.53	6.57	12.51	1.82	3.32	6.22	11.94	42
43	2.37	4.25	7.86	14.98	2.18	3.94	7.36	14.13	2.01	3.68	6.94	13.42	1.87	3.46	6.57	12.81	43
44	2.44	4.42	8.30	16.06	2.24	4.10	7.77	15.16	2.07	3.83	7.32	14.39	1.92	3.60	6.94	13.74	44
45	2.50	4.60	8.76	17.22	2.30	4.27	8.20	16.25	2.13	3.99	7.73	15.43	1.98	3.74	7.32	14.72	45
46	2.57	4.79	9.25	18.45	2.36	4.44	8.66	17.41	2.18	4.15	8.15	16.53	2.03	3.89	7.73	15.78	46
47	2.64	4.98	9.75	19.77	2.43	4.62	9.13	18.66	2.24	4.31	8.60	17.71	2.09	4.05	8.15	16.91	47
48	2.71	5.17	10.28	21.18	2.49	4.80	9.63	19.99	2.30	4.48	9.07	18.97	2.14	4.21	8.59	18.11	48
49	2.78	5.37	10.84	22.69	2.56	4.98	10.15	21.40	2.36	4.65	9.56	20.32	2.20	4.37	9.06	19.40	49
50	2.86	5.58	11.42	24.29	2.62	5.18	10.69	22.92	2.42	4.83	10.07	21.76	2.25	4.54	9.54	20.77	50

II. Retirement Planning where Salary Keeps Pace with Low 3% Inflation
Planned Retirement Age 59

Table 3 - 401(k) Contribution (% of Current Sal.) Needed to Replace 10% of Sal. at Retirement   II-59-3

Probable Life Expectancy at Retirement

	25.7 (Same as Male Avg.)				28.3 (Better than Male Avg.)				31 (Same as Female Avg.)				33.8 (Better than Female Avg.)				
	4% / 4%	6% / 5%	8% / 6%	10% / 7%	4% / 4%	6% / 5%	8% / 6%	10% / 7%	4% / 4%	6% / 5%	8% / 6%	10% / 7%	4% / 4%	6% / 5%	8% / 6%	10% / 7%	
Yrs. to Ret.			Expected Return		(Pre-Retirement/Post-Retirement)				(Pre-Retirement/Post-Retirement)				Expected Return				Yrs. to Ret.
0																	0
1	223.92	196.87	174.70	156.34	243.82	212.19	186.61	165.70	263.81	227.23	198.07	174.53	283.86	241.99	209.07	182.84	1
2	111.42	97.02	85.28	75.60	121.32	104.57	91.10	80.13	131.27	111.99	96.69	84.40	141.24	119.26	102.06	88.42	2
3	73.92	63.75	55.50	48.73	80.49	68.71	59.28	51.64	87.09	73.58	62.92	54.39	93.71	78.36	66.42	56.98	3
4	55.17	47.12	40.62	35.32	60.08	50.79	43.39	37.43	65.00	54.39	46.06	39.43	69.94	57.92	48.62	41.30	4
5	43.92	37.15	31.71	27.30	47.83	40.04	33.87	28.93	51.75	42.88	35.95	30.47	55.68	45.66	37.95	31.92	5
6	36.42	30.50	25.78	21.97	39.66	32.88	27.54	23.28	42.91	35.21	29.23	24.52	46.17	37.50	30.85	25.69	6
7	31.07	25.76	21.55	18.18	33.83	27.77	23.02	19.26	36.60	29.74	24.44	20.29	39.39	31.67	25.80	21.26	7
8	27.05	22.21	18.39	15.35	29.46	23.94	19.65	16.27	31.87	25.64	20.85	17.13	34.29	27.30	22.01	17.95	8
9	23.93	19.45	15.94	13.16	26.06	20.96	17.03	13.95	28.19	22.45	18.07	14.69	30.34	23.91	19.08	15.39	9
10	21.43	17.24	13.99	11.42	23.34	18.59	14.94	12.11	25.25	19.90	15.86	12.75	27.17	21.20	16.74	13.36	10
11	19.39	15.44	12.39	10.01	21.11	16.64	13.24	10.61	22.84	17.82	14.05	11.18	24.58	18.98	14.83	11.71	11
12	17.69	13.94	11.07	8.84	19.26	15.03	11.83	9.37	20.84	16.09	12.55	9.87	22.42	17.14	13.25	10.34	12
13	16.24	12.68	9.96	7.86	17.69	13.66	10.64	8.33	19.14	14.63	11.29	8.78	20.59	15.58	11.92	9.20	13
14	15.01	11.59	9.01	7.03	16.34	12.49	9.62	7.45	17.68	13.38	10.21	7.85	19.03	14.25	10.78	8.22	14
15	13.94	10.66	8.19	6.32	15.18	11.48	8.75	6.70	16.42	12.30	9.28	7.05	17.67	13.10	9.80	7.39	15
16	13.00	9.84	7.47	5.70	14.16	10.60	7.98	6.04	15.32	11.35	8.47	6.36	16.49	12.09	8.95	6.67	16
17	12.18	9.12	6.85	5.16	13.26	9.83	7.32	5.47	14.35	10.52	7.77	5.76	15.44	11.20	8.20	6.04	17
18	11.45	8.48	6.30	4.69	12.46	9.14	6.73	4.97	13.48	9.78	7.14	5.23	14.51	10.42	7.54	5.48	18
19	10.79	7.91	5.81	4.27	11.75	8.52	6.20	4.52	12.71	9.13	6.58	4.77	13.68	9.72	6.95	4.99	19
20	10.20	7.39	5.37	3.90	11.11	7.97	5.73	4.13	12.02	8.53	6.09	4.35	12.93	9.09	6.42	4.56	20
21	9.66	6.93	4.97	3.57	10.52	7.47	5.31	3.78	11.39	8.00	5.64	3.98	12.25	8.52	5.95	4.17	21
22	9.18	6.51	4.62	3.27	10.00	7.02	4.93	3.47	10.82	7.52	5.24	3.65	11.64	8.01	5.53	3.82	22
23	8.74	6.13	4.30	3.00	9.51	6.61	4.59	3.18	10.29	7.08	4.87	3.35	11.08	7.54	5.14	3.51	23
24	8.33	5.78	4.00	2.76	9.07	6.23	4.28	2.93	9.82	6.68	4.54	3.08	10.56	7.11	4.79	3.23	24
25	7.96	5.46	3.74	2.54	8.67	5.89	3.99	2.70	9.38	6.31	4.24	2.84	10.09	6.72	4.47	2.97	25
26	7.61	5.17	3.49	2.35	8.29	5.57	3.73	2.49	8.97	5.97	3.96	2.62	9.65	6.35	4.18	2.74	26
27	7.29	4.90	3.27	2.17	7.94	5.28	3.49	2.30	8.59	5.65	3.71	2.42	9.25	6.02	3.91	2.53	27
28	7.00	4.65	3.06	2.00	7.62	5.01	3.27	2.12	8.25	5.36	3.47	2.24	8.87	5.71	3.67	2.34	28
29	6.72	4.42	2.87	1.85	7.32	4.76	3.07	1.96	7.92	5.10	3.26	2.07	8.52	5.43	3.44	2.17	29
30	6.47	4.20	2.70	1.72	7.04	4.53	2.88	1.82	7.62	4.85	3.06	1.92	8.20	5.16	3.23	2.01	30
31	6.23	4.00	2.54	1.59	6.78	4.31	2.71	1.69	7.34	4.61	2.87	1.78	7.89	4.91	3.03	1.86	31
32	6.00	3.81	2.39	1.47	6.53	4.11	2.55	1.56	7.07	4.40	2.70	1.65	7.61	4.68	2.85	1.72	32
33	5.79	3.63	2.25	1.37	6.30	3.92	2.40	1.45	6.82	4.19	2.55	1.53	7.34	4.47	2.69	1.60	33
34	5.59	3.47	2.12	1.27	6.09	3.74	2.26	1.35	6.59	4.00	2.40	1.42	7.09	4.26	2.53	1.49	34
35	5.40	3.31	2.00	1.18	5.88	3.57	2.13	1.25	6.37	3.82	2.26	1.32	6.85	4.07	2.39	1.38	35
36	5.23	3.17	1.88	1.10	5.69	3.41	2.01	1.16	6.16	3.66	2.13	1.23	6.63	3.89	2.25	1.28	36
37	5.06	3.03	1.78	1.02	5.51	3.27	1.90	1.08	5.96	3.50	2.01	1.14	6.41	3.73	2.13	1.19	37
38	4.90	2.90	1.68	0.95	5.34	3.13	1.79	1.01	5.77	3.35	1.90	1.06	6.21	3.57	2.01	1.11	38
39	4.75	2.78	1.59	0.89	5.17	3.00	1.69	0.94	5.60	3.21	1.80	0.99	6.02	3.42	1.90	1.04	39
40	4.61	2.66	1.50	0.82	5.02	2.87	1.60	0.87	5.43	3.08	1.70	0.92	5.84	3.28	1.80	0.96	40
41	4.47	2.56	1.42	0.77	4.87	2.75	1.52	0.81	5.27	2.95	1.61	0.86	5.67	3.14	1.70	0.90	41
42	4.34	2.45	1.34	0.72	4.73	2.64	1.43	0.76	5.12	2.83	1.52	0.80	5.51	3.01	1.61	0.84	42
43	4.22	2.35	1.27	0.67	4.60	2.54	1.36	0.71	4.97	2.72	1.44	0.75	5.35	2.89	1.52	0.78	43
44	4.10	2.26	1.20	0.62	4.47	2.44	1.29	0.66	4.84	2.61	1.37	0.69	5.20	2.78	1.44	0.73	44
45	3.99	2.17	1.14	0.58	4.35	2.34	1.22	0.62	4.70	2.51	1.29	0.65	5.06	2.67	1.37	0.68	45
46	3.89	2.09	1.08	0.54	4.23	2.25	1.16	0.57	4.58	2.41	1.23	0.60	4.93	2.57	1.29	0.63	46
47	3.78	2.01	1.03	0.51	4.12	2.17	1.10	0.54	4.46	2.32	1.16	0.56	4.80	2.47	1.23	0.59	47
48	3.69	1.93	0.97	0.47	4.01	2.08	1.04	0.50	4.34	2.23	1.10	0.53	4.67	2.38	1.16	0.55	48
49	3.59	1.86	0.92	0.44	3.91	2.01	0.99	0.47	4.23	2.15	1.05	0.49	4.55	2.29	1.10	0.52	49
50	3.50	1.79	0.88	0.41	3.81	1.93	0.94	0.44	4.12	2.07	0.99	0.46	4.44	2.20	1.05	0.48	50

Appendix A

**II. Retirement Planning where Salary Keeps Pace with Low 3% Inflation
Planned Retirement Age 59**

Table 4 - Accumulation at Retirement (Multiple of Current Sal.) for 10% Sal. Replacement

Probable Life Expectancy at Retirement

Yrs. to Ret.	25.7 (Same as Male Avg.)				28.3 (Better than Male Avg.)				31 (Same as Female Avg.)				33.8 (Better than Female Avg.)				Yrs. to Ret.
	4%/4%	6%/5%	8%/6%	10%/7%	4%/4%	6%/5%	8%/6%	10%/7%	4%/4%	6%/5%	8%/6%	10%/7%	4%/4%	6%/5%	8%/6%	10%/7%	
	Expected Return				(Pre-Retirement/Post-Retirement)				(Pre-Retirement/Post-Retirement)				Expected Return				
0	2.24	1.97	1.75	1.56	2.44	2.12	1.87	1.66	2.64	2.27	1.98	1.75	2.84	2.42	2.09	1.83	0
1	2.31	2.03	1.80	1.61	2.51	2.19	1.92	1.71	2.72	2.34	2.04	1.80	2.92	2.49	2.15	1.88	1
2	2.38	2.09	1.85	1.66	2.59	2.25	1.98	1.76	2.80	2.41	2.10	1.85	3.01	2.57	2.22	1.94	2
3	2.45	2.15	1.91	1.71	2.66	2.32	2.04	1.81	2.88	2.48	2.16	1.91	3.10	2.64	2.28	2.00	3
4	2.52	2.22	1.97	1.76	2.74	2.39	2.10	1.87	2.97	2.56	2.23	1.96	3.19	2.72	2.35	2.06	4
5	2.60	2.28	2.03	1.81	2.83	2.46	2.16	1.92	3.06	2.63	2.30	2.02	3.29	2.81	2.42	2.12	5
6	2.67	2.35	2.09	1.87	2.91	2.53	2.23	1.98	3.15	2.71	2.37	2.08	3.39	2.89	2.50	2.18	6
7	2.75	2.42	2.15	1.92	3.00	2.61	2.30	2.04	3.24	2.79	2.44	2.15	3.49	2.98	2.57	2.25	7
8	2.84	2.49	2.21	1.98	3.09	2.69	2.36	2.10	3.34	2.88	2.51	2.21	3.60	3.07	2.65	2.32	8
9	2.92	2.57	2.28	2.04	3.18	2.77	2.43	2.16	3.44	2.96	2.58	2.28	3.70	3.16	2.73	2.39	9
10	3.01	2.65	2.35	2.10	3.28	2.85	2.51	2.23	3.55	3.05	2.66	2.35	3.81	3.25	2.81	2.46	10
11	3.10	2.73	2.42	2.16	3.38	2.94	2.58	2.29	3.65	3.15	2.74	2.42	3.93	3.35	2.89	2.53	11
12	3.19	2.81	2.49	2.23	3.48	3.03	2.66	2.36	3.76	3.24	2.82	2.49	4.05	3.45	2.98	2.61	12
13	3.29	2.89	2.57	2.30	3.58	3.12	2.74	2.43	3.87	3.34	2.91	2.56	4.17	3.55	3.07	2.69	13
14	3.39	2.98	2.64	2.36	3.69	3.21	2.82	2.51	3.99	3.44	3.00	2.64	4.29	3.66	3.16	2.77	14
15	3.49	3.07	2.72	2.44	3.80	3.31	2.91	2.58	4.11	3.54	3.09	2.72	4.42	3.77	3.26	2.85	15
16	3.59	3.16	2.80	2.51	3.91	3.41	2.99	2.66	4.23	3.65	3.18	2.80	4.56	3.88	3.35	2.93	16
17	3.70	3.25	2.89	2.58	4.03	3.51	3.08	2.74	4.36	3.76	3.27	2.88	4.69	4.00	3.46	3.02	17
18	3.81	3.35	2.97	2.66	4.15	3.61	3.18	2.82	4.49	3.87	3.37	2.97	4.83	4.12	3.56	3.11	18
19	3.93	3.45	3.06	2.74	4.28	3.72	3.27	2.91	4.63	3.98	3.47	3.06	4.98	4.24	3.67	3.21	19
20	4.04	3.56	3.16	2.82	4.40	3.83	3.37	2.99	4.76	4.10	3.58	3.15	5.13	4.37	3.78	3.30	20
21	4.17	3.66	3.25	2.91	4.54	3.95	3.47	3.08	4.91	4.23	3.68	3.25	5.28	4.50	3.89	3.40	21
22	4.29	3.77	3.35	3.00	4.67	4.07	3.58	3.18	5.05	4.35	3.80	3.34	5.44	4.64	4.01	3.50	22
23	4.42	3.89	3.45	3.09	4.81	4.19	3.68	3.27	5.21	4.48	3.91	3.44	5.60	4.78	4.13	3.61	23
24	4.55	4.00	3.55	3.18	4.96	4.31	3.79	3.37	5.36	4.62	4.03	3.55	5.77	4.92	4.25	3.72	24
25	4.69	4.12	3.66	3.27	5.11	4.44	3.91	3.47	5.52	4.76	4.15	3.65	5.94	5.07	4.38	3.83	25
26	4.83	4.25	3.77	3.37	5.26	4.58	4.02	3.57	5.69	4.90	4.27	3.76	6.12	5.22	4.51	3.94	26
27	4.97	4.37	3.88	3.47	5.42	4.71	4.15	3.68	5.86	5.05	4.40	3.88	6.31	5.38	4.64	4.06	27
28	5.12	4.50	4.00	3.58	5.58	4.85	4.27	3.79	6.04	5.20	4.53	3.99	6.49	5.54	4.78	4.18	28
29	5.28	4.64	4.12	3.68	5.75	5.00	4.40	3.90	6.22	5.35	4.67	4.11	6.69	5.70	4.93	4.31	29
30	5.44	4.78	4.24	3.79	5.92	5.15	4.53	4.02	6.40	5.52	4.81	4.24	6.89	5.87	5.07	4.44	30
31	5.60	4.92	4.37	3.91	6.10	5.30	4.67	4.14	6.60	5.68	4.95	4.36	7.10	6.05	5.23	4.57	31
32	5.77	5.07	4.50	4.03	6.28	5.46	4.81	4.27	6.79	5.85	5.10	4.49	7.31	6.23	5.38	4.71	32
33	5.94	5.22	4.63	4.15	6.47	5.63	4.95	4.40	7.00	6.03	5.25	4.63	7.53	6.42	5.55	4.85	33
34	6.12	5.38	4.77	4.27	6.66	5.80	5.10	4.53	7.21	6.21	5.41	4.77	7.75	6.61	5.71	5.00	34
35	6.30	5.54	4.92	4.40	6.86	5.97	5.25	4.66	7.42	6.39	5.57	4.91	7.99	6.81	5.88	5.14	35
36	6.49	5.71	5.06	4.53	7.07	6.15	5.41	4.80	7.65	6.59	5.74	5.06	8.23	7.01	6.06	5.30	36
37	6.68	5.88	5.22	4.67	7.28	6.33	5.57	4.95	7.88	6.78	5.91	5.21	8.47	7.22	6.24	5.46	37
38	6.88	6.05	5.37	4.81	7.50	6.52	5.74	5.10	8.11	6.99	6.09	5.37	8.73	7.44	6.43	5.62	38
39	7.09	6.24	5.53	4.95	7.72	6.72	5.91	5.25	8.35	7.20	6.27	5.53	8.99	7.66	6.62	5.79	39
40	7.30	6.42	5.70	5.10	7.95	6.92	6.09	5.41	8.61	7.41	6.46	5.69	9.26	7.89	6.82	5.96	40
41	7.52	6.61	5.87	5.25	8.19	7.13	6.27	5.57	8.86	7.63	6.65	5.86	9.54	8.13	7.02	6.14	41
42	7.75	6.81	6.05	5.41	8.44	7.34	6.46	5.73	9.13	7.86	6.85	6.04	9.82	8.37	7.24	6.33	42
43	7.98	7.02	6.23	5.57	8.69	7.56	6.65	5.91	9.40	8.10	7.06	6.22	10.12	8.63	7.45	6.52	43
44	8.22	7.23	6.41	5.74	8.95	7.79	6.85	6.08	9.69	8.34	7.27	6.41	10.42	8.88	7.68	6.71	44
45	8.47	7.44	6.61	5.91	9.22	8.02	7.06	6.27	9.98	8.59	7.49	6.60	10.73	9.15	7.91	6.91	45
46	8.72	7.67	6.80	6.09	9.50	8.26	7.27	6.45	10.28	8.85	7.71	6.80	11.06	9.43	8.14	7.12	46
47	8.98	7.90	7.01	6.27	9.78	8.51	7.49	6.65	10.58	9.12	7.95	7.00	11.39	9.71	8.39	7.34	47
48	9.25	8.14	7.22	6.46	10.08	8.77	7.71	6.85	10.90	9.39	8.18	7.21	11.73	10.00	8.64	7.56	48
49	9.53	8.38	7.44	6.65	10.38	9.03	7.94	7.05	11.23	9.67	8.43	7.43	12.08	10.30	8.90	7.78	49
50	9.82	8.63	7.66	6.85	10.69	9.30	8.18	7.26	11.57	9.96	8.68	7.65	12.44	10.61	9.17	8.02	50

II. Retirement Planning where Salary Keeps Pace with Low 3% Inflation
Planned Retirement Age 62

Table 1 - Percent of Salary Replaced by a 401(k) Account Equal to Current Annual Salary   II-62-1

Probable Life Expectancy at Retirement

	23.2 (Same as Male Avg.)				25.7 (Better than Male Avg.)				28.3 (Same as Female Avg.)				31 (Better than Female Avg.)				
	4% / 4%	6% / 5%	8% / 6%	10% / 7%	4% / 4%	6% / 5%	8% / 6%	10% / 7%	4% / 4%	6% / 5%	8% / 6%	10% / 7%	4% / 4%	6% / 5%	8% / 6%	10% / 7%	
Yrs. to Ret.	Expected Return				(Pre-Retirement/Post-Retirement)				(Pre-Retirement/Post-Retirement)				Expected Return				Yrs. to Ret.
0	4.90	5.52	6.16	6.83	4.47	5.08	5.72	6.40	4.10	4.71	5.36	6.03	3.79	4.40	5.05	5.73	0
1	4.95	5.68	6.46	7.30	4.51	5.23	6.00	6.83	4.14	4.85	5.62	6.45	3.83	4.53	5.29	6.12	1
2	5.00	5.84	6.78	7.79	4.55	5.38	6.29	7.30	4.18	4.99	5.89	6.88	3.86	4.66	5.55	6.54	2
3	5.05	6.01	7.10	8.32	4.60	5.54	6.60	7.79	4.22	5.14	6.18	7.35	3.90	4.80	5.82	6.98	3
4	5.09	6.19	7.45	8.89	4.64	5.70	6.92	8.32	4.26	5.29	6.48	7.85	3.94	4.94	6.10	7.45	4
5	5.14	6.37	7.81	9.49	4.69	5.86	7.25	8.89	4.30	5.44	6.79	8.39	3.98	5.08	6.40	7.96	5
6	5.19	6.55	8.19	10.14	4.73	6.03	7.61	9.49	4.35	5.60	7.12	8.96	4.02	5.23	6.71	8.50	6
7	5.24	6.75	8.59	10.83	4.78	6.21	7.97	10.14	4.39	5.76	7.47	9.56	4.06	5.38	7.03	9.08	7
8	5.29	6.94	9.00	11.56	4.82	6.39	8.36	10.83	4.43	5.93	7.83	10.21	4.09	5.54	7.37	9.70	8
9	5.35	7.14	9.44	12.35	4.87	6.58	8.77	11.56	4.47	6.10	8.21	10.91	4.13	5.70	7.73	10.36	9
10	5.40	7.35	9.90	13.19	4.92	6.77	9.19	12.35	4.52	6.28	8.60	11.65	4.17	5.86	8.11	11.06	10
11	5.45	7.57	10.38	14.09	4.97	6.96	9.64	13.19	4.56	6.46	9.02	12.44	4.22	6.03	8.50	11.81	11
12	5.50	7.79	10.88	15.05	5.01	7.17	10.10	14.09	4.61	6.65	9.46	13.29	4.26	6.21	8.91	12.62	12
13	5.56	8.01	11.41	16.07	5.06	7.38	10.59	15.04	4.65	6.84	9.92	14.19	4.30	6.39	9.35	13.48	13
14	5.61	8.24	11.96	17.16	5.11	7.59	11.11	16.07	4.69	7.04	10.40	15.16	4.34	6.58	9.80	14.39	14
15	5.66	8.48	12.54	18.33	5.16	7.81	11.65	17.16	4.74	7.25	10.90	16.19	4.38	6.77	10.27	15.37	15
16	5.72	8.73	13.15	19.57	5.21	8.04	12.21	18.33	4.79	7.46	11.43	17.29	4.42	6.96	10.77	16.42	16
17	5.78	8.99	13.79	20.91	5.26	8.27	12.80	19.57	4.83	7.67	11.99	18.47	4.47	7.17	11.29	17.53	17
18	5.83	9.25	14.45	22.33	5.31	8.51	13.43	20.90	4.88	7.90	12.57	19.72	4.51	7.38	11.84	18.72	18
19	5.89	9.52	15.16	23.85	5.36	8.76	14.08	22.32	4.93	8.13	13.18	21.06	4.55	7.59	12.42	20.00	19
20	5.94	9.79	15.89	25.47	5.42	9.02	14.76	23.84	4.97	8.36	13.82	22.50	4.60	7.81	13.02	21.36	20
21	6.00	10.08	16.66	27.20	5.47	9.28	15.48	25.46	5.02	8.61	14.49	24.03	4.64	8.04	13.65	22.81	21
22	6.06	10.37	17.47	29.05	5.52	9.55	16.23	27.19	5.07	8.86	15.19	25.66	4.69	8.27	14.31	24.36	22
23	6.12	10.67	18.32	31.02	5.58	9.83	17.01	29.04	5.12	9.12	15.93	27.40	4.73	8.51	15.01	26.02	23
24	6.18	10.98	19.21	33.13	5.63	10.11	17.84	31.02	5.17	9.38	16.70	29.27	4.78	8.76	15.73	27.79	24
25	6.24	11.30	20.14	35.39	5.68	10.41	18.70	33.13	5.22	9.65	17.51	31.26	4.83	9.02	16.50	29.68	25
26	6.30	11.63	21.11	37.79	5.74	10.71	19.61	35.38	5.27	9.94	18.36	33.38	4.87	9.28	17.30	31.69	26
27	6.36	11.97	22.14	40.36	5.80	11.02	20.56	37.79	5.32	10.22	19.25	35.65	4.92	9.55	18.14	33.85	27
28	6.42	12.32	23.21	43.11	5.85	11.34	21.56	40.36	5.37	10.52	20.18	38.08	4.97	9.83	19.02	36.15	28
29	6.48	12.68	24.34	46.04	5.91	11.67	22.60	43.10	5.43	10.83	21.16	40.67	5.02	10.11	19.94	38.61	29
30	6.55	13.05	25.52	49.17	5.97	12.01	23.70	46.03	5.48	11.14	22.19	43.43	5.06	10.41	20.90	41.24	30
31	6.61	13.43	26.75	52.51	6.02	12.36	24.85	49.16	5.53	11.47	23.26	46.38	5.11	10.71	21.92	44.04	31
32	6.67	13.82	28.05	56.08	6.08	12.72	26.06	52.51	5.59	11.80	24.39	49.54	5.16	11.02	22.98	47.03	32
33	6.74	14.22	29.41	59.90	6.14	13.09	27.32	56.08	5.64	12.14	25.58	52.91	5.21	11.34	24.10	50.23	33
34	6.81	14.63	30.84	63.97	6.20	13.47	28.64	59.89	5.69	12.50	26.82	56.51	5.26	11.67	25.26	53.65	34
35	6.87	15.06	32.34	68.32	6.26	13.86	30.03	63.96	5.75	12.86	28.12	60.35	5.31	12.01	26.49	57.30	35
36	6.94	15.50	33.90	72.97	6.32	14.27	31.49	68.31	5.81	13.24	29.48	64.45	5.37	12.36	27.78	61.19	36
37	7.00	15.95	35.55	77.93	6.38	14.68	33.02	72.96	5.86	13.62	30.91	68.83	5.42	12.72	29.12	65.35	37
38	7.07	16.41	37.27	83.23	6.45	15.11	34.62	77.92	5.92	14.02	32.41	73.51	5.47	13.09	30.53	69.80	38
39	7.14	16.89	39.08	88.89	6.51	15.55	36.30	83.21	5.98	14.43	33.98	78.51	5.52	13.47	32.02	74.54	39
40	7.21	17.38	40.97	94.93	6.57	16.00	38.06	88.87	6.03	14.85	35.63	83.85	5.58	13.86	33.57	79.61	40
41	7.28	17.89	42.96	101.39	6.63	16.47	39.90	94.92	6.09	15.28	37.36	89.55	5.63	14.27	35.20	85.03	41
42	7.35	18.41	45.05	108.28	6.70	16.96	41.84	101.37	6.15	15.72	39.17	95.64	5.69	14.68	36.90	90.81	42
43	7.42	18.94	47.23	115.64	6.76	17.44	43.87	108.26	6.21	16.18	41.07	102.15	5.74	15.11	38.69	96.98	43
44	7.49	19.49	49.52	123.51	6.83	17.95	46.00	115.63	6.27	16.65	43.06	109.09	5.80	15.55	40.57	103.58	44
45	7.57	20.06	51.92	131.90	6.90	18.47	48.23	123.49	6.33	17.13	45.15	116.51	5.85	16.00	42.54	110.62	45
46	7.64	20.65	54.44	140.87	6.96	19.00	50.57	131.89	6.39	17.63	47.34	124.44	5.91	16.47	44.60	118.14	46
47	7.71	21.25	57.08	150.45	7.03	19.56	53.02	140.85	6.46	18.15	49.63	132.90	5.97	16.94	46.76	126.18	47
48	7.79	21.86	59.85	160.68	7.10	20.13	55.59	150.43	6.52	18.67	52.04	141.93	6.02	17.44	49.03	134.76	48
49	7.87	22.50	62.75	171.61	7.17	20.71	58.29	160.66	6.58	19.22	54.57	151.59	6.08	17.95	51.41	143.92	49
50	7.94	23.16	65.80	183.28	7.24	21.32	61.11	171.59	6.65	19.78	57.21	161.89	6.14	18.47	53.90	153.71	50

Appendix A

II. Retirement Planning where Salary Keeps Pace with Low 3% Inflation
Planned Retirement Age 62

Table 2 - Percent of Salary Replaced by a 401(k) Contribution of 1% of Current Salary   II-62-2

Probable Life Expectancy at Retirement

Yrs. to Ret.	23.2 (Same as Male Avg.)				25.7 (Better than Male Avg.)				28.3 (Same as Female Avg.)				31 (Better than Female Avg.)				Yrs. to Ret.
	4%/4%	6%/5%	8%/6%	10%/7%	4%/4%	6%/5%	8%/6%	10%/7%	4%/4%	6%/5%	8%/6%	10%/7%	4%/4%	6%/5%	8%/6%	10%/7%	
	Expected Return				(Pre-Retirement/Post-Retirement)				(Pre-Retirement/Post-Retirement)				Expected Return				
0	0.00	0.00	0.00	0.00	0.00	0.00	0.00	0.00	0.00	0.00	0.00	0.00	0.00	0.00	0.00	0.00	0
1	0.05	0.06	0.06	0.07	0.04	0.05	0.06	0.06	0.04	0.05	0.05	0.06	0.04	0.04	0.05	0.06	1
2	0.10	0.11	0.13	0.14	0.09	0.10	0.12	0.13	0.08	0.10	0.11	0.12	0.08	0.09	0.10	0.12	2
3	0.15	0.17	0.19	0.22	0.14	0.16	0.18	0.21	0.12	0.15	0.17	0.19	0.11	0.14	0.16	0.18	3
4	0.20	0.23	0.27	0.30	0.18	0.21	0.25	0.28	0.17	0.20	0.23	0.27	0.15	0.18	0.22	0.25	4
5	0.25	0.29	0.34	0.39	0.23	0.27	0.32	0.37	0.21	0.25	0.30	0.35	0.19	0.23	0.28	0.33	5
6	0.30	0.36	0.42	0.49	0.27	0.33	0.39	0.46	0.25	0.30	0.36	0.43	0.23	0.28	0.34	0.41	6
7	0.35	0.42	0.50	0.59	0.32	0.39	0.46	0.55	0.30	0.36	0.43	0.52	0.27	0.34	0.41	0.49	7
8	0.41	0.49	0.59	0.70	0.37	0.45	0.54	0.65	0.34	0.42	0.51	0.61	0.31	0.39	0.48	0.58	8
9	0.46	0.56	0.68	0.81	0.42	0.51	0.63	0.76	0.38	0.48	0.59	0.72	0.35	0.45	0.55	0.68	9
10	0.51	0.63	0.77	0.94	0.47	0.58	0.71	0.88	0.43	0.54	0.67	0.83	0.40	0.50	0.63	0.78	10
11	0.57	0.70	0.87	1.07	0.52	0.65	0.81	1.00	0.47	0.60	0.76	0.94	0.44	0.56	0.71	0.89	11
12	0.62	0.78	0.97	1.21	0.57	0.72	0.90	1.13	0.52	0.67	0.85	1.07	0.48	0.62	0.80	1.01	12
13	0.68	0.86	1.08	1.36	0.62	0.79	1.00	1.27	0.57	0.73	0.94	1.20	0.52	0.68	0.89	1.14	13
14	0.73	0.94	1.20	1.52	0.67	0.86	1.11	1.42	0.61	0.80	1.04	1.34	0.57	0.75	0.98	1.27	14
15	0.79	1.02	1.31	1.69	0.72	0.94	1.22	1.58	0.66	0.87	1.14	1.49	0.61	0.81	1.08	1.42	15
16	0.84	1.10	1.44	1.87	0.77	1.02	1.34	1.75	0.71	0.94	1.25	1.66	0.65	0.88	1.18	1.57	16
17	0.90	1.19	1.57	2.07	0.82	1.10	1.46	1.94	0.75	1.02	1.37	1.83	0.70	0.95	1.29	1.74	17
18	0.96	1.28	1.71	2.28	0.87	1.18	1.59	2.13	0.80	1.09	1.49	2.01	0.74	1.02	1.40	1.91	18
19	1.02	1.37	1.85	2.50	0.93	1.26	1.72	2.34	0.85	1.17	1.61	2.21	0.79	1.10	1.52	2.10	19
20	1.08	1.47	2.01	2.74	0.98	1.35	1.86	2.57	0.90	1.25	1.74	2.42	0.83	1.17	1.64	2.30	20
21	1.14	1.57	2.16	3.00	1.03	1.44	2.01	2.80	0.95	1.34	1.88	2.65	0.88	1.25	1.77	2.51	21
22	1.20	1.67	2.33	3.27	1.09	1.54	2.17	3.06	1.00	1.42	2.03	2.89	0.92	1.33	1.91	2.74	22
23	1.26	1.77	2.51	3.56	1.14	1.63	2.33	3.33	1.05	1.51	2.18	3.14	0.97	1.41	2.05	2.98	23
24	1.32	1.88	2.69	3.87	1.20	1.73	2.50	3.62	1.10	1.60	2.34	3.42	1.02	1.50	2.20	3.24	24
25	1.38	1.99	2.88	4.20	1.26	1.83	2.68	3.93	1.15	1.70	2.51	3.71	1.07	1.59	2.36	3.52	25
26	1.44	2.10	3.08	4.55	1.31	1.93	2.86	4.26	1.21	1.79	2.68	4.02	1.11	1.68	2.53	3.82	26
27	1.50	2.22	3.29	4.93	1.37	2.04	3.06	4.62	1.26	1.89	2.86	4.36	1.16	1.77	2.70	4.14	27
28	1.57	2.34	3.52	5.33	1.43	2.15	3.26	4.99	1.31	2.00	3.06	4.71	1.21	1.86	2.88	4.47	28
29	1.63	2.46	3.75	5.77	1.49	2.26	3.48	5.40	1.37	2.10	3.26	5.09	1.26	1.96	3.07	4.84	29
30	1.70	2.59	3.99	6.23	1.55	2.38	3.71	5.83	1.42	2.21	3.47	5.50	1.31	2.06	3.27	5.22	30
31	1.76	2.72	4.25	6.72	1.61	2.50	3.94	6.29	1.48	2.32	3.69	5.93	1.36	2.17	3.48	5.63	31
32	1.83	2.85	4.51	7.24	1.67	2.63	4.19	6.78	1.53	2.44	3.92	6.40	1.41	2.27	3.70	6.07	32
33	1.90	2.99	4.79	7.80	1.73	2.75	4.45	7.31	1.59	2.55	4.17	6.89	1.47	2.38	3.93	6.54	33
34	1.96	3.13	5.09	8.40	1.79	2.88	4.73	7.87	1.64	2.68	4.42	7.42	1.52	2.50	4.17	7.05	34
35	2.03	3.28	5.40	9.04	1.85	3.02	5.01	8.47	1.70	2.80	4.69	7.99	1.57	2.61	4.42	7.58	35
36	2.10	3.43	5.72	9.73	1.91	3.16	5.31	9.11	1.76	2.93	4.97	8.59	1.62	2.73	4.69	8.16	36
37	2.17	3.58	6.06	10.46	1.98	3.30	5.63	9.79	1.82	3.06	5.27	9.24	1.68	2.86	4.96	8.77	37
38	2.24	3.74	6.41	11.23	2.04	3.45	5.96	10.52	1.87	3.20	5.58	9.92	1.73	2.99	5.25	9.42	38
39	2.31	3.91	6.79	12.07	2.10	3.60	6.30	11.30	1.93	3.34	5.90	10.66	1.79	3.12	5.56	10.12	39
40	2.38	4.08	7.18	12.96	2.17	3.75	6.67	12.13	1.99	3.48	6.24	11.44	1.84	3.25	5.88	10.87	40
41	2.45	4.25	7.59	13.90	2.24	3.91	7.05	13.02	2.05	3.63	6.60	12.28	1.90	3.39	6.22	11.66	41
42	2.53	4.43	8.02	14.92	2.30	4.08	7.45	13.97	2.11	3.78	6.97	13.18	1.95	3.53	6.57	12.51	42
43	2.60	4.61	8.47	16.00	2.37	4.25	7.86	14.98	2.18	3.94	7.36	14.13	2.01	3.68	6.94	13.42	43
44	2.67	4.80	8.94	17.16	2.44	4.42	8.30	16.06	2.24	4.10	7.77	15.16	2.07	3.83	7.32	14.39	44
45	2.75	5.00	9.44	18.39	2.50	4.60	8.76	17.22	2.30	4.27	8.20	16.25	2.13	3.99	7.73	15.43	45
46	2.82	5.20	9.95	19.71	2.57	4.79	9.25	18.45	2.36	4.44	8.66	17.41	2.18	4.15	8.15	16.53	46
47	2.90	5.40	10.50	21.12	2.64	4.98	9.75	19.77	2.43	4.62	9.13	18.66	2.24	4.31	8.60	17.71	47
48	2.98	5.62	11.07	22.63	2.71	5.17	10.28	21.18	2.49	4.80	9.63	19.99	2.30	4.48	9.07	18.97	48
49	3.06	5.84	11.67	24.23	2.78	5.37	10.84	22.69	2.56	4.98	10.15	21.40	2.36	4.65	9.56	20.32	49
50	3.13	6.06	12.30	25.95	2.86	5.58	11.42	24.29	2.62	5.18	10.69	22.92	2.42	4.83	10.07	21.76	50

II. Retirement Planning where Salary Keeps Pace with Low 3% Inflation
Planned Retirement Age 62

Table 3 - 401(k) Contribution (% of Current Sal.) Needed to Replace 10% of Sal. at Retirement   II-62-3

Probable Life Expectancy at Retirement

Yrs. to Ret.	23.2 (Same as Male Avg.)				25.7 (Better than Male Avg.)				28.3 (Same as Female Avg.)				31 (Better than Female Avg.)				Yrs. to Ret.
	4% / 4%	6% / 5%	8% / 6%	10% / 7%	4% / 4%	6% / 5%	8% / 6%	10% / 7%	4% / 4%	6% / 5%	8% / 6%	10% / 7%	4% / 4%	6% / 5%	8% / 6%	10% / 7%	
	Expected Return		(Pre-Retirement/Post-Retirement)				(Pre-Retirement/Post-Retirement)				Expected Return						
0																	0
1	204.04	181.23	162.26	146.37	223.92	196.87	174.70	156.34	243.82	212.19	186.61	165.70	263.81	227.23	198.07	174.53	1
2	101.53	89.31	79.21	70.78	111.42	97.02	85.28	75.60	121.32	104.57	91.10	80.13	131.27	111.99	96.69	84.40	2
3	67.36	58.68	51.55	45.62	73.92	63.75	55.50	48.73	80.49	68.71	59.28	51.64	87.09	73.58	62.92	54.39	3
4	50.27	43.38	37.73	33.06	55.17	47.12	40.62	35.32	60.08	50.79	43.39	37.43	65.00	54.39	46.06	39.43	4
5	40.02	34.20	29.45	25.55	43.92	37.15	31.71	27.30	47.83	40.04	33.87	28.93	51.75	42.88	35.95	30.47	5
6	33.19	28.08	23.95	20.56	36.42	30.50	25.78	21.97	39.66	32.88	27.54	23.28	42.91	35.21	29.23	24.52	6
7	28.31	23.72	20.02	17.02	31.07	25.76	21.55	18.18	33.83	27.77	23.02	19.26	36.60	29.74	24.44	20.29	7
8	24.65	20.45	17.08	14.37	27.05	22.21	18.39	15.35	29.46	23.94	19.65	16.27	31.87	25.64	20.85	17.13	8
9	21.81	17.90	14.81	12.32	23.93	19.45	15.94	13.16	26.06	20.96	17.03	13.95	28.19	22.45	18.07	14.69	9
10	19.53	15.87	12.99	10.69	21.43	17.24	13.99	11.42	23.34	18.59	14.94	12.11	25.25	19.90	15.86	12.75	10
11	17.67	14.22	11.51	9.37	19.39	15.44	12.39	10.01	21.11	16.64	13.24	10.61	22.84	17.82	14.05	11.18	11
12	16.12	12.83	10.28	8.28	17.69	13.94	11.07	8.84	19.26	15.03	11.83	9.37	20.84	16.09	12.55	9.87	12
13	14.80	11.67	9.25	7.36	16.24	12.68	9.96	7.86	17.69	13.66	10.64	8.33	19.14	14.63	11.29	8.78	13
14	13.68	10.67	8.37	6.58	15.01	11.59	9.01	7.03	16.34	12.49	9.62	7.45	17.68	13.38	10.21	7.85	14
15	12.70	9.81	7.60	5.91	13.94	10.66	8.19	6.32	15.18	11.48	8.75	6.70	16.42	12.30	9.28	7.05	15
16	11.85	9.05	6.94	5.34	13.00	9.84	7.47	5.70	14.16	10.60	7.98	6.04	15.32	11.35	8.47	6.36	16
17	11.10	8.39	6.36	4.83	12.18	9.12	6.85	5.16	13.26	9.83	7.32	5.47	14.35	10.52	7.77	5.76	17
18	10.43	7.80	5.85	4.39	11.45	8.48	6.30	4.69	12.46	9.14	6.73	4.97	13.48	9.78	7.14	5.23	18
19	9.83	7.28	5.39	4.00	10.79	7.91	5.81	4.27	11.75	8.52	6.20	4.52	12.71	9.13	6.58	4.77	19
20	9.29	6.81	4.99	3.65	10.20	7.39	5.37	3.90	11.11	7.97	5.73	4.13	12.02	8.53	6.09	4.35	20
21	8.81	6.38	4.62	3.34	9.66	6.93	4.97	3.57	10.52	7.47	5.31	3.78	11.39	8.00	5.64	3.98	21
22	8.36	6.00	4.29	3.06	9.18	6.51	4.62	3.27	10.00	7.02	4.93	3.47	10.82	7.52	5.24	3.65	22
23	7.96	5.64	3.99	2.81	8.74	6.13	4.30	3.00	9.51	6.61	4.59	3.18	10.29	7.08	4.87	3.35	23
24	7.59	5.32	3.72	2.59	8.33	5.78	4.00	2.76	9.07	6.23	4.28	2.93	9.82	6.68	4.54	3.08	24
25	7.25	5.03	3.47	2.38	7.96	5.46	3.74	2.54	8.67	5.89	3.99	2.70	9.38	6.31	4.24	2.84	25
26	6.94	4.76	3.24	2.20	7.61	5.17	3.49	2.35	8.29	5.57	3.73	2.49	8.97	5.97	3.96	2.62	26
27	6.65	4.51	3.04	2.03	7.29	4.90	3.27	2.17	7.94	5.28	3.49	2.30	8.59	5.65	3.71	2.42	27
28	6.38	4.28	2.84	1.87	7.00	4.65	3.06	2.00	7.62	5.01	3.27	2.12	8.25	5.36	3.47	2.24	28
29	6.13	4.06	2.67	1.73	6.72	4.42	2.87	1.85	7.32	4.76	3.07	1.96	7.92	5.10	3.26	2.07	29
30	5.89	3.87	2.51	1.61	6.47	4.20	2.70	1.72	7.04	4.53	2.88	1.82	7.62	4.85	3.06	1.92	30
31	5.67	3.68	2.36	1.49	6.23	4.00	2.54	1.59	6.78	4.31	2.71	1.69	7.34	4.61	2.87	1.78	31
32	5.47	3.51	2.22	1.38	6.00	3.81	2.39	1.47	6.53	4.11	2.55	1.56	7.07	4.40	2.70	1.65	32
33	5.28	3.34	2.09	1.28	5.79	3.63	2.25	1.37	6.30	3.92	2.40	1.45	6.82	4.19	2.55	1.53	33
34	5.09	3.19	1.97	1.19	5.59	3.47	2.12	1.27	6.09	3.74	2.26	1.35	6.59	4.00	2.40	1.42	34
35	4.92	3.05	1.85	1.11	5.40	3.31	2.00	1.18	5.88	3.57	2.13	1.25	6.37	3.82	2.26	1.32	35
36	4.76	2.92	1.75	1.03	5.23	3.17	1.88	1.10	5.69	3.41	2.01	1.16	6.16	3.66	2.13	1.23	36
37	4.61	2.79	1.65	0.96	5.06	3.03	1.78	1.02	5.51	3.27	1.90	1.08	5.96	3.50	2.01	1.14	37
38	4.47	2.67	1.56	0.89	4.90	2.90	1.68	0.95	5.34	3.13	1.79	1.01	5.77	3.35	1.90	1.06	38
39	4.33	2.56	1.47	0.83	4.75	2.78	1.59	0.89	5.17	3.00	1.69	0.94	5.60	3.21	1.80	0.99	39
40	4.20	2.45	1.39	0.77	4.61	2.66	1.50	0.82	5.02	2.87	1.60	0.87	5.43	3.08	1.70	0.92	40
41	4.08	2.35	1.32	0.72	4.47	2.56	1.42	0.77	4.87	2.75	1.52	0.81	5.27	2.95	1.61	0.86	41
42	3.96	2.26	1.25	0.67	4.34	2.45	1.34	0.72	4.73	2.64	1.43	0.76	5.12	2.83	1.52	0.80	42
43	3.85	2.17	1.18	0.62	4.22	2.35	1.27	0.67	4.60	2.54	1.36	0.71	4.97	2.72	1.44	0.75	43
44	3.74	2.08	1.12	0.58	4.10	2.26	1.20	0.62	4.47	2.44	1.29	0.66	4.84	2.61	1.37	0.69	44
45	3.64	2.00	1.06	0.54	3.99	2.17	1.14	0.58	4.35	2.34	1.22	0.62	4.70	2.51	1.29	0.65	45
46	3.54	1.92	1.00	0.51	3.89	2.09	1.08	0.54	4.23	2.25	1.16	0.57	4.58	2.41	1.23	0.60	46
47	3.45	1.85	0.95	0.47	3.78	2.01	1.03	0.51	4.12	2.17	1.10	0.54	4.46	2.32	1.16	0.56	47
48	3.36	1.78	0.90	0.44	3.69	1.93	0.97	0.47	4.01	2.08	1.04	0.50	4.34	2.23	1.10	0.53	48
49	3.27	1.71	0.81	0.41	3.59	1.86	0.92	0.44	3.91	2.01	0.99	0.47	4.23	2.15	1.05	0.49	49
50	3.19	1.65	0.81	0.39	3.50	1.79	0.88	0.41	3.81	1.93	0.94	0.44	4.12	2.07	0.99	0.46	50

II. Retirement Planning where Salary Keeps Pace with Low 3% Inflation
Planned Retirement Age 62

Table 4 - Accumulation at Retirement (Multiple of Current Sal.) for 10% Sal. Replacement
II-62-4

Probable Life Expectancy at Retirement

	23.2 (Same as Male Avg.)				25.7 (Better than Male Avg.)				28.3 (Same as Female Avg.)				31 (Better than Female Avg.)				
	4% / 4%	6% / 5%	8% / 6%	10% / 7%	4% / 4%	6% / 5%	8% / 6%	10% / 7%	4% / 4%	6% / 5%	8% / 6%	10% / 7%	4% / 4%	6% / 5%	8% / 6%	10% / 7%	
Yrs. to Ret.	Expected Return				(Pre-Retirement/Post-Retirement)				(Pre-Retirement/Post-Retirement)				Expected Return				Yrs. to Ret.
0	2.04	1.81	1.62	1.46	2.24	1.97	1.75	1.56	2.44	2.12	1.87	1.66	2.64	2.27	1.98	1.75	0
1	2.10	1.87	1.67	1.51	2.31	2.03	1.80	1.61	2.51	2.19	1.92	1.71	2.72	2.34	2.04	1.80	1
2	2.16	1.92	1.72	1.55	2.38	2.09	1.85	1.66	2.59	2.25	1.98	1.76	2.80	2.41	2.10	1.85	2
3	2.23	1.98	1.77	1.60	2.45	2.15	1.91	1.71	2.66	2.32	2.04	1.81	2.88	2.48	2.16	1.91	3
4	2.30	2.04	1.83	1.65	2.52	2.22	1.97	1.76	2.74	2.39	2.10	1.87	2.97	2.56	2.23	1.96	4
5	2.37	2.10	1.88	1.70	2.60	2.28	2.03	1.81	2.83	2.46	2.16	1.92	3.06	2.63	2.30	2.02	5
6	2.44	2.16	1.94	1.75	2.67	2.35	2.09	1.87	2.91	2.53	2.23	1.98	3.15	2.71	2.37	2.08	6
7	2.51	2.23	2.00	1.80	2.75	2.42	2.15	1.92	3.00	2.61	2.30	2.04	3.24	2.79	2.44	2.15	7
8	2.58	2.30	2.06	1.85	2.84	2.49	2.21	1.98	3.09	2.69	2.36	2.10	3.34	2.88	2.51	2.21	8
9	2.66	2.36	2.12	1.91	2.92	2.57	2.28	2.04	3.18	2.77	2.43	2.16	3.44	2.96	2.58	2.28	9
10	2.74	2.44	2.18	1.97	3.01	2.65	2.35	2.10	3.28	2.85	2.51	2.23	3.55	3.05	2.66	2.35	10
11	2.82	2.51	2.25	2.03	3.10	2.73	2.42	2.16	3.38	2.94	2.58	2.29	3.65	3.15	2.74	2.42	11
12	2.91	2.58	2.31	2.09	3.19	2.81	2.49	2.23	3.48	3.03	2.66	2.36	3.76	3.24	2.82	2.49	12
13	3.00	2.66	2.38	2.15	3.29	2.89	2.57	2.30	3.58	3.12	2.74	2.43	3.87	3.34	2.91	2.56	13
14	3.09	2.74	2.45	2.21	3.39	2.98	2.64	2.36	3.69	3.21	2.82	2.51	3.99	3.44	3.00	2.64	14
15	3.18	2.82	2.53	2.28	3.49	3.07	2.72	2.44	3.80	3.31	2.91	2.58	4.11	3.54	3.09	2.72	15
16	3.27	2.91	2.60	2.35	3.59	3.16	2.80	2.51	3.91	3.41	2.99	2.66	4.23	3.65	3.18	2.80	16
17	3.37	3.00	2.68	2.42	3.70	3.25	2.89	2.58	4.03	3.51	3.08	2.74	4.36	3.76	3.27	2.88	17
18	3.47	3.09	2.76	2.49	3.81	3.35	2.97	2.66	4.15	3.61	3.18	2.82	4.49	3.87	3.37	2.97	18
19	3.58	3.18	2.85	2.57	3.93	3.45	3.06	2.74	4.28	3.72	3.27	2.91	4.63	3.98	3.47	3.06	19
20	3.69	3.27	2.93	2.64	4.04	3.56	3.16	2.82	4.40	3.83	3.37	2.99	4.76	4.10	3.58	3.15	20
21	3.80	3.37	3.02	2.72	4.17	3.66	3.25	2.91	4.54	3.95	3.47	3.08	4.91	4.23	3.68	3.25	21
22	3.91	3.47	3.11	2.80	4.29	3.77	3.35	3.00	4.67	4.07	3.58	3.18	5.05	4.35	3.80	3.34	22
23	4.03	3.58	3.20	2.89	4.42	3.89	3.45	3.09	4.81	4.19	3.68	3.27	5.21	4.48	3.91	3.44	23
24	4.15	3.68	3.30	2.98	4.55	4.00	3.55	3.18	4.96	4.31	3.79	3.37	5.36	4.62	4.03	3.55	24
25	4.27	3.79	3.40	3.06	4.69	4.12	3.66	3.27	5.11	4.44	3.91	3.47	5.52	4.76	4.15	3.65	25
26	4.40	3.91	3.50	3.16	4.83	4.25	3.77	3.37	5.26	4.58	4.02	3.57	5.69	4.90	4.27	3.76	26
27	4.53	4.03	3.60	3.25	4.97	4.37	3.88	3.47	5.42	4.71	4.15	3.68	5.86	5.05	4.40	3.88	27
28	4.67	4.15	3.71	3.35	5.12	4.50	4.00	3.58	5.58	4.85	4.27	3.79	6.04	5.20	4.53	3.99	28
29	4.81	4.27	3.82	3.45	5.28	4.64	4.12	3.68	5.75	5.00	4.40	3.90	6.22	5.35	4.67	4.11	29
30	4.95	4.40	3.94	3.55	5.44	4.78	4.24	3.79	5.92	5.15	4.53	4.02	6.40	5.52	4.81	4.24	30
31	5.10	4.53	4.06	3.66	5.60	4.92	4.37	3.91	6.10	5.30	4.67	4.14	6.60	5.68	4.95	4.36	31
32	5.25	4.67	4.18	3.77	5.77	5.07	4.50	4.03	6.28	5.46	4.81	4.27	6.79	5.85	5.10	4.49	32
33	5.41	4.81	4.30	3.88	5.94	5.22	4.63	4.15	6.47	5.63	4.95	4.40	7.00	6.03	5.25	4.63	33
34	5.57	4.95	4.43	4.00	6.12	5.38	4.77	4.27	6.66	5.80	5.10	4.53	7.21	6.21	5.41	4.77	34
35	5.74	5.10	4.57	4.12	6.30	5.54	4.92	4.40	6.86	5.97	5.25	4.66	7.42	6.39	5.57	4.91	35
36	5.91	5.25	4.70	4.24	6.49	5.71	5.06	4.53	7.07	6.15	5.41	4.80	7.65	6.59	5.74	5.06	36
37	6.09	5.41	4.84	4.37	6.68	5.88	5.22	4.67	7.28	6.33	5.57	4.95	7.88	6.78	5.91	5.21	37
38	6.27	5.57	4.99	4.50	6.88	6.05	5.37	4.81	7.50	6.52	5.74	5.10	8.11	6.99	6.09	5.37	38
39	6.46	5.74	5.14	4.64	7.09	6.24	5.53	4.95	7.72	6.72	5.91	5.25	8.35	7.20	6.27	5.53	39
40	6.66	5.91	5.29	4.77	7.30	6.42	5.70	5.10	7.95	6.92	6.09	5.41	8.61	7.41	6.46	5.69	40
41	6.86	6.09	5.45	4.92	7.52	6.61	5.87	5.25	8.19	7.13	6.27	5.57	8.86	7.63	6.65	5.86	41
42	7.06	6.27	5.62	5.07	7.75	6.81	6.05	5.41	8.44	7.34	6.46	5.73	9.13	7.86	6.85	6.04	42
43	7.27	6.46	5.78	5.22	7.99	7.02	6.23	5.57	8.69	7.56	6.65	5.91	9.40	8.10	7.06	6.22	43
44	7.49	6.65	5.96	5.37	8.22	7.23	6.41	5.74	8.95	7.79	6.85	6.08	9.69	8.34	7.27	6.41	44
45	7.72	6.85	6.14	5.54	8.47	7.44	6.61	5.91	9.22	8.02	7.06	6.27	9.98	8.59	7.49	6.60	45
46	7.95	7.05	6.32	5.70	8.72	7.67	6.80	6.09	9.50	8.26	7.27	6.45	10.28	8.85	7.71	6.80	46
47	8.19	7.27	6.51	5.87	8.98	7.90	7.01	6.27	9.78	8.51	7.49	6.65	10.58	9.12	7.95	7.00	47
48	8.43	7.49	6.71	6.05	9.25	8.14	7.22	6.46	10.08	8.77	7.71	6.85	10.90	9.39	8.18	7.21	48
49	8.68	7.71	6.91	6.23	9.53	8.38	7.44	6.65	10.38	9.03	7.94	7.05	11.23	9.67	8.43	7.43	49
50	8.94	7.94	7.11	6.42	9.82	8.63	7.66	6.85	10.69	9.30	8.18	7.26	11.57	9.96	8.68	7.65	50

II. Retirement Planning where Salary Keeps Pace with Low 3% Inflation
Planned Retirement Age 65

Table 1 - Percent of Salary Replaced by a 401(k) Account Equal to Current Annual Salary

II-65-1

Probable Life Expectancy at Retirement

Yrs. to Ret.	20.7 (Same as Male Avg.)				23.2 (Better than Male Avg.)				25.7 (Same as Female Avg.)				28.3 (Better than Female Avg.)				Yrs. to Ret.
	4% / 4%	6% / 5%	8% / 6%	10% / 7%	4% / 4%	6% / 5%	8% / 6%	10% / 7%	4% / 4%	6% / 5%	8% / 6%	10% / 7%	4% / 4%	6% / 5%	8% / 6%	10% / 7%	
	Expected Return				(Pre-Retirement/Post-Retirement)				(Pre-Retirement/Post-Retirement)				Expected Return				
0	5.43	6.05	6.70	7.37	4.90	5.52	6.16	6.83	4.47	5.08	5.72	6.40	4.10	4.71	5.36	6.03	0
1	5.48	6.23	7.02	7.87	4.95	5.68	6.46	7.30	4.51	5.23	6.00	6.83	4.14	4.85	5.62	6.45	1
2	5.54	6.41	7.37	8.41	5.00	5.84	6.78	7.79	4.55	5.38	6.29	7.30	4.18	4.99	5.89	6.88	2
3	5.59	6.60	7.72	8.98	5.05	6.01	7.10	8.32	4.60	5.54	6.60	7.79	4.22	5.14	6.18	7.35	3
4	5.64	6.79	8.10	9.59	5.09	6.19	7.45	8.89	4.64	5.70	6.92	8.32	4.26	5.29	6.48	7.85	4
5	5.70	6.99	8.49	10.24	5.14	6.37	7.81	9.49	4.69	5.86	7.25	8.89	4.30	5.44	6.79	8.39	5
6	5.75	7.19	8.90	10.94	5.19	6.55	8.19	10.14	4.73	6.03	7.61	9.49	4.35	5.60	7.12	8.96	6
7	5.81	7.40	9.33	11.68	5.24	6.75	8.59	10.83	4.78	6.21	7.97	10.14	4.39	5.76	7.47	9.56	7
8	5.87	7.61	9.79	12.47	5.29	6.94	9.00	11.56	4.82	6.39	8.36	10.83	4.43	5.93	7.83	10.21	8
9	5.92	7.84	10.26	13.32	5.35	7.14	9.44	12.35	4.87	6.58	8.77	11.56	4.47	6.10	8.21	10.91	9
10	5.98	8.06	10.76	14.23	5.40	7.35	9.90	13.19	4.92	6.77	9.19	12.35	4.52	6.28	8.60	11.65	10
11	6.04	8.30	11.28	15.19	5.45	7.57	10.38	14.09	4.97	6.96	9.64	13.19	4.56	6.46	9.02	12.44	11
12	6.10	8.54	11.83	16.23	5.50	7.79	10.88	15.05	5.01	7.17	10.10	14.09	4.61	6.65	9.46	13.29	12
13	6.16	8.79	12.40	17.33	5.56	8.01	11.41	16.07	5.06	7.38	10.59	15.04	4.65	6.84	9.92	14.19	13
14	6.22	9.04	13.00	18.51	5.61	8.24	11.96	17.16	5.11	7.59	11.11	16.07	4.69	7.04	10.40	15.16	14
15	6.28	9.31	13.63	19.77	5.66	8.48	12.54	18.33	5.16	7.81	11.65	17.16	4.74	7.25	10.90	16.19	15
16	6.34	9.58	14.29	21.11	5.72	8.73	13.15	19.57	5.21	8.04	12.21	18.33	4.79	7.46	11.43	17.29	16
17	6.40	9.86	14.99	22.55	5.78	8.99	13.79	20.91	5.26	8.27	12.80	19.57	4.83	7.67	11.99	18.47	17
18	6.46	10.14	15.71	24.08	5.83	9.25	14.45	22.33	5.31	8.51	13.43	20.90	4.88	7.90	12.57	19.72	18
19	6.52	10.44	16.48	25.72	5.89	9.52	15.16	23.85	5.36	8.76	14.08	22.32	4.93	8.13	13.18	21.06	19
20	6.59	10.74	17.28	27.47	5.94	9.79	15.89	25.47	5.42	9.02	14.76	23.84	4.97	8.36	13.82	22.50	20
21	6.65	11.06	18.11	29.34	6.00	10.08	16.66	27.20	5.47	9.28	15.48	25.46	5.02	8.61	14.49	24.03	21
22	6.71	11.38	18.99	31.33	6.06	10.37	17.47	29.05	5.52	9.55	16.23	27.19	5.07	8.86	15.19	25.66	22
23	6.78	11.71	19.91	33.46	6.12	10.67	18.32	31.02	5.58	9.83	17.01	29.04	5.12	9.12	15.93	27.40	23
24	6.85	12.05	20.88	35.74	6.18	10.98	19.21	33.13	5.63	10.11	17.84	31.02	5.17	9.38	16.70	29.27	24
25	6.91	12.40	21.89	38.17	6.24	11.30	20.14	35.39	5.68	10.41	18.70	33.13	5.22	9.65	17.51	31.26	25
26	6.98	12.76	22.95	40.76	6.30	11.63	21.11	37.79	5.74	10.71	19.61	35.38	5.27	9.94	18.36	33.38	26
27	7.05	13.13	24.07	43.53	6.36	11.97	22.14	40.36	5.80	11.02	20.56	37.79	5.32	10.22	19.25	35.65	27
28	7.12	13.51	25.23	46.49	6.42	12.32	23.21	43.11	5.85	11.34	21.56	40.36	5.37	10.52	20.18	38.08	28
29	7.18	13.91	26.46	49.66	6.48	12.68	24.34	46.04	5.91	11.67	22.60	43.10	5.43	10.83	21.16	40.67	29
30	7.25	14.31	27.74	53.03	6.55	13.05	25.52	49.17	5.97	12.01	23.70	46.03	5.48	11.14	22.19	43.43	30
31	7.32	14.73	29.09	56.64	6.61	13.43	26.75	52.51	6.02	12.36	24.85	49.16	5.53	11.47	23.26	46.38	31
32	7.40	15.16	30.50	60.49	6.67	13.82	28.05	56.08	6.08	12.72	26.06	52.51	5.59	11.80	24.39	49.54	32
33	7.47	15.60	31.98	64.60	6.74	14.22	29.41	59.90	6.14	13.09	27.32	56.08	5.64	12.14	25.58	52.91	33
34	7.54	16.05	33.53	69.00	6.81	14.63	30.84	63.97	6.20	13.47	28.64	59.89	5.69	12.50	26.82	56.51	34
35	7.61	16.52	35.15	73.69	6.87	15.06	32.34	68.32	6.26	13.86	30.03	63.96	5.75	12.86	28.12	60.35	35
36	7.69	17.00	36.86	78.70	6.94	15.50	33.90	72.97	6.32	14.27	31.49	68.31	5.81	13.24	29.48	64.45	36
37	7.76	17.49	38.65	84.05	7.00	15.95	35.55	77.93	6.38	14.68	33.02	72.96	5.86	13.62	30.91	68.83	37
38	7.84	18.00	40.52	89.77	7.07	16.41	37.27	83.23	6.45	15.11	34.62	77.92	5.92	14.02	32.41	73.51	38
39	7.91	18.53	42.49	95.87	7.14	16.89	39.08	88.89	6.51	15.55	36.30	83.21	5.98	14.43	33.98	78.51	39
40	7.99	19.07	44.55	102.39	7.21	17.38	40.97	94.93	6.57	16.00	38.06	88.87	6.03	14.85	35.63	83.85	40
41	8.07	19.62	46.71	109.35	7.28	17.89	42.96	101.39	6.63	16.47	39.90	94.92	6.09	15.28	37.36	89.55	41
42	8.14	20.19	48.97	116.79	7.35	18.41	45.05	108.28	6.70	16.94	41.84	101.37	6.15	15.72	39.17	95.64	42
43	8.22	20.78	51.35	124.73	7.42	18.94	47.23	115.64	6.76	17.44	43.87	108.28	6.21	16.18	41.07	102.15	43
44	8.30	21.38	53.84	133.21	7.49	19.49	49.52	123.51	6.83	17.95	46.00	115.63	6.27	16.65	43.06	109.09	44
45	8.38	22.01	56.45	142.27	7.57	20.06	51.92	131.90	6.90	18.47	48.23	123.49	6.33	17.13	45.15	116.51	45
46	8.47	22.65	59.19	151.94	7.64	20.65	54.44	140.87	6.96	19.00	50.57	131.89	6.39	17.63	47.34	124.44	46
47	8.55	23.31	62.06	162.27	7.71	21.25	57.08	150.45	7.03	19.56	53.02	140.85	6.46	18.15	49.63	132.90	47
48	8.63	23.98	65.07	173.31	7.79	21.86	59.85	160.68	7.10	20.13	55.59	150.43	6.52	18.67	52.04	141.93	48
49	8.71	24.68	68.22	185.09	7.87	22.50	62.75	171.61	7.17	20.71	58.29	160.66	6.58	19.22	54.57	151.59	49
50	8.80	25.40	71.53	197.68	7.94	23.16	65.80	183.28	7.24	21.32	61.11	171.59	6.65	19.78	57.21	161.89	50

Appendix A

II. Retirement Planning where Salary Keeps Pace with Low 3% Inflation
Planned Retirement Age 65

Table 2 - Percent of Salary Replaced by a 401(k) Contribution of 1% of Current Salary — II-65-2

Probable Life Expectancy at Retirement

Yrs. to Ret.	20.7 (Same as Male Avg.)				23.2 (Better than Male Avg.)				25.7 (Same as Female Avg.)				28.3 (Better than Female Avg.)				Yrs. to Ret.
	4% / 4%	6% / 5%	8% / 6%	10% / 7%	4% / 4%	6% / 5%	8% / 6%	10% / 7%	4% / 4%	6% / 5%	8% / 6%	10% / 7%	4% / 4%	6% / 5%	8% / 6%	10% / 7%	
	Expected Return				(Pre-Retirement/Post-Retirement)				(Pre-Retirement/Post-Retirement)				Expected Return				
0	0.00	0.00	0.00	0.00	0.00	0.00	0.00	0.00	0.00	0.00	0.00	0.00	0.00	0.00	0.00	0.00	0
1	0.05	0.06	0.07	0.07	0.05	0.06	0.06	0.07	0.04	0.05	0.06	0.06	0.04	0.05	0.05	0.06	1
2	0.11	0.12	0.14	0.15	0.10	0.11	0.13	0.14	0.09	0.10	0.12	0.13	0.08	0.10	0.11	0.12	2
3	0.16	0.19	0.21	0.24	0.15	0.17	0.19	0.22	0.14	0.16	0.18	0.21	0.12	0.15	0.17	0.19	3
4	0.22	0.25	0.29	0.33	0.20	0.23	0.27	0.30	0.18	0.21	0.25	0.28	0.17	0.20	0.23	0.27	4
5	0.28	0.32	0.37	0.42	0.25	0.29	0.34	0.39	0.23	0.27	0.32	0.37	0.21	0.25	0.30	0.35	5
6	0.33	0.39	0.45	0.52	0.30	0.36	0.42	0.49	0.27	0.33	0.39	0.46	0.25	0.30	0.36	0.43	6
7	0.39	0.46	0.54	0.63	0.35	0.42	0.50	0.59	0.32	0.39	0.46	0.55	0.30	0.36	0.43	0.52	7
8	0.45	0.54	0.64	0.75	0.41	0.49	0.59	0.70	0.37	0.45	0.54	0.65	0.34	0.42	0.51	0.61	8
9	0.51	0.61	0.73	0.88	0.46	0.56	0.68	0.81	0.42	0.51	0.63	0.76	0.38	0.48	0.59	0.72	9
10	0.57	0.69	0.84	1.01	0.51	0.63	0.77	0.94	0.47	0.58	0.71	0.88	0.43	0.54	0.67	0.83	10
11	0.63	0.77	0.94	1.15	0.57	0.70	0.87	1.07	0.52	0.65	0.81	1.00	0.47	0.60	0.76	0.94	11
12	0.69	0.85	1.06	1.30	0.62	0.78	0.97	1.21	0.57	0.72	0.90	1.13	0.52	0.67	0.85	1.07	12
13	0.75	0.94	1.18	1.47	0.68	0.86	1.08	1.36	0.62	0.79	1.00	1.27	0.57	0.73	0.94	1.20	13
14	0.81	1.03	1.30	1.64	0.73	0.94	1.20	1.52	0.67	0.86	1.11	1.42	0.61	0.80	1.04	1.34	14
15	0.87	1.12	1.43	1.82	0.79	1.02	1.31	1.69	0.72	0.94	1.22	1.58	0.66	0.87	1.14	1.49	15
16	0.93	1.21	1.57	2.02	0.84	1.10	1.44	1.87	0.77	1.02	1.34	1.75	0.71	0.94	1.25	1.66	16
17	1.00	1.31	1.71	2.23	0.90	1.19	1.57	2.07	0.82	1.10	1.46	1.94	0.75	1.02	1.37	1.83	17
18	1.06	1.41	1.86	2.46	0.96	1.28	1.71	2.28	0.87	1.18	1.59	2.13	0.80	1.09	1.49	2.01	18
19	1.13	1.51	2.02	2.70	1.02	1.37	1.85	2.50	0.93	1.26	1.72	2.34	0.85	1.17	1.61	2.21	19
20	1.19	1.61	2.18	2.96	1.08	1.47	2.01	2.74	0.98	1.35	1.86	2.57	0.90	1.25	1.74	2.42	20
21	1.26	1.72	2.35	3.23	1.14	1.57	2.16	3.00	1.03	1.44	2.01	2.80	0.95	1.34	1.88	2.65	21
22	1.32	1.83	2.53	3.52	1.20	1.67	2.33	3.27	1.09	1.54	2.17	3.06	1.00	1.42	2.03	2.89	22
23	1.39	1.94	2.72	3.84	1.26	1.77	2.51	3.56	1.14	1.63	2.33	3.33	1.05	1.51	2.18	3.14	23
24	1.46	2.06	2.92	4.17	1.32	1.88	2.69	3.87	1.20	1.73	2.50	3.62	1.10	1.60	2.34	3.42	24
25	1.53	2.18	3.13	4.53	1.38	1.99	2.88	4.20	1.26	1.83	2.68	3.93	1.15	1.70	2.51	3.71	25
26	1.60	2.30	3.35	4.91	1.44	2.10	3.08	4.55	1.31	1.93	2.86	4.26	1.21	1.79	2.68	4.02	26
27	1.67	2.43	3.58	5.32	1.50	2.22	3.29	4.93	1.37	2.04	3.06	4.62	1.26	1.89	2.86	4.36	27
28	1.74	2.56	3.82	5.75	1.57	2.34	3.52	5.33	1.43	2.15	3.26	4.99	1.31	2.00	3.06	4.71	28
29	1.81	2.70	4.07	6.22	1.63	2.46	3.75	5.77	1.49	2.26	3.48	5.40	1.37	2.10	3.26	5.09	29
30	1.88	2.84	4.34	6.72	1.70	2.59	3.99	6.23	1.55	2.38	3.71	5.83	1.42	2.21	3.47	5.50	30
31	1.95	2.98	4.62	7.25	1.76	2.72	4.25	6.72	1.61	2.50	3.94	6.29	1.48	2.32	3.69	5.93	31
32	2.03	3.13	4.91	7.81	1.83	2.85	4.51	7.24	1.67	2.63	4.19	6.78	1.53	2.44	3.92	6.40	32
33	2.10	3.28	5.21	8.42	1.90	2.99	4.79	7.80	1.73	2.75	4.45	7.31	1.59	2.55	4.17	6.89	33
34	2.17	3.44	5.53	9.06	1.96	3.13	5.09	8.40	1.79	2.88	4.73	7.87	1.64	2.68	4.42	7.42	34
35	2.25	3.60	5.87	9.75	2.03	3.28	5.40	9.04	1.85	3.02	5.01	8.47	1.70	2.80	4.69	7.99	35
36	2.32	3.76	6.22	10.49	2.10	3.43	5.72	9.73	1.91	3.16	5.31	9.11	1.76	2.93	4.97	8.59	36
37	2.40	3.93	6.59	11.28	2.17	3.58	6.06	10.46	1.98	3.30	5.63	9.79	1.82	3.06	5.27	9.24	37
38	2.48	4.11	6.97	12.12	2.24	3.74	6.41	11.23	2.04	3.45	5.96	10.52	1.87	3.20	5.58	9.92	38
39	2.56	4.29	7.38	13.01	2.31	3.91	6.79	12.07	2.10	3.60	6.30	11.30	1.93	3.34	5.90	10.66	39
40	2.64	4.47	7.80	13.97	2.38	4.08	7.18	12.96	2.17	3.75	6.67	12.13	1.99	3.48	6.24	11.44	40
41	2.72	4.66	8.25	15.00	2.45	4.25	7.59	13.90	2.24	3.91	7.05	13.02	2.05	3.63	6.60	12.28	41
42	2.80	4.86	8.72	16.09	2.53	4.43	8.02	14.92	2.30	4.08	7.45	13.97	2.11	3.78	6.97	13.18	42
43	2.88	5.06	9.21	17.26	2.60	4.61	8.47	16.00	2.37	4.25	7.86	14.98	2.18	3.94	7.36	14.13	43
44	2.96	5.27	9.72	18.51	2.67	4.80	8.94	17.16	2.44	4.42	8.30	16.06	2.24	4.10	7.77	15.16	44
45	3.05	5.48	10.26	19.84	2.75	5.00	9.44	18.39	2.50	4.60	8.76	17.22	2.30	4.27	8.20	16.25	45
46	3.13	5.70	10.82	21.26	2.82	5.20	9.95	19.71	2.57	4.79	9.25	18.45	2.36	4.44	8.66	17.41	46
47	3.21	5.93	11.41	22.78	2.90	5.40	10.50	21.12	2.64	4.98	9.75	19.77	2.43	4.62	9.13	18.66	47
48	3.30	6.16	12.03	24.40	2.98	5.62	11.07	22.63	2.71	5.17	10.28	21.18	2.49	4.80	9.63	19.99	48
49	3.39	6.40	12.69	26.14	3.06	5.84	11.67	24.23	2.78	5.37	10.84	22.69	2.56	4.98	10.15	21.40	49
50	3.47	6.65	13.37	27.99	3.13	6.06	12.30	25.95	2.86	5.58	11.42	24.29	2.62	5.18	10.69	22.92	50

II. Retirement Planning where Salary Keeps Pace with Low 3% Inflation
Planned Retirement Age 65

Table 3 - 401(k) Contribution (% of Current Sal.) Needed to Replace 10% of Sal. at Retirement   II-65-3

Probable Life Expectancy at Retirement

Yrs. to Ret.	20.7 (Same as Male Avg.)				23.2 (Better than Male Avg.)				25.7 (Same as Female Avg.)				28.3 (Better than Female Avg.)				Yrs. to Ret.
	4% / 4%	6% / 5%	8% / 6%	10% / 7%	4% / 4%	6% / 5%	8% / 6%	10% / 7%	4% / 4%	6% / 5%	8% / 6%	10% / 7%	4% / 4%	6% / 5%	8% / 6%	10% / 7%	
	Expected Return				(Pre-Retirement/Post-Retirement)				(Pre-Retirement/Post-Retirement)				Expected Return				
0																	0
1	184.16	165.21	149.25	135.71	204.04	181.23	162.26	146.37	223.92	196.87	174.70	156.34	243.82	212.19	186.61	165.70	1
2	91.63	81.42	72.86	65.62	101.53	89.31	79.21	70.78	111.42	97.02	85.28	75.60	121.32	104.57	91.10	80.13	2
3	60.79	53.50	47.41	42.29	67.36	58.68	51.55	45.62	73.92	63.75	55.50	48.73	80.49	68.71	59.28	51.64	3
4	45.37	39.54	34.71	30.66	50.27	43.38	37.73	33.06	55.17	47.12	40.62	35.32	60.08	50.79	43.39	37.43	4
5	36.12	31.17	27.09	23.69	40.02	34.20	29.45	25.55	43.92	37.15	31.71	27.30	47.83	40.04	33.87	28.93	5
6	29.96	25.60	22.03	19.07	33.19	28.08	23.95	20.56	36.42	30.50	25.78	21.97	39.66	32.88	27.54	23.28	6
7	25.55	21.62	18.42	15.78	28.31	23.72	20.02	17.02	31.07	25.76	21.55	18.18	33.83	27.77	23.02	19.26	7
8	22.25	18.64	15.71	13.32	24.65	20.45	17.08	14.37	27.05	22.21	18.39	15.35	29.46	23.94	19.65	16.27	8
9	19.68	16.32	13.62	11.42	21.81	17.90	14.81	12.32	23.93	19.45	15.94	13.16	26.06	20.96	17.03	13.95	9
10	17.63	14.47	11.95	9.92	19.53	15.87	12.99	10.69	21.43	17.24	13.99	11.42	23.34	18.59	14.94	12.11	10
11	15.95	12.96	10.59	8.69	17.67	14.22	11.51	9.37	19.39	15.44	12.39	10.01	21.11	16.64	13.24	10.61	11
12	14.54	11.70	9.46	7.68	16.12	12.83	10.28	8.28	17.69	13.94	11.07	8.84	19.26	15.03	11.83	9.37	12
13	13.36	10.64	8.51	6.83	14.80	11.67	9.25	7.36	16.24	12.68	9.96	7.86	17.69	13.66	10.64	8.33	13
14	12.34	9.73	7.70	6.10	13.68	10.67	8.37	6.58	15.01	11.59	9.01	7.03	16.34	12.49	9.62	7.45	14
15	11.46	8.94	7.00	5.48	12.70	9.81	7.60	5.91	13.94	10.66	8.19	6.32	15.18	11.48	8.75	6.70	15
16	10.70	8.25	6.39	4.95	11.85	9.05	6.94	5.34	13.00	9.84	7.47	5.70	14.16	10.60	7.98	6.04	16
17	10.02	7.65	5.85	4.48	11.10	8.39	6.36	4.83	12.18	9.12	6.85	5.16	13.26	9.83	7.32	5.47	17
18	9.41	7.11	5.38	4.07	10.43	7.80	5.85	4.39	11.45	8.48	6.30	4.69	12.46	9.14	6.73	4.97	18
19	8.87	6.63	4.96	3.71	9.83	7.28	5.39	4.00	10.79	7.91	5.81	4.27	11.75	8.52	6.20	4.52	19
20	8.39	6.20	4.59	3.38	9.29	6.81	4.99	3.65	10.20	7.39	5.37	3.90	11.11	7.97	5.73	4.13	20
21	7.95	5.82	4.25	3.10	8.81	6.38	4.62	3.34	9.66	6.93	4.97	3.57	10.52	7.47	5.31	3.78	21
22	7.55	5.47	3.95	2.84	8.36	6.00	4.29	3.06	9.18	6.51	4.62	3.27	10.00	7.02	4.93	3.47	22
23	7.19	5.15	3.67	2.61	7.96	5.64	3.99	2.81	8.74	6.13	4.30	3.00	9.51	6.61	4.59	3.18	23
24	6.85	4.85	3.42	2.40	7.59	5.32	3.72	2.59	8.33	5.78	4.00	2.76	9.07	6.23	4.28	2.93	24
25	6.54	4.59	3.19	2.21	7.25	5.03	3.47	2.38	7.96	5.46	3.74	2.54	8.67	5.89	3.99	2.70	25
26	6.26	4.34	2.98	2.04	6.94	4.76	3.24	2.20	7.61	5.17	3.49	2.35	8.29	5.57	3.73	2.49	26
27	6.00	4.11	2.79	1.88	6.65	4.51	3.04	2.03	7.29	4.90	3.27	2.17	7.94	5.28	3.49	2.30	27
28	5.76	3.90	2.62	1.74	6.38	4.28	2.84	1.87	7.00	4.65	3.06	2.00	7.62	5.01	3.27	2.12	28
29	5.53	3.71	2.45	1.61	6.13	4.06	2.67	1.73	6.72	4.42	2.87	1.85	7.32	4.76	3.07	1.96	29
30	5.32	3.52	2.30	1.49	5.89	3.87	2.51	1.61	6.47	4.20	2.70	1.72	7.04	4.53	2.88	1.82	30
31	5.12	3.35	2.17	1.38	5.67	3.68	2.36	1.49	6.23	4.00	2.54	1.59	6.78	4.31	2.71	1.69	31
32	4.94	3.20	2.04	1.28	5.47	3.51	2.22	1.38	6.00	3.81	2.39	1.47	6.53	4.11	2.55	1.56	32
33	4.76	3.05	1.92	1.19	5.28	3.34	2.09	1.28	5.79	3.63	2.25	1.37	6.30	3.92	2.40	1.45	33
34	4.60	2.91	1.81	1.10	5.09	3.19	1.97	1.19	5.59	3.47	2.12	1.27	6.09	3.74	2.26	1.35	34
35	4.44	2.78	1.70	1.03	4.92	3.05	1.85	1.11	5.40	3.31	2.00	1.18	5.88	3.57	2.13	1.25	35
36	4.30	2.66	1.61	0.95	4.76	2.92	1.75	1.03	5.23	3.17	1.88	1.10	5.69	3.41	2.01	1.16	36
37	4.16	2.54	1.52	0.89	4.61	2.79	1.65	0.96	5.06	3.03	1.78	1.02	5.51	3.27	1.90	1.08	37
38	4.03	2.44	1.43	0.83	4.47	2.67	1.56	0.89	4.90	2.90	1.68	0.95	5.34	3.13	1.79	1.01	38
39	3.91	2.33	1.36	0.77	4.33	2.56	1.47	0.83	4.75	2.78	1.59	0.89	5.17	3.00	1.69	0.94	39
40	3.79	2.24	1.28	0.72	4.20	2.45	1.39	0.77	4.61	2.66	1.50	0.82	5.02	2.87	1.60	0.87	40
41	3.68	2.14	1.21	0.67	4.08	2.35	1.32	0.72	4.47	2.56	1.42	0.77	4.87	2.75	1.52	0.81	41
42	3.57	2.06	1.15	0.62	3.96	2.26	1.25	0.67	4.34	2.45	1.34	0.72	4.73	2.64	1.43	0.76	42
43	3.47	1.98	1.09	0.58	3.85	2.17	1.18	0.62	4.22	2.35	1.27	0.67	4.60	2.54	1.36	0.71	43
44	3.38	1.90	1.03	0.54	3.74	2.08	1.12	0.58	4.10	2.26	1.20	0.62	4.47	2.44	1.29	0.66	44
45	3.28	1.82	0.97	0.50	3.64	2.00	1.06	0.54	3.99	2.17	1.14	0.58	4.35	2.34	1.22	0.62	45
46	3.20	1.75	0.92	0.47	3.54	1.92	1.00	0.51	3.89	2.09	1.08	0.54	4.23	2.25	1.16	0.57	46
47	3.11	1.69	0.88	0.44	3.45	1.85	0.95	0.47	3.78	2.01	1.03	0.51	4.12	2.17	1.10	0.54	47
48	3.03	1.62	0.83	0.41	3.36	1.78	0.90	0.44	3.69	1.93	0.97	0.47	4.01	2.08	1.04	0.50	48
49	2.95	1.56	0.79	0.38	3.27	1.71	0.86	0.41	3.59	1.86	0.92	0.44	3.91	2.01	0.99	0.47	49
50	2.88	1.50	0.75	0.36	3.19	1.65	0.81	0.39	3.50	1.79	0.88	0.41	3.81	1.93	0.94	0.44	50

Appendix A

<table>
<tr><td colspan="18">II. Retirement Planning where Salary Keeps Pace with Low 3% Inflation
Planned Retirement Age 65</td></tr>
</table>

Table 4 - Accumulation at Retirement (Multiple of Current Sal.) for 10% Sal. Replacement   II-65-4

Probable Life Expectancy at Retirement

	20.7 (Same as Male Avg.)				23.2 (Better than Male Avg.)				25.7 (Same as Female Avg.)				28.3 (Better than Female Avg.)				
	4% / 4%	6% / 5%	8% / 6%	10% / 7%	4% / 4%	6% / 5%	8% / 6%	10% / 7%	4% / 4%	6% / 5%	8% / 6%	10% / 7%	4% / 4%	6% / 5%	8% / 6%	10% / 7%	
Yrs. to Ret.	Expected Return				(Pre-Retirement/Post-Retirement)				(Pre-Retirement/Post-Retirement)				Expected Return				Yrs. to Ret.
0	1.84	1.65	1.49	1.36	2.04	1.81	1.62	1.46	2.24	1.97	1.75	1.56	2.44	2.12	1.87	1.66	0
1	1.90	1.70	1.54	1.40	2.10	1.87	1.67	1.51	2.31	2.03	1.80	1.61	2.51	2.19	1.92	1.71	1
2	1.95	1.75	1.58	1.44	2.16	1.92	1.72	1.55	2.38	2.09	1.85	1.66	2.59	2.25	1.98	1.76	2
3	2.01	1.81	1.63	1.48	2.23	1.98	1.77	1.60	2.45	2.15	1.91	1.71	2.66	2.32	2.04	1.81	3
4	2.07	1.86	1.68	1.53	2.30	2.04	1.83	1.65	2.52	2.22	1.97	1.76	2.74	2.39	2.10	1.87	4
5	2.13	1.92	1.73	1.57	2.37	2.10	1.88	1.70	2.60	2.28	2.03	1.81	2.83	2.46	2.16	1.92	5
6	2.20	1.97	1.78	1.62	2.44	2.16	1.94	1.75	2.67	2.35	2.09	1.87	2.91	2.53	2.23	1.98	6
7	2.26	2.03	1.84	1.67	2.51	2.23	2.00	1.80	2.75	2.42	2.15	1.92	3.00	2.61	2.30	2.04	7
8	2.33	2.09	1.89	1.72	2.58	2.30	2.06	1.85	2.84	2.49	2.21	1.98	3.09	2.69	2.36	2.10	8
9	2.40	2.16	1.95	1.77	2.66	2.36	2.12	1.91	2.92	2.57	2.28	2.04	3.18	2.77	2.43	2.16	9
10	2.47	2.22	2.01	1.82	2.74	2.44	2.18	1.97	3.01	2.65	2.35	2.10	3.28	2.85	2.51	2.23	10
11	2.55	2.29	2.07	1.88	2.82	2.51	2.25	2.03	3.10	2.73	2.42	2.16	3.38	2.94	2.58	2.29	11
12	2.63	2.36	2.13	1.93	2.91	2.58	2.31	2.09	3.19	2.81	2.49	2.23	3.48	3.03	2.66	2.36	12
13	2.70	2.43	2.19	1.99	3.00	2.66	2.38	2.15	3.29	2.89	2.57	2.30	3.58	3.12	2.74	2.43	13
14	2.79	2.50	2.26	2.05	3.09	2.74	2.45	2.21	3.39	2.98	2.64	2.36	3.69	3.21	2.82	2.51	14
15	2.87	2.57	2.33	2.11	3.18	2.82	2.53	2.28	3.49	3.07	2.72	2.44	3.80	3.31	2.91	2.58	15
16	2.96	2.65	2.40	2.18	3.27	2.91	2.60	2.35	3.59	3.16	2.80	2.51	3.91	3.41	2.99	2.66	16
17	3.04	2.73	2.47	2.24	3.37	3.00	2.68	2.42	3.70	3.25	2.89	2.58	4.03	3.51	3.08	2.74	17
18	3.14	2.81	2.54	2.31	3.47	3.09	2.76	2.49	3.81	3.35	2.97	2.66	4.15	3.61	3.18	2.82	18
19	3.23	2.90	2.62	2.38	3.58	3.18	2.85	2.57	3.93	3.45	3.06	2.74	4.28	3.72	3.27	2.91	19
20	3.33	2.98	2.70	2.45	3.69	3.27	2.93	2.64	4.04	3.56	3.16	2.82	4.40	3.83	3.37	2.99	20
21	3.43	3.07	2.78	2.52	3.80	3.37	3.02	2.72	4.17	3.66	3.25	2.91	4.54	3.95	3.47	3.08	21
22	3.53	3.17	2.86	2.60	3.91	3.47	3.11	2.80	4.29	3.77	3.35	3.00	4.67	4.07	3.58	3.18	22
23	3.63	3.26	2.95	2.68	4.03	3.58	3.20	2.89	4.42	3.89	3.45	3.09	4.81	4.19	3.68	3.27	23
24	3.74	3.36	3.03	2.76	4.15	3.68	3.30	2.98	4.55	4.00	3.55	3.18	4.96	4.31	3.79	3.37	24
25	3.86	3.46	3.13	2.84	4.27	3.79	3.40	3.06	4.69	4.12	3.66	3.27	5.11	4.44	3.91	3.47	25
26	3.97	3.56	3.22	2.93	4.40	3.91	3.50	3.16	4.83	4.25	3.77	3.37	5.26	4.58	4.02	3.57	26
27	4.09	3.67	3.32	3.01	4.53	4.03	3.60	3.25	4.97	4.37	3.88	3.47	5.42	4.71	4.15	3.68	27
28	4.21	3.78	3.41	3.10	4.67	4.15	3.71	3.35	5.12	4.50	4.00	3.58	5.58	4.85	4.27	3.79	28
29	4.34	3.89	3.52	3.20	4.81	4.27	3.82	3.45	5.28	4.64	4.12	3.68	5.75	5.00	4.40	3.90	29
30	4.47	4.01	3.62	3.29	4.95	4.40	3.94	3.55	5.44	4.78	4.24	3.79	5.92	5.15	4.53	4.02	30
31	4.60	4.13	3.73	3.39	5.10	4.53	4.06	3.66	5.60	4.92	4.37	3.91	6.10	5.30	4.67	4.14	31
32	4.74	4.25	3.84	3.49	5.25	4.67	4.18	3.77	5.77	5.07	4.50	4.03	6.28	5.46	4.81	4.27	32
33	4.88	4.38	3.96	3.60	5.41	4.81	4.30	3.88	5.94	5.22	4.63	4.15	6.47	5.63	4.95	4.40	33
34	5.03	4.51	4.08	3.71	5.57	4.95	4.43	4.00	6.12	5.38	4.77	4.27	6.66	5.80	5.10	4.53	34
35	5.18	4.65	4.20	3.82	5.74	5.10	4.57	4.12	6.30	5.54	4.92	4.40	6.86	5.97	5.25	4.66	35
36	5.34	4.79	4.33	3.93	5.91	5.25	4.70	4.24	6.49	5.71	5.06	4.53	7.07	6.15	5.41	4.80	36
37	5.50	4.93	4.46	4.05	6.09	5.41	4.84	4.37	6.68	5.88	5.22	4.67	7.28	6.33	5.57	4.95	37
38	5.66	5.08	4.59	4.17	6.27	5.57	4.99	4.50	6.88	6.05	5.37	4.81	7.50	6.52	5.74	5.10	38
39	5.83	5.23	4.73	4.30	6.46	5.74	5.14	4.64	7.09	6.24	5.53	4.95	7.72	6.72	5.91	5.25	39
40	6.01	5.39	4.87	4.43	6.66	5.91	5.29	4.77	7.30	6.42	5.70	5.10	7.95	6.92	6.09	5.41	40
41	6.19	5.55	5.01	4.56	6.86	6.09	5.45	4.92	7.52	6.61	5.87	5.25	8.19	7.13	6.27	5.57	41
42	6.37	5.72	5.17	4.70	7.06	6.27	5.62	5.07	7.75	6.81	6.05	5.41	8.44	7.34	6.46	5.73	42
43	6.56	5.89	5.32	4.84	7.27	6.46	5.78	5.22	7.98	7.02	6.23	5.57	8.69	7.56	6.65	5.91	43
44	6.76	6.07	5.48	4.98	7.49	6.65	5.96	5.37	8.22	7.23	6.41	5.74	8.95	7.79	6.85	6.08	44
45	6.96	6.25	5.64	5.13	7.72	6.85	6.14	5.54	8.47	7.44	6.61	5.91	9.22	8.02	7.06	6.27	45
46	7.17	6.44	5.81	5.29	7.95	7.06	6.32	5.70	8.72	7.67	6.80	6.09	9.50	8.26	7.27	6.45	46
47	7.39	6.63	5.99	5.44	8.19	7.27	6.51	5.87	8.98	7.90	7.01	6.27	9.78	8.51	7.49	6.65	47
48	7.61	6.83	6.17	5.61	8.43	7.49	6.71	6.05	9.25	8.14	7.22	6.46	10.08	8.77	7.71	6.85	48
49	7.84	7.03	6.35	5.78	8.68	7.71	6.91	6.23	9.53	8.38	7.44	6.65	10.38	9.03	7.94	7.05	49
50	8.07	7.24	6.54	5.95	8.94	7.94	7.11	6.42	9.82	8.63	7.66	6.85	10.69	9.30	8.18	7.26	50

A-33

II. Retirement Planning where Salary Keeps Pace with Low 3% Inflation
Planned Retirement Age 68

Table 1 - Percent of Salary Replaced by a 401(k) Account Equal to Current Annual Salary II-68-1

Probable Life Expectancy at Retirement

	18.3 (Same as Male Avg.)				20.7 (Better than Male Avg.)				23.2 (Same as Female Avg.)				25.7 (Better than Female Avg.)				
	4% / 4%	6% / 5%	8% / 6%	10% / 7%	4% / 4%	6% / 5%	8% / 6%	10% / 7%	4% / 4%	6% / 5%	8% / 6%	10% / 7%	4% / 4%	6% / 5%	8% / 6%	10% / 7%	
Yrs. to Ret.	Expected Return				(Pre-Retirement/Post-Retirement)				(Pre-Retirement/Post-Retirement)				Expected Return				Yrs. to Ret.
0	6.08	6.71	7.36	8.03	5.43	6.05	6.70	7.37	4.90	5.52	6.16	6.83	4.47	5.08	5.72	6.40	0
1	6.14	6.91	7.72	8.58	5.48	6.23	7.02	7.87	4.95	5.68	6.46	7.30	4.51	5.23	6.00	6.83	1
2	6.20	7.11	8.09	9.16	5.54	6.41	7.37	8.41	5.00	5.84	6.78	7.79	4.55	5.38	6.29	7.30	2
3	6.26	7.31	8.49	9.79	5.59	6.60	7.72	8.98	5.05	6.01	7.10	8.32	4.60	5.54	6.60	7.79	3
4	6.32	7.53	8.90	10.45	5.64	6.79	8.10	9.59	5.09	6.19	7.45	8.89	4.64	5.70	6.92	8.32	4
5	6.38	7.75	9.33	11.16	5.70	6.99	8.49	10.24	5.14	6.37	7.81	9.49	4.69	5.86	7.25	8.89	5
6	6.44	7.97	9.78	11.92	5.75	7.19	8.90	10.94	5.19	6.55	8.19	10.14	4.73	6.03	7.61	9.49	6
7	6.50	8.20	10.26	12.73	5.81	7.40	9.33	11.68	5.24	6.75	8.59	10.83	4.78	6.21	7.97	10.14	7
8	6.57	8.44	10.76	13.60	5.87	7.61	9.79	12.47	5.29	6.94	9.00	11.56	4.82	6.39	8.36	10.83	8
9	6.63	8.69	11.28	14.52	5.92	7.84	10.26	13.32	5.35	7.14	9.44	12.35	4.87	6.58	8.77	11.56	9
10	6.70	8.94	11.82	15.51	5.98	8.06	10.76	14.23	5.40	7.35	9.90	13.19	4.92	6.77	9.19	12.35	10
11	6.76	9.20	12.40	16.57	6.04	8.30	11.28	15.19	5.45	7.57	10.38	14.09	4.97	6.96	9.64	13.19	11
12	6.83	9.47	13.00	17.69	6.10	8.54	11.83	16.23	5.50	7.79	10.88	15.05	5.01	7.17	10.10	14.09	12
13	6.89	9.74	13.63	18.90	6.16	8.79	12.40	17.33	5.56	8.01	11.41	16.07	5.06	7.38	10.59	15.04	13
14	6.96	10.03	14.29	20.18	6.22	9.04	13.00	18.51	5.61	8.24	11.96	17.16	5.11	7.59	11.11	16.07	14
15	7.03	10.32	14.98	21.55	6.28	9.31	13.63	19.77	5.66	8.48	12.54	18.33	5.16	7.81	11.65	17.16	15
16	7.10	10.62	15.71	23.02	6.34	9.58	14.29	21.11	5.72	8.73	13.15	19.57	5.21	8.04	12.21	18.33	16
17	7.16	10.93	16.47	24.58	6.40	9.86	14.99	22.55	5.78	8.99	13.79	20.91	5.26	8.27	12.80	19.57	17
18	7.23	11.25	17.27	26.26	6.46	10.14	15.71	24.08	5.83	9.25	14.45	22.33	5.31	8.51	13.43	20.90	18
19	7.30	11.57	18.11	28.04	6.52	10.44	16.48	25.72	5.89	9.52	15.16	23.85	5.36	8.76	14.08	22.32	19
20	7.37	11.91	18.99	29.95	6.59	10.74	17.28	27.47	5.94	9.79	15.89	25.47	5.42	9.02	14.76	23.84	20
21	7.45	12.26	19.91	31.99	6.65	11.06	18.11	29.34	6.00	10.08	16.66	27.20	5.47	9.28	15.48	25.46	21
22	7.52	12.61	20.87	34.16	6.71	11.38	18.99	31.33	6.06	10.37	17.47	29.05	5.52	9.55	16.23	27.19	22
23	7.59	12.98	21.88	36.48	6.78	11.71	19.91	33.46	6.12	10.67	18.32	31.02	5.58	9.83	17.01	29.04	23
24	7.66	13.36	22.95	38.96	6.85	12.05	20.88	35.74	6.18	10.98	19.21	33.13	5.63	10.11	17.84	31.02	24
25	7.74	13.75	24.06	41.61	6.91	12.40	21.89	38.17	6.24	11.30	20.14	35.39	5.68	10.41	18.70	33.13	25
26	7.81	14.15	25.23	44.44	6.98	12.76	22.95	40.76	6.30	11.63	21.11	37.79	5.74	10.71	19.61	35.38	26
27	7.89	14.56	26.45	47.47	7.05	13.13	24.07	43.53	6.36	11.97	22.14	40.36	5.80	11.02	20.56	37.79	27
28	7.97	14.98	27.73	50.69	7.12	13.51	25.23	46.49	6.42	12.32	23.21	43.11	5.85	11.34	21.56	40.36	28
29	8.04	15.42	29.08	54.14	7.18	13.91	26.46	49.66	6.48	12.68	24.34	46.04	5.91	11.67	22.60	43.10	29
30	8.12	15.87	30.49	57.82	7.25	14.31	27.74	53.03	6.55	13.05	25.52	49.17	5.97	12.01	23.70	46.03	30
31	8.20	16.33	31.97	61.75	7.32	14.73	29.09	56.64	6.61	13.43	26.75	52.51	6.02	12.36	24.85	49.16	31
32	8.28	16.80	33.52	65.95	7.40	15.16	30.50	60.49	6.67	13.82	28.05	56.08	6.08	12.72	26.06	52.51	32
33	8.36	17.29	35.14	70.44	7.47	15.60	31.98	64.60	6.74	14.22	29.41	59.90	6.14	13.09	27.32	56.08	33
34	8.44	17.80	36.85	75.23	7.54	16.05	33.53	69.00	6.81	14.63	30.84	63.97	6.20	13.47	28.64	59.89	34
35	8.52	18.31	38.63	80.34	7.61	16.52	35.15	73.69	6.87	15.06	32.34	68.32	6.26	13.86	30.03	63.96	35
36	8.61	18.85	40.51	85.81	7.69	17.00	36.86	78.70	6.94	15.50	33.90	72.97	6.32	14.27	31.49	68.31	36
37	8.69	19.40	42.47	91.64	7.76	17.49	38.65	84.05	7.00	15.95	35.55	77.93	6.38	14.68	33.02	72.96	37
38	8.77	19.96	44.53	97.87	7.84	18.00	40.52	89.77	7.07	16.41	37.27	83.23	6.45	15.11	34.62	77.92	38
39	8.86	20.54	46.69	104.53	7.91	18.53	42.49	95.87	7.14	16.89	39.08	88.89	6.51	15.55	36.30	83.21	39
40	8.94	21.14	48.96	111.64	7.99	19.07	44.55	102.39	7.21	17.38	40.97	94.93	6.57	16.00	38.06	88.87	40
41	9.03	21.75	51.33	119.23	8.07	19.62	46.71	109.35	7.28	17.89	42.96	101.39	6.63	16.47	39.90	94.92	41
42	9.12	22.39	53.82	127.33	8.14	20.19	48.97	116.79	7.35	18.41	45.05	108.28	6.70	16.94	41.84	101.37	42
43	9.21	23.04	56.43	135.99	8.22	20.78	51.35	124.73	7.42	18.94	47.23	115.64	6.76	17.44	43.87	108.26	43
44	9.30	23.71	59.17	145.24	8.30	21.38	53.84	133.21	7.49	19.49	49.52	123.51	6.83	17.95	46.00	115.63	44
45	9.39	24.40	62.04	155.12	8.38	22.01	56.45	142.27	7.57	20.06	51.92	131.90	6.90	18.47	48.23	123.49	45
46	9.48	25.11	65.05	165.67	8.47	22.65	59.19	151.94	7.64	20.65	54.44	140.87	6.96	19.00	50.57	131.89	46
47	9.57	25.84	68.20	176.93	8.55	23.31	62.06	162.27	7.71	21.25	57.08	150.45	7.03	19.56	53.02	140.85	47
48	9.66	26.59	71.51	188.96	8.63	23.98	65.07	173.31	7.79	21.86	59.85	160.68	7.10	20.13	55.59	150.43	48
49	9.76	27.36	74.98	201.81	8.71	24.68	68.22	185.09	7.87	22.50	62.75	171.61	7.17	20.71	58.29	160.66	49
50	9.85	28.16	78.61	215.53	8.80	25.40	71.53	197.68	7.94	23.16	65.80	183.28	7.24	21.32	61.11	171.59	50

Appendix A

II. Retirement Planning where Salary Keeps Pace with Low 3% Inflation
Planned Retirement Age 68

Table 2 - Percent of Salary Replaced by a 401(k) Contribution of 1% of Current Salary   II-68-2

Probable Life Expectancy at Retirement

Yrs. to Ret.	18.3 (Same as Male Avg.)				20.7 (Better than Male Avg.)				23.2 (Same as Female Avg.)				25.7 (Better than Female Avg.)				Yrs. to Ret.
	4% / 4%	6% / 5%	8% / 6%	10% / 7%	4% / 4%	6% / 5%	8% / 6%	10% / 7%	4% / 4%	6% / 5%	8% / 6%	10% / 7%	4% / 4%	6% / 5%	8% / 6%	10% / 7%	
	Expected Return				(Pre-Retirement/Post-Retirement)				(Pre-Retirement/Post-Retirement)				Expected Return				
0	0.00	0.00	0.00	0.00	0.00	0.00	0.00	0.00	0.00	0.00	0.00	0.00	0.00	0.00	0.00	0.00	0
1	0.06	0.07	0.07	0.08	0.05	0.06	0.07	0.07	0.05	0.06	0.06	0.07	0.04	0.05	0.06	0.06	1
2	0.12	0.14	0.15	0.17	0.11	0.12	0.14	0.15	0.10	0.11	0.13	0.14	0.09	0.10	0.12	0.13	2
3	0.18	0.21	0.23	0.26	0.16	0.19	0.21	0.24	0.15	0.17	0.19	0.22	0.14	0.16	0.18	0.21	3
4	0.25	0.28	0.32	0.36	0.22	0.25	0.29	0.33	0.20	0.23	0.27	0.30	0.18	0.21	0.25	0.28	4
5	0.31	0.36	0.41	0.46	0.28	0.32	0.37	0.42	0.25	0.29	0.34	0.39	0.23	0.27	0.32	0.37	5
6	0.37	0.43	0.50	0.57	0.33	0.39	0.45	0.52	0.30	0.36	0.42	0.49	0.27	0.33	0.39	0.46	6
7	0.44	0.51	0.60	0.69	0.39	0.46	0.54	0.63	0.35	0.42	0.50	0.59	0.32	0.39	0.46	0.55	7
8	0.50	0.59	0.70	0.82	0.45	0.54	0.64	0.75	0.41	0.49	0.59	0.70	0.37	0.45	0.54	0.65	8
9	0.57	0.68	0.81	0.95	0.51	0.61	0.73	0.88	0.46	0.56	0.68	0.81	0.42	0.51	0.63	0.76	9
10	0.64	0.77	0.92	1.10	0.57	0.69	0.84	1.01	0.51	0.63	0.77	0.94	0.47	0.58	0.71	0.88	10
11	0.70	0.86	1.04	1.25	0.63	0.77	0.94	1.15	0.57	0.70	0.87	1.07	0.52	0.65	0.81	1.00	11
12	0.77	0.95	1.16	1.42	0.69	0.85	1.06	1.30	0.62	0.78	0.97	1.21	0.57	0.72	0.90	1.13	12
13	0.84	1.04	1.29	1.60	0.75	0.94	1.18	1.47	0.68	0.86	1.08	1.36	0.62	0.79	1.00	1.27	13
14	0.91	1.14	1.43	1.79	0.81	1.03	1.30	1.64	0.73	0.94	1.20	1.52	0.67	0.86	1.11	1.42	14
15	0.98	1.24	1.57	1.99	0.87	1.12	1.43	1.82	0.79	1.02	1.31	1.69	0.72	0.94	1.22	1.58	15
16	1.05	1.34	1.72	2.20	0.93	1.21	1.57	2.02	0.84	1.10	1.44	1.87	0.77	1.02	1.34	1.75	16
17	1.12	1.45	1.88	2.43	1.00	1.31	1.71	2.23	0.90	1.19	1.57	2.07	0.82	1.10	1.46	1.94	17
18	1.19	1.56	2.04	2.68	1.06	1.41	1.86	2.46	0.96	1.28	1.71	2.28	0.87	1.18	1.59	2.13	18
19	1.26	1.67	2.22	2.94	1.13	1.51	2.02	2.70	1.02	1.37	1.85	2.50	0.93	1.26	1.72	2.34	19
20	1.33	1.79	2.40	3.22	1.19	1.61	2.18	2.96	1.08	1.47	2.01	2.74	0.98	1.35	1.86	2.57	20
21	1.41	1.91	2.59	3.52	1.26	1.72	2.35	3.23	1.14	1.57	2.16	3.00	1.03	1.44	2.01	2.80	21
22	1.48	2.03	2.79	3.84	1.32	1.83	2.53	3.52	1.20	1.67	2.33	3.27	1.09	1.54	2.17	3.06	22
23	1.56	2.15	2.99	4.18	1.39	1.94	2.72	3.84	1.26	1.77	2.51	3.56	1.14	1.63	2.33	3.33	23
24	1.63	2.28	3.21	4.55	1.46	2.06	2.92	4.17	1.32	1.88	2.69	3.87	1.20	1.73	2.50	3.62	24
25	1.71	2.42	3.44	4.94	1.53	2.18	3.13	4.53	1.38	1.99	2.88	4.20	1.26	1.83	2.68	3.93	25
26	1.79	2.56	3.68	5.35	1.60	2.30	3.35	4.91	1.44	2.10	3.08	4.55	1.31	1.93	2.86	4.26	26
27	1.87	2.70	3.94	5.80	1.67	2.43	3.58	5.32	1.50	2.22	3.29	4.93	1.37	2.04	3.06	4.62	27
28	1.95	2.84	4.20	6.27	1.74	2.56	3.82	5.75	1.57	2.34	3.52	5.33	1.43	2.15	3.26	4.99	28
29	2.02	2.99	4.48	6.78	1.81	2.70	4.07	6.22	1.63	2.46	3.75	5.77	1.49	2.26	3.48	5.40	29
30	2.11	3.15	4.77	7.32	1.88	2.84	4.34	6.72	1.70	2.59	3.99	6.23	1.55	2.38	3.71	5.83	30
31	2.19	3.31	5.07	7.90	1.95	2.98	4.62	7.25	1.76	2.72	4.25	6.72	1.61	2.50	3.94	6.29	31
32	2.27	3.47	5.39	8.52	2.03	3.13	4.91	7.81	1.83	2.85	4.51	7.24	1.67	2.63	4.19	6.78	32
33	2.35	3.64	5.73	9.18	2.10	3.28	5.21	8.42	1.90	2.99	4.79	7.80	1.73	2.75	4.45	7.31	33
34	2.43	3.81	6.08	9.88	2.17	3.44	5.53	9.06	1.96	3.13	5.09	8.40	1.79	2.88	4.73	7.87	34
35	2.52	3.99	6.45	10.63	2.25	3.60	5.87	9.75	2.03	3.28	5.40	9.04	1.85	3.02	5.01	8.47	35
36	2.60	4.17	6.83	11.44	2.33	3.76	6.22	10.49	2.10	3.43	5.72	9.73	1.91	3.16	5.31	9.11	36
37	2.69	4.36	7.24	12.30	2.40	3.93	6.59	11.28	2.17	3.58	6.06	10.46	1.98	3.30	5.63	9.79	37
38	2.78	4.55	7.66	13.21	2.48	4.11	6.97	12.12	2.24	3.74	6.41	11.23	2.04	3.45	5.96	10.52	38
39	2.87	4.75	8.11	14.19	2.56	4.29	7.38	13.01	2.31	3.91	6.79	12.07	2.10	3.60	6.30	11.30	39
40	2.95	4.96	8.58	15.24	2.64	4.47	7.80	13.97	2.38	4.08	7.18	12.96	2.17	3.75	6.67	12.13	40
41	3.04	5.17	9.07	16.35	2.72	4.66	8.25	15.00	2.45	4.25	7.59	13.90	2.24	3.91	7.05	13.02	41
42	3.13	5.39	9.58	17.54	2.80	4.86	8.72	16.09	2.53	4.43	8.02	14.92	2.30	4.08	7.45	13.97	42
43	3.22	5.61	10.12	18.82	2.88	5.06	9.21	17.26	2.60	4.61	8.47	16.00	2.37	4.25	7.86	14.98	43
44	3.32	5.84	10.68	20.18	2.96	5.27	9.72	18.51	2.67	4.80	8.94	17.16	2.44	4.42	8.30	16.06	44
45	3.41	6.08	11.27	21.63	3.05	5.48	10.26	19.84	2.75	5.00	9.44	18.39	2.50	4.60	8.76	17.22	45
46	3.50	6.32	11.89	23.18	3.13	5.70	10.82	21.26	2.82	5.20	9.95	19.71	2.57	4.79	9.25	18.45	46
47	3.60	6.57	12.54	24.84	3.21	5.93	11.41	22.78	2.90	5.40	10.50	21.12	2.64	4.98	9.75	19.77	47
48	3.69	6.83	13.23	26.61	3.30	6.16	12.03	24.40	2.98	5.62	11.07	22.63	2.71	5.17	10.28	21.18	48
49	3.79	7.10	13.94	28.50	3.39	6.40	12.69	26.14	3.06	5.84	11.67	24.23	2.78	5.37	10.84	22.69	49
50	3.89	7.37	14.69	30.51	3.47	6.65	13.37	27.99	3.13	6.06	12.30	25.95	2.86	5.58	11.42	24.29	50

II. Retirement Planning where Salary Keeps Pace with Low 3% Inflation
Planned Retirement Age 68

Table 3 - 401(k) Contribution (% of Current Sal.) Needed to Replace 10% of Sal. at Retirement   II-68-3

Probable Life Expectancy at Retirement

Yrs. to Ret.	18.3 (Same as Male Avg.)				20.7 (Better than Male Avg.)				23.2 (Same as Female Avg.)				25.7 (Better than Female Avg.)				Yrs. to Ret.
	4%/4%	6%/5%	8%/6%	10%/7%	4%/4%	6%/5%	8%/6%	10%/7%	4%/4%	6%/5%	8%/6%	10%/7%	4%/4%	6%/5%	8%/6%	10%/7%	
	Expected Return		(Pre-Retirement/Post-Retirement)				(Pre-Retirement/Post-Retirement)				Expected Return						
0																	0
1	164.48	149.01	135.81	124.46	184.16	165.21	149.25	135.71	204.04	181.23	162.26	146.37	223.92	196.87	174.70	156.34	1
2	81.85	73.44	66.30	60.19	91.63	81.42	72.86	65.62	101.53	89.31	79.21	70.78	111.42	97.02	85.28	75.60	2
3	54.30	48.25	43.14	38.79	60.79	53.50	47.41	42.29	67.36	58.68	51.55	45.62	73.92	63.75	55.50	48.73	3
4	40.53	35.67	31.58	28.12	45.37	39.54	34.71	30.66	50.27	43.38	37.73	33.06	55.17	47.12	40.62	35.32	4
5	32.26	28.12	24.65	21.73	36.12	31.17	27.09	23.69	40.02	34.20	29.45	25.55	43.92	37.15	31.71	27.30	5
6	26.76	23.09	20.04	17.49	29.96	25.60	22.03	19.07	33.19	28.08	23.95	20.56	36.42	30.50	25.78	21.97	6
7	22.82	19.50	16.76	14.47	25.55	21.62	18.42	15.78	28.31	23.72	20.02	17.02	31.07	25.76	21.55	18.18	7
8	19.87	16.81	14.30	12.22	22.25	18.64	15.71	13.32	24.65	20.45	17.08	14.37	27.05	22.21	18.39	15.35	8
9	17.58	14.72	12.39	10.48	19.68	16.32	13.62	11.42	21.81	17.90	14.81	12.32	23.93	19.45	15.94	13.16	9
10	15.74	13.05	10.87	9.09	17.63	14.47	11.95	9.92	19.53	15.87	12.99	10.69	21.43	17.24	13.99	11.42	10
11	14.24	11.69	9.63	7.97	15.95	12.96	10.59	8.69	17.67	14.22	11.51	9.37	19.39	15.44	12.39	10.01	11
12	12.99	10.55	8.61	7.04	14.54	11.70	9.46	7.68	16.12	12.83	10.28	8.28	17.69	13.94	11.07	8.84	12
13	11.93	9.59	7.74	6.26	13.36	10.64	8.51	6.83	14.80	11.67	9.25	7.36	16.24	12.68	9.96	7.86	13
14	11.03	8.77	7.00	5.60	12.34	9.73	7.70	6.10	13.68	10.67	8.37	6.58	15.01	11.59	9.01	7.03	14
15	10.24	8.06	6.37	5.03	11.46	8.94	7.00	5.48	12.70	9.81	7.60	5.91	13.94	10.66	8.19	6.32	15
16	9.55	7.45	5.81	4.54	10.70	8.25	6.39	4.95	11.85	9.05	6.94	5.34	13.00	9.84	7.47	5.70	16
17	8.95	6.90	5.32	4.11	10.02	7.65	5.85	4.48	11.10	8.39	6.36	4.83	12.18	9.12	6.85	5.16	17
18	8.41	6.42	4.90	3.73	9.41	7.11	5.38	4.07	10.43	7.80	5.85	4.39	11.45	8.48	6.30	4.69	18
19	7.93	5.98	4.51	3.40	8.87	6.63	4.96	3.71	9.83	7.28	5.39	4.00	10.79	7.91	5.81	4.27	19
20	7.49	5.60	4.17	3.10	8.39	6.20	4.59	3.38	9.29	6.81	4.99	3.65	10.20	7.39	5.37	3.90	20
21	7.10	5.25	3.87	2.84	7.95	5.82	4.25	3.10	8.81	6.38	4.62	3.34	9.66	6.93	4.97	3.57	21
22	6.74	4.93	3.59	2.60	7.55	5.47	3.95	2.84	7.96	6.00	4.29	3.06	9.18	6.51	4.62	3.27	22
23	6.42	4.64	3.34	2.39	7.19	5.15	3.67	2.61	7.96	5.64	3.99	2.81	8.74	6.13	4.30	3.00	23
24	6.12	4.38	3.11	2.20	6.85	4.85	3.42	2.40	7.59	5.32	3.72	2.59	8.33	5.78	4.00	2.76	24
25	5.85	4.14	2.90	2.03	6.54	4.59	3.19	2.21	7.25	5.03	3.47	2.38	7.96	5.46	3.74	2.54	25
26	5.59	3.91	2.72	1.87	6.26	4.34	2.98	2.04	6.94	4.76	3.24	2.20	7.61	5.17	3.49	2.35	26
27	5.36	3.71	2.54	1.72	6.00	4.11	2.79	1.88	6.65	4.51	3.04	2.03	7.29	4.90	3.27	2.17	27
28	5.14	3.52	2.38	1.59	5.76	3.90	2.62	1.74	6.38	4.28	2.84	1.87	7.00	4.65	3.06	2.00	28
29	4.94	3.34	2.23	1.47	5.53	3.71	2.45	1.61	6.13	4.06	2.67	1.73	6.72	4.42	2.87	1.85	29
30	4.75	3.18	2.10	1.37	5.32	3.52	2.30	1.49	5.89	3.87	2.51	1.61	6.47	4.20	2.70	1.72	30
31	4.57	3.03	1.97	1.27	5.12	3.35	2.17	1.38	5.67	3.68	2.36	1.49	6.23	4.00	2.54	1.59	31
32	4.41	2.88	1.85	1.17	4.94	3.20	2.04	1.28	5.47	3.51	2.22	1.38	6.00	3.81	2.39	1.47	32
33	4.25	2.75	1.75	1.09	4.76	3.05	1.92	1.19	5.28	3.34	2.09	1.28	5.79	3.63	2.25	1.37	33
34	4.11	2.63	1.65	1.01	4.60	2.91	1.81	1.10	5.09	3.19	1.97	1.19	5.59	3.47	2.12	1.27	34
35	3.97	2.51	1.55	0.94	4.44	2.78	1.70	1.03	4.92	3.05	1.85	1.11	5.40	3.31	2.00	1.18	35
36	3.84	2.40	1.46	0.87	4.30	2.66	1.61	0.95	4.76	2.92	1.75	1.03	5.23	3.17	1.88	1.10	36
37	3.72	2.29	1.38	0.81	4.16	2.54	1.52	0.89	4.61	2.79	1.65	0.96	5.06	3.03	1.78	1.02	37
38	3.60	2.20	1.30	0.76	4.03	2.44	1.43	0.83	4.47	2.67	1.56	0.89	4.90	2.90	1.68	0.95	38
39	3.49	2.10	1.23	0.70	3.91	2.33	1.36	0.77	4.33	2.56	1.47	0.83	4.75	2.78	1.59	0.89	39
40	3.39	2.02	1.17	0.66	3.79	2.24	1.28	0.72	4.20	2.45	1.39	0.77	4.61	2.66	1.50	0.82	40
41	3.29	1.93	1.10	0.61	3.68	2.14	1.21	0.67	4.08	2.35	1.32	0.72	4.47	2.56	1.42	0.77	41
42	3.19	1.86	1.04	0.57	3.57	2.06	1.15	0.62	3.96	2.26	1.25	0.67	4.34	2.45	1.34	0.72	42
43	3.10	1.78	0.99	0.53	3.47	1.98	1.09	0.58	3.85	2.17	1.18	0.62	4.22	2.35	1.27	0.67	43
44	3.01	1.71	0.94	0.50	3.38	1.90	1.03	0.54	3.74	2.08	1.12	0.58	4.10	2.26	1.20	0.62	44
45	2.93	1.65	0.89	0.46	3.28	1.82	0.97	0.50	3.64	2.00	1.06	0.54	3.99	2.17	1.14	0.58	45
46	2.85	1.58	0.84	0.43	3.20	1.75	0.92	0.47	3.54	1.92	1.00	0.51	3.89	2.09	1.08	0.54	46
47	2.78	1.52	0.80	0.40	3.11	1.69	0.88	0.44	3.45	1.85	0.95	0.47	3.78	2.01	1.03	0.51	47
48	2.71	1.46	0.76	0.38	3.03	1.62	0.83	0.41	3.36	1.78	0.90	0.44	3.69	1.93	0.97	0.47	48
49	2.64	1.41	0.72	0.35	2.95	1.56	0.79	0.38	3.27	1.71	0.86	0.41	3.59	1.86	0.92	0.44	49
50	2.57	1.36	0.68	0.33	2.88	1.50	0.75	0.36	3.19	1.65	0.81	0.39	3.50	1.79	0.88	0.41	50

Appendix A

II. Retirement Planning where Salary Keeps Pace with Low 3% Inflation
Planned Retirement Age 68

Table 4 - Accumulation at Retirement (Multiple of Current Sal.) for 10% Sal. Replacement   II-68-4

Probable Life Expectancy at Retirement

Yrs. to Ret.	18.3 (Same as Male Avg.)				20.7 (Better than Male Avg.)				23.2 (Same as Female Avg.)				25.7 (Better than Female Avg.)				Yrs. to Ret.
	4% / 4%	6% / 5%	8% / 6%	10% / 7%	4% / 4%	6% / 5%	8% / 6%	10% / 7%	4% / 4%	6% / 5%	8% / 6%	10% / 7%	4% / 4%	6% / 5%	8% / 6%	10% / 7%	
	Expected Return				(Pre-Retirement/Post-Retirement)				(Pre-Retirement/Post-Retirement)				Expected Return				
0	1.64	1.49	1.36	1.24	1.84	1.65	1.49	1.36	2.04	1.81	1.62	1.46	2.24	1.97	1.75	1.56	0
1	1.69	1.53	1.40	1.28	1.90	1.70	1.54	1.40	2.10	1.87	1.67	1.51	2.31	2.03	1.80	1.61	1
2	1.75	1.58	1.44	1.32	1.95	1.75	1.58	1.44	2.16	1.92	1.72	1.55	2.38	2.09	1.85	1.66	2
3	1.80	1.63	1.48	1.36	2.01	1.81	1.63	1.48	2.23	1.98	1.77	1.60	2.45	2.15	1.91	1.71	3
4	1.85	1.68	1.53	1.40	2.07	1.86	1.68	1.53	2.30	2.04	1.83	1.65	2.52	2.22	1.97	1.76	4
5	1.91	1.73	1.57	1.44	2.13	1.92	1.73	1.57	2.37	2.10	1.88	1.70	2.60	2.28	2.03	1.81	5
6	1.96	1.78	1.62	1.49	2.20	1.97	1.78	1.62	2.44	2.16	1.94	1.75	2.67	2.35	2.09	1.87	6
7	2.02	1.83	1.67	1.53	2.26	2.03	1.84	1.67	2.51	2.23	2.00	1.80	2.75	2.42	2.15	1.92	7
8	2.08	1.89	1.72	1.58	2.33	2.09	1.89	1.72	2.58	2.30	2.06	1.85	2.84	2.49	2.21	1.98	8
9	2.15	1.94	1.77	1.62	2.40	2.16	1.95	1.77	2.66	2.36	2.12	1.91	2.92	2.57	2.28	2.04	9
10	2.21	2.00	1.83	1.67	2.47	2.22	2.01	1.82	2.74	2.44	2.18	1.97	3.01	2.65	2.35	2.10	10
11	2.28	2.06	1.88	1.72	2.55	2.29	2.07	1.88	2.82	2.51	2.25	2.03	3.10	2.73	2.42	2.16	11
12	2.35	2.12	1.94	1.77	2.63	2.36	2.13	1.93	2.91	2.58	2.31	2.09	3.19	2.81	2.49	2.23	12
13	2.42	2.19	1.99	1.83	2.70	2.43	2.19	1.99	3.00	2.66	2.38	2.15	3.29	2.89	2.57	2.30	13
14	2.49	2.25	2.05	1.88	2.79	2.50	2.26	2.05	3.09	2.74	2.45	2.21	3.39	2.98	2.64	2.36	14
15	2.56	2.32	2.12	1.94	2.87	2.57	2.33	2.11	3.18	2.82	2.53	2.28	3.49	3.07	2.72	2.44	15
16	2.64	2.39	2.18	2.00	2.96	2.65	2.40	2.18	3.27	2.91	2.60	2.35	3.59	3.16	2.80	2.51	16
17	2.72	2.46	2.24	2.06	3.04	2.73	2.47	2.24	3.37	3.00	2.68	2.42	3.70	3.25	2.89	2.58	17
18	2.80	2.54	2.31	2.12	3.14	2.81	2.54	2.31	3.47	3.09	2.76	2.49	3.81	3.35	2.97	2.66	18
19	2.88	2.61	2.38	2.18	3.23	2.90	2.62	2.38	3.58	3.18	2.85	2.57	3.93	3.45	3.06	2.74	19
20	2.97	2.69	2.45	2.25	3.33	2.98	2.70	2.45	3.69	3.27	2.93	2.64	4.04	3.56	3.16	2.82	20
21	3.06	2.77	2.53	2.32	3.43	3.07	2.78	2.52	3.80	3.37	3.02	2.72	4.17	3.66	3.25	2.91	21
22	3.15	2.86	2.60	2.38	3.53	3.17	2.86	2.60	3.91	3.47	3.11	2.80	4.29	3.77	3.35	3.00	22
23	3.25	2.94	2.68	2.46	3.63	3.26	2.95	2.68	4.03	3.58	3.20	2.89	4.42	3.89	3.45	3.09	23
24	3.34	3.03	2.76	2.53	3.74	3.36	3.03	2.76	4.15	3.68	3.30	2.98	4.55	4.00	3.55	3.18	24
25	3.44	3.12	2.84	2.61	3.86	3.46	3.13	2.84	4.27	3.79	3.40	3.06	4.69	4.12	3.66	3.27	25
26	3.55	3.21	2.93	2.68	3.97	3.56	3.22	2.93	4.40	3.91	3.50	3.16	4.83	4.25	3.77	3.37	26
27	3.65	3.31	3.02	2.76	4.09	3.67	3.32	3.01	4.53	4.03	3.60	3.25	4.97	4.37	3.88	3.47	27
28	3.76	3.41	3.11	2.85	4.21	3.78	3.41	3.10	4.67	4.15	3.71	3.35	5.12	4.50	4.00	3.58	28
29	3.88	3.51	3.20	2.93	4.34	3.89	3.52	3.20	4.81	4.27	3.82	3.45	5.28	4.64	4.12	3.68	29
30	3.99	3.62	3.30	3.02	4.47	4.01	3.62	3.29	4.95	4.40	3.94	3.55	5.44	4.78	4.24	3.79	30
31	4.11	3.73	3.40	3.11	4.60	4.13	3.73	3.39	5.10	4.53	4.06	3.66	5.60	4.92	4.37	3.91	31
32	4.24	3.84	3.50	3.21	4.74	4.25	3.84	3.49	5.25	4.67	4.18	3.77	5.77	5.07	4.50	4.03	32
33	4.36	3.95	3.60	3.30	4.88	4.38	3.96	3.60	5.41	4.81	4.30	3.88	5.94	5.22	4.63	4.15	33
34	4.49	4.07	3.71	3.40	5.03	4.51	4.08	3.71	5.57	4.95	4.43	4.00	6.12	5.38	4.77	4.27	34
35	4.63	4.19	3.82	3.50	5.18	4.65	4.20	3.82	5.74	5.10	4.57	4.12	6.30	5.54	4.92	4.40	35
36	4.77	4.32	3.94	3.61	5.34	4.79	4.33	3.93	5.91	5.25	4.70	4.24	6.49	5.71	5.06	4.53	36
37	4.91	4.45	4.05	3.72	5.50	4.93	4.46	4.05	6.09	5.41	4.84	4.37	6.68	5.88	5.22	4.67	37
38	5.06	4.58	4.18	3.83	5.66	5.08	4.59	4.17	6.27	5.57	4.99	4.50	6.88	6.05	5.37	4.81	38
39	5.21	4.72	4.30	3.94	5.83	5.23	4.73	4.30	6.46	5.74	5.14	4.64	7.09	6.24	5.53	4.95	39
40	5.37	4.86	4.43	4.06	6.01	5.39	4.87	4.43	6.66	5.91	5.29	4.77	7.30	6.42	5.70	5.10	40
41	5.53	5.01	4.56	4.18	6.19	5.55	5.01	4.56	6.86	6.09	5.45	4.92	7.52	6.61	5.87	5.25	41
42	5.69	5.16	4.70	4.31	6.37	5.72	5.17	4.70	7.06	6.27	5.62	5.07	7.75	6.81	6.05	5.41	42
43	5.86	5.31	4.84	4.44	6.56	5.89	5.32	4.84	7.27	6.46	5.78	5.22	7.98	7.02	6.23	5.57	43
44	6.04	5.47	4.99	4.57	6.76	6.07	5.48	4.98	7.49	6.65	5.96	5.37	8.22	7.23	6.41	5.74	44
45	6.22	5.64	5.14	4.71	6.96	6.25	5.64	5.13	7.72	6.85	6.14	5.54	8.47	7.44	6.61	5.91	45
46	6.41	5.80	5.29	4.85	7.17	6.44	5.81	5.29	7.95	7.06	6.32	5.70	8.72	7.67	6.80	6.09	46
47	6.60	5.98	5.45	4.99	7.39	6.63	5.99	5.44	8.19	7.27	6.51	5.87	8.98	7.90	7.01	6.27	47
48	6.80	6.16	5.61	5.14	7.61	6.83	6.17	5.61	8.43	7.49	6.71	6.05	9.25	8.14	7.22	6.46	48
49	7.00	6.34	5.78	5.30	7.84	7.03	6.35	5.78	8.68	7.71	6.91	6.23	9.53	8.38	7.44	6.65	49
50	7.21	6.53	5.95	5.46	8.07	7.24	6.54	5.95	8.94	7.94	7.11	6.42	9.82	8.63	7.66	6.85	50

II. Retirement Planning where Salary Keeps Pace with Low 3% Inflation
Planned Retirement Age 71

Table 1 - Percent of Salary Replaced by a 401(k) Account Equal to Current Annual Salary   II-71-1

Probable Life Expectancy at Retirement

Yrs. to Ret.	16 (Same as Male Avg.)				18.3 (Better than Male Avg.)				20.7 (Same as Female Avg.)				23.2 (Better than Female Avg.)				Yrs. to Ret.
	4% / 4%	6% / 5%	8% / 6%	10% / 7%	4% / 4%	6% / 5%	8% / 6%	10% / 7%	4% / 4%	6% / 5%	8% / 6%	10% / 7%	4% / 4%	6% / 5%	8% / 6%	10% / 7%	
	Expected Return				(Pre-Retirement/Post-Retirement)				(Pre-Retirement/Post-Retirement)				Expected Return				
0	6.88	7.52	8.18	8.85	6.08	6.71	7.36	8.03	5.43	6.05	6.70	7.37	4.90	5.52	6.16	6.83	0
1	6.94	7.74	8.57	9.46	6.14	6.91	7.72	8.58	5.48	6.23	7.02	7.87	4.95	5.68	6.46	7.30	1
2	7.01	7.96	8.99	10.10	6.20	7.11	8.09	9.16	5.54	6.41	7.37	8.41	5.00	5.84	6.78	7.79	2
3	7.08	8.19	9.43	10.79	6.26	7.31	8.49	9.79	5.59	6.60	7.72	8.98	5.05	6.01	7.10	8.32	3
4	7.15	8.43	9.88	11.52	6.32	7.53	8.90	10.45	5.64	6.79	8.10	9.59	5.09	6.19	7.45	8.89	4
5	7.22	8.68	10.36	12.30	6.38	7.75	9.33	11.16	5.70	6.99	8.49	10.24	5.14	6.37	7.81	9.49	5
6	7.29	8.93	10.87	13.14	6.44	7.97	9.78	11.92	5.75	7.19	8.90	10.94	5.19	6.55	8.19	10.14	6
7	7.36	9.19	11.39	14.03	6.50	8.20	10.26	12.73	5.81	7.40	9.33	11.68	5.24	6.75	8.59	10.83	7
8	7.43	9.46	11.94	14.99	6.57	8.44	10.76	13.60	5.87	7.61	9.79	12.47	5.29	6.94	9.00	11.56	8
9	7.50	9.73	12.52	16.01	6.63	8.69	11.28	14.52	5.92	7.84	10.26	13.32	5.35	7.14	9.44	12.35	9
10	7.57	10.01	13.13	17.09	6.70	8.94	11.82	15.51	5.98	8.06	10.76	14.23	5.40	7.35	9.90	13.19	10
11	7.65	10.31	13.77	18.26	6.76	9.20	12.40	16.57	6.04	8.30	11.28	15.19	5.45	7.57	10.38	14.09	11
12	7.72	10.61	14.44	19.50	6.83	9.47	13.00	17.69	6.10	8.54	11.83	16.23	5.50	7.79	10.88	15.05	12
13	7.79	10.91	15.14	20.82	6.89	9.74	13.63	18.90	6.16	8.79	12.40	17.33	5.56	8.01	11.41	16.07	13
14	7.87	11.23	15.87	22.24	6.96	10.03	14.29	20.18	6.22	9.04	13.00	18.51	5.61	8.24	11.96	17.16	14
15	7.95	11.56	16.64	23.75	7.03	10.32	14.98	21.55	6.28	9.31	13.63	19.77	5.66	8.48	12.54	18.33	15
16	8.02	11.90	17.45	25.37	7.10	10.62	15.71	23.02	6.34	9.58	14.29	21.11	5.72	8.73	13.15	19.57	16
17	8.10	12.24	18.29	27.09	7.16	10.93	16.47	24.58	6.40	9.86	14.99	22.55	5.78	8.99	13.79	20.91	17
18	8.18	12.60	19.18	28.94	7.23	11.25	17.27	26.26	6.46	10.14	15.71	24.08	5.83	9.25	14.45	22.33	18
19	8.26	12.96	20.11	30.90	7.30	11.57	18.11	28.04	6.52	10.44	16.48	25.72	5.89	9.52	15.16	23.85	19
20	8.34	13.34	21.09	33.00	7.37	11.91	18.99	29.95	6.59	10.74	17.28	27.47	5.94	9.79	15.89	25.47	20
21	8.42	13.73	22.11	35.25	7.45	12.26	19.91	31.99	6.65	11.06	18.11	29.34	6.00	10.08	16.66	27.20	21
22	8.50	14.13	23.18	37.65	7.52	12.61	20.87	34.16	6.71	11.38	18.99	31.33	6.06	10.37	17.47	29.05	22
23	8.58	14.54	24.31	40.21	7.59	12.98	21.88	36.48	6.78	11.71	19.91	33.46	6.12	10.67	18.32	31.02	23
24	8.67	14.96	25.48	42.94	7.66	13.36	22.95	38.96	6.85	12.05	20.88	35.74	6.18	10.98	19.21	33.13	24
25	8.75	15.40	26.72	45.86	7.74	13.75	24.06	41.61	6.91	12.40	21.89	38.17	6.24	11.30	20.14	35.39	25
26	8.84	15.85	28.02	48.98	7.81	14.15	25.23	44.44	6.98	12.76	22.95	40.76	6.30	11.63	21.11	37.79	26
27	8.92	16.31	29.38	52.31	7.89	14.56	26.45	47.47	7.05	13.13	24.07	43.53	6.36	11.97	22.14	40.36	27
28	9.01	16.78	30.80	55.86	7.97	14.98	27.73	50.69	7.12	13.51	25.23	46.49	6.42	12.32	23.21	43.11	28
29	9.10	17.27	32.29	59.66	8.04	15.42	29.08	54.14	7.18	13.91	26.46	49.66	6.48	12.68	24.34	46.04	29
30	9.18	17.77	33.86	63.72	8.12	15.87	30.49	57.82	7.25	14.31	27.74	53.03	6.55	13.05	25.52	49.17	30
31	9.27	18.29	35.50	68.05	8.20	16.33	31.97	61.75	7.32	14.73	29.09	56.64	6.61	13.43	26.75	52.51	31
32	9.36	18.82	37.22	72.68	8.28	16.80	33.52	65.95	7.40	15.16	30.50	60.49	6.67	13.82	28.05	56.08	32
33	9.45	19.37	39.03	77.62	8.36	17.29	35.14	70.44	7.47	15.60	31.98	64.60	6.74	14.22	29.41	59.90	33
34	9.55	19.94	40.92	82.90	8.44	17.80	36.85	75.23	7.54	16.05	33.53	69.00	6.81	14.63	30.84	63.97	34
35	9.64	20.52	42.91	88.54	8.52	18.31	38.63	80.34	7.61	16.52	35.15	73.69	6.87	15.06	32.34	68.32	35
36	9.73	21.11	44.99	94.56	8.61	18.85	40.51	85.81	7.69	17.00	36.86	78.70	6.94	15.50	33.90	72.97	36
37	9.83	21.73	47.17	100.99	8.69	19.40	42.47	91.64	7.76	17.49	38.65	84.05	7.00	15.95	35.55	77.93	37
38	9.92	22.36	49.46	107.86	8.77	19.96	44.53	97.87	7.84	18.00	40.52	89.77	7.07	16.41	37.27	83.23	38
39	10.02	23.01	51.86	115.19	8.86	20.54	46.69	104.53	7.91	18.53	42.49	95.87	7.14	16.89	39.08	88.89	39
40	10.12	23.68	54.37	123.02	8.94	21.14	48.96	111.64	7.99	19.07	44.55	102.39	7.21	17.38	40.97	94.93	40
41	10.21	24.37	57.01	131.39	9.03	21.75	51.33	119.23	8.07	19.62	46.71	109.35	7.28	17.89	42.96	101.39	41
42	10.31	25.08	59.77	140.33	9.12	22.39	53.82	127.33	8.14	20.19	48.97	116.79	7.35	18.41	45.05	108.28	42
43	10.41	25.81	62.67	149.87	9.21	23.04	56.43	135.99	8.22	20.78	51.35	124.73	7.42	18.94	47.23	115.64	43
44	10.51	26.56	65.71	160.06	9.30	23.71	59.17	145.24	8.30	21.38	53.84	133.21	7.49	19.49	49.52	123.51	44
45	10.62	27.33	68.90	170.94	9.39	24.40	62.04	155.12	8.38	22.01	56.45	142.27	7.57	20.06	51.92	131.90	45
46	10.72	28.13	72.24	182.57	9.48	25.11	65.05	165.67	8.47	22.65	59.19	151.94	7.64	20.65	54.44	140.87	46
47	10.82	28.95	75.75	194.98	9.57	25.84	68.20	176.93	8.55	23.31	62.06	162.27	7.71	21.25	57.08	150.45	47
48	10.93	29.79	79.42	208.24	9.66	26.59	71.51	188.96	8.63	23.98	65.07	173.31	7.79	21.86	59.85	160.68	48
49	11.03	30.65	83.27	222.40	9.76	27.36	74.98	201.81	8.71	24.68	68.22	185.09	7.87	22.50	62.75	171.61	49
50	11.14	31.55	87.31	237.52	9.85	28.16	78.61	215.53	8.80	25.40	71.53	197.68	7.94	23.16	65.80	183.28	50

II. Retirement Planning where Salary Keeps Pace with Low 3% Inflation
Planned Retirement Age 71

Table 2 - Percent of Salary Replaced by a 401(k) Contribution of 1% of Current Salary   II-71-2

Probable Life Expectancy at Retirement

Yrs. to Ret.	16 (Same as Male Avg.)				18.3 (Better than Male Avg.)				20.7 (Same as Female Avg.)				23.2 (Better than Female Avg.)				Yrs. to Ret.
	4% / 4%	6% / 5%	8% / 6%	10% / 7%	4% / 4%	6% / 5%	8% / 6%	10% / 7%	4% / 4%	6% / 5%	8% / 6%	10% / 7%	4% / 4%	6% / 5%	8% / 6%	10% / 7%	
	Expected Return				(Pre-Retirement/Post-Retirement)				(Pre-Retirement/Post-Retirement)				Expected Return				
0	0.00	0.00	0.00	0.00	0.00	0.00	0.00	0.00	0.00	0.00	0.00	0.00	0.00	0.00	0.00	0.00	0
1	0.07	0.08	0.08	0.09	0.06	0.07	0.07	0.08	0.05	0.06	0.07	0.07	0.05	0.06	0.06	0.07	1
2	0.14	0.15	0.17	0.18	0.12	0.14	0.15	0.17	0.11	0.12	0.14	0.15	0.10	0.11	0.13	0.14	2
3	0.21	0.23	0.26	0.28	0.18	0.21	0.23	0.26	0.16	0.19	0.21	0.24	0.15	0.17	0.19	0.22	3
4	0.28	0.31	0.35	0.39	0.25	0.28	0.32	0.36	0.22	0.25	0.29	0.33	0.20	0.23	0.27	0.30	4
5	0.35	0.40	0.45	0.51	0.31	0.36	0.41	0.46	0.28	0.32	0.37	0.42	0.25	0.29	0.34	0.39	5
6	0.42	0.49	0.55	0.63	0.37	0.43	0.50	0.57	0.33	0.39	0.45	0.52	0.30	0.36	0.42	0.49	6
7	0.50	0.57	0.66	0.76	0.44	0.51	0.60	0.69	0.39	0.46	0.54	0.63	0.35	0.42	0.50	0.59	7
8	0.57	0.67	0.78	0.90	0.50	0.59	0.70	0.82	0.45	0.54	0.64	0.75	0.41	0.49	0.59	0.70	8
9	0.64	0.76	0.90	1.05	0.57	0.68	0.81	0.95	0.51	0.61	0.73	0.88	0.46	0.56	0.68	0.81	9
10	0.72	0.86	1.02	1.21	0.64	0.77	0.92	1.10	0.57	0.69	0.84	1.01	0.51	0.63	0.77	0.94	10
11	0.79	0.96	1.15	1.38	0.70	0.86	1.04	1.25	0.63	0.77	0.94	1.15	0.57	0.70	0.87	1.07	11
12	0.87	1.06	1.29	1.57	0.77	0.95	1.16	1.42	0.69	0.85	1.06	1.30	0.62	0.78	0.97	1.21	12
13	0.95	1.17	1.43	1.76	0.84	1.04	1.29	1.60	0.75	0.94	1.18	1.47	0.68	0.86	1.08	1.36	13
14	1.03	1.28	1.59	1.97	0.91	1.14	1.43	1.79	0.81	1.03	1.30	1.64	0.73	0.94	1.20	1.52	14
15	1.10	1.39	1.74	2.19	0.98	1.24	1.57	1.99	0.87	1.12	1.43	1.82	0.79	1.02	1.31	1.69	15
16	1.18	1.50	1.91	2.43	1.05	1.34	1.72	2.20	0.93	1.21	1.57	2.02	0.84	1.10	1.44	1.87	16
17	1.26	1.62	2.09	2.68	1.12	1.45	1.88	2.43	1.00	1.31	1.71	2.23	0.90	1.19	1.57	2.07	17
18	1.35	1.75	2.27	2.95	1.19	1.56	2.04	2.68	1.06	1.41	1.86	2.46	0.96	1.28	1.71	2.28	18
19	1.43	1.87	2.46	3.24	1.26	1.67	2.22	2.94	1.13	1.51	2.02	2.70	1.02	1.37	1.85	2.50	19
20	1.51	2.00	2.66	3.55	1.33	1.79	2.40	3.22	1.19	1.61	2.18	2.96	1.08	1.47	2.01	2.74	20
21	1.59	2.14	2.87	3.88	1.41	1.91	2.59	3.52	1.26	1.72	2.35	3.23	1.14	1.57	2.16	3.00	21
22	1.68	2.27	3.09	4.23	1.48	2.03	2.79	3.84	1.32	1.83	2.53	3.52	1.20	1.67	2.33	3.27	22
23	1.76	2.41	3.33	4.61	1.56	2.15	2.99	4.18	1.39	1.94	2.72	3.84	1.26	1.77	2.51	3.56	23
24	1.85	2.56	3.57	5.01	1.63	2.28	3.21	4.55	1.46	2.06	2.92	4.17	1.32	1.88	2.69	3.87	24
25	1.93	2.71	3.82	5.44	1.71	2.42	3.44	4.94	1.53	2.18	3.13	4.53	1.38	1.99	2.88	4.20	25
26	2.02	2.86	4.09	5.90	1.79	2.56	3.68	5.35	1.60	2.30	3.35	4.91	1.44	2.10	3.08	4.55	26
27	2.11	3.02	4.37	6.39	1.87	2.70	3.94	5.80	1.67	2.43	3.58	5.32	1.50	2.22	3.29	4.93	27
28	2.20	3.18	4.66	6.91	1.95	2.84	4.20	6.27	1.74	2.56	3.82	5.75	1.57	2.34	3.52	5.33	28
29	2.29	3.35	4.97	7.47	2.02	2.99	4.48	6.78	1.81	2.70	4.07	6.22	1.63	2.46	3.75	5.77	29
30	2.38	3.52	5.30	8.07	2.11	3.15	4.77	7.32	1.88	2.84	4.34	6.72	1.70	2.59	3.99	6.23	30
31	2.47	3.70	5.63	8.71	2.19	3.31	5.07	7.90	1.95	2.98	4.62	7.25	1.76	2.72	4.25	6.72	31
32	2.57	3.89	5.99	9.39	2.27	3.47	5.39	8.52	2.03	3.13	4.91	7.81	1.83	2.85	4.51	7.24	32
33	2.66	4.07	6.36	10.11	2.35	3.64	5.73	9.18	2.10	3.28	5.21	8.42	1.90	2.99	4.79	7.80	33
34	2.75	4.27	6.75	10.89	2.43	3.81	6.08	9.88	2.17	3.44	5.53	9.06	1.96	3.13	5.09	8.40	34
35	2.85	4.47	7.16	11.72	2.52	3.99	6.45	10.63	2.25	3.60	5.87	9.75	2.03	3.28	5.40	9.04	35
36	2.95	4.67	7.59	12.60	2.60	4.17	6.83	11.44	2.33	3.76	6.22	10.49	2.10	3.43	5.72	9.73	36
37	3.04	4.88	8.04	13.55	2.69	4.36	7.24	12.30	2.40	3.93	6.59	11.28	2.17	3.58	6.06	10.46	37
38	3.14	5.10	8.51	14.56	2.78	4.55	7.66	13.21	2.48	4.11	6.97	12.12	2.24	3.74	6.41	11.23	38
39	3.24	5.32	9.01	15.64	2.87	4.75	8.11	14.19	2.56	4.29	7.38	13.01	2.31	3.91	6.79	12.07	39
40	3.34	5.55	9.52	16.79	2.95	4.96	8.58	15.24	2.64	4.47	7.80	13.97	2.38	4.08	7.18	12.96	40
41	3.44	5.79	10.07	18.02	3.04	5.17	9.07	16.35	2.72	4.66	8.25	15.00	2.45	4.25	7.59	13.90	41
42	3.54	6.03	10.64	19.33	3.13	5.39	9.58	17.54	2.80	4.86	8.72	16.09	2.53	4.43	8.02	14.92	42
43	3.65	6.29	11.24	20.74	3.22	5.61	10.12	18.82	2.88	5.06	9.21	17.26	2.60	4.61	8.47	16.00	43
44	3.75	6.54	11.86	22.24	3.32	5.84	10.68	20.18	2.96	5.27	9.72	18.51	2.67	4.80	8.94	17.16	44
45	3.86	6.81	12.52	23.84	3.41	6.08	11.27	21.63	3.05	5.48	10.26	19.84	2.75	5.00	9.44	18.39	45
46	3.96	7.08	13.21	25.55	3.50	6.32	11.89	23.18	3.13	5.70	10.82	21.26	2.82	5.20	9.95	19.71	46
47	4.07	7.36	13.93	27.37	3.60	6.57	12.54	24.84	3.21	5.93	11.41	22.78	2.90	5.40	10.50	21.12	47
48	4.18	7.65	14.69	29.32	3.69	6.83	13.23	26.61	3.30	6.16	12.03	24.40	2.98	5.62	11.07	22.63	48
49	4.29	7.95	15.48	31.40	3.79	7.10	13.94	28.50	3.39	6.40	12.69	26.14	3.06	5.84	11.67	24.23	49
50	4.40	8.26	16.32	33.63	3.89	7.37	14.69	30.51	3.47	6.65	13.37	27.99	3.13	6.06	12.30	25.95	50

II. Retirement Planning where Salary Keeps Pace with Low 3% Inflation
Planned Retirement Age 71

Table 3 - 401(k) Contribution (% of Current Sal.) Needed to Replace 10% of Sal. at Retirement II-71-3

Probable Life Expectancy at Retirement

	16 (Same as Male Avg.)				18.3 (Better than Male Avg.)				20.7 (Same as Female Avg.)				23.2 (Better than Female Avg.)				
	4% / 4%	6% / 5%	8% / 6%	10% / 7%	4% / 4%	6% / 5%	8% / 6%	10% / 7%	4% / 4%	6% / 5%	8% / 6%	10% / 7%	4% / 4%	6% / 5%	8% / 6%	10% / 7%	
Yrs. to Ret.	Expected Return		(Pre-Retirement/Post-Retirement)				(Pre-Retirement/Post-Retirement)				Expected Return						Yrs. to Ret.
0																	0
1	145.45	133.02	122.28	112.94	164.48	149.01	135.81	124.46	184.16	165.21	149.25	135.71	204.04	181.23	162.26	146.37	1
2	72.37	65.56	59.69	54.61	81.85	73.44	66.30	60.19	91.63	81.42	72.86	65.62	101.53	89.31	79.21	70.78	2
3	48.02	43.08	38.85	35.20	54.30	48.25	43.14	38.79	60.79	53.50	47.41	42.29	67.36	58.68	51.55	45.62	3
4	35.84	31.84	28.43	25.51	40.53	35.67	31.58	28.12	45.37	39.54	34.71	30.66	50.27	43.38	37.73	33.06	4
5	28.53	25.10	22.20	19.72	32.26	28.12	24.65	21.73	36.12	31.17	27.09	23.69	40.02	34.20	29.45	25.55	5
6	23.66	20.61	18.05	15.87	26.76	23.09	20.04	17.49	29.96	25.60	22.03	19.07	33.19	28.08	23.95	20.56	6
7	20.18	17.41	15.09	13.13	22.82	19.50	16.76	14.47	25.55	21.62	18.42	15.78	28.31	23.72	20.02	17.02	7
8	17.57	15.01	12.87	11.09	19.87	16.81	14.30	12.22	22.25	18.64	15.71	13.32	24.65	20.45	17.08	14.37	8
9	15.54	13.14	11.16	9.51	17.58	14.72	12.39	10.48	19.68	16.32	13.62	11.42	21.81	17.90	14.81	12.32	9
10	13.92	11.65	9.79	8.25	15.74	13.05	10.87	9.09	17.63	14.47	11.95	9.92	19.53	15.87	12.99	10.69	10
11	12.59	10.43	8.67	7.23	14.24	11.69	9.63	7.97	15.95	12.96	10.59	8.69	17.67	14.22	11.51	9.37	11
12	11.49	9.42	7.75	6.39	12.99	10.55	8.61	7.04	14.54	11.70	9.46	7.68	16.12	12.83	10.28	8.28	12
13	10.55	8.57	6.97	5.68	11.93	9.59	7.74	6.26	13.36	10.64	8.51	6.83	14.80	11.67	9.25	7.36	13
14	9.75	7.83	6.30	5.08	11.03	8.77	7.00	5.60	12.34	9.73	7.70	6.10	13.68	10.67	8.37	6.58	14
15	9.06	7.20	5.73	4.56	10.24	8.06	6.37	5.03	11.46	8.94	7.00	5.48	12.70	9.81	7.60	5.91	15
16	8.45	6.65	5.23	4.12	9.55	7.45	5.81	4.54	10.70	8.25	6.39	4.95	11.85	9.05	6.94	5.34	16
17	7.91	6.16	4.79	3.73	8.95	6.90	5.32	4.11	10.02	7.65	5.85	4.48	11.10	8.39	6.36	4.83	17
18	7.43	5.73	4.41	3.39	8.41	6.42	4.90	3.73	9.41	7.11	5.38	4.07	10.43	7.80	5.85	4.39	18
19	7.01	5.34	4.06	3.08	7.93	5.98	4.51	3.40	8.87	6.63	4.96	3.71	9.83	7.28	5.39	4.00	19
20	6.62	5.00	3.76	2.82	7.49	5.60	4.17	3.10	8.39	6.20	4.59	3.38	9.29	6.81	4.99	3.65	20
21	6.28	4.68	3.48	2.58	7.10	5.25	3.87	2.84	7.95	5.82	4.25	3.10	8.81	6.38	4.62	3.34	21
22	5.96	4.40	3.23	2.36	6.74	4.93	3.59	2.60	7.55	5.47	3.95	2.84	8.36	6.00	4.29	3.06	22
23	5.68	4.14	3.01	2.17	6.42	4.64	3.34	2.39	7.19	5.15	3.67	2.61	7.96	5.64	3.99	2.81	23
24	5.41	3.91	2.80	2.00	6.12	4.38	3.11	2.20	6.85	4.85	3.42	2.40	7.59	5.32	3.72	2.59	24
25	5.17	3.69	2.62	1.84	5.85	4.14	2.90	2.03	6.54	4.59	3.19	2.21	7.25	5.03	3.47	2.38	25
26	4.95	3.49	2.44	1.69	5.59	3.91	2.72	1.87	6.26	4.34	2.98	2.04	6.94	4.76	3.24	2.20	26
27	4.74	3.31	2.29	1.56	5.36	3.71	2.54	1.72	6.00	4.11	2.79	1.88	6.65	4.51	3.04	2.03	27
28	4.55	3.14	2.14	1.45	5.14	3.52	2.38	1.59	5.76	3.90	2.62	1.74	6.38	4.28	2.84	1.87	28
29	4.37	2.98	2.01	1.34	4.94	3.34	2.23	1.47	5.53	3.71	2.45	1.61	6.13	4.06	2.67	1.73	29
30	4.20	2.84	1.89	1.24	4.75	3.18	2.10	1.37	5.32	3.52	2.30	1.49	5.89	3.87	2.51	1.61	30
31	4.04	2.70	1.77	1.15	4.57	3.03	1.97	1.27	5.12	3.35	2.17	1.38	5.67	3.68	2.36	1.49	31
32	3.90	2.57	1.67	1.07	4.41	2.88	1.85	1.17	4.94	3.20	2.04	1.28	5.47	3.51	2.22	1.38	32
33	3.76	2.45	1.57	0.99	4.25	2.75	1.75	1.09	4.76	3.05	1.92	1.19	5.28	3.34	2.09	1.28	33
34	3.63	2.34	1.48	0.92	4.11	2.63	1.65	1.01	4.60	2.91	1.81	1.10	5.09	3.19	1.97	1.19	34
35	3.51	2.24	1.40	0.85	3.97	2.51	1.55	0.94	4.44	2.78	1.70	1.03	4.92	3.05	1.85	1.11	35
36	3.40	2.14	1.32	0.79	3.84	2.40	1.46	0.87	4.30	2.66	1.61	0.95	4.76	2.92	1.75	1.03	36
37	3.29	2.05	1.24	0.74	3.72	2.29	1.38	0.81	4.16	2.54	1.52	0.89	4.61	2.79	1.65	0.96	37
38	3.18	1.96	1.17	0.69	3.60	2.20	1.30	0.76	4.03	2.44	1.43	0.83	4.47	2.67	1.56	0.89	38
39	3.09	1.88	1.11	0.64	3.49	2.10	1.23	0.70	3.91	2.33	1.36	0.77	4.33	2.56	1.47	0.83	39
40	2.99	1.80	1.05	0.60	3.39	2.02	1.17	0.66	3.79	2.24	1.28	0.72	4.20	2.45	1.39	0.77	40
41	2.91	1.73	0.99	0.55	3.29	1.93	1.10	0.61	3.68	2.14	1.21	0.67	4.08	2.35	1.32	0.72	41
42	2.82	1.66	0.94	0.52	3.19	1.86	1.04	0.57	3.57	2.06	1.15	0.62	3.96	2.26	1.25	0.67	42
43	2.74	1.59	0.89	0.48	3.10	1.78	0.99	0.53	3.47	1.98	1.09	0.58	3.85	2.17	1.18	0.62	43
44	2.67	1.53	0.84	0.45	3.01	1.71	0.94	0.50	3.38	1.90	1.03	0.54	3.74	2.08	1.12	0.58	44
45	2.59	1.47	0.80	0.42	2.93	1.65	0.89	0.46	3.28	1.82	0.97	0.50	3.64	2.00	1.06	0.54	45
46	2.52	1.41	0.76	0.39	2.85	1.58	0.84	0.43	3.20	1.75	0.92	0.47	3.54	1.92	1.00	0.51	46
47	2.46	1.36	0.72	0.37	2.78	1.52	0.80	0.40	3.11	1.69	0.88	0.44	3.45	1.85	0.95	0.47	47
48	2.39	1.31	0.68	0.34	2.71	1.46	0.76	0.38	3.03	1.62	0.83	0.41	3.36	1.78	0.90	0.44	48
49	2.33	1.26	0.65	0.32	2.64	1.41	0.72	0.35	2.95	1.56	0.79	0.38	3.27	1.71	0.86	0.41	49
50	2.27	1.21	0.61	0.30	2.57	1.36	0.68	0.33	2.88	1.50	0.75	0.36	3.19	1.65	0.81	0.39	50

A-40

Appendix A

II. Retirement Planning where Salary Keeps Pace with Low 3% Inflation
Planned Retirement Age 71

Table 4 - Accumulation at Retirement (Multiple of Current Sal.) for 10% Sal. Replacement — II-71-4

Probable Life Expectancy at Retirement

Yrs. to Ret.	16 (Same as Male Avg.) 4%/4%	6%/5%	8%/6%	10%/7%	18.3 (Better than Male Avg.) 4%/4%	6%/5%	8%/6%	10%/7%	20.7 (Same as Female Avg.) 4%/4%	6%/5%	8%/6%	10%/7%	23.2 (Better than Female Avg.) 4%/4%	6%/5%	8%/6%	10%/7%	Yrs. to Ret.
	Expected Return				(Pre-Retirement/Post-Retirement)				(Pre-Retirement/Post-Retirement)				Expected Return				
0	1.45	1.33	1.22	1.13	1.64	1.49	1.36	1.24	1.84	1.65	1.49	1.36	2.04	1.81	1.62	1.46	0
1	1.50	1.37	1.26	1.16	1.69	1.53	1.40	1.28	1.90	1.70	1.54	1.40	2.10	1.87	1.67	1.51	1
2	1.54	1.41	1.30	1.20	1.75	1.58	1.44	1.32	1.95	1.75	1.58	1.44	2.16	1.92	1.72	1.55	2
3	1.59	1.45	1.34	1.23	1.80	1.63	1.48	1.36	2.01	1.81	1.63	1.48	2.23	1.98	1.77	1.60	3
4	1.64	1.50	1.38	1.27	1.85	1.68	1.53	1.40	2.07	1.86	1.68	1.53	2.30	2.04	1.83	1.65	4
5	1.69	1.54	1.42	1.31	1.91	1.73	1.57	1.44	2.13	1.92	1.73	1.57	2.37	2.10	1.88	1.70	5
6	1.74	1.59	1.46	1.35	1.96	1.78	1.62	1.49	2.20	1.97	1.78	1.62	2.44	2.16	1.94	1.75	6
7	1.79	1.64	1.50	1.39	2.02	1.83	1.67	1.53	2.26	2.03	1.84	1.67	2.51	2.23	2.00	1.80	7
8	1.84	1.69	1.55	1.43	2.08	1.89	1.72	1.58	2.33	2.09	1.89	1.72	2.58	2.30	2.06	1.85	8
9	1.90	1.74	1.60	1.47	2.15	1.94	1.77	1.62	2.40	2.16	1.95	1.77	2.66	2.36	2.12	1.91	9
10	1.95	1.79	1.64	1.52	2.21	2.00	1.83	1.67	2.47	2.22	2.01	1.82	2.74	2.44	2.18	1.97	10
11	2.01	1.84	1.69	1.56	2.28	2.06	1.88	1.72	2.55	2.29	2.07	1.88	2.82	2.51	2.25	2.03	11
12	2.07	1.90	1.74	1.61	2.35	2.12	1.94	1.77	2.63	2.36	2.13	1.93	2.91	2.58	2.31	2.09	12
13	2.14	1.95	1.80	1.66	2.42	2.19	1.99	1.83	2.70	2.43	2.19	1.99	3.00	2.66	2.38	2.15	13
14	2.20	2.01	1.85	1.71	2.49	2.25	2.05	1.88	2.79	2.50	2.26	2.05	3.09	2.74	2.45	2.21	14
15	2.27	2.07	1.91	1.76	2.56	2.32	2.12	1.94	2.87	2.57	2.33	2.11	3.18	2.82	2.53	2.28	15
16	2.33	2.13	1.96	1.81	2.64	2.39	2.18	2.00	2.96	2.65	2.40	2.18	3.27	2.91	2.60	2.35	16
17	2.40	2.20	2.02	1.87	2.72	2.46	2.24	2.06	3.04	2.73	2.47	2.24	3.37	3.00	2.68	2.42	17
18	2.48	2.26	2.08	1.92	2.80	2.54	2.31	2.12	3.14	2.81	2.54	2.31	3.47	3.09	2.76	2.49	18
19	2.55	2.33	2.14	1.98	2.88	2.61	2.38	2.18	3.23	2.90	2.62	2.38	3.58	3.18	2.85	2.57	19
20	2.63	2.40	2.21	2.04	2.97	2.69	2.45	2.25	3.33	2.98	2.70	2.45	3.69	3.27	2.93	2.64	20
21	2.71	2.47	2.27	2.10	3.06	2.77	2.53	2.32	3.43	3.07	2.78	2.52	3.80	3.37	3.02	2.72	21
22	2.79	2.55	2.34	2.16	3.15	2.86	2.60	2.38	3.53	3.17	2.86	2.60	3.91	3.47	3.11	2.80	22
23	2.87	2.63	2.41	2.23	3.25	2.94	2.68	2.46	3.63	3.26	2.95	2.68	4.03	3.58	3.20	2.89	23
24	2.96	2.70	2.49	2.30	3.34	3.03	2.76	2.53	3.74	3.36	3.03	2.76	4.15	3.68	3.30	2.98	24
25	3.05	2.79	2.56	2.36	3.44	3.12	2.84	2.61	3.86	3.46	3.13	2.84	4.27	3.79	3.40	3.06	25
26	3.14	2.87	2.64	2.44	3.55	3.21	2.93	2.68	3.97	3.56	3.22	2.93	4.40	3.91	3.50	3.16	26
27	3.23	2.95	2.72	2.51	3.65	3.31	3.02	2.76	4.09	3.67	3.32	3.01	4.53	4.03	3.60	3.25	27
28	3.33	3.04	2.80	2.58	3.76	3.41	3.11	2.85	4.21	3.78	3.41	3.10	4.67	4.15	3.71	3.35	28
29	3.43	3.13	2.88	2.66	3.88	3.51	3.20	2.93	4.34	3.89	3.52	3.20	4.81	4.27	3.82	3.45	29
30	3.53	3.23	2.97	2.74	3.99	3.62	3.30	3.02	4.47	4.01	3.62	3.29	4.95	4.40	3.94	3.55	30
31	3.64	3.33	3.06	2.82	4.11	3.73	3.40	3.11	4.60	4.13	3.73	3.39	5.10	4.53	4.06	3.66	31
32	3.75	3.43	3.15	2.91	4.24	3.84	3.50	3.21	4.74	4.25	3.84	3.49	5.25	4.67	4.18	3.77	32
33	3.86	3.53	3.24	3.00	4.36	3.95	3.60	3.30	4.88	4.38	3.96	3.60	5.41	4.81	4.30	3.88	33
34	3.97	3.63	3.34	3.09	4.49	4.07	3.71	3.40	5.03	4.51	4.08	3.71	5.57	4.95	4.43	4.00	34
35	4.09	3.74	3.44	3.18	4.63	4.19	3.82	3.50	5.18	4.65	4.20	3.82	5.74	5.10	4.57	4.12	35
36	4.22	3.86	3.54	3.27	4.77	4.32	3.94	3.61	5.34	4.79	4.33	3.93	5.91	5.25	4.70	4.24	36
37	4.34	3.97	3.65	3.37	4.91	4.45	4.05	3.72	5.50	4.93	4.46	4.05	6.09	5.41	4.84	4.37	37
38	4.47	4.09	3.76	3.47	5.06	4.58	4.18	3.83	5.66	5.08	4.59	4.17	6.27	5.57	4.99	4.50	38
39	4.61	4.21	3.87	3.58	5.21	4.72	4.30	3.94	5.83	5.23	4.73	4.30	6.46	5.74	5.14	4.64	39
40	4.74	4.34	3.99	3.68	5.37	4.86	4.43	4.06	6.01	5.39	4.87	4.43	6.66	5.91	5.29	4.77	40
41	4.89	4.47	4.11	3.79	5.53	5.01	4.56	4.18	6.19	5.55	5.01	4.56	6.86	6.09	5.45	4.92	41
42	5.03	4.60	4.23	3.91	5.69	5.16	4.70	4.31	6.37	5.72	5.17	4.70	7.06	6.27	5.62	5.07	42
43	5.18	4.74	4.36	4.03	5.86	5.31	4.84	4.44	6.56	5.89	5.32	4.84	7.27	6.46	5.78	5.22	43
44	5.34	4.88	4.49	4.15	6.04	5.47	4.99	4.57	6.76	6.07	5.48	4.98	7.49	6.65	5.96	5.37	44
45	5.50	5.03	4.62	4.27	6.22	5.64	5.14	4.71	6.96	6.25	5.64	5.13	7.72	6.85	6.14	5.54	45
46	5.67	5.18	4.76	4.40	6.41	5.80	5.29	4.85	7.17	6.44	5.81	5.29	7.95	7.06	6.32	5.70	46
47	5.84	5.34	4.91	4.53	6.60	5.98	5.45	4.99	7.39	6.63	5.99	5.44	8.19	7.27	6.51	5.87	47
48	6.01	5.50	5.05	4.67	6.80	6.16	5.61	5.14	7.61	6.83	6.17	5.61	8.43	7.49	6.71	6.05	48
49	6.19	5.66	5.20	4.81	7.00	6.34	5.78	5.30	7.84	7.03	6.35	5.78	8.68	7.71	6.91	6.23	49
50	6.38	5.83	5.36	4.95	7.21	6.53	5.95	5.46	8.07	7.24	6.54	5.95	8.94	7.94	7.11	6.42	50

III. Retirement Planning where Salary Outpaces Low 3% Inflation
Planned Retirement Age 59

Table 1 - Percent of Salary Replaced by a 401(k) Account Equal to Current Annual Salary III-59-1

Probable Life Expectancy at Retirement

Yrs. to Ret.	25.7 (Same as Male Avg.) 4%/4%	6%/5%	8%/6%	10%/7%	28.3 (Better than Male Avg.) 4%/4%	6%/5%	8%/6%	10%/7%	31 (Same as Female Avg.) 4%/4%	6%/5%	8%/6%	10%/7%	33.8 (Better than Female Avg.) 4%/4%	6%/5%	8%/6%	10%/7%	Yrs. to Ret
	Expected Return				(Pre-Retirement/Post-Retirement)				(Pre-Retirement/Post-Retirement)				Expected Return				
0	4.47	5.08	5.72	6.40	4.10	4.71	5.36	6.03	3.79	4.40	5.05	5.73	3.52	4.13	4.78	5.47	0
1	4.47	5.18	5.94	6.77	4.10	4.80	5.57	6.38	3.79	4.49	5.24	6.06	3.52	4.21	4.97	5.78	1
2	4.47	5.28	6.17	7.16	4.10	4.90	5.78	6.75	3.79	4.57	5.45	6.41	3.52	4.29	5.16	6.12	2
3	4.47	5.38	6.41	7.57	4.10	4.99	6.00	7.14	3.79	4.66	5.65	6.78	3.52	4.38	5.36	6.47	3
4	4.47	5.48	6.66	8.01	4.10	5.09	6.23	7.55	3.79	4.75	5.87	7.17	3.52	4.46	5.56	6.84	4
5	4.47	5.59	6.91	8.47	4.10	5.18	6.47	7.99	3.79	4.84	6.10	7.58	3.52	4.54	5.78	7.24	5
6	4.47	5.69	7.18	8.96	4.10	5.28	6.72	8.45	3.79	4.93	6.33	8.02	3.52	4.63	6.00	7.66	6
7	4.47	5.80	7.46	9.47	4.10	5.38	6.98	8.94	3.79	5.03	6.58	8.49	3.52	4.72	6.23	8.10	7
8	4.47	5.91	7.74	10.02	4.10	5.49	7.25	9.45	3.79	5.12	6.83	8.97	3.52	4.81	6.47	8.57	8
9	4.47	6.03	8.04	10.60	4.10	5.59	7.53	10.00	3.79	5.22	7.09	9.49	3.52	4.90	6.72	9.06	9
10	4.47	6.14	8.35	11.21	4.10	5.70	7.82	10.58	3.79	5.32	7.37	10.04	3.52	5.00	6.98	9.58	10
11	4.47	6.26	8.67	11.86	4.10	5.81	8.12	11.19	3.79	5.42	7.65	10.62	3.52	5.09	7.25	10.14	11
12	4.47	6.38	9.01	12.54	4.10	5.92	8.43	11.83	3.79	5.53	7.94	11.23	3.52	5.19	7.53	10.72	12
13	4.47	6.50	9.35	13.26	4.10	6.03	8.76	12.51	3.79	5.64	8.25	11.88	3.52	5.29	7.82	11.34	13
14	4.47	6.63	9.71	14.03	4.10	6.15	9.09	13.24	3.79	5.74	8.57	12.57	3.52	5.39	8.12	11.99	14
15	4.47	6.76	10.09	14.84	4.10	6.27	9.44	14.00	3.79	5.85	8.90	13.29	3.52	5.50	8.43	12.69	15
16	4.47	6.89	10.48	15.69	4.10	6.39	9.81	14.81	3.79	5.97	9.24	14.06	3.52	5.60	8.75	13.42	16
17	4.47	7.02	10.88	16.60	4.10	6.51	10.19	15.66	3.79	6.08	9.60	14.87	3.52	5.71	9.09	14.19	17
18	4.47	7.15	11.30	17.56	4.10	6.64	10.58	16.57	3.79	6.20	9.97	15.73	3.52	5.82	9.44	15.01	18
19	4.47	7.29	11.73	18.57	4.10	6.76	10.98	17.52	3.79	6.32	10.35	16.63	3.52	5.93	9.80	15.88	19
20	4.47	7.43	12.19	19.64	4.10	6.89	11.41	18.53	3.79	6.44	10.75	17.59	3.52	6.04	10.18	16.79	20
21	4.47	7.57	12.65	20.77	4.10	7.03	11.85	19.60	3.79	6.56	11.16	18.61	3.52	6.16	10.57	17.76	21
22	4.47	7.72	13.14	21.97	4.10	7.16	12.30	20.73	3.79	6.69	11.59	19.68	3.52	6.28	10.98	18.79	22
23	4.47	7.87	13.65	23.24	4.10	7.30	12.78	21.93	3.79	6.82	12.04	20.82	3.52	6.40	11.40	19.87	23
24	4.47	8.02	14.17	24.58	4.10	7.44	13.27	23.19	3.79	6.95	12.50	22.02	3.52	6.52	11.84	21.02	24
25	4.47	8.17	14.72	26.00	4.10	7.58	13.78	24.53	3.79	7.08	12.98	23.29	3.52	6.65	12.30	22.23	25
26	4.47	8.33	15.29	27.50	4.10	7.73	14.31	25.95	3.79	7.22	13.48	24.64	3.52	6.78	12.77	23.52	26
27	4.47	8.49	15.87	29.09	4.10	7.88	14.86	27.44	3.79	7.35	14.00	26.06	3.52	6.91	13.26	24.87	27
28	4.47	8.65	16.49	30.77	4.10	8.03	15.43	29.03	3.79	7.50	14.54	27.56	3.52	7.04	13.77	26.31	28
29	4.47	8.82	17.12	32.54	4.10	8.18	16.03	30.70	3.79	7.64	15.10	29.15	3.52	7.17	14.31	27.82	29
30	4.47	8.99	17.78	34.42	4.10	8.34	16.64	32.47	3.79	7.79	15.68	30.83	3.52	7.31	14.86	29.43	30
31	4.47	9.16	18.46	36.40	4.10	8.50	17.28	34.35	3.79	7.94	16.29	32.61	3.52	7.45	15.43	31.13	31
32	4.47	9.34	19.17	38.51	4.10	8.66	17.95	36.33	3.79	8.09	16.91	34.49	3.52	7.59	16.02	32.92	32
33	4.47	9.51	19.91	40.73	4.10	8.83	18.64	38.43	3.79	8.24	17.56	36.48	3.52	7.74	16.64	34.82	33
34	4.47	9.70	20.68	43.08	4.10	9.00	19.36	40.64	3.79	8.40	18.24	38.59	3.52	7.89	17.28	36.83	34
35	4.47	9.88	21.48	45.56	4.10	9.17	20.10	42.99	3.79	8.56	18.94	40.81	3.52	8.04	17.94	38.96	35
36	4.47	10.07	22.30	48.19	4.10	9.35	20.88	45.47	3.79	8.73	19.67	43.17	3.52	8.19	18.64	41.21	36
37	4.47	10.27	23.16	50.97	4.10	9.53	21.68	48.09	3.79	8.89	20.43	45.66	3.52	8.35	19.35	43.58	37
38	4.47	10.46	24.05	53.91	4.10	9.71	22.52	50.87	3.79	9.07	21.21	48.30	3.52	8.51	20.10	46.10	38
39	4.47	10.66	24.98	57.02	4.10	9.89	23.38	53.80	3.79	9.24	22.03	51.08	3.52	8.68	20.87	48.76	39
40	4.47	10.87	25.94	60.31	4.10	10.08	24.28	56.91	3.79	9.42	22.88	54.03	3.52	8.84	21.68	51.57	40
41	4.47	11.08	26.94	63.79	4.10	10.28	25.22	60.19	3.79	9.60	23.76	57.15	3.52	9.01	22.51	54.55	41
42	4.47	11.29	27.98	67.48	4.10	10.48	26.19	63.66	3.79	9.78	24.68	60.44	3.52	9.19	23.38	57.70	42
43	4.47	11.51	29.05	71.37	4.10	10.68	27.20	67.34	3.79	9.97	25.63	63.93	3.52	9.36	24.28	61.03	43
44	4.47	11.73	30.17	75.49	4.10	10.88	28.25	71.22	3.79	10.16	26.61	67.62	3.52	9.54	25.21	64.55	44
45	4.47	11.95	31.33	79.84	4.10	11.09	29.33	75.33	3.79	10.36	27.64	71.52	3.52	9.72	26.18	68.27	45
46	4.47	12.18	32.53	84.45	4.10	11.30	30.46	79.68	3.79	10.56	28.70	75.65	3.52	9.91	27.19	72.21	46
47	4.47	12.42	33.79	89.32	4.10	11.52	31.64	84.28	3.79	10.76	29.81	80.01	3.52	10.10	28.24	76.38	47
48	4.47	12.66	35.09	94.48	4.10	11.74	32.85	89.14	3.79	10.96	30.95	84.63	3.52	10.30	29.32	80.78	48
49	4.47	12.90	36.44	99.93	4.10	11.97	34.12	94.28	3.79	11.17	32.14	89.51	3.52	10.49	30.45	85.44	49
50	4.47	13.15	37.85	105.69	4.10	12.20	35.43	99.72	3.79	11.39	33.38	94.68	3.52	10.69	31.63	90.37	50

Appendix A

III. Retirement Planning where Salary Outpaces Low 3% Inflation
Planned Retirement Age 59

Table 2 - Percent of Salary Replaced by a 401(k) Contribution of 1% of Current Salary   III-59-2

Probable Life Expectancy at Retirement

Yrs. to Ret.	25.7 (Same as Male Avg.)				28.3 (Better than Male Avg.)				31 (Same as Female Avg.)				33.8 (Better than Female Avg.)				Yrs. to Ret.
	4%/4%	6%/5%	8%/6%	10%/7%	4%/4%	6%/5%	8%/6%	10%/7%	4%/4%	6%/5%	8%/6%	10%/7%	4%/4%	6%/5%	8%/6%	10%/7%	
	Expected Return (Pre-Retirement/Post-Retirement)				(Pre-Retirement/Post-Retirement)				(Pre-Retirement/Post-Retirement)				Expected Return				
0	0.00	0.00	0.00	0.00	0.00	0.00	0.00	0.00	0.00	0.00	0.00	0.00	0.00	0.00	0.00	0.00	0
1	0.04	0.05	0.06	0.06	0.04	0.05	0.05	0.06	0.04	0.04	0.05	0.06	0.04	0.04	0.05	0.05	1
2	0.09	0.10	0.12	0.13	0.08	0.10	0.11	0.12	0.08	0.09	0.10	0.12	0.07	0.08	0.10	0.11	2
3	0.13	0.16	0.18	0.20	0.12	0.14	0.17	0.19	0.11	0.13	0.16	0.18	0.11	0.13	0.15	0.17	3
4	0.18	0.21	0.24	0.28	0.16	0.19	0.23	0.26	0.15	0.18	0.21	0.25	0.14	0.17	0.20	0.24	4
5	0.22	0.26	0.31	0.36	0.21	0.24	0.29	0.34	0.19	0.23	0.27	0.32	0.18	0.21	0.26	0.31	5
6	0.27	0.32	0.38	0.44	0.25	0.30	0.35	0.42	0.23	0.28	0.33	0.40	0.21	0.26	0.32	0.38	6
7	0.31	0.38	0.45	0.53	0.29	0.35	0.42	0.50	0.27	0.33	0.40	0.48	0.25	0.31	0.38	0.46	7
8	0.36	0.43	0.52	0.63	0.33	0.40	0.49	0.59	0.30	0.38	0.46	0.56	0.28	0.35	0.44	0.54	8
9	0.40	0.49	0.60	0.73	0.37	0.46	0.56	0.69	0.34	0.43	0.53	0.65	0.32	0.40	0.50	0.62	9
10	0.45	0.55	0.68	0.83	0.41	0.51	0.64	0.79	0.38	0.48	0.60	0.75	0.35	0.45	0.57	0.71	10
11	0.49	0.62	0.77	0.95	0.45	0.57	0.72	0.89	0.42	0.53	0.68	0.85	0.39	0.50	0.64	0.81	11
12	0.54	0.68	0.85	1.06	0.49	0.63	0.80	1.00	0.45	0.59	0.75	0.95	0.42	0.55	0.71	0.91	12
13	0.58	0.74	0.94	1.19	0.53	0.69	0.88	1.12	0.49	0.64	0.83	1.07	0.46	0.60	0.79	1.02	13
14	0.63	0.81	1.04	1.32	0.57	0.75	0.97	1.25	0.53	0.70	0.91	1.18	0.49	0.66	0.87	1.13	14
15	0.67	0.87	1.13	1.46	0.62	0.81	1.06	1.38	0.57	0.76	1.00	1.31	0.53	0.71	0.95	1.25	15
16	0.71	0.94	1.23	1.61	0.66	0.87	1.16	1.52	0.61	0.82	1.09	1.44	0.56	0.77	1.03	1.38	16
17	0.76	1.01	1.34	1.77	0.70	0.94	1.25	1.67	0.64	0.87	1.18	1.58	0.60	0.82	1.12	1.51	17
18	0.80	1.08	1.45	1.93	0.74	1.00	1.36	1.82	0.68	0.94	1.28	1.73	0.63	0.88	1.21	1.65	18
19	0.85	1.15	1.56	2.11	0.78	1.07	1.46	1.99	0.72	1.00	1.38	1.89	0.67	0.94	1.30	1.80	19
20	0.89	1.22	1.68	2.30	0.82	1.14	1.57	2.17	0.76	1.06	1.48	2.06	0.70	1.00	1.40	1.96	20
21	0.94	1.30	1.80	2.49	0.86	1.20	1.69	2.35	0.80	1.13	1.59	2.23	0.74	1.06	1.50	2.13	21
22	0.98	1.37	1.93	2.70	0.90	1.28	1.80	2.55	0.83	1.19	1.70	2.42	0.78	1.12	1.61	2.31	22
23	1.03	1.45	2.06	2.92	0.94	1.35	1.93	2.75	0.87	1.26	1.82	2.62	0.81	1.18	1.72	2.50	23
24	1.07	1.53	2.19	3.15	0.98	1.42	2.05	2.97	0.91	1.33	1.94	2.82	0.85	1.24	1.83	2.70	24
25	1.12	1.61	2.34	3.40	1.03	1.49	2.19	3.21	0.95	1.40	2.06	3.04	0.88	1.31	1.95	2.91	25
26	1.16	1.69	2.48	3.66	1.07	1.57	2.32	3.45	0.99	1.47	2.19	3.28	0.92	1.38	2.08	3.13	26
27	1.21	1.78	2.64	3.93	1.11	1.65	2.47	3.71	1.02	1.54	2.33	3.52	0.95	1.44	2.20	3.36	27
28	1.25	1.86	2.80	4.22	1.15	1.73	2.62	3.98	1.06	1.61	2.47	3.78	0.99	1.51	2.34	3.61	28
29	1.30	1.95	2.96	4.53	1.19	1.81	2.77	4.28	1.10	1.69	2.61	4.06	1.02	1.58	2.47	3.87	29
30	1.34	2.04	3.13	4.86	1.23	1.89	2.93	4.58	1.14	1.76	2.76	4.35	1.06	1.66	2.62	4.15	30
31	1.38	2.12	3.31	5.20	1.27	1.97	3.10	4.91	1.18	1.84	2.92	4.66	1.09	1.73	2.76	4.45	31
32	1.43	2.22	3.49	5.56	1.31	2.06	3.27	5.25	1.21	1.92	3.08	4.98	1.13	1.80	2.92	4.76	32
33	1.47	2.31	3.69	5.95	1.35	2.14	3.45	5.61	1.25	2.00	3.25	5.33	1.16	1.88	3.08	5.09	33
34	1.52	2.40	3.88	6.36	1.39	2.23	3.64	6.00	1.29	2.08	3.43	5.69	1.20	1.96	3.25	5.44	34
35	1.56	2.50	4.09	6.79	1.44	2.32	3.83	6.40	1.33	2.17	3.61	6.08	1.23	2.04	3.42	5.80	35
36	1.61	2.60	4.31	7.24	1.48	2.41	4.03	6.83	1.36	2.25	3.80	6.49	1.27	2.12	3.60	6.19	36
37	1.65	2.70	4.53	7.73	1.52	2.51	4.24	7.29	1.40	2.34	3.99	6.92	1.30	2.20	3.78	6.61	37
38	1.70	2.80	4.76	8.24	1.56	2.60	4.46	7.77	1.44	2.43	4.20	7.38	1.34	2.28	3.98	7.04	38
39	1.74	2.91	5.00	8.77	1.60	2.70	4.68	8.28	1.48	2.52	4.41	7.86	1.37	2.37	4.18	7.50	39
40	1.79	3.02	5.25	9.34	1.64	2.80	4.92	8.82	1.52	2.61	4.63	8.37	1.41	2.45	4.39	7.99	40
41	1.83	3.12	5.51	9.95	1.68	2.90	5.16	9.39	1.55	2.71	4.86	8.91	1.44	2.54	4.60	8.51	41
42	1.88	3.23	5.78	10.59	1.72	3.00	5.41	9.99	1.59	2.80	5.10	9.48	1.48	2.63	4.83	9.05	42
43	1.92	3.35	6.06	11.26	1.76	3.11	5.67	10.62	1.63	2.90	5.34	10.09	1.51	2.72	5.06	9.63	43
44	1.97	3.46	6.35	11.97	1.80	3.21	5.94	11.30	1.67	3.00	5.60	10.73	1.55	2.82	5.31	10.24	44
45	2.01	3.58	6.65	12.73	1.85	3.32	6.23	12.01	1.71	3.10	5.87	11.40	1.59	2.91	5.56	10.88	45
46	2.05	3.70	6.97	13.53	1.89	3.43	6.52	12.76	1.74	3.21	6.14	12.12	1.62	3.01	5.82	11.57	46
47	2.10	3.82	7.29	14.37	1.93	3.55	6.83	13.56	1.78	3.31	6.43	12.87	1.66	3.11	6.09	12.29	47
48	2.14	3.95	7.63	15.27	1.97	3.66	7.14	14.40	1.82	3.42	6.73	13.67	1.69	3.21	6.37	13.05	48
49	2.19	4.07	7.98	16.21	2.01	3.78	7.47	15.29	1.86	3.53	7.04	14.52	1.73	3.31	6.67	13.86	49
50	2.23	4.20	8.34	17.21	2.05	3.90	7.81	16.24	1.90	3.64	7.36	15.42	1.76	3.42	6.97	14.72	50

III. Retirement Planning where Salary Outpaces Low 3% Inflation
Planned Retirement Age 59

Table 3 - 401(k) Contribution (% of Current Sal.) Needed to Replace 10% of Sal. at Retirement   III-59-3

Probable Life Expectancy at Retirement

Yrs. to Ret.	25.7 (Same as Male Avg.)				28.3 (Better than Male Avg.)				31 (Same as Female Avg.)				33.8 (Better than Female Avg.)				Yrs. to Ret.
	4%/4%	6%/5%	8%/6%	10%/7%	4%/4%	6%/5%	8%/6%	10%/7%	4%/4%	6%/5%	8%/6%	10%/7%	4%/4%	6%/5%	8%/6%	10%/7%	
	Expected Return (Pre-Retirement/Post-Retirement)				(Pre-Retirement/Post-Retirement)				(Pre-Retirement/Post-Retirement)				Expected Return				
0																	0
1	223.92	196.87	174.70	156.34	243.82	212.19	186.61	165.70	263.81	227.23	198.07	174.53	283.86	241.99	209.07	182.84	1
2	111.96	97.50	85.70	75.98	121.91	105.09	91.54	80.53	131.90	112.54	97.16	84.82	141.93	119.84	102.56	88.86	2
3	74.64	64.38	56.05	49.22	81.27	69.39	59.87	52.17	87.94	74.31	63.54	54.95	94.62	79.13	67.07	57.56	3
4	55.98	47.82	41.23	35.86	60.96	51.54	44.04	38.01	65.95	55.20	46.75	40.03	70.96	58.78	49.34	41.94	4
5	44.78	37.89	32.35	27.86	48.76	40.84	34.56	29.53	52.76	43.73	36.68	31.10	56.77	46.57	38.72	32.58	5
6	37.32	31.27	26.44	22.54	40.64	33.70	28.24	23.89	43.97	36.09	29.97	25.17	47.31	38.44	31.64	26.37	6
7	31.99	26.55	22.22	18.76	34.83	28.61	23.73	19.88	37.69	30.64	25.19	20.94	40.55	32.63	26.59	21.94	7
8	27.99	23.00	19.06	15.93	30.48	24.79	20.36	16.88	32.98	26.55	21.61	17.78	35.48	28.27	22.81	18.63	8
9	24.88	20.25	16.61	13.74	27.09	21.82	17.74	14.56	29.31	23.37	18.83	15.33	31.54	24.89	19.88	16.06	9
10	22.39	18.05	14.65	11.99	24.38	19.45	15.65	12.71	26.38	20.83	16.61	13.38	28.39	22.18	17.54	14.02	10
11	20.36	16.24	13.05	10.57	22.17	17.51	13.94	11.20	23.98	18.75	14.80	11.80	25.81	19.97	15.62	12.36	11
12	18.66	14.74	11.73	9.39	20.32	15.89	12.53	9.96	21.98	17.02	13.30	10.49	23.65	18.12	14.03	10.98	12
13	17.22	13.48	10.61	8.40	18.76	14.53	11.33	8.91	20.29	15.55	12.03	9.38	21.84	16.57	12.69	9.83	13
14	15.99	12.39	9.65	7.56	17.42	13.35	10.31	8.01	18.84	14.30	10.94	8.44	20.28	15.23	11.55	8.84	14
15	14.93	11.45	8.82	6.84	16.25	12.34	9.42	7.24	17.59	13.22	10.00	7.63	18.92	14.07	10.56	7.99	15
16	13.99	10.63	8.10	6.21	15.24	11.45	8.65	6.58	16.49	12.27	9.18	6.93	17.74	13.06	9.70	7.26	16
17	13.17	9.90	7.47	5.66	14.34	10.67	7.98	5.99	15.52	11.43	8.47	6.31	16.70	12.17	8.94	6.61	17
18	12.44	9.26	6.91	5.17	13.55	9.98	7.38	5.48	14.66	10.69	7.83	5.77	15.77	11.38	8.27	6.05	18
19	11.79	8.68	6.41	4.74	12.83	9.36	6.84	5.02	13.88	10.02	7.26	5.29	14.94	10.67	7.67	5.54	19
20	11.20	8.17	5.96	4.36	12.19	8.80	6.36	4.62	13.19	9.43	6.76	4.86	14.19	10.04	7.13	5.09	20
21	10.66	7.70	5.56	4.01	11.61	8.30	5.93	4.25	12.56	8.89	6.30	4.48	13.52	9.46	6.65	4.69	21
22	10.18	7.28	5.19	3.70	11.08	7.84	5.54	3.93	11.99	8.40	5.88	4.14	12.90	8.94	6.21	4.33	22
23	9.74	6.89	4.86	3.43	10.60	7.42	5.19	3.63	11.47	7.95	5.51	3.82	12.34	8.47	5.81	4.01	23
24	9.33	6.53	4.56	3.17	10.16	7.04	4.87	3.36	10.99	7.54	5.17	3.54	11.83	8.03	5.45	3.71	24
25	8.96	6.21	4.28	2.94	9.75	6.69	4.57	3.12	10.55	7.17	4.85	3.29	11.35	7.63	5.12	3.44	25
26	8.61	5.91	4.03	2.73	9.38	6.37	4.30	2.90	10.15	6.82	4.57	3.05	10.92	7.26	4.82	3.20	26
27	8.29	5.63	3.79	2.54	9.03	6.07	4.05	2.70	9.77	6.50	4.30	2.84	10.51	6.92	4.54	2.97	27
28	8.00	5.38	3.58	2.37	8.71	5.79	3.82	2.51	9.42	6.20	4.06	2.64	10.14	6.61	4.28	2.77	28
29	7.72	5.14	3.38	2.21	8.41	5.54	3.61	2.34	9.10	5.93	3.83	2.46	9.79	6.31	4.04	2.58	29
30	7.46	4.91	3.19	2.06	8.13	5.30	3.41	2.18	8.79	5.67	3.62	2.30	9.46	6.04	3.82	2.41	30
31	7.22	4.71	3.02	1.92	7.87	5.07	3.23	2.04	8.51	5.43	3.43	2.15	9.16	5.78	3.62	2.25	31
32	7.00	4.51	2.86	1.80	7.62	4.86	3.06	1.90	8.24	5.21	3.25	2.01	8.87	5.55	3.43	2.10	32
33	6.79	4.33	2.71	1.68	7.39	4.67	2.90	1.78	7.99	5.00	3.08	1.88	8.60	5.32	3.25	1.97	33
34	6.59	4.16	2.57	1.57	7.17	4.48	2.75	1.67	7.76	4.80	2.92	1.76	8.35	5.11	3.08	1.84	34
35	6.40	4.00	2.44	1.47	6.97	4.31	2.61	1.56	7.54	4.61	2.77	1.64	8.11	4.91	2.93	1.72	35
36	6.22	3.85	2.32	1.38	6.77	4.14	2.48	1.46	7.33	4.44	2.63	1.54	7.88	4.73	2.78	1.61	36
37	6.05	3.70	2.21	1.29	6.59	3.99	2.36	1.37	7.13	4.27	2.50	1.44	7.67	4.55	2.64	1.51	37
38	5.89	3.57	2.10	1.21	6.42	3.84	2.24	1.29	6.94	4.12	2.38	1.36	7.47	4.38	2.51	1.42	38
39	5.74	3.44	2.00	1.14	6.25	3.71	2.14	1.21	6.76	3.97	2.27	1.27	7.28	4.23	2.39	1.33	39
40	5.60	3.32	1.90	1.07	6.10	3.57	2.03	1.13	6.60	3.83	2.16	1.19	7.10	4.08	2.28	1.25	40
41	5.46	3.20	1.81	1.01	5.95	3.45	1.94	1.07	6.43	3.69	2.06	1.12	6.92	3.93	2.17	1.18	41
42	5.33	3.09	1.73	0.94	5.81	3.33	1.85	1.00	6.28	3.57	1.96	1.05	6.76	3.80	2.07	1.10	42
43	5.21	2.99	1.65	0.89	5.67	3.22	1.76	0.94	6.14	3.45	1.87	0.99	6.60	3.67	1.98	1.04	43
44	5.09	2.89	1.57	0.84	5.54	3.11	1.68	0.89	6.00	3.33	1.79	0.93	6.45	3.55	1.88	0.98	44
45	4.98	2.79	1.50	0.79	5.42	3.01	1.61	0.83	5.86	3.22	1.70	0.88	6.31	3.43	1.80	0.92	45
46	4.87	2.70	1.44	0.74	5.30	2.91	1.53	0.78	5.73	3.12	1.63	0.83	6.17	3.32	1.72	0.86	46
47	4.76	2.62	1.37	0.70	5.19	2.82	1.47	0.74	5.61	3.02	1.56	0.78	6.04	3.22	1.64	0.81	47
48	4.66	2.53	1.31	0.66	5.08	2.73	1.40	0.69	5.50	2.93	1.49	0.73	5.91	3.12	1.57	0.77	48
49	4.57	2.46	1.25	0.62	4.98	2.65	1.34	0.65	5.38	2.83	1.42	0.69	5.79	3.02	1.50	0.72	49
50	4.48	2.38	1.20	0.58	4.88	2.57	1.28	0.62	5.28	2.75	1.36	0.65	5.68	2.93	1.43	0.68	50

Appendix A

III. Retirement Planning where Salary Outpaces Low 3% Inflation
Planned Retirement Age 59

Table 4 - Accumulation at Retirement (Multiple of Current Sal.) for 10% Sal. Replacement   III-59-4

Probable Life Expectancy at Retirement

Yrs. to Ret.	25.7 (Same as Male Avg.)				28.3 (Better than Male Avg.)				31 (Same as Female Avg.)				33.8 (Better than Female Avg.)				Yrs. to Ret.
	4%/4%	6%/5%	8%/6%	10%/7%	4%/4%	6%/5%	8%/6%	10%/7%	4%/4%	6%/5%	8%/6%	10%/7%	4%/4%	6%/5%	8%/6%	10%/7%	
	Expected Return		(Pre-Retirement/Post-Retirement)				(Pre-Retirement/Post-Retirement)				Expected Return						
0	2.24	1.97	1.75	1.56	2.44	2.12	1.87	1.66	2.64	2.27	1.98	1.75	2.84	2.42	2.09	1.83	0
1	2.33	2.05	1.82	1.63	2.54	2.21	1.94	1.72	2.74	2.36	2.06	1.82	2.95	2.52	2.17	1.90	1
2	2.42	2.13	1.89	1.69	2.64	2.30	2.02	1.79	2.85	2.46	2.14	1.89	3.07	2.62	2.26	1.98	2
3	2.52	2.21	1.97	1.76	2.74	2.39	2.10	1.86	2.97	2.56	2.23	1.96	3.19	2.72	2.35	2.06	3
4	2.62	2.30	2.04	1.83	2.85	2.48	2.18	1.94	3.09	2.66	2.32	2.04	3.32	2.83	2.45	2.14	4
5	2.72	2.40	2.13	1.90	2.97	2.58	2.27	2.02	3.21	2.76	2.41	2.12	3.45	2.94	2.54	2.22	5
6	2.83	2.49	2.21	1.98	3.09	2.68	2.36	2.10	3.34	2.88	2.51	2.21	3.59	3.06	2.65	2.31	6
7	2.95	2.59	2.30	2.06	3.21	2.79	2.46	2.18	3.47	2.99	2.61	2.30	3.74	3.18	2.75	2.41	7
8	3.06	2.69	2.39	2.14	3.34	2.90	2.55	2.27	3.61	3.11	2.71	2.39	3.88	3.31	2.86	2.50	8
9	3.19	2.80	2.49	2.23	3.47	3.02	2.66	2.36	3.75	3.23	2.82	2.48	4.04	3.44	2.98	2.60	9
10	3.31	2.91	2.59	2.31	3.61	3.14	2.76	2.45	3.90	3.36	2.93	2.58	4.20	3.58	3.09	2.71	10
11	3.45	3.03	2.69	2.41	3.75	3.27	2.87	2.55	4.06	3.50	3.05	2.69	4.37	3.73	3.22	2.81	11
12	3.58	3.15	2.80	2.50	3.90	3.40	2.99	2.65	4.22	3.64	3.17	2.79	4.54	3.87	3.35	2.93	12
13	3.73	3.28	2.91	2.60	4.06	3.53	3.11	2.76	4.39	3.78	3.30	2.91	4.73	4.03	3.48	3.04	13
14	3.88	3.41	3.03	2.71	4.22	3.67	3.23	2.87	4.57	3.93	3.43	3.02	4.92	4.19	3.62	3.17	14
15	4.03	3.55	3.15	2.82	4.39	3.82	3.36	2.98	4.75	4.09	3.57	3.14	5.11	4.36	3.77	3.29	15
16	4.19	3.69	3.27	2.93	4.57	3.97	3.50	3.10	4.94	4.26	3.71	3.27	5.32	4.53	3.92	3.42	16
17	4.36	3.83	3.40	3.05	4.75	4.13	3.63	3.23	5.14	4.43	3.86	3.40	5.53	4.71	4.07	3.56	17
18	4.54	3.99	3.54	3.17	4.94	4.30	3.78	3.36	5.34	4.60	4.01	3.54	5.75	4.90	4.24	3.70	18
19	4.72	4.15	3.68	3.29	5.14	4.47	3.93	3.49	5.56	4.79	4.17	3.68	5.98	5.10	4.40	3.85	19
20	4.91	4.31	3.83	3.43	5.34	4.65	4.09	3.63	5.78	4.98	4.34	3.82	6.22	5.30	4.58	4.01	20
21	5.10	4.49	3.98	3.56	5.56	4.84	4.25	3.78	6.01	5.18	4.51	3.98	6.47	5.51	4.76	4.17	21
22	5.31	4.67	4.14	3.71	5.78	5.03	4.42	3.93	6.25	5.39	4.69	4.14	6.73	5.73	4.95	4.33	22
23	5.52	4.85	4.31	3.85	6.01	5.23	4.60	4.08	6.50	5.60	4.88	4.30	7.00	5.96	5.15	4.51	23
24	5.74	5.05	4.48	4.01	6.25	5.44	4.78	4.25	6.76	5.82	5.08	4.47	7.28	6.20	5.36	4.69	24
25	5.97	5.25	4.66	4.17	6.50	5.66	4.97	4.42	7.03	6.06	5.28	4.65	7.57	6.45	5.57	4.87	25
26	6.21	5.46	4.84	4.33	6.76	5.88	5.17	4.59	7.31	6.30	5.49	4.84	7.87	6.71	5.80	5.07	26
27	6.46	5.68	5.04	4.51	7.03	6.12	5.38	4.78	7.61	6.55	5.71	5.03	8.18	6.98	6.03	5.27	27
28	6.71	5.90	5.24	4.69	7.31	6.36	5.60	4.97	7.91	6.81	5.94	5.23	8.51	7.26	6.27	5.48	28
29	6.98	6.14	5.45	4.88	7.60	6.62	5.82	5.17	8.23	7.09	6.18	5.44	8.85	7.55	6.52	5.70	29
30	7.26	6.39	5.67	5.07	7.91	6.88	6.05	5.37	8.56	7.37	6.42	5.66	9.21	7.85	6.78	5.93	30
31	7.55	6.64	5.89	5.27	8.22	7.16	6.29	5.59	8.90	7.66	6.68	5.89	9.57	8.16	7.05	6.17	31
32	7.86	6.91	6.13	5.48	8.55	7.44	6.55	5.81	9.25	7.97	6.95	6.12	9.96	8.49	7.33	6.41	32
33	8.17	7.18	6.37	5.70	8.90	7.74	6.81	6.05	9.62	8.29	7.23	6.37	10.36	8.83	7.63	6.67	33
34	8.50	7.47	6.63	5.93	9.25	8.05	7.08	6.29	10.01	8.62	7.52	6.62	10.77	9.18	7.93	6.94	34
35	8.84	7.77	6.89	6.17	9.62	8.37	7.36	6.54	10.41	8.97	7.82	6.89	11.20	9.55	8.25	7.22	35
36	9.19	8.08	7.17	6.42	10.01	8.71	7.66	6.80	10.83	9.33	8.13	7.16	11.65	9.93	8.58	7.50	36
37	9.56	8.40	7.46	6.67	10.41	9.06	7.96	7.07	11.26	9.70	8.45	7.45	12.12	10.33	8.92	7.80	37
38	9.94	8.74	7.75	6.94	10.82	9.42	8.28	7.36	11.71	10.09	8.79	7.75	12.60	10.74	9.28	8.12	38
39	10.34	9.09	8.06	7.22	11.26	9.80	8.61	7.65	12.18	10.49	9.14	8.06	13.10	11.17	9.65	8.44	39
40	10.75	9.45	8.39	7.51	11.71	10.19	8.96	7.96	12.67	10.91	9.51	8.38	13.63	11.62	10.04	8.78	40
41	11.18	9.83	8.72	7.81	12.17	10.59	9.32	8.27	13.17	11.35	9.89	8.71	14.17	12.08	10.44	9.13	41
42	11.63	10.22	9.07	8.12	12.66	11.02	9.69	8.60	13.70	11.80	10.29	9.06	14.74	12.57	10.86	9.49	42
43	12.09	10.63	9.43	8.44	13.17	11.46	10.08	8.95	14.25	12.27	10.70	9.43	15.33	13.07	11.29	9.87	43
44	12.58	11.06	9.81	8.78	13.69	11.92	10.48	9.31	14.82	12.76	11.12	9.80	15.94	13.59	11.74	10.27	44
45	13.08	11.50	10.20	9.13	14.24	12.39	10.90	9.68	15.41	13.27	11.57	10.19	16.58	14.13	12.21	10.68	45
46	13.60	11.96	10.61	9.50	14.81	12.89	11.34	10.07	16.03	13.80	12.03	10.60	17.24	14.70	12.70	11.11	46
47	14.15	12.44	11.04	9.88	15.40	13.41	11.79	10.47	16.67	14.36	12.51	11.03	17.93	15.29	13.21	11.55	47
48	14.71	12.94	11.48	10.27	16.02	13.94	12.26	10.89	17.33	14.93	13.01	11.47	18.65	15.90	13.74	12.01	48
49	15.30	13.45	11.94	10.68	16.66	14.50	12.75	11.32	18.03	15.53	13.53	11.93	19.40	16.54	14.29	12.49	49
50	15.91	13.99	12.42	11.11	17.33	15.08	13.26	11.78	18.75	16.15	14.08	12.40	20.17	17.20	14.86	12.99	50

A-45

III. Retirement Planning where Salary Outpaces Low 3% Inflation
Planned Retirement Age 62

Table 1 - Percent of Salary Replaced by a 401(k) Account Equal to Current Annual Salary   III-62-1

Probable Life Expectancy at Retirement

Yrs. to Ret.	23.2 (Same as Male Avg.)				25.7 (Better than Male Avg.)				28.3 (Same as Female Avg.)				31 (Better than Female Avg.)				Yrs. to Ret.
	4%/4%	6%/5%	8%/6%	10%/7%	4%/4%	6%/5%	8%/6%	10%/7%	4%/4%	6%/5%	8%/6%	10%/7%	4%/4%	6%/5%	8%/6%	10%/7%	
	Expected Return				(Pre-Retirement/Post-Retirement)				(Pre-Retirement/Post-Retirement)				Expected Return				
0	4.90	5.52	6.16	6.83	4.47	5.08	5.72	6.40	4.10	4.71	5.36	6.03	3.79	4.40	5.05	5.73	0
1	4.90	5.62	6.40	7.23	4.47	5.18	5.94	6.77	4.10	4.80	5.57	6.38	3.79	4.49	5.24	6.06	1
2	4.90	5.73	6.65	7.64	4.47	5.28	6.17	7.16	4.10	4.90	5.78	6.75	3.79	4.57	5.45	6.41	2
3	4.90	5.84	6.90	8.08	4.47	5.38	6.41	7.57	4.10	4.99	6.00	7.14	3.79	4.66	5.65	6.78	3
4	4.90	5.95	7.17	8.55	4.47	5.48	6.66	8.01	4.10	5.09	6.23	7.55	3.79	4.75	5.87	7.17	4
5	4.90	6.07	7.44	9.04	4.47	5.59	6.91	8.47	4.10	5.18	6.47	7.99	3.79	4.84	6.10	7.58	5
6	4.90	6.18	7.73	9.57	4.47	5.69	7.18	8.96	4.10	5.28	6.72	8.45	3.79	4.93	6.33	8.02	6
7	4.90	6.30	8.03	10.12	4.47	5.80	7.46	9.47	4.10	5.38	6.98	8.94	3.79	5.03	6.58	8.49	7
8	4.90	6.42	8.34	10.70	4.47	5.91	7.74	10.02	4.10	5.49	7.25	9.45	3.79	5.12	6.83	8.97	8
9	4.90	6.55	8.66	11.32	4.47	6.03	8.04	10.60	4.10	5.59	7.53	10.00	3.79	5.22	7.09	9.49	9
10	4.90	6.67	8.99	11.97	4.47	6.14	8.35	11.21	4.10	5.70	7.82	10.58	3.79	5.32	7.37	10.04	10
11	4.90	6.80	9.34	12.66	4.47	6.26	8.67	11.86	4.10	5.81	8.12	11.19	3.79	5.42	7.65	10.62	11
12	4.90	6.93	9.70	13.39	4.47	6.38	9.01	12.54	4.10	5.92	8.43	11.83	3.79	5.53	7.94	11.23	12
13	4.90	7.07	10.07	14.17	4.47	6.50	9.35	13.26	4.10	6.03	8.76	12.51	3.79	5.64	8.25	11.88	13
14	4.90	7.20	10.46	14.98	4.47	6.63	9.71	14.03	4.10	6.15	9.09	13.24	3.79	5.74	8.57	12.57	14
15	4.90	7.34	10.86	15.85	4.47	6.76	10.09	14.84	4.10	6.27	9.44	14.00	3.79	5.85	8.90	13.29	15
16	4.90	7.48	11.28	16.76	4.47	6.89	10.48	15.69	4.10	6.39	9.81	14.81	3.79	5.97	9.24	14.06	16
17	4.90	7.62	11.71	17.73	4.47	7.02	10.88	16.60	4.10	6.51	10.19	15.66	3.79	6.08	9.60	14.87	17
18	4.90	7.77	12.16	18.75	4.47	7.15	11.30	17.56	4.10	6.64	10.58	16.57	3.79	6.20	9.97	15.73	18
19	4.90	7.92	12.63	19.84	4.47	7.29	11.73	18.57	4.10	6.76	10.98	17.52	3.79	6.32	10.35	16.63	19
20	4.90	8.07	13.12	20.98	4.47	7.43	12.19	19.64	4.10	6.89	11.41	18.53	3.79	6.44	10.75	17.59	20
21	4.90	8.23	13.62	22.19	4.47	7.57	12.65	20.77	4.10	7.03	11.85	19.60	3.79	6.56	11.16	18.61	21
22	4.90	8.38	14.15	23.47	4.47	7.72	13.14	21.97	4.10	7.16	12.30	20.73	3.79	6.69	11.59	19.68	22
23	4.90	8.55	14.69	24.83	4.47	7.87	13.65	23.24	4.10	7.30	12.78	21.93	3.79	6.82	12.04	20.82	23
24	4.90	8.71	15.26	26.26	4.47	8.02	14.17	24.58	4.10	7.44	13.27	23.19	3.79	6.95	12.50	22.02	24
25	4.90	8.88	15.85	27.77	4.47	8.17	14.72	26.00	4.10	7.58	13.78	24.53	3.79	7.08	12.98	23.29	25
26	4.90	9.05	16.46	29.38	4.47	8.33	15.29	27.50	4.10	7.73	14.31	25.95	3.79	7.22	13.48	24.64	26
27	4.90	9.22	17.09	31.07	4.47	8.49	15.87	29.09	4.10	7.88	14.86	27.44	3.79	7.35	14.00	26.06	27
28	4.90	9.40	17.75	32.86	4.47	8.65	16.49	30.77	4.10	8.03	15.43	29.03	3.79	7.50	14.54	27.56	28
29	4.90	9.58	18.43	34.76	4.47	8.82	17.12	32.54	4.10	8.18	16.03	30.70	3.79	7.64	15.10	29.15	29
30	4.90	9.76	19.14	36.76	4.47	8.99	17.78	34.42	4.10	8.34	16.64	32.47	3.79	7.79	15.68	30.83	30
31	4.90	9.95	19.88	38.89	4.47	9.16	18.46	36.40	4.10	8.50	17.28	34.35	3.79	7.94	16.29	32.61	31
32	4.90	10.14	20.64	41.13	4.47	9.34	19.17	38.51	4.10	8.66	17.95	36.33	3.79	8.09	16.91	34.49	32
33	4.90	10.34	21.44	43.50	4.47	9.51	19.91	40.73	4.10	8.83	18.64	38.43	3.79	8.24	17.56	36.48	33
34	4.90	10.53	22.26	46.01	4.47	9.70	20.68	43.08	4.10	9.00	19.36	40.64	3.79	8.40	18.24	38.59	34
35	4.90	10.74	23.12	48.67	4.47	9.88	21.48	45.56	4.10	9.17	20.10	42.99	3.79	8.56	18.94	40.81	35
36	4.90	10.94	24.01	51.48	4.47	10.07	22.30	48.19	4.10	9.35	20.88	45.47	3.79	8.73	19.67	43.17	36
37	4.90	11.15	24.94	54.45	4.47	10.27	23.16	50.97	4.10	9.53	21.68	48.09	3.79	8.89	20.43	45.66	37
38	4.90	11.37	25.90	57.59	4.47	10.46	24.05	53.91	4.10	9.71	22.52	50.87	3.79	9.07	21.21	48.30	38
39	4.90	11.59	26.89	60.91	4.47	10.66	24.98	57.02	4.10	9.89	23.38	53.80	3.79	9.24	22.03	51.08	39
40	4.90	11.81	27.93	64.43	4.47	10.87	25.94	60.31	4.10	10.08	24.28	56.91	3.79	9.42	22.88	54.03	40
41	4.90	12.03	29.00	68.14	4.47	11.08	26.94	63.79	4.10	10.28	25.22	60.19	3.79	9.60	23.76	57.15	41
42	4.90	12.27	30.12	72.07	4.47	11.29	27.98	67.48	4.10	10.48	26.19	63.66	3.79	9.78	24.68	60.44	42
43	4.90	12.50	31.28	76.23	4.47	11.51	29.05	71.37	4.10	10.68	27.20	67.34	3.79	9.97	25.63	63.93	43
44	4.90	12.74	32.48	80.63	4.47	11.73	30.17	75.49	4.10	10.88	28.25	71.22	3.79	10.16	26.61	67.62	44
45	4.90	12.99	33.73	85.28	4.47	11.95	31.33	79.84	4.10	11.09	29.33	75.33	3.79	10.36	27.64	71.52	45
46	4.90	13.23	35.03	90.20	4.47	12.18	32.54	84.45	4.10	11.30	30.46	79.68	3.79	10.56	28.70	75.65	46
47	4.90	13.49	36.38	95.41	4.47	12.42	33.79	89.32	4.10	11.52	31.64	84.28	3.79	10.76	29.81	80.01	47
48	4.90	13.75	37.78	100.91	4.47	12.66	35.09	94.48	4.10	11.74	32.85	89.14	3.79	10.96	30.95	84.63	48
49	4.90	14.01	39.24	106.74	4.47	12.90	36.44	99.93	4.10	11.97	34.12	94.28	3.79	11.17	32.14	89.51	49
50	4.90	14.28	40.75	112.90	4.47	13.15	37.85	105.69	4.10	12.20	35.43	99.72	3.79	11.39	33.38	94.68	50

Appendix A

III. Retirement Planning where Salary Outpaces Low 3% Inflation
Planned Retirement Age 62

Table 2 - Percent of Salary Replaced by a 401(k) Contribution of 1% of Current Salary   III-62-2

Probable Life Expectancy at Retirement

	23.2 (Same as Male Avg.)				25.7 (Better than Male Avg.)				28.3 (Same as Female Avg.)				31 (Better than Female Avg.)			
	4% / 4%	6% / 5%	8% / 6%	10% / 7%	4% / 4%	6% / 5%	8% / 6%	10% / 7%	4% / 4%	6% / 5%	8% / 6%	10% / 7%	4% / 4%	6% / 5%	8% / 6%	10% / 7%	
Yrs. to Ret.			Expected Return		(Pre-Retirement/Post-Retirement)				(Pre-Retirement/Post-Retirement)				Expected Return				Yrs. to Ret.
0	0.00	0.00	0.00	0.00	0.00	0.00	0.00	0.00	0.00	0.00	0.00	0.00	0.00	0.00	0.00	0.00	0
1	0.05	0.06	0.06	0.07	0.04	0.05	0.06	0.06	0.04	0.05	0.05	0.06	0.04	0.04	0.05	0.06	1
2	0.10	0.11	0.13	0.14	0.09	0.10	0.12	0.13	0.08	0.10	0.11	0.12	0.08	0.09	0.10	0.12	2
3	0.15	0.17	0.19	0.22	0.13	0.16	0.18	0.20	0.12	0.14	0.17	0.19	0.11	0.13	0.16	0.18	3
4	0.20	0.23	0.26	0.30	0.18	0.21	0.24	0.28	0.16	0.19	0.23	0.26	0.15	0.18	0.21	0.25	4
5	0.25	0.29	0.33	0.38	0.22	0.26	0.31	0.36	0.21	0.24	0.29	0.34	0.19	0.23	0.27	0.32	5
6	0.29	0.35	0.41	0.47	0.27	0.32	0.38	0.44	0.25	0.30	0.35	0.42	0.23	0.28	0.33	0.40	6
7	0.34	0.41	0.48	0.57	0.31	0.38	0.45	0.53	0.29	0.35	0.42	0.50	0.27	0.33	0.40	0.48	7
8	0.39	0.47	0.56	0.67	0.36	0.43	0.52	0.63	0.33	0.40	0.49	0.59	0.30	0.38	0.46	0.56	8
9	0.44	0.54	0.65	0.78	0.40	0.49	0.60	0.73	0.37	0.46	0.56	0.69	0.34	0.43	0.53	0.65	9
10	0.49	0.60	0.73	0.89	0.45	0.55	0.68	0.83	0.41	0.51	0.64	0.79	0.38	0.48	0.60	0.75	10
11	0.54	0.67	0.82	1.01	0.49	0.62	0.77	0.95	0.45	0.57	0.72	0.89	0.42	0.53	0.68	0.85	11
12	0.59	0.74	0.92	1.14	0.54	0.68	0.85	1.06	0.49	0.63	0.80	1.00	0.45	0.59	0.75	0.95	12
13	0.64	0.81	1.02	1.27	0.58	0.74	0.94	1.19	0.53	0.69	0.88	1.12	0.49	0.64	0.83	1.07	13
14	0.69	0.88	1.12	1.41	0.63	0.81	1.04	1.32	0.57	0.75	0.97	1.25	0.53	0.70	0.91	1.18	14
15	0.74	0.95	1.22	1.56	0.67	0.87	1.13	1.46	0.62	0.81	1.06	1.38	0.57	0.76	1.00	1.31	15
16	0.78	1.02	1.33	1.72	0.71	0.94	1.23	1.61	0.66	0.87	1.16	1.52	0.61	0.82	1.09	1.44	16
17	0.83	1.10	1.44	1.89	0.76	1.01	1.34	1.77	0.70	0.94	1.25	1.67	0.64	0.87	1.18	1.58	17
18	0.88	1.17	1.56	2.07	0.80	1.08	1.45	1.93	0.74	1.00	1.36	1.82	0.68	0.94	1.28	1.73	18
19	0.93	1.25	1.68	2.25	0.85	1.15	1.56	2.11	0.78	1.07	1.46	1.99	0.72	1.00	1.38	1.89	19
20	0.98	1.33	1.81	2.45	0.89	1.22	1.68	2.30	0.82	1.14	1.57	2.17	0.76	1.06	1.48	2.06	20
21	1.03	1.41	1.94	2.66	0.94	1.30	1.80	2.49	0.86	1.20	1.69	2.35	0.80	1.13	1.59	2.23	21
22	1.08	1.49	2.07	2.88	0.98	1.37	1.93	2.70	0.90	1.28	1.80	2.55	0.83	1.19	1.70	2.42	22
23	1.13	1.58	2.22	3.12	1.03	1.45	2.06	2.92	0.94	1.35	1.93	2.75	0.87	1.26	1.82	2.62	23
24	1.18	1.66	2.36	3.37	1.07	1.53	2.19	3.15	0.98	1.42	2.05	2.97	0.91	1.33	1.94	2.82	24
25	1.23	1.75	2.52	3.63	1.12	1.61	2.34	3.40	1.03	1.49	2.19	3.21	0.95	1.40	2.06	3.04	25
26	1.27	1.84	2.67	3.91	1.16	1.69	2.48	3.66	1.07	1.57	2.32	3.45	0.99	1.47	2.19	3.28	26
27	1.32	1.93	2.84	4.20	1.21	1.78	2.64	3.93	1.11	1.65	2.47	3.71	1.02	1.54	2.33	3.52	27
28	1.37	2.02	3.01	4.51	1.25	1.86	2.80	4.22	1.15	1.73	2.62	3.98	1.06	1.61	2.47	3.78	28
29	1.42	2.11	3.19	4.84	1.30	1.95	2.96	4.53	1.19	1.81	2.77	4.28	1.10	1.69	2.61	4.06	29
30	1.47	2.21	3.37	5.19	1.34	2.04	3.13	4.86	1.23	1.89	2.93	4.58	1.14	1.76	2.76	4.35	30
31	1.52	2.31	3.56	5.56	1.38	2.12	3.31	5.20	1.27	1.97	3.10	4.91	1.18	1.84	2.92	4.66	31
32	1.57	2.41	3.76	5.94	1.43	2.22	3.49	5.56	1.31	2.06	3.27	5.25	1.21	1.92	3.08	4.98	32
33	1.62	2.51	3.97	6.36	1.47	2.31	3.69	5.95	1.35	2.14	3.45	5.61	1.25	2.00	3.25	5.33	33
34	1.67	2.61	4.18	6.79	1.52	2.40	3.88	6.36	1.39	2.23	3.64	6.00	1.29	2.08	3.43	5.69	34
35	1.72	2.72	4.40	7.25	1.56	2.50	4.09	6.79	1.44	2.32	3.83	6.40	1.33	2.17	3.61	6.08	35
36	1.76	2.83	4.64	7.74	1.61	2.60	4.31	7.24	1.48	2.41	4.03	6.83	1.36	2.25	3.80	6.49	36
37	1.81	2.93	4.88	8.25	1.65	2.70	4.53	7.73	1.52	2.51	4.24	7.29	1.40	2.34	3.99	6.92	37
38	1.86	3.05	5.13	8.80	1.70	2.80	4.76	8.24	1.56	2.60	4.46	7.77	1.44	2.43	4.20	7.38	38
39	1.91	3.16	5.38	9.37	1.74	2.91	5.00	8.77	1.60	2.70	4.68	8.28	1.48	2.52	4.41	7.86	39
40	1.96	3.28	5.65	9.98	1.79	3.02	5.25	9.34	1.64	2.80	4.92	8.82	1.52	2.61	4.63	8.37	40
41	2.01	3.39	5.93	10.63	1.83	3.12	5.51	9.95	1.68	2.90	5.16	9.39	1.55	2.71	4.86	8.91	41
42	2.06	3.51	6.22	11.31	1.88	3.23	5.78	10.59	1.72	3.00	5.41	9.99	1.59	2.80	5.10	9.48	42
43	2.11	3.64	6.52	12.03	1.92	3.35	6.06	11.26	1.76	3.11	5.67	10.62	1.63	2.90	5.34	10.09	43
44	2.16	3.76	6.84	12.79	1.97	3.46	6.35	11.97	1.80	3.21	5.94	11.30	1.67	3.00	5.60	10.73	44
45	2.21	3.89	7.16	13.60	2.01	3.58	6.65	12.73	1.85	3.32	6.23	12.01	1.71	3.10	5.87	11.40	45
46	2.25	4.02	7.50	14.45	2.05	3.70	6.97	13.53	1.89	3.43	6.52	12.76	1.74	3.21	6.14	12.12	46
47	2.30	4.15	7.85	15.35	2.10	3.82	7.29	14.37	1.93	3.55	6.83	13.56	1.78	3.31	6.43	12.87	47
48	2.35	4.29	8.21	16.31	2.14	3.95	7.63	15.27	1.97	3.66	7.14	14.40	1.82	3.42	6.73	13.67	48
49	2.40	4.42	8.59	17.31	2.19	4.07	7.98	16.21	2.01	3.78	7.47	15.29	1.86	3.53	7.04	14.52	49
50	2.45	4.56	8.98	18.38	2.23	4.20	8.34	17.21	2.05	3.90	7.81	16.24	1.90	3.64	7.36	15.42	50

A-47

III. Retirement Planning where Salary Outpaces Low 3% Inflation
Planned Retirement Age 62

Table 3 - 401(k) Contribution (% of Current Sal.) Needed to Replace 10% of Sal. at Retirement   III-62-3

Probable Life Expectancy at Retirement

Yrs. to Ret.	23.2 (Same as Male Avg.)				25.7 (Better than Male Avg.)				28.3 (Same as Female Avg.)				31 (Better than Female Avg.)				Yrs. to Ret.
	4%/4%	6%/5%	8%/6%	10%/7%	4%/4%	6%/5%	8%/6%	10%/7%	4%/4%	6%/5%	8%/6%	10%/7%	4%/4%	6%/5%	8%/6%	10%/7%	
	Expected Return				(Pre-Retirement/Post-Retirement)				(Pre-Retirement/Post-Retirement)				Expected Return				
0																	0
1	204.04	181.23	162.26	146.37	223.92	196.87	174.70	156.34	243.82	212.19	186.61	165.70	263.81	227.23	198.07	174.53	1
2	102.02	89.75	79.60	71.13	111.96	97.50	85.70	75.98	121.91	105.09	91.54	80.53	131.90	112.54	97.16	84.82	2
3	68.01	59.26	52.06	46.08	74.64	64.38	56.05	49.22	81.27	69.39	59.87	52.17	87.94	74.31	63.54	54.95	3
4	51.01	44.02	38.30	33.57	55.98	47.82	41.23	35.86	60.96	51.54	44.04	38.01	65.95	55.20	46.75	40.03	4
5	40.81	34.88	30.05	26.08	44.78	37.89	32.35	27.86	48.76	40.84	34.56	29.53	52.76	43.73	36.68	31.10	5
6	34.01	28.79	24.56	21.11	37.32	31.27	26.44	22.54	40.64	33.70	28.24	23.89	43.97	36.09	29.97	25.17	6
7	29.15	24.44	20.64	17.56	31.99	26.55	22.22	18.76	34.83	28.61	23.73	19.88	37.69	30.64	25.19	20.94	7
8	25.50	21.17	17.70	14.91	27.99	23.00	19.06	15.93	30.48	24.79	20.36	16.88	32.98	26.55	21.61	17.78	8
9	22.67	18.64	15.43	12.86	24.88	20.25	16.61	13.74	27.09	21.82	17.74	14.56	29.31	23.37	18.83	15.33	9
10	20.40	16.61	13.61	11.23	22.39	18.05	14.65	11.99	24.38	19.45	15.65	12.71	26.38	20.83	16.61	13.38	10
11	18.55	14.95	12.13	9.90	20.36	16.24	13.05	10.57	22.17	17.51	13.94	11.20	23.98	18.75	14.80	11.80	11
12	17.00	13.57	10.89	8.79	18.66	14.74	11.73	9.39	20.32	15.89	12.53	9.96	21.98	17.02	13.30	10.49	12
13	15.70	12.41	9.85	7.87	17.22	13.48	10.61	8.40	18.76	14.53	11.33	8.91	20.29	15.55	12.03	9.38	13
14	14.57	11.41	8.96	7.08	15.99	12.39	9.65	7.56	17.42	13.35	10.31	8.01	18.84	14.30	10.94	8.44	14
15	13.60	10.54	8.19	6.40	14.93	11.45	8.82	6.84	16.25	12.34	9.42	7.24	17.59	13.22	10.00	7.63	15
16	12.75	9.78	7.52	5.81	13.99	10.63	8.10	6.21	15.24	11.45	8.65	6.58	16.49	12.27	9.18	6.93	16
17	12.00	9.12	6.94	5.29	13.17	9.90	7.47	5.66	14.34	10.67	7.98	5.99	15.52	11.43	8.47	6.31	17
18	11.34	8.52	6.41	4.84	12.44	9.26	6.91	5.17	13.55	9.98	7.38	5.48	14.66	10.69	7.83	5.77	18
19	10.74	7.99	5.95	4.44	11.79	8.68	6.41	4.74	12.83	9.36	6.84	5.02	13.88	10.02	7.26	5.29	19
20	10.20	7.52	5.53	4.08	11.20	8.17	5.96	4.36	12.19	8.80	6.36	4.62	13.19	9.43	6.76	4.86	20
21	9.72	7.09	5.16	3.76	10.66	7.70	5.56	4.01	11.61	8.30	5.93	4.25	12.56	8.89	6.30	4.48	21
22	9.27	6.70	4.82	3.47	10.18	7.28	5.19	3.70	11.08	7.84	5.54	3.93	11.99	8.40	5.88	4.14	22
23	8.87	6.34	4.51	3.21	9.74	6.89	4.86	3.43	10.60	7.42	5.19	3.63	11.47	7.95	5.51	3.82	23
24	8.50	6.02	4.23	2.97	9.33	6.53	4.56	3.17	10.16	7.04	4.87	3.36	10.99	7.54	5.17	3.54	24
25	8.16	5.72	3.98	2.76	8.96	6.21	4.28	2.94	9.75	6.69	4.57	3.12	10.55	7.17	4.85	3.29	25
26	7.85	5.44	3.74	2.56	8.61	5.91	4.03	2.73	9.38	6.37	4.30	2.90	10.15	6.82	4.57	3.05	26
27	7.56	5.18	3.52	2.38	8.29	5.63	3.79	2.54	9.03	6.07	4.05	2.70	9.77	6.50	4.30	2.84	27
28	7.29	4.95	3.32	2.22	8.00	5.38	3.58	2.37	8.71	5.79	3.82	2.51	9.42	6.20	4.06	2.64	28
29	7.04	4.73	3.14	2.07	7.72	5.14	3.38	2.21	8.41	5.54	3.61	2.34	9.10	5.93	3.83	2.46	29
30	6.80	4.52	2.97	1.93	7.46	4.91	3.19	2.06	8.13	5.30	3.41	2.18	8.79	5.67	3.62	2.30	30
31	6.58	4.33	2.81	1.80	7.22	4.71	3.02	1.92	7.87	5.07	3.23	2.04	8.51	5.43	3.43	2.15	31
32	6.38	4.15	2.66	1.68	7.00	4.51	2.86	1.80	7.62	4.86	3.06	1.90	8.24	5.21	3.25	2.01	32
33	6.18	3.99	2.52	1.57	6.79	4.33	2.71	1.68	7.39	4.67	2.90	1.78	7.99	5.00	3.08	1.88	33
34	6.00	3.83	2.39	1.47	6.59	4.16	2.57	1.57	7.17	4.48	2.75	1.67	7.76	4.80	2.92	1.76	34
35	5.83	3.68	2.27	1.38	6.40	4.00	2.44	1.47	6.97	4.31	2.61	1.56	7.54	4.61	2.77	1.64	35
36	5.67	3.54	2.16	1.29	6.22	3.85	2.32	1.38	6.77	4.14	2.48	1.46	7.33	4.44	2.63	1.54	36
37	5.51	3.41	2.05	1.21	6.05	3.70	2.21	1.29	6.59	3.99	2.36	1.37	7.13	4.27	2.50	1.44	37
38	5.37	3.28	1.95	1.14	5.89	3.57	2.10	1.21	6.42	3.84	2.24	1.29	6.94	4.12	2.38	1.36	38
39	5.23	3.16	1.86	1.07	5.74	3.44	2.00	1.14	6.25	3.71	2.14	1.21	6.76	3.97	2.27	1.27	39
40	5.10	3.05	1.77	1.00	5.60	3.32	1.90	1.07	6.10	3.57	2.03	1.13	6.60	3.83	2.16	1.19	40
41	4.98	2.95	1.69	0.94	5.46	3.20	1.81	1.01	5.95	3.45	1.94	1.07	6.43	3.69	2.06	1.12	41
42	4.86	2.85	1.61	0.88	5.33	3.09	1.73	0.94	5.81	3.33	1.85	1.00	6.28	3.57	1.96	1.05	42
43	4.75	2.75	1.53	0.83	5.21	2.99	1.65	0.89	5.67	3.22	1.76	0.94	6.14	3.45	1.87	0.99	43
44	4.64	2.66	1.46	0.78	5.09	2.89	1.57	0.84	5.54	3.11	1.68	0.89	6.00	3.33	1.79	0.93	44
45	4.53	2.57	1.40	0.74	4.98	2.79	1.50	0.79	5.42	3.01	1.61	0.83	5.86	3.22	1.70	0.88	45
46	4.44	2.49	1.33	0.69	4.87	2.70	1.44	0.74	5.30	2.91	1.53	0.78	5.73	3.12	1.63	0.83	46
47	4.34	2.41	1.27	0.65	4.76	2.62	1.37	0.70	5.19	2.82	1.47	0.74	5.61	3.02	1.56	0.78	47
48	4.25	2.33	1.22	0.61	4.66	2.53	1.31	0.66	5.08	2.73	1.40	0.69	5.50	2.93	1.49	0.73	48
49	4.16	2.26	1.16	0.58	4.57	2.46	1.25	0.62	4.98	2.65	1.34	0.65	5.38	2.83	1.42	0.69	49
50	4.08	2.19	1.11	0.54	4.48	2.38	1.20	0.58	4.88	2.57	1.28	0.62	5.28	2.75	1.36	0.65	50

Appendix A

III. Retirement Planning where Salary Outpaces Low 3% Inflation
Planned Retirement Age 62

Table 4 - Accumulation at Retirement (Multiple of Current Sal.) for 10% Sal. Replacement   III-62-4

Probable Life Expectancy at Retirement

Yrs. to Ret.	23.2 (Same as Male Avg.)				25.7 (Better than Male Avg.)				28.3 (Same as Female Avg.)				31 (Better than Female Avg.)				Yrs. to Ret.
	4%/4%	6%/5%	8%/6%	10%/7%	4%/4%	6%/5%	8%/6%	10%/7%	4%/4%	6%/5%	8%/6%	10%/7%	4%/4%	6%/5%	8%/6%	10%/7%	
	Expected Return		(Pre-Retirement/Post-Retirement)				(Pre-Retirement/Post-Retirement)				Expected Return						
0	2.04	1.81	1.62	1.46	2.24	1.97	1.75	1.56	2.44	2.12	1.87	1.66	2.64	2.27	1.98	1.75	0
1	2.12	1.88	1.69	1.52	2.33	2.05	1.82	1.63	2.54	2.21	1.94	1.72	2.74	2.36	2.06	1.82	1
2	2.21	1.96	1.76	1.58	2.42	2.13	1.89	1.69	2.64	2.30	2.02	1.79	2.85	2.46	2.14	1.89	2
3	2.30	2.04	1.83	1.65	2.52	2.21	1.97	1.76	2.74	2.39	2.10	1.86	2.97	2.56	2.23	1.96	3
4	2.39	2.12	1.90	1.71	2.62	2.30	2.04	1.83	2.85	2.48	2.18	1.94	3.09	2.66	2.32	2.04	4
5	2.48	2.20	1.97	1.78	2.72	2.40	2.13	1.90	2.97	2.58	2.27	2.02	3.21	2.76	2.41	2.12	5
6	2.58	2.29	2.05	1.85	2.83	2.49	2.21	1.98	3.09	2.68	2.36	2.10	3.34	2.88	2.51	2.21	6
7	2.69	2.38	2.14	1.93	2.95	2.59	2.30	2.06	3.21	2.79	2.46	2.18	3.47	2.99	2.61	2.30	7
8	2.79	2.48	2.22	2.00	3.06	2.69	2.39	2.14	3.34	2.90	2.55	2.27	3.61	3.11	2.71	2.39	8
9	2.90	2.58	2.31	2.08	3.19	2.80	2.49	2.23	3.47	3.02	2.66	2.36	3.75	3.23	2.82	2.48	9
10	3.02	2.68	2.40	2.17	3.31	2.91	2.59	2.31	3.61	3.14	2.76	2.45	3.90	3.36	2.93	2.58	10
11	3.14	2.79	2.50	2.25	3.45	3.03	2.69	2.41	3.75	3.27	2.87	2.55	4.06	3.50	3.05	2.69	11
12	3.27	2.90	2.60	2.34	3.58	3.15	2.80	2.50	3.90	3.40	2.99	2.65	4.22	3.64	3.17	2.79	12
13	3.40	3.02	2.70	2.44	3.73	3.28	2.91	2.60	4.06	3.53	3.11	2.76	4.39	3.78	3.30	2.91	13
14	3.53	3.14	2.81	2.53	3.88	3.41	3.03	2.71	4.22	3.67	3.23	2.87	4.57	3.93	3.43	3.02	14
15	3.67	3.26	2.92	2.64	4.03	3.55	3.15	2.82	4.39	3.82	3.36	2.98	4.75	4.09	3.57	3.14	15
16	3.82	3.39	3.04	2.74	4.19	3.69	3.27	2.93	4.57	3.97	3.50	3.10	4.94	4.26	3.71	3.27	16
17	3.97	3.53	3.16	2.85	4.36	3.83	3.40	3.05	4.75	4.13	3.63	3.23	5.14	4.43	3.86	3.40	17
18	4.13	3.67	3.29	2.97	4.54	3.99	3.54	3.17	4.94	4.30	3.78	3.36	5.34	4.60	4.01	3.54	18
19	4.30	3.82	3.42	3.08	4.72	4.15	3.68	3.29	5.14	4.47	3.93	3.49	5.56	4.79	4.17	3.68	19
20	4.47	3.97	3.56	3.21	4.91	4.31	3.83	3.43	5.34	4.65	4.09	3.63	5.78	4.98	4.34	3.82	20
21	4.65	4.13	3.70	3.34	5.10	4.49	3.98	3.56	5.56	4.84	4.25	3.78	6.01	5.18	4.51	3.98	21
22	4.84	4.29	3.85	3.47	5.31	4.67	4.14	3.71	5.78	5.03	4.42	3.93	6.25	5.39	4.69	4.14	22
23	5.03	4.47	4.00	3.61	5.52	4.85	4.31	3.85	6.01	5.23	4.60	4.08	6.50	5.60	4.88	4.30	23
24	5.23	4.65	4.16	3.75	5.74	5.05	4.48	4.01	6.25	5.44	4.78	4.25	6.76	5.82	5.08	4.47	24
25	5.44	4.83	4.33	3.90	5.97	5.25	4.66	4.17	6.50	5.66	4.97	4.42	7.03	6.06	5.28	4.65	25
26	5.66	5.02	4.50	4.06	6.21	5.46	4.84	4.33	6.76	5.88	5.17	4.59	7.31	6.30	5.49	4.84	26
27	5.88	5.23	4.68	4.22	6.46	5.68	5.04	4.51	7.03	6.12	5.38	4.78	7.61	6.55	5.71	5.03	27
28	6.12	5.43	4.87	4.39	6.71	5.90	5.24	4.69	7.31	6.36	5.60	4.97	7.91	6.81	5.94	5.23	28
29	6.36	5.65	5.06	4.56	6.98	6.14	5.45	4.88	7.60	6.62	5.82	5.17	8.23	7.09	6.18	5.44	29
30	6.62	5.88	5.26	4.75	7.26	6.39	5.67	5.07	7.91	6.88	6.05	5.37	8.56	7.37	6.42	5.66	30
31	6.88	6.11	5.47	4.94	7.55	6.64	5.89	5.27	8.22	7.16	6.29	5.59	8.90	7.66	6.68	5.89	31
32	7.16	6.36	5.69	5.13	7.86	6.91	6.13	5.48	8.55	7.44	6.55	5.81	9.25	7.97	6.95	6.12	32
33	7.44	6.61	5.92	5.34	8.17	7.18	6.37	5.70	8.90	7.74	6.81	6.05	9.62	8.29	7.23	6.37	33
34	7.74	6.88	6.16	5.55	8.50	7.47	6.63	5.93	9.25	8.05	7.08	6.29	10.01	8.62	7.52	6.62	34
35	8.05	7.15	6.40	5.78	8.84	7.77	6.89	6.17	9.62	8.37	7.36	6.54	10.41	8.97	7.82	6.89	35
36	8.37	7.44	6.66	6.01	9.19	8.08	7.17	6.42	10.01	8.71	7.66	6.80	10.83	9.33	8.13	7.16	36
37	8.71	7.73	6.93	6.25	9.56	8.40	7.46	6.67	10.41	9.06	7.96	7.07	11.26	9.70	8.45	7.45	37
38	9.06	8.04	7.20	6.50	9.94	8.74	7.75	6.94	10.82	9.42	8.28	7.36	11.71	10.09	8.79	7.75	38
39	9.42	8.37	7.49	6.76	10.34	9.09	8.06	7.22	11.26	9.80	8.61	7.65	12.18	10.49	9.14	8.06	39
40	9.80	8.70	7.79	7.03	10.75	9.45	8.39	7.51	11.71	10.19	8.96	7.96	12.67	10.91	9.51	8.38	40
41	10.19	9.05	8.10	7.31	11.18	9.83	8.72	7.81	12.17	10.59	9.32	8.27	13.17	11.35	9.89	8.71	41
42	10.60	9.41	8.43	7.60	11.63	10.22	9.07	8.12	12.66	11.02	9.69	8.60	13.70	11.80	10.29	9.06	42
43	11.02	9.79	8.76	7.90	12.09	10.63	9.43	8.44	13.17	11.46	10.08	8.95	14.25	12.27	10.70	9.43	43
44	11.46	10.18	9.11	8.22	12.58	11.06	9.81	8.78	13.69	11.92	10.48	9.31	14.82	12.76	11.12	9.80	44
45	11.92	10.59	9.48	8.55	13.08	11.50	10.20	9.13	14.24	12.39	10.90	9.68	15.41	13.27	11.57	10.19	45
46	12.39	11.01	9.86	8.89	13.60	11.96	10.61	9.50	14.81	12.89	11.34	10.07	16.03	13.80	12.03	10.60	46
47	12.89	11.45	10.25	9.25	14.15	12.44	11.04	9.88	15.40	13.41	11.79	10.47	16.67	14.36	12.51	11.03	47
48	13.41	11.91	10.66	9.62	14.71	12.94	11.48	10.27	16.02	13.94	12.26	10.89	17.33	14.93	13.01	11.47	48
49	13.94	12.38	11.09	10.00	15.30	13.45	11.94	10.68	16.66	14.50	12.75	11.32	18.03	15.53	13.53	11.93	49
50	14.50	12.88	11.53	10.40	15.91	13.99	12.42	11.11	17.33	15.08	13.26	11.78	18.75	16.15	14.08	12.40	50

III. Retirement Planning where Salary Outpaces Low 3% Inflation
Planned Retirement Age 65

Table 1 - Percent of Salary Replaced by a 401(k) Account Equal to Current Annual Salary III-65-1

Probable Life Expectancy at Retirement

	20.7 (Same as Male Avg.)				23.2 (Better than Male Avg.)				25.7 (Same as Female Avg.)				28.3 (Better than Female Avg.)				
Yrs. to Ret.	4% / 4%	6% / 5%	8% / 6%	10% / 7%	4% / 4%	6% / 5%	8% / 6%	10% / 7%	4% / 4%	6% / 5%	8% / 6%	10% / 7%	4% / 4%	6% / 5%	8% / 6%	10% / 7%	Yrs. to Ret.
	Expected Return		(Pre-Retirement/Post-Retirement)						(Pre-Retirement/Post-Retirement)				Expected Return				
0	5.43	6.05	6.70	7.37	4.90	5.52	6.16	6.83	4.47	5.08	5.72	6.40	4.10	4.71	5.36	6.03	0
1	5.43	6.17	6.96	7.79	4.90	5.62	6.40	7.23	4.47	5.18	5.94	6.77	4.10	4.80	5.57	6.38	1
2	5.43	6.29	7.23	8.24	4.90	5.73	6.65	7.64	4.47	5.28	6.17	7.16	4.10	4.90	5.78	6.75	2
3	5.43	6.41	7.50	8.72	4.90	5.84	6.90	8.08	4.47	5.38	6.41	7.57	4.10	4.99	6.00	7.14	3
4	5.43	6.53	7.79	9.22	4.90	5.95	7.17	8.55	4.47	5.48	6.66	8.01	4.10	5.09	6.23	7.55	4
5	5.43	6.66	8.09	9.75	4.90	6.07	7.44	9.04	4.47	5.59	6.91	8.47	4.10	5.18	6.47	7.99	5
6	5.43	6.78	8.40	10.32	4.90	6.18	7.73	9.57	4.47	5.69	7.18	8.96	4.10	5.28	6.72	8.45	6
7	5.43	6.91	8.73	10.91	4.90	6.30	8.03	10.12	4.47	5.80	7.46	9.47	4.10	5.38	6.98	8.94	7
8	5.43	7.05	9.06	11.54	4.90	6.42	8.34	10.70	4.47	5.91	7.74	10.02	4.10	5.49	7.25	9.45	8
9	5.43	7.18	9.41	12.21	4.90	6.55	8.66	11.32	4.47	6.03	8.04	10.60	4.10	5.59	7.53	10.00	9
10	5.43	7.32	9.78	12.91	4.90	6.67	8.99	11.97	4.47	6.14	8.35	11.21	4.10	5.70	7.82	10.58	10
11	5.43	7.46	10.15	13.66	4.90	6.80	9.34	12.66	4.47	6.26	8.67	11.86	4.10	5.81	8.12	11.19	11
12	5.43	7.60	10.54	14.45	4.90	6.93	9.70	13.39	4.47	6.38	9.01	12.54	4.10	5.92	8.43	11.83	12
13	5.43	7.75	10.95	15.28	4.90	7.07	10.07	14.17	4.47	6.50	9.35	13.26	4.10	6.03	8.76	12.51	13
14	5.43	7.90	11.37	16.16	4.90	7.20	10.46	14.98	4.47	6.63	9.71	14.03	4.10	6.15	9.09	13.24	14
15	5.43	8.05	11.81	17.09	4.90	7.34	10.86	15.85	4.47	6.76	10.09	14.84	4.10	6.27	9.44	14.00	15
16	5.43	8.21	12.26	18.08	4.90	7.48	11.28	16.76	4.47	6.89	10.48	15.69	4.10	6.39	9.81	14.81	16
17	5.43	8.36	12.73	19.12	4.90	7.62	11.71	17.73	4.47	7.02	10.88	16.60	4.10	6.51	10.19	15.66	17
18	5.43	8.52	13.22	20.23	4.90	7.77	12.16	18.75	4.47	7.15	11.30	17.56	4.10	6.64	10.58	16.57	18
19	5.43	8.69	13.73	21.39	4.90	7.92	12.63	19.84	4.47	7.29	11.73	18.57	4.10	6.76	10.98	17.52	19
20	5.43	8.85	14.26	22.63	4.90	8.07	13.12	20.98	4.47	7.43	12.19	19.64	4.10	6.89	11.41	18.53	20
21	5.43	9.02	14.81	23.93	4.90	8.23	13.62	22.19	4.47	7.57	12.65	20.77	4.10	7.03	11.85	19.60	21
22	5.43	9.20	15.38	25.31	4.90	8.38	14.15	23.47	4.47	7.72	13.14	21.97	4.10	7.16	12.30	20.73	22
23	5.43	9.37	15.97	26.78	4.90	8.55	14.69	24.83	4.47	7.87	13.65	23.24	4.10	7.30	12.78	21.93	23
24	5.43	9.55	16.58	28.32	4.90	8.71	15.26	26.26	4.47	8.02	14.17	24.58	4.10	7.44	13.27	23.19	24
25	5.43	9.74	17.23	29.95	4.90	8.88	15.85	27.77	4.47	8.17	14.72	26.00	4.10	7.58	13.78	24.53	25
26	5.43	9.92	17.89	31.68	4.90	9.05	16.46	29.38	4.47	8.33	15.29	27.50	4.10	7.73	14.31	25.95	26
27	5.43	10.11	18.58	33.51	4.90	9.22	17.09	31.07	4.47	8.49	15.87	29.09	4.10	7.88	14.86	27.44	27
28	5.43	10.31	19.30	35.44	4.90	9.40	17.75	32.86	4.47	8.65	16.49	30.77	4.10	8.03	15.43	29.03	28
29	5.43	10.51	20.04	37.49	4.90	9.58	18.43	34.76	4.47	8.82	17.12	32.54	4.10	8.18	16.03	30.70	29
30	5.43	10.71	20.81	39.65	4.90	9.76	19.14	36.76	4.47	8.99	17.78	34.42	4.10	8.34	16.64	32.47	30
31	5.43	10.91	21.61	41.94	4.90	9.95	19.88	38.89	4.47	9.16	18.46	36.40	4.10	8.50	17.28	34.35	31
32	5.43	11.12	22.44	44.36	4.90	10.14	20.64	41.13	4.47	9.34	19.17	38.51	4.10	8.66	17.95	36.33	32
33	5.43	11.34	23.31	46.92	4.90	10.34	21.44	43.50	4.47	9.51	19.91	40.73	4.10	8.83	18.64	38.43	33
34	5.43	11.56	24.20	49.63	4.90	10.53	22.26	46.01	4.47	9.70	20.68	43.08	4.10	9.00	19.36	40.64	34
35	5.43	11.78	25.14	52.49	4.90	10.74	23.12	48.67	4.47	9.88	21.48	45.56	4.10	9.17	20.10	42.99	35
36	5.43	12.00	26.10	55.52	4.90	10.94	24.01	51.48	4.47	10.07	22.30	48.19	4.10	9.35	20.88	45.47	36
37	5.43	12.23	27.11	58.72	4.90	11.15	24.94	54.45	4.47	10.27	23.16	50.97	4.10	9.53	21.68	48.09	37
38	5.43	12.47	28.15	62.11	4.90	11.37	25.90	57.59	4.47	10.46	24.05	53.91	4.10	9.71	22.52	50.87	38
39	5.43	12.71	29.24	65.70	4.90	11.59	26.89	60.91	4.47	10.66	24.98	57.02	4.10	9.89	23.38	53.80	39
40	5.43	12.95	30.36	69.49	4.90	11.81	27.93	64.43	4.47	10.87	25.94	60.31	4.10	10.08	24.28	56.91	40
41	5.43	13.20	31.53	73.50	4.90	12.03	29.00	68.14	4.47	11.08	26.94	63.79	4.10	10.28	25.22	60.19	41
42	5.43	13.45	32.75	77.74	4.90	12.27	30.12	72.07	4.47	11.29	27.98	67.48	4.10	10.48	26.19	63.66	42
43	5.43	13.71	34.01	82.22	4.90	12.50	31.28	76.23	4.47	11.51	29.05	71.37	4.10	10.68	27.20	67.34	43
44	5.43	13.98	35.32	86.97	4.90	12.74	32.48	80.63	4.47	11.73	30.17	75.49	4.10	10.89	28.25	71.22	44
45	5.43	14.24	36.68	91.98	4.90	12.99	33.73	85.28	4.47	11.95	31.33	79.84	4.10	11.09	29.33	75.33	45
46	5.43	14.52	38.09	97.29	4.90	13.23	35.03	90.20	4.47	12.18	32.54	84.45	4.10	11.30	30.46	79.68	46
47	5.43	14.80	39.55	102.91	4.90	13.49	36.38	95.41	4.47	12.42	33.79	89.32	4.10	11.52	31.64	84.28	47
48	5.43	15.08	41.08	108.84	4.90	13.75	37.78	100.91	4.47	12.66	35.09	94.48	4.10	11.74	32.85	89.14	48
49	5.43	15.37	42.66	115.12	4.90	14.01	39.24	106.74	4.47	12.90	36.44	99.93	4.10	11.97	34.12	94.28	49
50	5.43	15.66	44.30	121.77	4.90	14.28	40.75	112.90	4.47	13.15	37.85	105.69	4.10	12.20	35.43	99.72	50

Appendix A

III. Retirement Planning where Salary Outpaces Low 3% Inflation
Planned Retirement Age 65

Table 2 - Percent of Salary Replaced by a 401(k) Contribution of 1% of Current Salary

Probable Life Expectancy at Retirement

	20.7 (Same as Male Avg.)				23.2 (Better than Male Avg.)				25.7 (Same as Female Avg.)				28.3 (Better than Female Avg.)				
	4% / 4%	6% / 5%	8% / 6%	10% / 7%	4% / 4%	6% / 5%	8% / 6%	10% / 7%	4% / 4%	6% / 5%	8% / 6%	10% / 7%	4% / 4%	6% / 5%	8% / 6%	10% / 7%	
Yrs. to Ret.	Expected Return				(Pre-Retirement/Post-Retirement)				(Pre-Retirement/Post-Retirement)				Expected Return				Yrs. to Ret.
0	0.00	0.00	0.00	0.00	0.00	0.00	0.00	0.00	0.00	0.00	0.00	0.00	0.00	0.00	0.00	0.00	0
1	0.05	0.06	0.07	0.07	0.05	0.06	0.06	0.07	0.04	0.05	0.06	0.06	0.04	0.05	0.05	0.06	1
2	0.11	0.12	0.14	0.15	0.10	0.11	0.13	0.14	0.09	0.10	0.12	0.13	0.08	0.10	0.11	0.12	2
3	0.16	0.19	0.21	0.23	0.15	0.17	0.19	0.22	0.13	0.16	0.18	0.20	0.12	0.14	0.17	0.19	3
4	0.22	0.25	0.28	0.32	0.20	0.23	0.26	0.30	0.18	0.21	0.24	0.28	0.16	0.19	0.23	0.26	4
5	0.27	0.31	0.36	0.41	0.25	0.29	0.33	0.38	0.22	0.26	0.31	0.36	0.21	0.24	0.29	0.34	5
6	0.33	0.38	0.44	0.51	0.29	0.35	0.41	0.47	0.27	0.32	0.38	0.44	0.25	0.30	0.35	0.42	6
7	0.38	0.45	0.53	0.61	0.34	0.41	0.48	0.57	0.31	0.38	0.45	0.53	0.29	0.35	0.42	0.50	7
8	0.43	0.52	0.61	0.72	0.39	0.47	0.56	0.67	0.36	0.43	0.52	0.63	0.33	0.40	0.49	0.59	8
9	0.49	0.59	0.70	0.84	0.44	0.54	0.65	0.78	0.40	0.49	0.60	0.73	0.37	0.46	0.56	0.69	9
10	0.54	0.66	0.80	0.96	0.49	0.60	0.73	0.89	0.45	0.55	0.68	0.83	0.41	0.51	0.64	0.79	10
11	0.60	0.73	0.90	1.09	0.54	0.67	0.82	1.01	0.49	0.62	0.77	0.95	0.45	0.57	0.72	0.89	11
12	0.65	0.81	1.00	1.23	0.59	0.74	0.92	1.14	0.54	0.68	0.85	1.06	0.49	0.63	0.80	1.00	12
13	0.71	0.88	1.10	1.37	0.64	0.81	1.02	1.27	0.58	0.74	0.94	1.19	0.53	0.69	0.88	1.12	13
14	0.76	0.96	1.21	1.52	0.69	0.88	1.12	1.41	0.63	0.81	1.04	1.32	0.57	0.75	0.97	1.25	14
15	0.81	1.04	1.33	1.69	0.74	0.95	1.22	1.56	0.67	0.87	1.13	1.46	0.62	0.81	1.06	1.38	15
16	0.87	1.12	1.44	1.86	0.78	1.02	1.33	1.72	0.71	0.94	1.23	1.61	0.66	0.87	1.16	1.52	16
17	0.92	1.20	1.57	2.04	0.83	1.10	1.44	1.89	0.76	1.01	1.34	1.77	0.70	0.94	1.25	1.67	17
18	0.98	1.29	1.69	2.23	0.88	1.17	1.56	2.07	0.80	1.08	1.45	1.93	0.74	1.00	1.36	1.82	18
19	1.03	1.37	1.83	2.43	0.93	1.25	1.68	2.25	0.85	1.15	1.56	2.11	0.78	1.07	1.46	1.99	19
20	1.09	1.46	1.96	2.64	0.98	1.33	1.81	2.45	0.89	1.22	1.68	2.30	0.82	1.14	1.57	2.17	20
21	1.14	1.55	2.11	2.87	1.03	1.41	1.94	2.66	0.94	1.30	1.80	2.49	0.86	1.20	1.69	2.35	21
22	1.19	1.64	2.26	3.11	1.08	1.49	2.07	2.88	0.98	1.37	1.93	2.70	0.90	1.28	1.80	2.55	22
23	1.25	1.73	2.41	3.36	1.13	1.58	2.22	3.12	1.03	1.45	2.06	2.92	0.94	1.35	1.93	2.75	23
24	1.30	1.82	2.57	3.63	1.18	1.66	2.36	3.37	1.07	1.53	2.19	3.15	0.98	1.42	2.05	2.97	24
25	1.36	1.92	2.73	3.91	1.23	1.75	2.52	3.63	1.12	1.61	2.34	3.40	1.03	1.49	2.19	3.21	25
26	1.41	2.02	2.91	4.21	1.27	1.84	2.67	3.91	1.16	1.69	2.48	3.66	1.07	1.57	2.32	3.45	26
27	1.47	2.12	3.09	4.53	1.32	1.93	2.84	4.20	1.21	1.78	2.64	3.93	1.11	1.65	2.47	3.71	27
28	1.52	2.22	3.27	4.87	1.37	2.02	3.01	4.51	1.25	1.86	2.80	4.22	1.15	1.73	2.62	3.98	28
29	1.57	2.32	3.46	5.22	1.42	2.11	3.19	4.84	1.30	1.95	2.96	4.53	1.19	1.81	2.77	4.28	29
30	1.63	2.42	3.66	5.60	1.47	2.21	3.37	5.19	1.34	2.04	3.13	4.86	1.23	1.89	2.93	4.58	30
31	1.68	2.53	3.87	5.99	1.52	2.31	3.56	5.56	1.38	2.12	3.31	5.20	1.27	1.97	3.10	4.91	31
32	1.74	2.64	4.09	6.41	1.57	2.41	3.76	5.94	1.43	2.22	3.49	5.56	1.31	2.06	3.27	5.25	32
33	1.79	2.75	4.31	6.85	1.62	2.51	3.97	6.36	1.47	2.31	3.69	5.95	1.35	2.14	3.45	5.61	33
34	1.85	2.87	4.55	7.32	1.67	2.61	4.18	6.79	1.52	2.40	3.88	6.36	1.39	2.23	3.64	6.00	34
35	1.90	2.98	4.79	7.82	1.72	2.72	4.40	7.25	1.56	2.50	4.09	6.79	1.44	2.32	3.83	6.40	35
36	1.95	3.10	5.04	8.35	1.76	2.83	4.64	7.74	1.61	2.60	4.31	7.24	1.48	2.41	4.03	6.83	36
37	2.01	3.22	5.30	8.90	1.81	2.93	4.88	8.25	1.65	2.70	4.53	7.73	1.52	2.51	4.24	7.29	37
38	2.06	3.34	5.57	9.49	1.86	3.05	5.13	8.80	1.70	2.80	4.76	8.24	1.56	2.60	4.46	7.77	38
39	2.12	3.47	5.85	10.11	1.91	3.16	5.38	9.37	1.74	2.91	5.00	8.77	1.60	2.70	4.68	8.28	39
40	2.17	3.59	6.15	10.77	1.96	3.28	5.65	9.98	1.79	3.02	5.25	9.34	1.64	2.80	4.92	8.82	40
41	2.23	3.72	6.45	11.46	2.01	3.39	5.93	10.63	1.83	3.12	5.51	9.95	1.68	2.90	5.16	9.39	41
42	2.28	3.85	6.77	12.20	2.06	3.51	6.22	11.31	1.88	3.23	5.78	10.59	1.72	3.00	5.41	9.99	42
43	2.33	3.99	7.09	12.97	2.11	3.64	6.52	12.03	1.92	3.35	6.06	11.26	1.76	3.11	5.67	10.62	43
44	2.39	4.13	7.43	13.80	2.16	3.76	6.84	12.79	1.97	3.46	6.35	11.97	1.80	3.21	5.94	11.30	44
45	2.44	4.27	7.79	14.66	2.21	3.89	7.16	13.60	2.01	3.58	6.65	12.73	1.85	3.32	6.23	12.01	45
46	2.50	4.41	8.15	15.58	2.25	4.02	7.50	14.45	2.05	3.70	6.97	13.53	1.89	3.43	6.52	12.76	46
47	2.55	4.55	8.53	16.56	2.30	4.15	7.85	15.35	2.10	3.82	7.29	14.37	1.93	3.55	6.83	13.56	47
48	2.61	4.70	8.93	17.59	2.35	4.29	8.21	16.31	2.14	3.95	7.63	15.27	1.97	3.66	7.14	14.40	48
49	2.66	4.85	9.34	18.67	2.40	4.42	8.59	17.31	2.19	4.07	7.98	16.21	2.01	3.78	7.47	15.29	49
50	2.72	5.01	9.77	19.83	2.45	4.56	8.98	18.38	2.23	4.20	8.34	17.21	2.05	3.90	7.81	16.24	50

A-51

III. Retirement Planning where Salary Outpaces Low 3% Inflation
Planned Retirement Age 65

Table 3 - 401(k) Contribution (% of Current Sal.) Needed to Replace 10% of Sal. at Retirement   III-65-3

Probable Life Expectancy at Retirement

	20.7 (Same as Male Avg.)				23.2 (Better than Male Avg.)				25.7 (Same as Female Avg.)				28.3 (Better than Female Avg.)				
	4% / 4%	6% / 5%	8% / 6%	10% / 7%	4% / 4%	6% / 5%	8% / 6%	10% / 7%	4% / 4%	6% / 5%	8% / 6%	10% / 7%	4% / 4%	6% / 5%	8% / 6%	10% / 7%	
Yrs. to Ret.	Expected Return				(Pre-Retirement/Post-Retirement)				(Pre-Retirement/Post-Retirement)				Expected Return				Yrs to Ret
0																	0
1	184.16	165.21	149.25	135.71	204.04	181.23	162.26	146.37	223.92	196.87	174.70	156.34	243.82	212.19	186.61	165.70	1
2	92.08	81.82	73.22	65.95	102.02	89.75	79.60	71.13	111.96	97.50	85.70	75.98	121.91	105.09	91.54	80.53	2
3	61.39	54.03	47.88	42.72	68.01	59.26	52.06	46.08	74.64	64.38	56.05	49.22	81.27	69.39	59.87	52.17	3
4	46.04	40.13	35.23	31.13	51.01	44.02	38.30	33.57	55.98	47.82	41.23	35.86	60.96	51.54	44.04	38.01	4
5	36.83	31.80	27.64	24.18	40.81	34.88	30.05	26.08	44.78	37.89	32.35	27.86	48.76	40.84	34.56	29.53	5
6	30.69	26.24	22.59	19.57	34.01	28.79	24.56	21.11	37.32	31.27	26.44	22.54	40.64	33.70	28.24	23.89	6
7	26.31	22.28	18.98	16.28	29.15	24.44	20.64	17.56	31.99	26.55	22.22	18.76	34.83	28.61	23.73	19.88	7
8	23.02	19.30	16.28	13.82	25.50	21.17	17.70	14.91	27.99	23.00	19.06	15.93	30.48	24.79	20.36	16.88	8
9	20.46	16.99	14.19	11.92	22.67	18.64	15.43	12.86	24.88	20.25	16.61	13.74	27.09	21.82	17.74	14.56	9
10	18.42	15.14	12.52	10.41	20.40	16.61	13.61	11.23	22.39	18.05	14.65	11.99	24.38	19.45	15.65	12.71	10
11	16.74	13.63	11.15	9.17	18.55	14.95	12.13	9.90	20.36	16.24	13.05	10.57	22.17	17.51	13.94	11.20	11
12	15.35	12.37	10.02	8.15	17.00	13.57	10.89	8.79	18.66	14.74	11.73	9.39	20.32	15.89	12.53	9.96	12
13	14.17	11.31	9.06	7.29	15.70	12.41	9.85	7.87	17.22	13.48	10.61	8.40	18.76	14.53	11.33	8.91	13
14	13.15	10.40	8.24	6.56	14.57	11.41	8.96	7.08	15.99	12.39	9.65	7.56	17.42	13.35	10.31	8.01	14
15	12.28	9.61	7.54	5.93	13.60	10.54	8.19	6.40	14.93	11.45	8.82	6.84	16.25	12.34	9.42	7.24	15
16	11.51	8.92	6.92	5.39	12.75	9.78	7.52	5.81	13.99	10.63	8.10	6.21	15.24	11.45	8.65	6.58	16
17	10.83	8.31	6.38	4.91	12.00	9.12	6.94	5.29	13.17	9.90	7.47	5.66	14.34	10.67	7.98	5.99	17
18	10.23	7.77	5.90	4.49	11.34	8.52	6.41	4.84	12.44	9.26	6.91	5.17	13.55	9.98	7.38	5.48	18
19	9.69	7.29	5.47	4.11	10.74	7.99	5.95	4.44	11.79	8.68	6.41	4.74	12.83	9.36	6.84	5.02	19
20	9.21	6.85	5.09	3.78	10.20	7.52	5.53	4.08	11.20	8.17	5.96	4.36	12.19	8.80	6.36	4.62	20
21	8.77	6.46	4.75	3.48	9.72	7.09	5.16	3.76	10.66	7.70	5.56	4.01	11.61	8.30	5.93	4.25	21
22	8.37	6.11	4.43	3.22	9.27	6.70	4.82	3.47	10.18	7.28	5.19	3.70	11.08	7.84	5.54	3.93	22
23	8.01	5.78	4.15	2.97	8.87	6.34	4.51	3.21	9.74	6.89	4.86	3.43	10.60	7.42	5.19	3.63	23
24	7.67	5.48	3.89	2.75	8.50	6.02	4.23	2.97	9.33	6.53	4.56	3.17	10.16	7.04	4.87	3.36	24
25	7.37	5.21	3.66	2.55	8.16	5.72	3.98	2.76	8.96	6.21	4.28	2.94	9.75	6.69	4.57	3.12	25
26	7.08	4.96	3.44	2.37	7.85	5.44	3.74	2.56	8.61	5.91	4.03	2.73	9.38	6.37	4.30	2.90	26
27	6.82	4.73	3.24	2.21	7.56	5.18	3.52	2.38	8.29	5.63	3.79	2.54	9.03	6.07	4.05	2.70	27
28	6.58	4.51	3.06	2.06	7.29	4.95	3.32	2.22	8.00	5.38	3.58	2.37	8.71	5.79	3.82	2.51	28
29	6.35	4.31	2.89	1.92	7.04	4.73	3.14	2.07	7.72	5.14	3.38	2.21	8.41	5.54	3.61	2.34	29
30	6.14	4.12	2.73	1.79	6.80	4.52	2.97	1.93	7.46	4.91	3.19	2.06	8.13	5.30	3.41	2.18	30
31	5.94	3.95	2.58	1.67	6.58	4.33	2.81	1.80	7.22	4.71	3.02	1.92	7.87	5.07	3.23	2.04	31
32	5.75	3.79	2.45	1.56	6.38	4.15	2.66	1.68	7.00	4.51	2.86	1.80	7.62	4.86	3.06	1.90	32
33	5.58	3.63	2.32	1.46	6.18	3.99	2.52	1.57	6.79	4.33	2.71	1.68	7.39	4.67	2.90	1.78	33
34	5.42	3.49	2.20	1.37	6.00	3.83	2.39	1.47	6.59	4.16	2.57	1.57	7.17	4.48	2.75	1.67	34
35	5.26	3.35	2.09	1.28	5.83	3.68	2.27	1.38	6.40	4.00	2.44	1.47	6.97	4.31	2.61	1.56	35
36	5.12	3.23	1.98	1.20	5.67	3.54	2.16	1.29	6.22	3.85	2.32	1.38	6.77	4.14	2.48	1.46	36
37	4.98	3.11	1.89	1.12	5.51	3.41	2.05	1.21	6.05	3.70	2.21	1.29	6.59	3.99	2.36	1.37	37
38	4.85	2.99	1.79	1.05	5.37	3.28	1.95	1.14	5.89	3.57	2.10	1.21	6.42	3.84	2.24	1.29	38
39	4.72	2.89	1.71	0.99	5.23	3.16	1.86	1.07	5.74	3.44	2.00	1.14	6.25	3.71	2.14	1.21	39
40	4.60	2.78	1.63	0.93	5.10	3.05	1.77	1.00	5.60	3.32	1.90	1.07	6.10	3.57	2.03	1.13	40
41	4.49	2.69	1.55	0.87	4.98	2.95	1.69	0.94	5.46	3.20	1.81	1.01	5.95	3.45	1.94	1.07	41
42	4.38	2.59	1.48	0.82	4.86	2.85	1.61	0.88	5.33	3.09	1.73	0.94	5.81	3.33	1.85	1.00	42
43	4.28	2.51	1.41	0.77	4.75	2.75	1.53	0.83	5.21	2.99	1.65	0.89	5.67	3.22	1.76	0.94	43
44	4.19	2.42	1.35	0.72	4.64	2.66	1.46	0.78	5.09	2.89	1.57	0.84	5.54	3.11	1.68	0.89	44
45	4.09	2.34	1.28	0.68	4.53	2.57	1.40	0.74	4.98	2.79	1.50	0.79	5.42	3.01	1.61	0.83	45
46	4.00	2.27	1.23	0.64	4.44	2.49	1.33	0.69	4.87	2.70	1.44	0.74	5.30	2.91	1.53	0.78	46
47	3.92	2.20	1.17	0.60	4.34	2.41	1.27	0.65	4.76	2.62	1.37	0.70	5.19	2.82	1.47	0.74	47
48	3.84	2.13	1.12	0.57	4.25	2.33	1.22	0.61	4.66	2.53	1.31	0.66	5.08	2.73	1.40	0.69	48
49	3.76	2.06	1.07	0.54	4.16	2.26	1.16	0.58	4.57	2.46	1.25	0.62	4.98	2.65	1.34	0.65	49
50	3.68	2.00	1.02	0.50	4.08	2.19	1.11	0.54	4.48	2.38	1.20	0.58	4.88	2.57	1.28	0.62	50

Appendix A

III. Retirement Planning where Salary Outpaces Low 3% Inflation
Planned Retirement Age 65

Table 4 - Accumulation at Retirement (Multiple of Current Sal.) for 10% Sal. Replacement III-65-4

Probable Life Expectancy at Retirement

Yrs. to Ret.	20.7 (Same as Male Avg.)				23.2 (Better than Male Avg.)				25.7 (Same as Female Avg.)				28.3 (Better than Female Avg.)				Yrs. to Ret.
	4% / 4%	6% / 5%	8% / 6%	10% / 7%	4% / 4%	6% / 5%	8% / 6%	10% / 7%	4% / 4%	6% / 5%	8% / 6%	10% / 7%	4% / 4%	6% / 5%	8% / 6%	10% / 7%	
	Expected Return		(Pre-Retirement/Post-Retirement)				(Pre-Retirement/Post-Retirement)				Expected Return						
0	1.84	1.65	1.49	1.36	2.04	1.81	1.62	1.46	2.24	1.97	1.75	1.56	2.44	2.12	1.87	1.66	0
1	1.92	1.72	1.55	1.41	2.12	1.88	1.69	1.52	2.33	2.05	1.82	1.63	2.54	2.21	1.94	1.72	1
2	1.99	1.79	1.61	1.47	2.21	1.96	1.76	1.58	2.42	2.13	1.89	1.69	2.64	2.30	2.02	1.79	2
3	2.07	1.86	1.68	1.53	2.30	2.04	1.83	1.65	2.52	2.21	1.97	1.76	2.74	2.39	2.10	1.86	3
4	2.15	1.93	1.75	1.59	2.39	2.12	1.90	1.71	2.62	2.30	2.04	1.83	2.85	2.48	2.18	1.94	4
5	2.24	2.01	1.82	1.65	2.48	2.20	1.97	1.78	2.72	2.40	2.13	1.90	2.97	2.58	2.27	2.02	5
6	2.33	2.09	1.89	1.72	2.58	2.29	2.05	1.85	2.83	2.49	2.21	1.98	3.09	2.68	2.36	2.10	6
7	2.42	2.17	1.96	1.79	2.69	2.38	2.14	1.93	2.95	2.59	2.30	2.06	3.21	2.79	2.46	2.18	7
8	2.52	2.26	2.04	1.86	2.79	2.48	2.22	2.00	3.06	2.69	2.39	2.14	3.34	2.90	2.55	2.27	8
9	2.62	2.35	2.12	1.93	2.90	2.58	2.31	2.08	3.19	2.80	2.49	2.23	3.47	3.02	2.66	2.36	9
10	2.73	2.45	2.21	2.01	3.02	2.68	2.40	2.17	3.31	2.91	2.59	2.31	3.61	3.14	2.76	2.45	10
11	2.84	2.54	2.30	2.09	3.14	2.79	2.50	2.25	3.45	3.03	2.69	2.41	3.75	3.27	2.87	2.55	11
12	2.95	2.65	2.39	2.17	3.27	2.90	2.60	2.34	3.58	3.15	2.80	2.50	3.90	3.40	2.99	2.65	12
13	3.07	2.75	2.49	2.26	3.40	3.02	2.70	2.44	3.73	3.28	2.91	2.60	4.06	3.53	3.11	2.76	13
14	3.19	2.86	2.58	2.35	3.53	3.14	2.81	2.53	3.88	3.41	3.03	2.71	4.22	3.67	3.23	2.87	14
15	3.32	2.98	2.69	2.44	3.67	3.26	2.92	2.64	4.03	3.55	3.15	2.82	4.39	3.82	3.36	2.98	15
16	3.45	3.09	2.80	2.54	3.82	3.39	3.04	2.74	4.19	3.69	3.27	2.93	4.57	3.97	3.50	3.10	16
17	3.59	3.22	2.91	2.64	3.97	3.53	3.16	2.85	4.36	3.83	3.40	3.05	4.75	4.13	3.63	3.23	17
18	3.73	3.35	3.02	2.75	4.13	3.67	3.29	2.97	4.54	3.99	3.54	3.17	4.94	4.30	3.78	3.36	18
19	3.88	3.48	3.14	2.86	4.30	3.82	3.42	3.08	4.72	4.15	3.68	3.29	5.14	4.47	3.93	3.49	19
20	4.04	3.62	3.27	2.97	4.47	3.97	3.56	3.21	4.91	4.31	3.83	3.43	5.34	4.65	4.09	3.63	20
21	4.20	3.76	3.40	3.09	4.65	4.13	3.70	3.34	5.10	4.49	3.98	3.56	5.56	4.84	4.25	3.78	21
22	4.36	3.92	3.54	3.22	4.84	4.29	3.85	3.47	5.31	4.67	4.14	3.71	5.78	5.03	4.42	3.93	22
23	4.54	4.07	3.68	3.34	5.03	4.47	4.00	3.61	5.52	4.85	4.31	3.85	6.01	5.23	4.60	4.08	23
24	4.72	4.23	3.83	3.48	5.23	4.65	4.16	3.75	5.74	5.05	4.48	4.01	6.25	5.44	4.78	4.25	24
25	4.91	4.40	3.98	3.62	5.44	4.83	4.33	3.90	5.97	5.25	4.66	4.17	6.50	5.66	4.97	4.42	25
26	5.11	4.58	4.14	3.76	5.66	5.02	4.50	4.06	6.21	5.46	4.84	4.33	6.76	5.88	5.17	4.59	26
27	5.31	4.76	4.30	3.91	5.88	5.23	4.68	4.22	6.46	5.68	5.04	4.51	7.03	6.12	5.38	4.78	27
28	5.52	4.95	4.48	4.07	6.12	5.43	4.87	4.39	6.71	5.90	5.24	4.69	7.31	6.36	5.60	4.97	28
29	5.74	5.15	4.65	4.23	6.36	5.65	5.06	4.56	6.98	6.14	5.45	4.88	7.60	6.62	5.82	5.17	29
30	5.97	5.36	4.84	4.40	6.62	5.88	5.26	4.75	7.26	6.39	5.67	5.07	7.91	6.88	6.05	5.37	30
31	6.21	5.57	5.03	4.58	6.88	6.11	5.47	4.94	7.55	6.64	5.89	5.27	8.22	7.16	6.29	5.59	31
32	6.46	5.80	5.24	4.76	7.16	6.36	5.69	5.13	7.86	6.91	6.13	5.48	8.55	7.44	6.55	5.81	32
33	6.72	6.03	5.45	4.95	7.44	6.61	5.92	5.34	8.17	7.18	6.37	5.70	8.90	7.74	6.81	6.05	33
34	6.99	6.27	5.66	5.15	7.74	6.88	6.16	5.55	8.50	7.47	6.63	5.93	9.25	8.05	7.08	6.29	34
35	7.27	6.52	5.89	5.36	8.05	7.15	6.40	5.78	8.84	7.77	6.89	6.17	9.62	8.37	7.36	6.54	35
36	7.56	6.78	6.13	5.57	8.37	7.44	6.66	6.01	9.19	8.08	7.17	6.42	10.01	8.71	7.66	6.80	36
37	7.86	7.05	6.37	5.79	8.71	7.73	6.93	6.25	9.56	8.40	7.46	6.67	10.41	9.06	7.96	7.07	37
38	8.17	7.33	6.63	6.02	9.06	8.04	7.20	6.50	9.94	8.74	7.75	6.94	10.82	9.42	8.28	7.36	38
39	8.50	7.63	6.89	6.26	9.42	8.37	7.49	6.76	10.34	9.09	8.06	7.22	11.26	9.80	8.61	7.65	39
40	8.84	7.93	7.17	6.52	9.80	8.70	7.79	7.03	10.75	9.45	8.39	7.51	11.71	10.19	8.96	7.96	40
41	9.20	8.25	7.45	6.78	10.19	9.05	8.10	7.31	11.18	9.83	8.72	7.81	12.17	10.59	9.32	8.27	41
42	9.56	8.58	7.75	7.05	10.60	9.41	8.43	7.60	11.63	10.22	9.07	8.12	12.66	11.02	9.69	8.60	42
43	9.95	8.92	8.06	7.33	11.02	9.79	8.76	7.90	12.09	10.63	9.43	8.44	13.17	11.46	10.08	8.95	43
44	10.34	9.28	8.38	7.62	11.46	10.18	9.11	8.22	12.58	11.06	9.81	8.78	13.69	11.92	10.48	9.31	44
45	10.76	9.65	8.72	7.93	11.92	10.59	9.48	8.55	13.08	11.50	10.20	9.13	14.24	12.39	10.90	9.68	45
46	11.19	10.04	9.07	8.24	12.39	11.01	9.86	8.89	13.60	11.96	10.61	9.50	14.81	12.89	11.34	10.07	46
47	11.63	10.44	9.43	8.57	12.89	11.45	10.25	9.25	14.15	12.44	11.04	9.88	15.40	13.41	11.79	10.47	47
48	12.10	10.86	9.81	8.92	13.41	11.91	10.66	9.62	14.71	12.94	11.48	10.27	16.02	13.94	12.26	10.89	48
49	12.58	11.29	10.20	9.27	13.94	12.38	11.09	10.00	15.30	13.45	11.94	10.68	16.66	14.50	12.75	11.32	49
50	13.09	11.74	10.61	9.64	14.50	12.88	11.53	10.40	15.91	13.99	12.42	11.11	17.33	15.08	13.26	11.78	50

III. Retirement Planning where Salary Outpaces Low 3% Inflation
Planned Retirement Age 68

Table 1 - Percent of Salary Replaced by a 401(k) Account Equal to Current Annual Salary

III-68-1

Probable Life Expectancy at Retirement

Yrs. to Ret.	18.3 (Same as Male Avg.)				20.7 (Better than Male Avg.)				23.2 (Same as Female Avg.)				25.7 (Better than Female Avg.)				Yrs. to Ret.
	4% / 4%	6% / 5%	8% / 6%	10% / 7%	4% / 4%	6% / 5%	8% / 6%	10% / 7%	4% / 4%	6% / 5%	8% / 6%	10% / 7%	4% / 4%	6% / 5%	8% / 6%	10% / 7%	
	Expected Return				(Pre-Retirement/Post-Retirement)				(Pre-Retirement/Post-Retirement)				Expected Return				
0	6.08	6.71	7.36	8.03	5.43	6.05	6.70	7.37	4.90	5.52	6.16	6.83	4.47	5.08	5.72	6.40	0
1	6.08	6.84	7.65	8.50	5.43	6.17	6.96	7.79	4.90	5.62	6.40	7.23	4.47	5.18	5.94	6.77	1
2	6.08	6.97	7.94	8.99	5.43	6.29	7.23	8.24	4.90	5.73	6.65	7.64	4.47	5.28	6.17	7.16	2
3	6.08	7.10	8.25	9.51	5.43	6.41	7.50	8.72	4.90	5.84	6.90	8.08	4.47	5.38	6.41	7.57	3
4	6.08	7.24	8.56	10.06	5.43	6.53	7.79	9.22	4.90	5.95	7.17	8.55	4.47	5.48	6.66	8.01	4
5	6.08	7.38	8.89	10.64	5.43	6.66	8.09	9.75	4.90	6.07	7.44	9.04	4.47	5.59	6.91	8.47	5
6	6.08	7.52	9.24	11.25	5.43	6.78	8.40	10.32	4.90	6.18	7.73	9.57	4.47	5.69	7.18	8.96	6
7	6.08	7.67	9.59	11.90	5.43	6.91	8.73	10.91	4.90	6.30	8.03	10.12	4.47	5.80	7.46	9.47	7
8	6.08	7.81	9.96	12.59	5.43	7.05	9.06	11.54	4.90	6.42	8.34	10.70	4.47	5.91	7.74	10.02	8
9	6.08	7.96	10.34	13.31	5.43	7.18	9.41	12.21	4.90	6.55	8.66	11.32	4.47	6.03	8.04	10.60	9
10	6.08	8.12	10.74	14.08	5.43	7.32	9.78	12.91	4.90	6.67	8.99	11.97	4.47	6.14	8.35	11.21	10
11	6.08	8.27	11.16	14.89	5.43	7.46	10.15	13.66	4.90	6.80	9.34	12.66	4.47	6.26	8.67	11.86	11
12	6.08	8.43	11.59	15.75	5.43	7.60	10.54	14.45	4.90	6.93	9.70	13.39	4.47	6.38	9.01	12.54	12
13	6.08	8.59	12.03	16.66	5.43	7.75	10.95	15.28	4.90	7.07	10.07	14.17	4.47	6.50	9.35	13.26	13
14	6.08	8.76	12.50	17.62	5.43	7.90	11.37	16.16	4.90	7.20	10.46	14.98	4.47	6.63	9.71	14.03	14
15	6.08	8.93	12.98	18.64	5.43	8.05	11.81	17.09	4.90	7.34	10.86	15.85	4.47	6.76	10.09	14.84	15
16	6.08	9.10	13.48	19.71	5.43	8.21	12.26	18.08	4.90	7.48	11.28	16.76	4.47	6.89	10.48	15.69	16
17	6.08	9.27	14.00	20.85	5.43	8.36	12.73	19.12	4.90	7.62	11.71	17.73	4.47	7.02	10.88	16.60	17
18	6.08	9.45	14.53	22.05	5.43	8.52	13.22	20.23	4.90	7.77	12.16	18.75	4.47	7.15	11.30	17.56	18
19	6.08	9.63	15.09	23.33	5.43	8.69	13.73	21.39	4.90	7.92	12.63	19.84	4.47	7.29	11.73	18.57	19
20	6.08	9.82	15.67	24.67	5.43	8.85	14.26	22.63	4.90	8.07	13.12	20.98	4.47	7.43	12.19	19.64	20
21	6.08	10.01	16.28	26.10	5.43	9.02	14.81	23.93	4.90	8.23	13.62	22.19	4.47	7.57	12.65	20.77	21
22	6.08	10.20	16.90	27.60	5.43	9.20	15.38	25.31	4.90	8.38	14.15	23.47	4.47	7.72	13.14	21.97	22
23	6.08	10.39	17.56	29.19	5.43	9.37	15.97	26.78	4.90	8.55	14.69	24.83	4.47	7.87	13.65	23.24	23
24	6.08	10.59	18.23	30.88	5.43	9.55	16.59	28.32	4.90	8.71	15.26	26.26	4.47	8.02	14.17	24.58	24
25	6.08	10.80	18.93	32.66	5.43	9.74	17.23	29.95	4.90	8.88	15.85	27.77	4.47	8.17	14.72	26.00	25
26	6.08	11.00	19.66	34.54	5.43	9.92	17.89	31.68	4.90	9.05	16.46	29.38	4.47	8.33	15.29	27.50	26
27	6.08	11.21	20.42	36.54	5.43	10.11	18.58	33.51	4.90	9.22	17.09	31.07	4.47	8.49	15.87	29.09	27
28	6.08	11.43	21.21	38.65	5.43	10.31	19.30	35.44	4.90	9.40	17.75	32.86	4.47	8.65	16.49	30.77	28
29	6.08	11.65	22.02	40.88	5.43	10.51	20.04	37.49	4.90	9.58	18.43	34.76	4.47	8.82	17.12	32.54	29
30	6.08	11.87	22.87	43.23	5.43	10.71	20.81	39.65	4.90	9.76	19.14	36.76	4.47	8.99	17.78	34.42	30
31	6.08	12.10	23.75	45.73	5.43	10.91	21.61	41.94	4.90	9.95	19.88	38.89	4.47	9.16	18.46	36.40	31
32	6.08	12.33	24.66	48.37	5.43	11.12	22.44	44.36	4.90	10.14	20.64	41.13	4.47	9.34	19.17	38.51	32
33	6.08	12.57	25.61	51.16	5.43	11.34	23.31	46.92	4.90	10.34	21.44	43.50	4.47	9.51	19.91	40.73	33
34	6.08	12.81	26.60	54.11	5.43	11.56	24.20	49.63	4.90	10.53	22.26	46.01	4.47	9.70	20.68	43.08	34
35	6.08	13.06	27.62	57.23	5.43	11.78	25.14	52.49	4.90	10.74	23.12	48.67	4.47	9.88	21.48	45.56	35
36	6.08	13.31	28.69	60.53	5.43	12.00	26.10	55.52	4.90	10.94	24.01	51.48	4.47	10.07	22.30	48.19	36
37	6.08	13.56	29.79	64.03	5.43	12.23	27.11	58.72	4.90	11.15	24.94	54.45	4.47	10.27	23.16	50.97	37
38	6.08	13.82	30.94	67.72	5.43	12.47	28.15	62.11	4.90	11.37	25.90	57.59	4.47	10.46	24.05	53.91	38
39	6.08	14.09	32.13	71.63	5.43	12.71	29.24	65.70	4.90	11.59	26.89	60.91	4.47	10.66	24.98	57.02	39
40	6.08	14.36	33.37	75.76	5.43	12.95	30.36	69.49	4.90	11.81	27.93	64.43	4.47	10.87	25.94	60.31	40
41	6.08	14.64	34.65	80.13	5.43	13.20	31.53	73.50	4.90	12.03	29.00	68.14	4.47	11.08	26.94	63.79	41
42	6.08	14.92	35.99	84.76	5.43	13.45	32.75	77.74	4.90	12.27	30.12	72.07	4.47	11.29	27.98	67.48	42
43	6.08	15.20	37.37	89.65	5.43	13.71	34.01	82.22	4.90	12.50	31.28	76.23	4.47	11.51	29.05	71.37	43
44	6.08	15.49	38.81	94.82	5.43	13.98	35.32	86.97	4.90	12.74	32.48	80.63	4.47	11.73	30.17	75.49	44
45	6.08	15.79	40.31	100.29	5.43	14.24	36.68	91.98	4.90	12.99	33.73	85.28	4.47	11.95	31.33	79.84	45
46	6.08	16.10	41.86	106.08	5.43	14.52	38.09	97.29	4.90	13.23	35.03	90.20	4.47	12.18	32.54	84.45	46
47	6.08	16.40	43.47	112.20	5.43	14.80	39.55	102.91	4.90	13.49	36.38	95.41	4.47	12.42	33.79	89.32	47
48	6.08	16.72	45.14	118.67	5.43	15.08	41.08	108.84	4.90	13.75	37.78	100.91	4.47	12.66	35.09	94.48	48
49	6.08	17.04	46.88	125.52	5.43	15.37	42.66	115.12	4.90	14.01	39.24	106.74	4.47	12.90	36.44	99.93	49
50	6.08	17.37	48.68	132.76	5.43	15.66	44.30	121.77	4.90	14.28	40.75	112.90	4.47	13.15	37.85	105.69	50

Appendix A

III. Retirement Planning where Salary Outpaces Low 3% Inflation
Planned Retirement Age 68

Table 2 - Percent of Salary Replaced by a 401(k) Contribution of 1% of Current Salary

Probable Life Expectancy at Retirement

Yrs. to Ret.	18.3 (Same as Male Avg.) 4%/4%	6%/5%	8%/6%	10%/7%	20.7 (Better than Male Avg.) 4%/4%	6%/5%	8%/6%	10%/7%	23.2 (Same as Female Avg.) 4%/4%	6%/5%	8%/6%	10%/7%	25.7 (Better than Female Avg.) 4%/4%	6%/5%	8%/6%	10%/7%	Yrs. to Ret.
	Expected Return				(Pre-Retirement/Post-Retirement)				(Pre-Retirement/Post-Retirement)				Expected Return				
0	0.00	0.00	0.00	0.00	0.00	0.00	0.00	0.00	0.00	0.00	0.00	0.00	0.00	0.00	0.00	0.00	0
1	0.06	0.07	0.07	0.08	0.05	0.06	0.07	0.07	0.05	0.06	0.06	0.07	0.04	0.05	0.06	0.06	1
2	0.12	0.14	0.15	0.17	0.11	0.12	0.14	0.15	0.10	0.11	0.13	0.14	0.09	0.10	0.12	0.13	2
3	0.18	0.21	0.23	0.26	0.16	0.19	0.21	0.23	0.15	0.17	0.19	0.22	0.13	0.16	0.18	0.20	3
4	0.24	0.28	0.31	0.35	0.22	0.25	0.28	0.32	0.20	0.23	0.26	0.30	0.18	0.21	0.24	0.28	4
5	0.30	0.35	0.40	0.45	0.27	0.31	0.36	0.41	0.25	0.29	0.33	0.38	0.22	0.26	0.31	0.36	5
6	0.36	0.42	0.49	0.56	0.33	0.38	0.44	0.51	0.29	0.35	0.41	0.47	0.27	0.32	0.38	0.44	6
7	0.43	0.50	0.58	0.67	0.38	0.45	0.53	0.61	0.34	0.41	0.48	0.57	0.31	0.38	0.45	0.53	7
8	0.49	0.57	0.67	0.79	0.43	0.52	0.61	0.72	0.39	0.47	0.56	0.67	0.36	0.43	0.52	0.63	8
9	0.55	0.65	0.77	0.91	0.49	0.59	0.70	0.84	0.44	0.54	0.65	0.78	0.40	0.49	0.60	0.73	9
10	0.61	0.73	0.88	1.05	0.54	0.66	0.80	0.96	0.49	0.60	0.73	0.89	0.45	0.55	0.68	0.83	10
11	0.67	0.81	0.99	1.19	0.60	0.73	0.90	1.09	0.54	0.67	0.82	1.01	0.49	0.62	0.77	0.95	11
12	0.73	0.90	1.10	1.34	0.65	0.81	1.00	1.23	0.59	0.74	0.92	1.14	0.54	0.68	0.85	1.06	12
13	0.79	0.98	1.21	1.49	0.71	0.88	1.10	1.37	0.64	0.81	1.02	1.27	0.58	0.74	0.94	1.19	13
14	0.85	1.07	1.33	1.66	0.76	0.96	1.21	1.52	0.69	0.88	1.12	1.41	0.63	0.81	1.04	1.32	14
15	0.91	1.15	1.46	1.84	0.81	1.04	1.33	1.69	0.74	0.95	1.22	1.56	0.67	0.87	1.13	1.46	15
16	0.97	1.24	1.59	2.02	0.87	1.12	1.44	1.86	0.78	1.02	1.33	1.72	0.71	0.94	1.23	1.61	16
17	1.03	1.33	1.72	2.22	0.92	1.20	1.57	2.04	0.83	1.10	1.44	1.89	0.76	1.01	1.34	1.77	17
18	1.09	1.43	1.86	2.43	0.98	1.29	1.69	2.23	0.88	1.17	1.56	2.07	0.80	1.08	1.45	1.93	18
19	1.16	1.52	2.01	2.65	1.03	1.37	1.83	2.43	0.93	1.25	1.68	2.25	0.85	1.15	1.56	2.11	19
20	1.22	1.62	2.16	2.88	1.09	1.46	1.96	2.64	0.98	1.33	1.81	2.45	0.89	1.22	1.68	2.30	20
21	1.28	1.72	2.32	3.13	1.14	1.55	2.11	2.87	1.03	1.41	1.94	2.66	0.94	1.30	1.80	2.49	21
22	1.34	1.82	2.48	3.39	1.19	1.64	2.26	3.11	1.08	1.49	2.07	2.88	0.98	1.37	1.93	2.70	22
23	1.40	1.92	2.65	3.67	1.25	1.73	2.41	3.36	1.13	1.58	2.22	3.12	1.03	1.45	2.06	2.92	23
24	1.46	2.02	2.82	3.96	1.30	1.82	2.57	3.63	1.18	1.66	2.36	3.37	1.07	1.53	2.19	3.15	24
25	1.52	2.13	3.01	4.27	1.36	1.92	2.73	3.91	1.23	1.75	2.52	3.63	1.12	1.61	2.34	3.40	25
26	1.58	2.24	3.19	4.59	1.41	2.02	2.91	4.21	1.27	1.84	2.67	3.91	1.16	1.69	2.48	3.66	26
27	1.64	2.35	3.39	4.94	1.47	2.12	3.09	4.53	1.32	1.93	2.84	4.20	1.21	1.78	2.64	3.93	27
28	1.70	2.46	3.60	5.31	1.52	2.22	3.27	4.87	1.37	2.02	3.01	4.51	1.25	1.86	2.80	4.22	28
29	1.76	2.57	3.81	5.69	1.57	2.32	3.46	5.22	1.42	2.11	3.19	4.84	1.30	1.95	2.96	4.53	29
30	1.82	2.69	4.03	6.10	1.63	2.42	3.66	5.60	1.47	2.21	3.37	5.19	1.34	2.04	3.13	4.86	30
31	1.88	2.81	4.26	6.53	1.68	2.53	3.87	5.99	1.52	2.31	3.56	5.56	1.38	2.12	3.31	5.20	31
32	1.95	2.93	4.49	6.99	1.74	2.64	4.09	6.41	1.57	2.41	3.76	5.94	1.43	2.22	3.49	5.56	32
33	2.01	3.05	4.74	7.47	1.79	2.75	4.31	6.85	1.62	2.51	3.97	6.36	1.47	2.31	3.69	5.95	33
34	2.07	3.18	5.00	7.99	1.85	2.87	4.55	7.32	1.67	2.61	4.18	6.79	1.52	2.40	3.88	6.36	34
35	2.13	3.31	5.26	8.53	1.90	2.98	4.79	7.82	1.72	2.72	4.40	7.25	1.56	2.50	4.09	6.79	35
36	2.19	3.44	5.54	9.10	1.95	3.10	5.04	8.35	1.76	2.83	4.64	7.74	1.61	2.60	4.31	7.24	36
37	2.25	3.57	5.83	9.70	2.01	3.22	5.30	8.90	1.81	2.93	4.88	8.25	1.65	2.70	4.53	7.73	37
38	2.31	3.70	6.12	10.34	2.06	3.34	5.57	9.49	1.86	3.05	5.13	8.80	1.70	2.80	4.76	8.24	38
39	2.37	3.84	6.43	11.02	2.12	3.47	5.85	10.11	1.91	3.16	5.38	9.37	1.74	2.91	5.00	8.77	39
40	2.43	3.98	6.75	11.74	2.17	3.59	6.15	10.77	1.96	3.28	5.65	9.98	1.79	3.02	5.25	9.34	40
41	2.49	4.13	7.09	12.50	2.23	3.72	6.45	11.46	2.01	3.39	5.93	10.63	1.83	3.12	5.51	9.95	41
42	2.55	4.27	7.43	13.30	2.28	3.85	6.77	12.20	2.06	3.51	6.22	11.31	1.88	3.23	5.78	10.59	42
43	2.61	4.42	7.79	14.14	2.33	3.99	7.09	12.97	2.11	3.64	6.52	12.03	1.92	3.35	6.06	11.26	43
44	2.68	4.58	8.17	15.04	2.39	4.13	7.43	13.80	2.16	3.76	6.84	12.79	1.97	3.46	6.35	11.97	44
45	2.74	4.73	8.56	15.99	2.44	4.27	7.79	14.66	2.21	3.89	7.16	13.60	2.01	3.58	6.65	12.73	45
46	2.80	4.89	8.96	16.99	2.50	4.41	8.15	15.58	2.25	4.02	7.50	14.45	2.05	3.70	6.97	13.53	46
47	2.86	5.05	9.38	18.05	2.55	4.55	8.53	16.56	2.30	4.15	7.85	15.35	2.10	3.82	7.29	14.37	47
48	2.92	5.21	9.81	19.17	2.61	4.70	8.93	17.59	2.35	4.29	8.21	16.31	2.14	3.95	7.63	15.27	48
49	2.98	5.38	10.26	20.36	2.66	4.85	9.34	18.67	2.40	4.42	8.59	17.31	2.19	4.07	7.98	16.21	49
50	3.04	5.55	10.73	21.62	2.72	5.01	9.77	19.83	2.45	4.56	8.98	18.38	2.23	4.20	8.34	17.21	50

III. Retirement Planning where Salary Outpaces Low 3% Inflation
Planned Retirement Age 68

Table 3 - 401(k) Contribution (% of Current Sal.) Needed to Replace 10% of Sal. at Retirement   III-68-3

Probable Life Expectancy at Retirement

	18.3 (Same as Male Avg.)				20.7 (Better than Male Avg.)				23.2 (Same as Female Avg.)				25.7 (Better than Female Avg.)			
	4% / 4%	6% / 5%	8% / 6%	10% / 7%	4% / 4%	6% / 5%	8% / 6%	10% / 7%	4% / 4%	6% / 5%	8% / 6%	10% / 7%	4% / 4%	6% / 5%	8% / 6%	10% / 7%
Yrs. to Ret.	Expected Return			(Pre-Retirement/Post-Retirement)				(Pre-Retirement/Post-Retirement)				Expected Return			Yrs. to Ret.
0																0
1	164.48	149.01	135.81	124.46	184.16	165.21	149.25	135.71	204.04	181.23	162.26	146.37	223.92	196.87	174.70	156.34	1
2	82.24	73.80	66.62	60.49	92.08	81.82	73.22	65.95	102.02	89.75	79.60	71.13	111.96	97.50	85.70	75.98	2
3	54.83	48.73	43.57	39.18	61.39	54.03	47.88	42.72	68.01	59.26	52.06	46.08	74.64	64.38	56.05	49.22	3
4	41.12	36.20	32.05	28.55	46.04	40.13	35.23	31.13	51.01	44.02	38.30	33.57	55.98	47.82	41.23	35.86	4
5	32.90	28.68	25.15	22.18	36.83	31.80	27.64	24.18	40.81	34.88	30.05	26.08	44.78	37.89	32.35	27.86	5
6	27.41	23.67	20.55	17.95	30.69	26.24	22.59	19.57	34.01	28.79	24.56	21.11	37.32	31.27	26.44	22.54	6
7	23.50	20.09	17.27	14.93	26.31	22.28	18.98	16.28	29.15	24.44	20.64	17.56	31.99	26.55	22.22	18.76	7
8	20.56	17.41	14.82	12.68	23.02	19.30	16.28	13.82	25.50	21.17	17.70	14.91	27.99	23.00	19.06	15.93	8
9	18.28	15.33	12.91	10.93	20.46	16.99	14.19	11.92	22.67	18.64	15.43	12.86	24.88	20.25	16.61	13.74	9
10	16.45	13.66	11.39	9.55	18.42	15.14	12.52	10.41	20.40	16.61	13.61	11.23	22.39	18.05	14.65	11.99	10
11	14.95	12.30	10.15	8.41	16.74	13.63	11.15	9.17	18.55	14.95	12.13	9.90	20.36	16.24	13.05	10.57	11
12	13.71	11.16	9.12	7.48	15.35	12.37	10.02	8.15	17.00	13.57	10.89	8.79	18.66	14.74	11.73	9.39	12
13	12.65	10.20	8.25	6.69	14.17	11.31	9.06	7.29	15.70	12.41	9.85	7.87	17.22	13.48	10.61	8.40	13
14	11.75	9.38	7.50	6.02	13.15	10.40	8.24	6.56	14.57	11.41	8.96	7.08	15.99	12.39	9.65	7.56	14
15	10.97	8.67	6.86	5.44	12.28	9.61	7.54	5.93	13.60	10.54	8.19	6.40	14.93	11.45	8.82	6.84	15
16	10.28	8.04	6.30	4.94	11.51	8.92	6.92	5.39	12.75	9.78	7.52	5.81	13.99	10.63	8.10	6.21	16
17	9.68	7.50	5.81	4.50	10.83	8.31	6.38	4.91	12.00	9.12	6.94	5.29	13.17	9.90	7.47	5.66	17
18	9.14	7.01	5.37	4.12	10.23	7.77	5.90	4.49	11.34	8.52	6.41	4.84	12.44	9.26	6.91	5.17	18
19	8.66	6.57	4.98	3.77	9.69	7.29	5.47	4.11	10.74	7.99	5.95	4.44	11.79	8.68	6.41	4.74	19
20	8.22	6.18	4.63	3.47	9.21	6.85	5.09	3.78	10.20	7.52	5.53	4.08	11.20	8.17	5.96	4.36	20
21	7.83	5.83	4.32	3.19	8.77	6.46	4.75	3.48	9.72	7.09	5.16	3.76	10.66	7.70	5.56	4.01	21
22	7.48	5.51	4.03	2.95	8.37	6.11	4.43	3.22	9.27	6.70	4.82	3.47	10.18	7.28	5.19	3.70	22
23	7.15	5.21	3.78	2.73	8.01	5.78	4.15	2.97	8.87	6.34	4.51	3.21	9.74	6.89	4.86	3.43	23
24	6.85	4.95	3.54	2.53	7.67	5.48	3.89	2.75	8.50	6.02	4.23	2.97	9.33	6.53	4.56	3.17	24
25	6.58	4.70	3.33	2.34	7.37	5.21	3.66	2.55	8.16	5.72	3.98	2.76	8.96	6.21	4.28	2.94	25
26	6.33	4.47	3.13	2.18	7.08	4.96	3.44	2.37	7.85	5.44	3.74	2.56	8.61	5.91	4.03	2.73	26
27	6.09	4.26	2.95	2.02	6.82	4.73	3.24	2.21	7.56	5.18	3.52	2.38	8.29	5.63	3.79	2.54	27
28	5.87	4.07	2.78	1.88	6.58	4.51	3.06	2.06	7.29	4.95	3.32	2.22	8.00	5.38	3.58	2.37	28
29	5.67	3.89	2.63	1.76	6.35	4.31	2.89	1.92	7.04	4.73	3.14	2.07	7.72	5.14	3.38	2.21	29
30	5.48	3.72	2.48	1.64	6.14	4.12	2.73	1.79	6.80	4.52	2.97	1.93	7.46	4.91	3.19	2.06	30
31	5.31	3.56	2.35	1.53	5.94	3.95	2.58	1.67	6.58	4.33	2.81	1.80	7.22	4.71	3.02	1.92	31
32	5.14	3.41	2.23	1.43	5.75	3.79	2.45	1.56	6.38	4.15	2.66	1.68	7.00	4.51	2.86	1.80	32
33	4.98	3.28	2.11	1.34	5.58	3.63	2.32	1.46	6.18	3.99	2.52	1.57	6.79	4.33	2.71	1.68	33
34	4.84	3.15	2.00	1.25	5.42	3.49	2.20	1.37	6.00	3.83	2.39	1.47	6.59	4.16	2.57	1.57	34
35	4.70	3.03	1.90	1.17	5.26	3.35	2.09	1.28	5.83	3.68	2.27	1.38	6.40	4.00	2.44	1.47	35
36	4.57	2.91	1.81	1.10	5.12	3.23	1.98	1.20	5.67	3.54	2.16	1.29	6.22	3.85	2.32	1.38	36
37	4.45	2.80	1.72	1.03	4.98	3.11	1.89	1.12	5.51	3.41	2.05	1.21	6.05	3.70	2.21	1.29	37
38	4.33	2.70	1.63	0.97	4.85	2.99	1.79	1.05	5.37	3.28	1.95	1.14	5.89	3.57	2.10	1.21	38
39	4.22	2.60	1.55	0.91	4.72	2.89	1.71	0.99	5.23	3.16	1.86	1.07	5.74	3.44	2.00	1.14	39
40	4.11	2.51	1.48	0.85	4.60	2.78	1.63	0.93	5.10	3.05	1.77	1.00	5.60	3.32	1.90	1.07	40
41	4.01	2.42	1.41	0.80	4.49	2.69	1.55	0.87	4.98	2.95	1.69	0.94	5.46	3.20	1.81	1.01	41
42	3.92	2.34	1.35	0.75	4.38	2.59	1.48	0.82	4.86	2.85	1.61	0.88	5.33	3.09	1.73	0.94	42
43	3.83	2.26	1.28	0.71	4.28	2.51	1.41	0.77	4.75	2.75	1.53	0.83	5.21	2.99	1.65	0.89	43
44	3.74	2.19	1.22	0.66	4.19	2.42	1.35	0.72	4.64	2.66	1.46	0.78	5.09	2.89	1.57	0.84	44
45	3.66	2.11	1.17	0.63	4.09	2.34	1.28	0.68	4.53	2.57	1.40	0.74	4.98	2.79	1.50	0.79	45
46	3.58	2.05	1.12	0.59	4.00	2.27	1.23	0.64	4.44	2.49	1.33	0.69	4.87	2.70	1.44	0.74	46
47	3.50	1.98	1.07	0.55	3.92	2.20	1.17	0.60	4.34	2.41	1.27	0.65	4.76	2.62	1.37	0.70	47
48	3.43	1.92	1.02	0.52	3.84	2.13	1.12	0.57	4.25	2.33	1.22	0.61	4.66	2.53	1.31	0.66	48
49	3.36	1.86	0.97	0.49	3.76	2.06	1.07	0.54	4.16	2.26	1.16	0.58	4.57	2.46	1.25	0.62	49
50	3.29	1.80	0.93	0.46	3.68	2.00	1.02	0.50	4.08	2.19	1.11	0.54	4.48	2.38	1.20	0.58	50

III. Retirement Planning where Salary Outpaces Low 3% Inflation
Planned Retirement Age 68

Table 4 - Accumulation at Retirement (Multiple of Current Sal.) for 10% Sal. Replacement   III-68-4

Probable Life Expectancy at Retirement

Yrs. to Ret.	18.3 (Same as Male Avg.) 4%/4%	6%/5%	8%/6%	10%/7%	20.7 (Better than Male Avg.) 4%/4%	6%/5%	8%/6%	10%/7%	23.2 (Same as Female Avg.) 4%/4%	6%/5%	8%/6%	10%/7%	25.7 (Better than Female Avg.) 4%/4%	6%/5%	8%/6%	10%/7%	Yrs. to Ret.
	Expected Return				(Pre-Retirement/Post-Retirement)				(Pre-Retirement/Post-Retirement)				Expected Return				
0	1.64	1.49	1.36	1.24	1.84	1.65	1.49	1.36	2.04	1.81	1.62	1.46	2.24	1.97	1.75	1.56	0
1	1.71	1.55	1.41	1.29	1.92	1.72	1.55	1.41	2.12	1.88	1.69	1.52	2.33	2.05	1.82	1.63	1
2	1.78	1.61	1.47	1.35	1.99	1.79	1.61	1.47	2.21	1.96	1.76	1.58	2.42	2.13	1.89	1.69	2
3	1.85	1.68	1.53	1.40	2.07	1.86	1.68	1.53	2.30	2.04	1.83	1.65	2.52	2.21	1.97	1.76	3
4	1.92	1.74	1.59	1.46	2.15	1.93	1.75	1.59	2.39	2.12	1.90	1.71	2.62	2.30	2.04	1.83	4
5	2.00	1.81	1.65	1.51	2.24	2.01	1.82	1.65	2.48	2.20	1.97	1.78	2.72	2.40	2.13	1.90	5
6	2.08	1.89	1.72	1.57	2.33	2.09	1.89	1.72	2.58	2.29	2.05	1.85	2.83	2.49	2.21	1.98	6
7	2.16	1.96	1.79	1.64	2.42	2.17	1.96	1.79	2.69	2.38	2.14	1.93	2.95	2.59	2.30	2.06	7
8	2.25	2.04	1.86	1.70	2.52	2.26	2.04	1.86	2.79	2.48	2.22	2.00	3.06	2.69	2.39	2.14	8
9	2.34	2.12	1.93	1.77	2.62	2.35	2.12	1.93	2.90	2.58	2.31	2.08	3.19	2.80	2.49	2.23	9
10	2.43	2.21	2.01	1.84	2.73	2.45	2.21	2.01	3.02	2.68	2.40	2.17	3.31	2.91	2.59	2.31	10
11	2.53	2.29	2.09	1.92	2.84	2.54	2.30	2.09	3.14	2.79	2.50	2.25	3.45	3.03	2.69	2.41	11
12	2.63	2.39	2.17	1.99	2.95	2.65	2.39	2.17	3.27	2.90	2.60	2.34	3.58	3.15	2.80	2.50	12
13	2.74	2.48	2.26	2.07	3.07	2.75	2.49	2.26	3.40	3.02	2.70	2.44	3.73	3.28	2.91	2.60	13
14	2.85	2.58	2.35	2.16	3.19	2.86	2.58	2.35	3.53	3.14	2.81	2.53	3.88	3.41	3.03	2.71	14
15	2.96	2.68	2.45	2.24	3.32	2.98	2.69	2.44	3.67	3.26	2.92	2.64	4.03	3.55	3.15	2.82	15
16	3.08	2.79	2.54	2.33	3.45	3.09	2.80	2.54	3.82	3.39	3.04	2.74	4.19	3.69	3.27	2.93	16
17	3.20	2.90	2.65	2.42	3.59	3.22	2.91	2.64	3.97	3.53	3.16	2.85	4.36	3.83	3.40	3.05	17
18	3.33	3.02	2.75	2.52	3.73	3.35	3.02	2.75	4.13	3.67	3.29	2.97	4.54	3.99	3.54	3.17	18
19	3.47	3.14	2.86	2.62	3.88	3.48	3.14	2.86	4.30	3.82	3.42	3.08	4.72	4.15	3.68	3.29	19
20	3.60	3.27	2.98	2.73	4.04	3.62	3.27	2.97	4.47	3.97	3.56	3.21	4.91	4.31	3.83	3.43	20
21	3.75	3.40	3.09	2.84	4.20	3.76	3.40	3.09	4.65	4.13	3.70	3.34	5.10	4.49	3.98	3.56	21
22	3.90	3.53	3.22	2.95	4.36	3.92	3.54	3.22	4.84	4.29	3.85	3.47	5.31	4.67	4.14	3.71	22
23	4.05	3.67	3.35	3.07	4.54	4.07	3.68	3.34	5.03	4.47	4.00	3.61	5.52	4.85	4.31	3.85	23
24	4.22	3.82	3.48	3.19	4.72	4.23	3.83	3.48	5.23	4.65	4.16	3.75	5.74	5.05	4.48	4.01	24
25	4.38	3.97	3.62	3.32	4.91	4.40	3.98	3.62	5.44	4.83	4.33	3.90	5.97	5.25	4.66	4.17	25
26	4.56	4.13	3.77	3.45	5.11	4.58	4.14	3.76	5.66	5.02	4.50	4.06	6.21	5.46	4.84	4.33	26
27	4.74	4.30	3.92	3.59	5.31	4.76	4.30	3.91	5.88	5.23	4.68	4.22	6.46	5.68	5.04	4.51	27
28	4.93	4.47	4.07	3.73	5.52	4.95	4.48	4.07	6.12	5.43	4.87	4.39	6.71	5.90	5.24	4.69	28
29	5.13	4.65	4.24	3.88	5.74	5.15	4.65	4.23	6.36	5.65	5.06	4.56	6.98	6.14	5.45	4.88	29
30	5.33	4.83	4.40	4.04	5.97	5.36	4.84	4.40	6.62	5.88	5.26	4.75	7.26	6.39	5.67	5.07	30
31	5.55	5.03	4.58	4.20	6.21	5.57	5.03	4.58	6.88	6.11	5.47	4.94	7.55	6.64	5.89	5.27	31
32	5.77	5.23	4.76	4.37	6.46	5.80	5.24	4.76	7.16	6.36	5.69	5.13	7.86	6.91	6.13	5.48	32
33	6.00	5.44	4.95	4.54	6.72	6.03	5.45	4.95	7.44	6.61	5.92	5.34	8.17	7.18	6.37	5.70	33
34	6.24	5.65	5.15	4.72	6.99	6.27	5.66	5.15	7.74	6.88	6.16	5.55	8.50	7.47	6.63	5.93	34
35	6.49	5.88	5.36	4.91	7.27	6.52	5.89	5.36	8.05	7.15	6.40	5.78	8.84	7.77	6.89	6.17	35
36	6.75	6.12	5.57	5.11	7.56	6.78	6.13	5.57	8.37	7.44	6.66	6.01	9.19	8.08	7.17	6.42	36
37	7.02	6.36	5.80	5.31	7.86	7.05	6.37	5.79	8.71	7.73	6.93	6.25	9.56	8.40	7.46	6.67	37
38	7.30	6.61	6.03	5.52	8.17	7.33	6.63	6.02	9.06	8.04	7.20	6.50	9.94	8.74	7.75	6.94	38
39	7.59	6.88	6.27	5.75	8.50	7.63	6.89	6.26	9.42	8.37	7.49	6.76	10.34	9.09	8.06	7.22	39
40	7.90	7.15	6.52	5.98	8.84	7.93	7.17	6.52	9.80	8.70	7.79	7.03	10.75	9.45	8.39	7.51	40
41	8.21	7.44	6.78	6.21	9.20	8.25	7.45	6.78	10.19	9.05	8.10	7.31	11.18	9.83	8.72	7.81	41
42	8.54	7.74	7.05	6.46	9.56	8.58	7.75	7.05	10.60	9.41	8.43	7.60	11.63	10.22	9.07	8.12	42
43	8.88	8.05	7.33	6.72	9.95	8.92	8.06	7.33	11.02	9.79	8.76	7.90	12.09	10.63	9.43	8.44	43
44	9.24	8.37	7.63	6.99	10.34	9.28	8.38	7.62	11.46	10.18	9.11	8.22	12.58	11.06	9.81	8.78	44
45	9.61	8.70	7.93	7.27	10.76	9.65	8.72	7.93	11.92	10.59	9.48	8.55	13.08	11.50	10.20	9.13	45
46	9.99	9.05	8.25	7.56	11.19	10.04	9.07	8.24	12.39	11.01	9.86	8.89	13.60	11.96	10.61	9.50	46
47	10.39	9.41	8.58	7.86	11.63	10.44	9.43	8.57	12.89	11.45	10.25	9.25	14.15	12.44	11.04	9.88	47
48	10.81	9.79	8.92	8.18	12.10	10.86	9.81	8.92	13.41	11.91	10.66	9.62	14.71	12.94	11.48	10.27	48
49	11.24	10.18	9.28	8.51	12.58	11.29	10.20	9.27	13.94	12.38	11.09	10.00	15.30	13.45	11.94	10.68	49
50	11.69	10.59	9.65	8.85	13.09	11.74	10.61	9.64	14.50	12.88	11.53	10.40	15.91	13.99	12.42	11.11	50

III. Retirement Planning where Salary Outpaces Low 3% Inflation
Planned Retirement Age 71

Table 1 - Percent of Salary Replaced by a 401(k) Account Equal to Current Annual Salary   III-71-1

Probable Life Expectancy at Retirement

Yrs. to Ret.	16 (Same as Male Avg.)				18.3 (Better than Male Avg.)				20.7 (Same as Female Avg.)				23.2 (Better than Female Avg.)				Yrs. to Ret.
	4% / 4%	6% / 5%	8% / 6%	10% / 7%	4% / 4%	6% / 5%	8% / 6%	10% / 7%	4% / 4%	6% / 5%	8% / 6%	10% / 7%	4% / 4%	6% / 5%	8% / 6%	10% / 7%	
	Expected Return				(Pre-Retirement/Post-Retirement)				(Pre-Retirement/Post-Retirement)				Expected Return				
0	6.88	7.52	8.18	8.85	6.08	6.71	7.36	8.03	5.43	6.05	6.70	7.37	4.90	5.52	6.16	6.83	0
1	6.88	7.66	8.49	9.36	6.08	6.84	7.65	8.50	5.43	6.17	6.96	7.79	4.90	5.62	6.40	7.23	1
2	6.88	7.81	8.82	9.91	6.08	6.97	7.94	8.99	5.43	6.29	7.23	8.24	4.90	5.73	6.65	7.64	2
3	6.88	7.96	9.16	10.48	6.08	7.10	8.25	9.51	5.43	6.41	7.50	8.72	4.90	5.84	6.90	8.08	3
4	6.88	8.11	9.51	11.08	6.08	7.24	8.56	10.06	5.43	6.53	7.79	9.22	4.90	5.95	7.17	8.55	4
5	6.88	8.27	9.88	11.72	6.08	7.38	8.89	10.64	5.43	6.66	8.09	9.75	4.90	6.07	7.44	9.04	5
6	6.88	8.43	10.26	12.40	6.08	7.52	9.24	11.25	5.43	6.78	8.40	10.32	4.90	6.18	7.73	9.57	6
7	6.88	8.59	10.65	13.11	6.08	7.67	9.59	11.90	5.43	6.91	8.73	10.91	4.90	6.30	8.03	10.12	7
8	6.88	8.75	11.06	13.87	6.08	7.81	9.96	12.59	5.43	7.05	9.06	11.54	4.90	6.42	8.34	10.70	8
9	6.88	8.92	11.49	14.67	6.08	7.96	10.34	13.31	5.43	7.18	9.41	12.21	4.90	6.55	8.66	11.32	9
10	6.88	9.09	11.93	15.52	6.08	8.12	10.74	14.08	5.43	7.32	9.78	12.91	4.90	6.67	8.99	11.97	10
11	6.88	9.27	12.39	16.41	6.08	8.27	11.16	14.89	5.43	7.46	10.15	13.66	4.90	6.80	9.34	12.66	11
12	6.88	9.44	12.87	17.36	6.08	8.43	11.59	15.75	5.43	7.60	10.54	14.45	4.90	6.93	9.70	13.39	12
13	6.88	9.63	13.36	18.36	6.08	8.59	12.03	16.66	5.43	7.75	10.95	15.28	4.90	7.07	10.07	14.17	13
14	6.88	9.81	13.88	19.42	6.08	8.76	12.50	17.62	5.43	7.90	11.37	16.16	4.90	7.20	10.46	14.98	14
15	6.88	10.00	14.41	20.54	6.08	8.93	12.98	18.64	5.43	8.05	11.81	17.09	4.90	7.34	10.86	15.85	15
16	6.88	10.19	14.97	21.72	6.08	9.10	13.48	19.71	5.43	8.21	12.26	18.08	4.90	7.48	11.28	16.76	16
17	6.88	10.39	15.54	22.98	6.08	9.27	14.00	20.85	5.43	8.36	12.73	19.12	4.90	7.62	11.71	17.73	17
18	6.88	10.59	16.14	24.30	6.08	9.45	14.53	22.05	5.43	8.52	13.22	20.23	4.90	7.77	12.16	18.75	18
19	6.88	10.79	16.76	25.71	6.08	9.63	15.09	23.33	5.43	8.69	13.73	21.39	4.90	7.92	12.63	19.84	19
20	6.88	11.00	17.41	27.19	6.08	9.82	15.67	24.67	5.43	8.85	14.26	22.63	4.90	8.07	13.12	20.98	20
21	6.88	11.21	18.08	28.76	6.08	10.01	16.28	26.10	5.43	9.02	14.81	23.93	4.90	8.23	13.62	22.19	21
22	6.88	11.42	18.78	30.42	6.08	10.20	16.90	27.60	5.43	9.20	15.38	25.31	4.90	8.38	14.15	23.47	22
23	6.88	11.64	19.50	32.17	6.08	10.39	17.56	29.19	5.43	9.37	15.97	26.78	4.90	8.55	14.69	24.83	23
24	6.88	11.87	20.25	34.03	6.08	10.59	18.23	30.88	5.43	9.55	16.59	28.32	4.90	8.71	15.26	26.26	24
25	6.88	12.09	21.03	35.99	6.08	10.80	18.93	32.66	5.43	9.74	17.23	29.95	4.90	8.88	15.85	27.77	25
26	6.88	12.33	21.84	38.07	6.08	11.00	19.66	34.54	5.43	9.92	17.89	31.68	4.90	9.05	16.46	29.38	26
27	6.88	12.56	22.68	40.27	6.08	11.21	20.42	36.54	5.43	10.11	18.58	33.51	4.90	9.22	17.09	31.07	27
28	6.88	12.80	23.55	42.59	6.08	11.43	21.21	38.65	5.43	10.31	19.30	35.44	4.90	9.40	17.75	32.86	28
29	6.88	13.05	24.46	45.05	6.08	11.65	22.02	40.88	5.43	10.51	20.04	37.49	4.90	9.58	18.43	34.76	29
30	6.88	13.30	25.40	47.65	6.08	11.87	22.87	43.23	5.43	10.71	20.81	39.65	4.90	9.76	19.14	36.76	30
31	6.88	13.56	26.38	50.39	6.08	12.10	23.75	45.73	5.43	10.91	21.61	41.94	4.90	9.95	19.88	38.89	31
32	6.88	13.82	27.39	53.30	6.08	12.33	24.66	48.37	5.43	11.12	22.44	44.36	4.90	10.14	20.64	41.13	32
33	6.88	14.08	28.45	56.38	6.08	12.57	25.61	51.16	5.43	11.34	23.31	46.92	4.90	10.34	21.44	43.50	33
34	6.88	14.35	29.54	59.63	6.08	12.81	26.60	54.11	5.43	11.56	24.20	49.63	4.90	10.53	22.26	46.01	34
35	6.88	14.63	30.68	63.07	6.08	13.06	27.62	57.23	5.43	11.78	25.14	52.49	4.90	10.74	23.12	48.67	35
36	6.88	14.91	31.86	66.71	6.08	13.31	28.69	60.53	5.43	12.00	26.10	55.52	4.90	10.94	24.01	51.48	36
37	6.88	15.19	33.09	70.56	6.08	13.56	29.79	64.03	5.43	12.23	27.11	58.72	4.90	11.15	24.94	54.45	37
38	6.88	15.49	34.36	74.63	6.08	13.82	30.94	67.72	5.43	12.47	28.15	62.11	4.90	11.37	25.90	57.59	38
39	6.88	15.78	35.69	78.94	6.08	14.09	32.13	71.63	5.43	12.71	29.24	65.70	4.90	11.59	26.89	60.91	39
40	6.88	16.09	37.06	83.49	6.08	14.36	33.37	75.76	5.43	12.95	30.36	69.49	4.90	11.81	27.93	64.43	40
41	6.88	16.39	38.49	88.31	6.08	14.64	34.65	80.13	5.43	13.20	31.53	73.50	4.90	12.03	29.00	68.14	41
42	6.88	16.71	39.97	93.40	6.08	14.92	35.99	84.76	5.43	13.45	32.75	77.74	4.90	12.27	30.12	72.07	42
43	6.88	17.03	41.51	98.79	6.08	15.20	37.37	89.65	5.43	13.71	34.01	82.22	4.90	12.50	31.28	76.23	43
44	6.88	17.36	43.10	104.49	6.08	15.49	38.81	94.82	5.43	13.98	35.32	86.97	4.90	12.74	32.48	80.63	44
45	6.88	17.69	44.76	110.52	6.08	15.79	40.31	100.29	5.43	14.24	36.68	91.98	4.90	12.99	33.73	85.28	45
46	6.88	18.03	46.49	116.90	6.08	16.10	41.86	106.08	5.43	14.52	38.09	97.29	4.90	13.23	35.03	90.20	46
47	6.88	18.38	48.28	123.65	6.08	16.40	43.47	112.20	5.43	14.80	39.55	102.91	4.90	13.49	36.38	95.41	47
48	6.88	18.73	50.14	130.78	6.08	16.72	45.14	118.67	5.43	15.08	41.08	108.84	4.90	13.75	37.78	100.91	48
49	6.88	19.09	52.07	138.33	6.08	17.04	46.88	125.52	5.43	15.37	42.66	115.12	4.90	14.01	39.24	106.74	49
50	6.88	19.46	54.07	146.31	6.08	17.37	48.68	132.76	5.43	15.66	44.30	121.77	4.90	14.28	40.75	112.90	50

Appendix A

III. Retirement Planning where Salary Outpaces Low 3% Inflation
Planned Retirement Age 71

Table 2 - Percent of Salary Replaced by a 401(k) Contribution of 1% of Current Salary   III-71-2

Probable Life Expectancy at Retirement

	16 (Same as Male Avg.)				18.3 (Better than Male Avg.)				20.7 (Same as Female Avg.)				23.2 (Better than Female Avg.)				
Yrs. to Ret.	4%/4%	6%/5%	8%/6%	10%/7%	4%/4%	6%/5%	8%/6%	10%/7%	4%/4%	6%/5%	8%/6%	10%/7%	4%/4%	6%/5%	8%/6%	10%/7%	Yrs. to Ret.
	Expected Return				(Pre-Retirement/Post-Retirement)				(Pre-Retirement/Post-Retirement)				Expected Return				
0	0.00	0.00	0.00	0.00	0.00	0.00	0.00	0.00	0.00	0.00	0.00	0.00	0.00	0.00	0.00	0.00	0
1	0.07	0.08	0.08	0.09	0.06	0.07	0.07	0.08	0.05	0.06	0.07	0.07	0.05	0.06	0.06	0.07	1
2	0.14	0.15	0.17	0.18	0.12	0.14	0.15	0.17	0.11	0.12	0.14	0.15	0.10	0.11	0.13	0.14	2
3	0.21	0.23	0.25	0.28	0.18	0.21	0.23	0.26	0.16	0.19	0.21	0.23	0.15	0.17	0.19	0.22	3
4	0.28	0.31	0.35	0.39	0.24	0.28	0.31	0.35	0.22	0.25	0.28	0.32	0.20	0.23	0.26	0.30	4
5	0.34	0.39	0.44	0.50	0.30	0.35	0.40	0.45	0.27	0.31	0.36	0.41	0.25	0.29	0.33	0.38	5
6	0.41	0.47	0.54	0.61	0.36	0.42	0.49	0.56	0.33	0.38	0.44	0.51	0.29	0.35	0.41	0.47	6
7	0.48	0.56	0.64	0.74	0.43	0.50	0.58	0.67	0.38	0.45	0.53	0.61	0.34	0.41	0.48	0.57	7
8	0.55	0.64	0.75	0.87	0.49	0.57	0.67	0.79	0.43	0.52	0.61	0.72	0.39	0.47	0.56	0.67	8
9	0.62	0.73	0.86	1.01	0.55	0.65	0.77	0.91	0.49	0.59	0.70	0.84	0.44	0.54	0.65	0.78	9
10	0.69	0.82	0.98	1.15	0.61	0.73	0.88	1.05	0.54	0.66	0.80	0.96	0.49	0.60	0.73	0.89	10
11	0.76	0.91	1.09	1.31	0.67	0.81	0.99	1.19	0.60	0.73	0.90	1.09	0.54	0.67	0.82	1.01	11
12	0.83	1.00	1.22	1.47	0.73	0.90	1.10	1.34	0.65	0.81	1.00	1.23	0.59	0.74	0.92	1.14	12
13	0.89	1.10	1.35	1.65	0.79	0.98	1.21	1.49	0.71	0.88	1.10	1.37	0.64	0.81	1.02	1.27	13
14	0.96	1.19	1.48	1.83	0.85	1.07	1.33	1.66	0.76	0.96	1.21	1.52	0.69	0.88	1.12	1.41	14
15	1.03	1.29	1.62	2.03	0.91	1.15	1.46	1.84	0.81	1.04	1.33	1.69	0.74	0.95	1.22	1.56	15
16	1.10	1.39	1.76	2.23	0.97	1.24	1.59	2.02	0.87	1.12	1.44	1.86	0.78	1.02	1.33	1.72	16
17	1.17	1.49	1.91	2.45	1.03	1.33	1.72	2.22	0.92	1.20	1.57	2.04	0.83	1.10	1.44	1.89	17
18	1.24	1.60	2.07	2.68	1.09	1.43	1.86	2.43	0.98	1.29	1.69	2.23	0.88	1.17	1.56	2.07	18
19	1.31	1.70	2.23	2.92	1.16	1.52	2.01	2.65	1.03	1.37	1.83	2.43	0.93	1.25	1.68	2.25	19
20	1.38	1.81	2.40	3.18	1.22	1.62	2.16	2.88	1.09	1.46	1.96	2.64	0.98	1.33	1.81	2.45	20
21	1.44	1.92	2.57	3.45	1.28	1.72	2.32	3.13	1.14	1.55	2.11	2.87	1.03	1.41	1.94	2.66	21
22	1.51	2.03	2.75	3.74	1.34	1.82	2.48	3.39	1.19	1.64	2.26	3.11	1.08	1.49	2.07	2.88	22
23	1.58	2.15	2.94	4.04	1.40	1.92	2.65	3.67	1.25	1.73	2.41	3.36	1.13	1.58	2.22	3.12	23
24	1.65	2.26	3.14	4.36	1.46	2.02	2.82	3.96	1.30	1.82	2.57	3.63	1.18	1.66	2.36	3.37	24
25	1.72	2.38	3.34	4.70	1.52	2.13	3.01	4.27	1.36	1.92	2.73	3.91	1.23	1.75	2.52	3.63	25
26	1.79	2.50	3.55	5.06	1.58	2.24	3.19	4.59	1.41	2.02	2.91	4.21	1.27	1.84	2.67	3.91	26
27	1.86	2.63	3.77	5.44	1.64	2.35	3.39	4.94	1.47	2.12	3.09	4.53	1.32	1.93	2.84	4.20	27
28	1.93	2.75	3.99	5.85	1.70	2.46	3.60	5.31	1.52	2.22	3.27	4.87	1.37	2.02	3.01	4.51	28
29	1.99	2.88	4.23	6.27	1.76	2.57	3.81	5.69	1.57	2.32	3.46	5.22	1.42	2.11	3.19	4.84	29
30	2.06	3.01	4.47	6.72	1.82	2.69	4.03	6.10	1.63	2.42	3.66	5.60	1.47	2.21	3.37	5.19	30
31	2.13	3.14	4.73	7.20	1.88	2.81	4.26	6.53	1.68	2.53	3.87	5.99	1.52	2.31	3.56	5.56	31
32	2.20	3.28	4.99	7.70	1.95	2.93	4.49	6.99	1.74	2.64	4.09	6.41	1.57	2.41	3.76	5.94	32
33	2.27	3.42	5.26	8.24	2.01	3.05	4.74	7.47	1.79	2.75	4.31	6.85	1.62	2.51	3.97	6.36	33
34	2.34	3.56	5.55	8.80	2.07	3.18	5.00	7.99	1.85	2.87	4.55	7.32	1.67	2.61	4.18	6.79	34
35	2.41	3.70	5.84	9.40	2.13	3.31	5.26	8.53	1.90	2.98	4.79	7.82	1.72	2.72	4.40	7.25	35
36	2.48	3.85	6.15	10.03	2.19	3.44	5.54	9.10	1.95	3.10	5.04	8.35	1.76	2.83	4.64	7.74	36
37	2.54	4.00	6.47	10.69	2.25	3.57	5.83	9.70	2.01	3.22	5.30	8.90	1.81	2.93	4.88	8.25	37
38	2.61	4.15	6.80	11.40	2.31	3.70	6.12	10.34	2.06	3.34	5.57	9.49	1.86	3.05	5.13	8.80	38
39	2.68	4.30	7.14	12.15	2.37	3.84	6.43	11.02	2.12	3.47	5.85	10.11	1.91	3.16	5.38	9.37	39
40	2.75	4.46	7.50	12.94	2.43	3.98	6.75	11.74	2.17	3.59	6.15	10.77	1.96	3.28	5.65	9.98	40
41	2.82	4.62	7.87	13.77	2.49	4.13	7.09	12.50	2.23	3.72	6.45	11.46	2.01	3.39	5.93	10.63	41
42	2.89	4.79	8.26	14.65	2.55	4.27	7.43	13.30	2.28	3.85	6.77	12.20	2.06	3.51	6.22	11.31	42
43	2.96	4.95	8.66	15.59	2.61	4.42	7.79	14.14	2.33	3.99	7.09	12.97	2.11	3.64	6.52	12.03	43
44	3.03	5.13	9.07	16.58	2.68	4.58	8.17	15.04	2.39	4.13	7.43	13.80	2.16	3.76	6.84	12.79	44
45	3.09	5.30	9.50	17.62	2.74	4.73	8.56	15.99	2.44	4.27	7.79	14.66	2.21	3.89	7.16	13.60	45
46	3.16	5.48	9.95	18.73	2.80	4.89	8.96	16.99	2.50	4.41	8.15	15.58	2.25	4.02	7.50	14.45	46
47	3.23	5.66	10.42	19.89	2.86	5.05	9.38	18.05	2.55	4.55	8.53	16.56	2.30	4.15	7.85	15.35	47
48	3.30	5.84	10.90	21.13	2.92	5.21	9.81	19.17	2.61	4.70	8.93	17.59	2.35	4.29	8.21	16.31	48
49	3.37	6.03	11.40	22.44	2.98	5.38	10.26	20.36	2.66	4.85	9.34	18.67	2.40	4.42	8.59	17.31	49
50	3.44	6.22	11.92	23.82	3.04	5.55	10.73	21.62	2.72	5.01	9.77	19.83	2.45	4.56	8.98	18.38	50

III. Retirement Planning where Salary Outpaces Low 3% Inflation
Planned Retirement Age 71

Table 3 - 401(k) Contribution (% of Current Sal.) Needed to Replace 10% of Sal. at Retirement   III-71-3

Probable Life Expectancy at Retirement

	16 (Same as Male Avg.)				18.3 (Better than Male Avg.)				20.7 (Same as Female Avg.)				23.2 (Better than Female Avg.)				
	4% /\n4%	6% /\n5%	8% /\n6%	10% /\n7%	4% /\n4%	6% /\n5%	8% /\n6%	10% /\n7%	4% /\n4%	6% /\n5%	8% /\n6%	10% /\n7%	4% /\n4%	6% /\n5%	8% /\n6%	10% /\n7%	
Yrs. to Ret.	Expected Return				(Pre-Retirement/Post-Retirement)				(Pre-Retirement/Post-Retirement)				Expected Return				Yrs. to Ret.
0																	0
1	145.45	133.02	122.28	112.94	164.48	149.01	135.81	124.46	184.16	165.21	149.25	135.71	204.04	181.23	162.26	146.37	1
2	72.72	65.88	59.99	54.89	82.24	73.80	66.62	60.49	92.08	81.82	73.22	65.95	102.02	89.75	79.60	71.13	2
3	48.48	43.50	39.23	35.56	54.83	48.73	43.57	39.18	61.39	54.03	47.88	42.72	68.01	59.26	52.06	46.08	3
4	36.36	32.31	28.86	25.91	41.12	36.20	32.05	28.55	46.04	40.13	35.23	31.13	51.01	44.02	38.30	33.57	4
5	29.09	25.60	22.64	20.13	32.90	28.68	25.15	22.18	36.83	31.80	27.64	24.18	40.81	34.88	30.05	26.08	5
6	24.24	21.13	18.51	16.29	27.41	23.67	20.55	17.95	30.69	26.24	22.59	19.57	34.01	28.79	24.56	21.11	6
7	20.78	17.94	15.55	13.55	23.50	20.09	17.27	14.93	26.31	22.28	18.98	16.28	29.15	24.44	20.64	17.56	7
8	18.18	15.54	13.34	11.51	20.56	17.41	14.82	12.68	23.02	19.30	16.28	13.82	25.50	21.17	17.70	14.91	8
9	16.16	13.68	11.63	9.92	18.28	15.33	12.91	10.93	20.46	16.99	14.19	11.92	22.67	18.64	15.43	12.86	9
10	14.54	12.19	10.26	8.66	16.45	13.66	11.39	9.55	18.42	15.14	12.52	10.41	20.40	16.61	13.61	11.23	10
11	13.22	10.98	9.14	7.64	14.95	12.30	10.15	8.41	16.74	13.63	11.15	9.17	18.55	14.95	12.13	9.90	11
12	12.12	9.96	8.21	6.79	13.71	11.16	9.12	7.48	15.35	12.37	10.02	8.15	17.00	13.57	10.89	8.79	12
13	11.19	9.11	7.42	6.07	12.65	10.20	8.25	6.69	14.17	11.31	9.06	7.29	15.70	12.41	9.85	7.87	13
14	10.39	8.37	6.75	5.46	11.75	9.38	7.50	6.02	13.15	10.40	8.24	6.56	14.57	11.41	8.96	7.08	14
15	9.70	7.74	6.18	4.94	10.97	8.67	6.86	5.44	12.28	9.61	7.54	5.93	13.60	10.54	8.19	6.40	15
16	9.09	7.18	5.67	4.48	10.28	8.04	6.30	4.94	11.51	8.92	6.92	5.39	12.75	9.78	7.52	5.81	16
17	8.56	6.69	5.23	4.09	9.68	7.50	5.81	4.50	10.83	8.31	6.38	4.91	12.00	9.12	6.94	5.29	17
18	8.08	6.26	4.83	3.73	9.14	7.01	5.37	4.12	10.23	7.77	5.90	4.49	11.34	8.52	6.41	4.84	18
19	7.66	5.87	4.48	3.42	8.66	6.57	4.98	3.77	9.69	7.29	5.47	4.11	10.74	7.99	5.95	4.44	19
20	7.27	5.52	4.17	3.15	8.22	6.18	4.63	3.47	9.21	6.85	5.09	3.78	10.20	7.52	5.53	4.08	20
21	6.93	5.20	3.89	2.90	7.83	5.83	4.32	3.19	8.77	6.46	4.75	3.48	9.72	7.09	5.16	3.76	21
22	6.61	4.92	3.63	2.68	7.48	5.51	4.03	2.95	8.37	6.11	4.43	3.22	9.27	6.70	4.82	3.47	22
23	6.32	4.65	3.40	2.47	7.15	5.21	3.78	2.73	8.01	5.78	4.15	2.97	8.87	6.34	4.51	3.21	23
24	6.06	4.42	3.19	2.29	6.85	4.95	3.54	2.53	7.67	5.48	3.89	2.75	8.50	6.02	4.23	2.97	24
25	5.82	4.20	3.00	2.13	6.58	4.70	3.33	2.34	7.37	5.21	3.66	2.55	8.16	5.72	3.98	2.76	25
26	5.59	3.99	2.82	1.98	6.33	4.47	3.13	2.18	7.08	4.96	3.44	2.37	7.85	5.44	3.74	2.56	26
27	5.39	3.81	2.66	1.84	6.09	4.26	2.95	2.02	6.82	4.73	3.24	2.21	7.56	5.18	3.52	2.38	27
28	5.19	3.63	2.50	1.71	5.87	4.07	2.78	1.88	6.58	4.51	3.06	2.06	7.29	4.95	3.32	2.22	28
29	5.02	3.47	2.36	1.59	5.67	3.89	2.63	1.76	6.35	4.31	2.89	1.92	7.04	4.73	3.14	2.07	29
30	4.85	3.32	2.24	1.49	5.48	3.72	2.48	1.64	6.14	4.12	2.73	1.79	6.80	4.52	2.97	1.93	30
31	4.69	3.18	2.12	1.39	5.31	3.56	2.35	1.53	5.94	3.95	2.58	1.67	6.58	4.33	2.81	1.80	31
32	4.55	3.05	2.00	1.30	5.14	3.41	2.23	1.43	5.75	3.79	2.45	1.56	6.38	4.15	2.66	1.68	32
33	4.41	2.93	1.90	1.21	4.98	3.28	2.11	1.34	5.58	3.63	2.32	1.46	6.18	3.99	2.52	1.57	33
34	4.28	2.81	1.80	1.14	4.84	3.15	2.00	1.25	5.42	3.49	2.20	1.37	6.00	3.83	2.39	1.47	34
35	4.16	2.70	1.71	1.06	4.70	3.03	1.90	1.17	5.26	3.35	2.09	1.28	5.83	3.68	2.27	1.38	35
36	4.04	2.60	1.63	1.00	4.57	2.91	1.81	1.10	5.12	3.23	1.98	1.20	5.67	3.54	2.16	1.29	36
37	3.93	2.50	1.55	0.94	4.45	2.80	1.72	1.03	4.98	3.11	1.89	1.12	5.51	3.41	2.05	1.21	37
38	3.83	2.41	1.47	0.88	4.33	2.70	1.63	0.97	4.85	2.99	1.79	1.05	5.37	3.28	1.95	1.14	38
39	3.73	2.32	1.40	0.82	4.22	2.60	1.55	0.91	4.72	2.89	1.71	0.99	5.23	3.16	1.86	1.07	39
40	3.64	2.24	1.33	0.77	4.11	2.51	1.48	0.85	4.60	2.78	1.63	0.93	5.10	3.05	1.77	1.00	40
41	3.55	2.16	1.27	0.73	4.01	2.42	1.41	0.80	4.49	2.69	1.55	0.87	4.98	2.95	1.69	0.94	41
42	3.46	2.09	1.21	0.68	3.92	2.34	1.35	0.75	4.38	2.59	1.48	0.82	4.86	2.85	1.61	0.88	42
43	3.38	2.02	1.16	0.64	3.83	2.26	1.28	0.71	4.28	2.51	1.41	0.77	4.75	2.75	1.53	0.83	43
44	3.31	1.95	1.10	0.60	3.74	2.19	1.22	0.66	4.19	2.42	1.35	0.72	4.64	2.66	1.46	0.78	44
45	3.23	1.89	1.05	0.57	3.66	2.11	1.17	0.63	4.09	2.34	1.28	0.68	4.53	2.57	1.40	0.74	45
46	3.16	1.83	1.00	0.53	3.58	2.05	1.12	0.59	4.00	2.27	1.23	0.64	4.44	2.49	1.33	0.69	46
47	3.09	1.77	0.96	0.50	3.50	1.98	1.07	0.55	3.92	2.20	1.17	0.60	4.34	2.41	1.27	0.65	47
48	3.03	1.71	0.92	0.47	3.43	1.92	1.02	0.52	3.84	2.13	1.12	0.57	4.25	2.33	1.22	0.61	48
49	2.97	1.66	0.88	0.45	3.36	1.86	0.97	0.49	3.76	2.06	1.07	0.54	4.16	2.26	1.16	0.58	49
50	2.91	1.61	0.84	0.42	3.29	1.80	0.93	0.46	3.68	2.00	1.02	0.50	4.08	2.19	1.11	0.54	50

Appendix A

III. Retirement Planning where Salary Outpaces Low 3% Inflation
Planned Retirement Age 71

Table 4 - Accumulation at Retirement (Multiple of Current Sal.) for 10% Sal. Replacement III-71-4

Probable Life Expectancy at Retirement

Yrs. to Ret.	16 (Same as Male Avg.) 4%/4%	6%/5%	8%/6%	10%/7%	18.3 (Better than Male Avg.) 4%/4%	6%/5%	8%/6%	10%/7%	20.7 (Same as Female Avg.) 4%/4%	6%/5%	8%/6%	10%/7%	23.2 (Better than Female Avg.) 4%/4%	6%/5%	8%/6%	10%/7%	Yrs. to Ret.
	Expected Return				(Pre-Retirement/Post-Retirement)				(Pre-Retirement/Post-Retirement)				Expected Return				
0	1.45	1.33	1.22	1.13	1.64	1.49	1.36	1.24	1.84	1.65	1.49	1.36	2.04	1.81	1.62	1.46	0
1	1.51	1.38	1.27	1.17	1.71	1.55	1.41	1.29	1.92	1.72	1.55	1.41	2.12	1.88	1.69	1.52	1
2	1.57	1.44	1.32	1.22	1.78	1.61	1.47	1.35	1.99	1.79	1.61	1.47	2.21	1.96	1.76	1.58	2
3	1.64	1.50	1.38	1.27	1.85	1.68	1.53	1.40	2.07	1.86	1.68	1.53	2.30	2.04	1.83	1.65	3
4	1.70	1.56	1.43	1.32	1.92	1.74	1.59	1.46	2.15	1.93	1.75	1.59	2.39	2.12	1.90	1.71	4
5	1.77	1.62	1.49	1.37	2.00	1.81	1.65	1.51	2.24	2.01	1.82	1.65	2.48	2.20	1.97	1.78	5
6	1.84	1.68	1.55	1.43	2.08	1.89	1.72	1.57	2.33	2.09	1.89	1.72	2.58	2.29	2.05	1.85	6
7	1.91	1.75	1.61	1.49	2.16	1.96	1.79	1.64	2.42	2.17	1.96	1.79	2.69	2.38	2.14	1.93	7
8	1.99	1.82	1.67	1.55	2.25	2.04	1.86	1.70	2.52	2.26	2.04	1.86	2.79	2.48	2.22	2.00	8
9	2.07	1.89	1.74	1.61	2.34	2.12	1.93	1.77	2.62	2.35	2.12	1.93	2.90	2.58	2.31	2.08	9
10	2.15	1.97	1.81	1.67	2.43	2.21	2.01	1.84	2.73	2.45	2.21	2.01	3.02	2.68	2.40	2.17	10
11	2.24	2.05	1.88	1.74	2.53	2.29	2.09	1.92	2.84	2.54	2.30	2.09	3.14	2.79	2.50	2.25	11
12	2.33	2.13	1.96	1.81	2.63	2.39	2.17	1.99	2.95	2.65	2.39	2.17	3.27	2.90	2.60	2.34	12
13	2.42	2.21	2.04	1.88	2.74	2.48	2.26	2.07	3.07	2.75	2.49	2.26	3.40	3.02	2.70	2.44	13
14	2.52	2.30	2.12	1.96	2.85	2.58	2.35	2.16	3.19	2.86	2.58	2.35	3.53	3.14	2.81	2.53	14
15	2.62	2.40	2.20	2.03	2.96	2.68	2.45	2.24	3.32	2.98	2.69	2.44	3.67	3.26	2.92	2.64	15
16	2.72	2.49	2.29	2.12	3.08	2.79	2.54	2.33	3.45	3.09	2.80	2.54	3.82	3.39	3.04	2.74	16
17	2.83	2.59	2.38	2.20	3.20	2.90	2.65	2.42	3.59	3.22	2.91	2.64	3.97	3.53	3.16	2.85	17
18	2.95	2.69	2.48	2.29	3.33	3.02	2.75	2.52	3.73	3.35	3.02	2.75	4.13	3.67	3.29	2.97	18
19	3.06	2.80	2.58	2.38	3.47	3.14	2.86	2.62	3.88	3.48	3.14	2.86	4.30	3.82	3.42	3.08	19
20	3.19	2.91	2.68	2.47	3.60	3.27	2.98	2.73	4.04	3.62	3.27	2.97	4.47	3.97	3.56	3.21	20
21	3.31	3.03	2.79	2.57	3.75	3.40	3.09	2.84	4.20	3.76	3.40	3.09	4.65	4.13	3.70	3.34	21
22	3.45	3.15	2.90	2.68	3.90	3.53	3.22	2.95	4.36	3.92	3.54	3.22	4.84	4.29	3.85	3.47	22
23	3.58	3.28	3.01	2.78	4.05	3.67	3.35	3.07	4.54	4.07	3.68	3.34	5.03	4.47	4.00	3.61	23
24	3.73	3.41	3.13	2.90	4.22	3.82	3.48	3.19	4.72	4.23	3.83	3.48	5.23	4.65	4.16	3.75	24
25	3.88	3.55	3.26	3.01	4.38	3.97	3.62	3.32	4.91	4.40	3.98	3.62	5.44	4.83	4.33	3.90	25
26	4.03	3.69	3.39	3.13	4.56	4.13	3.77	3.45	5.11	4.58	4.14	3.76	5.66	5.02	4.50	4.06	26
27	4.19	3.84	3.53	3.26	4.74	4.30	3.92	3.59	5.31	4.76	4.30	3.91	5.88	5.23	4.68	4.22	27
28	4.36	3.99	3.67	3.39	4.93	4.47	4.07	3.73	5.52	4.95	4.48	4.07	6.12	5.43	4.87	4.39	28
29	4.54	4.15	3.81	3.52	5.13	4.65	4.24	3.88	5.74	5.15	4.65	4.23	6.36	5.65	5.06	4.56	29
30	4.72	4.31	3.97	3.66	5.33	4.83	4.40	4.04	5.97	5.36	4.84	4.40	6.62	5.88	5.26	4.75	30
31	4.91	4.49	4.12	3.81	5.55	5.03	4.58	4.20	6.21	5.57	5.03	4.58	6.88	6.11	5.47	4.94	31
32	5.10	4.67	4.29	3.96	5.77	5.23	4.76	4.37	6.46	5.80	5.24	4.76	7.16	6.36	5.69	5.13	32
33	5.31	4.85	4.46	4.12	6.00	5.44	4.95	4.54	6.72	6.03	5.45	4.95	7.44	6.61	5.92	5.34	33
34	5.52	5.05	4.64	4.29	6.24	5.65	5.15	4.72	6.99	6.27	5.66	5.15	7.74	6.88	6.16	5.55	34
35	5.74	5.25	4.83	4.46	6.49	5.88	5.36	4.91	7.27	6.52	5.89	5.36	8.05	7.15	6.40	5.78	35
36	5.97	5.46	5.02	4.64	6.75	6.12	5.57	5.11	7.56	6.78	6.13	5.57	8.37	7.44	6.66	6.01	36
37	6.21	5.68	5.22	4.82	7.02	6.36	5.80	5.31	7.86	7.05	6.37	5.79	8.71	7.73	6.93	6.25	37
38	6.46	5.90	5.43	5.01	7.30	6.61	6.03	5.52	8.17	7.33	6.63	6.02	9.06	8.04	7.20	6.50	38
39	6.71	6.14	5.64	5.21	7.59	6.88	6.27	5.75	8.50	7.63	6.89	6.26	9.42	8.37	7.49	6.76	39
40	6.98	6.39	5.87	5.42	7.90	7.15	6.52	5.98	8.84	7.93	7.17	6.52	9.80	8.70	7.79	7.03	40
41	7.26	6.64	6.11	5.64	8.21	7.44	6.78	6.21	9.20	8.25	7.45	6.78	10.19	9.05	8.10	7.31	41
42	7.55	6.91	6.35	5.86	8.54	7.74	7.05	6.46	9.56	8.58	7.75	7.05	10.60	9.41	8.43	7.60	42
43	7.85	7.18	6.60	6.10	8.88	8.05	7.33	6.72	9.95	8.92	8.06	7.33	11.02	9.79	8.76	7.90	43
44	8.17	7.47	6.87	6.34	9.24	8.37	7.63	6.99	10.34	9.28	8.38	7.62	11.46	10.18	9.11	8.22	44
45	8.50	7.77	7.14	6.60	9.61	8.70	7.93	7.27	10.76	9.65	8.72	7.93	11.92	10.59	9.48	8.55	45
46	8.84	8.08	7.43	6.86	9.99	9.05	8.25	7.56	11.19	10.04	9.07	8.24	12.39	11.01	9.86	8.89	46
47	9.19	8.40	7.73	7.14	10.39	9.41	8.58	7.86	11.63	10.44	9.43	8.57	12.89	11.45	10.25	9.25	47
48	9.56	8.74	8.03	7.42	10.81	9.79	8.92	8.18	12.10	10.86	9.81	8.92	13.41	11.91	10.66	9.62	48
49	9.94	9.09	8.36	7.72	11.24	10.18	9.28	8.51	12.58	11.29	10.20	9.27	13.94	12.38	11.09	10.00	49
50	10.34	9.45	8.69	8.03	11.69	10.59	9.65	8.85	13.09	11.74	10.61	9.64	14.50	12.88	11.53	10.40	50

IV. Retirement Planning where Salary Falls Behind Moderate 6% Inflation
Planned Retirement Age 59

Table 1 - Percent of Salary Replaced by a 401(k) Account Equal to Current Annual Salary IV-59-1

Probable Life Expectancy at Retirement

Yrs. to Ret.	25.7 (Same as Male Avg.) 4%/4%	6%/5%	8%/6%	10%/7%	28.3 (Better than Male Avg.) 4%/4%	6%/5%	8%/6%	10%/7%	31 (Same as Female Avg.) 4%/4%	6%/5%	8%/6%	10%/7%	33.8 (Better than Female Avg.) 4%/4%	6%/5%	8%/6%	10%/7%	Yrs. to Ret.
	Expected Return				(Pre-Retirement/Post-Retirement)				(Pre-Retirement/Post-Retirement)				Expected Return				
0	2.87	3.36	3.89	4.45	2.54	3.01	3.53	4.08	2.26	2.72	3.22	3.77	2.01	2.46	2.96	3.50	0
1	2.85	3.40	4.00	4.66	2.52	3.04	3.63	4.28	2.23	2.74	3.32	3.95	1.99	2.49	3.04	3.67	1
2	2.82	3.43	4.11	4.88	2.49	3.07	3.73	4.48	2.21	2.77	3.41	4.14	1.98	2.51	3.13	3.85	2
3	2.79	3.46	4.23	5.11	2.47	3.10	3.84	4.69	2.19	2.80	3.51	4.34	1.96	2.53	3.22	4.03	3
4	2.77	3.49	4.35	5.36	2.44	3.13	3.95	4.92	2.17	2.82	3.61	4.54	1.94	2.56	3.31	4.22	4
5	2.74	3.53	4.48	5.61	2.42	3.16	4.06	5.15	2.15	2.85	3.71	4.76	1.92	2.58	3.41	4.42	5
6	2.71	3.56	4.60	5.88	2.40	3.19	4.18	5.40	2.13	2.88	3.82	4.99	1.90	2.61	3.51	4.63	6
7	2.69	3.59	4.74	6.16	2.38	3.22	4.30	5.65	2.11	2.90	3.93	5.22	1.88	2.63	3.61	4.85	7
8	2.66	3.63	4.87	6.45	2.35	3.25	4.42	5.92	2.09	2.93	4.04	5.47	1.87	2.66	3.71	5.08	8
9	2.64	3.66	5.01	6.76	2.33	3.28	4.55	6.21	2.07	2.96	4.15	5.73	1.85	2.68	3.82	5.33	9
10	2.61	3.70	5.15	7.08	2.31	3.31	4.68	6.50	2.05	2.99	4.27	6.01	1.83	2.71	3.92	5.58	10
11	2.59	3.73	5.30	7.42	2.29	3.35	4.81	6.81	2.03	3.02	4.40	6.29	1.81	2.73	4.04	5.85	11
12	2.56	3.77	5.45	7.77	2.26	3.38	4.95	7.13	2.01	3.04	4.52	6.59	1.80	2.76	4.15	6.12	12
13	2.54	3.80	5.61	8.14	2.24	3.41	5.09	7.47	1.99	3.07	4.65	6.90	1.78	2.79	4.27	6.42	13
14	2.51	3.84	5.77	8.53	2.22	3.44	5.24	7.83	1.97	3.10	4.78	7.23	1.76	2.81	4.39	6.72	14
15	2.49	3.88	5.93	8.93	2.20	3.47	5.39	8.20	1.95	3.13	4.92	7.58	1.74	2.84	4.52	7.04	15
16	2.47	3.91	6.10	9.36	2.18	3.51	5.54	8.59	1.94	3.16	5.06	7.94	1.73	2.87	4.65	7.38	16
17	2.44	3.95	6.28	9.80	2.16	3.54	5.70	9.00	1.92	3.19	5.21	8.32	1.71	2.89	4.78	7.73	17
18	2.42	3.99	6.46	10.27	2.14	3.57	5.86	9.43	1.90	3.22	5.35	8.71	1.70	2.92	4.92	8.09	18
19	2.40	4.03	6.64	10.76	2.12	3.61	6.03	9.88	1.88	3.25	5.51	9.13	1.68	2.95	5.06	8.48	19
20	2.37	4.06	6.83	11.27	2.10	3.64	6.20	10.35	1.86	3.28	5.67	9.56	1.66	2.98	5.20	8.88	20
21	2.35	4.10	7.03	11.81	2.08	3.68	6.38	10.84	1.85	3.32	5.83	10.02	1.65	3.00	5.35	9.31	21
22	2.33	4.14	7.23	12.37	2.06	3.71	6.56	11.36	1.83	3.35	5.99	10.49	1.63	3.03	5.50	9.75	22
23	2.31	4.18	7.44	12.96	2.04	3.75	6.75	11.90	1.81	3.38	6.17	10.99	1.62	3.06	5.66	10.21	23
24	2.29	4.22	7.65	13.58	2.02	3.78	6.94	12.46	1.79	3.41	6.34	11.52	1.60	3.09	5.82	10.70	24
25	2.26	4.26	7.87	14.22	2.00	3.82	7.14	13.06	1.78	3.44	6.52	12.06	1.59	3.12	5.99	11.21	25
26	2.24	4.30	8.09	14.90	1.98	3.86	7.35	13.68	1.76	3.48	6.71	12.64	1.57	3.15	6.16	11.74	26
27	2.22	4.34	8.32	15.61	1.96	3.89	7.56	14.33	1.74	3.51	6.90	13.24	1.56	3.18	6.34	12.30	27
28	2.20	4.38	8.56	16.35	1.94	3.93	7.77	15.01	1.73	3.54	7.10	13.87	1.54	3.21	6.52	12.89	28
29	2.18	4.43	8.81	17.13	1.93	3.97	7.99	15.73	1.71	3.58	7.30	14.53	1.53	3.24	6.71	13.50	29
30	2.16	4.47	9.06	17.95	1.91	4.00	8.22	16.48	1.69	3.61	7.51	15.22	1.51	3.27	6.90	14.14	30
31	2.14	4.51	9.32	18.80	1.89	4.04	8.46	17.26	1.68	3.64	7.73	15.95	1.50	3.30	7.09	14.82	31
32	2.12	4.55	9.58	19.70	1.87	4.08	8.70	18.08	1.66	3.68	7.95	16.71	1.48	3.33	7.30	15.52	32
33	2.10	4.60	9.86	20.63	1.85	4.12	8.95	18.94	1.65	3.71	8.17	17.50	1.47	3.37	7.51	16.26	33
34	2.08	4.64	10.14	21.62	1.84	4.16	9.20	19.84	1.63	3.75	8.41	18.33	1.46	3.40	7.72	17.03	34
35	2.06	4.68	10.43	22.64	1.82	4.20	9.47	20.79	1.62	3.78	8.65	19.21	1.44	3.43	7.94	17.84	35
36	2.04	4.73	10.73	23.72	1.80	4.24	9.74	21.78	1.60	3.82	8.90	20.12	1.43	3.46	8.17	18.69	36
37	2.02	4.77	11.04	24.85	1.78	4.28	10.02	22.81	1.58	3.86	9.15	21.08	1.41	3.49	8.40	19.58	37
38	2.00	4.82	11.35	26.03	1.77	4.32	10.30	23.90	1.57	3.89	9.41	22.08	1.40	3.53	8.64	20.52	38
39	1.98	4.86	11.68	27.27	1.75	4.36	10.60	25.04	1.55	3.93	9.68	23.13	1.39	3.56	8.89	21.49	39
40	1.96	4.91	12.01	28.57	1.73	4.40	10.90	26.23	1.54	3.97	9.96	24.23	1.37	3.60	9.14	22.52	40
41	1.94	4.96	12.35	29.93	1.72	4.44	11.21	27.48	1.53	4.01	10.24	25.39	1.36	3.63	9.41	23.59	41
42	1.93	5.00	12.71	31.36	1.70	4.48	11.53	28.79	1.51	4.04	10.54	26.60	1.35	3.66	9.67	24.71	42
43	1.91	5.05	13.07	32.85	1.68	4.53	11.86	30.16	1.50	4.08	10.84	27.86	1.34	3.70	9.95	25.89	43
44	1.89	5.10	13.44	34.41	1.67	4.57	12.20	31.59	1.48	4.12	11.15	29.19	1.32	3.73	10.24	27.12	44
45	1.87	5.15	13.83	36.05	1.65	4.61	12.55	33.10	1.47	4.16	11.47	30.58	1.31	3.77	10.53	28.41	45
46	1.85	5.20	14.22	37.77	1.64	4.66	12.91	34.67	1.45	4.20	11.79	32.03	1.30	3.81	10.83	29.76	46
47	1.84	5.25	14.63	39.56	1.62	4.70	13.28	36.32	1.44	4.24	12.13	33.56	1.29	3.84	11.14	31.18	47
48	1.82	5.30	15.05	41.45	1.61	4.75	13.66	38.05	1.43	4.28	12.48	35.16	1.27	3.88	11.46	32.66	48
49	1.80	5.35	15.48	43.42	1.59	4.79	14.05	39.86	1.41	4.32	12.83	36.83	1.26	3.91	11.79	34.22	49
50	1.78	5.40	15.92	45.49	1.58	4.84	14.45	41.76	1.40	4.36	13.20	38.58	1.25	3.95	12.12	35.85	50

IV. Retirement Planning where Salary Falls Behind Moderate 6% Inflation
Planned Retirement Age 59

Table 2 - Percent of Salary Replaced by a 401(k) Contribution of 1% of Current Salary   IV-59-2

Probable Life Expectancy at Retirement

Yrs. to Ret.	25.7 (Same as Male Avg.)				28.3 (Better than Male Avg.)				31 (Same as Female Avg.)				33.8 (Better than Female Avg.)				Yrs. to Ret.
	4% / 4%	6% / 5%	8% / 6%	10% / 7%	4% / 4%	6% / 5%	8% / 6%	10% / 7%	4% / 4%	6% / 5%	8% / 6%	10% / 7%	4% / 4%	6% / 5%	8% / 6%	10% / 7%	
	Expected Return (Pre-Retirement/Post-Retirement)								(Pre-Retirement/Post-Retirement)				Expected Return				
0	0.00	0.00	0.00	0.00	0.00	0.00	0.00	0.00	0.00	0.00	0.00	0.00	0.00	0.00	0.00	0.00	0
1	0.03	0.03	0.04	0.04	0.03	0.03	0.04	0.04	0.02	0.03	0.03	0.04	0.02	0.02	0.03	0.04	1
2	0.06	0.07	0.08	0.09	0.05	0.06	0.07	0.08	0.04	0.05	0.07	0.08	0.04	0.05	0.06	0.07	2
3	0.09	0.10	0.12	0.14	0.08	0.09	0.11	0.13	0.07	0.08	0.10	0.12	0.06	0.07	0.09	0.11	3
4	0.11	0.14	0.16	0.19	0.10	0.12	0.15	0.18	0.09	0.11	0.13	0.16	0.08	0.10	0.12	0.15	4
5	0.14	0.17	0.21	0.24	0.12	0.15	0.19	0.22	0.11	0.14	0.17	0.21	0.10	0.13	0.16	0.19	5
6	0.17	0.21	0.25	0.30	0.15	0.19	0.23	0.28	0.13	0.17	0.21	0.26	0.12	0.15	0.19	0.24	6
7	0.20	0.24	0.30	0.36	0.17	0.22	0.27	0.33	0.15	0.20	0.25	0.30	0.14	0.18	0.23	0.28	7
8	0.22	0.28	0.34	0.42	0.20	0.25	0.31	0.39	0.17	0.22	0.29	0.36	0.16	0.20	0.26	0.33	8
9	0.25	0.31	0.39	0.49	0.22	0.28	0.36	0.45	0.20	0.25	0.33	0.41	0.17	0.23	0.30	0.38	9
10	0.28	0.35	0.44	0.55	0.24	0.31	0.40	0.51	0.22	0.28	0.37	0.47	0.19	0.26	0.34	0.44	10
11	0.30	0.39	0.49	0.62	0.27	0.35	0.45	0.57	0.24	0.31	0.41	0.53	0.21	0.28	0.38	0.49	11
12	0.33	0.43	0.55	0.70	0.29	0.38	0.50	0.64	0.26	0.34	0.45	0.59	0.23	0.31	0.42	0.55	12
13	0.35	0.46	0.60	0.78	0.31	0.42	0.55	0.71	0.28	0.37	0.50	0.66	0.25	0.34	0.46	0.61	13
14	0.38	0.50	0.66	0.86	0.33	0.45	0.60	0.79	0.30	0.40	0.55	0.73	0.27	0.37	0.50	0.68	14
15	0.40	0.54	0.72	0.94	0.36	0.48	0.65	0.87	0.32	0.44	0.59	0.80	0.28	0.40	0.54	0.74	15
16	0.43	0.58	0.78	1.03	0.38	0.52	0.70	0.95	0.34	0.47	0.64	0.88	0.30	0.42	0.59	0.81	16
17	0.45	0.62	0.84	1.13	0.40	0.55	0.76	1.03	0.36	0.50	0.69	0.95	0.32	0.45	0.64	0.89	17
18	0.48	0.66	0.90	1.22	0.42	0.59	0.82	1.12	0.37	0.53	0.75	1.04	0.33	0.48	0.68	0.96	18
19	0.50	0.70	0.96	1.33	0.44	0.62	0.87	1.22	0.39	0.56	0.80	1.12	0.35	0.51	0.73	1.05	19
20	0.53	0.74	1.03	1.43	0.46	0.66	0.93	1.32	0.41	0.60	0.85	1.22	0.37	0.54	0.78	1.13	20
21	0.55	0.78	1.10	1.55	0.49	0.70	1.00	1.42	0.43	0.63	0.91	1.31	0.38	0.57	0.84	1.22	21
22	0.57	0.82	1.17	1.66	0.51	0.73	1.06	1.53	0.45	0.66	0.97	1.41	0.40	0.60	0.89	1.31	22
23	0.60	0.86	1.24	1.79	0.53	0.77	1.13	1.64	0.47	0.70	1.03	1.52	0.42	0.63	0.94	1.41	23
24	0.62	0.90	1.32	1.92	0.55	0.81	1.19	1.76	0.49	0.73	1.09	1.63	0.43	0.66	1.00	1.51	24
25	0.64	0.94	1.39	2.05	0.57	0.85	1.26	1.89	0.50	0.76	1.15	1.74	0.45	0.69	1.06	1.62	25
26	0.67	0.99	1.47	2.20	0.59	0.88	1.33	2.02	0.52	0.80	1.22	1.86	0.47	0.72	1.12	1.73	26
27	0.69	1.03	1.55	2.35	0.61	0.92	1.41	2.15	0.54	0.83	1.29	1.99	0.48	0.75	1.18	1.85	27
28	0.71	1.07	1.63	2.50	0.63	0.96	1.48	2.30	0.56	0.87	1.36	2.12	0.50	0.79	1.24	1.97	28
29	0.73	1.12	1.72	2.66	0.65	1.00	1.56	2.45	0.57	0.90	1.43	2.26	0.51	0.82	1.31	2.10	29
30	0.75	1.16	1.81	2.84	0.67	1.04	1.64	2.60	0.59	0.94	1.50	2.41	0.53	0.85	1.38	2.23	30
31	0.78	1.21	1.90	3.02	0.68	1.08	1.72	2.77	0.61	0.97	1.57	2.56	0.54	0.88	1.45	2.38	31
32	0.80	1.25	1.99	3.20	0.70	1.12	1.81	2.94	0.63	1.01	1.65	2.72	0.56	0.92	1.52	2.52	32
33	0.82	1.30	2.09	3.40	0.72	1.16	1.90	3.12	0.64	1.05	1.73	2.88	0.57	0.95	1.59	2.68	33
34	0.84	1.34	2.19	3.61	0.74	1.20	1.98	3.31	0.66	1.08	1.81	3.06	0.59	0.98	1.66	2.84	34
35	0.86	1.39	2.29	3.82	0.76	1.24	2.08	3.51	0.67	1.12	1.90	3.24	0.60	1.02	1.74	3.01	35
36	0.88	1.44	2.39	4.05	0.78	1.29	2.17	3.72	0.69	1.16	1.98	3.43	0.62	1.05	1.82	3.19	36
37	0.90	1.48	2.50	4.29	0.80	1.33	2.27	3.94	0.71	1.20	2.07	3.64	0.63	1.09	1.90	3.38	37
38	0.92	1.53	2.61	4.54	0.81	1.37	2.37	4.16	0.72	1.24	2.16	3.85	0.64	1.12	1.99	3.57	38
39	0.94	1.58	2.72	4.80	0.83	1.42	2.47	4.40	0.74	1.28	2.26	4.07	0.66	1.16	2.07	3.78	39
40	0.96	1.63	2.84	5.07	0.85	1.46	2.58	4.65	0.75	1.32	2.35	4.30	0.67	1.19	2.16	3.99	40
41	0.98	1.68	2.96	5.35	0.87	1.50	2.69	4.92	0.77	1.35	2.45	4.54	0.69	1.23	2.25	4.22	41
42	1.00	1.73	3.08	5.65	0.88	1.55	2.80	5.19	0.78	1.39	2.56	4.80	0.70	1.26	2.35	4.45	42
43	1.02	1.78	3.21	5.97	0.90	1.59	2.91	5.48	0.80	1.44	2.66	5.06	0.71	1.30	2.44	4.70	43
44	1.04	1.83	3.34	6.30	0.92	1.64	3.03	5.78	0.81	1.48	2.77	5.34	0.73	1.34	2.54	4.96	44
45	1.06	1.88	3.48	6.64	0.93	1.68	3.16	6.10	0.83	1.52	2.88	5.63	0.74	1.38	2.65	5.23	45
46	1.08	1.93	3.61	7.00	0.95	1.73	3.28	6.43	0.84	1.56	3.00	5.94	0.75	1.41	2.75	5.52	46
47	1.09	1.98	3.76	7.38	0.97	1.78	3.41	6.77	0.86	1.60	3.11	6.26	0.77	1.45	2.86	5.81	47
48	1.11	2.03	3.90	7.77	0.98	1.82	3.54	7.14	0.87	1.64	3.24	6.59	0.78	1.49	2.97	6.13	48
49	1.13	2.09	4.05	8.19	1.00	1.87	3.68	7.52	0.89	1.69	3.36	6.94	0.79	1.53	3.09	6.45	49
50	1.15	2.14	4.21	8.62	1.01	1.92	3.82	7.92	0.90	1.73	3.49	7.31	0.80	1.57	3.20	6.79	50

IV. Retirement Planning where Salary Falls Behind Moderate 6% Inflation
Planned Retirement Age 59

Table 3 - 401(k) Contribution (% of Current Sal.) Needed to Replace 10% of Sal. at Retirement IV-59-3

Probable Life Expectancy at Retirement

Yrs. to Ret.	25.7 (Same as Male Avg.)				28.3 (Better than Male Avg.)				31 (Same as Female Avg.)				33.8 (Better than Female Avg.)				Yrs. to Ret.
	4% / 4%	6% / 5%	8% / 6%	10% / 7%	4% / 4%	6% / 5%	8% / 6%	10% / 7%	4% / 4%	6% / 5%	8% / 6%	10% / 7%	4% / 4%	6% / 5%	8% / 6%	10% / 7%	
	Expected Return				(Pre-Retirement/Post-Retirement)				(Pre-Retirement/Post-Retirement)				Expected Return				
0																	0
1	347.88	297.27	257.23	224.84	393.78	331.68	283.38	244.91	443.29	367.89	310.25	265.08	496.67	405.97	337.84	285.32	1
2	174.77	147.93	126.80	109.81	197.83	165.06	139.69	119.61	222.71	183.08	152.94	129.46	249.52	202.03	166.54	139.35	2
3	117.07	98.16	83.34	71.49	132.52	109.52	91.81	77.87	149.18	121.47	100.51	84.28	167.14	134.05	109.45	90.72	3
4	88.22	73.27	61.61	52.35	99.86	81.75	67.88	57.03	112.42	90.67	74.31	61.72	125.95	100.06	80.92	66.44	4
5	70.91	58.34	48.59	40.89	80.27	65.09	53.52	44.54	90.36	72.19	58.60	48.20	101.24	79.67	63.81	51.88	5
6	59.37	48.38	39.91	33.26	67.21	53.98	43.96	36.22	75.66	59.88	48.13	39.21	84.77	66.07	52.41	42.20	6
7	51.13	41.27	33.71	27.82	57.88	46.05	37.14	30.30	65.16	51.08	40.66	32.80	73.00	56.36	44.28	35.30	7
8	44.95	35.94	29.07	23.75	50.88	40.10	32.03	25.87	57.28	44.48	35.06	28.00	64.18	49.08	38.18	30.14	8
9	40.15	31.80	25.47	20.59	45.44	35.48	28.05	22.43	51.16	39.35	30.71	24.28	57.32	43.42	33.45	26.13	9
10	36.30	28.48	22.58	18.08	41.09	31.78	24.88	19.69	46.26	35.24	27.24	21.31	51.83	38.89	29.66	22.94	10
11	33.16	25.77	20.23	16.03	37.53	28.75	22.29	17.46	42.25	31.89	24.40	18.89	47.34	35.19	26.57	20.34	11
12	30.54	23.50	18.27	14.32	34.57	26.23	20.13	15.60	38.91	29.09	22.04	16.89	43.60	32.10	24.00	18.18	12
13	28.32	21.59	16.61	12.89	32.06	24.09	18.30	14.04	36.09	26.72	20.04	15.20	40.43	29.49	21.82	16.36	13
14	26.42	19.95	15.20	11.66	29.91	22.26	16.74	12.71	33.67	24.69	18.33	13.75	37.72	27.25	19.96	14.80	14
15	24.77	18.53	13.97	10.61	28.04	20.68	15.39	11.56	31.57	22.94	16.85	12.51	35.37	25.31	18.35	13.46	15
16	23.33	17.29	12.90	9.69	26.41	19.29	14.21	10.56	29.73	21.40	15.56	11.43	33.31	23.61	16.95	12.30	16
17	22.06	16.20	11.96	8.89	24.97	18.07	13.18	9.68	28.11	20.04	14.43	10.48	31.50	22.12	15.71	11.27	17
18	20.93	15.22	11.13	8.17	23.70	16.98	12.26	8.90	26.68	18.84	13.42	9.64	29.89	20.79	14.61	10.37	18
19	19.92	14.35	10.38	7.54	22.55	16.01	11.43	8.21	25.39	17.76	12.52	8.89	28.45	19.60	13.63	9.57	19
20	19.02	13.57	9.71	6.97	21.53	15.14	10.70	7.60	24.23	16.79	11.71	8.22	27.15	18.53	12.75	8.85	20
21	18.19	12.86	9.11	6.47	20.60	14.35	10.03	7.04	23.18	15.91	10.98	7.62	25.98	17.56	11.96	8.21	21
22	17.45	12.21	8.56	6.01	19.75	13.63	9.43	6.54	22.23	15.11	10.32	7.08	24.91	16.68	11.24	7.62	22
23	16.77	11.63	8.06	5.59	18.98	12.97	8.88	6.09	21.36	14.39	9.72	6.59	23.94	15.88	10.59	7.10	23
24	16.14	11.09	7.60	5.21	18.27	12.37	8.38	5.68	20.57	13.72	9.17	6.15	23.05	15.14	9.99	6.62	24
25	15.57	10.59	7.19	4.87	17.62	11.82	7.92	5.30	19.84	13.11	8.67	5.74	22.23	14.46	9.44	6.18	25
26	15.04	10.13	6.80	4.55	17.02	11.31	7.49	4.96	19.16	12.54	8.20	5.37	21.47	13.84	8.93	5.78	26
27	14.55	9.71	6.45	4.26	16.47	10.83	7.10	4.65	18.54	12.02	7.78	5.03	20.77	13.26	8.47	5.41	27
28	14.09	9.32	6.12	4.00	15.95	10.40	6.74	4.36	17.96	11.53	7.38	4.71	20.12	12.72	8.04	5.07	28
29	13.67	8.95	5.81	3.75	15.47	9.99	6.40	4.09	17.42	11.08	7.01	4.42	19.51	12.23	7.64	4.76	29
30	13.27	8.61	5.53	3.53	15.02	9.61	6.09	3.84	16.91	10.66	6.67	4.16	18.95	11.76	7.26	4.47	30
31	12.90	8.29	5.27	3.32	14.60	9.25	5.80	3.61	16.44	10.26	6.35	3.91	18.42	11.32	6.92	4.21	31
32	12.56	7.99	5.02	3.12	14.21	8.92	5.53	3.40	16.00	9.89	6.06	3.68	17.93	10.92	6.59	3.96	32
33	12.23	7.71	4.79	2.94	13.84	8.61	5.28	3.20	15.59	9.54	5.78	3.47	17.46	10.53	6.29	3.73	33
34	11.92	7.45	4.57	2.77	13.50	8.31	5.04	3.02	15.20	9.22	5.52	3.27	17.02	10.17	6.01	3.52	34
35	11.64	7.20	4.37	2.62	13.17	8.03	4.82	2.85	14.83	8.91	5.27	3.08	16.61	9.83	5.74	3.32	35
36	11.36	6.96	4.18	2.47	12.86	7.77	4.61	2.69	14.48	8.62	5.04	2.91	16.22	9.51	5.49	3.13	36
37	11.11	6.74	4.00	2.33	12.57	7.52	4.41	2.54	14.15	8.34	4.83	2.75	15.86	9.21	5.25	2.96	37
38	10.86	6.53	3.83	2.21	12.30	7.29	4.22	2.40	13.84	8.08	4.62	2.60	15.51	8.92	5.03	2.80	38
39	10.63	6.33	3.67	2.09	12.04	7.07	4.05	2.27	13.55	7.84	4.43	2.46	15.18	8.65	4.82	2.65	39
40	10.41	6.14	3.52	1.97	11.79	6.86	3.88	2.15	13.27	7.60	4.25	2.33	14.87	8.39	4.62	2.50	40
41	10.20	5.96	3.38	1.87	11.55	6.65	3.72	2.03	13.00	7.38	4.07	2.20	14.57	8.14	4.44	2.37	41
42	10.01	5.79	3.24	1.77	11.33	6.46	3.57	1.93	12.75	7.17	3.91	2.09	14.29	7.91	4.26	2.24	42
43	9.82	5.63	3.11	1.68	11.11	6.28	3.43	1.83	12.51	6.97	3.76	1.98	14.02	7.69	4.09	2.13	43
44	9.64	5.47	2.99	1.59	10.91	6.11	3.30	1.73	12.28	6.77	3.61	1.87	13.76	7.48	3.93	2.02	44
45	9.46	5.33	2.88	1.51	10.71	5.94	3.17	1.64	12.06	6.59	3.47	1.78	13.51	7.27	3.78	1.91	45
46	9.30	5.18	2.77	1.43	10.53	5.78	3.05	1.56	11.85	6.41	3.34	1.68	13.28	7.08	3.63	1.81	46
47	9.14	5.05	2.66	1.36	10.35	5.63	2.93	1.48	11.65	6.25	3.21	1.60	13.05	6.89	3.50	1.72	47
48	8.99	4.92	2.56	1.29	10.18	5.49	2.82	1.40	11.46	6.09	3.09	1.52	12.84	6.71	3.37	1.63	48
49	8.85	4.79	2.47	1.22	10.01	5.35	2.72	1.33	11.27	5.93	2.98	1.44	12.63	6.54	3.24	1.55	49
50	8.71	4.67	2.38	1.16	9.86	5.21	2.62	1.26	11.10	5.78	2.87	1.37	12.43	6.38	3.12	1.47	50

Appendix A

IV. Retirement Planning where Salary Falls Behind Moderate 6% Inflation
Planned Retirement Age 59

Table 4 - Accumulation at Retirement (Multiple of Current Sal.) for 10% Sal. Replacement

Probable Life Expectancy at Retirement

Yrs. to Ret.	25.7 (Same as Male Avg.) 4%/4%	6%/5%	8%/6%	10%/7%	28.3 (Better than Male Avg.) 4%/4%	6%/5%	8%/6%	10%/7%	31 (Same as Female Avg.) 4%/4%	6%/5%	8%/6%	10%/7%	33.8 (Better than Female Avg.) 4%/4%	6%/5%	8%/6%	10%/7%	Yrs. to Ret.
	Expected Return				(Pre-Retirement/Post-Retirement)				(Pre-Retirement/Post-Retirement)				Expected Return				
0	3.48	2.97	2.57	2.25	3.94	3.32	2.83	2.45	4.43	3.68	3.10	2.65	4.97	4.06	3.38	2.85	0
1	3.65	3.12	2.70	2.36	4.13	3.48	2.98	2.57	4.65	3.86	3.26	2.78	5.22	4.26	3.55	3.00	1
2	3.84	3.28	2.84	2.48	4.34	3.66	3.12	2.70	4.89	4.06	3.42	2.92	5.48	4.48	3.72	3.15	2
3	4.03	3.44	2.98	2.60	4.56	3.84	3.28	2.84	5.13	4.26	3.59	3.07	5.75	4.70	3.91	3.30	3
4	4.23	3.61	3.13	2.73	4.79	4.03	3.44	2.98	5.39	4.47	3.77	3.22	6.04	4.93	4.11	3.47	4
5	4.44	3.79	3.28	2.87	5.03	4.23	3.62	3.13	5.66	4.70	3.96	3.38	6.34	5.18	4.31	3.64	5
6	4.66	3.98	3.45	3.01	5.28	4.44	3.80	3.28	5.94	4.93	4.16	3.55	6.66	5.44	4.53	3.82	6
7	4.90	4.18	3.62	3.16	5.54	4.67	3.99	3.45	6.24	5.18	4.37	3.73	6.99	5.71	4.75	4.01	7
8	5.14	4.39	3.80	3.32	5.82	4.90	4.19	3.62	6.55	5.44	4.58	3.92	7.34	6.00	4.99	4.22	8
9	5.40	4.61	3.99	3.49	6.11	5.15	4.40	3.80	6.88	5.71	4.81	4.11	7.70	6.30	5.24	4.43	9
10	5.67	4.84	4.19	3.66	6.41	5.40	4.62	3.99	7.22	5.99	5.05	4.32	8.09	6.61	5.50	4.65	10
11	5.95	5.08	4.40	3.85	6.74	5.67	4.85	4.19	7.58	6.29	5.31	4.53	8.49	6.94	5.78	4.88	11
12	6.25	5.34	4.62	4.04	7.07	5.96	5.09	4.40	7.96	6.61	5.57	4.76	8.92	7.29	6.07	5.12	12
13	6.56	5.61	4.85	4.24	7.43	6.25	5.34	4.62	8.36	6.94	5.85	5.00	9.37	7.66	6.37	5.38	13
14	6.89	5.89	5.09	4.45	7.80	6.57	5.61	4.85	8.78	7.28	6.14	5.25	9.83	8.04	6.69	5.65	14
15	7.23	6.18	5.35	4.67	8.19	6.90	5.89	5.09	9.22	7.65	6.45	5.51	10.33	8.44	7.02	5.93	15
16	7.59	6.49	5.62	4.91	8.60	7.24	6.19	5.35	9.68	8.03	6.77	5.79	10.84	8.86	7.37	6.23	16
17	7.97	6.81	5.90	5.15	9.03	7.60	6.50	5.61	10.16	8.43	7.11	6.08	11.38	9.30	7.74	6.54	17
18	8.37	7.15	6.19	5.41	9.48	7.98	6.82	5.89	10.67	8.85	7.47	6.38	11.95	9.77	8.13	6.87	18
19	8.79	7.51	6.50	5.68	9.95	8.38	7.16	6.19	11.20	9.30	7.84	6.70	12.55	10.26	8.54	7.21	19
20	9.23	7.89	6.83	5.97	10.45	8.80	7.52	6.50	11.76	9.76	8.23	7.03	13.18	10.77	8.96	7.57	20
21	9.69	8.28	7.17	6.26	10.97	9.24	7.89	6.82	12.35	10.25	8.64	7.39	13.84	11.31	9.41	7.95	21
22	10.18	8.70	7.52	6.58	11.52	9.70	8.29	7.16	12.97	10.76	9.08	7.75	14.53	11.88	9.88	8.35	22
23	10.69	9.13	7.90	6.91	12.10	10.19	8.70	7.52	13.62	11.30	9.53	8.14	15.26	12.47	10.38	8.76	23
24	11.22	9.59	8.30	7.25	12.70	10.70	9.14	7.90	14.30	11.86	10.01	8.55	16.02	13.09	10.90	9.20	24
25	11.78	10.07	8.71	7.61	13.33	11.23	9.60	8.29	15.01	12.46	10.51	8.98	16.82	13.75	11.44	9.66	25
26	12.37	10.57	9.15	7.99	14.00	11.79	10.08	8.71	15.76	13.08	11.03	9.43	17.66	14.43	12.01	10.15	26
27	12.99	11.10	9.60	8.39	14.70	12.38	10.58	9.14	16.55	13.74	11.58	9.90	18.54	15.16	12.61	10.65	27
28	13.64	11.65	10.08	8.81	15.44	13.00	11.11	9.60	17.38	14.42	12.16	10.39	19.47	15.91	13.24	11.19	28
29	14.32	12.24	10.59	9.25	16.21	13.65	11.66	10.08	18.25	15.14	12.77	10.91	20.44	16.71	13.91	11.74	29
30	15.04	12.85	11.12	9.72	17.02	14.34	12.25	10.59	19.16	15.90	13.41	11.46	21.47	17.55	14.60	12.33	30
31	15.79	13.49	11.67	10.20	17.87	15.05	12.86	11.11	20.12	16.70	14.08	12.03	22.54	18.42	15.33	12.95	31
32	16.58	14.16	12.26	10.71	18.76	15.80	13.50	11.67	21.12	17.53	14.78	12.63	23.67	19.34	16.10	13.60	32
33	17.41	14.87	12.87	11.25	19.70	16.59	14.18	12.25	22.18	18.41	15.52	13.26	24.85	20.31	16.90	14.28	33
34	18.28	15.62	13.51	11.81	20.69	17.42	14.89	12.87	23.29	19.33	16.30	13.93	26.09	21.33	17.75	14.99	34
35	19.19	16.40	14.19	12.40	21.72	18.30	15.63	13.51	24.45	20.29	17.11	14.62	27.40	22.39	18.64	15.74	35
36	20.15	17.22	14.90	13.02	22.81	19.21	16.41	14.18	25.67	21.31	17.97	15.35	28.77	23.51	19.57	16.53	36
37	21.16	18.08	15.64	13.67	23.95	20.17	17.23	14.89	26.96	22.37	18.87	16.12	30.20	24.69	20.55	17.35	37
38	22.21	18.98	16.43	14.36	25.14	21.18	18.09	15.64	28.31	23.49	19.81	16.93	31.71	25.92	21.57	18.22	38
39	23.32	19.93	17.25	15.08	26.40	22.24	19.00	16.42	29.72	24.67	20.80	17.77	33.30	27.22	22.65	19.13	39
40	24.49	20.93	18.11	15.83	27.72	23.35	19.95	17.24	31.21	25.90	21.84	18.66	34.97	28.58	23.78	20.09	40
41	25.72	21.97	19.01	16.62	29.11	24.52	20.95	18.10	32.77	27.19	22.93	19.59	36.71	30.01	24.97	21.09	41
42	27.00	23.07	19.97	17.45	30.56	25.74	21.99	19.01	34.41	28.55	24.08	20.57	38.55	31.51	26.22	22.15	42
43	28.35	24.23	20.96	18.32	32.09	27.03	23.09	19.96	36.13	29.98	25.28	21.60	40.48	33.09	27.53	23.25	43
44	29.77	25.44	22.01	19.24	33.70	28.38	24.25	20.96	37.93	31.48	26.55	22.68	42.50	34.74	28.91	24.42	44
45	31.26	26.71	23.11	20.20	35.38	29.80	25.46	22.01	39.83	33.06	27.88	23.82	44.63	36.48	30.36	25.64	45
46	32.82	28.05	24.27	21.21	37.15	31.29	26.73	23.11	41.82	34.71	29.27	25.01	46.86	38.30	31.87	26.92	46
47	34.46	29.45	25.48	22.27	39.01	32.86	28.07	24.26	43.91	36.44	30.73	26.26	49.20	40.22	33.47	28.26	47
48	36.18	30.92	26.76	23.39	40.96	34.50	29.47	25.47	46.11	38.27	32.27	27.57	51.66	42.23	35.14	29.68	48
49	37.99	32.47	28.09	24.56	43.01	36.22	30.95	26.75	48.41	40.18	33.88	28.95	54.24	44.34	36.90	31.16	49
50	39.89	34.09	29.50	25.78	45.16	38.04	32.50	28.09	50.83	42.19	35.58	30.40	56.96	46.55	38.74	32.72	50

IV. Retirement Planning where Salary Falls Behind Moderate 6% Inflation
Planned Retirement Age 62

Table 1 - Percent of Salary Replaced by a 401(k) Account Equal to Current Annual Salary — IV-62-1

Probable Life Expectancy at Retirement

Yrs. to Ret.	23.2 (Same as Male Avg.)				25.7 (Better than Male Avg.)				28.3 (Same as Female Avg.)				31 (Better than Female Avg.)				Yrs. to Ret.
	4% / 4%	6% / 5%	8% / 6%	10% / 7%	4% / 4%	6% / 5%	8% / 6%	10% / 7%	4% / 4%	6% / 5%	8% / 6%	10% / 7%	4% / 4%	6% / 5%	8% / 6%	10% / 7%	
	Expected Return				(Pre-Retirement/Post-Retirement)				(Pre-Retirement/Post-Retirement)				Expected Return				
0	3.28	3.78	4.32	4.88	2.87	3.36	3.89	4.45	2.54	3.01	3.53	4.08	2.26	2.72	3.22	3.77	0
1	3.25	3.82	4.44	5.11	2.85	3.40	4.00	4.66	2.52	3.04	3.63	4.28	2.23	2.74	3.32	3.95	1
2	3.21	3.85	4.57	5.36	2.82	3.43	4.11	4.88	2.49	3.07	3.73	4.48	2.21	2.77	3.41	4.14	2
3	3.18	3.89	4.70	5.61	2.79	3.46	4.23	5.11	2.47	3.10	3.84	4.69	2.19	2.80	3.51	4.34	3
4	3.15	3.93	4.83	5.88	2.77	3.49	4.35	5.36	2.44	3.13	3.95	4.92	2.17	2.82	3.61	4.54	4
5	3.12	3.96	4.97	6.16	2.74	3.53	4.48	5.61	2.42	3.16	4.06	5.15	2.15	2.85	3.71	4.76	5
6	3.09	4.00	5.11	6.45	2.71	3.56	4.60	5.88	2.40	3.19	4.18	5.40	2.13	2.88	3.82	4.99	6
7	3.06	4.04	5.26	6.76	2.69	3.59	4.74	6.16	2.38	3.22	4.30	5.65	2.11	2.90	3.93	5.22	7
8	3.04	4.08	5.41	7.08	2.66	3.63	4.87	6.45	2.35	3.25	4.42	5.92	2.09	2.93	4.04	5.47	8
9	3.01	4.12	5.56	7.42	2.64	3.66	5.01	6.76	2.33	3.28	4.55	6.21	2.07	2.96	4.15	5.73	9
10	2.98	4.16	5.72	7.77	2.61	3.70	5.15	7.08	2.31	3.31	4.68	6.50	2.05	2.99	4.27	6.01	10
11	2.95	4.20	5.88	8.14	2.59	3.73	5.30	7.42	2.29	3.35	4.81	6.81	2.03	3.02	4.40	6.29	11
12	2.92	4.24	6.05	8.53	2.56	3.77	5.45	7.77	2.26	3.38	4.95	7.13	2.01	3.04	4.52	6.59	12
13	2.89	4.28	6.23	8.94	2.54	3.80	5.61	8.14	2.24	3.41	5.09	7.47	1.99	3.07	4.65	6.90	13
14	2.87	4.32	6.40	9.36	2.51	3.84	5.77	8.53	2.22	3.44	5.24	7.83	1.97	3.10	4.78	7.23	14
15	2.84	4.36	6.59	9.81	2.49	3.88	5.93	8.93	2.20	3.47	5.39	8.20	1.95	3.13	4.92	7.58	15
16	2.81	4.40	6.78	10.27	2.47	3.91	6.10	9.36	2.18	3.51	5.54	8.59	1.94	3.16	5.06	7.94	16
17	2.79	4.44	6.97	10.76	2.44	3.95	6.28	9.80	2.16	3.54	5.70	9.00	1.92	3.19	5.21	8.32	17
18	2.76	4.48	7.17	11.28	2.42	3.99	6.46	10.27	2.14	3.57	5.86	9.43	1.90	3.22	5.35	8.71	18
19	2.73	4.52	7.37	11.81	2.40	4.03	6.64	10.76	2.12	3.61	6.03	9.88	1.88	3.25	5.51	9.13	19
20	2.71	4.57	7.58	12.38	2.37	4.06	6.83	11.27	2.10	3.64	6.20	10.35	1.86	3.28	5.67	9.56	20
21	2.68	4.61	7.80	12.96	2.35	4.10	7.03	11.81	2.08	3.68	6.38	10.84	1.85	3.32	5.83	10.02	21
22	2.66	4.65	8.02	13.58	2.33	4.14	7.23	12.37	2.06	3.71	6.56	11.36	1.83	3.35	5.99	10.49	22
23	2.63	4.70	8.25	14.23	2.31	4.18	7.44	12.96	2.04	3.75	6.75	11.90	1.81	3.38	6.17	10.99	23
24	2.61	4.74	8.49	14.90	2.29	4.22	7.65	13.58	2.02	3.78	6.94	12.46	1.79	3.41	6.34	11.52	24
25	2.58	4.79	8.73	15.61	2.26	4.26	7.87	14.22	2.00	3.82	7.14	13.06	1.78	3.44	6.52	12.06	25
26	2.56	4.83	8.98	16.36	2.24	4.30	8.09	14.90	1.98	3.86	7.35	13.68	1.76	3.48	6.71	12.64	26
27	2.53	4.88	9.24	17.14	2.22	4.34	8.32	15.61	1.96	3.89	7.56	14.33	1.74	3.51	6.90	13.24	27
28	2.51	4.93	9.50	17.95	2.20	4.38	8.56	16.35	1.94	3.93	7.77	15.01	1.73	3.54	7.10	13.87	28
29	2.48	4.97	9.78	18.81	2.18	4.43	8.81	17.13	1.93	3.97	7.99	15.73	1.71	3.58	7.30	14.53	29
30	2.46	5.02	10.06	19.70	2.16	4.47	9.06	17.95	1.91	4.00	8.22	16.48	1.69	3.61	7.51	15.22	30
31	2.44	5.07	10.34	20.64	2.14	4.51	9.32	18.80	1.89	4.04	8.46	17.26	1.68	3.64	7.73	15.95	31
32	2.41	5.12	10.64	21.62	2.12	4.55	9.58	19.70	1.87	4.08	8.70	18.08	1.66	3.68	7.95	16.71	32
33	2.39	5.17	10.94	22.65	2.10	4.60	9.86	20.63	1.85	4.12	8.95	18.79	1.65	3.71	8.17	17.50	33
34	2.37	5.21	11.26	23.73	2.08	4.64	10.14	21.62	1.84	4.16	9.20	19.84	1.63	3.75	8.41	18.33	34
35	2.35	5.26	11.58	24.86	2.06	4.68	10.43	22.64	1.82	4.20	9.47	20.79	1.62	3.78	8.65	19.21	35
36	2.32	5.31	11.91	26.04	2.04	4.73	10.73	23.72	1.80	4.24	9.74	21.78	1.60	3.82	8.90	20.12	36
37	2.30	5.36	12.25	27.28	2.02	4.77	11.04	24.85	1.78	4.28	10.02	22.81	1.58	3.86	9.15	21.08	37
38	2.28	5.42	12.60	28.58	2.00	4.82	11.35	26.03	1.77	4.32	10.30	23.90	1.57	3.89	9.41	22.08	38
39	2.26	5.47	12.96	29.94	1.98	4.86	11.68	27.27	1.75	4.36	10.60	25.04	1.55	3.93	9.68	23.13	39
40	2.24	5.52	13.33	31.37	1.96	4.91	12.01	28.57	1.73	4.40	10.90	26.23	1.54	3.97	9.96	24.23	40
41	2.22	5.57	13.71	32.86	1.94	4.96	12.35	29.93	1.72	4.44	11.21	27.48	1.53	4.01	10.24	25.39	41
42	2.19	5.62	14.10	34.42	1.93	5.00	12.71	31.36	1.70	4.48	11.53	28.79	1.51	4.04	10.54	26.60	42
43	2.17	5.68	14.51	36.06	1.91	5.05	13.07	32.85	1.68	4.53	11.86	30.16	1.50	4.08	10.84	27.86	43
44	2.15	5.73	14.92	37.78	1.89	5.10	13.44	34.41	1.67	4.57	12.20	31.59	1.48	4.12	11.15	29.19	44
45	2.13	5.79	15.35	39.58	1.87	5.15	13.83	36.05	1.65	4.61	12.55	33.10	1.47	4.16	11.47	30.58	45
46	2.11	5.84	15.79	41.46	1.85	5.20	14.22	37.77	1.64	4.66	12.91	34.67	1.45	4.20	11.79	32.03	46
47	2.09	5.90	16.24	43.43	1.84	5.25	14.63	39.56	1.62	4.70	13.28	36.32	1.44	4.24	12.13	33.56	47
48	2.07	5.95	16.71	45.50	1.82	5.30	15.05	41.45	1.61	4.75	13.66	38.05	1.43	4.28	12.48	35.16	48
49	2.05	6.01	17.18	47.67	1.80	5.35	15.48	43.42	1.59	4.79	14.05	39.86	1.41	4.32	12.83	36.83	49
50	2.03	6.07	17.67	49.94	1.78	5.40	15.92	45.49	1.58	4.84	14.45	41.76	1.40	4.36	13.20	38.58	50

Appendix A

IV. Retirement Planning where Salary Falls Behind Moderate 6% Inflation
Planned Retirement Age 62

Table 2 - Percent of Salary Replaced by a 401(k) Contribution of 1% of Current Salary   IV-62-2

Probable Life Expectancy at Retirement

Yrs. to Ret.	23.2 (Same as Male Avg.)				25.7 (Better than Male Avg.)				28.3 (Same as Female Avg.)				31 (Better than Female Avg.)				Yrs. to Ret.
	4% / 4%	6% / 5%	8% / 6%	10% / 7%	4% / 4%	6% / 5%	8% / 6%	10% / 7%	4% / 4%	6% / 5%	8% / 6%	10% / 7%	4% / 4%	6% / 5%	8% / 6%	10% / 7%	
	Expected Return				(Pre-Retirement/Post-Retirement)				(Pre-Retirement/Post-Retirement)				Expected Return				
0	0.00	0.00	0.00	0.00	0.00	0.00	0.00	0.00	0.00	0.00	0.00	0.00	0.00	0.00	0.00	0.00	0
1	0.03	0.04	0.04	0.05	0.03	0.03	0.04	0.04	0.03	0.03	0.04	0.04	0.02	0.03	0.03	0.04	1
2	0.07	0.08	0.09	0.10	0.06	0.07	0.08	0.09	0.05	0.06	0.07	0.08	0.04	0.05	0.07	0.08	2
3	0.10	0.11	0.13	0.15	0.09	0.10	0.12	0.14	0.08	0.09	0.11	0.13	0.07	0.08	0.10	0.12	3
4	0.13	0.15	0.18	0.21	0.11	0.14	0.16	0.19	0.10	0.12	0.15	0.18	0.09	0.11	0.13	0.16	4
5	0.16	0.19	0.23	0.27	0.14	0.17	0.21	0.24	0.12	0.15	0.19	0.22	0.11	0.14	0.17	0.21	5
6	0.19	0.23	0.28	0.33	0.17	0.21	0.25	0.30	0.15	0.19	0.23	0.28	0.13	0.17	0.21	0.26	6
7	0.22	0.27	0.33	0.39	0.20	0.24	0.30	0.36	0.17	0.22	0.27	0.33	0.15	0.20	0.25	0.30	7
8	0.25	0.31	0.38	0.46	0.22	0.28	0.34	0.42	0.20	0.25	0.31	0.39	0.17	0.22	0.29	0.36	8
9	0.28	0.35	0.44	0.53	0.25	0.31	0.39	0.49	0.22	0.28	0.36	0.45	0.20	0.25	0.33	0.41	9
10	0.31	0.39	0.49	0.61	0.28	0.35	0.44	0.55	0.24	0.31	0.40	0.51	0.22	0.28	0.37	0.47	10
11	0.34	0.44	0.55	0.69	0.30	0.39	0.49	0.62	0.27	0.35	0.45	0.57	0.24	0.31	0.41	0.53	11
12	0.37	0.48	0.61	0.77	0.33	0.43	0.55	0.70	0.29	0.38	0.50	0.64	0.26	0.34	0.45	0.59	12
13	0.40	0.52	0.67	0.85	0.35	0.46	0.60	0.78	0.31	0.42	0.55	0.71	0.28	0.37	0.50	0.66	13
14	0.43	0.56	0.73	0.94	0.38	0.50	0.66	0.86	0.33	0.45	0.60	0.79	0.30	0.40	0.55	0.73	14
15	0.46	0.61	0.79	1.03	0.40	0.54	0.72	0.94	0.36	0.48	0.65	0.87	0.32	0.44	0.59	0.80	15
16	0.49	0.65	0.86	1.13	0.43	0.58	0.78	1.03	0.38	0.52	0.70	0.95	0.34	0.47	0.64	0.88	16
17	0.52	0.69	0.93	1.24	0.45	0.62	0.84	1.13	0.40	0.55	0.76	1.03	0.36	0.50	0.69	0.95	17
18	0.54	0.74	1.00	1.34	0.48	0.66	0.90	1.22	0.42	0.59	0.82	1.12	0.37	0.53	0.75	1.04	18
19	0.57	0.78	1.07	1.46	0.50	0.70	0.96	1.33	0.44	0.62	0.87	1.22	0.39	0.56	0.80	1.12	19
20	0.60	0.83	1.14	1.57	0.53	0.74	1.03	1.43	0.46	0.66	0.93	1.32	0.41	0.60	0.85	1.22	20
21	0.63	0.87	1.22	1.70	0.55	0.78	1.10	1.55	0.49	0.70	1.00	1.42	0.43	0.63	0.91	1.31	21
22	0.65	0.92	1.30	1.83	0.57	0.82	1.17	1.66	0.51	0.73	1.06	1.53	0.45	0.66	0.97	1.41	22
23	0.68	0.97	1.38	1.96	0.60	0.86	1.24	1.79	0.53	0.77	1.13	1.64	0.47	0.70	1.03	1.52	23
24	0.71	1.01	1.46	2.11	0.62	0.90	1.32	1.92	0.55	0.81	1.19	1.76	0.49	0.73	1.09	1.63	24
25	0.73	1.06	1.54	2.25	0.64	0.94	1.39	2.05	0.57	0.85	1.26	1.89	0.50	0.76	1.15	1.74	25
26	0.76	1.11	1.63	2.41	0.67	0.99	1.47	2.20	0.59	0.88	1.33	2.02	0.52	0.80	1.22	1.86	26
27	0.78	1.16	1.72	2.57	0.69	1.03	1.55	2.35	0.61	0.92	1.41	2.15	0.54	0.83	1.29	1.99	27
28	0.81	1.21	1.81	2.75	0.71	1.07	1.63	2.50	0.63	0.96	1.48	2.30	0.56	0.87	1.36	2.12	28
29	0.83	1.26	1.91	2.93	0.73	1.12	1.72	2.66	0.65	1.00	1.56	2.45	0.57	0.90	1.43	2.26	29
30	0.86	1.31	2.01	3.11	0.75	1.16	1.81	2.84	0.67	1.04	1.64	2.60	0.59	0.94	1.50	2.41	30
31	0.88	1.36	2.11	3.31	0.78	1.21	1.90	3.02	0.68	1.08	1.72	2.77	0.61	0.97	1.57	2.56	31
32	0.91	1.41	2.21	3.52	0.80	1.25	1.99	3.20	0.70	1.12	1.81	2.94	0.63	1.01	1.65	2.72	32
33	0.93	1.46	2.32	3.73	0.82	1.30	2.09	3.40	0.72	1.16	1.90	3.12	0.64	1.05	1.73	2.88	33
34	0.96	1.51	2.43	3.96	0.84	1.34	2.19	3.61	0.74	1.20	1.98	3.31	0.66	1.08	1.81	3.06	34
35	0.98	1.56	2.54	4.20	0.86	1.39	2.29	3.82	0.76	1.24	2.08	3.51	0.67	1.12	1.90	3.24	35
36	1.00	1.61	2.66	4.45	0.88	1.44	2.39	4.05	0.78	1.29	2.17	3.72	0.69	1.16	1.98	3.43	36
37	1.03	1.67	2.77	4.71	0.90	1.48	2.50	4.29	0.80	1.33	2.27	3.94	0.71	1.20	2.07	3.64	37
38	1.05	1.72	2.90	4.98	0.92	1.53	2.61	4.54	0.81	1.37	2.37	4.16	0.72	1.24	2.16	3.85	38
39	1.07	1.77	3.02	5.26	0.94	1.58	2.72	4.80	0.83	1.42	2.47	4.40	0.74	1.28	2.26	4.07	39
40	1.09	1.83	3.15	5.56	0.96	1.63	2.84	5.07	0.85	1.46	2.58	4.65	0.75	1.32	2.35	4.30	40
41	1.12	1.88	3.29	5.88	0.98	1.68	2.96	5.35	0.87	1.50	2.69	4.92	0.77	1.35	2.45	4.54	41
42	1.14	1.94	3.42	6.21	1.00	1.73	3.08	5.65	0.88	1.55	2.80	5.19	0.78	1.39	2.56	4.80	42
43	1.16	2.00	3.56	6.55	1.02	1.78	3.21	5.97	0.90	1.59	2.91	5.48	0.80	1.44	2.66	5.06	43
44	1.18	2.05	3.71	6.91	1.04	1.83	3.34	6.30	0.92	1.64	3.03	5.78	0.81	1.48	2.77	5.34	44
45	1.20	2.11	3.86	7.29	1.06	1.88	3.48	6.64	0.93	1.68	3.16	6.10	0.83	1.52	2.88	5.63	45
46	1.23	2.17	4.01	7.68	1.08	1.93	3.61	7.00	0.95	1.73	3.28	6.43	0.84	1.56	3.00	5.94	46
47	1.25	2.23	4.17	8.10	1.09	1.98	3.76	7.38	0.97	1.78	3.41	6.77	0.86	1.60	3.11	6.26	47
48	1.27	2.29	4.33	8.53	1.11	2.03	3.90	7.77	0.98	1.82	3.54	7.14	0.87	1.64	3.24	6.59	48
49	1.29	2.35	4.50	8.99	1.13	2.09	4.05	8.19	1.00	1.87	3.68	7.52	0.89	1.69	3.36	6.94	49
50	1.31	2.41	4.67	9.46	1.15	2.14	4.21	8.62	1.01	1.92	3.82	7.92	0.90	1.73	3.49	7.31	50

IV. Retirement Planning where Salary Falls Behind Moderate 6% Inflation
Planned Retirement Age 62

Table 3 - 401(k) Contribution (% of Current Sal.) Needed to Replace 10% of Sal. at Retirement   IV-62-3

Probable Life Expectancy at Retirement

	23.2 (Same as Male Avg.)				25.7 (Better than Male Avg.)				28.3 (Same as Female Avg.)				31 (Better than Female Avg.)				
	4% / 4%	6% / 5%	8% / 6%	10% / 7%	4% / 4%	6% / 5%	8% / 6%	10% / 7%	4% / 4%	6% / 5%	8% / 6%	10% / 7%	4% / 4%	6% / 5%	8% / 6%	10% / 7%	
Yrs. to Ret.			Expected Return		(Pre-Retirement/Post-Retirement)				(Pre-Retirement/Post-Retirement)				Expected Return				Yrs. to Ret.
0																	0
1	305.23	264.50	231.73	204.82	347.88	297.27	257.23	224.84	393.78	331.68	283.38	244.91	443.29	367.89	310.25	265.08	1
2	153.34	131.62	114.23	100.03	174.77	147.93	126.80	109.81	197.83	165.06	139.69	119.61	222.71	183.08	152.94	129.46	2
3	102.72	87.33	75.08	65.12	117.07	98.16	83.34	71.49	132.52	109.52	91.81	77.87	149.18	121.47	100.51	84.28	3
4	77.40	65.19	55.51	47.69	88.22	73.27	61.61	52.35	99.86	81.75	67.88	57.03	112.42	90.67	74.31	61.72	4
5	62.22	51.90	43.77	37.24	70.91	58.34	48.59	40.89	80.27	65.09	53.52	44.54	90.36	72.19	58.60	48.20	5
6	52.09	43.05	35.95	30.29	59.37	48.38	39.91	33.26	67.21	53.98	43.96	36.22	75.66	59.88	48.13	39.21	6
7	44.86	36.72	30.37	25.34	51.13	41.27	33.71	27.82	57.88	46.05	37.14	30.30	65.16	51.08	40.66	32.80	7
8	39.44	31.98	26.19	21.63	44.95	35.94	29.07	23.75	50.88	40.10	32.03	25.87	57.28	44.48	35.06	28.00	8
9	35.22	28.29	22.94	18.76	40.15	31.80	25.47	20.59	45.44	35.48	28.05	22.43	51.16	39.35	30.71	24.28	9
10	31.85	25.34	20.34	16.47	36.30	28.48	22.58	18.08	41.09	31.78	24.88	19.69	46.26	35.24	27.24	21.31	10
11	29.09	22.92	18.22	14.60	33.16	25.77	20.23	16.03	37.53	28.75	22.29	17.46	42.25	31.89	24.40	18.89	11
12	26.79	20.91	16.46	13.05	30.54	23.50	18.27	14.32	34.57	26.23	20.13	15.60	38.91	29.09	22.04	16.89	12
13	24.85	19.21	14.97	11.74	28.32	21.59	16.61	12.89	32.04	24.09	18.30	14.04	36.09	26.72	20.04	15.20	13
14	23.18	17.75	13.69	10.63	26.42	19.95	15.20	11.66	29.91	22.26	16.74	12.71	33.67	24.69	18.33	13.75	14
15	21.74	16.49	12.59	9.66	24.77	18.53	13.97	10.61	28.04	20.68	15.39	11.56	31.57	22.94	16.85	12.51	15
16	20.47	15.38	11.62	8.83	23.33	17.29	12.90	9.69	26.41	19.29	14.21	10.56	29.73	21.40	15.56	11.43	16
17	19.36	14.41	10.78	8.09	22.06	16.20	11.96	8.89	24.97	18.07	13.18	9.68	28.11	20.04	14.43	10.48	17
18	18.37	13.54	10.02	7.44	20.93	15.22	11.13	8.17	23.70	16.98	12.26	8.90	26.68	18.84	13.42	9.64	18
19	17.48	12.77	9.35	6.87	19.92	14.35	10.38	7.54	22.55	16.01	11.43	8.21	25.39	17.76	12.52	8.89	19
20	16.68	12.07	8.75	6.35	19.02	13.57	9.71	6.97	21.53	15.14	10.70	7.60	24.23	16.79	11.71	8.22	20
21	15.96	11.44	8.20	5.89	18.19	12.86	9.11	6.47	20.60	14.35	10.03	7.04	23.18	15.91	10.98	7.62	21
22	15.31	10.87	7.71	5.47	17.45	12.21	8.56	6.01	19.75	13.63	9.43	6.54	22.23	15.11	10.32	7.08	22
23	14.71	10.34	7.26	5.09	16.77	11.63	8.06	5.59	18.98	12.97	8.88	6.09	21.36	14.39	9.72	6.59	23
24	14.16	9.86	6.85	4.75	16.14	11.09	7.60	5.21	18.27	12.37	8.38	5.68	20.57	13.72	9.17	6.15	24
25	13.66	9.42	6.47	4.44	15.57	10.59	7.19	4.87	17.62	11.82	7.92	5.30	19.84	13.11	8.67	5.74	25
26	13.19	9.02	6.13	4.15	15.04	10.13	6.80	4.55	17.02	11.31	7.49	4.96	19.16	12.54	8.20	5.37	26
27	12.76	8.64	5.81	3.88	14.55	9.71	6.45	4.26	16.47	10.83	7.10	4.65	18.54	12.02	7.78	5.03	27
28	12.36	8.29	5.51	3.64	14.09	9.32	6.12	4.00	15.95	10.40	6.74	4.36	17.96	11.53	7.38	4.71	28
29	11.99	7.96	5.24	3.42	13.67	8.95	5.81	3.75	15.47	9.99	6.40	4.09	17.42	11.08	7.01	4.42	29
30	11.64	7.66	4.98	3.21	13.27	8.61	5.53	3.53	15.02	9.61	6.09	3.84	16.91	10.66	6.67	4.16	30
31	11.32	7.38	4.74	3.02	12.90	8.29	5.27	3.32	14.60	9.25	5.80	3.61	16.44	10.26	6.35	3.91	31
32	11.02	7.11	4.52	2.84	12.56	7.99	5.02	3.12	14.21	8.92	5.53	3.40	16.00	9.89	6.06	3.68	32
33	10.73	6.86	4.31	2.68	12.23	7.71	4.79	2.94	13.84	8.61	5.28	3.20	15.59	9.54	5.78	3.47	33
34	10.46	6.63	4.12	2.53	11.92	7.45	4.57	2.77	13.50	8.31	5.04	3.02	15.20	9.22	5.52	3.27	34
35	10.21	6.41	3.94	2.38	11.64	7.20	4.37	2.62	13.17	8.03	4.82	2.85	14.83	8.91	5.27	3.08	35
36	9.97	6.20	3.77	2.25	11.36	6.96	4.18	2.47	12.86	7.77	4.61	2.69	14.48	8.62	5.04	2.91	36
37	9.75	6.00	3.60	2.13	11.11	6.74	4.00	2.33	12.57	7.52	4.41	2.54	14.15	8.34	4.83	2.75	37
38	9.53	5.81	3.45	2.01	10.86	6.53	3.83	2.21	12.30	7.29	4.22	2.40	13.84	8.08	4.62	2.60	38
39	9.33	5.63	3.31	1.90	10.63	6.33	3.67	2.09	12.04	7.07	4.05	2.27	13.55	7.84	4.43	2.46	39
40	9.14	5.47	3.17	1.80	10.41	6.14	3.52	1.97	11.79	6.86	3.88	2.15	13.27	7.60	4.25	2.33	40
41	8.95	5.31	3.04	1.70	10.20	5.96	3.38	1.87	11.55	6.65	3.72	2.03	13.00	7.38	4.07	2.20	41
42	8.78	5.15	2.92	1.61	10.01	5.79	3.24	1.77	11.33	6.46	3.57	1.93	12.75	7.17	3.91	2.09	42
43	8.61	5.01	2.81	1.53	9.82	5.63	3.11	1.68	11.11	6.28	3.43	1.83	12.51	6.97	3.76	1.98	43
44	8.46	4.87	2.70	1.45	9.64	5.47	2.99	1.59	10.91	6.11	3.30	1.73	12.28	6.77	3.61	1.87	44
45	8.30	4.74	2.59	1.37	9.46	5.33	2.88	1.51	10.71	5.94	3.17	1.64	12.06	6.59	3.47	1.78	45
46	8.16	4.61	2.49	1.30	9.30	5.18	2.77	1.43	10.53	5.78	3.05	1.56	11.85	6.41	3.34	1.68	46
47	8.02	4.49	2.40	1.23	9.14	5.05	2.66	1.36	10.35	5.63	2.93	1.48	11.65	6.25	3.21	1.60	47
48	7.89	4.37	2.31	1.17	8.99	4.92	2.56	1.29	10.18	5.49	2.82	1.40	11.46	6.09	3.09	1.52	48
49	7.76	4.26	2.22	1.11	8.85	4.79	2.47	1.22	10.01	5.35	2.72	1.33	11.27	5.93	2.98	1.44	49
50	7.64	4.16	2.14	1.06	8.71	4.67	2.38	1.16	9.86	5.21	2.62	1.26	11.10	5.78	2.87	1.37	50

IV. Retirement Planning where Salary Falls Behind Moderate 6% Inflation
Planned Retirement Age 62

Table 4 - Accumulation at Retirement (Multiple of Current Sal.) for 10% Sal. Replacement   IV-62-4

Probable Life Expectancy at Retirement

Yrs. to Ret.	23.2 (Same as Male Avg.) 4%/4%	6%/5%	8%/6%	10%/7%	25.7 (Better than Male Avg.) 4%/4%	6%/5%	8%/6%	10%/7%	28.3 (Same as Female Avg.) 4%/4%	6%/5%	8%/6%	10%/7%	31 (Better than Female Avg.) 4%/4%	6%/5%	8%/6%	10%/7%	Yrs. to Ret.
	Expected Return				(Pre-Retirement/Post-Retirement)				(Pre-Retirement/Post-Retirement)				Expected Return				
0	3.05	2.64	2.32	2.05	3.48	2.97	2.57	2.25	3.94	3.32	2.83	2.45	4.43	3.68	3.10	2.65	0
1	3.20	2.78	2.43	2.15	3.65	3.12	2.70	2.36	4.13	3.48	2.98	2.57	4.65	3.86	3.26	2.78	1
2	3.37	2.92	2.55	2.26	3.84	3.28	2.84	2.48	4.34	3.66	3.12	2.70	4.89	4.06	3.42	2.92	2
3	3.53	3.06	2.68	2.37	4.03	3.44	2.98	2.60	4.56	3.84	3.28	2.84	5.13	4.26	3.59	3.07	3
4	3.71	3.21	2.82	2.49	4.23	3.61	3.13	2.73	4.79	4.03	3.44	2.98	5.39	4.47	3.77	3.22	4
5	3.90	3.38	2.96	2.61	4.44	3.79	3.28	2.87	5.03	4.23	3.62	3.13	5.66	4.70	3.96	3.38	5
6	4.09	3.54	3.11	2.74	4.66	3.98	3.45	3.01	5.28	4.44	3.80	3.28	5.94	4.93	4.16	3.55	6
7	4.29	3.72	3.26	2.88	4.90	4.18	3.62	3.16	5.54	4.67	3.99	3.45	6.24	5.18	4.37	3.73	7
8	4.51	3.91	3.42	3.03	5.14	4.39	3.80	3.32	5.82	4.90	4.19	3.62	6.55	5.44	4.58	3.92	8
9	4.74	4.10	3.59	3.18	5.40	4.61	3.99	3.49	6.11	5.15	4.40	3.80	6.88	5.71	4.81	4.11	9
10	4.97	4.31	3.77	3.34	5.67	4.84	4.19	3.66	6.41	5.40	4.62	3.99	7.22	5.99	5.05	4.32	10
11	5.22	4.52	3.96	3.50	5.95	5.08	4.40	3.85	6.74	5.67	4.85	4.19	7.58	6.29	5.31	4.53	11
12	5.48	4.75	4.16	3.68	6.25	5.34	4.62	4.04	7.07	5.96	5.09	4.40	7.96	6.61	5.57	4.76	12
13	5.76	4.99	4.37	3.86	6.56	5.61	4.85	4.24	7.43	6.25	5.34	4.62	8.36	6.94	5.85	5.00	13
14	6.04	5.24	4.59	4.06	6.89	5.89	5.09	4.45	7.80	6.57	5.61	4.85	8.78	7.28	6.14	5.25	14
15	6.35	5.50	4.82	4.26	7.23	6.18	5.35	4.67	8.19	6.90	5.89	5.09	9.22	7.65	6.45	5.51	15
16	6.66	5.77	5.06	4.47	7.59	6.49	5.62	4.91	8.60	7.24	6.19	5.35	9.68	8.03	6.77	5.79	16
17	7.00	6.06	5.31	4.69	7.97	6.81	5.90	5.15	9.03	7.60	6.50	5.61	10.16	8.43	7.11	6.08	17
18	7.35	6.37	5.58	4.93	8.37	7.15	6.19	5.41	9.48	7.98	6.82	5.89	10.67	8.85	7.47	6.38	18
19	7.71	6.68	5.86	5.18	8.79	7.51	6.50	5.68	9.95	8.38	7.16	6.19	11.20	9.30	7.84	6.70	19
20	8.10	7.02	6.15	5.43	9.23	7.89	6.83	5.97	10.45	8.80	7.52	6.50	11.76	9.76	8.23	7.03	20
21	8.50	7.37	6.46	5.71	9.69	8.28	7.17	6.26	10.97	9.24	7.89	6.82	12.35	10.25	8.64	7.39	21
22	8.93	7.74	6.78	5.99	10.18	8.70	7.52	6.58	11.52	9.70	8.29	7.16	12.97	10.76	9.08	7.75	22
23	9.38	8.12	7.12	6.29	10.69	9.13	7.90	6.91	12.10	10.19	8.70	7.52	13.62	11.30	9.53	8.14	23
24	9.84	8.53	7.47	6.61	11.22	9.59	8.30	7.25	12.70	10.70	9.14	7.90	14.30	11.86	10.01	8.55	24
25	10.34	8.96	7.85	6.94	11.78	10.07	8.71	7.61	13.33	11.23	9.60	8.29	15.01	12.46	10.51	8.98	25
26	10.85	9.40	8.24	7.28	12.37	10.57	9.15	7.99	14.00	11.79	10.08	8.71	15.76	13.08	11.03	9.43	26
27	11.40	9.87	8.65	7.65	12.99	11.10	9.60	8.39	14.70	12.38	10.58	9.14	16.55	13.74	11.58	9.90	27
28	11.97	10.37	9.08	8.03	13.64	11.65	10.08	8.81	15.44	13.00	11.11	9.60	17.38	14.42	12.16	10.39	28
29	12.56	10.89	9.54	8.43	14.32	12.24	10.59	9.25	16.21	13.65	11.66	10.08	18.25	15.14	12.77	10.91	29
30	13.19	11.43	10.02	8.85	15.04	12.85	11.12	9.72	17.02	14.34	12.25	10.59	19.16	15.90	13.41	11.46	30
31	13.85	12.00	10.52	9.29	15.79	13.49	11.67	10.20	17.87	15.05	12.86	11.11	20.12	16.70	14.08	12.03	31
32	14.54	12.60	11.04	9.76	16.58	14.16	12.26	10.71	18.76	15.80	13.50	11.67	21.12	17.53	14.78	12.63	32
33	15.27	13.23	11.59	10.25	17.41	14.87	12.87	11.25	19.70	16.59	14.18	12.25	22.18	18.41	15.52	13.26	33
34	16.03	13.89	12.17	10.76	18.28	15.62	13.51	11.81	20.69	17.42	14.89	12.87	23.29	19.33	16.30	13.93	34
35	16.84	14.59	12.78	11.30	19.19	16.40	14.19	12.40	21.72	18.30	15.63	13.51	24.45	20.29	17.11	14.62	35
36	17.68	15.32	13.42	11.86	20.15	17.22	14.90	13.02	22.81	19.21	16.41	14.18	25.67	21.31	17.97	15.35	36
37	18.56	16.09	14.09	12.46	21.16	18.08	15.64	13.67	23.95	20.17	17.23	14.89	26.96	22.37	18.87	16.12	37
38	19.49	16.89	14.80	13.08	22.21	18.98	16.43	14.36	25.14	21.18	18.09	15.64	28.31	23.49	19.81	16.93	38
39	20.46	17.73	15.54	13.73	23.32	19.93	17.25	15.08	26.40	22.24	19.00	16.42	29.72	24.67	20.80	17.77	39
40	21.49	18.62	16.31	14.42	24.49	20.93	18.11	15.83	27.72	23.35	19.95	17.24	31.21	25.90	21.84	18.66	40
41	22.56	19.55	17.13	15.14	25.72	21.97	19.01	16.62	29.11	24.52	20.95	18.10	32.77	27.19	22.93	19.59	41
42	23.69	20.53	17.99	15.90	27.00	23.07	19.97	17.45	30.56	25.74	21.99	19.01	34.41	28.55	24.08	20.57	42
43	24.88	21.56	18.89	16.69	28.35	24.23	20.96	18.32	32.09	27.03	23.09	19.96	36.13	29.98	25.28	21.60	43
44	26.12	22.63	19.83	17.53	29.77	25.44	22.01	19.24	33.70	28.38	24.25	20.96	37.93	31.48	26.55	22.68	44
45	27.42	23.77	20.82	18.40	31.26	26.71	23.11	20.20	35.38	29.80	25.46	22.01	39.83	33.06	27.88	23.82	45
46	28.80	24.95	21.86	19.32	32.82	28.05	24.27	21.21	37.15	31.29	26.73	23.11	41.82	34.71	29.27	25.01	46
47	30.24	26.20	22.96	20.29	34.46	29.45	25.48	22.27	39.01	32.86	28.07	24.26	43.91	36.44	30.73	26.26	47
48	31.75	27.51	24.10	21.30	36.18	30.92	26.76	23.39	40.96	34.50	29.47	25.47	46.11	38.27	32.27	27.57	48
49	33.34	28.89	25.31	22.37	37.99	32.47	28.09	24.56	43.01	36.22	30.95	26.75	48.41	40.18	33.88	28.95	49
50	35.00	30.33	26.57	23.49	39.89	34.09	29.50	25.78	45.16	38.04	32.50	28.09	50.83	42.19	35.58	30.40	50

IV. Retirement Planning where Salary Falls Behind Moderate 6% Inflation Planned Retirement Age 65

| Table 1 - Percent of Salary Replaced by a 401(k) Account Equal to Current Annual Salary | IV-65-1 |

Probable Life Expectancy at Retirement

	20.7 (Same as Male Avg.)				23.2 (Better than Male Avg.)				25.7 (Same as Female Avg.)				28.3 (Better than Female Avg.)				
	4% / 4%	6% / 5%	8% / 6%	10% / 7%	4% / 4%	6% / 5%	8% / 6%	10% / 7%	4% / 4%	6% / 5%	8% / 6%	10% / 7%	4% / 4%	6% / 5%	8% / 6%	10% / 7%	
Yrs. to Ret.	Expected Return		(Pre-Retirement/Post-Retirement)				(Pre-Retirement/Post-Retirement)				Expected Return						Yrs. to Ret.
0	3.77	4.29	4.84	5.41	3.28	3.78	4.32	4.88	2.87	3.36	3.89	4.45	2.54	3.01	3.53	4.08	0
1	3.73	4.33	4.97	5.67	3.25	3.82	4.44	5.11	2.85	3.40	4.00	4.66	2.52	3.04	3.63	4.28	1
2	3.69	4.37	5.12	5.94	3.21	3.85	4.57	5.36	2.82	3.43	4.11	4.88	2.49	3.07	3.73	4.48	2
3	3.66	4.41	5.26	6.22	3.18	3.89	4.70	5.61	2.79	3.46	4.23	5.11	2.47	3.10	3.84	4.69	3
4	3.62	4.45	5.41	6.52	3.15	3.93	4.83	5.88	2.77	3.49	4.35	5.36	2.44	3.13	3.95	4.92	4
5	3.59	4.49	5.57	6.83	3.12	3.96	4.97	6.16	2.74	3.53	4.48	5.61	2.42	3.16	4.06	5.15	5
6	3.56	4.54	5.73	7.15	3.09	4.00	5.11	6.45	2.71	3.56	4.60	5.88	2.40	3.19	4.18	5.40	6
7	3.52	4.58	5.89	7.49	3.06	4.04	5.26	6.76	2.69	3.59	4.74	6.16	2.38	3.22	4.30	5.65	7
8	3.49	4.62	6.06	7.85	3.04	4.08	5.41	7.08	2.66	3.63	4.87	6.45	2.35	3.25	4.42	5.92	8
9	3.46	4.67	6.23	8.22	3.01	4.12	5.56	7.42	2.64	3.66	5.01	6.76	2.33	3.28	4.55	6.21	9
10	3.42	4.71	6.41	8.62	2.98	4.16	5.72	7.77	2.61	3.70	5.15	7.08	2.31	3.31	4.68	6.50	10
11	3.39	4.76	6.59	9.03	2.95	4.20	5.88	8.14	2.59	3.73	5.30	7.42	2.29	3.35	4.81	6.81	11
12	3.36	4.80	6.78	9.45	2.92	4.24	6.05	8.53	2.56	3.77	5.45	7.77	2.26	3.38	4.95	7.13	12
13	3.33	4.85	6.98	9.90	2.89	4.28	6.23	8.94	2.54	3.80	5.61	8.14	2.24	3.41	5.09	7.47	13
14	3.29	4.89	7.18	10.38	2.87	4.32	6.40	9.36	2.51	3.84	5.77	8.53	2.22	3.44	5.24	7.83	14
15	3.26	4.94	7.38	10.87	2.84	4.36	6.59	9.81	2.49	3.88	5.93	8.93	2.20	3.47	5.39	8.20	15
16	3.23	4.99	7.59	11.39	2.81	4.40	6.78	10.27	2.47	3.91	6.10	9.36	2.18	3.51	5.54	8.59	16
17	3.20	5.04	7.81	11.93	2.79	4.44	6.97	10.76	2.44	3.95	6.28	9.80	2.16	3.54	5.70	9.00	17
18	3.17	5.08	8.03	12.50	2.76	4.48	7.17	11.28	2.42	3.99	6.46	10.27	2.14	3.57	5.86	9.43	18
19	3.14	5.13	8.26	13.09	2.73	4.52	7.37	11.81	2.40	4.03	6.64	10.76	2.12	3.61	6.03	9.88	19
20	3.11	5.18	8.50	13.72	2.71	4.57	7.58	12.38	2.37	4.06	6.83	11.27	2.10	3.64	6.20	10.35	20
21	3.08	5.23	8.74	14.37	2.68	4.61	7.80	12.96	2.35	4.10	7.03	11.81	2.08	3.68	6.38	10.84	21
22	3.05	5.28	8.99	15.05	2.66	4.65	8.02	13.58	2.33	4.14	7.23	12.37	2.06	3.71	6.56	11.36	22
23	3.02	5.33	9.25	15.77	2.63	4.70	8.25	14.23	2.31	4.18	7.44	12.96	2.04	3.75	6.75	11.90	23
24	2.99	5.38	9.51	16.52	2.61	4.74	8.49	14.90	2.29	4.22	7.65	13.58	2.02	3.78	6.94	12.46	24
25	2.97	5.43	9.79	17.31	2.58	4.79	8.73	15.61	2.26	4.26	7.87	14.22	2.00	3.82	7.14	13.06	25
26	2.94	5.48	10.06	18.13	2.56	4.83	8.98	16.36	2.24	4.30	8.09	14.90	1.98	3.86	7.35	13.68	26
27	2.91	5.53	10.35	18.99	2.53	4.88	9.24	17.14	2.22	4.34	8.32	15.61	1.96	3.89	7.56	14.33	27
28	2.88	5.59	10.65	19.90	2.51	4.93	9.50	17.95	2.20	4.38	8.56	16.35	1.94	3.93	7.77	15.01	28
29	2.86	5.64	10.95	20.84	2.48	4.97	9.78	18.81	2.18	4.43	8.81	17.13	1.93	3.97	7.99	15.73	29
30	2.83	5.69	11.27	21.84	2.46	5.02	10.06	19.70	2.16	4.47	9.06	17.95	1.91	4.00	8.22	16.48	30
31	2.80	5.75	11.59	22.88	2.44	5.07	10.34	20.64	2.14	4.51	9.32	18.80	1.89	4.04	8.46	17.26	31
32	2.77	5.80	11.92	23.96	2.41	5.12	10.64	21.62	2.12	4.55	9.58	19.70	1.87	4.08	8.70	18.08	32
33	2.75	5.86	12.26	25.10	2.39	5.17	10.94	22.65	2.10	4.60	9.86	20.63	1.85	4.12	8.95	18.94	33
34	2.72	5.91	12.61	26.30	2.37	5.21	11.26	23.73	2.08	4.64	10.14	21.62	1.84	4.16	9.20	19.84	34
35	2.70	5.97	12.97	27.55	2.35	5.26	11.58	24.86	2.06	4.68	10.43	22.64	1.82	4.20	9.47	20.79	35
36	2.67	6.03	13.34	28.86	2.32	5.31	11.91	26.04	2.04	4.73	10.73	23.72	1.80	4.24	9.74	21.78	36
37	2.65	6.08	13.73	30.24	2.30	5.36	12.25	27.28	2.02	4.77	11.04	24.85	1.78	4.28	10.02	22.81	37
38	2.62	6.14	14.12	31.68	2.28	5.42	12.60	28.58	2.00	4.82	11.35	26.03	1.77	4.32	10.30	23.90	38
39	2.60	6.20	14.52	33.18	2.26	5.47	12.96	29.94	1.98	4.86	11.68	27.27	1.75	4.36	10.60	25.04	39
40	2.57	6.26	14.94	34.76	2.24	5.52	13.33	31.37	1.96	4.91	12.01	28.57	1.73	4.40	10.90	26.23	40
41	2.55	6.32	15.36	36.42	2.22	5.57	13.71	32.86	1.94	4.96	12.35	29.93	1.72	4.44	11.21	27.48	41
42	2.52	6.38	15.80	38.15	2.19	5.62	14.10	34.42	1.93	5.00	12.71	31.36	1.70	4.48	11.53	28.79	42
43	2.50	6.44	16.26	39.97	2.17	5.68	14.51	36.06	1.91	5.05	13.07	32.85	1.68	4.53	11.86	30.16	43
44	2.47	6.50	16.72	41.87	2.15	5.73	14.92	37.78	1.89	5.10	13.44	34.41	1.67	4.57	12.20	31.59	44
45	2.45	6.56	17.20	43.86	2.13	5.79	15.35	39.58	1.87	5.15	13.83	36.05	1.65	4.61	12.55	33.10	45
46	2.43	6.62	17.69	45.95	2.11	5.84	15.79	41.46	1.85	5.20	14.22	37.77	1.64	4.66	12.91	34.67	46
47	2.40	6.69	18.20	48.14	2.09	5.90	16.24	43.43	1.84	5.25	14.63	39.56	1.62	4.70	13.28	36.32	47
48	2.38	6.75	18.72	50.43	2.07	5.95	16.71	45.50	1.82	5.30	15.05	41.45	1.61	4.75	13.66	38.05	48
49	2.36	6.81	19.25	52.83	2.05	6.01	17.18	47.67	1.80	5.35	15.48	43.42	1.59	4.79	14.05	39.86	49
50	2.34	6.88	19.80	55.34	2.03	6.07	17.67	49.94	1.78	5.40	15.92	45.49	1.58	4.84	14.45	41.76	50

Appendix A

**IV. Retirement Planning where Salary Falls Behind Moderate 6% Inflation
Planned Retirement Age 65**

Table 2 - Percent of Salary Replaced by a 401(k) Contribution of 1% of Current Salary

Probable Life Expectancy at Retirement

Yrs. to Ret.	20.7 (Same as Male Avg.)				23.2 (Better than Male Avg.)				25.7 (Same as Female Avg.)				28.3 (Better than Female Avg.)				Yrs. to Ret.
	4% / 4%	6% / 5%	8% / 6%	10% / 7%	4% / 4%	6% / 5%	8% / 6%	10% / 7%	4% / 4%	6% / 5%	8% / 6%	10% / 7%	4% / 4%	6% / 5%	8% / 6%	10% / 7%	
	Expected Return				(Pre-Retirement/Post-Retirement)				(Pre-Retirement/Post-Retirement)				Expected Return				
0	0.00	0.00	0.00	0.00	0.00	0.00	0.00	0.00	0.00	0.00	0.00	0.00	0.00	0.00	0.00	0.00	0
1	0.04	0.04	0.05	0.05	0.03	0.04	0.04	0.05	0.03	0.03	0.04	0.04	0.03	0.03	0.04	0.04	1
2	0.07	0.09	0.10	0.11	0.07	0.08	0.09	0.10	0.06	0.07	0.08	0.09	0.05	0.06	0.07	0.08	2
3	0.11	0.13	0.15	0.17	0.10	0.11	0.13	0.15	0.09	0.10	0.12	0.14	0.08	0.09	0.11	0.13	3
4	0.15	0.17	0.20	0.23	0.13	0.15	0.18	0.21	0.11	0.14	0.16	0.19	0.10	0.12	0.15	0.18	4
5	0.18	0.22	0.26	0.30	0.16	0.19	0.23	0.27	0.14	0.17	0.21	0.24	0.12	0.15	0.19	0.22	5
6	0.22	0.26	0.31	0.37	0.19	0.23	0.28	0.33	0.17	0.21	0.25	0.30	0.15	0.19	0.23	0.28	6
7	0.26	0.31	0.37	0.44	0.22	0.27	0.33	0.39	0.20	0.24	0.30	0.36	0.17	0.22	0.27	0.33	7
8	0.29	0.35	0.43	0.51	0.25	0.31	0.38	0.46	0.22	0.28	0.34	0.42	0.20	0.25	0.31	0.39	8
9	0.33	0.40	0.49	0.59	0.28	0.35	0.44	0.53	0.25	0.31	0.39	0.49	0.22	0.28	0.36	0.45	9
10	0.36	0.45	0.55	0.67	0.31	0.39	0.49	0.61	0.28	0.35	0.44	0.55	0.24	0.31	0.40	0.51	10
11	0.40	0.49	0.61	0.76	0.34	0.44	0.55	0.69	0.30	0.39	0.49	0.62	0.27	0.35	0.45	0.57	11
12	0.43	0.54	0.68	0.85	0.37	0.48	0.61	0.77	0.33	0.43	0.55	0.70	0.29	0.38	0.50	0.64	12
13	0.46	0.59	0.75	0.94	0.40	0.52	0.67	0.85	0.35	0.46	0.60	0.78	0.31	0.42	0.55	0.71	13
14	0.50	0.64	0.82	1.04	0.43	0.56	0.73	0.94	0.38	0.50	0.66	0.86	0.33	0.45	0.60	0.79	14
15	0.53	0.69	0.89	1.15	0.46	0.61	0.79	1.03	0.40	0.54	0.72	0.94	0.36	0.48	0.65	0.87	15
16	0.56	0.74	0.96	1.26	0.49	0.65	0.86	1.13	0.43	0.58	0.78	1.03	0.38	0.52	0.70	0.95	16
17	0.59	0.79	1.04	1.37	0.52	0.69	0.93	1.24	0.45	0.62	0.84	1.13	0.40	0.55	0.76	1.03	17
18	0.63	0.84	1.12	1.49	0.54	0.74	1.00	1.34	0.48	0.66	0.90	1.22	0.42	0.59	0.82	1.12	18
19	0.66	0.89	1.20	1.61	0.57	0.78	1.07	1.46	0.50	0.70	0.96	1.33	0.44	0.62	0.87	1.22	19
20	0.69	0.94	1.28	1.74	0.60	0.83	1.14	1.57	0.53	0.74	1.03	1.43	0.46	0.66	0.93	1.32	20
21	0.72	0.99	1.37	1.88	0.63	0.87	1.22	1.70	0.55	0.78	1.10	1.55	0.49	0.70	1.00	1.42	21
22	0.75	1.04	1.45	2.03	0.65	0.92	1.30	1.83	0.57	0.82	1.17	1.66	0.51	0.73	1.06	1.53	22
23	0.78	1.10	1.54	2.18	0.68	0.97	1.38	1.96	0.60	0.86	1.24	1.79	0.53	0.77	1.13	1.64	23
24	0.81	1.15	1.64	2.33	0.71	1.01	1.46	2.11	0.62	0.90	1.32	1.92	0.55	0.81	1.19	1.76	24
25	0.84	1.20	1.73	2.50	0.73	1.06	1.54	2.25	0.64	0.94	1.39	2.05	0.57	0.85	1.26	1.89	25
26	0.87	1.26	1.83	2.67	0.76	1.11	1.63	2.41	0.67	0.99	1.47	2.20	0.59	0.88	1.33	2.02	26
27	0.90	1.31	1.93	2.85	0.78	1.16	1.72	2.57	0.69	1.03	1.55	2.35	0.61	0.92	1.41	2.15	27
28	0.93	1.37	2.03	3.04	0.81	1.21	1.81	2.75	0.71	1.07	1.63	2.50	0.63	0.96	1.48	2.30	28
29	0.96	1.42	2.14	3.24	0.83	1.26	1.91	2.93	0.73	1.12	1.72	2.66	0.65	1.00	1.56	2.45	29
30	0.99	1.48	2.25	3.45	0.86	1.31	2.01	3.11	0.75	1.16	1.81	2.84	0.67	1.04	1.64	2.60	30
31	1.02	1.54	2.36	3.67	0.88	1.36	2.11	3.31	0.78	1.21	1.90	3.02	0.68	1.08	1.72	2.77	31
32	1.04	1.59	2.48	3.90	0.91	1.41	2.21	3.52	0.80	1.25	1.99	3.20	0.70	1.12	1.81	2.94	32
33	1.07	1.65	2.60	4.14	0.93	1.46	2.32	3.73	0.82	1.30	2.09	3.40	0.72	1.16	1.90	3.12	33
34	1.10	1.71	2.72	4.39	0.96	1.51	2.43	3.96	0.84	1.34	2.19	3.61	0.74	1.20	1.98	3.31	34
35	1.13	1.77	2.85	4.65	0.98	1.56	2.54	4.20	0.86	1.39	2.29	3.82	0.76	1.24	2.08	3.51	35
36	1.15	1.83	2.98	4.93	1.00	1.61	2.66	4.45	0.88	1.44	2.39	4.05	0.78	1.29	2.17	3.72	36
37	1.18	1.89	3.11	5.22	1.03	1.67	2.77	4.71	0.90	1.48	2.50	4.29	0.80	1.33	2.27	3.94	37
38	1.21	1.95	3.25	5.52	1.05	1.72	2.90	4.98	0.92	1.53	2.61	4.54	0.81	1.37	2.37	4.16	38
39	1.23	2.01	3.39	5.83	1.07	1.77	3.02	5.26	0.94	1.58	2.72	4.80	0.83	1.42	2.47	4.40	39
40	1.26	2.07	3.53	6.17	1.09	1.83	3.15	5.56	0.96	1.63	2.84	5.07	0.85	1.46	2.58	4.65	40
41	1.28	2.14	3.68	6.51	1.12	1.88	3.29	5.88	0.98	1.68	2.96	5.35	0.87	1.50	2.69	4.92	41
42	1.31	2.20	3.84	6.88	1.14	1.94	3.42	6.21	1.00	1.73	3.08	5.65	0.88	1.55	2.80	5.19	42
43	1.33	2.26	3.99	7.26	1.16	2.00	3.56	6.55	1.02	1.78	3.21	5.97	0.90	1.59	2.91	5.48	43
44	1.36	2.33	4.16	7.66	1.18	2.05	3.71	6.91	1.04	1.83	3.34	6.30	0.92	1.64	3.03	5.78	44
45	1.38	2.39	4.32	8.08	1.20	2.11	3.86	7.29	1.06	1.88	3.48	6.64	0.93	1.68	3.16	6.10	45
46	1.41	2.46	4.49	8.52	1.23	2.17	4.01	7.68	1.08	1.93	3.61	7.00	0.95	1.73	3.28	6.43	46
47	1.43	2.53	4.67	8.98	1.25	2.23	4.17	8.10	1.09	1.98	3.76	7.38	0.97	1.78	3.41	6.77	47
48	1.46	2.59	4.85	9.46	1.27	2.29	4.33	8.53	1.11	2.03	3.90	7.77	0.98	1.82	3.54	7.14	48
49	1.48	2.66	5.04	9.96	1.29	2.35	4.50	8.99	1.13	2.09	4.05	8.19	1.00	1.87	3.68	7.52	49
50	1.50	2.73	5.23	10.49	1.31	2.41	4.67	9.46	1.15	2.14	4.21	8.62	1.01	1.92	3.82	7.92	50

IV. Retirement Planning where Salary Falls Behind Moderate 6% Inflation
Planned Retirement Age 65

Table 3 - 401(k) Contribution (% of Current Sal.) Needed to Replace 10% of Sal. at Retirement   IV-65-3

Probable Life Expectancy at Retirement

Yrs. to Ret.	20.7 (Same as Male Avg.)				23.2 (Better than Male Avg.)				25.7 (Same as Female Avg.)				28.3 (Better than Female Avg.)				Yrs. to Ret.
	4%/4%	6%/5%	8%/6%	10%/7%	4%/4%	6%/5%	8%/6%	10%/7%	4%/4%	6%/5%	8%/6%	10%/7%	4%/4%	6%/5%	8%/6%	10%/7%	
	Expected Return (Pre-Retirement/Post-Retirement)								(Pre-Retirement/Post-Retirement)				Expected Return				
0																	0
1	265.56	233.24	206.82	184.80	305.23	264.50	231.73	204.82	347.88	297.27	257.23	224.84	393.78	331.68	283.38	244.91	1
2	133.41	116.07	101.95	90.25	153.34	131.62	114.23	100.03	174.77	147.93	126.80	109.81	197.83	165.06	139.69	119.61	2
3	89.36	77.01	67.01	58.76	102.72	87.33	75.08	65.12	117.07	98.16	83.34	71.49	132.52	109.52	91.81	77.87	3
4	67.34	57.49	49.54	43.03	77.40	65.19	55.51	47.69	88.22	73.27	61.61	52.35	99.86	81.75	67.88	57.03	4
5	54.13	45.77	39.07	33.60	62.22	51.90	43.77	37.24	70.91	58.34	48.59	40.89	80.27	65.09	53.52	44.54	5
6	45.32	37.96	32.09	27.33	52.09	43.05	35.95	30.29	59.37	48.38	39.91	33.26	67.21	53.98	43.96	36.22	6
7	39.03	32.38	27.11	22.86	44.86	36.72	30.37	25.34	51.13	41.27	33.71	27.82	57.88	46.05	37.14	30.30	7
8	34.31	28.20	23.37	19.52	39.44	31.98	26.19	21.63	44.95	35.94	29.07	23.75	50.88	40.10	32.03	25.87	8
9	30.65	24.95	20.47	16.93	35.22	28.29	22.94	18.76	40.15	31.80	25.47	20.59	45.44	35.48	28.05	22.43	9
10	27.71	22.34	18.16	14.86	31.85	25.34	20.34	16.47	36.30	28.48	22.58	18.08	41.09	31.78	24.88	19.69	10
11	25.31	20.22	16.26	13.17	29.09	22.92	18.22	14.60	33.16	25.77	20.23	16.03	37.53	28.75	22.29	17.46	11
12	23.31	18.44	14.69	11.77	26.79	20.91	16.46	13.05	30.54	23.50	18.27	14.32	34.57	26.23	20.13	15.60	12
13	21.62	16.94	13.36	10.59	24.85	19.21	14.97	11.73	28.25	21.59	16.61	12.89	32.06	24.09	18.30	14.04	13
14	20.17	15.66	12.22	9.59	23.18	17.75	13.69	10.63	26.42	19.95	15.20	11.66	29.91	22.26	16.74	12.71	14
15	18.91	14.54	11.23	8.72	21.74	16.49	12.59	9.66	24.77	18.53	13.97	10.61	28.04	20.68	15.39	11.56	15
16	17.81	13.57	10.37	7.96	20.47	15.38	11.62	8.83	23.33	17.29	12.90	9.69	26.41	19.29	14.21	10.56	16
17	16.84	12.71	9.62	7.30	19.36	14.41	10.78	8.09	22.06	16.20	11.96	8.89	24.97	18.07	13.18	9.68	17
18	15.98	11.94	8.95	6.72	18.37	13.54	10.02	7.44	20.93	15.22	11.13	8.17	23.70	16.98	12.26	8.90	18
19	15.21	11.26	8.35	6.20	17.48	12.77	9.35	6.87	19.92	14.35	10.38	7.54	22.55	16.01	11.43	8.21	19
20	14.52	10.64	7.81	5.73	16.68	12.07	8.75	6.35	19.02	13.57	9.71	6.97	21.53	15.14	10.70	7.60	20
21	13.89	10.09	7.32	5.31	15.96	11.44	8.20	5.89	18.19	12.86	9.11	6.47	20.60	14.35	10.03	7.04	21
22	13.32	9.58	6.88	4.94	15.31	10.87	7.71	5.47	17.45	12.21	8.56	6.01	19.75	13.63	9.43	6.54	22
23	12.80	9.12	6.48	4.60	14.71	10.34	7.26	5.09	16.77	11.63	8.06	5.59	18.98	12.97	8.88	6.09	23
24	12.32	8.70	6.11	4.29	14.16	9.86	6.85	4.75	16.14	11.09	7.60	5.21	18.27	12.37	8.38	5.68	24
25	11.88	8.31	5.78	4.00	13.66	9.42	6.47	4.44	15.57	10.59	7.19	4.87	17.62	11.82	7.92	5.30	25
26	11.48	7.95	5.47	3.74	13.19	9.02	6.13	4.15	15.04	10.13	6.80	4.55	17.02	11.31	7.49	4.96	26
27	11.10	7.62	5.18	3.50	12.76	8.64	5.81	3.88	14.55	9.71	6.45	4.26	16.47	10.83	7.10	4.65	27
28	10.76	7.31	4.92	3.29	12.36	8.29	5.51	3.64	14.09	9.32	6.12	4.00	15.95	10.40	6.74	4.36	28
29	10.43	7.02	4.67	3.08	11.99	7.96	5.24	3.42	13.67	8.95	5.81	3.75	15.47	9.99	6.40	4.09	29
30	10.13	6.76	4.45	2.90	11.64	7.66	4.98	3.21	13.27	8.61	5.53	3.53	15.02	9.61	6.09	3.84	30
31	9.85	6.51	4.23	2.73	11.32	7.38	4.74	3.02	12.90	8.29	5.27	3.32	14.60	9.25	5.80	3.61	31
32	9.58	6.27	4.04	2.57	11.02	7.11	4.52	2.84	12.56	7.99	5.02	3.12	14.21	8.92	5.53	3.40	32
33	9.34	6.05	3.85	2.42	10.73	6.86	4.31	2.68	12.23	7.71	4.79	2.94	13.84	8.61	5.28	3.20	33
34	9.10	5.84	3.68	2.28	10.46	6.63	4.12	2.53	11.92	7.45	4.57	2.77	13.50	8.31	5.04	3.02	34
35	8.88	5.65	3.51	2.15	10.21	6.41	3.94	2.38	11.64	7.20	4.37	2.62	13.17	8.03	4.82	2.85	35
36	8.67	5.46	3.36	2.03	9.97	6.20	3.77	2.25	11.36	6.96	4.18	2.47	12.86	7.77	4.61	2.69	36
37	8.48	5.29	3.22	1.92	9.75	6.00	3.60	2.13	11.11	6.74	4.00	2.33	12.57	7.52	4.41	2.54	37
38	8.29	5.13	3.08	1.81	9.53	5.81	3.45	2.01	10.86	6.53	3.83	2.21	12.30	7.29	4.22	2.40	38
39	8.12	4.97	2.95	1.71	9.33	5.63	3.31	1.90	10.63	6.33	3.67	2.09	12.04	7.07	4.05	2.27	39
40	7.95	4.82	2.83	1.62	9.14	5.47	3.17	1.80	10.41	6.14	3.52	1.97	11.79	6.86	3.88	2.15	40
41	7.79	4.68	2.72	1.54	8.95	5.31	3.04	1.70	10.20	5.96	3.38	1.87	11.55	6.65	3.72	2.03	41
42	7.64	4.54	2.61	1.45	8.78	5.15	2.92	1.61	10.01	5.79	3.24	1.77	11.33	6.46	3.57	1.93	42
43	7.49	4.42	2.50	1.38	8.61	5.01	2.81	1.53	9.82	5.63	3.11	1.68	11.11	6.28	3.43	1.83	43
44	7.36	4.29	2.41	1.31	8.46	4.87	2.70	1.45	9.64	5.47	2.99	1.59	10.91	6.11	3.30	1.73	44
45	7.22	4.18	2.31	1.24	8.30	4.74	2.59	1.37	9.46	5.33	2.88	1.51	10.71	5.94	3.17	1.64	45
46	7.10	4.07	2.22	1.17	8.16	4.61	2.49	1.30	9.30	5.18	2.77	1.43	10.53	5.78	3.05	1.56	46
47	6.98	3.96	2.14	1.11	8.02	4.49	2.40	1.23	9.14	5.05	2.66	1.36	10.35	5.63	2.93	1.48	47
48	6.86	3.86	2.06	1.06	7.89	4.37	2.31	1.17	8.99	4.92	2.56	1.29	10.18	5.49	2.82	1.40	48
49	6.75	3.76	1.98	1.00	7.76	4.26	2.22	1.11	8.85	4.79	2.47	1.22	10.01	5.35	2.72	1.33	49
50	6.65	3.67	1.91	0.95	7.64	4.16	2.14	1.06	8.71	4.67	2.38	1.16	9.86	5.21	2.62	1.26	50

Appendix A

IV. Retirement Planning where Salary Falls Behind Moderate 6% Inflation
Planned Retirement Age 65

Table 4 - Accumulation at Retirement (Multiple of Current Sal.) for 10% Sal. Replacement IV-65-4

Probable Life Expectancy at Retirement

Yrs. to Ret.	20.7 (Same as Male Avg.)				23.2 (Better than Male Avg.)				25.7 (Same as Female Avg.)				28.3 (Better than Female Avg.)				Yrs. to Ret.
	4%/4%	6%/5%	8%/6%	10%/7%	4%/4%	6%/5%	8%/6%	10%/7%	4%/4%	6%/5%	8%/6%	10%/7%	4%/4%	6%/5%	8%/6%	10%/7%	
	Expected Return				(Pre-Retirement/Post-Retirement)				(Pre-Retirement/Post-Retirement)				Expected Return				
0	2.66	2.33	2.07	1.85	3.05	2.64	2.32	2.05	3.48	2.97	2.57	2.25	3.94	3.32	2.83	2.45	0
1	2.79	2.45	2.17	1.94	3.20	2.78	2.43	2.15	3.65	3.12	2.70	2.36	4.13	3.48	2.98	2.57	1
2	2.93	2.57	2.28	2.04	3.37	2.92	2.55	2.26	3.84	3.28	2.84	2.48	4.34	3.66	3.12	2.70	2
3	3.07	2.70	2.39	2.14	3.53	3.06	2.68	2.37	4.03	3.44	2.98	2.60	4.56	3.84	3.28	2.84	3
4	3.23	2.84	2.51	2.25	3.71	3.21	2.82	2.49	4.23	3.61	3.13	2.73	4.79	4.03	3.44	2.98	4
5	3.39	2.98	2.64	2.36	3.90	3.38	2.96	2.61	4.44	3.79	3.28	2.87	5.03	4.23	3.62	3.13	5
6	3.56	3.13	2.77	2.48	4.09	3.54	3.11	2.74	4.66	3.98	3.45	3.01	5.28	4.44	3.80	3.28	6
7	3.74	3.28	2.91	2.60	4.29	3.72	3.26	2.88	4.90	4.18	3.62	3.16	5.54	4.67	3.99	3.45	7
8	3.92	3.45	3.06	2.73	4.51	3.91	3.42	3.03	5.14	4.39	3.80	3.32	5.82	4.90	4.19	3.62	8
9	4.12	3.62	3.21	2.87	4.74	4.10	3.59	3.18	5.40	4.61	3.99	3.49	6.11	5.15	4.40	3.80	9
10	4.33	3.80	3.37	3.01	4.97	4.31	3.77	3.34	5.67	4.84	4.19	3.66	6.41	5.40	4.62	3.99	10
11	4.54	3.99	3.54	3.16	5.22	4.52	3.96	3.50	5.95	5.08	4.40	3.85	6.74	5.67	4.85	4.19	11
12	4.77	4.19	3.71	3.32	5.48	4.75	4.16	3.68	6.25	5.34	4.62	4.04	7.07	5.96	5.09	4.40	12
13	5.01	4.40	3.90	3.48	5.76	4.99	4.37	3.86	6.56	5.61	4.85	4.24	7.43	6.25	5.34	4.62	13
14	5.26	4.62	4.09	3.66	6.04	5.24	4.59	4.06	6.89	5.89	5.09	4.45	7.80	6.57	5.61	4.85	14
15	5.52	4.85	4.30	3.84	6.35	5.50	4.82	4.26	7.23	6.18	5.35	4.67	8.19	6.90	5.89	5.09	15
16	5.80	5.09	4.51	4.03	6.66	5.77	5.06	4.47	7.59	6.49	5.62	4.91	8.60	7.24	6.19	5.35	16
17	6.09	5.35	4.74	4.24	7.00	6.06	5.31	4.69	7.97	6.81	5.90	5.15	9.03	7.60	6.50	5.61	17
18	6.39	5.61	4.98	4.45	7.35	6.37	5.58	4.93	8.37	7.15	6.19	5.41	9.48	7.98	6.82	5.89	18
19	6.71	5.89	5.23	4.67	7.71	6.68	5.86	5.18	8.79	7.51	6.50	5.68	9.95	8.38	7.16	6.19	19
20	7.05	6.19	5.49	4.90	8.10	7.02	6.15	5.43	9.23	7.89	6.83	5.97	10.45	8.80	7.52	6.50	20
21	7.40	6.50	5.76	5.15	8.50	7.37	6.46	5.71	9.69	8.28	7.17	6.26	10.97	9.24	7.89	6.82	21
22	7.77	6.82	6.05	5.41	8.93	7.74	6.78	5.99	10.18	8.70	7.52	6.58	11.52	9.70	8.29	7.16	22
23	8.16	7.16	6.35	5.68	9.38	8.12	7.12	6.29	10.69	9.13	7.90	6.91	12.10	10.19	8.70	7.52	23
24	8.56	7.52	6.67	5.96	9.84	8.53	7.47	6.61	11.22	9.59	8.30	7.25	12.70	10.70	9.14	7.90	24
25	8.99	7.90	7.00	6.26	10.34	8.96	7.85	6.94	11.78	10.07	8.71	7.61	13.33	11.23	9.60	8.29	25
26	9.44	8.29	7.35	6.57	10.85	9.40	8.24	7.28	12.37	10.57	9.15	7.99	14.00	11.79	10.08	8.71	26
27	9.91	8.71	7.72	6.90	11.40	9.87	8.65	7.65	12.99	11.10	9.60	8.39	14.70	12.38	10.58	9.14	27
28	10.41	9.14	8.11	7.24	11.97	10.37	9.08	8.03	13.64	11.65	10.08	8.81	15.44	13.00	11.11	9.60	28
29	10.93	9.60	8.51	7.61	12.56	10.89	9.54	8.43	14.32	12.24	10.59	9.25	16.21	13.65	11.66	10.08	29
30	11.48	10.08	8.94	7.99	13.19	11.43	10.02	8.85	15.04	12.85	11.12	9.72	17.02	14.34	12.25	10.59	30
31	12.05	10.58	9.39	8.39	13.85	12.00	10.52	9.29	15.79	13.49	11.67	10.20	17.87	15.05	12.86	11.11	31
32	12.65	11.11	9.86	8.81	14.54	12.60	11.04	9.76	16.58	14.16	12.26	10.71	18.76	15.80	13.50	11.67	32
33	13.29	11.67	10.35	9.25	15.27	13.23	11.59	10.25	17.41	14.87	12.87	11.25	19.70	16.59	14.18	12.25	33
34	13.95	12.25	10.87	9.71	16.03	13.89	12.17	10.76	18.28	15.62	13.51	11.81	20.69	17.42	14.89	12.87	34
35	14.65	12.87	11.41	10.19	16.84	14.59	12.78	11.30	19.19	16.40	14.19	12.40	21.72	18.30	15.63	13.51	35
36	15.38	13.51	11.98	10.70	17.68	15.32	13.42	11.86	20.15	17.22	14.90	13.02	22.81	19.21	16.41	14.18	36
37	16.15	14.18	12.58	11.24	18.56	16.09	14.09	12.46	21.16	18.08	15.64	13.67	23.95	20.17	17.23	14.89	37
38	16.96	14.89	13.21	11.80	19.49	16.89	14.80	13.08	22.21	18.98	16.43	14.36	25.14	21.18	18.09	15.64	38
39	17.80	15.64	13.87	12.39	20.46	17.73	15.54	13.73	23.32	19.93	17.25	15.08	26.40	22.24	19.00	16.42	39
40	18.70	16.42	14.56	13.01	21.49	18.62	16.31	14.42	24.49	20.93	18.11	15.83	27.72	23.35	19.95	17.24	40
41	19.63	17.24	15.29	13.66	22.56	19.55	17.13	15.14	25.72	21.97	19.01	16.62	29.11	24.52	20.95	18.10	41
42	20.61	18.10	16.05	14.34	23.69	20.53	17.99	15.90	27.00	23.07	19.97	17.45	30.56	25.74	21.99	19.01	42
43	21.64	19.01	16.86	15.06	24.88	21.56	18.89	16.69	28.35	24.23	20.96	18.32	32.09	27.03	23.09	19.96	43
44	22.72	19.96	17.70	15.81	26.12	22.63	19.83	17.53	29.77	25.44	22.01	19.24	33.70	28.38	24.25	20.96	44
45	23.86	20.96	18.58	16.60	27.42	23.77	20.82	18.40	31.26	26.71	23.11	20.20	35.38	29.80	25.46	22.01	45
46	25.05	22.00	19.51	17.43	28.80	24.95	21.86	19.32	32.82	28.05	24.27	21.21	37.15	31.29	26.73	23.11	46
47	26.31	23.10	20.49	18.31	30.24	26.20	22.96	20.29	34.46	29.45	25.48	22.27	39.01	32.86	28.07	24.26	47
48	27.62	24.26	21.51	19.22	31.75	27.51	24.10	21.30	36.18	30.92	26.76	23.39	40.96	34.50	29.47	25.47	48
49	29.00	25.47	22.59	20.18	33.34	28.89	25.31	22.37	37.99	32.47	28.09	24.56	43.01	36.22	30.95	26.75	49
50	30.45	26.75	23.72	21.19	35.00	30.33	26.57	23.49	39.89	34.09	29.50	25.78	45.16	38.04	32.50	28.09	50

A-73

IV. Retirement Planning where Salary Falls Behind Moderate 6% Inflation
Planned Retirement Age 68

Table 1 - Percent of Salary Replaced by a 401(k) Account Equal to Current Annual Salary — IV-68-1

Probable Life Expectancy at Retirement

	18.3 (Same as Male Avg.)				20.7 (Better than Male Avg.)				23.2 (Same as Female Avg.)				25.7 (Better than Female Avg.)				
	4% / 4%	6% / 5%	8% / 6%	10% / 7%	4% / 4%	6% / 5%	8% / 6%	10% / 7%	4% / 4%	6% / 5%	8% / 6%	10% / 7%	4% / 4%	6% / 5%	8% / 6%	10% / 7%	
Yrs. to Ret.		Expected Return			(Pre-Retirement/Post-Retirement)				(Pre-Retirement/Post-Retirement)				Expected Return				Yrs. to Ret.
0	4.37	4.91	5.47	6.06	3.77	4.29	4.84	5.41	3.28	3.78	4.32	4.88	2.87	3.36	3.89	4.45	0
1	4.33	4.96	5.63	6.35	3.73	4.33	4.97	5.67	3.25	3.82	4.44	5.11	2.85	3.40	4.00	4.66	1
2	4.29	5.00	5.79	6.65	3.69	4.37	5.12	5.94	3.21	3.85	4.57	5.36	2.82	3.43	4.11	4.88	2
3	4.24	5.05	5.96	6.97	3.66	4.41	5.26	6.22	3.18	3.89	4.70	5.61	2.79	3.46	4.23	5.11	3
4	4.20	5.10	6.13	7.30	3.62	4.45	5.41	6.52	3.15	3.93	4.83	5.88	2.77	3.49	4.35	5.36	4
5	4.16	5.15	6.30	7.65	3.59	4.49	5.57	6.83	3.12	3.96	4.97	6.16	2.74	3.53	4.48	5.61	5
6	4.12	5.20	6.48	8.01	3.56	4.54	5.73	7.15	3.09	4.00	5.11	6.45	2.71	3.56	4.60	5.88	6
7	4.09	5.25	6.67	8.39	3.52	4.58	5.89	7.49	3.06	4.04	5.26	6.76	2.69	3.59	4.74	6.16	7
8	4.05	5.30	6.86	8.79	3.49	4.62	6.06	7.85	3.04	4.08	5.41	7.08	2.66	3.63	4.87	6.45	8
9	4.01	5.35	7.05	9.21	3.46	4.67	6.23	8.22	3.01	4.12	5.56	7.42	2.64	3.66	5.01	6.76	9
10	3.97	5.40	7.26	9.65	3.42	4.71	6.41	8.62	2.98	4.16	5.72	7.77	2.61	3.70	5.15	7.08	10
11	3.93	5.45	7.46	10.11	3.39	4.76	6.59	9.03	2.95	4.20	5.88	8.14	2.59	3.73	5.30	7.42	11
12	3.90	5.50	7.68	10.59	3.36	4.80	6.78	9.45	2.92	4.24	6.05	8.53	2.56	3.77	5.45	7.77	12
13	3.86	5.55	7.90	11.09	3.33	4.85	6.98	9.90	2.89	4.28	6.23	8.94	2.54	3.80	5.61	8.14	13
14	3.82	5.60	8.12	11.62	3.29	4.89	7.18	10.38	2.87	4.32	6.40	9.36	2.51	3.84	5.77	8.53	14
15	3.79	5.66	8.35	12.17	3.26	4.94	7.38	10.87	2.84	4.36	6.59	9.81	2.49	3.88	5.93	8.93	15
16	3.75	5.71	8.59	12.75	3.23	4.99	7.59	11.39	2.81	4.40	6.78	10.27	2.47	3.91	6.10	9.36	16
17	3.71	5.77	8.84	13.36	3.20	5.04	7.81	11.93	2.79	4.44	6.97	10.76	2.44	3.95	6.28	9.80	17
18	3.68	5.82	9.09	14.00	3.17	5.08	8.03	12.50	2.76	4.48	7.17	11.28	2.42	3.99	6.46	10.27	18
19	3.64	5.88	9.35	14.66	3.14	5.13	8.26	13.09	2.73	4.52	7.37	11.81	2.40	4.03	6.64	10.76	19
20	3.61	5.93	9.62	15.36	3.11	5.18	8.50	13.72	2.71	4.57	7.58	12.38	2.37	4.06	6.83	11.27	20
21	3.57	5.99	9.89	16.09	3.08	5.23	8.74	14.37	2.68	4.61	7.80	12.96	2.35	4.10	7.03	11.81	21
22	3.54	6.04	10.18	16.86	3.05	5.28	8.99	15.05	2.66	4.65	8.02	13.58	2.33	4.14	7.23	12.37	22
23	3.51	6.10	10.47	17.66	3.02	5.33	9.25	15.77	2.63	4.70	8.25	14.23	2.31	4.18	7.44	12.96	23
24	3.47	6.16	10.77	18.50	2.99	5.38	9.51	16.52	2.61	4.74	8.49	14.90	2.29	4.22	7.65	13.58	24
25	3.44	6.22	11.07	19.38	2.97	5.43	9.79	17.31	2.58	4.79	8.73	15.61	2.26	4.26	7.87	14.22	25
26	3.41	6.28	11.39	20.30	2.94	5.48	10.06	18.13	2.56	4.83	8.98	16.36	2.24	4.30	8.09	14.90	26
27	3.38	6.34	11.72	21.27	2.91	5.53	10.35	18.99	2.53	4.88	9.24	17.14	2.22	4.34	8.32	15.61	27
28	3.34	6.40	12.05	22.28	2.88	5.59	10.65	19.90	2.51	4.93	9.50	17.95	2.20	4.38	8.56	16.35	28
29	3.31	6.46	12.40	23.34	2.86	5.64	10.95	20.84	2.48	4.97	9.78	18.81	2.18	4.43	8.81	17.13	29
30	3.28	6.52	12.75	24.46	2.83	5.69	11.27	21.84	2.46	5.02	10.06	19.70	2.16	4.47	9.06	17.95	30
31	3.25	6.58	13.12	25.62	2.80	5.75	11.59	22.88	2.44	5.07	10.34	20.64	2.14	4.51	9.32	18.80	31
32	3.22	6.64	13.49	26.84	2.77	5.80	11.92	23.96	2.41	5.12	10.64	21.62	2.12	4.55	9.58	19.70	32
33	3.19	6.71	13.88	28.12	2.75	5.86	12.26	25.10	2.39	5.17	10.94	22.65	2.10	4.60	9.86	20.63	33
34	3.16	6.77	14.27	29.45	2.72	5.91	12.61	26.30	2.37	5.21	11.26	23.73	2.08	4.64	10.14	21.62	34
35	3.13	6.83	14.68	30.86	2.70	5.97	12.97	27.55	2.35	5.26	11.58	24.86	2.06	4.68	10.43	22.64	35
36	3.10	6.90	15.10	32.33	2.67	6.03	13.34	28.86	2.32	5.31	11.91	26.04	2.04	4.73	10.73	23.72	36
37	3.07	6.97	15.53	33.86	2.65	6.08	13.73	30.24	2.30	5.36	12.25	27.28	2.02	4.77	11.04	24.85	37
38	3.04	7.03	15.98	35.48	2.62	6.14	14.12	31.68	2.28	5.42	12.60	28.58	2.00	4.82	11.35	26.03	38
39	3.01	7.10	16.44	37.16	2.60	6.20	14.52	33.18	2.26	5.47	12.96	29.94	1.98	4.86	11.68	27.27	39
40	2.98	7.17	16.91	38.93	2.57	6.26	14.94	34.76	2.24	5.52	13.33	31.37	1.96	4.91	12.01	28.57	40
41	2.95	7.23	17.39	40.79	2.55	6.32	15.36	36.42	2.22	5.57	13.71	32.86	1.94	4.96	12.35	29.93	41
42	2.93	7.30	17.89	42.73	2.52	6.38	15.80	38.15	2.19	5.62	14.10	34.42	1.93	5.00	12.71	31.36	42
43	2.90	7.37	18.40	44.76	2.50	6.44	16.26	39.97	2.17	5.68	14.51	36.06	1.91	5.05	13.07	32.85	43
44	2.87	7.44	18.92	46.89	2.47	6.50	16.72	41.87	2.15	5.73	14.92	37.78	1.89	5.10	13.44	34.41	44
45	2.84	7.51	19.47	49.12	2.45	6.56	17.20	43.86	2.13	5.79	15.35	39.58	1.87	5.15	13.83	36.05	45
46	2.82	7.58	20.02	51.46	2.42	6.62	17.69	45.95	2.11	5.84	15.79	41.46	1.85	5.20	14.22	37.77	46
47	2.79	7.66	20.59	53.91	2.40	6.69	18.20	48.14	2.09	5.90	16.24	43.43	1.84	5.25	14.63	39.56	47
48	2.76	7.73	21.18	56.48	2.38	6.75	18.72	50.43	2.07	5.95	16.71	45.50	1.82	5.30	15.05	41.45	48
49	2.74	7.80	21.79	59.17	2.36	6.81	19.25	52.83	2.05	6.01	17.18	47.67	1.80	5.35	15.48	43.42	49
50	2.71	7.88	22.41	61.98	2.34	6.88	19.80	55.34	2.03	6.07	17.67	49.94	1.78	5.40	15.92	45.49	50

IV. Retirement Planning where Salary Falls Behind Moderate 6% Inflation
Planned Retirement Age 68

Table 2 - Percent of Salary Replaced by a 401(k) Contribution of 1% of Current Salary IV-68-2

Probable Life Expectancy at Retirement

Yrs. to Ret.	18.3 (Same as Male Avg.)				20.7 (Better than Male Avg.)				23.2 (Same as Female Avg.)				25.7 (Better than Female Avg.)				Yrs. to Ret.
	4% / 4%	6% / 5%	8% / 6%	10% / 7%	4% / 4%	6% / 5%	8% / 6%	10% / 7%	4% / 4%	6% / 5%	8% / 6%	10% / 7%	4% / 4%	6% / 5%	8% / 6%	10% / 7%	
	Expected Return				(Pre-Retirement/Post-Retirement)				(Pre-Retirement/Post-Retirement)				Expected Return				
0	0.00	0.00	0.00	0.00	0.00	0.00	0.00	0.00	0.00	0.00	0.00	0.00	0.00	0.00	0.00	0.00	0
1	0.04	0.05	0.05	0.06	0.04	0.04	0.05	0.05	0.03	0.04	0.04	0.05	0.03	0.03	0.04	0.04	1
2	0.09	0.10	0.11	0.12	0.07	0.09	0.10	0.11	0.07	0.08	0.09	0.10	0.06	0.07	0.08	0.09	2
3	0.13	0.15	0.17	0.19	0.11	0.13	0.15	0.17	0.10	0.11	0.13	0.15	0.09	0.10	0.12	0.14	3
4	0.17	0.20	0.23	0.26	0.15	0.17	0.20	0.23	0.13	0.15	0.18	0.21	0.11	0.14	0.16	0.19	4
5	0.21	0.25	0.29	0.33	0.18	0.22	0.26	0.30	0.16	0.19	0.23	0.27	0.14	0.17	0.21	0.24	5
6	0.26	0.30	0.35	0.41	0.22	0.26	0.31	0.37	0.19	0.23	0.28	0.33	0.17	0.21	0.25	0.30	6
7	0.30	0.35	0.42	0.49	0.26	0.31	0.37	0.44	0.22	0.27	0.33	0.39	0.20	0.24	0.30	0.36	7
8	0.34	0.41	0.48	0.57	0.29	0.35	0.43	0.51	0.25	0.31	0.38	0.46	0.22	0.28	0.34	0.42	8
9	0.38	0.46	0.55	0.66	0.33	0.40	0.49	0.59	0.28	0.35	0.44	0.53	0.25	0.31	0.39	0.49	9
10	0.42	0.51	0.62	0.75	0.36	0.45	0.55	0.67	0.31	0.39	0.49	0.61	0.28	0.35	0.44	0.55	10
11	0.46	0.57	0.70	0.85	0.40	0.49	0.61	0.76	0.34	0.44	0.55	0.69	0.30	0.39	0.49	0.62	11
12	0.50	0.62	0.77	0.95	0.43	0.54	0.68	0.85	0.37	0.48	0.61	0.77	0.33	0.43	0.55	0.70	12
13	0.54	0.68	0.85	1.06	0.46	0.59	0.75	0.94	0.40	0.52	0.67	0.85	0.35	0.46	0.60	0.78	13
14	0.58	0.73	0.93	1.17	0.50	0.64	0.82	1.04	0.43	0.56	0.73	0.94	0.38	0.50	0.66	0.86	14
15	0.61	0.79	1.01	1.28	0.53	0.69	0.89	1.15	0.46	0.61	0.79	1.03	0.40	0.54	0.72	0.94	15
16	0.65	0.84	1.09	1.41	0.56	0.74	0.96	1.26	0.49	0.65	0.86	1.13	0.43	0.58	0.78	1.03	16
17	0.69	0.90	1.18	1.53	0.59	0.79	1.04	1.37	0.52	0.69	0.93	1.24	0.45	0.62	0.84	1.13	17
18	0.73	0.96	1.27	1.67	0.63	0.84	1.12	1.49	0.54	0.74	1.00	1.34	0.48	0.66	0.90	1.22	18
19	0.76	1.02	1.36	1.81	0.66	0.89	1.20	1.61	0.57	0.78	1.07	1.46	0.50	0.70	0.96	1.33	19
20	0.80	1.08	1.45	1.95	0.69	0.94	1.28	1.74	0.60	0.83	1.14	1.57	0.53	0.74	1.03	1.43	20
21	0.84	1.14	1.55	2.11	0.72	0.99	1.37	1.88	0.63	0.87	1.22	1.70	0.55	0.78	1.10	1.55	21
22	0.87	1.19	1.64	2.27	0.75	1.04	1.45	2.03	0.65	0.92	1.30	1.83	0.57	0.82	1.17	1.66	22
23	0.91	1.26	1.75	2.44	0.78	1.10	1.54	2.18	0.68	0.97	1.38	1.96	0.60	0.86	1.24	1.79	23
24	0.94	1.32	1.85	2.61	0.81	1.15	1.64	2.33	0.71	1.01	1.46	2.11	0.62	0.90	1.32	1.92	24
25	0.98	1.38	1.96	2.80	0.84	1.20	1.73	2.50	0.73	1.06	1.54	2.25	0.64	0.94	1.39	2.05	25
26	1.01	1.44	2.07	2.99	0.87	1.26	1.83	2.67	0.76	1.11	1.63	2.41	0.67	0.99	1.47	2.20	26
27	1.04	1.50	2.18	3.20	0.90	1.31	1.93	2.85	0.78	1.16	1.72	2.57	0.69	1.03	1.55	2.35	27
28	1.08	1.57	2.30	3.41	0.93	1.37	2.03	3.04	0.81	1.21	1.81	2.75	0.71	1.07	1.63	2.50	28
29	1.11	1.63	2.42	3.63	0.96	1.42	2.14	3.24	0.83	1.26	1.91	2.93	0.73	1.12	1.72	2.66	29
30	1.14	1.69	2.55	3.86	0.99	1.48	2.25	3.45	0.86	1.31	2.01	3.11	0.75	1.16	1.81	2.84	30
31	1.18	1.76	2.67	4.11	1.02	1.54	2.36	3.67	0.88	1.36	2.11	3.31	0.78	1.21	1.90	3.02	31
32	1.21	1.83	2.80	4.37	1.04	1.59	2.48	3.90	0.91	1.41	2.21	3.52	0.80	1.25	1.99	3.20	32
33	1.24	1.89	2.94	4.63	1.07	1.65	2.60	4.14	0.93	1.46	2.32	3.73	0.82	1.30	2.09	3.40	33
34	1.27	1.96	3.08	4.91	1.10	1.71	2.72	4.39	0.96	1.51	2.43	3.96	0.84	1.34	2.19	3.61	34
35	1.31	2.03	3.22	5.21	1.13	1.77	2.85	4.65	0.98	1.56	2.54	4.20	0.86	1.39	2.29	3.82	35
36	1.34	2.10	3.37	5.52	1.15	1.83	2.98	4.93	1.00	1.61	2.66	4.45	0.88	1.44	2.39	4.05	36
37	1.37	2.16	3.52	5.84	1.18	1.89	3.11	5.22	1.03	1.67	2.77	4.71	0.90	1.48	2.50	4.29	37
38	1.40	2.23	3.67	6.18	1.21	1.95	3.25	5.52	1.05	1.72	2.90	4.98	0.92	1.53	2.61	4.54	38
39	1.43	2.30	3.83	6.53	1.23	2.01	3.39	5.83	1.07	1.77	3.02	5.26	0.94	1.58	2.72	4.80	39
40	1.46	2.38	4.00	6.91	1.26	2.07	3.53	6.17	1.09	1.83	3.15	5.56	0.96	1.63	2.84	5.07	40
41	1.49	2.45	4.17	7.30	1.28	2.14	3.68	6.51	1.12	1.88	3.29	5.88	0.98	1.68	2.96	5.35	41
42	1.52	2.52	4.34	7.70	1.31	2.20	3.84	6.88	1.14	1.94	3.42	6.21	1.00	1.73	3.08	5.65	42
43	1.55	2.59	4.52	8.13	1.33	2.26	3.99	7.26	1.16	2.00	3.56	6.55	1.02	1.78	3.21	5.97	43
44	1.58	2.67	4.70	8.58	1.36	2.33	4.16	7.66	1.18	2.05	3.71	6.91	1.04	1.83	3.34	6.30	44
45	1.61	2.74	4.89	9.05	1.38	2.39	4.32	8.08	1.20	2.11	3.86	7.29	1.06	1.88	3.48	6.64	45
46	1.63	2.82	5.09	9.54	1.41	2.46	4.49	8.52	1.23	2.17	4.01	7.68	1.08	1.93	3.61	7.00	46
47	1.66	2.89	5.29	10.05	1.43	2.53	4.67	8.98	1.25	2.23	4.17	8.10	1.09	1.98	3.76	7.38	47
48	1.69	2.97	5.49	10.59	1.46	2.59	4.85	9.46	1.27	2.29	4.33	8.53	1.11	2.03	3.90	7.77	48
49	1.72	3.05	5.71	11.16	1.48	2.66	5.04	9.96	1.29	2.35	4.50	8.99	1.13	2.09	4.05	8.19	49
50	1.75	3.12	5.92	11.75	1.50	2.73	5.23	10.49	1.31	2.41	4.67	9.46	1.15	2.14	4.21	8.62	50

IV. Retirement Planning where Salary Falls Behind Moderate 6% Inflation
Planned Retirement Age 68

Table 3 - 401(k) Contribution (% of Current Sal.) Needed to Replace 10% of Sal. at Retirement   IV-68-3

Probable Life Expectancy at Retirement

Yrs. to Ret.	18.3 (Same as Male Avg.)				20.7 (Better than Male Avg.)				23.2 (Same as Female Avg.)				25.7 (Better than Female Avg.)				Yrs. to Ret.
	4% / 4%	6% / 5%	8% / 6%	10% / 7%	4% / 4%	6% / 5%	8% / 6%	10% / 7%	4% / 4%	6% / 5%	8% / 6%	10% / 7%	4% / 4%	6% / 5%	8% / 6%	10% / 7%	
	Expected Return		(Pre-Retirement/Post-Retirement)				(Pre-Retirement/Post-Retirement)				Expected Return						
0																	0
1	228.94	203.70	182.74	165.00	265.56	233.24	206.82	184.80	305.23	264.50	231.73	204.82	347.88	297.27	257.23	224.84	1
2	115.02	101.37	90.08	80.58	133.41	116.07	101.95	90.25	153.34	131.62	114.23	100.03	174.77	147.93	126.80	109.81	2
3	77.04	67.26	59.20	52.46	89.36	77.01	67.01	58.76	102.72	87.33	75.08	65.12	117.07	98.16	83.34	71.49	3
4	58.06	50.20	43.77	38.42	67.34	57.49	49.54	43.03	77.40	65.19	55.51	47.69	88.22	73.27	61.61	52.35	4
5	46.67	39.97	34.52	30.01	54.13	45.77	39.07	33.60	62.22	51.90	43.77	37.24	70.91	58.34	48.59	40.89	5
6	39.07	33.15	28.35	24.41	45.32	37.96	32.09	27.33	52.09	43.05	35.95	30.29	59.37	48.38	39.91	33.26	6
7	33.65	28.28	23.95	20.41	39.03	32.38	27.11	22.86	44.86	36.72	30.37	25.34	51.13	41.27	33.71	27.82	7
8	29.58	24.63	20.65	17.43	34.31	28.20	23.37	19.52	39.44	31.98	26.19	21.63	44.95	35.94	29.07	23.75	8
9	26.42	21.79	18.09	15.11	30.65	24.95	20.47	16.93	35.22	28.29	22.94	18.76	40.15	31.80	25.47	20.59	9
10	23.89	19.51	16.04	13.27	27.71	22.34	18.16	14.86	31.85	25.34	20.34	16.47	36.30	28.48	22.58	18.08	10
11	21.82	17.65	14.37	11.76	25.31	20.22	16.26	13.17	29.09	22.92	18.22	14.60	33.16	25.77	20.23	16.03	11
12	20.10	16.11	12.98	10.51	23.31	18.44	14.69	11.77	26.79	20.91	16.46	13.05	30.54	23.50	18.27	14.32	12
13	18.64	14.80	11.80	9.46	21.62	16.94	13.36	10.59	24.85	19.21	14.97	11.74	28.32	21.59	16.61	12.89	13
14	17.39	13.67	10.80	8.56	20.17	15.66	12.22	9.59	23.18	17.75	13.69	10.63	26.42	19.95	15.20	11.66	14
15	16.30	12.70	9.93	7.79	18.91	14.54	11.23	8.72	21.74	16.49	12.59	9.66	24.77	18.53	13.97	10.61	15
16	15.36	11.85	9.17	7.11	17.81	13.57	10.37	7.96	20.47	15.38	11.62	8.83	23.33	17.29	12.90	9.69	16
17	14.52	11.10	8.50	6.52	16.84	12.71	9.62	7.30	19.36	14.41	10.78	8.09	22.06	16.20	11.96	8.89	17
18	13.78	10.43	7.90	6.00	15.98	11.94	8.95	6.72	18.37	13.54	10.02	7.44	20.93	15.22	11.13	8.17	18
19	13.11	9.83	7.37	5.53	15.21	11.26	8.35	6.20	17.48	12.77	9.35	6.87	19.92	14.35	10.38	7.54	19
20	12.51	9.30	6.90	5.12	14.52	10.64	7.81	5.73	16.68	12.07	8.75	6.35	19.02	13.57	9.71	6.97	20
21	11.97	8.81	6.47	4.75	13.89	10.09	7.32	5.31	15.96	11.44	8.20	5.89	18.19	12.86	9.11	6.47	21
22	11.48	8.37	6.08	4.41	13.32	9.58	6.88	4.94	15.31	10.87	7.71	5.47	17.45	12.21	8.56	6.01	22
23	11.03	7.97	5.73	4.10	12.80	9.12	6.48	4.60	14.71	10.34	7.26	5.09	16.77	11.63	8.06	5.59	23
24	10.62	7.60	5.40	3.83	12.32	8.70	6.11	4.29	14.16	9.86	6.85	4.75	16.14	11.09	7.60	5.21	24
25	10.24	7.26	5.10	3.57	11.88	8.31	5.78	4.00	13.66	9.42	6.47	4.44	15.57	10.59	7.19	4.87	25
26	9.90	6.94	4.83	3.34	11.48	7.95	5.47	3.74	13.19	9.02	6.13	4.15	15.04	10.13	6.80	4.55	26
27	9.57	6.65	4.58	3.13	11.10	7.62	5.18	3.50	12.76	8.64	5.81	3.88	14.55	9.71	6.45	4.26	27
28	9.27	6.38	4.35	2.93	10.76	7.31	4.92	3.29	12.36	8.29	5.51	3.64	14.09	9.32	6.12	4.00	28
29	8.99	6.13	4.13	2.75	10.43	7.02	4.67	3.08	11.99	7.96	5.24	3.42	13.67	8.95	5.81	3.75	29
30	8.73	5.90	3.93	2.59	10.13	6.76	4.45	2.90	11.64	7.66	4.98	3.21	13.27	8.61	5.53	3.53	30
31	8.49	5.68	3.74	2.43	9.85	6.51	4.23	2.73	11.32	7.38	4.74	3.02	12.90	8.29	5.27	3.32	31
32	8.26	5.48	3.57	2.29	9.58	6.27	4.04	2.57	11.02	7.11	4.52	2.84	12.56	7.99	5.02	3.12	32
33	8.05	5.28	3.40	2.16	9.34	6.05	3.85	2.42	10.73	6.86	4.31	2.68	12.23	7.71	4.79	2.94	33
34	7.85	5.10	3.25	2.03	9.10	5.84	3.68	2.28	10.46	6.63	4.12	2.53	11.92	7.45	4.57	2.77	34
35	7.66	4.93	3.11	1.92	8.88	5.65	3.51	2.15	10.21	6.41	3.94	2.38	11.64	7.20	4.37	2.62	35
36	7.48	4.77	2.97	1.81	8.67	5.46	3.36	2.03	9.97	6.20	3.77	2.25	11.36	6.96	4.18	2.47	36
37	7.31	4.62	2.84	1.71	8.48	5.29	3.22	1.92	9.75	6.00	3.60	2.13	11.11	6.74	4.00	2.33	37
38	7.15	4.48	2.72	1.62	8.29	5.13	3.08	1.81	9.53	5.81	3.45	2.01	10.86	6.53	3.83	2.21	38
39	7.00	4.34	2.61	1.53	8.12	4.97	2.95	1.71	9.33	5.63	3.31	1.90	10.63	6.33	3.67	2.09	39
40	6.85	4.21	2.50	1.45	7.95	4.82	2.83	1.62	9.14	5.47	3.17	1.80	10.41	6.14	3.52	1.97	40
41	6.72	4.09	2.40	1.37	7.79	4.68	2.72	1.54	8.95	5.31	3.04	1.70	10.20	5.96	3.38	1.87	41
42	6.58	3.97	2.30	1.30	7.64	4.54	2.61	1.45	8.78	5.15	2.92	1.61	10.01	5.79	3.24	1.77	42
43	6.46	3.86	2.21	1.23	7.49	4.42	2.50	1.38	8.61	5.01	2.81	1.53	9.82	5.63	3.11	1.68	43
44	6.34	3.75	2.13	1.17	7.36	4.29	2.41	1.31	8.46	4.87	2.70	1.45	9.64	5.47	2.99	1.59	44
45	6.23	3.65	2.04	1.11	7.22	4.18	2.31	1.24	8.30	4.74	2.59	1.37	9.46	5.33	2.88	1.51	45
46	6.12	3.55	1.97	1.05	7.10	4.07	2.22	1.17	8.16	4.61	2.49	1.30	9.30	5.18	2.77	1.43	46
47	6.02	3.46	1.89	0.99	6.98	3.96	2.14	1.11	8.02	4.49	2.40	1.23	9.14	5.05	2.66	1.36	47
48	5.92	3.37	1.82	0.94	6.86	3.86	2.06	1.06	7.89	4.37	2.31	1.17	8.99	4.92	2.56	1.29	48
49	5.82	3.28	1.75	0.90	6.75	3.76	1.98	1.00	7.76	4.26	2.22	1.11	8.85	4.79	2.47	1.22	49
50	5.73	3.20	1.69	0.85	6.65	3.67	1.91	0.95	7.64	4.16	2.14	1.06	8.71	4.67	2.38	1.16	50

**IV. Retirement Planning where Salary Falls Behind Moderate 6% Inflation
Planned Retirement Age 68**

Table 4 - Accumulation at Retirement (Multiple of Current Sal.) for 10% Sal. Replacement   IV-68-4

Probable Life Expectancy at Retirement

Yrs. to Ret.	18.3 (Same as Male Avg.)				20.7 (Better than Male Avg.)				23.2 (Same as Female Avg.)				25.7 (Better than Female Avg.)				Yrs. to Ret.
	4% / 4%	6% / 5%	8% / 6%	10% / 7%	4% / 4%	6% / 5%	8% / 6%	10% / 7%	4% / 4%	6% / 5%	8% / 6%	10% / 7%	4% / 4%	6% / 5%	8% / 6%	10% / 7%	
	Expected Return (Pre-Retirement/Post-Retirement)												Expected Return				
0	2.29	2.04	1.83	1.65	2.66	2.33	2.07	1.85	3.05	2.64	2.32	2.05	3.48	2.97	2.57	2.25	0
1	2.40	2.14	1.92	1.73	2.79	2.45	2.17	1.94	3.20	2.78	2.43	2.15	3.65	3.12	2.70	2.36	1
2	2.52	2.25	2.01	1.82	2.93	2.57	2.28	2.04	3.37	2.92	2.55	2.26	3.84	3.28	2.84	2.48	2
3	2.65	2.36	2.12	1.91	3.07	2.70	2.39	2.14	3.53	3.06	2.68	2.37	4.03	3.44	2.98	2.60	3
4	2.78	2.48	2.22	2.01	3.23	2.84	2.51	2.25	3.71	3.21	2.82	2.49	4.23	3.61	3.13	2.73	4
5	2.92	2.60	2.33	2.11	3.39	2.98	2.64	2.36	3.90	3.38	2.96	2.61	4.44	3.79	3.28	2.87	5
6	3.07	2.73	2.45	2.21	3.56	3.13	2.77	2.48	4.09	3.54	3.11	2.74	4.66	3.98	3.45	3.01	6
7	3.22	2.87	2.57	2.32	3.74	3.28	2.91	2.60	4.29	3.72	3.26	2.88	4.90	4.18	3.62	3.16	7
8	3.38	3.01	2.70	2.44	3.92	3.45	3.06	2.73	4.51	3.91	3.42	3.03	5.14	4.39	3.80	3.32	8
9	3.55	3.16	2.83	2.56	4.12	3.62	3.21	2.87	4.74	4.10	3.59	3.18	5.40	4.61	3.99	3.49	9
10	3.73	3.32	2.98	2.69	4.33	3.80	3.37	3.01	4.97	4.31	3.77	3.34	5.67	4.84	4.19	3.66	10
11	3.92	3.48	3.13	2.82	4.54	3.99	3.54	3.16	5.22	4.52	3.96	3.50	5.95	5.08	4.40	3.85	11
12	4.11	3.66	3.28	2.96	4.77	4.19	3.71	3.32	5.48	4.75	4.16	3.68	6.25	5.34	4.62	4.04	12
13	4.32	3.84	3.45	3.11	5.01	4.40	3.90	3.48	5.76	4.99	4.37	3.86	6.56	5.61	4.85	4.24	13
14	4.53	4.03	3.62	3.27	5.26	4.62	4.09	3.66	6.04	5.24	4.59	4.06	6.89	5.89	5.09	4.45	14
15	4.76	4.23	3.80	3.43	5.52	4.85	4.30	3.84	6.35	5.50	4.82	4.26	7.23	6.18	5.35	4.67	15
16	5.00	4.45	3.99	3.60	5.80	5.09	4.51	4.03	6.66	5.77	5.06	4.47	7.59	6.49	5.62	4.91	16
17	5.25	4.67	4.19	3.78	6.09	5.35	4.74	4.24	7.00	6.06	5.31	4.69	7.97	6.81	5.90	5.15	17
18	5.51	4.90	4.40	3.97	6.39	5.61	4.98	4.45	7.35	6.37	5.58	4.93	8.37	7.15	6.19	5.41	18
19	5.79	5.15	4.62	4.17	6.71	5.89	5.23	4.67	7.71	6.68	5.86	5.18	8.79	7.51	6.50	5.68	19
20	6.07	5.40	4.85	4.38	7.05	6.19	5.49	4.90	8.10	7.02	6.15	5.43	9.23	7.89	6.83	5.97	20
21	6.38	5.67	5.09	4.60	7.40	6.50	5.76	5.15	8.50	7.37	6.46	5.71	9.69	8.28	7.17	6.26	21
22	6.70	5.96	5.35	4.83	7.77	6.82	6.05	5.41	8.93	7.74	6.78	5.99	10.18	8.70	7.52	6.58	22
23	7.03	6.26	5.61	5.07	8.16	7.16	6.35	5.68	9.38	8.12	7.12	6.29	10.69	9.13	7.90	6.91	23
24	7.38	6.57	5.89	5.32	8.56	7.52	6.67	5.96	9.84	8.53	7.47	6.61	11.22	9.59	8.30	7.25	24
25	7.75	6.90	6.19	5.59	8.99	7.90	7.00	6.26	10.34	8.96	7.85	6.94	11.78	10.07	8.71	7.61	25
26	8.14	7.24	6.50	5.87	9.44	8.29	7.35	6.57	10.85	9.40	8.24	7.28	12.37	10.57	9.15	7.99	26
27	8.55	7.60	6.82	6.16	9.91	8.71	7.72	6.90	11.40	9.87	8.65	7.65	12.99	11.10	9.60	8.39	27
28	8.97	7.99	7.16	6.47	10.41	9.14	8.11	7.24	11.97	10.37	9.08	8.03	13.64	11.65	10.08	8.81	28
29	9.42	8.38	7.52	6.79	10.93	9.60	8.51	7.61	12.56	10.89	9.54	8.43	14.32	12.24	10.59	9.25	29
30	9.89	8.80	7.90	7.13	11.48	10.08	8.94	7.99	13.19	11.43	10.02	8.85	15.04	12.85	11.12	9.72	30
31	10.39	9.24	8.29	7.49	12.05	10.58	9.39	8.39	13.85	12.00	10.52	9.29	15.79	13.49	11.67	10.20	31
32	10.91	9.71	8.71	7.86	12.65	11.11	9.86	8.81	14.54	12.60	11.04	9.76	16.58	14.16	12.26	10.71	32
33	11.45	10.19	9.14	8.26	13.29	11.67	10.35	9.25	15.27	13.23	11.59	10.25	17.41	14.87	12.87	11.25	33
34	12.03	10.70	9.60	8.67	13.95	12.25	10.87	9.71	16.03	13.89	12.17	10.76	18.28	15.62	13.51	11.81	34
35	12.63	11.24	10.08	9.10	14.65	12.87	11.41	10.19	16.84	14.59	12.78	11.30	19.19	16.40	14.19	12.40	35
36	13.26	11.80	10.58	9.56	15.38	13.51	11.98	10.70	17.68	15.32	13.42	11.86	20.15	17.22	14.90	13.02	36
37	13.92	12.39	11.11	10.03	16.15	14.18	12.58	11.24	18.56	16.09	14.09	12.46	21.16	18.08	15.64	13.67	37
38	14.62	13.01	11.67	10.54	16.96	14.89	13.21	11.80	19.49	16.89	14.80	13.08	22.21	18.98	16.43	14.36	38
39	15.35	13.66	12.25	11.06	17.80	15.64	13.87	12.39	20.46	17.73	15.54	13.73	23.32	19.93	17.25	15.08	39
40	16.12	14.34	12.86	11.62	18.70	16.42	14.56	13.01	21.49	18.62	16.31	14.42	24.49	20.93	18.11	15.83	40
41	16.92	15.06	13.51	12.20	19.63	17.24	15.29	13.66	22.56	19.55	17.13	15.14	25.72	21.97	19.01	16.62	41
42	17.77	15.81	14.18	12.81	20.61	18.10	16.05	14.34	23.69	20.53	17.99	15.90	27.00	23.07	19.97	17.45	42
43	18.66	16.60	14.89	13.45	21.64	19.01	16.86	15.06	24.88	21.56	18.89	16.69	28.35	24.23	20.96	18.32	43
44	19.59	17.43	15.64	14.12	22.72	19.96	17.70	15.81	26.12	22.63	19.83	17.53	29.77	25.44	22.01	19.24	44
45	20.57	18.30	16.42	14.83	23.86	20.96	18.58	16.60	27.42	23.77	20.82	18.40	31.26	26.71	23.11	20.20	45
46	21.60	19.22	17.24	15.57	25.05	22.00	19.51	17.43	28.80	24.95	21.86	19.32	32.82	28.05	24.27	21.21	46
47	22.68	20.18	18.10	16.35	26.31	23.10	20.49	18.31	30.24	26.20	22.96	20.29	34.46	29.45	25.48	22.27	47
48	23.81	21.19	19.01	17.16	27.62	24.26	21.51	19.22	31.75	27.51	24.10	21.30	36.18	30.92	26.76	23.39	48
49	25.00	22.25	19.96	18.02	29.00	25.47	22.59	20.18	33.34	28.89	25.31	22.37	37.99	32.47	28.09	24.56	49
50	26.25	23.36	20.96	18.92	30.45	26.75	23.72	21.19	35.00	30.33	26.57	23.49	39.89	34.09	29.50	25.78	50

IV. Retirement Planning where Salary Falls Behind Moderate 6% Inflation
Planned Retirement Age 71

Table 1 - Percent of Salary Replaced by a 401(k) Account Equal to Current Annual Salary   IV-71-1

Probable Life Expectancy at Retirement

	16 (Same as Male Avg.)				18.3 (Better than Male Avg.)				20.7 (Same as Female Avg.)				23.2 (Better than Female Avg.)			
	4% / 4%	6% / 5%	8% / 6%	10% / 7%	4% / 4%	6% / 5%	8% / 6%	10% / 7%	4% / 4%	6% / 5%	8% / 6%	10% / 7%	4% / 4%	6% / 5%	8% / 6%	10% / 7%	
Yrs. to Ret.	Expected Return				(Pre-Retirement/Post-Retirement)				(Pre-Retirement/Post-Retirement)				Expected Return				Yrs. to Ret.
0	5.11	5.67	6.25	6.86	4.37	4.91	5.47	6.06	3.77	4.29	4.84	5.41	3.28	3.78	4.32	4.88	0
1	5.06	5.73	6.43	7.18	4.33	4.96	5.63	6.35	3.73	4.33	4.97	5.67	3.25	3.82	4.44	5.11	1
2	5.01	5.78	6.62	7.52	4.29	5.00	5.79	6.65	3.69	4.37	5.12	5.94	3.21	3.85	4.57	5.36	2
3	4.97	5.84	6.81	7.88	4.24	5.05	5.96	6.97	3.66	4.41	5.26	6.22	3.18	3.89	4.70	5.61	3
4	4.92	5.89	7.00	8.26	4.20	5.10	6.13	7.30	3.62	4.45	5.41	6.52	3.15	3.93	4.83	5.88	4
5	4.87	5.95	7.20	8.65	4.16	5.15	6.30	7.65	3.59	4.49	5.57	6.83	3.12	3.96	4.97	6.16	5
6	4.83	6.00	7.41	9.06	4.12	5.20	6.48	8.01	3.56	4.54	5.73	7.15	3.09	4.00	5.11	6.45	6
7	4.78	6.06	7.62	9.49	4.09	5.25	6.67	8.39	3.52	4.58	5.89	7.49	3.06	4.04	5.26	6.76	7
8	4.73	6.12	7.84	9.95	4.05	5.30	6.86	8.79	3.49	4.62	6.06	7.85	3.04	4.08	5.41	7.08	8
9	4.69	6.18	8.06	10.42	4.01	5.35	7.05	9.21	3.46	4.67	6.23	8.22	3.01	4.12	5.56	7.42	9
10	4.64	6.24	8.29	10.91	3.97	5.40	7.26	9.65	3.42	4.71	6.41	8.62	2.98	4.16	5.72	7.77	10
11	4.60	6.29	8.53	11.43	3.93	5.45	7.46	10.11	3.39	4.76	6.59	9.03	2.95	4.20	5.88	8.14	11
12	4.56	6.35	8.77	11.98	3.90	5.50	7.68	10.59	3.36	4.80	6.78	9.45	2.92	4.24	6.05	8.53	12
13	4.51	6.41	9.02	12.55	3.86	5.55	7.90	11.09	3.33	4.85	6.98	9.90	2.89	4.28	6.23	8.94	13
14	4.47	6.48	9.28	13.15	3.82	5.60	8.12	11.62	3.29	4.89	7.18	10.38	2.87	4.32	6.40	9.36	14
15	4.43	6.54	9.55	13.77	3.79	5.66	8.35	12.17	3.26	4.94	7.38	10.87	2.84	4.36	6.59	9.81	15
16	4.39	6.60	9.82	14.43	3.75	5.71	8.59	12.75	3.23	4.99	7.59	11.39	2.81	4.40	6.78	10.27	16
17	4.34	6.66	10.10	15.11	3.71	5.77	8.84	13.36	3.20	5.04	7.81	11.93	2.79	4.44	6.97	10.76	17
18	4.30	6.73	10.39	15.83	3.68	5.82	9.09	14.00	3.17	5.08	8.03	12.50	2.76	4.48	7.17	11.28	18
19	4.26	6.79	10.69	16.59	3.64	5.88	9.35	14.66	3.14	5.13	8.26	13.09	2.73	4.52	7.37	11.81	19
20	4.22	6.85	10.99	17.38	3.61	5.93	9.62	15.36	3.11	5.18	8.50	13.72	2.71	4.57	7.58	12.38	20
21	4.18	6.92	11.31	18.20	3.57	5.99	9.89	16.09	3.08	5.23	8.74	14.37	2.68	4.61	7.80	12.96	21
22	4.14	6.98	11.63	19.07	3.54	6.04	10.18	16.86	3.05	5.28	8.99	15.05	2.66	4.65	8.02	13.58	22
23	4.10	7.05	11.96	19.98	3.51	6.10	10.47	17.66	3.02	5.33	9.25	15.77	2.63	4.70	8.25	14.23	23
24	4.06	7.12	12.30	20.93	3.47	6.16	10.77	18.50	2.99	5.38	9.51	16.52	2.61	4.74	8.49	14.90	24
25	4.02	7.19	12.66	21.93	3.44	6.22	11.07	19.38	2.97	5.43	9.79	17.31	2.58	4.79	8.73	15.61	25
26	3.99	7.25	13.02	22.97	3.41	6.28	11.39	20.30	2.94	5.48	10.06	18.13	2.56	4.83	8.98	16.36	26
27	3.95	7.32	13.39	24.06	3.38	6.34	11.72	21.27	2.91	5.53	10.35	18.99	2.53	4.88	9.24	17.14	27
28	3.91	7.39	13.77	25.21	3.34	6.40	12.05	22.28	2.88	5.59	10.65	19.90	2.51	4.93	9.50	17.95	28
29	3.87	7.46	14.17	26.41	3.31	6.46	12.40	23.34	2.86	5.64	10.95	20.84	2.48	4.97	9.78	18.81	29
30	3.84	7.53	14.57	27.66	3.28	6.52	12.75	24.45	2.83	5.69	11.27	21.84	2.46	5.02	10.06	19.70	30
31	3.80	7.60	14.99	28.98	3.25	6.58	13.12	25.62	2.80	5.75	11.59	22.88	2.44	5.07	10.34	20.64	31
32	3.76	7.68	15.42	30.36	3.22	6.64	13.49	26.84	2.77	5.80	11.92	23.96	2.41	5.12	10.64	21.62	32
33	3.73	7.75	15.86	31.81	3.19	6.71	13.88	28.12	2.75	5.86	12.26	25.10	2.39	5.17	10.94	22.65	33
34	3.69	7.82	16.31	33.32	3.16	6.77	14.27	29.45	2.72	5.91	12.61	26.30	2.37	5.21	11.26	23.73	34
35	3.66	7.90	16.78	34.91	3.13	6.83	14.68	30.86	2.70	5.97	12.97	27.55	2.35	5.26	11.58	24.86	35
36	3.62	7.97	17.26	36.57	3.10	6.90	15.10	32.33	2.67	6.03	13.34	28.86	2.32	5.31	11.91	26.04	36
37	3.59	8.05	17.75	38.31	3.07	6.97	15.53	33.86	2.65	6.08	13.73	30.24	2.30	5.36	12.25	27.28	37
38	3.56	8.13	18.26	40.13	3.04	7.03	15.98	35.48	2.62	6.14	14.12	31.68	2.28	5.42	12.60	28.58	38
39	3.52	8.20	18.78	42.04	3.01	7.10	16.44	37.16	2.60	6.20	14.52	33.18	2.26	5.47	12.96	29.94	39
40	3.49	8.28	19.32	44.04	2.98	7.17	16.91	38.93	2.57	6.26	14.94	34.76	2.24	5.52	13.33	31.37	40
41	3.45	8.36	19.87	46.14	2.95	7.23	17.39	40.79	2.55	6.32	15.36	36.42	2.22	5.57	13.71	32.86	41
42	3.42	8.44	20.44	48.34	2.93	7.30	17.89	42.73	2.52	6.38	15.80	38.15	2.19	5.62	14.10	34.42	42
43	3.39	8.52	21.02	50.64	2.90	7.37	18.40	44.76	2.50	6.44	16.26	39.97	2.17	5.68	14.51	36.06	43
44	3.36	8.60	21.63	53.05	2.87	7.44	18.92	46.89	2.47	6.50	16.72	41.87	2.15	5.73	14.92	37.78	44
45	3.33	8.68	22.24	55.57	2.84	7.51	19.47	49.12	2.45	6.56	17.20	43.86	2.13	5.79	15.35	39.58	45
46	3.29	8.76	22.88	58.22	2.82	7.58	20.02	51.46	2.43	6.62	17.69	45.95	2.11	5.84	15.79	41.46	46
47	3.26	8.85	23.53	60.99	2.79	7.66	20.59	53.91	2.40	6.69	18.20	48.14	2.09	5.90	16.24	43.43	47
48	3.23	8.93	24.21	63.89	2.76	7.73	21.18	56.48	2.38	6.75	18.72	50.43	2.07	5.95	16.71	45.50	48
49	3.20	9.02	24.90	66.93	2.74	7.80	21.79	59.17	2.36	6.81	19.25	52.83	2.05	6.01	17.18	47.67	49
50	3.17	9.10	25.61	70.12	2.71	7.88	22.41	61.98	2.34	6.88	19.80	55.34	2.03	6.07	17.67	49.94	50

IV. Retirement Planning where Salary Falls Behind Moderate 6% Inflation
Planned Retirement Age 71

Table 2 - Percent of Salary Replaced by a 401(k) Contribution of 1% of Current Salary IV-71-2

Probable Life Expectancy at Retirement

Yrs. to Ret.	16 (Same as Male Avg.)				18.3 (Better than Male Avg.)				20.7 (Same as Female Avg.)				23.2 (Better than Female Avg.)				Yrs. to Ret.
	4% / 4%	6% / 5%	8% / 6%	10% / 7%	4% / 4%	6% / 5%	8% / 6%	10% / 7%	4% / 4%	6% / 5%	8% / 6%	10% / 7%	4% / 4%	6% / 5%	8% / 6%	10% / 7%	
	Expected Return		(Pre-Retirement/Post-Retirement)				(Pre-Retirement/Post-Retirement)				Expected Return						
0	0.00	0.00	0.00	0.00	0.00	0.00	0.00	0.00	0.00	0.00	0.00	0.00	0.00	0.00	0.00	0.00	0
1	0.05	0.06	0.06	0.07	0.04	0.05	0.05	0.06	0.04	0.04	0.05	0.05	0.03	0.04	0.04	0.05	1
2	0.10	0.11	0.13	0.14	0.09	0.10	0.11	0.12	0.07	0.09	0.10	0.11	0.07	0.08	0.09	0.10	2
3	0.15	0.17	0.19	0.22	0.13	0.15	0.17	0.19	0.11	0.13	0.15	0.17	0.10	0.11	0.13	0.15	3
4	0.20	0.23	0.26	0.29	0.17	0.20	0.23	0.26	0.15	0.17	0.20	0.23	0.13	0.15	0.18	0.21	4
5	0.25	0.29	0.33	0.38	0.21	0.25	0.29	0.33	0.18	0.22	0.26	0.30	0.16	0.19	0.23	0.27	5
6	0.30	0.35	0.40	0.46	0.26	0.30	0.35	0.41	0.22	0.26	0.31	0.37	0.19	0.23	0.28	0.33	6
7	0.35	0.41	0.48	0.55	0.30	0.35	0.42	0.49	0.26	0.31	0.37	0.44	0.22	0.27	0.33	0.39	7
8	0.40	0.47	0.55	0.65	0.34	0.41	0.48	0.57	0.29	0.35	0.43	0.51	0.25	0.31	0.38	0.46	8
9	0.44	0.53	0.63	0.75	0.38	0.46	0.55	0.66	0.33	0.40	0.49	0.59	0.28	0.35	0.44	0.53	9
10	0.49	0.59	0.71	0.85	0.42	0.51	0.62	0.75	0.36	0.45	0.55	0.67	0.31	0.39	0.49	0.61	10
11	0.54	0.65	0.80	0.96	0.46	0.57	0.70	0.85	0.40	0.49	0.61	0.76	0.34	0.44	0.55	0.69	11
12	0.58	0.72	0.88	1.08	0.50	0.62	0.77	0.95	0.43	0.54	0.68	0.85	0.37	0.48	0.61	0.77	12
13	0.63	0.78	0.97	1.20	0.54	0.68	0.85	1.06	0.46	0.59	0.75	0.94	0.40	0.52	0.67	0.85	13
14	0.67	0.85	1.06	1.32	0.58	0.73	0.93	1.17	0.50	0.64	0.82	1.04	0.43	0.56	0.73	0.94	14
15	0.72	0.91	1.15	1.45	0.61	0.79	1.01	1.28	0.53	0.69	0.89	1.15	0.46	0.61	0.79	1.03	15
16	0.76	0.98	1.25	1.59	0.65	0.84	1.09	1.41	0.56	0.74	0.96	1.26	0.49	0.65	0.86	1.13	16
17	0.81	1.04	1.34	1.73	0.69	0.90	1.18	1.53	0.59	0.79	1.04	1.37	0.52	0.69	0.93	1.24	17
18	0.85	1.11	1.45	1.89	0.73	0.96	1.27	1.67	0.63	0.84	1.12	1.49	0.54	0.74	1.00	1.34	18
19	0.89	1.18	1.55	2.04	0.76	1.02	1.36	1.81	0.66	0.89	1.20	1.61	0.57	0.78	1.07	1.46	19
20	0.93	1.24	1.66	2.21	0.80	1.08	1.45	1.95	0.69	0.94	1.28	1.74	0.60	0.83	1.14	1.57	20
21	0.98	1.31	1.77	2.38	0.84	1.14	1.55	2.11	0.72	0.99	1.37	1.88	0.63	0.87	1.22	1.70	21
22	1.02	1.38	1.88	2.57	0.87	1.19	1.64	2.27	0.75	1.04	1.45	2.03	0.65	0.92	1.30	1.83	22
23	1.06	1.45	2.00	2.76	0.91	1.26	1.75	2.44	0.78	1.10	1.54	2.18	0.68	0.97	1.38	1.96	23
24	1.10	1.52	2.12	2.96	0.94	1.32	1.85	2.61	0.81	1.15	1.64	2.33	0.71	1.01	1.46	2.11	24
25	1.14	1.59	2.24	3.17	0.98	1.38	1.96	2.80	0.84	1.20	1.73	2.50	0.73	1.06	1.54	2.25	25
26	1.18	1.66	2.37	3.39	1.01	1.44	2.07	2.99	0.87	1.26	1.83	2.67	0.76	1.11	1.63	2.41	26
27	1.22	1.74	2.50	3.61	1.04	1.50	2.18	3.20	0.90	1.31	1.93	2.85	0.78	1.16	1.72	2.57	27
28	1.26	1.81	2.63	3.86	1.08	1.57	2.30	3.41	0.93	1.37	2.03	3.04	0.81	1.21	1.81	2.75	28
29	1.30	1.88	2.77	4.11	1.11	1.63	2.42	3.63	0.96	1.42	2.14	3.24	0.83	1.26	1.91	2.93	29
30	1.34	1.96	2.91	4.37	1.14	1.69	2.55	3.86	0.99	1.48	2.25	3.45	0.86	1.31	2.01	3.11	30
31	1.38	2.03	3.05	4.65	1.18	1.76	2.67	4.11	1.02	1.54	2.36	3.67	0.88	1.36	2.11	3.31	31
32	1.42	2.11	3.20	4.94	1.21	1.83	2.80	4.37	1.04	1.59	2.48	3.90	0.91	1.41	2.21	3.52	32
33	1.45	2.19	3.36	5.24	1.24	1.89	2.94	4.63	1.07	1.65	2.60	4.14	0.93	1.46	2.32	3.73	33
34	1.49	2.26	3.52	5.56	1.27	1.96	3.08	4.91	1.10	1.71	2.72	4.39	0.96	1.51	2.43	3.96	34
35	1.53	2.34	3.68	5.89	1.31	2.03	3.22	5.21	1.13	1.77	2.85	4.65	0.98	1.56	2.54	4.20	35
36	1.56	2.42	3.85	6.24	1.34	2.10	3.37	5.52	1.15	1.83	2.98	4.93	1.00	1.61	2.66	4.45	36
37	1.60	2.50	4.02	6.61	1.37	2.16	3.52	5.84	1.18	1.89	3.11	5.22	1.03	1.67	2.77	4.71	37
38	1.64	2.58	4.20	6.99	1.40	2.23	3.67	6.18	1.21	1.95	3.25	5.52	1.05	1.72	2.90	4.98	38
39	1.67	2.66	4.38	7.39	1.43	2.30	3.83	6.53	1.23	2.01	3.39	5.83	1.07	1.77	3.02	5.26	39
40	1.71	2.74	4.57	7.81	1.46	2.38	4.00	6.91	1.26	2.07	3.53	6.17	1.09	1.83	3.15	5.56	40
41	1.74	2.83	4.76	8.25	1.49	2.45	4.17	7.30	1.28	2.14	3.68	6.51	1.12	1.88	3.29	5.88	41
42	1.78	2.91	4.96	8.71	1.52	2.52	4.34	7.70	1.31	2.20	3.84	6.88	1.14	1.94	3.42	6.21	42
43	1.81	3.00	5.16	9.20	1.55	2.59	4.52	8.13	1.33	2.26	3.99	7.26	1.16	2.00	3.56	6.55	43
44	1.84	3.08	5.37	9.70	1.58	2.67	4.70	8.58	1.36	2.33	4.16	7.66	1.18	2.05	3.71	6.91	44
45	1.88	3.17	5.59	10.23	1.61	2.74	4.89	9.05	1.38	2.39	4.32	8.08	1.20	2.11	3.86	7.29	45
46	1.91	3.25	5.81	10.79	1.63	2.82	5.09	9.54	1.41	2.46	4.49	8.52	1.23	2.17	4.01	7.68	46
47	1.94	3.34	6.04	11.37	1.66	2.89	5.29	10.05	1.43	2.53	4.67	8.98	1.25	2.23	4.17	8.10	47
48	1.98	3.43	6.28	11.98	1.69	2.97	5.49	10.59	1.46	2.59	4.85	9.46	1.27	2.29	4.33	8.53	48
49	2.01	3.52	6.52	12.62	1.72	3.05	5.71	11.16	1.48	2.66	5.04	9.96	1.29	2.35	4.50	8.99	49
50	2.04	3.61	6.77	13.29	1.75	3.12	5.92	11.75	1.50	2.73	5.23	10.49	1.31	2.41	4.67	9.46	50

IV. Retirement Planning where Salary Falls Behind Moderate 6% Inflation
Planned Retirement Age 71

Table 3 - 401(k) Contribution (% of Current Sal.) Needed to Replace 10% of Sal. at Retirement   IV-71-3

Probable Life Expectancy at Retirement

Yrs. to Ret.	16 (Same as Male Avg.)				18.3 (Better than Male Avg.)				20.7 (Same as Female Avg.)				23.2 (Better than Female Avg.)				Yrs. to Ret.
	4% / 4%	6% / 5%	8% / 6%	10% / 7%	4% / 4%	6% / 5%	8% / 6%	10% / 7%	4% / 4%	6% / 5%	8% / 6%	10% / 7%	4% / 4%	6% / 5%	8% / 6%	10% / 7%	
	Expected Return		(Pre-Retirement/Post-Retirement)				(Pre-Retirement/Post-Retirement)				Expected Return						
0																	0
1	195.71	176.28	159.91	145.86	228.94	203.70	182.74	165.00	265.56	233.24	206.82	184.80	305.23	264.50	231.73	204.82	1
2	98.32	87.72	78.83	71.24	115.02	101.37	90.08	80.58	133.41	116.07	101.95	90.25	153.34	131.62	114.23	100.03	2
3	65.86	58.21	51.81	46.38	77.04	67.26	59.20	52.46	89.36	77.01	67.01	58.76	102.72	87.33	75.08	65.12	3
4	49.63	43.45	38.30	33.96	58.06	50.20	43.77	38.42	67.34	57.49	49.54	43.03	77.40	65.19	55.51	47.69	4
5	39.89	34.59	30.20	26.52	46.67	39.97	34.52	30.01	54.13	45.77	39.07	33.60	62.22	51.90	43.77	37.24	5
6	33.40	28.69	24.81	21.57	39.07	33.15	28.35	24.41	45.32	37.96	32.09	27.33	52.09	43.05	35.95	30.29	6
7	28.77	24.47	20.96	18.05	33.65	28.28	23.95	20.41	39.03	32.38	27.11	22.86	44.86	36.72	30.37	25.34	7
8	25.29	21.31	18.07	15.41	29.58	24.63	20.65	17.43	34.31	28.20	23.37	19.52	39.44	31.98	26.19	21.63	8
9	22.58	18.85	15.83	13.36	26.42	21.79	18.09	15.11	30.65	24.95	20.47	16.93	35.22	28.29	22.94	18.76	9
10	20.42	16.89	14.04	11.73	23.89	19.51	16.04	13.27	27.71	22.34	18.16	14.86	31.85	25.34	20.34	16.47	10
11	18.65	15.28	12.58	10.40	21.82	17.65	14.37	11.76	25.31	20.22	16.26	13.17	29.09	22.92	18.22	14.60	11
12	17.18	13.94	11.36	9.29	20.10	16.11	12.98	10.51	23.31	18.44	14.69	11.77	26.79	20.91	16.46	13.05	12
13	15.93	12.80	10.33	8.36	18.64	14.80	11.80	9.46	21.62	16.94	13.36	10.59	24.85	19.21	14.97	11.74	13
14	14.86	11.83	9.45	7.57	17.39	13.67	10.80	8.56	20.17	15.66	12.22	9.59	23.18	17.75	13.69	10.63	14
15	13.94	10.99	8.69	6.88	16.30	12.70	9.93	7.79	18.91	14.54	11.23	8.72	21.74	16.49	12.59	9.66	15
16	13.13	10.25	8.02	6.29	15.36	11.85	9.17	7.11	17.81	13.57	10.37	7.96	20.47	15.38	11.62	8.83	16
17	12.41	9.60	7.44	5.76	14.52	11.10	8.50	6.52	16.84	12.71	9.62	7.30	19.36	14.41	10.78	8.09	17
18	11.78	9.03	6.92	5.30	13.78	10.43	7.90	6.00	15.98	11.94	8.95	6.72	18.37	13.54	10.02	7.44	18
19	11.21	8.51	6.45	4.89	13.11	9.83	7.37	5.53	15.21	11.26	8.35	6.20	17.48	12.77	9.35	6.87	19
20	10.70	8.04	6.04	4.52	12.51	9.30	6.90	5.12	14.52	10.64	7.81	5.73	16.68	12.07	8.75	6.35	20
21	10.24	7.62	5.66	4.19	11.97	8.81	6.47	4.75	13.89	10.09	7.32	5.31	15.96	11.44	8.20	5.89	21
22	9.82	7.24	5.32	3.90	11.48	8.37	6.08	4.41	13.32	9.58	6.88	4.94	15.31	10.87	7.71	5.47	22
23	9.43	6.89	5.01	3.63	11.03	7.97	5.73	4.10	12.80	9.12	6.48	4.60	14.71	10.34	7.26	5.09	23
24	9.08	6.57	4.73	3.38	10.62	7.60	5.40	3.83	12.32	8.70	6.11	4.29	14.16	9.86	6.85	4.75	24
25	8.76	6.28	4.47	3.16	10.24	7.26	5.10	3.57	11.88	8.31	5.78	4.00	13.66	9.42	6.47	4.44	25
26	8.46	6.01	4.23	2.95	9.90	6.94	4.83	3.34	11.48	7.95	5.47	3.74	13.19	9.02	6.13	4.15	26
27	8.18	5.76	4.01	2.77	9.57	6.65	4.58	3.13	11.10	7.62	5.18	3.50	12.76	8.64	5.81	3.88	27
28	7.93	5.53	3.80	2.59	9.27	6.38	4.35	2.93	10.76	7.31	4.92	3.29	12.36	8.29	5.51	3.64	28
29	7.69	5.31	3.61	2.43	8.99	6.13	4.13	2.75	10.43	7.02	4.67	3.08	11.99	7.96	5.24	3.42	29
30	7.47	5.11	3.44	2.29	8.73	5.90	3.93	2.59	10.13	6.76	4.45	2.90	11.64	7.66	4.98	3.21	30
31	7.26	4.92	3.27	2.15	8.49	5.68	3.74	2.43	9.85	6.51	4.23	2.73	11.32	7.38	4.74	3.02	31
32	7.06	4.74	3.12	2.03	8.26	5.48	3.57	2.29	9.58	6.27	4.04	2.57	11.02	7.11	4.52	2.84	32
33	6.88	4.57	2.98	1.91	8.05	5.28	3.40	2.16	9.34	6.05	3.85	2.42	10.73	6.86	4.31	2.68	33
34	6.71	4.42	2.84	1.80	7.85	5.10	3.25	2.03	9.10	5.84	3.68	2.28	10.46	6.63	4.12	2.53	34
35	6.55	4.27	2.72	1.70	7.66	4.93	3.11	1.92	8.88	5.65	3.51	2.15	10.21	6.41	3.94	2.38	35
36	6.39	4.13	2.60	1.60	7.48	4.77	2.97	1.81	8.67	5.46	3.36	2.03	9.97	6.20	3.77	2.25	36
37	6.25	4.00	2.49	1.51	7.31	4.62	2.84	1.71	8.48	5.29	3.22	1.92	9.75	6.00	3.60	2.13	37
38	6.11	3.87	2.38	1.43	7.15	4.48	2.72	1.62	8.29	5.13	3.08	1.81	9.53	5.81	3.45	2.01	38
39	5.98	3.76	2.28	1.35	7.00	4.34	2.61	1.53	8.12	4.97	2.95	1.71	9.33	5.63	3.31	1.90	39
40	5.86	3.64	2.19	1.28	6.85	4.21	2.50	1.45	7.95	4.82	2.83	1.62	9.14	5.47	3.17	1.80	40
41	5.74	3.54	2.10	1.21	6.72	4.09	2.40	1.37	7.79	4.68	2.72	1.54	8.95	5.31	3.04	1.70	41
42	5.63	3.44	2.02	1.15	6.58	3.97	2.30	1.30	7.64	4.54	2.61	1.45	8.78	5.15	2.92	1.61	42
43	5.52	3.34	1.94	1.09	6.46	3.86	2.21	1.23	7.49	4.42	2.50	1.38	8.61	5.01	2.81	1.53	43
44	5.42	3.25	1.86	1.03	6.34	3.75	2.13	1.17	7.36	4.29	2.41	1.31	8.46	4.87	2.70	1.45	44
45	5.32	3.16	1.79	0.98	6.23	3.65	2.04	1.11	7.22	4.18	2.31	1.24	8.30	4.74	2.59	1.37	45
46	5.23	3.07	1.72	0.93	6.12	3.55	1.97	1.05	7.10	4.07	2.22	1.17	8.16	4.61	2.49	1.30	46
47	5.14	2.99	1.65	0.88	6.02	3.46	1.89	0.99	6.98	3.96	2.14	1.11	8.02	4.49	2.40	1.23	47
48	5.06	2.92	1.59	0.83	5.92	3.37	1.82	0.94	6.86	3.86	2.06	1.06	7.89	4.37	2.31	1.17	48
49	4.98	2.84	1.53	0.79	5.82	3.28	1.75	0.90	6.75	3.76	1.98	1.00	7.76	4.26	2.22	1.11	49
50	4.90	2.77	1.48	0.75	5.73	3.20	1.69	0.85	6.65	3.67	1.91	0.95	7.64	4.16	2.14	1.06	50

IV. Retirement Planning where Salary Falls Behind Moderate 6% Inflation
Planned Retirement Age 71

Table 4 - Accumulation at Retirement (Multiple of Current Sal.) for 10% Sal. Replacement   IV-71-4

Probable Life Expectancy at Retirement

	16 (Same as Male Avg.)				18.3 (Better than Male Avg.)				20.7 (Same as Female Avg.)				23.2 (Better than Female Avg.)			
	4% / 4%	6% / 5%	8% / 6%	10% / 7%	4% / 4%	6% / 5%	8% / 6%	10% / 7%	4% / 4%	6% / 5%	8% / 6%	10% / 7%	4% / 4%	6% / 5%	8% / 6%	10% / 7%	
Yrs. to Ret.	Expected Return		(Pre-Retirement/Post-Retirement)				(Pre-Retirement/Post-Retirement)				Expected Return						Yrs. to Ret.
0	1.96	1.76	1.60	1.46	2.29	2.04	1.83	1.65	2.66	2.33	2.07	1.85	3.05	2.64	2.32	2.05	0
1	2.05	1.85	1.68	1.53	2.40	2.14	1.92	1.73	2.79	2.45	2.17	1.94	3.20	2.78	2.43	2.15	1
2	2.16	1.94	1.76	1.61	2.52	2.25	2.01	1.82	2.93	2.57	2.28	2.04	3.37	2.92	2.55	2.26	2
3	2.27	2.04	1.85	1.69	2.65	2.36	2.12	1.91	3.07	2.70	2.39	2.14	3.53	3.06	2.68	2.37	3
4	2.38	2.14	1.94	1.77	2.78	2.48	2.22	2.01	3.23	2.84	2.51	2.25	3.71	3.21	2.82	2.49	4
5	2.50	2.25	2.04	1.86	2.92	2.60	2.33	2.11	3.39	2.98	2.64	2.36	3.90	3.38	2.96	2.61	5
6	2.62	2.36	2.14	1.95	3.07	2.73	2.45	2.21	3.56	3.13	2.77	2.48	4.09	3.54	3.11	2.74	6
7	2.75	2.48	2.25	2.05	3.22	2.87	2.57	2.32	3.74	3.28	2.91	2.60	4.29	3.72	3.26	2.88	7
8	2.89	2.60	2.36	2.16	3.38	3.01	2.70	2.44	3.92	3.45	3.06	2.73	4.51	3.91	3.42	3.03	8
9	3.04	2.73	2.48	2.26	3.55	3.16	2.83	2.56	4.12	3.62	3.21	2.87	4.74	4.10	3.59	3.18	9
10	3.19	2.87	2.60	2.38	3.73	3.32	2.98	2.69	4.33	3.80	3.37	3.01	4.97	4.31	3.77	3.34	10
11	3.35	3.02	2.74	2.49	3.92	3.48	3.13	2.82	4.54	3.99	3.54	3.16	5.22	4.52	3.96	3.50	11
12	3.51	3.17	2.87	2.62	4.11	3.66	3.28	2.96	4.77	4.19	3.71	3.32	5.48	4.75	4.16	3.68	12
13	3.69	3.32	3.02	2.75	4.32	3.84	3.45	3.11	5.01	4.40	3.90	3.48	5.76	4.99	4.37	3.86	13
14	3.87	3.49	3.17	2.89	4.53	4.03	3.62	3.27	5.26	4.62	4.09	3.66	6.04	5.24	4.59	4.06	14
15	4.07	3.66	3.32	3.03	4.76	4.23	3.80	3.43	5.52	4.85	4.30	3.84	6.35	5.50	4.82	4.26	15
16	4.27	3.85	3.49	3.18	5.00	4.45	3.99	3.60	5.80	5.09	4.51	4.03	6.66	5.77	5.06	4.47	16
17	4.49	4.04	3.67	3.34	5.25	4.67	4.19	3.78	6.09	5.35	4.74	4.24	7.00	6.06	5.31	4.69	17
18	4.71	4.24	3.85	3.51	5.51	4.90	4.40	3.97	6.39	5.61	4.98	4.45	7.35	6.37	5.58	4.93	18
19	4.95	4.45	4.04	3.69	5.79	5.15	4.62	4.17	6.71	5.89	5.23	4.67	7.71	6.68	5.86	5.18	19
20	5.19	4.68	4.24	3.87	6.07	5.40	4.85	4.38	7.05	6.19	5.49	4.90	8.10	7.02	6.15	5.43	20
21	5.45	4.91	4.46	4.06	6.38	5.67	5.09	4.60	7.40	6.50	5.76	5.15	8.50	7.37	6.46	5.71	21
22	5.73	5.16	4.68	4.27	6.70	5.96	5.35	4.83	7.77	6.82	6.05	5.41	8.93	7.74	6.78	5.99	22
23	6.01	5.41	4.91	4.48	7.03	6.26	5.61	5.07	8.16	7.16	6.35	5.68	9.38	8.12	7.12	6.29	23
24	6.31	5.69	5.16	4.70	7.38	6.57	5.89	5.32	8.56	7.52	6.67	5.96	9.84	8.53	7.47	6.61	24
25	6.63	5.97	5.42	4.94	7.75	6.90	6.19	5.59	8.99	7.90	7.00	6.26	10.34	8.96	7.85	6.94	25
26	6.96	6.27	5.69	5.19	8.14	7.24	6.50	5.87	9.44	8.29	7.35	6.57	10.85	9.40	8.24	7.28	26
27	7.31	6.58	5.97	5.45	8.55	7.60	6.82	6.16	9.91	8.71	7.72	6.90	11.40	9.87	8.65	7.65	27
28	7.67	6.91	6.27	5.72	8.97	7.99	7.16	6.47	10.41	9.14	8.11	7.24	11.97	10.37	9.08	8.03	28
29	8.06	7.26	6.58	6.00	9.42	8.38	7.52	6.79	10.93	9.60	8.51	7.61	12.56	10.89	9.54	8.43	29
30	8.46	7.62	6.91	6.30	9.89	8.80	7.90	7.13	11.48	10.08	8.94	7.99	13.19	11.43	10.02	8.85	30
31	8.88	8.00	7.26	6.62	10.39	9.24	8.29	7.49	12.05	10.58	9.39	8.39	13.85	12.00	10.52	9.29	31
32	9.33	8.40	7.62	6.95	10.91	9.71	8.71	7.86	12.65	11.11	9.86	8.81	14.54	12.60	11.04	9.76	32
33	9.79	8.82	8.00	7.30	11.45	10.19	9.14	8.26	13.29	11.67	10.35	9.25	15.27	13.23	11.59	10.25	33
34	10.28	9.26	8.40	7.66	12.03	10.70	9.60	8.67	13.95	12.25	10.87	9.71	16.03	13.89	12.17	10.76	34
35	10.80	9.72	8.82	8.05	12.63	11.24	10.08	9.10	14.65	12.87	11.41	10.19	16.84	14.59	12.78	11.30	35
36	11.34	10.21	9.26	8.45	13.26	11.80	10.58	9.56	15.38	13.51	11.98	10.70	17.68	15.32	13.42	11.86	36
37	11.90	10.72	9.72	8.87	13.92	12.39	11.11	10.03	16.15	14.18	12.58	11.24	18.56	16.09	14.09	12.46	37
38	12.50	11.26	10.21	9.31	14.62	13.01	11.67	10.54	16.96	14.89	13.21	11.80	19.49	16.89	14.80	13.08	38
39	13.12	11.82	10.72	9.78	15.35	13.66	12.25	11.06	17.80	15.64	13.87	12.39	20.46	17.73	15.54	13.73	39
40	13.78	12.41	11.26	10.27	16.12	14.34	12.86	11.62	18.70	16.42	14.56	13.01	21.49	18.62	16.31	14.42	40
41	14.47	13.03	11.82	10.78	16.92	15.06	13.51	12.20	19.63	17.24	15.29	13.66	22.56	19.55	17.13	15.14	41
42	15.19	13.68	12.41	11.32	17.77	15.81	14.18	12.81	20.61	18.10	16.05	14.34	23.69	20.53	17.99	15.90	42
43	15.95	14.37	13.03	11.89	18.66	16.60	14.89	13.45	21.64	19.01	16.86	15.06	24.88	21.56	18.89	16.69	43
44	16.75	15.08	13.68	12.48	19.59	17.43	15.64	14.12	22.72	19.96	17.70	15.81	26.12	22.63	19.83	17.53	44
45	17.58	15.84	14.37	13.11	20.57	18.30	16.42	14.83	23.86	20.96	18.58	16.60	27.42	23.77	20.82	18.40	45
46	18.46	16.63	15.08	13.76	21.60	19.22	17.24	15.57	25.05	22.00	19.51	17.43	28.80	24.95	21.86	19.32	46
47	19.39	17.46	15.84	14.45	22.68	20.18	18.10	16.35	26.31	23.10	20.49	18.31	30.24	26.20	22.96	20.29	47
48	20.36	18.34	16.63	15.17	23.81	21.19	19.01	17.16	27.62	24.26	21.51	19.22	31.75	27.51	24.10	21.30	48
49	21.37	19.25	17.46	15.93	25.00	22.25	19.96	18.02	29.00	25.47	22.59	20.18	33.34	28.89	25.31	22.37	49
50	22.44	20.22	18.34	16.73	26.25	23.36	20.96	18.92	30.45	26.75	23.72	21.19	35.00	30.33	26.57	23.49	50

Appendix B
IRS Tables of
Expected Return Multiples

Table V--Ordinary Life Annuities
One Life -- Expected Return Multiples

Age	Multiple	Age	Multiple	Age	Multiple
5	76.6	42	40.6	79	10.0
6	75.6	43	39.6	80	9.5
7	74.7	44	38.7	81	8.9
8	73.7	45	37.7	82	8.4
9	72.7	46	36.8	83	7.9
10	71.7	47	35.9	84	7.4
11	70.7	48	34.9	85	6.9
12	69.7	49	34.0	86	6.5
13	68.8	50	33.1	87	6.1
14	67.8	51	32.2	88	5.7
15	66.8	52	31.3	89	5.3
16	65.8	53	30.4	90	5.0
17	64.8	54	29.5	91	4.7
18	63.9	55	28.6	92	4.4
19	62.9	56	27.7	93	4.1
20	61.9	57	26.8	94	3.9
21	60.9	58	25.9	95	3.7
22	59.9	59	25.0	96	3.4
23	59.0	60	24.2	97	3.2
24	58.0	61	23.3	98	3.0
25	57.0	62	22.5	99	2.8
26	56.0	63	21.6	100	2.7
27	55.1	64	20.8	101	2.5
28	54.1	65	20.0	102	2.3
29	53.1	66	19.2	103	2.1
30	52.2	67	18.4	104	1.9
31	51.2	68	17.6	105	1.8
32	50.2	69	16.8	106	1.6
33	49.3	70	16.0	107	1.4
34	48.3	71	15.3	108	1.3
35	47.3	72	14.6	109	1.1
36	46.4	73	13.9	110	1.0
37	45.4	74	13.2	111	0.9
38	44.4	75	12.5	112	0.8
39	43.5	76	11.9	113	0.7
40	42.5	77	11.2	114	0.6
41	41.5	78	10.6	115	0.5

Table VI--Ordinary Joint Life & Last Survivor Annuities
Two Lives--Expected Return Multiples

Ages	5	6	7	8	9	10	11	12	13	14
5............	83.8	83.3	82.8	82.4	82.0	81.6	81.2	80.9	80.6	80.3
6............	83.3	82.8	82.3	81.8	81.4	81.0	80.6	80.3	79.9	79.6
7............	82.8	82.3	81.8	81.3	80.9	80.4	80.0	79.6	79.3	78.9
8............	82.4	81.8	81.3	80.8	80.3	79.9	79.4	79.0	78.6	78.3
9............	82.0	81.4	80.9	80.3	79.8	79.3	78.9	78.4	78.0	77.6
10............	81.6	81.0	80.4	79.9	79.3	78.8	78.3	77.9	77.4	77.0
11............	81.2	80.6	80.0	79.4	78.9	78.3	77.8	77.3	76.9	76.4
12............	80.9	80.3	79.6	79.0	78.4	77.9	77.3	76.8	76.3	75.9
13............	80.6	79.9	79.3	78.6	78.0	77.4	76.9	76.3	75.8	75.3
14............	80.3	79.6	78.9	78.3	77.6	77.0	76.4	75.9	75.3	74.8
15............	80.0	79.3	78.6	77.9	77.3	76.6	76.0	75.4	74.9	74.3
16............	79.8	79.0	78.3	77.6	76.9	76.3	75.6	75.0	74.4	73.9
17............	79.5	78.8	78.0	77.3	76.6	75.9	75.3	74.6	74.0	73.4
18............	79.3	78.5	77.8	77.0	76.3	75.6	74.9	74.3	73.6	73.0
19............	79.1	78.3	77.5	76.8	76.0	75.3	74.6	73.9	73.3	72.6
20............	78.9	78.1	77.3	76.5	75.8	75.0	74.3	73.6	72.9	72.3
21............	78.7	77.9	77.1	76.3	75.5	74.8	74.0	73.3	72.6	71.9
22............	78.6	77.7	76.9	76.1	75.3	74.5	73.8	73.0	72.3	71.6
23............	78.4	77.6	76.7	75.9	75.1	74.3	73.5	72.8	72.0	71.3
24............	78.3	77.4	76.6	75.7	74.9	74.1	73.3	72.6	71.8	71.1
25............	78.2	77.8	76.4	75.6	74.8	73.9	73.1	72.3	71.6	70.8
26............	78.0	77.2	76.3	75.4	74.6	73.8	72.9	72.1	71.3	70.6
27............	77.9	77.1	76.2	75.3	74.4	73.6	72.8	71.9	71.1	70.3
28............	77.8	76.9	76.1	75.2	74.3	73.4	72.6	71.8	70.9	70.1
29............	77.7	76.8	76.0	75.1	74.2	73.3	72.5	71.6	70.8	70.0
30............	77.7	76.8	75.9	75.0	74.1	73.2	72.3	71.5	70.6	69.8
31............	77.6	76.7	75.8	74.9	74.0	73.1	72.2	71.3	70.5	69.6
32............	77.5	76.6	75.7	74.8	73.9	73.0	72.1	71.2	70.3	69.5
33............	77.5	76.5	75.6	74.7	73.8	72.9	72.0	71.1	70.2	69.3
34............	77.4	76.5	75.5	74.6	73.7	72.8	71.9	71.0	70.1	69.2
35............	77.3	76.4	75.5	74.5	73.6	72.7	71.8	70.9	70.0	69.1
36............	77.3	76.3	75.4	74.5	73.5	72.6	71.7	70.8	69.9	69.0
37............	77.2	76.3	75.4	74.4	73.5	72.6	71.6	70.7	69.8	68.9
38............	77.2	76.2	75.3	74.4	73.4	72.5	71.6	70.6	69.7	68.8
39............	77.2	76.2	75.3	74.3	73.4	72.4	71.5	70.6	69.6	68.7
40............	77.1	76.2	75.2	74.3	73.3	72.4	71.4	70.5	69.6	68.6
41............	77.1	76.1	75.2	74.2	73.3	72.3	71.4	70.4	69.5	68.6
42............	77.0	76.1	75.1	74.2	73.2	72.3	71.3	70.4	69.4	68.5
43............	77.0	76.1	75.1	74.1	73.2	72.2	71.3	70.3	69.4	68.5
44............	77.0	76.0	75.1	74.1	73.1	72.2	71.2	70.3	69.3	68.4
45............	77.0	76.0	75.0	74.1	73.1	72.2	71.2	70.2	69.3	68.4
46............	76.9	76.0	75.0	74.0	73.1	72.1	71.2	70.2	69.3	68.3
47............	76.9	75.9	75.0	74.0	73.1	72.1	71.1	70.2	69.2	68.3
48............	76.9	75.9	75.0	74.0	73.0	72.1	71.1	70.1	69.2	68.2
49............	76.9	75.9	74.9	74.0	73.0	72.0	71.1	70.1	69.1	68.2
50............	76.9	75.9	74.9	73.9	73.0	72.0	71.0	70.1	69.1	68.2
51............	76.8	75.9	74.9	73.9	73.0	72.0	71.0	70.1	69.1	68.1
52............	76.8	75.9	74.9	73.9	72.9	72.0	71.0	70.0	69.1	68.1
53............	76.8	75.8	74.9	73.9	72.9	71.9	71.0	70.0	69.0	68.1
54............	76.8	75.8	74.8	73.9	72.9	71.9	71.0	70.0	69.0	68.1
55............	76.8	75.8	74.8	73.9	72.9	71.9	70.9	70.0	69.0	68.0
56............	76.8	75.8	74.8	73.8	72.9	71.9	70.9	69.9	69.0	68.0
57............	76.8	75.8	74.8	73.8	72.9	71.9	70.9	69.9	69.0	68.0
58............	76.8	75.8	74.8	73.8	72.8	71.9	70.9	69.9	68.9	68.0
59............	76.7	75.8	74.8	73.8	72.8	71.9	70.9	69.9	68.9	68.0

Table VI--Ordinary Joint Life & Last Survivor Annuities
Two Lives--Expected Return Multiples

Ages	5	6	7	8	9	10	11	12	13	14
60..........	76.7	75.8	74.8	73.8	72.8	71.8	70.9	69.9	68.9	67.9
61..........	76.7	75.7	74.8	73.8	72.8	71.8	70.9	69.9	68.9	67.9
62..........	76.7	75.7	74.8	73.8	72.8	71.8	70.8	69.9	68.9	67.9
63..........	76.7	75.7	74.8	73.8	72.8	71.8	70.8	69.9	68.9	67.9
64..........	76.7	75.7	74.7	73.8	72.8	71.8	70.8	69.8	68.9	67.9
65..........	76.7	75.7	74.7	73.8	72.8	71.8	70.8	69.8	68.9	67.9
66..........	76.7	75.7	74.7	73.7	72.8	71.8	70.8	69.8	68.9	67.9
67..........	76.7	75.7	74.7	73.7	72.8	71.8	70.8	69.8	68.8	67.9
68..........	76.7	75.7	74.7	73.7	72.8	71.8	70.8	69.8	68.8	67.9
69..........	76.7	75.7	74.7	73.7	72.7	71.8	70.8	69.8	68.8	67.8
70..........	76.7	75.7	74.7	73.7	72.7	71.8	70.8	69.8	68.8	67.8
71..........	76.7	75.7	74.7	73.7	72.7	71.8	70.8	69.8	68.8	67.8
72..........	76.7	75.7	74.7	73.7	72.7	71.8	70.8	69.8	68.8	67.8
73..........	76.7	75.7	74.7	73.7	72.7	71.7	70.8	69.8	68.8	67.8
74..........	76.7	75.7	74.7	73.7	72.7	71.7	70.8	69.8	68.8	67.8
75..........	76.7	75.7	74.7	73.7	72.7	71.7	70.8	69.8	68.8	67.8
76..........	76.6	75.7	74.7	73.7	72.7	71.7	70.8	69.8	68.8	67.8
77..........	76.6	75.7	74.7	73.7	72.7	71.7	70.8	69.8	68.8	67.8
78..........	76.6	75.7	74.7	73.7	72.7	71.7	70.7	69.8	68.8	67.8
79..........	76.6	75.7	74.7	73.7	72.7	71.7	70.7	69.8	68.8	67.8
80..........	76.6	75.7	74.7	73.7	72.7	71.7	70.7	69.8	68.8	67.8
81..........	76.6	75.7	74.7	73.7	72.7	71.7	70.7	69.8	68.8	67.8
82..........	76.6	75.7	74.7	73.7	72.7	71.7	70.7	69.8	68.8	67.8
83..........	76.6	75.7	74.7	73.7	72.7	71.7	70.7	69.8	68.8	67.8
84..........	76.6	75.7	74.7	73.7	72.7	71.7	70.7	69.8	68.8	67.8
85..........	76.6	75.7	74.7	73.7	72.7	71.7	70.7	69.8	68.8	67.8
86..........	76.6	75.7	74.7	73.7	72.7	71.7	70.7	69.8	68.8	67.8
87..........	76.6	75.7	74.7	73.7	72.7	71.7	70.7	69.8	68.8	67.8
88..........	76.6	75.7	74.7	73.7	72.7	71.7	70.7	69.8	68.8	67.8
89..........	76.6	75.7	74.7	73.7	72.7	71.7	70.7	69.7	68.8	67.8
90..........	76.6	75.6	74.7	73.7	72.7	71.7	70.7	69.7	68.8	67.8
91..........	76.6	75.6	74.7	73.7	72.7	71.7	70.7	69.7	68.8	67.8
92..........	76.6	75.6	74.7	73.7	72.7	71.7	70.7	69.7	68.8	67.8
93..........	76.6	75.6	74.7	73.7	72.7	71.7	70.7	69.7	68.8	67.8
94..........	76.6	75.6	74.7	73.7	72.7	71.7	70.7	69.7	68.8	67.8
95..........	76.6	75.6	74.7	73.7	72.7	71.7	70.7	69.7	68.8	67.8
96..........	76.6	75.6	74.7	73.7	72.7	71.7	70.7	69.7	68.8	67.8
97..........	76.6	75.6	74.7	73.7	72.7	71.7	70.7	69.7	68.8	67.8
98..........	76.6	75.6	74.7	73.7	72.7	71.7	70.7	69.7	68.8	67.8
99..........	76.6	75.6	74.7	73.7	72.7	71.7	70.7	69.7	68.8	67.8
100..........	76.6	75.6	74.7	73.7	72.7	71.7	70.7	69.7	68.8	67.8
101..........	76.6	75.6	74.7	73.7	72.7	71.7	70.7	69.7	68.8	67.8
102..........	76.6	75.6	74.7	73.7	72.7	71.7	70.7	69.7	68.8	67.8
103..........	76.6	75.6	74.7	73.7	72.7	71.7	70.7	69.7	68.8	67.8
104..........	76.6	75.6	74.7	73.7	72.7	71.7	70.7	69.7	68.8	67.8
105..........	76.6	75.6	74.7	73.7	72.7	71.7	70.7	69.7	68.8	67.8
106..........	76.6	75.6	74.7	73.7	72.7	71.7	70.7	69.7	68.8	67.8
107..........	76.6	75.6	74.7	73.7	72.7	71.7	70.7	69.7	68.8	67.8
108..........	76.6	75.6	74.7	73.7	72.7	71.7	70.7	69.7	68.8	67.8
109..........	76.6	75.6	74.7	73.7	72.7	71.7	70.7	69.7	68.8	67.8
110..........	76.6	75.6	74.7	73.7	72.7	71.7	70.7	69.7	68.8	67.8
111..........	76.6	75.6	74.7	73.7	72.7	71.7	70.7	69.7	68.8	67.8
112..........	76.6	75.6	74.7	73.7	72.7	71.7	70.7	69.7	68.8	67.8
113..........	76.6	75.6	74.7	73.7	72.7	71.7	70.7	69.7	68.8	67.8
114..........	76.6	75.6	74.7	73.7	72.7	71.7	70.7	69.7	68.8	67.8
115..........	76.6	75.6	74.7	73.7	72.7	71.7	70.7	69.7	68.8	67.8

Table VI--Ordinary Joint Life & Last Survivor Annuities
Two Lives--Expected Return Multiples

Ages	15	16	17	18	19	20	21	22	23	24
15............	73.8	73.3	72.9	72.4	72.0	71.6	71.3	70.9	70.6	70.3
16............	73.3	72.8	72.3	71.9	71.4	71.0	70.7	70.3	70.0	69.6
17............	72.9	72.3	71.8	71.3	70.9	70.5	70.0	69.7	69.3	69.0
18............	72.4	71.9	71.3	70.8	70.4	69.0	69.5	69.9	68.7	68.3
19............	72.0	71.4	70.9	70.4	69.8	69.4	68.9	68.5	68.1	67.7
20............	71.6	71.0	70.5	69.9	69.4	68.8	68.4	67.9	67.5	67.1
21............	71.3	70.7	70.0	69.5	68.9	68.4	67.9	67.4	66.9	66.5
22............	70.9	70.3	69.7	69.0	68.5	67.9	67.4	66.9	66.4	65.9
23............	70.6	70.0	69.3	68.7	68.1	67.5	66.9	66.4	65.9	65.4
24............	70.3	69.6	69.0	68.3	67.7	67.1	66.5	65.9	65.4	64.9
25............	70.1	69.3	68.6	68.0	67.3	66.7	66.1	65.5	64.9	64.4
26............	69.8	69.1	68.3	67.6	67.0	66.3	65.7	65.1	64.5	63.9
27............	69.6	68.8	68.1	67.3	66.7	66.0	65.3	64.7	64.1	63.5
28............	69.3	68.6	67.8	67.1	66.4	65.7	65.0	64.3	63.7	63.1
29............	69.1	68.4	67.6	66.8	66.1	65.4	64.7	64.0	63.3	62.7
30............	69.0	68.2	67.4	66.6	65.8	65.1	64.4	63.7	63.0	62.3
31............	68.8	68.0	67.2	66.4	65.6	64.8	64.1	63.4	62.7	62.0
32............	68.6	67.8	67.0	66.2	65.4	64.6	63.8	63.1	62.4	61.7
33............	68.5	67.6	66.8	66.0	65.2	64.4	63.6	62.8	62.1	61.4
34............	68.3	67.5	66.6	65.8	65.0	64.2	63.4	62.6	61.9	61.1
35............	68.2	67.4	66.5	65.6	64.8	64.0	63.2	62.4	61.6	60.9
36............	68.1	67.2	66.4	65.5	64.7	63.8	63.0	62.2	61.4	60.6
37............	68.0	67.1	66.2	65.4	64.5	63.7	62.8	62.0	61.2	60.4
38............	67.9	67.0	66.1	65.2	64.4	63.5	62.7	61.8	61.0	60.2
39............	67.8	66.9	66.0	65.1	64.2	63.4	62.5	61.7	60.8	60.0
40............	67.7	66.8	65.9	65.0	64.1	63.3	62.4	61.5	60.7	59.9
41............	67.7	66.7	65.8	64.9	64.0	63.1	62.3	61.4	60.5	59.7
42............	67.6	66.7	65.7	64.8	63.9	63.0	62.2	61.3	60.4	59.6
43............	67.5	66.6	65.7	64.8	63.8	62.9	62.1	61.2	60.3	59.4
44............	67.5	66.5	65.6	64.7	63.8	62.9	62.0	61.1	60.2	59.3
45............	67.4	66.5	65.5	64.6	63.7	62.8	61.9	61.0	60.1	59.2
46............	67.4	66.4	65.4	64.6	63.6	62.7	61.8	60.9	60.0	59.1
47............	67.3	66.4	65.4	64.5	63.6	62.6	61.7	60.8	59.9	59.0
48............	67.3	66.3	65.4	64.4	63.5	62.6	61.6	60.7	59.8	58.9
49............	67.2	66.3	65.3	64.4	63.5	62.5	61.6	60.7	59.7	58.8
50............	67.2	66.2	65.3	64.3	63.4	62.5	61.5	60.6	59.7	58.8
51............	67.2	66.2	65.3	64.3	63.4	62.4	61.5	60.5	59.6	58.7
52............	67.1	66.2	65.2	64.3	63.3	62.4	61.4	60.5	59.6	58.6
53............	67.1	66.2	65.2	64.2	63.3	62.3	61.4	60.4	59.5	58.6
54............	67.1	66.1	65.2	64.2	63.2	62.3	61.3	60.4	59.5	58.5
55............	67.1	66.1	65.1	64.2	63.2	62.3	61.3	60.4	59.4	58.5
56............	67.0	66.1	65.1	64.1	63.2	62.2	61.3	60.3	59.4	58.4
57............	67.0	66.1	65.1	64.1	63.2	62.2	61.2	60.3	59.3	58.4
58............	67.0	66.0	65.1	64.1	63.1	62.2	61.2	60.3	59.3	58.4
59............	67.0	66.0	65.0	64.1	63.1	62.1	61.2	60.2	59.3	58.3
60............	67.0	66.0	65.0	64.1	63.1	62.1	61.2	60.2	59.2	58.3
61............	67.0	66.0	65.0	64.0	63.1	62.1	61.1	60.2	59.2	58.3
62............	66.9	66.0	65.0	64.0	63.1	62.1	61.1	60.2	59.2	58.2
63............	66.9	66.0	65.0	64.0	63.0	62.1	61.1	60.1	59.2	58.2
64............	66.9	65.9	65.0	64.0	63.0	62.1	61.1	60.1	59.2	58.2

Table VI--Ordinary Joint Life & Last Survivor Annuities
Two Lives--Expected Return Multiples

Ages	15	16	17	18	19	20	21	22	23	24
65............	66.9	65.9	65.0	64.0	63.0	62.0	61.1	60.1	59.1	58.2
66............	66.9	65.9	64.9	64.0	63.0	62.0	61.1	60.1	59.1	58.2
67............	66.9	65.9	64.9	64.0	63.0	62.0	61.1	60.1	59.1	58.1
68............	66.9	65.9	64.9	64.0	63.0	62.0	61.0	60.1	59.1	58.1
69............	66.9	65.9	64.9	63.9	63.0	62.0	61.0	60.0	59.1	58.1
70............	66.9	65.9	64.9	63.9	63.0	62.0	61.0	60.0	59.1	58.1
71............	66.9	65.9	64.9	63.9	62.9	62.0	61.0	60.0	59.1	58.1
72............	66.9	65.9	64.9	63.9	62.9	62.0	61.0	60.0	59.0	58.1
73............	66.8	65.9	64.9	63.9	62.9	62.0	61.0	60.0	59.0	58.1
74............	66.8	65.9	64.9	63.9	62.9	62.0	61.0	60.0	59.0	58.1
75............	66.8	65.9	64.9	63.9	62.9	61.9	61.0	60.0	59.0	58.1
76............	66.8	65.9	64.9	63.9	62.9	61.9	61.0	60.0	59.0	58.0
77............	66.8	65.9	64.9	63.9	63.9	62.9	61.0	60.0	59.0	58.0
78............	66.8	65.8	64.9	63.9	62.9	61.9	61.0	60.0	59.0	58.0
79............	66.8	65.8	64.9	63.9	62.9	61.9	61.0	60.0	59.0	58.0
80............	66.8	65.9	64.9	63.9	62.9	61.9	60.9	60.0	59.0	58.0
81............	66.8	65.8	64.9	63.9	62.9	61.9	60.9	60.0	59.0	58.0
82............	66.8	65.8	64.9	63.9	62.9	61.9	60.9	60.0	59.0	58.0
83............	66.8	65.8	64.9	63.9	62.9	61.9	60.9	60.0	59.0	58.0
84............	66.8	65.8	64.8	63.9	62.9	61.9	60.9	60.0	59.0	58.0
85............	66.8	65.8	64.8	63.9	62.9	61.9	60.9	60.0	59.0	58.0
86............	66.8	65.8	64.8	63.9	62.9	61.9	60.9	60.0	59.0	58.0
87............	66.8	65.8	64.8	63.9	62.9	61.9	60.9	60.0	59.0	58.0
88............	66.8	65.8	64.8	63.9	62.9	61.9	60.9	60.0	59.0	58.0
89............	66.8	65.8	64.8	63.9	62.9	61.9	60.9	60.0	59.0	58.0
90............	66.8	65.8	64.8	63.9	62.9	61.9	60.9	60.0	59.0	58.0
91............	66.8	65.8	64.8	63.9	62.9	61.9	60.9	60.0	59.0	58.0
92............	66.8	65.8	64.8	63.9	62.9	61.9	60.9	59.9	59.0	58.0
93............	66.8	65.8	64.8	63.9	62.9	61.9	60.9	59.9	59.0	58.0
94............	66.8	65.8	64.8	63.9	62.9	61.9	60.9	59.9	59.0	58.0
95............	66.8	65.8	64.8	63.9	62.9	61.9	60.9	59.9	59.0	58.0
96............	66.8	65.8	64.8	63.9	62.9	61.9	60.9	59.9	59.0	58.0
97............	66.8	65.8	64.8	63.9	62.9	61.9	60.9	59.9	59.0	58.0
98............	66.8	65.8	64.8	63.9	62.9	61.9	60.9	59.9	59.0	58.0
99............	66.8	65.8	64.8	63.9	62.9	61.9	60.9	59.9	59.0	58.0
100............	66.8	65.8	64.8	63.9	62.9	61.9	60.9	59.9	59.0	58.0
101............	66.8	65.8	64.8	63.9	62.9	61.9	60.9	59.9	59.0	58.0
102............	66.8	65.8	64.8	63.9	62.9	61.9	60.9	59.9	59.0	58.0
103............	66.8	65.8	64.8	63.9	62.9	61.9	60.9	59.9	59.0	58.0
104............	66.8	65.8	64.8	63.9	62.9	61.9	60.9	59.9	59.0	58.0
105............	66.8	65.8	64.8	63.9	62.9	61.9	60.9	59.9	59.0	58.0
106............	66.8	65.8	64.8	63.9	62.9	61.9	60.9	59.9	59.0	58.0
107............	66.8	65.8	64.8	63.9	62.9	61.9	60.9	59.9	59.0	58.0
108............	66.8	65.8	64.8	63.9	62.9	61.9	60.9	59.9	59.0	58.0
109............	66.8	65.8	64.8	63.9	62.9	61.9	60.9	59.9	59.0	58.0
110............	66.8	65.8	64.8	63.9	62.9	61.9	60.9	59.9	59.0	58.0
111............	66.8	65.8	64.8	63.9	62.9	61.9	60.9	59.9	59.0	58.0
112............	66.8	65.8	64.8	63.9	62.9	61.9	60.9	59.9	59.0	58.0
113............	66.8	65.8	64.8	63.9	62.9	61.9	60.9	59.9	59.0	58.0
114............	66.8	65.8	64.8	63.9	62.9	61.9	60.9	59.9	59.0	58.0
115............	66.8	65.8	64.8	63.9	62.9	61.9	60.9	59.9	59.0	58.0

Table VI--Ordinary Joint Life & Last Survivor Annuities
Two Lives--Expected Return Multiples

Ages	25	26	27	28	29	30	31	32	33	34
25............	63.9	63.4	62.9	62.5	62.1	61.7	61.3	61.0	60.7	60.4
26............	63.4	62.9	62.4	61.9	61.5	61.1	60.7	60.4	60.0	59.7
27............	62.9	62.4	61.9	61.4	60.9	60.5	60.1	59.7	59.4	59.0
28............	62.5	61.9	61.4	60.9	60.4	60.0	59.5	59.1	58.7	58.4
29............	62.1	61.5	60.9	60.4	59.9	59.4	59.0	58.5	58.1	57.7
30............	61.7	61.1	60.5	60.0	59.4	58.9	58.4	58.0	57.5	57.1
31............	61.3	60.7	60.1	59.5	59.0	58.4	57.9	57.4	57.0	56.5
32............	61.0	60.4	59.7	59.1	58.5	58.0	57.4	56.9	56.4	56.0
33............	60.7	60.0	59.4	58.7	58.1	57.5	57.0	56.4	55.9	55.5
34............	60.4	59.7	59.0	58.4	57.7	57.1	56.5	56.0	55.5	54.9
35............	60.1	59.4	58.7	58.0	57.4	56.7	56.1	55.6	55.0	54.5
36............	59.9	59.1	58.4	57.7	57.0	56.4	55.8	55.1	54.6	54.0
37............	59.6	58.9	58.1	57.4	56.7	56.0	55.4	54.8	54.2	53.6
38............	59.4	58.6	57.9	57.9	56.4	55.7	55.1	54.4	53.8	53.2
39............	59.2	58.4	57.7	56.9	56.2	55.4	54.7	54.1	53.4	52.8
40............	59.0	58.2	57.4	56.7	55.9	55.2	54.5	53.8	53.1	52.4
41............	58.9	58.0	57.2	56.4	55.7	54.9	54.2	53.5	52.8	52.1
42............	58.7	57.9	57.1	56.2	55.5	54.7	53.9	53.2	52.5	51.8
43............	58.6	57.7	56.9	56.1	55.3	54.5	53.7	52.9	52.2	51.5
44............	58.4	57.6	56.7	55.9	55.1	54.3	53.5	52.7	52.0	51.2
45............	58.3	57.4	56.6	55.7	54.9	54.1	53.3	52.5	51.7	51.0
46............	58.2	57.3	56.5	55.6	54.8	53.9	53.1	52.3	51.5	50.7
47............	58.1	57.2	56.3	55.5	54.6	53.8	52.9	52.1	51.3	50.5
48............	58.0	57.1	56.2	55.3	54.5	53.6	52.8	51.9	51.1	50.3
49............	57.9	57.0	56.1	55.2	54.4	53.5	52.6	51.8	51.0	50.1
50............	57.8	56.9	56.0	55.1	54.2	53.4	52.5	51.7	50.8	50.0
51............	57.8	56.9	55.9	55.0	54.1	53.3	52.4	51.5	50.7	49.8
52............	57.7	56.8	55.9	55.0	54.1	53.2	52.3	51.4	50.5	49.7
53............	57.6	56.7	55.8	54.9	54.0	53.1	52.2	51.3	50.4	49.6
54............	57.6	56.7	55.7	54.8	53.9	53.0	52.1	51.2	50.3	49.4
55............	57.5	56.6	55.7	54.7	53.8	52.9	52.0	51.1	40.2	49.3
56............	57.5	56.5	55.6	54.7	53.8	52.8	51.9	51.0	50.1	49.2
57............	57.4	56.5	55.6	54.6	53.7	52.8	51.9	50.9	50.0	49.1
58............	57.4	56.5	55.5	54.6	53.6	52.7	51.8	50.9	50.0	49.1
59............	57.4	56.4	55.5	54.5	53.6	52.7	51.7	50.8	49.9	49.0
60............	57.3	56.4	55.4	54.5	53.6	52.6	51.7	50.8	49.8	48.9
61............	57.3	56.4	55.4	54.5	53.5	52.6	51.6	50.7	49.8	48.9
62............	57.3	56.3	55.4	54.4	53.5	52.5	51.6	50.7	49.7	48.8
63............	57.3	56.3	55.3	54.4	53.4	52.5	51.6	50.6	49.7	48.7
64............	57.2	56.3	55.3	54.4	53.4	52.5	51.5	50.6	49.6	48.7
65............	57.2	56.3	55.3	54.3	53.4	52.4	51.5	50.5	49.6	48.7
66............	57.2	56.2	55.3	54.3	53.4	52.4	51.5	50.5	49.6	48.6
67............	57.2	56.2	55.3	54.3	53.3	52.4	51.4	50.5	49.5	48.6
68............	57.2	56.2	55.2	54.3	53.3	52.4	51.4	50.4	49.5	48.6
69............	57.1	56.2	55.2	54.3	53.3	52.3	51.4	50.4	49.5	48.5

Table VI--Ordinary Joint Life & Last Survivor Annuities
Two Lives--Expected Return Multiples

Ages	25	26	27	28	29	30	31	32	33	34
70...........	57.1	56.2	55.2	54.2	53.3	52.3	51.4	50.4	49.4	48.5
71...........	57.1	56.2	55.2	54.2	53.3	52.3	51.3	50.4	49.4	48.5
72...........	57.1	56.1	55.2	54.2	53.2	52.3	51.3	50.4	49.4	48.5
73...........	57.1	56.1	55.2	54.2	53.2	52.3	51.3	50.3	49.4	48.4
74...........	57.1	56.1	55.2	54.2	53.2	52.3	51.3	50.3	49.4	48.4
75...........	57.1	56.1	55.1	54.2	53.2	52.2	51.3	50.3	49.4	48.4
76...........	57.1	56.1	55.1	54.2	53.2	52.2	51.3	50.3	49.3	48.4
77...........	57.1	56.1	55.1	54.2	53.2	52.2	51.3	50.3	49.3	48.4
78...........	57.1	56.1	55.1	54.2	53.2	52.2	51.3	50.3	49.3	48.4
79...........	57.1	56.1	55.1	54.1	53.2	52.2	51.2	50.3	49.3	48.4
80...........	57.1	56.1	55.1	54.1	53.2	52.2	51.2	50.3	49.3	48.3
81...........	57.0	56.1	55.1	54.1	53.2	52.2	51.2	50.3	49.3	48.3
82...........	57.0	56.1	55.1	54.1	53.2	52.2	51.2	50.3	49.3	48.3
83...........	57.0	56.1	55.1	54.1	53.2	52.2	51.2	50.3	49.3	48.3
84...........	57.0	56.1	55.1	54.1	53.2	52.2	51.2	50.3	49.3	48.3
85...........	57.0	56.1	55.1	54.1	53.2	52.2	51.2	50.2	49.3	48.3
86...........	57.0	56.1	55.1	54.1	53.1	52.2	51.2	50.2	49.3	48.3
87...........	57.0	56.1	55.1	54.1	53.1	52.2	51.2	50.2	49.3	48.3
88...........	57.0	56.1	55.1	54.1	53.1	52.2	51.2	50.2	49.3	48.3
89...........	57.0	56.1	55.1	54.1	53.1	52.2	51.2	50.2	49.3	48.3
90...........	57.0	56.1	55.1	54.1	53.1	52.2	51.2	50.2	49.3	48.3
91...........	57.0	56.1	55.1	54.1	53.1	52.2	51.2	50.2	49.3	48.3
92...........	57.0	56.1	55.1	54.1	53.1	52.2	51.2	50.2	49.3	48.3
93...........	57.0	56.1	55.1	54.1	53.1	52.2	51.2	50.2	49.3	48.3
94...........	57.0	56.0	55.1	54.1	53.1	52.2	51.2	50.2	49.3	48.3
95...........	57.0	56.0	55.1	54.1	53.1	52.2	51.2	50.2	49.3	48.3
96...........	57.0	56.0	55.1	54.1	53.1	52.2	51.2	50.2	49.3	48.3
97...........	57.0	56.0	55.1	54.1	53.1	52.2	51.2	50.2	49.3	48.3
98...........	57.0	56.0	55.1	54.1	53.1	52.2	51.2	50.2	49.3	48.3
99...........	57.0	56.0	55.1	54.1	53.1	52.2	51.2	50.2	49.3	48.3
100...........	57.0	56.0	55.1	54.1	53.1	52.2	51.2	50.2	49.3	48.3
101...........	57.0	56.0	55.1	54.1	53.1	52.2	51.2	50.2	49.3	48.3
102...........	57.0	56.0	55.1	54.1	53.1	52.2	51.2	50.2	49.3	48.3
103...........	57.0	56.0	55.1	54.1	53.1	52.2	51.2	50.2	49.3	48.3
104...........	57.0	56.0	55.1	54.1	53.1	52.2	51.2	50.2	49.3	48.3
105...........	57.0	56.0	55.1	54.1	53.1	52.2	51.2	50.2	49.3	48.3
106...........	57.0	56.0	55.1	54.1	53.1	52.2	51.2	50.2	49.3	48.3
107...........	57.0	56.0	55.1	54.1	53.1	52.2	51.2	50.2	49.3	48.3
108...........	57.0	56.0	55.1	54.1	53.1	52.2	51.2	50.2	49.3	48.3
109...........	57.0	56.0	55.1	54.1	53.1	52.2	51.2	50.2	49.3	48.3
110...........	57.0	56.0	55.1	54.1	53.1	52.2	51.2	50.2	49.3	48.3
111...........	57.0	56.0	55.1	54.1	53.1	52.2	51.2	50.2	49.3	48.3
112...........	57.0	56.0	55.1	54.1	53.1	52.2	51.2	50.2	49.3	48.3
113...........	57.0	56.0	55.1	54.1	53.1	52.2	51.2	50.2	49.3	48.3
114...........	57.0	56.0	55.1	54.1	53.1	52.2	51.2	50.2	49.3	48.3
115...........	57.0	56.0	55.1	54.1	53.1	52.2	51.2	50.2	49.3	48.3

Table VI--Ordinary Joint Life & Last Survivor Annuities
Two Lives--Expected Return Multiples

Ages	35	36	37	38	39	40	41	42	43	44
35............	54.0	53.5	53.0	52.6	52.2	51.8	51.4	51.1	50.8	50.5
36............	53.5	53.0	52.5	52.0	51.6	51.2	50.8	50.4	50.1	49.8
37............	53.0	52.5	52.0	51.5	51.0	50.6	50.2	49.8	49.5	49.1
38............	52.6	52.0	51.5	51.0	50.5	50.0	49.6	49.2	48.8	48.5
39............	52.2	51.6	51.0	50.5	50.0	49.5	49.1	48.6	48.2	47.8
40............	51.8	51.2	50.6	50.0	49.5	49.0	48.5	48.1	47.6	47.2
41............	51.4	50.8	50.2	49.6	49.1	48.5	48.0	47.5	47.1	46.7
42............	51.1	50.4	49.8	49.2	48.6	48.1	47.5	47.0	46.6	46.1
43............	50.8	50.1	49.5	48.8	48.2	47.6	47.1	46.6	46.0	45.6
44............	50.5	49.8	49.1	48.5	47.8	47.2	46.7	46.1	45.6	45.1
45............	50.2	49.5	48.8	48.1	47.5	46.9	46.3	45.7	45.1	44.6
46............	50.0	49.2	48.5	47.8	47.2	46.5	45.9	45.3	44.7	44.1
47............	49.7	49.0	48.3	47.5	46.8	46.2	45.5	44.9	44.3	43.7
48............	49.5	48.8	48.0	47.3	46.6	45.9	45.2	44.5	43.9	43.3
49............	49.3	48.5	47.8	47.0	46.3	45.6	44.9	44.2	43.6	42.9
50............	49.2	48.4	47.6	46.8	46.0	45.3	44.6	43.9	43.2	42.6
51............	49.0	48.2	47.4	46.6	45.8	45.1	44.3	43.6	42.9	44.2
52............	48.8	48.0	47.2	46.4	45.6	44.8	44.1	43.3	42.6	41.9
53............	48.7	47.9	47.0	46.2	45.4	44.6	43.9	43.1	42.4	41.7
54............	48.6	47.7	46.9	46.0	45.2	44.4	43.6	42.9	42.1	41.4
55............	48.5	47.6	46.7	45.9	45.1	44.2	43.4	42.7	41.9	41.2
56............	48.3	47.5	46.6	45.8	44.9	44.1	43.3	42.5	41.7	40.9
57............	48.3	47.4	46.5	45.6	44.8	43.9	43.1	42.3	41.5	40.7
58............	48.2	47.3	46.4	45.5	44.7	43.8	43.0	42.1	41.3	40.5
59............	48.1	47.2	46.3	45.4	44.5	43.7	42.8	42.0	41.2	40.4
60............	48.0	47.1	46.2	45.3	44.4	43.6	42.7	41.9	41.0	40.2
61............	47.9	47.0	46.1	45.2	44.3	43.5	42.6	41.7	40.9	40.0
62............	47.9	47.0	46.0	45.1	44.2	43.4	42.5	41.6	40.8	39.9
63............	47.8	46.9	46.0	45.1	44.2	43.3	42.4	41.5	40.6	39.8
64............	47.8	46.8	45.9	45.0	44.1	43.2	42.3	41.4	40.5	39.7
65............	47.7	46.8	45.9	44.9	44.0	43.1	42.2	41.3	40.4	39.6
66............	47.7	46.7	45.8	44.9	44.0	43.1	42.2	41.3	40.4	39.5
67............	47.6	46.7	45.8	44.8	43.9	43.0	42.1	41.2	40.3	39.4
68............	47.6	46.7	45.7	44.8	43.9	42.9	42.0	41.1	40.2	39.3
69............	47.6	46.6	45.7	44.8	43.8	42.9	42.0	41.1	40.2	39.3
70............	47.5	46.6	45.7	44.7	43.8	42.9	41.9	41.0	40.1	39.2
71............	47.5	46.6	45.6	44.7	43.8	42.8	41.9	41.0	40.1	39.1
72............	47.5	46.6	45.6	44.7	43.7	42.8	41.9	40.9	40.0	39.1
73............	47.5	46.5	45.6	44.6	43.7	42.8	41.8	40.9	40.0	39.0
74............	47.5	46.5	45.6	44.6	43.7	42.7	41.8	40.9	39.9	39.0

Table VI--Ordinary Joint Life & Last Survivor Annuities
Two Lives--Expected Return Multiples

Ages	35	36	37	38	39	40	41	42	43	44
75............	47.4	46.5	45.5	44.6	43.6	42.7	41.8	40.8	39.9	39.0
76............	47.4	46.5	45.5	44.6	43.6	42.7	41.7	40.8	39.9	38.9
77............	47.4	46.5	45.5	44.6	43.6	42.7	41.7	40.8	39.8	38.9
78............	47.4	46.4	45.5	44.5	43.6	42.6	41.7	40.7	39.8	38.9
79............	47.4	46.4	45.5	44.5	43.6	42.6	41.7	40.7	39.8	38.9
80............	47.4	46.4	45.5	44.5	43.6	42.6	41.7	40.7	39.8	38.8
81............	47.4	46.4	45.5	44.5	43.5	42.6	41.6	40.7	39.8	38.8
82............	47.4	46.4	45.4	44.5	43.5	42.6	41.6	40.7	39.7	38.8
83............	47.4	46.4	45.4	44.5	43.5	42.6	41.6	40.7	39.7	38.8
84............	47.4	46.4	45.4	44.5	43.5	42.6	41.6	40.7	39.7	38.8
85............	47.4	46.4	45.4	44.5	43.5	42.6	41.6	40.7	39.7	38.8
86............	47.3	46.4	45.4	44.5	43.5	42.5	41.6	40.6	39.7	38.8
87............	47.3	46.4	45.4	44.5	43.5	42.5	41.6	40.6	39.7	38.7
88............	47.3	46.4	45.4	44.5	43.5	42.5	41.6	40.6	39.7	38.7
89............	47.3	46.4	45.4	44.4	43.5	42.5	41.6	40.6	39.7	38.7
90............	47.3	46.4	45.4	44.4	43.5	42.5	41.6	40.6	39.7	38.7
91............	47.3	46.4	45.4	44.4	43.5	42.5	41.6	40.6	39.7	39.7
92............	47.3	46.4	45.4	44.4	44.4	43.5	42.5	41.6	40.6	38.7
92..[rev]...					[43.5]	[42.5]	[41.6]	[40.6]	[38.7]	
93............	47.3	46.4	45.4	43.5	42.5	41.6	40.6	39.7	39.7	38.7
93..[rev]...				[44.4]	[43.5]	[42.5]	[41.6]	[40.6]		
94............	47.3	46.4	45.4	44.4	43.5	42.5	41.6	40.6	39.7	38.7
95............	47.3	46.4	45.4	44.4	43.5	42.5	41.6	40.6	39.7	38.7
96............	47.3	46.4	45.4	44.4	43.5	42.5	41.6	40.6	39.7	38.7
97............	47.3	46.4	45.4	44.4	43.5	42.5	41.6	40.6	39.6	38.7
98............	47.3	46.4	45.4	44.4	43.5	42.5	41.6	40.6	39.6	38.7
99............	47.3	46.4	45.4	44.4	43.5	42.5	41.5	40.6	39.6	38.7
100..........	47.3	46.4	45.4	44.4	43.5	42.5	41.5	40.6	39.6	38.7
101..........	47.3	46.4	45.4	44.4	43.5	42.5	41.5	40.6	39.6	38.7
102..........	47.3	46.4	45.4	44.4	43.5	42.5	41.5	40.6	39.6	38.7
103..........	47.3	46.4	45.4	44.4	43.5	42.5	41.5	40.6	39.6	38.7
104..........	47.3	46.4	45.4	44.4	43.5	42.5	41.5	40.6	39.6	38.7
105..........	47.3	46.4	45.4	44.4	43.5	42.5	41.5	40.6	39.6	38.7
106..........	47.3	46.4	45.4	44.4	43.5	42.5	41.5	40.6	39.6	38.7
107..........	47.3	46.4	45.4	44.4	43.5	42.5	41.5	40.6	39.6	38.7
108..........	47.3	46.4	45.4	44.4	43.5	42.5	41.5	40.6	39.6	38.7
109..........	47.3	46.4	45.4	44.4	43.5	42.5	41.5	40.6	39.6	38.7
110..........	47.3	46.4	45.4	44.4	43.5	42.5	41.5	40.6	39.6	38.7
111..........	47.3	46.4	45.4	44.4	43.5	42.5	41.5	40.6	39.6	38.7
112..........	47.3	46.4	45.4	44.4	43.5	42.5	41.5	40.6	39.6	38.7
113..........	47.3	46.4	45.4	44.4	43.5	42.5	41.5	40.6	39.6	38.7
114..........	47.3	46.4	45.4	44.4	43.5	42.5	41.5	40.6	39.6	38.7
115..........	47.3	46.4	45.4	44.4	43.5	42.5	41.5	40.6	39.6	38.7

Table VI--Ordinary Joint Life & Last Survivor Annuities
Two Lives--Expected Return Multiples

Ages	45	46	47	48	49	50	51	52	53	54
45............	44.1	43.6	43.2	42.7	42.3	42.0	41.6	41.3	41.0	40.7
46............	43.6	43.1	42.6	42.2	41.8	41.4	41.0	40.6	40.3	40.0
47............	43.2	42.6	42.1	41.7	41.2	40.8	40.4	40.0	39.7	39.3
48............	42.7	42.2	41.7	41.2	40.7	40.2	39.8	39.4	39.0	38.7
49............	42.3	41.8	41.2	40.7	40.2	39.7	39.3	38.8	38.4	38.1
50............	42.0	41.4	40.8	40.2	39.7	39.2	38.7	38.3	37.9	37.5
51............	41.6	41.0	40.4	39.8	39.3	38.7	38.2	37.8	37.3	36.9
52............	41.3	40.6	40.0	39.4	38.8	38.3	37.8	37.3	36.8	36.4
53............	41.0	40.3	39.7	39.0	38.4	37.9	37.3	36.8	36.3	35.8
54............	40.7	40.0	39.3	38.7	38.1	37.5	36.9	36.4	35.8	35.3
55............	40.4	39.7	39.0	38.4	37.7	37.1	36.5	35.9	35.4	34.9
56............	40.2	39.5	38.7	38.1	37.4	36.8	36.1	35.6	35.0	34.4
57............	40.0	39.2	38.5	37.8	37.1	36.4	35.8	35.2	34.6	34.0
58............	39.7	39.0	38.2	37.5	36.8	36.1	35.5	34.8	34.2	33.6
59............	39.6	38.8	38.0	37.3	36.6	35.9	35.2	34.5	33.9	33.3
60............	39.4	38.6	37.8	37.1	36.3	35.6	34.9	34.2	33.6	32.9
61............	39.2	38.4	37.6	36.9	36.1	35.4	34.6	33.9	33.3	32.6
62............	39.1	38.3	37.5	36.7	35.9	35.1	34.4	33.7	33.0	32.3
63............	38.9	38.1	37.3	36.5	35.7	34.9	34.2	33.5	32.7	32.0
64............	38.8	38.0	37.2	36.3	35.5	34.8	34.0	33.2	32.5	31.8
65............	38.7	37.9	37.0	36.2	35.4	34.6	33.8	33.0	32.3	31.6
66............	38.6	37.8	36.9	36.1	35.2	34.4	33.6	32.9	32.1	31.4
67............	38.5	37.7	36.8	36.0	35.1	34.3	33.5	32.7	31.9	31.2
68............	38.4	37.6	36.7	35.8	35.0	34.2	33.4	32.5	31.8	31.0
69............	38.4	37.5	36.6	35.7	34.9	34.1	33.2	32.4	31.6	30.8
70............	38.3	37.4	36.5	35.7	34.8	34.0	33.1	32.3	31.5	30.7
71............	38.2	37.3	36.5	35.6	34.7	33.9	33.0	32.2	31.4	30.5
72............	38.2	37.3	36.4	35.5	34.6	33.8	32.9	32.1	31.2	30.4
73............	38.1	37.2	36.3	35.4	34.6	33.7	32.8	32.0	31.1	30.3
74............	38.1	37.2	36.3	35.4	34.5	33.6	32.8	31.9	31.1	30.2
75............	38.1	37.1	36.2	35.3	34.5	33.6	32.7	31.8	31.0	30.1
76............	38.0	37.1	36.2	35.3	34.4	33.5	32.6	31.8	30.9	30.1
77............	38.0	37.1	36.2	35.3	34.4	33.5	32.6	31.7	30.8	30.0
78............	38.0	37.0	36.1	35.2	34.3	33.4	32.5	31.7	30.8	29.9
79............	37.9	37.0	36.1	35.2	34.3	33.4	32.5	31.6	30.7	29.9

Table VI--Ordinary Joint Life & Last Survivor Annuities
Two Lives--Expected Return Multiples

Ages	45	46	47	48	49	50	51	52	53	54
80...........	37.9	37.0	36.1	35.2	34.2	33.4	32.5	31.6	30.7	29.8
81...........	37.9	37.0	36.0	35.1	34.2	33.3	32.4	31.5	30.7	29.8
82...........	37.9	36.9	36.0	35.1	34.2	33.3	32.4	31.5	30.6	29.7
83...........	37.9	36.9	36.0	35.1	34.2	33.3	32.4	31.5	30.6	29.7
84...........	37.8	36.9	36.9	35.0	34.2	33.2	32.3	31.4	30.6	29.7
85...........	37.8	36.9	36.0	35.1	34.1	33.2	32.3	31.4	30.5	29.6
86...........	38.8	36.9	36.0	35.0	34.1	33.2	32.3	31.4	30.5	29.6
87...........	37.8	36.9	35.9	35.0	34.1	33.2	32.3	31.4	30.5	29.6
88...........	37.8	36.9	35.9	35.0	34.1	33.2	32.3	31.4	30.5	29.6
89...........	37.8	36.9	35.9	35.0	34.1	33.2	32.3	31.3	30.5	29.6
90...........	37.8	36.9	35.9	35.0	34.1	33.2	32.3	31.3	30.5	29.6
91...........	37.8	36.8	35.9	35.0	34.1	33.2	32.2	31.3	30.4	29.5
92...........	37.8	36.8	35.9	35.0	34.1	33.2	32.2	31.3	30.4	29.5
93...........	37.8	36.8	35.9	35.0	34.1	33.1	32.2	31.3	30.4	29.5
94...........	37.8	36.8	35.9	35.0	34.1	33.1	32.2	31.3	30.4	29.5
95...........	37.8	36.8	35.9	35.0	34.0	33.1	32.2	31.3	30.4	29.5
96...........	37.8	36.8	35.9	35.0	34.0	33.1	32.2	31.3	30.4	29.5
97...........	37.8	36.8	35.9	35.0	34.0	33.1	32.2	31.3	30.4	29.5
98...........	37.8	36.8	35.9	35.0	34.0	33.1	32.2	31.3	30.4	29.5
99...........	37.8	36.8	35.9	35.0	34.0	33.1	32.2	31.3	30.4	29.5
101...........	37.8	36.8	35.9	35.0	34.0	33.1	32.2	31.3	30.4	29.5
102...........	37.8	36.8	35.9	35.0	34.0	33.1	32.2	31.3	30.4	29.5
103...........	37.7	36.8	35.9	34.9	34.0	33.1	32.2	31.3	30.4	29.5
104...........	37.7	36.8	35.9	34.9	34.0	33.1	32.2	31.3	30.4	29.5
105...........	37.7	36.8	35.9	34.9	34.0	33.1	32.2	31.3	30.4	29.5
106...........	37.7	36.8	35.9	34.9	34.0	33.1	32.2	31.3	30.4	29.5
107...........	37.7	36.8	35.9	34.9	34.0	33.1	32.2	31.3	30.4	29.5
108...........	37.7	36.8	35.9	34.9	34.0	33.1	32.2	31.3	30.4	29.5
109...........	37.7	36.8	35.9	34.9	34.0	33.1	32.2	31.3	30.4	29.5
110...........	37.7	36.8	35.9	34.9	34.0	33.1	32.2	31.3	30.4	29.5
111...........	37.7	36.8	35.9	34.9	34.0	33.1	32.2	31.3	30.4	29.5
112...........	37.7	36.8	35.9	34.9	34.0	33.1	32.2	31.3	30.4	29.5
113...........	37.7	36.8	35.9	34.9	34.0	33.1	32.2	31.3	30.4	29.5
114...........	37.7	36.8	35.9	34.9	34.0	33.1	32.2	31.3	30.4	29.5
115...........	37.7	36.8	35.9	34.9	34.0	33.1	32.2	31.3	30.4	29.5

Table VI--Ordinary Joint Life & Last Survivor Annuities
Two Lives--Expected Return Multiples

Ages	55	56	57	58	59	60	61	62	63	64
55..........	34.4	33.9	33.5	33.1	32.7	32.3	32.0	31.7	31.4	31.1
56..........	33.9	33.4	33.0	32.5	32.1	31.7	31.4	31.0	30.7	30.4
57..........	33.5	33.0	32.5	32.0	31.6	31.2	30.8	30.4	30.1	29.8
58..........	33.1	32.5	32.0	31.5	31.1	30.6	30.2	29.9	29.5	29.2
59..........	32.7	32.1	31.6	31.1	30.6	30.1	29.7	29.3	28.9	28.6
60..........	32.3	31.7	31.2	30.6	30.1	29.7	29.2	28.8	28.4	28.0
61..........	32.0	31.4	30.8	30.2	29.7	29.2	28.7	28.3	27.8	27.4
62..........	31.7	31.0	30.4	29.9	29.3	28.8	28.3	27.8	27.3	26.9
63..........	31.4	30.7	30.1	29.5	28.9	28.4	27.8	27.3	26.9	26.4
64..........	31.1	30.4	29.8	29.2	28.6	28.0	27.4	26.9	26.4	25.9
65..........	30.9	30.2	29.5	28.9	28.2	27.6	27.1	26.5	26.0	25.5
66..........	30.6	29.9	29.2	28.6	27.9	27.3	26.7	26.1	25.6	25.1
67..........	30.4	29.7	29.0	28.3	27.6	27.0	26.4	25.8	25.2	24.7
68..........	30.2	29.5	28.8	28.1	27.4	26.7	26.1	25.5	24.9	24.3
69..........	30.1	29.3	28.6	27.8	27.1	26.5	25.8	25.2	24.6	24.0
70..........	29.9	29.1	28.4	27.6	26.9	26.2	25.6	24.9	24.3	23.7
71..........	29.7	29.0	28.2	27.5	26.7	26.0	25.3	24.7	24.0	23.4
72..........	29.6	28.8	28.1	27.3	26.5	25.8	25.1	24.4	23.8	23.1
73..........	29.5	28.7	27.9	27.1	26.4	25.6	24.9	24.2	23.5	22.9
74..........	29.4	28.6	27.8	27.0	26.2	25.5	24.7	24.0	23.3	22.7
75..........	29.3	28.5	27.7	26.9	26.1	25.3	24.6	23.8	23.1	22.4
76..........	29.2	28.4	27.6	26.8	26.0	25.2	24.4	23.7	23.0	22.3
77..........	29.1	28.3	27.5	26.7	25.9	25.1	24.3	23.6	22.8	22.1
78..........	29.1	28.2	27.4	26.6	25.8	25.0	24.2	23.4	22.7	21.9
79..........	29.0	28.2	27.3	26.5	25.7	24.9	24.1	23.3	22.6	21.8
80..........	29.0	28.1	27.3	26.4	25.6	24.8	24.0	23.2	22.4	21.7
81..........	28.9	28.1	27.2	26.4	25.5	24.7	23.9	23.1	22.3	21.6
82..........	28.9	28.0	27.2	26.3	25.5	24.6	23.8	23.0	22.3	21.5
83..........	28.8	28.0	27.1	26.3	25.4	24.6	23.8	23.0	22.2	21.4
84..........	28.8	27.9	27.1	26.2	25.4	24.5	23.7	22.9	22.1	21.3

Table VI--Ordinary Joint Life & Last Survivor Annuities
Two Lives--Expected Return Multiples

Ages	55	56	57	58	59	60	61	62	63	64
85............	28.8	27.9	27.0	26.2	25.3	24.5	23.7	22.8	22.0	21.3
86............	28.7	27.9	27.0	26.1	25.3	24.5	23.6	22.8	22.0	21.2
87............	28.7	27.8	27.0	26.1	25.3	24.4	23.6	22.8	21.9	21.1
88............	28.7	27.8	27.0	26.1	25.2	24.4	23.5	22.7	21.9	21.1
89............	28.7	27.8	26.9	26.1	25.2	24.4	23.5	22.7	21.9	21.1
90............	28.7	27.8	26.9	26.1	25.2	24.3	23.5	22.7	21.8	21.0
91............	28.7	27.8	26.9	26.0	25.2	24.3	23.5	22.6	21.8	21.0
92............	28.6	27.8	26.9	26.0	25.2	24.3	23.5	22.6	21.8	21.0
93............	28.6	27.8	26.9	26.0	25.1	24.3	23.4	22.6	21.8	20.9
94............	28.6	27.7	26.9	26.0	25.1	24.3	23.4	22.6	21.7	20.9
95............	28.6	27.7	26.9	26.0	25.1	24.3	23.4	22.6	21.7	20.9
96............	28.6	27.7	26.9	26.0	25.1	24.2	23.4	22.6	21.7	20.9
97............	28.6	27.7	26.8	26.0	25.1	24.2	23.4	22.5	21.7	20.9
98............	28.6	27.7	26.8	26.0	25.1	24.2	23.4	22.5	21.7	20.9
99............	28.6	27.7	26.8	26.0	25.1	24.2	23.4	22.5	21.7	20.9
100............	28.6	27.7	26.8	26.0	25.1	24.2	23.4	22.5	21.7	20.8
101............	28.6	27.7	26.8	25.9	25.1	24.2	23.4	22.5	21.7	20.8
102............	28.6	27.7	26.8	25.9	25.1	24.2	23.3	22.5	21.7	20.8
103............	28.6	27.7	26.8	25.9	25.1	24.2	23.3	22.5	21.7	20.8
104............	28.6	27.7	26.8	25.9	25.1	24.2	23.3	22.5	21.6	20.8
105............	28.6	27.7	26.8	25.9	25.1	24.2	23.3	22.5	21.6	20.8
106............	28.6	27.7	26.8	25.9	25.1	24.2	23.3	22.5	21.6	20.8
107............	28.6	27.7	26.8	25.9	25.1	24.2	23.3	22.5	21.6	20.8
108............	28.6	27.7	26.8	25.9	25.1	24.2	23.3	22.5	21.6	20.8
109............	28.6	27.7	26.8	25.9	25.1	24.2	23.3	22.5	21.6	20.8
110............	28.6	27.7	26.8	25.9	25.1	24.2	23.3	22.5	21.6	20.8
111............	28.6	27.7	26.8	25.9	25.0	24.2	23.3	22.5	21.6	20.8
112............	28.6	27.7	26.8	25.9	25.0	24.2	23.3	22.5	21.6	20.8
113............	28.6	27.7	26.8	25.9	25.0	24.2	23.3	22.5	21.6	20.8
114............	28.6	27.7	26.8	25.9	25.0	24.2	23.3	22.5	21.6	20.8
115............	28.6	27.7	26.8	25.9	25.0	24.2	23.3	22.5	21.6	20.8

Table VI--Ordinary Joint Life & Last Survivor Annuities
Two Lives--Expected Return Multiples

Ages	65	66	67	68	69	70	71	72	73	74
65............	25.0	24.6	24.2	23.8	23.4	23.1	22.8	22.5	22.2	22.0
66............	24.6	24.1	23.7	23.3	22.9	22.5	22.2	21.9	21.6	21.4
67............	24.2	23.7	23.2	22.8	22.4	22.0	21.7	21.3	21.0	20.8
68............	23.8	23.3	22.8	22.3	21.9	21.5	21.2	20.8	20.5	20.2
69............	23.4	22.9	22.4	21.9	21.5	21.1	20.7	20.3	20.0	19.6
70............	23.1	22.5	22.0	21.5	21.1	20.6	20.2	19.8	19.4	19.1
71............	22.8	22.2	21.7	21.2	20.7	20.2	19.8	19.4	19.0	18.6
72............	22.5	21.9	21.3	20.8	20.3	19.8	19.4	18.9	18.5	18.2
73............	22.2	21.6	21.0	20.5	20.0	19.4	19.0	18.5	18.1	17.7
74............	22.0	21.4	20.8	20.2	19.6	19.1	18.6	18.2	17.7	17.3
75............	21.8	21.1	20.5	19.9	19.3	18.8	18.3	17.8	17.3	16.9
76............	21.6	20.9	20.3	19.7	19.1	18.5	18.0	17.5	17.0	16.5
77............	21.4	20.7	20.1	19.4	18.8	18.3	17.7	17.2	16.7	16.2
78............	21.2	20.5	19.9	19.2	18.6	18.0	17.5	16.9	16.4	15.9
79............	21.1	20.4	19.7	19.0	18.4	17.8	17.2	16.7	16.1	15.6
80............	21.0	20.2	19.5	18.9	18.2	17.6	17.0	16.4	15.9	15.4
81............	20.8	20.1	19.4	18.7	18.1	17.4	16.8	16.2	15.7	15.1
82............	20.7	20.0	19.3	18.6	17.9	17.3	16.6	16.0	15.5	14.9
83............	20.6	19.9	19.2	18.5	17.8	17.1	16.5	15.9	15.3	14.7
84............	20.5	19.8	19.1	18.4	17.7	17.0	16.3	15.7	15.1	14.5
85............	20.5	19.7	19.0	18.3	17.6	16.9	16.2	15.6	15.0	14.4
86............	20.4	19.6	18.9	18.2	17.5	16.8	16.1	15.5	14.8	14.2
87............	20.4	19.6	18.8	18.1	17.4	16.7	16.0	15.4	14.7	14.1
88............	20.3	19.5	18.8	18.0	17.3	16.6	15.9	15.3	14.6	14.0
89............	20.3	19.5	18.7	18.0	17.2	16.5	15.8	15.2	14.5	13.9
90............	20.2	19.4	18.7	17.9	17.2	16.5	15.8	15.1	14.5	13.8
91............	20.2	19.4	18.6	17.9	17.1	16.4	15.7	15.0	14.4	13.7
92............	20.2	19.4	18.6	17.8	17.1	16.4	15.7	15.0	14.3	13.7
93............	20.1	19.3	18.6	17.8	17.1	16.3	15.6	14.9	14.3	13.6
94............	20.1	19.3	18.5	17.8	17.0	16.3	15.6	14.9	14.2	13.6
95............	20.1	19.3	18.5	17.8	17.0	16.3	15.6	14.9	14.2	13.5
96............	20.1	19.3	18.5	17.7	17.0	16.2	15.5	14.8	14.2	13.5
97............	20.1	19.3	18.5	17.7	17.0	16.2	15.5	14.8	14.1	13.5
98............	20.1	19.3	18.5	17.7	16.9	16.2	15.5	14.8	14.1	13.4
99............	20.0	19.2	18.5	17.7	16.9	16.2	15.5	14.7	14.1	13.4
100............	20.0	19.2	18.4	17.7	16.9	16.2	15.4	14.7	14.0	13.4
101............	20.0	19.2	18.4	17.7	16.9	16.1	15.4	14.7	14.0	13.3
102............	20.0	19.2	18.4	17.6	16.9	16.1	15.4	14.7	14.0	13.3
103............	20.0	19.2	18.4	17.6	16.9	16.1	15.4	14.7	14.0	13.3
104............	20.0	19.2	18.4	17.6	16.9	16.1	15.4	14.7	14.0	13.3
105............	20.0	19.2	18.4	17.6	16.8	16.1	15.4	14.6	13.9	13.3
106............	20.0	19.2	18.4	17.6	16.8	16.1	15.3	14.6	13.9	13.3
107............	20.0	19.2	18.4	17.6	16.8	16.1	15.3	14.6	13.9	13.2
108............	20.0	19.2	18.4	17.6	16.8	16.1	15.3	14.6	13.9	13.2
109............	20.0	19.2	18.4	17.6	16.8	16.1	15.3	14.6	13.9	13.2
110............	20.0	19.2	18.4	17.6	16.8	16.1	15.3	14.6	13.9	13.2
111............	20.0	19.2	18.4	17.6	16.8	16.0	15.3	14.6	13.9	13.2
112............	20.0	19.2	18.4	17.6	16.8	16.0	15.3	14.6	13.9	13.2
113............	20.0	19.2	18.4	17.6	16.8	16.0	15.3	14.6	13.9	13.2
114............	20.0	19.2	18.4	17.6	16.8	16.0	15.3	14.6	13.9	13.2
115............	20.0	19.2	18.4	17.6	16.8	16.0	15.3	14.6	13.9	13.2

Table VI--Ordinary Joint Life & Last Survivor Annuities
Two Lives--Expected Return Multiples

Ages	75	76	77	78	79	80	81	82	83	84
75............	16.5	16.1	15.8	15.4	15.1	14.9	14.6	14.4	14.2	14.0
76............	16.1	15.7	15.4	15.0	14.7	14.4	14.1	13.9	13.7	13.5
77............	15.8	15.4	15.0	14.6	14.3	14.0	13.7	13.4	13.2	13.0
78............	15.4	15.0	14.6	14.2	13.9	13.5	13.2	13.0	12.7	12.5
79............	15.1	14.7	14.3	13.9	13.5	13.2	12.8	12.5	12.3	12.0
80............	14.9	14.4	14.0	13.5	13.2	12.8	12.5	12.2	11.9	11.6
81............	14.6	14.1	13.7	13.2	12.8	12.5	12.1	11.8	11.5	11.2
82............	14.4	13.9	13.4	13.0	12.5	12.2	11.8	11.5	11.1	10.9
83............	14.2	13.7	13.2	12.7	12.3	11.9	11.5	11.1	10.8	10.5
84............	14.0	13.5	13.0	12.5	12.0	11.6	11.2	10.9	10.5	10.2
85............	13.8	13.3	12.8	12.3	11.8	11.4	11.0	10.6	10.2	9.9
86............	13.7	13.1	12.6	12.1	11.6	11.2	10.8	10.4	10.0	9.7
87............	13.5	13.0	12.4	11.9	11.4	11.0	10.6	10.1	9.8	9.4
88............	13.4	12.8	12.3	11.8	11.3	10.8	10.4	10.0	9.6	9.2
89............	13.3	12.7	12.2	11.6	11.1	10.7	10.2	9.8	9.4	9.0
90............	13.2	12.6	12.1	11.5	11.0	10.5	10.1	9.6	9.2	8.8
91............	13.1	12.5	12.0	11.4	10.9	10.4	9.9	9.5	9.1	8.7
92............	13.1	12.5	11.9	11.3	10.8	10.3	9.8	9.4	8.9	8.5
93............	13.0	12.4	11.8	11.3	10.7	10.2	9.7	9.3	8.8	8.4
94............	12.9	12.3	11.7	11.2	10.6	10.1	9.6	9.2	8.7	8.3
95............	12.9	12.3	11.7	11.1	10.6	10.1	9.6	9.1	8.6	8.2
96............	12.9	12.2	11.6	11.1	10.5	10.0	9.5	9.0	8.5	8.1
97............	12.8	12.2	11.6	11.0	10.5	9.9	9.4	8.9	8.5	8.0
98............	12.8	12.2	11.5	11.0	10.4	9.9	9.4	8.9	8.4	8.0
99............	12.7	12.1	11.5	10.9	10.4	9.8	9.3	8.8	8.3	7.9
100...........	12.7	12.1	11.5	10.9	10.3	9.8	9.2	8.7	8.3	7.8
101...........	12.7	12.1	11.4	10.8	10.3	9.7	9.2	8.7	8.2	7.8
102...........	12.7	12.0	11.4	10.8	10.2	9.7	9.2	8.7	8.2	7.7
103...........	12.6	12.0	11.4	10.8	10.2	9.7	9.1	8.6	8.1	7.7
104...........	12.6	12.0	11.4	10.8	10.2	9.6	9.1	8.6	8.1	7.6
105...........	12.6	12.0	11.3	10.7	10.2	9.6	9.1	8.5	8.0	7.6
106...........	12.6	11.9	11.3	10.7	10.1	9.6	9.0	8.5	8.0	7.5
107...........	12.6	11.9	11.3	10.7	10.1	9.6	9.0	8.5	8.0	7.5
108...........	12.6	11.9	11.3	10.7	10.1	9.5	9.0	8.5	8.0	7.5
109...........	12.6	11.9	11.3	10.7	10.1	9.5	9.0	8.4	7.9	7.5
110...........	12.6	11.9	11.3	10.7	10.1	9.5	9.0	8.4	7.9	7.4
111...........	12.5	11.9	11.3	10.7	10.1	9.5	8.9	8.4	7.9	7.4
112...........	12.5	11.9	11.3	10.6	10.1	9.5	8.9	8.4	7.9	7.4
113...........	12.5	11.9	11.2	10.6	10.0	9.5	8.9	8.4	7.9	7.4
114...........	12.5	11.9	11.2	10.6	10.0	9.5	8.9	8.4	7.9	7.4
115...........	12.5	11.9	11.2	10.6	10.0	9.5	8.9	8.4	7.9	7.4

Table VI--Ordinary Joint Life & Last Survivor Annuities
Two Lives--Expected Return Multiples

Ages	85	86	87	88	89	90	91	92	93	94
85............	9.6	9.3	9.1	8.9	8.7	8.5	8.3	8.2	8.0	7.9
86............	9.3	9.1	8.8	8.6	8.3	8.2	8.0	7.8	7.7	7.6
87............	9.1	8.8	8.5	8.3	8.1	7.9	7.7	7.5	7.4	7.2
88............	8.9	8.6	8.3	8.0	7.8	7.6	7.4	7.2	7.1	6.9
89............	8.7	8.3	8.1	7.8	7.5	7.3	7.1	6.9	6.8	6.6
90............	8.5	8.2	7.9	7.6	7.3	7.1	6.9	6.7	6.5	6.4
91............	8.3	8.0	7.7	7.4	7.1	6.9	6.7	6.5	6.3	6.2
92............	8.2	7.8	7.5	7.2	6.9	6.7	6.5	6.3	6.1	5.9
93............	8.0	7.7	7.4	7.1	6.8	6.5	6.3	6.1	5.9	5.8
94............	7.9	7.6	7.2	6.9	6.6	6.4	6.2	5.9	5.8	5.6
95............	7.8	7.5	7.1	6.8	6.5	6.3	6.0	5.8	5.6	5.4
96............	7.7	7.3	7.0	6.7	6.4	6.1	5.9	5.7	5.5	5.3
97............	7.6	7.3	6.9	6.6	6.3	6.0	5.8	5.5	5.3	5.1
98............	7.6	7.2	6.8	6.5	6.2	5.9	5.6	5.4	5.2	5.0
99............	7.5	7.1	6.7	6.4	6.1	5.8	5.5	5.3	5.1	4.9
100............	7.4	7.0	6.6	6.3	6.0	5.7	5.4	5.2	5.0	4.8
101............	7.3	6.9	6.6	6.2	5.9	5.6	5.3	5.1	4.9	4.7
102............	7.3	6.9	6.5	6.2	5.8	5.5	5.3	5.0	4.8	4.6
103............	7.2	6.8	6.4	6.1	5.8	5.5	5.2	4.9	4.7	4.5
104............	7.2	6.8	6.4	6.0	5.7	5.4	5.1	4.8	4.6	4.4
105............	7.1	6.7	6.3	6.0	5.6	5.3	5.0	4.8	4.5	4.3
106............	7.1	6.7	6.3	5.9	5.6	5.3	5.0	4.7	4.5	4.2
107............	7.1	6.6	6.2	5.9	5.5	5.2	4.9	4.6	4.4	4.2
108............	7.0	6.6	6.2	5.8	5.5	5.2	4.9	4.6	4.3	4.1
109............	7.0	6.6	6.2	5.8	5.5	5.1	4.8	4.5	4.3	4.1
110............	7.0	6.6	6.2	5.8	5.4	5.1	4.8	4.5	4.3	4.0
111............	7.0	6.5	6.1	5.7	5.4	5.1	4.8	4.5	4.2	4.0
112............	7.0	6.5	6.1	5.7	5.4	5.0	4.7	4.4	4.2	3.9
113............	6.9	6.5	6.1	5.7	5.4	5.0	4.7	4.4	4.2	3.9
114............	6.9	6.5	6.1	5.7	5.3	5.0	4.7	4.4	4.1	3.9
115............	6.9	6.5	6.1	5.7	5.3	5.0	4.7	4.4	4.1	3.9

Ages	95	96	97	98	99	100	101	102	103	104
95............	5.3	5.1	5.0	4.8	4.7	4.6	4.5	4.4	4.3	4.2
96............	5.1	5.0	4.8	4.7	4.5	4.4	4.3	4.2	4.1	4.0
97............	5.0	4.8	4.7	4.5	4.4	4.3	4.1	4.0	3.9	3.8
98............	4.8	4.7	4.5	4.4	4.2	4.1	4.0	3.9	3.8	3.7
99............	4.7	4.5	4.4	4.2	4.1	4.0	3.8	3.7	3.6	3.5
100............	4.6	4.4	4.3	4.1	4.0	3.8	3.7	3.6	3.5	3.3
101............	4.5	4.3	4.1	4.0	3.8	3.7	3.6	3.4	3.3	3.2
102............	4.4	4.2	4.0	3.9	3.7	3.6	3.4	3.3	3.2	3.1
103............	4.3	4.1	3.9	3.8	3.6	3.5	3.3	3.2	3.0	2.9
104............	4.2	4.0	3.8	3.7	3.5	3.3	3.2	3.1	2.9	2.8
105............	4.1	3.9	3.7	3.6	3.4	3.2	3.1	2.9	2.8	2.7
106............	4.0	3.8	3.6	3.5	3.3	3.1	3.0	2.8	2.7	2.5
107............	4.0	3.8	3.6	3.4	3.2	3.1	2.9	2.7	2.6	2.4
108............	3.9	3.7	3.5	3.3	3.1	3.0	2.8	2.7	2.5	2.3
109............	3.8	3.6	3.4	3.3	3.1	2.9	2.7	2.6	2.4	2.3
110............	3.8	3.6	3.4	3.2	3.0	2.8	2.7	2.5	2.3	2.2
111............	3.8	3.5	3.3	3.2	3.0	2.8	2.6	2.4	2.3	2.1
112............	3.7	3.5	3.3	3.1	2.9	2.8	2.6	2.4	2.2	2.1
113............	3.7	3.5	3.3	3.1	2.9	2.7	2.5	2.4	2.2	2.0
114............	3.7	3.5	3.3	3.1	2.9	2.7	2.5	2.3	2.1	2.0
115............	3.7	3.4	3.2	3.0	2.8	2.7	2.5	2.3	2.1	1.9

Table VI--Ordinary Joint Life & Last Survivor Annuities
Two Lives--Expected Return Multiples

Ages	105	106	107	108	109	110	111	112	113	114	115
105............	2.5	2.4	2.3	2.2	2.1	2.0	2.0	1.9	1.8	1.8	1.8
106............	2.4	2.3	2.2	2.1	2.0	1.9	1.8	1.7	1.7	1.6	1.6
107............	2.3	2.2	2.1	1.9	1.8	1.7	1.7	1.6	1.5	1.5	1.4
108............	2.2	2.1	1.9	1.8	1.7	1.6	1.5	1.5	1.4	1.3	1.3
109............	2.1	2.0	1.8	1.7	1.6	1.5	1.4	1.3	1.3	1.2	1.1
110............	2.0	1.9	1.7	1.6	1.5	1.4	1.3	1.2	1.1	1.1	1.0
111............	2.0	1.8	1.7	1.5	1.4	1.3	1.2	1.1	1.0	0.9	0.9
112............	1.9	1.7	1.6	1.5	1.3	1.2	1.1	1.0	0.9	0.8	0.8
113............	1.8	1.7	1.5	1.4	1.3	1.1	1.0	0.9	0.8	0.7	0.7
114............	1.8	1.6	1.5	1.3	1.2	1.1	0.9	0.8	0.7	0.6	0.6
115............	1.8	1.6	1.4	1.3	1.1	1.0	0.9	0.8	0.7	0.6	0.5

Glossary

ABP Test: See **Average Benefit Percentage Test**.

Accrued Benefit: The portion of the retirement benefit that has been earned since an employee began to participate in a plan. In a defined contribution plan (including a 401(k) plan), the accrued benefit for a participant is the value of all accounts maintained on behalf of the participant, including the value of insurance contracts on the life of the participant. In a defined benefit plan, the accrued benefit is the portion of the benefit payable at normal retirement age that the participant has currently earned.

ACP Test: See **Actual Contribution Percentage Test**.

Actual Contribution Percentage Test (ACP Test): A test that measures whether employer matching contributions and employee after-tax contributions discriminate in favor of highly compensated employees.

Actual Deferral Percentage Test (ADP Test): A test that measures whether elective contributions (salary deferrals) in a 401(k) plan discriminate in favor of highly compensated employees.

Actuarial Equivalence: A form of benefit that differs in time, period, or manner of payment from the normal form of benefit provided by the plan, but is equivalent in value to the normal form of benefit. For example, a 401(k) plan provides a lump sum as the normal form of benefit and the participant has an account balance of $100,000. Depending on the factors in the plan, the actuarially equivalent life annuity benefit may provide the participant with an annual annuity for life equal to $12,200 commencing at age 65.

Administrative Policy Regarding Self-Correction (APRSC): A program for correcting operational (but not document) defects by the end of the second plan year following the year in which the defect arose (or later, if, given all the facts and circumstances, the defects are considered insignificant). No fees or filings with the IRS are required. It cannot be used to correct violations of the exclusive benefit rule or violations such as might occur in the Section 410(b) minimum coverage rules arising from shifts in demographics. (See also **EPCRS**.)

ADP Test: See **Actual Deferral Percentage Test**.

Affiliated Service Group: A group of organizations that, by virtue of business relationships, are treated for various employee benefit requirements as a single employer but do not share sufficient common ownership to be a controlled group.

Age-Weighted Profit-Sharing Plan: A type of profit-sharing plan in which contributions are allocated to participants on a basis that considers both age and compensation.

Alternate Payee: Any spouse, former spouse, child, or other dependent of a participant who is recognized by a domestic relations order as having a right to receive all, or a portion of, the participant's accrued benefit.

Annual Additions: Amounts that are credited to a participant's account during the limitation year, exclusive of interest, earnings, and rollovers.

Annuity: A series of monthly or annual payments, generally for the life of the participant. Annuity payments may be level or may be subject to an annual cost-of-living adjustment. (See **Joint and Survivor Annuity**.)

Anti-Assignment Rule: The portion of the Internal Revenue Code that restricts the accrued benefits of participants from being pledged or assigned, either voluntarily or involuntarily.

Anti-Cutback Rule: A provision in the Internal Revenue Code that prohibits an employer from reducing accrued benefits.

APRSC: See **Administrative Policy Regarding Self-Correction**.

Asset Allocation: The process of deciding how investment dollars will be apportioned among available asset classes.

Asset Class: A grouping of investment types that share similar risk and return characteristics. The three primary asset classes are stocks, bonds, and cash investments.

Audit CAP: A program under which a qualified plan negotiates a penalty with the IRS as an alternative to plan disqualification on account of plan document or operational defects identified by the IRS during a plan audit. It also covers demographic failures (i.e., failure to satisfy minimum coverage requirements), but is not available for violations relating to the diversion or misuse of plan assets. (See also **Walk-in Cap** and **EPCRS**.)

Average Benefit Percentage (ABP) Test: One of two tests necessary to determine whether a plan meets the Average Benefit Test. (See **Nondiscriminatory Classification Test**.)

Average Benefit Test: One of two alternative tests used for purposes of determining whether a plan meets the minimum coverage requirements.

Balance Forward Accounting: See **Pooled Accounting**.

Beneficiary: The person to whom a share of a deceased participant's account balance is payable.

Bond: A type of debt instrument issued by corporations, governments, and government agencies. The issuer makes regular interest payments and promises to pay back, or redeem, the face value of the bond at a specified time called the maturity date.

Bonus Deferral: An election to defer taxation on a bonus payment made no later than 2½ months following the close of the plan year. A bonus deferral is included in the ADP test. (See **Actual Deferral Percentage Test**.)

Bundled Services: A package of complete administrative and investment services provided to 401(k) plan sponsors by a single entity.

C Corporation: A regular corporation that elects to be taxed at the corporate, rather than individual, level. (See **S Corporation**.)

Cafeteria Plan: A plan that allows employees to choose between taxable and non-taxable benefits; also known as a Section 125 or flexible benefits plan. Typical non-taxable benefits would include health insurance, group term life, and dental benefits. Taxable benefits would always include the option to choose cash, although a taxable benefit such as auto or homeowner's insurance could be offered. A 401(k) plan may be offered as an option under a cafeteria plan.

CAP: Closing Agreement Program. (See **Audit CAP** and **Walk-in Cap**.)

Cash-Balance Plan: A defined benefit plan in which the accrued benefit is defined in terms of a hypothetical account balance that is increased yearly by hypothetical contributions and earnings.

Cash-or-Deferred Arrangement (CODA): Generally known as a 401(k) plan, a qualified profit-sharing or stock bonus plan that allows participants to elect to receive cash or to have the employer contribute amounts on their behalf to a plan.

Closely Held Corporation: A corporation that has a small number of shareholders and whose stock is not traded on a public stock exchange.

CODA: See **Cash-or-Deferred Arrangement**.

Code: The Internal Revenue Code of 1986, as amended.

Collectively Bargained Plans: Retirement plans that are established and maintained pursuant to a collective bargaining agreement. If more than one employer is required to contribute to the plan, the plan is usually treated as a multiemployer plan.

Common-Law Employee: An individual who performs services for the employer in an employment relationship; partners in a partnership and sole proprietors are not common-law employees.

Commonly Controlled Businesses: All partnerships, sole proprietorships, and other businesses under common control are treated as a commonly controlled business. Also, all corporations that are members of a controlled group are treated as a commonly controlled business. Commonly controlled businesses are treated as a single employer for certain employee benefit requirements.

Compensation: The amount of a participant's taxable and non-taxable remuneration that is considered for purposes of certain employee benefit requirements. Different definitions are used for deduction purposes, for calculation of maximum benefits and contributions, and for nondiscrimination purposes.

Conduit IRA: A rollover individual retirement account that is used to temporarily hold funds from a qualified plan until the employee chooses to roll funds into the qualified plan of another employer.

Contributory Plan: A qualified plan that mandates employee contributions as a condition of participation; may be in the form of a defined benefit or defined contribution plan.

Controlled Group of Corporations: Two or more corporations, that, by virtue of common ownership, are treated as a single entity for purposes of certain employee benefit requirements.

Corrective Distribution: A mechanism for distributing excess deferrals, excess contributions, and excess aggregate contributions in order to satisfy statutory limits or ADP, ACP, and multiple use tests. Corrective distributions provide a fail-safe mechanism for a plan to avoid disqualification.

Cost Recovery: A method for a participant to recoup previously taxed amounts from a qualified plan.

Daily Recordkeeping: See **On-Demand Accounting**.

Death Benefit: The portion of a participant's accrued benefit that is payable to a named beneficiary upon the participant's death.

Deficit Reduction Act of 1984 (DEFRA): An act of Congress passed to reduce the budget deficit. A portion of this bill contained the Tax Reform Act of 1984.

Defined Benefit Plan: A retirement plan that promises a specific benefit at retirement usually defined in terms of such factors as salary and years of service. Since the benefit is not determined solely by allocated contributions and investment earnings as in a defined contribution plan, the sponsor—not the employee—bears the investment risk.

Defined Contribution Plan: A type of qualified plan in which a participant's benefits are based solely on the participant's account balance; the account balance depends on the level of employer and employee contributions and the earnings on those contributions.

DEFRA: See **Deficit Reduction Act of 1984**.

Department of Labor (DOL): One of the government agencies responsible for the enforcement of ERISA.

Determination Letter: A letter issued by the IRS that states whether a submitted plan meets the qualification requirements of the Internal Revenue Code.

Direct Rollover: Payment of an eligible rollover distribution directly to the trustee of an eligible retirement plan.

Discretionary Contributions: Any employer contributions to a 401(k) or profit-sharing plan that are not mandated by the terms of the plan.

Discrimination: The undue favoring of highly compensated employees in plan provisions or operations.

Disqualification: The IRS sanction for failure to satisfy the qualification requirements of the Internal Revenue Code. Penalties for disqualification may include loss of tax-exempt status of the trust, loss of tax deductions, and taxable income to employees.

Disqualified Person: The Internal Revenue Code term for an individual who is prohibited from engaging in certain transactions with the plan. (See **Party in Interest**.)

DOL: Department of Labor

Earmarking: The ability of an employee to select investment choices for his or her account balance.

Elective Deferral (Contributions): The amount of a participant's voluntary reduction in pay; otherwise known as salary deferrals. An election to defer pay must be made in advance. The employer then contributes the deferral to the 401(k) plan.

Eligible Employee: Any employee who is eligible to become a participant in the plan pursuant to the terms of the plan document.

Eligible Retirement Plan: An individual retirement account (IRA) or a qualified plan that will accept a direct rollover of an eligible rollover distribution.

Eligible Rollover Distribution: A distribution of all or part of a participant's interest in a plan except for certain periodic distributions, minimum distributions, and the portion of a distribution representing a return of employee contributions.

Employee: Any individual employed by the employer maintaining the plan or any affiliated employer required to be aggregated with the employer under Code Sections 414(b), 414(c), 414(m), and 414(o). A leased employee may also be deemed an employee for purposes of these rules. (See **Affiliated Service Group** and **Leased Employee**.)

Employee Contributions: Contributions made by an employee to a qualified plan that have previously been taxed. (See **Mandatory Contribution** and **Voluntary Contributions**.)

Employee-Directed Plan: A plan that permits employees to select investment choices for their account balances.

Employee Plans Compliance Resolution System (EPCRS): An IRS created system of correction programs that allow sponsors of qualified retirement plans to correct document, operational, and demographic defects that would otherwise result in disqualification. EPCRS incorporates the older programs: Audit CAP, Walk-in CAP, APRSC, VCR, and SVP.

Employee Retirement Income Security Act of 1974 (ERISA): An act of Congress encompassing both Internal Revenue Code provisions, which determine when a plan is tax qualified, and Department of Labor provisions, which govern the rights of participants and beneficiaries and the obligations of plan fiduciaries.

Employee Stock Ownership Plan (ESOP): A plan designed to invest primarily in employer securities. Unlike other types of qualified plans, an ESOP may borrow funds to acquire employer securities.

Employer-Sponsored IRA: An IRA program for employees that is set up and maintained by the employer. (See **Individual Retirement Account**.)

Employer Securities: Shares of stock, bonds, or debentures issued by a corporation sponsoring the plan, including securities of a parent or subsidiary.

EPCRS: See **Employee Plans Compliance Resolution System**.

ERISA: See **Employment Retirement Income Security Act of 1974**.

ESOP: See **Employee Stock Ownership Plan**.

Excess Aggregate Contributions: The amount by which matching contributions and voluntary employee contributions made on behalf of highly compensated employees exceeds the amount permitted by the ACP nondiscrimination test contained in Code Section 401(m).

Excess Contributions: The amount by which elective contributions made on behalf of highly compensated employees exceeds the amount permitted by the ADP nondiscrimination test contained in Code Section 401(k).

Excess Deferrals: The amount by which elective deferrals made on behalf of an employee by all employers exceeds the annual cap in effect for that taxable year.

Excise Tax: A nondeductible tax imposed on the occurrence of an event.

Excludable Employee: An employee who does not need to be counted when performing a test on the plan.

Family Aggregation: The treatment of highly compensated employees and family members, prior to plan years beginning in 1997, as a single highly compensated employee for purposes of the ADP and ACP tests, as well as the Section 410(b) coverage tests. A family member is any employee who is the spouse, lineal descendent or spouse thereof, or lineal ascendent or spouse thereof, of a highly compensated employee who is a 5 percent owner or is one of the ten highly compensated employees with the highest compensation.

Federal Insurance Contributions Act (FICA): An act of Congress requiring employers and employees to pay into a federal fund that provides for retirement and welfare benefits.

Federal Unemployment Tax Act (FUTA): An act of Congress that imposes a tax on employers to fund cash benefits to former employees undergoing temporary periods of unemployment.

FICA: See **Federal Insurance Contributions Act**.

5 Percent Owner: An employee who owns, directly or indirectly, more than 5 percent of the value or voting power of the stock of the employer or, if the employer is not a corporation, more than 5 percent of the capital or profits interest. A 5 percent owner is both a highly compensated employee and a key employee.

Floor Plan: A defined benefit plan that provides a minimum level of benefits for all participants in conjunction with a defined contribution plan.

Forfeitures: The portion of a participant's benefit that may be lost if the participant separates from service before becoming 100 percent vested.

Frozen Plan: A qualified plan that holds benefits for future distribution but does not permit current contributions or accruals other than top-heavy minimum accruals for a frozen defined benefit plan.

FUTA: See **Federal Unemployment Tax Act.**

Hardship Withdrawal: An in-service withdrawal from a 401(k) plan because of the immediate and heavy financial need of a participant that cannot be satisfied from other resources. The conditions for a hardship withdrawal of elective contributions can be determined through either a safe harbor or a facts-and-circumstances method.

HCE: See **Highly Compensated Employee.**

Highly Compensated Employee (HCE):   An employee who, during either the determination year or lookback year, was a 5 percent owner of the employer or, during the lookback year, earned more than $80,000 and (optionally) was in the top-paid group.

Individual Account Plan: A plan in which individual accounts are established for each participant. A participant's benefit is determined solely on the basis of contributions to his or her account and the investment experience of those contributions. Participants are not guaranteed any particular benefit amount. (See **Defined Contribution Plan.**)

Individual Retirement Account (IRA):   An individual retirement account or an individual retirement annuity that holds assets on a tax-deferred basis. [IRC § 408]

Individually Designed Plan: A plan tailored specifically to an individual employer that is not part of a master or prototype plan, regional prototype plan, or volume submitter program.

In-House Administration: The performance of plan administration services by employees of the entity sponsoring the plan.

In-Service Withdrawal: A withdrawal of plan benefits prior to separation from service with the employer.

Integrated Plan: A plan that makes adjustments in contributions or benefits for amounts available through Social Security. (See **Permitted Disparity**.)

Interested Parties: Individuals who must be notified when application is made for a determination letter on a plan. This includes all employees of the sponsoring entity.

Internal Revenue Service (IRS): The agency of the Treasury Department with the responsibility for administering, interpreting, and enforcing the Internal Revenue Code.

IRA: See **Individual Retirement Account**.

IRC: Internal Revenue Code of 1986, as amended.

IRRA: See **IRS Restructuring and Reform Act of 1998**.

IRS: See **Internal Revenue Service**.

IRS Restructuring and Reform Act of 1998 (IRRA): Act containing technical corrections to TRA '97 and SBJPA, many of which deal with Roth IRAs.

Joint and Survivor Annuity: An annuity that is paid for the life of a participant, with a survivor annuity available for the life of his or her spouse. A qualified joint and survivor annuity must offer a survivor benefit that is not less than 50 percent nor more than 100 percent of the annuity received by the participant.

Keogh Plan: A qualified retirement plan covering a self-employed person.

Key Employee: A participant who at any time during the five preceding years: (1) earned at least one-half the defined benefit dollar limit and was an officer, (2) earned more than $30,000 and was one of the top ten employees owning the largest interest in the employer, (3) owned more than 5 percent of the employer, or (4) earned more than $150,000 and owned more than 1 percent of the employer. The dollar limits in (1) and (2) are adjusted for cost of living on an annual basis.

KSOP: A stock bonus plan in which elective contributions or employer matching contributions may be invested in employer stock.

Leased Employee: An individual (not an employee) who provides services under the primary direction and control of the employer pursuant to an agreement with the employer, on a substantially full-time basis for a period of at least one year. Leased employees are counted as employees for purposes of the coverage and minimum participation rules, as well as determining key employees and highly compensated employees.

Leveraged ESOP: An employee stock ownership plan that takes out a loan to purchase employer stock.

Life Cycle Plan: See **Retirement Bonus Plan**.

Limited Liability Company (LLC): A corporation designed to be taxed as a partnership. For 401(k) plan purposes, the members of the LLC are treated like partners and the non-members are treated like partnership employees.

Lookback Rules: Rules used in determining who is a highly compensated or key employee. Under the highly compensated rules, the lookback period is one year. For key employees, the lookback period is five years. Employees who meet the definition of a highly compensated or key employee for a lookback year will be counted as current highly compensated or key employees in the current year.

Look-Through Fund: A fund in which the underlying assets of a pooled fund are taken into account in determining whether ERISA's diversification requirements have been satisfied.

Lump-Sum Distribution: A distribution that qualifies for forward averaging. The basic requirements are that the distribution be made within one taxable year of the recipient, that it include the entire balance to the credit of the employee, and that it be made on account of the employee's death, attainment of age 59½, separation from service (except for the self-employed), or disability (self-employed persons only). [IRC § 402(e)(4)(A)]

Lump Sum Plan: See **Retirement Bonus Plan**.

Mandatory Aggregation: Plans, or portions of plans, that must be tested together when applying the average benefit percentage test.

Mandatory Contribution: An after-tax employee contribution required as a condition of participation in qualified plans.

Mandatory Disaggregation: Portions of plans that must be tested separately under the minimum participation and coverage rules. Mandatory disaggregation is required for collectively bargained plans, multiple employer plans, plans of different contribution types (coverage only), and ESOPs.

Master Plan: A plan sponsored by a bank, insurance company, credit union, trade union, professional organization or individual approved by the IRS. Master plans are funded using a pooled trust with a corporate trustee. This type of plan can be adopted by an employer by completing an adoption agreement that tailors the plan to the needs of the individual employer. (See **Prototype Plan**.)

Matching Contribution: An employer contribution in a 401(k) plan that is linked to an elective deferral contribution. For example, an employer might match elective contributions up to 4 percent of pay on a dollar-for-dollar basis.

Minimum Distribution Requirements: Rules governing when distributions from a qualified plan must commence and the maximum time period over which benefit payments can be made. Generally, distributions must commence by April 1 of the year following the later of the calendar year in which the employee attains age 70½ or retires (the delay until retirement is only for non-5 percent owners) and must be paid over a period not to exceed the life expectancy of the employee and his or her designated beneficiary.

Money Purchase Plan: An individual account plan in which the employer has a fixed obligation to make annual contributions to the plan, usually based on a percentage of pay.

Multiemployer Plan: A plan maintained under a collective bargaining agreement that covers employees of different employers within the same industry.

Multiple Employer Plan: A plan sponsored by a group of employers that do not have sufficient common ownership to be considered a controlled group or affiliated service group. Not subject to a collective bargaining agreement as is the case with a multiemployer plan.

Multiple Use Limitation: A rule that prevents an employer from using the alternative limitation in both the actual deferral percentage test and the actual contribution percentage test for the same testing year.

Mutual Fund: An investment company that combines the money of its numerous shareholders to invest in a variety of securities in an effort to achieve a specific objective over time.

NHCE: See **Non-Highly Compensated Employee**.

Noncontributory Plan: A plan to which employees do not make contributions.

Nondiscrimination: A requirement that a qualified plan not unduly favor highly compensated employees. The nondiscrimination requirements of the Code are found in Code Sections 401(a)(4), 401(a)(26), 401(k), 401(m), and 410(b).

Nondiscriminatory Classification Test: A component test of the average benefits test under Code Section 410(b). The nondiscriminatory classification test requires a plan to benefit a class of employees that is both reasonable and nondiscriminatory. (See **Average Benefit Percentage Test**.)

Nonelective Contributions: Employer contributions (other than matching contributions) made without regard to elective contributions.

Nonforfeitable Benefits: Benefits under a plan to which a participant has an unconditional right.

Non-Highly Compensated Employee (NHCE): An employee who is not a highly compensated employee.

Non-Key Employee: An employee who is not a key employee.

Nonqualified Deferred Compensation Plan: A retirement plan to which the advantages of qualification do not apply. To avoid ERISA's eligibility, vesting, and accrued benefit requirements, these plans are unfunded and made available only to a select group of management or highly compensated employees.

OASDI: See **Old Age, Survivors, and Disability Insurance**.

OBRA '87: The Omnibus Budget Reconciliation Act of 1987.

Officer: An employee who is an administrative executive in regular and continued service. An officer may be a key employee.

Old Age, Survivors, and Disability Insurance (OASDI): A program under Social Security. Also refers to that portion of the employment taxes paid under Chapter 21 of the Code used to fund this program. (See **FICA**.)

On-Demand Accounting: A system of accounting that provides for the allocation of earnings and losses to a participant's account on a daily basis.

1 Percent Owner: An employee who owns, directly or indirectly, more than 1 percent of the value or voting power of the stock of an employer, or, if the employer is not a corporation, more than 1 percent of the capital or profits interest. A 1 percent owner who has compensation in excess of $150,000 is considered a key employee.

Optional Forms of Benefit: Distribution alternatives available for the payment of an employee's benefit.

Owner-Employee: A self-employed individual who owns more than 10 percent of a noncorporate employer.

Paired Plans: Two or more standardized plans maintained by the same sponsor which are designed to satisfy automatically the top-heavy requirements and the contribution limitations under Code Section 415.

Partial Termination: The exclusion, either by plan amendment or severance from service with the employer, of a group of employees who are covered by a plan.

Participant: An employee or former employee who has an accrued benefit under the plan.

Participant Directed Plan: A plan under which participants determine the investment of their account balance.

Participant Loan: A loan from the plan to a participant.

Party-in-Interest: An ERISA term referring to certain parties who have a close relationship to the plan and, as a consequence, are prohibited from engaging in certain transactions with the plan in the absence of a statutory or an administrative exemption. (See **Disqualified Person.**)

Pension Simplification Act of 1996: Contained in the Small Business Job Protection Act of 1996.

Permitted Disparity: Rules under Code Section 401(l) that permit a plan to recognize the Social Security contributions made by the employer on behalf of employees in determining the allocation of nonelective contributions. Permitted disparity allows a greater share of such contributions to be allocated to highly paid participants. (See **Integrated Plan.**)

Plan Administration: The tasks required to be performed in order to operate the plan in accordance with its terms.

Plan Year: The period for which the records of the plan are kept.

Pooled Accounting: A system of accounting that provides for the allocation of earnings and losses to a participant's accounts on an annual or more frequent basis.

Pooled Fund: A fund that is managed by a registered investment company, bank, or insurance company and that is offered as an investment choice in a participant-directed plan.

Profit Sharing Plan: A plan under which contributions made by the employer are allocated to participants pursuant to a definite predetermined formula. Contributions are generally discretionary and may be made without regard to profits. [Treas Reg § 1.401-1(b)(1)(ii); IRC § 401(a)(27)]

Prohibited Transaction: A transaction between the plan and a party-in-interest (disqualified person).

Prohibited Transaction Exemptions: Statutory or administrative exemptions that permit transactions between plans and parties-in-interest to occur that would otherwise be prohibited.

Protected Benefit Rights and Features: Optional forms of benefits and other features of a plan that are of more than insignificant value.

Prototype Plan: An IRS-approved plan generally sponsored by a bank, insurance company, or mutual fund that is made available for adoption by the clients of the sponsor.

PS–58 Cost: The taxable value of the pure life insurance protection in a plan that provides for insured death benefits. [Treas Reg § 1.72-16]

QDRO: See **Qualified Domestic Relations Order**.

QMACs: See **Qualified Matching Contributions**.

QNECs: See **Qualified Nonelective Contributions**.

QSLOB: See **Qualified Separate Line of Business**.

Qualified Domestic Relations Order (QDRO): A domestic relations order that entitles an alternate payee to receive some or all of a participant's benefits under a plan.

Qualified Matching Contributions (QMACs): Matching contributions that are 100 percent vested at all times and that are subject to the same restrictions on distributability as elective contributions.

Qualified Nonelective Contributions (QNECs): Nonelective contributions that are 100 percent vested at all times and that are subject to the same restrictions on distributability as elective contributions.

Qualified Plan: A plan the provisions of which satisfy Code Section 401(a). Sometimes used more broadly to include plans that qualify under other Code sections.

Qualified Separate Line of Business (QSLOB): A line of business that meets certain IRS requirements and thus may be treated as a distinct unit for purposes of applying certain nondiscrimination requirements.

Recharacterization: A mechanism that treats excess contributions as employee contributions in order to correct an ADP test that does not meet the requirements of the law.

Regional Prototype Plan: An IRS-approved plan generally sponsored by a plan administration firm or law firm that is made available for adoption by their clients.

Retirement Bonus Plan: Also known as lump-sum plan or life cycle plan. A type of defined benefit plan where the accrued benfit is specified to be a lump sum equal to accumulated service credits times final average salary.

Reversion of Employer Contributions: The return of plan assets to the employer. A reversion can occur only under limited circumstances.

Rollover: A plan contribution made by an employee, attributable to a distribution from a qualified plan or a conduit IRA.

Rollover IRA Account: An individual retirement account that is funded with an eligible distribution from a qualified plan. A rollover IRA account may or may not function as a conduit IRA.

Roth IRA: A type of IRA funded with after-tax dollars, qualifying distributions from which are excludable from income tax.

S Corporation: A small business corporation in which the shareholders elect to be taxed like a partnership with profits and losses passing directly through to the shareholders. Income is not taxed at the corporate level. (See **C Corporation**.) [IRC §§ 1361 et seq.]

Safe Harbor 401(k) Plan: A 401(k) plan exempt from nondiscrimination testing of elective and/or matching contributions in exchange for providing certain minimum levels of matching or nonelective contributions. Permitted for plan years beginning after December 31, 1998.

Safe Harbor Rules: Regulations that specify plan provisions or plan operational characteristics by virtue of which more complex rules or tests need not be considered.

Salary Reduction Arrangement: A cash-or-deferred arrangement under which an employee elects to reduce a portion of his or her regular salary or wages and to have that portion contributed by the employer to a 401(k) plan.

Salary Reduction Simplified Employee Pension Plan (SARSEP): A simplified employee pension under Section 408(k) that permits employees to make elective contributions to their IRAs. New SARSEPs may not be established after December 31, 1996.

SAR: See **Summary Annual Report**.

SARSEP: See **Salary Reduction Simplified Employee Pension Plan**.

Savings or Thrift Plan: A contributory defined contribution plan where the employer's obligation to make contributions depends on whether the employee makes a required contribution out of after-tax compensation. Thrift plans are subject to the Section 401(m) nondiscrimination requirements.

SBJPA: See **Small Business Job Protection Act of 1996**.

SEC: Securities and Exchange Commission.

Section 401(k) Plan: A plan in which employees may elect to make pre-tax contributions to an employer-sponsored plan in lieu of receiving taxable income. (See **Cash-or-Deferred Arrangement**.)

Section 403(b) Plan: An elective contribution arrangement available to employees of government schools and to employees of entities that are tax exempt under Code Section 501(c)(3). A 403(b) plan may also provide for employer contributions. Also available to tribal governments, but not to governmental entities generally. (See **Tax Sheltered Annuities**.)

Section 457 Plan: An elective contribution arrangement available to states, political subdivisions of a state, or any agency or instrumentality of a state under Code Section 457.

Self-Directed Option: An investment option permitting participants to invest their plan assets in an unlimited number of investment options through either a full brokerage account or a mutual fund window.

Self-Employed Person: An individual who has net earnings from self-employment with respect to a trade or business in which the personal services of the individual are a material income-producing factor. [IRC § 401(c)(1)]

SEP: See **Simplified Employee Pension Plan**.

Separate Line of Business (SLOB):   A line of business that is organized and operated separately from the remaining businesses of the employer and that meets certain requirements.

Shareholder-Employee: An employee who owns more than 5 percent of the capital stock of a corporation that is taxed as a Subchapter S small business corporation.

SIMPLE 401(k) Plan: A 401(k) plan for the small employer exempt from ADP and ACP testing and the top-heavy rules in exchange for prescribed employer contributions and a lower limit on salary deferrals. Cannot be used in conjunction with any other active qualified plan covering the same employees.

SIMPLE IRA Plan.   Also called SIMPLE retirement account plan. A salary deferral plan for small employers exempt from discrimination testing and top-heavy rules but subject to prescribed employer contributions and a $6,000 (indexed) cap on deferrals. All contributions are made to IRAs. Cannot be used in conjunction with any other active qualified plan of the same sponsor(s).

Simplified Employee Pension Plan (SEP):   A retirement plan where contributions are made to the individual retirement accounts (IRAs) of the participants.

SLOB: See **Separate Line of Business**.

Small Business Job Protection Act of 1996 (SBJPA):   Contains the Pension Simplification Act of 1996.

Sole Proprietor: The owner of 100 percent of an unincorporated business.

SPD: See **Summary Plan Description**.

Split-Funded Plan: A plan that is funded by a combination of insurance contracts and a separate trust fund.

Spousal IRA: An additional IRA contribution made by a working spouse on behalf of a nonworking spouse. The deductible limit is increased to $4,000 if both spouses file a joint return; however, no more than $2,000 may be contributed to one spouse's account.

Standardized Plan: A prototype plan that is designed to satisfy automatically the Code's minimum coverage and nondiscrimination requirements.

Standardized VCR Program (SVP):   A variant of the VCR program that applies only to seven specified defects each of which must be cured by a method set forth by the IRS. (See also **EPCRS**.)

Stock: A security that represents part ownership, or equity, in a corporation.

Stock Bonus Plan: A defined contribution plan similar to a profit-sharing plan except that distributions must generally be made in company stock. A stock bonus plan may contain a cash-or-deferred arrangement.

Summary Annual Report (SAR):   A report of overall plan financial information provided to each participant in a format published by the DOL. The information is derived from the Form 5500 series annual report.

Summary Plan Description (SPD):   A written description of the plan designed to provide a participant or beneficiary with a comprehensive but understandable overview of how the plan operates.

SVP: See **Standardized VCR Program**.

TAMRA: Technical and Miscellaneous Revenue Act of 1988.

Tax Equity and Fiscal Responsibility Act of 1982 (TEFRA):   Created minimum distribution requirements, reduced the limits on contributions and benefits in plans, established parity between corporate and noncorporate or Keogh plans, treated certain plan loans as taxable distributions, and added the top-heavy rules.

Taxable Year: The 12-month period selected by an employer to report income for tax purposes.

Tax Reform Act of 1984 (TRA '84): See **Deficit Reduction Act of 1984.**

Tax Reform Act of 1986 (TRA '86): The first wholesale revision of the tax code since 1954. The Code is now named the "Internal Revenue Code of 1986."

Taxpayer Relief Act of 1997 (TRA '97): Act containing a number of retirement plan provisions simplifying plan administration and creating new retirement planning options—notably the Roth IRA.

Tax-Sheltered Annuities (TSA): Also known as 403(b) annuities. This is currently the mechanism for employees of certain not-for-profit organizations to elect to defer compensation in a qualified retirement plan.

TEFRA: See **Tax Equity and Fiscal Responsibility Act of 1982.**

Third-Party Administrator: A plan administrator who is unrelated to the sponsoring employer.

Top-Heavy Plan: A qualified retirement plan in which more than 60 percent of the benefits are for key employees. Top-heavy plans must provide accelerated vesting and minimum benefits or contributions for non-key employees.

TRA '84: See **Deficit Reduction Act of 1984.**

TRA '86: See **Tax Reform Act of 1986.**

TRA '97: See **Taxpayer Relief Act of 1997.**

Treasury Regulations: Regulations written by the IRS interpreting the Internal Revenue Code are technically Treasury Regulations. The IRS is part of the Department of the Treasury, and the Code authorizes the Secretary of the Treasury to promulgate regulations.

Trust: A legal entity established under state law that holds and administers plan assets for the benefit of participants.

Trustees: The parties named in a trust document who have responsibility to hold assets for the participants. Some plan documents also give investment responsibility to the trustees.

Truth-in-Lending: Federal law governing consumer credit transactions that provides for uniform disclosure of annual credit cost, finance charges, amount financed, and total payments to be made.

TSA: See **Tax-Sheltered Annuities.**

Unincorporated Business: A business organization that is not a corporation, such as a partnership or sole proprietorship.

User Fees: The fees charged by the IRS to review determination letter applications as to the qualified status of the form of retirement plans.

VCR: See **Voluntary Compliance Resolution**.

Vested Benefits: Benefits that become nonforfeitable with respect to a participant as the result of the passage of time or the occurrence of an event such as retirement or plan termination.

Volume Submitter: A type of individually designed retirement plan document for which a specimen plan is submitted to the IRS for approval. The submitter must certify that at least 30 employers will adopt the plan. The user fees are less than for a regular, individually designed document.

Voluntary Compliance Resolution (VCR): A program that enables a plan sponsor to cure non-egregious operational defects by paying a flat fee and requesting a compliance statement from the IRS. (See also **EPCRS**.)

Voluntary Contributions: Participant contributions made to a plan on an after-tax basis. These contributions are treated as Section 415 annual additions and are subject to Section 401(m) nondiscrimination requirements.

Walk-in CAP: A program initiated voluntarily by the sponsor of a qualified plan prior to an audit. Except for situations relating to the diversion or misuse of plan assets, the program is available to cure all document and operational defects. Unlike **Audit Cap**, where a penalty amount is negotiated with the IRS, Walk-in CAP provides for the payment of a fee. (See also **EPCRS**.)

Year of Service: A 12-month period in which an employee completes a specified number of hours of service, commonly at least 1,000 hours; however, the plan document can provide a lesser requirement.

Tables

Internal Revenue Code

[References are to questions.]

Key Code Sections

401(a): The basic requirements for a retirement plan to be qualified for special treatment under the Internal Revenue Code. (See chapter 2.)

401(a)(4): The general nondiscrimination rule. A qualified plan may not discriminate in favor of highly compensated employees with respect to contributions or benefits. (See chapter 11.)

401(a)(17): Cap on compensation that may be considered in determining benefits under a qualified retirement plan. (See chapter 9.)

401(a)(26): The minimum participation requirement. Each plan must benefit the lesser of 50 employees or 40 percent of all employees of the employer. It no longer applies to 401(k) and other defined contribution plans. (See 10:1–10:9.)

401(a)(31): The requirement that distributees must be offered a direct rollover election on all eligible rollover distributions. (See chapter 15.)

401(k): The requirements for a qualified cash-or-deferred arrangement that must be followed in order to give participants a choice between receiving currently taxable cash compensation or deferring tax by electing to contribute amounts to a profit sharing or stock bonus plan. (See especially chapters 1 and 2.)

401(m): The nondiscrimination test for employer matching contributions and after-tax employee contributions. (See chapter 12.)

402(g): The limit on the amount of elective deferrals a participant may exclude from current taxation. The limit is adjusted annually for cost of living increases; for 1998 it is $10,000. This section also describes the mechanism for returning elective deferrals that exceed the limit. (See chapter 8.)

[References are to questions.]

403(b): Describes how employees of certain tax-exempt nonprofit organizations can defer receipt of currently taxable compensation by means of salary deferrals (also known as tax-sheltered annuities). (See chapter 21.)

410(b): The specific minimum coverage requirements for a qualified retirement plan. Consists of two alternate tests, the ratio-percentage test and the average benefit test. (See chapter 10.)

411(d): The anti-cutback rules that protect a participant from having rights or benefits accrued under a plan being taken away. (See chapter 15.)

415: The overall maximum limits on contributions and benefits with respect to participants under qualified plans. (See chapter 8.)

416: The top-heavy rules requiring accelerated vesting and minimum benefit or contribution standards in the event that more than 60 percent of a plan's benefits are for key employees. (See chapter 13.)

417: The minimum survivor annuity requirements, which affect the form and timing of distributions and provide for spousal consent to distributions from the plan. (See chapter 16.)

457: Deferred compensation arrangements for employees and independent contractors of state and local governments. (See chapter 21.)

3405: Income tax withholding on 401(k) plan distributions, including the 20 percent withholding requirements. (See chapter 15.)

[References are to questions.]

IRC §		IRC §	
401(a)(4) ..	1:45, 2:31, 2:43–2:44, 2:46, 2:48, 2:50, 2:60, 3:21, 6:39, 6:55–6:56, 6:92, 8:27, 9:37, 9:108, 10:8, 10:14, 10:39, 13:6, 21:53, 21:77, 21:100, 21:114, 21:118	401(k)(4)(A)	2:31
401(a)(5)	21:118	401(k)(4)(B)	1:18
401(a)(9)	12:65, 15:14–15:15, 15:50, 15:53, 15:97, 17:80, 19:20, 21:97	401(k)(8)(C)	12:20
		401(k)(11)	2:28, 2:33, 2:131, 12:1
401(a)(9)(A)	15:37	401(k)(11)(B)(ii)	2:135
401(a)(9)(C)	15:23, 21:136	401(k)(12)	2:29, 2:33, 2:143, 2:146, 12:1
401(a)(9)(C)(ii)(I)	15:26	401(l)	11:15, 21:27, 21:70
401(a)(11) . . .	15:16, 15:35, 15:70	401(m) ..	2:8, 2:57, 17:58, 21:100, 21:114, 21:118
401(a)(12)	2:74		
401(a)(13)	2:70	401(m)(2)(A)	12:41
401(a)(17)	2:15, 2:77, 2:135, 9:37, 9:104, 9:109–9:112, 12:11, 21:37–21:38, 21:114, 21:118	401(m)(4)(A)	2:26
		401(m)(6)(C)	12:55
		401(m)(10)	2:131, 12:1
		401(m)(11) . . .	2:143, 21:146, 12:1
401(a)(17)(A)	9:109	402	17:26
401(a)(17)(B)	9:110	402(b)(2)	10:7
401(a)(26)	9:37, 9:59, 10:6, 10:9, 21:71, 21:118	402(c)(1)	15:46
		402(c)(4)	1:47, 15:49–15:50
401(a)(26)(H)	1:45	402(c)(6)	15:56
401(a)(27)	2:81	402(c)(8)	15:91
401(a)(28)	6:48	402(c)(9)	17:34
401(a)(30)	2:80, 8:18	402(d)(4)(A)	17:15
401(a)(31)	2:83, 15:59–15:60, 21:118	402(d)(4)(B)	17:20
		402(d)(4)(C)	17:17–17.18
401(a)(31)(A)	15:54	402(d)(4)(D)	17:23
401(b)(2)	10:38	402(d)(4)(F)	17:15
401(c)	9:60	402(d)(4)(H)	17:18
401(c)(1)	9:81	402(d)(4)(J)	16:39, 17:21
401(c)(3)	14:1, 21:117	402(e)(1)	17:34
401(d)(1)(C)	17:24	402(e)(1)(A)	16:39
401(f)	2:65, 4:4, 21:107	402(e)(1)(B)	16:39
401(k)	9:59, 21:101	402(e)(4)	17:29
401(k)(1)	1:21, 6:48	402(e)(4)(A)(iii)	21:140
401(k)(2)(B)	2:161, 2:162	402(e)(4)(E)	17:30
401(k)(2)(B)(i)(IV)	1:47	402(e)(5)	2:65
401(k)(3)	1:45	402(f)	15:72
401(k)(3)(A)(ii)	12:4, 12:5	402(g)	2:155, 2:157, 2:162, 19:20
401(k)(3)(F)	12:37		
		402(g)(3)	1:45
		402(g)(3)(C)	1:19
		402(g)(8)	21:102
		402(h)(1)	21:30

[References are to questions.]

[References are to questions.]

[References are to questions.]

[References are to questions.]

United States Code

[References are to questions.]

ERISA

[References are to questions.]

Key ERISA Sections

404(c): This provision relieves plan fiduciaries from some fiduciary responsibility for plan investments if participants have a certain amount of control over the assets in their accounts. (See chapter 6.)

[References are to questions.]

Tax Equity and Fiscal Responsibility Act

[References are to questions.]

Bankruptcy Code

[References are to questions.]

Small Business Job Protection Act of 1996

[References are to questions.]

Taxpayer Relief Act of 1997

[References are to questions.]

IRS Restructuring
and Reform Act of 1998

[References are to questions.]

Cases

[References are to questions.]

Code of Federal Regulations

[References are to questions.]

Treasury Regulations

[References are to questions.]

T-29

[References are to questions.]

[References are to questions.]

[References are to questions.]

[References are to questions.]

[References are to questions.]

[References are to questions.]

[References are to questions.]

[References are to questions.]

Department of Labor Regulations

[References are to questions.]

[References are to questions.]

DOL Interpretive Bulletins

[References are to questions.]

Miscellaneous Announcements, Notices, Memoranda, Rulings, Procedures, and Opinions

[References are to questions.]

[References are to questions.]

IRS Notices

97-45, 1997-33 IRB 7, Q&A 8   15:24
97-75, 1997-51 IRB 18   15:45, 15:53
98-1, 1998-3 IRB 42 . . . . . .   2:144,
    12:4–12:6, 12:8–12:9, 12:14,
       12:41–12:44, 12:67
98-29, 1998-22 IRB 8 . . . . .   20:25
98-52, 1998-46 IRB 16   2:143, 13:39
99-1, 1999-2 IRB 8 . . .   1:49, 15:17,
    15:19
99-5, 1999-3 IRB 10 . .   1:47, 14:39,
    15:50, 15:85
99-11, 1999-8 IRB 56 . .   1:42, 1:49

Memorandum

General Counsel Memorandum
    39344 (Oct 16, 1984) . .   20:16

Private Letter Rulings

8103063 . . . .   14:21
8741069 . . . .   21:97
8920040 . . . .   9:109
8921027 . . . .   9:109
8933018 . . . .   14:26
9007001 . . . .   21:94
9124034 . . . .   4:44
9124035 . . . .   4:44
9124036 . . . .   4:44
9124037 . . . .   4:44
9144041 . . . .   2:69

Revenue Rulings

55-747 . . . .   17:46
56-497, 1956-2 CB 284 . . . . . .   1:1
60-31, 1960-1 CB 174 . . . . .   21:87
61-164, 1961-2 CB 99 . . . . . .   2:66
63-180, 1963-2 CB 189 . . . . . .   1:1
65-295, 1965-2 CB 148 . . . . .   8:51
66-110, 1966-1 CB 12 . . . . .   17:46

Revenue Rulings

66-274, 1966-2 CB 446 . . . .   21:93
67-290, 1967-2 CB 198 . . . .   21:93
68-24, 1968-1 CB 150 . . . . .   14:45
68-89, 1968-1 CB 402 . . . .   1:1
68-116, 1968-1 CB 177 . . . . .   21:94
69-494, 1969-2 CB 88 . . . . . .   6:39
69-502, 1969-2 CB 89 . . . . .   21:68
69-569, 1969-2 CB 91 . . . . . .   2:68
70-411, 1970-2 CB 91 . . . . .   2:68
71-90, 1971-1 CB 115 . . . . . .   2:64
71-224, 1971-1 CB 124 . . . .   14:46
71-295, 1971-2 CB 184 . . . .   14:45
72-439, 1972-2 CB 223 . . . .   20:16
73-284, 1973-2 CB 139 . . . .   20:16
74-466, 1974-2 CB 131 . . . . .   2:63
76-259, 1976-2 CB 111 . . . .   13:42,
    21:68
80-145, 1980-1 CB 89 . . . . . .   8:49
80-155, 1980-1 CB 84 . .   6:39, 6:93
86-103, 1986-2 CB 62 . . . .   21:139
89-14, 1989-1 CB 111 . . . . .   14:14
90-105, 1990-2 CB 69 . . . . . .   8:57
91-4, 1991-1 CB 57 . . . .   2:69
98-30, 1998-25 IRB 8 . . . . . .   1:48

Revenue Procedures

89-9, 1989-1 CB 780, §6 . . . .   3:23
89-9, 1989-1 CB 780 . . . .   3:2
89-13, 1989-1 CB 801, §11 . . .   3:23
89-13, 1989-1 CB 801 . . . .   3:8
92-93, 1992-2 CB 505 . . . . . .   8:28
95-4, 1995-1 CB 397 . . . . .   21:110
95-24, 1995-1 CB 694 . . . .   21:109
97-9, 1997-1 CB 624 . . . . . .   2:142
98-22, 1998-12 IRB 11 . .   1:49, 19:2,
    19:20, 19:21, 19:24,
    19:25, 19:26, 19:28
98-22, 1998-12 IRB 11, §12.03 .   19:21,
    19:24
98-22, 1998-12 IRB 11, §13.05(2)   19.26
98-22, 1998-12 IRB 11, §15.02   19:28

[References are to questions.]

Index

[References are to question numbers.]

[References are to question numbers.]

[References are to question numbers.]

[References are to question numbers.]

[References are to question numbers.]

[References are to question numbers.]

[*References are to question numbers.*]

[References are to question numbers.]

[References are to question numbers.]

[References are to question numbers.]

[References are to question numbers.]

[References are to question numbers.]

[References are to question numbers.]